West's Law School
Advisory Board

CYBERLAW

PROBLEMS OF POLICY AND JURISPRUDENCE IN THE INFORMATION AGE

Third Edition

By

Patricia L. Bellia
Lilly Endowment Associate Professor of Law
Notre Dame Law School

Paul Schiff Berman
Jesse Root Professor of Law
University of Connecticut School of Law

David G. Post
I. Herman Stern Professor of Law
Beasley School of Law, Temple University

AMERICAN CASEBOOK SERIES®

THOMSON
WEST

Mat #40438400

American Casebook Series and West Group are trademarks
registered in the U.S. Patent and Trademark Office.

© West, a Thomson business, 2003–2004
© 2007 West, a Thomson business
      610 Opperman Drive
      P.O. Box 64526
      St. Paul, MN 55164–0526
      1–800–328–9352

Printed in the United States of America

ISBN–13: 978–0–314–16687–6
ISBN–10: 0–314–16687–4

TEXT IS PRINTED ON 10% POST
CONSUMER' RECYCLED PAPER

Acknowledgments

In preparing this casebook, we have benefitted from the input of cyberlaw colleagues too numerous to mention individually, both for their illuminating discussions with us, online and off-, concerning the issues addressed in this book, and, in the case of a number of colleagues who taught from the text, for their specific comments about strengths and weaknesses of our treatment of those issues. In addition, we thank Brooke Bennett, Tamara Dugan, Gretchen Heinze, Jeffery Houin, and Nathaniel Pollock for excellent research assistance, and Annemarie Bridy and Arthur Denner for help with translating the *Yahoo!* materials in Chapter Three.

A Note on the Editing: We have omitted citations and footnotes within court opinions and commentary without so specifying; other omissions or alterations are indicated by asterisks or brackets. We have not indicated omissions at the beginning or the end of an excerpt or where the omission is otherwise obvious from context. We have altered paragraph structure to facilitate readability. Numbered footnotes are from the original materials; lettered footnotes are ours.

We are grateful to the following sources for their permission to reprint excerpts from their work:

Tom W. Bell, *Fair Use vs. Fared Use: The Impact of Automated Rights Management on Copyright's Fair Use Doctrine*, 76 North Carolina Law Review 557 (1998). Copyright © 1998, North Carolina Law Review. Reprinted by permission.

Yochai Benkler, *Net Regulation: Taking Stock and Looking Forward*, 71 The University of Colorado Law Review 1203 (2000). Copyright © 2000, Yochai Benkler. Reprinted by permission.

Dan L. Burk & Julie E. Cohen, *Fair Use Infrastructure for Rights Management Systems*, 15 Harvard Journal of Law & Technology 41 (2001). Copyright © 2001, Harvard Journal of Law & Technology. Reprinted by permission.

Anupam Chander, *Whose Republic?*, 69 The University of Chicago Law Review 1479 (2002). Copyright © 2002, The University of Chicago Law Review. Reprinted by permission.

Julie E. Cohen, *Examined Lives, Informational Privacy and the Subject as Object*, 52 Stanford Law Review 1373 (2000). Copyright © 2000, Stanford Law Review. Reprinted by permission.

Julie E. Cohen, *Lochner in Cyberspace: The New Economic Orthodoxy of "Rights Management"*, 97 Michigan Law Review 462 (1998). Copyright © 1998, Julie E. Cohen. Reprinted by permission of the publisher and author.

Frank H. Easterbrook, *Cyberspace and the Law of the Horse*, 1996 The University of Chicago Legal Forum 207. Copyright © 1996, Frank H. Easterbrook. Reprinted by permission.

Owen M. Fiss, *Why the State?*, 100 Harvard Law Review 781 (1987). Copyright © 1987, Harvard Law Review. Reprinted with the permission of the publisher and author.

A. Michael Froomkin, *Wrong Turn in Cyberspace: Using ICANN to Route Around the APA and the Constitution*, 50 Duke Law Journal 17 (2000). Copyright © 2000, A. Michael Froomkin. Reprinted by permission.

Jack L. Goldsmith, *The Internet and the Legitimacy of Remote Cross-Border Searches*, 2001 The University of Chicago Legal Forum 103. Copyright © 2001, The University of Chicago Legal Forum. Reprinted by permission.

Jack L. Goldsmith, *Against Cyberanarchy*, 65 The University of Chicago Law Review 1199 (1998). Copyright © 1998, The University of Chicago Law Review. Reprinted by permission.

Jack L. Goldsmith, *The Internet and the Abiding Significance of Territorial Sovereignty*, 5 Indiana Journal of Global Legal Studies 475 (1998). Copyright © 1998, Indiana Journal of Global Legal Studies. Reprinted by permission.

James Grimmelmann, *Virtual Worlds as Comparative Law*, 2004-05 New York Law School Law Review 147. Copyright © 2004-05, James Grimmelmann. Reprinted by permission.

Lawrence Lessig, Code and Other Laws of Cyberspace (1999). Copyright © 1999 by Lawrence Lessig. Reprinted by permission of Basic Books, a member of Perseus Books, L.L.C.

Lawrence Lessig, *The Law of the Horse: What Cyberlaw Might Teach*, 113 Harvard Law Review 501 (1999). Copyright © 1999, Harvard Law Review. Reprinted with the permission of the publisher and author.

Lawrence Lessig, *The Spam Wars*, The Industry Standard, December 31, 1998. Copyright © 1998, Lawrence Lessig. Reprinted by permission.

Robert McChesney, *So Much for the Magic of Technology and the Free Market*, in The World Wide Web and Contemporary Cultural Theory 7 (2000). Copyright © 2000 From The World Wide Web and Contemporary Cultural Theory by Andrew Herman & Thomas Swiss eds. Reproduced by permission of Routledge, Inc., part of The Taylor & Francis Group.

Frank Pasquale, *Rankings, Reductionism, and Responsibility*, 54 Cleveland State Law Review 115 (2006). Copyright © 2006, Frank Pasquale. Reprinted by permission.

Margaret Jane Radin, *Regulation by Contract, Regulation by Machine*, 160 Journal of Institutional and Theoretical Economics 142 (2004). Copyright © 2004, Margaret Jane Radin. Reprinted by permission.

Jonathan Rosen, The Talmud and the Internet: A Journey Between Worlds (2000). Copyright © 2000, Farrar, Straus and Giroux. Reprinted by permission.

Paul M. Schwartz, *Privacy and Democracy in Cyberspace*, 52 Vanderbilt Law Review 1609 (1999). Copyright © 1999 Vanderbilt Law Review. Reprinted by permission.

Daniel J. Solove, *Conceptualizing Privacy*, 90 California Law Review 1087 (2002). Copyright © 2002 by the California Law Review. Reprinted by permission of the California Law Review, Inc.

Sherry Turkle, Life on the Screen (1994). Reprinted by permission of Simon & Schuster Adult Publishing Group from LIFE ON THE SCREEN: Identity in the Age of the Internet by Sherry Turkle. Copyright © 1995 by Sherry Turkle.

Jonathan Weinberg, *Rating the Net*, 19 Hastings Communications and Entertainment Law Journal 453 (1997). Copyright © 1997 by University of California, Hastings College of Law. Reprinted from Hastings Communications and Entertainment Law Journal, Volume 19, Number 2, Winter 1997, 453-482, by permission.

Philip J. Weiser, *Internet Governance, Standard Setting, and Self-Regulation*, 28 Northern Kentucky Law Review 822 (2001). Copyright © 2001, Northern Kentucky Law Review. Reprinted by permission.

Michele Wilson, *Community in the Abstract: A Political and Ethical Dilemma?*, in The Cybercultures Reader 644 (2000). Copyright © 2000, Thomson Publishing Services. Reprinted by permission.

Alfred C. Yen, *Western Frontier or Feudal Society?: Metaphors and Perceptions of Cyberspace*, 17 Berkeley Technology Law Journal 1207 (2002). Copyright © 2002, Alfred C. Yen. Reprinted by permission.

Christopher S. Yoo & Tim Wu, *Keeping the Internet Neutral?,* Legal Affairs Debate Club, May 1, 2006. Copyright © 2006 Christopher S. Yoo & Tim Wu. Reprinted by permission.

Jonathan Zittrain, *The Generative Internet*, 119 Harvard Law Review 1974 (2006). Exclusive License held by Harvard Law Review. Reprinted by Permission.

Summary of Contents

		Page
ACKNOWLEDGMENTS		iii
TABLE OF CASES		xix
TABLE OF AUTHORITIES		xxvii

Chapter

1. **Introduction** --- 1
   - A. Why Cyberlaw? --- 2
   - B. Our Approach -- 12
   - C. Internet Basics --- 13
2. **Problems of Metaphor and Analogy:**
   Introductory Case Studies -------------------------------- 21
   - Introduction --- 21
   - A. Trespass to Chattels in Cyberspace ---------------------- 23
   - B. Consumer Confusion and Online Trademarks --------------- 44
   - C. Internet Access and Content Filtering in Public Libraries ---- 57
3. **Problems of Geography and Sovereignty** ---------------------- 63
   - Introduction --- 63
   - A. The Theoretical Debate ---------------------------------- 65
   - B. Jurisdiction To Prescribe ------------------------------- 83
   - C. Jurisdiction to Adjudicate ------------------------------ 112
   - D. Judgment Recognition and the Power of Persuasion -------- 137
   - E. Extraterritorial Law Enforcement Activity -------------- 149
   - F. A Case Study in the Internationalization of Legal Regimes: 166
4. **Problems of Legal versus Technological Regulation** ---------- 195
   - Introduction --- 195
   - A. The Effect of Technological Change on Legal Rules ------- 196
   - B. The Use of Technology to Supplant Legal Rules ---------- 211
   - C. The Effect of Legal Rules on Technological Innovation ----- 238
   - D. A Case Study on the Interaction of Law and Technology:
     - Domain Names and the Market for Search Tools --------- 284
5. **Problems of "Public" versus "Private" Regulation** ---------- 295
   - Introduction --- 295
   - A. The Role of Private Regulatory Entities in Cyberspace ----- 296
   - B. Constitutional Responses to "Private" Regulatory Power --- 327
   - C. Legislative Responses to "Private" Regulatory Power ------ 351
6. **Problems of Speech Regulation** ----------------------------- 389
   - A. Government Regulation of Sexually Explicit Speech -------- 390
   - B. Private Filtering of Sexually Explicit Speech ----------- 426
   - C. Filtering Technology and the First Amendment ----------- 440

7. **Problems of Intermediaries** ----------------------------------- 481
   Introduction --- 481
   A. Intermediary Liability for Online Conduct ---------------------- 482
   B. Intermediary Control of Information --------------------------- 532
8. **Problems of Privacy and Surveillance** ------------------------- 561
   Introduction --- 561
   A. Framing Privacy --- 563
   B. Government Surveillance -------------------------------------- 575
   C. Private Acquisition of Communications and Data ------------ 648
9. **Problems of Information Enclosure** --------------------------- 679
   Introduction --- 679
   A. The "Cyberproperty" Controversy ----------------------------- 680
   B. State Law Claims: Trespass and Contract --------------------- 686
   C. The Computer Fraud and Abuse Act --------------------------- 698
   D. The Digital Millennium Copyright Act's Anti-Circumvention
      and Anti-Trafficking Restrictions ----------------------------- 714
10. **Problems of Cultural Change** -------------------------------- 733
   Introduction --- 733
   A. Cyberspace as Metaphor -------------------------------------- 734
   B. Cyberspace, Community, and Globalization -------------------- 753
   C. Cyberspace and the Formation of Law and Policy ------------ 776

INDEX --- 799

Table of Contents

	Page
ACKNOWLEDGMENTS	iii
TABLE OF CASES	xix
TABLE OF AUTHORITIES	xxvii

Chapter One: Introduction ------- 1
  A. Why Cyberlaw? ------- 2
    Frank H. Easterbrook, Cyberspace and the Law of the Horse ------ 2
    Lawrence Lessig, The Law of the Horse: What Cyberlaw
      Might Teach ------- 4
    Notes and Questions ------- 10
  B. Our Approach ------- 12
  C. Internet Basics ------- 13

Chapter Two: Problems of Metaphor and Analogy:
Introductory Case Studies ------- 21
  Introduction ------- 21
  A. Trespass to Chattels in Cyberspace ------- 23
    eBay, Inc. v. Bidder's Edge, Inc. ------- 23
    Notes and Questions ------- 28
    Intel Corporation v. Hamidi ------- 30
    Notes and Questions ------- 42
  B. Consumer Confusion and Online Trademarks ------- 44
    Brookfield Communications, Inc. v. West Coast
      Entertainment Corp. ------- 44
    Notes and Questions ------- 51
    People for the Ethical Treatment of Animals v. Doughney ------- 54
    Notes and Questions ------- 56
  C. Internet Access and Content Filtering in Public Libraries ------- 57
    Mainstream Loudoun v. Board of Trustees of the Loudoun
      County Public Library ------- 57
    Notes and Questions ------- 61

Chapter Three: Problems of Geography and Sovereignty ------- 63
  Introduction ------- 63
  A. The Theoretical Debate ------- 65
    David R. Johnson and David G. Post, Law and Borders—The
      Rise of Law in Cyberspace ------- 65
    Jack L. Goldsmith, The Internet and the Abiding
      Significance of Territorial Sovereignty ------- 70

Jack L. Goldsmith, Against Cyberanarchy ------------------------------ 75
David G. Post, Against "Against Cyberanarchy" --------------------- 77
Notes and Questions --- 82
B. Jurisdiction To Prescribe --- 83
Note on Jurisdiction --- 83
1. Extraterritorial Regulation of Speech ------------------------------ 84
American Civil Liberties Union v. Reno ---------------------------- 85
Ashcroft v. American Civil Liberties Union ----------------------- 89
Notes and Questions --- 93
La Ligue Contre le Racisme et l'Antisémitisme v. Yahoo!, Inc. 94
Notes and Questions --- 96
2. The "Dormant" Commerce Clause -------------------------------- 98
American Libraries Association v. Pataki -------------------------- 98
Washington v. Heckel --- 104
Notes and Questions --- 109
Note on Center for Democracy and Technology v. Pappert --- 111
C. Jurisdiction to Adjudicate --- 112
1. The United States Personal Jurisdiction Inquiry ------------- 112
Introductory Note --- 112
Calder v. Jones -- 115
Notes and Questions --- 117
2. Jurisdiction Based on Online Interaction ----------------------- 117
Zippo Manufacturing Co. v. Zippo Dot Com, Inc. -------------- 119
Notes and Questions --- 122
Amway Corp. v. The Procter & Gamble Company -------------- 125
Notes and Questions --- 127
Young v. New Haven Advocate ------------------------------------- 129
Notes and Questions --- 132
Paul Schiff Berman, The Globalization of Jurisdiction ------- 134
Notes and Questions --- 136
D. Judgment Recognition and the Power of Persuasion -------------- 137
Yahoo!, Inc. v. La Ligue Contre le Racisme et l'Antisémitisme - 138
Notes and Questions --- 143
Citron v. Zündel --- 145
Notes and Questions --- 148
E. Extraterritorial Law Enforcement Activity --------------------------- 149
Patricia L. Bellia, Chasing Bits Across Borders -------------------- 149
Jack L. Goldsmith, The Internet and the Legitimacy of Remote
   Cross-Border Searches --- 153
Notes and Questions --- 156
United States v. Verdugo-Urquidez --------------------------------- 157
Notes and Questions --- 162
United States v. Gorshkov --- 163
Notes and Questions --- 165
F. A Case Study in the Internationalization of Legal Regimes:
Governing the Domain Name System ---------------------------------- 166
1. An Introduction to the Domain Name System ------------------ 167

2. Domain Names as Trademarks and the Extraterritorial
Application of Trademark Law ------------------------------ 169
Cable News Network L.P. v. Cnnews.com ----------------------- 171
Notes and Questions --- 174
GlobalSantaFe Corp. v. Globalsantafe.com ---------------------- 175
Notes & Questions -- 184
3. Non-Territorial Administration of the Domain Name
System --- 186
David G. Post, Governing Cyberspace, or Where is James
Madison When We Need Him? ---------------------------- 187
Notes and Questions --- 192

**Chapter Four: Problems of Legal versus
Technological Regulation** ----------------------------------- 195
Introduction -- 195
A. The Effect of Technological Change on Legal Rules -------------- 196
Olmstead v. United States ------------------------------------- 198
Katz v. United States --- 201
Notes and Questions --- 204
Kyllo v. United States --- 205
Notes and Questions --- 210
B. The Use of Technology to Supplant Legal Rules ------------------ 211
1. Automated Standardized Contracts ---------------------------- 211
ProCD, Inc. v. Zeidenberg ------------------------------------ 211
Notes and Questions --- 214
Specht v. Netscape Communications Corp. --------------------- 215
Notes and Questions --- 220
Margaret Jane Radin, Regulation by Contract, Regulation
by Machine -- 222
Notes and Questions --- 226
2. Technological Protection Measures --------------------------- 228
Dan L. Burk & Julie E. Cohen, Fair Use Infrastructure
for Rights Management Systems ---------------------------- 231
Tom W. Bell, Fair Use vs. Fared Use: The Impact of
Automated Rights Management on Copyright's
Fair Use Doctrine --------------------------------------- 232
Julie E. Cohen, *Lochner* in Cyberspace: The New
Economic Orthodoxy of "Rights Management" ------------- 234
Notes and Questions --- 236
C. The Effect of Legal Rules on Technological Innovation --------- 238
1. Home Video Recording Devices ------------------------------ 239
Sony Corporation of America v. Universal City Studios, Inc. 239
Notes and Questions --- 245
Section 1201 of the Digital Millennium Copyright Act ------- 246
Real Networks, Inc. v. Streambox, Inc. ----------------------- 248
Notes and Questions --- 253
2. Peer-to-Peer File Sharing ---------------------------------- 255

A & M Records, Inc. v. Napster, Inc. -------------------------------- 255

    Notes and Questions -- 264

Metro-Goldwyn-Mayer Studios Inc. v. Grokster, Ltd. --------- 265

    Notes and Questions -- 281

    3. Telecommunications Devices ------------------------------------- 282

D. A Case Study on the Interaction of Law and Technology:

     Domain Names and the Market for Search Tools ------------- 284

    Anticybersquatting Consumer Protection Act --------------------- 285

    Notes and Questions -- 287

    Yochai Benkler, Net Regulation: Taking Stock and

     Looking Forward -- 289

    Notes and Questions -- 292

Chapter Five: Problems of "Public" versus

"Private" Regulation --- 295

Introduction --- 295

A. The Role of Private Regulatory Entities in Cyberspace ---------- 296

    1. Standard-Setting Bodies --- 297

    Philip J. Weiser, Internet Governance, Standard Setting,

     and Self-Regulation -- 297

    Notes and Questions -- 300

    2. ICANN -- 300

    A. Michael Froomkin, Wrong Turn in Cyberspace: Using

     ICANN to Route Around the APA and the Constitution ----- 301

    Notes and Questions -- 306

    3. Corporate Regulation -- 308

    Search King, Inc. v. Google Technology, Inc. ------------------ 308

    Frank Pasquale, Rankings, Reductionism,

     and Responsibility --- 310

    Notes and Questions -- 316

    4. Individual and Collective Regulation ----------------------------- 317

    Media3 Technologies, LLC v. Mail Abuse Prevention

     System, LLC -- 318

    Lawrence Lessig, The Spam Wars -------------------------------- 320

    David G. Post, Of Black Holes and Decentralized

     Law-Making in Cyberspace ------------------------------- 322

    Notes and Questions -- 325

B. Constitutional Responses to "Private" Regulatory Power ------- 327

    Marsh v. Alabama --- 329

    Notes and Questions -- 332

    Amalgamated Food Employees Union v. Logan Valley

     Plaza, Inc. -- 333

    Lloyd Corporation v. Tanner ------------------------------------ 337

    Hudgens v. National Labor Relations Board ----------------- 343

    Notes and Questions -- 346

    Paul Schiff Berman, Cyberspace and the "State Action"

    Debate: The Cultural Value of Applying Constitutional

Norms to "Private" Regulation ------------------------------------- 348
Notes and Questions --- 350
C. Legislative Responses to "Private" Regulatory Power ----------- 351
  1. Regulation of Media Entities ------------------------------- 351
   Red Lion Broadcasting Co. v. FCC ----------------------------- 352
   Notes and Questions --- 356
   Miami Herald Publishing Co. v. Tornillo ----------------------- 357
   Notes and Questions --- 361
   Note on Must-Carry Requirements ----------------------------- 361
   Turner Broadcasting System, Inc. v. FCC --------------------- 362
   Notes and Questions --- 371
   Owen M. Fiss, Why the State? ----------------------------------- 373
   Notes and Questions --- 377
  2. Open Access Requirements ----------------------------------- 377
  3. Net Neutrality Requirements -------------------------------- 380
   Keeping the Internet Neutral?: Christopher S. Yoo
    and Tim Wu Debate --- 381
   Notes and Questions --- 385

Chapter Six: Problems of Speech Regulation --------------------- 389
Introduction -- 389
A. Government Regulation of Sexually Explicit Speech ------------- 390
  Ginsberg v. New York --- 391
  FCC v. Pacifica Foundation ------------------------------------ 394
  Notes and Questions --- 400
  Sable Communications of California, Inc. v. FCC --------------- 401
  Notes and Questions --- 405
  Renton v. Playtime Theatres, Inc. ----------------------------- 406
  Notes and Questions --- 409
  Reno v. American Civil Liberties Union ----------------------- 409
  Notes and Questions --- 425
B. Private Filtering of Sexually Explicit Speech ---------------------- 426
  Jonathan Weinberg, Rating the Net ------------------------------ 427
  Notes and Questions --- 433
  Lawrence Lessig, Code and Other Laws of Cyberspace ----------- 435
  Notes and Questions --- 438
C. Filtering Technology and the First Amendment ------------------ 440
  Ashcroft v. American Civil Liberties Union ------------------- 441
  Notes and Questions --- 450
  The Children's Internet Protection Act --------------------------- 452
  United States v. American Library Association, Inc. ----------- 453
  Notes and Questions --- 465
  Pennsylvania Internet Child Pornography Act --------------------- 466
  Center for Democracy and Technology v. Pappert -------------- 468
  Notes and Questions --- 478

Chapter Seven: Problems of Intermediaries ------------------------ 481
  Introduction -- 481
  A. Intermediary Liability for Online Conduct -------------------------- 482
      Ira S. Bushey & Sons, Inc. v. United States ---------------------- 483
      Notes and Questions --- 485
      1. Liability for Defamatory Content ------------------------------ 486
          Cubby, Inc. v. CompuServe, Inc. ---------------------------- 486
          Stratton Oakmont, Inc. v. Prodigy Services Co. ------------- 489
          Notes and Questions --------------------------------------- 491
          Section 230 of the Communications Decency Act -------------- 492
          Zeran v. America Online, Inc. ----------------------------- 494
          Blumenthal v. Drudge -------------------------------------- 500
          Notes and Questions --------------------------------------- 503
          Batzel v. Smith --- 505
          Notes and Questions --------------------------------------- 511
      2. Copyright Liability --- 511
          *Religious Technology Center v. Netcom On-Line
              Communication Services* --------------------------------- 512
          Notes and Questions --------------------------------------- 519
          Section 512 of the Digital Millennium Copyright Act -------- 520
          Notes and Questions --------------------------------------- 525
      3. Trademark Liability --- 527
          Gucci America, Inc. v. Hall & Associates ------------------ 527
          Notes and Questions --------------------------------------- 531
  B. Intermediary Control of Information ------------------------------- 532
      1. Individual Identity and Anonymity ----------------------------- 532
          In re Subpoena Duces Tecum to America Online, Inc. ------- 534
          Doe v. 2TheMart.com Inc. --------------------------------- 537
          Notes and Questions --------------------------------------- 541
          Subsection 512(h) of the Digital Millennium Copyright Act   542
          *Recording Industry Ass'n of Am., Inc. v. Verizon
              Internet Servs., Inc.* ---------------------------------- 543
          Notes and Questions --------------------------------------- 549
          Sony Music Entertainment, Inc. v. Does 1-40 -------------- 550
          Notes and Questions --------------------------------------- 554
          Section 2702 of the Stored Communications Act -------------- 555
          Notes and Questions --------------------------------------- 557
      2. Communications Privacy -- 558

Chapter Eight: Problems of Privacy and Surveillance ---------- 561
  Introduction -- 561
  A. Framing Privacy -- 563
      Daniel J. Solove, Conceptualizing Privacy ------------------------ 563
      Notes and Questions --- 569
      Paul M. Schwartz, Privacy and Democracy in Cyberspace ------ 570
      Julie E. Cohen, Examined Lives: Informational Privacy
          and the Subject as Object ------------------------------------ 572

Notes and Questions -- 574
B. Government Surveillance --------------------------------------- 575
   1. Prospective Acquisition of Contents ------------------------------ 577
     Berger v. New York --- 577
     Notes and Questions -- 579
     Interception of Wire, Oral, and Electronic Communications 579
     Notes and Questions -- 582
   2. Retrospective Acquisition of Stored Communications ------- 583
     United States v. Miller ------------------------------------- 584
     United States v. Barr --------------------------------------- 586
     Notes and Questions -- 589
     Stored Communications and Transactional Records Access 590
     a. What Constitutes an "Interception"? ------------------------ 593
      United States v. Smith ------------------------------------ 593
      Notes and Questions -------------------------------------- 598
      Konop v. Hawaiian Airlines, Inc. -------------------------- 598
      Konop v. Hawaiian Airlines, Inc. -------------------------- 603
     b. What Constitutes "Electronic Storage"? -------------------- 608
      U.S. Department of Justice, Criminal Division,
      Computer Crime and Intellectual Property Section,
      Searching and Seizing Computers and Obtaining
      Electronic Evidence in Criminal Investigations ------------ 608
      Fraser v. Nationwide Mutual Ins. Co. ---------------------- 609
      Theofel v. Farey-Jones ------------------------------------ 611
      Notes and Questions -------------------------------------- 615
   3. Acquisition of Noncontent Information ------------------------- 616
     Smith v. Maryland -- 617
     Notes and Questions -- 621
     Pen Registers and Trap and Trace Devices --------------------- 622
     Notes and Questions -- 624
     *Note on the Customer Records Provisions of the
     Stored Communications Act* ---------------------------------- 624
   4. National Security Investigations ------------------------------- 625
     *United States v. United States District Court for the
     Eastern District of Michigan* -------------------------------- 627
     Notes and Questions -- 632
     Foreign Intelligence Surveillance, Subchapter I,
     Electronic Surveillance -------------------------------------- 632
     Notes and Questions -- 636
     *Note on Acquisition of Stored Communications and
     Non-Content Information in National Security
     Investigations* -- 639
     Doe v. Ashcroft --- 642
     Notes and Questions -- 647
C. Private Acquisition of Communications and Data ------------------ 648
   1. Employer Monitoring -- 648
     Fraser v. Nationwide Mutual Insurance Co. ------------------ 649

Smyth v. Pillsbury Co. ---- 651
Notes and Questions ---- 653
Konop v. Hawaiian Airlines, Inc. ---- 654
Notes and Questions ---- 656
2. Transaction-Based Monitoring: Online Profiling and
the Collection and Use of Personal Data ---- 656
Online Profiling: A Report to Congress ---- 658
Notes and Questions ---- 661
In re DoubleClick Inc. Privacy Litigation ---- 662
Notes and Questions ---- 669
Dwyer v. American Express Co. ---- 670
Notes and Questions ---- 672
Note on the Federal Trade Commission Act and the
Children's Online Privacy Protection Act ---- 672
Notes and Questions ---- 674

Chapter Nine: Problems of Information Enclosure ---- 679
Introduction ---- 679
A. The "Cyberproperty" Controversy ---- 680
Patricia L. Bellia, Defending Cyberproperty ---- 680
B. State Law Claims: Trespass and Contract ---- 686
Ticketmaster Corporation v. Tickets.com, Inc. ---- 687
Register.com, Inc. v. Verio, Inc. ---- 692
Notes and Questions ---- 697
C. The Computer Fraud and Abuse Act ---- 698
United States v. Morris ---- 703
Notes and Questions ---- 706
America Online, Inc. v. LCGM, Inc. ---- 707
Notes and Questions ---- 709
EF Cultural Travel BV v. Explorica, Inc. ---- 709
Notes and Questions ---- 713
D. The Digital Millennium Copyright Act's Anti-Circumvention
and Anti-Trafficking Restrictions ---- 714
Lexmark International, Inc. v. Static Control
Components, Inc. ---- 715
Notes and Questions ---- 723
Davidson & Assoc. v. Jung ---- 724
Notes and Questions ---- 731

Chapter Ten: Problems of Cultural Change ---- 733
Introduction ---- 733
A. Cyberspace as Metaphor ---- 734
Sherry Turkle, Life on the Screen ---- 735
Notes and Questions ---- 739
Alfred C. Yen, Western Frontier or Feudal Society?:
Metaphors and Perceptions of Cyberspace ---- 739
Notes and Questions ---- 745

Jonathan Rosen, The Talmud and the Internet -------------------- 746
Notes and Questions -- 752
B. Cyberspace, Community, and Globalization ------------------------ 753
Paul Schiff Berman, The Globalization of Jurisdiction ---------- 754
Anupam Chander, Whose Republic? --------------------------------- 758
Michele Wilson, Community in the Abstract: A Political
and Ethical Dilemma? -- 762
James Grimmelmann, Virtual Worlds as Comparative Law ---- 765
Notes and Questions -- 775
C. Cyberspace and the Formation of Law and Policy ---------------- 776
Jonathan Zittrain, The Generative Internet ----------------------- 777
Notes and Questions -- 787
David G. Post, Governing Cyberspace ------------------------------- 788
Notes and Questions -- 790
Robert McChesney, So Much for the Magic of Technology
and the Free Market: The World Wide Web and the
Corporate Media System --- 791
Notes and Questions -- 797

INDEX -- 799

Table of Cases

The principal cases are in bold type. Cases cited or discussed in the text are roman type. References are to pages.

1-800 Contacts v. WhenU.com, Inc., 414 F.3d 400 (2d Cir. 2005), 53, 532

A & M Records, Inc. v. Napster, Inc., 239 F.3d 1004 (9th Cir. 2001), **255**

Abrams v. United States, 250 U.S. 616, 630 (1919), 390

Agnello v. United States, 269 U.S. 20 (1925), 203

Aimster Copyright Litigation, In re, 334 F.3d 643 (7th Cir. 2003), 264, 282

Alexander v. United States, 509 U.S. 544 (1993), 476

Allstate Ins. Co. v. Hague, 449 U.S. 302 (1981), 76

ALS Scan v. RemarQ Communities, Inc., 239 F.3d 619 (4th Cir. 2001), 525

ALS Scan, Inc. v. Digital Serv. Consultants, Inc., 293 F.3d 707 (2002), 129, 131, 132

Amalgamated Food Employees Union v. Logan Valley Plaza, Inc., 391 U.S. 308 (1968), **333**, 337-342, 344, 346

America Online v. Superior Court, 108 Cal. Rptr. 2d 699 (2001), 227

America Online, Inc. v. Aol.org, 259 F. Supp. 2d 449 (E.D. Va. 2003), 185

America Online, Inc. v. Huang, 106 F. Supp.2d 848 (E.D. Va. 2000), 177

America Online, Inc. v. LCGM, Inc., 46 F. Supp. 2d 444 (E.D. Va. 1998), **707**

America Online, Inc. v. Pasieka, 870 So.2d 170 (Fl. App. Ct. 2004), 227

America Online, Inc., v. Anonymous Publicly Traded Co., 542 S.E.2d 377 (Va. 2001), 541

American Civil Liberties Union v. Ashcroft, 322 F.3d 240 (3d Cir. 2003), 94

American Civil Liberties Union v. Johnson, 194 F.3d 1149 (10th Cir. 1999), 110

American Civil Liberties Union v. Reno, 217 F.3d 162 (3d Cir. 2000), **85**

American Civil Liberties Union v. Reno, 31 F. Supp. 2d 473 (E.D. Pa. 1999), 441

American Civil Liberties Union v. Reno, 929 F. Supp. 824, 832 (E.D. Pa. 1996), 15, 427, 432

American Libraries Ass'n v. Pataki, 969 F. Supp. 160 (S.D.N.Y. 1997), **88, 98**, 108, 109

American Library Ass'n, Inc. United States v., 539 U.S. 194 (2003), 62, 445, 447, **453**

Amway Corp. v. The Procter & Gamble Co., No. 1:98-CV-726, 2000 WL 33725105 (W.D. Mich. Jan 6, 2000), **125**, 136

Andersen Consulting LLP v. UOP, 991 F. Supp. 1042 (N.D. Ill. 1998), 558

Arden v. Columbia Pictures Indus., Inc., 908 F. Supp. 1248 (S.D.N.Y. 1995), 552

Arista Records v. Sakfield Holding Co., 314 F. Supp. 2d 27 (D.D.C. 2004), 118

Arizona v. Hicks, 480 U.S. 321 (1987), 208

Arkansas Ed. Television Comm'n v. Forbes, 523 U. S. 666 (1998), 455

Armstrong v. United States, 364 U.S. 40 (1960), 352

Ashcroft v. American Civil Liberties Union, 535 U.S. 564 (2002), **89**, 111, 118, 442

Ashcroft v. American Civil Liberties Union, 542 U.S. 656 (2004), 94, **441**

Associated Press v. United States, 326 U.S. 1 (1945), 355, 359, 360

AT & T Techs., Inc. v. Communications Workers of Am., 475 U.S. 643 (1986), 218

Bailey, United States v., (In re Subpoena Duces Tecum), 228 F.3d 341 (4th Cir. 2000), 644

Baker v. General Motors, 522 U.S. 222 (1998), 143

Balsys, United States v., 524 U.S. 666 (1998), 163

Bancroft & Masters Inc. v. Augusta Nat'l Inc., 223 F.3d 1082 (9th Cir. 2000), 128

Bangoura v. Washington Post, 235 D.L.R. (4th) 564 (Ontario Super. Ct. Justice 2004), 97

Barcelona.com Inc. v. Excelentisimo Ayuntamiento de Barcelona, 330 F.3d 617 (4th Cir. 2003), 186

Barona, United States v., 56 F.3d 1087 (9th Cir. 1995), 162

Barr, United States v., , 605 F. Supp. 114 (S.D.N.Y. 1985), **586**

Barrett v. Rosenthal, 9 Cal. Rptr. 3d 142 (Cal. App. 1st Dist. 2004), *review granted*, 12 Cal. Rptr. 3d 48 (2004), 504

Barrett v. Rosenthal,___ Cal. Rptr. 3d ___, 2006 WL 3346218 (Nov. 20, 2006), 504

Barrows, People v., 177 Misc. 2d 712, 677 N.Y.S.2d 672 (N.Y. 1998), 86

Batzel v. Smith, 333 F.3d 1018 (9th Cir. 2003), 504, **505**

Ben Ezra, Weinstein, & Co. v. America Online, 206 F.3d 980 (10th Cir. 2000), 504, 505

Berger v. New York, 388 U.S. 41 (1967), **577**

Berlin Democratic Club v. Rumsfeld, 410 F. Supp. 114 (D.D.C. 1976), 162

Blumenthal v. Drudge, 992 F. Supp. 44 (D.D.C. 1998), **500**

Board of Comm'rs, Wabaunsee Cty. v. Umbehr, 518 U. S. 668 (1996), 457

Board of Educ. v. Pico, 457 U.S. 853 (1982), 58-60, 463, 465

Bohach v. City of Reno, 932 F. Supp. 1232 (D. Nev. 1996), 595, 650

Bolger v. Youngs Drug Products Corp., 463 U.S. 60 (1983), 404, 417

Borse v. Piece Goods Shop, Inc., 963 F.2d 611 (3d Cir. 1992), 652, 653

Bowers v. Baystate Technologies, Inc., 320 F.3d 1317 (Fed. Cir. 2003), 214, 728

Boyd v. United States, 116 U.S. 616 (1886), 206, 585

Branzburg v. Hayes, 408 U.S. 665 (1972), 360

Broadrick v. Oklahoma, 413 U.S. 601 (1973), 396

Brockett v. Spokane Arcades, Inc., 472 U.S. 491 (1985), 424

Brookfield Communications, Inc. v. West Coast Entm't Corp., 174 F.3d 1036 (9th Cir. 1999), **44**

Brown v. Grand Hotel Eden, No. 00 Civ. 7346 (NRB), 2003 WL 21496756 (S.D.N.Y. June 30, 2003), 124

Buckley v. American Const'l Law Found., 525 U.S. 182 (1999), 538

Burger King Corp. v. Rudzewicz, 471 U.S. 462 (1985), 114, 122

Burkholder v. Hutchison, 403 Pa. Super. 498, 589 A.2d 721 (1991), 652

Burnham v. Superior Court of California, 495 U.S. 604 (1990), 175

Butler v. Michigan, 352 U.S. 380 (1957), 392, 403, 405, 422

Cable News Network L.P. v. Cnnews. com, 162 F. Supp. 2d 484 (E.D. Va. 2001), **171**

Cable/Home Communication Corp. v. Network Prods., Inc., 902 F.2d 829 (11th Cir. 1990), 260

Calder v. Jones, 465 U.S. 783 (1984), **115**, 131

California Bankers Assn. v. Shultz, 416 U.S. 21 (1974), 585

California v. Ciraolo, 476 U.S. 207 (1986), 207

California v. Greenwood, 486 U.S. 35 (1988), 582

Campbell v. Acuff-Rose Music, Inc., 510 U.S. 569 (1994), 258, 690

Canda v. Michigan Malleable Iron Co.,124 F. 486 (6th Cir. 1903), 271

Carafano v. Metrosplash.com, Inc., 207 F. Supp. 2d 1055 (C.D. Cal. 2002), 505, 511

Carefirst of Maryland v. Carefirst Pregnancy Centers, 334 F.3d 390, 401 (2003), 133

Carlin Communications, Inc. v. FCC, 837 F.2d 546, cert. denied, 488 U.S. 924 (1988), 402

Carroll v. United States, 267 U.S. 132 (1925), 209

Caterpillar, Inc. v. Miskin Scraper Works, Inc., 256 F. Supp. 2d 849 (C.D. Ill. 2003), 124

CBS v. Democratic National Committee, 412 U.S. 94 (1973), 361

Center for Democracy and Technology v. Pappert, 337 F. Supp. 2d 505 (E.D. Pa. 2004), 98, 111, **468**

Century Communications Corp. v. FCC, 835 F.2d 292 (D.C. Cir. 1987), *clarified*, 837 F.2d 517 (D.C. Cir. 1988), 362

Chamberlain Group, Inc. v. Skylink Technologies, 381 F.3d 1178 (Fed. Cir. 2004), 724

Chance v. Avenue A, 165 F. Supp. 2d 1153 (W.D. Wash. 2001), 670

Chaplinsky v. New Hampshire, 315 U.S. 568 (1942), 397

Cianci v. New Times Publ'g Co., 639 F.2d 54 (2d Cir. 1980), 487

Citron v. Zündel, T.D. 1/02 2002/01/18 (Canadian Human Rights Trib. Jan. 18, 2002), **145**

City of Ladue v. Gilleo, 512 U.S. 43 (1994), 92

Cliffs Notes, Inc. v. Bantam Doubleday Dell Publ'g Group, Inc., 886 F.2d 490 (2d Cir. 1989), 55

Cohen v. California, 403 U.S. 15 (1971), 397, 399, 400

Columbia Ins. Co. v. Seescandy.com, 185 F.R.D. 573 (N.D. Cal. 1999), 538, 539

Commercial Factors Corp. v. Kurtzman Bros., 131 Cal. App. 2d 133 (1955), 218

Community Television of Southern California v. Gottfried, 459 U.S. 498 (1983), 244

CompuServe, Inc. v. Cyber Promotions, Inc., 962 F. Supp. 1015 (S.D. Ohio 1997), 27, 33, 38, 43, 681

Consolidated Cigar Corp. v. Reilly, 218 F.3d 30 (1st Cir. 2000), 110

Consumer Product Safety Comm'n v. GTE Sylvania, Inc., 447 U.S. 102 (1980), 607

Cornelius v. NAACP Legal Defense & Ed. Fund, Inc., 473 U. S. 788 (1985), 455

CoStar v. LoopNet, Inc., 373 F.3d 544 (4th Cir. 2004), 519, 525

Cubby, Inc. v. CompuServe Inc., 776 F. Supp. 135 (S.D.N.Y. 1991), **486**, 490, 498, 503, 511

Cyber Promotions, Inc. v. America Online, 948 F. Supp. 456 (E.D. Pa. 1996), 789

Cybersell, Inc. v. Cybersell, Inc., 130 F.3d 414 (9th Cir. 1997), 126

Cyberspace Communications v. Engler, 55 F. Supp. 2d 737 (E.D. Mich. 1999), 110

Daas, United States v., 198 F.3d 1167 (9th Cir.1999), 655

David White Instruments, LLC v. TLZ, Inc., No. 02 C 7156, 2003 WL 21148224 (N.D. Ill. May 16, 2003), 124

Davidson & Assoc. v. Jung, 422 F.3d 630 (8th Cir. 2005), **724**

Dawson Chemical Co. v. Rohm & Hass Co., 448 U.S. 176 (1980), 241

Dendrite Int'l v. Doe, 775 A.2d 756 (N.J. App. Div. 2001), 541

Denver Area Ed. Telecommunications Consortium, Inc. v. FCC, 518 U.S. 727 (1996), 415

Diageo plc v. Zuccarini, WIPO Case No. D2000-0996 (Oct. 22, 2000), *available at* http://arbiter.wipo.int/domains/decisions/html/2000/d2000-0996.html, 288

Dionisio, United States v., 410 U.S. 1 (1973), 587

DKT Memorial Fund Ltd. v. Agency for Int'l Dev., 887 F.2d 275 (D.C. Cir. 1989), 163

Doe v. 2TheMart.com Inc., 140 F. Supp. 2d 1088 (W.D. Wash. 2001), **537**, 541, 554

Doe v. Ashcroft, 334 F. Supp. 2d 471 (S.D.N.Y. 2004), *vacated on other grounds*, 449 F.3d 415 (2d Cir. 2006), **642**

Doe v. GTE Corp., 347 F.3d 655 (7th Cir. 2003), 504

Doran v. Salem Inn, *Inc.*, 422 U.S. 922, 931 (1975), 443

Dow Jones & Co., Inc. v. Gutnick, HCA 56 (Austl. 2002), 97, 133

Dwyer v. American Express Co., 652 N.E.2d 1351 (Ill. App. Ct. 1995), **670**

Dyer v. Northwest Airlines Corps., 334 F. Supp. 2d 1196 (D.N.D. 2004), 557

eBay v. Bidder's Edge, Inc., 100 F. Supp. 2d 1058 (N.D. Cal. 2000), **23**, 33, 39

Edelman v. N2H2, No. Civ. A.02CV 11503RGS (D. Mass. Apr. 7, 2003), 255

Edgar v. MITE Corp., 457 U.S. 624 (1982), 108

Edmonson v. Leesville Concrete Co., 500 U.S. 614 (1991), 347

EF Cultural Travel BV v. Explorica, Inc., 274 F.3d 577 (1st Cir. 2001), **709**

EF Cultural Travel BV v. Zefer Corp., 318 F.3d 58 (1st Cir. 2003), 713

Ellison v. Robertson, 357 F.3d 1072 (9th Cir. 2004), 526

Erznoznik v. Jacksonville, 422 U.S. 205 (1975), 400, 409

ESAB Group, Inc. v. Centricut, Inc., 126 F.3d 617 (4th Cir. 1997), 131

Euclid v. Ambler Realty Co., 272 U.S. 365 (1926), 398

Evans v. Newton, 382 U.S. 296 (1966), 346

F.M. Corp. v. Corporate Aircraft Mgmt., 626 F. Supp. 1533 (D .Mass. 1985), 320

FCC v. Pacifica Foundation, 438 U.S. 726 (1978), **394**, 402-404, 412-414, 418

Feist Publications v. Rural Tel. Serv. Co., 499 U.S. 340 (1991), 689

Felten v. Recording Industry Ass'n of Am., No. 01 CV 2669 (D.N.J. Nov. 28, 2001), 255

Fleetboston Fin. Corp. v. Fleetbostonfinancial.com, 138 F. Supp. 2d 121 (D. Mass. 2001), 174

Fonovisa, Inc. v. Cherry Auction, Inc., 847 F. Supp. 1492 (E.D. Cal. 1994), 260, 262, 516, 529

Fort Wayne Books, Inc. v. Indiana, 489 U.S. 46 (1989), 476

Franks & Son v. Washington, 966 P.2d 1232 (Wash. 1998), 106

Fraser v. Nationwide Mutual Ins. Co., 135 F. Supp. 2d 623 (E.D. Pa. 2001), *rev'd on other grounds*, 352 F.3d 107 (3rd Cir.

2003), **609**, 612

Fraser v. Nationwide Mutual Ins. Co., 352 F.3d 107 (3d Cir. 2003), **649**

Freedman v. America Online, Inc., 329 F. Supp. 2d 745 (E.D. Va. 2004), 558

Freedman v. Maryland, 380 U.S. 51, 58 (1965), 476

Garrison v. Louisiana, 379 U.S. 64 (1964), 355

GeoCities, In the Matter of, FTC Docket No. C-3850 (1999), 673

Gershwin Publ'g Corp. v. Columbia Artists Mgmt., Inc., 443 F.2d 1159 (2d Cir. 1971), 260, 515, 516

Gibbons v. Ogden, 9 Wheat. 1 (1824), 99

Gimbel v. Federal Deposit Ins. Corp. (In re Gimbel), 77 F.3d 593 (2d Cir. 1996), 644

Ginsberg v. New York, 390 U.S. 629 (1968), **391**, 398, 403, 412, 418, 422, 424, 425, 435, 436

GlobalSantaFe Corp. v. Globalsantafe. com, 250 F. Supp. 2d 610 (E.D. Va. 2003), **175**

Goldman v. United States, 316 U.S. 129 (1942), 202, 203

Gorman v. Ameritrade Holding Corp., 293 F.3d 506 (D.C. Cir. 2002), 123

Gorshkov, United States v., 2001 WL 1024026 (W.D. Wash., May 23, 2001), 163, 165

Green v. America Online, 318 F.3d 465 (3d Cir. 2003), 504

Gucci America, Inc. v. Hall & Associates, 135 F. Supp. 2d 409 (S.D.N.Y. 2001), **527**

Hale v. Henkel, 201 U.S. 43 (1906), 587

Hamling v. United States, 418 U.S. 87 (1974), 88

Handelsblatt v. Paperboy, Federal Supreme Court of Germany (Bundesgerichtshof), 698

Hanson v. Denckla, 357 U.S. 235 (1958), 114, 120

Hard Rock Cafe Licensing Corp. v. Concession Servs., Inc., 955 F.2d 1143 (7th Cir. 1992), 529

Harrods Ltd. v. Sixty Internet Domain Names, 302 F.3d 214 (4th Cir. 2002), 175

Hendrickson v. Amazon.com, Inc., 298 F. Supp. 2d 914 (C.D. Cal. 2003), 526

Henry v. A.B. Dick Co., 224 U.S. 1 (1912), overruled on other grounds, Motion Picture Patents Co. v. Universal Film Mfg. Co., 243 U.S. 502 (1917), 241

Henry v. Pittsburgh & Lake Erie Railroad Co., 139 Pa. 289, 21 A. 157 (1891), 651

Heroes, Inc. v. Heroes Found., 958 F. Supp. 1 (D.D.C. 1996), 118

Hilton v. Guyot, 159 U.S. 113 (1895), 142

Hodge v. Mountain States Tel. & Tel. Co., 555 F.2d 254 (9th Cir. 1977), 619

Hoffa v. United States, 385 U.S. 293 (1966), 584

Holiday Inns v. 800 Reservation, 86 F.3d 619 (6th Cir. 1997), 50

Hudgens v. National Labor Relations Board, 424 U.S. 507 (1976), **343**

Humphrey v. Granite Gate Resorts, Inc., 568 N.W.2d 715 (Minn. 1997), 118

Hustler Magazine v. Falwell, 485 U.S. 46, 53 (1988), 309

Hy Cite Corp. v. Badbusinessbureau.com, 297 F. Supp. 2d 1154 (W.D. Wis. 2004), 125

Illinois Bd. of Elections v. Socialist Workers Party, 440 U.S. 173 (1979), 450

Illinois v. McArthur, 531 U.S. 326 (2001), 165

IMO Indus., Inc. v. Kiekert, AG, 155 F.3d 254 (3d Cir. 1998), 127

In re Charter Communications, Inc., 393 F.3d 771 (8th Cir. 2005), 549

In re DoubleClick Inc. Privacy Litigation, 154 F. Supp. 2d 497 (S.D.N.Y. 2001), 612, **662**

Inquiry into Section 73.1910, In re, 102 F.C.C.2d 143 (1985), 357

INS v. Lopez-Mendoza, 468 U.S. 1032 (1984), 160

Inset Systems, Inc. v. Instruction Set, Inc., 937 F. Supp. 161 (D. Conn. 1996), 118

Instructional Sys., Inc. v. Computer Curriculum Corp., 35 F.3d 813 (3d Cir. 1994), 108

Intel Corporation v. Hamidi, 71 P.3d 296 (Cal. 2003), **30**

Interactive Products Corp. v. a2z Mobile Office Solutions, 326 F.3d 687 (6th Cir. 2003), 57

International Shoe Co. v. Washington, 326 U.S. 310 (1945), 114, 116, 174, 175, 177

International Soc. for Krishna Consciousness, Inc. v. Lee, 505 U.S. 672 (1992), 455

Intuit Privacy Litigation, In re, 138 F. Supp. 2d 1272 (C.D. Cal. 2001), 670

Inwood Labs., Inc. v. Ives Labs., Inc., 456 U.S. 844 (1982), 528

Ira S. Bushey & Sons, Inc. v. United States, 398 F.2d 167 (1968), **483**

J.K. Harris & Co. v. Kassel, 253 F. Supp. 2d 1120 (N.D. Ca. 2003), 56

Jackson v. Metropolitan Edison, 419 U.S. 345 (1974), 347

Jarecki v. G.D. Searle & Co., 367 U.S. 303 (1961), 596

Jefferson County Sch. Dist. No. R-1 v. Moody's Investor's Services, Inc., 175 F.3d 848 (10th Cir. 1999), 309

Jordache Enters., Inc. v. Hogg Wyld, Ltd., 828 F.2d 1482 (10th Cir. 1987), 55

Juda, United States v., 46 F.3d 961 (9th Cir. 1995), 162

Kalem Co. v. Harper Brothers, 222 U.S. 55 (1911), 240

Karo, United States v., 468 U.S. 705 (1984), 208

Katz v. United States, 389 U.S. 347 (1967), **201**, 205, 206, 565, 575, 585, 587, 618, 620, 625

Kelly v. Arriba Soft Corp., 280 F.3d 934 (9th Cir. 2002), 691, 698

Kelly v. Arriba Soft Corp., 336 F.3d 811 (9th Cir. 2003), 697, 698

Konop v. Hawaiian Airlines, Inc., 236 F.3d 1035 (9th Cir. 2001), *withdrawn*, 262 F.3d 972, *superseded*, 302 F.3d 868 (9th Cir. 2002), **598**

Konop v. Hawaiian Airlines, Inc., 302 F.3d 868 (9th Cir. 2002), **603, 654**

Kungys v. United States, 485 U.S. 759 (1988), 596

Kyllo v. United States, 533 U.S. 27 (2001), **205**

L.L. Bean, Inc. v. Drake Publishers, Inc., 811 F.2d 26 (1st Cir. 1987), 55

La Ligue Contre le Racisme et l'Antisémitisme v. Yahoo!, Inc. (Super. Court of Paris, May 22, 2000), **94**, 109

Lebron v. Nat'l R.R. Passenger Corp., 513 U.S. 374 (1995), 348

Lehman v. Shaker Heights, 418 U.S. 298 (1974), 400

Lerman v. Chuckleberry Publishing, Inc., 521 F. Supp. 228 (S.D.N.Y. 1981), 488

Lerman v. Flynt Distributing Co., 745 F.2d 123 (2d Cir. 1984), 488

Lewis v. King, [2004] EWCA Civ 1329 (Eng.), 97, 128

Lexmark Int'l Inc. v. Static Control Components, Inc., 387 F.3d 522 (6th Cir. 2004), **715**, 729

Lloyd Corp. v. Tanner, 407 U.S. 551 (1972), **337**, 344, 345, 351

Lockheed Martin Corp. v. Network Solutions, Inc., 985 F. Supp. 949 (C.D. Cal. 1997), 529, 531

Long, United States v., 64 M.J. 57 (C.A.A.F. 2006), 589

Lorillard Tobacco Co. v. Reilly, 121 S. Ct.

2404 (2001), 111

Los Angeles v. Preferred Communications, Inc., 476 U.S. 488 (1986), 364

Mainstream Loudoun v. Board of Trustees of the Loudoun County Public Library, 2 F. Supp. 2d 783 (E.D. Va. 1998), **57**, 465

Marin Storage & Trucking, Inc. v. Benco Trucking & Eng'g, Inc., 107 Cal. Rptr. 2d 645 (Ct. App. 2001), 219

Maritz v. CyberGold, Inc., 947 F. Supp. 1328 (E.D. Mo. 1996), 117

Marsh v. Alabama, 326 U.S. 501 (1946), **329**, 334, 336-341, 343, 344

Matthew Bender & Co. v. West Publ'g Co., 158 F.3d 693 (2d Cir. 1998), 260

Maxwell, United States v., 45 M.J. 406 (C.A.A.F. 1996), 589

McAvoy v. Shufrin, 401 Mass. 593 (1987), 320

McIntyre v. Ohio Elections Comm'n, 514 U.S. 334 (1995), 532, 535, 538

McVeigh v. Cohen, 983 F. Supp. 215 (D.D.C. 1998), 558

Media3 Technologies, LLC v. Mail Abuse Prevention System, LLC, No. 00-CV-12524-MEL, 2001 WL 92389 (D. Mass. Jan. 2, 2001), **318**

Meese v. Keene, 481 U.S. 465 (1987), 434

Metro-Goldwyn-Mayer Studios Inc. v. Grokster, Ltd., 545 U.S. 913 (2005), **265**

Meyer v. Nebraska, 262 U.S. 390 (1923), 393

Miami Herald Publishing Company v. Tornillo, 418 U.S. 241 (1974), **357**, 364-366, 368-370, 397

Miller v. California, 413 U.S. 15 (1975), 84, 86-88, 91

Miller, United States v., 425 U.S. 435 (1976), **584**, 587, 620

Milliken v. Meyer, 311 U.S. 457 (1940), 116

Mink v. AAAA Dev., L.L.C., 190 F.3d 333 (5th Cir. 1999), 123

Mobil Oil Corp. v. Pegasus Petroleum Corp., 818 F.2d 254 (2d Cir. 1987), 49

Morris, United States v., 928 F.2d 504 (2d Cir. 1991), **703**

Morton Salt Co., United States v., 338 U.S. 632 (1950), 644

Moshe D., In re (Court of Cassation, Italy, Jan. 10, 2001), 96

Munn v. Illinois, 94 U.S. 113 (1877), 346

National Broadcasting Co. v. United States, 319 U.S. 190 (1943), 354, 364

National Cable & Telecommunications Ass'n v. Brand X Internet Services, 545 U.S. 967 (2005), 379

National Endowment for Arts v. Finley, 524 U. S. 569 (1998), 455, 462

National Football League v. TVRadioNow Corp., 53 U.S.P.Q.2d 1831 (W.D. Pa. 2000), 123

NBA Properties v. Untertainment Records LLC, 1999 WL 335147 (S.D.N.Y. May 26, 1999), 531

Near v. Minnesota, 283 U.S. 697 (1931), 477

Nelson v. American-West African Line, 86 F.2d 730 (2d Cir. 1936), 484

New York Tel. Co., United States v., 434 U.S. 159 (1977), 283, 619

New York Times Co. v. Sullivan, 376 U.S. 254 (1964), 360, 373, 530

Noble State Bank v. Haskell, 219 U.S. 104 (1911), 393

Official Airline Guides, Inc. v. Goss, 6 F.3d 1385 (9th Cir. 1993), 48

Olmstead v. United States, 277 U.S. 438 (1928), **198**, 202-204

Online Policy Group v. Diebold, Inc., 337 F. Supp. 2d 1195 (N.D. Cal. 2004), 527

OptInRealBig.com v. IronPort Systems, Inc., 323 F. Supp. 2d 1037 (N.D. Cal. 2004), 511

Osborn v. United States, 385 U.S. 323 (1967), 203

O'Brien, United States v., 391 U.S. 367 (1968), 368, 370, 407, 475

Pacific Gas & Elec. Co. v. Public Util. Comm'n of Cal., 475 U.S. 1 (1986), 368-370

Panavision Int'l L.P. v. Toeppen, 141 F.3d 1316 (9th Cir. 1998), 169

Payton v. New York, 445 U.S. 573 (1980), 208

Pennoyer v. Neff, 95 U.S. 714 (1877), 113

People for the Ethical Treatment of Animals v. Doughney, 263 F.3d 359 (4th Cir. 2001), **54**, 288

Perez v. Brownell, 356 U.S. 44 (1958), 160

Peterson, United States v., 812 F.2d 486 (9th Cir. 1987), 162

Pharmatrak, Inc. Privacy Litigation, In re, 220 F. Supp. 2d 4 (D. Mass. 2002), 670

Pharmatrak, Inc. Privacy Litigation, In re, 329 F.3d 9 (1st Cir. 2003), 670

Phillips Petroleum Co. v. Shutts, 472 U.S. 797 (1985), 76

Pike v. Bruce Church, Inc., 397 U.S. 137 (1970), 102, 106-108, 110

Planned Parenthood Fed'n of Am. v. Bucci, 42 U.S.P.Q.2d 1430 (S.D.N.Y. 1997), 54

Playboy Enterprises, Inc. v. Netscape Communications Corp., 354 F.3d 1020 (9th Cir. 2004), 52

Playboy Entm't Group, Inc., United States v., 529 U.S. 803 (2000), 442, 445, 450, 473, 474

Police Dept. of Chicago v. Mosley, 408 U.S. 92 (1972), 408

Polito v. AOL Time Warner, No. Civ.A. 03CV3218, 2004 WL 3768897 (Ct. Com. Pl. Pa. Jan. 28, 2004), 541

Porsche Cars North Amer., Inc. v. Porsche.net et al., 302 F.3d 248 (4th Cir. 2002), 175

Powell v. Zuckert, 366 F.2d 634 (D.C. Cir. 1966), 162

Prince v. Massachusetts, 321 U.S. 158 (1944), 393

ProCD, Inc. v. Zeidenberg, 86 F.3d 1447 (7th Cir. 1996), **211**, 220, 222

PruneYard Shopping Center v. Robins, 447 U.S. 74 (1980), 351

PSINet, Inc. v. Chapman, 362 F.3d 227 (4th Cir. 2004), 110

Qualitex Co. v. Jacobson Products Co., Inc., 514 U.S. 159 (1995), 48

Quincy Cable TV, Inc. v. FCC, 768 F.2d 1434 (D.C. Cir. 1985), 361

Re, United States v., 313 F. Supp. 442 (S.D.N.Y. 1970), 587

Real Networks, Inc. v. Streambox, Inc., 2000 WL 127311 (W.D. Wash. 2000), 248, 731

Recording Indus. Ass'n of Am. v. Diamond Multimedia Sys., Inc., 180 F.3d 1072 (9th Cir. 1999), 259

Recording Industry Ass'n of Am., Inc. v. Verizon Internet Servs., Inc., 351 F.3d 1229 (D.C. Cir. 2003), **543**, 552

Recording Industry Ass'n of America, Inc. v. Verizon Internet Servs., Inc., 257 F. Supp. 2d 244 (D.D.C. 2003), 552

Red Lion Broadcasting Co. v. FCC, 395 U.S. 367 (1969), **352**, 364, 365

Register.com v. Verio, 356 F.3d 393 (2d Cir. 2004), 221, **692**

Register.com, Inc. v. Verio, Inc., 126 F. Supp. 2d 238 (S.D.N.Y. 2000), 33

Reid v. Covert, 354 U.S. 1 (1957), 159, 161

Religious Technology Ctr. v. Netcom On-line Communication Servs., 923 F. Supp. 1231 (N.D. Cal. 1995), 519

Religious Technology Ctr. v. Netcom On-Line Communication Servs., 907 F. Supp. 1361 (N.D. Cal. 1995), 261, 262, **512**, 528, 529

Reno v. American Civil Liberties Union, 521 U.S. 844 (1997), 5, 60, 61, 85, 88, **409**, 426, 441, 445, 461, 492

Renton v. Playtime Theatres, Inc., 475 U.S. 41 (1986), **406**, 412, 414

Rescuecom Corp. v. Google, Inc., __ F. Supp. 2d __, 2006 WL 2811711 (N.D.N.Y. Sep. 28, 2006), 532

Revell v. Lidov, 317 F.3d 467 (5th Cir. 2002), 123

Reyes, United States v., 922 F. Supp. 818 (S.D.N.Y.1996), 596

Richardson v. Schwarzenegger, [2004] EWHC 2422 (QB) (Eng.), 97

Riley v. National Federation of Blind of N.C., Inc., 487 U.S. 781 (1988), 364, 433

Rosenberger v. Rector and Visitors of Univ. of Va., 515 U. S. 819 (1995), 456

Rossi v. Motion Picture Ass'n of America, No. Civ. 0200239 (D. Hawaii, Apr. 29, 2003), 527

Rust v. Sullivan, 500 U. S. 173 (1991), 458, 461

Sable Comm'ns of Cal. v. FCC, 492 U.S. 115 (1989), 88, 371, **401**, 414, 421, 446

Sante Fe Natural Tobacco Co., Inc. v. Spitzer, 00CIV7274 (LAP) (S.D.N.Y. 2001), 111

Schad v. Mount Ephraim, 452 U.S. 61 (1981), 409

Schaumburg v. Citizens for a Better Environment, 444 U.S. 620 (1980), 403

Schneider v. Amazon.com, 31 P.3d 37 (Wash. App. Div. 1 2001), 511

Sealed Case, In re, 310 F.3d 717 (For. Intell. Surv. Ct. Rev. 2002), 638

Search King, Inc. v. Google Technology, Inc., 2003 WL 21464568 (W.D. Okl. 2003), **308**, 310, 313

Sec. and Exch. Comm'n v. Banner Fund Int'l, 211 F.3d 602 (D.C. Cir. 2000), 184

See v. City of Seattle, 387 U.S. 541 (1967), 644

Sega Enters. v. Accolade, Inc., 977 F.2d 1510 (9th Cir. 1992), 689

Select Theatres Corp. v. Ronzoni Macaroni Corp., 59 U.S.P.Q. 288 (S.D.N.Y. 1943), 517

Shaffer v. Heitner, 433 U.S. 186 (1977), 116, 173-175

Shelley v. Kraemer, 334 U.S. 1 (1948), 143

Silverman v. United States, 365 U.S. 505 (1961), 202, 206, 207

Smith v. Maryland, 442 U.S. 735 (1979), **617**, 621

Smith, United States v., 151 F.3d 1051 (9th Cir. 1998), **593**, 599, 600, 604, 606, 607

Smyth v. Pillsbury, 914 F. Supp. 97 (E.D. Pa. 1996), **651**

Sony Computer Entm't, Inc. v. Connectix

Corp., 203 F.3d 596 (9th Cir. 2000), 689

Sony Corp. of America v. Universal City Studios, Inc., 464 U.S. 417 (1984), **239**, 252, 259-262, 264, 269-272, 275, 276, 278-281, 515

Sony Music Entertainment, Inc. v. Does 1-40, 326 F. Supp. 2d 556 (S.D.N.Y. 2004), **550**

South Dakota v. Dole, 483 U. S. 203 (1987), 454

Southeastern Promotions, Ltd. v. Conrad, 420 U.S. 546 (1975), 87, 414

Specht v. Netscape Comm'ns Corp., 306 F.3d 17 (2d Cir. 2002), **215**, 695, 696

Stanley v. Georgia, 394 U.S. 557 (1969), 399

State of New York v. Network Associates, 758 N.Y.S.2d 466 (N.Y. Sup. Ct. 2003), 214

Step-Saver Data Systems, Inc. v. Wyse Technology, 939 F.2d 91 (3d Cir. 1991), 222

Steve Jackson Games, Inc. v. United States Secret Service, 36 F.3d 457 (5th Cir.1994), 594-596, 599, 601, 603, 604, 612

Stratton Oakmont, Inc. v. Prodigy Services Co., 1995 WL 323710 (N.Y. Sup. Ct. May 24, 1995), **489**, 494, 497, 498, 511

Streifel, United States v., 665 F.2d 414 (2d Cir. 1981), 643

Strick Corp. v. Strickland, 162 F. Supp. 2d 372 (E.D. Pa. 2001), 52

Subpoena Duces Tecum to America Online, Inc., In re, 52 Va. Cir. 26, 2000 WL 1210372 (Va. 2000), **534**, 539, 554

Syracuse Peace Council, 2 F.C.C. Rcd. 5043 (1987), 357

Talley v. California, 362 U.S. 60 (1960), 532

Telco Communications v. An Apple a Day, 977 F. Supp. 404 (E.D. Va. 1997), 118

Theofel v. Farey-Jones, 359 F.3d 1066 (9th Cir. 2004), **611**

Thrifty-Tel, Inc. v. Bezenek, 54 Cal. Rptr. 2d 468 (1996), 26, 31, 32, 40

Ticketmaster Corp. v. Tickets.com, Inc., 2000 WL 1887522 (C.D. Cal. 2000), 33

Ticketmaster Corp. v. Tickets.com, Inc., 2000 WL 525390 (C.D. Cal. 2000), 221, 696

Ticketmaster Corporation v. Tickets. com, Inc., 2003 U.S. Dist. LEXIS 6483 (C.D. Cal. 2003), **687**

Tiede, United States v., 86 F.R.D. 227 (U.S. Ct. Berlin 1979), 162

Toys "R" Us, Inc. v. Step Two, S.A., 318 F.3d 446 (3d Cir. 2003), 128, 133

Turk, United States v., 526 F.2d 654 (5th Cir.1976), 595, 599, 600, 603, 607

Turner Broadcasting Sys., Inc. v. FCC, 516 U.S. 1110 (1996), **373**

Turner Broadcasting Sys., Inc. v. FCC, 910 F.

Supp. 734 (D.D.C. 1995), 372

Turner Broadcasting System, Inc. v. FCC, 512 U.S. 622 (1994), 362

United States v. _____ (see opposing party)

United States District Court for the Eastern District of Michigan, United States v., 407 U.S. 297 (1972), **627**

Universal City Studios, Inc. v. Corley, 273 F.3d 429 (2d Cir. 2001), 254, 722, 731

Vance v. Universal Amusement Co., 445 U.S. 308 (1980), 477

Vault v. Quaid Software Ltd., 847 F.2d 255 (5th Cir. 1988), 727

Verdugo-Urquidez, United States v., 494 U.S. 259 (1990), 157, 163, 165

Virginia Pharmacy Bd. v. Virginia Citizens Consumer Council, Inc., 425 U.S. 748 (1976), 408

Wal-Mart Stores, Inc. v. wallmart canadasucks.com, Case No. D2000-1104, 6(A) (Nov. 23, 2000), http://arbiter.wipo.int/domains/decisions/html/2000/d2000-1104.html (Perritt, Arb.), 288

Ward v. Rock Against Racism, 491 U.S. 781 (1989), 370

Warden v. Hayden, 387 U.S. 294 (1967), 202, 585

Washington v. Heckel, 24 P.3d. 404 (Wash. 2001), **104**, 109, 110

Watchtower Bible & Tract Soc. of N. Y., Inc. v. Village of Stratton, 536 U.S. 150 (2002), 461

Wesley College v. Pitts, 974 F. Supp. 375 (D. Del. 1997), 595

Windsor Mills, Inc. v. Collins & Aikman Corp., 25 Cal. App. 3d 987 (1972), 218, 219

Wong Sun v. United States, 371 U.S. 471 (1963), 203

World Wrestling Fed'n v. Posters, Inc., 2000 WL 1409831 (N.D. Ill. Sept. 26, 2000), 531

World-Wide Volkswagen Corp. v. Woodson, 444 U.S. 286 (1980), 114, 121, 122

Yahoo!, Inc. v. La Ligue Contre le Racisme et l'Antisémitisme, 169 F. Supp. 2d 1181 (N.D. Cal. 2001), **138**

Yahoo!, Inc. v. La Ligue Contre le Racisme et l'Antisémitisme, 433 F.3d 1199 (9th Cir. 2006) (en banc), 144

Young v. American Mini Theatres, Inc., 427 U.S. 50 (1976), 407, 408, 414, 757

Young v. New Haven Advocate, 315 F.3d 256 (4th Cir. 2002), **129**, 136

Zeran v. America Online, Inc., 129 F.3d 327 (4th Cir. 1997), **494**, 503

Zippo Mfg. Co. v. Zippo Dot Com, Inc., 952 F. Supp. 1191 (W.D. Pa. 1997), **119**, 122, 124, 126-128, 136

Table of Authorities

If excerpts have been taken, the page numbers appear
in bold; all others are roman.

Abbate, Janet, *Inventing the Internet* (MIT Press 2000), 20

Adler, R., *Reckless Disregard* (1986), 375

Allen, Anita L., *Uneasy Access: Privacy for Women in a Free Society* (1988), 564

American Bar Association, *Achieving Legal and Business Order in Cyberspace: A Report on Global Jurisdiction Issues Created by the Internet* (2000), 133

American Library Ass'n, Inc. v. United States, 201 F. Supp. 2d 401 (E.D. Pa. 2002), 453, 454

Appiah, Kwame Anthony, *Cosmopolitan Patriots*, in *Cosmopolitics: Thinking and Feeling Beyond the Nation* 91 (Pheng Cheah & Bruce Robbins eds., 1998), 757

Baker, C. Edwin, Turner Broadcasting: *Content-Based Regulation of Persons and Presses*, 1994 Sup. Ct. Rev. 57, 372

Barber, Benjamin R., *A Place for Us: How to Make Society Civil and Democracy Strong* (1998), 571

Battelle, John, *How Google and Its Rivals Rewrote the Rules of Business and Transformed Our Culture* (2005), 315

Bell, Tom W., *Escape from Copyright: Market Success vs. Statutory Failure in the Protection of Expressive Works*, 69 U. Cin. L. Rev. 741 (2001), 237

Bell, Tom W., *Fair Use vs. Fared Use: The Impact of Automated Rights Management on Copyright's Fair Use Doctrine*, 76 N.C. L. Rev. 557 (1998), 29, 230, 232

Bell, Tom W., *Free Speech, Strict Scrutiny, and Self-Help: How Technology Upgrades Constitutional Jurisprudence*, 87 Minn. L. Rev. 743 (2003), 451

Bellia, Patricia L., *Chasing Bits Across Borders*, 2001 U. Chi. Legal F. 35, 149, 166

Bellia, Patricia L., *Spyware and the Limits of Surveillance Law*, 20 Berkeley Tech. L.J. 1283 (2005), 608, 670

Bellia, Patricia L., *Surveillance Law Through Cyberlaw's Lens*, 72 Geo. Wash. L. Rev. 1375 (2004), 582

Bellia, Patricia L, *Defending Cyberproperty*, 79 N.Y.U. L. Rev. 2164 (2004) 699, 714

Bellia, Patricia L, *The "Lone Wolf" Amendment and the Future of Foreign Intelligence Surveillance Law*, 50 Vill. L. Rev. 425 (2005), 636, 638

Benkler, Yochai, *Free as the Air to Common Use: First Amendment Constraints on Enclosure of the Public Domain*, 74 N.Y.U. L. Rev. 354 (1999), 724

Benkler, Yochai, *Net Regulation: Taking Stock and Looking Forward*, 71 U. Colo. L. Rev. 1203 (2000), 289

Berman, Paul Schiff, *Cyberspace and the "State Action" Debate: The Cultural Value of Applying Constitutional Norms to "Private" Regulation*, 71 U. Colo. L. Rev. 1263 (2000), 348

Berman, Paul Schiff, *The Globalization of Jurisdiction*, 31 U. Pa. L. Rev. 311 (2002), 134, 754

Bloustein, Edward J., *Privacy as an Aspect of Human Dignity: An Answer to Dean Prosser*, 39 N.Y.U. L. Rev. 962 (1964), 566

Borchers, Patrick J., *Internet Libel: The Consequences of a Non-Rule Approach to Personal Jurisdiction*, 98 Nw. U. L. Rev. 473 (2004), 123

Boyle, James, *Foucault in Cyberspace: Surveillance, Sovereignty, and Hardwired Censors*, 66 U. Cin. L. Rev. 177 (1997), 451

Boyle, James, *Shamans, Software, and Spleens: Law and the Construction of the Information Society* (1996), 733

Burk, Dan L. & Julie E. Cohen, *Fair Use*

Infrastructure for Rights Management Systems, 15 Harv. J.L. & Tech. 41 (2001), **231**

Burk, Dan L., *Federalism in Cyberspace,* 28 Conn. L. Rev. 1095 (1996), 111

Burk, Dan L., *The Trouble with Trespass,* 4 J. Small & Emerging Bus. L. 27 (2000), 29, 42

Calabresi, Guido, The Decision for Accidents: An Approach to Non-fault Allocation of Costs, 78 Harv. L. Rev. 713 (1965), 484

Cardozo, Benjamin, *The Nature of the Judicial Process* (1921), 42

Carr, James G. & Patricia L. Bellia, *The Law of Electronic Surveillance* (West Group 2005), 557

Cerf, Vinton G., *Computer Networking: Global Infrastructure for the 21st Century, at* http://www.isoc.org/internet/infrastructure /, 20

Chander, Anupam, *Whose Republic?,* 69 U. Chi. L. Rev. 1479 (2002), 440, **758**

Coase, Ronald H., *The Institutional Structure of Production, in* Coase, *Essays on Economics and Economists* (1994), 233

Cohen, Julie E., *A Right To Read Anonymously: A Closer Look at "Copyright Management" in Cyberspace,* 28 Conn. L. Rev. 981 (1996), 237

Cohen, Julie E., *Examined Lives: Informational Privacy and the Subject as Object,* 52 Stan. L. Rev. 1373 (2000), **562,** 572, 677

Cohen, Julie E., Lochner *in Cyberspace: The New Economic Orthodoxy of "Rights Management"*, 97 Mich. L. Rev. 462 (1998), 29, **234**

Cooley, Thomas M., *Law of Torts* (2d ed. 1888), 563

Crawford, Susan P., *The Ambulance, the Squad Car, & the Internet,* 21 Berkeley Tech. L.J. 873 (2006), 283

Davison, Ruth, *Privacy and the Limits of Law,* 89 Yale L.J. 421 (1980), 567

Dinwoodie, Graeme, *Private International Aspects of the Protection of Trademarks* (2001) (WIPO Doc. No. WIPO/PIL/01/4), 170

Doheny-Farina, Stephen, *The Wired Neighborhood* (1996), 571

Easterbrook, Frank H., *Cyberspace and the Law of the Horse,* 1996 U. Chi. Legal F. 207, **2**

Elkin-Koren, Niva, *Let the Crawlers Crawl: On Virtual Gatekeepers and the Right to Exclude Indexing,* 49 J. Copyright Soc'y 165 (2001), 28

Epstein, Richard A., *Cybertrespass,* 70 U. Chi. L. Rev. 73 (2003) 29

Farber, Daniel A., *Book Review, Privacy, Intimacy, and Isolation by Julie C. Inness,* 10 Const. Comment. 510 (1993), 567

Federal Trade Comm'n, *Online Profiling: A Report to Congress, Part 2 (Recommendations)* (July 2000), 674

Federal Trade Comm'n, *Online Profiling: A Report to Congress* (June 2000), **658**

Fiss, Owen M., *Why the State?,* 100 Harv. L. Rev. 781 (1987), **373**

Freiwald, Susan, *Comparative Institutional Analysis in Cyberspace: The Case of Intermediary Liability for Defamation,* 14 Harv. J. L. & Tech. 569 (2001), 494, 504

Freiwald, Susan, *Online Surveillance: Remembering the Lessons of the Wiretap Act,* 56 Ala. L. Rev. 9 (2004), 589, 608, 616

Freund, Paul, *American Law Institute, 52nd Annual Meeting* (1975), 566

Froomkin, A. Michael, *Wrong Turn in Cyberspace, Using ICANN to Route Around the APA and the Constitution,* 50 Duke L.J. 17 (2000), **301**

Galbraith, Christine D., *Access Denied: Improper Use of the Computer Fraud and Abuse Act to Control Information on Publicly Accessible Internet Websites,* 63 Md. L. Rev. 320, 324 (2004), 714

Garth, Bryant G. & Austin Sarat, *Justice and Power in Law and Society Research: On the Contested Careers of Core Concepts, in Justice and Power in Sociolegal Studies* (Bryant G. Garth & Austin Sarat eds., 1997), 733

Geist, Michael, *Fair.com?: An Examination of the Allegations of Systemic Unfairness in the ICANN UDRP,* 27 Brooklyn J. Int'l L. 903 (2002), 187

Geist, Michael, *Is There a There There? Toward Greater Certainty for Internet Jurisdiction,* 16 Berkeley Tech. L.J. 1345 (2001), 128

Giddens, Anthony, *The Consequences of Modernity* (1990), 755

Goldsmith, Jack L. & Alan O. Sykes, *The Internet and the Dormant Commerce Clause,* 110 Yale L.J. 785 (2001), 107, 111

Goldsmith, Jack L., *Against Cyberanarchy,* 65 U. Chi. L. Rev. 1199 (1998), **75,** 77, 80

Goldsmith, Jack L., *The Internet and*

the Abiding Significance of Territorial Sovereignty, 5 Indiana J. Global Legal Stud. 475 (1998), **70**

Goldsmith, Jack L., *The Internet and the Legitimacy of Remote Cross-Border Searches*, 2001 U. Chi. Legal F. 103, **153**

Goldstein, Paul, *Copyright's Highway* (1994), 234

Greenberg, Thomas, *E-Mail and Voice Mail: Employee Privacy and the Federal Wiretap Statute*, 44 Am. U.L.Rev. 219 (1994), 602

Griffiths, Richard T., *History of the Internet, the Internet for Historians, at* http://www.let.leidenuniv.nl/history/ivh/frame_theorie.html, 20

Grimmelmann, James, *Virtual Worlds as Comparative Law*, 2004-05 N.Y. L. Sch. L. Rev. 147, **765**

Gupta, Akhil & James Ferguson, *Culture, Power, Place: Ethnography at the End of an Era,* in *Culture, Power, Place: Explorations in Critical Anthropology* 1 (Akhil Gupta & James Ferguson eds., 1997), 754

Gupta, Akhil, *The Song of the Nonaligned World: Transnational Identities and the Reinscription of Space in Late Capitalism,* in *Culture, Power, Place: Explorations in Critical Anthropology* 179 (Akhil Gupta & James Ferguson eds., 1997), 755

Gurak, Laura J., *Persuasion and Privacy in Cyberspace: The Online Protests over Lotus Marketplace and the Clipper Chip* (1997), 571

Hardy, I. Trotter, *Property (and Copyright) in Cyberspace*, 1996 U. Chi. Legal F. 217, 29

Heller, Michael A., *The Tragedy of the Anticommons: Property in the Transition from Marx to Markets*, 111 Harv. L. Rev. 621 (1998), 29

Horrigan, John B., *Online Communities, Networks That Nurture Long-Distance Relationships and Local Ties* (2001), available at http://www.pewInternet.org/reports/pdfs/PIP_Communities_Report.pdf., 753

Hunter, Dan, *Cyberspace as Place and the Tragedy of the Digital Anticommons*, 91 Cal. L. Rev. 439 (2003), 22

Hunter, Dan, *ICANN and the Concept of Democratic Deficit*, 36 Loy. L.A. L. Rev. 1087 (2003), 307

Hwang, Francis, *Do Domain Names Matter?*, July 25, 2003, http://fhwang.net/writing/do_domain_names_matter.html, 293

Johnson, David R., & David Post, *Law and Borders—The Rise of Law in Cyberspace,* 48 Stan. L. Rev. 1367 (1996), 63, **65**, 70, 73

Kahn, Paul, *The Cultural Study of Law: Reconstructing Legal Scholarship* (1999), 734

Kang, Jerry, *Information Privacy in Cyberspace*, 50 Stan. L. Rev. 1193 (1998), 657

Kaplan, David H., *Territorial Identities and Geographic Scale,* in *Nested Identities: Nationalism, Territory, and Scale* 31 (Guntram H. Herb & David H. Kaplan eds., 1999), 754

Kay, Richard S., *The State Action Doctrine, the Public-Private Distinction, and the Independence of Constitutional Law*, 10 Const. Comment. 329 (1993), 349

Keller, Bruce P., *The Game's the Same: Why Gambling in Cyberspace Violates Federal Law*, 108 Yale L.J. 1569 (1999), 111

Kerr, Orin S., *A User's Guide to the Stored Communications Act, and a Legislator's Guide to Amending It*, 72 Geo. Wash. L. Rev. 1208 (2004), 616

Kerr, Orin S., *Cybercrime's Scope: Interpreting "Access" and "Authorization" in Computer Misuse Statutes*, 78 N.Y.U. L. Rev. 1596 (2003), 714

Kerr, Orin S., *The Fourth Amendment and New Technologies: Constitutional Myths and the Case for Caution*, 102 Mich. L. Rev. 801 (2004), 211

Kleinwoechter, Wolfgang, *From Self-Governance to Public-Private Partnership: The Changing Role of Governments in the Management of the Internet's Core Resources*, 36 Loy. L.A. L. Rev. 1103 (2003), 307

Koren, Niva Elkin, *Copyrights in Cyberspace—Rights Without Laws?*, 73 Chi.-Kent L. Rev. 1155 (1998), 323

Kraakman, Reinier, *Gatekeepers: The Anatomy of a Third-Party Enforcement Strategy*, J. L. & Econ. 53 (1986), 483

Leiner et al., Barry M. *A Brief History of the Internet, at* http://www.isoc.org/internet/history/brief.shtml, 20

Lessig, Lawrence, *Code and Other Laws of Cyberspace* (1999), 195, 232, **435**, 676

Lessig, Lawrence, *Reading the Constitution in Cyberspace*, 45 Emory L.J. 869, 886 (1996), 422, 423

Lessig, Lawrence, *The Law of the Horse: What Cyberlaw Might Teach*, 113 Harv. L. Rev. 501 (1999), **4**

Lessig, Lawrence, *The Spam Wars, In-

dustry Standard (Dec. 31, 1998), **320**

Lewis, Peter H., *Microsoft Backs Ratings System for Internet, N.Y. Times*, Mar. 1, 1996, at D5, 427

Lidsky, Lyrissa Barrett, Silencing John Doe: Defamation and Discourse in Cyberspace, 49 Duke L.J. 855 (2000), 534

Massey, Doreen, *Space, Place, and Gender* (1994), 135

McChesney, Robert, *So Much for the Magic of Technology and the Free Market: The World Wide Web and the Corporate Media System*, in *The World Wide Web and Contemporary Cultural Theory* (Andrew Herman & Thomas Swiss eds., 2000), **791**

McGowan, David, *Website Access: The Case for Consent*, 35 Loy. Chi. L. Rev. 341 (2003) 29

Michel man, Frank, *How Can the People Ever Make the Laws? A Critique of Deliberative Democracy*, in *Deliberative Democracy: Essays on Reason and Politics* 145 (James Bowman & William Rehg eds., 1997), 570

Mulligan, Deirdre K., *Reasonable Expectations in Electronic Communications: A Critical Analysis*, 72 Geo. Wash. L. Rev. 1557 (2004), 560

Murphy, Richard S., *Property Rights in Personal Information: An Economic Defense of Privacy*, 84 Geo. L. Rev. 2381 (1996), 658

National Research Council, *The Internet's Coming of Age* (Nat'l Acad. Press 2001), 20

Negroponte, Nicholas, *Being Digital* (1995), 439

Nimmer on Copyright (1999 Supp.), 252

Nussbaum, Martha C., *Patriotism and Cosmopolitanism,* in Martha C. Nussbaum et al., *For Love of Country: Debating the Limits of Patriotism* 3 (Joshua Cohen ed., 1996), 756, 757

Olsen, Frances E., *The Myth of State Intervention in the Family*, 18 Mich. J.L. Reform 835 (1985), 349

Ong, Aihwa, *Flexible Citizenship: The Cultural Logics of Transnationality* (1999), 758

Orwell, George, *1984* (Penguin Books 1954) (1949), 572

O'Rourke, Maureen A., *Copyright Preemption After the ProCD Case: A Market-Based Approach*, 12 Berkeley Tech. L.J. 53 (1997), 236

Pasquale, Frank, *Rankings, Reduction- ism, and Responsibility*,54 Cleve. St. L. Rev. 115 (2006), **310**

Perritt, Henry H., *Economic and Other Barriers to Electronic Commerce*, 21 U. Pa. J. of Int'l Econ. L. 563, 573 (2000), 128

Posner, Richard A., The Economics of Justice (1981), 564

Posner, Richard A., *The Right of Privacy*, 12 Ga. L. Rev. 393 (1978), 658

Post, David G., *Against "Against Cyberanarchy"*, 17 Berkeley Tech. L.J. 1363 (2002), **77**

Post, David G., *Governing Cyberspace*, 43 Wayne L. Rev. 155 (1997), **788**

Post, David G., *Governing Cyberspace, or Where is James Madison When We Need Him?*, June 1999, available at http://www.temple.edu/lawschool/dpost/icann/comment1.html, **187**

Post, David G., *Of Black Holes and Decentralized Law-Making in Cyberspace*, 2 Vand. J. Ent. L. & Prac. 70 (2000), **322**

Prosser and Keeton, *Torts* (5th ed. 1984), 31

Radin, Margaret J., & R. Polk Wagner, *The Myth of Private Ordering: Rediscovering Legal Realism in Cyberspace*, 73 Chi.-Kent L. Rev. 1295 (1998), 296

Radin, Margaret Jane, & R. Polk Wagner, *The Myth of Private Ordering: Rediscovering Legal Realism in Cyberspace*, 73 Chi.-Kent L. Rev. 1295 (1998), 289

Radin, Margaret Jane, *Regulation by Contract, Regulation by Machine*, 160 J. of Inst'l & Theoretical Econ. 142 (2004), **222**, 228

Redish, Martin H., & Kirk J. Kaludis, *The Right of Expressive Access in First Amendment Theory: Redistributive Values and the Democratic Dilemma*, 93 Nw. U. L. Rev. 1083 (1999), 377

Redman, Jeffrey H., *Privacy, Intimacy, and Personhood,* in Philosophical Dimensions of Privacy 300, 314 (Ferdinand David Schoeman ed., 1984), 566

Reidenberg, Joel R., *Lex Informatica*, 76 Tex. L. Rev. 553 (1998), 232

Reisman, Michael, *Lining Up: The Micro legal System of Queues*, 54 U. Cin. L. Rev. 417 (1985), 326

Reisman, Michael, *Looking, Staring and Glaring: Microlegal Systems and Public Order*, 12 Denv. J. Int'l L. & Pol'y 165 (1983), 326

Reisman, Michael, *Rapping and Talking to*

the Boss: The Microlegal System of Two People Talking, in Conflict and Integration: Comparative Law in the World Today 61 (Institute of Comparative Law in Japan ed., 1988), 326

Restatement (Second) of Torts (1965), 31, 32, 37, 40

Restatement (Third) of the Foreign Relations Law of the United States (1987), 83, 149

Reynolds, Glenn Harlan, Virtual Reality and "Virtual Welters": A Note on the Commerce Clause Implications of Regulating Cyberporn, 82 Va. L. Rev. 535 (1996), 111

Ribstein, Larry, and Bruce Kobayashi, State Regulation of Electronic Commerce, 51 Emory L.J. 1 (2002), 111

Robbins, Bruce, Introduction Part I: Actually Existing Cosmopolitanism, in Cosmopolitics: Thinking and Feeling Beyond the Nation 1 (Pheng Cheah & Bruce Robbins eds., 1998), 756-758

Rosen, Jonathan, The Talmud and the Internet (2000), 746

Rosen, Mark, Exporting the Constitution, 53 Emory L.J. 171 (2004), 143

Rotenberg, Marc, Fair Information Practices and the Architecture of Privacy (What Larry Doesn't Get), 2001 Stan. Tech. L. Rev. 1, 676

Rubenfeld, Jed, The Right of Privacy, 102 Harv. L. Rev. 737 (1989), 567

Salus, Peter, The Net: A Brief History of Origins, 38 Jurimetrics 671 (1998), 20

Samuelson, Pamela, & Suzanne Scotchmer, The Law and Economics of Reverse Engineering, 111 Yale L.J. 1575 (2002), 285, 724

Samuelson, Pamela, Intellectual Property and the Digital Economy: Why the Anti-Circumvention Regulations Need To Be Revised, 14 Berkeley Tech. L.J. 519 (1999), 253

Schwartz, Paul M., Privacy and Democracy in Cyberspace, 52 Vand. L. Rev. 1609 (1999), 570

Shapiro, Andrew J., The Control Revolution (1999), 377

Shuler, Rus, How Does the Internet Work?, at http://www.theshulers.com/whitepapers, 20

Solove, Daniel J., Conceptualizing Privacy, 90 Cal. L. Rev. 1087 (2002), 563

Solove, Daniel J., Digital Dossiers and the Dissipation of Fourth Amendment Privacy, 75 S. Cal. L. Rev. 1083 (2002), 562

Sorkin, Andrew Ross, Software Bullet is Sought to Kill Musical Piracy, New York Times, May 4, 2003, at 1, 237

Stein, Allan R., Personal Jurisdiction and the Internet: Seeing Due Process Through the Lens of Regulatory Precision, 98 Nw. L. Rev. 411 (2004), 124

Stigler, George J., An Introduction to Privacy in Economics and Politics, 9 J. Legal Stud. 623 (1980), 658

Story, Joseph, Commentaries on the Conflict of Laws, Foreign and Domestic (Little, Brown 2d ed 1841), 154

Struve, Catherine T. & R. Polk Wagner, Realspace Sovereigns in Cyberspace: Problems with the Anticybersquatting Consumer Protection Act, 17 Berkeley Tech. L.J. 989 (2002), 170

Struve, Catherine T. & R. Polk Wagner, Realspace Sovereigns in Cyberspace: Problems with the Anticybersquatting Consumer Protection Act, 17 Berkeley Tech. L.J. 989 (2002), 185

Sunstein, Cass R., The First Amendment in Cyberspace, 104 Yale L.J. 1757, 1774 (1995), 372

Sunstein, Cass, Republic.com (2001), 377, 439

Swire, Peter P., Katz is Dead. Long Live Katz, 102 Mich. L. Rev. 904 (2004), 211

Swire, Peter P., The System of Foreign Intelligence Surveillance Law, 72 Geo. Wash. L. Rev. 1306 (2004), 575

Thomson, Judith Jarvis, The Right to Privacy, in Philosophical Dimensions of Privacy: An Anthology 272 (Ferdinand David Schoeman ed., 1984), 658

Tomlinson, John, Globalization and Culture (1999), 755

Tribe, Laurence A., American Constitutional Law (2d ed. 1988), 143

Turkle, Sherry, Life on the Screen (1995), 1, 11, 735

Turner, Frederick Jackson, The Significance of the Frontier in American History, in Report of the American Historical Association for 1893 (1894), reprinted in Frederick Jackson Turner, The Frontier in American History (1st ed. Henry Holt & Co. 1920), 741

U.S. Internet Service Provider Association, Electronic Evidence Compliance—A Guide for Internet Service Providers, 18 Berkeley Tech. L.J. 945 (2003), 640

Wagner, R. Polk, Filters and the First Amendment, 83 Minn. L. Rev. 755 (1999),

434

Wallace, Jonathan, *Why I Will Not Rate My Site* (visited Feb. 7, 1997), http://www. spectacle.org/cda/rate.html#report>, 429

Warner, Richard, *Border Disputes: Trespass to Chattels on the Internet*, 47 Vill. L. Rev. 117 (2002), 29

Warren, Samuel D. & Louis D. Brandeis, *The Right to Privacy*, 4 Harv. L. Rev. 193 (1890), 563

Weinberg, Jonathan, *Rating the Net*, 19 Hastings Comm/Ent L.J. 453 (1997), **427,** 434

Weiser, Philip J., *Internet Governance, Standard Setting, and Self-Regulation*, 28 N. Ky. L. Rev. 822 (2001), **297**

Westin, Alan F., Privacy and Freedom (1967), 565

Weyrauch, Walter Otto, & Maureen Anne Bell, *Autonomous Lawmaking: The Case of the "Gypsies"*, 103 Yale L.J. 323 (1993), 327

Wilson, Michele, *Community in the Abstract: A Political and Ethical Dilemma?*, in *The Cybercultures Reader* (David Bell & Barbara M. Kennedy eds., 2000), **762**

Wriston, Walter, *The Twilight of Sovereignty* (1992), 788

Wu, Tim, *Application-Centered Internet Analysis*, 85 Va. L. Rev. 1163 (1999), 17

Wu, Tim, Why You Should Care About Net Neutrality, Slate, May 1, 2006, *available at* http://www.slate.com/id/2140850/, 386

Yen, Alfred C., *Western Frontier or Feudal Society?: Metaphors and Perceptions of Cyberspace*, 17 Berkeley Tech. L.J. 1207 (2002), **739**

Yoo, Christopher S. & Tim Wu, Keeping the Internet Neutral?, Legal Affairs Debate Club, May 1, 2006, http://www. legalaffairs.org/webexclusive/debateclub_ net-neutrality0506.msp 381

Young, Iris Marion, *The Ideal of Community and the Politics of Difference*, in *Feminism/Postmodernism* 300 (Linda J. Nicholson ed., 1990), 757

Zittrain, Jonathan, *Internet Points of Control*, 44 B.C. L. Rev 653 (2003), 98, 468, 479, 481

Zittrain, Jonathan, *The Generative Internet*, 119 Harv. L. Rev. 1974 (2006), 238, 715, **777**

Chapter One

INTRODUCTION

The emergence of a global network of interconnected computers able to access, store, process, and transmit vast amounts of information in digital form has already altered our cultural landscape and, in the decades to come, may help to transform many of our assumptions about communication, knowledge, invention, information, sovereignty, identity, and community. Inevitably, these tremendous cultural changes bring with them new legal challenges and new legal questions, not only about how law is to be applied to a new technology, but, more fundamentally, about what law is, how it is formed, and its relation to the culture of which it is a part.

It is by now no secret that law students around the country are flocking to courses exploring these sorts of questions. Indeed, nearly every law school now offers some course touching on the Internet, and many schools provide multiple options. One reason for cyberlaw's popularity is obvious: students see an opportunity to learn a body of law that will be necessary for them to understand as they enter legal practice in the 21st century. But another aspect of cyberlaw's importance may not be so apparent: studying cyberspace legal issues forces us to rethink established legal doctrines that many people (professors as well as students) may have taken for granted, and to question some of the premises that underlie our thinking about the law and the way that the law operates.

Cyberlaw, in other words, is not simply a set of legal rules governing online interaction; it is a lens through which broader conceptual debates can be re-examined, challenged, and potentially reconceived. As Sherry Turkle observed in 1995, computers have become our "test objects"[a]—metaphors through which we come to understand reality, and as a result a whole range of classic jurisprudential conundrums might fruitfully be revisited through the prism of cyberlaw.

Because nearly every area of legal activity now involves online interaction in some way, cyberlaw (if it is to be a useful field of study)

---

a. SHERRY TURKLE, LIFE ON THE SCREEN 22 (1995).

cannot simply encompass every legal case or statute that involves online interaction. We believe what is needed is an approach that will identify a set of concerns that runs throughout the various topics that Internet law can cover, a set of principles that can unify the inquiry into such diverse topics as jurisdiction, free speech, computer crime, intellectual property, and privacy, as applied to conduct on the global network.

Accordingly, this casebook has as its explicit aim the synthesis of a coherent field of study by emphasizing the broad conceptual debates that cut across the specific areas of doctrine touched by cyberspace. In addition, we will use the rise of the Internet to encourage you to reconsider various assumptions in traditional legal doctrine. We expect that this dual focus will provide broad-based and sophisticated training in Internet-related legal issues while also helping to shape cyberlaw as a coherent and useful field of study.

We begin by examining our central thesis: in what sense *is* cyberlaw a separate field of study? Why not simply focus on constitutional law, or civil procedure, or contracts, or administrative law, and apply the principles underlying those domains to the problems posed by online communication? What benefit might there be to thinking about so-called cyberlaw issues in an integrated way?

SECTION A. WHY CYBERLAW?

Frank H. Easterbrook,
Cyberspace and the Law of the Horse
1996 U. Chi. Legal F. 207

When he was dean of [the University of Chicago School of Law], Gerhard Casper was proud that the [school] did not offer a course in "The Law of the Horse." He did not mean by this that Illinois specializes in grain rather than livestock. His point, rather, was that "Law and . . ." courses should be limited to subjects that could illuminate the entire law * * * [and] that the best way to learn the law applicable to specialized endeavors is to study general rules. Lots of cases deal with sales of horses; others deal with people kicked by horses; still more deal with the licensing and racing of horses, or with the care veterinarians give to horses, or with prizes at horse shows. Any effort to collect these strands into a course on "The Law of the Horse" is doomed to be shallow and to miss unifying principles. Teaching 100 percent of the cases on people kicked by horses will not convey the law of torts very well. Far better for most students—better, even, for those who plan to go into the horse trade—to take courses in property, torts, commercial transactions, and the like, adding to the diet of horse cases a smattering of transactions in cucumbers, cats, coal, and cribs. Only by putting the law of the horse in the context of broader rules about commercial endeavors could one really understand the law about horses.

Now you can see the meaning of my title. When asked to talk about "Property in Cyberspace," my immediate reaction was, "Isn't this just the law of the horse?" I don't know much about cyberspace; what I do know will be outdated in five years (if not five months!); and my predictions about the direction of change are worthless, making any effort to tailor the law to the subject futile. And if I did know something about computer networks, all I could do in discussing "Property in Cyberspace" would be to isolate the subject from the rest of the law of intellectual property, making the assessment weaker.

This leads directly to my principal conclusion: Develop a sound law of intellectual property, then apply it to computer networks. Problem: we do not know whether many features of existing law are optimal. Why seventeen years for patents, a lifetime plus some for copyrights, and forever for trademarks? Should these rights be strengthened or weakened? Why does copyright have the particular form it does? What sense can one make of the fuzzball factors for fair use? How can one make these rights more precise, and therefore facilitate * * * bargains? Until we have answers to these questions, we cannot issue prescriptions for applications to computer networks.

Cyberspace reduces the effective cost of copying. This continues a trend that began when Gutenberg invented movable type and gave rise to political demand for what has become copyright law. Yet how can we tackle the question whether copying has become too easy, and therefore should be met by countervailing changes, when we have not solved the problems posed by yesterday's technology? Consider the plain-paper photocopier. People can run off scholarly articles. To what extent may researchers copy articles from increasingly expensive journals to create a stockpile for their own future endeavors? This is a question about fair use; yet the fair-use criteria are so ambulatory that no one can give a general answer. * * *

If we are so far behind in matching law to a well-understood technology such as photocopiers—if we have not even managed to create well-defined property rights so that people can adapt their own conduct to maximize total wealth—what chance do we have for a technology such as computers that is mutating faster than the virus in *The Andromeda Strain*?

Well, then, what can we do? By and large, nothing. If you don't know what is best, let people make their own arrangements.

Next after nothing is: keep doing what you have been doing. Most behavior in cyberspace is easy to classify under current property principles. What people freely make available is freely copyable. When people attach strings, they must be respected, and the tough question when someone copies commercial software will be whether the person making copies is a direct infringer or only a contributory infringer, and whether the remedy should be civil damages or time in prison. Lower costs of copying may make violations of the law more attractive, which suggests the allocation of additional prosecutorial resources, but movement along a cost continuum does not call for change in legal substance. * * *

Error in legislation is common, and never more so than when the technology is galloping forward. Let us not struggle to match an imperfect legal system to an evolving world that we understand poorly. Let us instead do what is essential to permit the participants in this evolving world to make their own decisions. That means three things: make rules clear; create property rights where now there are none; and facilitate the formation of bargaining institutions. Then let the world of cyberspace evolve as it will, and enjoy the benefits.

Lawrence Lessig, *The Law of the Horse: What Cyberlaw Might Teach*

113 HARV. L. REV. 501 (1999)

A few years ago, at a conference on the "Law of Cyberspace" held at the University of Chicago, Judge Frank Easterbrook told the assembled listeners, a room packed with "cyberlaw" devotees, * * * that there was no more a "law of cyberspace" than there was a "Law of the Horse"; that the effort to speak as if there were such a law would just muddle rather than clarify; and that legal academics * * * should just stand aside as judges and lawyers and technologists worked through the quotidian problems that this souped-up telephone would present. "Go home," in effect, was Judge Easterbrook's welcome. * * *

Easterbrook's concern is a fair one. Courses in law school, Easterbrook argued, "should be limited to subjects that could illuminate the entire law." "[T]he best way to learn the law applicable to specialized endeavors," he argued, "is to study general rules." This "the law of cyberspace," conceived of as torts in cyberspace, contracts in cyberspace, property in cyberspace, etc., was not.

My claim is to the contrary. I agree that our aim should be courses that "illuminate the entire law," but unlike Easterbrook, I believe that there is an important general point that comes from thinking in particular about how law and cyberspace connect.

This general point is about the limits on law as a regulator and about the techniques for escaping those limits. This escape, both in real space and in cyberspace, comes from recognizing the collection of tools that a society has at hand for affecting constraints upon behavior. Law in its traditional sense—an order backed by a threat directed at primary behavior—is just one of these tools. The general point is that law can affect these other tools—that they constrain behavior themselves, and can function as tools of the law. The choice among tools obviously depends upon their efficacy. But importantly, the choice will also raise a question about values. By working through these examples of law interacting with cyberspace, we will throw into relief a set of general questions about law's regulation outside of cyberspace.

I do not argue that any specialized area of law would produce the same insight. I am not defending the law of the horse. My claim is specific to cyberspace. We see something when we think about the regulation of cyberspace that other areas would not show us. * * *

Consider two cyber-spaces, and the problems that each creates for two different social goals. Both spaces have different problems of "information"—in the first, there is not enough; in the second, too much. Both problems come from a fact about *code*—about the software and hardware that make each cyber-space the way it is. * * * [T]he central regulatory challenge in the context of cyberspace is how to make sense of this effect of code. * * *

1. Zoning Speech.—Porn in real space is zoned from kids. Whether because of laws (banning the sale of porn to minors), or norms (telling us to shun those who do sell porn to minors), or the market (porn costs money), it is hard in real space for kids to buy porn. In the main, not everywhere; hard, not impossible. But on balance the regulations of real space have an effect. That effect keeps kids from porn.

These real-space regulations depend upon certain features in the "design" of real space. It is hard in real space to hide that you are a kid. Age in real space is a self-authenticating fact. Sure—a kid may try to disguise that he is a kid; he may don a mustache or walk on stilts. But costumes are expensive, and not terribly effective. And it is hard to walk on stilts. Ordinarily a kid transmits that he is a kid; ordinarily, the seller of porn knows a kid is a kid, and so the seller of porn, either because of laws or norms, can at least identify underage customers. Self-authentication makes zoning in real space easy.

In cyberspace, age is not similarly self-authenticating. Even if the same laws and norms did apply in cyberspace, and even if the constraints of the market were the same (as they are not), any effort to zone porn in cyberspace would face a very difficult problem. Age is extremely hard to certify. To a website accepting traffic, all requests are equal. There is no simple way for a website to distinguish adults from kids, and, likewise, no easy way for an adult to establish that he is an adult. This *feature* of the space makes zoning speech there costly—so costly, the Supreme Court concluded in *Reno v. ACLU* that the Constitution may prohibit it.

2. Protected Privacy.—If you walked into a store, and the guard at the store recorded your name; if cameras tracked your every step, noting what items you looked at and what items you ignored; if an employee followed you around, calculating the time you spent in any given aisle; if before you could purchase an item you selected, the cashier demanded that you reveal who you were—if any or all of these things happened in real space, you would notice. You would notice and could then make a choice about whether you wanted to shop in such a store. Perhaps the vain enjoy the attention; perhaps the thrifty are attracted by the resulting lower prices. They might have no problem with this data collection regime. But at least you would know. Whatever the reason, whatever the consequent choice, you would know enough in real space to know to make a choice.

In cyberspace, you would not. You would not notice such monitoring because such tracking in cyberspace is not similarly visible. * * * [W]hen you enter a store in cyberspace, the store can record who you are; click monitors (watching what you choose with your mouse) will track where you browse, how long you view a particular page; an "employee" (if only a bot) can follow you around, and when you make a purchase, it can record who you are and from where you came. All this happens in cyberspace—invisibly. Data is collected, but without your knowledge. Thus you cannot (at least not as easily) choose whether you will participate in or consent to this surveillance. In cyberspace, surveillance is not self-authenticating. Nothing reveals whether you are being watched, so there is no real basis upon which to consent.

These examples mirror each other, and present a common pattern. In each, some bit of data is missing, which means that in each, some end cannot be pursued. In the first case, that end is collective (zoning porn); in the second, it is individual (choosing privacy). But in both, it is a feature of cyberspace that interferes with the particular end. And hence in both, law faces a choice—whether to regulate to change this architectural feature, or to leave cyberspace alone and disable this collective or individual goal. Should the law change in response to these differences? Or should the law try to change the features of cyberspace, to make them conform to the law? And if the latter, then what constraints should there be on the law's effort to change cyberspace's "nature"? What principles should govern the law's mucking about with this space? Or, again, how should law *regulate*? * * *

To many this question will seem very odd. Many believe that cyberspace simply cannot be regulated. * * * The anonymity and multi-jurisdictionality of cyberspace makes control by government in cyberspace impossible. The nature of the space makes behavior there *unregulable*.

This belief about cyberspace is wrong, but wrong in an interesting way. It assumes either that the nature of cyberspace is fixed—that its architecture, and the control it enables, cannot be changed—or that government cannot take steps to change this architecture.

Neither assumption is correct. Cyberspace has no nature; it has no particular architecture that cannot be changed. Its architecture is a function of its design—or * * * its code. This code can change, either because it evolves in a different way, or because government or business pushes it to evolve in a particular way. And while particular versions of cyberspace do resist effective regulation, it does not follow that every version of cyberspace does so as well. Or alternatively, there are versions of cyberspace where behavior can be regulated, and the government can take steps to increase this regulability.

To see just how, we should think more broadly about the question of regulation. What does it mean to say that someone is "regulated"? How is that regulation achieved? * * *

Behavior, we might say, is regulated by four kinds of constraints. Law is just one of those constraints. Law (in at least one of its aspects) orders people to behave in certain ways; it threatens punishment if they do not obey. The law tells me not to buy certain drugs, not to sell cigarettes without a license, and not to trade across international borders without first filing a customs form. It promises strict punishments if these orders are not followed. In this way, we say that law regulates.

But not only law regulates in this sense. Social norms do as well. Norms control where I can smoke; they affect how I behave with members of the opposite sex; they limit what I may wear; they influence whether I will pay my taxes. Like law, norms regulate by threatening punishment ex post. But unlike law, the punishments of norms are not centralized. Norms are enforced (if at all) by a community, not by a government. In this way, norms constrain, and therefore regulate.

Markets, too, regulate. They regulate by price. The price of gasoline limits the amount one drives—more so in Europe than in the United States. The price of subway tickets affects the use of public transportation—more so in Europe than in the United States. Of course the market is able to constrain in this manner only because of other constraints of law and social norms: property and contract law govern markets; markets operate within the domain permitted by social norms. But given these norms, and given this law, the market presents another set of constraints on individual and collective behavior.

And finally, there is a fourth feature of real space that regulates behavior—"architecture." By "architecture" I mean the physical world as we find it, even if *"as we find it"* is simply *how it has already been made.* That a highway divides two neighborhoods limits the extent to which the neighborhoods integrate. That a town has a square, easily accessible with a diversity of shops, increases the integration of residents in that town. That Paris has large boulevards limits the ability of revolutionaries to protest. That the Constitutional Court in Germany is in Karlsruhe, while the capital is in Berlin, limits the influence of one branch of government over the other. These constraints function in a way that shapes behavior. In this way, they too regulate.

These four modalities regulate together. The "net regulation" of any particular policy is the sum of the regulatory effects of the four modalities together. A policy trades off among these four regulatory tools. It selects its tool depending upon what works best.

So understood, this model describes the regulation of cyberspace as well. There, too, we can describe four modalities of constraint.

Law regulates behavior in cyberspace—copyright, defamation, and obscenity law all continue to threaten ex post sanctions for violations. How efficiently law regulates behavior in cyberspace is a separate question—in some cases it does so more efficiently, in others not. Better or not, law continues to threaten an expected return. Legislatures enact, prosecutors threaten, courts convict.

Norms regulate behavior in cyberspace as well: talk about democratic politics in the alt.knitting newsgroup, and you open yourself up to "flaming" (an angry, text-based response). "Spoof" another's identity in a "MUD" (a text-based virtual reality), and you may find yourself "toadied" (your character removed). Talk too much on a discussion list, and you are likely to wind up on a common "bozo" filter (blocking messages from you). In each case norms constrain behavior, and, as in real space, the threat of ex post (but decentralized) sanctions enforce these norms.

Markets regulate behavior in cyberspace too. Prices structures often constrain access, and if they do not, then busy signals do. (America Online (AOL) learned this lesson when it shifted from an hourly to a flat-rate pricing plan.) Some sites on the web charge for access, as on-line services like AOL have for some time. Advertisers reward popular sites; on-line services drop unpopular forums. These behaviors are all a function of market constraints and market opportunity, and they all reflect the regulatory role of the market.

And finally the architecture of cyberspace, or its *code*, regulates behavior in cyberspace. The code, or the software and hardware that make cyberspace the way it is, constitutes a set of constraints on how one can behave. The substance of these constraints varies—cyberspace is not one place. But what distinguishes the architectural constraints from other constraints is how they are experienced. As with the constraints of architecture in real space—railroad tracks that divide neighborhoods, bridges that block the access of buses, constitutional courts located miles from the seat of the government—they are experienced as conditions on one's access to areas of cyberspace. The conditions, however, are different. In some places, one must enter a password before one gains access; in other places, one can enter whether identified or not. In some places, the transactions that one engages in produce traces, or "mouse droppings," that link the transactions back to the individual; in other places, this link is achieved only if the individual consents. In some places, one can elect to speak a language that only the recipient can understand (through encryption); in other places, encryption is not an option. Code sets these features; they are features selected by code writers; they constrain some behavior (for example, electronic eavesdropping) by making other behavior possible (encryption). They embed certain values, or they make the realization of certain values impossible. In this sense, these features of cyberspace also regulate, just as architecture in real space regulates.

These four constraints—both in real space and in cyberspace—operate together. For any given policy, their interaction may be cooperative, or competitive. Thus, to understand how a regulation might succeed, we must view these four modalities as acting on the same field, and understand how they interact.

The two problems from the beginning of this section are a simple example of this point:

(a) Zoning Speech.—If there is a problem zoning speech in cyberspace, it is a problem traceable (at least in part) to a difference in the architecture of that place. In real space, age is (relatively) self-authenticating. In cyberspace, it is not. The basic architecture of cyberspace permits users' attributes to remain invisible. So norms, or laws, that turn upon a consumer's age are more difficult to enforce in cyberspace. Law and norms are disabled by this different architecture.

(b) Protecting Privacy.—A similar story can be told about the "problem" of privacy in cyberspace. Real-space architecture makes surveillance generally self-authenticating. Ordinarily, we can notice if we are being followed, or if data from an identity card is being collected. Knowing this enables us to decline giving information if we do not want that information known. Thus, real space interferes with non-consensual collection of data. Hiding that one is spying is relatively hard.

The architecture of cyberspace does not similarly flush out the spy. We wander through cyberspace, unaware of the technologies that gather and track our behavior. We cannot function in life if we assume that everywhere we go such information is collected. Collection practices differ, depending on the site and its objectives. To consent to being tracked, we must know that data is being collected. But the architecture disables (relative to real space) our ability to know when we are being monitored, and to take steps to limit that monitoring. * * *

I noted earlier the general perception that cyberspace was unregulable—that its nature made it so and that this nature was fixed. I argued that whether cyberspace can be regulated is not a function of Nature. It depends, instead, upon its architecture, or its code. Its regulability, that is, is a function of its design. There are designs where behavior within the Net is beyond government's reach; and there are designs where behavior within the Net is fully within government's reach. My claim * * * is that government can take steps to alter the Internet's design. It can take steps, that is, to affect the regulability of the Internet. * * *

[R]egulability * * * depends upon the architecture of the space, and * * * this architecture can be changed. The code of cyberspace might disable government choice, but the code can disable individual choice as well. There is no natural and general alignment between bottom-up regulation and the existing architecture of the Internet. Enabling *individual* choice may require collective modification of the architecture of cyberspace, just as enabling *collective* choice may require modification of this architecture. The architecture of cyberspace is neutral; it can enable or disable either kind of choice. The choice about which to enable, however, is not in any sense neutral. * * *

[A]rchitectures of cyberspace can enable or disable the values implicit in law; law, acting on architectures in cyberspace, can enable or disable the values implicit in code. As one displaces the other, a competition could develop. Authors of code might develop code that displaces law; authors of law might respond with law that displaces code.

East Coast Code (written in Washington, published in the U.S. Code) can thus compete with West Coast Code (written in Silicon Valley, or Redmond, published in bits burned in plastic). Likewise authors of East Coast Code can cooperate with authors of West Coast Code. It is not clear which code one should fear more. The conflict displaces values in both spheres, but cooperation threatens values as well. * * *

This conflict between code and law should push us to consider principle. We should think again about the values that should guide, or constrain, this conflict between authorities. * * * [C]yberspace is not inherently unregulable; * * * its regulability is a function of its design. Some designs make behavior more refutable; others make behavior less regulable. Government * * * can influence the design of cyberspace in ways that enhance government's ability to regulate. * * *

Judge Easterbrook argued that there was no reason to teach the "law of cyberspace," any more than there was reason to teach the "law of the horse," because neither, he suggested, would "illuminate the entire law." This essay has been a respectful disagreement. The threats to values implicit in the law—threats raised by changes in the architecture of code—are just particular examples of a more general point: that more than law alone enables legal values, and law alone cannot guarantee them. If our objective is a world constituted by these values, then it is as much these other regulators—code, but also norms and the market—that must be addressed. Cyberspace makes plain not just how this interaction takes place, but also the urgency of understanding how to affect it.

Notes and Questions

1. Why does Judge Easterbrook believe that cyberlaw is not a distinct field of study? Why does he think courses in torts or property are more appropriate?

2. Judge Easterbrook argues that law does a poor job adjusting to changes in technology. While it is certainly true that such changes often raise difficult questions, what is the appropriate response for judges and legislators? Should they get out of the way, as Judge Easterbrook suggests, and "let the world of cyberspace evolve as it will"? What are the consequences of such a choice? Are the consequences different in cyberspace than in other areas of law?

3. Why *didn't* the University of Chicago Law School offer a course in the "Law of the Horse," anyway? Thirty or forty years ago, few law schools recognized "family law," or "elder law," or "environmental law" as valid sub-fields worthy of study, yet most do now. Is "cyberspace law" more like family law or the "law of the horse"?

4. What does Lessig mean when he talks of "East Coast Code" and "West Coast Code?" What is the relationship between "code" and law?

5. Think about the two examples cited by Lessig: controlling indecent material and protecting privacy. How might altering "code" affect these problems in the online environment? What might Judge Easterbrook think of using code to "solve" online problems?

6. What role should government play in influencing the "code" of cyberspace? What role *can* it play? Lessig declares his disagreement with those who believe that cyberspace cannot be regulated by territorial sovereign governments; we will explore these questions when we discuss problems of geography and sovereignty in Chapter Three.

7. In what ways might cyberspace not only permit us to revisit problems of jurisprudence, but also cause us to change our concepts of self and community? Consider the following excerpt:

> Writing in his diary in 1832, Ralph Waldo Emerson reflected that "Dreams and beasts are two keys by which we are to find out the secrets of our nature . . . they are our test objects." Emerson was prescient. Freud and his heirs would insist that we measure human nature against nature itself—the world of the beasts seen as our forbears and kin. If Emerson had lived at the end of the twentieth century, he would surely have seen the computer as a new test object. Like dreams and beasts, the computer stands on the margins. It is a mind that is not yet a mind. It is inanimate yet interactive. It does not think, yet neither is it external to thought. It is an object, ultimately a mechanism, but it behaves, interacts, and seems in a certain sense to know. It confronts us with an uneasy sense of kinship. After all, we too behave, interact, and seem to know, and yet are ultimately made of matter and programmed DNA. We think we can think. But can *it* think? Could it have the capacity to feel? Could it ever be said to be alive? * * * The computer is an evocative object that causes old boundaries to be renegotiated.

SHERRY TURKLE, LIFE ON THE SCREEN 22 (1995).

What does Professor Turkle mean when she refers to computers as "test objects"? Can you think of ways in which the pervasiveness of the computer, the common reference to virtual realities such as "desktops" or "folders" on a screen, and the use of various forms of online interaction (e-mail, web-based communities, hypertext linking, multi-player games and virtual worlds, etc.) might change the way we think of ourselves and the world? For example, if we become used to interacting with simulated objects and with manipulating multiple screens at once, does that change our conceptions of what makes something "real," or what distinguishes human beings from computers, or what makes a self coherent? If we are used to linking from one website to another, picking and choosing bits of information to read, does that change our sense of whether ideas are linear or whether individual authorship is possible, or whether ownership of intellectual property is sensible? If we daily interact by e-mail or in virtual communities, does that change our conception of distance or the importance of territorial boundaries or geographically based communities? Can you think of any other long-term cultural effects of the information age that might usefully be viewed through the lens of cyberlaw?

SECTION B. OUR APPROACH

We believe that cyberspace presents us with an opportunity to view general problems of policy, jurisprudence, and culture in a new and useful way. We will not, therefore, approach online legal issues along traditional doctrinal lines—First Amendment, jurisdiction, copyright, contracts, and so on—for to do so would presuppose precisely what we intend to question: that traditional doctrinal approaches map neatly and simply onto online phenomena. Instead, we have organized the material that follows according to a set of conceptual issues that extends across the spectrum of cyberspace legal dilemmas. This approach is meant both to illuminate the legal conundrums posed by online activity and to encourage you to explore more general topics such as: the role of analogy in developing legal rules for new social contexts such as the rise of cyberspace; the difficulties territorially based sovereign entities face in attempting to regulate *any* online activity, whether it involves gambling, or the transmission of sexually explicit material, or the distribution of copyrighted material, or the like; the possibility of alternative models of Internet governance; the ways in which law and technological architecture conflict with, or reinforce, each other as regulatory tools; the role played by the competing rhetorics of anarchy and control in debates about online regulation; the rise of so-called "private ordering" approaches to the creation of law and social norms; the complicated position of "intermediaries" (such as Internet service providers) within regulatory regimes, and many others. While all of the "traditional" subject matter areas of cyberlaw will be addressed, they will be placed in a new framework—one that asks you to consider what it is that cyberlaw has to teach us about law more generally.

In addition, this casebook will focus on the way legal and cultural norms interact and shape one another. Most casebooks study the role of law solely as a mechanism for resolving disputes, or meting out punishment, or creating incentives, or regulating behavior. This view emphasizes the instrumental role of law; that is, the role of law as a rational effort to *do* something to affect society. But that is not all there is to law. Law is also a discourse for conceptualizing reality, or, as anthropologist Clifford Geertz put it, a way of "imagining the real,"[b] a mechanism through which we construct meaning from the world around us. It is a "complex of characterizations and imaginings, stories about events cast in imagery about principles."[c] These stories provide a framework to interpret what we experience and a language for describing reality.

Because law does not exist in a vacuum, any particular cyberlaw regime will inevitably have tremendous impact on the distribution of power

---

b. Clifford Geertz, *Local Knowledge: Fact and Law in Comparative Perspective, in* LOCAL KNOWLEDGE: FURTHER ESSAYS IN INTERPRETIVE ANTHROPOLOGY 167, 173 (1983).

c. *Id.* at 215.

in society as a whole, our understanding of terms such as free speech, intellectual property, and jurisdiction, as well as our fundamental conceptions of how behavior is regulated both online and off. Thus, this casebook will provide not simply an introduction to legal issues involving online interaction, but a chance to consider and challenge core ideas about the role of law more generally. Finally, because we must try to understand the *cultural* significance of cyberspace in all its variety before we impose any single *legal* category on the experience of being "online," we will devote a chapter to the psychological, social, and political ramifications of cyberspace.

In order to structure your thinking, you may wish to consider five fundamental questions that will recur throughout the book:

- Does the rise of a global network present a new paradigm that requires a completely different way of thinking about law, or is it just a matter of adapting current legal categories to new technology?

- Is it best to allow law in cyberspace to evolve internally, through indigenous legal regimes, or must a uniform regime be imposed from outside? And is it even possible for cyberspace to have an "internal" legal regime totally divorced from more traditional "outside" legal systems?

- To what extent will regulation in cyberspace be accomplished through its technical architecture, and to what extent does this form of regulation affect how we develop policy on cyberspace issues?

- In what ways does the rise of online interaction alter the balance of power among individuals, corporations, and government, and how should our choice of legal regime be influenced by these changes?

- How does thinking about cyberspace legal issues help illuminate more general issues of policy and jurisprudence?

SECTION C. INTERNET BASICS

Professor Lessig suggests that "technical" questions and "legal" questions—questions about "code" and questions about "law"—will interact in complex ways, and may often substantially overlap, in cyberspace. While one does not have to be a systems engineer to understand and analyze the legal issues posed by online interaction, some understanding of the underlying technologies will be useful; even Judge Easterbrook, we suspect, would agree that one has to know *something* about how cyberspace is constituted in order to apply the "general principles" to which he refers in the online context, just as a knowledge of horse behavior or anatomy would be useful in order to apply the general principle, say, of "reasonable care" to the horse owner.

The Internet, as most people know by now, is not a physical entity but rather a network of networks—an inter-network, a set of communications links and communications rules (known as "protocols") allowing computer networks to exchange information with one another. It is only one of many thousands of such inter-networks out there; numerous businesses, for example, operate private inter-networks linking their remote office or retail locations together. The Internet had its origins in 1969 as an experimental networking project supported and managed by the Advanced Research Project Agency ("ARPA") of the U.S. Department of Defense. Known then as the "ARPANET," it linked together computers and computer networks owned by the military, defense contractors, and university laboratories conducting defense-related research. On January 1, 1983, the networks comprising the ARPANET—then numbering under one thousand—switched over to the TCP/IP protocol suite ("Transmission Control Protocol/Internet Protocol") to manage network communications, and the network that was to become "the Internet" was born. By 2006, the TCP/IP network had over 400 million individual "hosts"—computers, or computer networks, capable of exchanging messages with one another.

What made the TCP/IP inter-network so successful? Why did *this* particular set of networking protocols spawn "the Internet," *i.e.,* the vast, global communications medium? "Much of the answer," the National Research Council wrote in a recent study,

> lies in the combination of two factors: functionality and lower costs. The new functionality stems from the Internet's unique design principles and features that make connection, interconnection, and innovation in both facilities and services relatively easy. The Internet's characteristics have also made it possible to use the underlying communications infrastructure more efficiently, thereby setting a lower price point for the communications it enables.

NATIONAL RESEARCH COUNCIL, THE INTERNET'S COMING OF AGE 34 (Nat'l Acad. Press 2001).

Although the technical architecture of the Internet is always subject to change, it is worth reflecting on what aspects of the Internet's design have made it particularly useful as a communications medium. Such "unique design principles and features" may or may not be considered part of the Internet's "nature," but to the extent that we acknowledge how successful the Internet has been, we might at least want to think twice before disabling fundamental features about the Internet that have fueled its growth. Some of those design features are:

A. *Decentralized Control.* Unlike many other networks (most office LANs and university networks, for instance), TCP/IP networks like the Internet have no central "server" responsible for managing network traffic and seeing to it that messages reach their intended destinations. Instead, messages make their way from one network host to another by traversing the network one "hop" at a time:

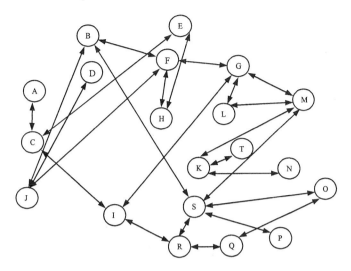

A message from Network A—say, in Austin, Texas—can thus take any one of a large number of alternate paths to reach its destination at Network P (Paris, France); it might travel via routers in Atlanta, Philadelphia, Newfoundland, and Stockholm before reaching its destination, or, alternatively, if that path were for some reason unavailable, via Chicago, Denver, Mexico City, Mumbai, and Brussels. This feature—known to the engineers as *redundancy*—allows the Internet to continue to function notwithstanding damage to, or failure by, a portion of the network; messages can be routed around the damaged portion and through alternate paths. By contrast, with more centralized designs, damage to the central server renders the entire network inoperable. This was one of the features that first appealed to the Department of Defense, because it seemed to insure the survivability of the inter-network in the face of attack.

> No single entity—academic, corporate, governmental, or non-profit— administers the Internet. It exists and functions as a result of the fact that hundreds of thousands of separate operators of computers and computer networks independently decided to use common data transfer protocols to exchange communications and information with other computers (which in turn exchange communications and information with still other computers). There is no centralized storage location, control point, or communications channel for the Internet, and it would not be technically feasible for a single entity to control all of the information conveyed on the Internet.

American Civil Liberties Union v. Reno, 929 F. Supp. 824, 832 (E.D. Pa. 1996), *aff'd,* 521 U.S. 844 (1997).

B. *Openness.* The Internet is an "open" network in several senses. First, the TCP/IP protocols themselves, which are required in order to send and to receive messages over the Internet, are publicly-accessible and non-proprietary (see the collection of "Internet Standards" at http://www.ietf.org); this has allowed hardware and software providers to implement the required standards relatively easily. Second, the Internet is "open" in the sense that it is easy to join; with no central server that must be informed of a new network participant, in order to communicate with others over the Internet one need only obtain the necessary software and arrange for a connection to any one of the thousands of Internet service providers worldwide. Third, the Internet is open in the sense that it can inter-connect networks that may themselves use different operating systems and underlying technologies.

C. *Packet-switching.* The Internet is a "packet-switched" network (as contrasted with *circuit-switched* networks such as the telephone network). Packet-switching means that before being transmitted over the inter-network, a message is broken up into small, fixed-length blocks (or "packets"), and each of the packets is then routed independently of the others to the recipient machine. That recipient machine is then responsible for re-assembling all of the packets—which are likely to arrive out of order, given the different routes they have taken—back into a single message. As a consequence, the physical communications lines connecting any two users on the Internet can be performing that same task for thousands, or hundreds of thousands, of users more-or-less simultaneously, as packet follows packet follows packet across the wires. By contrast, a circuit-switched network—like the telephone network—identifies a single line between sender and recipient and keeps that line "open," dedicated exclusively to that one connection, until the communication between the two is completed. Packet-switching not only makes it more difficult to intercept and interpret messages traveling over the network (because messages have been disassembled before transmission)—another feature of the Internet's design that appealed to military planners—it allows for a much more efficient use of available transmission capacity, allowing many more communications between many more users to travel over the same physical facilities, compared to circuit-switched networks.

D. *Digital Information.* The inter-network transmits information only in digital form, as on-off pulses of electrical energy representing the binary digits "1" and "0". Physical distance is thus largely irrelevant to online communications; digital information can move nearly as quickly across the globe as across town, with no significant degradation in quality. From a technical perspective, there is no music, or pornography, or message boards, or virtual worlds, or books for sale, etc. on the Internet; there are only massive strings of 1s and 0s. And because digital information can be copied instantly and (virtually) without error (compared to analog information), copying is an essential part of the architecture itself. For example, messages are reproduced each time they move from one router to another across the network. Similarly, every time one accesses a website, a copy of the requested page is produced on one's own computer.

E. *Layered Architecture.* Professor Tim Wu offers this helpful analogy to describe the Internet's "layered" design:

What it means for a network to have a layered architecture, viewed all at once, can be at first difficult to grasp, yet the idea is so clever that it merits understanding. A network communication between computers is a very complex operation. The essence of network layering is a grand simplification by delegation to functional submodules, the layers. Dividing one large task among several layers has numerous advantages—it allows specialized efficiency, organizational coherency, and future flexibility—and is something we constantly see in the real world yet consider unremarkable.

Consider, as a way to understand this, what happens when one lawyer uses the postal system to mail a legal argument to another lawyer. The postal system is structured so that no one in the postal system needs to understand law (the language of the lawyers) for the message to be successfully delivered. And, similarly, neither lawyer need do anything more than understand the rules on addressing and postage. This makes for a simple two-layer network. The function of understanding the contents of the letter has been delegated to a "higher" layer (in this case lawyers), and the function of delivering the letter has been delegated to a "lower" layer (the postal system).

In this example, the postal level is called "lower" because it can be seen as more fundamental. The lawyers need the postal system or they cannot communicate at all; yet if the lawyers did not exist, the postal system would continue to carry mail for doctors, scientists and other interpreters of strange lingo. Notice also that the postal system is more fundamental in the sense that it can set standards that apply to everyone in the higher levels, regardless of who they are. For example, the postal service could require that all envelopes be blue. The higher-level users of the system would have no choice but to comply.

Notice several things about a network so structured. First, it allows an efficient specialization: That the postal system need not understand law (or the content of any of the messages it carries) dramatically reduces the burden on the post office and allows it to focus on one task: delivering mail. Second, the system is very flexible: The postal system can carry any type of message, and the communication will be successful, provided that the person on the other side understands it. This makes the postal system useful for a wide variety of applications. Finally, the layers are modular: Were the postal system to begin using spaceships to deliver its mail, the lawyers would be unaffected so long as the rules for postage and writing addresses remained the same.

Tim Wu, *Application-Centered Internet Analysis*, 85 VA. L. REV. 1163, 1189–91 (1999).

The Internet shares this same basic layered structure—though with four, rather than two, layers.

POSTAL SYSTEM LAYERS   INTERNET LAYERS

User layer [rules for interpreting delivered mail]   Application

                                              Transport

Postal Service [addressing rules]   Network

                                              Physical

To see roughly how Internet layering operates, suppose that you are sitting in a law school classroom, connected via a fiber optic cable to your school's local area network and, through that connection, to the Internet, and you have just sent a request for a web page located at http://www.aclu.org. The protocols used at the *physical layer* determine how the electrical transmissions produced by your computer are to be converted into bit strings by the LAN server; most (but by no means all) LANs use the Ethernet protocol suite for this task. (This layer is absent from the postal system Professor Wu describes above—although one might perhaps think of the rules governing the conversion of otherwise meaningless blotches of ink on paper into meaningful "letters" as operating at the equivalent of the "physical layer" of the postal system.)

The protocol at the *network layer* is the direct analogue of the postal service layer in Professor Wu's example; it determines how the bit-strings that you have sent to your LAN server are to be addressed so that they can be routed over the inter-network to the correct recipient("www.aclu.org"). On the Internet, the *Internet Protocol* is used for these tasks.

As mentioned above, the Internet Protocol requires that all messages (including your file request to www.aclu.org) be broken up into fixed-length packets before transmission over the Internet. Protocols at the *transport layer* govern the way in which messages are re-assembled when delivered to the recipient machines. Many different transport layer protocols are used for Internet communication, although TCP ("Transmission Control Protocol") is the most common. Typically, transport layer protocols provide for error-correction and quality control (*i.e.,* some way for the recipient machine to know that all of the packets comprising a single message have arrived, to check for transmission errors, and to request re-transmission of missing or damaged packets). (There is no equivalent of the transport layer in the postal system; we would need a transport layer, and a transport layer protocol, if the postal service required, for example, that all letters had to be torn up into one-inch square fragments before they could be delivered.)

Finally, there is the *application layer*. Just as lawyers in Professor Wu's example use the rules of English (or, perhaps, that strange dialect known as "legalese") to interpret and to give meaning to the messages that the postal service delivers, so, too, the recipient of your message has to decode and interpret it—to determine whether it is a request for a copy of a particular file residing on the recipient's computer, or an e-mail message, or a voice communication, or something else. The communication you sent to www.aclu.org—having been converted into a bit-string by some physical layer protocol (*e.g.,* Ethernet), broken up into packets and addressed using a network protocol (IP), transmitted to and re-assembled by the recipient machine (TCP)—uses HTTP (the "hypertext transfer protocol") as the application layer protocol; this tells the recipient machine that this is indeed a request for the transmission of a copy of the file "Index.html" residing on the machine at the www.aclu.org address.

This architecture, as in the postal system example, allows specialization at each layer of the protocol stack; protocols at each layer operate independently of the protocols in the other layers. The network layer protocols can be designed to route packets from one place to another as quickly and as efficiently as possible, without having to know anything about what the bit-strings that are being routed "mean." Similarly, applications can interpret the data they send to each other without worrying about how it got there—just as plumbers, doctors, lawyers, chemists, and insurance salesmen can develop and all use their own specialized lingoes for communication, secure in the knowledge the postal service will deliver their letters correctly.

F. *End-to-End Design.* The end-to-end design principle is closely linked to the principle of layered architecture; it holds that, wherever possible, functions should be placed at the *higher* layers of the protocol stack, *i.e.,* that as much as possible should be left to software running in the *applications* layer—at the user "end" rather than in the network "center." The lower-level protocols are kept as simple and unobtrusive as possible, focused only on the minimal function of transmitting data. End-to-end design means that the physical, network, and transport layer protocols will deliver a network user's bits wherever directed—what happens to them after that point is of no concern to the network itself but is controlled entirely by the applications running on the user's machine.

So while the basic network protocol (IP), for example, *could* do much more than just addressing and routing—checking for malicious code, for instance, or more aggressive security and authentication of sender identity, or any number of other functions—end-to-end leaves these functions for users to implement if they wish (or not).

End-to-end design has profound implications for the Internet's growth and utilization. It grants the maximum possible autonomy to applications running "on top" of the basic network protocols themselves, giving application-writers the freedom to achieve their goals in whatever manner they see fit, and to innovate whenever and however they like. Virtually all of the network's "intelligence"—the processing required to *interpret* the bit-strings delivered over the Internet by the lower level protocols—is located in the software running in the applications layer. Bits are bits; the network will move them around for you as directed no matter what they mean, or what they are intended to do when they reach their destination. Innovation comes in the form of new applications—e-mail, or instant messaging, or the World Wide Web, or VoIP (Voice over Internet Protocol), or peer-to-peer file-sharing—developed and deployed at the edges of the network, not the center; the center need not participate in (nor even have any information about) those new applications. At the same time, by confining the lower level protocols to simple functions, the design avoids blocking out future applications that may be unknown and unpredictable at the time of design.

This is, again, in stark contrast to the telephone network, which was designed to allow very simple devices at the edges—telephones—to connect to a very sophisticated central processing core:

> Its relatively rapid responsiveness to users and other design attributes distinguish the Internet from other parts of the information infrastructure, such as the * * * telephone network or the television networks (cable and broadcast). The design of those other networks is more focused on the center, and greater functionality is located *within* the networks. They have been more centrally developed and managed and historically have limited what users can do with them. In contrast, the Internet's design is effectively neutral to what services operate across the network. This enables a relatively unrestricted set of applications to run over it without the need for changes to be made within the network.

NATIONAL RESEARCH COUNCIL, THE INTERNET'S COMING OF AGE 34 (Nat'l Acad. Press 2001).

The above is, of course, a simplified version of the full story, and we urge the student seeking to understand, or to practice in, this area of law to consult one or more of the excellent (and eminently readable) descriptions of Internet history, architecture, and operating principles. We particularly recommend KATIE HAFNER & MATTHEW LYON, WHERE WIZARDS STAY UP LATE (Simon & Schuster 1996) (with a companion website at http://www.simonsays.com/titles/0684812010/); JANET ABBATE, INVENTING THE INTERNET (MIT Press 2000); Barry M. Leiner et al., *A Brief History of the Internet*, http://www.isoc.org/internet/history/brief.shtml; NATIONAL RESEARCH COUNCIL, THE INTERNET'S COMING OF AGE (Nat'l Acad. Press 2001); Internet History, http://www.livinginternet.com/i/ii.htm; Peter Salus, *The Net: A Brief History of Origins*, 38 JURIMETRICS 671 (1998); Rus Shuler, *How Does the Internet Work?*, http://www.theshulers.com/whitepapers; Vinton G. Cerf, *Computer Networking: Global Infrastructure for the 21st Century*, http://www.isoc.org/internet/infrastructure/; Richard T. Griffiths, *History of the Internet, the Internet for Historians*, http://www.let.leidenuniv.nl/history/ivh/frame_theorie.html.

Chapter Two

PROBLEMS OF METAPHOR AND ANALOGY: INTRODUCTORY CASE STUDIES

INTRODUCTION

By the time they finish the first year of law school, most students have become familiar with the process by which common-law judges reach solutions to new cases by analogizing from precedent: gleaning relevant principles from past cases and applying those principles to new settings. This kind of reasoning can, of course, create difficulties; not only may it not always be apparent which analogy is the "right" one for a given case, but the principles established in analogous cases may not always be well suited for the new context.

These difficulties are hardly unique to cyberspace; every case, online or off, is in *some* ways "new," presenting "new" facts. These problems of metaphor and analogy, of finding the right language to describe the particular constellation of facts in any given case and of finding the most closely analogous case or cases from those that have been decided previously, are therefore implicit in *all* judicial decision-making. All legal reasoning involves identifying the relevant precedents and deciding whether a new case can satisfactorily be resolved by analogy to prior cases or, instead, requires some newly developed legal principle for its resolution.

But while they may not be unique to cyberspace, these problems of metaphor and analogy do become especially prominent in cases involving online conduct, and we will encounter them frequently (albeit indirectly) throughout this book. In this chapter we focus on them directly. Before judges can simply apply old common-law doctrines to the online context, they must ask a series of questions: Is this merely an old legal issue dressed up in high-tech packaging? Or is there something about the online context that changes the nature of the question such that the old precedent cannot simply be applied without further reflection? What are the guiding assumptions underlying the line of precedent? What balances did the precedent seek to strike? Are those guiding premises still valid in this new context? Might applying the precedent actually upset the balances rather than maintain them?

Furthermore, we must be acutely aware of the metaphors that lawyers and judges employ when thinking about Internet legal issues. For example, consider the variety of metaphors drawn from the physical world that are habitually (and often unconsciously) used to talk about events, transactions, and systems that exist or occur online:

> At its most fundamental, think of the term WEB, an allusion to the "web-like" connections between computers. Then there is the NET, referring to the network of connections as well as the net-like character of the material caught in the network. We SURF this WEB, MOVING from one SITE to the next, ENTERING or VISITING the site, or, in the slightly old-fashioned nomenclature, we access someone's HOMEPAGE. We HANG OUT IN CHATROOMS communicating with our ONLINE buddies. We ROAM AROUND Multiple User DUNGEONS and DOMAINS. * * * Software programs called ROBOTS, AGENTS, or SPIDERS are allowed to CRAWL over websites unless they are barred by terms and conditions of ENTRY or ACCESS, or by the robot EXCLUSION standard. We NAVIGATE the WEB using computer programs with names like NAVIGATOR and EXPLORER. We use Uniform Resource LOCATORS ("URLs") and DOMAIN names to find our way. Information is sent to us using hypertext TRANSPORT protocol ("http") or simple mail TRANSPORT protocol. We use email ADDRESSES to send messages to others, and the machines themselves use Internet Protocol ("IP") ADDRESSES to locate other computers. We log INTO or log ONTO our Internet Service Provider ("ISP"). Malignant wrongdoers ACCESS our accounts by hacking INTO the system using BACKDOORS, TRAPDOORS, or stolen KEYS * * *.

Dan Hunter, *Cyberspace as Place and the Tragedy of the Digital Anticommons*, 91 CAL. L. REV. 439, 453-54 (2003). As Hunter points out, the metaphor of place has been a dominant trope in thinking about the Internet. And if, as cognitive scientists increasingly believe, metaphor shapes our thinking in subtle but significant ways, then this focus on the Internet as a place may have important consequences. Consider the following argument:

> Thinking of cyberspace as a place has led judges, legislators, and legal scholars to apply physical assumptions about property in this new, abstract space. Owners of Internet resources think of their systems as their own little claims in cyberspace, which must be protected against the typical encroachments that we find in the physical property world. This has led to a series of cases and statutes that enshrine the idea of property interests in cyberspace. The effect of

this is to take the hitherto commons-like character of cyberspace and splinter it into millions of tiny landholdings.

Id. at 443.

Thus, at the very least, we must think about how metaphors and analogies are used in legal decisions and then evaluate the degree to which those metaphors and analogies illuminate or distort the legal issues in dispute. The materials in this chapter—which address three different areas of legal doctrine surrounding online communication—provide a first opportunity for such consideration. With regard to each issue, the judges must determine whether to apply various "real-space" analogies and metaphors to reach their decisions and, if so, how the applicable legal precedent should be applied. Ask yourself what dilemmas the judges deciding these cases faced and how you would have dealt with the arguably relevant precedents.

SECTION A. TRESPASS TO CHATTELS IN CYBERSPACE

eBay, Inc. v. Bidder's Edge, Inc.

United States District Court for the Northern District of California, 2000
100 F. Supp. 2d 1058

WHYTE, District Judge.

I. BACKGROUND

eBay is an Internet-based, person-to-person trading site. eBay offers sellers the ability to list items for sale and prospective buyers the ability to search those listings and bid on items. The seller can set the terms and conditions of the auction. The item is sold to the highest bidder. The transaction is consummated directly between the buyer and seller without eBay's involvement. A potential purchaser looking for a particular item can access the eBay site and perform a key word search for relevant auctions and bidding status. eBay has also created category listings that identify items in over 2500 categories, such as antiques, computers, and dolls. Users may browse these category listing pages to identify items of interest.

Users of the eBay site must register and agree to the eBay User Agreement. Users agree to the seven page User Agreement by clicking on an "I Accept" button located at the end of the User Agreement. The current version of the User Agreement prohibits the use of "any robot, spider, other automatic device, or manual process to monitor or copy our web pages or the content contained herein without our prior expressed written permission." It is not clear that the version of the User Agreement in effect at the time [Bidder's Edge (BE)] began searching the eBay site prohibited such activity, or that BE ever agreed to comply with the User Agreement.

eBay currently has over 7 million registered users. Over 400,000 new items are added to the site every day. Every minute, 600 bids are placed on almost 3 million items. Users currently perform, on average, 10 million searches per day on eBay's database. Bidding for and sales of items are continuously ongoing in millions of separate auctions.

A software robot is a computer program which operates across the Internet to perform searching, copying and retrieving functions on the web sites of others. A software robot is capable of executing thousands of instructions per minute, far in excess of what a human can accomplish. Robots consume the processing and storage resources of a system, making that portion of the system's capacity unavailable to the system owner or other users. Consumption of sufficient system resources will slow the processing of the overall system and can overload the system such that it will malfunction or "crash." A severe malfunction can cause a loss of data and an interruption in services.

The eBay site employs "robot exclusion headers." A robot exclusion header is a message, sent to computers programmed to detect and respond to such headers, that eBay does not permit unauthorized robotic activity. * * * eBay identifies robotic activity on its site by monitoring the number of incoming requests from each particular [Internet Protocol (IP)] address. Once eBay identifies an IP address believed to be involved in robotic activity, an investigation into the identity, origin and owner of the IP address may be made in order to determine if the activity is legitimate or authorized. If an investigation reveals unauthorized robotic activity, eBay may attempt to ignore ("block") any further requests from that IP address. Attempts to block requests from particular IP addresses are not always successful. * * *

Bidder's Edge [BE] is a company with 22 employees that was founded in 1997. The BE web site debuted in November 1998. BE does not host auctions. BE is an auction aggregation site designed to offer on-line auction buyers the ability to search for items across numerous on-line auctions without having to search each host site individually. As of March 2000, the BE web site contained information on more that five million items being auctioned on more than one hundred auction sites. BE also provides its users with additional auction-related services and information. The information available on the BE site is contained in a database of information that BE compiles through access to various auction sites such as eBay. When a user enters a search for a particular item at BE, BE searches its database and generates a list of every item in the database responsive to the search, organized by auction closing date and time. Rather than going to each host auction site one at a time, a user who goes to BE may conduct a single search to obtain information about that item on every auction site tracked by BE. It is important to include information regarding eBay auctions on the BE site because eBay is by far the biggest consumer to consumer on-line auction site. * * *

In early 1998, eBay gave BE permission to include information regarding eBay-hosted auctions for Beanie Babies and Furbies in the BE database. In early 1999, BE added to the number of person-to-person auction sites it covered and started covering a broader range of items hosted by those sites, including eBay. On April 24, 1999, eBay verbally approved BE crawling the eBay web site for a period of 90 days. The parties contemplated that during this period they would reach a formal licensing agreement. They were unable to do so. * * *

III. ANALYSIS

* * * According to eBay, the load on its servers resulting from BE's web crawlers represents between 1.11% and 1.53% of the total load on eBay's listing servers. eBay alleges both economic loss from BE's current activities and potential harm resulting from the total crawling of BE and others. In alleging economic harm, eBay's argument is that eBay has expended considerable time, effort and money to create its computer system, and that BE should have to pay for the portion of eBay's system BE uses. eBay attributes a pro rata portion of the costs of maintaining its entire system to the BE activity. However, eBay does not indicate that these expenses are incrementally incurred because of BE's activities, nor that any particular service disruption can be attributed to BE's activities. eBay provides no support for the proposition that the pro rata costs of obtaining an item represent the appropriate measure of damages for unauthorized use. In contrast, California law appears settled that the appropriate measure of damages is the actual harm inflicted by the conduct * * * .

eBay's right to injunctive relief is * * * based upon a much stronger argument. If BE's activity is allowed to continue unchecked, it would encourage other auction aggregators to engage in similar recursive searching of the eBay system such that eBay would suffer irreparable harm from reduced system performance, system unavailability, or data losses. BE does not appear to seriously contest that reduced system performance, system unavailability or data loss would inflict irreparable harm on eBay consisting of lost profits and lost customer goodwill. Harm resulting from lost profits and lost customer goodwill is irreparable because it is neither easily calculable, nor easily compensable and is therefore an appropriate basis for injunctive relief. * * *

BE correctly observes that there is a dearth of authority supporting a preliminary injunction based on an ongoing to trespass to chattels. In contrast, it is black letter law in California that an injunction is an appropriate remedy for a continuing trespass to real property. If eBay were a brick and mortar auction house with limited seating capacity, eBay would appear to be entitled to reserve those seats for potential bidders, to refuse entrance to individuals (or robots) with no intention of bidding on any of the items, and to seek preliminary injunctive relief against non-customer trespassers eBay was physically unable to exclude. The analytic difficulty is that a wrongdoer can commit an ongoing trespass of a computer system that is more akin to the traditional notion of a trespass to real property, than the traditional notion of a trespass to chattels, because even though it is ongoing, it will probably never amount to a conversion. The court concludes that under the circumstances present here, BE's ongoing violation of eBay's fundamental property right to exclude others from its computer system potentially causes sufficient irreparable harm to support a preliminary injunction. * * *

Trespass to chattels "lies where an intentional interference with the possession of personal property has proximately caused injury." *Thrifty-Tel v. Bezenek*, 54 Cal. Rptr. 2d 468, 473 (1996). Trespass to chattels "although seldom employed as a tort theory in California" was recently applied to cover the unauthorized use of long distance telephone lines. *Id.* Specifically, the court noted "the electronic signals generated by the [defendants'] activities were sufficiently tangible to support a trespass cause of action." *Id.* at n. 6. Thus, it appears likely that the electronic signals sent by BE to retrieve information from eBay's computer system are also sufficiently tangible to support a trespass cause of action.

In order to prevail on a claim for trespass based on accessing a computer system, the plaintiff must establish: (1) defendant intentionally and without authorization interfered with plaintiff's possessory interest in the computer system; and (2) defendant's unauthorized use proximately resulted in damage to plaintiff. Here, eBay has presented evidence sufficient to establish a strong likelihood of proving both prongs and ultimately prevailing on the merits of its trespass claim.

a.   BE's Unauthorized Interference

eBay argues that BE's use was unauthorized and intentional. eBay is correct. BE does not dispute that it employed an automated computer program to connect with and search eBay's electronic database. BE admits that, because other auction aggregators were including eBay's auctions in their listing, it continued to "crawl" eBay's web site even after eBay demanded BE terminate such activity.

BE argues that it cannot trespass eBay's web site because the site is publicly accessible. BE's argument is unconvincing. eBay's servers are private property, conditional access to which eBay grants the public. eBay does not generally permit the type of automated access made by BE. In fact, eBay explicitly notifies automated visitors that their access is not permitted. * * *

Even if BE's web crawlers were authorized to make individual queries of eBay's system, BE's web crawlers exceeded the scope of any such consent when they began acting like robots by making repeated queries. Moreover, eBay repeatedly and explicitly notified BE that its use of eBay's computer system was unauthorized. * * * The court concludes that BE's activity is sufficiently outside of the scope of the use permitted by eBay that it is unauthorized for the purposes of establishing a trespass.

eBay argues that BE interfered with eBay's possessory interest in its computer system. Although eBay appears unlikely to be able to show a substantial interference at this time, such a showing is not required. Conduct that does not amount to a substantial interference with possession, but which consists of intermeddling with or use of another's personal property, is sufficient to establish a cause of action for trespass to chattel. Although the court admits some uncertainty as to the precise level of possessory interference required to constitute an intermeddling, there does not appear to be any dispute that eBay can show that BE's conduct amounts to use of eBay's computer systems. Accordingly, eBay has made a strong showing that it is likely to prevail on the merits of its assertion that BE's use of eBay's computer system was an unauthorized and intentional interference with eBay's possessory interest.

b. *Damage to eBay's Computer System*

A trespasser is liable when the trespass diminishes the condition, quality or value of personal property. *See CompuServe, Inc. v. Cyber Promotions*, 962 F. Supp. 1015 (S.D. Ohio 1997). The quality or value of personal property may be "diminished even though it is not physically damaged by defendant's conduct." *Id.* at 1022. * * *

eBay is likely to be able to demonstrate that BE's activities have diminished the quality or value of eBay's computer systems. BE's activities consume at least a portion of plaintiff's bandwidth and server capacity. Although there is some dispute as to the percentage of queries on eBay's site for which BE is responsible, BE admits that it sends some 80,000 to 100,000 requests to plaintiff's computer systems per day. Although eBay does not claim that this consumption has led to any physical damage to eBay's computer system, nor does eBay provide any evidence to support the claim that it may have lost revenues or customers based on this use, eBay's claim is that BE's use is appropriating eBay's personal property by using valuable bandwidth and capacity, and necessarily compromising eBay's ability to use that capacity for its own purposes.

BE argues that its searches represent a negligible load on plaintiff's computer systems, and do not rise to the level of impairment to the condition or value of eBay's computer system required to constitute a trespass. However, it is undisputed that eBay's server and its capacity are personal property, and that BE's searches use a portion of this property. Even if, as BE argues, its searches use only a small amount of eBay's computer system capacity, BE has nonetheless deprived eBay of the ability to use that portion of its personal property for its own purposes. The law recognizes no such right to use another's personal property. Accordingly, BE's actions appear to have caused injury to eBay and appear likely to continue to cause injury to eBay. If the court were to hold otherwise, it would likely encourage other auction aggregators to crawl the eBay site, potentially to the point of denying effective access to eBay's customers. If preliminary injunctive relief were denied, and other aggregators began to crawl the eBay site, there appears to be little doubt that the load on eBay's computer system would qualify as a substantial impairment of condition or value. California law does not require eBay to wait for such a disaster before applying to this court for relief. The court concludes that eBay has made a strong showing that it is likely to prevail on the merits of its trespass claim, and that there is at least a possibility that it will suffer irreparable harm if preliminary injunctive relief is not granted. eBay is therefore entitled to preliminary injunctive relief.

Notes and Questions

1. Assume Denise's Drugs is a "brick and mortar" drug store. Dave's Discount Pharmacy opens a discount store next door. Each week, an employee of Dave's enters Denise's, walks around the store, and writes down the prices Denise's charges for various items, perhaps purchasing a couple of items as well so as to appear like a regular customer. Armed with this information, Dave's offers many of the same products at a lower price. If Denise finds out about this practice, can she sue Dave on a trespass theory? What if all Dave does is stand on the sidewalk and look at the sale prices displayed in Denise's window? Are these useful analogies to the online context? Why or why not?

2. What about the argument that Internet users have an interest in low-cost, worldwide communication and unimpeded access to information? Indeed, such low-cost communication and open access to information arguably have been critical to the rapid growth and vitality of both the Internet and e-commerce. Does a decision such as *Bidder's Edge* impede this sort of access to information? If so, what is the appropriate solution? For a discussion of these issues, see Niva Elkin-Koren, *Let the Crawlers Crawl: On Virtual Gatekeepers and the Right to Exclude Indexing*, 49 J. COPYRIGHT SOC'Y 165 (2001).

3. Consider arguments based on economics and market efficiency. Some have argued that decisions such as the one in *Bidder's Edge*, by impeding access to information, make the market less efficient:

> The Internet has the potential to approximate a perfectly efficient information medium because it can allow buyers to cheaply, easily and quickly search for items they want. The role of product comparison sites is critical to the benefits of e-commerce. Aggregators of product and price information, "shop-bots" that automate the price comparison process, and comparative product evaluators like Consumer Reports and its online equivalents all reduce transactions costs and improve competition by helping consumers get fast, cheap and accurate information about products and prices. Because search technology and so-called "shop-bots" allow consumers to automatically identify goods in which they are interested, the match between sellers and buyers can approach perfect efficiency. In addition, because there is no practical limit to the number of servers that can be connected to the Internet, there is virtually no upper limit to the number of sellers that can participate in what promises to be near-perfect competition.

Brief of Amici Curiae Mark A. Lemley *et al.*, *eBay, Inc. v. Bidder's Edge, Inc.*, No. 00-15995 (9th Cir. filed June 22, 2000).

On the other hand, granting sites like eBay the right to exclude aggregators does not necessarily mean that such aggregators will vanish from the scene; rather, they may negotiate license agreements with the auction sites and then continue to offer the same information to consumers. Indeed, some have argued that, by creating a clear property right to exclude unauthorized users from a website, the law would facilitate efficient bargaining between the parties. *See, e.g.*, Richard A. Epstein, *Cybertrespass*, 70 U. CHI. L. REV. 73 (2003); David McGowan, *Website Access: The Case for Consent*, 35 LOY. CHI. L. REV. 341 (2003); Richard Warner, *Border Disputes: Trespass to Chattels on the Internet*, 47 VILL. L. REV. 117 (2002). Nevertheless, can you think of any possible barriers to the creation of such licensing agreements?

4. What about search engines? They use crawlers of various sorts to search websites and index content. Should they be required to negotiate licenses with every site they index? If not, can you think of how you might craft an exception to the rule enunciated in *Bidder's Edge*? Might the law infer an implied license to index unless sites specifically disclaim permission? Would such an implied license scheme be practical?

5. Is there a danger of "over-propertization" of the online environment? Michael Heller has written of the dilemma that arises when property rights are so finely divided that it becomes essentially impossible to conduct any type of business. *See* Michael A. Heller, *The Tragedy of the Anticommons: Property in the Transition from Marx to Markets*, 111 HARV. L. REV. 621 (1998). In such highly fragmented property systems, myriad licenses must be obtained from many, many owners before any type of large-scale project can be undertaken. The transaction costs involved in locating the rights holders and negotiating separate licenses with each of them might tend to deter complex endeavors. *See* Dan L. Burk, *The Trouble with Trespass*, 4 J. SMALL & EMERGING BUS. L. 27, 49 (2000).

On the other hand, it might be possible to reduce these transaction costs online through automation. Users would then be able electronically to enter into licensing negotiations with the owners of ever more finely-grained levels of network property and then keep track of all the agreements through digital certificates. *See* Trotter Hardy, *Property (and Copyright) in Cyberspace*, 1996 U. CHI. LEGAL F. 217; *see also* Tom W. Bell, *Fair Use vs. Fared Use: The Impact of Automated Rights Management on Copyright's Fair Use Doctrine*, 76 N.C. L. REV. 557 (1998). *But see* Julie E. Cohen, Lochner *in Cyberspace: The New Economic Orthodoxy of "Rights Management"*, 97 MICH. L. REV. 462 (1998) (offering a critique of this view).

Are either of these visions convincing?

6. Should online trespass actions be based only on the harms arising from increased traffic over computer lines? For example, if company X has greater server capacity than company Y, should it be less able to pursue a trespass action? If not, then are these trespass actions more concerned simply with the right of those who own computer servers or websites to control access, rather than fears about damage to computer systems?

7. Even if a plaintiff must show harm to be entitled to *damages* under a trespass theory, should a claim for *injunctive* relief be successful in the absence of any allegation of harm, on the theory that, as in the real property context,

a system owner should have the right to exclude unwanted uses? Does *Bidder's Edge* implicitly rely on a real property analogy? Is such an analogy appropriate? Consider the following case.

Intel Corporation v. Hamidi

Supreme Court of California, 2003
71 P.3d 296

WERDEGAR, J.

Intel Corporation (Intel) maintains an electronic mail system, connected to the Internet, through which messages between employees and those outside the company can be sent and received, and permits its employees to make reasonable nonbusiness use of this system. On six occasions over almost two years, Kourosh Kenneth Hamidi, a former Intel employee, sent e-mails criticizing Intel's employment practices to numerous current employees on Intel's electronic mail system. * * * The messages criticized Intel's employment practices, warned employees of the dangers those practices posed to their careers, suggested employees consider moving to other companies, solicited employees' participation in [an organization Hamidi and others founded, Former and Current Employees of Intel (FACE-Intel)], and urged employees to inform themselves further by visiting FACE-Intel's Web site. The messages stated that recipients could, by notifying the sender of their wishes, be removed from FACE-Intel's mailing list; Hamidi did not subsequently send messages to anyone who requested removal.

Each message was sent to thousands of addresses (as many as 35,000 according to FACE-Intel's Web site), though some messages were blocked by Intel before reaching employees. Intel's attempt to block internal transmission of the messages succeeded only in part; Hamidi later admitted he evaded blocking efforts by using different sending computers. When Intel, in March 1998, demanded in writing that Hamidi and FACE-Intel stop sending e-mails to Intel's computer system, Hamidi asserted the organization had a right to communicate with willing Intel employees; he sent a new mass mailing in September 1998.

The summary judgment record contains no evidence Hamidi breached Intel's computer security in order to obtain the recipient addresses for his messages; indeed, internal Intel memoranda show the company's management concluded no security breach had occurred. Hamidi stated he created the recipient address list using an Intel directory on a floppy disk anonymously sent to him. Nor is there any evidence that the receipt or internal distribution of Hamidi's electronic messages damaged Intel's computer system or slowed or impaired its functioning. Intel did present uncontradicted evidence, however, that many employee recipients asked a company official to stop the messages and that staff time was consumed in attempts to block further messages from FACE-Intel. According to the FACE-Intel Web site, moreover, the messages had prompted discussions between "[e]xcited and nervous managers" and the company's human resources department.

Intel sued Hamidi and FACE-Intel, pleading * * * trespass to chattels * * * . [The trial court] granted Intel's motion for summary judgment, permanently enjoining Hamidi, FACE-Intel, and their agents from sending unsolicited e-mail to addresses on Intel's computer systems. * * * The Court of Appeal, with one justice dissenting, affirmed the grant of injunctive relief. The majority took the view that the use of or intermeddling with another's personal property is actionable as a trespass to chattels without proof of any actual injury to the personal property; even if Intel could not show any damages resulting from Hamidi's sending of messages, it showed he was disrupting its business by using its property and therefore is entitled to injunctive relief based on a theory of trespass to chattels. The dissenting justice warned that the majority's application of the trespass to chattels tort to unsolicited electronic mail that causes no harm to the private computer system that receives it would expand the tort of trespass to chattel in untold ways and to unanticipated circumstances.

We granted Hamidi's petition for review.

DISCUSSION

I. Current California Tort Law

* * * [T]he tort of trespass to chattels allows recovery for interferences with possession of personal property not sufficiently important to be classed as conversion, and so to compel the defendant to pay the full value of the thing with which he has interfered. PROSSER & KEETON, TORTS § 14, at 85-86 (5th ed. 1984). Though not amounting to conversion, the defendant's interference must, to be actionable, have caused some injury to the chattel or to the plaintiff's rights in it. Under California law, trespass to chattels lies where an intentional interference with the possession of personal property *has proximately caused injury*. *Thrifty-Tel, Inc. v. Bezenek*, 46 Cal. App. 4th 1559, 1566, 54 Cal. Rptr. 2d 468 (1996) (italics added).

The Restatement, too, makes clear that some actual injury must have occurred in order for a trespass to chattels to be actionable. Under section 218 of the Restatement Second of Torts, dispossession alone, without further damages, is actionable, *see id.*, par. (a) & com. d, at 420-421, but other forms of interference require some additional harm to the personal property or the possessor's interests in it. *Id.*, pars. (b)-(d).

> The interest of a possessor of a chattel in its inviolability, unlike the similar interest of a possessor of land, is not given legal protection by an action for nominal damages for harmless intermeddlings with the chattel. In order that an actor who interferes with another's chattel may be liable, his conduct must affect some other and more important interest of the possessor. *Therefore, one who intentionally intermeddles with another's chattel is subject to liability only if his intermeddling is harmful to the possessor's materially valuable interest*

in the physical condition, quality, or value of the chattel, or if the possessor is deprived of the use of the chattel for a substantial time, or some other legally protected interest of the possessor is affected as stated in Clause (c). Sufficient legal protection of the possessor's interest in the mere inviolability of his chattel is afforded by his privilege to use reasonable force to protect his possession against even harmless interference.

Id., com. e, at 421-422 (italics added). * * *

The dispositive issue in this case, therefore, is whether the undisputed facts demonstrate Hamidi's actions caused or threatened to cause damage to Intel's computer system, or injury to its rights in that personal property, such as to entitle Intel to judgment as a matter of law. To review, the undisputed evidence revealed no actual or threatened damage to Intel's computer hardware or software and no interference with its ordinary and intended operation. Intel was not dispossessed of its computers, nor did Hamidi's messages prevent Intel from using its computers for any measurable length of time. Intel presented no evidence its system was slowed or otherwise impaired by the burden of delivering Hamidi's electronic messages. Nor was there any evidence transmission of the messages imposed any marginal cost on the operation of Intel's computers. In sum, no evidence suggested that in sending messages through Intel's Internet connections and internal computer system Hamidi used the system in any manner in which it was not intended to function or impaired the system in any way. * * *

Relying on a line of decisions, most from federal district courts, applying the tort of trespass to chattels to various types of unwanted electronic contact between computers, Intel contends that, while its computers were not damaged by receiving Hamidi's messages, its interest in the physical condition, quality or value of the computers was harmed. We disagree. The cited line of decisions does not persuade us that the mere sending of electronic communications that assertedly cause injury only because of their contents constitutes an actionable trespass to a computer system through which the messages are transmitted. Rather, the decisions finding electronic contact to be a trespass to computer systems have generally involved some actual or threatened interference with the computers' functioning.

In *Thrifty-Tel, Inc. v. Bezenek, supra,* 46 Cal. App. 4th at 1566-1567, 54 Cal. Rptr. 2d 468 *(Thrifty-Tel),* the California Court of Appeal held that evidence of automated searching of a telephone carrier's system for authorization codes supported a cause of action for trespass to chattels. The defendant's automated dialing program overburdened the [plaintiff's] system, denying some subscribers access to phone lines, *Thrifty-Tel, supra,* 46 Cal. App. 4th at 1564, 54 Cal. Rptr. 2d 468, showing the requisite injury.

Following *Thrifty-Tel,* a series of federal district court decisions held that sending [unsolicited commercial e-mail (UCE)] through an ISP's equipment may constitute trespass to the ISP's computer system. * * * In each of these spamming cases, the plaintiff showed, or was prepared to show, some interference with the efficient functioning of its computer system. In [the leading case, *CompuServe, Inc. v. Cyber Promotions, Inc.*, for example], the plaintiff ISP's mail equipment monitor stated that mass UCE mailings, especially from nonexistent addresses such as those used by the defendant, placed "a tremendous burden" on the ISP's equipment, using "disk space and drain[ing] the processing power," making those resources unavailable to serve subscribers. 962 F. Supp. 1015, 1021-22 (S.D. Ohio 1997). * * *

Building on the spamming cases, in particular *CompuServe,* three even more recent district court decisions addressed whether unauthorized robotic data collection from a company's publicly accessible Web site is a trespass on the company's computer system. *eBay, Inc. v. Bidder's Edge, Inc.*, 100 F. Supp. 2d 1058, 1069-1072 (N.D. Cal. 2000) (*eBay*); *Register.com, Inc. v. Verio, Inc.*, 126 F. Supp. 2d 238, 248-251 (S.D.N.Y. 2000); *Ticketmaster Corp. v. Tickets.com, Inc.*, 2000 WL 1887522, at *4 (C.D. Cal. 2000). The two district courts that found such automated data collection to constitute a trespass relied, in part, on the deleterious impact this activity could have, especially if replicated by other searchers, on the functioning of a Web site's computer equipment.

In the leading case, *eBay,* the defendant Bidder's Edge (BE), operating an auction aggregation site, accessed the eBay Web site about 100,000 times per day, accounting for between 1 and 2 percent of the information requests received by eBay and a slightly smaller percentage of the data transferred by eBay. The district court rejected eBay's claim that it was entitled to injunctive relief because of the defendant's unauthorized presence alone, or because of the incremental cost the defendant had imposed on operation of the eBay site, but found sufficient proof of *threatened* harm in the potential for others to imitate the defendant's activity: "If BE's activity is allowed to continue unchecked, it would encourage other auction aggregators to engage in similar recursive searching of the eBay system such that eBay would suffer irreparable harm from reduced system performance, system unavailability, or data losses." 100 F. Supp. 2d at 1066. * * * Here, * * * Intel has demonstrated neither any appreciable effect on the operation of its computer system from Hamidi's messages, nor any likelihood that Hamidi's actions will be replicated by others if found not to constitute a trespass.

That Intel does not claim the type of functional impact that spammers and robots have been alleged to cause is not surprising in light of the differences between Hamidi's activities and those of a commercial enterprise that uses sheer quantity of messages as its communications strategy. Though Hamidi sent thousands of copies of the same message on six occasions over 21 months, that number is minuscule compared to the amounts of mail sent by commercial operations. * * *

Intel relies on language in the *eBay* decision suggesting that unauthorized use of another's chattel is actionable even without any showing of injury: "Even if, as [defendant] BE argues, its searches use only a small amount of eBay's computer system capacity, BE has nonetheless deprived eBay of the ability to use that portion of its personal property for its own purposes. The law recognizes no such right to use another's personal property." *eBay,* 100 F. Supp. 2d at 1071. But as the *eBay* court went on immediately to find that the defendant's conduct, if widely replicated, *would* likely impair the functioning of the plaintiff's system, we do not read the quoted remarks as expressing the court's complete view of the issue. In isolation, moreover, they would not be a correct statement of California or general American law on this point. While one may have no *right* temporarily to use another's personal property, such use is actionable as a trespass only if it has proximately caused injury. * * * That Hamidi's messages temporarily used some portion of the Intel computers' processors or storage is, therefore, not enough; Intel must, but does not, demonstrate some measurable loss from the use of its computer system.

In addition to impairment of system functionality, *CompuServe* and its progeny also refer to the ISP's loss of business reputation and customer goodwill, resulting from the inconvenience and cost that spam causes to its members, as harm to the ISP's legally protected interests in its personal property. Intel argues that its own interest in employee productivity, assertedly disrupted by Hamidi's messages, is a comparable protected interest in its computer system. We disagree.

Whether the economic injuries identified in *CompuServe* were properly considered injuries to the ISP's possessory interest in its personal property, the type of property interest the tort is primarily intended to protect, has been questioned. * * * But even if the loss of goodwill identified in *CompuServe* were the type of injury that would give rise to a trespass to chattels claim under California law, Intel's position would not follow, for Intel's claimed injury has even less connection to its personal property than did CompuServe's.

CompuServe's customers were annoyed because the system was inundated with unsolicited commercial messages, making its use for personal communication more difficult and costly. Their complaint, which allegedly led some to cancel their CompuServe service, was about *the functioning of CompuServe's electronic mail service.* Intel's workers, in contrast, were allegedly distracted from their work not because of the frequency or quantity of Hamidi's messages, but because of assertions and opinions the messages conveyed. Intel's complaint is thus about *the contents of the messages* rather than the functioning of the company's e-mail system. Even accepting *CompuServe'* s economic injury rationale, therefore, Intel's position represents a further extension of the trespass to chattels tort, fictionally recharacterizing the allegedly injurious effect of a communication's *contents* on recipients as an impairment to the device which transmitted the message. * * *

While unwelcome communications, electronic or otherwise, can cause a variety of injuries to economic relations, reputation and emotions, those interests are protected by other branches of tort law; in order to address them, we need not create a fiction of injury to the communication system. Nor may Intel appropriately assert a *property* interest in its employees' time. * * * Whatever interest Intel may have in preventing its employees from receiving disruptive communications, it is not an interest in personal property, and trespass to chattels is therefore not an action that will lie to protect it. Nor, finally, can the fact Intel staff spent time attempting to block Hamidi's messages be bootstrapped into an injury to Intel's possessory interest in its computers. To quote, again, from the dissenting opinion in the Court of Appeal: "[I]t is circular to premise the damage element of a tort solely upon the steps taken to prevent the damage." * * *

Intel connected its e-mail system to the Internet and permitted its employees to make use of this connection both for business and, to a reasonable extent, for their own purposes. In doing so, the company necessarily contemplated the employees' receipt of unsolicited as well as solicited communications from other companies and individuals. That some communications would, because of their contents, be unwelcome to Intel management was virtually inevitable. Hamidi did nothing but use the e-mail system for its intended purpose—to communicate with employees. The system worked as designed, delivering the messages without any physical or functional harm or disruption. These occasional transmissions cannot reasonably be viewed as impairing the quality or value of Intel's computer system. We conclude, therefore, that Intel has not presented undisputed facts demonstrating an injury to its personal property, or to its legal interest in that property, that support, under California tort law, an action for trespass to chattels.

II. Proposed Extension of California Tort Law

We next consider whether California common law should be *extended* to cover, as a trespass to chattels, an otherwise harmless electronic communication whose contents are objectionable. We decline to so expand California law. Intel, of course, was not the recipient of Hamidi's messages, but rather the owner and possessor of computer servers used to relay the messages, and it bases this tort action on that ownership and possession. The property rule proposed is a rigid one, under which the sender of an electronic message would be strictly liable to the owner of equipment through which the communication passes—here, Intel—for any consequential injury flowing from the *contents* of the communication. The arguments of amici curiae and academic writers on this topic, discussed below, leave us highly doubtful whether creation of such a rigid property rule would be wise.

Writing on behalf of several industry groups appearing as amici curiae, Professor Richard A. Epstein of the University of Chicago urges us to excuse the required showing of injury to personal property in cases of unauthorized electronic contact between computers, extending the rules of trespass to real property to all interactive Web sites and servers. The court is thus urged to recognize, for owners of a particular species of personal property, computer servers, the same interest in inviolability as is generally accorded a possessor of land. In effect, Professor Epstein suggests that a company's server should be its castle, upon which any unauthorized intrusion, however harmless, is a trespass.

Epstein's argument derives, in part, from the familiar metaphor of the Internet as a physical space, reflected in much of the language that has been used to describe it: cyberspace, the information superhighway, e-mail addresses, and the like. Of course, * * * [a] major component of the Internet is the World Wide Web, a descriptive term suggesting neither personal nor real property, and cyberspace itself has come to be known by the oxymoronic phrase virtual reality, which would suggest that any real property located in cyberspace must be virtually real property. Metaphor is a two-edged sword. * * *[7]

More substantively, Professor Epstein argues that a rule of computer server inviolability will, through the formation or extension of a market in computer-to-computer access, create the right social result. In most circumstances, he predicts, companies with computers on the Internet will continue to authorize transmission of information through e-mail, Web site searching, and page linking because they benefit by that open access. When a Web site owner does deny access to a particular sending, searching, or linking computer, a system of simple one-on-one negotiations will arise to provide the necessary individual licenses.

Other scholars are less optimistic about such a complete propertization of the Internet. Professor Mark Lemley of the University of California, Berkeley, writing on behalf of an amici curiae group of professors of intellectual property and computer law, observes that under a property rule of server inviolability, each of the hundreds of millions of [Internet] users must get permission in advance from anyone with whom they want to communicate and anyone who owns a server through which their message may travel. The consequence for e-mail could be a substantial reduction in the freedom of electronic communication, as the owner of each computer

---

7. The tort law discussion in Justice Brown's dissenting opinion similarly suffers from an overreliance on metaphor and analogy. Attempting to find an actionable trespass, Justice Brown analyzes Intel's e-mail system as comparable to the exterior of an automobile, a plot of land, the interior of an automobile, a toothbrush, a head of livestock, and a mooring buoy, while Hamidi is characterized as a vandal damaging a school building or a prankster unplugging and moving employees' computers. These colorful analogies tend to obscure the plain fact that this case involves communications equipment, used by defendant to communicate. Intel's e-mail system was equipment designed for speedy communication between employees and the outside world; Hamidi communicated with Intel employees over that system in a manner entirely consistent with its design; and Intel objected not because of an offense against the integrity or dignity of its computers, but because the communications themselves affected employee-recipients in a manner Intel found undesirable. The proposal that we extend trespass to chattels to cover any communication that the owner of the communications equipment considers annoying or distracting raises, moreover, concerns about control over the flow of information and views that would not be presented by, for example, an injunction against chasing another's cattle or sleeping in her car.

through which an electronic message passes could impose its own limitations on message content or source. * * *

We discuss this debate among the amici curiae and academic writers only to note its existence and contours, not to attempt its resolution. Creating an absolute property right to exclude undesired communications from one's e-mail and Web servers might help force spammers to internalize the costs they impose on ISP's and their customers. But such a property rule might also create substantial new costs, to e-mail and e-commerce users and to society generally, in lost ease and openness of communication and in lost network benefits. In light of the unresolved controversy, we would be acting rashly to adopt a rule treating computer servers as real property for purposes of trespass law. * * * We therefore decline to create an exception * * * to the general rule that a trespass to chattels is not actionable if it does not involve actual or threatened injury to the personal property or to the possessor's legally protected interest in the personal property. No such injury having been shown on the undisputed facts, Intel was not entitled to summary judgment in its favor.

We concur: KENNARD, MORENO, JJ., and PERREN, J.

[Concurring opinion of Justice Kennard omitted.]

Dissenting opinion of BROWN, J.

Candidate A finds the vehicles that candidate B has provided for his campaign workers, and A spray paints the water soluble message, "Fight corruption, vote for A" on the bumpers. The majority's reasoning would find that notwithstanding the time it takes the workers to remove the paint and the expense they incur in altering the bumpers to prevent further unwanted messages, candidate B does not deserve an injunction unless the paint is so heavy that it reduces the cars' gas mileage or otherwise depreciates the cars' market value. Furthermore, candidate B has an obligation to permit the paint's display, because the cars are driven by workers and not B personally, because B allows his workers to use the cars to pick up their lunch or retrieve their children from school, or because the bumpers display B's own slogans. I disagree.

Intel has invested millions of dollars to develop and maintain a computer system. It did this not to act as a public forum but to enhance the productivity of its employees. Kourosh Kenneth Hamidi sent as many as 200,000 e-mail messages to Intel employees. The time required to review and delete Hamidi's messages diverted employees from productive tasks and undermined the utility of the computer system. "There may . . . be situations in which the value to the owner of a particular type of chattel may be impaired by dealing with it in a manner that does not affect its physical condition." REST. 2D TORTS, § 218, com. h, at 422. This is such a case. * * *

The majority refuses to protect Intel's interest in maintaining the integrity of its own system, contending that: (1) Hamidi's mailings did not physically injure the system; (2) Intel receives many unwanted messages, of which Hamidi's are but a small fraction; (3) Intel must have contemplated that it would receive some unwanted messages; and (4) Hamidi used the e-mail system for its intended purpose, to communicate with employees. * * *

Intel had the right to exclude the unwanted speaker from its property, which Hamidi does not dispute; he does not argue that he has a to right force unwanted messages on Intel. The instant case thus turns on the question of whether Intel deserves a remedy for the continuing violation of its rights. I believe it does, and as numerous cases have demonstrated, an injunction to prevent a trespass to chattels is an appropriate means of enforcement. * * *

HARMLESS TRESPASSES TO CHATTELS MAY BE PREVENTED

* * * Regardless of whether property is real or personal, it is beyond dispute that an individual has the right to have his personal property free from interference. There is some division among authorities regarding the available remedy, particularly whether a harmless trespass supports a claim for nominal damages. * * * But the Restatement expressly refutes defendant's assertion that only real property is inviolable. From the modest distinction holding that only victims of a trespass to land may profit in the form of damages exceeding actual harm, defendant offers the position that only trespasses to land may be *prevented*. The law is to the contrary; numerous cases have authorized injunctive relief to safeguard the inviolability of personal property. * * *

The *CompuServe* court * * * authoriz[ed] an injunction to prevent the delivery of unwanted e-mail messages. The majority summarily distinguishes *CompuServe* and its progeny by noting "there the plaintiff showed, or was prepared to show, some interference with the efficient functioning of its computer system." But although *CompuServe* did note the impairment imposed by the defendant's unsolicited e-mail, this was not part of its holding. Just before beginning its analysis, the court summarized its ruling without mentioning impairment. "[T]his Court holds that where defendants engaged in a course of conduct of transmitting a substantial volume of electronic data in the form of unsolicited e-mail to plaintiff's proprietary computer equipment, where defendants continued such practice after repeated demands to cease and desist, and where defendants deliberately evaded plaintiff's affirmative efforts to protect its computer equipment from such use, plaintiff has a viable claim for trespass to personal property and is entitled to injunctive relief to protect its property." *CompuServe*, 962 F. Supp. at 1017. The cited criteria apply fully to Hamidi's conduct. Likewise, the conclusion of *CompuServe's* analysis fully applies here: "Defendants' intentional use of plaintiff's proprietary computer equipment exceeds plaintiff's consent and, indeed, continued after repeated demands that defendants cease. Such use is an actionable trespass to plaintiff's chattel." *Id.* at p. 1027.

Post-*CompuServe* case law has emphasized that unauthorized use of another's property establishes a trespass, even without a showing of physical damage. "Although eBay appears unlikely to be able to show a substantial interference at this time, such a showing is not required. Conduct that does not amount to a substantial interference with possession, but which consists of intermeddling with or use of another's personal property, is sufficient to establish a cause of action for trespass to chattel." *eBay, Inc. v. Bidder's Edge, Inc.* 100 F. Supp. 2d 1058, 1070 (N.D. Cal. 2000). While the *eBay* decision could be read to require an interference that was more than negligible, * * * this Court concludes that *eBay,* in fact, imposes no such requirement. Ultimately, the court in that case concluded that the defendant's conduct was sufficient to establish a cause of action for trespass not because the interference was "substantial" but simply because the defendant's conduct amounted to "use" of Plaintiff's computer. An intruder is not entitled to sleep in his neighbor's car, even if he does not chip the paint.

Hamidi concedes Intel's legal entitlement to block the unwanted messages. The problem is that although Intel has resorted to the cyberspace version of reasonable force, it has so far been unsuccessful in determining how to resist the unwanted use of its system. Thus, while Intel has the legal right to exclude Hamidi from its system, it does not have the physical ability. It *may* forbid Hamidi's use, but it *can* not prevent it.

To the majority, Hamidi's ability to outwit Intel's cyber defenses justifies denial of Intel's claim to exclusive use of its property. Under this reasoning, it is not right but might that determines the extent of a party's possessory interest. Although the world often works this way, the legal system should not.

INTEL SUFFERED INJURY

Even if *CompuServe* and its progeny deem injury a prerequisite for injunctive relief, such injury occurred here. Intel suffered not merely an affront to its dignitary interest in ownership but tangible economic loss. Furthermore, notwithstanding the calendar's doubts, it is entirely consistent with the Restatement and case law to recognize a property interest in the subjective utility of one's property. Finally, case law further recognizes as actionable the loss that occurs when one party maintains property for its own use and another party uses it, even if the property does not suffer damage as a result.

Intel Suffered Economic Loss

Courts have recognized the tangible costs imposed by the receipt of unsolicited bulk e-mail (UBE). * * * Although Hamidi claims he sent only six e-mails, he sent them to between 8,000 and 35,000 employees, thus sending from 48,000 to 210,000 messages. Since it is the effect on Intel that is determinative, it is the number of messages received, not sent, that matters. In any event, Hamidi *sent* between 48,000 and 210,000 messages; the six refers only to the number of distinct texts Hamidi sent. Even if it takes little time to determine the author of a message and then delete it, this process, multiplied hundreds of thousands of times, amounts to a substantial loss of employee time, and thus work product. If Intel received

200,000 messages, and each one could be skimmed and deleted in six seconds, it would take approximately 333 hours, or 42 business days, to delete them all. In other words, if Intel hired an employee to remove all unwanted mail, it would take that individual two entire months to finish.

Intel's Injury is Properly Related to the Chattel

The majority does not dispute that Intel suffered a loss of work product as a matter of fact, so much as it denies that this loss may constitute the requisite injury as a matter of law. According to the majority, the reduced utility of the chattel to the owner does not constitute a sufficiently cognizable injury, which exists only where the chattel itself suffers injury, i.e., its market value falls. The Restatement and related case law are to the contrary.

The Restatement recognizes that the measure of impairment may be subjective; a cognizable injury may occur not only when the trespass reduces the chattel's market value but also when the trespass affects its value to the owner. * * * *CompuServe* is in accord, as it observed how a bundle of unwanted messages decreased the utility of the server. Here, Intel maintains a possessory interest in the efficient and productive use of its system—which it spends millions of dollars to acquire and maintain. Hamidi's conduct has impaired the system's optimal functioning for Intel's business purposes. As the Restatement supports liability where "harm is caused to . . . some . . . thing in which the possessor has a legally protected interest," REST. 2D TORTS, § 218, subd. (d), Hamidi has trespassed upon Intel's chattel.

The Unlawful Use of Another's Property is a Trespass, Regardless of Its Effect on the Property's Utility to the Owner

Finally, even if Hamidi's interference did not affect the server's utility to Intel, it would still amount to a trespass. Intel has poured millions of dollars into a resource that Hamidi has now appropriated for his own use. * * * Intel has paid for thousands of computers, as well as the costs of maintaining a server. * * * Hamidi has * * * acted as a free rider in enjoying the use of not only Intel's computer system but the extra storage capacity needed to accommodate his messages. * * * Hamidi has thus unlawfully shifted the costs of his speaking to Intel.

Moreover, even such free ridership is not necessary to establish a trespass to chattels. * * * *"[N]either injury to the trespassee nor benefit to the trespasser is an element of trespass to chattel.* [T]respass to chattel has evolved considerably from its original common law application—concerning the asportation of another's tangible property—to include even the unauthorized *use* of personal property." *Thrifty Tel, supra,* 46 Cal. App. 4th at 1566, 54 Cal. Rptr. 2d 468.

As in those cases in which courts have granted injunctions to prevent the delivery of unwanted mail, paper or electronic, Intel is not attempting to *profit* from its trespass action by receiving nominal damages. Rather, it seeks an injunction to *prevent* further trespass. Moreover, Intel suffered the requisite injury by losing a great deal of work product, a harm properly related to the property itself, as well as the money it spent in maintaining the system, which Hamidi wrongfully expropriated.

CONCLUSION

Those who have contempt for grubby commerce and reverence for the rarified heights of intellectual discourse may applaud today's decision, but even the flow of ideas will be curtailed if the right to exclude is denied. * * * The principles of both personal liberty and social utility should counsel us to usher the common law of property into the digital age.

Dissenting Opinion by MOSK, J.

In my view, the repeated transmission of bulk e-mails by appellant * * * Hamidi to the employees of Intel * * * on its proprietary confidential e-mail lists, despite Intel's demand that he cease such activities, constituted an actionable trespass to chattels. The majority fail to distinguish open communication in the public commons of the Internet from unauthorized intermeddling on a private, proprietary intranet. Hamidi is not communicating in the equivalent of a town square or of an unsolicited junk mailing through the United States Postal Service. His action, in crossing from the public Internet into a private intranet, is more like intruding into a private office mailroom, commandeering the mail cart, and dropping off unwanted broadsides on 30,000 desks. Because Intel's security measures have been circumvented by Hamidi, the majority leave Intel, which has exercised all reasonable self-help efforts, with no recourse unless he causes a malfunction or systems crash. Hamidi's repeated intrusions did more than merely prompt[ ] discussions between "[e]xcited and nervous managers" and the company's human resource department; they also constituted a misappropriation of Intel's private computer system contrary to its intended use and against Intel's wishes. * * *

The majority suggest that Intel is not entitled to injunctive relief because it chose to allow its employees access to e-mail through the Internet and because Hamidi has apparently told employees that he will remove them from his mailing list if they so request. They overlook the proprietary nature of Intel's intranet system; Intel's system is not merely a conduit for messages to its employees. As the owner of the computer system, it is Intel's request that Hamidi stop that must be respected. The fact that, like most large businesses, Intel's intranet includes external e-mail access for essential business purposes does not logically mean, as the majority suggest, that Intel has forfeited the right to determine who has access to its system. Its intranet is not the equivalent of a common carrier or public communications licensee that would be subject to requirements to provide service and access. Just as Intel can, and does, regulate the use of its computer system by its employees, it should be entitled to control its use by outsiders and to seek injunctive relief when self-help fails. * * *

As discussed above, I believe that existing legal principles are adequate to support Intel's request for injunctive relief. But even if the injunction in this case amounts to an extension of the traditional tort of trespass to chattels, this is one of those cases in which, as Justice Cardozo suggested, "[t]he creative element in the judicial process finds its opportunity and power in the development of the law." CARDOZO, NATURE OF THE JUDICIAL PROCESS 165 (1921).

The law has evolved to meet economic, social, and scientific changes in society. The industrial revolution, mass production, and new transportation and communication systems all required the adaptation and evolution of legal doctrines. The age of computer technology and cyberspace poses new challenges to legal principles. * * * The court must now grapple with proprietary interests, privacy, and expression arising out of computer-related disputes. * * * That the Legislature has dealt with some aspects of commercial unsolicited bulk e-mail should not inhibit the application of common law tort principles to deal with e-mail transgressions not covered by the legislation.

Before the computer, a person could not easily cause significant disruption to another's business or personal affairs through methods of communication without significant cost. With the computer, by a mass mailing, one person can at no cost disrupt, damage, and interfere with another's property, business, and personal interests. Here, the law should allow Intel to protect its computer-related property from the unauthorized, harmful, free use by intruders.

Notes and Questions

1. The common law actions for trespass to land and trespass to chattels are distinctly different. As one commentator has pointed out:

> Conflating these two types of trespass has serious consequences; they may share a common history, and even a common name, but they secure entirely different interests. Trespass to chattels exists as "the little brother of conversion." The gravamen of both actions lies in the dispossession of the property from its owner. In conversion, the dispossession is total; in trespass to chattels, the dispossession is only partial. Neither entails the interest in inviolability that attends trespass to land. Indeed, even in the context of real property, impinging ephemeral substances such as smoke, or intangibles such as sound or light, typically have been addressed under doctrines of nuisance rather than doctrines of trespass.

Dan L. Burk, *The Trouble with Trespass*, 4 J. SMALL & EMERGING BUS. L. 27, 33 (2000). Thus, there is at least some question whether electronic signals sent via e-mail are sufficiently "tangible" to qualify as "interference" with a computer system, quite apart from the issue of what harm, if any, is required to sustain a claim for injunctive relief.

2. The broader question is whether the idea of trespass should be applied to the *Hamidi* case. In what ways do you find the analogy to trespass to chattels useful? Is the analogy to trespass to real property more persuasive? What about common law nuisance? Would that be a better analogy, or does it replicate the problems of trespass?

3. Notice that the majority and dissenting opinions disagree both about the extent of harm Intel suffered as a result of Hamidi's e-mail and whether Intel even needs to show harm at all. What are the possible harms to Intel that the dissents identify? Why does the majority reject these allegations of harm? Should a showing of harm be required for Intel to secure injunctive relief? Why or why not?

4. How does the *Hamidi* court attempt to distinguish the *eBay* case? Is its effort persuasive? If a case with facts similar to *eBay* again arose in California, would it be decided the same way?

5. Notice the variety of metaphors employed by the three *Hamidi* opinions excerpted above. Are any of these metaphors useful or persuasive? Or would the justices be better off saying that this is simply a new kind of harm that tort law either should or should not protect?

6. Are there other available ways, short of legal action, for Intel to stop Hamidi? The majority appears to conclude that Intel would be free to use self-help to block Hamidi's e-mails. What kinds of "self-help" alternatives are open to Intel? How effective are these alternatives? Suppose that Intel could take a very simple action—putting one line of code into its mail server's routing program—that would make it impossible for Hamidi to get his e-mail onto that server; should that affect the court's decision about whether Intel also has a legal right of action against Hamidi?

7. Is there any reason to treat e-mail differently from other forms of trespass? Can you think of specific attributes of e-mail communication that make the need to stop people like Hamidi more pressing? How about specific attributes of e-mail that make the need to stop people like Hamidi *less* pressing?

8. Why do the dissenting justices find it important that Intel created a private intranet system for its own employees and did not "open up" such a system to the public? If indeed it is important to analyze the degree to which a system is open to the public, would that mean that Bidder's Edge did *not* trespass (because eBay was open to the public)?

9. As discussed in *Hamidi*, courts have used trespass theories to enjoin the sending of unsolicited business e-mails (also known as "spam") over computer networks. For example, in *CompuServe v. Cyber Promotions*, 962 F. Supp. 1015 (S.D. Ohio 1997), CompuServe was granted an injunction preventing Cyber Promotions from sending bulk e-mail over CompuServe's system. Should Hamidi's e-mail messages be treated differently from commercial bulk e-mail? If so, is there any way to draw a useful distinction? Is the majority's effort to distinguish *CompuServe* persuasive?

10. One possible concern is that a private trespass action will permit website operators and service providers to stifle speech. For example, if trespass can be used to clear a system of spam, one could imagine an ISP similarly deciding to clear its networks of undesirable Internet web content, such as transmissions from pornographic or white supremacist websites (or even sites espousing political views with which the CEO of the ISP disagrees). Do you think this is a problem? Or do you think such speech restrictions are permissible because the websites are sending electronic signals over the ISP's

"private" property? Although such actions might raise free speech concerns, the First Amendment has often been interpreted to reach only governmental censorship rather than censorship by private property owners. Should cyberspace be deemed private property or has it replaced the traditional town square, making it effectively public? This issue is explored in more detail in Chapter Five.

SECTION B. CONSUMER CONFUSION AND ONLINE TRADEMARKS

Trademark law protects words, symbols, and other means of identifying the source of goods and services. At the federal level, the main source of trademark protection is the Lanham Act. Two of the most important provisions of that statute are section 32 (15 U.S.C. § 1114), governing infringement of a registered mark, and section 43(a) (15 U.S.C. § 1125(a)), governing unfair competition. Both provisions prohibit the use of a competitor's mark in commerce in connection with the offering of goods and services in a manner that is likely to cause confusion. Although protection against confusingly similar uses of a mark is the essence of trademark law, in 1995 Congress provided additional federal protection for "famous" marks, by prohibiting "dilution" of such marks even when a particular use would be unlikely to cause confusion and the defendant is not in competition with the owner of the mark. *See* 15 U.S.C. §§ 1125(c), 1127.

One of the functions of a trademark is to reduce a consumer's search costs, by providing information about the price, quality, and location of a particular product. Obviously the Internet drastically reduces such search costs. Should consumer confusion in the online context therefore be treated differently? Consider the following case.

Brookfield Communications, Inc. v. West Coast Entertainment Corp.

United States Court of Appeals for the Ninth Circuit, 1999
174 F.3d 1036

O'SCANNLAIN, Circuit Judge.

We must venture into cyberspace to determine whether federal trademark and unfair competition laws prohibit a video rental store chain from using an entertainment-industry information provider's trademark in the domain name of its web site and in its web site's metatags.

Brookfield Communications, Inc. ("Brookfield") appeals the district court's denial of its motion for a preliminary injunction prohibiting West Coast Entertainment Corporation ("West Coast") from using in commerce terms confusingly similar to Brookfield's trademark, "MovieBuff." Brookfield gathers and sells information about the entertainment industry.

Founded in 1987 for the purpose of creating and marketing software and services for professionals in the entertainment industry, Brookfield initially offered software applications featuring information such as recent film submissions, industry credits, professional contacts, and future projects. These offerings targeted major Hollywood film studios, independent production companies, agents, actors, directors, and producers.

Brookfield expanded into the broader consumer market with computer software featuring a searchable database containing entertainment-industry related information marketed under the "MovieBuff" mark around December 1993. Brookfield's "MovieBuff" software now targets smaller companies and individual consumers who are not interested in purchasing Brookfield's professional level alternative, The Studio System, and includes comprehensive, searchable, entertainment-industry databases and related software applications containing information such as movie credits, box office receipts, films in development, film release schedules, entertainment news, and listings of executives, agents, actors, and directors.   This "MovieBuff" software comes in three versions—(1) the MovieBuff Pro Bundle, (2) the MovieBuff Pro, and (3) MovieBuff—and is sold through various retail stores, such as Borders, Virgin Megastores, Nobody Beats the Wiz, The Writer's Computer Store, Book City, and Samuel French Bookstores.

Sometime in 1996, Brookfield attempted to register the World Wide Web ("the Web") domain name "moviebuff.com" with Network Solutions, Inc. ("Network Solutions"), but was informed that the requested domain name had already been registered by West Coast. Brookfield subsequently registered "brookfieldcomm.com" in May 1996 and "moviebuffonline.com" in September 1996. Sometime in 1996 or 1997, Brookfield began using its web sites to sell its "MovieBuff" computer software and to offer an Internet-based searchable database marketed under the "MovieBuff" mark. Brookfield sells its "MovieBuff" computer software through its "brookfieldcomm.com" and "moviebuffonline.com" web sites and offers subscribers online access to the MovieBuff database itself at its "inhollywood.com" web site.

On August 19, 1997, Brookfield applied to the Patent and Trademark Office (PTO) for federal registration of "MovieBuff" as a mark to designate both goods and services. Its trademark application describes its product as "computer software providing data and information in the field of the motion picture and television industries." Its service mark application describes its service as "providing multiple-user access to an on-line network database offering data and information in the field of the motion picture and television industries." Both federal trademark registrations issued on September 29, 1998. Brookfield had previously obtained a California state trademark registration for the mark "MovieBuff" covering "computer software" in 1994.

In October 1998, Brookfield learned that West Coast—one of the nation's largest video rental store chains with over 500 stores—intended to launch a web site at "moviebuff.com" containing, *inter alia*, a searchable entertainment database similar to "MovieBuff." West Coast had registered "moviebuff.com" with Network Solutions on February 6, 1996 and claims that it chose the domain name because the term "Movie Buff" is part of its service mark, "The Movie Buff's Movie Store," on which a federal registration issued in 1991 covering "retail store services featuring video cassettes and video game cartridges" and "rental of video cassettes and video game cartridges." West Coast notes further that, since at least 1988, it has also used various phrases including the term "Movie Buff" to promote goods and services available at its video stores in Massachusetts * * * .

On November 10, Brookfield delivered to West Coast a cease-and-desist letter alleging that West Coast's planned use of the "moviebuff.com" would violate Brookfield's trademark rights; as a "courtesy" Brookfield attached a copy of a complaint that it threatened to file if West Coast did not desist.

The next day, West Coast issued a press release announcing the imminent launch of its web site full of "movie reviews, Hollywood news and gossip, provocative commentary, and coverage of the independent film scene and films in production." The press release declared that the site would feature "an extensive database, which aids consumers in making educated decisions about the rental and purchase of" movies and would also allow customers to purchase movies, accessories, and other entertainment-related merchandise on the web site. * * *

To resolve the legal issues before us, we must first understand the basics of the * * * World Wide Web. * * * Each web page has a corresponding domain address, which is an identifier somewhat analogous to a telephone number or street address. Domain names consist of a second-level domain—simply a term or series of terms (e.g., westcoastvideo)—followed by a top-level domain, many of which describe the nature of the enterprise. Top-level domains include ".com" (commercial), ".edu" (educational), ".org" (non-profit and miscellaneous organizations), ".gov" (government), ".net" (networking provider), and ".mil" (military). Commercial entities generally use the ".com" top-level domain, which also serves as a catchall top-level domain. To obtain a domain name, an individual or entity files an application with Network Solutions listing the domain name the applicant wants. Because each web page must have an unique domain name, Network Solution checks to see whether the requested domain name has already been assigned to someone else. If so, the applicant must choose a different domain name. Other than requiring an applicant to make certain representations, Network Solutions does not make an independent determination about a registrant's right to use a particular domain name.

Using a Web browser, such as Netscape's Navigator or Microsoft's Internet Explorer, a cyber "surfer" may navigate the Web—searching for, communicating with, and retrieving information from various web sites. A specific web site is most easily located by using its domain name. Upon entering a domain name into the web browser, the corresponding web site will quickly appear on the computer screen. Sometimes, however, a Web surfer will not know the domain name of the site he is looking for, whereupon he has two principal options: trying to guess the domain name or seeking the assistance of an Internet "search engine."

Oftentimes, an Internet user will begin by hazarding a guess at the domain name, especially if there is an obvious domain name to try. Web users often assume, as a rule of thumb, that the domain name of a particular company will be the company name followed by ".com." For example, one looking for Kraft Foods, Inc. might try "kraftfoods.com," and indeed this web site contains information on Kraft's many food products. Sometimes, a trademark is better known than the company itself, in which case a Web surfer may assume that the domain address will be "'trademark'.com." One interested in today's news would do well visiting "usatoday.com," which features, as one would expect, breaking stories from Gannett's USA Today. Guessing domain names, however, is not a risk-free activity. The Web surfer who assumes that "'X'.com" will always correspond to the web site of company X or trademark X will, however, sometimes be misled. One looking for the latest information on Panavision, International, L.P., would sensibly try "panavision.com." Until recently, that Web surfer would have instead found a web site owned by Dennis Toeppen featuring photographs of the City of Pana, Illinois. Having registered several domain names that logically would have corresponded to the web sites of major companies such as Panavision, Delta Airlines, Neiman Marcus, Lufthansa, Toeppen sought to sell "panavision.com" to Panavision, which gives one a taste of some of the trademark issues that have arisen in cyberspace.

A Web surfer's second option when he does not know the domain name is to utilize an Internet search engine, such as Yahoo, Altavista, or Lycos. When a keyword is entered, the search engine processes it through a self-created index of web sites to generate a (sometimes long) list relating to the entered keyword. Each search engine uses its own algorithm to arrange indexed materials in sequence, so the list of web sites that any particular set of keywords will bring up may differ depending on the search engine used. Search engines look for keywords in places such as domain names, actual text on the web page, and metatags. Metatags are [Hypertext Markup Language (HTML)] code intended to describe the contents of the web site. There are different types of metatags, but those of principal concern to us are the "description" and "keyword" metatags. The description metatags are intended to describe the web site; the keyword metatags, at least in theory, contain keywords relating to the contents of the web site. The more often a term appears in the metatags and in the text of the web page, the more likely it is that the web page will be "hit" in a search for that keyword and the higher on the list of "hits" the web page will appear.

With this basic understanding of the * * * Web, we may now analyze the legal issues before us. * * *

To establish a trademark infringement claim under section 32 of the Lanham Act or an unfair competition claim under section 43(a) of the Lanham Act, Brookfield must establish that West Coast is using a mark confusingly similar to a valid, protectable trademark of Brookfield's. * * *

[The court first determined that Brookfield has a valid, protectable trademark interest in the "MovieBuff" mark and marketed "MovieBuff" products well before West Coast began using "moviebuff.com" in commerce.]

Brookfield must also show that the public is likely to be somehow confused about the source or sponsorship of West Coast's "moviebuff.com" web site—and somehow to associate that site with Brookfield. The Supreme Court has described "the basic objectives of trademark law" as follows: "trademark law, by preventing others from copying a source-identifying mark, 'reduce[s] the customer's costs of shopping and making purchasing decisions,' for it quickly and easily assures a potential customer that this item—the item with this mark—is made by the same producer as other similarly marked items that he or she liked (or disliked) in the past. At the same time, the law helps assure a producer that it (and not an imitating competitor) will reap the financial, reputation-related rewards associated with a desirable product." *Qualitex Co. v. Jacobson Products Co., Inc.*, 514 U.S. 159, 163-64 (1995) (internal citations omitted). Where two companies each use a different mark and the simultaneous use of those marks does not cause the consuming public to be confused as to who makes what, granting one company exclusive rights over both marks does nothing to further the objectives of the trademark laws; in fact, prohibiting the use of a mark that the public has come to associate with a company would actually contravene the intended purposes of the trademark law by making it *more* difficult to identify and to distinguish between different brands of goods.

"The core element of trademark infringement is the likelihood of confusion, i.e., whether the similarity of the marks is likely to confuse customers about the source of the products." *Official Airline Guides, Inc. v. Goss*, 6 F.3d 1385, 1391 (9th Cir. 1993) (quotation marks omitted). We look to the following factors for guidance in determining the likelihood of confusion: similarity of the conflicting designations; relatedness or proximity of the two companies' products or services; strength of Brookfield's mark; marketing channels used; degree of care likely to be exercised by purchasers in selecting goods; West Coast's intent in selecting its mark; evidence of actual confusion; and likelihood of expansion in product lines. * * *

[Applying these factors, the court determined that that Brookfield had demonstrated a likelihood of success on its claim that West Coast's use of "moviebuff.com" infringed Brookfield's trademark.]

At first glance, our resolution of the infringement issues in the domain name context would appear to dictate a similar conclusion of likelihood of confusion with respect to West Coast's use of "moviebuff.com" in its metatags. Indeed, all eight likelihood of confusion factors outlined [above]—with the possible exception of purchaser care, which we discuss below—apply here as they did in our analysis of domain names; we are, after all, dealing with the same marks, the same products and services, the same consumers, etc. Disposing of the issue so readily, however, would ignore the fact that the likelihood of confusion in the domain name context resulted largely from the associational confusion between West Coast's domain name "moviebuff.com" and Brookfield's trademark "MovieBuff." The question in the metatags context is quite different. Here, we must determine whether West Coast can use "MovieBuff" or "moviebuff.com" in the metatags of its web site at "westcoastvideo.com" or at any other domain address *other than* "moviebuff.com" (which we have determined that West Coast may not use).

Although entering "MovieBuff" into a search engine is likely to bring up a list including "westcoastvideo.com" if West Coast has included that term in its metatags, the resulting confusion is not as great as where West Coast uses the "moviebuff.com" domain name. First, when the user inputs "MovieBuff" into an Internet search engine, the list produced by the search engine is likely to include both West Coast's and Brookfield's web sites. Thus, in scanning such list, the Web user will often be able to find the particular web site he is seeking. Moreover, even if the Web user chooses the web site belonging to West Coast, he will see that the domain name of the web site he selected is "westcoastvideo.com." Since there is no confusion resulting from the domain address, and since West Coast's initial web page prominently displays its own name, it is difficult to say that a consumer is likely to be confused about whose site he has reached or to think that Brookfield somehow sponsors West Coast's web site.

Nevertheless, West Coast's use of "moviebuff.com" in metatags will still result in what is known as initial interest confusion. Web surfers looking for Brookfield's "MovieBuff" products who are taken by a search engine to "westcoastvideo.com" will find a database similar enough to "MovieBuff" such that a sizeable number of consumers who were originally looking for Brookfield's product will simply decide to utilize West Coast's offerings instead. Although there is no source confusion in the sense that consumers know they are patronizing West Coast rather than Brookfield, there is nevertheless initial interest confusion in the sense that, by using "moviebuff.com" or "MovieBuff" to divert people looking for "MovieBuff" to its web site, West Coast improperly benefits from the goodwill that Brookfield developed in its mark. * * *

[D]iversion of consumers' initial interest is a form of confusion against which the Lanham Act protects * * * . [For example, in *Mobil Oil Corp. v. Pegasus Petroleum Corp.*, 818 F.2d 254 (2d Cir. 1987),] Mobil Oil Corporation ("Mobil") asserted a federal trademark infringement claim against Pegasus Petroleum, alleging that Pegasus Petroleum's use of "Pegasus" was likely to cause confusion with Mobil's trademark, a flying horse symbol in the form of the Greek mythological Pegasus. Mobil established that "potential purchasers would be misled into an initial interest in Pegasus Petroleum" because they thought that Pegasus

Petroleum was associated with Mobil. *Id.* at 260. But these potential customers would generally learn that Pegasus Petroleum was unrelated to Mobil well before any actual sale was consummated. Nevertheless, the Second Circuit held that "[s]uch initial confusion works a sufficient trademark injury." *Id.* * * *

Using another's trademark in one's metatags is much like posting a sign with another's trademark in front of one's store. Suppose West Coast's competitor (let's call it "Blockbuster") puts up a billboard on a highway reading—"West Coast Video: 2 miles ahead at Exit 7"—where West Coast is really located at Exit 8 but Blockbuster is located at Exit 7. Customers looking for West Coast's store will pull off at Exit 7 and drive around looking for it. Unable to locate West Coast, but seeing the Blockbuster store right by the highway entrance, they may simply rent there. Even consumers who prefer West Coast may find it not worth the trouble to continue searching for West Coast since there is a Blockbuster right there. Customers are not confused in the narrow sense: they are fully aware that they are purchasing from Blockbuster and they have no reason to believe that Blockbuster is related to, or in any way sponsored by, West Coast. Nevertheless, the fact that there is only initial consumer confusion does not alter the fact that Blockbuster would be misappropriating West Coast's acquired goodwill.

The few courts to consider whether the use of another's trademark in one's metatags constitutes trademark infringement have ruled in the affirmative. For example, in a case in which Playboy Enterprises, Inc. ("Playboy") sued AsiaFocus International, Inc. ("AsiaFocus") for trademark infringement resulting from AsiaFocus's use of the federally registered trademarks "Playboy" and "Playmate" in its HTML code, a district court granted judgment in Playboy's favor, reasoning that AsiaFocus intentionally misled viewers into believing that its Web site was connected with, or sponsored by, Playboy. * * *

[W]e conclude that the Lanham Act bars West Coast from including in its metatags any term confusingly similar with Brookfield's mark. West Coast argues that our holding conflicts with *Holiday Inns*, in which the Sixth Circuit held that there was no trademark infringement where an alleged infringer merely took advantage of a situation in which confusion was likely to exist and did not affirmatively act to create consumer confusion. *See Holiday Inns, Inc. v. 800 Reservation*, 86 F.3d 619, 622 (6th Cir. 1997) (holding that the use of "1-800-405-4329"—which is equivalent to "1-800-H[zero]LIDAY"—did not infringe Holiday Inn's trademark, "1-800-HOLIDAY"). Unlike the defendant in *Holiday Inns*, however, West Coast was not a passive figure; instead, it acted affirmatively in placing Brookfield's trademark in the metatags of its web site, thereby *creating* the initial interest confusion. Accordingly, our conclusion comports with *Holiday Inns*.

Contrary to West Coast's contentions, we are not in any way restricting West Coast's right to use terms in a manner which would constitute fair use under the Lanham Act. It is well established that the Lanham Act does not prevent one from using a competitor's mark truthfully to identify the competitor's goods, or in comparative advertisements. This fair use doctrine applies in cyberspace as it does in the real world. * * *

We agree that West Coast can legitimately use an appropriate descriptive term in its metatags. But "MovieBuff" is not such a descriptive term. Even though it differs from "Movie Buff" by only a single space, that difference is pivotal. The term "Movie Buff" is a descriptive term, which is routinely used in the English language to describe a movie devotee. "MovieBuff" is not. The term "MovieBuff" is not in the dictionary. Nor has that term been used in any published federal or state court opinion. In light of the fact that it is not a word in the English language, when the term "MovieBuff" *is* employed, it is used to refer to Brookfield's products and services, rather than to mean "motion picture enthusiast." The proper term for the "motion picture enthusiast" is "Movie Buff," which West Coast certainly *can* use. It cannot, however, omit the space.

Moreover, West Coast is not absolutely barred from using the term "MovieBuff." As we explained above, that term can be legitimately used to describe Brookfield's product. For example, its web page might well include an advertisement banner such as "Why pay for MovieBuff when you can get the same thing here for FREE?" which clearly employs "MovieBuff" to refer to Brookfield's products. West Coast, however, presently uses Brookfield's trademark not to reference Brookfield's products, but instead to describe its own product (in the case of the domain name) and to attract people to its web site in the case of the metatags. That is not fair use.

Notes and Questions

1. With respect to West Coast's use of the domain name "moviebuff.com," what if consumers who go to the site are immediately greeted with the following message: "THIS IS THE WEBSITE OF WEST COAST VIDEO. IT IS **NOT** THE SITE OF BROOKFIELD COMMUNICATIONS." Would that cure the confusion? Does your answer change if, in addition to the disclaimer, West Coast's site also provides a link to Brookfield's site?

2. The court of appeals distinguishes as follows between the confusion caused by West Coast's use of the moviebuff.com domain name and the confusion caused by West Coast's use of "MovieBuff" in its metatags: "[T]he resulting confusion is not as great as where West Coast uses the 'moviebuff.com' domain name. * * * [A] list produced by a search engine is likely to include both West Coast's and Brookfield's web site. Thus, in scanning such list, the Web user will often be able to find the particular web site he is seeking." The court then points out that the Lanham Act has been interpreted to encompass "initial interest confusion." Thus, it can be a violation if consumers are initially diverted to a competitor even if, by the time of purchase, customers are no longer confused as to the source of goods purchased. The rationale for this doctrine is aptly summarized in the court's hypothetical about Blockbuster Video erecting a misleading sign by the

highway. Go back to the opinion and read this discussion again. Do you agree with the court that the use of a competitor's mark as part of a metatag should be treated the same as use of a competitor's mark on a road sign? Can you think of any important differences? For example, how long do you think it takes consumers misdirected to a competitor's website to realize the error? How difficult is it for them to then re-direct their browser to the website they intended? Compare that to the highway exit example. Does the rationale for initial interest confusion still hold in cyberspace? Why or why not?

3. For comparison, consider a later case ruling that initial interest confusion—whereby "consumers will realize they are at the wrong site and go to an Internet search engine to find the right one—is not substantial enough to be legally cognizable." According to the court, "Internet surfers are inured to the false starts and excursions awaiting them" and are "unlikely to be dissuaded, or unnerved" when, after "tak[ing] a stab at what they think is the most likely domain name for a particular web site" guess wrong and bring up another's web page. *Strick Corp. v. Strickland*, 162 F. Supp. 2d 372, 377 (E.D. Pa. 2001) (internal quotation marks and citations omitted). Note that the *Strick Corp.* case involved use of a domain name by a defendant not in competition with the trademark holder, rather than the use of a domain name or metatags by a competitor. Is this enough to distinguish the case from *Brookfield*? For a case adopting *Brookfield*'s logic in the metatag context, see *Promatek Industries, Ltd. v. Equitrac Corp.*, 300 F.3d 808 (7th Cir. 2002).

4. How should *Brookfield*'s logic apply to other kinds of search confusion? After all, there are at least three types of search confusion that have generated trademark infringement suits. First, competitors may use trademarks in their own domain names. Second, competitors may use trademarks in their metatags, which results in more hits for the competitor whenever a customer runs a search for the trademarked site. Third, search engines themselves can—for a price—key trademarked terms to advertisements for rival websites.

Should these three scenarios be treated differently from each other? For example, consider a case in which a search engine keyed the trademarked terms "playboy" and "playmate" to websites seeking to compete with Playboy Enterprises, Inc. (the holder of the trademarks). On the one hand, as a competitor's use of a domain name, the advertisers appear to be taking advantage of the familiarity of Playboy's trademarked terms and the goodwill Playboy has developed. On the other hand, there is far less likelihood of actual consumer confusion because the user must actively decide to click on the advertised site, and there is no reason the user would necessarily think the site was connected to Playboy Enterprises.

That fact, however, does not necessarily distinguish the use of a keyed search term from use of a metatag. After all, in both types of cases, the trademarked term nowhere appears to the customer and is only used to influence the results of the search. In the metatag cases, unlike the keyed search term cases, the alleged infringer puts the trademarked name onto its own website as opposed to paying a search engine to use the trademarked term in its searches. But should that difference matter? For a case raising these issues, see *Playboy Enterprises, Inc. v. Netscape Communications Corp.*, 354 F.3d 1020 (9th Cir. 2004) (reversing district court's summary judgment ruling in favor of Netscape after finding issues of material fact concerning Playboy's trademark claim). How would you resolve each type of case?

5.   The Lanham Act also requires that the trademark be used "in commerce" by the alleged infringer. If a competitor pays a search engine to key online advertisements to trademarked terms, is that a "use in commerce," given that customers never see the way the trademarked term is used and the advertisements appear in separately marked windows? At least one court of appeals has found no use in commerce in this circumstance. *See 1-800-Contacts, Inc. v. WhenU.com, Inc.*, 414 F.3d 400 (2d Cir. 2005). Would you distinguish *Brookfield*'s initial interest confusion logic in this way?

In considering the *Brookfield* court's analogy, we might think of other, alternative "brick and mortar" comparisons that might apply. For example, what if Brookfield had a store on a street in a town, and West Coast purposely bought the lot right next door in order to lure away customers going to Brookfield. This is not at all an unlikely scenario. Indeed, Freeport, Maine has blossomed into an entire town filled with factory outlet stores largely because Freeport is home to the popular retailer L.L. Bean. Certainly, if one of those stores put a sign out front saying "We're better and cheaper than L.L. Bean–Shop Here!" it would be clear that the store was piggy-backing on both L.L. Bean's reputation and its customers' desire to go to the L.L. Bean store. But it is equally certain that this would not be a trademark violation. Are West Coast Video's actions in *Brookfield* relevantly different, or is using trademarks in domain names, metatags, or keyed search terms merely the cyber-equivalent of "locating" oneself in the "neighborhood" of a more famous competitor in the hope of picking off customers? On the other hand, perhaps the mere fact that one can only view a single website at a time makes the Internet version of "locating next door" more problematic. Or, perhaps it is sufficient, as discussed in notes 4-5 above, to allow competitors to key advertising to trademarked search terms, while prohibiting them (as in *Brookfield*) from using trademarks in the domain names (or metatags) themselves. But does that distinction make logical sense?

Might there be a free speech component to the question? For example, in the physical world, anti-abortion protesters often locate their protests near Planned Parenthood clinics in order to give information to women entering the clinic. Assuming that the protestors do not trespass on Planned Parenthood's property and their activities remain merely informational (for these purposes, we leave aside the extensive litigation concerning efforts to physically intimidate women), the mere fact that the protestors located themselves near Planned Parenthood would not normally be legally objectionable. Should the analysis be different if an anti-abortion group registers www.plannedparenthood.org and uses the site to provide arguments against abortion?

This was the subject of a 1997 case in which a federal district court found that an anti-abortion activist using www.plannedparenthood.org had infringed Planned Parenthood's trademark. In that case, however, the alleged infringer configured his website to deceive users into thinking they had actually reached Planned Parenthood's site. *See Planned Parenthood Federation of Am. v. Bucci*, 42 U.S.P.Q.2d 1430 (S.D.N.Y. 1997). But what if such deception were not present? Should political opponents be able to target an organization's potential "customers" the way they might in the physical world? Consider the following case.

People for the Ethical Treatment of Animals v. Doughney

United States Court of Appeals for the Fourth Circuit, 2001
263 F.3d 359

GREGORY, Circuit Judge.

People for the Ethical Treatment of Animals (PETA) * * * is an animal rights organization with more than 600,000 members worldwide. PETA "is dedicated to promoting and heightening public awareness of animal protection issues and it opposes the exploitation of animals for food, clothing, entertainment and vivisection."

Doughney is a former internet executive who has registered many domain names since 1995. * * * At the time the district court issued its summary judgment ruling, Doughney owned 50-60 domain names.

Doughney registered the domain name *peta.org* in 1995 with Network Solutions, Inc. ("NSI"). * * * After registering the *peta.org* domain name, Doughney used it to create a website purportedly on behalf of "People Eating Tasty Animals." Doughney claims he created the website as a parody of PETA. A viewer accessing the website would see the title "People Eating Tasty Animals" in large, bold type. Under the title, the viewer would see a statement that the website was a "resource for those who enjoy eating meat, wearing fur and leather, hunting, and the fruits of scientific research." The website contained links to various meat, fur, leather, hunting, animal research, and other organizations, all of which held views generally antithetical to PETA's views. Another statement on the website asked the viewer whether he/she was "Feeling lost? Offended? Perhaps you should, like, *exit immediately.*" The phrase *"exit immediately"* contained a hyperlink to PETA's official website. * * *

A plaintiff alleging causes of action for trademark infringement and unfair competition must prove (1) that it possesses a mark; (2) that the defendant used the mark; (3) that the defendant's use of the mark occurred "in commerce"; (4) that the defendant used the mark "in connection with the sale, offering for sale, distribution, or advertising" of goods or services; and (5) that the defendant used the mark in a manner likely to confuse consumers. 15 U.S.C. §§ 1114, 1125(a).

There is no dispute here that PETA owns the "PETA" Mark, that Doughney used it, and that Doughney used the Mark "in commerce." * * * To use PETA's Mark "in connection with" goods or services, Doughney need not have actually sold or advertised goods or services on the *www.peta.org* website. Rather, Doughney need only have prevented users from obtaining or using PETA's goods or services, or need only have connected the website to other's goods or services. * * * Moreover, Doughney's web site provides links to more than 30 commercial operations offering goods and services. By providing links to these commercial operations, Doughney's use of PETA's Mark is "in connection with" the sale of goods or services.

The unauthorized use of a trademark infringes the trademark holder's rights if it is likely to confuse an "ordinary consumer" as to the source or sponsorship of the goods. To determine whether a likelihood of confusion exists, a court should not consider "how closely a fragment of a given use duplicates the trademark," but must instead consider "whether the use in its entirety creates a likelihood of confusion."

Doughney does not dispute that the *peta.org* domain name engenders a likelihood of confusion between his web site and PETA. Doughney claims, though, that the inquiry should not end with his domain name. Rather, he urges the Court to consider his website in conjunction with the domain name because, together, they purportedly parody PETA and, thus, do not cause a likelihood of confusion.

A "parody" is defined as a "simple form of entertainment conveyed by juxtaposing the irreverent representation of the trademark with the idealized image created by the mark's owner." *L.L. Bean, Inc. v. Drake Publishers, Inc.*, 811 F. 2d 26, 34 (1st Cir.1987). A parody must "convey two simultaneous—and contradictory—messages: that it is the original, but also that it is *not* the original and is instead a parody." *Cliffs Notes, Inc. v. Bantam Doubleday Dell Publ. Group, Inc.*, 886 F. 2d 490, 494 (2d Cir.1989). To the extent that an alleged parody conveys only the first message, "it is not only a poor parody but also vulnerable under trademark law, since the customer will be confused." *Id.* While a parody necessarily must engender some initial confusion, an effective parody will diminish the risk of consumer confusion "by conveying [only] just enough of the original design to allow the consumer to appreciate the point of parody." *Jordache Enterprises, Inc. v. Hogg Wyld, Ltd.*, 828 F.2d 1482, 1486 (10th Cir.1987).

Looking at Doughney's domain name alone, there is no suggestion of a parody. The domain name *peta.org* simply copies PETA's Mark, conveying the message that it is related to PETA. The domain name does not convey the second, contradictory message needed to establish a parody—a message that the domain name is not related to PETA, but that it is a parody of PETA.

Doughney claims that this second message can be found in the content of his website. Indeed, the website's content makes it clear that it is not related to PETA. However, this second message is not conveyed *simultaneously* with the first message, as required to be considered a parody. The domain name conveys the first message; the second message is conveyed only when the viewer reads the content of the website. As the district court explained, "an internet user would not realize that they were not on an official PETA web site until after they had used PETA's Mark to access the web page 'www.peta.org.'" Thus, the messages are not conveyed simultaneously and do not constitute a parody. The district court properly rejected Doughney's parody defense and found that Doughney's use of the *peta.org* domain name engenders a likelihood of confusion.

Notes and Questions

1. On what basis does the court determine that the website at issue is sufficiently "commercial" so that the various provisions of the Lanham Act apply? Are these reasons convincing to you? Is there any way Doughney could have configured his website so as to be non-commercial under the court's criteria?

2. Judge Gregory rejects Doughney's argument that his use of the peta.org domain name would not cause confusion because the text of his site clearly identifies his opposition to PETA's cause. Why isn't the text sufficient to cure any possible confusion about the sites?

3. Consider again the introductory text immediately preceding this case. Assume that Doughney decides to open an office right next to a PETA location. He admits that he located his office specifically so that he can hand out literature to people who are drawn to the office next door and who might not otherwise come into contact with his communicative message. Do you think that would be a trademark violation? Why or why not? Is this analogy an appropriate one to apply to the domain name context? Why or why not?

4. Assume that Doughney gives up the disputed domain name, but continues to operate a website under his own name. Would it violate the Lanham Act for him to use the name "People for the Ethical Treatment of Animals" as a metatag? Or to pay a search engine to have his site listed every time people searched for PETA? Could the rationale in *Brookfield Communications* be distinguished? And if metatags and keyed search terms would also be impermissible, is there any way for Doughney to reach his target audiences online? If not, is that a cause for concern? In this regard, consider the following situation. Two companies are direct business competitors. Company X repeatedly uses Company Y's trade name on its site and in metatags so that, when users run a search for Company X, Company Y's site gets prominently listed in the search results as well. If Company Y is successful at diverting business to its site in this way, is there a trademark violation? In a case raising this question, a court distinguished *Brookfield* on the ground that the company using the competitor's trade name on its site was doing so in order to criticize that company, and there would be no way to criticize the company without using its name. *See J.K. Harris & Co. v. Kassel*, 253 F. Supp. 2d 1120 (N.D. Cal. 2003). The logic of this decision seems to imply that, if Doughney registers a new domain name, but then uses the words "People for the Ethical

Treatment of Animals" many times on his site in order both to criticize PETA and to divert traffic, such use might be permissible. Is this a sensible result?

5. What if Doughney registered a domain name, www.doughney.com, and placed the material critical of PETA on a page labeled www.doughney.com/peta? Does the existence of a trademark in a "post-domain path" create sufficient likelihood of confusion? At least one federal appellate court has rejected a trademark infringement claim under these circumstances. *See Interactive Products Corp. v. a2z Mobile Office Solutions*, 326 F.3d 687 (6th Cir. 2003).

SECTION C. INTERNET ACCESS AND CONTENT FILTERING IN PUBLIC LIBRARIES

Mainstream Loudoun v. Board of Trustees of the Loudoun County Public Library

United States District Court for the Eastern District of Virginia, 1998
2 F. Supp. 2d 783

BRINKEMA, District Judge.

I. Background

The plaintiffs in this case are an association, Mainstream Loudoun, and ten individual plaintiffs, all of whom are both members of Mainstream Loudoun and adult patrons of Loudoun County public libraries. Defendants are the Board of Trustees of the Loudoun County Public Library, five individual Board members, and Douglas Henderson, Loudoun County's Director of Library Services. The Loudoun County public library system has six branches and provides patrons with access to the Internet and the World Wide Web. Under state law, the "management and control" of this library system is vested in a Board of Trustees (the "Library Board"). * * *

On October 20, 1997, the Library Board voted to adopt a "Policy on Internet Sexual Harassment" (the "Policy"), which requires that "[s]ite-blocking software . . . be installed on all [library] computers" so as to: "a. block child pornography and obscene material (hard core pornography)"; and "b. block material deemed Harmful to Juveniles under applicable Virginia statutes and legal precedents (soft core pornography)." To implement the Policy, the Library Board chose "X-Stop," a commercial software product intended to limit access to sites deemed to violate the Policy.

Plaintiffs allege that the Policy impermissibly blocks their access to protected speech such as the Quaker Home Page, the Zero Population Growth website, and the site for the American Association of University Women–Maryland. They also claim that there are no clear criteria for blocking decisions and that defendants maintain an unblocking policy that unconstitutionally chills plaintiffs' receipt of constitutionally protected materials.

Based on the above allegations, plaintiffs bring this action under 42 U.S.C. § 1983 against the Library Board and against five individual Library Board members in both their personal and official capacities, and Director of Library Services Douglas Henderson in his official capacity. Plaintiffs allege that the Policy imposes an unconstitutional restriction on their right to access protected speech on the Internet, and seek declaratory and injunctive relief, as well as costs and attorneys' fees pursuant to 42 U.S.C. § 1988. [The defendants sought dismissal of the complaint or, in the alternative, summary judgment.] * * *

IV. Plaintiffs' First Amendment Claim

* * * [D]efendants concede that the Policy prohibits access to speech on the basis of its content. However, defendants argue that the "First Amendment does not in any way limit the decisions of a public library on whether to provide access to information on the Internet." Indeed, at oral argument, defendants went so far as to claim that a public library could constitutionally prohibit access to speech simply because it was authored by African-Americans, or because it espoused a particular political viewpoint, for example pro-Republican. Thus, the central question before this Court is whether a public library may, without violating the First Amendment, enforce content-based restrictions on access to Internet speech.

No cases directly address this issue. However, the parties agree that the most analogous authority on this issue is *Board of Education v. Pico*, 457 U.S. 853 (1982), in which the Supreme Court reviewed the decision of a local board of education to remove certain books from a high school library based on the board's belief that the books were "anti-American, anti-Christian, anti-Sem[i]tic, and just plain filthy." *Id.* at 856. The Second Circuit had reversed the district court's grant of summary judgment to the school board on plaintiff's First Amendment claim. A sharply-divided Court voted to affirm the Court of Appeal's decision to remand the case for a determination of the school board's motives. However, the Court did not render a majority opinion. Justice Brennan, joined by three Justices, [concluded] that the First Amendment necessarily limits the government's right to remove materials on the basis of their content from a high school library. Justice Brennan reasoned that the right to receive information is inherent in the right to speak and that "the State may not, consistently with the spirit of the First Amendment, contract the spectrum of available knowledge." *Id.* at 866 (plurality op.). Justice Brennan explained that this principle was particularly important given the special role of the school's library as a locus for free and independent inquiry. At the same time, Justice Brennan recognized that public high schools play a crucial inculcative role in "the preparation of individuals for participation as citizens" and are therefore entitled to great discretion "to establish and apply their curriculum in such a way as to transmit community values." *Id.* at 863-64. Accordingly, Justice Brennan held that the school board members could not remove books "simply because they dislike the ideas contained [in them]," thereby "prescrib[ing] what shall be orthodox in politics, nationalism, religion, or other matters of opinion," but that the board might remove books for reasons of educational suitability, for example pervasive vulgarity. *Id.* at 872.

In a concurring opinion, Justice Blackmun focused not on the right to receive information recognized by the plurality, but on the school board's discrimination against disfavored ideas. Justice Blackmun explicitly recognized that *Pico* 's facts invoked two significant, competing interests: the inculcative mission of public high schools and the First Amendment's core proscription against content-based regulation of speech. See id. at 876-79 (Blackmun, J., concurring). Justice Blackmun noted that the State must normally demonstrate a compelling reason for content-based regulation, but that a more limited form of protection should apply in the context of public high schools. Balancing the two principles above, Justice Blackmun agreed with the plurality that the school board could not remove books based on mere disapproval of their content but could limit its collection for reasons of educational suitability or budgetary constraint. Dissenting, Chief Justice Burger, joined by three Justices, concluded that any First Amendment right to receive speech did not affirmatively obligate the government to provide such speech in high school libraries. *See id.* at 888 (Burger, C.J., dissenting). Chief Justice Burger reasoned that although the State could not constitutionally prohibit a speaker from reaching an intended audience, nothing in the First Amendment requires public high schools to act as a conduit for particular speech. Chief Justice Burger explained that such an obligation would be inconsistent with public high schools' inculcative mission, which necessarily requires schools to make content-based choices among competing ideas in order to establish a curriculum and educate students.

Defendants contend that the *Pico* plurality opinion has no application to this case because it addressed only decisions to remove materials from libraries and specifically declined to address library decisions to acquire materials. Defendants liken the Internet to a vast Interlibrary Loan system, and contend that restricting Internet access to selected materials is merely a decision not to acquire such materials rather than a decision to remove them from a library's collection. As such, defendants argue, the instant case is outside the scope of the *Pico* plurality.

In response, plaintiffs argue that, unlike a library's collection of individual books, the Internet is a "single, integrated system." As plaintiffs explain, "[t]hough information on the Web is contained in individual computers, the fact that each of these computers is connected to the Internet through [World Wide Web] protocols allows all of the information to become part of a single body of knowledge." Accordingly, plaintiffs analogize the Internet to a set of encyclopedias, and the Library Board's enactment of the Policy to a decision to "black out" selected articles considered inappropriate for adult and juvenile patrons.

After considering both arguments, we conclude that defendants have misconstrued the nature of the Internet. By purchasing Internet access, each Loudoun library has made all Internet publications instantly accessible to its patrons. Unlike an Interlibrary loan or outright book purchase, no appreciable expenditure of library time or resources is required to make a particular Internet publication available to a library patron. In contrast, a library must actually expend resources to restrict Internet access to a publication that is otherwise immediately available. In effect, by purchasing one such publication, the library has purchased them all. The Internet therefore more closely resembles plaintiffs' analogy of a collection of encyclopedias from which defendants have laboriously redacted portions deemed unfit for library patrons. As such, the Library Board's action is more appropriately characterized as a removal decision. We therefore conclude that the principles discussed in the *Pico* plurality are relevant and apply to the Library Board's decision to promulgate and enforce the Policy. * * *

To the extent that *Pico* applies to this case, we conclude that it stands for the proposition that the First Amendment applies to, and limits, the discretion of a public library to place content-based restrictions on access to constitutionally protected materials within its collection. * * * Furthermore, the factors which justified giving high school libraries broad discretion to remove materials in *Pico* are not present in this case. * * * [A]dults are deemed to have acquired the maturity needed to participate fully in a democratic society, and their right to speak and receive speech is entitled to full First Amendment protection. Accordingly, adults are entitled to receive categories of speech, for example "pervasively vulgar" speech, which may be inappropriate for children. *See Reno v. ACLU*, 521 U.S. 844, 874 (1997). * * * [T]he tension Justice Blackmun recognized between the inculcative role of high schools and the First Amendment's prohibition on content-based regulation of speech does not exist here. * * * [N]o curricular motive justifies a public library's decision to restrict access to Internet materials on the basis of their content. Finally, the unique advantages of Internet speech eliminate any resource-related rationale libraries might otherwise have for engaging in content-based discrimination. * * *

In sum, there is "no basis for qualifying the level of First Amendment scrutiny" that must be applied to a public library's decision to restrict access to Internet publications. *Reno*, 521 U.S. at 870. We are therefore left with the First Amendment's central tenet that content-based restrictions on speech must be justified by a compelling governmental interest and must be narrowly tailored to achieve that end. This principle was recently affirmed within the context of Internet speech. *See id.* at 868-79. Accordingly, we hold that the Library Board may not adopt and enforce content-based restrictions on access to protected Internet speech absent a compelling state interest and means narrowly drawn to achieve that end.

This holding does not obligate defendants to act as unwilling conduits of information, because the Library Board need not provide access to the

Internet at all. Having chosen to provide access, however, the Library Board may not thereafter selectively restrict certain categories of Internet speech because it disfavors their content. * * *

[The court concluded that plaintiffs had stated a valid First Amendment claim and that several material factual issues remained, and therefore denied in relevant part the defendants' motion to dismiss and motion for summary judgment.]

Notes and Questions

1. This excerpt focuses primarily on the question of whether to treat library filtering as an acquisition or removal decision. There is, of course, a further issue as to whether and under what circumstances such filtering (at least in a public library) may be constitutionally permissible. That question will be taken up in Chapter Six.

2. Notice that while the parties agree that *Pico* was "the most analogous authority" on the issue presented in the instant case, the court still had to choose between very different interpretations of that case—a task made more difficult by the fact that the *Pico* court did not issue a majority opinion. Judge Brinkema takes a rather narrow view of the *Pico* decision; it stands, in her interpretation, "for the proposition that the First Amendment applies to, and limits, the discretion of a public library to place content-based restrictions on access to constitutionally protected materials *within its collection*" (emphasis added)—*i.e.*, it applies to library *removal* decisions, but not necessarily to library *acquisition* decisions. Does that distinction make sense? Are there reasons why the First Amendment might not apply, or might not apply in the same way, to a library's acquisition decision? It is true that the *Pico* case involved a challenge to a removal, not an acquisition, decision, but what makes that fact especially pertinent to the court's reading of the *Pico* opinions? If the Library Board in *Pico* had made its decision on a Tuesday, nobody would argue that the *Pico* opinion does not apply to library decisions made on Thursdays, would they? So what makes the court think that the removal/acquisition distinction is a meaningful one?

3. Having decided what *Pico* stands for, the court then has to apply the *Pico* principle to the case at hand. Why does the court reject defendant's argument that the Internet is a "vast Interlibrary Loan system," and, therefore, that restricting Internet access is equivalent to deciding not to acquire material for the library's patrons. What makes plaintiffs' analogy—that the Internet is like "a set of encyclopedias," a "single, integrated system," with the Board's policy equivalent to deciding to black out or remove articles it deems inappropriate—more persuasive? If the Internet is like an interlibrary loan system (in some ways), and it is like a set of encyclopedias (in some ways), how does the court decide which analogy is best for this case?

4. The court notes that "[u]nlike an Interlibrary loan or outright book purchase, no appreciable expenditure of library time or resources is required to make a particular Internet publication available to a library patron." Suppose the Loudoun County Library Board were offered a special discount deal on new computers that already had the filtering software pre-installed, and

that an "expenditure of library time or resources" would be required to un-install that software; would that change the result in this case? Should it?

5. The court notes that, "[b]y purchasing Internet access, each Loudoun library has made all Internet publications instantly accessible to its patrons." Is that a factual conclusion? A legal conclusion? Both?

6. According to the court, its holding "does not obligate defendants to act as unwilling conduits of information, because the Library Board need not provide access to the Internet at all." Is that a sensible policy choice—all or nothing? To what extent does this conclusion follow from the court's characterization of the Internet as a "single, integrated system"?

7. In *United States v. American Library Association, Inc.*, 539 U.S. 194 (2003), the Supreme Court considered the constitutionality of the Children's Internet Protection Act, a statute that made the use of filtering software by public libraries a condition of the receipt of funds under certain federal programs. The Court rejected a facial challenge to the statute, and the Justices' views on whether the decision to use filtering software constituted an "acquisition" or "removal" decision were crucial to their views on the statute's constitutionality. Chief Justice Rehnquist's plurality opinion in favor of upholding the constitutionality of the statute focused on a library's broad discretion in "selecting the materials it provides to its patrons." *Id.* at 205 (plurality opinion). Justice Souter's dissent, in contrast, characterized the use of filtering software as the equivalent of removing materials from a library's collection—"buying a book and then keeping it from adults lacking an acceptable 'purpose,' or * * * buying an encyclopedia and then cutting out pages with anything thought to be unsuitable for all adults." *Id.* at 237 (Souter, J., dissenting). We discuss the case further in Chapter Six.

8. The three topics explored in this chapter—trespass, consumer confusion in domain names and metatags, and the application of the First Amendment to a library's decision to filter Internet access—provide only examples of a problem that will be encountered throughout this course: how well do analogies from old precedents really fit the online context? In every setting, we cannot simply apply old rules reflexively; thus, you must always question whether the metaphors and analogies judges choose are truly apt. In what cases is the existence of an online component irrelevant to the basic analysis, and in what cases is there truly a new set of issues to be addressed? Moreover, though it is easy to understand why these are important issues with regard to a new technology such as the Internet, if you think about your other law school courses, you may be surprised to discover that the same questions must be asked across the spectrum of common-law legal doctrines.

Chapter Three

PROBLEMS OF GEOGRAPHY AND SOVEREIGNTY

INTRODUCTION

In the past decade, the terms "cyberspace" and "globalization" have become buzzwords of a new generation. And it is not surprising that the two have entered the lexicon simultaneously. The Internet from its beginning heralded a new world order of interconnection and decentralization, while the word globalization conjured for many the specter both of increasing transnational and supranational governance and increasing mobility of persons and capital across geographical boundaries. Thus, both terms reflect a perception that territorial borders might no longer be as significant as they once were.

In a provocative early article, David Johnson and David Post argued that cyberspace could not legitimately be governed by territorially based sovereigns and that the online world should be seen as its own legal jurisdiction (or multiple jurisdictions).[a] Predictably, nation-states pushed in the opposite direction, passing a slew of laws purporting to regulate almost any conceivable online activity from gambling to chat rooms to auction sites, and seeking to enforce territorially based rules regarding trademarks, contractual relations, privacy norms, "indecent" content, and crime, among others.

These assertions of national authority have raised many of the legal conundrums regarding nation-state sovereignty, territorial borders, and legal jurisdiction that Johnson and Post predicted. For example, if a person posts content online that is legal where posted but illegal in some place where it is viewed, can that person be subject to suit in the far-off location? Is online activity sufficient to make one "present" in a jurisdiction for tax

---

a. *See* David R. Johnson & David G. Post, *Law and Borders—The Rise of Law in Cyberspace*, 48 STAN. L. REV. 1367 (1996).

purposes? Is a patchwork of national copyright laws feasible given the ability to transfer digital information around the globe instantaneously? How might national rules regarding the definition and investigation of crimes complicate efforts to combat international computer crime? Should the law of trademarks, which historically has permitted two firms to retain the same name as long as they operated in different geographical areas, be expanded to provide an international cause of action regarding the ownership of an easily identifiable domain name? And, if so, should such a system be enforced by national courts (and in which country) or by an international body (and how should such a body be constituted)? And on and on.

All of these questions, though they arise in a variety of doctrinal areas and involve a wide range of different legal and policy concerns, nevertheless have at least one common element: the idea of legal *jurisdiction*, the circumstances under which a juridical body can assert authority to adjudicate or apply its legal norms to a dispute. And, in each of these cases, the question is complicated by the fact that jurisdiction may be asserted in one physical location over activities or parties located in another physical location (and perhaps within the boundaries of a different sovereign). The issue of jurisdiction is thus deeply enmeshed with precisely the fixed conception of territorial boundaries that contemporary events are challenging.

The "problem," of course, from a jurisdictional perspective, is that local geographically based communities are now far more likely to be affected by activities and entities with no local presence. Cross-border interaction obviously is not a new phenomenon, but in an electronically connected world the effects of any given action may immediately be felt elsewhere with no relationship to physical geography at all. It is thus not surprising that local communities might feel the need to assert jurisdiction over extraterritorial activities because of the local harms such activities cause. On the other hand, assertions of jurisdiction on this basis will almost inevitably tend towards a system of universal jurisdiction, because so many activities will have effects far beyond their immediate geographical boundaries. Such a system, for better or worse, would appear to jettison any idea that the application of legal norms to a party depends in some way on the party having consented to be governed by those norms.

In this chapter, we explore these and related problems of geography and sovereignty. Online interaction challenges fundamental assumptions about the feasibility and legitimacy of regulation by geographically based sovereign entities. And, as in the introductory case studies in Chapter Two, we must ask whether these challenges can adequately be addressed through existing legal regimes, or whether we need to think about our territorially based rules in fundamentally new ways. At the very least, we may be able to illuminate some legal doctrines familiar to you from other law school classes—"community standards," "minimum contacts," the "dormant Commerce Clause"—when we look at the way in which these doctrines are put under stress in the online context.

SECTION A. THE THEORETICAL DEBATE

David R. Johnson and David G. Post, *Law and Borders—The Rise of Law in Cyberspace*

48 STAN. L. REV. 1367 (1996)

Global computer-based communications cut across territorial borders, creating a new realm of human activity and undermining the feasibility— and legitimacy—of laws based on geographic boundaries. While these electronic communications play havoc with geographic boundaries, a new boundary, made up of the screens and passwords that separate the virtual world from the "real world" of atoms, emerges. This new boundary defines a distinct Cyberspace that needs and can create its own law and legal institutions. Territorially based law-makers and law-enforcers find this new environment deeply threatening. But established territorial authorities may yet learn to defer to the self-regulatory efforts of Cyberspace participants who care most deeply about this new digital trade in ideas, information, and services. Separated from doctrine tied to territorial jurisdictions, new rules will emerge to govern a wide range of new phenomena that have no clear parallel in the nonvirtual world. These new rules will play the role of law by defining legal personhood and property, resolving disputes, and crystallizing a collective conversation about online participants' core values.

We take for granted a world in which geographical borders—lines separating physical spaces—are of primary importance in determining legal rights and responsibilities. Territorial borders, generally speaking, delineate areas within which different sets of legal rules apply. There has until now been a general correspondence between borders drawn in physical space (between nation states or other political entities) and borders in "law space." For example, if we were to superimpose a "law map" (delineating areas where different rules apply to particular behaviors) onto a political map of the world, the two maps would overlap to a significant degree, with clusters of homogeneous applicable law and legal institutions fitting within existing physical borders. * * *

Physical borders are not, of course, simply arbitrary creations. Although they may be based on historical accident, geographic borders for law make sense in the real world. Their logical relationship to the development and enforcement of legal rules is based on a number of related considerations.

Power. Control over physical space, and the people and things located in that space, is a defining attribute of sovereignty and statehood. Law-making requires some mechanism for law enforcement, which in turn depends on the ability to exercise physical control over, and impose coercive sanctions on, law-violators. For example, the U.S. government does not impose its trademark law on a Brazilian business operating in Brazil, at least in part because imposing sanctions on the Brazilian business would require assertion of physical control over business owners. Such an assertion of control would conflict with the Brazilian government's recognized monopoly on the use of force over its citizens.

Effects. The correspondence between physical boundaries and "law space" boundaries also reflects a deeply rooted relationship between physical proximity and the effects of any particular behavior. That is, Brazilian trademark law governs the use of marks in Brazil because that use has a more direct impact on persons and assets within Brazil than anywhere else. For example, a large sign over "Jones' Restaurant" in Rio de Janeiro is unlikely to have an impact on the operation of "Jones' Restaurant" in Oslo, Norway, for we may assume that there is no substantial overlap between the customers, or competitors, of these two entities. Protection of the former's trademark does not—and probably should not—affect the protection afforded the latter's.

Legitimacy. We generally accept the notion that the persons within a geographically defined border are the ultimate source of law-making authority for activities within that border. The "consent of the governed" implies that those subject to a set of laws must have a role in their formulation. By virtue of the preceding considerations, those people subject to a sovereign's laws, and most deeply affected by those laws, are the individuals who are located in particular physical spaces. Similarly, allocation of responsibility among levels of government proceeds on the assumption that, for many legal problems, physical proximity between the responsible authority and those most directly affected by the law will improve the quality of decision making, and that it is easier to determine the will of those individuals in physical proximity to one another.

Notice. Physical boundaries are also appropriate for the delineation of "law space" in the physical world because they can give notice that the rules change when the boundaries are crossed. Proper boundaries have signposts that provide warning that we will be required, after crossing, to abide by different rules, and physical boundaries—lines on the geographical map—are generally well-equipped to serve this signpost function.

Cyberspace radically undermines the relationship between legally significant (online) phenomena and physical location. The rise of the global computer network is destroying the link between geographical location and: (1) the power of local governments to assert control over online behavior; (2) the effects of online behavior on individuals or things; (3) the legitimacy of a local sovereign's efforts to regulate global phenomena; and (4) the ability of physical location to give notice of which sets of rules apply. The Net thus radically subverts the system of rule-making based on borders between physical spaces, at least with respect to the claim that Cyberspace should naturally be governed by territorially defined rules.

Cyberspace has no territorially based boundaries, because the cost and speed of message transmission on the Net is almost entirely independent of physical location. Messages can be transmitted from one physical location to any other location without degradation, decay, or substantial delay, and without any physical cues or barriers that might otherwise keep certain geographically remote places and people separate from one another. The Net enables transactions between people who do not know, and in many cases cannot know, each other's physical location. Location remains vitally important, but only location within a virtual space consisting of the "addresses" of the machines between which messages and information are routed. The system is indifferent to the physical location of those machines, and there is no necessary connection between an Internet address and a physical jurisdiction. Although the domain name initially assigned to a given machine may be associated with an Internet Protocol address that corresponds to that machine's physical location (for example, a ".uk" domain name extension), the machine may be physically moved without affecting its domain name. Alternatively, the owner of the domain name might request that the name become associated with an entirely different machine, in a different physical location. Thus, a server with a ".uk" domain name need not be located in the United Kingdom, a server with a ".com" domain name may be anywhere, and users, generally speaking, are not even aware of the location of the server that stores the content that they read.

The power to control activity in Cyberspace has only the most tenuous connections to physical location. Nonetheless, many governments' first response to electronic communications crossing their territorial borders is to try to stop or regulate that flow of information. Rather than permitting self-regulation by participants in online transactions, many governments establish trade barriers, attempt to tax border-crossing cargo, and respond especially sympathetically to claims that information coming into the jurisdiction might prove harmful to local residents. As online information becomes more important to local citizens, these efforts increase. In particular, resistance to "transborder data flow" (TDF) reflects the concerns of sovereign nations that the development and use of TDF's will undermine their "informational sovereignty," will impinge upon the privacy of local citizens, and will upset private property interests in information. Even local governments in the United States have expressed concern about their loss of control over information and transactions flowing across their borders.

But efforts to control the flow of electronic information across physical borders—to map local regulation and physical boundaries onto Cyberspace—are likely to prove futile, at least in countries that hope to participate in global commerce. Individual [electronic impulses] can easily, and without any realistic prospect of detection, "enter" any sovereign's territory. The volume of electronic communications crossing territorial boundaries is just too great in relation to the resources available to government authorities. United States Customs officials have generally given up. They assert jurisdiction only over the physical goods that cross the geographic borders they guard and claim no right to force declarations of the value of materials transmitted by modem. Banking and securities regulators seem likely to lose their battle to impose local regulations on a global financial marketplace. And state attorneys general face serious challenges in seeking to intercept the [electronic signals] that transmit the kinds of consumer fraud that, if conducted physically within the local jurisdiction, would be easier to shut down.

Faced with their inability to control the flow of [electronic signals] across physical borders, some authorities strive to inject their boundaries into the new electronic medium through filtering mechanisms and the establishment of electronic barriers. Others have been quick to assert the right to regulate all online trade insofar as it might adversely affect local citizens. The Attorney General of Minnesota, for example, has asserted the right to regulate gambling that occurs on a foreign web page that a local resident accessed and "brought into" the state. The New Jersey securities regulatory agency has similarly asserted the right to shut down any offending Web page accessible from within the state.

But such protective schemes will likely fail as well. First, the determined seeker of prohibited communications can simply reconfigure his connection so as to appear to reside in a location outside the particular locality, state, or country. Because the Net is engineered to work on the basis of "logical," not geographical, locations, any attempt to defeat the independence of messages from physical locations would be as futile as an effort to tie an atom and a bit together. And, moreover, assertions of law-making authority over Net activities on the ground that those activities constitute "entry into" the physical jurisdiction can just as easily be made by any territorially-based authority. If Minnesota law applies to gambling operations conducted on the World Wide Web because such operations foreseeably affect Minnesota residents, so, too, must the law of any physical jurisdiction from which those operations can be accessed. By asserting a right to regulate whatever its citizens may access on the Net, these local authorities are laying the predicate for an argument that Singapore or Iraq or any other sovereign can regulate the activities of U.S. companies operating in Cyberspace from a location physically within the United States. All such Web-based activity, in this view, must be subject simultaneously to the laws of all territorial sovereigns.

Nor are the effects of online activities tied to geographically proximate locations. Information available on the World Wide Web is available simultaneously to anyone with a connection to the global network. The notion that the effects of an activity taking place on that Web site radiate from a physical location over a geographic map in concentric circles of decreasing intensity, however sensible that may be in the nonvirtual world, is incoherent when applied to Cyberspace. A Web site physically located in Brazil, to continue with that example, has no more of an effect on individuals in Brazil than does a Web site physically located in Belgium or Belize that is accessible in Brazil. Usenet discussion groups, to take another example, consist of continuously changing collections of messages that are routed from one network to another, with no centralized location at all. They exist, in effect, everywhere, nowhere in particular, and only on the Net.

Territorial regulation of online activities serves neither the legitimacy nor the notice justifications. There is no geographically localized set of constituents with a stronger and more legitimate claim to regulate it than any other local group. The strongest claim to control comes from the participants themselves, and they could be anywhere. And in Cyberspace, physical borders no longer function as signposts informing individuals of the obligations assumed by entering into a new, legally significant, place. Individuals are unaware of the existence of those borders as they move through virtual space.

The rise of an electronic medium that disregards geographical boundaries throws the law into disarray by creating entirely new phenomena that need to become the subject of clear legal rules but that cannot be governed, satisfactorily, by any current territorially based sovereign. For example, although privacy on the Net may be a familiar concept, analogous to privacy doctrine for mail systems, telephone calls, and print publications, electronic communications create serious questions regarding the nature and adequacy of geographically based privacy protections. Communications that create vast new transactional records may pass through or even simultaneously exist in many different territorial jurisdictions. What substantive law should we apply to protect this new, vulnerable body of transactional data? May a French policeman lawfully access the records of communications traveling across the Net from the United States to Japan? Similarly, whether it is permissible for a commercial entity to publish a record of all of any given individual's postings to Usenet newsgroups, or whether it is permissible to implement an interactive Web page application that inspects a user's "bookmarks" to determine which other pages that user has visited, are questions not readily addressed by existing legal regimes—both because the phenomena are novel and because any given local territorial sovereign cannot readily control the relevant, globally dispersed, actors and actions.

Because events on the Net occur everywhere but nowhere in particular, are engaged in by online personae who are both "real" (possessing reputations, able to perform services, and deploy intellectual assets) and "intangible" (not necessarily or traceably tied to any particular person in the physical sense), and concern "things" (messages, databases, standing relationships) that are not necessarily separated from one another by any physical boundaries, no physical jurisdiction has a more compelling claim than any other to subject these events exclusively to its laws. * * *

We know that the activities that have traditionally been the subject of regulation must still be engaged in by real people who are, after all, at distinct physical locations. But the interactions of these people now somehow transcend those physical locations. The Net enables forms of interaction in which the shipment of tangible items across geographic boundaries is irrelevant and in which the location of the participants does not matter. Efforts to determine "where" the events in question occur are decidedly misguided, if not altogether futile.

Jack L. Goldsmith, *The Internet and the Abiding Significance of Territorial Sovereignty*

5 IND. J. GLOBAL LEGAL STUD. 475 (1998)

More than any other technology, the Internet facilitates cheap, fast, and difficult-to-detect multi-jurisdictional transactions. This in a nutshell is why so many believe that the Internet "undermin[es] the feasibility—and legitimacy—of laws based on geographical boundaries." See David R. Johnson & David G. Post, *Law and Borders-The Rise of Law in Cyberspace*, 48 STAN. L. REV. 1367, 1367 (1996). * * * This essay attempts * * * to show that from the perspective of jurisdiction and choice of law, territorial regulation of the Internet is no less feasible and no less legitimate than territorial regulation of non-Internet transactions. * * *

Territorial sovereignty is relevant to Internet regulation in a straightforward fashion. The Internet is not, as many suggest, a separate place removed from our world. Like the telephone, the telegraph, and the smoke signal, the Internet is a medium through which people in real space in one jurisdiction communicate with people in real space in another jurisdiction. Territorial sovereignty supports national regulation of persons within the territory who use the Internet. It also supports national regulation of the means of communication—Internet hardware and software—located in the territory. Finally, a nation's prerogative to control events within its territory entails the power to regulate the local effects of extraterritorial acts. When a person abroad uses the Internet to produce harmful local effects, the local sovereign is justified in regulating these local effects. These various forms of legitimate territorial regulation enable nations to significantly raise the cost of, and thus to regulate, proscribed Internet transactions.

The arguments against this view * * * [involve] three basic [claims]. First, territorial regulation of the Internet is not feasible because the source of Internet transactions can easily be located outside of the regulating sovereign's territory. Second, unilateral territorial regulation of the Internet leads to overlapping and often inconsistent regulation of the same transaction. Third, unilateral territorial regulation of the Internet produces significant, normatively problematic spillover effects. I consider each argument in turn.

The first argument against territorial regulation of the Internet concerns regulatory leakage. This is an argument about the infeasibility of territorial regulation of the Internet. Because Internet information flows cross territorial borders without detection, and because Internet content providers can shift with relative ease the source of their information flows outside of any regulating territory, much of the content of the Internet is beyond the regulatory scope of any particular territorial sovereignty.

It is true that it is costly (but not impossible) to arrest the flow of Internet protocol packets over territorial borders. It is also true that these information flows often have an extraterritorial source. But these features do not distinguish the Internet from real space transnational transactions for which territorial regulation is a common and effective tool. Persons acting abroad often do things that cause adverse effects within the regulating jurisdiction that cannot be intercepted at the border. For example, when English reinsurers conspire in England to limit the types of reinsurance sold in the United States, U.S. customs officials cannot stop the harm to American insurers and insureds at the border. The local economic harm of foreign activity is similarly impossible to stop at the border when a foreign corporation makes a fraudulent tender offer on foreign soil for a foreign corporation owned in very small part by Americans. In the modern interdependent international economy, these economic effects are oblivious to border control. The point is not limited to economic effects. Harmful pollution that wafts from one state into another is also difficult to intercept at the state line.

Does the inability of governments to stop these harmful effects at the border mean that the extraterritorial sources of these local harms are beyond local regulation? Of course not. Some harmful effects cannot be intercepted at the border and thus must be regulated *ex post* through legal sanctions (or *ex ante* through the threat of such sanctions). In each of the three non-Internet examples above, for example, the jurisdiction that suffered the harmful effects applied its laws to the extraterritorial activity. Internet activities are functionally identical to these non-Internet activities. People in one jurisdiction do something—upload pornography, facilitate gambling, offer a fraudulent security, send spam, etc.—that is costly to stop at another jurisdiction's border and that produces effects within that jurisdiction deemed illegal there. The territorial effects rationale for regulating these harms is the same as the rationale for regulating similar harms in the non Internet cases. The medium by which the harm is transmitted into the regulating jurisdiction—be it economic interdependence, postal mail, wind currents, or the Internet—is not relevant to the justification for regulating it.

The effects criterion tells us that it is legitimate for a nation to apply its regulation to an extraterritorial act with harmful local effects. It does not tell us whether such a regulation will be efficacious. In most instances, regulation of extraterritorial activity is efficacious only to the extent that the agents of the acts have a local presence or local property against which local laws can be enforced. In this sense, the concept of extraterritoriality can be misleading. It does not (usually) mean that a nation enforces its law abroad. Rather, it means that a nation uses the threat of force against local persons or property to punish, and thus regulate, extraterritorial acts that cause local harms. If the extraterritorial source has no local presence or property, the efficacy of the local regulation is diminished (but, as we shall see in a moment, not eliminated). In this sense the enforceable scope of a local regulation is much more significant than its putative scope. And the enforceable scope is largely limited by the old-fashioned conception of territorial sovereignty: a nation has plenary enforcement jurisdiction over persons and property within its borders but little if any beyond.

The relative importance of the enforceable (as opposed to the putative) scope of a regulation is often not noticed with respect to extraterritorial regulation of non-Internet activities. Nor are the largely territorial limitations on this scope. This is probably because in non-Internet cases the extraterritorial source of local harm is frequently a firm with some local presence (property, employees, business contracts) against which the local regulating jurisdiction can assert leverage in trying to alter extraterritorial behavior. For example, the United States can apply its antitrust laws to alter the acts of English reinsurers in London because these reinsurers have widespread contractual relations with American firms that they want to preserve. Similarly, the European Community can impose strict and almost deal-breaking conditions on a Federal Trade Commission–approved merger between two U.S. companies with no manufacturing facilities in Europe because of the many offices, agents, and contracts that the U.S. companies have in Europe. In both cases the foreign company subject to local regulation has a local business presence that is more beneficial than the costs of local regulation; otherwise, the foreign company would eliminate its presence in the regulating jurisdiction and avoid the regulation.

At first glance, the architecture of the Internet transactions appears to differ from real space in a way that makes regulatory leakage a more serious problem. For the Internet makes it very easy and very inexpensive for individuals outside the regulating jurisdiction to send harmful content into the regulating jurisdiction that is difficult to intercept at the border. Since individuals abroad rarely have local presence or assets, it appears that many local regulations of Internet activity will be inefficacious. * * *

This phenomenon—which we might label offshore regulation evasion—is not limited to the Internet. For example, corporations reincorporate in jurisdictions with favorable internal affairs laws, and drug lords send cocaine into the United States from South America. Closer to point, offshore regulation evasion has been a prominent characteristic of other communication media. For example, Radio-Free Europe broadcast into the U.S.S.R. but lacked a regulatory presence there; television signals are sometimes broadcast from abroad by an entity with no local presence; and a person living in one country can libel a person in another via telephone. Like the content source of many Internet transactions, the extraterritorial source of these and many other non-Internet activities is often beyond the enforceable scope of local regulation. However, this does not mean that local regulation is inefficacious. In cyberspace, as in real space, offshore regulation evasion does not prevent a nation from indirectly regulating extraterritorial activity that has local effects.

The reason once again has to do with territorial sovereignty as traditionally conceived. A nation retains the ability to regulate the extraterritorial sources of local harms through regulation of persons and property within its territory. This form of indirect extraterritorial regulation is how nations have, with various degrees of success, regulated local harms caused by other communications media with offshore sources and no local presence. It is also how nations have begun to regulate local harms caused on the Internet by extraterritorial content providers. For example, nations penalize in-state end-users who obtain and use illegal content or who otherwise participate in an illegal cyberspace transaction. They also regulate the local means through which foreign content is transmitted. For example, they regulate in-state entities that supply or transmit information. Or they regulate in-state hardware and software through which Internet transmissions are received. These and related local regulations affect the cost and feasibility within the regulating nation of obtaining content from, or participating with, offshore regulation evaders. In these ways, local regulations indirectly regulate extraterritorial content supply.

In both the Internet and non-Internet contexts, such indirect regulation will rarely be perfect in the sense of eliminating evasion. But of course few if any regulations are perfect in this sense. And regulation need not be perfect to be effective. The question is always whether the regulation will heighten the costs of the activity sufficiently to achieve its acceptable control from whatever normative perspective is deemed appropriate. Whether indirect regulation of Internet content transmitted from abroad will achieve acceptable control depends on one's normative commitments and on empirical and technological questions that remain unresolved. * * *

I have focused thus far on the claim that territorial regulation of the Internet is unfeasible. My arguments might appear to support a somewhat different type of anti-regulation claim. This is the claim that because Internet content can simultaneously appear in every territorial jurisdiction in the world, all Internet activity is simultaneously subject to all national regulations. This appears to lead to the normatively problematic conclusion that all "Web-based activity. . . . must be subject simultaneously to the laws of all territorial sovereigns." Johnson & Post, *supra*, at 1374.

It is worth noting, however, that * * * [a] government's regulation of the harmful local effects of an Internet transaction does not become less legitimate because the effects of the same transaction are regulated differently in other jurisdictions where these effects appear. These multiple regulation scenarios raise a normative concern because of the spillover effects of each nation's Internet regulation. * * * [T]hese spillovers might call for multijurisdictional harmonization. But by themselves they do not make unilateral regulation illegitimate. * * *

The problem of notice presents another apparent normative quagmire for Internet regulation. Many fear that content providers do not know where in the world their information goes, and thus do not have notice of the laws they might be violating. This problem too is greatly exaggerated. First, the limits on enforcement jurisdiction mean that most individual content providers never have to worry about violating foreign laws. Second, content providers can take steps—such as conditioning access to content on presentation of geographical identification—to control content flows geographically. As digital signature and filtering technology continues to develop to facilitate such geographical identification, the Internet content provider will look like any other "real space" content provider who must take care not to send his content into a jurisdiction where it is illegal. Third, even in the absence of such technology, a content provider is on notice that his information might flow into a jurisdiction where it is illegal. It is a complicated question beyond the scope of this essay whether this notice suffices to make it fair to impose an obligation on the content provider to learn whether this information is illegal in the regulating territory. Ignoring for the moment the limits on enforcement jurisdiction and the availability of geographical flow control devices, such a regime places enormous burden on content providers that might significantly curtail Internet activity. But there is nothing sacrosanct about Internet speed, or about a foreign content provider's right to send information everywhere in the world with impunity. From the perspective of the regulating jurisdiction, the content provider is knowingly sending information into a jurisdiction; like all persons who do the same in real space, the content provider benefits from this in-state activity, is deemed to know the law of the territory, and is subject to penalties for non-compliance (assuming that enforcement is possible).

In any event, this quagmire is much less significant than it appears. The claim that unilateral national regulation of the Internet invariably leads to simultaneous (and oft-conflicting) regulation of the Internet is as exaggerated as the claim about the unfeasibility of territorial regulation of the Internet. And for the same reason: traditional territorial sovereignty. As explained above, a nation cannot enforce its laws against an individual content provider from another country unless the content provider has a local presence. The vast majority of individuals who transact on the Internet have no presence or assets in the jurisdictions that wish to regulate their information flows. Such regulations will apply mainly to service providers and users with a physical presence in the regulating jurisdiction. And indeed this has been the focus of regulation to date. * * *

Even assuming the worst about the feasibility of geographic content control of Internet information flows, spillover effects caused by territorial regulation of the Internet do not undermine the legitimacy of such regulation. * * * [S]pillover effects are an inevitable consequence of unilateral territorial regulation of transnational transactions. * * * Spillovers are present when activity deemed legal in one country causes harm deemed illegal in another, regardless of which nation's law applies. These spillovers can be diminished through international harmonization. But they can only be eliminated by abolishing national (as opposed to international) lawmaking entities altogether, or by eliminating transnational activity. Neither option is remotely plausible. In this sense the spillovers from territorial regulation of the Internet are inevitable.

Jack L. Goldsmith, *Against Cyberanarchy*

65 U. CHI. L. REV. 1199 (1998)

Consider the predicament of one of the scores of companies that offer, sell, and deliver products on the World Wide Web. Assume that the web page of a fictional Seattle-based company, Digitalbook.com, offers digital books for sale and delivery over the Web. One book it offers for sale is *Lady Chatterley's Lover*. This offer extends to, and can be accepted by, computer users in every country with access to the Web. Assume that in Singapore the sale and distribution of pornography is criminal, and that Singapore deems *Lady Chatterley's Lover* to be pornographic. Assume further that Digitalbook.com's terms of sale contain a term that violates English consumer protection laws, and that the publication of Digitalbook.com's *Lady Chatterley's Lover* in England would infringe upon the rights of the novel's English copyright owner. Digitalbook.com sells and sends copies of *Lady Chatterley's Lover* to two people whose addresses (say, anonymous@ aol.com and anonymous@msn.com) do not reveal their physical location but who, unbeknownst to Digitalbook.com, live and receive the book in Singapore and London, respectively.

The skeptics claim that it is difficult for courts in Singapore or England to regulate disputes involving these transactions in accordance with geographical choice-of-law rules. In addition, they argue that English and Singaporean regulations will expose Digitalbook.com to potentially inconsistent obligations. Finally, the skeptics claim that Digitalbook.com can easily evade the Singaporean and English regulations by sending unstoppable digital information into these countries from a locale beyond their enforcement jurisdiction.

On the normative side, the skeptics are concerned that the application of English and Singaporean law to regulate Digitalbook.com's transactions constitutes an impermissible extraterritorial regulation of a U.S. corporation. Because Digitalbook.com might bow to the English and Singaporean regulations, and because the company cannot limit its cyberspace information flows by geography, the English and Singaporean regulations might cause it to withdraw *Lady Chatterley's Lover* everywhere or to raise its price. The English and Singaporean regulations would thus affect Digitalbook.com's behavior in the United States and adversely affect the purchasing opportunities of parties in other countries. The skeptics believe these negative spillover effects of the national regulations are illegitimate. They also think it is unfair for England and Singapore to apply their laws in this situation because Digitalbook.com had no way of knowing that it sold and delivered a book to consumers in these countries. * * *

The skeptics are in the grip of a nineteenth century territorialist conception of how "real space" is regulated and how "real-space" conflicts of law are resolved. This conception was repudiated in the middle of this century. The skeptics' first mistake, therefore, is to measure the feasibility and legitimacy of national regulation of cyberspace against a repudiated yardstick. * * * Changes in transportation, communication, and in the scope of corporate activity led to an unprecedented increase in multijurisdictional activity. These changes put pressure on the rigid territorialist conception, which purported to identify a single legitimate governing law for transborder activity based on discrete territorial contacts. So too did the rise of the regulatory state, which led to more caustic public policy differences among jurisdictions, and which pressured the interested forum to apply local regulations whenever possible. * * *

Today, the Constitution permits a state to apply its law if it has a "significant contact or significant aggregation of contacts, creating state interests, such that choice of its law is neither arbitrary nor fundamentally unfair." *Phillips Petroleum Co v. Shutts*, 472 U.S. 797, 818 (1985) (quoting *Allstate Insurance Co v. Hague*, 449 U.S. 302, 312-13 (1981)). In practice, this standard is notoriously easy to satisfy. It prohibits the application of local law only when the forum state has no interest in the case because the substance of the lawsuit has no relationship to the state. Customary international law limits on a nation's regulation of extraterritorial events are less clear because there are few international decisions on point, and because state practice does not reveal a settled custom. Nonetheless, it seems clear that customary international law, like the United States Constitution, permits a nation to apply its law to extraterritorial behavior with substantial local effects. In addition, both the Constitution and international law permit a nation or state to regulate the extraterritorial conduct of a citizen or domiciliary. In short, in modern times a transaction can legitimately be regulated by the jurisdiction where the transaction occurs, the jurisdictions where significant effects of the transaction are felt, and the jurisdictions where the parties burdened by the regulation are from. * * *

A nation can purport to regulate activity that takes place anywhere. The Island of Tobago can enact a law that purports to bind the rights of the whole world. But the effective scope of this law depends on Tobago's ability to enforce it. And in general a nation can only enforce its laws against: (i) persons with a presence or assets in the nation's territory; (ii) persons over whom the nation can obtain personal jurisdiction and enforce a default judgment against abroad; or (iii) persons whom the nation can successfully extradite.

A defendant's physical presence or assets within the territory remains the primary basis for a nation or state to enforce its laws. The large majority of persons who transact in cyberspace have no presence or assets in the jurisdictions that wish to regulate their information flows in cyberspace. Such regulations are thus likely to apply primarily to Internet service providers and Internet users with a physical presence in the regulating jurisdiction. Cyberspace users in other territorial jurisdictions will indirectly feel the effect of the regulations to the extent that they are dependent on service or content providers with a presence in the regulating jurisdiction. But for almost all users, there will be no threat of extraterritorial legal liability because of a lack of presence in the regulating jurisdictions. * * *

[T]he * * * choice-of-law problems implicated by cyberspace are * * * no more complex than the same issues in real space. They also are no more complex or challenging than similar issues presented by increasingly prevalent real-space events such as airplane crashes, mass torts, multistate insurance coverage, or multinational commercial transactions, all of which form the bread and butter of modern conflict of laws. Indeed, they are no more complex than a simple products liability suit arising from a two-car accident among residents of the same state, which can implicate the laws of several states, including the place of the accident, the states where the car and tire manufacturers are headquartered, the states where the car and tires were manufactured, and the state where the car was purchased. Resolution of choice-of-law problems in these contexts is challenging. But the skeptics overstate the challenge.

David G. Post, *Against "Against Cyberanarchy"*
17 BERKELEY TECH. L.J. 1365 (2002)

Goldsmith's position—what I term "Unexceptionalism"—is straightforward. However difficult and complicated Digitalbooks.com's problems may be, they are no *more* difficult or complicated because the underlying transactions take place "in cyberspace." * * * Those who think otherwise—Goldsmith calls them "regulation skeptics," though I prefer the less loaded and more symmetrical term "Exceptionalists"—believe that cyberspace *is* somehow different, that it matters, for purposes of understanding these jurisdictional questions, that Digitalbooks.com is operating on the World Wide Web and not in a brick-and-mortar realspace storefront. * * *

[At the core of the Unexceptionalist position is] a simple, but very powerful, syllogism:

> Transnational activities of an ordinary, brick-and-mortar bookstore—"Analogbooks, Inc."—are subject to "settled principles" of "customary international law."

> These settled principles hold that if Analogbooks' realspace activities produce "substantial local effects" in Singapore, or in England, those activities can "legitimately be regulated" by those governments.

> Digitalbooks' activities are "functionally identical" to Analogbooks' activities.

Therefore, if Digitalbooks' cyberspace activities produce "substantial local effects" in Singapore, or in England, those activities can "legitimately be regulated" by those governments. The logic is unassailable: If X is true in environment 1, and if environment 2 is "functionally identical" to environment 1, then X is true in environment 2. The argument, however, is not quite as persuasive as it might appear at first glance.

Take, for instance, the Unexceptionalists' reliance upon settled principles of customary international law. Even accepting Professor Goldsmith's assertion that these principles "are settled"—in particular, the "uncontested assumptions" that, at least in modern times, transactions "can legitimately be regulated by . . . the jurisdictions where significant effects of the transaction are felt," and that "a nation's right to control events within its territory and to protect its citizens permits it to regulate the local effects of extratteritorial acts"—it is clear that this "modern view" of international jurisdiction is itself the product of profound changes in the world over the past century or so (as Goldsmith himself points out).

These now-settled principles were, in other words, once themselves in conflict with then-settled principles. It was once "settled" law that a state *cannot* regulate extraterritorial acts, the "substantial local effects" of those acts notwithstanding, and that therefore Analogbooks' activities could not "legitimately be regulated" in either Singapore or England. The Unexceptionalists of one hundred, or even fifty, years ago might have made an argument very much like Goldsmith's, arguing that rail transport, the telephone, or radio broadcasting, would (and should) have no effect on our analysis of jurisdictional problems. We can imagine the following colloquy:

> Scene: A New York street corner, circa 1900. Two law professors, Professor E and Professor U, meet.
>
> Professor E: "Have you noticed? This telegraph thing changes everything! I can step inside a Western Union office in New York and execute a contract in San Francisco *instantaneously*! Incredible, eh?"
>
> Professor U: "Well, I suppose it is. But what of it?"
>
> E: "What of it? Surely you jest. The world as we know it will never be the same. We're going to need new principles of law to deal with this phenomenon. Our jurisdictional principles—especially that one that requires *physical presence* for the exercise of "jurisdiction to prescribe"—must yield to this new context, no?"
>
> U: "Not at all. Transactions completed by telegraph are functionally identical to those completed by mail or by smoke signal; they all involve real people in one territorial jurisdiction either (i) transacting with real people in other territorial jurisdictions or (ii) engaging in activity in one jurisdiction that causes real-world effects in another territorial jurisdiction. It is settled law that the people of California *cannot* reach people and transactions occurring outside of its borders. Why would we need to adjust those principles now?"

* * * Looking backwards, of course, we know that events proved *those* Unexceptionalists wrong. Though it was surely difficult to see at the time, the world was changing profoundly, and settled understandings were becoming unsettled because of that change. * * *

The world, sometimes, does that—changes profoundly. When it does, settled understandings sometimes change with it. Unless we think that for some reason this cannot happen again, questions about the legitimate scope of a nation's jurisdictional reach cannot rest on the notion that those questions are somehow already, and forever, "settled."

That the world *can* change so as to unsettle settled principles does not, of course, mean that it has done so in ways that are relevant to the questions at hand. The Unexceptionalists say that it has not; activity in cyberspace is *"functionally identical to transnational activity mediated by other means, such as mail or telephone or smoke signal."*

What could that possibly mean? It does not take a great deal of insight or deep thinking to come up with ways in which activity in cyberspace is functionally not identical to activity in realspace. For example, in cyberspace, I can communicate an offer to sell some product or service

- instantaneously (or nearly so);

- at zero marginal cost (or nearly so);

- to several million people;

- with near-zero probability of error in the reproduction or distribution of that offer;

- which can be stored, retrieved, and translated into another language, by each of the recipients (instantaneously, and at zero marginal cost); and

- to recipients who have the capability to respond to my offer (instantaneously, and at zero marginal cost).

I surely cannot engage in a transaction having *all* of those features simultaneously using mail, or telephones, or smoke signals. * * *

It is true that events and transactions in realspace and cyberspace are identical in many ways, and can be treated identically for many purposes. Transactions between human beings are still transactions between human beings, whether they take place via e-mail, postcards, telegraph, or smoke signal. Whatever it is that motivates human beings to engage in one transaction or another—love, hate, greed, curiosity, fear, etc.—remains the same, on or off the Internet. * * *

Digitalbooks.com and Analogbooks will thus have many identical characteristics. Digitalbooks.com, just like Analogbooks, provides: a forum where buyers and sellers can exchange consideration for goods; a system for making sure that those goods get shipped from seller to buyer after a transaction is consummated; rules for identifying the winners and losers of individual auctions; and means for obtaining payment for its services, accounting for those payments, and transferring money to its suppliers. * * *

However, it is also true that events and transactions in realspace and cyberspace are *not* identical in many other ways. For example, transactions in cyberspace can take place at much greater physical remove; they are consummated by means of the movement of bits rather than atoms; they are digitally encoded; they are unaffected by the participants' sense of smell; they are embedded in and mediated by software; they travel at the speed of light, etc. * * *

The question we need to be addressing, then, is this one: are Digitalbooks.com's and Analogbooks' transactions identical—or, at least, sufficiently similar—to one another *with respect to the relevant principles of international choice of law and prescriptive jurisdiction?* If so, it is reasonable to ignore the many differences between them; if not, it is not.

To the Unexceptionalist, Digitalbooks.com's and Analogbooks' transactions *are* identical with respect to the relevant principles of international choice of law. The issues raise by application of these principles and prescriptive jurisdiction to Digitalbooks.com's cyberspace transactions, they say,

> . . . are no more complex than the same issues in real space. They also are no more complex or challenging than similar issues presented by increasingly prevalent real-space events such as airplane crashes, mass torts, multistate insurance coverage, or multinational commercial transactions, all of which form the bread and butter of modern conflict of laws. Indeed, they are no more complex than a simple products liability suit arising from a two-car accident among residents of the same state, which can implicate the laws of several states, including the place of the accident, the states where the car and tire manufacturers are headquartered, the states where the car and tires were manufactured, and the state where the car was purchased.

Goldsmith, *Against Cyberanarchy, supra,* at 1234.

This may well be true. Digitalbooks.com's sale of an individual book to a customer in Singapore, in isolation, is no more "complex or challenging" as a matter of international law than Analogbooks' sale of the same book to the same customer.

To stop the analysis there, however, is to miss the forest for the trees. Scale matters; the biologists and the engineers know this. * * * A tree is one thing; the forest, though it is nothing more than a large number of trees, is another, more "complex and challenging," phenomenon. The movement of a single clump of dirt down a slope is one thing; an avalanche, though it is nothing more than the movement of a lot of individual pieces of dirt down a slope, is another, more "complex and challenging," event. * * *

Therefore, although Digitalbooks.com and Analogbooks each may be doing the "same" things, the *systems* within which they operate are not necessarily the same as a consequence of that identity. *Scale matters.* Differences in degree sometimes become differences in kind; quantitative changes can become qualitative changes. Rules and principles that may be quite reasonable at one scale may be incoherent and unreasonable at another. * * *

We live in a world of inter-connected and geographically complex causes and effects * * * . Imagine for the moment something we might call an "effects map." To construct such a map, we mark the location of every event taking place at any specific moment, the "effects" of which will be felt in, say Singapore. An "effects map" would look something like the familiar nighttime satellite images of "The Earth from Space" * * * . Each point of light on the "effects map," however, would represent not an actual source of illumination but rather the location of an event or transaction whose effects were felt by some person, or institution, in Singapore.

Consider an effects map depicting a moment in 1450. Inasmuch as the effects of most activity taking place in 1450 declined rapidly with increasing geographical distance, most events or transactions having an effect in Singapore would themselves take place in, or around, Singapore. Our effects map would therefore show the territory around Singapore itself as a dense concentration of points, a small patch of intense light, with the remainder of the globe in almost total darkness.

An effects map for 1950 would undoubtedly show greater relative "brightness" *outside* of Singapore's borders, reflecting changes in communication and transportation technologies over the past several centuries, and the increased numbers of border-crossing events and transactions with widely dispersed geographical effects—"airplane crashes, mass torts, multistate insurance coverage, or multinational commercial transactions." Goldsmith, *Against Cyberanarchy*, *supra*, at 1234.

But the 1950 map would, I submit, retain its geographical coherence because the effects of most human activity in 1950, notwithstanding "mail, the telephone, and smoke signals," remained geographically constrained. There would still be a bright cluster of points down on the southern tip of the Malaysian peninsula. On the basis of this patch of relative brightness alone, we would probably be able to reconstruct those boundaries with reasonable accuracy without too much trouble, even if Singapore's actual political boundaries were omitted from our effects map.

However, an effects map plotting events and transactions taking place today in *cyberspace* would look very different from this. A plot of the location of all events and transactions taking place in cyberspace that have an effect on persons and property in Singapore will have virtually no geographical structure at all; points of light will be wildly scattered about the map, seemingly at random. It's a cliché, but it's true nonetheless: On the global network all points are (virtually) equidistant from one another, irrespective of their location in real space * * * . We would have much, much more trouble reconstructing Singapore's actual boundaries from a map limited to cyberspace events and transactions in 2002 than in any of our previous maps.

With respect to the "Effects Principle" at the heart of the Unexceptionalist argument * * * the world *has* changed, rather dramatically. Border-crossing events and transactions, previously at the margins of the legal system, of sufficient rarity to be cabined off into a small corner of the legal universe ("airplane crashes, mass torts, multistate insurance coverage, or multinational commercial transactions") have migrated, in cyberspace, to the core of that system. * * *

A world in which virtually *all* events and transactions have border-crossing effects is surely not "functionally identical" to a world in which most do not, at least not with respect to the application of a principle that necessarily requires consideration of the distribution of those effects. A world in which Effects Principle returns the result "No Substantial Effects Outside the Borders" when applied to the vast majority of events and transactions is not "functionally identical" to a world in which application of the same principle to the vast majority of events and transactions returns the opposite result. A world in which, on occasion, bullets are fired from one jurisdiction into another is not "functionally identical" to a world in which all jurisdictions are constantly subjected to shrapnel from a thousand different directions.

Notes and Questions

1. Johnson and Post, and other "cyberspace exceptionalists" (or "regulation skeptics," as Professor Goldsmith calls them), make two fundamentally different arguments. First, they make a *descriptive* claim that online transactions *cannot* effectively be regulated by territorial sovereigns because of the ease with which cyberspace actors can relocate their activities beyond the reach of the enforcing sovereign. Thus, if a state wanted to regulate online gambling, a website devoted to gambling could simply relocate in another state (or outside the country) and still reach the same audience within the state. Second, they make a *normative* claim that it is *illegitimate* for territorial sovereigns to regulate activities beyond their borders. Do you agree with either or both claims? What are Goldsmith's responses to each claim?

2. If Johnson and Post are correct that territorial regulation will be impossible or normatively undesirable, what sort of entities will regulate online transactions? Would Johnson's and Post's answer be different from Goldsmith's?

3. Goldsmith argues that "it is legitimate for a nation to apply its regulation to an extraterritorial act with harmful local effects." Is this an adequate response to the challenge Johnson and Post raise?

4. Johnson and Post contend that content providers in cyberspace may be subject to multiple regulation in multiple jurisdictions around the globe. What is Goldsmith's answer to this problem? Is geographical tracking software the answer to the problem? How does a website operator—even assuming she could determine the location of all users—monitor access to the site so that it accords with every different local law? Does Goldsmith recognize this as a problem? How would he respond?

5. Goldsmith argues that cyberspace poses no new legal jurisdictional difficulties, given that cross-border interaction has been a reality for some time. What is Post's response to this argument? Which side do you find more convincing? Why?

6. Goldsmith argues that we need not fear extraterritorial regulation of online activity by remote governments because those governments will have no way to enforce any judgments they issue. Is that a sufficient answer? Assume that you are the CEO of Digitalbooks.com, and Singapore prosecuted you in absentia for distributing *Lady Chatterley's Lover* "in" Singapore. It is true that, if you had no assets in Singapore, there might be no means of enforcement. But what about if you subsequently vacationed in Singapore? Or flew to Indonesia through Singapore's airspace? Or traveled to a country that was willing to honor Singapore's extradition request?

7. Are Goldsmith's arguments consistent? On the one hand he argues that we need not worry about extraterritorial regulation of online activities because of a variety of limitations regarding enforcement. On the other hand, he argues that such extraterritorial regulation is legitimate because online activity creates harmful effects—for example subjecting people in state x to content that state x has deemed inappropriate. But if enforcement is not possible in most circumstances, then there is no remedy for the harmful effects. And if enforcement *is* possible, then isn't such enforcement extraterritorial?

8. Goldsmith argues that, even if a nation cannot regulate a distant online actor, it can control the local effects by prosecuting end users or (more likely) local intermediaries such as service providers. For example, the federal Unlawful Internet Gambling Enforcement Act of 2006, Pub. L. No. 109-347, §§ 801-803, 120 Stat. 1952, acknowledges that "traditional law enforcement mechanisms are often inadequate" in this area and therefore focuses instead on banks, credit card companies, and other payment providers. The Act forbids such institutions from knowingly processing payments, fund transfers, and the like made in connection with Internet gambling. Is that form of indirect regulation likely to be more effective?

9. What effect might regulatory activity aimed at Internet service providers have on such intermediaries? We will explore this question in more detail in Chapter Seven.

SECTION B. JURISDICTION TO PRESCRIBE

Note on Jurisdiction

When discussing problems connected with territorial regulation of online activity, it is important to differentiate between three different forms of legal authority. First, the *jurisdiction to prescribe* describes a community's right to apply its legal *norms* to a given dispute. (In the United States, this inquiry is often referred to as "choice of law.") Second, the *jurisdiction to adjudicate*—"personal jurisdiction"—is the ability to subject persons or things to legal *process*. Third, judgment recognition refers to the circumstances under which one legal authority will choose to enforce the judgment of another legal authority. This is also sometimes called *jurisdiction to enforce*. RESTATEMENT (THIRD) OF THE FOREIGN RELATIONS LAW OF THE UNITED STATES § 401 (1987).

We will look at each of these in turn. It is, though, important to recognize that these inquiries are often linked. For example, as a practical matter, the jurisdiction to prescribe or adjudicate may be ineffectual if the legal norms prescribed and adjudicated cannot actually be enforced. Moreover, because enforcement often depends on the willingness of another court or governing body to recognize the original judgment, it is significant that a court is less likely to recognize another court's judgment if it believes the first court did not have proper adjudicatory jurisdiction over the suit in question.

1. Extraterritorial Regulation of Speech

In *Miller v. California*, 413 U.S. 15 (1973), the Supreme Court held that a state could constitutionally prohibit "obscene" speech. *Miller* approved a test for obscenity that still controls today:

> (a) whether the average person, applying contemporary community standards would find that the work, taken as a whole, appeals to the prurient interest;
> (b) whether the work depicts or describes, in a patently offensive way, sexual conduct specifically defined by the applicable state law; and
> (c) whether the work, taken as a whole, lacks serious literary, artistic, political, or scientific value.

Id. at 24 (internal quotation marks and citations omitted).

Based on *Miller*, attempts to regulate sexually explicit speech at the federal or local level often tie the legality of the speech to whether it is consistent with "contemporary community standards." When a defendant challenges the government's ability to use such a test to regulate online speech, the issue is not, strictly speaking, whether the government has "jurisdiction to prescribe." For example, in the case of a federal law regulating sexually explicit speech, the government may seek merely to apply its law to speech originating within the United States; its power to do so as a matter of jurisdiction is undisputed. But to the extent that such a regulation relies on "contemporary community standards," it raises a directly analogous issue: in what circumstances can one community apply its legal norms to speech originating in a different community? To avoid liability under such a statute, would a speaker have to tailor his or her speech to the standards of the least tolerant community? If so, would such a statute unconstitutionally burden protected speech?

American Civil Liberties Union v. Reno

United States Court of Appeals for the Third Circuit, 2000
217 F.3d 162

[Note: In 1997, the Supreme Court, in *Reno v. American Civil Liberties Union*, 521 U.S. 844, struck down as unconstitutional a federal statute that made it unlawful to use a telecommunications device or interactive computer service to transmit or display "indecent" or "patently offensive" material to persons under the age of eighteen. (We will examine that case in detail in Chapter Six, Section A.) In response to that decision, Congress passed the Child Online Protection Act (COPA), which was immediately challenged by a coalition of plaintiffs, again on the grounds that the statute was unconstitutional under the First Amendment.]

GARTH, Circuit Judge.

[The Child Online Protection Act (COPA)] prohibits an individual or entity from:

> knowingly and with knowledge of the character of the material, in interstate or foreign commerce by means of the World Wide Web, mak[ing] any communication for commercial purposes that is available to any minor and that includes any material that is harmful to minors.

47 U.S.C. § 231(a)(1). * * * Under COPA, whether material published on the Web is "harmful to minors" is governed by a three-part test, *each* of which must be found before liability can attach:

> (A) the average person, applying *contemporary community standards*, would find, taking the material as a whole and with respect to minors, is designed to appeal to, or is designed to pander to, the prurient interest;

> (B) depicts, describes, or represents, in a manner patently offensive with respect to minors, an actual or simulated sexual act or sexual contact, an actual or simulated normal or perverted sexual act, or a lewd exhibition of the genitals or post-pubescent female breast; and

> (C) taken as a whole, lacks serious, literary, artistic, political, or scientific value for minors.

47 U.S.C. § 231(e)(6) (emphasis added). The parties conceded at oral argument that this "contemporary community standards" test applies to those communities within the United States, and not to foreign communities. Therefore, the more liberal community standards of Amsterdam or the more restrictive community standards of Tehran would not impact upon the analysis of whether material is "harmful to minors" under COPA.

COPA also provides Web publishers subject to the statute with affirmative defenses. If a Web publisher "has restricted access by minors to material that is harmful to minors" through the use of a "credit card, debit account, adult access code, or adult personal identification number . . . a digital certificate that verifies age . . . or by any other reasonable measures that are feasible under available technology," then no liability will attach to the Web publisher even if a minor should nevertheless gain access to restricted material under COPA. 47 U.S.C. § 231(c)(1). COPA violators face both criminal (maximum fines of $50,000 and a maximum prison term of six months, or both) and civil (fines of up to $50,000 for each day of violation) penalties. * * *

Because the Internet has an "international, geographically borderless nature," *People v. Barrows*, 177 Misc. 2d 712, 729, 677 N.Y.S.2d 672 (N.Y. 1998), with the proper software every Web site is accessible to all other Internet users worldwide. * * * [As the district court noted,] under *current* technology, Web publishers "cannot prevent [their site's] content from entering any geographic community." As such, Web publishers cannot prevent Internet users in certain geographic locales from accessing their site; and in fact the Web publisher will not even know the geographic location of visitors to its site. Similarly, a Web publisher cannot modify the content of its site so as to restrict different geographic communities to access of only certain portions of their site. Thus, once published on the Web, existing technology does not permit the published material to be restricted to particular states or jurisdictions. * * *

It is undisputed that the government has a compelling interest in protecting children from material that is harmful to them, even if not obscene by adult standards. At issue is whether, in achieving this compelling objective, Congress has articulated a constitutionally permissible means to achieve its objective without curtailing the protected free speech rights of adults. * * *

We base our particular determination of COPA's likely unconstitutionality * * * on COPA's reliance on "contemporary community standards" in the context of the electronic medium of the Web to identify material that is harmful to minors. The overbreadth of COPA's definition of "harmful to minors" applying a "contemporary community standards" clause * * * so concerns us that we are persuaded that this aspect of COPA, without reference to its other provisions, must lead inexorably to a holding of a likelihood of unconstitutionality of the entire COPA statute. Hence we base our opinion entirely on the basis of the likely unconstitutionality of this clause, even though the District Court relied on numerous other grounds. * * *

Previously, in addressing the mailing of unsolicited sexually explicit material in violation of a California obscenity statute, the Supreme Court held that the fact-finder must determine whether "'the average person, applying contemporary community standards' would find the work taken as a whole, [to appeal] to the prurient interest." *Miller v. California*, 413 U.S. 15, 24 (1973). * * * Congress incorporated into COPA this *Miller* test * * *. Even in so doing, Congress remained cognizant of the fact that "the application of community standards in the context of the Web is controversial." H.R. REP. No. 107-775, at 28 (1998). Nevertheless, in defending the constitutionality of COPA's use of the *Miller* test, the government insists that "there is nothing dispositive about the fact that [in COPA] commercial distribution of such [harmful] materials occurs through an online, rather than a brick and mortar outlet."

Despite the government's assertion, "[e]ach medium of expression 'must be assessed for First Amendment purposes by standards suited to it, for each may present its own problems.'" *American Civil Liberties Union v. Reno*, 31 F. Supp. 2d 473, 495 (E.D. Pa. 1999) (quoting *Southeastern Promotions, Ltd. v. Conrad*, 420 U.S. 546, 557 (1975)). In considering "the unique factors that affect communication in the new and technology-laden medium of the Web," we are convinced that there are crucial differences between a "brick and mortar outlet" and the online Web that dramatically affect a First Amendment analysis. *Id.*

Unlike a "brick and mortar outlet" with a specific geographic locale, and unlike the voluntary physical mailing of material from one geographic location to another, as in *Miller*, the uncontroverted facts indicate that the Web is *not geographically constrained.* Indeed, and of extreme significance, is the fact, as found by the District Court, that Web publishers are without any means to limit access to their sites based on the geographic location of particular Internet users. As soon as information is published on a Web site, it is accessible to all other Web visitors. Current technology prevents Web publishers from circumventing particular jurisdictions or limiting their site's content "from entering any [specific] geographic community." *Id.* at 484. This key difference necessarily affects our analysis in attempting to define what contemporary community standards should or could mean in a medium without geographic boundaries. * * *

[T]o avoid liability under COPA, affected Web publishers would either need to severely censor their publications or implement an age or credit card verification system whereby any material that might be deemed harmful by the most puritan of communities in any state is shielded behind such a verification system. Shielding such vast amounts of material behind verification systems would prevent access to protected material by any adult seventeen or over without the necessary age verification credentials. Moreover, it would completely bar access to those materials to all minors under seventeen—even if the material would not otherwise have been deemed "harmful" to them in their respective geographic communities.

The government argues that subjecting Web publishers to varying community standards is not constitutionally problematic or, for that matter, unusual. The government notes that there are numerous cases in which the courts have already subjected the same conduct to varying community standards, depending on the community in which the conduct occurred. For example, the Supreme Court has stated that "distributors of allegedly obscene materials may be subjected to varying community standards in the various federal judicial districts into which they transmit the material [but that] does not render a federal statute unconstitutional because of the failure of the application of uniform national standards of obscenity." *Hamling v. United States*, 418 U.S. 87, 106 (1974). Similarly, the government cites to the "dial-a-porn" cases in which the Supreme Court has held that even if the "audience is comprised of different communities with different local standards" the company providing the obscene material "ultimately bears the burden of complying with the prohibition on obscene messages" under each community's respective standard. *Sable Communications of California v. F.C.C.*, 492 U.S. 115, 125-26 (1989).

These cases, however, are easily distinguished from the present case. In each of those cases, the defendants had the ability to control the distribution of controversial material with respect to the geographic communities into which they released it. Therefore, the defendants could limit their exposure to liability by avoiding those communities with particularly restrictive standards, while continuing to provide the controversial material in more liberal-minded communities. For example, the pornographer in *Hamling* could have chosen not to mail unsolicited sexually explicit material to certain communities while continuing to mail them to others. Similarly, the telephone pornographers ("dial-a-porn") in *Sable* could have screened their incoming calls and then only accepted a call if its point of origination was from a community with standards of decency that were not offended by the content of their pornographic telephone messages.

By contrast, Web publishers have no such comparable control. Web publishers cannot restrict access to their site based on the geographic locale of the Internet user visiting their site. In fact, "an Internet user cannot foreclose access to . . . work from certain states or send differing versions of . . . communication[s] to different jurisdictions . . . The Internet user has no ability to bypass any particular state." *American Libraries Ass'n v. Pataki*, 969 F. Supp. 160, 183 (S.D.N.Y. 1997). As a result, unlike telephone or postal mail pornographers, Web publishers of material that may be harmful to minors must "comply with the regulation imposed by the State with the most stringent standard or [entirely] forego Internet communication of the message that might or might not subject [the publisher] to prosecution." *Id*. * * *

Our concern with COPA's adoption of *Miller*'s "contemporary community standards" test by which to determine whether material is harmful to minors is with respect to its overbreadth in the context of the Web medium. Because no technology *currently* exists by which Web publishers may avoid liability, such publishers would necessarily be compelled to abide by the "standards of the community most likely to be offended by the message," *Reno v. American Civil Liberties Union*, 521 U.S. 844, 877-78 (1997), even if the same material would not have been deemed harmful to minors in all other communities. Moreover, by restricting their publications to meet the more stringent standards of less liberal communities, adults whose constitutional rights permit them to view such materials would be unconstitutionally deprived of those rights. Thus, this result imposes an overreaching burden and restriction on constitutionally protected speech.

Ashcroft v. American Civil Liberties Union

Supreme Court of the United States, 2002
535 U.S. 564

[JUSTICE THOMAS announced the judgment of the Court and delivered an opinion that, with respect to the portions excerpted below, was joined by THE CHIEF JUSTICE and JUSTICE SCALIA.]

The Court of Appeals * * * concluded that this Court's prior community standards jurisprudence "has no applicability to the Internet and the Web" because "Web publishers are *currently* without the ability to control the geographic scope of the recipients of their communications." We therefore must decide whether this technological limitation renders COPA's reliance on community standards constitutionally infirm.

A

In addressing this question, the parties first dispute the nature of the community standards that jurors will be instructed to apply when assessing, in prosecutions under COPA, whether works appeal to the prurient interest of minors and are patently offensive with respect to minors. Respondents contend that jurors will evaluate material using "local community standards," while petitioner maintains that jurors will not consider the community standards of any particular geographic area, but rather will be "instructed to consider the standards of the adult community as a whole, without geographic specification."

In the context of this case, which involves a facial challenge to a statute that has never been enforced, we do not think it prudent to engage in speculation as to whether certain hypothetical jury instructions would or would not be consistent with COPA, and deciding this case does not require us to do so. It is sufficient to note that community standards need not be defined by reference to a precise geographic area. Absent geographic specification, a juror applying community standards will inevitably draw upon personal "knowledge of the community or vicinage from which he comes." *Hamling v. United States*, 418 U.S. 87, 105 (1974). Petitioner concedes the latter point, and admits that, even if jurors were instructed under COPA to apply the standards of the adult population as a whole, the variance in community standards across the country could still cause juries in different locations to reach inconsistent conclusions as to whether a particular work is "harmful to minors."

B

Because juries would apply different standards across the country, and Web publishers currently lack the ability to limit access to their sites on a geographic basis, the Court of Appeals feared that COPA's "community standards" component would effectively force all speakers on the Web to

abide by the "most puritan" community's standards.   And such a
requirement, the Court of Appeals concluded, "imposes an overreaching
burden and restriction on constitutionally protected speech." * * *

C

When the scope of an obscenity statute's coverage is sufficiently
narrowed by a "serious value" prong and a "prurient interest" prong, we
have held that requiring a speaker disseminating material to a national
audience to observe varying community standards does not violate the First
Amendment. * * * While JUSTICE KENNEDY and JUSTICE STEVENS question
the applicability of this Court's community standards jurisprudence to the
Internet, we do not believe that the medium's "unique characteristics"
justify adopting a different approach * * * . If a publisher chooses to send
its material into a particular community, this Court's jurisprudence teaches
that it is the publisher's responsibility to abide by that community's
standards.   The publisher's burden does not change simply because it
decides to distribute its material to every community in the Nation.   Nor
does it change because the publisher may wish to speak only to those in a
community where avant garde culture is the norm, but nonetheless utilizes
a medium that transmits its speech from coast to coast.   If a publisher
wishes for its material to be judged only by the standards of particular
communities, then it need only take the simple step of utilizing a medium
that enables it to target the release of its material into those
communities.[14] * * * [W]e have no reason to believe that the practical effect
of varying community standards under COPA, given the statute's definition
of "material that is harmful to minors," is significantly greater than the
practical effect of varying community standards under federal obscenity
statutes.   It is noteworthy, for example, that respondents fail to point out
even a single exhibit in the record as to which coverage under COPA would
depend upon which community in the country evaluated the material.   As
a result, if we were to hold COPA unconstitutional *because of* its use of
community standards, federal obscenity statutes would likely also be
unconstitutional as applied to the Web * * * .

The scope of our decision today is quite limited.   We hold only that
COPA's reliance on community standards to identify "material that is
harmful to minors" does not *by itself* render the statute substantially
overbroad for purposes of the First Amendment.   We do not express any
view as to whether COPA suffers from substantial overbreadth for other
reasons, whether the statute is unconstitutionally vague, or whether the
District Court correctly concluded that the statute likely will not survive
strict scrutiny analysis once adjudication of the case is completed below.
While respondents urge us to resolve these questions at this time, prudence

---

14. In addition, COPA does not, as JUSTICE KENNEDY suggests, "foreclose an entire
medium of expression." While JUSTICE KENNEDY and JUSTICE STEVENS repeatedly imply that
COPA banishes from the Web material deemed harmful to minors by reference to community
standards, the statute does no such thing. It only requires that such material be placed behind
adult identification screens.

dictates allowing the Court of Appeals to first examine these difficult issues. * * *

JUSTICE O'CONNOR, concurring in part and concurring in the judgment.

I agree with the plurality that even if obscenity on the Internet is defined in terms of local community standards, respondents have not shown that the Child Online Protection Act (COPA) is overbroad solely on the basis of the variation in the standards of different communities. * * * I write separately to express my views on the constitutionality and desirability of adopting a national standard for obscenity for regulation of the Internet.

The plurality's opinion argues that, even under local community standards, the variation between the most and least restrictive communities is not so great with respect to the narrow category of speech covered by COPA as to, alone, render the statute substantially overbroad. I agree, given respondents' failure to provide examples of materials that lack literary, artistic, political, and scientific value for minors, which would nonetheless result in variation among communities judging the other elements of the test. Respondents' examples of material for which community standards would vary include such things as the appropriateness of sex education and the desirability of adoption by same-sex couples. Material addressing the latter topic, however, seems highly unlikely to be seen to appeal to the prurient interest in any community, and educational material like the former must, on any objective inquiry, have scientific value for minors. * * *

[Nevertheless,] given Internet speakers' inability to control the geographic location of their audience, expecting them to bear the burden of controlling the recipients of their speech * * * may be entirely too much to ask, and would potentially suppress an inordinate amount of expression. For these reasons, adoption of a national standard is necessary in my view for any reasonable regulation of Internet obscenity. * * *

To be sure, the Court in *Miller* * * * stated that a national standard might be "unascertainable," *Miller v. California*, 413 U.S. 15, 31 (1973), and "[un]realistic," *id.* at 32. But where speech on the Internet is concerned, I do not share that skepticism. It is true that our Nation is diverse, but many local communities encompass a similar diversity. For instance, in *Miller* itself, the jury was instructed to consider the standards of the entire State of California, a large * * * and diverse State that includes both Berkeley and Bakersfield. If the *Miller* Court believed generalizations about the standards of the people of California were possible, and that jurors would be capable of assessing them, it is difficult to believe that similar generalizations are not also possible for the Nation as a whole. Moreover, the existence of the Internet, and its facilitation of national dialogue, has itself made jurors more aware of the views of adults in other parts of the United States. Although jurors asked to evaluate the obscenity of speech based on a national standard will inevitably base their assessments to some extent on their experience of their local communities, * * * the lesser degree of variation that would result is inherent in the jury system and does not necessarily pose a First Amendment problem. In my view, a national standard is not only constitutionally permissible, but also reasonable.

JUSTICE KENNEDY, with whom JUSTICE SOUTER and JUSTICE GINSBURG join, concurring in the judgment.

The Court of Appeals found that COPA in effect subjects every Internet speaker to the standards of the most puritanical community in the United States. This concern is a real one, but it alone cannot suffice to invalidate COPA without careful examination of the speech and the speakers within the ambit of the Act. For this reason, I join the judgment of the Court vacating the opinion of the Court of Appeals and remanding for consideration of the statute as a whole. Unlike JUSTICE THOMAS, however, I would not assume that the Act is narrow enough to render the national variation in community standards unproblematic. Indeed, if the District Court correctly construed the statute across its other dimensions, then the variation in community standards might well justify enjoining enforcement of the Act. * * *

The economics and technology of Internet communication differ in important ways from those of telephones and mail. Paradoxically, as the District Court found, it is easy and cheap to reach a worldwide audience on the Internet, but expensive if not impossible to reach a geographic subset. A Web publisher in a community where avant garde culture is the norm may have no desire to reach a national market; he may wish only to speak to his neighbors; nevertheless, if an eavesdropper in a more traditional, rural community chooses to listen in, there is nothing the publisher can do. As a practical matter, COPA makes the eavesdropper the arbiter of propriety on the Web. And it is no answer to say that the speaker should "take the simple step of utilizing a [different] medium." *Ante* (principal opinion of THOMAS, J.). "Our prior decisions have voiced particular concern with laws that foreclose an entire medium of expression . . . . [T]he danger they pose to the freedom of speech is readily apparent—by eliminating a common means of speaking, such measures can suppress too much speech." *City of Ladue v. Gilleo*, 512 U.S. 43, 55 (1994). * * *

[T]he Court of Appeals was correct to focus on COPA's incorporation of varying community standards; and it may have been correct as well to conclude that in practical effect COPA imposes the most puritanical community standard on the entire country. * * * The national variation in community standards constitutes a particular burden on Internet speech. * * *

The question that remains is whether this observation "*by itself*" suffices to enjoin the Act. I agree with the Court that it does not. We cannot know whether variation in community standards renders the Act substantially overbroad without first assessing the extent of the speech covered and the variations in community standards with respect to that speech.

First, the breadth of the Act itself will dictate the degree of overbreadth caused by varying community standards. * * * Second, community standards may have different degrees of variation depending on the question posed to the community. * * * On the one hand, the Court of Appeals found "no evidence to suggest that adults *everywhere* in America would share the same standards for determining what is harmful to minors." On the other hand, JUSTICE THOMAS finds "no reason to believe that the practical effect of varying community standards under COPA . . . is significantly greater than the practical effect of varying standards under federal obscenity statutes." When a key issue has "no evidence" on one side and "no reason to believe" the other, it is a good indication that we should vacate for further consideration.

[Opinions of Justice Breyer, concurring in part and concurring in the judgment, and Justice Stevens, dissenting, omitted.]

Notes and Questions

1. The Third Circuit seemed to have embraced what Professor Post called the "Exceptionalist" position: "[W]e are convinced that there are crucial differences between a 'brick and mortar outlet' and the online Web that dramatically affect a First Amendment analysis." (What might those differences be?) Three Justices (Thomas, Rehnquist, and Scalia) are clearly in the Unexceptionalist camp on this issue; inasmuch as it is constitutional to "requir[e] a speaker disseminating material to a national audience" by traditional means to "observe varying community standards," it is similarly constitutional to require an online speaker to do so as well. Where do the other Justices come out on this question? In what ways is the Internet the same as, and in what ways is it different from, magazines or "dial-a-porn" services with a nationwide distribution?

2. Justice Thomas concludes that "[i]f a publisher chooses to send its material into a particular community, this Court's jurisprudence teaches that it is the publisher's responsibility to abide by that community's standards." Is it accurate to say that a website operator "sends" her material to every community in the country (or the world)? Couldn't one just as easily say that the website remains in one place, and people in various communities "travel to" the site to gather information? And what about Justice Kennedy's idea that those who view websites not intended for them are like eavesdroppers? How can one choose between these metaphorical formulations? What might be the legal consequences that flow from the choice of metaphors? Are there other metaphors that might be appropriate?

3. Justice O'Connor advocates a national obscenity standard. Is such a standard feasible? What are the difficulties that one might encounter in crafting such a standard? And, if a standard were developed, would it apply only to online material?

4. What do you think Professor Post would say about COPA's community standards language? Would he embrace Justice O'Connor's position? Justice Thomas's? Justice Kennedy's?

5. Several of the opinions in this case stress the fact that, using current technology, it is difficult or impossible for a website operator to limit access based on the geographical location of the end user. Why do you think this is so difficult? Assuming geographical tracking software were perfected, should that change the analysis?

6. Think about the "spillover effects" that Johnson and Post and Goldsmith discussed. Would the existence of varying community standards create regulatory spillover from one jurisdiction to another? Why? On the other hand, wouldn't there also be "spillover effects" if COPA had been drafted so that only the community standards of the server location were considered?

7. On remand, the Third Circuit again ruled that COPA violated the First Amendment, relying on various aspects of the Act beyond simply the "community standards" language discussed here. *See American Civil Liberties Union v. Ashcroft*, 322 F.3d 240 (3d Cir. 2003). The Supreme Court subsequently affirmed, though the Court suggested that the Third Circuit had unnecessarily construed various statutory definitions not considered by the district court. *Ashcroft v. American Civil Liberties Union*, 542 U.S. 656 (2004). Accordingly, the Court limited itself to ruling that the district court did not abuse its discretion in granting preliminary injunctive relief. *Id.* at 673. For further discussion, see *infra* p. 441.

8. Although Justice O'Connor seeks to solve the problem of content regulation through a uniform national rule, such an approach would not address the possibility of conflicting standards for speech internationally. The next case raises the international issue.

La Ligue Contre le Racisme et l'Antisémitisme v. Yahoo!, Inc.

Superior Court of Paris, May 22, 2000

[The Yahoo.com website included an auctions page through which various private parties could purchase items from each other. Among other items available on the auctions page were Nazi relics, insignias, emblems, flags, and other objects. Yahoo.com also provided links to other pages on which various Nazi texts—such as *Mein Kampf* and *The Protocols of the Elders of Zion*—were available for sale. These same sites also included "Holocaust revisionist" material, such as photographs purporting to "prove" that reports of gas chambers were fictitious. L'Union des Etudiants Juif de France (Jewish Students' Union of France, or UEJF) and La Ligue Contre le Racisme et l'Antisémitisme (League Against Racism and Antisemitism, or LICRA) sued Yahoo!, alleging violations of article R. 645-1 of the French Penal Code, which prohibits the public display of Nazi-related objects.]

JEAN-JACQUES GOMEZ, Presiding Justice.

Whereas it is not contested that a surfer who accesses Yahoo.com from French territory, directly or by virtue of the link that Yahoo.fr provides, can view on his computer screen pages, services, and sites to which Yahoo.com gives access, in particular the auction service (Auctions) hosted by Geocities.com, Yahoo! Inc.'s hosting service, notably its listings of Nazi items;

Whereas the exhibition of Nazi items for sale constitutes a violation of French law (Article R. [645-1] of the Penal Code) but even more an insult to the collective memory of a country deeply wounded by the atrocities that were committed by and in the name of the Nazi criminal organization against its nationals, and especially against its Jewish nationals;

Whereas by allowing the viewing of these items in France and by allowing the eventual participation of a surfer in France in such an exhibition-sale, Yahoo! Inc. commits a wrong on French territory—the unintentional nature of which is apparent, but which causes the damage to LICRA and the UEJF, both of which have as their mission to pursue in France any form of trivialization of Nazism—notwithstanding that the activity at issue is marginal in relation to the general activity of the auction service that Yahoo.com offers on its site;

Whereas the damage was suffered in France, and we are therefore competent to exercise jurisdiction over the present dispute * * * ;

Whereas Yahoo! Inc. argues that it is technically impossible for it to control access to the auction service or to other services and, as a result, to prevent a surfer accessing the Internet from France from viewing these services on his screen;

Whereas Yahoo! Inc. wishes to emphasize that it warns any visitor against using its services for purposes "worthy of reprobation for any reason whatsoever," notably for purposes of racial or ethnic discrimination (see its users' charter);

But whereas Yahoo! Inc. has the capability to identify the geographical origin of the site that accesses its services, based on the [Internet Protocol] address of the surfer, which should allow Yahoo! Inc. to use appropriate means to prevent surfers in France from accessing services and sites the viewing of which on a screen in France * * * can be considered [punishable under French law], as is obviously the case with the display of uniforms, badges, and emblems that recall the ones worn or displayed by the Nazis;

Whereas with regard to surfers who access its services through sites that ensure anonymity, Yahoo! Inc. has less ability to control access, but nevertheless can do so, for example, by systematically refusing access to any visitor who does not reveal his geographical origin;

Whereas the real difficulties encountered by Yahoo! Inc. thus do not constitute insurmountable obstacles; * * *

[We order] Yahoo! Inc. to take all such measures as would dissuade and prevent any access through Yahoo.com to the auction service for Nazi items or any other site or service that constitutes an apology for Nazism or questions Nazi crimes[.]

Notes and Questions

1. Yahoo! claimed that it could not, as a technological matter, selectively block access to prohibited sites based on the geographical location of the user. Should that matter to the French court? If Yahoo! cannot distinguish French users from others, would compliance with the court's order here necessarily mean withholding the proscribed material to everyone around the globe? This is the same technological limitation that we discussed in reference to the community standards issue above; see note 5, page 94. If technology becomes readily available that would allow Yahoo! to identify user location, should it be required to use that technology to comply with the demands of the French court?

2. Would Professor Goldsmith support the French court's decision to assert its "jurisdiction to prescribe" in regard to Yahoo!'s website? How will the French plaintiffs enforce the court's order? If enforcement poses difficulties, does that support Goldsmith's point that extraterritorial regulation is nothing to worry about?

3. Why wasn't there any dispute that the French court could order the removal of offensive material from Yahoo.fr? Why do you think such removal was insufficient from the point of view of the French complainants?

4. It is worth noting that, under French jurisdictional law, the French court could have asserted jurisdiction based on a (then-existing) provision that extended jurisdiction over anyone, anywhere in the world, so long as there was a French plaintiff. However, because of the controversial nature of such a jurisdictional assertion, this provision has rarely been invoked and was not discussed by the court in this case (and the provision has since been struck down by France's highest court). Nevertheless, Yahoo!'s argument was essentially that even the court's more limited assertion of jurisdiction was tantamount to an assertion of universal jurisdiction over any website viewable in France. Do you agree?

5. Should the mere fact that Yahoo!'s servers are not located in France be sufficient to deny the French court jurisdiction? What criteria should be used for determining whether a company such as Yahoo! should face liability in France? Professor Joel Reidenberg points out, for example, that Yahoo! is a sophisticated, multinational operator, with a business plan aimed at reaching web users worldwide, a marketing strategy touting its "global footprint," and a French subsidiary in which it owns a seventy-percent ownership stake. Reidenberg argues that Yahoo! exerted substantial control over this subsidiary, dictating some of the links and content of the site and requiring the subsidiary to maintain links to its United States–based site. Moreover, Yahoo! routinely profiled French users in order to target them with advertisements written in French. All of this, he suggests, is more than sufficient to justify France's assertion of jurisdiction over Yahoo! *See* Joel R. Reidenberg, *Yahoo and Democracy on the Internet*, 42 JURIMETRICS J. 261 (2002). Do you agree?

6. Shortly after the French court ruling, Italy's highest court, in an appeal of an online defamation case, ruled that Italian courts can assert jurisdiction over foreign-based websites and shut them down if they do not abide by Italian law. *See In re Moshe D.* (Court of Cassation, Italy, Dec. 27, 2000), English translation available at http://www.cdt.org/speech/international/

001227italiandecision.pdf. The court determined, as in the *Yahoo!* case, that Italian courts have jurisdiction both when an act or omission has actually been committed on Italian territory *and* when simply the *effects* or consequences of an act are felt in Italy. Likewise, Germany's second-highest court ruled that an Australian website owner—whose website questioning the Holocaust is illegal in Germany but not in Australia—could be jailed for violating German speech laws. *See Australian Faces Trial for Holocaust Denial*, REUTERS (Dec. 14, 2000). The High Court of Australia similarly ruled that Australian courts could assert jurisdiction over an American publisher for publishing on its website an article allegedly defaming an Australian citizen, *see Dow Jones & Co., Inc. v. Gutnick*, HCA 56 (Austl. 2002), and the Court of Appeal of England and Wales ruled that allegedly defamatory materials posted on a U.S.-based website were nevertheless "published" for purposes of a libel action in the jurisdiction where they were downloaded, *see Lewis v. King*, [2004] EWCA Civ 1329 (Eng.); *see also Richardson v. Schwarzenegger*, [2004] EWHC 2422 (QB) (Eng.) (relying on *Lewis* to assert jurisdiction over a libel suit arising from an article in the *Los Angeles Times* that was available online); *Bangoura v. Washington Post*, 235 D.L.R. (4th) 564 (Ontario Super. Ct. Justice 2004) (asserting jurisdiction over a libel suit concerning materials on a U.S.-based website accessible in Canada).

7. In our discussion of local "community standards," we encountered the "lowest common denominator" argument: if websites are subject to the laws of *all* jurisdictions from which they can be accessed, the legal norms of the *most restrictive* community will prevail. But what about the flipside of that argument: If foreign courts cannot reach websites located in other jurisdictions, will the legal norms of the *least restrictive* community prevail? In the context of the *Yahoo!* case, if foreign courts cannot reach U.S.-based entities, has the United States then imposed its (relatively unrestrictive) First Amendment on global Internet speech? If so, is that problematic? The *Yahoo!* case raises the possibility that other countries might begin to challenge America's legal dominance by advancing alternative normative visions about the shape of online regulation. Is this a "democratizing" of Internet regulation, or a recipe for local chaos? Or both?

8. Suppose the plaintiffs in the Yahoo! case could have obtained, under French law, an order requiring French ISPs to block French subscribers' access to the offending content on Yahoo!'s auction site (rather than an injunction against the foreign website itself). Wouldn't that "solve" the extraterritoriality problem (while still serving the law's purpose of eliminating the "public display" of Nazi-related material) inasmuch as French law would be applied to the conduct of French, rather than foreign, entities? In February 2002, the Commonwealth of Pennsylvania enacted the Internet Child Pornography Act, 18 Pa. Cons. Stat. §§ 7621-7630, which took just this approach to the control of unlawful content on the Internet. The Pennsylvania statute required Internet service providers to "disable access" to "child pornography items"—defined elsewhere in the statute—"residing on or accessible through its service in a manner accessible to persons located within Pennsylvania" after notification from the Pennsylvania Attorney General that there was probable cause to believe such material could be accessed from within Pennsylvania over the ISP's facilities. By its terms, the statute was directed entirely at *within-*

state activities; the statute left the offending websites, which might be physically located anywhere in the world, completely undisturbed, only ISPs *serving Pennsylvania subscribers* were subject to the court's orders, and compliance with the statute only required them to make the offending websites inaccessible to their subscribers *in Pennsylvania.*

From the standpoint of the "jurisdiction to prescribe," does Pennsylvania's approach successfully avoid the charge that Pennsylvania is attempting to reach out beyond its borders to control the behavior of individuals or entities outside of its jurisdiction? In *Center for Democracy and Technology v. Pappert*, 337 F. Supp. 2d 606 (E.D. Pa. 2004), a federal court struck down the Pennsylvania statute on the grounds that it violated both the First Amendment and the "dormant" Commerce Clause; we discuss this case in Section B.2 of this Chapter, *infra* p. 111, and in Section C of Chapter Six, *infra* p. 468. *See also* Jonathan Zittrain, *Internet Points of Control*, 44 B.C. L. REV 653 (2003).

9. If you were a U.S. judge asked to enforce the French court's order, would you do so? Why or why not? Yahoo! did in fact file suit in the United States seeking a declaration that enforcement of the French judgment would violate the U.S. Constitution. We examine that case later in this chapter.

2. The "Dormant" Commerce Clause

American Libraries Association v. Pataki

United States District Court for the Southern District of New York, 1997
969 F. Supp. 160

PRESKA, District Judge.

The Internet may well be the premier technological innovation of the present age. Judges and legislators faced with adapting existing legal standards to the novel environment of cyberspace struggle with terms and concepts that the average American five-year-old tosses about with breezy familiarity. Not surprisingly, much of the legal analysis of Internet-related issues has focused on seeking a familiar analogy for the unfamiliar. * * * I find, as described more fully below, that the Internet is analogous to a highway or railroad. This determination means that the phrase "information superhighway" is more than a mere buzzword; it has legal significance, because the similarity between the Internet and more traditional instruments of interstate commerce leads to analysis under the Commerce Clause.

The plaintiffs in the present case filed this action challenging New York Penal Law § 235.21(3) (the "Act" or the "New York Act"), seeking declaratory and injunctive relief. Plaintiffs contend that the Act is unconstitutional both because it unduly burdens free speech in violation of the First Amendment and because it unduly burdens interstate commerce in violation of the Commerce Clause. * * *

The Act in question amended N.Y. Penal Law § 235.21 by adding a new subdivision. The amendment makes it a crime for an individual:

Knowing the character and content of the communication which, in whole or in part, depicts actual or simulated nudity, sexual conduct or sado-masochistic abuse, and which is harmful to minors, [to] intentionally use[] any computer communication system allowing the input, output, examination or transfer, of computer data or computer programs from one computer to another, to initiate or engage in such communication with a person who is a minor.

Violation of the Act is a Class E felony, punishable by one to four years of incarceration. The Act applies to both commercial and non-commercial disseminations of material. * * *

The borderless world of the Internet raises profound questions concerning the relationship among the several states and the relationship of the federal government to each state, questions that go to the heart of "our federalism." The Act at issue in the present case is only one of many efforts by state legislators to control the chaotic environment of the Internet. * * * Further, states have adopted widely varying approaches in the application of general laws to communications taking place over the Internet. * * *

The unique nature of the Internet highlights the likelihood that a single actor might be subject to haphazard, uncoordinated, and even outright inconsistent regulation by states that the actor never intended to reach and possibly was unaware were being accessed. Typically, states' jurisdictional limits are related to geography; geography, however, is a virtually meaningless construct on the Internet. The menace of inconsistent state regulation invites analysis under the Commerce Clause of the Constitution, because that clause represented the framers' reaction to overreaching by the individual states that might jeopardize the growth of the nation—and in particular, the national infrastructure of communications and trade—as a whole.

The Commerce Clause is more than an affirmative grant of power to Congress. As long ago as 1824, Justice Johnson in his concurring opinion in *Gibbons v. Ogden*, 9 Wheat. 1, 231-32, 239 (1824), recognized that the Commerce Clause has a negative sweep as well. In what commentators have come to term its negative or "dormant" aspect, the Commerce Clause restricts the individual states' interference with the flow of interstate commerce in two ways. The Clause prohibits discrimination aimed directly at interstate commerce and bars state regulations that, although facially nondiscriminatory, unduly burden interstate commerce. Moreover, courts have long held that state regulation of those aspects of commerce that by their unique nature demand cohesive national treatment is offensive to the Commerce Clause.

Thus, as will be discussed in more detail below, the New York Act is concerned with interstate commerce and contravenes the Commerce Clause for three reasons. First, the Act represents an unconstitutional projection of New York law into conduct that occurs wholly outside New York. Second, the Act is invalid because although protecting children from indecent material is a legitimate and indisputably worthy subject of state legislation, the burdens on interstate commerce resulting from the Act clearly exceed any local benefit derived from it. Finally, the Internet is one of those areas of commerce that must be marked off as a national preserve to protect users from inconsistent legislation that, taken to its most extreme, could paralyze development of the Internet altogether. Thus, the Commerce Clause ordains that only Congress can legislate in this area, subject, of course, to whatever limitations other provisions of the Constitution (such as the First Amendment) may require.

A.   The Act Concerns Interstate Commerce

At oral argument, the defendants advanced the theory that the Act is aimed solely at intrastate conduct. This argument is unsupportable in light of the text of the statute itself, its legislative history, and the reality of Internet communications. The section in question contains no such limitation * * * . By its terms, the Act applies to any communication, intrastate or interstate, that fits within the prohibition and over which New York has the capacity to exercise criminal jurisdiction.

Further, the legislative history of the Act clearly evidences the legislators' understanding and intent that the Act would apply to communications between New Yorkers and parties outside the State, despite occasional glib references to the Act's "intrastate" applicability. * * *

The conclusion that the Act must apply to interstate as well as intrastate communications receives perhaps its strongest support from the nature of the Internet itself. The Internet is wholly insensitive to geographic distinctions. In almost every case, users of the Internet neither know nor care about the physical location of the Internet resources they access. Internet protocols were designed to ignore rather than document geographic location; while computers on the network do have "addresses," they are logical addresses on the network rather than geographic addresses in real space. The majority of Internet addresses contain no geographic clues and, even where an Internet address provides such a clue, it may be misleading. * * *

Moreover, no aspect of the Internet can feasibly be closed off to users from another state. An Internet user who posts a Web page cannot prevent New Yorkers or Oklahomans or Iowans from accessing that page and will not even know from what state visitors to that site hail. Nor can a participant in a chat room prevent other participants from a particular state from joining the conversation. Someone who uses a mail exploder is similarly unaware of the precise contours of the mailing list that will ultimately determine the recipients of his or her message, because users can add or remove their names from a mailing list automatically. Thus, a person could choose a list believed not to include any New Yorkers, but an after-added New Yorker would still receive the message.

E-mail, because it is a one-to-one messaging system, stands on a slightly different footing than the other aspects of the Internet. Even in the context of e-mail, however, a message from one New Yorker to another New Yorker may well pass through a number of states en route. * * *

The system is further complicated by two Internet practices: packet switching and caching. "Packet switching" protocols subdivide individual messages into smaller packets that are then sent independently to the destination, where they are automatically reassembled by the receiving computer. If computers along the route become overloaded, packets may be rerouted to computers with greater capacity. A single message may—but does not always—travel several different pathways before reaching the receiving computer. "Caching" is the Internet practice of storing partial or complete duplicates of materials from frequently accessed sites to avoid repeatedly requesting copies from the original server. The recipient has no means of distinguishing between the cached materials and the original. Thus, the user may be accessing materials at the original site, or he may be accessing copies of those materials cached on a different machine located anywhere in the world.

The New York Act, therefore, cannot effectively be limited to purely intrastate communications over the Internet because no such communications exist. No user could reliably restrict her communications only to New York recipients. Moreover, no user could avoid liability under the New York Act simply by directing his or her communications elsewhere, given that there is no feasible way to preclude New Yorkers from accessing a Web site, receiving a mail exploder message or a newsgroup posting, or participating in a chat room. Similarly, a user has no way to ensure that an e-mail does not pass through New York even if the ultimate recipient is not located there, or that a message never leaves New York even if both sender and recipient are located there. * * *

The Act is therefore necessarily concerned with interstate communications. The next question that requires an answer as a threshold matter is whether the types of communication involved constitute "commerce" within the meaning of the Clause.

The definition of commerce in the Supreme Court's decisions has been notably broad. * * * The Supreme Court has expressly held that the dormant commerce clause is applicable to activities undertaken without a profit motive. * * * [In addition,] courts have long recognized that railroads, trucks, and highways are themselves "instruments of commerce," because they serve as conduits for the transport of products and services. The Internet is more than a means of communication; it also serves as a conduit for transporting digitized goods, including software, data, music, graphics, and videos which can be downloaded from the provider's site to the Internet user's computer. * * *

The inescapable conclusion is that the Internet represents an instrument of interstate commerce, albeit an innovative one; the novelty of the technology should not obscure the fact that regulation of the Internet impels traditional Commerce Clause considerations. The New York Act is therefore closely concerned with interstate commerce, and scrutiny of the Act under the Commerce Clause is entirely appropriate. As discussed in the following sections, the Act cannot survive such scrutiny, because it places an undue burden on interstate traffic, whether that traffic be in goods, services, or ideas.

B.   *New York Has Overreached by Enacting a Law That Seeks To Regulate Conduct Occurring Outside its Borders*

* * * The nature of the Internet makes it impossible to restrict the effects of the New York Act to conduct occurring within New York. An Internet user may not intend that a message be accessible to New Yorkers, but lacks the ability to prevent New Yorkers from visiting a particular Website or viewing a particular newsgroup posting or receiving a particular mail exploder. Thus, conduct that may be legal in the state in which the user acts can subject the user to prosecution in New York and thus subordinate the user's home state's policy—perhaps favoring freedom of expression over a more protective stance—to New York's local concerns. New York has deliberately imposed its legislation on the Internet and, by doing so, projected its law into other states whose citizens use the Net. This encroachment upon the authority which the Constitution specifically confers upon the federal government and upon the sovereignty of New York's sister states is per se violative of the Commerce Clause.

C.   *The Burdens the Act Imposes on Interstate Commerce Exceed Any Local Benefit*

Even if the Act were not a per se violation of the Commerce Clause by virtue of its extraterritorial effects, the Act would nonetheless be an invalid indirect regulation of interstate commerce, because the burdens it imposes on interstate commerce are excessive in relation to the local benefits it confers. The Supreme Court set forth the balancing test applicable to indirect regulations of interstate commerce in *Pike v. Bruce Church, Inc.*, 397 U.S. 137, 142 (1970). *Pike* requires a two-fold inquiry. The first level of examination is directed at the legitimacy of the state's interest. The next, and more difficult, determination weighs the burden on interstate commerce in light of the local benefit derived from the statute.

In the present case, I accept that the protection of children against pedophilia is a quintessentially legitimate state objective—a proposition with which I believe even the plaintiffs have expressed no quarrel. * * * Even with the fullest recognition that the protection of children from sexual exploitation is an indisputably valid state goal, however, the present statute cannot survive even the lesser scrutiny to which indirect regulations of interstate commerce are subject under the Constitution. The State cannot avoid the second stage of the inquiry simply by invoking the legitimate state interest underlying the Act.

The local benefits likely to result from the New York Act are not overwhelming. The Act can have no effect on communications originating outside the United States. * * * Further, in the present case, New York's

prosecution of parties from out of state who have allegedly violated the Ac
but whose only contact with New York occurs via the Internet, is beset wit
practical difficulties, even if New York is able to exercise crimin
jurisdiction over such parties. The prospect of New York bounty huntei
dragging pedophiles from the other 49 states into New York is not
consistent with traditional concepts of comity. * * *

The Act is, of course, not the only law in New York's statute books
designed to protect children against sexual exploitation. The State is able
to protect children through vigorous enforcement of the existing laws
criminalizing obscenity and child pornography. Moreover, plaintiffs do not
challenge the sections of the statute that criminalize the sale of obscene
materials to children, over the Internet or otherwise, and prohibit adults
from luring children into sexual contact by communicating with them via
the Internet. The local benefit to be derived from the challenged section of
the statute is therefore confined to that narrow class of cases that does not
fit within the parameters of any other law. * * *

Balanced against the limited local benefits resulting from the Act is an
extreme burden on interstate commerce. The New York Act casts its net
worldwide; moreover, the chilling effect that it produces is bound to exceed
the actual cases that are likely to be prosecuted, as Internet users will steer
clear of the Act by significant margin. * * * Moreover, * * * the costs
associated with Internet users' attempts to comply with the terms of the
defenses that the Act provides are excessive. * * * These costs of compliance, coupled with the threat of serious criminal sanctions for failure to
comply, could drive some Internet users off the Internet altogether.

The severe burden on interstate commerce resulting from the New
York statute is not justifiable in light of the attenuated local benefits arising
from it. The alternative analysis of the Act as an indirect regulation on
interstate commerce therefore also mandates the issuance of the
preliminary injunction sought by plaintiffs.

D.   *The Act Unconstitutionally Subjects Interstate Use of the Internet to
     Inconsistent Regulations*

Finally, a third mode of Commerce Clause analysis further confirms
that the plaintiffs are likely to succeed on the merits of their claim that the
New York Act is unconstitutional. The courts have long recognized that
certain types of commerce demand consistent treatment and are therefore
susceptible to regulation only on a national level. The Internet represents
one of those areas; effective regulation will require national, and more likely
global, cooperation. Regulation by any single state can only result in chaos,
because at least some states will likely enact laws subjecting Internet users
to conflicting obligations. Without the limitations imposed by the
Commerce Clause, these inconsistent regulatory schemes could paralyze the
development of the Internet altogether. * * *

The Internet, like the rail and highway traffic at issue in [earlier
Supreme Court] cases, requires a cohesive national scheme of regulation so
that users are reasonably able to determine their obligations. Regulation

on a local level, by contrast, will leave users lost in a welter of inconsistent laws, imposed by different states with different priorities. New York is not the only state to enact a law purporting to regulate the content of communications on the Internet. * * *

An Internet user cannot foreclose access to her work from certain states or send differing versions of her communication to different jurisdictions. In this sense, the Internet user is in a worse position than the truck driver or train engineer who can steer around Illinois or Arizona, or change the mudguard or train configuration at the state line; the Internet user has no ability to bypass any particular state. The user must thus comply with the regulation imposed by the state with the most stringent standard or forego Internet communication of the message that might or might not subject her to prosecution. * * *

Further development of the Internet requires that users be able to predict the results of their Internet use with some degree of assurance. Haphazard and uncoordinated state regulation can only frustrate the growth of cyberspace. The need for uniformity in this unique sphere of commerce requires that New York's law be stricken as a violation of the Commerce Clause.

Washington v. Heckel

Supreme Court of Washington, 2001
24 P.3d 404

OWENS, J.

BACKGROUND

As early as February 1996, defendant Jason Heckel, an Oregon resident doing business as Natural Instincts, began sending unsolicited commercial e-mail (UCE), or "spam," over the Internet. In 1997, Heckel developed a 46 page on-line booklet entitled "How to Profit from the Internet." The booklet described how to set up an on-line promotional business, acquire free e-mail accounts, and obtain software for sending bulk e-mail. From June 1998, Heckel marketed the booklet by sending between 100,000 and 1,000,000 UCE messages per week. To acquire the large volume of e-mail addresses, Heckel used the Extractor Pro software program, which harvests e-mail addresses from various on-line sources and enables a spammer to direct a bulk-mail message to those addresses by entering a simple command. The Extractor Pro program requires the spammer to enter a return e-mail address, a subject line, and the text of the message to be sent. The text of Heckel's UCE was a lengthy sales pitch that included testimonials from satisfied purchasers and culminated in an order form that the recipient could download and print. The order form included the Salem, Oregon, mailing address for Natural Instincts. Charging $39.95 for the booklet, Heckel made 30 to 50 sales per month.

In June 1998, the Consumer Protection Division of the Washington State Attorney General's Office received complaints from Washington recipients of Heckel's UCE messages. The complaints alleged that Heckel's messages contained misleading subject lines and false transmission paths. Responding to the June complaints, David Hill, an inspector from the Consumer Protection Division, sent Heckel a letter advising him of the existence of [Washington's commercial electronic mail act]. The Act provides that anyone sending a commercial e-mail message from a computer located in Washington or to an e-mail address [that the sender knows or has reason to know is] held by a Washington resident may not use a third-party's domain name without permission, misrepresent or disguise in any other way the message's point of origin or transmission path, or use a misleading subject line. * * *

Responding to Hill's letter, Heckel telephoned Hill on or around June 25, 1998. According to Hill, he discussed with Heckel the provisions of the Act and the procedures bulk e-mailers can follow to identify e-mail addressees who are Washington residents. Nevertheless, the Attorney General's Office continued to receive consumer complaints alleging that Heckel's bulk e-mailings from Natural Instincts appeared to contain misleading subject lines, false or unusable return e-mail addresses, and false or misleading transmission paths. Between June and September 1998, the Consumer Protection Division of the Attorney General's Office documented 20 complaints from 17 recipients of Heckel's UCE messages.

On October 22, 1998, the State filed suit against Heckel. * * *

ISSUE

Does the Act, which prohibits misrepresentation in the subject line or transmission path of any commercial e-mail message sent to Washington residents or from a Washington computer, unconstitutionally burden interstate commerce?

ANALYSIS

* * * The Commerce Clause grants Congress the "power . . . [t]o regulate commerce with foreign nations, and among the several states." U.S. CONST. art. I, § 8, cl. 3. Implicit in this affirmative grant is the negative or "dormant" Commerce Clause—the principle that the states impermissibly intrude on this federal power when they enact laws that unduly burden interstate commerce. Analysis of a state law under the dormant Commerce Clause generally follows a two-step process. We first determine whether the state law openly discriminates against interstate commerce in favor of intrastate economic interests. If the law is facially neutral, applying impartially to in-state and out-of-state businesses, the analysis moves to the second step, a balancing of the local benefits against the interstate burdens:

> Where the statute regulates evenhandedly to effectuate a legitimate local public interest, and its effects on interstate commerce are only incidental, it will be upheld unless the burden imposed on such

commerce is clearly excessive in relation to the putative local benefits. If a legitimate local purpose is found, then the question becomes one of degree. And the extent of the burden that will be tolerated will of course depend on the nature of the local interest involved, and on whether it could be promoted as well with a lesser impact on interstate activities. . . .

Franks & Son, Inc. v. Washington, 966 P.2d 1232, 1241 (Wash. 1998) (quoting *Pike v. Bruce Church, Inc.*, 397 U.S. 137, 142 (1970)).

The Act is not facially discriminatory. The Act applies evenhandedly to in-state and out-of-state spammers: *"No person"* may transmit the proscribed commercial e-mail messages "from a computer located in Washington or to an electronic mail address that the sender knows, or has reason to know, is held by a Washington resident." RCW 19.190.020(1) (emphasis added). Thus, just as the statute applied to Heckel, an Oregon resident, it is enforceable against a Washington business engaging in the same practices.

Because we conclude that the Act's local benefits surpass any alleged burden on interstate commerce, the statute likewise survives the *Pike* balancing test. The Act protects the interests of three groups—ISPs, actual owners of forged domain names, and e-mail users. * * * To handle the increased e-mail traffic attributable to deceptive spam, ISPs must invest in more computer equipment. Operational costs likewise increase as ISPs hire more customer service representatives to field spam complaints and more system administrators to detect accounts being used to send spam.

Along with ISPs, the owners of impermissibly used domain names and e-mail addresses suffer economic harm. For example, the registered owner of "localhost.com" alleged that his computer system was shut down for three days by 7,000 responses to a bulk-mail message in which the spammer had forged the e-mail address "nobody@localhost.com" into his spam's header.

Deceptive spam harms individual Internet users as well. When a spammer distorts the point of origin or transmission path of the message, e-mail recipients cannot promptly and effectively respond to the message (and thereby opt out of future mailings); their efforts to respond take time, cause frustration, and compound the problems that ISPs face in delivering and storing the bulk messages. And the use of false or misleading subject lines further hampers an individual's ability to use computer time most efficiently. When spammers use subject lines such as "Hi There!," "Information Request," and "Your Business Records," it becomes virtually impossible to distinguish spam from legitimate personal or business messages. Individuals who do not have flat-rate plans for Internet access but pay instead by the minute or hour are harmed more directly, but all Internet users (along with their ISPs) bear the cost of deceptive spam.

This cost-shifting—from deceptive spammers to businesses and e-mail users—has been likened to sending junk mail with postage due or making telemarketing calls to someone's pay-per-minute cellular phone. * * * We thus recognize that the Act serves the "legitimate local purpose" of banning the cost-shifting inherent in the sending of deceptive spam.

Under the *Pike* balancing test, "[i]f a legitimate local purpose is found, then the question becomes one of degree." 397 U.S. at 142. In the present case, the trial court questioned whether the Act's requirement of truthfulness (in the subject lines and header information) would redress the costs associated with bulk e-mailings. As legal commentators have observed, however, "the truthfulness requirements (such as the requirement not to misrepresent the message's Internet origin) make spamming unattractive to the many fraudulent spammers, thereby reducing the volume of spam." Jack L. Goldsmith & Alan O. Sykes, *The Internet and the Dormant Commerce Clause*, 110 YALE L.J. 785, 819 (2001). Calling "simply wrong" the trial court's view "that truthful identification in the subject header would do little to relieve the annoyance of spam," the commentators assert that "[t]his identification alone would allow many people to delete the message without opening it (which takes time) and perhaps being offended by the content." *Id.* The Act's truthfulness requirements thus appear to advance the Act's aim of protecting ISPs and consumers from the problems associated with commercial bulk e-mail.

To be weighed against the Act's local benefits, the only burden the Act places on spammers is the requirement of truthfulness, a requirement that does not burden commerce at all but actually "facilitates it by eliminating fraud and deception." *Id.* Spammers must use an accurate, nonmisleading subject line, and they must not manipulate the transmission path to disguise the origin of their commercial messages. While spammers incur no costs in complying with the Act, they do incur costs for noncompliance, because they must take steps to introduce forged information into the header of their message. In finding the Act "unduly burdensome," the trial court apparently focused not on what spammers must do to comply with the Act but on what they must do if they choose to use deceptive subject lines or to falsify elements in the transmission path. To initiate *deceptive* spam without violating the Act, a spammer must weed out Washington residents by contacting the registrant of the domain name contained in the recipient's e-mail address. This focus on the burden of *non*compliance is contrary to the approach in the *Pike* balancing test, where the United States Supreme Court assessed the cost of compliance with a challenged statute. Indeed, the trial court could have appropriately considered the filtering requirement a burden only if Washington's statute had banned outright the sending of UCE messages to Washington residents. We therefore conclude that Heckel has failed to prove that "the burden imposed on . . . commerce [by the Act] is *clearly excessive* in relation to the putative local benefits." *Pike*, 397 U.S. at 142 (emphasis added).

* * * Heckel contended that the Act (1) created inconsistency among the states and (2) regulated conduct occurring wholly outside of Washington. The inconsistent-regulations test and the extraterritoriality analysis are appropriately regarded as facets of the *Pike* balancing test. The Act survives both inquiries. At present, 17 other states have passed

legislation regulating electronic solicitations. The truthfulness requirements of the Act do not conflict with any of the requirements in the other states' statutes, and it is inconceivable that any state would ever pass a law requiring spammers to use misleading subject lines or transmission paths. Some states' statutes do include additional requirements; for example, some statutes require spammers to provide contact information (for opt-out purposes) or to introduce subject lines with such labels as "ADV" or "ADV-ADLT." But because such statutes "merely create additional, but not irreconcilable, obligations," they "are not considered to be 'inconsistent'" for purposes of the dormant Commerce Clause analysis. *Instructional Sys., Inc. v. Computer Curriculum Corp.*, 35 F.3d 813, 826 (3d Cir. 1994). The inquiry under the dormant Commerce Clause is not whether the states have enacted different anti-spam statutes but whether those differences create compliance costs that are "clearly excessive in relation to the putative local benefits." *Pike*, 397 U.S. at 142. We do not believe that the differences between the Act and the anti-spam laws of other states impose extraordinary costs on businesses deploying spam.[17]

Nor does the Act violate the extraterritoriality principle in the dormant Commerce Clause analysis. Here, there is no "sweeping extraterritorial effect" that would outweigh the local benefits of the Act. *Edgar v. MITE Corp.*, 457 U.S. 624, 642 (1982). Heckel offers the hypothetical of a Washington resident who downloads and reads the deceptive spam while in Portland or Denver. He contends that the dormant Commerce Clause is offended because the Act would regulate the recipient's conduct while out of state. However, the Act does not burden interstate commerce by regulating when or where recipients may open the proscribed UCE messages. Rather, the Act addresses the conduct of spammers in targeting Washington consumers. Moreover, the hypothetical mistakenly presumes that the Act must be construed to apply to Washington residents when they are out of state, a construction that creates a jurisdictional question not at issue in this case.

In sum, we reject the trial court's conclusion that the Act violates the dormant Commerce Clause. Although the trial court found particularly persuasive *American Libraries Association v. Pataki*, 969 F. Supp. 160 (S.D.N.Y. 1997), that decision—the first to apply the dormant Commerce Clause to a state law on Internet use—is distinguishable in a key respect. At issue in *American Libraries* was a New York statute that made it a crime to use a computer to distribute harmful, sexually explicit content to minors. The statute applied not just to initiation of e-mail messages but to all Internet activity, including the creation of websites. Thus, under the New York statute, a website creator in California could inadvertently violate the law simply because the site could be viewed in New York. * * * In contrast

---

17. As the State notes, "[p]resently, mail and phone solicitors are expected to abide by different states' telemarketing laws and other consumer protection laws. E-mail solicitors should not be excused from the burden of complying with a state's law simply because of the ease of sending bulk e-mail solicitations in relation to other forms of commercial solicitation."

to the New York statute, which could reach all content posted on the Internet and therefore subject individuals to liability based on unintended access, the Act reaches only those deceptive UCE messages directed to a Washington resident or initiated from a computer located in Washington; in other words, the Act does not impose liability for messages that are merely routed through Washington or that are read by a Washington resident who was not the actual addressee.

CONCLUSION

The Act limits the harm that deceptive commercial e-mail causes Washington businesses and citizens. The Act prohibits e-mail solicitors from using misleading information in the subject line or transmission path of any commercial e-mail message sent to Washington residents or from a computer located in Washington. We find that the local benefits of the Act outweigh any conceivable burdens the Act places on those sending commercial e-mail messages. Consequently, we hold that the Act does not violate the dormant Commerce Clause of the United States Constitution.

Notes and Questions

1. In *American Libraries*, Judge Preska likens the Internet to a highway or railroad, while the Washington court compares e-mail to "mail and phone solicitation." Are these metaphors apt? Do they affect the courts' analyses in particular ways?

2. Recall the *Yahoo!* case; in what ways is France's attempt to regulate Internet content different from (or similar to) New York's attempt or Washington's attempts to do so? There is, of course, no "dormant Commerce Clause" analysis at the international level; but should there be? Are the same considerations that apply to the efficacy and legitimacy of state regulation in the domestic context applicable to national regulation in the international context?

3. Notice that Judge Preska's analysis in *American Libraries* depends in part on the fact that an e-mail message sent from one state to another may travel over wires in New York en route, and that, by and large, users cannot control the routing of their messages. The court in *Washington v. Heckel* seized upon this to distinguish *American Libraries*, pointing out that while the New York statute applied to "all Internet activity," the Washington statute did not impose liability "for messages that are merely routed through Washington." Is that distinction persuasive? Or are the two decisions irreconcilable?

4. The Washington Supreme Court rules that, unlike an outright ban on unsolicited commercial e-mail, the Washington law does not conflict with the regulations of other states because "it is inconceivable that any state would ever pass a law requiring spammers to use misleading subject lines or transmission paths." Is this the correct inquiry? What if a state decided it wanted to attract more business by becoming a haven for telemarketers and commercial e-mailers? Although this state might not *require* "misleading subject lines or transmission paths," it might make the affirmative choice to

permit such e-mail to be sent from within its borders. Does the Washington statute conflict with this aim?

5. The Washington court concludes that, in weighing the burden on interstate commerce, the focus must be on the cost of compliance with the law, rather than the cost of non-compliance. Is this a helpful distinction? How do you think a focus on compliance would have affected the outcome in *American Libraries*?

6. The U.S. Supreme Court's decision in *Pike v. Bruce Church Inc.*, 397 U.S. 137 (1970), asks courts to balance the local regulatory interest against the burdens placed on interstate activity. The trial court in *Washington v. Heckel* had struck down the state statute in part on the ground that the local benefits of the statute were minimal. How does the Washington Supreme Court explain its disagreement with this determination? On the other hand, why isn't New York's interest in combating pedophilia overwhelming? To what degree do both courts' conclusions about the strength of the state's interests turn on their analysis of the effectiveness of the statutes in question?

7. One solution to the dormant Commerce Clause problem, of course, is national harmonization. After all, Congress, unlike the states, *does* have the constitutional power to regulate interstate commerce and therefore could enact laws meant to deter unsolicited e-mail. Congress has attempted such legislation, enacting the Controlling the Assault of Non-Solicited Pornography and Marketing Act of 2003 (CAN SPAM Act), codified at 15 U.S.C. §§ 7701ff. The law allows marketers to send unsolicited commercial e-mail only if the message contains an opt-out provision, a legitimate return address, a valid subject line that indicates it is an advertisement, and the sender's physical address. However, it may be that even national regulation will have little effect on businesses that can still locate their servers offshore or take other measures to avoid prosecution.

8. Might there be technological, rather than statutory, means of fighting spam? For example, the "Sender Policy Framework" creates a way for the owner of an Internet domain, such as aol.com, to specify which computers are authorized to send e-mail with aol.com return addresses. Such an identification would allow a recipient's e-mail system to determine whether a message being represented as coming from someone at aol.com really is from that address. In what ways might such technology-based approaches to the problem of spam be more effective than government statutes? Are there nevertheless concerns about such approaches?

9. The dormant Commerce Clause has been applied in a number of other cases to invalidate state regulation of sexually explicit material on the Internet. *See, e.g., PSINet, Inc. v. Chapman*, 362 F.3d 227 (4th Cir. 2004) (Virginia law regulating pornographic communications); *American Civil Liberties Union v. Johnson*, 194 F.3d 1149 (10th Cir. 1999) (New Mexico statute criminalizing dissemination by computer of materials harmful to minors); *Cyberspace Communications, Inc. v. Engler*, 55 F. Supp. 2d 737 (E.D. Mich. 1999) (Michigan statute criminalizing the use of computers to distribute sexually explicit materials to minors). Other cases have extended the reach of the dormant Commerce Clause to state regulation of online communication more broadly. *See, e.g., Consolidated Cigar Corp. v. Reilly*, 218 F.3d 30 (1st Cir.

2000), *aff'd in part, rev'd in part on other grounds, Lorillard Tobacco Co. v. Reilly*, 121 S. Ct. 2404 (2001) (Massachusetts cigar advertising law, if applied to Internet advertising, would violate the dormant Commerce Clause); *Sante Fe Natural Tobacco Co., Inc. v. Spitzer*, 00 Civ. 7274 (LAP) (S.D.N.Y. 2001) (permanently enjoining, on dormant Commerce Clause grounds, state law that effectively prohibited Internet and mail order sales of cigarettes). What is the proper role for state regulation of Internet activities? Recall the arguments for and against a national obscenity standard in *Ashcroft v. American Civil Liberties Union* above. What role *should* local jurisdictions have in regulating online expression and online conduct? Is there any limit to the dormant Commerce Clause analysis, or are *all* local regulations of online activity impermissible? Like the courts, scholars have divided on the question. *Compare, e.g.*, Dan L. Burk, *Federalism in Cyberspace*, 28 CONN. L. REV. 1095, 1123-34 (1996); Bruce P. Keller, *The Game's the Same: Why Gambling in Cyberspace Violates Federal Law*, 108 YALE L.J. 1569, 1593-96 (1999); *and* Glenn Harlan Reynolds, *Virtual Reality and "Virtual Welters": A Note on the Commerce Clause Implications of Regulating Cyberporn*, 82 VA. L. REV. 535, 537-42 (1996), *with* Jack L. Goldsmith & Alan O. Sykes, *The Internet and the Dormant Commerce Clause*, 110 YALE L.J. 785 (2001) *and* Larry Ribstein & Bruce Kobayashi, *State Regulation of Electronic Commerce*, 51 EMORY L.J. 1 (2002).

Note on Center for Democracy and Technology v. Pappert

The difficulties that states may have trying to regulate Internet conduct within the constraints of the dormant Commerce Clause are illustrated by the result in *Center for Democracy and Technology v. Pappert*, 337 F. Supp. 2d 606 (E.D. Pa. 2004). In that case, the court struck down the Pennsylvania Internet Child Pornography Act, 18 Pa. Cons. Stat. Ann. §§ 7621-7630, discussed earlier in this chapter, *see supra* note 8, p. 97, which authorized the Pennsylvania Attorney General, upon obtaining probable cause to believe that an Internet site contains child pornography (as defined in the Pennsylvania criminal code), to obtain a court order requiring Internet service providers to make the site inaccessible to all of their Pennsylvania subscribers.

Although the statute expressly authorized enforcement actions only against ISPs serving within-state users, the court concluded both that the statute was a *per se* violation of the Commerce Clause, and that it failed the *Pike* balancing test. In its lengthy factual findings, the court found that ISPs did not have reasonable technical means at their disposal to block access to the offending websites only for their Pennsylvania subscribers; instead, when they received an order to block access to a specific URL, they would remove the offending IP address of the website from their message-routing databases, which had the effect of making the website unavailable to *all* of their subscribers, whether located in Pennsylvania or elsewhere. As a result, subscribers in *other* states would find that the offending sites were inaccessible to them:

This Act has the practical effect of exporting Pennsylvania's domestic policies. As an example, a WorldCom witness testified that a customer in Minnesota would not be able to access a website hosted in Georgia if an IP Address was blocked by a Pennsylvania order.

Id. at 662. Performing the *Pike* balancing, the court reasoned that the act had minimal local benefit, because those interested in "obtaining or providing child pornography can evade blocking efforts using a number of different methods," and that the act substantially burdened interstate commerce, because providers seeking to comply with the act were forced to disable sites that did not in fact contain child pornography. *Id.*

Should the state of ISP filtering technology matter for the dormant commerce clause analysis? If users in New Jersey, or Florida, are unable to access particular Internet sites because of Pennsylvania law, does that constitute an attempt by Pennsylvania, in the words of the *Pataki* case, to unconstitutionally "impose[] its legislation on the Internet and * * * project[ ] its law into other states whose citizens use the Net"?

SECTION C. JURISDICTION TO ADJUDICATE

1. The United States Personal Jurisdiction Inquiry

Introductory Note

Once a plaintiff has decided to initiate a civil action, one of the first questions to be asked is: where to sue? To which courthouse should the plaintiff proceed? In order to answer this question, the plaintiff must determine which court has jurisdiction (and therefore the proper adjudicatory authority) over the claim. In the United States, this jurisdictional inquiry breaks down into two categories: subject matter jurisdiction and personal jurisdiction.

In this section, we will focus on the second issue—personal jurisdiction. With personal jurisdiction, the inquiry is this: assuming the plaintiff has found the right *type* of court, where, *geographically*, can the lawsuit be brought?

The answer to this question, at least in the United States, was originally grounded in the territorial power of the sovereign. Each sovereign was deemed to have jurisdiction, exclusive of all other sovereigns, to bind persons and things present within its territorial boundaries. This conception of jurisdiction implicitly adopted an idea of "community" as a local territorial unit ruled by a single power. Over the past two hundred years, changes in commerce, transportation, and communications technology have repeatedly challenged both this idea of community and its accompanying jurisdictional rules.

In the nineteenth century, the United States Supreme Court determined that a territorially based conception of jurisdiction was an inherent part of constitutional due process itself. In *Pennoyer v. Neff*, 95 U.S. 714, 720 (1877), the Court ruled that "[t]he authority of every tribunal is necessarily restricted by the territorial limits of the State in which it is established. Any attempt to exercise authority beyond those limits would be deemed in every other forum . . . an illegitimate assumption of power, and be resisted as mere abuse." According to the Court, although "every State possesses exclusive jurisdiction and sovereignty over persons and property within its territory . . . . no State can exercise direct jurisdiction and authority over persons and property without its territory." *Id.* at 722. The *Pennoyer* decision reflected a conception of jurisdiction based on territorial borders and pure power. The underlying message was: if a state can "tag" you, it can have power over you; if it can "tag" your property, it can have power over your property. Under this formulation, the limits of judicial power were rigidly defined by the boundaries of each state.

By the early twentieth century, growth of interstate commerce and transportation put pressure on the idea that a state's judicial power extended only to its territorial boundary. In particular, the invention of the automobile and the development of the modern corporation meant that far-away entities could inflict harm within a state without actually being present there at the time of a lawsuit. In response, a number of states enacted statutes based on a theory of "consent" to jurisdiction, a theory that the *Pennoyer* Court had recognized as valid.

For example, a Massachusetts statute decreed that an out-of-state motorist using the state's highways would be deemed to have consented to Massachusetts jurisdiction in actions arising from accidents on those highways. The United States Supreme Court ultimately upheld this rather strained notion of consent in 1927. *Hess v. Pawloski*, 274 U.S. 352 (1927). Similarly, most states enacted statutes essentially requiring out-of-state corporations to agree to jurisdiction within the state as a condition of conducting business there. Moreover, even if the corporation did not explicitly agree, it was often viewed as having implicitly consented to state jurisdiction simply by transacting business in the state.[b] Alternatively, courts sometimes ruled that corporations were physically "present" in any state in which that corporation was "doing business," making the corporations subject to jurisdiction regardless of their consent.[c] While allowing more flexibility in the jurisdictional calculus, the concepts of "consent" and "presence" were analytically unsatisfying, in large part because corporations have neither individual wills nor physical reality.

---

b. *See, e.g., Smolik v. Philadelphia & Reading Co.*, 222 F. 148 (S.D.N.Y. 1915).

c. *See, e.g., Philadelphia & Reading Ry. Co. v. McKibbin*, 243 U.S. 264, 265 (1917) ("A foreign corporation is amenable to process to enforce a personal liability, in the absence of consent, only if it is doing business within the State in such a manner and to such extent as to warrant the inference that it is present there.").

Speaking of "consent" to jurisdiction and "presence" in a state was no more than a legal fiction invented to cope with changing economic reality.

Perhaps in response to these societal changes, the U.S. Supreme Court, in the 1945 case of *International Shoe Co. v. Washington*, 326 U.S. 310 (1945), adopted a new test for analyzing jurisdiction. The Court replaced the strict territorial rules of *Pennoyer* with a more flexible due process inquiry based on whether the defendant had sufficient contact with the relevant state such that jurisdiction would be consistent with "traditional notions of fair play and substantial justice." *Id.* at 316. This "minimum contacts" test would be satisfied as long as the "quality and nature of the activity" of the defendant within the state was sufficient "in relation to the fair and orderly administration of the laws which it was the purpose of the due process clause to insure." *Id.* at 319.

Since the decision in *International Shoe*, the minimum contacts test has provided the framework for determining the outer limits of personal jurisdiction under the United States Constitution. Although the test's flexibility is its greatest strength, such flexibility means that the minimum contacts analysis does not provide a clearly defined rule, relying instead on a highly particularized, fact-specific inquiry. Accordingly, it is difficult to be certain in advance how many and what sort of contacts will be enough for a state to exercise jurisdiction under the federal Constitution. The Supreme Court has variously looked to whether defendants have "purposely availed" themselves of the state, *Hanson v. Denckla*, 357 U.S. 235, 253 (1958), whether they could "reasonably anticipate" that they would be sued there, *World-Wide Volkswagen Corp. v. Woodson*, 444 U.S. 286, 297 (1980), or whether the interests of the plaintiff and the forum state in adjudicating a dispute outweighed the defendant's concerns about increased cost, inconvenience, or potential bias, *see Burger King v. Rudzewicz*, 471 U.S. 462, 476-77 (1985).

For example, in *World-Wide Volkswagen Corporation v. Woodson*, decided in 1980, the defendant, a car dealership, sold a car in New York to a New York resident. Later, the purchaser was injured in an accident while driving the car in Oklahoma. The purchaser filed suit in Oklahoma, naming as defendants the New York dealership and regional distributor, among others. The United States Supreme Court ruled that neither the dealership nor the regional distributor could be sued in Oklahoma because they had no contacts with the state and because it was not reasonably foreseeable that they would be haled into court there. In so doing, the Court rejected the argument that, because an automobile is mobile by its very design and purpose, it was therefore foreseeable that the car could cause injury beyond the boundaries of the state where it was sold. Instead, the Court held that "the mere unilateral activity of those who claim some relationship with a nonresident defendant cannot satisfy the requirement of contact with the forum State." *World-Wide Volkswagen*, 444 U.S. at 298 (internal quotation marks omitted).

Providers of content have always been particularly concerned about the jurisdictional inquiry because content created in one place can so easily travel elsewhere, leaving the content provider potentially subject to a broad jurisdictional net. Consider the following case.

Calder v. Jones

Supreme Court of the United States, 1984
465 U.S. 783

JUSTICE REHNQUIST delivered the opinion of the Court.

Respondent Shirley Jones * * * lives and works in California. She and her husband brought this suit against the National Enquirer, Inc., its local distributing company, and petitioners for libel, invasion of privacy, and intentional infliction of emotional harm. The Enquirer is a Florida corporation with its principal place of business in Florida. It publishes a national weekly newspaper with a total circulation of over 5 million. About 600,000 of those copies, almost twice the level of the next highest State, are sold in California. Respondent's and her husband's claims were based on an article that appeared in the Enquirer's October 9, 1979 issue. Both the Enquirer and the distributing company answered the complaint and made no objection to the jurisdiction of the California court.

Petitioner South is a reporter employed by the Enquirer. He is a resident of Florida, though he frequently travels to California on business. South wrote the first draft of the challenged article, and his byline appeared on it. He did most of his research in Florida, relying on phone calls to sources in California for the information contained in the article. Shortly before publication, South called respondent's home and read to her husband a draft of the article so as to elicit his comments upon it. Aside from his frequent trips and phone calls, South has no other relevant contacts with California.

Petitioner Calder is also a Florida resident. He has been to California only twice—once, on a pleasure trip, prior to the publication of the article and once after to testify in an unrelated trial. Calder is president and editor of the Enquirer. He "oversee[s] just about every function of the Enquirer." He reviewed and approved the initial evaluation of the subject of the article and edited it in its final form. He also declined to print a retraction requested by respondent. Calder has no other relevant contacts with California.

In considering petitioners' motion to quash service of process, the superior court surmised that the actions of petitioners in Florida, causing injury to respondent in California, would ordinarily be sufficient to support an assertion of jurisdiction over them in California. But the court felt that special solicitude was necessary because of the potential "chilling effect" on reporters and editors which would result from requiring them to appear in remote jurisdictions to answer for the content of articles upon which they worked. The court also noted that respondent's rights could be "fully satisfied" in her suit against the publisher without requiring petitioners to appear as parties. The superior court, therefore, granted the motion.

* * * The Due Process Clause of the Fourteenth Amendment to the United States Constitution permits personal jurisdiction over a defendant in any State with which the defendant has "certain minimum contacts . . . such that the maintenance of the suit does not offend 'traditional notions of fair play and substantial justice.' *Milliken v. Meyer,* 311 U.S. 457, 463 [(1940)]." *International Shoe Co. v. Washington,* 326 U.S. 310, 316 (1945). In judging minimum contacts, a court properly focuses on "the relationship among the defendant, the forum, and the litigation." *Shaffer v. Heitner,* 433 U.S. 186, 204 (1977). * * *

The allegedly libelous story concerned the California activities of a California resident. It impugned the professionalism of an entertainer whose television career was centered in California. The article was drawn from California sources, and the brunt of the harm, in terms both of respondent's emotional distress and the injury to her professional reputation, was suffered in California. In sum, California is the focal point both of the story and of the harm suffered. Jurisdiction over petitioners is therefore proper in California based on the "effects" of their Florida conduct in California.

Petitioners argue that they are not responsible for the circulation of the article in California. A reporter and an editor, they claim, have no direct economic stake in their employer's sales in a distant State. Nor are ordinary employees able to control their employer's marketing activity. The mere fact that they can "foresee" that the article will be circulated and have an effect in California is not sufficient for an assertion of jurisdiction. * * * Petitioners liken themselves to a welder employed in Florida who works on a boiler which subsequently explodes in California. Cases which hold that jurisdiction will be proper over the manufacturer, should not be applied to the welder who has no control over and derives no direct benefit from his employer's sales in that distant State.

Petitioners' analogy does not wash. Whatever the status of their hypothetical welder, petitioners are not charged with mere untargeted negligence. Rather, their intentional, and allegedly tortious, actions were expressly aimed at California. Petitioner South wrote and petitioner Calder edited an article that they knew would have a potentially devastating impact upon respondent. And they knew that the brunt of that injury would be felt by respondent in the State in which she lives and works and in which the *National Enquirer* has its largest circulation. Under the circumstances, petitioners must "reasonably anticipate being haled into court there" to answer for the truth of the statements made in their article. An individual injured in California need not go to Florida to seek redress from persons who, though remaining in Florida, knowingly cause the injury in California.

* * * We also reject the suggestion that First Amendment concerns enter into the jurisdictional analysis. The * * * potential chill on protected

First Amendment activity stemming from libel and defamation actions is already taken into account in the constitutional limitations on the substantive law governing such suits. To reintroduce those concerns at the jurisdictional stage would be a form of double counting.

Notes and Questions

1. Is the *Calder* decision best conceptualized as an "effects" test or a "targeting" test? In other words, does the Court conclude that the *Enquirer*'s editor and writer "targeted" California because the article concerned a California resident, or is California jurisdiction appropriate merely because some of the effects of the article were felt in California? Can you imagine situations where behavior that does nothing to target a jurisdiction nevertheless has significant effects there?

2. Is the Court correct that the author and editor of the Enquirer article "targeted" California? Presumably the article on Jones was meant to have a nationwide readership. Why should the location of the subject of an article be the determinant of jurisdiction? If someone writes an article about Mount McKinley, should that person necessarily be subject to suit in Alaska?

3. What if Jones had chosen to sue in New York (or any other state where the *Enquirer* is distributed, for that matter), on the ground that the article harmed her reputation there just as surely as it did in California? If the analysis turns on the effects of a publication, what principled justification is there for limiting the assertion of jurisdiction to the actual state of citizenship of the subject of the article?

4. If, on the other hand, the *Calder* test turns on targeting, rather than effects, might jurisdiction be permissible anywhere the *Enquirer* is advertised, on the ground that the *Enquirer* deliberately sought sales in the jurisdiction?

5. Note that the publisher of the *Enquirer* did not contest jurisdiction. Should the analysis for jurisdiction over the publisher differ from the analysis concerning the writer or editor of the article at issue? The answer to this question may be significant when discussing websites, where the distinctions among author, editor, and publisher are frequently blurred.

2. Jurisdiction Based on Online Interaction

Should the Internet context change the *Calder* inquiry? Given that websites are, at least in theory, accessible anywhere, an analysis that focuses on effects may result in the potential for far-ranging jurisdictional assertions. And indeed when judges were initially faced with Internet-based jurisdictional issues in the 1990s, many took the position that a website was akin to a 24-hour advertisement directly aimed at customers in every state. Accordingly, a series of decisions held that website operators were subject to jurisdiction anywhere their site was viewed. For example, in *Maritz Inc. v. CyberGold, Inc.*, 947 F. Supp. 1328 (E.D. Mo. 1996), the court found jurisdiction in Missouri over a California corporation. Although defendant's web server was located in California, the court noted that the disputed website was "continually accessible to every Internet-connected computer in Missouri." *Id.* at 1330. According to the court, "CyberGold has consciously decided to transmit advertising information to all Internet users, knowing that such information will be transmitted globally. Thus, CyberGold's contacts are of such a quality and nature, albeit a very new quality and nature for personal jurisdiction jurisprudence, that they favor the exercise of personal jurisdiction over defendant." *Id.* at 1333. Similarly, in *Humphrey v. Granite Gate Resorts, Inc.*, 568 N.W.2d 715 (Minn. 1997), the Minnesota Supreme Court ruled that the state Attorney General's office could sue an online gambling service in Minnesota even though the service was based outside of the state. Relying in part on *Maritz*, the court determined that the defendants had "purposefully availed themselves of the privilege of doing business in Minnesota," *id.* at 721, based on a finding that "computers located throughout the United States, including Minnesota, accessed appellants' websites," *id.* at 718. *See also, e.g., Telco Communications v. An Apple a Day*, 977 F. Supp. 404, 407 (E.D. Va. 1997) (a website available twenty-four hours a day in the forum state constituted "a persistent course of conduct" in the state); *Heroes, Inc. v. Heroes Found.*, 958 F. Supp. 1, 5 (D.D.C. 1996) (suggesting that the existence of a website might be deemed a sustained contact with the forum because "it has been possible for a . . . resident [of the forum] to gain access to it at any time since it was first posted"); *Inset Systems, Inc. v. Instruction Set, Inc.*, 937 F. Supp. 161 (D. Conn. 1996) (ruling that the website of a Massachusetts corporation constitutes a continuous advertisement in Connecticut, thus justifying the assertion of jurisdiction). *Cf. Arista Records v. Sakfield Holding Co.*, 314 F. Supp. 2d 27 (D.D.C. 2004) (Spanish website allowing users to download 25 free songs before subscribing was actively soliciting business in Washington, D.C. if D.C. residents downloaded songs from the site, even if no D.C. resident actually ended up subscribing). These opinions are similar to Justice Thomas's position in *Ashcroft v. American Civil Liberties Union, supra* p. 89, that website operators should be subject to the standards of decency applicable in any community where the site is accessible.

Interestingly, such a view either implicitly or explicitly conceptualizes a website as a foreign entity that "enters" or is "directed at" other jurisdictions. Yet, one could just as plausibly say that a website is not directed anywhere, but is instead simply sitting in a location waiting for people to "visit." In the end, however, neither formulation has proved satisfactory. The first tends toward broad assertions of jurisdiction that lead to theoretical concerns about legitimacy and practical concerns about exposure of websites to legal process in far-flung jurisdictions. The second, in contrast, creates the potential for regulatory evasion by allowing sites simply to "locate" in the most convivial jurisdiction and force all suits concerning the site to be brought there.

Not surprisingly, therefore, courts have sought various "middle ground" positions. But such positions have been difficult to articulate in a conceptually satisfying manner. Consider the following attempt.

Zippo Manufacturing Co. v. Zippo Dot Com, Inc.

United States District Court for the Western District of Pennsylvania, 1997
952 F. Supp. 1119

McLAUGHLIN, District Judge.

This is an Internet domain name dispute. * * * Plaintiff Zippo Manufacturing Corporation ("Manufacturing") has filed a five count complaint against Zippo Dot Com, Inc. ("Dot Com") alleging trademark dilution, infringement, and false designation under the Federal Trademark Act, 15 U.S.C. §§ 1051-1127. * * *

The facts relevant to this motion are as follows. Manufacturing is a Pennsylvania corporation with its principal place of business in Bradford, Pennsylvania. Manufacturing makes, among other things, well known "Zippo" tobacco lighters. Dot Com is a California corporation with its principal place of business in Sunnyvale, California. Dot Com operates an Internet Web site and an Internet news service and has obtained the exclusive right to use the domain names "zippo.com", "zippo.net" and "zipponews.com" on the Internet.

Dot Com's Web site contains information about the company, advertisements and an application for its Internet news service. The news service itself consists of three levels of membership—public/free, "Original" and "Super." Each successive level offers access to a greater number of Internet newsgroups. A customer who wants to subscribe to either the "Original" or "Super" level of service, fills out an on-line application that asks for a variety of information including the person's name and address. Payment is made by credit card over the Internet or the telephone. The application is then processed and the subscriber is assigned a password which permits the subscriber to view and/or download Internet newsgroup messages that are stored on the Defendant's server in California.

Dot Com's contacts with Pennsylvania have occurred almost exclusively over the Internet. Dot Com's offices, employees and Internet servers are located in California. Dot Com maintains no offices, employees or agents in Pennsylvania. Dot Com's advertising for its service to Pennsylvania residents involves posting information about its service on its Web page, which is accessible to Pennsylvania residents via the Internet. Defendant has approximately 140,000 paying subscribers worldwide. Approximately two percent (3,000) of those subscribers are Pennsylvania residents. These subscribers have contracted to receive Dot Com's service by visiting its Web site and filling out the application. Additionally, Dot Com has entered into agreements with seven Internet access providers in

Pennsylvania to permit their subscribers to access Dot Com's news service. Two of these providers are located in the Western District of Pennsylvania.

The basis of the trademark claims is Dot Com's use of the word "Zippo" in the domain names it holds, in numerous locations in its Web site and in the heading of Internet newsgroup messages that have been posted by Dot Com subscribers. When an Internet user views or downloads a newsgroup message posted by a Dot Com subscriber, the word "Zippo" appears in the "Message–Id" and "Organization" sections of the heading. The news message itself, containing text and/or pictures, follows. Manufacturing points out that some of the messages contain adult oriented, sexually explicit subject matter. * * *

In *Hanson v. Denckla*, the Supreme Court noted that "[a]s technological progress has increased the flow of commerce between States, the need for jurisdiction has undergone a similar increase." 357 U.S. 235, 250-51 (1958). Twenty seven years later, the Court observed that jurisdiction could not be avoided "merely because the defendant did not physically enter the forum state." *Burger King Corp. v. Rudzewicz*, 471 U.S. 462, 476 (1985). The Court observed that:

> [I]t is an inescapable fact of modern commercial life that a substantial amount of commercial business is transacted solely by mail and wire communications across state lines, thus obviating the need for physical presence within a State in which business is conducted.

Id. * * *

The Internet makes it possible to conduct business throughout the world entirely from a desktop. With this global revolution looming on the horizon, the development of the law concerning the permissible scope of personal jurisdiction based on Internet use is in its infant stages. The cases are scant. Nevertheless, our review of the available cases and materials reveals that the likelihood that personal jurisdiction can be constitutionally exercised is directly proportionate to the nature and quality of commercial activity that an entity conducts over the Internet. This sliding scale is consistent with well developed personal jurisdiction principles. At one end of the spectrum are situations where a defendant clearly does business over the Internet. If the defendant enters into contracts with residents of a foreign jurisdiction that involve the knowing and repeated transmission of computer files over the Internet, personal jurisdiction is proper. At the opposite end are situations where a defendant has simply posted information on an Internet Web site which is accessible to users in foreign jurisdictions. A passive Web site that does little more than make information available to those who are interested in it is not grounds for the exercise personal jurisdiction. The middle ground is occupied by interactive Web sites where a user can exchange information with the host computer. In these cases, the exercise of jurisdiction is determined by examining the level of interactivity and commercial nature of the exchange of information that occurs on the Web site.

Traditionally, when an entity intentionally reaches beyond its boundaries to conduct business with foreign residents, the exercise of specific jurisdiction is proper. Different results should not be reached simply because business is conducted over the Internet. * * * Dot Com has contracted with approximately 3,000 individuals and seven Internet access providers in Pennsylvania. The intended object of these transactions has been the downloading of the electronic messages that form the basis of this suit in Pennsylvania.

We find Dot Com's efforts to characterize its conduct as falling short of purposeful availment of doing business in Pennsylvania wholly unpersuasive. At oral argument, Defendant repeatedly characterized its actions as merely "operating a Web site" or "advertising." Dot Com also cites to a number of cases from this Circuit which, it claims, stand for the proposition that merely advertising in a forum, without more, is not a sufficient minimal contact. This argument is misplaced. Dot Com has done more than advertise on the Internet in Pennsylvania. Defendant has sold passwords to approximately 3,000 subscribers in Pennsylvania and entered into seven contracts with Internet access providers to furnish its services to their customers in Pennsylvania. * * *

Defendant argues that it has not "actively" solicited business in Pennsylvania and that any business it conducts with Pennsylvania residents has resulted from contacts that were initiated by Pennsylvanians who visited the Defendant's Web site. The fact that Dot Com's services have been consumed in Pennsylvania is not "fortuitous" within the meaning of *World-Wide Volkswagen v. Woodson*, 444 U.S. 286, 295 (1980). In *World-Wide Volkswagen*, a couple that had purchased a vehicle in New York, while they were New York residents, were injured while driving that vehicle through Oklahoma and brought suit in an Oklahoma state court. The manufacturer did not sell its vehicles in Oklahoma and had not made an effort to establish business relationships in Oklahoma. The Supreme Court characterized the manufacturer's ties with Oklahoma as fortuitous because they resulted entirely out the fact that the plaintiffs had driven their car into that state.

Here, Dot Com argues that its contacts with Pennsylvania residents are fortuitous because Pennsylvanians happened to find its Web site or heard about its news service elsewhere and decided to subscribe. This argument misconstrues the concept of fortuitous contacts embodied in *World-Wide Volkswagen*. Dot Com's contacts with Pennsylvania would be fortuitous within the meaning of *World-Wide Volkswagen* if it had no Pennsylvania subscribers and an Ohio subscriber forwarded a copy of a file he obtained from Dot Com to a friend in Pennsylvania or an Ohio subscriber brought his computer along on a trip to Pennsylvania and used it to access Dot Com's service. That is not the situation here. Dot Com repeatedly and consciously chose to process Pennsylvania residents' applications and to assign them passwords. Dot Com knew that the result of these contracts would be the transmission of electronic messages into Pennsylvania. The transmission of these files was entirely within its control. Dot Com cannot maintain that these contracts are "fortuitous" or "coincidental" within the meaning of World-Wide Volkswagen. When a defendant makes a conscious choice to conduct business with the residents of a forum state, "it has clear notice that it is subject to suit there." *World-Wide Volkswagen*, 444 U.S. at 297. Dot Com was under no obligation to sell its services to Pennsylvania residents. It freely chose to do so, presumably in order to profit from those transactions. If a corporation determines that the risk of being subject to personal jurisdiction in a particular forum is too great, it can choose to sever its connection to the state. If Dot Com had not wanted to be amenable to jurisdiction in Pennsylvania, the solution would have been simple—it could have chosen not to sell its services to Pennsylvania residents.

Next, Dot Com argues that its forum-related activities are not numerous or significant enough to create a "substantial connection" with Pennsylvania. Defendant points to the fact that only two percent of its subscribers are Pennsylvania residents. However, the Supreme Court has made clear that even a single contact can be sufficient. The test has always focused on the "nature and quality" of the contacts with the forum and not the quantity of those contacts. *International Shoe Co. v. Washington*, 326 U.S. 310, 320 (1945). * * *

In the instant case, both a significant amount of the alleged infringement and dilution, and resulting injury have occurred in Pennsylvania. The object of Dot Com's contracts with Pennsylvania residents is the transmission of the messages that Plaintiff claims dilute and infringe upon its trademark. When these messages are transmitted into Pennsylvania and viewed by Pennsylvania residents on their computers, there can be no question that the alleged infringement and dilution occur in Pennsylvania. Moreover, since Manufacturing is a Pennsylvania corporation, a substantial amount of the injury from the alleged wrongdoing is likely to occur in Pennsylvania. Thus, we conclude that the cause of action arises out of Dot Com's forum-related activities.

Finally, Dot Com argues that the exercise of jurisdiction would be unreasonable in this case. We disagree. There can be no question that Pennsylvania has a strong interest in adjudicating disputes involving the alleged infringement of trademarks owned by resident corporations. We must also give due regard to the Plaintiff's choice to seek relief in Pennsylvania. These concerns outweigh the burden created by forcing the Defendant to defend the suit in Pennsylvania, especially when Dot Com consciously chose to conduct business in Pennsylvania, pursuing profits from the actions that are now in question. The Due Process Clause is not a "territorial shield to interstate obligations that have been voluntarily assumed." *Burger King*, 471 U.S. at 474.

Notes and Questions

1. The *Zippo* court finds that jurisdiction is reasonable in part because "Dot Com repeatedly and consciously chose to process Pennsylvania residents'

applications and to assign them passwords." Is this an accurate description of Dot Com's activities? After all, the Pennsylvania users merely filled out a form on Dot Com's website in order to receive a password. What if the form included no inquiry as to the user's state of residence? In addition, given that the password process is likely to be an automated computer-to-computer transaction, does it make sense for the court to say that Dot Com "consciously chose" to sell to Pennsylvania subscribers?

2. Assume that Dot Com posts on its website a disclaimer that no citizens of Pennsylvania are permitted to access the site and advises users that, in filling out the online form, anyone listing a Pennsylvania address will be denied a password. Further assume that the same 3,000 Pennsylvania residents access the site anyway, using a fictitious, non-Pennsylvania address. Would jurisdiction be proper under the *Zippo* analysis?

3. The problem of geographical exclusion based on self-identification has also arisen in the copyright context. In 1999, iCraveTV.com began offering online a streaming version of seventeen Canadian and American broadcast television stations uncut and uninterrupted, arguing that such retransmission was permitted under Canadian copyright law and that the site was intended for Canadian viewers only. Nevertheless, the steps taken by the site to block access to Americans were trivially easy to circumvent. First, a potential user was required to enter his or her local area code. If the user entered an area code that was not Canadian, the user was denied access to the service. Users who negotiated the first step were then confronted with two icons: "I'm in Canada" and "Not in Canada" and were asked to click one. Ultimately, a federal judge in Pittsburgh ruled that "acts of [United States copyright] infringement are committed within the United States when United States citizens received and viewed defendants' streaming of the copyrighted materials." *National Football League v. TVRadioNow Corp.*, 53 U.S.P.Q.2d 1831, 1834-35 (W.D. Pa. 2000). The judge issued a temporary restraining order against the Internet company, which subsequently settled the case and later went out of business.

4. According to one commentator, "Zippo has earned a place in history as one of the most-cited district court opinions ever." Patrick J. Borchers, *Internet Libel: The Consequences of a Non-Rule Approach to Personal Jurisdiction*, 98 Nw. U. L. Rev. 473, 478 (2004). Moreover, at least one court of appeals has even used *Zippo* to rule that maintaining an interactive website, by itself, constitutes "continuous and systematic" contacts so as to justify *general* jurisdiction over a cause of action unrelated to those contacts. *See Gorman v. Ameritrade Holding Corp.*, 293 F.3d 506 (D.C. Cir. 2002); *see also Mink v. AAAA Dev., L.L.C.*, 190 F.3d 333 (5th Cir. 1999) (adopting *Zippo* framework to analyze general jurisdiction). *But see Revell v. Lidov*, 317 F.3d 467, 471 (5th Cir. 2002) (acknowledging *Mink*, but suggesting that the *Zippo* test "is not well adapted to the general jurisdiction inquiry").

5. Nevertheless, *Zippo*'s sliding-scale test has been subject to strong criticism. According to one scholar, *Zippo*'s passive/interactive distinction is "an egregious failure of legal imagination. Lacking an adequate conceptual account of why purposeful availment matters, the courts have reverted to thinking about jurisdiction in. . . physical terms: the interactive website looks

like the defendant is really operating a branch store in the forum. If defendant is simply conveying information, he is not 'really' there." Allan R. Stein, *Personal Jurisdiction and the Internet: Seeing Due Process Through the Lens of Regulatory Precision*, 98 NW. L. REV. 411, 430 (2004). Do you agree that this passive/interactive distinction is unworkable?

6. Assuming it is workable, how does one draw the distinction between a passive and an interactive site? For example, if a website includes only a list of all the poems a given website author has written, that site appears to be passive under the *Zippo* analysis. If the author then includes a sentence on the site inviting readers to e-mail their comments about the poems, or providing links to other sites where the related poems can be found, is the addition of that extra material enough to transform the passive site into an interactive one?

7. Does the *Zippo* test create bizarre incentives? Might a web operator wishing to avoid jurisdictional exposure be encouraged to limit the utility of its web page? "For instance, rather than facilitate an online order of merchandise, a risk-averse seller will simply provide product information on its website, but require a follow-up phone call to finalize the order. . . . It is hard to imagine how any state or person would benefit from encouraging such behavior." Allan R. Stein, *Personal Jurisdiction and the Internet: Seeing Due Process Through the Lens of Regulatory Precision*, 98 NW. L. REV. 411, 431 (2004). Moreover, while the interactive/passive distinction was difficult to draw in 1997, when *Zippo* was decided, the line between interactive and passive sites is even more blurry now and is likely to become increasingly so in the future, as websites grow ever more complex and sophisticated. Ultimately, many sites probably will fall into the middle ground.

8. Turning to the middle ground of the *Zippo* framework, what does it mean to examine "the level of interactivity and commercial nature of the exchange of information"? Assume a site that is not otherwise interactive sells advertising based on the number of "hits" the sites receives or collects and markets data about users. Do such activities render the sites sufficiently interactive to justify the assertion of jurisdiction under the *Zippo* framework? This is a crucial question because few large organizations or corporations will spend the money necessary to create a sophisticated website without including some mechanism to earn money back from the site. Are all such sites to be deemed interactive? If so, mightn't the *Zippo* test result in just the sort of broad-based assertions of jurisdiction that it seems intended to restrain?

9. Perhaps because of these concerns, courts have been reluctant to find that websites are sufficiently interactive to justify the assertion of jurisdiction. *See, e.g., Caterpillar, Inc. v. Miskin Scraper Works, Inc.*, 256 F. Supp. 2d 849 (C.D. Ill. 2003) (website that promotes products, but does not provide for "direct contractual relationships," insufficiently interactive to support jurisdiction); *Brown v. Grand Hotel Eden*, No. 00 Civ. 7346 (NRB), 2003 WL 21496756 (S.D.N.Y. June 30, 2003) (interactivity of website that allowed users to check hotel room availability, but required phone call to make reservation, insufficiently interactive to sustain jurisdiction in personal injury case); *David White Instruments, LLC v. TLZ, Inc.*, No. 02 C 7156, 2003 WL 21148224 (N.D. Ill. May 16, 2003) (website promoting products that infringed plaintiff's patent

not sufficiently interactive where site merely located local retailer based on consumer's zip code); see also Michael Geist, *Is There a There There? Toward Greater Certainty for Internet Jurisdiction*, 16 BERKELEY TECH. L.J. 1345, 1379 (2001) (noting trend away from finding websites sufficiently interactive to support jurisdiction).

10. More fundamentally, why is the degree to which a website is interactive relevant to the question of jurisdiction? Would an interactive website be sufficient to support the assertion of jurisdiction in Pennsylvania even if the site had never actually been accessed there? For example, as one court has noted,

> it is not clear why a website's level of interactivity should be determinative on the issue of personal jurisdiction. . . [A] court cannot determine whether personal jurisdiction is appropriate simply by deciding whether a website is "passive" or "interactive" (assuming that websites can be readily classified into one category or the other). Even a "passive" website may support a finding of jurisdiction if the defendant used its website intentionally to harm the plaintiff in the forum state. Similarly, an "interactive" or commercial website may not be sufficient to support jurisdiction if it is not aimed at residents in the forum state. Moreover, regardless how interactive a website is, it cannot form the basis for personal jurisdiction unless a nexus exists between the website and the cause of action or unless the contacts through the website are so substantial that they may be considered "systematic and continuous" for the purpose of general jurisdiction. Thus, a rigid adherence to the *Zippo* test is likely to lead to erroneous results.

Hy Cite Corp. v. Badbusinessbureau.com, 297 F. Supp. 2d 1154, 1160 (W.D. Wis. 2004) (citations omitted).

11. How can *Zippo*'s emphasis on the degree of interactivity be squared with *Calder*'s focus on effects? Consider the following case.

Amway Corp. v. The Procter & Gamble Company

United States District Court for the Western District of Michigan, 2000
2000 WL 33725105

BELL, District Judge.

Plaintiff Amway has filed suit against Defendant Sidney Schwartz, alleging in its third amended complaint tortious interference with contract and with actual and prospective business relations. Defendant Schwartz, who is a resident of the State of Oregon, has filed a motion to dismiss for lack of personal jurisdiction.

* * * Plaintiff's * * * contention is that Defendant Schwartz's maintenance of the Internet web site entitled "Amway: the Untold Story," was intended to and did cause consequences in Michigan, sufficient to constitute the necessary minimum contacts with the forum state. Sidney Schwartz resides in Oregon. He has created a Web site where he posts information about Amway that he has collected, and e-mail responses from

those who have visited his Web site. Defendant Schwartz's Web site is accessible to people in every state and all over the globe.

The issue of what type of Internet activity is sufficient to establish personal jurisdiction in a particular forum is a relatively new issue. Most courts that have considered the issue have adopted the "sliding scale" approach set forth in *Zippo Mfg. Co. v. Zippo Dot Com. Inc.*, 952 F. Supp. 1119 (W.D. Pa. 1997). * * * Defendant Schwartz contends that his Web page is a passive Web site that does little more than make information available to those who are interested in it, and that therefore, [it] * * * is not grounds for the exercise of personal jurisdiction. "[N]o court has ever held that an Internet advertisement alone is sufficient to subject the advertiser to jurisdiction in the plaintiff's home state ." *Cybersell, Inc. v. Cybersell, Inc.*, 130 F.3d 414, 418 (9th Cir. 1997). If jurisdiction were based upon a defendant's mere presence on the Internet, a defendant would be subjected to jurisdiction on a worldwide basis and the personal jurisdiction requirements as they currently exist would be eviscerated. Accordingly, in each case where personal jurisdiction has been exercised, there has been "something more" to indicate that the defendant purposefully (albeit electronically) directed his activity in a substantial way to the forum state.

That "something more" may be satisfied by the "effects doctrine." * * * In tort cases, jurisdiction may attach if the defendant's conduct is aimed at or has an effect in the forum state. * * * Plaintiff's third amended complaint focuses on Defendants' allegedly intentional tortious activity of placing defamatory statements on the Web site with the intent that it would cause harm to Plaintiff in Michigan. Allegations that a defendant intentionally directed its tortious Internet activities at the forum state are analyzed under the "effects test" articulated in *Calder v. Jones*, 465 U.S. 783, 788-90 (1984). * * *

Plaintiff Amway has alleged that Defendant Schwartz "has committed and is committing tortious acts with the intent and effect of harming Amway in Michigan." Plaintiff alleges that * * * Defendant Schwartz is the author of a web site which has been "devoted to making malicious attacks against Amway" and "foments hate rhetoric about Amway, its employees, and its distributors." Plaintiff alleges that Defendant Schwartz has broadcasted "vulgar, false, and defamatory statements about Amway, its officers, its business practices, and its products," all "calculated to paint Amway in a false and negative light." Plaintiff's complaint clearly meets the first prong of the "effects" test. Plaintiff has alleged that Defendant committed an intentional tort.

The second prong of the test requires Plaintiff to show that it felt the brunt of the harm in the forum such that the forum can be said to be the focal point of the harm suffered by the plaintiff as a result of that tort. Although it has been noted a corporation typically does not suffer harm in a particular geographic location in the same sense that an individual does, there is nothing in the case law that would preclude a determination that a corporation suffers the brunt of harm in its principal place of business. * * * Amway is a Michigan corporation with its principal place of business in Ada, Michigan. The business was founded in Michigan and its headquarters remain in Michigan. Because the complaint alleges interference with business relations through the dissemination of false and defamatory statements about Amway, its officers, its business practices, and its products, Plaintiff has adequately made a prima facie showing that Plaintiff felt the brunt of the harm in Michigan.

In order to make out the third prong of the *Calder* "effects" test, "the plaintiff must show that the defendant knew that the plaintiff would suffer the brunt of the harm caused by the tortious conduct in the forum, and point to specific activity indicating that the defendant expressly aimed its tortious conduct at the forum." *IMO Indus., Inc. v. Kiekert, AG*, 155 F.3d 254, 266 (3d Cir. 1998). Defendant Schwartz was an Amway distributor for a period of time so that he could get informational mailing from Amway. Because he had an insider's knowledge of Amway, and because Plaintiff is alleging that he was using his Web page to target not only Amway, but its officers as well, there is no question that Michigan was the focal point of the allegedly tortious activity.

Considering the pleadings in the light most favorable to the Plaintiff, this Court concludes that the allegations in Plaintiff's third amended complaint, together with the excerpts of Defendant Schwartz's deposition, are sufficient to make out a prima facie showing of personal jurisdiction over Defendant Schwartz under the effects doctrine. Plaintiff has made a prima facie showing that Defendant Schwartz has taken intentional actions, aimed at the forum state, and that these actions cause harm, the brunt of which is suffered, and which the defendant knew was likely to be suffered, in the forum state. * * *

Notes and Questions

1. How would the jurisdictional question in this case be approached under *Zippo*? Does Judge Bell reject that framework?

2. Was the degree of interactivity of the defendant's website a relevant factor in the jurisdictional inquiry?

3. The court rejects the idea that jurisdiction could be based on plaintiff's mere presence on the Internet. Yet, isn't the court's decision to assert jurisdiction over Schwartz ultimately based only on the existence of Schwartz's website? If so, then does the "effects" principle offer a useful limitation on jurisdiction when applied to websites?

4. The court's assertion of jurisdiction seems to rest largely on the fact that defamation is an intentional tort, meaning that the alleged effects were, in a sense, deliberately "aimed at" Amway in Michigan. Would the same analysis apply if Schwartz were accused of violating Amway's trademark? Or if Schwartz had allegedly engaged in unfair competition? What if Schwartz had violated Amway's copyright?

5. As in the *Amway* decision, many courts have shifted away from the *Zippo* approach (even as they often continue to cite *Zippo*) towards a test based

on *Calder* and the effects of the activity within the jurisdiction. Yet, an effects analysis may not offer any real limitation on the reach of jurisdiction, given that a website can easily cause effects elsewhere. Accordingly, another possible approach has been to focus not on the interactivity of the website or the ultimate effect a defendant's activities may cause in a jurisdiction, but on whether a defendant deliberately *targets* individuals in any particular state. One commentator, advocating a targeting inquiry, has argued:

> Unlike the *Zippo* approach, a targeting analysis would seek to identify the intentions of the parties and to assess the steps taken to either enter or avoid a particular jurisdiction. Targeting would also lessen the reliance on effects-based analysis, the source of considerable uncertainty since Internet-based activity can ordinarily be said to create some effects in most jurisdictions.

Michael Geist, *Is There a There There? Toward Greater Certainty for Internet Jurisdiction*, 16 BERKELEY TECH. L.J. 1345, 1345-46 (2001); *see also* Henry H. Perritt, Jr., *Economic and Other Barriers to Electronic Commerce*, 21 U. PA. J. OF INT'L ECON. L. 563, 573 (2000) ("The concept of targeting is the best solution to the theoretical challenge presented by difficulties in localizing conduct in Internet markets.").

On the other hand, the Court of Appeal of England and Wales has specifically rejected any reliance on whether or not the site in question targeted viewers in a specific jurisdiction. According to the court,

> it makes little sense to distinguish between one jurisdiction and another in order to decide which the defendant has "targeted", when in truth he has "targeted" every jurisdiction where his text may be downloaded. Further, if the exercise required the ascertainment of what it was the defendant subjectively intended to "target", it would in our judgment be liable to manipulation and uncertainty, and much more likely to diminish than enhance the interests of justice.

Lewis v. King, [2004] EWCA Civ 1329 (Eng.), at ¶ 34. Do you find this reasoning convincing? If so, is there any way for judges to devise a test that would help combat such manipulation? Recall that in *Calder* itself, the Court determined that the allegedly libelous acts of the writer and editor were "aimed at" California. Does the use of such a capacious conception of targeting support the British court's judgment that a targeting inquiry does not provide a useful limiting principle?

6. At least three federal courts of appeals have explicitly embraced a targeting analysis. In *Bancroft & Masters Inc. v. Augusta Nat'l Inc.*, 223 F.3d 1082 (9th Cir. 2000), the Ninth Circuit ruled that jurisdiction is proper "when the defendant is alleged to have engaged in wrongful conduct targeted at a plaintiff whom the defendant knows to be a resident of the forum state." *Id.* at 1087. Similarly, the Third Circuit has concluded that "there must be evidence that the defendant 'purposefully availed' itself of conducting activity in the forum state, by directly targeting its web site to the state, knowingly interacting with residents of the forum state via its web site, or through sufficient related contacts." *Toys "R" Us, Inc. v. Step Two, S.A.*, 318 F.3d 446, 454 (3d Cir. 2003). And the Fourth Circuit has held that jurisdiction is proper only if the defendant "(1) directs electronic activity into the State, (2) with the

manifested intent of engaging in business or other interactions within the State, and (3) that activity creates, in a person within the State, a potential cause of action cognizable in the State's courts." *ALS Scan, Inc. v. Digital Serv. Consultants, Inc.*, 293 F.3d 707, 714 (4th Cir. 2002). Likewise, OECD Consumer Protection Guidelines, Securities and Exchange Commission regulations on Internet-based offerings, and the American Bar Association Internet Jurisdiction Project all include references to targeting as a touchstone for the exercise of jurisdiction.

7. If courts ultimately embrace this approach, however, they will need to identify criteria to be used in assessing whether a website has actually targeted a particular jurisdiction (and they will need to reconcile the approach with the language of effects in *Calder*). Consider the following case.

Young v. New Haven Advocate

United States Court of Appeals for the Fourth Circuit, 2002
315 F.3d 256

MICHAEL, Circuit Judge.

Sometime in the late 1990s the State of Connecticut was faced with substantial overcrowding in its maximum security prisons. To alleviate the problem, Connecticut contracted with the Commonwealth of Virginia to house Connecticut prisoners in Virginia's correctional facilities. Beginning in late 1999 Connecticut transferred about 500 prisoners, mostly African-American and Hispanic, to the Wallens Ridge State Prison, a "supermax" facility in Big Stone Gap, Virginia. The plaintiff, Stanley Young, is the warden at Wallens Ridge. Connecticut's arrangement to incarcerate a sizeable number of its offenders in Virginia prisons provoked considerable public debate in Connecticut. Several Connecticut legislators openly criticized the policy, and there were demonstrations against it at the state capitol in Hartford.

Connecticut newspapers, including defendants the New Haven Advocate (the Advocate) and the Hartford Courant (the Courant), began reporting on the controversy. On March 30, 2000, the Advocate published a news article, written by one of its reporters, defendant Camille Jackson, about the transfer of Connecticut inmates to Wallens Ridge. The article discussed the allegedly harsh conditions at the Virginia prison and pointed out that the long trip to southwestern Virginia made visits by prisoners' families difficult or impossible. In the middle of her lengthy article, Jackson mentioned a class action that inmates transferred from Connecticut had filed against Warden Young and the Connecticut Commissioner of Corrections. The inmates alleged a lack of proper hygiene and medical care and the denial of religious privileges at Wallens Ridge. Finally, a paragraph at the end of the article reported that a Connecticut state senator had expressed concern about the presence of Confederate Civil War memorabilia in Warden Young's office. At about the same time the Courant published three columns, written by defendant-reporter Amy Pagnozzi, questioning the practice of relocating Connecticut inmates to Virginia prisons. The columns reported on letters written home by inmates who alleged cruelty by prison guards. In one column Pagnozzi called Wallens Ridge a "cut-rate gulag." Warden Young was not mentioned in any of the Pagnozzi columns.

On May 12, 2000, Warden Young sued the two newspapers, their editors * * * , and the two reporters for libel in a diversity action filed in the Western District of Virginia. He claimed that the newspapers' articles imply that he "is a racist who advocates racism" and that he "encourages abuse of inmates by the guards" at Wallens Ridge. Young alleged that the newspapers circulated the allegedly defamatory articles throughout the world by posting them on their Internet websites.

The newspaper defendants filed motions to dismiss the complaint under Federal Rule of Civil Procedure 12(b)(2) on the ground that the district court lacked personal jurisdiction over them. In support of the motions the editor and reporter from each newspaper provided declarations establishing the following undisputed facts. The Advocate is a free newspaper published once a week in New Haven, Connecticut. It is distributed in New Haven and the surrounding area, and some of its content is published on the Internet. The Advocate has a small number of subscribers, and none of them [is] in Virginia. The Courant is published daily in Hartford, Connecticut. The newspaper is distributed in and around Hartford, and some of its content is published on the Internet. When the articles in question were published, the Courant had eight mail subscribers in Virginia. Neither newspaper solicits subscriptions from Virginia residents. No one from either newspaper, not even the reporters, traveled to Virginia to work on the articles about Connecticut's prisoner transfer policy. * * * The newspapers do not have offices or employees in Virginia, and they do not regularly solicit or do business in Virginia. Finally, the newspapers do not derive any substantial revenue from goods used or services rendered in Virginia. * * *

Warden Young argues that the district court has specific personal jurisdiction over the newspaper defendants (hereafter, the "newspapers") because of the following contacts between them and Virginia: (1) the newspapers, knowing that Young was a Virginia resident, intentionally discussed and defamed him in their articles, (2) the newspapers posted the articles on their websites, which were accessible in Virginia, and (3) the primary effects of the defamatory statements on Young's reputation were felt in Virginia. Young emphasizes that he is not arguing that jurisdiction is proper in any location where defamatory Internet content can be accessed, which would be anywhere in the world. Rather, Young argues that personal jurisdiction is proper in Virginia because the newspapers understood that their defamatory articles, which were available to Virginia residents on the Internet, would expose Young to public hatred, contempt, and ridicule in Virginia, where he lived and worked. As the district court put it, "[t]he defendants were all well aware of the fact that the plaintiff was employed as a warden within the Virginia correctional system and resided in Virginia," and they "also should have been aware that any harm suffered by Young from the circulation of these articles on the Internet would primarily occur in Virginia."

Young frames his argument in a way that makes one thing clear: if the newspapers' contacts with Virginia were sufficient to establish personal jurisdiction, those contacts arose solely from the newspapers' Internet-based activities. Recently, in *ALS Scan* we discussed the challenges presented in applying traditional jurisdictional principles to decide when "an out-of-state citizen, through electronic contacts, has conceptually 'entered' the State via the Internet for jurisdictional purposes." *ALS Scan, Inc. v. Digital Serv. Consultants, Inc.*, 293 F.3d 707, 713 (2002). There, we held that "specific jurisdiction in the Internet context may be based only on an out-of-state person's Internet activity directed at [the forum state] and causing injury that gives rise to a potential claim cognizable in [that state]." *Id.* at 714. We noted that this standard for determining specific jurisdiction based on Internet contacts is consistent with the one used by the Supreme Court in *Calder v. Jones*, 465 U.S. 783 (1984). *ALS Scan*, 293 F.3d at 714. *Calder*, though not an Internet case, has particular relevance here because it deals with personal jurisdiction in the context of a libel suit. In *Calder* a California actress brought suit there against, among others, two Floridians, a reporter and an editor who wrote and edited in Florida a National Enquirer article claiming that the actress had a problem with alcohol. The Supreme Court held that California had jurisdiction over the Florida residents because "California [was] the focal point both of the story and of the harm suffered." *Calder*, 465 U.S. at 789. The writers' "actions were expressly aimed at California," the Court said, "[a]nd they knew that the brunt of [the potentially devastating] injury would be felt by [the actress] in the State in which she lives and works and in which the National Enquirer has its largest circulation," 600,000 copies. *Calder*, 465 U.S. at 789-90.

Warden Young argues that *Calder* requires a finding of jurisdiction in this case simply because the newspapers posted articles on their Internet websites that discussed the warden and his Virginia prison, and he would feel the effects of any libel in Virginia, where he lives and works. *Calder* does not sweep that broadly, as we have recognized. For example, in *ESAB Group, Inc. v. Centricut, Inc.*, 126 F.3d 617, 625-26 (4th Cir. 1997), we emphasized how important it is in light of *Calder* to look at whether the defendant has expressly aimed or directed its conduct toward the forum state. We said that "[a]lthough the place that the plaintiff feels the alleged injury is plainly relevant to the [jurisdictional] inquiry, it must ultimately be accompanied by the defendant's own [sufficient minimum] contacts with the state if jurisdiction . . . is to be upheld." *Id.* at 626. We thus had no trouble in concluding in *ALS Scan* that application of *Calder* in the Internet context requires proof that the out-of-state defendant's Internet activity is expressly targeted at or directed to the forum state. *ALS Scan*, 293 F.3d at 714. In *ALS Scan* we went on to adapt the traditional standard * * * for establishing specific jurisdiction so that it makes sense in the Internet context. We "conclude[d] that a State may, consistent with due process, exercise judicial power over a person outside of the State when that person (1) directs electronic activity into the State, (2) with the manifested intent of engaging in business or other interactions within the State, and (3) that activity creates, in a person within the State, a potential cause of action cognizable in the State's courts." *ALS Scan*, 293 F.3d at 714.

* * * We thus ask whether the newspapers manifested an intent to direct their website content—which included certain articles discussing conditions in a Virginia prison—to a Virginia audience. * * * [T]he fact that the newspapers' websites could be accessed anywhere, including Virginia, does not by itself demonstrate that the newspapers were intentionally directing their website content to a Virginia audience. * * * The newspapers must, through the Internet postings, manifest an intent to target and focus on Virginia readers.

* * * The overall content of [the newspapers'] websites is decidedly local, and neither newspaper's website contains advertisements aimed at a Virginia audience. For example, the website that distributes the Courant, ctnow.com, provides access to local (Connecticut) weather and traffic information and links to websites for the University of Connecticut and Connecticut state government. The Advocate's website features stories focusing on New Haven, such as one entitled "The Best of New Haven." In sum, it appears that these newspapers maintain their websites to serve local readers in Connecticut, to expand the reach of their papers within their local markets, and to provide their local markets with a place for classified ads. The websites are not designed to attract or serve a Virginia audience.

We also examine the specific articles Young complains about to determine whether they were posted on the Internet with the intent to target a Virginia audience. The articles included discussions about the allegedly harsh conditions at the Wallens Ridge prison, where Young was warden. One article mentioned Young by name and quoted a Connecticut state senator who reported that Young had Confederate Civil War memorabilia in his office. The focus of the articles, however, was the Connecticut prisoner transfer policy and its impact on the transferred prisoners and their families back home in Connecticut. The articles reported on and encouraged a public debate in Connecticut about whether the transfer policy was sound or practical for that state and its citizens. Connecticut, not Virginia, was the focal point of the articles. * * *

The facts in this case establish that the newspapers' websites, as well as the articles in question, were aimed at a Connecticut audience. The newspapers did not post materials on the Internet with the manifest intent of targeting Virginia readers. Accordingly, * * * the newspapers do not have sufficient Internet contacts with Virginia to permit the district court to exercise specific jurisdiction over them.

Notes and Questions

1. How does the court distinguish the facts of this case from those in *Calder*? Why is an article about a California actress sufficiently targeted to

California, while an article about a Virginia prison warden is not sufficiently targeted to Virginia? Would it have made a difference if Young had been able to show that many Virginia residents had downloaded the articles in question?

2. The court relies in part on the fact that the articles focused on Connecticut policy and were therefore directed at Connecticut, not Virginia. Is that sufficient? After all, many defamatory acts are directed at third parties rather than at the person allegedly defamed. Does the choice of conversational partner change the scope of the harm caused?

3. How would one determine whether a generally accessible website is targeting a particular jurisdiction? Would it matter, for example, how many web hits the site received from that jurisdiction? Or is the determination properly based only on the content of the site? For example, the *Young* court relied on the fact that the sites in question primarily contain regional news. What if the site contained *both* local and international news? How does one determine whether or not a site is of predominantly local character?

4. In a subsequent case, the Fourth Circuit similarly refused to permit the exercise of jurisdiction in Maryland over a Chicago-based company with a "generally accessible, semi-interactive Internet website." *Carefirst of Maryland v. Carefirst Pregnancy Centers*, 334 F.3d 390, 401 (2003). As in *Young*, the court focused on the "local character" of the website, which sought to provide assistance to "'women and families *in the Chicago area.*'" *Id.* (emphasis in original). Although the site generally solicited donations and there was evidence that at least one Maryland resident had in fact donated to the company, the court deemed such contact insufficient because there was no "manifest intent of engaging in business or other interactions within that state in particular." *Id.*

5. In *Dow Jones & Company Inc. v. Gutnick*, HCA 56 (Austl. 2002), Australia's highest court ruled that a local businessman could pursue a defamation suit against U.S.-based Dow Jones & Co. because of an article Dow Jones posted on its website. As one of the judges observed, "[a] publisher, particularly one carrying on the business of publishing, does not act to put matter on the Internet in order for it to reach a small target. It is its ubiquity which is one of the main attractions to users of it." Do you agree? Is there a way of distinguishing the Dow Jones site from the sites at issue in *Young*?

6. Are there other ways of determining whether a website is targeting a particular jurisdiction? The American Bar Association Internet Jurisdiction Project, a global study on Internet jurisdiction released in 2000, referred to the language of the site as a potentially significant way of determining whether a site operator has targeted a particular jurisdiction. AMERICAN BAR ASSOCIATION, ACHIEVING LEGAL AND BUSINESS ORDER IN CYBERSPACE: A REPORT ON GLOBAL JURISDICTION ISSUES CREATED BY THE INTERNET (2000). For example, the Third Circuit has refused to assert jurisdiction over a Spanish company, despite the interactivity of its website, in large part because the text of the site was in Spanish, the goods were priced in euros and pesetas, and the form on which buyers listed their phone numbers did not have room for a country access code. Under these circumstances, the court found insufficient evidence of an intent to service the U.S. market to sustain jurisdiction. *See Toys "R" Us, Inc. v. Step Two, S.A.*, 318 F. 3d 446, 450 (3d Cir. 2003). While

this seems to be a sensible result, such clear demarcations based on language may become unsustainable over time, given the development of language translation capabilities that allow a website owner to create her site in any language she wishes, knowing that a user will automatically be able to view the site in the user's chosen language.

7.   To the extent that courts focus on targeting and are therefore scrutinizing the local (or international) character of websites, can we really say that courts are analyzing the *contacts* with the forum state as *International Shoe* instructs? And does it really make sense to try to adapt the *International Shoe* minimum contacts test to the online environment at all? Consider this argument.

Paul Schiff Berman, *The Globalization of Jurisdiction*
131 U. PA. L. REV. 311 (2002)

[C]onceptions of legal jurisdiction (by which I mean to include both the jurisdiction to decide a dispute and the determination that a jurisdiction's law will apply) are more than simply ideas about the appropriate boundaries for state regulation or the efficient allocation of governing authority. Jurisdiction is the locus for debates about community definition, sovereignty, and legitimacy. Moreover, the idea of legal jurisdiction both reflects and reinforces social conceptions of space, distance, and identity. Too often, however, contemporary frameworks for thinking about jurisdictional authority unreflectively accept the assumption that nation-states defined by fixed territorial borders remain the relevant jurisdictional entities, without examining how people actually experience allegiance to community or understand their relationship to geographical distance and territorial borders. * * *

Indeed, even a cursory examination reveals that our current territorially based rules for jurisdiction (and conflict of laws) were developed in an era when physical geography was more meaningful than it is today and during a brief historical moment when the ideas of nation and state were being joined by a hyphen to create an historically contingent Westphalian order.[24] Yet if the ideas of geographical territory and the nation-state are no longer treated as givens for defining community, an entirely new set of questions can be asked. How are communities appropriately defined in today's world? In what ways might we say that the nation-state is an *imagined* community, and what other imaginings are possible? How do people actually experience the idea of membership in multiple, overlapping communities? Should citizenship be theorized as one of the many subject positions occupied by people as members of diverse, sometimes non-territorial, collectivities? In what ways is our sense of place

---

24. The Peace of Westphalia ended the Thirty Years War. Westphalia is generally thought to have ushered in an international legal order based on individual state sovereignty. * * *

and community membership constructed through social forces? And if i(such as "place", "community", "member", "nation", "citizen", "bound; and "stranger" are not natural and inevitable, but are instead constru imagined, and (sometimes) imposed, what does that say about the pres¹ "naturalness" of our geographically based jurisdiction and choice of law rules? * * *

Moreover, by analyzing the social meaning of our affiliations across space, we can think about alternative conceptions of community that are subnational, transnational, supranational, or cosmopolitan. Such an analysis provides a better understanding of the world of experience on which the legal world is mapped and is therefore essential in order to develop a richer descriptive account of what it means for a juridical body to assert jurisdiction over a controversy.

In addition, moving from the descriptive to the normative, I * * * argue that, just as a rigidly territorial conception of jurisdiction eventually gave way in the first part of the twentieth century to the idea of jurisdiction based on contacts with a sovereign entity, so too a contacts-based approach must now yield to a conception of jurisdiction based on community definition. * * * I offer one such conception, which I call a cosmopolitan pluralist conception of jurisdiction.

A *cosmopolitan* approach would allow us to think of community not as a geographically determined territory circumscribed by fixed boundaries, but as "articulated moments in networks of social relations and understandings."[30] This dynamic understanding of the relationship between the "local" community and other forms of community affiliation (regional, national, transnational, international, cosmopolitan) permits us to conceptualize legal jurisdiction in terms of social interactions that are fluid processes, not motionless demarcations frozen in time and space. A court in one country might therefore appropriately assert community dominion over a legal dispute even if its territorially based contacts with the dispute are minimal. Or conversely, a country that might have certain "contacts" with a dispute might nevertheless not be able to establish a tie between a local community and a distant defendant sufficient to justify asserting its dominion.

A cosmopolitan interrogation of conceptions of community, therefore, might rein in some assertions of jurisdiction over distant acts while permitting other extraterritorial assertions of jurisdiction that are currently unrecognized. Accordingly, the cosmopolitan pluralist conception of jurisdiction I propose seeks to capture a middle ground between strict territorialism on the one hand, and a system of complete universal jurisdiction on the other. In any event, the jurisdictional inquiry would no longer be based on a reified counting of contacts with, effects on, or interests of, a territorially-bounded population. Rather, courts would take seriously the multiple definitions of community that might be available, the

---

30. DOREEN MASSEY, SPACE, PLACE, AND GENDER 154 (1994).

symbolic significance of asserting jurisdiction over an actor, and the normative desirability of conceptualizing the parties before the court as members of the same legal jurisdiction.

In addition, if the nation-state is an imagined, historically contingent community defined by admittedly arbitrary geographical boundaries, and if those nation-states—because of transnational flows of information, capital, and people—no longer define a unified community (if they ever did), then there is no conceptual justification for conceiving of nation-states as possessing a monopoly on the assertion of jurisdiction. Instead, any comprehensive theory of jurisdiction must acknowledge that *non-state* communities also assert various claims to jurisdictional authority and articulate alternative norms that are often incorporated into more "official" legal regimes. This *pluralist* understanding of jurisdiction helps us to see that law is not merely the coercive command of a sovereign power, but a language for imagining alternative future worlds. Moreover, various norm-generating communities (not just the sovereign) are always contesting the shape of such worlds.

Notes and Questions

1. Professor Berman argues first and foremost that jurisdiction is not so much about efficient legal regulation as it is about various communities asserting dominion over an event or actor. Is this a convincing account? Can you think of occasions when the assertion of jurisdiction seems to serve primarily symbolic (or even therapeutic) purposes?

2. Is Berman right that physical geography is less meaningful in today's world than it was fifty or a hundred or three hundred years ago? Would Professor Post agree? What about Professor Goldsmith?

3. Think about the various communities with which you feel affiliated: your family, your friends, your race, your ethnicity, your religion, your law school, your local area, your sports team, your fellow hiking enthusiasts, etc. How many of these communities can be defined in territorial terms? How many of them cross state or national boundaries? Should the law recognize some or all of those affiliations? How does one choose which affiliations should be legally cognizable and which should not?

4. Does it matter that only official governmental communities have police forces or armies with which to enforce their assertions of jurisdiction? Or should we think of adjudicatory authority as something different from the ability to enforce a judgment?

5. Consider *Zippo*, *Amway*, and *Young*. Does it really make sense in those cases to try to count web-based "contacts" with a geographically defined place? On the other hand, does a cosmopolitan pluralist approach change the analysis? If so, how?

6. Even assuming that the nation-state is as historically contingent and arbitrary as Berman thinks, it would be difficult to deny that national loyalty has great power for many people. After all, people are far more willing to die

for their country than, say, for their bowling leagues. Why shouldn't the nation-state hold a monopoly on the exercise of legal jurisdiction?

7. On the other hand, how does a state-sanctioned court exercise its authority? What if a court adjudicated a dispute, and the police refused to enforce the order? If courts ultimately derive their power from the ability to persuade others of the legitimacy of their rulings, then is a state-sanctioned court truly different from any other purported community that attempts to exercise jurisdiction?

Keep these questions in mind as we approach the issue of judgment recognition and enforcement more directly.

SECTION D. JUDGMENT RECOGNITION AND THE POWER OF PERSUASION

In each of the civil cases considered above, the main issue was whether a court had the authority to apply a local law or adjudicate a dispute involving a defendant from outside of the local jurisdiction. It is crucial to remember, however, that the mere assertion of jurisdiction does not necessarily entail the ability to *enforce* the judgment reached. After all, a court in one location may issue a judgment against a foreign defendant, but may have no way to carry out its edict. Instead, it must rely on courts or other governmental authorities with more coercive power over the defendant.

The assertion of jurisdiction, therefore, is in part simply the ability to assert community dominion, articulate norms, and thereby generate debate. This jurisdictional assertion may have an important symbolic or rhetorical value in and of itself, even if the judgment rendered does not initially persuade other communities to enforce the norms articulated. Indeed, the assertion of jurisdiction is in part a mechanism for opening up space so that debate about community affiliation and substantive norms can occur. Such norms, even if they are not able to persuade others in the near term, may gain traction over time and may ultimately come to be accepted more broadly. In contrast, if jurisdiction is not asserted at all, courts cannot reach the "merits," and no substantive norms are articulated.

Thus, if a community asserts jurisdiction but cannot itself enforce its judgment, it must convince other jurisdictions of the justice of its ruling (and the legitimacy of its assertion of community). As a result, jurisdiction becomes the rhetorical site for discussions of multiple overlapping and shifting conceptions of community, and recognition of judgments becomes the terrain on which these alternative conceptions of community vie for persuasive power and legitimacy. Think about these questions of rhetorical persuasion and enforcement as you consider the following two cases.

Yahoo!, Inc. v. La Ligue Contre le Racisme et l'Antisémitisme

United States District Court for the Northern District of California, 2001
169 F. Supp. 2d 1181

FOGEL, District Judge.

I. PROCEDURAL HISTORY

Defendants La Ligue Contre Le Racisme Et l'Antisemitisme ("LICRA") and L'Union Des Etudiants Juifs De France, citizens of France, are non-profit organizations dedicated to eliminating anti-Semitism. Plaintiff Yahoo!, Inc. ("Yahoo!") is a corporation organized under the laws of Delaware with its principal place of business in Santa Clara, California. Yahoo! is an Internet service provider that operates various Internet websites and services that any computer user can access at the Uniform Resource Locator ("URL") *http://www.yahoo.com.* Yahoo! services ending in the suffix, ".com," without an associated country code as a prefix or extension (collectively, "Yahoo!'s U.S. Services") use the English language and target users who are residents of, utilize servers based in and operate under the laws of the United States. Yahoo! subsidiary corporations operate regional Yahoo! sites and services in twenty other nations, including, for example, Yahoo! France, Yahoo! India, and Yahoo! Spain. Each of these regional web sites contains the host nation's unique two-letter code as either a prefix or a suffix in its URL (e.g., Yahoo! France is found at *http://www.yahoo.fr* and Yahoo! Korea at *http://www.yahoo.kr*). Yahoo!'s regional sites use the local region's primary language, target the local citizenry, and operate under local laws.

Yahoo! provides a variety of means by which people from all over the world can communicate and interact with one another over the Internet. Examples include an Internet search engine, e-mail, an automated auction site, personal web page hostings, shopping services, chat rooms, and a listing of clubs that individuals can create or join. Any computer user with Internet access is able to post materials on many of these Yahoo! sites, which in turn are instantly accessible by anyone who logs on to Yahoo!'s Internet sites. As relevant here, Yahoo!'s auction site allows anyone to post an item for sale and solicit bids from any computer user from around the globe. Yahoo! records when a posting is made and after the requisite time period lapses sends an e-mail notification to the highest bidder and seller with their respective contact information. Yahoo! is never a party to a transaction, and the buyer and seller are responsible for arranging privately for payment and shipment of goods. Yahoo! monitors the transaction through limited regulation by prohibiting particular items from being sold (such as stolen goods, body parts, prescription and illegal drugs, weapons, and goods violating U.S. copyright laws or the Iranian and Cuban embargos) and by providing a rating system through which buyers and sellers have their transactional behavior evaluated for the benefit of future consumers. Yahoo! informs auction sellers that they must comply with

Yahoo!'s policies and may not offer items to buyers in jurisdictions in which the sale of such item violates the jurisdiction's applicable laws. Yahoo! does not actively regulate the content of each posting, and individuals are able to post, and have in fact posted, highly offensive matter, including Nazi-related propaganda and Third Reich memorabilia, on Yahoo!'s auction sites.

On or about April 5, 2000, LICRA sent a "cease and desist" letter to Yahoo!'s Santa Clara headquarters informing Yahoo! that the sale of Nazi and Third Reich related goods through its auction services violates French law. LICRA threatened to take legal action unless Yahoo! took steps to prevent such sales within eight days. Defendant subsequently * * * filed a civil complaint against Yahoo! in the Tribunal de Grande Instance de Paris (the "French Court").

The French Court found that approximately 1,000 Nazi and Third Reich related objects, including Adolf Hitler's *Mein Kampf, The Protocol of the Elders of Zion* (an infamous anti-Semitic report produced by the Czarist secret police in the early 1900's), and purported "evidence" that the gas chambers of the Holocaust did not exist were being offered for sale on Yahoo.com's auction site. Because any French citizen is able to access these materials on Yahoo.com directly or through a link on Yahoo.fr, the French Court concluded that the Yahoo.com auction site violates Section R645-1 of the French Criminal Code, which prohibits exhibition of Nazi propaganda and artifacts for sale. On [May 22, 2000], the French Court entered an order requiring Yahoo! to (1) eliminate French citizens' access to any material on the Yahoo.com auction site that offers for sale any Nazi objects, relics, insignia, emblems, and flags; (2) eliminate French citizens' access to web pages on Yahoo.com displaying text, extracts, or quotations from *Mein Kampf* and *Protocol of the Elders of Zion;* (3) post a warning to French citizens on Yahoo.fr that any search through Yahoo.com may lead to sites containing material prohibited by Section R645-1 of the French Criminal Code, and that such viewing of the prohibited material may result in legal action against the Internet user; (4) remove from all browser directories accessible in the French Republic index headings entitled "negationists" and from all hypertext links the equation of "negationists" under the heading "Holocaust." The order subjects Yahoo! to a penalty of 100,000 [Francs] for each day that it fails to comply with the order. The order concludes:

> We order the Company YAHOO! Inc. to take all necessary measures to dissuade and render impossible any access via Yahoo.com to the Nazi artifact auction service and to any other site or service that may be construed as constituting an apology for Nazism or a contesting of Nazi crimes.

The French Court set a return date in July 2000 for Yahoo! to demonstrate its compliance with the order.

Yahoo! asked the French Court to reconsider the terms of the order, claiming that although it easily could post the required warning on

Yahoo.fr, compliance with the order's requirements with respect to Yahoo.com was technologically impossible. The French Court sought expert opinion on the matter and on November 20, 2000 "reaffirmed" its order of May 22. The French Court ordered Yahoo! to comply with the May 22 order within three (3) months or face a penalty of 100,000 Francs (approximately U.S. $13,300) for each day of non-compliance. The French Court also provided that penalties assessed against Yahoo! Inc. may not be collected from Yahoo! France. * * *

Yahoo! subsequently posted the required warning and prohibited postings in violation of Section R645-1 of the French Criminal Code from appearing on Yahoo.fr. Yahoo! also amended the auction policy of Yahoo.com to prohibit individuals from auctioning:

> Any item that promotes, glorifies, or is directly associated with groups or individuals known principally for hateful or violent positions or acts, such as Nazis or the Ku Klux Klan. Official government-issue stamps and coins are not prohibited under this policy. Expressive media, such as books and films, may be subject to more permissive standards as determined by Yahoo! in its sole discretion.

Yahoo Auction Guidelines (visited Oct. 23, 2001) <http://user.auctions. Yahoo.com/html/guidelines.html>. Notwithstanding these actions, the Yahoo.com auction site still offers certain items for sale (such as stamps, coins, and a copy of *Mein Kampf)* which appear to violate the French Order. While Yahoo! has removed the *Protocol of the Elders of Zion* from its auction site, it has not prevented access to numerous other sites which reasonably "may be construed as constituting an apology for Nazism or a contesting of Nazi crimes."

Yahoo! claims that because it lacks the technology to block French citizens from accessing the Yahoo.com auction site to view materials which violate the French Order or from accessing other Nazi-based content of websites on Yahoo.com, it cannot comply with the French order without banning Nazi-related material from Yahoo.com altogether. Yahoo! contends that such a ban would infringe impermissibly upon its rights under the First Amendment to the United States Constitution. Accordingly, Yahoo! filed a complaint in this Court seeking a declaratory judgment that the French Court's orders are neither cognizable nor enforceable under the laws of the United States. * * *

II. OVERVIEW

As this Court and others have observed, the instant case presents novel and important issues arising from the global reach of the Internet. Indeed, the specific facts of this case implicate issues of policy, politics, and culture that are beyond the purview of one nation's judiciary. Thus it is critical that the Court define at the outset what is and is not at stake in the present proceeding.

This case is *not* about the moral acceptability of promoting the symbols or propaganda of Nazism. Most would agree that such acts are profoundly offensive. By any reasonable standard of morality, the Nazis were responsible for one of the worst displays of inhumanity in recorded history. This Court is acutely mindful of the emotional pain reminders of the Nazi era cause to Holocaust survivors and deeply respectful of the motivations of the French Republic in enacting the underlying statutes and of the defendant organizations in seeking relief under those statutes. Vigilance is the key to preventing atrocities such as the Holocaust from occurring again.

Nor is this case about the right of France or any other nation to determine its own law and social policies. A basic function of a sovereign state is to determine by law what forms of speech and conduct are acceptable within its borders. In this instance, as a nation whose citizens suffered the effects of Nazism in ways that are incomprehensible to most Americans, France clearly has the right to enact and enforce laws such as those relied upon by the French Court here.

What *is* at issue here is whether it is consistent with the Constitution and laws of the United States for another nation to regulate speech by a United States resident within the United States on the basis that such speech can be accessed by Internet users in that nation. In a world in which ideas and information transcend borders and the Internet in particular renders the physical distance between speaker and audience virtually meaningless, the implications of this question go far beyond the facts of this case. The modern world is home to widely varied cultures with radically divergent value systems. There is little doubt that Internet users in the United States routinely engage in speech that violates, for example, China's laws against religious expression, the laws of various nations against advocacy of gender equality or homosexuality, or even the United Kingdom's restrictions on freedom of the press. If the government or another party in one of these sovereign nations were to seek enforcement of such laws against Yahoo! or another U.S.-based Internet service provider, what principles should guide the court's analysis?

The Court has stated that it must and will decide this case in accordance with the Constitution and laws of the United States. It recognizes that in so doing, it necessarily adopts certain value judgments embedded in those enactments, including the fundamental judgment expressed in the First Amendment that it is preferable to permit the non-violent expression of offensive viewpoints rather than to impose viewpoint-based governmental regulation upon speech. The government and people of France have made a different judgment based upon their own experience. In undertaking its inquiry as to the proper application of the laws of the United States, the Court intends no disrespect for that judgment or for the experience that has informed it. * * *

IV. LEGAL ISSUES

* * *

3. *Abstention*

Defendants * * * argue that this Court should abstain from deciding the instant case because Yahoo! simply is unhappy with the outcome of the French litigation and is trying to obtain a more favorable result here. * * *

In the present case, the French court has determined that Yahoo!'s auction site and website hostings on Yahoo.com violate French law. Nothing in Yahoo!'s suit for declaratory relief in this Court appears to be an attempt to relitigate or disturb the French court's application of French law or its orders with respect to Yahoo!'s conduct in France. Rather, the purpose of the present action is to determine whether a United States court may enforce the French order without running afoul of the First Amendment. The actions involve distinct legal issues, and as this Court concluded in its jurisdictional order, a United States court is best situated to determine the application of the United States Constitution to the facts presented. No basis for abstention has been established.

4. *Comity*

No legal judgment has any effect, of its own force, beyond the limits of the sovereignty from which its authority is derived. However, the United States Constitution and implementing legislation require that full faith and credit be given to judgments of sister states, territories, and possessions of the United States. U.S. CONST. art. IV, § 1, cl. 1; 28 U.S.C. § 1738. The extent to which the United States, or any state, honors the judicial decrees of foreign nations is a matter of choice, governed by "the comity of nations." *Hilton v. Guyot*, 159 U.S. 113, 163 (1895). Comity "is neither a matter of absolute obligation, on the one hand, nor of mere courtesy and good will, upon the other." *Id.* at 163-64. United States courts generally recognize foreign judgments and decrees unless enforcement would be prejudicial or contrary to the country's interests.

As discussed previously, the French order's content and viewpoint-based regulation of the web pages and auction site on Yahoo.com, while entitled to great deference as an articulation of French law, clearly would be inconsistent with the First Amendment if mandated by a court in the United States. What makes this case uniquely challenging is that the Internet in effect allows one to speak in more than one place at the same time. Although France has the sovereign right to regulate what speech is permissible in France, this Court may not enforce a foreign order that violates the protections of the United States Constitution by chilling protected speech that occurs simultaneously within our borders. * * * Absent a body of law that establishes international standards with respect to speech on the Internet and an appropriate treaty or legislation addressing enforcement of such standards to speech originating within the United States, the principle of comity is outweighed by the Court's obligation to uphold the First Amendment.

Notes and Questions

1. Although the district court ultimately declined to enforce the French order, it did *not* rule that the French court had acted without proper jurisdiction in the first place. Why not? Is there any advantage to allowing the French jurisdictional assertion but disagreeing with the substantive rule articulated by the French court?

2. Should the district court have considered international standards regarding hate speech and not just the First Amendment? If so, how would it have gone about determining precisely what those standards are? To the extent that the First Amendment is in tension with those standards, should that be relevant in a case involving the enforcement of a foreign judgment?

3. Judge Fogel appears to assume that it would actually be *unconstitutional* for a U.S. court to enforce the French judgment simply because that judgment could not constitutionally have been issued by a U.S. court. But does that necessarily follow? After all, the concerns involved in simply enforcing another jurisdiction's judgment are quite different from those involved when a court is ruling in the first instance. Indeed, the whole idea of full faith and credit in the domestic context rests on the premise that there is a value in states enforcing other states' judgments even if those judgments are contrary to the public policies of the enforcing state. *See, e.g., Baker v. General Motors*, 522 U.S. 222, 233 (1998) (describing the full faith and credit obligation as "exacting"). Mightn't the same be true internationally? *See, e.g.*, Mark Rosen, *Exporting the Constitution*, 53 EMORY L.J. 171 (2004) (arguing that, even if foreign judgments are "'Un-American' insofar as they come from non-American polities and reflect political values that are at variance with American constitutional law, neither the foreign judgments themselves nor their enforcement by an American court is unconstitutional").

Moreover, it is unclear whether or not the mere enforcement of a foreign order should be deemed sufficient state action to trigger constitutional scrutiny. In *Shelley v. Kraemer*, 334 U.S. 1 (1948), the U.S. Supreme Court ruled that judicial enforcement of racially restrictive covenants would violate the Equal Protection Clause of the Fourteenth Amendment, U.S. CONST. amend. XIV, § 1. *Shelley*, 334 U.S. at 20-21. On the other hand, *Shelley*'s logic "consistently applied, would require individuals to conform their private agreements to constitutional standards whenever, as almost always, the individuals might later seek the security of potential judicial enforcement." LAURENCE H. TRIBE, AMERICAN CONSTITUTIONAL LAW 1697 (2d ed. 1988). This issue implicates longstanding debates about the coherence of trying to draw a distinction between "private" and "public" action for constitutional purposes. We will take up such questions in Chapter Five.

4. If the U.S. court refuses to enforce the French judgment, does France have any recourse? And, if not, has the United States then "imposed" the First Amendment on France? On the other hand, if the U.S. court enforces the French judgment, would France then be "imposing" its hate speech laws on the United States? Earlier in this chapter we encountered the argument that if local communities have the authority to reach out beyond their borders and impose their law on Internet speech, Internet speakers will be forced to comply with the most restrictive local ordinances; on the other hand, if local

communities do *not* have such authority, does that mean that the *least* restrictive law will prevail? Is there any way out of this dilemma? Does Goldsmith's discussion of regulatory spillover help here? What about Post's notion that rule-sets should be internal to cyberspace? Or Berman's cosmopolitan pluralist approach?

5. The district court's opinion was subsequently reversed by the United States Court of Appeals for the Ninth Circuit. *See Yahoo!, Inc. v. La Ligue Contre le Racisme et l'Antisémitisme*, 433 F.3d 1199 (9th Cir. 2006) (en banc). The appeals court declined to reach the First Amendment question, however. Instead, a majority of the *en banc* court agreed that the case should be dismissed, though the judges disagreed on the rationale for the dismissal. Some wanted to dismiss for lack of jurisdiction over the French defendants because the defendants had insufficient contact with California. Others saw it as a ripeness problem, because part of the reason the French complainants had insufficient contact with California is that they had chosen not to seek an enforcement order in the United States. Whatever the rationale, however, the effect of the ruling was to prevent Yahoo!'s claim from going forward unless and until a U.S. court is actually asked to enforce the French order. At that point, the controversy would become ripe for review, and at the same time jurisdiction would presumably no longer be a problem.

6. When a court is called upon to enforce a foreign judgment, its task is complicated by the fact that it must decipher precisely what obligations the foreign court has imposed on the party seeking to avoid enforcement. The *Yahoo!* case illustrates the difficulties that a court might face. In the California case, Yahoo! argued that it lacked the means to comply with the obligations the French court had imposed upon it. But what obligations, precisely, did the French court impose? Compare the translation of the concluding paragraph of the French court order that the district court adopts here with the one appearing on page 95. The question is how to interpret the crucial language "Ordonnons à la Société YAHOO ! Inc. de prendre toutes les mesures de nature à dissuader et à rendre impossible toute consultation sur Yahoo.com . . . ." Here, the court accepts the translation offered by Yahoo!: "We order the Company YAHOO! Inc. to take *all necessary measures to dissuade and render impossible* any access via Yahoo.com . . . ." The alternative translation on page 95 would understand the French court to have ordered Yahoo! "to take *all such measures as would dissuade and prevent* any access." The passage might also be translated as "to take *all normal measures to dissuade and prevent* any access." Are there substantive differences between these formulations? How might the choice of one translation or another affect the court's decision whether to enforce the judgment?

7. The *Yahoo!* case raises the possibility that other countries might begin to challenge America's legal dominance by advancing alternative normative visions about the shape of online regulation. If multiple communities are affected by online activity (and almost inevitably multiple communities *will* be affected), then giving the court systems of those communities greater latitude to weigh in on the best regulatory approach may be desirable. The French jurisdictional assertion therefore creates an opportunity for ongoing international debate about the appropriate rules for speech in online interaction. This debate is important (and might have long-term consequences)

even if in this particular instance a U.S. court decides not to enforce the French order.

Citron v. Zündel

Canadian Human Rights Tribunal, 2002
T.D. 1/02 2002/01/18

Access to the Internet has revolutionized global communication and has had a profound impact on modern society. With its promise of readily accessible information and the explosion in use of the Internet, serious concerns have been raised about the content found on many sites. The relationship of the Internet to existing regulatory frameworks, such as restrictions on the display of pornography, the protection of individual privacy, and the limits of permissible commerce are all the subject of significant legal debate and public controversy.

As we begin to explore the legal limits of the use of the Internet for the mass distribution of information, fundamental issues are raised regarding the preservation of legitimate free speech interests. At the same time, the proliferation of alleged "hate sites" on the World Wide Web has been particularly disturbing for the equality seeking community. This case, for the first time, raises squarely the application of the Canadian Human Rights Act to sites on the World Wide Web, and yet again exposes the constant tension between competing social interests.

The complaints now before us seek to apply §13(1) of the Canadian Human Rights Act to communication via the Internet.[d] It is alleged that by posting material to the Zundelsite, the Respondent, Ernst Zündel [a German-Canadian citizen currently living in the United States], caused repeated telephonic communication that was likely to expose Jews to hatred or contempt. We are therefore asked to determine whether it is a discriminatory practice to post material on a Website if the material is likely to expose a person to hatred or contempt. What limits, if any, are to be applied to repeated communication of hate messages via the Internet? Finally, if applied to the Internet, is this a permissible restriction on freedom of speech under the Charter of Rights and Freedoms? * * *

The particulars of this complaint allege that from October 10, 1995 onward, Ernst Zündel offered a Homepage on the World Wide Web that repeatedly provided pamphlets and publications that were likely to expose

---

d. Section 13(1) of the Canadian Human Rights Act provides:

It is a discriminatory practice for a person or a group of persons acting in concert to communicate telephonically or to cause to be so communicated, repeatedly, in whole or in part by means of the facilities of a telecommunication undertaking within the legislative authority of Parliament, any matter that is likely to expose a person or persons to hatred or contempt by reason of the fact that that person or those persons are identifiable on the basis of a prohibited ground of discrimination.

persons of the Jewish faith and ethnic origin to hatred and contempt. Examples of these messages were cited in, and attached to the Complaint form and included the following publications: "Did Six Million Really Die", "66 Questions and Answers on the Holocaust", and "Jewish Soap." * * *

The central thesis of [the complaint] is that the Respondent, Ernst Zündel, was engaged in a discriminatory practise when he caused to be communicated, via the World Wide Web and the Internet, material that was likely to expose Jews to hatred and contempt. It is alleged that, by posting material on the Zundelsite the Respondent has caused the repeated telephonic communication of hate messages. * * *

In proceeding with this analysis it is important to begin with the proposition that §13(1) aims at controlling messages that are likely to expose individuals to hatred and contempt, within a realm that is open to Parliament to control, that is, facilities of a telecommunication undertaking. The Canadian Human Rights Act, at its foundation, assumes that individuals are equal, that groups are equal, and that mere membership in a religious, ethnic, or racial group does not carry with it any positive or negative characteristics and should not be the basis for a generalized prejudice hatred or contempt. * * *

In our opinion, changes in technology that alter and expand the means of telephonic communication cannot diminish the importance of the purpose found in §13(1) to prevent messages of hatred and contempt directed at identifiable groups that undermine the dignity and self-worth of those individuals. The Internet, as a technology, is capable of purveying and transmitting the same kind of hate messages restrained under §13(1). * * *

We conclude therefore that while the Internet introduces a different context from the traditional use of the telephone, * * * Parliament's intent to prevent serious harms caused by hate propaganda remains a matter of pressing and substantial importance * * *. As the new phenomenon of the Internet evolves, perceived at the beginning, as one writer has put it, as being everywhere yet nowhere and as free floating as a cloud, it has become apparent that it too is subject to the rule of law in diverse ways. * * *

As a society, our disapproval of hate messages does not depend narrowly on whether they are found on a telephone-answering device. Parliament has spoken. If the telephone is ideally suited to the effective transmission of prejudicial beliefs as part of a campaign to affect public beliefs and attitudes, how much more effective and ideally suited is the Internet to the efficient transmission of such detrimental beliefs. We see no basis for a distinction based on the facts of this case that would allow us, in a free and democratic society, to withdraw our commitment to protecting minority groups from the intolerance and psychological pain caused by the expression of hate propaganda.

In view of the focused purpose of §13(1) as an instrument of national policy and from the perspective of international commitments, it is, in our view, inappropriate to say that hate propaganda is licit because it has found expression through another medium, the Internet. Once it is accepted that hate propaganda is antithetical to Charter values, the means of expression, in our view, is not a controlling factor so long as it is within the constitutional jurisdiction of Parliament.

Freedom of expression also continues to be impaired as minimally as possible by §13(1). The definition of "hatred", "contempt" and "likely to expose" remains the same and has been found [in previous Canadian Supreme Court cases] not to be overly broad. Since the focus of §13(1) is on "repeated" telephonic messages that are likely to expose persons to hatred or contempt, attention is directed to large scale, public schemes for the dissemination of hate propaganda. The structure of Internet communications makes it especially susceptible to this analysis. It is difficult for us to see why the Internet, with its pervasive influence and accessibility, should be available to spread messages that are likely to expose persons to hatred or contempt. One can conceive that this new medium of the Internet is a much more effective and well-suited vehicle for the dissemination of hate propaganda. * * *

In our view, the use of §13(1) of the Act to deal with hateful telephonic messages on the Internet remains a restriction on the Respondent's freedom of speech which is reasonable and justified in a free and democratic society. * * *

It was suggested during the course of the hearing that a cease and desist order issued against the Respondent would have virtually no effect in eliminating this material from the World Wide Web. * * * One of the unique features of the Internet is the ease with which strangers to the creator of a particular site can access material and, if they choose, replicate the entire site at another web address. The evidence before us supports the contention that "mirror" sites already exist that duplicate in their totality the material currently found on the Zundelsite. We also accept that some individuals, in an attempt to rebuff efforts to limit speech or regulate the Internet, might be prompted to create mirror sites in direct response to an Order issued by this Tribunal. As there is no evidence that these sites are under the control of Mr. Zündel, it was submitted that even if we find that there has been a contravention of §13(1) of the Act, it would be totally ineffectual to issue a cease and desist order. Notwithstanding any Order that we might issue, the material found on the Zundelsite, which we have determined offends §13(1) of the Act, will remain accessible to anyone in Canada who can find a mirror site. * * *

We are extremely conscious of the limits of the remedial power available in this case. There always exists the possibility that an individual, wholly unrelated to a named respondent, will engage in a similar discriminatory practise. The technology involved in the posting of materials to the Internet, however, magnifies this problem and arguably makes it much easier to avoid the ultimate goal of eliminating the material from telephonic communication.

Nonetheless, as a Tribunal we are charged with the responsibility of determining the complaints referred to us, and then making an Order if we find that the Respondent has engaged in a discriminatory practise. We cannot be unduly influenced in this case by what others might do once we issue our Order. The Commission, or individual complainants, can elect to file other complaints, or respond in any other manner that they consider appropriate should they believe that there has been a further contravention of the Act.

Any remedy awarded by this, or any, Tribunal will inevitably serve a number of purposes: prevention and elimination of discriminatory practises is only one of the outcomes flowing from an Order issued as a consequence of these proceedings. There is also a significant symbolic value in the public denunciation of the actions that are the subject of this complaint. Similarly, there is the potential educative and ultimately larger preventative benefit that can be achieved by open discussion of the principles enunciated in this or any Tribunal decision.

Parliament, on behalf of all Canadians, has determined that the telephonic communication of hate messages is not to be tolerated in our society. In our view, the victims of hate are entitled to obtain the benefit of the full weight of our authority.

We have determined that the Respondent Ernst Zündel has engaged in a discriminatory practise by posting material to his website that is likely to expose Jews to hatred or contempt, and the granting of the remedy requested is warranted and appropriate.

We therefore order that the Respondent, Ernst Zündel, and any other individuals who act in the name of, or in concert with Ernst Zündel cease the discriminatory practise of communicating telephonically or causing to be communicated telephonically by means of the facilities of a telecommunication undertaking within the legislative authority of Parliament, matters of the type * * * found on the Zundelsite, or any other messages of a substantially similar form or content that are likely to expose a person or persons to hatred or contempt by reason of the fact that that person or persons are identifiable on the basis of a prohibited ground of discrimination, contrary to §13(1) of the Canadian Human Rights Act.

Notes and Questions

1. Why is the Canadian Human Rights Tribunal without power to enforce its order? Why doesn't the acknowledged lack of enforcement power deprive the Tribunal of adjudicatory jurisdiction as well?

2. The Tribunal acknowledges it may well be unable to prevent the material on Zündel's site from being disseminated on the Internet. Given that admission, is there any point to issuing the order? What is the "symbolic value" to which the opinion refers? Did the French *Yahoo!* decision have similar symbolic value?

SECTION E. EXTRATERRITORIAL LAW ENFORCEMENT ACTIVITY

We have already considered how the judicial branch addresses concerns about extraterritoriality in deciding whether or not to assert jurisdiction in cases concerning online interaction. But concerns about extraterritoriality also arise when the executive branch—through the exercise of the police power—seeks to "enter" another state in order to investigate its own domestic crimes (or arrest criminals accused of violating its own domestic laws).

Such concerns are present, of course, whenever a state is investigating any crime with an international component. Crimes involving computers, however, add an extra layer of complexity. The fact that the Internet cuts across international borders means that computer-related crimes can easily involve conduct occurring or evidence stored in another jurisdiction; at the same time, the Internet makes it possible for a state to conduct some of its investigatory activities remotely, perhaps interfering with the property or privacy protections of the foreign state but never physically crossing into its territory. The materials below address the international law and domestic law implications of "remote cross-border searches"—that is, a state's use of a computer within its territory to access data physically stored outside of its territory. As you read the materials, think back to the theoretical debate introduced earlier in the chapter. Does the fact that a state may pursue criminal investigations across territorial borders make states' attempts to regulate Internet transactions cutting across borders more or less legitimate? Is it possible to determine where a remote cross-border search occurs, or, as Johnson and Post suggested in a different context, is it true that "[e]fforts to determine 'where' the events in question occur are decidedly misguided, if not altogether futile"? *Supra* p. 69. Is it necessary to assign a geographic location to the search to assess its legality under international or domestic law? And what does the debate over the legality of remote cross-border searches tell us about how jurisdictional rules develop?

Patricia L. Bellia, *Chasing Bits Across Borders*

2001 U. CHI. LEGAL F. 35

Although a state may have jurisdiction to prescribe rules limiting certain extraterritorial conduct, it generally may not enforce its law— whether through actions of its courts or actions of its executive officials— outside of its territory. As the Restatement (Third) of the Foreign Relations Law explains, "A state's law enforcement officers may exercise their functions in the territory of another state only with the consent of the other state, given by duly authorized officials of that state."[40] In the criminal context, then, customary international law generally prohibits law enforcement officials from one country from exercising their functions—such as conducting searches or making arrests—in the territory of another state without that state's permission. * * * States have dealt with this gap between their ability to prescribe laws governing extraterritorial conduct and their ability to investigate such conduct through a variety of legal assistance mechanisms[, including bilateral Mutual Legal Assistance Treaties (MLATs) obligating states to produce persons or evidence located within their territories]. * * * These traditional arrangements, however, are unlikely to prove effective in computer crime investigations.

Although transnational crimes are becoming more common even outside of the computer context, cases in which evidence is primarily located abroad still remain the exception rather than the rule. In computer crime cases, a country with a strong interest in investigating a transaction will often find that crucial evidence is beyond its borders. Indeed, evidence may be stored across international borders even when a crime has no other international element. Consider the simplest case—where law enforcement officials seek to obtain evidence that is stored on a computer. For papers to be useful in crime, they generally must be physically located near the criminal. Electronic information, in contrast, need not be physically stored nearby in order to be useful to a criminal. The physical location of electronic evidence therefore often depends upon the fortuity of network architecture: an American subsidiary of a French corporation may house all of its data on a server that is physically located in France; two Japanese citizens might subscribe to America Online and have their electronic mail stored on AOL's Virginia servers. Alternatively, a criminal might deliberately store files on a foreign server to take advantage of the privacy protections of an off-shore data haven. Traditional cooperative arrangements do not contemplate evidence of domestic crime routinely being found only abroad.

The second problem that law enforcement officials relying on traditional legal assistance arrangements will face is that electronic evidence can so easily be lost or destroyed. Electronic evidence located in one country may be readily accessible to a criminal in another, who can remove, alter, or destroy the evidence with a few keystrokes from thousands of miles away. The United States has defended FBI agents' recent cross-border search of data on Russian servers in part on the ground that data otherwise would have been lost. Even when evidence is not deliberately destroyed, it might be unavailable after a short period. Suppose, for example, that a hacker seeks to extract proprietary information from a corporate computer system linked to the Internet. Investigating officials may find that the attack originates from a computer outside of the United

---

40. Restatement (Third) of the Foreign Relations Law of the United States § 432(2) (1987).

States and may seek information from a foreign internet service provider. The investigating officials may secure the cooperation of foreign officials in contacting the service provider, only to find that the provider's system no longer holds the relevant information. Because traditional cooperative arrangements require time to execute requests for assistance, they are likely to be ineffective with respect to evidence that is fleeting. * * *

The difficulties that law enforcement officials have in coping with electronic evidence have prompted states to move beyond traditional legal assistance arrangements in computer crime cases. * * * Some states claim a unilateral power to search and seize data remotely, without assistance from the country in which the data is stored; the United States recently acknowledged that it exercised such a power in connection with an investigation of a Russian hacking ring. * * *

The starting point for analyzing the legality of unilateral cross-border searches is the principle * * * that one state generally has no power to conduct a law enforcement investigation within the territory of another state without that state's permission. This limitation reflects a well established rule of customary international law. * * * The question is whether a principle generally barring a state from conducting law enforcement activities in another state's territory applies when the investigating officials never physically enter the other state, but rather remotely search or manipulate data found on servers within that state. * * *

[T]he modern conception of territorial sovereignty permits a state to regulate activities having harmful effects wherever the activities occur. At first glance, this approach would seem to suggest that territorial sovereignty likewise empowers a state to protect property or persons within its territory against the actions of a foreign state, even when foreign officials never set foot in the target state's territory. * * * [But] the matter is not so simple. Just as the target state would likely argue that it can legitimately prevent or respond to a foreign state's remote search because of the harm the search would cause within its borders, the searching state would likely argue that its actions are simply a response to conduct occurring in the target state but causing harm within its borders. In other words, the view that states have the power to conduct remote cross-border searches presents a conflict between two claimed sovereignty interests: the interest of the target state in regulating the harm caused by the extraterritorial conduct of the searching state's officials; and the interest of the searching state in regulating the harm giving rise to the search.

* * * How do we resolve this conflict? Do the competing sovereignty claims at issue in cross-border search situations render the general customary international law rule against performing law enforcement activities in the territory of another state inapplicable? We can approach these questions by noting that this same conflict exists when foreign officials physically enter another state to conduct investigative activities. The searching state may believe that international law permits it to regulate certain activities, and the power to enforce its regulations is a

necessary incident to this power even when doing so would interfere with another state's sovereignty. This approach, of course, is not consistent with the distinction typically drawn between a state's jurisdiction to regulate and a state's jurisdiction to enforce; while a state can regulate extraterritorial conduct, it generally cannot take enforcement actions extraterritorially. * * *

[What accounts for the distinction between a state's jurisdiction to regulate and a state's jurisdiction to enforce is that a regulating state's interference with a foreign state's sovereignty is] largely indirect. Nothing prevents a state from adopting its own regulatory scheme and applying it where its sovereignty permits. An extraterritorial regulation may frustrate certain policy goals by forcing private parties within one state's territory to adjust their activities to conform to a foreign state's law. But the primary purpose of such regulation is likely to be the advancement of certain regulatory goals within the regulating state; frustration of the foreign state's policy goals is merely a byproduct of the regulating state's action. The interference with the sovereignty of the state in which the regulated conduct occurs is relatively minor, in the sense that the regulating state's actions are not specifically directed toward interfering with the other state's sovereign interests. [In contrast, when] a foreign state's officials enter a state's territory to perform investigative functions, the interference with sovereignty is in no sense indirect: the investigating state specifically intends to interfere with the target state's ability to exert exclusive control over persons and property within its borders. * * *

There are three potential bases for arguing that a remote cross-border search, like mere regulation, presents only an indirect affront to another state's sovereignty and that states should therefore have more freedom to conduct remote cross-border searches than they do to enter the target state and conduct physical searches. First, it could be argued that a remote search is less invasive than a physical search. It is not clear, however, why this is so. If the sovereignty interest at issue is the target state's power to protect persons and property within its borders, it does not matter whether interference with that power comes from inside or outside of the target state. If this interference were irrelevant to the sovereignty analysis, then a foreign state could, without objection, rely upon persons already legitimately within the target state's territory to conduct its investigative activities. And in the case of a remote cross-border search in which the searching state knows where the data is located, this interference is not merely a byproduct of a policy intended to operate both within and without its borders, but an intentional harm directed at the target state's territory.

Second, in some circumstances it will not be possible for a searching state to know where the data it seeks is located. Even if this observation is correct, it does not lead to the broad conclusion that states are free to engage in cross-border searches in all circumstances; at most, it suggests that an accidental search of data in a foreign state does not have the sort of direct, intended effect on state sovereignty that justifies the distinction between jurisdiction to regulate and jurisdiction to enforce, not that all cross-border searches fail to produce such effects.

Third, the architecture of the internet is such that the location of data may be fortuitous. The target state's interest in protecting persons and property within its borders is therefore likely to be attenuated in some circumstances. A searching state may have a stronger interest in the data than the state in which the data is stored. For example, if two French citizens communicate by e-mail, their communications may be stored in the United States. But it is easy to imagine analogous circumstances in which a foreign state has a much stronger interest in physically acquiring persons or property than the target state has in sheltering such persons or property. For example, a person facing criminal charges in one state may flee to another. Though the second state may have an obligation to return the accused to the first state, the first state's officials are not free to enter the target state's territory merely because of its stronger interest in bringing the accused to justice or because of the target state's lack of interest in sheltering the individual. Relatedly, the possibility that an individual will deliberately store data so as to take advantage of a favorable legal regime does not justify a departure from the customary international rule against conducting searches in the territory of another state. Bank secrecy jurisdictions present similar problems, and states do not take the view that they can physically seize evidence within such jurisdictions merely because of the interest they may have in retrieving the evidence.

This discussion suggests that the customary international law rule against one state conducting investigative activities in another state's territory provides a strong basis for states to object to remote cross-border searches of data within their territory. Of course, it may be that over time states come to accept such searches as legitimate. Customary international law, after all, is formed through the practice of states. But to the extent that states seek to conform their actions to perceptions of applicable international law rules, there is a strong argument that the general rule against conducting investigative activities in the territory of another sovereign applies even when the searching state's officials do not enter the target state's territory, but merely interfere with the target state's power to provide privacy or property protections there.

Jack L. Goldsmith, *The Internet and the Legitimacy of Remote Cross-Border Searches*

2001 U. Chi. Legal F. 103

Does territorial sovereignty limit one nation's ability to search, seize, and freeze data related to a crime that is located in another country where the crime originates? * * *

Begin with some old and simple principles of jurisdiction. Joseph Story famously stated the classical principles of territorial sovereignty as lows. First, "every nation possesses an exclusive sovereignty and isdiction within its own territory."[26] Second,

> no state or nation can, by its laws, *directly* affect, or bind property out of its territory, or bind persons not resident therein . . . . This is a natural consequence of the first proposition; for it would be wholly incompatible with the equality and exclusiveness of the sovereignty of all nations, that any one nation should be at liberty to regulate either persons or things not within its own territory.[27]

The key word here is "directly." Even a territorialist like Story realized that through purely territorial exercises of power, one nation can indirectly regulate persons and property abroad. Indirect regulation works because the regulating nation brings force to bear on persons and property within its territory, and this purely local force (or threat of force) can have effects on behavior abroad. If an offshore person or firm causes local harm from abroad, the local government can indirectly regulate the harmful foreign activity by threatening to seize the offshore firm's local assets. The United States is able to apply its securities laws, antitrust laws, and criminal laws to activities abroad because many offshore entities have a U.S. presence (assets, employees, debts, etc.) that the United States can threaten to seize in response to non-compliance with its regulations. * * *

Nations have always exercised indirect extraterritorial regulation of this sort. They have always exercised territorial power in ways that changed behavior in other nations. Indeed, indirect extraterritorial regulation of this sort is inevitable in a world of decentralized lawmaking and trans-jurisdictional transactions. One nation's regulation of a cross-border transaction will always have consequences in other nations to which the transaction is connected.

What has changed in modern times is not indirect extraterritorial regulation per se, but rather the scope of indirect extraterritorial influence. Throughout modern history, the permissible scope of a nation's extraterritorial influence has expanded pursuant to the following inexorable logic. Technological and related exogenous changes lower the costs of cross-border communication and travel. These changes increase cross-border activity, and make it easier for activity originating in jurisdiction A to have effects (including harmful effects) in jurisdiction B. The government of B, responsible for protecting local interests, takes increasingly aggressive steps within its territory to redress these new local harms from A. These steps expand the indirect extraterritorial effect, in A, of B's purely territorial assertions of authority. The result is a change in our conception of what "territorial sovereignty" permits.

---

26. *See* JOSEPH STORY, COMMENTARIES ON THE CONFLICT OF LAWS, FOREIGN AND DOMESTIC, IN REGARD TO CONTRACTS, RIGHTS AND REMEDIES, AND ESPECIALLY IN REGARD TO MARRIAGES, DIVORCES, WILLS, SUCCESSIONS, AND JUDGMENTS § 18 at 19 (Little, Brown 2d ed 1841).

27. *Id.* at § 20 (emphasis added).

This in a nutshell is the logic and historical pattern of jurisdictional change. Note several important characteristics of this logic. First, changes in technology expand extraterritorial influence in both directions. Both the source nation and the target nation, acting within their territory (where "acting" includes permitting activity within the territory), have increasing influence abroad. Second, the influence of territorial power simultaneously expands and contracts, along different dimensions, through time. In the example above, A at first glance seems empowered by technological change, because activity within it (whether prohibited or authorized by A's government) increasingly has effects abroad. For the same reason, B initially seems weakened by technological change. But B fights back with its own in-state acts, and these acts, in part facilitated by the technological change that has increased cross-border activity in the first place, has heightened extraterritorial effects in A. In both directions, technological change alters the extraterritorial influence of purely territorial action. * * *

[C]onsider an example that clearly involves enforcement jurisdiction and is directly analogous to remote cross-border searches on the internet. At one time, the United States refused to order firms with a U.S. presence to disclose documents abroad [in response to a grand jury subpoena] if doing so violated foreign bank secrecy law. These courts reasoned that such disclosure orders exceeded the limits of enforcement jurisdiction and were inconsistent with international comity. U.S. courts began to change their tune, however, in the face of technological changes that made it easier to avoid liability for local harms by transferring and hiding illegal funds and transactions in banks and institutions abroad. Many U.S. courts have ordered a U.S. branch office to disclose documents in a parent or branch abroad, even if doing so violates foreign law. Such orders are obeyed because of the court's credible threat to seize or fine local assets. These judicial orders clearly have the direct and immediate effect of revealing information from abroad, even though the court's power technically extends only to its territorial border. * * *

[W]e can add a different but related [example] that also sheds light on cross-border internet searches. Nations have long gathered information located in other nations without physically entering the territory of those nations. For hundreds of years, ships on the high seas have used binoculars, spyglasses, telescopes, and periscopes to learn what's going on inside a country. Balloon aerial surveillance dates to the French revolution, and was frequently employed in the American Civil War. Airplane reconnaissance dates to the 1911 Italo-Turkish War, and remains an important means of cross-border surveillance. During the last fifty years the United States has made tens of thousands of flights in international air space to gather reconnaissance information inside other countries. At least half a dozen countries (not to mention scores of private firms) employ orbital reconnaissance satellites to monitor activities within other countries. The most sophisticated of these satellites can distinguish objects that are as small as six inches, and digital data provided by these satellites can be further manipulated by local computers to provide even more detailed three-dimensional images. * * *

With these examples and principles in mind, we return to remote cross-border searches on the internet. Many analogize these cross-border searches to physical invasion of police forces into another territory. But the analogy is not persuasive. Such searches are, instead, better analogized to the grand jury orders and spy techniques outlined above. Cross-border searches and seizures are like grand jury orders because they leverage power in the United States to achieve disclosure of information abroad. And they are like spy techniques because they use a universal medium to observe events in another country. Seen this way, remote cross-border searches fit into the long-accepted practice of officials in one nation acting within their territory (or from public spaces) to extract information from another.

These analogies are not perfect, of course. The costs of cross-border internet searches are lower than many other exercises of extraterritorial influence. As a result, one might worry that the potential for abuse in the se of internet cross-border searches and seizures is higher than more traditional counterparts, like grand jury orders. The point so far has been simply to show that international law principles of enforcement jurisdiction do not clearly prohibit such searches, and that the concept of "territorial sovereignty" by itself does little, if any, analytical work in determining the validity of such searches under international law. There is little doubt that if such searches prove necessary to redress cross-border internet attacks, international law will adapt to permit them in some circumstances. As we have seen, the history of international jurisdiction is one of the law accommodating the nations' felt needs to take steps within their borders to redress local harms caused from abroad that cannot otherwise be addressed.

Notes and Questions

1. On what grounds might a state object to another state's remote cross-border investigative activities? Suppose that a state lacks privacy or property protections that prohibit such activities. Could the searched state still object? Are state sovereignty concerns implicated?

2. Return to the materials in Section A of this chapter setting forth the theoretical debate over whether states can and should regulate Internet activities. What views about the relationship between state power and territory underlie the different positions in that debate? What light do these views shed on the permissible scope of enforcement activities?

3. Consider Professor Post's arguments that a state cannot control the flow of data across its borders and that a state generally should not apply its laws to extraterritorial Internet conduct, even if that conduct causes local harm. How, if at all, does a remote cross-border search differ from other forms of extraterritorial conduct that Post believes states should not regulate?

4. In his discussion of enforcement jurisdiction, Professor Goldsmith acknowledges a change in "the scope of extraterritorial influence" that results

in "a change in our conception of what 'territorial sovereignty' permits." Are Professor Goldsmith's positions on prescriptive jurisdiction and enforcement jurisdiction consistent? How might you reconcile them?

5. The excerpts above reflect disagreement over whether a remote cross-border search has "direct" or "indirect" effects on persons and property within the searched state. Which view is more persuasive? Although the authors disagree over where the line between direct and indirect effects should be drawn, both attach legal significance to that line. Do you agree that the legality of a cross-border search should depend on where this line is drawn? Recall the personal jurisdiction discussion in Section B above. In what ways is the determination of whether a cross-border search is a direct or an indirect affront to sovereignty similar to the inquiry into whether a website owner has "targeted" a particular jurisdiction? What other approaches could be taken to assess the legality of cross-border searches?

6. Professor Goldsmith argues that remote cross-border searches are analogous to grand jury orders, because "they leverage power in the United States to achieve disclosure of information abroad," and analogous to spy techniques, because they "use a universal medium to observe events in another country." Are these analogies persuasive? Why or why not?

7. Professor Bellia suggests that remote cross-border searches are less problematic if the searching state does not know where the data it seeks is located. Is this argument persuasive? Why or why not?

However one views remote cross-border searches as a matter of international law, such searches also raise a difficult question of U.S. law. The Fourth Amendment to the U.S. Constitution constrains the manner in which U.S. officials conduct searches within U.S. borders. In particular, if an individual has a reasonable expectation of privacy in certain data and no exigent circumstances are present, U.S. officials generally can search that data only after obtaining a warrant issued by a neutral and detached magistrate based on probable cause to believe that the data reflects evidence of a crime. If U.S. officials situated within the United States remotely search or seize data that is physically located in another country, does the Fourth Amendment similarly limit their conduct?

United States v. Verdugo-Urquidez

Supreme Court of the United States, 1990
494 U.S. 259

CHIEF JUSTICE REHNQUIST delivered the opinion of the Court.

The question presented by this case is whether the Fourth Amendment applies to the search and seizure by United States agents of property that is owned by a nonresident alien and located in a foreign country. We hold that it does not.

Respondent Rene Martin Verdugo-Urquidez is a citizen and resident of Mexico. He is believed by the United States Drug Enforcement Agency (DEA) to be one of the leaders of a large and violent organization in Mexico that smuggles narcotics into the United States. Based on a complaint charging respondent with various narcotics-related offenses, the Government obtained a warrant for his arrest on August 3, 1985. In January 1986, Mexican police officers, after discussions with United States marshals, apprehended Verdugo-Urquidez in Mexico and transported him to the United States Border Patrol station in Calexico, California. There, United States marshals arrested respondent and eventually moved him to a correctional center in San Diego, California, where he remains incarcerated pending trial. Following respondent's arrest, Terry Bowen, a DEA agent assigned to the Calexico DEA office, decided to arrange for searches of Verdugo-Urquidez's Mexican residences located in Mexicali and San Felipe. * * * DEA agents working in concert with [Mexican officers] searched respondent's properties in Mexicali and San Felipe and seized certain documents. * * *

The District Court granted respondent's motion to suppress evidence seized during the searches, concluding that the Fourth Amendment applied to the searches and that the DEA agents had failed to justify searching respondent's premises without a warrant. A divided panel of the Court of Appeals for the Ninth Circuit affirmed[,] * * * conclud[ing] that "[t]he Constitution imposes substantive constraints on the federal government, even when it operates abroad." * * * Having concluded that the Fourth Amendment applied to the searches of respondent's properties, the court went on to decide that the searches violated the Constitution because the DEA agents failed to procure a search warrant. Although recognizing that "an American search warrant would be of no legal validity in Mexico," the majority deemed it sufficient that a warrant would have "substantial constitutional value in this country," because it would reflect a magistrate's determination that there existed probable cause to search and would define the scope of the search. * * *

The Fourth Amendment provides:

"The right of the people to be secure in their persons, houses, papers, and effects, against unreasonable searches and seizures, shall not be violated, and no Warrants shall issue, but upon probable cause, supported by Oath or affirmation, and particularly describing the place to be searched, and the persons or things to be seized."

That text, by contrast with the Fifth and Sixth Amendments, extends its reach only to "the people." Contrary to the suggestion of *amici curiae* that the Framers used this phrase "simply to avoid [an] awkward rhetorical redundancy," "the people" seems to have been a term of art employed in select parts of the Constitution. The Preamble declares that the Constitution is ordained and established by "the People of the United States." The

Second Amendment protects "the right of the people to keep and bear Arms," and the Ninth and Tenth Amendments provide that certain rights and powers are retained by and reserved to "the people." See also U.S. Const., Amdt. 1 ("Congress shall make no law . . . abridging . . . *the right of the people* peaceably to assemble") (emphasis added). While this textual exegesis is by no means conclusive, it suggests that "the people" protected by the Fourth Amendment, and by the First and Second Amendments, and to whom rights and powers are reserved in the Ninth and Tenth Amendments, refers to a class of persons who are part of a national community or who have otherwise developed sufficient connection with this country to be considered part of that community. * * *

What we know of the history of the drafting of the Fourth Amendment also suggests that its purpose was to restrict searches and seizures which might be conducted by the United States in domestic matters. * * * The available historical data show * * * that the purpose of the Fourth Amendment was to protect the people of the United States against arbitrary action by their own Government; it was never suggested that the provision was intended to restrain the actions of the Federal Government against aliens outside of the United States territory. * * *

To support his all-encompassing view of the Fourth Amendment, respondent points to language from the plurality opinion in *Reid v. Covert*, 354 U.S. 1 (1957). *Reid* involved an attempt by Congress to subject the wives of American servicemen to trial by military tribunals without the protection of the Fifth and Sixth Amendments. The Court held that it was unconstitutional to apply the Uniform Code of Military Justice to the trials of the American women for capital crimes. Four Justices "reject[ed] the idea that when the United States acts *against citizens* abroad it can do so free of the Bill of Rights." *Id.*, at 5 (emphasis added). The plurality went on to say:

"The United States is entirely a creature of the Constitution. Its power and authority have no other source. It can only act in accordance with all the limitations imposed by the Constitution. When the Government reaches out to punish *a citizen* who is abroad, the shield which the Bill of Rights and other parts of the Constitution provide to protect his life and liberty should not be stripped away just because he happens to be in another land." *Id.*, at 5-6 (emphasis added; footnote omitted).

Respondent urges that we interpret this discussion to mean that federal officials are constrained by the Fourth Amendment wherever and against whomever they act. But the holding of *Reid* stands for no such sweeping proposition: it decided that United States citizens stationed abroad could invoke the protection of the Fifth and Sixth Amendments. The concurrences by Justices Frankfurter and Harlan in *Reid* resolved the case on much narrower grounds than the plurality and declined even to hold that United States citizens were entitled to the full range of constitutional protections in all overseas criminal prosecutions. * * * Since respondent is not a United States citizen, he can derive no comfort from the *Reid* holding.

Verdugo-Urquidez also relies on a series of cases in which we have held that aliens enjoy certain constitutional rights. These cases, however, establish only that aliens receive constitutional protections when they have come within the territory of the United States and developed substantial connections with this country. Respondent is an alien who has had no previous significant voluntary connection with the United States, so these cases avail him not.

JUSTICE STEVENS' concurrence in the judgment takes the view that even though the search took place in Mexico, it is nonetheless governed by the requirements of the Fourth Amendment because respondent was "lawfully present in the United States . . . even though he was brought and held here against his will." But this sort of presence—lawful but involuntary—is not of the sort to indicate any substantial connection with our country. The extent to which respondent might claim the protection of the Fourth Amendment if the duration of his stay in the United States were to be prolonged—by a prison sentence, for example—we need not decide. When the search of his house in Mexico took place, he had been present in the United States for only a matter of days. We do not think the applicability of the Fourth Amendment to the search of premises in Mexico should turn on the fortuitous circumstance of whether the custodian of its nonresident alien owner had or had not transported him to the United States at the time the search was made.

The Court of Appeals found some support for its holding in our decision in *INS v. Lopez-Mendoza*, 468 U.S. 1032 (1984), where a majority of Justices assumed that the Fourth Amendment applied to illegal aliens in the United States. * * * Even assuming such aliens would be entitled to Fourth Amendment protections, their situation is different from respondent's. The illegal aliens in *Lopez-Mendoza* were in the United States voluntarily and presumably had accepted some societal obligations; but respondent had no voluntary connection with this country that might place him among "the people" of the United States. * * *

We think that the text of the Fourth Amendment, its history, and our cases discussing the application of the Constitution to aliens and extraterritorially require rejection of respondent's claim. At the time of the search, he was a citizen and resident of Mexico with no voluntary attachment to the United States, and the place searched was located in Mexico. Under these circumstances, the Fourth Amendment has no application. For better or for worse, we live in a world of nation-states in which our Government must be able to "functio[n] effectively in the company of sovereign nations." *Perez v. Brownell*, 356 U.S. 44, 57 (1958). Some who violate our laws may live outside our borders under a regime quite different from that which obtains in this country. Situations threatening to important American interests may arise half-way around the globe, situations which in the view of the political branches of our

Government require an American response with armed force. If there are to be restrictions on searches and seizures which occur incident to such American action, they must be imposed by the political branches through diplomatic understanding, treaty, or legislation.

JUSTICE KENNEDY, concurring.

I cannot place any weight on the reference to "the people" in the Fourth Amendment as a source of restricting its protections. With respect, I submit these words do not detract from its force or its reach. Given the history of our Nation's concern over warrantless and unreasonable searches, explicit recognition of "the right of the people" to Fourth Amendment protection may be interpreted to underscore the importance of the right, rather than to restrict the category of persons who may assert it. The restrictions that the United States must observe with reference to aliens beyond its territory or jurisdiction depend, as a consequence, on general principles of interpretation, not on an inquiry as to who formed the Constitution or a construction that some rights are mentioned as being those of "the people."

I take it to be correct, as the plurality opinion in *Reid v. Covert* sets forth, that the Government may act only as the Constitution authorizes, whether the actions in question are foreign or domestic. See 354 U.S., at 6. But this principle is only a first step in resolving this case. The question before us then becomes what constitutional standards apply when the Government acts, in reference to an alien, within its sphere of foreign operations. * * * [W]e must interpret constitutional protections in light of the undoubted power of the United States to take actions to assert its legitimate power and authority abroad. * * * Justice Harlan made this observation in his opinion concurring in the judgment in *Reid v. Covert:*

> "I cannot agree with the suggestion that every provision of the Constitution must always be deemed automatically applicable to American citizens in every part of the world. * * * [T]here is no rigid and abstract rule that Congress, as a condition precedent to exercising power over Americans overseas, must exercise it subject to all the guarantees of the Constitution, no matter what the conditions and considerations are that would make adherence to a specific guarantee altogether impracticable and anomalous." 354 U.S., at 74.

The conditions and considerations of this case would make adherence to the Fourth Amendment's warrant requirement impracticable and anomalous. * * * [T]he Constitution does not require United States agents to obtain a warrant when searching the foreign home of a nonresident alien. If the search had occurred in a residence within the United States, I have little doubt that the full protections of the Fourth Amendment would apply. But that is not this case. The absence of local judges or magistrates available to issue warrants, the differing and perhaps unascertainable conceptions of reasonableness and privacy that prevail abroad, and the need to cooperate with foreign officials all indicate that the Fourth Amendment's warrant requirement should not apply in Mexico as it does in this country.

For this reason, in addition to the other persuasive justifications stated by the Court, I agree that no violation of the Fourth Amendment has occurred in the case before us. The rights of a citizen, as to whom the United States has continuing obligations, are not presented by this case.

JUSTICE STEVENS, concurring in the judgment.

In my opinion aliens who are lawfully present in the United States are among those "people" who are entitled to the protection of the Bill of Rights, including the Fourth Amendment. Respondent is surely such a person even though he was brought and held here against his will. I therefore cannot join the Court's sweeping opinion. I do agree, however, with the Government's submission that the search conducted by the United States agents with the approval and cooperation of the Mexican authorities was not "unreasonable" as that term is used in the first Clause of the Amendment. I do not believe the Warrant Clause has any application to searches of noncitizens' homes in foreign jurisdictions because American magistrates have no power to authorize such searches. I therefore concur in the Court's judgment.

[Dissenting opinions of Justice Brennan and Justice Blackmun omitted.]

Notes and Questions

1. *Verdugo* makes clear that U.S. officials can conduct a search in a foreign country without meeting Fourth Amendment requirements if the searched party lacks any substantial, voluntary connection to the United States. Should the Fourth Amendment apply when U.S. officials search the foreign property of a person who does have a substantial connection, such as a citizen or resident alien? If the Fourth Amendment does apply, does it require officials to obtain a warrant based on probable cause, or merely to act reasonably? Who would have the power to issue such a warrant? If the Fourth Amendment would require only reasonableness, is reasonableness to be determined by compliance with foreign law or by some other standard? For cases considering these questions, see *United States v. Barona*, 56 F.3d 1087 (9th Cir. 1995); *United States v. Juda*, 46 F.3d 961 (9th Cir. 1995); *United States v. Peterson*, 812 F.2d 486 (9th Cir. 1987); *Berlin Democratic Club v. Rumsfeld*, 410 F. Supp. 114 (D.D.C. 1976); *Powell v. Zuckert*, 366 F.2d 634 (D.C. Cir. 1966).

2. Should American officials be required to obey the U.S. Constitution no matter where in the world they act? Consider *United States v. Tiede*, 86 F.R.D. 227 (U.S. Ct. Berlin 1979). In that case, a foreign national accused of hijacking a Polish aircraft abroad was tried under German substantive law in Berlin in a court created by the United States. The U.S. court held that, despite the use of German substantive law, the foreign national was entitled to a jury trial as a matter of U.S. constitutional right because the U.S. court must act in accordance with the Constitution even when situated beyond U.S. territorial borders. According to the court, "[i]t is a first principle of American life—not only life at home but life abroad—that everything American public officials do is governed by, measured against, and must be authorized by the United States

Constitution." *Id.* at 244; *see also DKT Memorial Fund Ltd. v. Agency for Int'l Dev.*, 887 F.2d 275, 307-308 (D.C. Cir. 1989) (R.B. Ginsburg, J., concurring in part and dissenting in part) ("[J]ust as our flag carries its message . . . both at home and abroad, so does our Constitution and the values it expresses") (citation and internal quotation marks omitted); *cf. United States v. Balsys*, 524 U.S. 666, 701-02 (1998) (Ginsburg, J., dissenting) (expressing view that "the Fifth Amendment privilege against self-incrimination prescribes a rule of conduct generally to be followed by our Nation's officialdom," and "should command the respect of United States interrogators, whether the prosecution reasonably feared by the examinee is domestic or foreign.").

3. Among the arguments advanced in *Verdugo* for not applying the warrant requirement to U.S. searches wholly conducted abroad is that no U.S. court can issue or supervise the execution of such a warrant. Do the same concerns apply in the case of a remote cross-border search launched from the United States?

4. Is the *Verdugo* exception to the application of Fourth Amendment principles useful in the context of computer searches? How should U.S. officials seeking data proceed if they cannot determine where the data is located, or whether a suspect has a substantial voluntary connection with the United States? Moreover, if *Verdugo* holds that the Fourth Amendment does not apply to a search occurring outside of U.S. borders, does the legality of a cross-border search as a matter of domestic law turn on assigning a physical location to the search? Consider the following case.

United States v. Gorshkov

United States District Court for the Western District of Washington, 2001
2001 WL 1024026

COUGHENOUR, J.

This matter comes before the Court on Defendant's Motion to Suppress Seized Computer Data. * * * Following an extensive national investigation of a series of computer hacker intrusions into the computer systems of businesses in the United States emanating from Russia, Alexey Ivanov was identified as one of the intruders. Around June, 2000, the FBI set up Invita, a "sting" computer security company in Seattle. On or about November 10, 2000, Mr. Ivanov, along with his "business partner," Defendant Vasiliy Gorshkov, flew from Russia to Sea-Tac.

In Seattle, the two men met with undercover FBI agents at the Invita office. * * * During the meeting and at the behest of the FBI, Defendant Gorshkov used an FBI IBM Thinkpad computer ("IBM") ostensibly to demonstrate his computer hacking and computer security skills and to access his computer system, "tech.net.ru," in Russia. After the meeting and demonstration, both Gorshkov and Ivanov were arrested. Following the Defendants' arrest, without Defendant Gorshkov's knowledge or consent, the FBI searched and seized the IBM and all key strokes made by the Defendant while he used it, by means of a "sniffer" program which allowed the FBI to track and store the information. The FBI thereby obtained the Defendant's computer user name and password that he had used to access the Russian computer.

Armed with this information the FBI logged onto the subject computer(s) located in Russia. Faced with the possibility that a confederate of the defendant could destroy the files in the Russian computer, the FBI decided to download the file contents of the subject computer(s). This was done without reading same until after a search warrant was obtained. * * *

The * * * issue is whether the FBI violated the Fourth Amendment by using the password to access the Russian computers and downloading the data. The Court finds that the Fourth Amendment was inapplicable to the accessing of the Russian computer and the downloading of the data. Moreover, the Court determines that even if the accessing of the Russian computers and the downloading of the data was a search and seizure for purposes of the Fourth Amendment, the FBI's actions were reasonable under the exigent circumstances and therefore no constitutional violation occurred.

1.   *Fourth Amendment Does Not Apply*

The use of the password to access the Russian computers and download the data did not constitute a Fourth Amendment violation. The Fourth Amendment does not apply to the agents' extraterritorial access to computers in Russia and their copying of data contained thereon. First, the Russian computers are not protected by the Fourth Amendment because they are property of a non-resident and located outside the territory of the United States. Under *United States v. Verdugo-Urquidez*, 494 U.S. 259 (1990), the Fourth Amendment does not apply to a search or seizure of a non-resident alien's property outside the territory of the United States. In this case, the computers accessed by the agents were located in Russia, as was the data contained on those computers that the agents copied. Until the copied data was transmitted to the United States, it was outside the territory of this country and not subject to the protections of the Fourth Amendment.

Defendant attempts to distinguish *Verdugo* by first noting that the defendant in that case was found not to have significant contacts with the United States because he involuntarily entered the country after his arrest, while in this case Defendant Gorshkov voluntarily entered the country. The Court finds, however, that a single entry into the United States that is made for a criminal purpose is hardly the sort of voluntary association with this country that should qualify Defendant as part of our national community for purposes of the Fourth Amendment. * * *

2.   *Even if the Fourth Amendment Applied, the Search and Seizure Were Reasonable*

Even if the Fourth Amendment were to apply to the Government's actions, the Court finds that those actions were reasonable under all of the circumstances and therefore met Fourth Amendment requirements. The Supreme Court recently stated "We have found no case in which this Court has held unlawful a temporary seizure that was supported by probable cause and was designed to prevent the loss of evidence while the police diligently obtained a warrant in a reasonable period of time." *Illinois v. McArthur*, 531 U.S. 326, 334 (2001). In *McArthur*, the Court held that it was "reasonable"—and thus consistent with the Fourth Amendment—for police to prevent someone from entering his trailer home until a search warrant could be obtained, based on the risk that evidence might be destroyed otherwise. In the context of pressing or urgent law enforcement needs such as exigent circumstances, the Fourth Amendment requires courts to "balance the privacy-related and law enforcement related concerns to determine if the intrusion was reasonable." *Id.* at 331. * * *

[I]n the present case[,] [t]he Government's agents had probable cause to believe that the Russian computers contained evidence of crimes. The agents had good reason to fear that if they did not copy the data, Defendant's coconspirators would destroy the evidence, or make it unavailable before any assistance could be obtained from Russian authorities. The agents made "reasonable efforts" to reconcile their needs with Defendant's privacy interest by copying the data, without altering it or examining its contents until a search warrant could be obtained. Finally, the agents imposed no "restraint" on Defendant's data, and obtained a search warrant as soon as diplomatic notification was made to Russia's government. Therefore, under the law of the Fourth Amendment, because the agents were acting under exigent circumstances, the agents' actions in accessing the Russian computers and downloading the data without a warrant were fully legal and the evidence should not be suppressed.

Notes and Questions

1. The *Gorshkov* court rejects the defendant's attempt to distinguish *Verdugo* on the ground that Verdugo's presence in the United States was involuntary. Is the court's reasoning persuasive? What constitutes a sufficient voluntary connection with the United States to trigger the application of the Fourth Amendment?

2. Even if Gorshkov lacked any substantial connection to the United States, why wasn't the presence of U.S. officials within U.S. borders enough to trigger the Fourth Amendment, even if their actions were directed at the foreign state?

3. Assume that in the Gorshkov investigation U.S. officials had reviewed the Russian data, rather than merely collecting it and applying for a warrant. Would the result in the case have been the same? Why or why not?

4. The *Gorshkov* court sustains the collection of data in the absence of a warrant based in part on a theory of exigent circumstances—that data would have been lost if officials had not secured it. If electronic evidence is by its nature capable of being disposed of quickly, are there any limits on the applicability of the exigent circumstances exception in computer investigations?

5. As in the debate over the legality of cross-border searches under international law, it is difficult to determine precisely where a cross-border

search occurs—in the territory from which the search is launched, or in the territory in which the search's effects are felt. Do the different conceptions of the relationship between power and territory discussed earlier in this chapter shed any light on this question? Is it necessary to determine where the search occurs in order to assess its legality?

6. In 2001, the Committee of Ministers of the Council of Europe, with the United States participating as an observer, adopted a Convention on Cyber-Crime containing extensive procedural provisions addressing states' obligations to exchange data physically located within their borders. Among other things, the Convention would require states to "adopt such legislative and other measures as may be necessary to enable its competent authorities to order or similarly obtain the expeditious preservation" of stored computer data in response to a request from a foreign state. Council of Europe Committee of Ministers, 109th Sess., Convention on Cyber-Crime art. 29 (opened for signature Nov. 23, 2001). Will such provisions eliminate the need for states to engage in remote cross-border searches?

The Convention contains limited provisions authorizing remote cross-border searches, specifically in the case of "open-source" (publicly available) data and data the searching state obtains the lawful consent to search. *Id.* art. 32. Assume that continuing concerns about the legality of remote cross-border searches prompt states to incorporate broader cross-border search provisions into future multilateral and bilateral arrangements. Are there any domestic law constraints on the United States' entry into such arrangements? For example, could the United States permit a foreign state to conduct a search of data located within the United States based on foreign law standards lower than those of the Fourth Amendment? For a discussion of this issue, see Patricia L. Bellia, *Chasing Bits Across Borders*, 2001 U. CHI. LEGAL F. 35, 80-99.

SECTION F. A CASE STUDY IN THE INTERNATIONALIZATION OF LEGAL REGIMES: GOVERNING THE DOMAIN NAME SYSTEM

Having spent this chapter exploring issues of geography, sovereignty, and various possible forms of governance in the online context, we conclude with a case study. The system of domain names provides the crucial "address book" of the Internet, matching hard-to-remember strings of digits with easier-to-remember names. In the early years of the Internet, the task of administering the system could be performed by a single computer programmer. By the early to mid-1990s, however, as corporations and entrepreneurs began to understand the potential value of a recognizable domain name, pressure increased to create trademark rights in domain names and to develop a more bureaucratized forum for administering the system. In this concluding section, we consider each of these efforts in turn and we explore the problem of extraterritorial (or nonterritorial) governance that have resulted.

1. An Introduction to the Domain Name System

Computers connected to the Internet are identified by unique, 32-bit numbers known as Internet Protocol (IP) addresses. Such addresses are usually represented as four sets of numbers, converted into decimal form and separated by periods, such as 129.74.0.1. Because these addresses are somewhat cumbersome, researchers developed a way for IP addresses to be associated with alphanumeric "domain names."

The domain name system (DNS) essentially creates a hierarchical name structure. At the top level of that structure are "top-level" or "first-level" domains, often referred to as TLDs. Examples of TLDs include the familiar generic TLDs, such as .com, .org., .edu, and .net, as well as country code TLDs, such as .us, .uk, and .fr. Within every TLD, there are large numbers of "second-level" domains. Although every second-level domain name within a particular TLD must be unique, there can be duplication across TLDs. Within particular second-level domains, there can be third-level domains, and so on. Although up to 127 levels are possible, it is rare for a domain name to have more than four levels. In any domain name, the left-most portion is the "host" name, which specifies a machine with a particular IP address. In the example www.yahoo.com, ".com" is the top-level domain, "yahoo" is the second-level domain, and "www" identifies a particular web server within the yahoo.com domain.

For domain names to be useful, of course, there must be a means of translating domain names into corresponding IP addresses. That translation function is performed by machines known as "domain name servers," which are part of a distributed database that replicates the structure of the domain name system itself. At the top of the hierarchy are thirteen "root servers," each of which holds a list of IP addresses of domain name servers that contain authoritative information for each of the TLDs. In turn, the TLD name servers hold lists of IP addresses for domain name servers containing authoritative information for the second-level domains within that TLD.

Every time an Internet-connected computer needs to resolve a domain name into an IP address, its client software queries a default local domain name server. Assume the user wishes to connect to the site "www.yahoo.com." The local domain name server checks its cache to determine whether it already holds the IP address corresponding to the particular domain name; if not, it queries another domain name server. The local domain name server contains a file holding the IP addresses of each of the root servers. The local domain name server can query one of the root servers to find the IP address of a name server that holds authoritative information for the .com domain. Once the local server receives that information, it queries the .com name server to find the IP address of a second-level domain name server holding authoritative information for the yahoo.com domain. It then contacts that second-level domain name server, which returns the IP address for the host machine www.yahoo.com. The diagram below represents this process graphically:

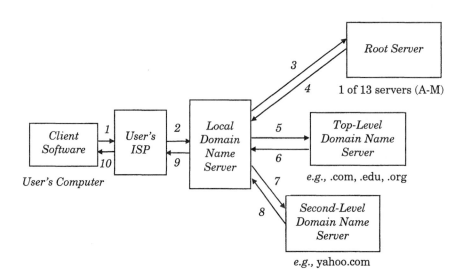

Process of Resolving a Domain Name into an IP Address.

As a practical matter, in most cases a local domain name server need not consult the root server first. When a local domain name server contacts the root server for the first time, and the root server returns the IP address of the .com name server, the local domain name server caches the address of that server. Thus, a local domain name server moves through the domain name servers in its cache before consulting the root server.

With regard to trademarks in domain names, the structure of the domain name system is significant for at least two reasons. First, for domain names to be properly resolved into IP addresses, each domain name must be unique. Accordingly, for each domain name level there must be some entity controlling the list of domain names and preventing duplication. For TLDs, the entity controlling the list of domain names is known as the "registry." It is important to distinguish between this single "registry" and the multiple "registrars" that are authorized to register domain names on behalf of users. An individual wishing to reserve a domain name contacts one of these many registrars, and the registrar passes the relevant information on to the single registry for that TLD. The registry for the .com domain name is a Virginia corporation known as VeriSign, the successor to Network Solutions, Inc. (NSI). At one time, NSI was also the sole registrar for the .com TLD. NSI and VeriSign figure prominently in some of cases that follow.

Second, at each level, the ability to modify (or to refuse to modify) the files that contain domain name information is a significant power. For example, if the entity that controls the root servers refuses to add to the file information on a particular country code top-level domain, that domain will be invisible to users. Similarly, the registry that maintains the list of second-level domain names within any TLD has the ability (unconstrained by technology, though perhaps constrained by law) to determine who among parties disputing "ownership" of a domain name is entitled to use the domain name, because the entity maintaining the list essentially decides what second-level domain name servers to "point" to.

2. Domain Names as Trademarks and the Extraterritorial Application of Trademark Law

Historically, the boundaries of trademark law have been delineated in part by reference to physical geography. Thus, if you own a store in Los Angeles called "Sally's," you cannot, as a general matter, prevent a person in Australia from opening a store that is also called "Sally's," even if you have previously established a trademark in the name. The idea is that customers would not be likely to confuse the two stores because they are in markets that are spatially distinct. In the online world such clear spatial boundaries are collapsed because, as the domain name system is currently organized, there can be only one sallys.com domain name, and it can only point to one of the two stores.

As noted previously, the rise of the commercial Internet in the 1990s brought with it increased calls to create trademark rights in domain names. For example, one early Internet domain name dispute involved the Panavision Corporation, which holds a trademark in the name "Panavision." In 1995, Panavision attempted to establish a website with the domain name panavision.com, but found that the name had already been registered to Dennis Toeppen. When contacted by Panavision, Toeppen offered to relinquish the name in exchange for $13,000. Panavision sued, arguing that Toeppen's registration violated trademark law despite the fact that Toeppen's Panavision site (which included photographs of the City of Pana, Illinois) could hardly be confused with the Panavision Corporation. The district court and the Ninth Circuit concluded that Toeppen had violated the Federal Trademark Dilution Act, because Panavision's inability to use the panavision.com website diminished the "'capacity of the Panavision marks to identify and distinguish Panavision's goods and services on the Internet.'" *See Panavision Int'l v. Toeppen*, 141 F.3d 1316 (9th Cir. 1998). In so doing, the court was, in effect, expanding the geographical reach of trademark law, at least with regard to domain names. While you still could not sue Sally's store in Australia for violating your trademark by choosing a confusingly similar name for its store, you might now have a cause of action concerning the sallys.com domain name if the Australian store registered the name ahead of you.

The U.S. Congress subsequently enacted legislation confirming this expansion of trademark law. Under pressure from trademark holders,

Congress passed the Anticybersquatting Consumer Protection Act (ACPA), which provides an explicit federal remedy to combat so-called "cybersquatting." According to the congressional reports, the ACPA is meant to address cases like *Panavision*, where non-trademark holders register well-known trademarks as domain names and then try to "ransom" the names back to the trademark owners.

We take up the question of whether it makes sense to apply trademark law to domain names in Chapter Four. Here we focus on the way in which the application of trademark law to domain names has unmoored trademark law from physical geography. Thus, in the online context, trademark law is now far more likely to operate extraterritorially. Potentially, even those who are legitimately using a website that happens to bear the name of a famous mark held by an entity across the globe could be forced to relinquish the name.[e] In addition, as several commentators have noted, this unmooring of trademarks from territory creates the possibility that individual countries will interpret their trademark laws expansively, thereby reducing trademark rights to their most destructive form: the mutual ability to block (or at least interfere with) the online use of marks recognized in other countries.[f]

Finally, each of the parties claiming ownership in a trademark could sue in a different country and, because of differences in substantive law, each party could win. Thus, with the increasing scope of trademark law in cyberspace, the next question becomes: how shall any domain name decision be enforced?

The federal Anticybersquatting Consumer Protection Act attempts to address this problem. To combat the difficulty of asserting jurisdiction over a distant entity that registers an allegedly infringing domain name, the Act effectively globalizes its scope by providing for *in rem* jurisdiction over the domain name itself. 15 U.S.C. § 1125(d)(2) provides that

> (A) The owner of a mark may file an in rem civil action against a domain name in the judicial district in which the domain name registrar, domain name registry, or other domain name authority that registered or assigned the domain name is located if

---

e. In response to this problem, the World Intellectual Property Organization adopted, in the fall of 2001, a Joint Recommendation calling for a definition of "use" for purposes of trademark law that would protect legitimate users of marks who disclaimed any intent to engage in commerce in a particular country. See Joint Recommendation Concerning Provisions on the Protection of Marks, and Other Industrial Property Rights in Signs, on the Internet (Sep. 24-Oct. 3, 2001), *available at* http://www.wipo.org/about-ip/en/index.html?wipo_content_frame=/about-ip/en/trademarks.html.

f. *See*, e.g., Graeme Dinwoodie, *Private International Aspects of the Protection of Trademarks* (2001) (WIPO Doc. No. WIPO/PIL/01/4); Catherine T. Struve & R. Polk Wagner, *Realspace Sovereigns in Cyberspace: Problems with the Anticybersquatting Consumer Protection Act*, 17 BERKELEY TECH. L.J. 989 (2002).

(i) the domain name violates any right of the owner of a mark registered in the Patent and Trademark Office, or protected under subsection (a) or (c); and

(ii) the court finds that the owner—

(I) is not able to obtain in personam jurisdiction over a person who would have been a defendant in a civil action under paragraph (1); or

(II) through due diligence was not able to find a person who would have been a defendant in a civil action under paragraph (1) * * *

(C) In an in rem action under this paragraph, a domain name shall be deemed to have its situs in the judicial district in which

(i) the domain name registrar, registry, or other domain name authority that registered or assigned the domain name is located; or

(ii) documents sufficient to establish control and authority regarding the disposition of the registration and use of the domain name are deposited with the court.

(D)(i) The remedies in an in rem action under this paragraph shall be limited to a court order for the forfeiture or cancellation of the domain name or the transfer of the domain name to the owner of the mark. * * *

The idea is that the disputed property, the domain name, is "located" where it is registered and that this property can form the basis for jurisdiction even if there is insufficient basis for jurisdiction over the defendant personally. Thus, for example, the ACPA permits a trademark owner to file suit in Virginia to recover a domain name registered online with NSI, even if the owner of the domain name has never set foot in Virginia and did not know that NSI was located there. Does such a jurisdictional provision run afoul of the Due Process Clause requirement, articulated in *International Shoe*, that defendants have "minimum contacts" with a state before jurisdiction can be asserted?

Cable News Network L.P. v. Cnnews.com

United States District Court for the Eastern District of Virginia, 2001
162 F. Supp. 2d 484, *aff'd in relevant part*, 2003 WL 152846 (4th Cir. Jan. 27, 2003)

ELLIS, District Judge.

I.

Plaintiff, Cable News Network L.P., L.L.L.P., is a Delaware limited liability limited partnership with its principal place of business in Atlanta, Georgia. It is engaged in the business of providing news and information services throughout the world via a variety of electronic media. It is also the owner of the trademark "CNN," which plaintiff has registered in this country and dozens of others, including China. Since at least 1980, plaintiff has used its registered CNN trademark in connection with providing news and information services to people worldwide through a variety of cable and satellite television networks, private networks, radio networks, websites, and syndicated news services. Some of these services are accessible in China and provided in the Chinese language. Since adopting the CNN mark, plaintiff has used the mark "CNN" in the names of all of its broadcast networks, the best known of which include CNN Headline News, CNN En Espanol, CNNSI, CNNFN, and CNN International. Plaintiff's services are also accessible worldwide via the internet at the domain name "cnn.com." There can be no doubt that plaintiff's CNN mark is famous.

Maya Online Broadband Network (HK) Co. Ltd. ("Maya") is a Chinese company that is a subsidiary of a second Chinese company, Shanghai Online Broadband Network Co. Ltd. On November 12, 1999, Maya's general manager, Heyu Wang, registered the domain name "cnnews.com" with Network Solutions, Inc. ("NSI"), a domain name registrar and registry, located in Herndon, Virginia.

Maya operates the cnnews.com website, which is designed to provide news and information to Chinese-speaking individuals worldwide. This website is part of Maya's comprehensive on-line services system that includes video on demand, broadband services, and a variety of e-business services. The cnnews.com website is one of many sites linked to Maya's main website, cnmaya.com. The "cn" prefix apparently refers to "China," where the characters "cn" are widely used and understood as an abbreviation for the country name "China." The top level Internet domain for China is "cn." Given this, Maya, the respondent in this action, asserts that its choice of the domain name cnnews.com was entirely reasonable and that it did not select or use this domain name in bad faith. And Maya further points out that most people who access the cnnews.com website in China likely have never heard of CNN, as most Chinese citizens lack access to plaintiff's television stations and websites.

Maya asserts that the target audience of its online services, including cnnews.com, is located entirely within China. Maya also asserts that it does not advertise any of its services outside of China, sells no products or services to persons outside of China, does not ship goods outside of China, or accept payments from any source outside of China. In confirmation of these assertions, Maya proffers statistics reflecting that 99.5% of the registered users of Maya's websites are located within Chinese cities. It appears, moreover, that all of Maya's business is conducted in the Chinese language and that it transacts no business in the United States.

Plaintiff acted promptly on discovering that Wang had registered the cnnews.com domain name with NSI and that Maya had posted news information on that site. First, plaintiff notified Wang of its service mark rights and demanded that he transfer the domain name cnnews.com to plaintiff. Plaintiff also warned that it would pursue an ACPA *in rem* action in the Eastern District of Virginia to acquire control over the cnnews.com domain name if he failed to comply. Maya responded to plaintiff's communications with Wang, indicating that it did not intend to comply with plaintiff's demands. Next, plaintiff suggested that Maya change the domain name of its news website to "cn-news.com" and use the new domain name only in Chinese characters. Maya rejected this proposal and plaintiff subsequently filed this complaint. * * *

II.

At the outset, it is necessary to confirm that this action meets the ACPA criteria for an *in rem* action. These criteria, found in 15 U.S.C. §1125(d)(2)(A), make clear that the owner of a mark, like plaintiff, may maintain an *in rem* action against an infringing domain name (i) if the action is brought in the jurisdiction where the registrar or registry of the infringing domain name is located, and (ii) if *in personam* jurisdiction over the registrant does not exist. This action fits squarely within these criteria. The registry for the allegedly infringing domain name is located in this jurisdiction and it is clear on this record that there is no *in personam* jurisdiction over Wang or Maya, the former and current registrants of cnnews.com. Thus, *in rem* jurisdiction is proper.

But the analysis cannot end here, for if it is clear that this action meets the ACPA criteria for an *in rem* action against a domain name, it is less clear that such an action comports with due process in light of *Shaffer v. Heitner*, 433 U.S. 186 (1977). Put another way, the question is whether judicial disposition of an absent registrant's substantive rights to an infringing domain name in an ACPA *in rem* action is consistent with due process.

III.

More than twenty years ago, the Supreme Court, in a close and controversial decision, cast doubt on the constitutionality of certain *in rem* proceedings. *See Shaffer v. Heitner*, 433 U.S. 186 (1977). Properly understood, *Shaffer* is no bar to an ACPA *in rem* action.

In *Shaffer*, the Supreme Court held unconstitutional a Delaware statute that provided *in rem* jurisdiction by allowing the sequestration of stock of a Delaware corporation so as to compel the personal appearance of nonresident corporate managers who owned shares of the stock and were facing a shareholders' derivative lawsuit in Delaware state court. In *Shaffer, in rem* jurisdiction was invoked solely to compel the appearance of the defendants in a matter unrelated to the property upon which *in rem* jurisdiction was based.

To understand *Shaffer*, it is necessary to distinguish three types of *in rem* actions * * * and then to understand *Shaffer's* effect on each type. The first of the three, usually called simply *"in rem"* or "true *in rem*," arises when a court adjudicates the property rights corresponding to a particular *res* for every potential rights holder, whether each rights holder is named in the proceeding or not. ACPA *in rem* actions, including the case at bar, are of the "true *in rem*" genre because they involve the rights of a disputed mark for every potential rights holder. The second type of *in rem* action is the "quasi *in rem*" or "quasi *in rem* I" action, which allocates property rights as against particular named persons. Examples of this type of litigation include actions to remove a cloud on a land title or actions seeking quiet title against another individual's claim. The third type of *in rem* proceeding, "quasi *in rem* II," concerns the rights of a particular person or persons in a thing, but is distinguished from quasi *in rem* I claims because the underlying claim in a quasi *in rem* II matter is unrelated to the *res* that provides jurisdiction. *Shaffer* was a quasi *in rem* II matter because the suit itself (a shareholders' derivative action alleging misconduct against a corporation's directors and officers) was unrelated to the *res* that established jurisdiction (the stock certificates owned by the managers of the corporation).

Shaffer clearly holds that quasi *in rem* II and *in personam* proceedings require the same minimum contacts so as to satisfy due process, as discussed in *International Shoe Co. v. Washington*, 326 U.S. 310, 316 (1945). It is less clear, however, how, if at all, *Shaffer* affects true *in rem* and quasi *in rem* I cases. To be sure, there is language in *Shaffer* that could be read to require that *all in rem* cases conform to the same due process constraints as *in personam* cases. For instance, the *Shaffer* opinion states that "[t]he standard for determining whether an exercise of jurisdiction over the interest of persons is consistent with the Due Process Clause is the minimum-contacts standard elucidated in *International Shoe*." *Shaffer*, 433 U.S. at 207. Some courts, therefore, have held that *Shaffer* commands that all types of *in rem* actions must have the same minimum contacts as required for *in personam* actions. *See, e.g., Fleetboston Financial Corp. v. Fleetbostonfinancial.com*, 138 F. Supp. 2d 121, 133-34 (D. Mass. 2001). Yet, the greater weight of (and more persuasive) authority holds that the language of *Shaffer* requires minimum contacts only for quasi *in rem* II-type cases. * * * Thus, where, as here, the action is properly categorized as "true *in rem*," there is no requirement that the owner or claimant of the *res* have minimum contacts with the forum. More particularly, in an ACPA *in rem* action, it is not necessary that the allegedly infringing registrant have minimum contacts with the forum; it is enough, as here, that the registry is located in the forum.

Notes and Questions

1. Given that nearly all of Maya's business activities are focused on China, is it fair to subject it to suit in Virginia based only on its having registered a domain name using an online form?

2. Does it make sense to treat the domain name registration as property that is "located" in Virginia? Will such a rule permit U.S. courts to adjudicate domain name disputes throughout the world? What if the plaintiff in this case were not CNN, but a Saudi Arabian corporation? Would such a case still appropriately be adjudicated in Virginia?

3. As the *CNN* court recognized, the resolution of this question under American constitutional law probably rests ultimately on whether courts interpret the U.S. Supreme Court's decision in *Shaffer v. Heitner*, 433 U.S. 186 (1977), to have extended the constitutional requirements of *International Shoe* to all *in rem* actions (or at least those that do not involve real property). Some courts read *Shaffer* narrowly, as the *CNN* court does here. For example, the Fourth Circuit subsequently took the same approach, determining that *in rem* jurisdiction, as authorized by the ACPA, is not a violation of the Due Process Clause of the Constitution if "the property itself is the source of the underlying controversy between the plaintiff and defendant," and jurisdiction is assigned "based on the location of the property." *See Porsche Cars North Amer., Inc. v. Porsche.net et al.*, 302 F.3d 248, 260 (4th Cir. 2002). Even some members of the U.S. Supreme Court have read *Shaffer* narrowly. *See Burnham v. Superior Court of California*, 495 U.S. 604, 620-21 (1990) (plurality opinion of Scalia, J.).

On the other hand, dicta in *Shaffer* suggests that the Supreme Court intended its holding to extend the minimum contacts test of *International Shoe* to all assertions of *in rem* jurisdiction, not solely to the subcategory of *in rem* cases specifically at issue. *See, e.g., Shaffer*, 433 U.S. at 212 (stating that, henceforth, "*all* assertions of state-court jurisdiction must be evaluated according to the standards set forth in *International Shoe* and its progeny."); *id.* ("The fiction that an assertion of jurisdiction over property is anything but an assertion of jurisdiction over the owner of the property supports an ancient form without substantial modern justification.") Thus, *Shaffer* may be taken to stand for the proposition that Congress cannot avoid the constitutional requirements of fair play and substantial justice simply by calling an action *in rem*, and by limiting recovery to the *res* itself. The U.S. Supreme Court has not yet resolved the question, although (as noted above) the Fourth Circuit has upheld the constitutionality of the ACPA's *in rem* provisions. *See Harrods, Ltd. v. Sixty Internet Domain Names*, 302 F.3d 214 (4th Cir. 2002).

4. What if South Korea enacted a provision giving its courts jurisdiction to hear any domain name dispute so long as the registrar corporation was South Korean? Assume that Maya's general manager, instead of registering cnnews.com with Network Solutions, used a South Korean registrar. Then, in response to an American court order that the South Korean registrar release the domain name to CNN pursuant to the ACPA, a Korean court issued a contrary order, enjoining the registrar from doing so. Consider the following case, which raises this convoluted scenario.

GlobalSantaFe Corp. v. Globalsantafe.com

United States District Court for the Eastern District of Virginia, 2003
250 F. Supp. 2d 610

ELLIS, District Judge.

Prior to their merger, Global Marine Inc. ("Global Marine") and Santa Fe International Corporation ("Santa Fe") were both involved in the business of contract drilling and related services. Global Marine was a major international offshore drilling contractor, and the world's largest provider of drilling management services, while Santa Fe was a leading international offshore and land contract driller and also provided drilling-related services to the petroleum industry. Since 1958, Global Marine had conducted business under its GLOBAL MARINE mark and in 1969 Global Marine was issued a federal trademark for the mark. While Santa Fe's mark was not registered, the company had used its SANTA FE mark in conducting and promoting its services since 1946, and customers and others came to associate the mark with Santa Fe's services.

On September 3, 2001, Global Marine and Santa Fe publicly announced their agreement to merge into an entity to be known as GlobalSantaFe Corporation. Less than one day later, Jongsun Park registered the domain name <globalsantafe.com> with the Korean registrar Hangang Systems, Inc. ("Hangang"). The domain name was subsequently transferred to Fanmore Corporation, a Korean entity, with Jong Ha Park ("Park") listed as the administrative, billing and technical contact. The web site currently linked to the domain name is simply a placeholder site marked "under construction."

On October 5, 2001, just over one month after the announcement and Jongsun Park's registration of the <globalsantafe.com> domain name, Global Marine and Santa Fe filed this [Anticybersquatting Consumer Protection Act (ACPA)] *in rem* action against the domain name. Service was perfected as required under the ACPA by sending notice of the alleged violation and the pending *in rem* action to the postal and email addresses of the listed registrant and by publishing notice of the action in two Korean newspapers. *See* 15 U.S.C. § 1125(d)(2)(A)(ii)(aa) & (bb). In the meantime, on November 20, 2001, the merger of the two companies became effective, resulting in the publicly traded GlobalSantaFe company with a market value of approximately $6 billion. On November 15, 2001, GlobalSantaFe applied for a federal trademark registration for the GLOBALSANTAFE mark under four separate categories, and those applications are pending. On December 20, 2001 the registrar, Hangang, deposited the registrar certificate for the domain name with the Clerk of this Court, and by doing so "tender[ed] to the Court complete control and authority over the registration" for <globalsantafe.com>, as required by the ACPA, 15 U.S.C. § 1125(d)(2)(D)(i)(I). The registrant failed to appear, either in person or through pleadings, to defend its right to use the domain name.

In response to the registrant's apparent default, * * * this Court * * * ordered * * * both Hangang and VeriSign Global Registry Services ("VeriSign") to "take all appropriate steps to transfer the domain name" to GlobalSantaFe.[9]

---

9. VeriSign, the ".com" registry, is the single entity that maintains all official records worldwide for registrations in the " .com" top level domain, while Hangang, as the registrar for <globalsantafe.com>, is one of several entities that is authorized to register ".com" domain names for registrants.

On April 9, 2002, Park filed an application for an injunction in the District Court of Seoul, Korea, requesting that court to issue an injunction prohibiting Hangang from transferring the domain name as ordered by this Court. The District Court of Seoul provisionally granted this injunction by order dated September 17, 2002, finding that this Court likely lacked jurisdiction over the matter. In light of these proceedings and the Korean court's order, it appears that Hangang has refused to transfer the domain name as directed by Order of this Court. GlobalSantaFe, therefore, now seeks [an] amended judgment, which not only directs Hangang and VeriSign to transfer the domain name, but additionally directs VeriSign, the registry, to cancel the infringing domain name pursuant to the ACPA until the domain name is transferred to GlobalSantaFe. * * *

In rem ACPA suits must meet several jurisdictional requirements. First, the ACPA allows a trademark owner to file an *in rem* action only in specific jurisdictions, namely "in the judicial district in which the domain name registrar, domain name registry, or other domain name authority that registered or assigned the domain name is located." 15 U.S.C. § 1125(d)(2)(A). This statutory requirement is satisfied here because the domain name registry in this case, VeriSign, is located within this district in Dulles, Virginia.

Second, *in rem* actions under the ACPA are appropriate only if there is no personal jurisdiction over the registrant in any district. *See* ACPA, § 1125(d)(2)(A)(ii)(I). This requirement is also plainly met, as there is no evidence that Park or Fanmore have conducted or transacted business in any district in the United States, nor is there any evidence that their actions constitute sufficient minimum contacts to support personal jurisdiction in the United States. *See International Shoe Co. v. Washington,* 326 U.S. 310, 316 (1945). While it is true that the infringing domain name is included in the VeriSign registry, this is not enough to establish minimum contacts; indeed, even if the registrar were also located in this district, the resultant contacts would still be too minimal to support jurisdiction. *See America Online, Inc., et al. v. Huang,* 106 F. Supp.2d 848, 856-58 (E.D. Va. 2000). Nor does the nature of the website operating at <globalsantafe.com> provide a jurisdictional nexus; it is a passive, placeholder site, consisting largely of the notice that the site is "under construction," and therefore is not itself a basis for jurisdiction over the registrant. Thus, there is no personal jurisdiction over Park or Fanmore in this district or, it appears, in any district in this country.

Third, GlobalSantaFe has properly perfected service, as required by the ACPA, by sending notice to the registrant's listed email and postal addresses and by publishing notice in Korean newspapers as directed by Order dated October 23, 2002. *See* 15 U.S.C § 1125(d)(2)(A)(ii)(aa) & (bb).

The substantive merits of GlobalSantaFe's ACPA claim are manifest. * * * [T]he domain name <globalsantafe.com> is confusingly similar to the marks of Global Marine and Santa Fe, and identical to the mark of the merged entity GlobalSantaFe. * * * [T]he record shows that the original registrant clearly registered the <globalsantafe.com> domain name after, and in response to, GlobalSantaFe's use of the GLOBALSANTAFE mark in its merger announcement. Furthermore, there is no indication of any prior use of the GLOBALSANTAFE mark, legitimate or otherwise, by the original registrant, Fanmore, or Park. * * * Thus, the registration of <globalsantafe.com> was in clear violation of the ACPA, and GlobalSantaFe is accordingly entitled to transfer or cancellation of the domain name under § 1125(d)(2)(D)(i).

The [original order] issued on April 1, 2002 directs both VeriSign and Hangang to take all steps necessary to transfer the domain name to plaintiffs within 10 days of receipt of the order. Yet Hangang, the registrar, has not complied with the Order, presumably because it is subject to a Korean court order arising from a case filed by Park shortly after the April 1 Order. It is understandable that the registrar would obey the order of a domestic court despite an order of this court. Notably, while Hangang was named as the defendant in the Korean proceeding, it has not been formally joined as a party in this matter. Further, there is no evidence in the record that Hangang operates in the United States or has sufficient minimum contacts with the United States to satisfy the due process requirements for personal jurisdiction; thus it does not appear on this record that Hangang could be hailed into this Court or any other court in the United States for the purpose of enforcing this Court's order.

* * * Although * * * the registrar and the registrant are beyond the jurisdiction of this Court, the use of the infringing domain name on the Internet will infringe GlobalSantaFe's trademark rights in the United States every time it is accessed here. Furthermore, the operation of the domain name relies on the VeriSign registry, an entity located within this district. Accordingly, the instant motion requests that the Judgment Order be amended to direct VeriSign to take the steps necessary unilaterally to cancel the domain name <globalsantafe.com> pending its transfer by Hangang and VeriSign to GlobalSantaFe as ordered. * * *

There are at least three [principal] means to achieve cancellation of a domain name. First, the current registrar of the domain name can cancel a domain name by directing the registry to delete the registration information from the Registry Database. Second, the registry for the pertinent top-level domain can disable the domain name in that top-level domain by placing it on "hold" status and rendering it inactive. Third, the pertinent registry can cancel a domain name by acting unilaterally to delete the registration information without the pertinent registrar's cooperation. The technical and practical implications of each of these cancellation means merit exploration. As a predicate to this, it is necessary to review the * * * roles of the registrars and the registry with regard to transfer and cancellation of a domain name. * * *

The [domain name system (DNS)] allows an individual user to identify a computer using an easier-to-remember alphanumeric "domain name," such as "www.globalsantafe.com," rather than the numerical IP address.

The DNS "resolves" the domain name by identifying the particular IP address associated with each domain name.

Significantly, the DNS is not a single master file in one location containing all the registered domain names and the corresponding IP addresses, but rather a hierarchical and distributed system, with each "name server" providing information for its "zone." Under this hierarchical system, the domain name "space" is divided into top-level domains ("TLDs"), such as ".com" and ".net."[20] Each TLD name server provides the information necessary to direct domain name queries to the second-level domain (SLD) name server responsible for the domain name in question. Thus, VeriSign, as the registry for all domain names ending in ".com," is responsible for directing domain name queries regarding the "globalsantafe.com" second level domain to the appropriate SLD name server. This SLD name server, in turn, matches the domain name, e.g. "www.globalsantafe.com," with its specific numeric IP address. In other words, the ".com" TLD zone file maintained by VeriSign contains a list of all second level domains within the ".com" zone linked to the IP addresses of the SLD name servers for those second level domains, while the "globalsantafe.com" SLD name server maintains the file which matches all domain names in the "globalsantafe.com" SLD zone to the IP addresses of the individual host computers.

Registering, transferring, or deleting a domain name typically involves interaction between the registrar and the registry. The relationship between the registry and the registrars is governed by several contracts, including the Registry-Registrar Agreement, the Registrar Accreditation Agreement, and the .com Registration Agreement.[24] These contracts allocate the responsibilities of a registry and related registrars and establish the processes for domain name registration. The registrars handle the retail side of domain name registration, selling domain names to individual domain name registrants. The registry, in turns, performs a central but more limited function, namely maintaining and operating the unified Registry Database, which contains all domain names registered by all registrants and registrars in a given top level domain, as well as the associated TLD zone file used to resolve domain name queries in that domain. Thus, for each domain name in the ".com" TLD, VeriSign, the ".com" registry, is responsible for maintaining and propagating the following information: (i) the domain name, (ii) the IP addresses of the primary and secondary name server for that domain name, (iii) the name

---

20. There is a limited set of TLDs. The list of seven "generic" TLDs, which included ".com," ".edu," ".gov", ".int", ".mil", ".net", and ".org," was expanded by the November 2000 selection of seven new generic TLDs including ".biz," ".info," ".name," and ".pro." In addition, there are over 240 "country-code" TLDs, e.g. ".us" for the United States, and ".kr" for the Republic of Korea.

24. VeriSign operates as the exclusive registry for ".com" domain names pursuant to a contract with the U.S. Department of Commerce and the Internet Corporation for Assigned Names and Numbers ("ICANN"), and also enters into standard contracts with the various ".com" registrars. * * *

of the registrar for the domain name, and (iv) the expiration date for the registration. Hangang, in turn, as one of many ".com" registrars, maintains the same information for each domain name it sells to a registrant, and in addition, maintains records containing the name and address of the registrant as well as information regarding a technical and administrative contact for each domain name.[25]

Interaction between registrars and the registry is highly structured and automated. Registrar-registry communications occur over a secure electronic connection. The registry's role is almost entirely passive, namely to process the registrar's orders while checking to ensure that there are no conflicts within the central Registry Database such as duplicate domain name registrations. Registrars initiate virtually all changes to the Registry Database, by issuing automated commands to the registry, such as ADD, CHECK, RENEW, DEL (delete), MOD (modify), and TRANSFER.[26]

There are contractual restrictions in VeriSign's authorizing contracts which generally bar VeriSign from changing the information in the Registry Database on its own initiative. First, VeriSign's authorizing contract specifies that it can only register domain names in response to requests from registrars, and that it cannot act as a registrar with respect to the registry's TLD. However, exceptions permit VeriSign to register a limited number of specified domain names for its own use and for ICANN's use. Second, the standard form Registry-Registrar Agreement grants VeriSign only a limited license to use the registration data submitted by the registrar "for propagation of and the provision of authorized access to the TLD zone files." Thus, as contemplated in the agreements, transfer or cancellation of a domain name normally requires the approval or initiative of the current registrar.

With this general background regarding the domain name system and the registrar-registry relationship, the three principal means of cancelling a domain name can be meaningfully explored.

Under normal procedures, a domain name is canceled by the issuance of a delete command by the domain name's current registrar. The current registrar uses the DEL command to instruct the registry to delete all information regarding the domain name from the Registry Database and the TLD zone file. The removal of this information completely and effectively cancels the domain name. This is so, because any attempt to use

---

25. Thus, while VeriSign's Registry Database provides information as to which *registrar* registered a given domain name, it does not include information identifying who the individual *registrant* for a domain name is, or where the registrant is located. Only the registrar maintains that information.

26. For example, in order to register a new domain name for an individual end user, the registrar sends to the registry the ADD command as well as the information the registry needs to populate its database, namely the domain name, the IP addresses of the local name servers for that domain name, the registrar, and the expiration date for the registration. The registry, in turn, either enters this information into the central Registry Database and the TLD zone file, or returns an error message if, for example, the domain name is already registered.

the domain name will fail, owing to the removal of the pertinent information from the registry's TLD zone file. Importantly, because the registration information has been deleted from the Registry Database, the individual domain name will once again be available for registration to any registrant on a first-come, first-served basis. This method of cancellation also has the virtue of using the established channels for registrar-registry communication to effectuate complete cancellation of the domain name. Yet, this approach requires cooperation by the current registrar, and thus may not be effective in situations where, as here, the registrar has declined to cooperate and is beyond the jurisdiction of United States courts.

The second means of cancellation does not require the approval or initiative of the current registrar. Although VeriSign is not contractually authorized to delete a domain name registration on its own initiative, the registry may nonetheless unilaterally disable a domain name. VeriSign can render a domain name "inactive" by placing the domain name in REGISTRY-HOLD status. When a domain name is placed on REGISTRY-HOLD status, the domain name is removed from the TLD zone file but the information in the Registry Database is otherwise unchanged. The practical effect of this type of cancellation is twofold. On the one hand, the removal of the domain name from the TLD zone file renders it functionally useless, as attempts to locate the domain name and an associated IP address in the DNS will fail. On the other hand, the domain name remains registered to the current, infringing registrant and cannot be registered by the trademark holder or anyone else. Thus, the infringing domain name is rendered "inactive" but remains registered. In other words, if the domain name <globalsantafe.com> were disabled in this manner, individual users who attempted to access the domain name on the Internet would receive an error message indicating that the domain name could not be found, yet GlobalSantaFe could not register the domain name for its own use because it would still be registered by Park and Fanmore.

This disabling approach offers less than a complete cancellation remedy, yet it has a significant advantage over cancellation pursuant to a registrar's command; namely that VeriSign is contractually authorized to take this action unilaterally without the cooperation of the current registrar. Thus, this disabling approach may be preferable in circumstances where, as here, a recalcitrant registrar is beyond a court's jurisdiction. Unfortunately, where the current registrant is simply holding the domain name rather than putting it to any practical use, as is true here, disabling the domain name will have minimal practical effect—the trademark holder will still not be able to use the domain name, and the cybersquatter can continue squatting on the domain name as long as he keeps the registration active.

A third means of cancellation involves a court order directing VeriSign to act unilaterally to cancel the domain name by deleting the registration information in the Registry Database and removing the domain name from the TLD zone file, without regard to the current registrar's lack of cooperation and the normal contractual procedures for cancellation. * * *

VeriSign's maintenance and control of the central Registry Database and the vital .com TLD zone file effectively enables VeriSign to transfer control of any ".com" domain name. Similarly, it is apparent that VeriSign's physical control of these files enables VeriSign to cancel any ".com" domain name by deleting the relevant information in the Registry Database and the TLD zone file. It may be that taking such a step would require a change in VeriSign's procedures and programming to allow the registry to delete the information without approval by the current registrar. Yet, nothing in the record indicates cancelling a domain name without the current registrar's consent is beyond VeriSign's physical or technical capabilities.

With regard to unilateral cancellation or transfer, it should be noted that VeriSign has indicated that it would oppose an order directing VeriSign unilaterally to transfer or cancel a domain name on grounds that such an order would require VeriSign to violate its contracts with the registrar and with ICANN and to interfere with the registrar-registrant contract. Yet, it is not clear that VeriSign would, in fact, be acting in violation of its authorizing contract, as transferring or canceling a domain name pursuant to a direct court order does not constitute "acting as a registrar" in contravention of the authorizing contract from ICANN. Furthermore, * * * VeriSign's contractual agreements with ICANN and Hangang cannot serve to limit the trademark rights and remedies granted to GlobalSantaFe by federal law under the Lanham Act and the ACPA. While the ACPA expressly authorizes a "court order for the . . . cancellation of the domain name," it does not require that such orders be directed only at the current registrar, nor does it shield the registry from cancellation orders. 15 U.S.C. § 1125(d)(2)(D)(i). Thus, VeriSign's contracts with ICANN and with the registrar should not be read to limit GlobalSantaFe's federal trademark rights and remedies. Simply put, the interest in vindicating congressionally provided trademark rights trumps contract. In any event, for the reasons that follow, it is not necessary to reach the question of unilateral transfer or deletion of a domain name by the registry in this case.

In sum, all three means of cancellation may be appropriate means of carrying out the cancellation remedy granted by the ACPA. To be sure, it is normally appropriate to direct a cancellation order primarily at the current domain name registrar and to direct that cancellation proceed through the usual channels. However, in situations, where, as here, such an order has proven ineffective at achieving cancellation, it becomes necessary to direct the registry to act unilaterally to carry out the cancellation remedy authorized under the ACPA. In this regard, a court is not limited merely to the disabling procedure envisioned by VeriSign's contractual agreements, but may also order the registry to delete completely a domain name registration pursuant to the court's order, just as the registry would in response to a registrar's request. Indeed, in order to vindicate the purposes of the ACPA, disabling alone in many cases may not be sufficient, for it does not oust the cybersquatter from his perch, but rather allows the cybersquatter to remain in possession of the name in violation of the trademark holder's rights.

In this regard, the physical location of the ".com" registry within this district is quite significant, for it is the location of the registry here which establishes the situs of the power to transfer or cancel the domain name within this district, pursuant to the ACPA, even if the registrar has not submitted a registrar certificate granting the court authority over the disputed domain name. Significantly, if the infringing domain name were registered in a top-level domain whose registry was outside the United States, jurisdiction in the United States might be avoided entirely, provided the registrar is also foreign and the individual registrant lacks sufficient contacts with the forum to meet the due process requirements for personal jurisdiction. In other words, there is a significant gap in the ACPA's trademark enforcement regime for domain names registered under top-level domain names, such as the foreign country code domain names, whose registry is located outside the United States.

The current ability to assert jurisdiction over a large number of domain names in this district pursuant to the ACPA hinges on two factors, (i) the location of VeriSign within this district and (ii) the current popularity of the ".com" and ".net" top-level domain names, particularly for commercial Internet operations. Either factor may change in the future. Indeed, * * * an aggressive assertion of United States jurisdiction and control over the domain name system based on its essentially arbitrary physical geography may have the unintended consequence of causing a segmentation of the domain name system as other countries seek to assert their own control over the Internet by establishing competing and conflicting systems physically located outside the United States. Even absent such segmentation, a desire to avoid United States jurisdiction may cause foreign registrants to choose to use domain names within their respective country code top-level domains, whose registries are located in and operated by the foreign countries, rather than the currently popular "generic" domain names such as ".com" and ".net." The result may be an increasing number of domain names registered out of the reach of United States jurisdiction, but accessible to United States users through the universal domain name system, which in turn will pose a serious challenge to the enforcement of United States trademark rights on the Internet.

In any event, in this case, the narrow issue presented is whether the circumstances justify * * * an order directing VeriSign to cancel the domain name by disabling it. Given the nature of the specific relief requested by GlobalSantaFe, it is unnecessary to consider whether complete cancellation of the domain name by VeriSign is appropriate here. As discussed *supra*, cancellation of the infringing domain name is clearly authorized as a remedy under the ACPA, and disabling the domain name through removal of the pertinent information from the TLD zone file is the least intrusive practical means of achieving cancellation without the cooperation of the registrar. Thus, the amended judgment order requested by GlobalSantaFe in this matter is legally valid and practically appropriate.

The remaining question * * * is whether concerns of international comity dictate deference to the injunction issued by the Korean court. In this regard, neither the general law regarding abstention in favor of a foreign court's adjudication of *in rem* actions, nor the specific concerns raised by the facts of this case counsel against the requested cancellation remedy.

The law regarding competing jurisdiction in *in rem* actions is clear: "[A]ccording to longstanding precedent and practice, the first court seized of jurisdiction over property, or asserting jurisdiction in a case requiring control over property, may exercise that jurisdiction to the exclusion of any other court." *See Sec. and Exch. Comm'n v. Banner Fund Int'l,* 211 F.3d 602, 611 (D.C. Cir. 2000). This doctrine, * * * applies only to *in rem* or *quasi in rem* cases, and requires federal courts to decline jurisdiction over a particular property or *res* over which another court has already asserted jurisdiction. Although originally developed in the context of federalism, the first-in-time rule has since been applied to federal cases with parallel proceedings underway in another country.

With regard to the first-in-time rule, the facts clearly establish that this Court was the first to assert jurisdiction over the domain name. Park's application for an injunction was filed with the District Court of Seoul on April 9, 2002, six months after GlobalSantaFe's filing of the *in rem* action in this Court. * * * Clearly, then, this Court is not obligated * * * to cede jurisdiction over the domain name in light of the subsequent order issued by the Korean court.

As noted in *Banner Fund,* acquiescence to a foreign court is not only not required in this instance, it is also not appropriate:

> True, we cannot require a foreign court to yield when the United States court was the first to assume jurisdiction, but neither can we acquiesce in a rule under which the United States court recedes regardless of its priority in time. That rule would empower a defendant in the United States to oust our courts of *in rem* jurisdiction merely by filing its own action in the courts of any hospitable country—of which there would be no shortage if that were our rule.

Id. at 611-12. * * * [Moreover,] there is clearly no basis for abstention on comity grounds where, as here (i) the proceedings are not concurrent, the Korean proceeding having been commenced in an effort to block enforcement of the already issued judgment in this case, (ii) the foreign court proceeding is intended to frustrate the enforcement of the Judgment of this Court, and (iii) that Judgment supports significant public policies under United States law. Thus, comity concerns do not bar the amendment of the Judgment Order to grant GlobalSantaFe the additional remedy of cancellation to which it is entitled under the ACPA.

Notes & Questions

1. If, as the court notes, both the registrar (Hangang) and the registrant (Park) are beyond the court's jurisdiction, what is there in the United States for the court to have power over? What is it that VeriSign "possesses" in the

United States? Should that be sufficient to support the court's assertion of jurisdiction in this case?

2. In reviewing the various ways that a domain name may be cancelled, the district court notes that merely placing the name on hold—removing the name from the zone file, but leaving the registry database unchanged—may not be of any practical benefit to the trademark holder because the holder will still not be able to register or use the disputed domain name. Yet, later in the opinion, the court notes that this is precisely the relief that GlobalSantaFe is requesting. Why do you think GlobalSantaFe did not go farther and request that the name be removed from the database altogether?

3. Although the district court in this case was not asked to order that VeriSign go so far as to transfer the domain name at issue to the trademark holder, the same court subsequently extended the holding of *GlobalSantaFe* to include such a remedy, at least in cases where the registrar has refused or failed to do so after notice of an appropriate order. *See America Online, Inc. v. Aol.org*, 259 F. Supp. 2d 449 (E.D. Va. 2003).

4. Because the registry companies for the three most popular top-level domains—".com", ".org", and ".edu"—are all located in the United States, the *Globalsantafe* ruling would mean that most domain name trademark disputes could be adjudicated in the United States under the ACPA, regardless of where and with whom the domain was registered. Is this an appropriate or just outcome? On the other hand, if the ACPA could *not* be applied to such a dispute, what would prevent domain name registrars from simply locating in jurisdictions that are less strict in enforcing trademark rights?

5. The court expresses concern that aggressive assertion of United States jurisdiction and control over the domain name system may have the unintended consequence of causing a segmentation of the domain name system. What is the danger of such segmentation? Why would such segmentation occur? Which top-level domains would be beyond the reach of the ACPA? For a discussion of these issues, see Catherine T. Struve & R. Polk Wagner, *Realspace Sovereigns in Cyberspace: Problems with the Anticybersquatting Consumer Protection Act*, 17 BERKELEY TECH. L.J. 989 (2002).

6. Recall the U.S. court decision in the *Yahoo!* case earlier in this chapter, in which the court ruled that the French judgment was unenforceable in the United States. Is such a ruling any different from the ruling of the South Korean court in this case?

7. In its discussion of potential comity concerns, the court emphasizes that it asserted jurisdiction and adjudicated the trademark claim *prior* to the order of the South Korean court. But should "first in time" really matter? What if Park, knowing that GlobalSantaFe was likely to file an ACPA action in the United States, had gone into court in South Korea and sought, in advance, a declaratory judgment stating that the registration was permissible under South Korean trademark law? If such a judgment had issued before the U.S. case were filed, do you think the district court would have abstained from adjudicating the ACPA claim on comity grounds? Should it?

8. In *GlobalSantaFe*, the U.S. court issued the initial order, followed by the South Korean court. But what should a U.S. court do if the foreign court

order comes first? In *Hawes v. Network Solutions, Inc.*, 337 F.3d 377 (4th Cir. 2003), the Fourth Circuit addressed such a situation. After Hawes had registered the domain name lorealcomplaints.com, the French hair color company L'Oreal obtained an injunction from a French court requiring that the domain name be turned over to the company pursuant to French trademark law. Hawes responded by bringing an action in the United States under the ACPA, contending that his domain name did *not* violate L'Oreal's trademark rights under U.S. law and that he should therefore retain control over the name. While declining to rule on the merits, the Fourth Circuit decided that the ACPA claim against L'Oreal could in fact proceed in a U.S. court under U.S. law. Is such a result consistent with *GlobalSantaFe*?

9. Another case, *Barcelona.com Inc. v. Excelentisimo Ayuntamiento de Barcelona*, 330 F.3d 617 (4th Cir. 2003), raises a similar issue. A U.S. corporation registered barcelona.com in the United States and then, after its ownership of the domain name was challenged by the City Council of Barcelona, Spain, sought a declaratory judgment that such registration was lawful under the ACPA. The U.S. district court, however, chose to apply Spanish trademark law (rather than the ACPA), and ruled in favor of the city. The Fourth Circuit reversed, ruling both that the ACPA applied and that, under the ACPA, the domain name registration was permissible. Is the district court's solution—asserting jurisdiction but applying Spanish law—an appropriate way to resolve the competing international interests at stake? Or is the Fourth Circuit right to apply U.S. law? Is there any basis for choosing whether to apply the law of the country where the alleged trademark holder resides rather than the law of the country of the alleged infringer? On the Fourth Circuit's theory in *Barcelona.com*, should the *GlobalSantaFe* court have applied South Korean law because it was the law of the domain name registrant? Or should a court in an Internet dispute always simply apply its own law and let whichever court has actual power over the registry "win"?

10. What role should physical geography play in adjudicating domain name trademark disputes? Should it be the case that whichever country happens to host a registry database gets to apply its trademark law? Is there any other way to resolve potential stalemates between national courts like the one in this case? Should there be an international body to adjudicate domain name disputes (and resolve other related technical and governance issues)? If so, how should such a body be structured? The next section takes up such questions.

3. Non-Territorial Administration of the Domain Name System

Given that the domain name system (with its embedded protocols) operates across territorial borders, it is not surprising that the increasing importance of domain names was accompanied not only by broader national assertions of jurisdiction, but also by efforts to create bureaucratic governance bodies that could operate transnationally. Since 1998, the Internet Corporation for Assigned Names and Numbers (ICANN), a California-based not-for-profit corporation, has administered the domain name system under contract with the U.S. Department of Commerce. In addition to addressing questions such as whether to create more top-level domains, ICANN, along with the World Intellectual Property Organization (WIPO), a United Nations administrative body, administers a dispute resolution process for resolving domain name disputes. While the ability of these organizations to govern domain names is not hemmed in by geographical borders, they face their own legitimacy problems because they are entities exercising *de facto* governing power over the Internet without structures of democratic accountability or transparency that some think necessary. For example, a study of ICANN's and WIPO's dispute resolution process suggests that the arbitration system is fundamentally biased in favor of trademark holders.[g] Thus, even this alternative to the problem of territorially based Internet governance faces substantial challenges. Consider the discussion of ICANN below. Is it a model for non-territorial governance of online interaction or a nightmare of unaccountable private regulation? To what extent should a private entity be allowed to establish rules that govern the entire Internet community?

David G. Post, *Governing Cyberspace, or Where is James Madison When We Need Him?*

June 1999, *available at* http://www.temple.edu/lawschool/dpost/icann/comment1.html

In a column last Fall I suggested that the pending reorganization of the Internet's domain name system (DNS) had the potential to become cyberspace's own "constitutional moment," a profound and thorough transformation of the institutions and processes responsible for law-making and regulation on the global electronic network. Over the last several months, the shadowy outlines of a new kind of constitutional structure for cyberspace have indeed begun to emerge. The consequences of these developments for the Internet's future could not be more profound, and the picture that is emerging is not always a pretty one. Not many people are paying close attention to these developments; they should. Not to be an alarmist, but to boil a frog alive, the parable tells us, you need just to turn up the heat by increments so small that the frog never notices—never pays attention to—the rising temperature until it is too late to do anything about it (like jump out of the pot). Well, the temperature on the Internet is starting to rise.

1. *(A bit of) Background*

For the Internet to exist as a single coherent network, there must be a way to be sure that a message sent from any point on the network to *janedoe@xyz.com*, or a request to view the webpage at *www.school.edu*, is routed to the "right" machine; that is, each of those addresses (*xyz.com* or *www.school.edu*) must be associated unambiguously with a particular machine if message traffic is to move in a predictable way.

---

g. *See* Michael Geist, *Fair.com?: An Examination of the Allegations of Systemic Unfairness in the ICANN UDRP*, 27 BROOKLYN J. INT'L L. 903 (2002).

To make an extremely long story short, the global network we call "the Internet" manages this by, first, requiring that each machine on the network have a unique numerical address [e.g., 123.45.67.89]; indeed, to be "on the Internet" means to have (or to be connected to) a machine to which such an address has been assigned. For your message to *www.school.edu* to be routed correctly, your computer must somehow be able to find the numerical address corresponding to the machine named *www.school.edu*. This is accomplished, on the Internet, by means of what Tony Rutkowski calls a "magical mystery tour."

When you send off a message requesting a copy of the *www.school.edu* home page ("*http://www.school.edu*"), the message first stops off at a machine known as a "DNS [Domain Name System] server." It is the job of the DNS server, which is usually operated by your Internet Service Provider, to find the correct numerical address for your message. The DNS server reads, in effect, from right to left; seeing that this is a message destined for some machine in the EDU domain, it needs to find out where addresses in the EDU domain are stored. It does this by asking a different machine (known as the "root server") that very question: "Who is responsible for the EDU domain?" The root server replies with the numerical address of a different machine (known as the "EDU domain server"). Your DNS server then asks the EDU domain server the question: "Who is responsible for *school.edu*?" The EDU domain server replies with another numerical address [or with "Not Found" if it cannot find an entry for "*school.edu*" in its database of names and addresses]. Your DNS server then asks this machine: "Who is responsible for *www.school.edu*?" School.edu replies with yet another numerical address, and now your DNS server has completed its task; once it receives the address for www.school.edu, it places that address into your message and sends it on its way.

How does this all work as smoothly as it does? Who is in charge of the root server? How does the operator of the root server decide which machines are the "authorized" domain servers for EDU, or COM, or ORG, or any of the other top-level domains? Who controls those machines (and the database of names and addresses contained in them)? And how is this whole scheme enforced? That is, what makes the root server "the" root server? Why do the many thousands of Internet Service Providers, operating the many thousands of DNS servers worldwide, all use the same root server?

In the early days of the Internet, of course—through, say, the early 90s—no one outside the small cadre of engineers that was putting the system together cared very much about the answers to these questions. There were, of course, answers to them all. The United States government had long operated the root server (a holdover from the days that the Internet was a Defense Department project), and had worked with something known as the Internet Assigned Numbering Authority (IANA)—a group of engineers led by the late Jon Postel—to organize the necessary data and to see that the various domain servers were being properly managed.

As long as it all seemed to be working smoothly enough; who cared what was going on behind the Wizard's curtain? And who noticed when, in 1992, as the extraordinary growth of the network began to outstrip the management capacity of this (largely volunteer) operation, the U.S. government engaged a private firm, Network Solutions, Inc. (NSI), to manage and maintain the databases and domain servers for the COM, ORG, and NET domains?

But slowly, as more and more people began to realize that the Internet was a Really Big Deal (and that these funny "domain name" things might actually be of real value), more and more people started to pay attention to all of this, and this arrangement began to come under increasing fire from many quarters. The government and NSI found themselves increasingly under attack from within and without the Net community—by those challenging NSI's apparent monopoly control over these increasingly valuable top-level domains, by trademark owners concerned about domain names that appeared to infringe upon their valuable trademark rights, and others.

As the expiration date of the government's contract with NSI approached last June, the Commerce Department announced that the government wanted to get out of the DNS management business entirely. Citing "widespread dissatisfaction about the absence of competition in domain name registration," and the need for a "more formal and robust management structure," the government proposed transferring responsibility for management and operation of the DNS to a private non-profit corporation. This new corporation, to be formed by "Internet stakeholders" on a global basis, would take over responsibility for overseeing the operation of the authoritative Internet root server.

2. *Um, What Does This Have To Do With "Internet Governance"?*

This new corporation—ICANN, the Internet Corporation for Assigned Names and Numbers—has, over the past several months, set up shop and gotten to work. It's been a busy time. It has begun to establish "Supporting Organizations," new coalitions comprising various Internet constituencies (*e.g.*, domain name registrars, trademark owners) who will be responsible for electing certain members of the ICANN Board of Directors and for formulating aspects of domain name policy. It has accredited five companies * * * to begin issuing registrations in the COM, ORG, and NET, domains during a two-month test period (along with twenty-nine other entities who can begin accepting registrations in these domains once the test phase is completed). It commissioned, and recently adopted (in part), a report from the World Intellectual Property Organization (WIPO) outlining the procedures to be used in cases involving "cybersquatting" (the intentional "warehousing" of domain names for later sale). * * *

My goal here is not to discuss any of these specific actions; there is much here to digest and debate, pro and con * * * . Rather, [it] is just to suggest that notwithstanding the government's (and ICANN's) protestations to the contrary, this is about nothing less than Internet governance writ large. The Commerce Department took pains to characterize it in other terms; this new corporation would be responsible only for "technical management of the DNS," the "narrow issues of management and administration of Internet names and numbers on an ongoing basis"—sort of what the International Telecommunications Union does with respect to managing interconnections on the international telephone network. This new framework for managing the DNS

. . . does not set out a system of Internet "governance." Existing human rights and free speech protections will not be disturbed and, therefore, need not be specifically included in the core principles for DNS management. In addition, this policy is not intended to displace other legal regimes (international law, competition law, tax law and principles of international taxation, intellectual property law, etc.) that may already apply. The continued applicability of these systems as well as the principle of representation should ensure that DNS management proceeds in the interest of the Internet community as a whole."

United States Department of Commerce, *The Management of Internet Names and Addresses* (June 5, 1998).

It is all well and good to say that this new institution will not be engaged in Internet governance—but words will not make it so. Any entity exercising control over the DNS will be subject to immense pressure to do more than mere "technical management," because, bizarre as it may seem at first glance, the root server, and the various domain servers to which it points, constitute the very heart of the Internet, the Archimedean point on which this vast global network balances.

To appreciate that, imagine for the moment that you had control over operation of the root server. You alone get to decide which machines are "authoritative" domain servers for the COM, NET, ORG, EDU, and the other top-level domains, the machines to which all Internet users worldwide will be directed when they try to send any message to any address in those domains. You have the power, therefore, to determine who gets an address in those domains—who gets a passport without which passage across the border into cyberspace is impossible. You can say "From now on, we will use the data in machine X as the authoritative list of COM names and addresses, but only so long as the operator of that machine complies with the following conditions," and then you can list—well, just about anything you'd like, I suppose. It's your root server, after all. You can require that all domain server operators pay you a certain fee, or provide you with particular kinds of information about the people to whom they have handed out specific names and addresses, or only allow transmission of files in a specified format, or abide by a particular set of laws or rules or regulations. And you can demand that they "flow through" these conditions (or others) to anyone whom they list in their authoritative databases, that they revoke any name given to anyone who does not pay the required fee, or provide the required information, or use the specified file format, or comply with the specified rules and regulations.

This is quite literally a kind of life-or-death power over the global network itself, *because presence in (or absence from) this chain of interlocking servers and databases is a matter of [network] life or death: If your name and address cannot be found on the "authoritative" server, you simply do not exist—at least, not on the Internet.* Eliminate the entry for *xyz.com* from the COM domain server, and *xyz.com* vanishes entirely from cyberspace; designate as the new COM domain server a machine that does not have an entry for *xyz.com* in its database, and you have imposed the electronic equivalent of the death penalty on *xyz.com*.

Anyone interested in controlling the rules under which activities on the Internet take place—and many commercial interests, who now realize the huge economic stake they have in this medium, and many governments, who have spent the last few years worrying about how they would ever get back their taxing and regulatory authority over Internet transactions, find that they are indeed quite interested in that now—is likely to find the existing of a single controlling point awfully tempting. Anyone with a vision of how the Internet can be made a "better" place—by making it safer for the exploitation of intellectual property rights, say, or by eliminating the capability to engage in anonymous transactions, or by making it more difficult for children to get access to indecent material—is likely to view control over the root server as the means to impose its particular vision on Internet users worldwide. After all the talk over the past few years about how difficult it will be to regulate conduct on the Internet, the domain name system looks like the Holy Grail, the *one place* where enforceable Internet policy can be promulgated without any of the messy enforcement and jurisdictional problems that bedevil ordinary law-making exercises on the Net.

And that is why these are *governance* questions, why any reorganization of this system, far from being an arcane technical detail of Internet engineering, is inherently of constitutional significance. Power corrupts, absolute power corrupts absolutely—on the Internet as elsewhere. Questions about constraining any form of absolute power are constitutional questions of the highest order, and "governance" means nothing more (and nothing less) than the search for mechanisms to insure that absolute power is not exercised in an unjust or oppressive manner. How can we be assured that ICANN will be able to resist pressures to stray beyond this limited "technical" mandate? Where are the checks on the new corporation's exercise of its powers?

You think, perhaps, that I exaggerate the significance of these developments, and perhaps I do. But let me point to a few dark clouds on the horizon that make me very, very nervous about what ICANN is up to. Remember all those things you could do if you were in control of the root? Like " require that domain server operators pay you a certain fee"? Well, ICANN has imposed the requirement that each accredited registrar pay ICANN a fee of $1 for each new domain name they hand out—can anyone say "taxation without representation"? Or "provide you with particular kinds of information about the people to whom they have handed out specific names and addresses"? ICANN, having now endorsed the WIPO Report referenced earlier, is about to impose a requirement on all domain name registrars that they collect and make available "accurate and reliable contact details of domain name holders," and that they agree to "cancel the domain name registrations" wherever those contact details are shown to be "inaccurate and unreliable."—a move with grave consequences for the continued viability of anonymous communications on the Internet. Or "abide by a particular set of laws or rules or regulations"? The WIPO Report, again, envisions that all claims by trademark holders that a domain name registrant registered an infringing name "in bad faith" be submitted to a single, uniform, worldwide dispute resolution process for adjudication.

Now, some, or even all, of these may be good ideas. But this is already way beyond the realm of technical "standards-setting," and we really must ask whether we really want or need this kind of global Internet policy and whether this is the way it should be put together.   When did the affected constituency—all Internet users worldwide—decide that they want a global policy-making organ of this kind?   Who decided that the bottom-up, decentralized, consensus-based governance structures under which the Internet grew and flourished are incompatible with its continued growth and development?   When are we going to get a chance to ratify these new arrangements?

There are hard questions here, but one thing is clear; we need to disabuse ourselves of the notion that this is somehow *not* about Internet governance if we are going to make any serious headway on them. We know something about how institutions that possess life and death power can be constrained, about constitutions and constitutionalism, about the fragmentation of power and the need for checks on the exercise of power, and we better start thinking about this problem in these terms before too much more time elapses.

Oh—and about James Madison? Madison not only thought more clearly and more insightfully about these questions than anyone before or since, he understood the necessity for public discussion and debate about issues of this kind; the Federalist Papers, in which he and Alexander Hamilton (and a somewhat recalcitrant John Jay) laid out the arguments for (and against) the constitutional structure put together in Philadelphia in 1787, began life, let us not forget, as newspaper columns appearing weekly in the New York press. We could do worse than to start thinking about updating that for the new cyber world we are building now.

Notes and Questions

1. Earlier in this chapter, we encountered Post's argument in opposition to the regulation of online activity by territorially based sovereign entities. Why isn't ICANN the appropriate response to his concerns? Why does Post oppose ICANN as well?

2. What are the advantages to resolving domain name disputes through a body such as ICANN rather than through territorially based courts? For example, does ICANN solve the jurisdictional problems discussed earlier with regard to the Anticybersquatting Consumer Protection Act? On the other hand, what are the disadvantages Post identifies?

3. Why does Post view ICANN as a form of government? What differentiates ICANN from a technical standard-setting body?

4. Would it be better if control over the domain name system were held by a body at the United Nations rather than a private corporation? At a 2003 U.N. meeting on Internet issues, representatives of various countries expressed concern about the extent of ICANN's power, particularly given the fact that the corporation, though nominally private, was created at the behest of the U.S. government. A U.N. working group subsequently issued a Report on Internet Governance seeking to identify principles by which such governance should be exercised. An International Internet Governance Forum has also included calls to loosen the tie between ICANN and the U.S. government and to explore forms of Internet governance that would involve multiple national

participation. Do you think such international oversight is a good idea? What do you think Post would say?

5. Post argues for constitutionally based thinking about the best way to structure ICANN's authority. Does it matter that ICANN is not officially a governmental entity? The question of whether such nominally "private" actors should be thought of (and perhaps treated) as governmental will be discussed in Chapter Five.

Chapter Four

PROBLEMS OF LEGAL VERSUS TECHNOLOGICAL REGULATION

INTRODUCTION

In Chapter Three, we examined the scholarly debate over whether national and state governments can and should regulate Internet activities, and, if so, how they might do so. We saw arguments on both sides of the debate being played out in a range of concrete disputes—over states' power to regulate speech, to hale a defendant into court, to investigate crime, and so on.

Our discussion focused mainly on the state's ability to exercise its power by applying its law, taking the state of technology largely as a given. But the relationship between law and technology is a complex one. Recall Professor Lessig's observation that the "code" of cyberspace—its architecture and the software and hardware implementing that architecture—can act as an important constraint on behavior:

> Cyberspace presents something new for those who think about regulation and freedom. It demands a new understanding of how regulation works and of what regulates life there. It compels us to look beyond the traditional lawyer's scope—beyond laws, regulations, and norms. It requires an account of a newly salient regulator.
>
> That regulator is * * * Code. In real space we recognize how laws regulate—through constitutions, statutes, and other legal codes. In cyberspace we must understand how code regulates—how the software and hardware that make cyberspace what it is regulate cyberspace as it is. As William Mitchell puts it, this code is cyberspace's "law." *Code is law*.

LAWRENCE LESSIG, CODE AND OTHER LAWS OF CYBERSPACE 6 (1999).

In this chapter, we explore in greater detail the relationship between law and technology (or "code," if you will). This relationship turns out to be dynamic and multi-faceted. Indeed, there are at least three ways in which law and technology interact, and we will consider each in turn.

First, we examine the ways in which *technological advances often necessitate changes in law*. As technology enables individuals, corporations, or governmental actors to perform tasks that were previously impossible (or impractical), there is always a question of how law should respond to the new capability. Although there are countless doctrinal areas in which to observe this dynamic, we focus on one where the interplay is particularly evident: changes over time in the law and technology of government surveillance.

Second, we turn to the possibility that *technological measures can be used to replace or supplant the balances struck by formal legal regulation*. Here the concern is that automated standardized contracts backed by "code" can become a perfectly enforced private law that regulates behavior, regardless of what legal rules might permit. This section explores one prominent example of such code-based regulation: the use of technological protection measures to enforce contractual terms.

Third, we examine ways in which *legal rules can themselves affect the technological options that may be made available* in the first place. Indeed, although technology can certainly destabilize law, it is equally true that the legal environment can have a strong impact on what sorts of new technology gets developed and distributed. We consider such impacts by examining how law has shaped incentives in three areas: the development of home video recording devices, the use of online peer-to-peer file sharing networks, and the design of new telecommunications technologies.

Finally, as in Chapter Three, we use the domain name system as a case study. This time, we consider an argument that the Anticybersquatting Consumer Protection Act, in attempting to adjust trademark law to respond to the technological changes of the Internet era, has adversely affected the development of beneficial search engine and aggregation technology that would actually benefit users. As such, this final section allows us to see both the way that law responds to technological change and the way that law may, in its response, unwittingly (and perhaps unwisely) shape the market for future technological innovation.

SECTION A. THE EFFECT OF
TECHNOLOGICAL CHANGE ON LEGAL RULES

When considering the scope of individual freedoms, we often focus on the way in which we (and others) are constrained by the regulatory force of law. The provisions of the Bill of Rights, for example, are rightly seen as crucial to limiting the potential for governmental overreaching. But the state of existing technology is often just as important—or even more important—in determining what the precise contours of regulation might be at any given moment in history. For example, before the invention of high-quality directional microphones, people could be reasonably confident that those out of earshot were simply unable to overhear a private conversation, regardless of the law regarding such eavesdropping. Thus, our regulatory environment is always determined by a combination of the legal rules that dictate what is *permissible* and the technological (or physical) realities that dictate what is *possible* (or practical). Moreover, the current state of technology is particularly significant in the surveillance context because courts determine whether or not the government has engaged in an unreasonable search and seizure prohibited by the Fourth Amendment by analyzing the extent of intrusion upon a "reasonable expectation of privacy." And the law alone cannot create expectations of privacy; those expectations are also shaped by what ordinary people assume that technology can and cannot do.

Changes in technology, then, almost inevitably destabilize the existing regulatory environment, whether we are talking about surveillance law, or the allocation of the radio spectrum in an era of wireless communications, or the response of copyright or trademark law to the rise of digital communications, or the scope of First Amendment protections given to online bloggers, and on and on. As we saw in Chapter Two, even the venerable law of trespass has been challenged to respond to the phenomenon of electrical impulses traveling over computer systems. In short, there is almost no area of law that is not at least potentially affected by changes in technology.

So, how should law respond? This section takes up this question, using changes in government surveillance technology as a case study for considering how law responds to technological change more generally. Fundamentally, there are always two basic ways that law can approach the issue of technological change. On the one hand, one can assume that the prior regulatory environment was simply an accident of the particular combination of law and technological architecture that then existed and therefore accept that technological change inevitably creates a new regulatory environment. Taking such an approach, one might conclude, to take our previous microphone example, that after the invention of long-distance surveillance technology, whatever privacy we took for granted in the previous technological environment no longer applies. On the other hand, one might take steps to adjust law in order to maintain the regulatory environment that was previously taken for granted. Thus, surveillance law could be altered to try to regulate uses of the new technology. Which of these approaches seems more appropriate to you? And how would you decide on the best response to any given change of technology? As to the Fourth Amendment inquiry, how would you apply the "reasonable expectation of privacy" test? Should the development and widespread public use of technologies that facilitate government surveillance effectively shrink the scope of the Fourth Amendment's protection because the new technology inevitably changes people's idea of what is reasonably expected? Or is the whole idea of a "reasonable expectation of privacy" unhelpful, because it relies upon (and is affected by) the particular state of technological and legal regulation in effect at any given moment? Keep these questions in mind as you consider the cases that follow.

Olmstead v. United States

Supreme Court of the United States, 1928
277 U.S. 438

MR. CHIEF JUSTICE TAFT delivered the opinion of the Court.

The petitioners were convicted in the District Court for the Western District of Washington of a conspiracy to violate the National Prohibition Act by unlawfully possessing, transporting and importing intoxicating liquors and maintaining nuisances, and by selling intoxicating liquors. * * * The evidence in the records discloses a conspiracy of amazing magnitude to import, possess, and sell liquor unlawfully. * * * Olmstead was the leading conspirator and the general manager of the business. * * *

The information which led to the discovery of the conspiracy and its nature and extent was largely obtained by intercepting messages on the telephones of the conspirators by four federal prohibition officers. Small wires were inserted along the ordinary telephone wires from the residences of four of the petitioners and those leading from the chief office. The insertions were made without trespass upon any property of the defendants. They were made in the basement of the large office building. The taps from house lines were made in the streets near the houses. * * *

The Fourth Amendment provides—"The right of the people to be secure in their persons, houses, papers, and effects, against unreasonable searches and seizures, shall not be violated, and no warrants shall issue, but upon probable cause, supported by oath or affirmation, and particularly describing the place to be searched, and the persons or things to be seized." * * * The well known historical purpose of the Fourth Amendment, directed against general warrants and writs of assistance, was to prevent the use of governmental force to search a man's house, his person, his papers, and his effects, and to prevent their seizure against his will. * * * Here we have testimony only of voluntary conversations secretly overheard.

The Amendment itself shows that the search is to be of material things—the person, the house, his papers, or his effects. * * * By the invention of the telephone fifty years ago, and its application for the purpose of extending communications, one can talk with another at a far distant place. The language of the Amendment cannot be extended and expanded to include telephone wires, reaching to the whole world from the defendant's house or office. The intervening wires are not part of his house or office, any more than are the highways along which they are stretched. * * *

Congress may, of course, protect the secrecy of telephone messages by making them, when intercepted, inadmissible in evidence in federal criminal trials, by direct legislation, and thus depart from the common law of evidence. But the courts may not adopt such a policy by attributing an enlarged and unusual meaning to the Fourth Amendment. The reasonable view is that one who installs in his house a telephone instrument with connecting wires intends to project his voice to those quite outside, and that the wires beyond his house, and messages while passing over them, are not within the protection of the Fourth Amendment. Here those who intercepted the projected voices were not in the house of either party to the conversation.

Neither the cases we have cited nor any of the many federal decisions brought to our attention hold the Fourth Amendment to have been violated as against a defendant, unless there has been an official search and seizure of his person or such a seizure of his papers or his tangible material effects or an actual physical invasion of his house "or curtilage" for the purpose of making a seizure. We think, therefore, that the wire tapping here disclosed did not amount to a search or seizure within the meaning of the Fourth Amendment.

MR. JUSTICE BRANDEIS (dissenting).

The Government makes no attempt to defend the methods employed by its officers. Indeed, it concedes that, if wire tapping can be deemed a search and seizure within the Fourth Amendment, such wire tapping as was practiced in the case at bar was an unreasonable search and seizure, and that the evidence thus obtained was inadmissible. But it relies on the language of the amendment, and it claims that the protection given thereby cannot properly be held to include a telephone conversation.

"We must never forget," said Mr. Chief Justice Marshall in *McCulloch v. Maryland*, 4 Wheat. 316, 407 (1819), "that it is a Constitution we are expounding." Since then this Court has repeatedly sustained the exercise of power by Congress, under various clauses of that instrument, over objects of which the Fathers could not have dreamed. We have likewise held that general limitations on the powers of Government, like those embodied in the due process clauses of the Fifth and Fourteenth Amendments, do not forbid the United States or the states from meeting modern conditions by regulations which "a century ago, or even half a century ago, probably would have been rejected as arbitrary and oppressive." *Village of Euclid v. Ambler Realty Co.*, 272 U. S. 365, 387 (1926). Clauses guaranteeing to the individual protection against specific abuses of power, must have a similar capacity of adaptation to a changing world. * * *

When the Fourth and Fifth Amendments were adopted, "the form that evil had theretofore taken," *Weems v. United States*, 217 U.S. 349, 373 (1910), had been necessarily simple. Force and violence were then the only means known to man by which a Government could directly effect self-incrimination. It could compel the individual to testify—a compulsion effected, if need be, by torture. It could secure possession of his papers and other articles incident to his private life—a seizure effected, if need be, by breaking and entry. Protection against such invasion of "the sanctities of a man's home and the privacies of life" was provided in the Fourth and Fifth Amendments by specific language. *Boyd v. United States*, 116 U. S. 616, 630 (1886). But "time works changes, brings into existence new conditions and purposes." Subtler and more far-reaching means of invading privacy have become available to the Government. Discovery and invention have made it possible for the Government, by means far more effective than stretching upon the rack, to obtain disclosure in court of what is whispered in the closet.

Moreover, "in the application of a constitution, our contemplation cannot be only of what has been, but of what may be." *Weems*, 217 U.S. at 373. The progress of science in furnishing the Government with means of espionage is not likely to stop with wire tapping. Ways may some day be developed by which the Government, without removing papers from secret drawers, can reproduce them in court, and by which it will be enabled to expose to a jury the most intimate occurrences of the home. Advances in the psychic and related sciences may bring means of exploring unexpressed beliefs, thoughts and emotions. "That places the liberty of every man in the hands of every petty officer" was said by James Otis of much lesser intrusions than these. To Lord Camden, a far slighter intrusion seemed "subversive of all the comforts of society." Can it be that the Constitution affords no protection against such invasions of individual security? * * *

In *Ex parte Jackson*, 96 U. S. 727 (1877), it was held that a sealed letter intrusted to the mail is protected by the Amendments. The mail is a public service furnished by the Government. The telephone is a public service furnished by its authority. There is, in essence, no difference between the sealed letter and the private telephone message. As Judge Rudkin said below: "True, the one is visible, the other invisible; the one is tangible, the other intangible; the one is sealed, and the other unsealed; but these are distinctions without a difference."

The evil incident to invasion of the privacy of the telephone is far greater than that involved in tampering with the mails. Whenever a telephone line is tapped, the privacy of the persons at both ends of the line is invaded, and all conversations between them upon any subject, and although proper, confidential, and privileged, may be overheard. Moreover, the tapping of one man's telephone line involves the tapping of the telephone of every other person whom he may call, or who may call him. As a means of espionage, writs of assistance and general warrants are but puny instruments of tyranny and oppression when compared with wire-tapping.

Time and again, this Court, in giving effect to the principle underlying the Fourth Amendment, has refused to place an unduly literal construction upon it. * * * No court which looked at the words of the Amendment rather than at its underlying purpose would hold, as this Court did in *Ex parte Jackson*, 96 U.S. 727, 733 (1877), that its protection extended to letters in the mails. * * * Decisions of this Court * * * have settled [that] * * *

[u]njustified search and seizure violates the Fourth Amendment, whatever the character of the paper; whether the paper when taken by the federal officers was in the home, in an office, or elsewhere; whether the taking was effected by force, by fraud, or in the orderly process of a court's procedure. From these decisions, it follows necessarily that the Amendment is violated by the officer's reading the paper without a physical seizure, without his even touching it * * * .

Applying to the Fourth * * * Amendment[] the established rule of construction, the defendants' objections to the evidence obtained by wiretapping must, in my opinion, be sustained. It is, of course, immaterial where the physical connection with the telephone wires leading into the defendants' premises was made. And it is also immaterial that the intrusion was in aid of law enforcement. Experience should teach us to be most on our guard to protect liberty when the Government's purposes are beneficent. Men born to freedom are naturally alert to repel invasion of their liberty by evil-minded rulers. The greatest dangers to liberty lurk in insidious encroachment by men of zeal, well-meaning but without understanding.

[Dissenting opinions of Justice Holmes, Justice Butler, and Justice Stone omitted.]

Katz v. United States

Supreme Court of the United States, 1967
389 U.S. 347

MR. JUSTICE STEWART delivered the opinion of the Court.

The petitioner was convicted in the District Court for the Southern District of California under an eight-count indictment charging him with transmitting wagering information by telephone from Los Angeles to Miami and Boston in violation of a federal statute. At trial the Government was permitted, over the petitioner's objection, to introduce evidence of the petitioner's end of telephone conversations, overheard by FBI agents who had attached an electronic listening and recording device to the outside of the public telephone booth from which he had placed his calls. In affirming his conviction, the Court of Appeals rejected the contention that the recordings had been obtained in violation of the Fourth Amendment, because "[t]here was no physical entrance into the area occupied by, [the petitioner]." We granted certiorari in order to consider the constitutional questions thus presented. * * *

[T]he parties have attached great significance to the characterization of the telephone booth from which the petitioner placed his calls. The petitioner has strenuously argued that the booth was a "constitutionally protected area." The Government has maintained with equal vigor that it was not. But this effort to decide whether or not a given "area," viewed in the abstract, is "constitutionally protected" deflects attention from the problem presented by this case. For the Fourth Amendment protects people, not places. What a person knowingly exposes to the public, even in his own home or office, is not a subject of Fourth Amendment protection. But what he seeks to preserve as private, even in an area accessible to the public, may be constitutionally protected.

The Government stresses the fact that the telephone booth from which the petitioner made his calls was constructed partly of glass, so that he was as visible after he entered it as he would have been if he had remained outside. But what he sought to exclude when he entered the booth was not the intruding eye—it was the uninvited ear. He did not shed his right to do so simply because he made his calls from a place where he might be seen. No less than an individual in a business office, in a friend's apartment, or in a taxicab, a person in a telephone booth may rely upon the protection of the Fourth Amendment. One who occupies it, shuts the door behind him, and pays the toll that permits him to place a call is surely entitled to assume that the words he utters into the mouthpiece will not be broadcast to the world. To read the Constitution more narrowly is to ignore the vital role that the public telephone has come to play in private communication.

The Government contends, however, that the activities of its agents in this case should not be tested by Fourth Amendment requirements, for the surveillance technique they employed involved no physical penetration of the telephone booth from which the petitioner placed his calls. It is true that the absence of such penetration was at one time thought to foreclose further Fourth Amendment inquiry, *Olmstead v. United States*, 277 U.S. 438 (1928); *Goldman v. United States*, 316 U.S. 129, 134-136 (1942), for that Amendment was thought to limit only searches and seizures of tangible property. But "[t]he premise that property interests control the right of the Government to search and seize has been discredited." *Warden v. Hayden*, 387 U.S. 294, 304 (1967). Thus, although a closely divided Court supposed in *Olmstead* that surveillance without any trespass and without the seizure of any material object fell outside the ambit of the Constitution, we have since departed from the narrow view on which that decision rested. Indeed, we have expressly held that the Fourth Amendment governs not only the seizure of tangible items, but extends as well to the recording of oral statements overheard without any "technical trespass under * * * local property law." *Silverman v. United States*, 365 U.S. 505, 511 (1961). Once this much is acknowledged, and once it is recognized that the Fourth Amendment protects people—and not simply "areas"—against unreasonable searches and seizures, it becomes clear that the reach of that Amendment cannot turn upon the presence or absence of a physical intrusion into any given enclosure.

We conclude that the underpinnings of *Olmstead* and *Goldman* have been so eroded by our subsequent decisions that the "trespass" doctrine there enunciated can no longer be regarded as controlling. The Government's activities in electronically listening to and recording the petitioner's words violated the privacy upon which he justifiably relied while using the telephone booth and thus constituted a "search and seizure" within the meaning of the Fourth Amendment. The fact that the electronic device employed to achieve that end did not happen to penetrate the wall of the booth can have no constitutional significance.

The question remaining for decision, then, is whether the search and seizure conducted in this case complied with constitutional standards. In that regard, the Government's position is that its agents acted in an entirely defensible manner: They did not begin their electronic surveillance until investigation of the petitioner's activities had established a strong probability that he was using the telephone in question to transmit gambling information to persons in other States, in violation of federal law. Moreover, the surveillance was limited, both in scope and in duration, to the specific purpose of establishing the contents of the petitioner's unlawful telephonic communications. The agents confined their surveillance to the brief periods during which he used the telephone booth, and they took great care to overhear only the conversations of the petitioner himself.

Accepting this account of the Government's actions as accurate, it is clear that this surveillance was so narrowly circumscribed that a duly authorized magistrate, properly notified of the need for such investigation, specifically informed of the basis on which it was to proceed, and clearly apprised of the precise intrusion it would entail, could constitutionally have authorized, with appropriate safeguards, the very limited search and seizure that the Government asserts in fact took place. Only last Term we sustained the validity of such an authorization [in *Osborn v. United States*, 385 U.S. 323 (1967)]. * * *

The Government urges that, because its agents relied upon the decisions in *Olmstead* and *Goldman*, and because they did no more here than they might properly have done with prior judicial sanction, we should retroactively validate their conduct. That we cannot do. It is apparent that the agents in this case acted with restraint. Yet the inescapable fact is that this restraint was imposed by the agents themselves, not by a judicial officer. They were not required, before commencing the search, to present their estimate of probable cause for detached scrutiny by a neutral magistrate. They were not compelled, during the conduct of the search itself, to observe precise limits established in advance by a specific court order. Nor were they directed, after the search had been completed, to notify the authorizing magistrate in detail of all that had been seized. In the absence of such safeguards, this Court has never sustained a search upon the sole ground that officers reasonably expected to find evidence of a particular crime and voluntarily confined their activities to the least intrusive means consistent with that end. Searches conducted without warrants have been held unlawful "notwithstanding facts unquestionably showing probable cause," *Agnello v. United States*, 269 U.S. 20, 33 (1925), for the Constitution requires "that the deliberate, impartial judgment of a judicial officer . . . be interposed between the citizen and the police . . . ." *Wong Sun v. United States*, 371 U.S. 471, 481-482 (1963). * * *

[The] considerations [requiring prior judicial authorization by a magistrate upon a showing of probable cause] do not vanish when the search in question is transferred from the setting of a home, an office, or a hotel room to that of a telephone booth. Wherever a man may be, he is entitled to know that he will remain free from unreasonable searches and seizures. The government agents here ignored "the procedure of antecedent justification . . . that is central to the Fourth Amendment," *Osborn*, 385 U.S. at 330, a procedure that we hold to be a constitutional precondition of the kind of electronic surveillance involved in this case. Because the surveillance here failed to meet that condition, and because it led to the petitioner's conviction, the judgment must be reversed.

MR. JUSTICE MARSHALL took no part in the consideration or decision of this case.

MR. JUSTICE HARLAN, concurring:

As the Court's opinion states, "the Fourth Amendment protects people, not places." The question, however, is what protection it affords to those people. Generally, as here, the answer to that question requires reference to a "place." My understanding of the rule that has emerged from prior decisions is that there is a twofold requirement, first that a person have exhibited an actual (subjective) expectation of privacy and, second, that the expectation be one that society is prepared to recognize as "reasonable." Thus a man's home is, for most purposes, a place where he expects privacy, but objects, activities, or statements that he exposes to the "plain view" of outsiders are not "protected" because no intention to keep them to himself has been exhibited. On the other hand, conversations in the open would not be protected against being overheard, for the expectation of privacy under the circumstances would be unreasonable.

[Concurring opinions of Justice Douglas and Justice White and dissenting opinion of Justice Black omitted.]

Notes and Questions

1. Why did the *Olmstead* majority hold that government officials violate the Fourth Amendment only when their conduct would amount to a common law trespass to land? Recall the discussion in Chapter Two about the circumstances in which it is appropriate for a judge to adapt common law principles to changing technology. Would it have been appropriate to conclude that wiretapping itself can constitute a trespass? Why or why not?

2. Justice Brandeis explicitly concedes in *Olmstead* that the literal language of the Fourth Amendment does not prohibit wiretapping. Do you agree?

3. When is it legitimate for courts to account for changes in technology by giving effect to the underlying purpose of an Amendment rather than its precise language? How should courts discern that purpose? To what extent should a court seek to strike the same balance of protection between law and

technology as that which prevailed at the time of the Fourth Amendment's adoption?

4. In shifting the definition of what constitutes a search from the invasion of a constitutionally protected area to the invasion of the privacy on which an individual "justifiably relie[s]," does the *Katz* Court adequately give effect to the purpose of the Fourth Amendment? Can you think of any circumstances in which the trespass doctrine the Court abandons may actually be *more* protective than the privacy doctrine the Court embraces?

5. What, in Justice Harlan's view, is a reasonable expectation of privacy? To what extent is the reasonableness of an expectation affected by the availability of surveillance-facilitating technology? Consider the following case.

Kyllo v. United States

Supreme Court of the United States, 2001
533 U.S. 27

JUSTICE SCALIA delivered the opinion of the Court.

This case presents the question whether the use of a thermal-imaging device aimed at a private home from a public street to detect relative amounts of heat within the home constitutes a "search" within the meaning of the Fourth Amendment.

I

In 1991 Agent William Elliott of the United States Department of the Interior came to suspect that marijuana was being grown in the home belonging to petitioner Danny Kyllo, part of a triplex on Rhododendron Drive in Florence, Oregon. Indoor marijuana growth typically requires high-intensity lamps. In order to determine whether an amount of heat was emanating from petitioner's home consistent with the use of such lamps, at 3:20 a.m. on January 16, 1992, Agent Elliott and Dan Haas used an Agema Thermovision 210 thermal imager to scan the triplex. Thermal imagers detect infrared radiation, which virtually all objects emit but which is not visible to the naked eye. The imager converts radiation into images based on relative warmth—black is cool, white is hot, shades of gray connote relative differences; in that respect, it operates somewhat like a video camera showing heat images. The scan of Kyllo's home took only a few minutes and was performed from the passenger seat of Agent Elliott's vehicle across the street from the front of the house and also from the street in back of the house. The scan showed that the roof over the garage and a side wall of petitioner's home were relatively hot compared to the rest of the home and substantially warmer than neighboring homes in the triplex. Agent Elliott concluded that petitioner was using halide lights to grow marijuana in his house, which indeed he was. Based on tips from informants, utility bills, and the thermal imaging, a Federal Magistrate Judge issued a warrant authorizing a search of petitioner's home, and the agents found an indoor growing operation involving more than 100 plants. Petitioner was indicted on one count of manufacturing marijuana, in violation of 21 U.S.C. § 841(a)(1). He unsuccessfully moved to suppress the evidence seized from his home and then entered a conditional guilty plea. The Court of Appeals for the Ninth Circuit [affirmed]. * * *

II

The Fourth Amendment provides that "[t]he right of the people to be secure in their persons, houses, papers, and effects, against unreasonable searches and seizures, shall not be violated." "At the very core" of the Fourth Amendment "stands the right of a man to retreat into his own home and there be free from unreasonable governmental intrusion." *Silverman v. United States*, 365 U.S. 505, 511 (1961). With few exceptions, the question whether a warrantless search of a home is reasonable and hence constitutional must be answered no.

On the other hand, the antecedent question of whether or not a Fourth Amendment "search" has occurred is not so simple under our precedent. The permissibility of ordinary visual surveillance of a home used to be clear because, well into the 20th century, our Fourth Amendment jurisprudence was tied to common-law trespass. Visual surveillance was unquestionably lawful because "'the * * * eye cannot by the laws of England be guilty of a trespass.'" *Boyd v. United States*, 116 U.S. 616, 628 (1886) (quoting *Entick v. Carrington*, 19 How. St. Tr. 1029, 95 Eng. Rep. 807 (K.B.1765)). We have since decoupled violation of a person's Fourth Amendment rights from trespassory violation of his property, but the lawfulness of warrantless visual surveillance of a home has still been preserved.

One might think that the new validating rationale would be that examining the portion of a house that is in plain public view, while it is a "search" despite the absence of trespass, is not an "unreasonable" one under the Fourth Amendment. But in fact we have held that visual observation is no "search" at all—perhaps in order to preserve somewhat more intact our doctrine that warrantless searches are presumptively unconstitutional. In assessing when a search is not a search, we have applied somewhat in reverse the principle first enunciated in *Katz v. United States*, 389 U.S. 347 (1967). *Katz* involved eavesdropping by means of an electronic listening device placed on the outside of a telephone booth—a location not within the catalog ("persons, houses, papers, and effects") that the Fourth Amendment protects against unreasonable searches. We held that the Fourth Amendment nonetheless protected Katz from the warrantless eavesdropping because he "justifiably relied" upon the privacy of the telephone booth. *Id.*, at 353. As Justice Harlan's oft-quoted concurrence described it, a Fourth Amendment search occurs when the government violates a subjective expectation of privacy that society recognizes as reasonable. See *id.*, at 361. We have subsequently applied this principle to hold that a Fourth Amendment search does *not* occur—even when the explicitly protected location of a *house* is concerned—unless "the individual manifested a subjective expectation of privacy in the object of the challenged search," and "society [is] willing to recognize that expectation as reasonable." *California v. Ciraolo*, 476 U.S. 207, 211 (1986). * * *

The present case involves officers on a public street engaged in more than naked-eye surveillance of a home. We have previously reserved judgment as to how much technological enhancement of ordinary perception from such a vantage point, if any, is too much. While we upheld enhanced aerial photography of an industrial complex in *Dow Chemical Co. v. United States*, we noted that we found "it important that this is *not* an area immediately adjacent to a private home, where privacy expectations are most heightened," 476 U.S. 227, 237, n. 4 (1986) (emphasis in original).

III

It would be foolish to contend that the degree of privacy secured to citizens by the Fourth Amendment has been entirely unaffected by the advance of technology. For example, as the cases discussed above make clear, the technology enabling human flight has exposed to public view (and hence, we have said, to official observation) uncovered portions of the house and its curtilage that once were private. See *Ciraolo*, *supra*, at 215. The question we confront today is what limits there are upon this power of technology to shrink the realm of guaranteed privacy.

The *Katz* test—whether the individual has an expectation of privacy that society is prepared to recognize as reasonable—has often been criticized as circular, and hence subjective and unpredictable. While it may be difficult to refine *Katz* when the search of areas such as telephone booths, automobiles, or even the curtilage and uncovered portions of residences are at issue, in the case of the search of the interior of homes—the prototypical and hence most commonly litigated area of protected privacy—there is a ready criterion, with roots deep in the common law, of the minimal expectation of privacy that *exists*, and that is acknowledged to be *reasonable*. To withdraw protection of this minimum expectation would be to permit police technology to erode the privacy guaranteed by the Fourth Amendment. We think that obtaining by sense-enhancing technology any information regarding the interior of the home that could not otherwise have been obtained without physical "intrusion into a constitutionally protected area," *Silverman*, 365 U.S., at 512, constitutes a search—at least where (as here) the technology in question is not in general public use. This assures preservation of that degree of privacy against government that existed when the Fourth Amendment was adopted. On the basis of this criterion, the information obtained by the thermal imager in this case was the product of a search.

The Government maintains, however, that the thermal imaging must be upheld because it detected "only heat radiating from the external surface of the house." * * * But just as a thermal imager captures only heat emanating from a house, so also a powerful directional microphone picks up only sound emanating from a house—and a satellite capable of scanning from many miles away would pick up only visible light emanating from a house. We rejected such a mechanical interpretation of the Fourth

Amendment in *Katz*, where the eavesdropping device picked up only sound waves that reached the exterior of the phone booth. Reversing that approach would leave the homeowner at the mercy of advancing technology—including imaging technology that could discern all human activity in the home. While the technology used in the present case was relatively crude, the rule we adopt must take account of more sophisticated systems that are already in use or in development.[3] * * *

The Government also contends that the thermal imaging was constitutional because it did not "detect private activities occurring in private areas." It points out that in *Dow Chemical* we observed that the enhanced aerial photography did not reveal any "intimate details." 476 U.S., at 238. *Dow Chemical*, however, involved enhanced aerial photography of an industrial complex, which does not share the Fourth Amendment sanctity of the home. The Fourth Amendment's protection of the home has never been tied to measurement of the quality or quantity of information obtained. In *Silverman*, for example, we made clear that any physical invasion of the structure of the home, "by even a fraction of an inch," was too much, 365 U.S., at 512 and there is certainly no exception to the warrant requirement for the officer who barely cracks open the front door and sees nothing but the nonintimate rug on the vestibule floor. In the home, our cases show, *all* details are intimate details, because the entire area is held safe from prying government eyes. Thus, in *United States v. Karo*, 468 U.S. 705 (1984), the only thing detected was a can of ether in the home; and in *Arizona v. Hicks*, 480 U.S. 321 (1987), the only thing detected by a physical search that went beyond what officers lawfully present could observe in "plain view" was the registration number of a phonograph turntable. These were intimate details because they were details of the home, just as was the detail of how warm—or even how relatively warm—Kyllo was heating his residence. * * *

We have said that the Fourth Amendment draws "a firm line at the entrance to the house," *Payton v. New York*, 445 U.S. 573, 590 (1980). That line, we think, must be not only firm but also bright—which requires clear specification of those methods of surveillance that require a warrant. While it is certainly possible to conclude from the videotape of the thermal imaging that occurred in this case that no "significant" compromise of the homeowner's privacy has occurred, we must take the long view, from the original meaning of the Fourth Amendment forward.

"The Fourth Amendment is to be construed in the light of what was deemed an unreasonable search and seizure when it was adopted, and

---

3. The ability to "see" through walls and other opaque barriers is a clear, and scientifically feasible, goal of law enforcement research and development. The National Law Enforcement and Corrections Technology Center, a program within the United States Department of Justice, features on its Internet Website projects that include a "Radar-Based Through-the-Wall Surveillance System," "Handheld Ultrasound Through the Wall Surveillance," and a "Radar Flashlight" that "will enable law officers to detect individuals through interior building walls." www.nlectc.org/techproj/ (visited May 3, 2001).

in a manner which will conserve public interests as well as the interests and rights of individual citizens." *Carroll v. United States*, 267 U.S. 132, 149 (1925).

Where, as here, the Government uses a device that is not in general public use, to explore details of the home that would previously have been unknowable without physical intrusion, the surveillance is a "search" and is presumptively unreasonable without a warrant.

JUSTICE STEVENS, with whom THE CHIEF JUSTICE, JUSTICE O'CONNOR, and JUSTICE KENNEDY join, dissenting.

There is, in my judgment, a distinction of constitutional magnitude between "through-the-wall surveillance" that gives the observer or listener direct access to information in a private area, on the one hand, and the thought processes used to draw inferences from information in the public domain, on the other hand. The Court has crafted a rule that purports to deal with direct observations of the inside of the home, but the case before us merely involves indirect deductions from "off-the-wall" surveillance, that is, observations of the exterior of the home. Those observations were made with a fairly primitive thermal imager that gathered data exposed on the outside of petitioner's home but did not invade any constitutionally protected interest in privacy. Moreover, I believe that the supposedly "bright-line" rule the Court has created in response to its concerns about future technological developments is unnecessary, unwise, and inconsistent with the Fourth Amendment. * * *

II

Instead of trying to answer the question whether the use of the thermal imager in this case was even arguably unreasonable, the Court has fashioned a rule that is intended to provide essential guidance for the day when "more sophisticated systems" gain the "ability to 'see' through walls and other opaque barriers." The newly minted rule encompasses "obtaining [1] by sense-enhancing technology [2] any information regarding the interior of the home [3] that could not otherwise have been obtained without physical intrusion into a constitutionally protected area . . . [4] at least where (as here) the technology in question is not in general public use." In my judgment, the Court's new rule is at once too broad and too narrow, and is not justified by the Court's explanation for its adoption. As I have suggested, I would not erect a constitutional impediment to the use of sense-enhancing technology unless it provides its user with the functional equivalent of actual presence in the area being searched.

Despite the Court's attempt to draw a line that is "not only firm but also bright," the contours of its new rule are uncertain because its protection apparently dissipates as soon as the relevant technology is "in general public use." Yet how much use is general public use is not even hinted at by the Court's opinion, which makes the somewhat doubtful assumption that the thermal imager used in this case does not satisfy that criterion. In any event, putting aside its lack of clarity, this criterion is somewhat perverse because it seems likely that the threat to privacy will grow, rather than recede, as the use of intrusive equipment becomes more readily available.

It is clear, however, that the category of "sense-enhancing technology" covered by the new rule is far too broad. It would, for example, embrace potential mechanical substitutes for dogs trained to react when they sniff narcotics. But in *United States v. Place*, 462 U.S. 696, 707 (1983), we held that a dog sniff that "discloses only the presence or absence of narcotics" does "not constitute a 'search' within the meaning of the Fourth Amendment," and it must follow that sense-enhancing equipment that identifies nothing but illegal activity is not a search either. Nevertheless, the use of such a device would be unconstitutional under the Court's rule * * * .

The application of the Court's new rule to "any information regarding the interior of the home" is also unnecessarily broad. If it takes sensitive equipment to detect an odor that identifies criminal conduct and nothing else, the fact that the odor emanates from the interior of a home should not provide it with constitutional protection. * * * Because the new rule applies to information regarding the "interior" of the home, it is too narrow as well as too broad. Clearly, a rule that is designed to protect individuals from the overly intrusive use of sense-enhancing equipment should not be limited to a home. * * *

The final requirement of the Court's new rule, that the information "could not otherwise have been obtained without physical intrusion into a constitutionally protected area," also extends too far as the Court applies it. * * * [T]he Court effectively treats the mental process of analyzing data obtained from external sources as the equivalent of a physical intrusion into the home. * * * [T]he process of drawing inferences from data in the public domain should not be characterized as a search. * * *

III

Although the Court is properly and commendably concerned about the threats to privacy that may flow from advances in the technology available to the law enforcement profession, it has unfortunately failed to heed the tried and true counsel of judicial restraint. Instead of concentrating on the rather mundane issue that is actually presented by the case before it, the Court has endeavored to craft an all-encompassing rule for the future. It would be far wiser to give legislators an unimpeded opportunity to grapple with these emerging issues rather than to shackle them with prematurely devised constitutional constraints.

Notes and Questions

1. When, under the rule the Court announces in *Kyllo*, will police use of sense-enhancing technology violate the Fourth Amendment?

2. If thermal imaging becomes widely used, will its use by law enforcement officials be upheld in future cases? Should it be? Why or why not?

3. To what extent does the Court's opinion resurrect the notion, abandoned in *Katz*, that a Fourth Amendment violation occurs when the government invades a "constitutionally protected area"?

4. How would the Court's reasoning apply to the use of sense-enhancing technologies not directed at the home, such as technology designed to detect whether a suspect is carrying concealed weapons? How would the reasoning apply to technologies used to retrieve communications stored outside of the home, such as e-mail held on the servers of an Internet service provider?

5. With respect to surveillance techniques, should the task of moderating the balance between law enforcement and privacy interests fall to the courts, through interpretation of the Fourth Amendment, or to legislatures, through enactment of privacy laws? Congress has adopted protections governing the interception of communications, the retrieval stored communications, and the acquisition of source and destination information in connection with communications. We discuss those provisions in greater detail in Chapter Eight. For different perspectives on the appropriate roles of Congress and the courts, see, e.g., Orin S. Kerr, *The Fourth Amendment and New Technologies: Constitutional Myths and the Case for Caution*, 102 MICH. L. REV. 801 (2004); Peter P. Swire, *Katz is Dead. Long Live* Katz, 102 MICH. L. REV. 904 (2004).

SECTION B. THE USE OF TECHNOLOGY TO SUPPLANT LEGAL RULES

In the previous section, we explored ways in which law responds to technological change. Now, we turn to another problem raised by technology: the possibility that legislative compromises may be supplanted altogether by a combination of automated standardized contracts and technologically-based enforcement of them.

1. Automated Standardized Contracts

ProCD, Inc. v. Zeidenberg

United States Court of Appeals for the Seventh Circuit, 1996
86 F.3d 1447

EASTERBROOK, Circuit Judge.

Must buyers of computer software obey the terms of shrinkwrap licenses? The district court held not, for two reasons: first, they are not contracts because the licenses are inside the box rather than printed on the outside; second, federal law forbids enforcement even if the licenses are contracts. The parties and numerous amici curiae have briefed many other issues, but these are the only two that matter—and we disagree with the district judge's conclusion on each. Shrinkwrap licenses are enforceable unless their terms are objectionable on grounds applicable to contracts in general (for example, if they violate a rule of positive law, or if they are unconscionable). Because no one argues that the terms of the license at issue here are troublesome, we remand with instructions to enter judgment for the plaintiff.

I

ProCD, the plaintiff, has compiled information from more than 3,000 telephone directories into a computer database. We may assume that this database cannot be copyrighted * * * . ProCD sells a version of the database, called SelectPhone (trademark), on CD-ROM discs. * * * A proprietary method of compressing the data serves as effective encryption too. Customers decrypt and use the data with the aid of an application program that ProCD has written. This program, which is copyrighted, searches the database in response to users' criteria (such as "find all people named Tatum in Tennessee, plus all firms with 'Door Systems' in the corporate name"). The resulting lists (or, as ProCD prefers, "listings") can be read and manipulated by other software, such as word processing programs. * * *

[ProCD makes a commercial version of the product and a less expensive consumer version.] Every box containing its consumer product declares that the software comes with restrictions stated in an enclosed license. This license, which is encoded on the CD-ROM disks as well as printed in the manual, and which appears on a user's screen every time the software runs, limits use of the application program and listings to non-commercial purposes.

Matthew Zeidenberg bought a consumer package of SelectPhone in 1994 from a retail outlet in Madison, Wisconsin, but decided to ignore the license. He formed Silken Mountain Web Services, Inc., to resell the information in the SelectPhone database. The corporation makes the database available on the Internet to anyone willing to pay its price—which, needless to say, is less than ProCD charges its commercial customers. * * * ProCD filed this suit seeking an injunction against further dissemination that exceeds the rights specified in the licenses * * * .

II

Following the district court, we treat the licenses as ordinary contracts accompanying the sale of products, and therefore as governed by the common law of contracts and the Uniform Commercial Code. * * * Zeidenberg [argues], and the district court held, that placing the package of software on the shelf is an "offer," which the customer "accepts" by paying the asking price and leaving the store with the goods. In Wisconsin, as elsewhere, a contract includes only the terms on which the parties have agreed. One cannot agree to hidden terms, the judge concluded. So far, so good—but one of the terms to which Zeidenberg agreed by purchasing the software is that the transaction was subject to a license. Zeidenberg's position therefore must be that the printed terms on the outside of a box are the parties' contract—except for printed terms that refer to or incorporate other terms. But why would Wisconsin fetter the parties' choice in this way? Vendors can put the entire terms of a contract on the outside of a box only by using microscopic type, removing other information that buyers might find more useful (such as what the software does, and on which computers it works), or both. The "Read Me" file included with most software, describing system requirements and potential incompatibilities, may be equivalent to ten pages of type; warranties and license restrictions take still more space. Notice on the outside, terms on the inside, and a right to return the software for a refund if the terms are unacceptable (a right that the license expressly extends), may be a means of doing business valuable to buyers and sellers alike. * * *

III

The district court held that, even if Wisconsin treats shrinkwrap licenses as contracts, § 301(a) of the Copyright Act, 17 U.S.C. § 301(a), prevents their enforcement. The relevant part of § 301(a) preempts any "legal or equitable rights [under state law] that are equivalent to any of the exclusive rights within the general scope of copyright as specified by section 106 in works of authorship that are fixed in a tangible medium of expression and come within the subject matter of copyright as specified by sections 102 and 103." * * * One function of § 301(a) is to prevent states from giving special protection to works of authorship that Congress has decided should be in the public domain * * * .

But are rights created by contract "equivalent to any of the exclusive rights within the general scope of copyright"? * * * Rights "equivalent to any of the exclusive rights within the general scope of copyright" are rights established *by law*—rights that restrict the options of persons who are strangers to the author. Copyright law forbids duplication, public performance, and so on, unless the person wishing to copy or perform the work gets permission; silence means a ban on copying. A copyright is a right against the world. Contracts, by contrast, generally affect only their parties; strangers may do as they please, so contracts do not create "exclusive rights." Someone who found a copy of SelectPhone on the street would not be affected by the shrinkwrap license—though the federal copyright laws of their own force would limit the finder's ability to copy or transmit the application program. * * *

A law student uses the LEXIS database, containing public-domain documents, under a contract limiting the results to educational endeavors; may the student resell his access to this database to a law firm from which LEXIS seeks to collect a much higher hourly rate? Suppose ProCD hires a firm to scour the nation for telephone directories, promising to pay $100 for each that ProCD does not already have. The firm locates 100 new directories, which it sends to ProCD with an invoice for $10,000. ProCD incorporates the directories into its database; does it have to pay the bill? Surely yes; * * * promises to pay for intellectual property may be enforced even though federal law * * * offers no protection against third-party uses of that property. But these illustrations are what our case is about. ProCD offers software and data for two prices: one for personal use, a higher price for commercial use. Zeidenberg wants to use the data without paying the seller's price; if the law student * * * could not do that, neither can Zeidenberg.

Although Congress possesses power to preempt even the enforcement of contracts about intellectual property * * * courts usually read preemption clauses to leave private contracts unaffected. * * * Section 301(a) * * * prevents states from substituting their own regulatory systems for those of the national government. Just as § 301(a) does not itself interfere with private transactions in intellectual property, so it does not prevent states from respecting those transactions. * * * [W]e think it prudent to refrain from adopting a rule that anything with the label "contract" is necessarily outside the preemption clause: the variations and possibilities are too numerous to foresee. * * * But general enforcement of shrinkwrap licenses of the kind before us does not create such interference.

Notes and Questions

1. Courts have often been willing to enforce contractual provisions even when they potentially conflict with federal copyright law. For example, in *Bowers v. Baystate Technologies, Inc.*, 320 F.3d 1317 (Fed. Cir. 2003), the Federal Circuit, following *ProCD*, ruled that a shrinkwrap agreement could prevent a purchaser of computer software from "reverse engineering" it to view the source code, even though the very same court had previously held such reverse engineering to be fair use under the Copyright Act. Yet if state contract law is not preempted by federal copyright law, then are there no rights granted under copyright law that cannot be given away pursuant to contract? For example, what if a software license included a provision that prevented the user from writing a review of the product in any trade publication or general interest magazine or newspaper? Such a provision surely would run afoul of the fair use provisions of the Copyright Act. But would the provision nevertheless be enforceable pursuant to state contract law? At least one court has disallowed such a provision. *See State of New York v. Network Associates*, 758 N.Y.S.2d 466 (N.Y. Sup. Ct. 2003).

2. How far do you think the court's reasoning extends? The court notes that the terms of the license were inside the box and that the license provided a right to return the software for a refund if the user objected to the terms. How important do you think these aspects of the holding were? What if there had been no opportunity to see the terms even after purchase? Or what if the terms were included inside the box, but there was no provision for returning the product? Do you think the court would have resolved the case the same way?

3. Although *ProCD* establishes that substantive contract terms embodied in shrinkwrap licenses are generally enforceable, there may be circumstances under which courts will find that such terms have not been "accepted" by the consumer. Consider the following case.

Specht v. Netscape Communications Corp.

United States Court of Appeals for the Second Circuit, 2002
306 F.3d 17

SOTOMAYOR, Circuit Judge.

This is an appeal from a judgment of the Southern District of New York denying a motion by defendants-appellants Netscape Communications Corporation and its corporate parent, America Online, Inc. (collectively, "defendants" or "Netscape"), to compel arbitration and to stay court proceedings. In order to resolve the central question of arbitrability presented here, we must address issues of contract formation in cyberspace. Principally, we are asked to determine whether plaintiffs-appellees ("plaintiffs"), by acting upon defendants' invitation to download free software made available on defendants' webpage, agreed to be bound by the software's license terms (which included the arbitration clause at issue), even though plaintiffs could not have learned of the existence of those terms unless, prior to executing the download, they had scrolled down the webpage to a screen located below the download button. We agree with the district court that a reasonably prudent Internet user in circumstances such as these would not have known or learned of the existence of the license terms before responding to defendants' invitation to download the free software, and that defendants therefore did not provide reasonable notice of the license terms. In consequence, plaintiffs' bare act of downloading the software did not unambiguously manifest assent to the arbitration provision contained in the license terms. * * *

BACKGROUND

In three related putative class actions, plaintiffs alleged that, unknown to them, their use of SmartDownload transmitted to defendants private information about plaintiffs' downloading of files from the Internet, thereby effecting an electronic surveillance of their online activities in violation of two federal statutes, the Electronic Communications Privacy Act, 18 U.S.C. §§ 2510 *et seq.*, and the Computer Fraud and Abuse Act, 18 U.S.C. § 1030.

Specifically, plaintiffs alleged that when they first used Netscape's Communicator—a software program that permits Internet browsing—the program created and stored on each of their computer hard drives a small text file known as a "cookie" that functioned "as a kind of electronic identification tag for future communications" between their computers and Netscape. Plaintiffs further alleged that when they installed SmartDownload—a separate software "plug-in" that served to enhance Communicator's browsing capabilities—SmartDownload created and stored on their computer hard drives another string of characters, known as a "Key," which similarly functioned as an identification tag in future communications with Netscape. According to the complaints in this case, each time a computer user employed Communicator to download a file from the Internet, SmartDownload "assume[d] from Communicator the task of downloading" the file and transmitted to Netscape the address of the file being downloaded together with the cookie created by Communicator and the Key created by SmartDownload. These processes, plaintiffs claim, constituted unlawful "eavesdropping" on users of Netscape's software products as well as on Internet websites from which users employing SmartDownload downloaded files.

In the time period relevant to this litigation, Netscape offered on its website various software programs, including Communicator and SmartDownload, which visitors to the site were invited to obtain free of charge. It is undisputed that five of the six named plaintiffs—Michael Fagan, John Gibson, Mark Gruber, Sean Kelly, and Sherry Weindorf—downloaded Communicator from the Netscape website. These plaintiffs acknowledge that when they proceeded to initiate installation of Communicator, they were automatically shown a scrollable text of that program's license agreement and were not permitted to complete the installation until they had clicked on a "Yes" button to indicate that they accepted all the license terms. If a user attempted to install Communicator without clicking "Yes," the installation would be aborted. All five named user plaintiffs expressly agreed to Communicator's license terms by clicking "Yes." The Communicator license agreement that these plaintiffs saw made no mention of SmartDownload or other plug-in programs, and stated that "[t]hese terms apply to Netscape Communicator and Netscape Navigator" and that "all disputes relating to this Agreement (excepting any dispute relating to intellectual property rights)" are subject to "binding arbitration in Santa Clara County, California." * * *

The signal difference between downloading Communicator and downloading SmartDownload was that no clickwrap presentation accompanied the latter operation. Instead, once plaintiffs * * * had clicked on the "Download" button located at or near the bottom of their screen, and the downloading of SmartDownload was complete, these plaintiffs encountered no further information about the plug-in program or the existence of license terms governing its use. The sole reference to SmartDownload's license terms on the "SmartDownload Communicator" webpage was located in text that would have become visible to plaintiffs only if they had scrolled down to the next screen.

Had plaintiffs scrolled down instead of acting on defendants' invitation to click on the "Download" button, they would have encountered the following invitation: "Please review and agree to the terms of the *Netscape SmartDownload software license agreement* before downloading and using the software." Plaintiffs Gibson, Gruber, Kelly, and Weindorf averred in their affidavits that they never saw this reference to the SmartDownload license agreement when they clicked on the "Download" button. They also testified during depositions that they saw no reference to license terms when they clicked to download SmartDownload, although under questioning by defendants' counsel, some plaintiffs added that they could not "remember" or be "sure" whether the screen shots of the SmartDownload page attached to their affidavits reflected precisely what they had seen on their computer screens when they downloaded SmartDownload.

In sum, plaintiffs Gibson, Gruber, Kelly, and Weindorf allege that the process of obtaining SmartDownload contrasted sharply with that of obtaining Communicator. Having selected SmartDownload, they were required neither to express unambiguous assent to that program's license agreement nor even to view the license terms or become aware of their existence before proceeding with the invited download of the free plug-in program. Moreover, once these plaintiffs had initiated the download, the existence of SmartDownload's license terms was not mentioned while the software was running or at any later point in plaintiffs' experience of the product.

Even for a user who, unlike plaintiffs, did happen to scroll down past the download button, SmartDownload's license terms would not have been immediately displayed in the manner of Communicator's clickwrapped terms. Instead, if such a user had seen the notice of SmartDownload's terms and then clicked on the underlined invitation to review and agree to the terms, a hypertext link would have taken the user to a separate webpage entitled "License & Support Agreements." The first paragraph on this page read, in pertinent part:

> The use of each Netscape software product is governed by a license agreement. You must read and agree to the license agreement terms BEFORE acquiring a product. Please click on the appropriate link below to review the current license agreement for the product of interest to you before acquisition. For products available for download, you must read and agree to the license agreement terms BEFORE you install the software. If you do not agree to the license terms, do not download, install or use the software.

Below this paragraph appeared a list of license agreements, the first of which was "*License Agreement for Netscape Navigator and Netscape Communicator Product Family* (Netscape Navigator, Netscape Communicator and Netscape SmartDownload)." If the user clicked on that link, he or she would be taken to yet another webpage that contained the full text of a license agreement that was identical in every respect to the Communicator license agreement except that it stated that its "terms apply to Netscape Communicator, Netscape Navigator, and Netscape SmartDownload." The license agreement granted the user a nonexclusive license to use and reproduce the software, subject to certain terms:

> BY CLICKING THE ACCEPTANCE BUTTON OR INSTALLING OR USING NETSCAPE COMMUNICATOR, NETSCAPE NAVIGATOR, OR NETSCAPE SMARTDOWNLOAD SOFTWARE (THE "PRODUCT"), THE INDIVIDUAL OR ENTITY LICENSING THE PRODUCT ("LICENSEE") IS CONSENTING TO BE BOUND BY AND IS BECOMING A PARTY TO THIS AGREEMENT. IF LICENSEE DOES NOT AGREE TO ALL OF THE TERMS OF THIS AGREEMENT, THE BUTTON INDICATING NON-ACCEPTANCE MUST BE SELECTED, AND LICENSEE MUST NOT INSTALL OR USE THE SOFTWARE.

Among the license terms was a provision requiring virtually all disputes relating to the agreement to be submitted to arbitration:

> Unless otherwise agreed in writing, all disputes relating to this Agreement (excepting any dispute relating to intellectual property rights) shall be subject to final and binding arbitration in Santa Clara County, California, under the auspices of JAMS/EndDispute, with the losing party paying all costs of arbitration.

* * *

DISCUSSION

The [Federal Arbitration Act (FAA)] provides that a "written provision in any . . . contract evidencing a transaction involving commerce to settle by arbitration a controversy thereafter arising out of such contract or transaction . . . shall be valid, irrevocable, and enforceable, save upon such grounds as exist at law or in equity for the revocation of any contract." 9 U.S.C. § 2. It is well settled that a court may not compel arbitration until it has resolved "the question of the very existence" of the contract embodying the arbitration clause. "[A]rbitration is a matter of contract and a party cannot be required to submit to arbitration any dispute which he has not agreed so to submit." *AT & T Techs., Inc. v. Communications Workers of Am.*, 475 U.S. 643, 648 (1986) (quotation marks omitted). * * *

Whether governed by the common law or by Article 2 of the Uniform Commercial Code ("UCC"), a transaction, in order to be a contract, requires a manifestation of agreement between the parties. Mutual manifestation of assent, whether by written or spoken word or by conduct, is the touchstone of contract. Although an onlooker observing the disputed transactions in this case would have seen each of the user plaintiffs click on the SmartDownload "Download" button, a consumer's clicking on a download button does not communicate assent to contractual terms if the offer did not make clear to the consumer that clicking on the download button would signify assent to those terms. California's common law is clear that "an offeree, regardless of apparent manifestation of his consent, is not bound by inconspicuous contractual provisions of which he is unaware, contained in a document whose contractual nature is not obvious." *Windsor Mills, Inc. v. Collins & Aikman Corp.*, 25 Cal. App. 3d 987, 992 (1972).

Arbitration agreements are no exception to the requirement of manifestation of assent. * * * Clarity and conspicuousness of arbitration terms are important in securing informed assent. "If a party wishes to bind in writing another to an agreement to arbitrate future disputes, such purpose should be accomplished in a way that each party to the arrangement will fully and clearly comprehend that the agreement to arbitrate exists and binds the parties thereto." *Commercial Factors Corp. v. Kurtzman Bros.*, 131 Cal. App. 2d 133, 134-35 (1955) (internal quotation marks omitted). Thus, California contract law measures assent by an objective standard that takes into account both what the offeree said, wrote, or did and the transactional context in which the offeree verbalized or acted.

Defendants argue that plaintiffs must be held to a standard of reasonable prudence and that, because notice of the existence of SmartDownload license terms was on the next scrollable screen, plaintiffs were on "inquiry notice" of those terms. We disagree with the proposition that a reasonably prudent offeree in plaintiffs' position would necessarily have known or learned of the existence of the SmartDownload license agreement prior to acting, so that plaintiffs may be held to have assented to that agreement with constructive notice of its terms. It is true that "[a] party cannot avoid the terms of a contract on the ground that he or she failed to read it before signing." *Marin Storage & Trucking, Inc. v. Benco Trucking & Eng'g, Inc.*, 107 Cal. Rptr. 2d 645, 651 (Cal. App. 1st Dist. 2001). But courts are quick to add: "An exception to this general rule exists when the writing does not appear to be a contract and the terms are not called to the attention of the recipient. In such a case, no contract is formed with respect to the undisclosed term." *Id.*

Most of the cases cited by defendants in support of their inquiry-notice argument are drawn from the world of paper contracting. * * * [R]eceipt of a physical document containing contract terms or notice thereof is frequently deemed, in the world of paper transactions, a sufficient circumstance to place the offeree on inquiry notice of those terms. * * * These principles apply equally to the emergent world of online product delivery, pop-up screens, hyperlinked pages, clickwrap licensing, scrollable documents, and urgent admonitions to "Download Now!". What plaintiffs saw when they were being invited by defendants to download this fast, free plug-in called SmartDownload was a screen containing praise for the product and, at the very bottom of the screen, a "Download" button. Defendants argue that under the principles set forth in the cases cited above, a "fair and prudent person using ordinary care" would have been on inquiry notice of SmartDownload's license terms.

We are not persuaded that a reasonably prudent offeree in these circumstances would have known of the existence of license terms. Plaintiffs were responding to an offer that did not carry an immediately visible notice of the existence of license terms or require unambiguous manifestation of assent to those terms. Thus, plaintiffs' "apparent manifestation of . . . consent" was to terms "contained in a document whose contractual nature [was] not obvious." *Windsor Mills*, 101 Cal. Rptr. at 351. Moreover, the fact that, given the position of the scroll bar on their computer screens, plaintiffs may have been aware that an unexplored portion of the Netscape webpage remained below the download button does not mean that they reasonably should have concluded that this portion contained a notice of license terms. In their deposition testimony, plaintiffs variously stated that they used the scroll bar "[o]nly if there is something that I feel I need to see that is on—that is off the page," or that the elevated position of the scroll bar suggested the presence of "mere[] formalities, standard lower banner links" or "that the page is bigger than what I can see." Plaintiffs testified, and defendants did not refute, that plaintiffs were in fact unaware that defendants intended to attach license terms to the use of SmartDownload.

We conclude that in circumstances such as these, where consumers are urged to download free software at the immediate click of a button, a reference to the existence of license terms on a submerged screen is not sufficient to place consumers on inquiry or constructive notice of those terms. * * * Internet users may have, as defendants put it, "as much time as they need[]" to scroll through multiple screens on a webpage, but there is no reason to assume that viewers will scroll down to subsequent screens simply because screens are there. When products are "free" and users are invited to download them in the absence of reasonably conspicuous notice that they are about to bind themselves to contract terms, the transactional circumstances cannot be fully analogized to those in the paper world of arm's-length bargaining. * * *

In *ProCD, Inc. v. Zeidenberg*, the [Seventh Circuit] held that where an individual purchased software in a box containing license terms which were displayed on the computer screen every time the user executed the software program, the user had sufficient opportunity to review the terms and to return the software, and so was contractually bound after retaining the product. *ProCD*, 86 F.3d 1447, 1452 (7th Cir. 1996). * * * Insofar as the purchaser in *ProCD* was confronted with conspicuous, mandatory license terms every time he ran the software on his computer, that case actually undermines defendants' contention that downloading in the absence of conspicuous terms is an act that binds plaintiffs to those terms. * * * [Other] cases in which courts have found contracts arising from Internet use do not assist defendants, because in those circumstances there was much clearer notice than in the present case that a user's act would manifest assent to contract terms. * * *

After reviewing the California common law and other relevant legal authority, we conclude that under the circumstances here, plaintiffs' downloading of SmartDownload did not constitute acceptance of defendants' license terms. Reasonably conspicuous notice of the existence of contract terms and unambiguous manifestation of assent to those terms by consumers are essential if electronic bargaining is to have integrity and credibility. We hold that a reasonably prudent offeree in plaintiffs' position would not have known or learned, prior to acting on the invitation to download, of the reference to SmartDownload's license terms hidden below the "Download" button on the next screen. We affirm the district court's conclusion that the user plaintiffs * * * are not bound by the arbitration clause contained in those terms.

Notes and Questions

1. The *Specht* court distinguishes *ProCD* on the ground that the license terms in *ProCD* were more conspicuous. Does the different outcome merely reflect the difference between shrinkwrap and "browsewrap" licenses? As one court has noted, a "'shrink-wrap license agreement' is open and obvious and in

fact hard to miss," whereas terms and conditions on a website are often "set forth so that the customer needs to scroll down the home page to find and read them." Given this difference, the court concluded, "[i]t cannot be said that merely putting the terms and conditions in this fashion necessarily creates a contract with any one using the website." *Ticketmaster Corp. v. Tickets.com, Inc.*, 2000 WL 525390, *3 (C.D. Cal. 2000).

2. Such "browsewrap" licenses can be distinguished from "clickwrap" licenses, which actually require the user to click a button labeled "I agree" before proceeding to the next screen. Do such procedures solve the notice problems identified in *Specht*? If so, why should the two different procedures lead to completely different outcomes? Does it matter whether or not the user actually reads the license prior to clicking "I agree"? At least one federal court of appeals has indicated that the enforcement of online terms of use should *not* be dependent on a specific act of assent by the user. In *Register.com, Inc. v. Verio, Inc.*, 356 F.3d 393 (2d Cir. 2004), the Second Circuit noted that "[i]t is standard contract doctrine that when a benefit is offered subject to stated conditions, and the offeree makes a decision to take the benefit with knowledge of the terms of the offer, the taking constitutes an acceptance of the terms, which accordingly become binding on the offeree." *Id.* at 403.

3. How important to the analysis is the perceived fairness/appropriateness of the substantive contractual term? In *Specht*, although the court does not address the substance of the arbitration clause directly, do you think that concerns about the fairness of mandatory arbitration informed the decision? To test this idea, consider a suit regarding a provision of the license agreement that might be far less controversial, say, a small fee for a late payment. Should it matter that most consumers would have accepted the provision and that there is no substantive unfairness? Should the provision nevertheless be deemed unenforceable because of a lack of notice?

4. By requiring evidence of assent, is the *Specht* court likely to make browsing websites more cumbersome for users? After all, in the wake of this decision, sites are more likely to insist that users scroll down to the end of every license agreement and click "I agree." Such requirements slow down users and lessen the efficiency and speed of online activity. Is this a price worth bearing, or could courts achieve the same ends simply by refusing to enforce unconscionable contract terms rather than resting enforcement decisions on formal notice?

5. Might the entire language of contract be inappropriate to describe these forms of private regulation? After all, by changing the inquiry from *consent* to *assent*, we have already moved a fair distance from the classic model of contract as bargained-for exchange. "Shrinkwrap," "browsewrap," and "clickwrap" arrangements go farther still. Is it a cause for concern when the "law of the state" is effectively replaced by the "law of the firm" through the use of such purported agreements? Are there any substantive limitations on the possible terms that could be enforceable? Consider this argument.

Margaret Jane Radin, *Regulation by Contract, Regulation by Machine*

160 J. OF INST'L & THEORETICAL ECON. 142 (2004)

Introduction

Property and contract form the legal infrastructure for what is known as private ordering. Actually "private ordering" is a misleading term, if those who use it mean ordering without state regulation. Ordering by property and contract has significant regulatory dimensions, because whether or not entitlements and transactions are valid and efficacious depends on state definition and enforcement of the rules that comprise the legal infrastructure. The state's structuring of the contours of property rights delimits the list of recognized entitlements and the possible range of exploitation of them. The state's structuring of what counts as contract separates legitimate from illegitimate redistributions of those entitlements.

In this essay I want to consider what is happening to property and contract in the world of networked computers and digitized content. * * *

Replacing the Law of the State with the "Law" of the Firm

The original form of shrink-wrap contract, usually called a shrink-wrap license, came with software marketed in boxes covered with transparent plastic shrink-wrap film. The terms were either printed on the shrink-wrap, or on the box beneath, or on a card between the box and the shrink-wrap. The terms stated that by breaking the shrink-wrap the purchaser was signifying acceptance of the terms. In this type of procedure the purchaser could have seen the terms before purchasing—though whether in fact anyone ever actually read them is unknown but doubtful. The term shrink-wrap was later extended to refer to a procedure that has come to be known as "money-now-terms-later." In this situation what is printed on the box or on the card under the shrink-wrap states that there are additional terms inside the box. Here the terms cannot be seen before purchase. They are on a separate sheet or in a separate envelope containing the diskettes or CD in which the software is fixed, and/or they are shown on the start-up screen when the user runs the program. The terms usually state that using the software constitutes acceptance of the terms, and that if the buyer wants to reject the terms he must return the software and will receive a refund.[3]

The term click-wrap has nothing to do with wrapping, other than the functional resemblance—the proponent's desire to achieve legally binding commitment—to procedures called shrink-wrap. Click-wrap just means that the user or customer is asked to signify acceptance of terms by clicking with her mouse in a box on her computer screen. Similarly, the term

---

3. A celebrated case enforcing a shrink-wrap license of the second kind is *ProCD v. Zeidenberg*, 86 F. 3d 1447 (7th Cir. 1996). Other courts have been doubtful. See, e.g., *Step-Saver Data Systems, Inc. v. Wyse Technology*, 939 F.2d 91 (3d Cir. 1991).

browse-wrap has nothing to do with wrapping either. This locution refers to terms on an interior page of a website, which the viewer, who is browsing, will not see unless he chooses to click on the small print of a link at the bottom of a home page. usually labeled "Terms" or "Terms of Use" or sometimes merely "Legal Notices." The terms commonly say that continuing to use the site—whether or not the user ever clicks on or even sees the link that would reveal the terms—binds the user to these terms and such new terms as the site owner may post from time to time. Thus the terms declare themselves binding on anyone accessing the site, regardless of whether anyone ever opens the link that reveals them.

It is clear that these "-wrap" procedures are not "agreements" in accord with the traditional rhetoric of "consent" and "meeting of the minds," but neither are most contracts in the contemporary offline world. Although the principles to be applied in these cases are not fully developed, U.S. law inclines in the direction of finding contractual obligation in many or most of them. The controversial proposed UCITA (Uniform Computer Information Transactions Act) would validate them explicitly in a broad range of cases.[6] It is my impression that non-U.S. jurisdictions are much less likely than U.S. states to find binding commitment vis-à-vis a consumer in cases involving standardized purported contracts of this kind. What should ultimately be the appropriate legal position(s) on validity and enforceability of these purported contracts? That is a complex question, and an urgent one, because if e-commerce is to flourish we will need more harmonization and more certainty of contract. We will need it all the more because, as this essay argues, contract is displacing intellectual property law as the main source of rules governing distribution of rights among content owners, licensees or purchasers, and the general public.

Nevertheless, I am going to bracket the question of validity and enforceability for now, in order to explore the world these contracts would create. So let us assume all of these contracts are efficacious. By efficacious I mean that the regimes of rules laid down in the contracts govern the actual behavior of parties in the world. By assuming the contracts are efficacious in this sense, I am assuming that all of the state's rules of entitlement are default rules, and that the courts will not use contract-limiting doctrines such as unconscionability to preclude enforcement. The assumption that all entitlements recognized and laid down by the state are default rules means that all legal rights granted or protected by the constitution, all legal rules enacted by legislatures, and all doctrines worked out by the courts can he waived or altered by contract. The assumption that the courts will not use contract-limiting doctrines means that the

---

6. The proposed UCITA has been enacted in two states, but three states have enacted "bomb shelter" legislation to prevent its being applied to their residents. The National Commissioners on Uniform State Laws (NCCUSL), after several years of championing (and redrafting) UCITA, has now put it on hold. UCITA has been opposed by the American Law Institute (ALI) and about half of the states' attorneys general. For information on UCITA, see www.ncusi.org.

traditional limits built into contract law, such as unconscionability, will not be used to alter the terms as written. * * *

In the hypothetical world of contractual efficaciousness and default rules, a standardized mass-market contract creates its own regime of liberties and obligations, in which the constitutional, legislative or judicial rules engendered by the state are superseded by the contractual regime. * * * If the AOL TOS ("Terms of Service") were to provide that the recipient shall not bring a class action, then a regime without class actions prevails in this social world, even if the legislature has seen fit to provide the polity with class action remedies. If the Microsoft EULA ("End User License Agreement") were to provide that anyone using the software is precluded from publishing a critical review of it, then in this regime the First Amendment is inoperative and superseded. If eBay's TOS were to decree that data made available to the public on the site could only be used by consumers for personal and noncommercial purposes, then the U.S. constitutional holding[10] that facts are not propertizable under copyright law is irrelevant. I am going to call these regimes "efficacious promulgated superseding entitlement regimes"—EPSER's. They are "superseding" because they replace the law of the state with the "law" of the company: "promulgated" because they are developed and "enacted" by the company without negotiation or input from the recipient and "regimes" because they are widespread, governing many millions of people.

Toward the Irrelevance of the Property Regime

Now I want to examine what happens to property in this hypothetical world of EPSER's. The exact contouring of property entitlement—what specific package of rights constitutes a property interest recognized by the state—is evolutionary and is a balancing enterprise undertaken by the polity. By delimiting property rights the entities of the state also limit propertization, and limit the extent of control propertization confers on owners. Propertization has a democratic component, because the entities of the state are, at least ideally, responsive to democratic input.

Consider this perspective on copyright law. Suppose that after extensive and expensive political debate and maneuvering, extensive consideration of the arguments of all parties, the U.S. Congress arrives at a regime of intellectual property entitlements representing various incentives, trade-offs, balances, deals, respect for property ideology and culture, express or inherent constitutional commitments, and so forth. Suppose the regime as thus constructed looks like the U.S. Copyright Act of 1976, as interpreted by the federal courts. In that regime, property in information is limited to expression of ideas; ideas are non-property. Expression can also be non-property in special situations where others need to use it for their business. Property in expression expires after a fixed term, albeit a long one. Thus, older information is non-property, and property does not include the right to extend monopoly control past the

---

10. *Feist Publications, Inc. v. Rural Telephone Service Co, Inc.*, 499 U.S. 340 (1991).

enacted term. Property in information is limited to expression that is original (exhibits some modicum of creativity); unoriginal information, such as facts, is non-property. Infringement against property can be excused on a case-by-case basis in certain circumstances labeled fair use. Whatever activity in derogation of rights of the copyright holder that is adjudicated fair use becomes non-property, just as whatever activity of a landowner is adjudicated nuisance becomes non-property. Copyright law also contains an exhaustion provision (known as the first-sale doctrine), such that when the owner passes a tangible object in which a work is fixed to a new owner, the new owner is free to pass on the object subsequently. Property in information does not include the right to restrain alienation of information-containing objects, nor thereby to preclude subsequent transferees from accessing or using the information. Property in information does not include the right to leverage the monopoly against would-be competitors in ways that courts interpret as copyright misuse.

Next consider a widespread promulgated contractual regime of the sort I described earlier and assumed to be efficacious, an EPSER. Let's assume that a term of the contract says that no copying of information—software or other content—will be permitted. This provision supersedes copyright law by extending control of the property owner to information that the copyright law delimits as non-property: information consisting of fact, or consisting of ideas, or older than the duration of propertization, etc. Let's assume that another term says that the recipient is precluded from exercising fair use rights, for example by performing intermediate copying for the purpose of reverse engineering. This provision supersedes copyright law by extending control of the property owner to foreclose a legislatively enacted safety valve, which the legislature deliberately left open to those who were willing to infringe and turn the matter over to a court to adjudicate as non-actionable. Let's assume that still another term says that the recipient is precluded from passing to anyone else the tangible object in which the information is embodied. This provision supersedes copyright law by extending control of the property owner to include a restraint on alienation that the legislature denied.

If we continue assuming, as I have been doing, that the mass-market contractual regime is efficacious, then it is obvious that for a large subset of the social order, copyright, the law of the state, has been superseded by the promulgated contractual regime, the "law" of the firm. In the limiting case, in which the entire society has become subject to the extended propertization regime, the official constitutional/legislative/judicial regime is completely irrelevant. In situations short of the limiting case, but in which large numbers of people are subject to these superseding regimes, the official constitutional/legislative/judicial regime is severely eroded or marginalized.[12]

Moreover, it is also obvious that these promulgated regimes extend propertization far beyond the level engendered by the law of the state. The propertization extension regime is promulgated for a firm, for the firm's own benefit. In the limiting case, the regime, for the firm's private benefit, has superseded the state regime of property, which exists for the benefit of the public as a whole. The propertization extension regime is not subject to democratic input and debate. The propertization extension regime was not arrived at by balancing conflicting interests against each other, nor (by hypothesis) will it be subject to continuing rebalancing and checking by the courts. Sovereignty has been abrogated in favor of whatever firm has promulgated the regime.

Notes and Questions

1.   Professor Radin writes that these "–wrap" procedures are not "agreements" in accord with traditional notions of contract. Should that matter? Should the lack of true bargaining mean that these contracts should be deemed unenforceable? Or does the need for harmonization and certainty in online transactions render concerns about contract quaint?

2.   More fundamentally, Radin worries about a world in which standardized sets of terms supplant the balances and compromises struck through the legislative process. Do you share her concern? Do you think we can count on market forces to make sure that unfair terms do not thrive?

3. If Radin's most significant concern is with the actual substantive terms found in these purported contracts, can you think of ways in which law might respond? For example, courts could strike certain terms as unconscionable. *See Comb v. Pay Pal*, 218 F. Supp. 2d 1165 (ruling the terms of an arbitration clause unconscionable). On the other hand, such ad hoc, litigation-based, regulation necessarily undermines the goals of uniformity and predictability that the standardized contractual regime is meant to achieve. Another possibility is government regulation. For example, the Federal Trade Commission could declare that certain types of contractual provisions are unenforceable. In form, such rules would not be so different from current doctrines that prevent people from contracting themselves into slavery or

---

12. To the extent that those who held entitlements allocated by the regime of the state can be understood to have bargained them away for something of value to them, the regime of the state is not irrelevant in that it provided the entitlement-holders something with which to bargain. Even if we understand there to have been such a bargain, if the bargain is a one-time relinquishment then the state's regime looks irrelevant going forward, even if it played a role in bringing about the current situation of regulation by EPSER's. The state's regime is less irrelevant, even under a regime of EPSER's, if we assume that entitlement holders are continually trading off, in an ongoing manner, their state-engendered entitlements to the firms that promulgate EPSER's.

selling their body parts. What are the strengths and weaknesses of this approach?

4. Assuming either courts or regulators step in to police these sorts of standardized contracts, what types of contractual terms should be deemed unenforceable? Certainly most standardized consumer contracts contain terms that favor the corporate entity. Should all such terms be unenforceable? How does one determine at what point a contractual provision is so unfair that it should be invalid? Are there certain categories of provisions that might be deemed beyond the pale? For example, provisions that impair fundamental rights, like free speech, could be held unenforceable. Such an approach would render invalid provisions that purport to stifle criticism of the product. Other provisions that might be deemed out-of-bounds are those that force consumers to contract away their right to neutral third-party review. But, if one took that approach, would it invalidate all arbitration clauses? Or only ones that force consumers to pursue such arbitration under expensive or onerous conditions? Or should arbitration presumptively be considered a sufficient form of third-party review? Finally, one might be concerned about rights that people tend to contract away because it is difficult for them to gauge the true cost of doing so. For example, people often easily contract away privacy rights because each individual incursion on privacy rarely seems significant on its own. Should regulation prevent the enforcement of terms that affect such rights?

5. What about forum selection clauses? The U.S. Supreme Court has ruled that such provisions are generally enforceable, even if it is likely that the consumer was unaware of them. *See Carnival Cruise Lines, Inc. v. Shute*, 499 U.S. 585 (1991). However, there is no doubt that such clauses in many instances deny consumers the benefit of their own state's consumer protection laws. Indeed, several state courts have at times refused to honor forum selection clauses contained in online Terms of Service agreements precisely for this reason. *See, e.g., America Online, Inc. v. Pasieka*, 870 So.2d 170 (Fl. App. Ct. 2004); *America Online v. Superior Court,* 108 Cal. Rptr. 2d 699 (2001). Do you agree that such forum selection clauses should be invalidated?

6. Is the need for forum selection clauses more significant in the online context? After all, as discussed in Chapter Three, website operators might well wish to limit their exposure so that they are not subject to suit in every jurisdiction their site is viewed. On the other hand, consider the *Yahoo!* case discussed in Chapter Three. If Yahoo! had included in its terms of use a forum selection clause designating California as the proper forum for all suits concerning material accessed on its site, would that have rendered the French court's assertion of jurisdiction less legitimate? If so, are geographically based sovereigns impotent to adjudicate cases that concern public policies if the website at issue contains a forum selection clause?

7. What if courts in different jurisdictions take different positions as to whether online agreements are enforceable? For example, some countries may determine that such agreements are enforceable while others might view them as not being true bargains because the bargaining power among the participants might be unequal. Or, as noted above, some states might determine that consumer protection issues implicate public values that cannot

simply be contracted away by parties to a transaction. If so, which jurisdiction's consumer protection law should apply? And does the uncertainty defeat the purpose of such contractual provisions in the first place?

2. Technological Protection Measures

Although contracts of the sort discussed in the previous section might at least sometimes be invalidated by courts or regulators, firms ultimately may seek to avoid even this remote possibility by using technological protection measures (TPMs) to control access to content, with no recourse to law possible at all. Such TPMs are essentially programs that limit distribution and use of a particular item of digital content (text, video, music, software, etc.). A TPM "could prevent content from being copied, or allow it to be copied once and sent to one recipient, but deleted from the original recipient's hard drive. It could delete content automatically after a set time period. It could link a copy to a particular computer, so that it would not be playable anywhere else." Margaret Jane Radin, *Regulation by Contract, Regulation by Machine*, 160 J. OF INST'L & THEORETICAL ECON. 142, 152 (2004). And there are potentially no limitations on the types of limitations encoded.

These TPMs will attempt to accomplish through technology what was previously accomplished through contract. For example, a shrink-wrap license that prohibits copying can be replaced by software code that simply prevents such copying. Likewise, a TPM can be configured to make a video unplayable after a certain period of time or on someone else's machine, and so on. Thus, TPMs potentially bypass the state's structuring of contract law. As one commentator has argued, TPMs function as

> an infallible "injunction" controlled completely by one party. The recipient has no option to breach and pay damages; efficient breach is therefore "repealed." The recipient has no option to infringe and then argue fair use to a court; the safety valve of fair use is "repealed" . . . No entity of the state will balance the hardships and look for irreprable harm before issuing an injunction. . . . The recipient cannot ask the court to consider reliance, reasonable expectation, economic durress, and so forth. In other words, [TPMs] will make even non-waivable rights irrelevant, unless legal limitations on the operation of machine "injunctions" come into existence.

Id. (footnotes omitted).

Should we be concerned about the deployment of TPMs? On the one hand, we might view TPMs as an appropriate self-help mechanism to insure that content providers can control access to their work in the digital age. On the other, TPMs threaten to supplant important balances struck by current law. In order to explore this debate, we will focus on TPMs and copyright law.

The Constitution authorizes Congress "[t]o promote the Progress of Science and useful Arts, by securing for limited Times to Authors and Inventors the exclusive Right to their respective Writings and Discoveries." U.S. CONST. art. I., sec. 8, cl. 8. Congress has used this power to grant copyright protection to "original works of authorship fixed in any tangible medium of expression." 17 U.S.C. § 102. Copyright protection extends to, among other things, literary works, musical works, dramatic works, sound recordings, and audiovisual works. To qualify for this protection, a work must be "original" in the sense that it represents its author's intellectual creation, but it need not be particularly inventive. Copyright protection does not extend to an idea, concept, or principle; rather, it extends to the expression of that idea in a tangible medium. *Id.* § 102(b).

In essence, copyright law grants an author a limited monopoly over the fruits of his or her creative efforts. The public, in return, gains limited rights to use the copyrighted work during the copyright period as well as unlimited rights to use it once its term of protection expires. Among the exclusive rights the law secures to a copyright holder are the rights to reproduce, distribute, display, and perform the work, and to prepare derivative works based upon the copyrighted work. *Id.* § 106. The copyright statute, however, limits the author's exclusive rights by reserving to the public the right to make a "fair use" of a copyrighted work—as for purposes such as criticism, comment, or education. This limitation, developed at common law and codified in the 1976 Copyright Act, creates an affirmative defense to a claim of infringement. *See id.* § 107. In addition, under the copyright law's "first sale doctrine," a person who lawfully acquires a copyrighted work generally can give it to someone else, resell it, or destroy it. *See* 17 U.S.C. § 109. Finally, protection of a copyrighted work does not extend indefinitely. For works created on or after the effective date of the current statute, January 1, 1978, the term of protection is the life of the author plus 70 years. Works of institutional authors are protected for a period of 95 years from the date of publication or 120 years from the date of creation, whichever is shorter. When the term of protection ends, a work passes into the public domain.

Until the development and widespread use of digital technology, an author could be reasonably assured that others seeking to exploit his or her work could not cheaply produce and distribute successive high-quality copies of the work. An analog recording of music, for example, can be re-recorded, but subject to degradation in the quality of sound. The quality of successive generation copies would likewise degrade, and mass distribution would be quite costly.

The development of digital technology arguably removed this layer of protection. As the federal government recognized in its 1995 document *Intellectual Property and the National Information Infrastructure*, widely known as the "White Paper," technology posed two challenges for copyright holders. First, digital copies of intellectual property can be perfect copies— intellectual property in digital form is made up of strings of zeros and ones, and those strings can be precisely duplicated. Second, the development of the Internet makes distribution of intellectual property in digital form much less costly. Thus, some have seen the Internet as a giant copy machine and have argued for increased legal protections lest copyright law be rendered irrelevant by changes in technology.

TPMs (backed by legal restrictions against circumvention) offer a possible response to these developments by providing owners of content with a set of tools to protect their assets. In that sense, proponents of TPMs argue, they are not unlike the way in which owners of more tangible property deploy fences or locks. The only difference is that here the "fences" and "locks" are built into computer hardware and software and implemented via firewalls, encryption, and passwords. TPMs enable a "pay-per-use" world, where content providers can offer encrypted files for sale one at a time. At its most powerful, a TPM enables the "'superdistribution' of proprietary information. In other words, it allows information providers to market documents that disallow certain types of uses (e.g., copying) and provide continuing revenue (e.g., charging 2 cents per access) regardless of who holds the document (e.g., including someone who obtained it post-first sale)." Tom W. Bell, *Fair Use vs. Fared Use: The Impact of Automated Rights Management on Copyright's Fair Use Doctrine*, 76 N.C. L. REV. 557, 566-67 (1998). Thus, we might view TPMs as a useful and necessary way to make digital content more accessible, by ensuring that content providers will be able to enforce copyright or trade secret claims and define contractual rights without resorting to costly and unpredictable litigation.

Yet, this is only one half of the story. TPMs give content providers the means to more perfectly restrict access to materials. Thus, a copy-protected compact disc prevents a teacher from making a copy even if the copyright law might have deemed the copying a fair use. Likewise, although the first sale doctrine permits users to transfer or resell their copies, TPMs could technologically prevent these actions. Thus, TPMs can be used to foreclose activities that the background public legal regime has made the right of the user.

Accordingly, while technology changes many of the assumptions underlying copyright law, it is far from clear whether such changes result in an expansion or contraction of control over content. As a result, it is difficult to determine how copyright law should adapt. Do content providers need new legal tools to combat the increased ease of digital copying? Or do there need to be new *limits* on the increased ability of content providers to block public access to information? Or are the policies underlying copyright sufficiently served by a purely market-based approach—that is, by allowing an arms race of sorts between infringement-facilitating and infringement-blocking technologies?

The materials below attempt to lay out the basic arguments on both sides concerning the use of TPMs, focusing in particular on the interaction between TPMs and copyright law. As you read the arguments, consider how enforcement of the choices embedded in TPMs affect the balance of rights between providers and users of content that copyright law seeks to strike. Will enforcement of authors' choices about which uses of a work to permit lead to a balance of rights preferable to the one the copyright statute seeks to achieve? Or does the use of TPMs improperly supplant the law of the state with the "law" of the firm?

Throughout, we use the term "technological protection measures" or "TPMs" to refer to the use of technological means to restrict access to content. These TPMs are sometimes referred to by others as "digital rights management systems," "automated rights management systems," or "copyright management systems." We believe that using a formulation that includes the word "rights" distorts the discussion because a crucial part of the debate is whether what is technologically protected is necessarily being protected as of right. Thus, we prefer the more neutral term "technological protection measures." Nevertheless, in the excerpts below we have retained the formulations used by the authors.

Dan L. Burk & Julie E. Cohen, *Fair Use Infrastructure for Rights Management Systems*

15 HARV. J.L. & TECH. 41 (2001)

Together with technology experts, the copyright industries have developed secure packaging and delivery software designed to prevent purchasers and third parties from making unauthorized uses of digital works. As envisioned by the copyright industries, these "rights management systems" will be capable of controlling, monitoring, and metering almost every conceivable use of a digital work. This increased control, however, will allow copyright owners to appropriate far more protection than copyright law now provides. Of particular significance for this paper, copyright law allows some copying of protected expression under the fair use doctrine (and also under a variety of other exceptions designed to serve the public interest) and allows any use after the term of copyright protection has expired. Rights management systems, in contrast, can insist that permission be sought, and a fee paid, for any use. This is so, moreover, whether or not the underlying information is still (or was ever) protected by copyright. * * *

The development of rights management systems powerfully demonstrates the ability of technology to regulate behavior. Much as physical barriers and spatial relations constrain behavior in actual space, technical standards constrain behavior in cyberspace. In the physical world, people cannot walk through solid walls, occupy two spaces simultaneously, or carry skyscrapers away in their pockets. Similarly, there are certain activities that simply cannot be performed on a particular computer system because the system is not built to accommodate the behavior—the system may be programmed to deny access without a password, prevent logging on simultaneously from two terminals, or prohibit alteration of a file that is designated "read-only." At first consideration, the observation that the technology will only do what the technology will do may seem blatantly obvious, even tautological. But as Larry Lessig and Joel Reidenberg have pointed out, technical standards are within the control of the designer and so confer upon the designer the power to govern behavior with regard to that system.[27] Once constraints on behavior are built into the technical standards governing a technology, the technical standards effectively become a new method for governing use of that technology—in essence, the technical standards become a type of law. Such technical rule sets may supplement or even supplant the legal rule sets designed to govern the same behavior. * * *

In the case of rights management systems, copyright owners determine the rules that are embedded into the technological controls. By implementing technical constraints on access to and use of digital information, a copyright owner can effectively supersede the rules of intellectual property law. For example, as described above, the copyright owner may decide that the technological controls will not permit any copying of the controlled content, whether or not the copying would be fair use. If the integrity of the controls is backed by the state, * * * the legal enforcement of rights also shifts its focus from penalties for unauthorized infringement to penalties for access unauthorized by the rightsholder.

The implications of these developments are stark: Where technological constraints substitute for legal constraints, control over the design of information rights is shifted into the hands of private parties, who may or may not honor the public policies that animate public access doctrines such as fair use. Rightsholders can effectively write their own intellectual property statute in computer code.

Tom W. Bell, *Fair Use vs. Fared Use: The Impact of Automated Rights Management on Copyright's Fair Use Doctrine*

76 N.C. L. REV. 557 (1998)

As courts and commentators often have noted, the Constitution demands a public benefit as the price for the limited statutory privileges that copyright creates. In contrast to the view that the fair use doctrine represents a second-best response to pervasive market failure, therefore, some commentators regard the doctrine as an integral part of this constitutional quid pro quo. On this view, fair use provides a public benefit—unbilled access to copyrighted works—to balance the State's grant of a limited monopoly.

Automated rights management at first appears to threaten this bargain. It seems as if ARM restricts the public's access to copyrighted works in digital intermedia without offering a benefit in return. As this

---

27. LAWRENCE LESSIG, CODE AND OTHER LAWS OF CYBERSPACE (1999); Joel R. Reidenberg, *Lex Informatica*, 76 TEX. L. REV. 553 (1998).

subsection's consideration of the issue shows, however, friends of fair use should not assume that ARM will leave the public worse off. To the contrary, it appears likely to provide a net benefit to the public.

By reducing transaction costs throughout the market for copyrighted expressions, ARM benefits the public both directly and indirectly. Having emanated from an intentionally vague statute and developed in various, occasionally contradictory cases, the fair use doctrine necessarily blurs the boundary between valid and invalid copyright claims. High risks of "theft"—here, infringement—increase the insecurity of copyright's protection. Though the resultant uncertainty obviously harms producers and sellers of copyrighted works, it also harms consumers. Academics, artists, commentators, and others desirous of reusing copyrighted works without authorization must borrow at their peril, consult experts on fair use, or, sadly, forgo such reuse altogether. ARM's clarifying power directly benefits those who would reuse copyrighted works—and through them their public audiences—by creating harbors safe from the threat of copyright litigation.

Moreover, ARM benefits the public indirectly by increasing the transactional efficiency of the market for expressive works. Like other markets, the market for expressive works does not constitute a zero sum game. And, as Coase observed of markets in general,

> [i]t is obviously desirable that rights should be assigned to those who can use them most productively and with incentives that lead them to do so. It is also desirable that, to discover (and maintain) such a distribution of rights, the costs of their transference should be low, through clarity in the law and by making the legal requirements for such transfers less onerous.[137]

ARM, by its systemic improvement of copyright's transactional efficiency, helps us discover and maintain a distribution of rights to expressive works that will increase net social wealth. ARM thus stands to benefit both producers and consumers.

In particular, because it increases the *value* of expressive works, ARM will put deflationary pressure on the *price* of accessing them. In general, an asset's current price internalizes the value of its future income stream. Copyrights therefore commonly lose present value because, with the passage of time and their wider distribution, they prove increasingly vulnerable to uncompensated uses. Because it reduces such risks, ARM tends to increase the value of copyrights. But although this windfall might initially accrue to copyright owners, competition among information providers would force access prices downward, toward the marginal costs of obtaining and distributing expressive works. Directly or indirectly, such price pressure would similarly affect the prices that copyright owners can demand. Gains

---

137. Ronald H. Coase, *The Institutional Structure of Production*, in COASE, ESSAYS ON ECONOMICS AND ECONOMISTS 3, 11 (1994).

that ARM provides to copyright owners would thus pass on to consumers in the form of reduced access fees.

Because ARM will increase the value of copyrighted works, moreover, it will encourage their greater production and improved distribution. Consumers will thus benefit from better access to information. Access providers will improve the information itself, too, increasing its quantity and making it better organized, verified, interlinked, diverse, up-to-date, and relevant. Although this cornucopia of information may at first come only for a fee, some of it eventually will fall into the public domain. To judge from current implementations of ARM, copyright owners might very well offer limited free access to their wares in an attempt to draw more extensive (and expensive) uses. Entrepreneurs will undoubtedly create other services, at present utterly and inevitably unforeseen, to attract and satisfy consumers of information.

* * * Because automated rights management creates well-defined and readily transferable property rights to information, it puts the power of the market in the service of consumer demand. As Professor Goldstein explains, "there is no better way for the public to indicate what they want than through the price they are willing to pay in the marketplace. Uncompensated use inevitably dilutes these signals."[150] Fared use therefore probably will provide better public access to copyrighted works in digital intermedia than fair use does or could. At any rate, no one can plausibly claim that fared use necessarily would serve the public interest any less well than the existing quid pro quo.

Julie E. Cohen, Lochner *in Cyberspace: The New Economic Orthodoxy of "Rights Management"*
97 Mich. L. Rev. 462 (1998)

[Those who argue for] the relative superiority (as compared with copyright) of common law property and contract rules for protecting and disseminating digital works * * * present their private-law models for digital property rights as the logical products of neutral, incontestable axioms. Upon closer inspection, however, the economic arguments they assert are neither especially neutral nor particularly compelling. Rather, they embody a socially determined "natural law" of the market that takes the private-law institutions of property and contract as exogenous. Although the conceptualism of the *Lochner* era no longer dominates legal thought, the mode of economic analysis practiced by the cybereconomists, and implicit in the arguments offered by copyright owners to support strengthening their proprietary rights, rests upon a conceptualism of a different sort. "Contract," "market," and "property"—the efficient building blocks of the new social order—have talismanic significance, with the result that private-

---

150. Paul Goldstein, Copyright's Highway 217 (1994).

law forms of regulation are advocated absent any proof that they would produce the best regime, or even a good one, for disseminating information and promoting ongoing creative progress. * * *

The cybereconomists' belief in the superiority of contract for allocating usage rights in digital works rests on two points. First, they argue that granting more control to the purveyors of digital works will make creative and informational works more accessible in the long run (which, it is assumed, will result in more progress) as the natural result of competition in the consumer market. Second, they assert that the legislative process is comparatively unsuited to accomplish these ends because it is coercive and controlled by special interests. Neither of these points survives more thorough scrutiny. Even assuming that a market based on voluntary, informed bargaining over rights in digital works would work as the cybereconomists say it would, the conditions for such bargaining do not exist in the market we have. As a result, it is impossible to say with certainty that the market would be better at promoting access and progress than the existing system of public ordering via the legislative process.

Two fundamental requirements of the neoclassical model of social ordering through private exchange are knowledge of contract terms and meaningful (i.e., voluntary and fully informed) assent. Both are necessary (though not sufficient) requirements for an "unregulated" market to reach the efficient equilibrium point; the absence of either or both may signal a market failure justifying some form of adjustment. Under the proposed digital [copyright management system (CMS)] regime, however, consumer transactions relating to digital works will bear little resemblance to the paradigmatic bargained-for exchange. Instead, much like the typical software purchase today, they will be governed by standard form "licenses" that include provisions regarding permissible and impermissible uses. Digital CMS enable the use of such "click-through" contracts to require acceptance of usage restrictions for any type of work that is made available online. A critical question is whether this sort of transaction, in aggregate, can or will produce the near-perfect, self-equilibrating market that, for the neoclassically-grounded economist, constitutes the pinnacle of social ordering. * * *

[Some cybereconomists] evade this question. * * * They argue that * * * copyright law * * * constitutes the onerous standard form contract and market ordering * * * constitutes the flexible, policy-sensitive instrument. * * * The market is the realm of consent, while the legislative process is the realm of interest-group opposition. * * * [T]he cybereconomists compare the legislative process with the market-generated collective licensing institutions, and find the market superior. Both legislative and market actions reflect the pursuit of self-interest, but the self-interest manifested in the market is (so the reasoning appears to go) uncomplicated by distorting interest-group effects, undiminished by administrative costs, and subject to the market's wealth-maximizing power of correction. But that is disingenuous, and far too simple. * * * [T]he comparison is misdirected. The legislative process may (indeed must) be imperfect, but it does not follow that the market is always preferable. An * * * important lesson of institutional economics is that all real-world institutions, including market-based ones, are imperfect, and that it is real-world institutions that must be compared. * * * [T]he market we have is not the pure neoclassical market the cybereconomists posit.

Notes and Questions

1. What can a content provider achieve through TPMs that he or she cannot achieve through copyright law? Why might a TPM system be objectionable even if it sought only to mirror the rights and exceptions reflected in the copyright law?

2. Why does Professor Bell believe that TPMs will improve public access to copyrighted works, even if those systems embody choices about access different from those reflected in the copyright statute? Other commentators make different economic arguments about why contract is presumptively more efficient than copyright at promoting the dissemination of creative works. For example, some argue that a contract-based approach will allow content owners to engage in price discrimination—to charge private individuals lower rates in exchange for subjecting them to use restrictions—and that a content owner's strengthened ability to recoup his or her investment will make it more likely that the content owner will produce the work in the first place. *See, e.g.,* Maureen A. O'Rourke, *Copyright Preemption After the ProCD Case: A Market-Based Approach*, 12 BERKELEY TECH. L.J. 53 (1997). How does Professor Cohen respond to these arguments? Which analysis do you find more persuasive?

3. As Professors Burk and Cohen point out, TPMs can be used not only in connection with works protected under copyright law, but also in connection with works, or portions of works, that never were eligible for or that no longer have copyright protection. Assume they are correct about the negative effects of TPMs on the public's right of access to copyrighted works. What are some possible solutions to the problem? Burk and Cohen consider a combination of two. First, the government might mandate or encourage the development of TPMs that are specifically designed to allow purchasers to make fair use of content. Second, the government might condition the availability of anti-circumvention protection under the law on the deposit of an access key with a third party, who would issue the key to a party seeking to make a fair use (without evaluating the merits of the access application). Will these approaches be able to accommodate fair use as formulated in current copyright law? Are they desirable as a policy matter?

4. In 1998, Congress passed the Digital Millennium Copyright Act (DMCA), which, among other things, restricts the dissemination and use of tools that can be used to circumvent access and copy controls that a copyright holder uses to protect his or her work. These provisions make it unlawful to disable or circumvent a TPM of the sort discussed above or to traffic in technology that facilitates such disabling or circumvention. Do you think such provisions are a good idea? Do you think they will be effective? We discuss the effect of the DMCA's anti-circumvention and anti-trafficking provisions on technological innovation in the next section, and return in Chapter Nine to

questions about whether the DMCA allows content providers to "enclose" too much information.

5. Note that Professor Bell, writing before the passage of the DMCA, does not argue that TPMs should receive special statutory protections beyond those that the common law provides. *Cf.* Tom W. Bell, *Escape from Copyright: Market Success vs. Statutory Failure in the Protection of Expressive Works*, 69 U. CIN. L. REV. 741, 749-50 (2001) (distinguishing between common law protection and DMCA protection of TPMs). How would an economic defense of applying the DMCA to enforce a copyright owner's choices about use of a work proceed differently from an economic defense of applying contract principles to enforce a copyright owner's choices about use of a work?

6. Do TPMs compromise a user's ability to read with anonymity? Consider the following perspective:

> The same technologies that enable readers to access digitally stored works * * * also will enable copyright owners to generate precise and detailed records of such access. Copyright owners can then use that data, together with other new technological tools, to monitor on a continuing basis, and extract additional royalties for, readers' subsequent uses of the work they have acquired. * * * In addition to using new digital technologies to exert continuing control over readers' uses of digital works, some copyright owners may use the transaction records generated by their copyright management systems to learn more about their customers through a process known as "profiling." * * * [P]rofiling in the digital age holds out, for the first time, the tantalizing promise of "perfect" information, because digital communications can be structured to create detailed records of consumer purchases and reading activities.

Julie E. Cohen, *A Right To Read Anonymously: A Closer Look at "Copyright Management" in Cyberspace*, 28 CONN. L. REV. 981 (1996).

7. What do you think about content providers employing technological self-help to combat online copying? For example, the music industry has developed software programs that would sabotage the computers and Internet connections of people who download pirated music. *See, e.g.*, Andrew Ross Sorkin, *Software Bullet is Sought to Kill Musical Piracy*, N.Y. TIMES, at 1 (May 4, 2003). Is this an appropriate and commensurate response to online file-sharing, or a problematic escalation in an unhealthy technological arms race? How, if at all, should law respond to such uses of technology?

8. Finally, having debated the pros and cons of TPMs, it is worth asking whether they are really as much of a threat to the availability of online content as critics fear. Consider this argument:

> The notion that code is law undergirds a powerful theory, but some of its most troubling empirical predictions about the use of code to restrict individual freedom have not yet come to pass. * * * To be sure, since the DMCA's passage a number of unobtrusive rights management schemes have entered wide circulation. Yet only a handful of cases have been brought against those who have cracked such schemes, and there has been little if any decrease in consumers' capacity to copy digital works, whether for fair use or for wholesale piracy. Programmers have

historically been able to crack nearly every PC protection scheme, and those less technically inclined can go to the trouble of generating a fresh copy of a digital work without having to crack the scheme, exploiting the "analog hole" by, for example, filming a television broadcast or recording a playback of a song. Once an unprotected copy is generated, it can then be shared freely on Internet file-sharing networks that run on generative PCs at the behest of their content-hungry users.

Thus, the * * * fears of digital lockdown through trusted systems may seem premature or unfounded. As a practical matter, any scheme designed to protect content finds itself rapidly hacked, and the hack (or the content protected) in turn finds itself shared with technically unsophisticated PC owners. Alternatively, the analog hole can be used to create a new, unprotected master copy of protected content. The fact remains that so long as code can be freely written by anyone and easily distributed to run on PC platforms, [TPMs] can serve as no more than speed bumps or velvet ropes—barriers that the public circumvents should they become more than mere inconveniences. Apple's iTunes Music Store is a good example of this phenomenon: music tracks purchased through iTunes are encrypted with Apple's proprietary scheme, and there are some limitations on their use that, although unnoticeable to most consumers, are designed to prevent the tracks from immediately circulating on peer-to-peer networks. But the scheme is easily circumvented by taking music purchased from the store, burning it onto a standard audio CD, and then re-ripping the CD into an unprotected format, such as MP3.

Jonathan Zittrain, *The Generative Internet*, 119 HARV. L. REV. 1974, 1997-2000 (2006). Do you agree that we can rely on programmers to circumvent TPMs? Does the DMCA's threat of criminal prosecution change this calculus? What would Zittrain say?

SECTION C. THE EFFECT OF LEGAL RULES ON TECHNOLOGICAL INNOVATION

In the last section, we explored ways in which the deployment of technology can undermine or supplant the balances struck by law. But it would be a mistake to think that law is simply powerless in the face of technological change. To the contrary, legal rules can privilege some technological innovations over others, they can influence what sorts of technologies become widely distributed, and they can help to generate social norms that affect how technology is developed and used.

The examples below allow us to consider these sorts of effects in three different contexts: the market for home video recording devices, the deployment and use of peer-to-peer file sharing networks, and the design of telecommunications technologies. In each case, ask yourself how the legal rule enunciated by Congress or the courts is likely to change the environment for the development and distribution of technological innovation. Do you think law's impact is salutary or not?

1. Home Video Recording Devices

Although the Copyright Act does not expressly render anyone liable for facilitating an act of infringement by another, courts have applied common law principles to impose liability in certain circumstances. In particular, courts will hold contributorily liable one who knows or has reason to know of infringing activity and who materially contributes to that activity. We examine these principles in greater depth in Chapter Seven, as they relate to the liability and incentives of Internet service providers and other intermediaries whose users engage in infringing activities. For now, focus on how Congress has treated infringement-facilitating technologies in the digital age.

Sony Corporation of America v. Universal City Studios, Inc.

Supreme Court of the United States, 1984
464 U.S. 417

JUSTICE STEVENS delivered the opinion of the Court.

Petitioners manufacture and sell home video tape recorders. Respondents own the copyrights on some of the television programs that are broadcast on the public airwaves. * * * Respondents commenced this copyright infringement action against petitioners in the United States District Court for the Central District of California in 1976. Respondents alleged that some individuals had used Betamax video tape recorders (VTR's) to record some of respondents' copyrighted works which had been exhibited on commercially sponsored television and contended that these individuals had thereby infringed respondents' copyrights. Respondents further maintained that petitioners were liable for the copyright infringement allegedly committed by Betamax consumers because of petitioners' marketing of the Betamax VTR's. * * * After a lengthy trial, the District Court denied respondents all the relief they sought and entered judgment for petitioners. The United States Court of Appeals for the Ninth Circuit reversed the District Court's judgment on respondent's copyright claim, holding petitioners liable for contributory infringement and ordering the District Court to fashion appropriate relief. * * *

III

The Copyright Act does not expressly render anyone liable for infringement committed by another. In contrast, the Patent Act expressly brands anyone who "actively induces infringement of a patent" as an infringer, 35 U.S.C. § 271(b), and further imposes liability on certain individuals labeled "contributory" infringers, § 271(c). The absence of such express language in the copyright statute does not preclude the imposition of liability for copyright infringements on certain parties who have not themselves engaged in the infringing activity. For vicarious liability is imposed in virtually all areas of the law, and the concept of contributory infringement is merely a species of the broader problem of identifying the circumstances in which it is just to hold one individual accountable for the actions of another. * * *

Such circumstances were plainly present in *Kalem Co. v. Harper Brothers*, 222 U.S. 55 (1911), the copyright decision of this Court on which respondents place their principal reliance. In *Kalem*, the Court held that the producer of an unauthorized film dramatization of the copyrighted book Ben Hur was liable for his sale of the motion picture to jobbers, who in turn arranged for the commercial exhibition of the film. * * * Respondents argue that *Kalem* stands for the proposition that supplying the "means" to accomplish an infringing activity and encouraging that activity through advertisement are sufficient to establish liability for copyright infringement. This argument rests on a gross generalization that cannot withstand scrutiny. The producer in *Kalem* did not merely provide the "means" to accomplish an infringing activity; the producer supplied the work itself, albeit in a new medium of expression. Sony in the instant case does not supply Betamax consumers with respondents' works; respondents do. Sony supplies a piece of equipment that is generally capable of copying the entire range of programs that may be televised: those that are uncopyrighted, those that are copyrighted but may be copied without objection from the copyright holder, and those that the copyright holder would prefer not to have copied. The Betamax can be used to make authorized or unauthorized uses of copyrighted works, but the range of its potential use is much broader than the particular infringing use of the film *Ben Hur* involved in *Kalem*. *Kalem* does not support respondents' novel theory of liability.

Justice Holmes stated [in *Kalem*] that the producer had "contributed" to the infringement of the copyright, and the label "contributory infringement" has been applied in a number of lower court copyright cases involving an ongoing relationship between the direct infringer and the contributory infringer at the time the infringing conduct occurred. In such cases, as in other situations in which the imposition of vicarious liability is manifestly just, the "contributory" infringer was in a position to control the use of copyrighted works by others and had authorized the use without permission from the copyright owner. This case, however, plainly does not fall in that category. The only contact between Sony and the users of the Betamax that is disclosed by this record occurred at the moment of sale. The District Court expressly found that "no employee of Sony, Sonam or DDBI had either direct involvement with the allegedly infringing activity or direct contact with purchasers of Betamax who recorded copyrighted works off-the-air." And it further found that "there was no evidence that any of the copies made by Griffiths or the other individual witnesses in this suit were influenced or encouraged by [Sony's] advertisements." * * *

In the Patent Code both the concept of infringement and the concept of contributory infringement are expressly defined by statute. The prohibition against contributory infringement is confined to the knowing sale of a component especially made for use in connection with a particular patent. There is no suggestion in the statute that one patentee may object to the sale of a product that might be used in connection with other patents. Moreover, the Act expressly provides that the sale of a "staple article or commodity of commerce suitable for substantial noninfringing use" is not contributory infringement. 35 U.S.C. § 271(c).

When a charge of contributory infringement is predicated entirely on the sale of an article of commerce that is used by the purchaser to infringe a patent, the public interest in access to that article of commerce is necessarily implicated. A finding of contributory infringement does not, of course, remove the article from the market altogether; it does, however, give the patentee effective control over the sale of that item. Indeed, a finding of contributory infringement is normally the functional equivalent of holding that the disputed article is within the monopoly granted to the patentee.

For that reason, in contributory infringement cases arising under the patent laws the Court has always recognized the critical importance of not allowing the patentee to extend his monopoly beyond the limits of his specific grant. These cases deny the patentee any right to control the distribution of unpatented articles unless they are "unsuited for any commercial noninfringing use." *Dawson Chemical Co. v. Rohm & Hass Co.*, 448 U.S. 176, 198 (1980). Unless a commodity "has no use except through practice of the patented method," *id.*, at 199, the patentee has no right to claim that its distribution constitutes contributory infringement. "To form the basis for contributory infringement the item must almost be uniquely suited as a component of the patented invention." P. ROSENBERG, PATENT LAW FUNDAMENTALS § 17.02[2] (1982). "[A] sale of an article which though adapted to an infringing use is also adapted to other and lawful uses, is not enough to make the seller a contributory infringer. Such a rule would block the wheels of commerce." *Henry v. A.B. Dick Co.*, 224 U.S. 1, 48 (1912), overruled on other grounds, *Motion Picture Patents Co. v. Universal Film Mfg. Co.*, 243 U.S. 502, 517 (1917).

We recognize there are substantial differences between the patent and copyright laws. But in both areas the contributory infringement doctrine is grounded on the recognition that adequate protection of a monopoly may require the courts to look beyond actual duplication of a device or publication to the products or activities that make such duplication possible. The staple article of commerce doctrine must strike a balance between a copyright holder's legitimate demand for effective—not merely symbolic—protection of the statutory monopoly, and the rights of others freely to engage in substantially unrelated areas of commerce. Accordingly, the sale of copying equipment, like the sale of other articles of commerce, does not constitute contributory infringement if the product is widely used for legitimate, unobjectionable purposes. Indeed, it need merely be capable of substantial noninfringing uses.

IV

The question is thus whether the Betamax is capable of commercially significant noninfringing uses. In order to resolve that question, we need not explore *all* the different potential uses of the machine and determine whether or not they would constitute infringement. Rather, we need only consider whether on the basis of the facts as found by the district court a significant number of them would be non-infringing. Moreover, in order to resolve this case we need not give precise content to the question of how much use is commercially significant. For one potential use of the Betamax plainly satisfies this standard, however it is understood: private, noncommercial time-shifting in the home. It does so both (A) because respondents have no right to prevent other copyright holders from authorizing it for their programs, and (B) because the District Court's factual findings reveal that even the unauthorized home time-shifting of respondents' programs is legitimate fair use.

A.   *Authorized Time-Shifting*

Each of the respondents owns a large inventory of valuable copyrights, but in the total spectrum of television programming their combined market share is small. The exact percentage is not specified, but it is well below 10%. If they were to prevail, the outcome of this litigation would have a significant impact on both the producers and the viewers of the remaining 90% of the programming in the Nation. No doubt, many other producers share respondents' concern about the possible consequences of unrestricted copying. Nevertheless the findings of the District Court make it clear that time-shifting may enlarge the total viewing audience and that many producers are willing to allow private time-shifting to continue, at least for an experimental time period.

> The District Court found:
>
> "Even if it were deemed that home-use recording of copyrighted material constituted infringement, the Betamax could still legally be used to record noncopyrighted material or material whose owners consented to the copying. An injunction would deprive the public of the ability to use the Betamax for this noninfringing off-the-air recording."
>
> "Defendants introduced considerable testimony at trial about the potential for such copying of sports, religious, educational and other programming." * * *

In addition to the religious and sports officials identified explicitly by the District Court, two items in the record deserve specific mention. * * *

Second is the testimony of Fred Rogers, president of the corporation that produces and owns the copyright on Mister Rogers' Neighborhood. The program is carried by more public television stations than any other program. Its audience numbers over 3,000,000 families a day. He testified that he had absolutely no objection to home taping for noncommercial use and expressed the opinion that it is a real service to families to be able to record children's programs and to show them at appropriate times.

If there are millions of owners of VTR's who make copies of televised sports events, religious broadcasts, and educational programs such as Mister Rogers' Neighborhood, and if the proprietors of those programs welcome the practice, the business of supplying the equipment that makes such copying feasible should not be stifled simply because the equipment is used by some individuals to make unauthorized reproductions of respondents' works. The respondents do not represent a class composed of all copyright holders. Yet a finding of contributory infringement would inevitably frustrate the interests of broadcasters in reaching the portion of their audience that is available only through time-shifting.

Of course, the fact that other copyright holders may welcome the practice of time-shifting does not mean that respondents should be deemed to have granted a license to copy their programs. Third-party conduct would be wholly irrelevant in an action for direct infringement of respondents' copyrights. But in an action for *contributory* infringement against the seller of copying equipment, the copyright holder may not prevail unless the relief that he seeks affects only his programs, or unless he speaks for virtually all copyright holders with an interest in the outcome. In this case, the record makes it perfectly clear that there are many important producers of national and local television programs who find nothing objectionable about the enlargement in the size of the television audience that results from the practice of time-shifting for private home use. The seller of the equipment that expands those producers' audiences cannot be a contributory infringer if, as is true in this case, it has had no direct involvement with any infringing activity.

B.   *Unauthorized Time-Shifting*

Even unauthorized uses of a copyrighted work are not necessarily infringing. An unlicensed use of the copyright is not an infringement unless it conflicts with one of the specific exclusive rights conferred by the copyright statute. Moreover, the definition of exclusive rights in § 106 of the present Act is prefaced by the words "subject to sections 107 through 118." Those sections describe a variety of uses of copyrighted material that "are not infringements of copyright" "notwithstanding the provisions of § 106." The most pertinent in this case is § 107, the legislative endorsement of the doctrine of "fair use."

That section identifies various factors that enable a Court to apply an "equitable rule of reason" analysis to particular claims of infringement. Although not conclusive, the first factor requires that "the commercial or nonprofit character of an activity" be weighed in any fair use decision. If the Betamax were used to make copies for a commercial or profit-making purpose, such use would presumptively be unfair. The contrary presumption is appropriate here, however, because the District Court's findings plainly establish that time-shifting for private home use must be characterized as a noncommercial, nonprofit activity. Moreover, when one considers the nature of a televised copyrighted audiovisual work, and that time-shifting merely enables a viewer to see such a work which he had been invited to witness in its entirety free of charge, the fact that the entire work is reproduced does not have its ordinary effect of militating against a finding of fair use.

This is not, however, the end of the inquiry because Congress has also directed us to consider "the effect of the use upon the potential market for or value of the copyrighted work." The purpose of copyright is to create incentives for creative effort. Even copying for noncommercial purposes may impair the copyright holder's ability to obtain the rewards that Congress intended him to have. But a use that has no demonstrable effect upon the potential market for, or the value of, the copyrighted work need not be prohibited in order to protect the author's incentive to create. The prohibition of such noncommercial uses would merely inhibit access to ideas without any countervailing benefit. * * *

[T]o the extent time-shifting expands public access to freely broadcast television programs, it yields societal benefits. Earlier this year, in *Community Television of Southern California v. Gottfried*, 459 U.S. 498, 508 n. 12 (1983), we acknowledged the public interest in making television broadcasting more available. Concededly, that interest is not unlimited. But it supports an interpretation of the concept of "fair use" that requires the copyright holder to demonstrate some likelihood of harm before he may condemn a private act of time-shifting as a violation of federal law.

JUSTICE BLACKMUN, with whom JUSTICE MARSHALL, JUSTICE POWELL, and JUSTICE REHNQUIST join, dissenting:

Sony argues that the manufacturer or seller of a product used to infringe is absolved from liability whenever the product can be put to any substantial noninfringing use. The District Court so held, borrowing the "staple article of commerce" doctrine governing liability for contributory infringement of patents. * * * I do not agree that this technical judge-made doctrine of patent law, based in part on considerations irrelevant to the field of copyright, should be imported wholesale into copyright law. * * *

I recognize, however, that many of the concerns underlying the "staple article of commerce" doctrine are present in copyright law as well. As the District Court noted, if liability for contributory infringement were imposed on the manufacturer or seller of every product used to infringe—a typewriter, a camera, a photocopying machine—the "wheels of commerce" would be blocked. I therefore conclude that if a *significant* portion of the product's use is *noninfringing*, the manufacturers and sellers cannot be held contributorily liable for the product's infringing uses. If virtually all of the product's use, however, is to infringe, contributory liability may be imposed; if no one would buy the product for noninfringing purposes alone, it is clear that the manufacturer is purposely profiting from the infringement, and that liability is appropriately imposed. In such a case, the copyright owner's monopoly would not be extended beyond its proper bounds; the manufacturer of such a product contributes to the infringing activities of others and profits directly thereby, while providing no benefit to the public sufficient to justify the infringement. * * *

The Court explains that a manufacturer of a product is not liable for contributory infringement as long as the product is "*capable* of substantial noninfringing uses." Such a definition essentially eviscerates the concept of contributory infringement. Only the most unimaginative manufacturer would be unable to demonstrate that a image-duplicating product is "capable" of substantial noninfringing uses. Surely Congress desired to prevent the sale of products that are used almost exclusively to infringe copyrights; the fact that noninfringing uses exist presumably would have little bearing on that desire.

Notes and Questions

1. According to the Court, what distinguishes the actions of a defendant who manufactures and sells products capable of being used to infringe a copyright from the actions of the defendant in a case like *Kalem*?

2. In the patent code, Congress specifically provided that the sale of a staple article of commerce that is suitable for substantial noninfringing use does not constitute contributory infringement. What policy considerations does the Court identify as supporting this exception?

3. No similar exception exists in the copyright statute. Is it appropriate for the Court to fashion an exception in that context? Why or why not? Are the relevant policy considerations the same as in the patent context?

4. When will the sale of a product capable of being used to infringe a copyright be found not to constitute contributory infringement? Does the test the Court establishes match the test it describes for patent cases? How does the test differ from the one the dissent would adopt?

5. Should it matter that VCRs are *capable* of substantial noninfringing uses, if it were found that in fact most uses of VCRs were infringing?

6. What do you think would have happened to the home video market if this decision had gone the other way? Do you think that the respondents would have been better off if they had won, or worse off? Should courts consider such questions in deciding cases involving new technologies?

As discussed in the previous section, technological developments not only make copying and disseminating copyrighted works in digital form easier, they also enable copyright holders to use technical means to restrict access to or copying of protected works. In the last days of the 1998 legislative session, Congress passed the Digital Millennium Copyright Act ("DMCA"), enacting sweeping changes to the Copyright Act. The most controversial of the DMCA's provisions are those restricting the dissemination and use of tools that can be used to circumvent access and copy controls that a copyright holder uses to protect his or her work.

Section 1201 of the Digital Millennium Copyright Act
17 U.S.C. § 1201

§ 1201. Circumvention of copyright protection systems

(a) **Violations regarding circumvention of technological measures.**—(1)(A) No person shall circumvent a technological measure that effectively controls access to a work protected under this title. * * *

(2) No person shall manufacture, import, offer to the public, provide, or otherwise traffic in any technology, product, service, device, component, or part thereof, that—

(A) is primarily designed or produced for the purpose of circumventing a technological measure that effectively controls access to a work protected under this title;

(B) has only limited commercially significant purpose or use other than to circumvent a technological measure that effectively controls access to a work protected under this title; or

(C) is marketed by that person or another acting in concert with that person with that person's knowledge for use in circumventing a technological measure that effectively controls access to a work protected under this title.

(3) As used in this subsection—

(A) to "circumvent a technological measure" means to descramble a scrambled work, to decrypt an encrypted work, or otherwise to avoid, bypass, remove, deactivate, or impair a technological measure, without the authority of the copyright owner; and

(B) a technological measure "effectively controls access to a work" if the measure, in the ordinary course of its operation, requires the application of information, or a process or a treatment, with the authority of the copyright owner, to gain access to the work.

(b) **Additional violations.**—(1) No person shall manufacture, import, offer to the public, provide, or otherwise traffic in any technology, product, service, device, component, or part thereof, that—

(A) is primarily designed or produced for the purpose of circumventing protection afforded by a technological measure that effectively protects a right of a copyright owner under this title in a work or a portion thereof;

(B) has only limited commercially significant purpose or use other than to circumvent protection afforded by a technological measure that effectively protects a right of a copyright owner under this title in a work or a portion thereof; or

(C) is marketed by that person or another acting in concert with that person with that person's knowledge for use in circumventing protection afforded by a technological measure that effectively protects a right of a copyright owner under this title in a work or a portion thereof.

(2) As used in this subsection—

(A) to "circumvent protection afforded by a technological measure" means avoiding, bypassing, removing, deactivating, or otherwise impairing a technological measure; and

(B) a technological measure "effectively protects a right of a copyright owner under this title" if the measure, in the ordinary course of its operation, prevents, restricts, or otherwise limits the exercise of a right of a copyright owner under this title.

(c) Other rights, etc., not affected.—(1) Nothing in this section shall affect rights, remedies, limitations, or defenses to copyright infringement, including fair use, under this title.

(2) Nothing in this section shall enlarge or diminish vicarious or contributory liability for copyright infringement in connection with any technology, product, service, device, component, or part thereof. * * *

§ 1203. Civil remedies

(a) Civil actions.—Any person injured by a violation of section 1201 or 1202 may bring a civil action in an appropriate United States district court for such violation. * * *

§ 1204. Criminal Offenses and penalties

(a) In general.—Any person who violates section 1201 or 1202 willfully and for purposes of commercial advantage or private financial gain—

(1) shall be fined not more than $500,000 or imprisoned for not more than 5 years, or both, for the first offense; and

(2) shall be fined not more than $1,000,000 or imprisoned for not more than 10 years, or both, for any subsequent offense.

Several exceptions to the statute are worth noting. First, the statute authorizes the Librarian of Congress to exempt certain classes of works from subsection 1201(a)(1)'s ban on the act of circumventing technical protection systems that control access to a protected work. The exemption applies to those classes of works as to which the Librarian determines the prohibition on circumvention will "adversely affect[]" users "in their ability to make noninfringing uses." 17 U.S.C. § 1201(a)(1)(C). Second, the Act specifically allows certain acts of circumvention, including law enforcement activities, steps taken to reverse-engineer a program to achieve interoperability with other programs, legitimate encryption research, steps taken to protect personally identifying information, and security testing activities. The exceptions to the anti-trafficking prohibitions of subsections 1201(a)(2) and 1201(b)(1) are narrower, but they still allow the development of circumvention technology in connection with law enforcement, reverse engineering, encryption research, and security testing activities.

To what extent do the anti-circumvention and anti-trafficking provisions alter, or even displace, copyright law? As you read the cases that follow, keep in mind the scope of the *Sony* defense to contributory infringement for the manufacture and sale of products that may facilitate infringement. How does the statute alter that defense with respect to circumvention technology? What impact might such changes have for the development and distribution of new video recording technology?

Real Networks, Inc. v. Streambox, Inc.

Western District of Washington, 2000
2000 WL 127311

PECHMAN, J.

INTRODUCTION

Plaintiff RealNetworks, Inc. ("RealNetworks") filed this action on December 21, 1999. RealNetworks claims that Defendant Streambox has violated provisions of the Digital Millennium Copyright Act ("DMCA"), 17 U.S.C. § 1201 et seq., by distributing and marketing [a product] known as the Streambox VCR * * * . The Court, having considered the papers and pleadings filed herein and having heard oral argument from the parties, concludes that a preliminary injunction should be entered to enjoin the manufacture, distribution, and sale of the Streambox VCR * * * during the pendency of this action. * * *

FINDINGS OF FACT

* * * RealNetworks offers products that enable consumers to access audio and video content over the Internet through a process known as "streaming." When an audio or video clip is "streamed" to a consumer, no trace of the clip is left on the consumer's computer, unless the content owner has permitted the consumer to download the file. Streaming is to be contrasted with "downloading," a process by which a complete copy of an audio or video clip is delivered to and stored on a consumer's computer. Once a consumer has downloaded a file, he or she can access the file at will, and can generally redistribute copies of that file to others.

In the digital era, the difference between streaming and downloading is of critical importance. A downloaded copy of a digital audio or video file is essentially indistinguishable from the original, and such copies can often be created at the touch of a button. A user who obtains a digital copy may supplant the market for the original by distributing copies of his or her own. To guard against the unauthorized copying and redistribution of their content, many copyright owners do not make their content available for downloading, and instead distribute the content using streaming technology in a manner that does not permit downloading.

A large majority of all Internet Web pages that deliver streaming music or video use the RealNetworks' format. * * * Owners of audio or video content may choose to use a RealNetworks product to encode their digital content into RealNetworks' format. Once encoded in that format, the media files are called RealAudio or RealVideo (collectively "RealMedia") files. After a content owner has encoded its content into the RealMedia format, it may decide to use a "RealServer" to send that content to consumers. A RealServer is software program that resides on a content owner's computer that holds RealMedia files and "serves" them to consumers through streaming. To download streaming content distributed by a RealServer, * * * a consumer must employ a "RealPlayer." The RealPlayer is a software program that resides on an end-user's computer and must be used to access and play a streaming RealMedia file that is sent from a RealServer. * * *

RealNetworks' products can be used to enable owners of audio and video content to make their content available for consumers to listen to or view, while at the same time securing the content against unauthorized access or copying. The first of these measures, called the "Secret Handshake" by RealNetworks, ensures that files hosted on a RealServer will only be sent to a RealPlayer. The Secret Handshake is an authentication sequence which only RealServers and RealPlayers know. By design, unless this authentication sequence takes place, the RealServer does not stream the content it holds. By ensuring that RealMedia files hosted on a RealServer are streamed only to RealPlayers, RealNetworks can ensure that a second security measure, which RealNetworks calls the "Copy Switch," is given effect. The Copy Switch is a piece of data in all RealMedia files that contains the content owner's preference regarding whether or not the stream may be copied by end-users. RealPlayers are designed to read this Copy Switch and obey the content owner's wishes. If a content owner turns on the Copy Switch in a particular RealMedia file, when that file is streamed, an end-user can use the RealPlayer to save a copy of that RealMedia file to the user's computer. If a content owner does not turn on the Copy Switch in a RealMedia file, the RealPlayer will not allow an end-user to make a copy of that file. The file will simply "evaporate" as the user listens to or watches it stream.

Through the use of the Secret Handshake and the Copy Switch, owners of audio and video content can prevent the unauthorized copying of their content if they so choose. * * * RealNetworks' success as a company is due in significant part to the fact that it has offered copyright owners a successful means of protecting against unauthorized duplication and distribution of their digital works. * * *

The Streambox VCR enables end-users to access and download copies of RealMedia files that are streamed over the Internet. * * * In order to gain access to RealMedia content located on a RealServer, the VCR mimics a RealPlayer and circumvents the authentication procedure, or Secret Handshake, that a RealServer requires before it will stream content. In other words, the Streambox VCR is able to convince the RealServer into thinking that the VCR is, in fact, a RealPlayer. Having convinced a RealServer to begin streaming content, the Streambox VCR, like the RealPlayer, acts as a receiver. However, unlike the RealPlayer, the VCR ignores the Copy Switch that tells a RealPlayer whether an end-user is allowed to make a copy of (i.e., download) the RealMedia file as it is being streamed. The VCR thus allows the end-user to download RealMedia files even if the content owner has used the Copy Switch to prohibit end-users from downloading the files.

The only reason for the Streambox VCR to circumvent the Secret Handshake and interact with a RealServer is to allow an end-user to access and make copies of content that a copyright holder has placed on a RealServer in order to secure it against unauthorized copying. In this way, the Streambox VCR acts like a "black box" which descrambles cable or satellite broadcasts so that viewers can watch pay programming for free. Like the cable and satellite companies that scramble their video signals to control access to their programs, RealNetworks has employed technological measures to ensure that only users of the RealPlayer can access RealMedia content placed on a RealServer. RealNetworks has gone one step further than the cable and satellite companies, not only controlling access, but also allowing copyright owners to specify whether or not their works can be copied by end-users, even if access is permitted. The Streambox VCR circumvents both the access control and copy protection measures. * * * Once an unauthorized, digital copy of a RealMedia file is created it can be redistributed to others at the touch of a button. * * *

Conclusions of Law

* * * The DMCA prohibits the manufacture, import, offer to the public, or trafficking in any technology, product, service, device, component, or part thereof that: (1) is primarily designed or produced for the purpose of circumventing a technological measure that effectively "controls access to" a copyrighted work or "protects a right of a copyright owner;" (2) has only limited commercially significant purpose or use other than to circumvent such technological protection measures; or (3) is marketed for use in circumventing such technological protection measures. 17 U.S.C. §§ 1201(a)(2), 1201(b). Under the DMCA, the Secret Handshake that must take place between a RealServer and a RealPlayer before the RealServer will begin streaming content to an end-user appears to constitute a "technological measure" that "effectively controls access" to copyrighted works. *See* 17 U.S.C. § 1201(a)(3)(B) (measure "effectively controls access" if it "requires the application of information or a process or a treatment, with the authority of the copyright holder, to gain access to the work"). To gain access to a work protected by the Secret Handshake, a user must

employ a RealPlayer, which will supply the requisite information to the RealServer in a proprietary authentication sequence.

In conjunction with the Secret Handshake, the Copy Switch is [also] a "technological measure" that effectively protects the right of a copyright owner to control the unauthorized copying of its work. *See* 17 U.S.C. § 1201(b)(2)(B) (measure "effectively protects" right of copyright holder if it "prevents, restricts or otherwise limits the exercise of a right of a copyright owner"). To access a RealMedia file distributed by a RealServer, a user must use a RealPlayer. The RealPlayer reads the Copy Switch in the file. If the Copy Switch in the file is turned off, the RealPlayer will not permit the user to record a copy as the file is streamed. Thus, the Copy Switch may restrict others from exercising a copyright holder's exclusive right to copy its work.

Under the DMCA, a product or part thereof "circumvents" protections afforded a technological measure by "avoiding, bypassing, removing, deactivating or otherwise impairing" the operation of that technological measure. 17 U.S.C. §§ 1201(b)(2)(A), 1201(a)(3)(A). Under that definition, at least a part of the Streambox VCR circumvents the technological measures RealNetworks affords to copyright owners. Where a RealMedia file is stored on a RealServer, the VCR "bypasses" the Secret Handshake to gain access to the file. The VCR then circumvents the Copy Switch, enabling a user to make a copy of a file that the copyright owner has sought to protect.

Given the circumvention capabilities of the Streambox VCR, Streambox violates the DMCA if the product or a part thereof: (i) is primarily designed to serve this function; (ii) has only limited commercially significant purposes beyond the circumvention; or (iii) is marketed as a means of circumvention. 17 U.S.C. §§ 1201(a)(2)(A-C), 1201(b)(1)(A-C). These three tests are disjunctive. A product that meets only one of the three independent bases for liability is still prohibited. Here, the VCR meets at least the first two.

The Streambox VCR meets the first test for liability under the DMCA because at least a part of the Streambox VCR is primarily, if not exclusively, designed to circumvent the access control and copy protection measures that RealNetworks affords to copyright owners. The second basis for liability is met because the portion of the VCR that circumvents the Secret Handshake so as to avoid the Copy Switch has no significant commercial purpose other than to enable users to access and record protected content. There does not appear to be any other commercial value that this capability affords.

Streambox's primary defense to Plaintiff's DMCA claims is that the VCR has legitimate uses. In particular, Streambox claims that the VCR allows consumers to make "fair use" copies of RealMedia files, notwithstanding the access control and copy protection measures that a copyright owner may have placed on that file.

The portions of the VCR that circumvent the secret handshake and copy switch permit consumers to obtain and redistribute perfect digital copies of audio and video files that copyright owners have made clear they do not want copied. For this reason, Streambox's VCR is not entitled to the same "fair use" protections the Supreme Court afforded to video cassette recorders used for "time-shifting" in *Sony Corp. v. Universal City Studios, Inc.*, 464 U.S. 417 (1984). The *Sony* decision turned in large part on a finding that substantial numbers of copyright holders who broadcast their works either had authorized or would not object to having their works time-shifted by private viewers. Here, by contrast, copyright owners have specifically chosen to prevent the copying enabled by the Streambox VCR by putting their content on RealServers and leaving the Copy Switch off.

Moreover, the *Sony* decision did not involve interpretation of the DMCA. Under the DMCA, product developers do not have the right to distribute products that circumvent technological measures that prevent consumers from gaining unauthorized access to or making unauthorized copies of works protected by the Copyright Act. Instead, Congress specifically prohibited the distribution of the tools by which such circumvention could be accomplished. The portion of the Streambox VCR that circumvents the technological measures that prevent unauthorized access to and duplication of audio and video content therefore runs afoul of the DMCA.

This point is underscored by the leading treatise on copyright, which observes that the enactment of the DMCA means that "those who manufacture equipment and products generally can no longer gauge their conduct as permitted or forbidden by reference to the *Sony* doctrine. For a given piece of machinery might qualify as a staple item of commerce, with a substantial noninfringing use, and hence be immune from attack under Sony's construction of the Copyright Act—but nonetheless still be subject to suppression under Section 1201." 1 NIMMER ON COPYRIGHT (1999 Supp.), § 12A.18[B]. As such, "[e]quipment manufacturers in the twenty-first century will need to vet their products for compliance with Section 1201 in order to avoid a circumvention claim, rather than under Sony to negate a copyright claim." *Id.*

Streambox also argues that the VCR does not violate the DMCA because the Copy Switch that it avoids does not "effectively protect" against the unauthorized copying of copyrighted works as required by § 1201(a)(3)(B). Streambox claims this "effective" protection is lacking because an enterprising end-user could potentially use other means to record streaming audio content as it is played by the end-user's computer speakers. This argument fails because the Copy Switch, in the ordinary course of its operation when it is on, restricts and limits the ability of people to make perfect digital copies of a copyrighted work. The Copy Switch therefore constitutes a technological measure that effectively protects a copyright owner's rights under section. 1201(a)(3)(B). In addition, the argument ignores the fact that before the Copy Switch is even implicated, the Streambox VCR has already circumvented the Secret Handshake to gain access to a unauthorized RealMedia file. That alone is sufficient for liability under the DMCA. * * *

RealNetworks has demonstrated that it would likely suffer irreparable harm if the Streambox VCR is distributed. The VCR circumvents RealNetworks' security measures, and will necessarily undermine the confidence that RealNetworks' existing and potential customers have in those measures. It would not be possible to determine how many of RealNetworks' existing or potential customers declined to use the company's products because of the perceived security problems created by the VCR's ability to circumvent RealNetworks' security measures. An injunction against the VCR also would serve the public interest because the VCR's ability to circumvent RealNetworks' security measures would likely reduce the willingness of copyright owners to make their audio and video works accessible to the public over the Internet.

Notes and Questions

1. How does section 1201 define illegal conduct? Does the provision change the traditional standard that applies to devices that facilitate infringement? Is the definition of illegal conduct closer to that of the majority or the dissent in *Sony*?

2. The statute purports not to affect any rights, remedies, limitations, or defenses under copyright law. *See* 17 U.S.C. § 1201(c)(1). But does the DMCA condition the illegality of trafficking in a circumvention technology or the illegality of circumvention itself on proof that the user has violated the copyright laws? Can one who circumvents a technological protection measure controlling access to a protected work claim that he or she did so to make lawful use of the work—for example, to engage in fair use—and thereby escape liability under the DMCA?

3. Note that, in addition to prohibiting trafficking in circumvention technology, section 1201 prohibits circumvention of measures that control access to a protected work, but not measures that prevent copying of a protected work. *See* 17 U.S.C. § 1201(a)(1)(A). In other words, the statute ostensibly would allow one to circumvent copy controls (but not access controls) to make a fair use of a protected work. Is this distinction between access controls and copy controls justified? Assuming that the statute does not prohibit circumvention of copy controls, how would one obtain the technology necessary to accomplish the circumvention?

4. The DMCA's anti-circumvention and anti-trafficking provisions were ostensibly intended to bring the United States into compliance with the 1996 World Intellectual Property Organization ("WIPO") Copyright Treaty, which requires contracting parties to "provide adequate legal protection and effective legal remedies against the circumvention of effective technological measures that are used by authors in connection with the exercise of their rights" under international copyright agreements. WIPO Treaty, Apr. 12, 1997, art. 11, S. Treaty Doc. No. 105-17 (1997). For an argument that the anti-circumvention and anti-trafficking provisions went beyond what the treaty required, see Pamela Samuelson, *Intellectual Property and the Digital Economy: Why the*

Anti-Circumvention Regulations Need To Be Revised, 14 BERKELEY TECH. L.J. 519, 521-24 (1999).

5. Note that section 1201(a)(1)(A) of the DMCA requires the content provider to employ a technological measure that "effectively controls access" to a work. We take up the question of what counts as an effective access control in Chapter Nine.

6. How might you argue that the anti-circumvention and anti-trafficking provisions of the DMCA are a needed response to the ease of copying and distributing digital works? What would happen if circumvention devices were merely subject to the *Sony* test?

7. What if Streambox had simply posted on a website information about how to circumvent the Real Networks Secret Handshake? In a case raising this question with regard to circumvention of TPMs encoded onto DVDs, the Second Circuit ruled that disseminating computer code that would enable circumvention itself violates the DMCA. Further, the court held that, although software code can be protected speech under the First Amendment, it is only protected to the extent that the code conveys information to a human being. In contrast, according to the court, the code at issue violated the DMCA "solely because of its capacity to instruct a computer," making regulation permissible under the First Amendment. *See Universal City Studios v. Corley*, 273 F.3d 429 (2d Cir. 2001). Does the distinction between the speech and non-speech elements of software code make sense? Also, if someone supplied a link to a website that provided circumvention information, do you think that the linker should also be deemed to violate the DMCA? *See id.* (upholding district court's injunction against linking to offending site).

8. In addition to providing for civil liability, the DMCA imposes criminal penalties for violations that are willful and committed for purposes of commercial advantage or private financial gain. This provision was first invoked against the development of computer software in the controversial case of Russian programmer Dmitry Skylarov and his employer, Russian software manufacturer ElcomSoft Ltd. The indictment alleged that Skylarov and ElcomSoft manufactured a program called Advanced eBook Processor (AEBPR), which allegedly removes the technological protection from electronic books that are in Adobe's eBook format and thereby allows them to be used in more ways than Adobe's eBook Reader permits. Although Skylarov and ElcomSoft produced the program in Russia, where it was legal to do so, the indictment alleged that Skylarov and ElcomSoft caused AEBPR to be marketed from Internet services based in Washington and Illinois. Skylarov was arrested in July 2001 after traveling to the United States and presenting a paper at a conference on the weaknesses in Adobe's eBook software. In May 2002, a district court denied ElcomSoft's motion to dismiss the case for lack of jurisdiction, concluding that AEBPR was offered for sale from servers in the United States and that payments were directed to an entity in the United States. In December 2002, a jury acquitted ElcomSoft of all charges.

9. To what extent does the DMCA chill legitimate research activities? As previously noted, the anti-circumvention and anti-trafficking provisions each exempt legitimate encryption-related research, security testing, and certain other activities. Nevertheless, two controversial cases have raised questions

about the DMCA's effect on research. The first involved Princeton University professor Edward Felten and several other scientists. Felten and his team participated in a challenge run by the Secure Digital Music Initiative (SDMI) Foundation, a consortium of record companies and technology companies, to test the strength of watermarking technology designed to protect digital music. Felten's team claimed to defeat the the SDMI watermarking system. When Felten sought to present an academic paper on SDMI's weaknesses, the Recording Industry Association of America (RIAA) and the SDMI Foundation warned that discussing the details of his team's efforts could subject his team to suit under the DMCA. Felten and his team filed suit in federal court against the RIAA, the SDMI Foundation, and the United States, seeking a declaratory judgment that the DMCA could not constitutionally be applied to their activities. The district court dismissed the suit as nonjusticiable after the RIAA and SDMI Foundation claimed not to oppose release of Felten's research and Felten published the results of his research without retribution. *Felten v. Recording Industry Ass'n of Am.*, No. 01 CV 2669 (D.N.J. Nov. 28, 2001).

The second case involved Ben Edelman, a computer consultant who claimed that he was unable to test the operations of an Internet filtering program without the threat of a lawsuit based on the DMCA's anti-circumvention provisions. The American Civil Liberties Union filed suit on Edelman's behalf, seeking a declaration that the DMCA cannot constitutionally be applied to his activities. The district court dismissed the case on the ground that Edelman had not shown a sufficiently imminent "injury" to satisfy constitutional standing requirements. *Edelman v. N2H2*, No. Civ. A.02CV 11503RGS (D. Mass. Apr. 7, 2003).

Would the research activities involved in either of these cases have violated the DMCA?

10. What might the impact of the DMCA be on the development of technologies such as Streambox? If such technological innovation is shut down, would that be a good thing? Will the DMCA prevent home recording in the digital era? Why are newer products such as TiVo not illegal under the DMCA? Does the widespread adoption of TiVo and similar digital video recorders suggest that concerns about the DMCA stifling technological innovation are misplaced? Or are there still concerns about the DMCA's impact on new technology?

2. Peer-to-Peer File Sharing

A & M Records, Inc. v. Napster, Inc.

United States Court of Appeals for the Ninth Circuit, 2001
239 F.3d 1004

BEEZER, Circuit Judge.

Plaintiffs are engaged in the commercial recording, distribution and sale of copyrighted musical compositions and sound recordings. The complaint alleges that Napster, Inc. ("Napster") is a contributory and vicarious copyright infringer. * * * The district court preliminarily enjoined

Napster "from engaging in, or facilitating others in copying, downloading, uploading, transmitting, or distributing plaintiffs' copyrighted musical compositions and sound recordings, protected by either federal or state law, without express permission of the rights owner." * * * We entered a temporary stay of the preliminary injunction pending resolution of this appeal. * * * We affirm in part, reverse in part and remand.

I

* * * Napster facilitates the transmission of MP3 files between and among its users. Through a process commonly called "peer-to-peer" file sharing, Napster allows its users to: (1) make MP3 music files stored on individual computer hard drives available for copying by other Napster users; (2) search for MP3 music files stored on other users' computers; and (3) transfer exact copies of the contents of other users' MP3 files from one computer to another via the Internet. These functions are made possible by Napster's MusicShare software, available free of charge from Napster's Internet site, and Napster's network servers and server-side software. Napster provides technical support for the indexing and searching of MP3 files, as well as for its other functions, including a "chat room," where users can meet to discuss music, and a directory where participating artists can provide information about their music.

A.   *Accessing the System*

In order to copy MP3 files through the Napster system, a user must first access Napster's Internet site and download the MusicShare software to his individual computer. Once the software is installed, the user can access the Napster system. A first-time user is required to register with the Napster system by creating a "user name" and password.

B.   *Listing Available Files*

If a registered user wants to list available files stored in his computer's hard drive on Napster for others to access, he must first create a "user library" directory on his computer's hard drive. The user then saves his MP3 files in the library directory, using self-designated file names. He next must log into the Napster system using his user name and password. His MusicShare software then searches his user library and verifies that the available files are properly formatted. If in the correct MP3 format, the names of the MP3 files will be uploaded from the user's computer to the Napster servers. The content of the MP3 files remains stored in the user's computer.

Once uploaded to the Napster servers, the user's MP3 file names are stored in a server-side "library" under the user's name and become part of a "collective directory" of files available for transfer during the time the user is logged onto the Napster system. The collective directory is fluid; it tracks users who are connected in real time, displaying only file names that are immediately accessible.

C. *Searching For Available Files*

Napster allows a user to locate other users' MP3 files in two ways: through Napster's search function and through its "hotlist" function.

Software located on the Napster servers maintains a "search index" of Napster's collective directory. To search the files available from Napster users currently connected to the network servers, the individual user accesses a form in the MusicShare software stored in his computer and enters either the name of a song or an artist as the object of the search. The form is then transmitted to a Napster server and automatically compared to the MP3 file names listed in the server's search index. Napster's server compiles a list of all MP3 file names pulled from the search index which include the same search terms entered on the search form and transmits the list to the searching user. The Napster server does not search the contents of any MP3 file; rather, the search is limited to "a text search of the file names indexed in a particular cluster. Those file names may contain typographical errors or otherwise inaccurate descriptions of the content of the files since they are designated by other users."

To use the "hotlist" function, the Napster user creates a list of other users' names from whom he has obtained MP3 files in the past. When logged onto Napster's servers, the system alerts the user if any user on his list (a "hotlisted user") is also logged onto the system. If so, the user can access an index of all MP3 file names in a particular hotlisted user's library and request a file in the library by selecting the file name. The contents of the hotlisted user's MP3 file are not stored on the Napster system.

D. *Transferring Copies of an MP3 file*

To transfer a copy of the contents of a requested MP3 file, the Napster server software obtains the Internet address of the requesting user and the Internet address of the "host user" (the user with the available files). The Napster servers then communicate the host user's Internet address to the requesting user. The requesting user's computer uses this information to establish a connection with the host user and downloads a copy of the contents of the MP3 file from one computer to the other over the Internet, "peer-to-peer." A downloaded MP3 file can be played directly from the user's hard drive using Napster's MusicShare program or other software. The file may also be transferred back onto an audio CD if the user has access to equipment designed for that purpose. In both cases, the quality of the original sound recording is slightly diminished by transfer to the MP3 format. * * *

III

Plaintiffs claim Napster users are engaged in the wholesale reproduction and distribution of copyrighted works, all constituting direct infringement. The district court agreed. We note that the district court's conclusion that plaintiffs have presented a prima facie case of direct infringement by Napster users is not presently appealed by Napster. * * * Napster [instead] asserts an affirmative defense to the charge that its users directly infringe plaintiffs' copyrighted musical compositions and sound recordings[, contending] that its users do not directly infringe plaintiffs' copyrights because the users are engaged in fair use of the material. *See* 17 U.S.C. § 107 ("[T]he fair use of a copyrighted work . . . is not an infringement of copyright."). * * *

[In analyzing the Napster system generally, the] district court considered factors listed in 17 U.S.C. § 107, which guide a court's fair use determination. These factors are: (1) the purpose and character of the use; (2) the nature of the copyrighted work; (3) the "amount and substantiality of the portion used" in relation to the work as a whole; and (4) the effect of the use upon the potential market for the work or the value of the work. *See* 17 U.S.C. § 107. [The district court concluded that all factors cut against a finding of fair use. In assessing the purpose and character of the use, the court reasoned that because Napster users create no new work through downloading and avoid the expense of purchasing authorized copies, the use is "nontransformative," *see Campbell v. Acuff-Rose Music, Inc.*, 510 U.S. 569, 579 (1994), and "commercial." With respect to the remaining factors, the district court concluded that the copyrighted works are creative in nature and therefore "closer to the core of intended copyright protection," *Campbell*, 510 U.S. at 586; that Napster users engage in wholesale copying of the copyrighted works; and that Napster harms the market for plaintiffs' works by reducing sales among college students and raising barriers to the plaintiffs' entry into the market for digital downloads.]

[The district court did not abuse its discretion] in reaching the above fair use conclusions, nor were the findings of fact with respect to fair use considerations clearly erroneous. [Napster maintains that the district court nevertheless erred in excluding specific fair uses it identified:] sampling, where users make temporary copies of a work before purchasing; space-shifting, where users access a sound recording through the Napster system that they already own in audio CD format; and permissive distribution of recordings by both new and established artists. * * *]

a.   *Sampling*

Napster contends that its users download MP3 files to "sample" the music in order to decide whether to purchase the recording. * * *

The district court determined that sampling remains a commercial use even if some users eventually purchase the music. We find no error in the district court's determination. Plaintiffs have established that they are likely to succeed in proving that even authorized temporary downloading of individual songs for sampling purposes is commercial in nature. The record supports a finding that free promotional downloads are highly regulated by the record company plaintiffs and that the companies collect royalties for song samples available on retail Internet sites. Evidence relied on by the district court demonstrates that the free downloads provided by the record companies consist of thirty-to-sixty second samples or are full songs programmed to "time out," that is, exist only for a short time on the downloader's computer. In comparison, Napster users download a full, free and permanent copy of the recording. The determination by the district court as to the commercial purpose and character of sampling is not clearly erroneous.

The district court further found that both the market for audio CDs and market for online distribution are adversely affected by Napster's service. * * * [T]he district court determined that "[e]ven if the type of sampling supposedly done on Napster were a non-commercial use, plaintiffs have demonstrated a substantial likelihood that it would adversely affect the potential market for their copyrighted works if it became widespread." The record supports the district court's preliminary determinations that: (1) the more music that sampling users download, the less likely they are to eventually purchase the recordings on audio CD; and (2) even if the audio CD market is not harmed, Napster has adverse effects on the developing digital download market. * * *

b. *Space-Shifting*

Napster also maintains that space-shifting is a fair use. Space-shifting occurs when a Napster user downloads MP3 music files in order to listen to music he already owns on audio CD. Napster asserts that we have already held that space-shifting of musical compositions and sound recordings is a fair use. *See Recording Indus. Ass'n of Am. v. Diamond Multimedia Sys., Inc.*, 180 F.3d 1072, 1079 (9th Cir. 1999) ("Rio [a portable MP3 player] merely makes copies in order to render portable, or 'space-shift,' those files that already reside on a user's hard drive. . . . Such copying is a paradigmatic noncommercial personal use."). *See also generally Sony Corp. v. Universal City Studios*, 464 U.S. 417, 423 (1984) (holding that "time-shifting," where a video tape recorder owner records a television show for later viewing, is a fair use).

We conclude that the district court did not err when it refused to apply the "shifting" analyses of *Sony* and *Diamond*. Both *Diamond* and *Sony* are inapposite because the methods of shifting in these cases did not also simultaneously involve distribution of the copyrighted material to the general public; the time or space-shifting of copyrighted material exposed the material only to the original user. * * *

c. *Other Uses*

Permissive reproduction by either independent or established artists is the final fair use claim made by Napster. The district court noted that plaintiffs did not seek to enjoin this and any other noninfringing use of the Napster system, including: chat rooms, message boards and Napster's New Artist Program. Plaintiffs do not challenge these uses on appeal.

We find no error in the district court's determination that plaintiffs will likely succeed in establishing that Napster users do not have a fair use defense. Accordingly, we next address whether Napster is secondarily liable for the direct infringement under two doctrines of copyright law: contributory copyright infringement and vicarious copyright infringement.

IV

We first address plaintiffs' claim that Napster is liable for contributory copyright infringement. Traditionally, "one who, with knowledge of the infringing activity, induces, causes or materially contributes to the infringing conduct of another, may be held liable as a 'contributory' infringer." *Gershwin Publ'g Corp. v. Columbia Artists Mgmt., Inc.*, 443 F.2d 1159, 1162 (2d Cir.1971); *see also Fonovisa, Inc. v. Cherry Auction, Inc.*, 76 F.3d 259, 264 (9th Cir. 1996). Put differently, liability exists if the defendant engages in "personal conduct that encourages or assists the infringement." *Matthew Bender & Co. v. West Publ'g Co.*, 158 F.3d 693, 706 (2d Cir. 1998).

The district court determined that plaintiffs in all likelihood would establish Napster's liability as a contributory infringer. The district court did not err; Napster, by its conduct, knowingly encourages and assists the infringement of plaintiffs' copyrights.

A.   *Knowledge*

Contributory liability requires that the secondary infringer "know or have reason to know" of direct infringement. *Cable/Home Communication Corp. v. Network Prods., Inc.*, 902 F.2d 829, 845 & 846 n. 29 (11th Cir. 1990). The district court found that Napster had both actual and constructive knowledge that its users exchanged copyrighted music. The district court also concluded that the law does not require knowledge of "specific acts of infringement" and rejected Napster's contention that because the company cannot distinguish infringing from noninfringing files, it does not "know" of the direct infringement.

It is apparent from the record that Napster has knowledge, both actual and constructive, of direct infringement. Napster claims that it is nevertheless protected from contributory liability by the teaching of *Sony Corp. v. Universal City Studios, Inc.*, 464 U.S. 417 (1984). We disagree. We observe that Napster's actual, specific knowledge of direct infringement renders *Sony*'s holding of limited assistance to Napster. * * *

The *Sony* Court refused to hold the manufacturer and retailers of video tape recorders liable for contributory infringement despite evidence that such machines could be and were used to infringe plaintiffs' copyrighted television shows. *Sony* stated that if liability "is to be imposed on petitioners in this case, it must rest on the fact that *they have sold equipment with constructive knowledge of the fact that their customers may use that equipment to make unauthorized copies* of copyrighted material." *Id.* at 439. The *Sony* Court declined to impute the requisite level of knowledge where the defendants made and sold equipment capable of both infringing and "substantial noninfringing uses." *Id.* at 442

We are bound to follow *Sony*, and will not impute the requisite level of knowledge to Napster merely because peer-to-peer file sharing technology may be used to infringe plaintiffs' copyrights. *See* 464 U.S. at 436 (rejecting argument that merely supplying the "'means' to accomplish an infringing activity" leads to imposition of liability). We depart from the reasoning of the district court that Napster failed to demonstrate that its system is capable of commercially significant noninfringing uses. The district court improperly confined the use analysis to current uses, ignoring the system's capabilities. *See generally Sony*, 464 U.S. at 442-43 (framing inquiry as whether the video tape recorder is "*capable* of commercially significant noninfringing uses") (emphasis added). Consequently, the district court placed undue weight on the proportion of current infringing use as compared to current and future noninfringing use. Nonetheless, whether we might arrive at a different result is not the issue here. * * *

Regardless of the number of Napster's infringing versus noninfringing uses, the evidentiary record here supported the district court's finding that plaintiffs would likely prevail in establishing that Napster knew or had reason to know of its users' infringement of plaintiffs' copyrights. This analysis is similar to that of *Religious Technology Center v. Netcom On-Line Communication Services, Inc.*, 907 F. Supp. 1361 (N.D. Cal. 1995), which suggests that in an online context, evidence of actual knowledge of specific acts of infringement is required to hold a computer system operator liable for contributory copyright infringement. *Netcom* considered the potential contributory copyright liability of a computer bulletin board operator whose system supported the posting of infringing material. The court, in denying Netcom's motion for summary judgment of noninfringement * * * , found that a disputed issue of fact existed as to whether the operator had sufficient knowledge of infringing activity. The court determined that for the operator to have sufficient knowledge, the copyright holder must "provide the necessary documentation to show there is likely infringement." 907 F. Supp. at 1374. If such documentation was provided, the court reasoned that Netcom would be liable for contributory infringement because its failure to remove the material "and thereby stop an infringing copy from being distributed worldwide constitutes substantial participation" in distribution of copyrighted material. *Id.*

We agree that if a computer system operator learns of specific infringing material available on his system and fails to purge such material from the system, the operator knows of and contributes to direct infringement. Conversely, absent any specific information which identifies infringing activity, a computer system operator cannot be liable for contributory infringement merely because the structure of the system allows for the exchange of copyrighted material. *See Sony*, 464 U.S. at 436, 442-43. To enjoin simply because a computer network allows for infringing use would, in our opinion, violate *Sony* and potentially restrict activity unrelated to infringing use.

We nevertheless conclude that sufficient knowledge exists to impose contributory liability when linked to demonstrated infringing use of the Napster system. The record supports the district court's finding that Napster has *actual* knowledge that *specific* infringing material is available using its system, that it could block access to the system by suppliers of the infringing material, and that it failed to remove the material.

B. *Material Contribution*

Under the facts as found by the district court, Napster materially contributes to the infringing activity. Relying on *Fonovisa*, the district court concluded that "[w]ithout the support services defendant provides, Napster users could not find and download the music they want with the ease of which defendant boasts." We agree that Napster provides "the site and facilities" for direct infringement. *See Fonovisa*, 76 F.3d at 264; *cf. Netcom*, 907 F. Supp. at 1372 ("Netcom will be liable for contributory infringement since its failure to cancel [a user's] infringing message and thereby stop an infringing copy from being distributed worldwide constitutes substantial participation."). The district court correctly applied the reasoning in *Fonovisa*, and properly found that Napster materially contributes to direct infringement.

We affirm the district court's conclusion that plaintiffs have demonstrated a likelihood of success on the merits of the contributory copyright infringement claim. We will address the scope of the injunction in part VIII of this opinion.

V

We turn to the question whether Napster engages in vicarious copyright infringement. Vicarious copyright liability is an "outgrowth" of respondeat superior. *Fonovisa*, 76 F.3d at 262. In the context of copyright law, vicarious liability extends beyond an employer/employee relationship to cases in which a defendant "has the right and ability to supervise the infringing activity and also has a direct financial interest in such activities." *Id.*

Before moving into this discussion, we note that *Sony*'s "staple article of commerce" analysis has no application to Napster's potential liability for vicarious copyright infringement. *See Sony*, 464 U.S. at 434-435. The issues of Sony's liability under the "doctrines of 'direct infringement' and 'vicarious liability'" were not before the Supreme Court, although the Court recognized that the "lines between direct infringement, contributory infringement, and vicarious liability are not clearly drawn." *Id.* at 435 n.17. Consequently, when the *Sony* Court used the term "vicarious liability," it did so broadly and outside of a technical analysis of the doctrine of vicarious copyright infringement. *Id.* at 435.

A. *Financial Benefit*

The district court determined that plaintiffs had demonstrated they would likely succeed in establishing that Napster has a direct financial interest in the infringing activity. We agree. Financial benefit exists where the availability of infringing material "acts as a 'draw' for customers." *Fonovisa*, 76 F.3d at 263-64. Ample evidence supports the district court's finding that Napster's future revenue is directly dependent upon "increases in userbase." More users register with the Napster system as the "quality and quantity of available music increases." We conclude that the district court did not err in determining that Napster financially benefits from the availability of protected works on its system.

B. *Supervision*

The district court determined that Napster has the right and ability to supervise its users' conduct. We agree in part.

The ability to block infringers' access to a particular environment for any reason whatsoever is evidence of the right and ability to supervise. Here, plaintiffs have demonstrated that Napster retains the right to control access to its system. Napster has an express reservation of rights policy, stating on its website that it expressly reserves the "right to refuse service and terminate accounts in [its] discretion, including, but not limited to, if Napster believes that user conduct violates applicable law . . . or for any reason in Napster's sole discretion, with or without cause."

To escape imposition of vicarious liability, the reserved right to police must be exercised to its fullest extent. Turning a blind eye to detectable acts of infringement for the sake of profit gives rise to liability. The district court correctly determined that Napster had the right and ability to police its system and failed to exercise that right to prevent the exchange of copyrighted material. The district court, however, failed to recognize that the boundaries of the premises that Napster "controls and patrols" are limited. Put differently, Napster's reserved "right and ability" to police is cabined by the system's current architecture. As shown by the record, the Napster system does not "read" the content of indexed files, other than to check that they are in the proper MP3 format.

Napster, however, has the ability to locate infringing material listed on its search indices, and the right to terminate users' access to the system. The file name indices, therefore, are within the "premises" that Napster has the ability to police. We recognize that the files are user-named and may not match copyrighted material exactly (for example, the artist or song could be spelled wrong). For Napster to function effectively, however, file names must reasonably or roughly correspond to the material contained in the files, otherwise no user could ever locate any desired music. As a practical matter, Napster, its users and the record company plaintiffs have equal access to infringing material by employing Napster's "search function."

Our review of the record requires us to accept the district court's conclusion that plaintiffs have demonstrated a likelihood of success on the merits of the vicarious copyright infringement claim. Napster's failure to police the system's "premises," combined with a showing that Napster financially benefits from the continuing availability of infringing files on its system, leads to the imposition of vicarious liability. We address the scope of the injunction in part VIII of this opinion. * * *

VIII

The district court correctly recognized that a preliminary injunction against Napster's participation in copyright infringement is not only warranted but required. We believe, however, that the scope of the injunction needs modification in light of our opinion. Specifically, we reiterate that contributory liability may potentially be imposed only to the extent that Napster: (1) receives reasonable knowledge of specific infringing files with copyrighted musical compositions and sound recordings; (2) knows or should know that such files are available on the Napster system; and (3) fails to act to prevent viral distribution of the works. The mere existence of the Napster system, absent actual notice and Napster's demonstrated failure to remove the offending material, is insufficient to impose contributory liability. *See Sony*, 464 U.S. at 442-43.

Conversely, Napster may be vicariously liable when it fails to affirmatively use its ability to patrol its system and preclude access to potentially infringing files listed in its search index. Napster has both the ability to use its search function to identify infringing musical recordings and the right to bar participation of users who engage in the transmission of infringing files.

The preliminary injunction which we stayed is overbroad because it places on Napster the entire burden of ensuring that no "copying, downloading, uploading, transmitting, or distributing" of plaintiffs' works occur on the system. As stated, we place the burden on plaintiffs to provide notice to Napster of copyrighted works and files containing such works available on the Napster system before Napster has the duty to disable access to the offending content. Napster, however, also bears the burden of policing the system within the limits of the system. Here, we recognize that this is not an exact science in that the files are user named. In crafting the injunction on remand, the district court should recognize that Napster's system does not currently appear to allow Napster access to users' MP3 files. * * *

X

We affirm in part, reverse in part and remand.

Notes and Questions

1. Look back at the excerpt from the *Sony* case above. Do you agree with the *Napster* court that the *Sony* defense does not apply when a service provider has actual knowledge of specific instances of infringement? How does Napster's knowledge of its user's infringing activities differ from Sony's knowledge?

The Seventh Circuit rejected the *Napster* court's conclusion that actual knowledge of infringing use is sufficient, in and of itself, for contributory infringement. *See In re Aimster Copyright Litigation*, 334 F.3d 643 (7th Cir. 2003). According to the *Aimster* court, it was surely apparent that VCRs were being used for infringing as well as noninfringing purposes at the time of the *Sony* litigation, and yet the Supreme Court "was unwilling to allow copyright holders to prevent infringement effectuated by means of a new technology at the price of possibly denying noninfringing consumers the benefit of the technology." *Id.* at 649. Nevertheless, the Seventh Circuit ruled that, because Aimster had failed to show that its file-sharing service had ever been used for *any* noninfringing purposes, a preliminary injunction based on a theory of contributory copyright liability was still justified.

2. Should a court always decline to "impute" knowledge of infringing activity to a service provider whose system is capable of noninfringing uses? Why or why not?

3. Why is the *Sony* defense unavailable against a claim of vicarious liability?

4. To what degree is the scope of the *Napster* decision limited to the particular technological architecture that Napster employed? Consider the following case, which addresses more decentralized peer-to-peer networks.

Metro-Goldwyn-Mayer Studios Inc. v. Grokster, Ltd.

Supreme Court of the United States, 2005
125 S. Ct. 2764

JUSTICE SOUTER delivered the opinion of the Court.

The question is under what circumstances the distributor of a product capable of both lawful and unlawful use is liable for acts of copyright infringement by third parties using the product. We hold that one who distributes a device with the object of promoting its use to infringe copyright, as shown by clear expression or other affirmative steps taken to foster infringement, is liable for the resulting acts of infringement by third parties.

I

A

Respondents, Grokster, Ltd., and StreamCast Networks, Inc., defendants in the trial court, distribute free software products that allow computer users to share electronic files through peer-to-peer networks, so called because users' computers communicate directly with each other, not through central servers. The advantage of peer-to-peer networks over information networks of other types shows up in their substantial and growing popularity. Because they need no central computer server to mediate the exchange of information or files among users, the high-bandwidth communications capacity for a server may be dispensed with, and the need for costly server storage space is eliminated. Since copies of a file (particularly a popular one) are available on many users' computers, file requests and retrievals may be faster than on other types of networks, and since file exchanges do not travel through a server, communications can take place between any computers that remain connected to the network without risk that a glitch in the server will disable the network in its entirety. Given these benefits in security, cost, and efficiency, peer-to-peer networks are employed to store and distribute electronic files by universities, government agencies, corporations, and libraries, among others.

Other users of peer-to-peer networks include individual recipients of Grokster's and StreamCast's software, and although the networks that they enjoy through using the software can be used to share any type of digital file, they have prominently employed those networks in sharing copyrighted music and video files without authorization. A group of copyright holders

(MGM for short, but including motion picture studios, recording companies, songwriters, and music publishers) sued Grokster and StreamCast for their users' copyright infringements, alleging that they knowingly and intentionally distributed their software to enable users to reproduce and distribute the copyrighted works in violation of the Copyright Act. MGM sought damages and an injunction.

Discovery during the litigation revealed the way the software worked, the business aims of each defendant company, and the predilections of the users. Grokster's eponymous software employs what is known as FastTrack technology, a protocol developed by others and licensed to Grokster. StreamCast distributes a very similar product except that its software, called Morpheus, relies on what is known as Gnutella technology. A user who downloads and installs either software possesses the protocol to send requests for files directly to the computers of others using software compatible with FastTrack or Gnutella. On the FastTrack network opened by the Grokster software, the user's request goes to a computer given an indexing capacity by the software and designated a supernode, or to some other computer with comparable power and capacity to collect temporary indexes of the files available on the computers of users connected to it. The supernode (or indexing computer) searches its own index and may communicate the search request to other supernodes. If the file is found, the supernode discloses its location to the computer requesting it, and the requesting user can download the file directly from the computer located. The copied file is placed in a designated sharing folder on the requesting user's computer, where it is available for other users to download in turn, along with any other file in that folder.

In the Gnutella network made available by Morpheus, the process is mostly the same, except that in some versions of the Gnutella protocol there are no supernodes. In these versions, peer computers using the protocol communicate directly with each other. When a user enters a search request into the Morpheus software, it sends the request to computers connected with it, which in turn pass the request along to other connected peers. The search results are communicated to the requesting computer, and the user can download desired files directly from peers' computers. As this description indicates, Grokster and StreamCast use no servers to intercept the content of the search requests or to mediate the file transfers conducted by users of the software, there being no central point through which the substance of the communications passes in either direction.

Although Grokster and StreamCast do not therefore know when particular files are copied, a few searches using their software would show what is available on the networks the software reaches. MGM commissioned a statistician to conduct a systematic search, and his study showed that nearly 90% of the files available for download on the FastTrack system were copyrighted works. Grokster and StreamCast dispute this figure, raising methodological problems and arguing that free copying even of copyrighted works may be authorized by the rightholders. They also argue that potential noninfringing uses of their software are significant in kind, even if infrequent in practice. Some musical performers, for example, have gained new audiences by distributing their copyrighted works for free across peer-to-peer networks, and some distributors of unprotected content have used peer-to-peer networks to disseminate files, Shakespeare being an example. Indeed, StreamCast has given Morpheus users the opportunity to download the briefs in this very case, though their popularity has not been quantified.

As for quantification, the parties' anecdotal and statistical evidence entered thus far to show the content available on the FastTrack and Gnutella networks does not say much about which files are actually downloaded by users, and no one can say how often the software is used to obtain copies of unprotected material. But MGM's evidence gives reason to think that the vast majority of users' downloads are acts of infringement, and because well over 100 million copies of the software in question are known to have been downloaded, and billions of files are shared across the FastTrack and Gnutella networks each month, the probable scope of copyright infringement is staggering.

Grokster and StreamCast concede the infringement in most downloads, and it is uncontested that they are aware that users employ their software primarily to download copyrighted files, even if the decentralized FastTrack and Gnutella networks fail to reveal which files are being copied, and when. From time to time, moreover, the companies have learned about their users' infringement directly, as from users who have sent e-mail to each company with questions about playing copyrighted movies they had downloaded, to whom the companies have responded with guidance. And MGM notified the companies of 8 million copyrighted files that could be obtained using their software.

Grokster and StreamCast are not, however, merely passive recipients of information about infringing use. The record is replete with evidence that from the moment Grokster and StreamCast began to distribute their free software, each one clearly voiced the objective that recipients use it to download copyrighted works, and each took active steps to encourage infringement.

After the notorious file-sharing service, Napster, was sued by copyright holders for facilitation of copyright infringement, StreamCast gave away a software program of a kind known as OpenNap, designed as compatible with the Napster program and open to Napster users for downloading files from other Napster and OpenNap users' computers. Evidence indicates that "[i]t was always [StreamCast's] intent to use [its OpenNap network] to be able to capture email addresses of [its] initial target market so that [it] could promote [its] StreamCast Morpheus interface to them," App. 861; indeed, the OpenNap program was engineered "'to leverage Napster's 50 million user base,'" id., at 746.

StreamCast monitored both the number of users downloading its OpenNap program and the number of music files they downloaded. It also used the resulting OpenNap network to distribute copies of the Morpheus software and to encourage users to adopt it. Internal company documents indicate that StreamCast hoped to attract large numbers of former Napster users if that company was shut down by court order or otherwise, and that StreamCast planned to be the next Napster. A kit developed by StreamCast to be delivered to advertisers, for example, contained press articles about StreamCast's potential to capture former Napster users, and it introduced itself to some potential advertisers as a company "which is similar to what Napster was." It broadcast banner advertisements to users of other Napster-compatible software, urging them to adopt its OpenNap. An internal e-mail from a company executive stated: "'We have put this network in place so that when Napster pulls the plug on their free service . . . or if the Court orders them shut down prior to that . . . we will be positioned to capture the flood of their 32 million users that will be actively looking for an alternative.'"

Thus, StreamCast developed promotional materials to market its service as the best Napster alternative. One proposed advertisement read: "Napster Inc. has announced that it will soon begin charging you a fee. That's if the courts don't order it shut down first. What will you do to get around it?" Another proposed ad touted StreamCast's software as the "# 1 alternative to Napster" and asked "[w]hen the lights went off at Napster . . . where did the users go?" StreamCast even planned to flaunt the illegal uses of its software; when it launched the OpenNap network, the chief technology officer of the company averred that "[t]he goal is to get in trouble with the law and get sued. It's the best way to get in the new[s]."

The evidence that Grokster sought to capture the market of former Napster users is sparser but revealing, for Grokster launched its own OpenNap system called Swaptor and inserted digital codes into its Web site so that computer users using Web search engines to look for "Napster" or "[f]ree filesharing" would be directed to the Grokster Web site, where they could download the Grokster software. And Grokster's name is an apparent derivative of Napster.

StreamCast's executives monitored the number of songs by certain commercial artists available on their networks, and an internal communication indicates they aimed to have a larger number of copyrighted songs available on their networks than other file-sharing networks. The point, of course, would be to attract users of a mind to infringe, just as it would be with their promotional materials developed showing copyrighted songs as examples of the kinds of files available through Morpheus. Morpheus in fact allowed users to search specifically for "Top 40" songs, which were inevitably copyrighted. Similarly, Grokster sent users a newsletter promoting its ability to provide particular, popular copyrighted materials.

In addition to this evidence of express promotion, marketing, and intent to promote further, the business models employed by Grokster and StreamCast confirm that their principal object was use of their software to download copyrighted works. Grokster and StreamCast receive no revenue from users, who obtain the software itself for nothing. Instead, both companies generate income by selling advertising space, and they stream the advertising to Grokster and Morpheus users while they are employing the programs. As the number of users of each program increases, advertising opportunities become worth more. While there is doubtless some demand for free Shakespeare, the evidence shows that substantive volume is a function of free access to copyrighted work. Users seeking Top 40 songs, for example, or the latest release by Modest Mouse, are certain to be far more numerous than those seeking a free Decameron, and Grokster and StreamCast translated that demand into dollars.

Finally, there is no evidence that either company made an effort to filter copyrighted material from users' downloads or otherwise impede the sharing of copyrighted files. Although Grokster appears to have sent e-mails warning users about infringing content when it received threatening notice from the copyright holders, it never blocked anyone from continuing to use its software to share copyrighted files. StreamCast not only rejected another company's offer of help to monitor infringement, but blocked the Internet Protocol addresses of entities it believed were trying to engage in such monitoring on its networks.

B

After discovery, the parties on each side of the case cross-moved for summary judgment. * * * The District Court held that those who used the Grokster and Morpheus software to download copyrighted media files directly infringed MGM's copyrights, a conclusion not contested on appeal, but the court nonetheless granted summary judgment in favor of Grokster and StreamCast as to any liability arising from distribution of the then current versions of their software. * * * The Court of Appeals affirmed. In the court's analysis, a defendant was liable as a contributory infringer when it had knowledge of direct infringement and materially contributed to the infringement. But the court read *Sony Corp. of America v. Universal City Studios, Inc.*, 464 U.S. 417 (1984), as holding that distribution of a commercial product capable of substantial noninfringing uses could not give rise to contributory liability for infringement unless the distributor had actual knowledge of specific instances of infringement and failed to act on that knowledge. The fact that the software was capable of substantial noninfringing uses in the Ninth Circuit's view meant that Grokster and StreamCast were not liable, because they had no such actual knowledge, owing to the decentralized architecture of their software. The court also held that Grokster and StreamCast did not materially contribute to their users' infringement because it was the users themselves who searched for, retrieved, and stored the infringing files, with no involvement by the defendants beyond providing the software in the first place.

The Ninth Circuit also considered whether Grokster and StreamCast could be liable under a theory of vicarious infringement. The court held against liability because the defendants did not monitor or control the use of the software, had no agreed-upon right or current ability to supervise its use, and had no independent duty to police infringement. We granted certiorari.

II

A

MGM and many of the *amici* fault the Court of Appeals's holding for upsetting a sound balance between the respective values of supporting creative pursuits through copyright protection and promoting innovation in new communication technologies by limiting the incidence of liability for copyright infringement. The more artistic protection is favored, the more technological innovation may be discouraged; the administration of copyright law is an exercise in managing the trade-off.

The tension between the two values is the subject of this case, with its claim that digital distribution of copyrighted material threatens copyright holders as never before, because every copy is identical to the original, copying is easy, and many people (especially the young) use file-sharing software to download copyrighted works. This very breadth of the software's use may well draw the public directly into the debate over copyright policy, and the indications are that the ease of copying songs or movies using software like Grokster's and Napster's is fostering disdain for copyright protection. As the case has been presented to us, these fears are said to be offset by the different concern that imposing liability, not only on infringers but on distributors of software based on its potential for unlawful use, could limit further development of beneficial technologies.

The argument for imposing indirect liability in this case is, however, a powerful one, given the number of infringing downloads that occur every day using StreamCast's and Grokster's software. When a widely shared service or product is used to commit infringement, it may be impossible to enforce rights in the protected work effectively against all direct infringers, the only practical alternative being to go against the distributor of the copying device for secondary liability on a theory of contributory or vicarious infringement.

One infringes contributorily by intentionally inducing or encouraging direct infringement and infringes vicariously by profiting from direct infringement while declining to exercise a right to stop or limit it.[9] Although "[t]he Copyright Act does not expressly render anyone liable for infringement committed by another," *Sony Corp. v. Universal City Studios,* 464 U.S., at 434, these doctrines of secondary liability emerged from common law principles and are well established in the law.

B

Despite the currency of these principles of secondary liability, this Court has dealt with secondary copyright infringement in only one recent case, and because MGM has tailored its principal claim to our opinion there,

---

9. * * * In the present case MGM has argued a vicarious liability theory, which allows imposition of liability when the defendant profits directly from the infringement and has a right and ability to supervise the direct infringer, even if the defendant initially lacks knowledge of the infringement. Because we resolve the case based on an inducement theory, there is no need to analyze separately MGM's vicarious liability theory.

a look at our earlier holding is in order. In *Sony Corp. v. Universal City Studios,* this Court addressed a claim that secondary liability for infringement can arise from the very distribution of a commercial product. There, the product, novel at the time, was what we know today as the videocassette recorder or VCR. Copyright holders sued Sony as the manufacturer, claiming it was contributorily liable for infringement that occurred when VCR owners taped copyrighted programs because it supplied the means used to infringe, and it had constructive knowledge that infringement would occur. At the trial on the merits, the evidence showed that the principal use of the VCR was for "'time-shifting,'" or taping a program for later viewing at a more convenient time, which the Court found to be a fair, not an infringing, use. There was no evidence that Sony had expressed an object of bringing about taping in violation of copyright or had taken active steps to increase its profits from unlawful taping. Although Sony's advertisements urged consumers to buy the VCR to "'record favorite shows'" or "'build a library'" of recorded programs, 464 U.S. at 459 (Blackmun, J., dissenting), neither of these uses was necessarily infringing.

On those facts, with no evidence of stated or indicated intent to promote infringing uses, the only conceivable basis for imposing liability was on a theory of contributory infringement arising from its sale of VCRs to consumers with knowledge that some would use them to infringe. But because the VCR was "capable of commercially significant noninfringing uses," we held the manufacturer could not be faulted solely on the basis of its distribution. *Id.,* at 442.

This analysis reflected patent law's traditional staple article of commerce doctrine, now codified, that distribution of a component of a patented device will not violate the patent if it is suitable for use in other ways. * * * [W]here an article is "good for nothing else" but infringement, *Canda v. Michigan Malleable Iron Co.,* 124 F. 486, 489 (C.A.6 1903), there is no legitimate public interest in its unlicensed availability, and there is no injustice in presuming or imputing an intent to infringe. Conversely, the doctrine absolves the equivocal conduct of selling an item with substantial lawful as well as unlawful uses, and limits liability to instances of more acute fault than the mere understanding that some of one's products will be misused. It leaves breathing room for innovation and a vigorous commerce.

The parties and many of the *amici* in this case think the key to resolving it is the *Sony* rule and, in particular, what it means for a product to be "capable of commercially significant noninfringing uses." MGM advances the argument that granting summary judgment to Grokster and StreamCast as to their current activities gave too much weight to the value of innovative technology, and too little to the copyrights infringed by users of their software, given that 90% of works available on one of the networks was shown to be copyrighted. Assuming the remaining 10% to be its noninfringing use, MGM says this should not qualify as "substantial," and the Court should quantify *Sony* to the extent of holding that a product used "principally" for infringement does not qualify. As mentioned before, Grokster and StreamCast reply by citing evidence that their software can be used to reproduce public domain works, and they point to copyright holders who actually encourage copying. Even if infringement is the principal practice with their software today, they argue, the noninfringing uses are significant and will grow.

We agree with MGM that the Court of Appeals misapplied *Sony*, which it read as limiting secondary liability quite beyond the circumstances to which the case applied. *Sony* barred secondary liability based on presuming or imputing intent to cause infringement solely from the design or distribution of a product capable of substantial lawful use, which the distributor knows is in fact used for infringement. The Ninth Circuit has read *Sony's* limitation to mean that whenever a product is capable of substantial lawful use, the producer can never be held contributorily liable for third parties' infringing use of it; it read the rule as being this broad, even when an actual purpose to cause infringing use is shown by evidence independent of design and distribution of the product, unless the distributors had "specific knowledge of infringement at a time at which they contributed to the infringement, and failed to act upon that information." Because the Circuit found the StreamCast and Grokster software capable of substantial lawful use, it concluded on the basis of its reading of *Sony* that neither company could be held liable, since there was no showing that their software, being without any central server, afforded them knowledge of specific unlawful uses.

This view of *Sony*, however, was error, converting the case from one about liability resting on imputed intent to one about liability on any theory. Because *Sony* did not displace other theories of secondary liability, and because we find below that it was error to grant summary judgment to the companies on MGM's inducement claim, we do not revisit *Sony* further, as MGM requests, to add a more quantified description of the point of balance between protection and commerce when liability rests solely on distribution with knowledge that unlawful use will occur. It is enough to note that the Ninth Circuit's judgment rested on an erroneous understanding of *Sony* and to leave further consideration of the *Sony* rule for a day when that may be required.

C

Sony's rule limits imputing culpable intent as a matter of law from the characteristics or uses of a distributed product. But nothing in *Sony* requires courts to ignore evidence of intent if there is such evidence, and the case was never meant to foreclose rules of fault-based liability derived from the common law. Thus, where evidence goes beyond a product's characteristics or the knowledge that it may be put to infringing uses, and shows statements or actions directed to promoting infringement, *Sony's* staple-article rule will not preclude liability.

The classic case of direct evidence of unlawful purpose occurs when one induces commission of infringement by another, or "entic[es] or persuad[es] another" to infringe, Black's Law Dictionary 790 (8th ed.2004), as by advertising. * * * [O]ne who distributes a device with the object of promoting its use to infringe copyright, as shown by clear expression or other affirmative steps taken to foster infringement, is liable for the resulting acts of infringement by third parties. We are, of course, mindful of the need to keep from trenching on regular commerce or discouraging the development of technologies with lawful and unlawful potential. Accordingly, just as *Sony* did not find intentional inducement despite the knowledge of the VCR manufacturer that its device could be used to infringe, mere knowledge of infringing potential or of actual infringing uses would not be enough here to subject a distributor to liability. Nor would ordinary acts incident to product distribution, such as offering customers technical support or product updates, support liability in themselves. The inducement rule, instead, premises liability on purposeful, culpable expression and conduct, and thus does nothing to compromise legitimate commerce or discourage innovation having a lawful promise.

III

A

The only apparent question about treating MGM's evidence as sufficient to withstand summary judgment under the theory of inducement goes to the need on MGM's part to adduce evidence that StreamCast and Grokster communicated an inducing message to their software users. The classic instance of inducement is by advertisement or solicitation that broadcasts a message designed to stimulate others to commit violations. MGM claims that such a message is shown here. It is undisputed that StreamCast beamed onto the computer screens of users of Napster-compatible programs ads urging the adoption of its OpenNap program, which was designed, as its name implied, to invite the custom of patrons of Napster, then under attack in the courts for facilitating massive infringement. Those who accepted StreamCast's OpenNap program were offered software to perform the same services, which a factfinder could conclude would readily have been understood in the Napster market as the ability to download copyrighted music files. Grokster distributed an electronic newsletter containing links to articles promoting its software's ability to access popular copyrighted music. And anyone whose Napster or free file-sharing searches turned up a link to Grokster would have understood Grokster to be offering the same file-sharing ability as Napster, and to the same people who probably used Napster for infringing downloads; that would also have been the understanding of anyone offered Grokster's suggestively named Swaptor software, its version of OpenNap. And both companies communicated a clear message by responding affirmatively to requests for help in locating and playing copyrighted materials.

In StreamCast's case, of course, the evidence just described was supplemented by other unequivocal indications of unlawful purpose in the internal communications and advertising designs aimed at Napster users ("When the lights went off at Napster . . . where did the users go?") Whether the messages were communicated is not to the point on this record. The function of the message in the theory of inducement is to prove by a defendant's own statements that his unlawful purpose disqualifies him from claiming protection (and incidentally to point to actual violators likely to be found among those who hear or read the message). Proving that a message was sent out, then, is the preeminent but not exclusive way of showing that active steps were taken with the purpose of bringing about infringing acts, and of showing that infringing acts took place by using the device distributed. Here, the summary judgment record is replete with other evidence that Grokster and StreamCast, unlike the manufacturer and distributor in *Sony*, acted with a purpose to cause copyright violations by use of software suitable for illegal use.

Three features of this evidence of intent are particularly notable. First, each company showed itself to be aiming to satisfy a known source of demand for copyright infringement, the market comprising former Napster users. StreamCast's internal documents made constant reference to Napster, it initially distributed its Morpheus software through an OpenNap program compatible with Napster, it advertised its OpenNap program to Napster users, and its Morpheus software functions as Napster did except that it could be used to distribute more kinds of files, including copyrighted movies and software programs. Grokster's name is apparently derived from Napster, it too initially offered an OpenNap program, its software's function is likewise comparable to Napster's, and it attempted to divert queries for Napster onto its own Web site. Grokster and StreamCast's efforts to supply services to former Napster users, deprived of a mechanism to copy and distribute what were overwhelmingly infringing files, indicate a principal, if not exclusive, intent on the part of each to bring about infringement.

Second, this evidence of unlawful objective is given added significance by MGM's showing that neither company attempted to develop filtering tools or other mechanisms to diminish the infringing activity using their software. While the Ninth Circuit treated the defendants' failure to develop such tools as irrelevant because they lacked an independent duty to monitor their users' activity, we think this evidence underscores Grokster's and StreamCast's intentional facilitation of their users' infringement.[12]

Third, there is a further complement to the direct evidence of unlawful objective. It is useful to recall that StreamCast and Grokster make money by selling advertising space, by directing ads to the screens of computers employing their software. As the record shows, the more the software is used, the more ads are sent out and the greater the advertising revenue becomes. Since the extent of the software's use determines the gain to the distributors, the commercial sense of their enterprise turns on high-volume use, which the record shows is infringing. This evidence alone would not

---

12. Of course, in the absence of other evidence of intent, a court would be unable to find contributory infringement liability merely based on a failure to take affirmative steps to prevent infringement, if the device otherwise was capable of substantial noninfringing uses. Such a holding would tread too close to the *Sony* safe harbor.

justify an inference of unlawful intent, but viewed in the context of the entire record its import is clear.

The unlawful objective is unmistakable.

B

In addition to intent to bring about infringement and distribution of a device suitable for infringing use, the inducement theory of course requires evidence of actual infringement by recipients of the device, the software in this case. As the account of the facts indicates, there is evidence of infringement on a gigantic scale, and there is no serious issue of the adequacy of MGM's showing on this point in order to survive the companies' summary judgment requests. Although an exact calculation of infringing use, as a basis for a claim of damages, is subject to dispute, there is no question that the summary judgment evidence is at least adequate to entitle MGM to go forward with claims for damages and equitable relief. * * *

The judgment of the Court of Appeals is vacated, and the case is remanded for further proceedings consistent with this opinion.

It is so ordered.

JUSTICE GINSBURG, with whom THE CHIEF JUSTICE and JUSTICE KENNEDY join, concurring

I concur in the Court's decision, which vacates in full the judgment of the Court of Appeals for the Ninth Circuit, and write separately to clarify why I conclude that the Court of Appeals misperceived, and hence misapplied, our holding in *Sony Corp. of America v. Universal City Studios, Inc.,* 464 U.S. 417 (1984). There is here at least a "genuine issue as to [a] material fact," Fed. Rule Civ. Proc. 56(c), on the liability of Grokster or StreamCast, not only for actively inducing copyright infringement, but also or alternatively, based on the distribution of their software products, for contributory copyright infringement. On neither score was summary judgment for Grokster and StreamCast warranted.

At bottom, however labeled, the question in this case is whether Grokster and StreamCast are liable for the direct infringing acts of others. Liability under our jurisprudence may be predicated on actively encouraging (or inducing) infringement through specific acts (as the Court's opinion develops) or on distributing a product distributees use to infringe copyrights, if the product is not capable of "substantial" or "commercially significant" noninfringing uses. *Sony,* 464 U.S., at 442. While the two categories overlap, they capture different culpable behavior. * * *

In *Sony,* the Court considered Sony's liability for selling the Betamax video cassette recorder. It did so enlightened by a full trial record. * * * [T]o resolve the *Sony* case, the Court explained, it had to determine "whether the Betamax is capable of commercially significant noninfringing uses." *Id.* at 442. To answer that question, the Court considered whether "a significant number of [potential uses of the Betamax were] noninfringing." *Ibid.* The Court homed in on one potential use—private, noncommercial time-shifting of television programs in the home (*i.e.*, recording a broadcast TV program for later personal viewing). Time-shifting was noninfringing, the Court concluded, because in some cases trial testimony showed it was authorized by the copyright holder and in others it qualified as legitimate fair use. Most purchasers used the Betamax principally to engage in time-shifting, a use that "plainly satisfie[d]" the Court's standard. *Id.,* at 442. Thus, there was no need in *Sony* to "give precise content to the question of how much [actual or potential] use is commercially significant." *Ibid.* Further development was left for later days and cases. * * *

This case differs markedly from *Sony.* Here, there has been no finding of any fair use and little beyond anecdotal evidence of noninfringing uses. In finding the Grokster and StreamCast software products capable of substantial noninfringing uses, the District Court and the Court of Appeals appear to have relied largely on declarations submitted by the defendants. These declarations include assertions (some of them hearsay) that a number of copyright owners authorize distribution of their works on the Internet and that some public domain material is available through peer-to-peer networks including those accessed through Grokster's and StreamCast's software. * * * These declarations do not support summary judgment in the face of evidence, proffered by MGM, of overwhelming use of Grokster's and StreamCast's software for infringement.

Even if the absolute number of noninfringing files copied using the Grokster and StreamCast software is large, it does not follow that the products are therefore put to substantial noninfringing uses and are thus immune from liability. The number of noninfringing copies may be reflective of, and dwarfed by, the huge total volume of files shared. * * *

In sum, when the record in this case was developed, there was evidence that Grokster's and StreamCast's products were, and had been for some time, overwhelmingly used to infringe, and that this infringement was the overwhelming source of revenue from the products. Fairly appraised, the evidence was insufficient to demonstrate, beyond genuine debate, a reasonable prospect that substantial or commercially significant noninfringing uses were likely to develop over time. On this record, the District Court should not have ruled dispositively on the contributory infringement charge by granting summary judgment to Grokster and StreamCast.

If, on remand, the case is not resolved on summary judgment in favor of MGM based on Grokster and StreamCast actively inducing infringement, the Court of Appeals, I would emphasize, should reconsider, on a fuller record, its interpretation of *Sony's* product distribution holding.

JUSTICE BREYER, with whom JUSTICE STEVENS and JUSTICE O'CONNOR join, concurring.

I agree with the Court that the distributor of a dual-use technology may be liable for the infringing activities of third parties where he or she actively seeks to advance the infringement. I further agree that, in light of our holding today, we need not now "revisit" *Sony Corp. of America v. Universal City Studios, Inc.,* 464 U.S. 417 (1984). Other Members of the Court, however, take up the *Sony* question: whether Grokster's product is "capable of 'substantial' or 'commercially significant' noninfringing uses." (GINSBURG, J., concurring) (quoting *Sony, supra,* at 442). And they answer that question by stating that the Court of Appeals was wrong when it granted summary judgment on the issue in Grokster's favor. I write to explain why I disagree with them on this matter.

I

The Court's opinion in *Sony* and the record evidence (as described and analyzed in the many briefs before us) together convince me that the Court of Appeals' conclusion has adequate legal support.

A

I begin with *Sony's* standard. In *Sony,* the Court considered the potential copyright liability of a company that did not itself illegally copy protected material, but rather sold a machine—a Video Cassette Recorder (VCR)—that could be used to do so. A buyer could use that machine for *non*infringing purposes, such as recording for later viewing (sometimes called "time-shifting") uncopyrighted television programs or copyrighted programs with a copyright holder's permission. The buyer could use the machine for infringing purposes as well, such as building libraries of taped copyrighted programs. Or, the buyer might use the machine to record copyrighted programs under circumstances in which the legal status of the act of recording was uncertain (*i.e.,* where the copying may, or may not, have constituted a "fair use." Sony knew many customers would use its VCRs to engage in unauthorized copying and "'library-building.'" *Id.,* at 458-459 (Blackmun, J., dissenting). But that fact, said the Court, was insufficient to make Sony itself an infringer. And the Court ultimately held that Sony was not liable for its customers' acts of infringement.

In reaching this conclusion, the Court recognized the need for the law, in fixing *secondary* copyright liability, to "strike a balance between a copyright holder's legitimate demand for effective—not merely symbolic—protection of the statutory monopoly, and the rights of others freely to engage in substantially unrelated areas of commerce." *Id.,* at 442. * * * The Court ultimately characterized the legal "question" in the particular case as "whether [Sony's VCR] is *capable of commercially significant noninfringing uses*" (while declining to give "precise content" to these terms).

It then applied this standard. The Court had before it a survey (commissioned by the District Court and then prepared by the respondents) showing that roughly 9% of all VCR recordings were of the type—namely, religious, educational, and sports programming—owned by producers and distributors testifying on Sony's behalf who did not object to time-shifting. * * * A much higher percentage of VCR *users* had at one point taped an authorized program, in addition to taping unauthorized programs. And the plaintiffs—not a large class of content providers as in this case—owned only a small percentage of the total available *un*authorized programming. But of all the taping actually done by Sony's customers, only around 9% was of the sort the Court referred to as authorized.

The Court found that the magnitude of authorized programming was "significant," and it also noted the "significant potential for future authorized copying." 464 U.S., at 444. The Court supported this conclusion by referencing the trial testimony of professional sports league officials and a religious broadcasting representative. *Id.*, at 444, and n. 24. It also discussed (1) a Los Angeles educational station affiliated with the Public Broadcasting Service that made many of its programs available for home taping, and (2) Mr. Rogers' Neighborhood, a widely watched children's program. *Id.*, at 445. On the basis of this testimony and other similar evidence, the Court determined that producers of this kind had authorized duplication of their copyrighted programs "in significant enough numbers to create a *substantial* market for a noninfringing use of the" VCR. *Id.*, at 447, n. 28 (emphasis added).

The Court, in using the key word "substantial," indicated that these circumstances alone constituted a sufficient basis for rejecting the imposition of secondary liability. Nonetheless, the Court buttressed its conclusion by finding separately that, in any event, *un*authorized timeshifting often constituted not infringement, but "fair use." *Id.*, at 447–456.

B

When measured against *Sony's* underlying evidence and analysis, the evidence now before us shows that Grokster passes *Sony's* test—that is, whether the company's product is capable of substantial or commercially significant noninfringing uses. For one thing, petitioners' (hereinafter MGM) own expert declared that 75% of current files available on Grokster are infringing and 15% are "likely infringing." That leaves some number of files near 10% that apparently are noninfringing, a figure very similar to the 9% or so of authorized time-shifting uses of the VCR that the Court faced in *Sony.* * * * [I]t is reasonable to infer quantities of current lawful use roughly approximate to those at issue in *Sony.* At least, MGM has offered no evidence sufficient to survive summary judgment that could plausibly demonstrate a significant quantitative difference. To be sure, in quantitative terms these uses account for only a small percentage of the total number of uses of Grokster's product. But the same was true in *Sony,* which characterized the relatively limited authorized copying market as "substantial."

Importantly, *Sony* also used the word "capable," asking whether the product is "*capable of* "substantial noninfringing uses. Its language and analysis suggest that a figure like 10%, if fixed for all time, might well prove insufficient, but that such a figure serves as an adequate foundation where there is a reasonable prospect of expanded legitimate uses over time. See *ibid.* (noting a "significant potential for future authorized copying"). And its language also indicates the appropriateness of looking to potential future uses of the product to determine its "capability."

Here the record reveals a significant future market for noninfringing uses of Grokster-type peer-to-peer software. Such software permits the exchange of *any* sort of digital file—whether that file does, or does not, contain copyrighted material. As more and more uncopyrighted information is stored in swappable form, it seems a likely inference that lawful peer-to-peer sharing will become increasingly prevalent. There may be other now-unforeseen noninfringing uses that develop for peer-to-peer software, just as the home-video rental industry (unmentioned in *Sony*) developed for the VCR. But the foreseeable development of such uses, when taken together with an estimated 10% noninfringing material, is sufficient to meet *Sony's* standard. And while *Sony* considered the record following a trial, there are no facts asserted by MGM in its summary judgment filings that lead me to believe the outcome after a trial here could be any different. The lower courts reached the same conclusion.

Of course, Grokster itself may not want to develop these other noninfringing uses. But *Sony's* standard seeks to protect not the Groksters of this world (which in any event may well be liable under today's holding), but the development of technology more generally. And Grokster's desires in this respect are beside the point.

II

The real question here, I believe, is not whether the record evidence satisfies *Sony*. As I have interpreted the standard set forth in that case, it does. * * * Instead, the real question is whether we should modify the *Sony* standard, as MGM requests, or interpret *Sony* more strictly, as I believe JUSTICE GINSBURG's approach would do in practice. * * * *Sony* itself sought to "strike a balance between a copyright holder's legitimate demand for effective—not merely symbolic—protection of the statutory monopoly, and the rights of others freely to engage in substantially unrelated areas of commerce." *Id.*, at 442. Thus, to determine whether modification, or a strict interpretation, of *Sony* is needed, I would ask whether MGM has shown that *Sony* incorrectly balanced copyright and new-technology interests. In particular: (1) Has *Sony* (as I interpret it) worked to protect new technology? (2) If so, would modification or strict interpretation significantly weaken that protection? (3) If so, would new or necessary copyright-related benefits outweigh any such weakening?

A

The first question is the easiest to answer. *Sony's* rule, as I interpret it, has provided entrepreneurs with needed assurance that they will be shielded from copyright liability as they bring valuable new technologies to market.

Sony's rule is clear. That clarity allows those who develop new products that are capable of substantial noninfringing uses to know, *ex ante,* that distribution of their product will not yield massive monetary liability. At the same time, it helps deter them from distributing products that have no other real function than—or that are specifically intended for—copyright infringement, deterrence that the Court's holding today reinforces (by adding a weapon to the copyright holder's legal arsenal).

Sony's rule is strongly technology protecting. The rule deliberately makes it difficult for courts to find secondary liability where new technology is at issue. It establishes that the law will not impose copyright liability upon the distributors of dual-use technologies (who do not themselves engage in unauthorized copying) unless the product in question will be used *almost exclusively* to infringe copyrights (or unless they actively induce infringements as we today describe). * * *

Sony's rule is forward looking. It does not confine its scope to a static snapshot of a product's current uses (thereby threatening technologies that have undeveloped future markets). Rather, as the VCR example makes clear, a product's market can evolve dramatically over time. And *Sony*—by referring to a *capacity* for substantial noninfringing uses—recognizes that fact. * * *

Sony's rule is mindful of the limitations facing judges where matters of technology are concerned. Judges have no specialized technical ability to answer questions about present or future technological feasibility or commercial viability where technology professionals, engineers, and venture capitalists themselves may radically disagree and where answers may differ depending upon whether one focuses upon the time of product development or the time of distribution. * * *

B

The second, more difficult, question is whether a modified *Sony* rule (or a strict interpretation) would significantly weaken the law's ability to protect new technology. JUSTICE GINSBURG's approach would require defendants to produce considerably more concrete evidence—more than was presented here—to earn *Sony's* shelter. That heavier evidentiary demand, and especially the more dramatic (case-by-case balancing) modifications that MGM and the Government seek, would, I believe, undercut the protection that *Sony* now offers. * * *

C

The third question—whether a positive copyright impact would outweigh any technology-related loss—I find the most difficult of the three. I do not doubt that a more intrusive *Sony* test would generally provide greater revenue security for copyright holders. But it is harder to conclude that the gains on the copyright swings would exceed the losses on the technology roundabouts. * * *

Unauthorized copying likely diminishes industry revenue, though it is not clear by how much. The extent to which related production has actually and resultingly declined remains uncertain, though there is good reason to believe that the decline, if any, is not substantial. More importantly, copyright holders at least potentially have other tools available to reduce piracy and to abate whatever threat it poses to creative production. As today's opinion makes clear, a copyright holder may proceed against a technology provider where a provable specific intent to infringe (of the kind the Court describes) is present. Services like Grokster may well be liable under an inducement theory. In addition, a copyright holder has always had the legal authority to bring a traditional infringement suit against one who wrongfully copies. * * *

Further, copyright holders may develop new technological devices that will help curb unlawful infringement. Some new technology, called "digital 'watermarking' " and "digital fingerprint[ing]," can encode within the file information about the author and the copyright scope and date, which "fingerprints" can help to expose infringers. At the same time, advances in technology have discouraged unlawful copying by making *lawful* copying (*e.g.*, downloading music with the copyright holder's permission) cheaper and easier to achieve. * * *

Finally, as *Sony* recognized, the legislative option remains available. Courts are less well suited than Congress to the task of "accommodat[ing] fully the varied permutations of competing interests that are inevitably implicated by such new technology." *Sony,* 464 U.S., at 431.

I do not know whether these developments and similar alternatives will prove sufficient, but I am reasonably certain that, given their existence, a strong demonstrated need for modifying *Sony* (or for interpreting *Sony's* standard more strictly) has not yet been shown. That fact, along with the added risks that modification (or strict interpretation) would impose upon technological innovation, leads me to the conclusion that we should maintain *Sony,* reading its standard as I have read it. As so read, it requires affirmance of the Ninth Circuit's determination of the relevant aspects of the *Sony* question.

Notes and Questions

1. The Court bases its conclusion that Grokster and StreamCast actively sought to induce infringement on three factors: evidence that the services targeted Napster's customers, the services' advertising-based business model, and the absence of any efforts to filter noninfringing uses. What weight should each of these factors have received? Would the last two factors have mattered in the absence of evidence that the services targeted Napster's customers? If not, has the Court simply constructed an inducement rule that is trivially easy to avoid?

2. Assume that the Court had not been presented with evidence of Grokster's and StreamCast's intent to induce infringing activity. How should it have resolved the case? How are courts likely to resolve future challenges to peer-to-peer technology where such evidence does not exist?

3. Do the concurring opinions diverge solely in their evaluation of the quantum of evidence MGM presented concerning infringing and noninfringing uses, or do they reflect fundamentally different interpretations of *Sony*?

4. What triggered the *Sony* Court's conclusion that the Betamax was capable of substantial noninfringing uses? Note that Justice Ginsburg views *Sony* as holding that authorized copying and time-shifting that is unauthorized but a fair use, taken together, make up the noninfringing uses that the *Sony* Court deemed substantial or significant. Justice Breyer, in contrast, appears to

suggest that authorized copying alone, which amounted to some nine percent of the Betamax's use, constituted a substantial noninfringing use. Which interpretation of *Sony* is correct? Which approach would be preferable as a matter of policy?

5. Assuming that courts are confronted in the future with the question of how to apply *Sony* to peer-to-peer technologies, how should courts determine when such technologies are capable of substantial noninfringing uses? By comparing the commercial significance of the noninfringing uses to the commercial significance of the infringing ones? By examining the economically feasible alternatives to the claimed noninfringing uses, and discounting such uses if alternatives do exist? Should *Sony*'s test be replaced by a different analysis, such as whether it would be disproportionately costly for the distributor of a technology to reduce or eliminate the infringing uses? *Cf. In re Aimster Copyright Litigation*, 334 F.3d 643, 653 (7th Cir. 2003).

6. All three of the *Grokster* opinions express concern about the impact the Court's decision might have in stifling the development of new technologies that could have both infringing and noninfringing uses. Do you think the Court successfully addressed this concern? Is an intent standard sufficient not to chill technological development? What legal advice would you provide to companies seeking to develop other peer-to-peer technologies on how to avoid liability?

3. Telecommunications Devices

Earlier in this chapter, we explored ways in which the Supreme Court's Fourth Amendment privacy jurisprudence has been forced to respond to changes in technology. But, as we have seen, law can also be used to influence how technology develops. For example, certain telecommunications technologies undoubtedly make it easier for law enforcement officials to conduct surveillance operations, while others make such operations more difficult. Not surprisingly then, Congress has at times used law to influence how such telecommunications systems are designed.

For example, following the Supreme Court's decision in *Katz v. United States* (discussed earlier in this chapter), Congress adopted procedures for law enforcement officials to follow to obtain appropriate judicial authorization for wiretapping and eavesdropping activities. These procedures, enacted as Title III of the Omnibus Crime Control and Safe Streets Act of 1968 ("Title III") are codified as amended at 18 U.S.C. §§ 2510-2522.

Law enforcement officials traditionally conducted court-authorized surveillance of telephone conversations under Title III by attaching equipment to the "local loop"—the wires running from a telephone company's switching equipment to an individual subscriber's home. Following the breakup of the Bell system, however, officials claimed that the development of digital telephone technology and the proliferation of new communications services (such as call forwarding, call waiting, and the like) complicated the execution of court-ordered wiretaps. In hearings and submissions to Congress in 1994, the FBI identified "specific instances in which law enforcement agencies were precluded due to technological impediments from fully implementing authorized electronic surveillance." H.R. REP. 103-827, at 14, *reprinted in* 1994 U.S.C.C.A.N. 3489, 3494. Since 1970, Title III itself has required telephone companies and others to furnish "all information, facilities, and technical assistance necessary to accomplish" a court-ordered interception. 18 U.S.C. § 2518(4); *see United States v. New York Tel.* Co., 434 U.S. 159, 177 (1977). Nothing in the statute, however, imposed a direct obligation on providers to design their systems so as not to impede lawful interceptions.

In 1994, Congress passed the Communications Assistance for Law Enforcement Act ("CALEA"), which required telecommunications carriers to ensure that their systems are technically capable of "expeditiously isolating and enabling the government, pursuant to a court order or other lawful authorization," to intercept wire and electronic communications concurrently with their transmission to the subscriber and to access call-identifying information reasonably available to the carrier. 47 U.S.C. § 1002(a)(1), (2). The statute authorized the telecommunications industry, in consultation with law enforcement agencies, to develop its own technical standards for meeting the statutory requirements. If a government agency believed industry standards were deficient, it could petition the Federal Communications Commission to establish technical standards by rule. Industry efforts to meet the statutory requirements led to a protracted dispute between the Department of Justice and telecommunications providers over what capabilities the law required providers to embed in their switching equipment. *See United States Telecom Ass'n v. FCC*, 227 F.3d 450 (D.C. Cir. 2000).

The dispute between the Justice Department and telecommunications carriers has now spilled over to the Internet. By its terms, CALEA does not apply to entities insofar as they provide "information services," by offering "a capability for generating, acquiring, storing, transforming, processing, utilizing, or making available information via telecommunications." 47 U.S.C. § 1001(6), (8). It thus excludes various Internet services, including e-mail services. In response to a Justice Department request for clarification, however, the FCC issued an order in August 2005 concluding that CALEA's mandate extends to providers of interconnected Voice over Internet Protocol (VoIP) services. *See In re* Communications Assistance for Law Enforcement Act and Broadband Access Servs., 20 F.C.C.R. 14,989 (Aug. 5, 2005).[a] The order requires that VoIP services comply with CALEA by May 2007 by making their applications and facilities capable of isolating communications for government interception.

Is it legitimate for law enforcement authorities to ask Congress and industry for surveillance capabilities to keep pace with technological

---

a. For an illuminating discussion of the FCC's decision, see Susan P. Crawford, *The Ambulance, the Squad Car, & the Internet*, 21 BERKELEY TECH. L.J. 873 (2006).

changes? Is the approach the government took here—seeking legislation requiring providers to make their systems capable of executing wiretap orders—appropriate? Consider the following perspective:

> The question that regulators faced was [whether the telephone network should adopt an architecture that made tapping a phone difficult, or one that made tapping a phone easier]. And the difference between versions is just a choice of code. Some codes cost more than others, and some codes protect privacy better than others. So the choice among codes becomes a choice among values. Congress asked whether this choice should be solely private (made by telephone engineers) or partially public (influenced by Congress). It chose the latter. * * *
>
> No doubt CALEA's ultimate aim in requiring this architecture is to reduce crime, but it pursues this aim indirectly, by modifying the code to constrain individuals who might want to engage in crime. Because the government can once again tap when it has authority to tap, digital networks are no longer as helpful to criminals. Hence, the payoff from crime is reduced.
>
> This is law regulating code. Its indirect effect is to improve law enforcement, but it does so by modifying code-based constraints on law enforcement. It selects an architecture that distributes the burdens of code in a collectively valued way.

LAWRENCE LESSIG, CODE AND OTHER LAWS OF CYBERSPACE 44-45 (1999). What dangers arise when the government requires providers to hardwire surveillance-facilitating mechanisms into their technology—when the government regulates "code"?

SECTION D. A CASE STUDY ON THE INTERACTION OF LAW AND TECHNOLOGY: DOMAIN NAMES AND THE MARKET FOR SEARCH TOOLS

In this chapter, we have explored multiple ways in which law and technology interact. As we have seen, technological change often spurs legal responses, but legal responses also affect future technological innovation. The federal government's treatment of encryption technology provides a ready example. In response to concerns about crime that arose with the rise of strong encryption technology, the government severely restricted the export of strong encryption products in the mid-1990s. But, because of those restrictions, producers of mass-market software were slow to incorporate strong encryption technology into their products. Similarly, we have previously considered claims that the anti-circumvention and anti-trafficking provisions of the DMCA could chill research activities or reverse engineering efforts, notwithstanding the exclusion of some such activities from the prohibitions of the statute. In addition to these relatively predictable effects of legal policy choices upon technology, it is possible to identify more surprising effects. In the case of the DMCA, for example, Professors Pamela Samuelson and Suzanne Scotchmer argue that prohibiting circumvention of access controls will actually curtail the development of truly effective technological measures designed to prevent access to protected works, because content owners can rely instead on marginally effective measures backed by the protections of the DMCA. *See* Pamela Samuelson & Suzanne Scotchmer, *The Law and Economics of Reverse Engineering*, 111 YALE L.J. 1575, 1639, 1646 (2002).

In order to bring together these various ideas about legal and technological regulation, we again use the domain name system as a concluding case study, and we explore the complex dance between law and technology that has accompanied the rise of "dot com" in the public lexicon. As discussed in Chapter Two, trademark law protects words, symbols, and other means of identifying the source of goods and services. One of the functions of a trademark is to reduce a consumer's search costs, by providing information about the price, quality, and location of a particular product. Thus, it is not surprising that, because familiar and recognizable domain names can help consumers to find particular websites, the rise of the Internet domain name system created pressure for law to respond by creating trademarks in domain names. As you consider Congress' efforts in this regard and the critique that follows it, ask yourself whether, overall, you think creating trademarks in domain names was a good idea.

Anticybersquatting Consumer Protection Act

15 U.S.C. § 1125(d)

§ 1125. False designations of origin, false descriptions, and dilution forbidden

* * *

(d) Cyberpiracy prevention

(1)(A) A person shall be liable in a civil action by the owner of a mark, including a personal name which is protected as a mark under this section, if, without regard to the goods or services of the parties, that person

(i) has a bad faith intent to profit from that mark, including a personal name which is protected as a mark under this section; and

(ii) registers, traffics in, or uses a domain name that--

(I) in the case of a mark that is distinctive at the time of registration of the domain name, is identical or confusingly similar to that mark;

(II) in the case of a famous mark that is famous at the time of registration of the domain name, is identical or confusingly similar to or dilutive of that mark; or

(III) is a trademark, word, or name protected by reason of section 706 of Title 18 or section 220506 of Title 36.

(B)(i) In determining whether a person has a bad faith intent described under subparagraph (a), a court may consider factors such as, but not limited to

(I) the trademark or other intellectual property rights of the person, if any, in the domain name;

(II) the extent to which the domain name consists of the legal name of the person or a name that is otherwise commonly used to identify that person;

(III) the person's prior use, if any, of the domain name in connection with the bona fide offering of any goods or services;

(IV) the person's bona fide noncommercial or fair use of the mark in a site accessible under the domain name;

(V) the person's intent to divert consumers from the mark owner's online location to a site accessible under the domain name that could harm the goodwill represented by the mark, either for commercial gain or with the intent to tarnish or disparage the mark, by creating a likelihood of confusion as to the source, sponsorship, affiliation, or endorsement of the site;

(VI) the person's offer to transfer, sell, or otherwise assign the domain name to the mark owner or any third party for financial gain without having used, or having an intent to use, the domain name in the bona fide offering of any goods or services, or the person's prior conduct indicating a pattern of such conduct;

(VII) the person's provision of material and misleading false contact information when applying for the registration of the domain name, the person's intentional failure to maintain accurate contact information, or the person's prior conduct indicating a pattern of such conduct;

(VIII) the person's registration or acquisition of multiple domain names which the person knows are identical or confusingly similar to marks of others that are distinctive at the time of registration of such domain names, or dilutive of famous marks of others that are famous at the time of registration of such domain names, without regard to the goods or services of the parties; and

(IX) the extent to which the mark incorporated in the person's domain name registration is or is not distinctive and famous within the meaning of subsection (c) of this section.

(ii) Bad faith intent described under subparagraph (A) shall not be found in any case in which the court determines that the person believed and had reasonable grounds to believe that the use of the domain name was a fair use or otherwise lawful.

(C) In any civil action involving the registration, trafficking, or use of a domain name under this paragraph, a court may order the forfeiture or cancellation of the domain name or the transfer of the domain name to the owner of the mark.

(D) A person shall be liable for using a domain name under subparagraph (A) only if that person is the domain name registrant or that registrant's authorized licensee.

(E) As used in this paragraph, the term "traffics in" refers to transactions that include, but are not limited to, sales, purchases, loans, pledges, licenses, exchanges of currency, and any other transfer for consideration or receipt in exchange for consideration.

Notes and Questions

1. The ACPA is not the only avenue for a trademark holder to combat cybersquatting. In October 1999, the Internet Corporation for Assigned Names and Numbers (ICANN), the entity responsible for developing policies for the domain name system, adopted a Uniform Dispute Resolution Policy (UDRP) to govern domain name disputes. The company originally responsible for registering most domain names, Network Solutions Inc. (NSI), had earlier incorporated a dispute policy into its registration agreements. NSI would place a registration on "hold" if the owner of a nationally registered trademark claimed that its mark was identical to a subsequently registered domain name. The UDRP supplanted this policy, and accredited domain name registrars now incorporate the UDRP into their registration agreements. Under the UDRP, a registrant must submit to an administrative proceeding before an ICANN-approved dispute resolution provider if a complainant alleges that:

(i) [the registrant's] domain name is identical or confusingly similar to a trademark or service mark in which the complainant has rights; and

(ii) [the registrant has] no rights or legitimate interests in respect of the domain name; and

(iii) [the registrant's] domain name has been registered and is being used in bad faith.

ICANN, Uniform Dispute Resolution Policy, para. 4(a) (Oct. 24, 1999), *available at* http://www.icann.org/udrp/udrp-policy-24oct99.htm. Rules accompanying the UDRP contain specific time limitations designed to expedite resolution of disputes. The only remedies available under the UDRP are forfeiture and transfer of the domain name.

How does the substantive standard of the UDRP differ from that of the ACPA? From that of the NSI dispute policy?

2. The ACPA and the UDRP, of course, are designed to make it easier for trademark holders to recover domain names from cybersquatters. How, if at all,

do these legal regimes affect disputes between trademark holders and their competitors? Between trademark holders and those who might have a legitimate interest in the use of a domain name incorporating a trademark? To what extent can a trademark holder use the threat of litigation or arbitration to "hijack" a domain name from one with a legitimate interest in the use of that name?

For example, several cases have raised the question of whether websites that are supposedly dedicated to criticism of the trademark holder may use the domain name trademarksucks.com, or whether such a domain name is confusingly similar to the trademark. There appears to be a split of opinion among UDRP arbitrators on this issue. On one side arbitrators reason that a domain name including "sucks" is obviously a critical site and could never be confusingly similar to the trademark to which "sucks" is appended. *See, e.g., Wal-Mart Stores, Inc. v. wallmartcanadasucks.com*, Case No. D2000-1104, 6(A) (Nov. 23, 2000), *available at* http://arbiter.wipo.int/domains/decisions/html/2000/ d2000-1104.html (Perritt, Arb.). On the other side, arbitrators have concluded that any domain name that includes a trademarked term is confusingly similar to the trademark itself. *See, e.g., Diageo plc v. Zuccarini*, WIPO Case No. D2000-0996 (Oct. 22, 2000), *available at* http://arbiter.wipo.int/domains/ decisions/html/2000/d2000-0996.html (Bridgeman, Arb.). Do these cases raise the possibility that application of trademark law could hinder free speech? In this regard, consider *People for the Ethical Treatment of Animals v. Doughney*, 263 F.3d 359 (4th Cir. 2001), discussed in Chapter Two. Why didn't the court think that the "People Eating Tasty Animals" site was an obvious parody, thereby removing any possibility of consumer confusion? Should the same reasoning apply to trademarksucks.com cases?

The Anticybersquatting Consumer Protection Act (ACPA) was Congress' attempt to respond to the rise of the domain name system by making sure that domain names would be linked to pre-existing trademarks. And certainly consumers may benefit from being able to type in a domain name using a familiar trademark. But what effects might the existence of the ACPA have on the development of succeeding generations of online technology? After all, in responding to the perceived "threat" to trademarks, Congress ignored the fact that the online environment and tools such as search engines dramatically reduce a consumer's search costs. Significantly, this technological reality points in exactly the opposite direction from the concerns that animated the ACPA in the first place. If searching is easy and most people come to use search engines, recognizable domain names become *less* important because people no longer expect to look for a site by typing www.trademarkedname.com. As two commentators speculated in 1998: "One thing that seems likely to happen is that domain names are going to become relatively less valuable. * * * [T]he importance of domain names could subside: sophisticated search engines, 'smart browsers,' agent applications, or other technological innovations may perhaps render them largely irrelevant." Margaret Jane Radin & R. Polk Wagner, *The Myth of Private Ordering: Rediscovering Legal Realism in Cyberspace*, 73 CHI.-KENT L. REV. 1295, 1303 (1998).

Ironically, the accuracy of such a prediction ultimately depends on the state of the law and its effect on technology. To the extent that the law preserves the value of domain names containing trademarks—by granting trademark owners the power to control the use of their trademarks in domain names—sophisticated search tools become relatively less important. As a result, in responding to new technology by creating trademark rights in domain names, Congress, perhaps unwittingly, affected the degree to which domain names would retain importance and the degree to which new search technologies would be developed. Consider the following argument.

Yochai Benkler, *Net Regulation: Taking Stock and Looking Forward*

71 U. COLO. L. REV. 1203 (2000)

II. MAPPING NET REGULATION

[One] cluster of issues on Congress's legislative agenda during the 1990s directly concerns control over information. These efforts at regulation respond to radical changes that the Net has wrought on traditional structures of control over information flows. Where doors and locked bureaus could once protect privacy, data-mining and encryption now do battle over whether there will be more privacy than in the pre-Net environment, or less. Where clearly-demarcated copies of information goods—like books or records—once defined the boundaries of control that intellectual property owners had over their products, technological protection measures and licenses do battle with digital duplication and transmission to determine whether owners or users will gain more control over the information products they own, or use, respectively. Where brown paper wraps, the watchful eye of the store keeper or the parent, and government and social regulation once controlled access to "dangerous materials," kids more technologically attuned than their parents and users who seek out or provide "dangerous materials" can now produce and access these materials at lower cost, and much freer of the traditional means of social surveillance, than ever before. This   * * *   cluster is a series of laws attempting to establish the terms of control over information flows, given the shake-up of the technological parameters that defined the boundaries of control before the Net. * * *

III. DISTRIBUTING CONTROL OVER INFORMATION

[These laws] all perceive a destabilizing effect that the Net has on the pre-Net equilibrium of control over certain kinds of information, and all intervene to settle the lack of equilibrium by setting the parameters for a new pattern of control over the information flows on the Net. * * *

A. *Destabilization*

        * * *

5.   Trademarks and Domain Names

The destabilizing effect of the Net on trademarks is a result of the radical reduction in the cost of searching for information on the Net. In the physical business environment, searching for products to compare, say, price and quality, is costly. Brand names and trademarks reduce search costs by declaring location and price/quality information in easily-accessible ways. The mass mediated information environment works well with this role of trademarks, for it provides a relatively costly way of communicating this self-designation of price and quality. Such a costly method excludes many potential competitors—who would crowd the attention of consumers with competing marks—and permits a relatively small number of businesses to acquire instant, human-memory-based recognition as carrying certain attributes of the price/quality tradeoff. Hence the emergence of the category of "famous marks" that is increasingly receiving property-like, rather than consumer-protection-like, protection, as in the Anti-Dilution Act of 1995.

The Net radically reduces the transaction costs involved in obtaining multiple quotes and offers. It makes possible software-based comparison shopping, and facilitates the acquisition of price/quality tradeoff information on a purchase-by-purchase rather than vendor-by-vendor basis. It allows for the development of services like CNET, that collect information, review it, make price comparisons, and link to vendors. While this may be good news for consumers and for aggregate social welfare, it is very bad news for the owners of famous brand names. The value of their brand names—premised on the happy accident that their social-welfare-increasing investments in saving consumers search costs also made competition more difficult from non-brand name producers, and hence gave them the ability to exercise some discipline on prices and quality—was undermined. The result of this destabilization is seen in the trademark/domain name debate. * * *

B. *Possible Approaches to Stabilization*

        * * *

5.   Trademarks and Domain Names

The concern over trademarks in domain names represents a destabilization of the value of trademarks as search-cost reducing mechanisms. One response could be an attempt to transfer the value of trademarks from the high search cost bricks-and-mortar plus mass media environment to the low search cost digitally networked environment. The other approach would be to accept the declining importance of trademarks, to limit legal protection to situations where competitors try to use a mark to confuse consumers, and to abandon the notion of dilution as protection of goodwill, which developed to protect the famous marks most useful in the old environment. This would result in some decline in the importance and value of famous marks, and would instead increase the importance of search engines, rating services, and other methods of reducing search costs.

C. *Regulatory Choices Made*

* * *

5.   Trademarks and Domain Names

The resolution of the destabilization of trademarks has gone in the direction of trying to maintain the value of brand names at the expense of the efficiency of electronic commerce.   Whether this position is the (relatively) more moderate approach taken in the Internet Corporation for Assigned Names and Numbers ("ICANN") rules,[242] or the more aggressive approach taken by Congress,[243] the basic approach has been to do the following three things.   First, the resolution assumes that consumers will seek out products on the Net by taking their knowledge base from the mass-mediated environment and deciding that the way to acquire the most appropriate product given the consumer's preferred price, quality, and terms is to seek a recognizable brand name from the mass media environment to fit that preference, rather than to go to a search engine or a product review site. Second, it assumes that this reliance on an existing knowledge base will be translated into a consumer typing into their browser a uniform resource locator ("URL") such as http:// www.brandname.com as their primary way to access products. Third, it gives owners of trademarks the power to control the use of the alphanumeric string that is a part of their trademark as a second level domain name, the place represented by "brandname" in our example.

It is not clear, however, that this resolution will be effective. It assumes that browsers will continue to be as they are, that search-and-compare shopping software and review services will continue to play second fiddle to brand recognition, along with a variety of other technological and market assumptions that may or may not turn out to be true. But what is important here is to see that the regulatory effort identified an opportunity to negate the destabilizing effect, and secured it for the stakeholders prior to the destabilizing event. In this case, if consumers, rather than going to a search engine, shopping software, or review site, hunt around for http://www. brandname.com, or http://www.brand-name.com, or http://www.brandname. net, then they continue to depend on their relatively limited ability to remember brand names, and the investments made in building name recognition to capture consumers is not lost.   To make this possible, it is absolutely necessary that this way of seeking information be a viable approach to searching at least for those branded products, and for that purpose the control of brand-name owners on the second level domain space must be more or less complete.   It also suggests, as we in fact see in early 2000, resistance on the part of brand name owners to an expansion of the

---

242. *See* ICANN, Uniform Domain Name Dispute Resolution Policy (As Approved by ICANN on October 24, 1999) (last modified Jan. 3, 2000) <http://www.icann.org/udrp/udrp-policy-24oct99.htm>.

243. *See* Anticybersquatting Consumer Protection Act, Pub. L. No. 106- 113, § 3001, 1999 U.S.C.C.A.N. (113 Stat.) 1501.

generic top level domain ("gTLD") space. The very strong dilution/goodwill, rather than confusion-based, protection offered in many of the cases, the [Anticybersquatting Consumer Protection] Act, and the ICANN policy is consistent with the attempt to transfer the value of brand names from the real-space, mass-mediated environment to the digital environment. This is the appropriate regulatory means to maximize the probability that this outcome will obtain in the market.

Whether it is in fact sensible—as a matter of social policy—to saddle electronic commerce with the baggage of an imperfect approach to saving search costs from the mass-mediated, real-world environment is a different question. The private stakes for those corporations who have invested in building brand recognition and plan to recoup their investments by exercising some price discipline using the value of their brand name as a search-cost saving device for consumers are obvious. The public benefits of protecting these costs by encouraging consumers not to take advantage of the reduced search costs in the electronic commerce environment are more questionable. But the methodological point is the important one for this article. This is an instance in which the policy choice was to counteract the destabilizing effect of the reduction in search costs associated with electronic commerce and the solution is in fact appropriate to provide at least the legal infrastructure necessary to permit people to engage in electronic commerce without taking advantage of its reduced search costs, relying instead on the real-world, mass media stand-in for actual comparison—brand name recognition.

Notes and Questions

1. According to Benkler, what effect has law had on the development of search engine technology? What are the consequences of recognizing strong trademark rights with regard to domain name addresses?

2. What would happen if trademark holders could *not* bring actions to secure domain names associated with the trademark (absent deception)?

3. Would end-users benefit from a system where domain names did not necessarily correspond to corporate identification? On the one hand, Benkler's approach might simply make domain names function like addresses in the physical world: as a way to *get to* a location, but not usually as a way of *identifying the entity* to be found at that location. Most people do not find such a world particularly difficult to navigate. On the other hand, if domain names do not necessarily relate to the name of the entity at the address, then there seems little reason to have domain names at all. We could simply return to using the numeric string of the IP address.

4. Should it matter that end-users may find typing www.brandname.com a convenient way to access a site? Benkler argues that this is simply how users have used the Internet *at one moment in time* and that trademark law is improperly seeking to stabilize the way users currently look for sites rather than allowing that system to become destabilized by advances in technology. Benkler believes such destabilization might well lead to better ways of seeking

information online. Of course, law often seeks to impose status quo stability in shifting environments. Is such an impulse always to be resisted? Mightn't destabilization itself impose costs on end-users and websites during the period of transition? Finally, how do we know, *ex ante*, what would happen in a world without trademark rights in domain names? And if we don't know, is that a reason to resist such a change or allow a period of destabilization in return for the possibility of innovation? For an argument that new tools for finding information or accessing sites are rendering domain names increasingly unimportant, see Francis Hwang, *Do Domain Names Matter?*, http://fhwang.net/writing/do_domain_names_matter.html.

Chapter Five

PROBLEMS OF "PUBLIC" VERSUS "PRIVATE" REGULATION

———

INTRODUCTION

As we have already seen, much regulation in cyberspace is and will be conducted by non-governmental entities, through the use of technological protection measures, private regulatory bodies (such as the Internet Corporation for Assigned Names and Numbers (ICANN)), and contract and property law regimes. Thus, if an access screen requires a user to click "OK" to contractual terms, and those terms obligate the reader to pay a dollar per page viewed at a given website, then the dollar fee becomes the "law" of that website, even if the copyright law would have permitted the use for free. Similarly, if an Internet service provider wishes to censor a user's speech from its chatrooms, it can simply eliminate the user's online privileges, regardless of whether the First Amendment would protect that speech. Or if Google decides not to list a particular site in response to a search request, that site becomes effectively non-existent, with no right to appeal the judgment. And, perhaps most importantly, because the technical standard-setting bodies of cyberspace are non-governmental, they may face no real oversight at all. Such non-governmental law-making has two distinct advantages over the sort of legal rules you may be more familiar with from your legal study. First, it is perhaps more flexible because it does not rely on top-down governmental solutions. Second, it is less likely to be subject to the problems of geography and sovereignty discussed earlier.

Nevertheless, if private entities will play an increasingly large role in regulating cyberspace, we might wish to ask whether those entities are subject to any of the checks and balances that we usually associate with democratic governance. For example, what role should the Constitution play, if any, in regulating those private entities? And are there arguments about governmental legitimacy, accountability, and transparency that can be brought to bear on these entities? And even if constitutional norms do not apply, might governments impose regulatory standards via statute?

This unit will ask questions about the line between public and private regulation and consider whether the public/private distinction can be maintained in cyberspace. Moreover, we will ask whether, as a normative matter, there *should* be any constitutional or other checks on private regulation online.

SECTION A. THE ROLE OF PRIVATE REGULATORY ENTITIES IN CYBERSPACE

As discussed in Chapter Three, some commentators have suggested both that cyberspace is inherently unregulable by territorially based sovereigns and that, as a normative matter, such a failure is to be celebrated because it will usher in the promise of "bottom-up" regulation by non-state actors. In this *laissez faire* vision, private entities will be free to generate their own law—the "law" of eBay, for example, or the Terms of Service imposed by America Online. Such private law will, in effect, create a free market in law. People will vote with their browsers by flocking to those sites or providers whose law they find acceptable.

In response to this perspective, others have revived old arguments about the public-private distinction, contending that all legal relationships are "public" and that, therefore, there can be no such thing as a "private" law. As one article puts it, "[c]ontrary to *laissez-faire* ideology, the 'private' legal regimes of property and contract presuppose a 'public' regime of enforcement and policing, a baseline of background rights."[a] Accordingly, such commentators challenge the entire distinction between "bottom-up" and "top-down" ordering. They argue that such a distinction is incoherent because, to the extent the "private" ordering in cyberspace depends on rules of property and contract, it is relying upon norms created and enforced by the state. Moreover, they contend that categorizing any particular regime as truly top-down or bottom-up, public or private, is difficult and perhaps impossible: "To some, nuisance law is unwanted top-down regulation; to others it is a needed limitation on property titles arrived at by bottom-up coordination among neighbors."[b]

Nevertheless, it seems clear that non-governmental entities will continue to exert a strong regulatory force in cyberspace. After all, in cyberspace, one uses privately owned browsers to access privately owned online service providers, with messages traveling over privately owned routers to privately owned websites. Moreover, the governance of the domain name system is currently in the hands of a private not-for-profit

---

a. Margaret J. Radin & R. Polk Wagner, *The Myth of Private Ordering: Rediscovering Legal Realism in Cyberspace*, 73 CHI.-KENT L. REV. 1295, 1295 (1998).

b. *Id.* at 1298.

corporation, ICANN. And, the "code writers" of cyberspace, who have functioned to this point through relatively independent bodies of experts setting policy by means of open meetings and consensus decision making, are now at risk of being captured by competitive market interests.

This section describes some of these entities. As you think about such "private" regulation, ask yourself whether any of these entities should be subject to forms of public oversight and regulation, constitutional or otherwise. Or might we prefer that governing norms online be constructed by such regulatory bodies instead of more official governmental bodies, such as legislatures and courts?

1. Standard-Setting Bodies

Philip J. Weiser, *Internet Governance, Standard Setting, and Self-Regulation*

28 N. Ky. L. Rev. 822 (2001)

The most formidable regulatory regime that has governed the Internet to date is the institution of open standards that has allowed the Internet to grow exponentially as a network of networks. * * * [A] series of open protocols, such as the basic protocol that facilitates data transport, the Transmission Control Protocol/Internet Protocol (TCP/IP) and others such as HTML, have gained wide acceptance, enabling millions to use the Internet. These standards, in large part because they were open and endorsed by trusted standard-setting committees, helped drive the development of new applications and encourage the increased usage of the Internet.

The close relationship between the Internet's success and voluntary standard-setting organizations reflect a happy coincidence of events. During the formative years when individuals in the scientific, research, and governmental communities began envisioning the emergence of what would become the Internet, the telecommunications establishment—then represented by the AT&T monopoly—viewed the Internet skeptically and rejected an offer to manage its infrastructure. In retrospect, the fact that the Defense Department's Advanced Research Projects Administration (ARPA), along with individuals in the academic community, developed the basic architecture for the Internet meant that no one owned the Internet's protocols or had to pay a license for their use. Thus, the Internet's standards were open and approved by standard-setting bodies like the Internet Engineering Task Force (IETF) and were not proprietary ones held by AT&T.

The Internet's openness created a virtuous cycle where members of the Internet community continued to improve upon its basic architecture by adding new functionalities that were placed in the public domain, thereby making the Internet a more valuable network. On the supply side, a culture emerged whereby developers would work with one another and rely on open standards rather than compete with one another to establish the basic architecture that supports the Internet. Because trusted standard-setting organizations adopted these key standards and made them open, developers did not have to worry about these standards being ignored and defeated, thereby undermining the value of any applications built off of those standards. * * *

The positive feedback loop experienced on the supply side of the Internet's development also drove the demand side growth of the Internet as well. As economists have explained, the economics of information goods, like those supplied on the Internet, differ markedly from traditional industrial goods. For starters, information goods are often expensive to produce, but very cheap to copy (particularly if they are in a digital format); thus, as an economist would put it, when the marginal cost of a product is very close to zero, people should not be surprised when companies adopt unconventional strategies like giving products away for free. The other key dynamic, which reinforces the value of giving away information goods for free, is that companies supplying such products are often concerned about establishing a dominant network. As on the supply side, the demand side also benefits from the virtuous cycle that the more users who join a network, the more valuable it is. Thus, whether the network is AOL instant messaging users, eBay auction customers, or Napster users, the more individuals who use the product, the more valuable it is. Significantly, provided that the basic platform of the Internet is open and accessible, the various applications that ride on top of it—instant messaging, auctions, or digital music—can all enhance the value of the Internet itself, particularly because its open protocols assures both users and developers that it will be a stable standard.

The supply side and demand side developments stemming from the Internet's open platform have contributed greatly to the Internet's popularity and increased use. On today's Internet, individuals, whether as developers or users, benefit from what engineers have called the Internet's "end-to-end" architecture principle. In short, "end to end" means a commitment to (1) openness (both in terms of its basic standards and in the culture of the standard-setting organizations themselves); (2) modularity and protocol layering; and (3) the shifting of intelligence and control to the edge of the network. Significantly, the norm of end-to-end architecture reflected a particular policy that facilitated open access to applications made available on the Internet. Whether and how Internet standards follow this principle in the future will impact greatly on matters ranging from privacy to security policy. Thus, policymakers cannot afford to ignore the work of technical standard-setting committees.

Numerous commentators have championed the role of government in maintaining a communications commons and preserving the Internet's end-to-end architecture * * * . The shift in the Internet from an entirely open standards-based model to one where there are increasing uses of proprietary standards for critical functions raises a serious question for Internet governance. As long as the basic standards were in the public domain, the Internet's architecture contained a form of self-control that ensured that individuals and developers could easily access critical functions. But as the Internet moved to accommodate commerce, the incentives for developing proprietary applications—and the increased difficulty in maintaining a categorical commitment to openness—were going to be difficult to contain. Indeed, the larger the Internet community becomes, the more difficult it is to maintain a completely "commons" model. The dynamics introduced by the transformation of the Internet from a public commons to a growing private marketplace thus creates challenges both for the existing standard-setting committees and, where critical standards remain proprietary, for government as well. * * *

In 1995, before the Internet became big business, private standard-setting bodies like the IETF could focus on the technical merits of proposed standards without the distorting influence of private companies that would benefit depending on the ultimate outcome. As the stakeholders in the future of the Internet become more diverse and more concerned with the impact of the Internet's development on their profits, stable, open, and end-to-end-based standards may well become the exception, not the norm. Take the case of instant messaging, for example. Instant Messaging, or IM, relies on the Internet transport protocols and adds a Names and Presence Directory to facilitate real-time communication. Unlike email, IM providers have yet to agree on an open, interoperable protocol that enables all users of the service to reach one another. But with the high stakes in a battle to "win" this new network market, AOL has not been eager to share its [protocol] with others. AOL claims that its actions reflect legitimate concerns about privacy and security, but others, including the FCC, have concluded that AOL is "dragging its feet" to maintain a dominant position that might suffer in a world where IM was an interoperable service.

Although direct government oversight of the deliberations or outcome of Internet standard setting would be quite controversial, antitrust oversight of the setting of Internet standards will undoubtedly increase as the area becomes ripe for anticompetitive conduct. In particular, antitrust enforcers (and courts) should guard against two particular concerns: (1) the use of standard-setting bodies to freeze technology, either through delay or refusal to certify a new technology; and (2) the non-disclosure of information that enables a company to control key proprietary technology used in a purportedly open standard. But as antitrust can only safeguard a fair competitive process, it will be up to government regulators to decide whether to condone de facto, proprietary standards or to enforce some form of open access regime to preserve the Internet's commitment to open standards for its key functions. In so doing, government regulators will have to be mindful of the difficulty of superintending open access regimes, not to mention setting technical standards.

Notes and Questions

1. Why is it important to have uniform technical standards? What are the benefits of having those standards remain "open"?

2. In what way do technical standards "regulate" online behavior? Can you think of examples of how such "regulations" work?

3. Should standard-setting bodies be deemed governmental? Is there an argument that, because they regulate an essential governmental function—communication—they should be subject to constitutional norms? What if the IETF adopted a new technical protocol that made it easier for individual users to censor speech online? Even if the users were not subject to the First Amendment, is there any argument that the IETF should be?

4. If the Constitution does not apply to technical standard-setting bodies directly, is there any argument that the government should aim to assure open access? What form might such governmental oversight take? Do you think Professor Weiser would advocate stronger governmental oversight of the standard-setting process? Why or why not?

5. If open standards are as beneficial as Weiser argues, why would corporations ever seek to institute proprietary standards? For example, why would America Online want to keep Instant Messaging proprietary? How about Apple's decision to render music downloaded from its iTunes unplayable on other companies' devices? Are there downsides to such a strategy? To the extent the interests of corporate standard-setters and the public diverge, should the government play a role?

6. Might the government pass laws to ensure access to seemingly private property? For example, what if a state passed a law (or a state constitutional provision) *requiring* owners of shopping malls to permit leafleting? Would such a law violate either the free speech or property rights of the owners? Are there any constitutional constraints on such governmental action? Such questions will be addressed in more detail later in the chapter.

2. ICANN

Next we turn to the Internet Corporation for Assigned Names and Numbers (ICANN), the body currently administering the domain-name system. Chapter Three introduced the concern that ICANN is making important policy decisions without sufficient oversight. The excerpt that follows goes farther and asks whether ICANN's activities actually constitute *governance*. This is a particularly knotty question because of ICANN's ongoing ties to the U.S. government. Indeed, one might even go so far as to think that ICANN should be deemed an arm of the U.S. government itself. In any event, given ICANN's important quasi-governmental power, it is important to consider how, if at all, such power should be delimited and checked.

A. Michael Froomkin, *Wrong Turn in Cyberspace: Using ICANN to Route Around the APA and the Constitution*

50 DUKE L.J. 17 (2000)

For almost two years, the Internet Corporation for Assigned Names and Numbers (ICANN) has been making domain name policy under contract with the Department of Commerce (DoC). ICANN is formally a private nonprofit California corporation created, in response to a summoning by U.S. government officials, to take regulatory actions that DoC was unable or unwilling to take directly. * * *

Despite being famously decentralized and un-hierarchical, the Internet relies on an underlying centralized hierarchy built into the domain name system (DNS). Domain names (such as "www.law.miami.edu") are the unique identifiers that people depend on to route e-mail, find web pages, and connect to other Internet resources. The need to enforce uniqueness, that is, to prevent two people from attempting to use the exact same domain name, creates a need for some sort of body to monitor or allocate naming. However, control over the DNS confers substantial power over the Internet. Whoever controls the DNS decides what new families of "top-level" domain names can exist (e.g., new suffixes like .xxx or .union) and how names and essential routing numbers will be assigned to websites and other Internet resources. The power to create is also the power to destroy, and the power to destroy carries in its train the power to attach conditions to the use of a domain name. Currently, this power is used to require domain name registrants to publish their addresses and telephone numbers on a worldwide readable list and to agree that any trademark holder in the world aggrieved by their registration can demand arbitration regarding ownership of the name under an eccentric set of rules and standards. In theory, the power conferred by control of the DNS could be used to enforce many kinds of regulation of the Internet; it could, for example, be used to impose content controls on the World Wide Web (WWW), although there are no signs that anyone intends this at present.

Without meaning to at first, the United States government found itself controlling this unique Internet chokepoint. When the Internet was small, the DNS was run by a combination of volunteers, the National Science Foundation (NSF), and U.S. government civilian and military contractors and grant recipients. As the paymaster for these contractors, the U.S. government became the de facto ruler of the DNS, although it barely exercised—and for a long time may not in any real sense have been aware of—its power. The Internet's exponential growth placed strains on the somewhat ad hoc system for managing the DNS, and what had been primarily technical issues became political, legal, and economic problems that attracted high-level official attention. In particular, as attractive domain names in .com began to become scarce, disputes over attractive names became increasingly common, and pressure mounted for the creation of new "top-level" domain suffixes such as .shop or .web. Although technically trivial to implement, the proposals ran into intense counter-pressure from intellectual property rights holders who already faced mounting problems with cybersquatters—speculators who registered domain names corresponding to trademarks and held them for profit. Meanwhile, foreign governments, notably the European Union, began to express understandable concern about the United States' control of a critical element of a global communication and commercial resource on which they foresaw their economies and societies becoming ever-more dependent.

As the DNS issue, and especially the relationship between domain names and trademarks, grew in importance, the conflicting pressures on the federal government for action grew as well. In June 1998, DoC and an interagency task force headed by Presidential Senior Adviser Ira Magaziner responded with the Statement of policy on the Privatization of Internet Domain Name System, known as the DNS White Paper. Abandoning earlier hopes of issuing a substantive rule, which requires statutory authorization and is subject to judicial review, the policy statement instead set out goals that the administration thought could be achieved without rulemaking. Embracing the rhetoric of privatization, the DNS White Paper called for the creation of a private nonprofit corporation to take over the DNS and institute various reforms. Shortly thereafter, an international group incorporated ICANN as a private nonprofit California corporation, and, after some negotiation, DoC lent ICANN much of its authority over management of the DNS. * * *

Almost as soon as it was in place, the ICANN board undertook major decisions, beginning with the agenda set out in the White Paper. ICANN pushed Network Solutions, Inc. (NSI), the monopoly registry and dominant registrar, to allow more competition among registrars. ICANN also instituted mandatory arbitration of trademark claims. ICANN's "Uniform Dispute Resolution Policy" (UDRP) requires every registrant in .com, .org, or .net to agree to arbitration before ICANN-selected arbitration providers if any trademark owners anywhere in the world feel aggrieved by their registration of a term similar to that trademark.

As a result of this policy, registrants are now subject to an idiosyncratic set of arbitration rules and procedures that benefit third-party trademark holders at the expense of registrants and do not necessarily conform to U.S. trademark law. ICANN also chose to keep in place and step up enforcement of some policies that it inherited, notably NSI's anti-privacy rule requiring that every registrant of a domain name agree to have his name, address, e-mail, and telephone number placed in a database readable by any Internet user in the world.

Since ostensibly handing the policy baton to ICANN, DoC has * * * made, or acquiesced in ICANN's making, some of the most important decisions relating to the near-term future of the Internet via research contracts rather than agency adjudication or rulemaking, thus evading notice, comment, due process, and judicial review. Government outsourcing and privatization often is premised on the theory that private enterprise can provide some goods and services more efficiently than the public sector. DoC's reliance on ICANN is different from the classic model of privatization, because rather than privatizing a revenue-generating function, the government is "privatizing" a policy-generating function. Furthermore, the "privatization" is subject to sufficient strings to make ICANN's actions fairly chargeable to the government. Although the ICANN-DoC contracts speak of cooperation and research, some of the most significant outputs from ICANN are government regulation in all but name. It is time to call them what they are.

However one chooses to characterize the U.S. government's interest in the root file or the DNS as a whole, there is little debate that (1) DoC derives at least part of whatever authority it has from its ability to instruct a U.S. government contractor, NSI, regarding the content of the root file, and (2) whatever authority ICANN holds at present emanates from, and remains subject to, DoC's ultimate authority. The U.S. government's continuing control of the DNS has legal consequences that have not been well understood * * * . Chief among these legal consequences is that to the extent that DoC relies on ICANN to regulate in its stead—and this reliance appears to be quite substantial—DoC's relationship with ICANN violates fundamental U.S. policies that are designed to ensure democratic control over the use of government power. DoC's relationship with ICANN is, therefore, illegal. * * *

The ICANN issue is unique in a number of ways. * * * The issue [usually] is whether Congress's attempt to vest power in an agency or a private body is constitutional. In the case of ICANN, there is no statute. Congress at no time determined that the DNS should be privatized, or, indeed, legislated anything about national DNS policy. Instead, DoC itself chose to delegate the DNS functions to ICANN, relying on its general authority to enter into contracts. ICANN is also a very unusual corporation. There are many government contractors, both profit-making and nonprofit. But it is unusual for a nonprofit corporation to be created for the express purpose of taking over a government regulatory function.

There is a danger, however, that ICANN may not be unique for long. One administration spokesperson has already suggested that ICANN should be a model for regulation of other Internet-related issues such as accreditation standards for distance learning and e-commerce over business-to-business "closed" networks. The specter of a series of ICANN clones in the United States or in cyberspace should give one pause, because ICANN is a very bad model, one that undermines the procedural values that motivate * * * the Due Process Clause of the Constitution. * * *

Both ICANN and DoC deny that ICANN is engaged in either regulation or governance. Instead they proffer the *standard-setting* view, in which ICANN is engaged in nothing more than routine standard setting or perhaps technical coordination. Thus, ICANN maintains that it "has no statutory or regulatory 'authority' of any kind." It has, it says, "only the power of the consensus that it represents," since root servers not run by or under contract to the U.S. government could at any time choose to point to a different root, albeit at the cost of causing the very fragmentation most root server operators oppose. * * *

To the extent that ICANN really is engaged in mere technical standard setting—the Internet equivalent of deciding how insulated a wire must be to be safe—the *standard-setting story* has merit. The assignment of IP numbers, the maintenance of unique protocol numbers for various Internet functions—these and other semi-ministerial tasks are indeed just standard setting * * *. Yet both ICANN's conduct and the various agreements it has entered into reveal that a substantial fraction of ICANN's activities go far beyond the setting of technical standards. Choosing [top-level domain names such as .com, .gov., .edu, .net, etc.] on the basis of social utility from among multiple technically qualified providers, fixing the business models of registrars, enforcing dispute resolution procedures on millions of unwilling business and consumers, accrediting dispute resolution providers, writing substantive and procedural rules for the disputes—not one of these tasks is "technical" standard setting in any routinely meaningful sense of the word.

The most glaring example of ICANN's policymaking to date is surely its promulgation of the Uniform Dispute Resolution Policy (UDRP). * * * ICANN imposed on all current and future registrants in .com, .org, and .net a requirement that they agree to a third-party beneficiary clause in favor of any person, anywhere, who believes that the registrant's domain name registration infringed the complainant's trademark right. This clause was not optional: pursuant to the Registrar Agreement, ICANN required domain registrars to include this clause in every registration contract and to modify existing contracts with their customers; and, pursuant to the Registry Agreement, ICANN required NSI to agree to refuse to list registrations from any registrar who failed to do so.

The UDRP offers a great deal to trademark registrants seeking to claim domain names from registrants, as the proceeding can cost under $1000 and runs on a fast track, with each side (ordinarily) entering only exhibits and one short pleading and no live witnesses or arguments. But the UDRP reduces registrants' legal rights in at least three ways.

First, complainants choose the arbitral tribunal from a small list of approved providers maintained by ICANN, which gives the providers an economic incentive to compete by being "complainant-friendly." The first fruits of this competition can be seen in the decision of one of the competing providers * * * to offer plaintiffs a chance to file an extra brief after the ordinary close of pleadings for $150. Respondents have no say in which provider will manage the case, and no peremptory challenges to block arbitrators whom they may fear are biased. Respondents can, however, pick one member of a three-person panel—at their own expense if the complainant opted for a single panelist and the respondent decides three are needed. The choice of the provider determines who will be the arbitrators.

For one-person panels the arbitrator must come from the provider's lists, and for three-person panels, each side provides a list of choices for one arbitrator, and the provider picks the chair.

Second, unlike court proceedings, the UDRP does not require actual notice to defendants, only attempted notice for a relatively short period of time. Proceedings normally take forty-five days or less. After the complainant selects an ICANN-approved dispute provider and files a complaint, the dispute provider has three days to check it for formal compliance and forward it to the respondent. The respondent has twenty days *from the date this notice is sent* (not received) to respond. The provider then ordinarily has five days to appoint the arbitrator(s). The panel then has fourteen days to make its decision. The provider has three more days to communicate the decision to the parties. If the respondent loses, he has ten days to file a challenge in a competent court, or the domain name is transferred to the complainant. It can be seen from this chronology that, barring exceptional circumstances, the longest a proceeding can take from filing of complaint to decision is forty-five days, with another ten days before a decision to transfer takes effect. The decision to forgo requiring actual notice in absolutely all cases is understandable, given the efforts that the sleaziest registrants make to hide their contact details in shady registrations. The short deadlines, on the other hand, are completely unfair. Defendants who happen to take a month's vacation without e-mail can lose their chance to explain why they should keep their domain name without ever knowing it was endangered.

Third, and most significantly, the consequences of the arbitration are highly asymmetric and discriminate against registrants. UDRP decisions are not "binding"; if the plaintiff loses, the arbitration does not preclude an attempt to bring the case in court. This alone is a desirable feature, because a summary procedure, in which each side has only one submission, and in which there is neither testimony, cross-examination, briefing, nor argument cannot by itself hope to make reliable credibility determinations or sort out complex competing claims. If the system by design can resolve only clear cases of trademark infringement, it follows that plaintiffs with more complex cases should lose but still be entitled to have their day in court— where sometimes they will deserve to prevail.

The unfairness comes in comparison to what happens if the defendant loses. First, the registrant now has to sue to keep the name, taking on the burden of proof, and possibly being subject to different courts, rules of procedure, language, and choice of law than if the trademark complainant had been forced into litigation where the registrant resides. Worse, under the UDRP, a defendant is given only ten days to file an action in a court with jurisdiction over the plaintiff—or in the jurisdiction where the registrar is located—to halt the transfer of the domain name. No injunction is required, as filing suffices to stop the clock, but this still means that either the losing defendant must have hired and probably paid a lawyer in advance, or the loser will need to find representation in a great hurry. This contrasts very unfavorably with the position of the losing plaintiff, who has as much time as statutes of limitations or laches will allow. The rule has particularly harsh effects in legal systems that do not provide for amendment of pleadings as of right, or at all.

* * * ICANN's objective in promoting mandatory domain name arbitration was to produce a rapid, lightweight, and inexpensive process that would allow victims of cybersquatting to vindicate their rights far more cheaply and quickly that would be possible in most courts. To the extent that this reduced the settlement value of clearly meritless defenses by persons infringing trademarks online, this was surely a very laudable objective. But it was not in any sense "technical coordination" of the Internet. Rather, it represents a clear policy choice to sacrifice the interests of (some) domain name registrants in favor of (some) trademark registrants for the communal good. While this policy choice is surely one that a legislature could make, it is not at all evident that Congress has delegated power over trademark policy to DoC. And, even if this sort of policy choice is within DoC's mandate, there can be no grounds by which DoC could outsource policymaking discretion of this sort to ICANN. * * *

ICANN is currently able to take measures such as the UDRP because it is formally independent from DoC. ICANN is a California nonprofit corporation. It is not a federal agency. It has a board of directors, a staff, and a budget. As a formal matter there is no question that ICANN has an independent legal existence and personality. Form, however, is not everything; substance matters.

Notes and Questions

1. Why does Professor Froomkin reject the argument that ICANN is not making policy decisions, but is merely a technical standard-setting body of the sort described in the previous section? Do you agree that instituting a dispute resolution process is policy-making? Does it matter that agreeing to use the UDRP is a voluntary contractual decision? On the other hand, is it truly voluntary, given that a registrar cannot be accredited unless it adopts the UDRP, and end users cannot register domain names unless they agree to the UDRP's terms? Recall the discussion in Chapter Four concerning whether similar sorts of online "agreements" should be deemed valid as a matter of contract law.

2. Does it matter that the UDRP process of which Froomkin complains was not itself enacted pursuant to a governmental command? Thus, even if ICANN came into being at the behest of the Commerce Department, ICANN's particular policy choices might not derive from government. Does this mean that ICANN should be treated as public for some purposes and private for others? Can such distinctions usefully be drawn?

3. Is ICANN more governmental than a technical standard-setting body? Why or why not? Is ICANN's governance model more legitimate than those of the standard-setting bodies discussed in the last section? Which is more democratic? Why?

4. ICANN's relationship with governmental entities has grown even more complicated since its inception. In 2002, ICANN revised its bylaws to give governments what one commentator has called "something akin to veto power." Wolfgang Kleinwoechter, *From Self-Governance to Public-Private Partnership: The Changing Role of Governments in the Management of the Internet's Core Resources*, 36 LOY. L.A. L. REV. 1103, 1121 (2003). Although no governmental official may serve as an ICANN director, a "Government Advisory Committee" (GAC) must be informed "of any proposal raising public policy issues on which it or any of ICANN's supporting organizations or advisory committees seeks public comment, and [ICANN] shall take duly into account any timely response to that notification prior to taking action." ICANN, Bylaws for Internet Corporation for Assigned Names and Numbers (2002), art. IX, sec. 2.1.h. Moreover, the GAC "may put issues to the Board directly, either by way of comment or prior advice, or by way of specifically recommending action or new policy development or revision to existing policies." *Id.* sec. 2.1.i. The Board must take GAC recommendations "duly * * * into account, both in the formulation and adoption of policies," and if the Board wishes to reject a GAC recommendation it must enter into a mediation-like process. *Id.* sec. 2.1.j.

Is this type of public-private partnership desirable? Does such a close relationship jeopardize ICANN's purported role as a form of Internet self-governance? Are the interests of end-users more likely to be represented by an independent ICANN, or is governmental oversight necessary to protect public interests? Does the increased power of governments in the governance of ICANN render ICANN sufficiently governmental to implicate state action? For further discussion of the ICANN bylaws, see generally *Symposium, ICANN Governance*, 36 LOY. L.A. L. REV. 1087 (2003). The bylaws themselves are available at http://www.icann.org/general/bylaws.htm.

5. If ICANN *were* treated as a governmental entity, it might fail standards of democratic accountability. Although the Board of Directors originally included "at-large" members to be chosen from the "Internet community," an online election resulted in very low participation rates, and (perhaps in response to concerns of corporate and governmental stakeholders) the idea of at-large members has now been scrapped. Without such at-large members (or perhaps even with them), can we plausibly say that ICANN has democratic legitimacy as a regulatory entity? Does the involvement of governmental entities through the GAC resolve the "democratic deficit"? Or is the romantic idea of participatory democracy an empty concept when considering online regulatory governance? *See, e.g.*, Dan Hunter, *ICANN and the Concept of Democratic Deficit*, 36 LOY. L.A. L. REV. 1087, 1149 (2003).

6. Go back to Professor Post's criticism of ICANN in Chapter Three. Are Professor Post's arguments the same as Professor Froomkin's? Recall Post's reference to "the bottom-up, decentralized, consensus-based governance structures under which the Internet grew and flourished." What sorts of governance structures do you suppose Post has in mind? Why isn't ICANN an example of such a governance structure?

3. Corporate Regulation

Search King, Inc. v. Google Technology, Inc.

United States District Court for the Western District of Oklahoma, 2003
2003 WL 21464568

MILES-LAGRANGE, District Judge.

Google operates an Internet search engine. Every search engine is controlled by a mathematical algorithm. One component of Google's mathematical algorithm produces a "PageRank," which is a numerical representation of the relative significance of a particular web site as it corresponds to a search query. The PageRank is derived from a combination of factors that include text-matching and the number of links from other web sites that point to the PageRanked web site. The higher the PageRank, the more closely the web site in question ostensibly matches the search query, and vice versa. Google does not sell PageRanks, and the web sites that are ranked have no power to determine where they are ranked, or indeed whether they are included on Google's search engine at all.

Notwithstanding the fact that PageRanks cannot be purchased, they do have value. For example, highly-ranked web sites can charge a premium for advertising space. PR Ad Network ("PRAN," and together with Search King, "Search King"), which was introduced by Search King in August of 2002, capitalizes on this benefit by acting as a middleman, charging its clients a fee for locating highly-ranked web sites receptive to the idea of advertising on their sites, and in turn compensating those highly-ranked web sites with a portion of its fee. PRAN's fee is based, in part, on the PageRank assigned to the web site on which its client's advertisement and/or link is placed.

This action is based upon a PageRank reduction. From approximately February of 2001 until July of 2002, Search King's PageRank was 7. In July of 2002, Search King's PageRank was increased to 8. Before it was decreased, PRAN's PageRank was 2. In August or September of 2002, Search King's PageRank dropped to 4; PRAN's PageRank was eliminated completely, resulting in "no rank." The devaluation is alleged to have adversely impacted the business opportunities available to Search King and PRAN to an indeterminate degree by limiting their exposure on Google's search engine.

* * * Search King alleges Google purposefully and maliciously decreased the PageRanks previously assigned to Search King, PRAN, and certain unidentified, affiliated web sites on Google's Internet search engine in August or September of 2002. Search King asserts the devaluation occurred after and because Google learned that PRAN was competing with Google and that it was profiting by selling advertising space on web sites ranked highly by Google's PageRank system. Google asserts it is immune

from tort liability arising out of the devaluation because PageRanks constitute protected speech.

Search King asserts a single cause of action—tortious interference with contractual relations. Under Oklahoma law, such an action requires a plaintiff to demonstrate: (1) the defendant interfered with a business or contractual relationship of the plaintiff; (2) the interference was malicious and wrongful, and was not justified, privileged, or excusable; and (3) the plaintiff suffered injury as a proximate result of the interference. The parties concede that this case turns on the second factor. The Court must, therefore, determine whether Google's manual decrease of Search King's PageRank was malicious and wrongful, and was not justified, privileged, or excusable. Google asserts that its actions cannot be considered wrongful because PageRanks constitute opinions protected by the First Amendment. In support of that proposition, Google relies on *Jefferson County Sch. Dist. No. R-1 v. Moody's Investor's Services, Inc.*, 175 F.3d 848 (10th Cir. 1999).

In *Jefferson County,* the Tenth Circuit, relying on the Supreme Court's holding that "a statement of opinion relating to matters of public concern which does not contain a provably false factual connotation will receive full constitutional protection," *Jefferson County,* 175 F.3d at 852, held that First Amendment protection extended to a financial rating service's unfavorable review of the value of a school district's refunding bonds. At the same time, the court dispensed with the school district's allegation that Moody's acted intentionally and with malice, noting that "even when a speaker or writer is motivated by hatred or illwill his expression [is] protected by the First Amendment." *Id.* at 857-58 (quoting *Hustler Magazine v. Falwell,* 485 U.S. 46, 53 (1988) (alteration in original)). Based in large part on the constitutional protection afforded the review, the Tenth Circuit affirmed the district court order granting Moody's motion to dismiss the school district's claims for intentional interference with contract, intentional interference with business relations, and publication of an injurious falsehood. * * *

Two questions remain. First, are PageRanks constitutionally protected opinions? Second, if PageRanks fall within the scope of protection afforded by the First Amendment, is the publication of PageRanks *per se* lawful under Oklahoma law, thereby precluding tort liability premised on the intentional and even malicious manipulation of PageRanks by Google? The Court answers both questions in the affirmative. * * * Google argues that PageRanks are subjective opinions, not unlike Moody's review of the school district's refunding bonds in *Jefferson County.* * * * Here, the process, which involves the application of the PageRank algorithm, is objective in nature. In contrast, the result, which is the PageRank—or the numerical representation of relative significance of a particular web site—is fundamentally subjective in nature. This is so because every algorithm employed by every search engine is different, and will produce a different representation of the relative significance of a particular web site depending on the various factors, and the weight of the factors, used to determine whether a web site corresponds to a search query. In the case at bar, it is the subjective result, the PageRank, which was modified, and which forms the basis for Search King's tort action. * * *

In view of the foregoing discussion, the Court concludes that *Jefferson County* is analogous to the case at bar. Like the review in *Jefferson County*, the Court finds that PageRanks relate to matters of public concern, in this case, via the "World Wide Web." In addition, the Court finds that PageRanks do not contain provably false connotations. PageRanks are opinions—opinions of the significance of particular web sites as they correspond to a search query. Other search engines express different opinions, as each search engine's method of determining relative significance is unique. The Court simply finds there is no conceivable way to prove that the relative significance assigned to a given web site is false. Accordingly, the Court concludes that Google's PageRanks are entitled to "full constitutional protection." *Jefferson County*, 175 F.3d at 852 (quoting *Milkovich*, 497 U.S. at 20).

Having determined that PageRanks are constitutionally protected opinions, the Court must now consider whether, under Oklahoma law, Google is immune from tort liability arising out of the intentional manipulation of PageRanks. In *Jefferson County*, the Tenth Circuit concluded that under Colorado law, protected speech cannot constitute improper interference in the context of a claim for tortious interference with contractual relations. The Court finds that Oklahoma law compels the same conclusion in this case. * * * [U]nder Oklahoma law, protected speech—in this case, PageRanks—cannot give rise to a claim for tortious interference with contractual relations because it cannot be considered wrongful, even if the speech is motivated by hatred or ill will. Accordingly, the Court finds that Search King has failed to state a claim upon which relief may be granted.

Frank Pasquale, *Rankings, Reductionism, and Responsibility*

54 CLEVE. ST. L. REV. 115 (2006)

In *SearchKing v. Google*, a federal district court dismissed various unfair competition complaints on the grounds that search engine results are protected under the First Amendment. In *SearchKing*, the court simultaneously called the automation of search results an important reason not to hold search engines accountable for them, and yet reached out to immunize Google's acknowledged human intervention to bury results referring to a potential competitor. Admittedly, the plaintiff in the case was not terribly sympathetic, and the court may just have been trying to avoid the chaotic consequences of exposing search engines to all manner of state laws governing business torts. Nevertheless, one need not reject the court's conclusion that a business tort occurred here in order to agree that some accountability for search engine results is increasingly necessary as they become the primary portal for net users. * * *

Search engines work by gathering a great deal of information and then providing responses to search queries. Once a search engine has indexed a set of web pages and other information resources, it can generate responses to searchers' queries. For example, if I were to type in "plastic Christmas trees" to the Yahoo! search engine, I would receive a page with several pieces of information. First, the most prominently displayed materials are two "paid listings" from major retailers who sell such trees. Paid listings border the page, and are permitted a variety of attention-getting design strategies. Below them appear the search results: several web pages commenting on Christmas trees, and some from sellers of such trees. The top right hand corner indicates that this initial page is displaying merely ten of the 3,540,000 potentially relevant pages. Theoretically, an obsessive searcher could review all of them (ten sites at a time) merely by clicking the next button on the bottom right hand corner of the page 354,000 times; in practice, the number of results initially "claimed" tends to decline as one clicks toward lower-ranked results.

As that fanciful idea suggests, actual human inspection plays a very small role in search engine's sorting and ranking of webpages. Rather, software does nearly all the work. Although they have long tried to keep their ranking algorithms a "black box" to preserve competitive advantage, search engines have begun to reveal the basics of how their searches work. The basic strategy is to index pages on two axes: 1) relevance to the query; and 2) overall importance. Step one, relevance, compares the searcher's query with the text on the webpage, the "metatags" embedded in the coding of the page, and other aspects of the page. Step two, importance, relies on a number of heuristics, the most important being the number of other pages that link to the page, the number of pages that link to the linking pages, and so on, recursively.

* * * [The] next generation of "ranking" controversies * * * will likely arise around two contrasting demands: 1) by those seeking privacy (who want search engines to remove links to sensitive, misleading, or false information); and 2) by those seeking publicity (who want to become more highly ranked in response to relevant queries). Currently the law does little to hold search engines accountable on either score.

Keeping Material From Being Highly Ranked

The "privacy" or "reputational" challenges to keep materials off search results come from individuals, corporations, and even countries. Some are amusing—one New York Times reporter recently recounted her unsuccessful effort to keep a webpage featuring an unflattering photograph of herself from appearing as a high-ranked web result when her name was queried on Google. More troubling was Yahoo's failure to hide a webpage that featured the pictures, name, phone number, and address of a woman whose ex-boyfriend had posted them in order to spite and humiliate her. Corporations have also tried to control their presentation on the web, trying to keep critical websites from appearing atop a websearch including their company names.

Search engines' general policy is to refuse to intervene in situations like this. For example, in response to the query "Can you remove my information from Google's search results?," Google answers, "We'd like to assist you, but information in our search results is actually located on third-party publicly available webpages. In order to remove your information from our search results, you'll need to contact the webmaster of this third-party site."* * *

Given the immensity of the World Wide Web, it is easy to sympathize with Google's plight. It is certainly in no position to review individually all new content put on the web. * * * Nevertheless, the pleas of impotence here are a bit disingenuous. When confronted by important enough entities, Google does intervene in search results. For example, due to a number of anti-Semites' efforts to manipulate search rankings (a process known colloquially as "Google-bombing"), a Holocaust-denial site routinely appeared in the top ten results for the query "Jew." In response to a number of complaints from the Anti-Defamation League, Google added a headline titled, "An explanation of our search results" to the top of the page. The linked webpage explains the reasons why the anti-Semitic site appeared so high in the relevant ranking and distances Google from the result.

* * * It is not the place of this paper to assess whether Google's response in this particular controversy was adequate. However, the very fact that there was a response at all raises some interesting questions. Do search engines have an obligation to assure that material appearing on the web fairly, accurately, or otherwise constructively relates to the query at issue? Are certain types or sites or particularly sensitive information by their very nature undeserving of the type of publicity high-ranked results provide? Consider, for instance, a hapless man whose name generates a highly-ranked result linked to a page on the site "Don't Date Him, Girl," (which permits disgruntled ex-wives and ex-girlfriends to post in great detail the shortcomings of their former husbands or boyfriends). If it is true, or "merely" an opinion, he can't sue the poster for defamation. But should this be the end of the story—his web presence forever compromised by a virtual "scarlet letter" attached to his name?

Search engines like to advise individuals and companies who don't like the current highly-ranked results associated with them to engage in self-help—by trying to persuade the offending poster to take down or modify their site, by creating their own highly ranked information, and by purchasing "adwords" to assure highly ranked "paid results" above and to the side of unpaid results. For example, if WalMart is deeply unhappy that two critical sites come up in the top five responses to the query "Walmart," it could eventually create a group of well-connected "supportive" sites that eventually displace "Walmart Watch" and the "Walmart Movie." It could also purchase several relevant "adwords" (such as "sex discrimination" or "low wages") to assure that such sites appear in "paid results" listings near results listings generated by queries for critical sites. Search engines give a number of tips on how those concerned with search results can attempt to secure better placement for their sites—and, in turn, displace unflattering material or contextualize it with purchased links.

Getting Material Highly Ranked

So far, search engines' laissez-faire approach to complaints about ranking results may appear well-founded. They claim to be merely directories of websites and not to generate content themselves. Those dissatisfied with results can put up their own rival content or pay for an advertisement connected to key queries. Given these opportunities, search engines claim that they are just one more forum in the "marketplace of ideas" which give the disgruntled more than adequate opportunity to respond to or reconfigure search results they dislike.

However, efforts to displace unfavorable information may ultimately increase its visibility, as "important" websites may be drawn to comment on the efforts themselves. Search engines do not want website publishers to get too adept at manipulating the rankings, and routinely punish those who they say unfairly influence their results. Although Google gives webmasters a number of general suggestions on how to increase the rank of their websites, they warn against hiring certain unsavory "Search Engine Optimizers" ("SEO's") companies which attempt to increase one's rank in response to relevant (and sometimes not-so-relevant) queries. As litigation recently revealed, at least one search engine "buried" the website of a Search Engine Optimizer under dozens of other listings in order to punish the company for manipulating page rankings. After becoming aware of the SEO SearchKing's strategy to increase its clients' ranking, "Google knowingly and intentionally decreased the PageRanks assigned to ... SearchKing," greatly diminishing potential clients' ability to find SearchKing via a Google search.[43]

At first glance, this seems like perfectly reasonable behavior—the search engine's unpaid rankings are both a public service and the foundation of its commercial enterprises, and it has a right to maintain its integrity. Moreover, the unpaid rankings are only commercially feasible given the paid rankings, and not many website owners would pay for rankings if they could easily assure top placement via other means. Yet search engines' secrecy regarding the way they rank pages makes the whole idea of "fair" or "unfair" ranking manipulation exceptionally vague. If site owners have only a vague idea of what counts as a legitimate factor in webpage ranking, they have little idea of whether their tactics are a brilliant maneuver that will lead to cyberfame or a censured ploy that will consign them to anonymity.

Despite these paradoxes, the Search King controversy ultimately gave search engines little to worry about. Following earlier decisions that deemed bond rating agencies' assessment of firms' creditworthiness protected speech, the court found that Google's page rankings were an

---

43. Search King, Inc. v. Google, Inc., 2003 WL 21464568, at *2.

opinion protected under the First Amendment. Google, and by implication other search engines, had no obligation to assure that their published results were actually generated by the "objective," unmanipulated algorithm that they claim produces them.

There are several reasons to object to such blanket protection for search results. The court may call rankings opinions, but the world does not treat them as such; rather, the more dominant a search engine is, the more its ranking is treated as (and becomes) a fact about the relevance, quality, and prominence of the ranked. Given that the purported "objectivity" of rankings and lack of human intervention is the main reason why search engines refuse to review or remove links to the material mentioned above, the legal protection of their capacity to alter results at will, and secretly, is curious at best. Search engines serve valuable social functions, but indiscriminate application of First Amendment immunities to their results provides unnecessarily expansive protections.* * * As search engines become more authoritative, encompassing more and more sources of data, they are also likely to become more important sources of information in our daily lives. If an individual has some rights to control personally identifiable information in the transfer of bank, medical, and video store records, shouldn't similar protections apply to search results? Moreover, in a world where dates, employers, and even casual acquaintances "google" the individuals they meet and companies they do business with, shouldn't the "googled" have some opportunity to present their side of the story in response to potentially misleading, biased, or merely cruel links? Finally, if search engines can evade responsibility in the foregoing scenarios by pointing to the automation of their services, shouldn't they also have some legal obligation to actually follow the algorithms they claim to adhere to? Internet policymakers should address each of these concerns in coming years. * * * [Search engine] providers are not merely one among many voices on the World Wide Web. They organize and rank all the rest, acting as a "public good" as indispensable as phone books, traffic signals, or lighthouses. We all gain when authoritative, comprehensive search engines can refer us to all the webpages, books, and other media relating to the topics that interest us. Yet we all stand to lose if increasingly authoritative search engines do not act responsibly when publishing and disseminating the information they gather.

* * * [Moreover,] the economics of search predict that, in any given market for information, there are enormous returns to scale—individuals are going to seek out the most comprehensive and authoritative source of information, and the very fact that this occurs gives the leading source enormous leverage to assure that information sources will want to appear (and be highly ranked) on its search results. Growing numbers of searches on a given service give that service ever more data to refine and improve its index. The "rich get richer," making the search and rankings field a very difficult one to enter.

To the extent that search is a natural monopoly or oligopoly, government must try to assure that search engines are responsible for their results. * * * The Federal Trade Commission (FTC) took an important first step in this direction by warning search engines to clearly distinguish between paid and unpaid search listings, lest the former constitute a form of false advertising. The FTC could further advance fair competition in the search market by requiring large search engines to put in place basic procedural protections for those potentially harmed by query results.

Just as major credit bureaus must respond to consumers' allegations that a piece of information on their credit report is false or misleading, complaints about false or misleading search results on major search engines should lead to more than polite advice about self-help or a price list for adwords. When meritorious, such complaints should result in the right to give one's own side of the story. A small asterisk next to the offending result, linked to the complainant's own website, would accomplish this at minimal cost to the affected search engine.

* * * [S]earch engine results can [also] be arbitrary and capricious, suddenly dropping individuals who built their livelihoods and reputations on high rankings. Sometimes drops in ranking result from understandable efforts to assure the integrity of ranking algorithms. However, more suspect manipulations have also been documented. John Battelle relates the following stunning turn of events in the *American Blinds* case:

> September 17, 2004 was the day the San Jose District Court was to hear arguments in the American Blinds case [regarding a dispute over the trademarked adwords "American Blinds"]. . . . Google had filed a motion to dismiss. . . . [When a] member of American Blinds' legal team . . . [attempted to] test the system, he brought up Google and entered what had become a habitual search query: "American Blinds." . . . . Every [other] time someone entered "American Blinds" into Google's search field, competitors to American Blinds came up on the screen.
>
> Only this morning, for some reason, they did not.
>
> The lawyer suspected Google had changed its results, and called colleagues in other parts of the country. Sure enough, searches in other regions returned different results, including the potentially infringing advertisements . . . . The lawyer quickly documented his findings.[94] * * *

As long as ranking algorithms are a "black box," such potentially troubling practices are likely to continue—and perhaps become more undetectable. Given the strength of IP protection of search algorithms, it is unlikely that proposals to make ranking methods transparent can succeed. However, those hurt by sudden changes in ranking should have some opportunity to learn about what caused the change. Just as credit bureaus must report to consumers the nature of "adverse information" that

---

94. JOHN BATTELLE, HOW GOOGLE AND ITS RIVALS REWROTE THE RULES OF BUSINESS AND TRANSFORMED OUR CULTURE 184 (2005).

makes their credit reports less than perfect, search engines should have some responsibility to reveal the reasons for their re-rankings to those adversely affected. Though such information may prove anodyne at first, scrutiny might eventually reveal any overly self-serving or unfair manipulations of rank. Moreover, search engines cannot complain that these minor revelations would overly burden their business—the credit rating agencies still manages to keep the exact nature of their most important scoring mechanisms (such as the FICO score) a tightly-held secret. * * * Courts have largely failed to hold [the search engine] process up to normative scrutiny, preferring instead to view search engine results as both 1) unregulable speech that is but one more contribution to the marketplace of ideas; and 2) an automated result not susceptible to the kind of moral judgment we usually reserve for humans. This piece argues that neither justification for leaving search engine results unregulated is convincing. Search engines are not merely one more voice in a pluralistic public dialogue, but are poised to become the chief organizer and forum for research, public discussion, and commercial competition among internet users. Moreover, the same automated processes that make search engine results so rapid, useful, and flexible can also be deployed to make them more fair and responsible. Rather than hiding behind the mechanical application of First Amendment protections, new public fora like search engines should promote the First Amendment goal of open public forums.

Notes and Questions

1. On what basis does Judge Miles-LaGrange conclude that Google is immune from liability? Do you agree that rankings decisions should be protected speech under the First Amendment?

2. Why does Professor Pasquale think that search engines should be regulated? What role does he see search engines playing in society? Do you agree? For an influential article exploring the significant societal role search engines play, see Lucas D. Introna & Helen Nissenbaum, *Shaping the Web: Why the Politics of Search Engines Matters*, 16 INFORMATION SOC'Y, no. 3, at 1 (2000).

3. If Pasquale is right about the role of search engines, then aren't there First Amendment interests on the other side as well? After all, a website that receives a low ranking (or no ranking at all) is effectively silenced because few will find the website in question. This gives Google the power to exert its rankings power to squelch speech with which it disagrees. Is this cause for concern? What if, as in China, Google alters search results based on the wishes of state actors?

4. What sort of regulation does Pasquale favor? Do you think such regulation would chill the activities of search engines?

5. Both Judge Miles-LaGrange and Pasquale liken Google to actors in the financial services companies that do bond and credit rating. Why then do they draw opposite conclusions from their analogies? Is either analogy persuasive to you?

6. Should Google's size and market share matter? Pasquale points out that economies of scale will make it difficult for new competitors to enter the market. If that is true, and Google is therefore likely to maintain a dominant position, does it make sense to view Google's rankings decisions as quasi-governmental and thereby subject them to increased scrutiny?

7. Consider the Federal Trade Commission's ruling, discussed by Pasquale, that search engines must clearly distinguish advertisements from other search results. How can such regulation be justified if search engines have the First Amendment right to organize search results as they see fit? And if you think that the FTC's action is justifiable, why isn't Search King's suit similarly justifiable? On the other hand, is there a way to distinguish between permissible and impermissible forms of search engine regulation? How would you draw the line? What line would Pasquale draw?

8. Should companies such as Google be entitled to First Amendment protection in the first place? What about a cable TV operator that chooses which channels to include on its service and which to exclude? Is that also an editorial decision, similar to rankings? Or should Congress be able to regulate such decisions by, say, requiring cable TV operators to carry local public access channels? And what about newspapers? Can they be required to give equal space to both candidates in a political contest? We will take up these issues later in the chapter.

4. Individual and Collective Regulation

Are the questions of "private" regulation online any different when it is not a single corporation, but a collection of individuals engaging in forms of regulation or censorship? For example, if people construct mechanisms for regulating unwanted online behavior, is that an example of effective decentralized governance or is it vigilante justice?

In order to consider such questions, we return to the problem of unsolicited commercial e-mail, or spam. We have already twice encountered governmental efforts to regulate spam. First, in Chapter Two we saw that the doctrine of trespass to chattels might be extended to provide individuals or corporations with a cause of action for e-mail sent over one's wires or servers. Second, in Chapter Three we considered whether the State of Washington's anti-spam statute might violate the dormant Commerce Clause. Both of these approaches raise certain practical and legal difficulties. Might there be other ways to regulate spam that are less obviously "governmental"? If so, are these alternative forms of regulation more or less effective than the approaches we have encountered thus far? And, even if they are effective, do you think they are a wise way to create public policy? Does the Constitution have anything to say about these self-help efforts? And, even if not, should these efforts be regulated by courts or legislatures?

Media3 Technologies, LLC v. Mail Abuse Prevention System, LLC

United States District Court for the District of Massachusetts, 2001
2001 WL 92389

LASKER, J.

Media3 is an Internet "web-hosting" company based in Pembroke, Massachusetts, that offers services in creating and maintaining websites to those who wish to conduct electronic commerce. As a "web-hosting" company, Media3 is the owner of forty-two "Class C network address blocks." Each block is capable of holding approximately 254 "Internet protocol addresses" on which websites may be placed. Media3 rents Internet protocol addresses on these Class C networks to individuals and organizations who wish to create websites. Often with Media3's help, these customers then build websites which Media3 also assists in maintaining.

Before agreeing to host a website, Media3 follows the standard industry practice of requiring its customers to sign an Acceptable Use Policy for conducting business on the Internet. This policy contains provisions which are standard in the industry, including an "anti-spam" provision.

Spam is the industry term used to describe unwanted e-mail that is often sent en masse to e-mail addresses for commercial purposes. For obvious reasons, spam is unpopular with many in the Internet community. One not so obvious, but critically important reason why spam is unpopular, is that while it is free to send it costs money to receive. Media3's Acceptable Use Policy prohibits not only the transmission of spam, but also the support of spam through the development of software which could be used to hide the origin of a person sending spam.

Although Media3's Acceptable Use Policy bars websites it hosts from supporting spam in some ways, it does not prohibit its hosted websites from providing other services which appear to be used primarily by spammers. These services include the sale of lists of hundreds of thousands and even millions of e-mail addresses and computer software programs which can "harvest" similar lists from the Internet. While the vast majority of Media3's customers do not offer such "spam support" services, a few do.

In May of 2000, the offending websites were brought to the attention of MAPS. MAPS is a non-profit Internet service provider based in California which, like other Internet service providers (such as America Online), provides Internet and e-mail access to its subscribers. While MAPS is organized like an ordinary ISP, its mission and role in the Internet community is distinct. MAPS's stated purpose is to combat spam. Its primary means for combating spam is its "Realtime Blackhole List." The blackhole list is a constantly updated list of the websites which, in MAPS's view, either send or support the sending of spam. When MAPS places a website on the blackhole list, it blocks transmission between the website and addresses in its system. MAPS has made its popular blackhole list available to other Internet service providers, sometimes for a fee. It is a popular product and approximately 40 percent of all internet addresses, including those of several Massachusetts enterprises, use MAPS's blackhole list as a spam filter.

In May of 2000, when MAPS learned that Media3 was hosting ten websites on one of its Class C networks which allegedly "supported spam," it contacted Media3 and requested that Media3: (1) terminate its hosting agreements with the contested websites; and (2) revise its Acceptable Use Policy to expressly prohibit the provision of "spam support" services such as the harvesting of e-mail addresses described above. If Media3 did not comply, MAPS informed Media3 that it would place on the blackhole list not only the ten contested websites but also any other websites that were on the same Class C network as the contested websites. This prospect was of some concern to Media3 because, as a hosting company, one of the primary services that it provides to its customers is ensuring that their websites are freely accessible and can easily access the Internet. Inclusion on MAPS's blackhole list would threaten Media3's ability to deliver good access to the Internet. After some exchange back and forth via e-mail and telephone between MAPS, in California, and Media3, in Massachusetts, Media3 refused to comply with MAPS's requests. MAPS then listed the disputed websites and any other websites on the same Class C network on the blackhole list.

In October and November of 2000, a similar exchange between MAPS and Media3 occurred. MAPS asserted that seven websites, on five different Class C networks hosted by Media3, were providing spam support. Once again, after several communications back and forth, Media3 refused to terminate the disputed websites and MAPS then added five more Class C networks hosted by Media3 to the blackhole list. At present, six Class C networks, containing over 1,500 websites hosted by Media3, remain on MAPS's blackhole list. * * *

Preliminary injunctive relief may be granted only upon a showing:

(1) that plaintiff will suffer irreparable injury if the injunction is not granted;

(2) that such injury outweighs any harm which granting injunctive relief would inflict on the defendant;

(3) that plaintiff has exhibited a likelihood of success on the merits; and

(4) that the public interest will not be adversely affected by the granting of the injunction.

Although it has made serious claims which may entitle it to ultimate relief, Media3 has failed to establish a likelihood of success on the merits or that it is suffering irreparable injury. Accordingly, Media3's motion for preliminary relief is denied. * * *

Business defamation is committed when a false and defamatory statement is communicated which "prejudice[s] [the plaintiff] in the conduct of its business and deter[s] others from dealing with it." *F.M. Corp. v. Corporate Aircraft Mgmt.*, 626 F. Supp. 1533 (D .Mass. 1985). In all other respects, the elements of a business defamation claim are those of ordinary defamation, that is, that the defendant published "a false and defamatory written communication of and concerning the plaintiff." *McAvoy v. Shufrin,* 401 Mass. 593, 597 (1987).

* * * There is no dispute among the parties that calling an Internet business a "spammer," or "spam-friendly," discredits the enterprise in the minds of a considerable segment of the Internet community. However, even if the statement is subject to a defamatory construction, truth is a complete defense. It is the defendant's burden to prove truth as an affirmative defense. MAPS has labeled Media3 as a "spam-friendly" organization. Media3 contends that the label is false. In attempting to prove the falsity of the statement, Media3 relies heavily on its "Acceptable Use Policy," which it requires all its hosted websites to sign. This "Acceptable Use Policy" contains an "anti-spam" provision. MAPS responds that its assertion that Media3 is "spam-friendly" is true because Media3 does, in fact, host companies that provide services exclusively to spammers.

Media3 has not established a likelihood that it will prevail on the merits of its defamation claim because, on the present record, MAPS has made a strong showing that its characterization of Media3 as "spam-friendly," is true. Media3's actions may well be found to outweigh its "Acceptable Use Policy." As described above, Media3 hosts several websites which provide support services that are used either exclusively or predominantly by spammers. These services include the sale of hundreds of thousands and even millions of e-mail addresses which are sold without any indication whatsoever that they are sold with the permission of the e-mail user. As the record stands, there is a serious question whether MAPS's assertion that Media3 is "spam-friendly" is defamatory because the statement appears to be accurate. * * *

Lawrence Lessig, *The Spam Wars*

THE INDUSTRY STANDARD, December 31, 1998

A war of sorts was avoided last month—an Internet war. It was avoided by accident, and in time, the crisis is certain to recur.

The looming conflict is a spam war. A spam war is not the battle to clear our in-boxes of uninvited junk. A spam war is the battle that will be fought as spam vigilantes flex their muscles and ISPs resist. The result won't be pretty, and the terms of a possible peace aren't obvious.

This skirmish began at MIT. In November, Jeff Schiller, MIT's network administrator, began receiving e-mail from people complaining that mail sent outside the MIT domain had been blocked. It took little effort to discover the mail was being blocked because an antispam vigilante, Open Relay Blocking System, had decided MIT had "bad e-mail practices."

Without notice, MIT was placed on the ORBS list, and subscribers to ORBS began excluding MIT mail automatically.

No one likes to be accused of "bad e-mail practices," especially not an MIT type. It was salt in the wound when Hewlett-Packard confirmed its policy of blocking according to the ORBS list. MIT was told that mail from MIT to HP would not go through until MIT changed its network policy.

But MIT was not to be bullied. In Schiller's view, the institute's decision not to block all "third-party relay" e-mail (e-mail sent through the MIT server without authentication that the sender is associated with MIT) made sense. MIT is not pro-spam. Its network has measures to limit spam, in particular by policing the use of its third-party relay facility. But MIT's methods are not the methods of ORBS, which made MIT an ORBS enemy.

Rather than cave to the pressure of ORBS, Schiller decided to fight it out with HP. The plan was to bounce all e-mail from HP until HP stopped bouncing e-mail from MIT. So it would have gone, had not a network god of sorts intervened. Responding to complaints from other ISPs, ORBS' network services provider, BC Tel, decided that ORBS' "unauthorized relay testing" was a violation of its own network policy agreement. BC Tel bumped ORBS off its network, and mail from MIT flowed again to HP. * * *

These battles will not go away. The power of the vigilantes will no doubt increase, as they hold out the ever-more-appealing promise of a world without spam. But the conflicts with these vigilantes will increase as well. Network service providers will struggle with antispam activists even as activists struggle with spam.

There's something wrong with this picture. This policy question will fundamentally affect the architecture of e-mail. The ideal solution would involve a mix of rules about spam and code to implement the rules. But there's little agreement about what the spam rules should be, and even less agreement about how they might be enforced. * * * The real problem is that vigilantes and network service providers are deciding fundamental policy questions about how the Net will work—each group from its own perspective.

This is policy-making by the "invisible hand." It's not that policy is not being made, but that those making the policy are unaccountable. The self-righteous spam police may or may not be right about the solution to spam; that's not the point. The problem is that policy is being made by people who threaten that if you complain or challenge their boycotts through the legal system, then you will suffer their boycott all the more forcibly. * * *

This is not how policy should be made. We know this, but we don't know what could replace it. We imagine policy decisions made in a context where dissent can be expressed without punishment, where collective decisions can be made. But no such context exists in cyberspace, nor in our imagination about what cyberspace might become.

The Net has thrived because decisions have been made from the bottom up, but wars also thrive under those circumstances. What's needed is an institution that can mesh the best of the bottom-up culture with a top-down perspective. If necessity is the mother of invention, then one might hope, that these struggles will bring some sensible sort of Internet governance. But I've yet to see such a creature around these parts.

David G. Post, *Of Black Holes and Decentralized Law-Making in Cyberspace*

2 VAND. J. ENT. L. & PRAC. 70 (2000)

What are we to make of things like the [MAPS] Realtime Blackhole List (RBL)? Here we have a problem—the proliferation of unsolicited mass e-mailing operations—that is, we might agree, a serious, or at least a non-trivial, one. At just the moment that e-mail has become an indispensable form of communication, of incalculable commercial and non-commercial importance for a substantial and ever-growing segment of the world community, its value is being undermined by a barrage of unwanted and unsolicited communications. But is the RBL a reasonable means of addressing this problem? To what extent can we, and should we, rely on things like the RBL to devise a "solution" (however we might define a solution) to that problem?

The question is, I think, both an interesting and an important one. Legal scholars have recently discovered—or re-discovered—the important role played by informal systems of decentralized, consensus-based social control in shaping human social behavior. It is becoming increasingly clear that systems of rules and sanctions created and administered without reliance on State "authority," and outside of any formal State-managed process—"norms"—are powerful determinants of behavior in many contexts. And what is the RBL if not a textbook example of an informal, decentralized, norm-creation process? The MAPS operators propose a norm, a description of behavior that they consider, for whatever reason, unacceptable—allowing open mail relay systems, for example, or providing "spam support services." They offer to serve as your agent—or, more accurately, as the agent for your network administrator or ISP—in identifying those who are violating this norm. They offer to keep you informed of those identifications (via the RBL). They propose to sanction norm-violators. The sanction they have in mind is the Ur-Sanction of informal social control processes: shunning. Those who choose to apply the sanction simply turn their backs on offenders, ceasing all (electronic) communication with them. MAPS helpfully provides you with the means to accomplish this sanction—software that will configure your system to delete e-mail to or from blackholed addresses. * * * Neither the decision to join (or not join) the group shunning exercise (i.e., to subscribe to the RBL in the first place), nor the shunning sanction imposed on violators of the norm, relies on access to (formal) State-supported enforcement devices or

State-imposed legal sanctions, and the decision whether to join that exercise is in the hands of a (relatively large) number of independently-acting agents. * * *

The debate over the normative implications of these informal processes has become a lively one indeed. In one corner are commentators, myself included, who find these systems normatively attractive, on both "legitimacy" and "efficiency" grounds. Legitimacy justifications rest on the view that informal private ordering schemes like the RBL are a "superior alternative to centralized government models in that [they are] the most consistent with autonomy and freedom."[24] By these lights, MAPS is normatively attractive inasmuch as it constrains individuals' behavior only to the extent, and precisely to the extent, that others share MAPS' views on the definition of wrongdoing, the choice of appropriate sanction, the identity of the wrongdoers, etc; the MAPS operators can persuade, cajole, and beg the thousands of ISPs to subscribe to the RBL, but they cannot force them to do so in any meaningful sense of that term. Efficiency justifications rest on the extraordinary power of decentralized systems to generate, by means of repeated trial-and-error and the pull-and-tug of competing rules and counter-rules, solutions to complex problems that can be found no other way.

Others disagree, both with particular reference to institutions like the RBL and in general, arguing both that the efficiency benefits of these cyberspace norm-creation processes are overblown and that such processes systematically exclude "public values" from being incorporated into the norms they generate. * * *

We like to think, at least at a conceptual level, that we conduct this debate by placing decentralized rule-making processes (like the RBL) on the table, dissecting their features, and comparing them, on whatever normative or descriptive criteria we choose, with alternative processes. But there are serious impediments to our ability to do that, impediments that skew the inquiry into the virtues (or lack thereof) of decentralized processes. Let me try to explain the sorts of things I have in mind.

First, I would suggest that *we understand little—far less than we need to—about the processes of self-ordering and informal coordination.* The rise of the Internet itself shows us, I think, how little we know about the ways that decentralized, trial-and-error, consensual processes can build stable structures of literally unimaginable complexity and power. If cyberspace did not exist, we would all probably agree that it could not exist. How, after all, would we go about building something as ridiculously complex as a single interconnected global communications network? Who would we place in charge of such a project? How would we solve the seemingly impossible coordination problem facing anyone trying to construct that global

---

24. Niva Elkin-Koren, *Copyrights in Cyberspace—Rights Without Laws?*, 73 CHI.-KENT L. REV. 1155, 1172 (1998).

network—constructing, and getting large numbers of people to adopt, what amounts to a single global language?

Of course, we did, somehow, solve it, without any "authority" in charge of bringing it into being, in a remarkably short period of time, and to the surprise of virtually everyone. A decentralized process of developing consensus among larger and larger numbers of geographically-dispersed individuals somehow managed to get us here. Emergent institutions like the Internet Engineering Task Force (whose motto, "We reject Kings, Presidents, and voting; we seek rough consensus and working code," aptly captures its decentralized orientation), the World Wide Web Consortium, the Internet Assigned Numbering Authority, and the like—institutions with no authority whatsoever to act on anyone's behalf, no fixed address or membership, no formal legal existence—somehow got hundreds of millions of individuals across the globe to agree on a common syntax for their electronic conversations. The protocols of the global network, like the natural languages they so closely resemble, emerged from a process that was at its core unplanned and undirected. Though we can certainly point *ex post* to many individuals and institutions who played particularly important roles in its emergence, *ex ante* there was no one we could have pointed to as charged with "creating" the set of rules we now know as the Internet, any more than we can point to any one individual or institution charged with creating the set of rules for English syntax. Could it have been built any other way? My instinct is that it could not have, that only an "authority-free" process of this kind could have constructed this system, that *no one with the authority to build the Internet could have done so.*

Second, and relatedly, I believe that *conditions in cyberspace make it difficult to specify the alternative processes with which decentralized processes are to be compared as part of this policy calculus.* No one, of course, suggests that decentralized processes like the one of which the RBL is a part constitute rule-making Nirvana. The relevant normative question is always whether processes of this kind are better—however one chooses to define "better"—than available alternatives.

We need, in other words, to be debating whether the process of which RBL is a part is better than—than what? * * * What *are* the alternative rule-making processes or institutions that should be placed on the analytic table alongside the RBL? The problems posed by the borderless features of this new medium for traditional rule-making institutions, faced with the problem of mapping territorially-based legal regimes onto a medium in which physical location is of little significance, have long since passed into cliche; but that doesn't mean that they are not real problems. Whose rules regarding spam should we be comparing to MAPS'? The Virginia legislature's? The United States Congress'? The International Telecommunications Union's? UNESCO's? ICANN's? * * *

Third and finally, if all this weren't confusing enough, *decentralized processes are fundamentally, and irreducibly, unpredictable.* No one can say ex ante what kind of anti-spam rules will emerge from the RBL process, or how the domain name allocation system would today be operating had the Commerce Department chosen to step aside in 1998, because that information does not exist unless and until the process itself generates it. No one can say whether MAPS' initiative will, or will not, cause open mail relay systems to disappear, because that depends upon the response of thousands of individual system administrators; no one can say whether alternative and as yet untried and perhaps unthought-of means of deterring spammers will prove more popular than MAPS; no one can say how spammers will react to the absence of open-mail relay (or to these other alternatives) or how the anti-spammers will react to those reactions, etc.

Because we can not see, or imagine, where the RBL might take us—the rule(s) of spamming that the RBL and its variants could produce—we cannot lay these rules side-by-side with their centralized alternatives for purposes of analysis, deliberation, and debate. Our analytic table contains only, as it were, the bad news: the inherently disordered and aggravating messiness of decentralized processes, mail that doesn't reach its intended destination, disruptions of service, and the like.

It all makes for an apparently simple policy choice: order versus chaos. * * * My fear is that this leads to a policy-making catastrophe of significant proportions. A "stable" Internet is one locked in place, incapable of generating innovative responses to the very problems that it is itself bringing into existence. The very existence of the Internet should caution us against dismissing too quickly the notion that there are some problems that are best solved by these messy, disordered, semi-chaotic, unplanned, decentralized systems, and that the costs that necessarily accompany such unplanned disorder may sometimes be worth bearing. But which problems? How can we know?

Notes and Questions

1. Although Judge Lasker denies Media3 Technologies' motion for a preliminary injunction, he nowhere suggests that MAPS might be immune from suit on First Amendment grounds. Thus, unlike in the case involving Google in the last section, the court actually addresses the merits of the claim and rules that MAPS' decision to place the websites at issue on its RBL was justified. Given this distinction, do you think that Search King should have alleged that Google's rankings devaluation decision was defamatory? Would the claim have been any more successful? Should it have been? Aside from the doctrinal differences in the claims raised in the two cases, do you think that Google and MAPS should be treated differently from each other for constitutional or regulatory purposes? Why or why not?

2. What are the advantages of MAPS' approach to the problem of unsolicited commercial e-mail? Why does Professor Post advocate such an approach? Does it solve some of the problems with other forms of spam regulation we encountered previously? Is the RBL likely to be more effective than a statutory or judicial approach? Why or why not?

3. Although a decentralized, technology-based approach like an RBL seems to solve certain enforcement problems associated with legislative or judicial approaches, bulk marketers have fought back against RBLs through technological means, launching so-called "denial of service" attacks against RBL operators by clogging their servers with thousands of e-mail messages. Indeed, from September 25 to October 3, 2003, four different RBL operators closed their operations in response to crippling denial of service attacks. Does the existence of such a technological arms race support Lessig's argument that this is simply unaccountable vigilante law-making? Or, does it support Post's point that we cannot (and need not) know what will ultimately emerge from this organic system of action and reaction?

4. What are Professor Lessig's objections to the RBL? What does he find objectionable about policy making by the "invisible hand"? With regard to the problem of spam, are there any other options? What do you think Lessig would advocate?

5. In the previous section we considered private "censorship" as practiced by a Google. Is the RBL more or less troubling to you? Does it matter to you how widespread the RBL becomes? What if ninety percent of all Internet service providers subscribe to the RBL? A hundred percent? Or do you think the RBL is less troubling because individual service providers are always free to unsubscribe? Is this different from Google?

6. Given that the court in this case essentially authorizes MAPS to keep the websites at issue on the RBL, thereby denying those operators the ability to send e-mail to certain users, might MAPS be treated as a kind of state-authorized censor? Is MAPS fulfilling any governmental functions? Should constitutional norms apply to MAPS' decisions about whom to include on the RBL? Should MAPS be regulated by statute? Or is court oversight for defamatory listings sufficient? Are there any other checks on the RBL's power? Are those checks sufficient?

7. Consider the idea of decentralized norm-creation more generally. Can you think of off-line examples of such norm-creation? Indeed, isn't much of our daily life "regulated" by such social norms? Is it appropriate to think of such norms as a form of law? For example, Michael Riesman has described social norms as "microlegal systems." *See* Michael Reisman, *Lining Up: The Microlegal System of Queues*, 54 U. CIN. L. REV. 417 (1985); Michael Reisman, *Looking, Staring and Glaring: Microlegal Systems and Public Order*, 12 DENV. J. INT'L L. & POL'Y 165 (1983); Michael Reisman, *Rapping and Talking to the Boss: The Microlegal System of Two People Talking*, in CONFLICT AND INTEGRATION: COMPARATIVE LAW IN THE WORLD TODAY 61 (Institute of Comparative Law in Japan ed., 1988). According to this view, law is found not only in the formal decisions of judges, legislators, and administrators, but also

> any place and any time that a group gathers together to pursue an objective. The rules, open or covert, by which they govern themselves, and the methods and techniques by which these rules are enforced is the law of the group. Judged by this broad standard, most law-making is too ephemeral to be even noticed. But when conflict within the group ensues, and it is forced to decide between conflicting claims, law arises in an overt

and relatively conspicuous fashion. The challenge forces decision, and decisions make law.

Walter Otto Weyrauch & Maureen Anne Bell, *Autonomous Lawmaking: The Case of the "Gypsies"*, 103 YALE L.J. 323, 328 (1993) (quoting Thomas A. Cowan & Donald A. Strickland, *The Legal Structure of a Confined Microsociety*, at *i* (Space Sciences Laboratory, University of California, Berkeley, Internal Working Paper No. 34, 1965)). Is this a helpful formulation? Does thinking about these social norms as a kind of law change the way we evaluate the use of such norms to control social behavior?

8. Is there any reason to believe that the sort of decentralized norm-creation represented by the RBL might actually be more effective in cyberspace than elsewhere? Can you imagine similar approaches to other online problems? Could such approaches actually replace more conventional law-making online? Would that be a good thing? Are there any problems that are not susceptible to such an approach?

9. What about Post's and Lessig's more general views about order and chaos? Why does Lessig oppose what he describes as vigilantism? Why does Post embrace this sort of decentralized lawmaking? If Post is right that decentralized systems, by their nature, are impossible to predict, how do we determine in advance whether such law-making is likely to be beneficial? Is the uncertainty about how informal norms will evolve itself a reason to prefer more formal law-making approaches? Do you think Post would see any role at all for formal governmental bodies in regulating the Internet? On the other hand, what about Post's concern that an overly stable Internet will not evolve effective solutions to social problems? Can you see ways in which governmental rules concerning, for example, unsolicited commercial e-mail or encryption technology might ultimately retard the growth of new technologies that might be beneficial?

10. Post argues that the creation of the Internet itself is an example of a decentralized emergent system. But is that really true? For example, what are we to make of the fact that the Internet was first developed under the auspices of the United States Defense Department? Might this fact have influenced the technical architecture of the Internet? Are there any other centralized forces at work in the construction of technical protocols for online activity? Does the existence of such governmental forces in the background challenge the idea that the development of "private" regulation is truly non-governmental?

SECTION B. CONSTITUTIONAL RESPONSES TO "PRIVATE" REGULATORY POWER

In the previous section, we encountered a variety of nominally private actors who wield tremendous regulatory power over online activities. Given that these actors may exercise such power in objectionable ways, the next logical question is whether there is any form of oversight available. One form of oversight, of course, is simply the marketplace. If people think

Google's rankings are inappropriate, they can switch to a different search engine. Likewise, if ISPs don't like the work of the RBL or programmers don't like the work of the Internet Engineering Task Force, they can establish (or subscribe to) rival organizations. Unfortunately, such alternatives might not always be viable, either because barriers to entry in the market render competition difficult or because governmental involvement prevents (or at least strongly deters) competition. It would be difficult for a rival domain name authority to get much traction, for example, given the U.S. government's backing of ICANN.

If, for whatever reason, the market is not deemed sufficient to effectively monitor or discipline these forms of "private" regulation, two alternatives present themselves. First, there is the possibility that U.S. constitutional norms might be applied to check the activities of these entities. Second, we might explore oversight mechanisms that could be adopted by legislatures. This section explores the first of these options, and the next section explores the second.

Turning to the possibility of constitutionally-based oversight, the question of how to apply constitutional norms to "private" entities implicates the so-called "state action" doctrine. Having its genesis in an 1883 Supreme Court decision overturning Reconstruction-era civil rights legislation, the state action doctrine, in its least nuanced form, rests on the observation that most constitutional commandments proscribe only the conduct of governmental actors. For example, the Fourteenth Amendment provides that "No *state* shall. . . ." And the First Amendment begins: "*Congress* shall make no law . . ." As a result, the Supreme Court has often refused to apply these constitutional provisions to what it deems to be "private action." Thus—and again to express the doctrine in its least subtle form—the state cannot constitutionally exclude African Americans from a government housing facility, but the Constitution is silent with regard to an individual's choice to exclude African Americans from his or her home. Similarly in cyberspace, so the doctrine might go, the activities of private corporations, such as Google or America Online or ICANN, or the Internet Engineering Task Force, are not subject to the Constitution because they are not state actors.

Some commentators have argued, however, that the state action doctrine rests on the illusory hope that we can draw a clear and coherent line between what constitutes public as opposed to private behavior. Indeed, Supreme Court decisions about state action have been uncertain and often inconsistent. And scholars frequently have criticized the state action doctrine both as a matter of historical fidelity and public policy. On the other hand, just because a line is difficult to draw does not necessarily mean there should not be *any* line. And, as a practical matter, most of us experience a difference between public and private acts in our daily lives and therefore might find it counterintuitive to conflate the two.

The "state action" doctrine requires a court to ask when the conduct of a private party is fairly attributable to the government for constitutional purposes. Although the Supreme Court's approach to state action questions has shifted over time, the cases of the last five decades present recurrent themes. First, courts often look to whether the private party is performing a "public function"—that is, whether the private party is sufficiently state-like to be treated as the state for purposes of applying constitutional guarantees. Second, courts examine the points of contact between the government and the private party to assess whether there is a sufficient nexus between the two to justify imposing constitutional restraints on the private actor—as, for example, where the government jointly participates in or compels the private party's conduct.

Both approaches to state action are relevant to questions about private control over online behavior. The cases we consider below focus mainly on the public function approach. As you read the cases, consider not only the doctrine that emerges, but also whether the shifts in the Supreme Court's approach are legitimate. Finally, ask yourself what the cases reveal about the power of private parties to control behavior, both in real space and in cyberspace. Should the "private" entities considered so far in this chapter be deemed state actors for constitutional purposes?

Marsh v. Alabama

Supreme Court of the United States, 1946
326 U.S. 501

MR. JUSTICE BLACK delivered the opinion of the Court.

In this case we are asked to decide whether a State, consistently with the First and Fourteenth Amendments, can impose criminal punishment on a person who undertakes to distribute religious literature on the premises of a company-owned town contrary to the wishes of the town's management. The town, a suburb of Mobile, Alabama, known as Chickasaw, is owned by the Gulf Shipbuilding Corporation. Except for that it has all the characteristics of any other American town. The property consists of residential buildings, streets, a system of sewers, a sewage disposal plant and a "business block" on which business places are situated. A deputy of the Mobile County Sheriff, paid by the company, serves as the town's policeman. Merchants and service establishments have rented the stores and business places on the business block and the United States uses one of the places as a post office from which six carriers deliver mail to the people of Chickasaw and the adjacent area. The town and the surrounding neighborhood, which can not be distinguished from the Gulf property by anyone not familiar with the property lines, are thickly settled, and according to all indications the residents use the business block as their regular shopping center. To do so, they now, as they have for many years, make use of a company-owned paved street and sidewalk located alongside the store fronts in order to enter and leave the stores and the post office. Intersecting company-owned roads at each end of the business block lead into a four-lane public highway which runs parallel to the business block at a distance of thirty feet. There is nothing to stop highway traffic from coming onto the business block and upon arrival a traveler may make free use of the facilities available there. In short the town and its shopping district are accessible to and freely used by the public in general and there is nothing to distinguish them from any other town and shopping center except the fact that the title to the property belongs to a private corporation.

Appellant, a Jehovah's Witness, came onto the sidewalk we have just described, stood near the post-office and undertook to distribute religious literature. In the stores the corporation had posted a notice which read as follows: "This Is Private Property, and Without Written Permission, No Street, or House Vendor, Agent or Solicitation of Any Kind Will Be Permitted." Appellant was warned that she could not distribute the literature without a permit and told that no permit would be issued to her. She protested that the company rule could not be constitutionally applied so as to prohibit her from distributing religious writings. When she was asked to leave the sidewalk and Chickasaw she declined. The deputy sheriff arrested her and she was charged in the state court with violating [a state statute] which makes it a crime to enter or remain on the premises of another after having been warned not to do so. Appellant contended that to construe the state statute as applicable to her activities would abridge her right to freedom of press and religion contrary to the First and Fourteenth Amendments to the Constitution. This contention was rejected and she was convicted. * * *

Had the title to Chickasaw belonged not to a private but to a municipal corporation and had appellant been arrested for violating a municipal ordinance rather than a ruling by those appointed by the corporation to manage a company town it would have been clear that appellant's conviction must be reversed. * * * Our question then narrows down to this: Can those people who live in or come to Chickasaw be denied freedom of press and religion simply because a single company has legal title to all the town? For it is the state's contention that the mere fact that all the property interests in the town are held by a single company is enough to give that company power, enforceable by a state statute, to abridge these freedoms.

We do not agree that the corporation's property interests settle the question. The State urges in effect that the corporation's right to control the inhabitants of Chickasaw is coextensive with the right of a homeowner to regulate the conduct of his guests. We can not accept that contention. Ownership does not always mean absolute dominion. The more an owner, for his advantage, opens up his property for use by the public in general, the more do his rights become circumscribed by the statutory and constitutional rights of those who use it. Thus, the owners of privately held bridges, ferries, turnpikes and railroads may not operate them as freely as a farmer does his farm. Since these facilities are built and operated primarily to benefit the public and since their operation is essentially a public function, it is subject to state regulation. * * *

Whether a corporation or a municipality owns or possesses the town the public in either case has an identical interest in the functioning of the community in such manner that the channels of communication remain free. As we have heretofore stated, the town of Chickasaw does not function differently from any other town. The "business block" serves as the community shopping center and is freely accessible and open to the people in the area and those passing through. The managers appointed by the corporation cannot curtail the liberty of press and religion of these people consistently with the purposes of the Constitutional guarantees, and a state statute, as the one here involved, which enforces such action by criminally punishing those who attempt to distribute religious literature clearly violates the First and Fourteenth Amendments to the Constitution.

Many people in the United States live in company-owned towns. These people, just as residents of municipalities, are free citizens of their State and country. Just as all other citizens they must make decisions which affect the welfare of community and nation. To act as good citizens they must be informed. In order to enable them to be properly informed their information must be uncensored. There is no more reason for depriving these people of the liberties guaranteed by the First and Fourteenth Amendments than there is for curtailing these freedoms with respect to any other citizen.

When we balance the Constitutional rights of owners of property against those of the people to enjoy freedom of press and religion, as we must here, we remain mindful of the fact that the latter occupy a preferred position. * * * In our view the circumstance that the property rights to the premises where the deprivation of liberty, here involved, took place, were held by others than the public, is not sufficient to justify the State's permitting a corporation to govern a community of citizens so as to restrict their fundamental liberties and the enforcement of such restraint by the application of a State statute.

MR. JUSTICE JACKSON took no part in the consideration or decision of this case.

[Concurring opinion of Justice Frankfurter omitted.]

MR. JUSTICE REED, dissenting.

Former decisions of this Court have interpreted generously the Constitutional rights of people in this Land to exercise freedom of religion, of speech and of the press. It has never been held and is not now by this opinion of the Court that these rights are absolute and unlimited either in respect to the manner or the place of their exercise. What the present decision establishes as a principle is that one may remain on private property against the will of the owner and contrary to the law of the state so long as the only objection to his presence is that he is exercising an asserted right to spread there his religious views. * * *

Both Federal and Alabama law permit, so far as we are aware, company towns. By that we mean an area occupied by numerous houses, connected by passways, fenced or not, as the owners may choose. These communities may be essential to furnish proper and convenient living conditions for employees on isolated operations in lumbering, mining, production of high explosives and large-scale farming. The restrictions imposed by the owners upon the occupants are sometimes galling to the employees and may appear unreasonable to outsiders. Unless they fall under the prohibition of some legal rule, however, they are a matter for adjustment between owner and licensee, or by appropriate legislation. * * *

Our Constitution guarantees to every man the right to express his views in an orderly fashion. An essential element of "orderly" is that the man shall also have a right to use the place he chooses for his exposition. The rights of the owner, which the Constitution protects as well as the right of free speech, are not outweighed by the interests of the trespasser, even though he trespasses in behalf of religion or free speech. We cannot say that Jehovah's Witnesses can claim the privilege of a license, which has never been granted, to hold their meetings in other private places, merely because the owner has admitted the public to them for other limited purposes. Even though we have reached the point where this Court is required to force private owners to open their property for the practice there of religious activities or propaganda distasteful to the owner, because of the public interest in freedom of speech and religion, there is no need for the application of such a doctrine here. Appellant, as we have said, was free to engage in such practices on the public highways, without becoming a trespasser on the company's property.

THE CHIEF JUSTICE and MR. JUSTICE BURTON join in this dissent.

Notes and Questions

1. What are the specific attributes of Chickasaw that make the majority view it as essentially governmental? Are the facts of this case generalizable to any other situation?

2. Can the opinion be read to stand for the proposition that states may not escape constitutional restraints by "delegating" to private parties functions traditionally performed by the state? If so, does the opinion make clear what those limits on delegation might be?

3. The majority writes that "[t]he more an owner, for his advantage, opens up his property for use by the public in general, the more do his rights become circumscribed by the statutory and constitutional rights of those who use it." Do you agree? Might this doctrine hurt the general public by encouraging property owners *not* to open their property up to public use?

4. Consider the shopping centers and malls now so common in American life. Are they similar to Chickasaw? After all, they often include retail stores, restaurants, entertainment events, movie theaters, "parks," and many other attributes we might associate with town squares or municipal centers. Ought such spaces be deemed quasi-governmental and therefore subject to constitutional strictures? Consider the following three cases, which take up these questions.

Amalgamated Food Employees Union v.
Logan Valley Plaza, Inc.

Supreme Court of the United States, 1968
391 U.S. 308

MR. JUSTICE MARSHALL delivered the opinion of the Court.

This case presents the question whether peaceful picketing of a business enterprise located within a shopping center can be enjoined on the ground that it constitutes an unconsented invasion of the property rights of the owners of the land on which the center is situated. We granted certiorari to consider petitioners' contentions that the decisions of the state courts enjoining their picketing as a trespass are violative of their rights under the First and Fourteenth Amendments of the United States Constitution. We reverse.

Logan Valley Plaza, Inc. (Logan), one of the two respondents herein, owns a large, newly developed shopping center complex, known as the Logan Valley Mall, located near the City of Altoona, Pennsylvania. * * *

At the time of the events in this case, Logan Valley Mall was occupied by two businesses, Weis Markets, Inc. (Weis), the other respondent herein, and Sears, Roebuck and Co. (Sears), although other enterprises were then expected and have since moved into the center. Weis operates a supermarket and Sears operates both a department store and an automobile service center. The Weis property consists of the enclosed supermarket building, an open but covered porch along the front of the building, and an approximately five-foot-wide parcel pickup zone that runs 30 to 40 feet along the porch. The porch functions as a sidewalk in front of the building and the pickup zone is used as a temporary parking place for the loading of purchases into customers' cars by Weis employees. * * *

On December 8, 1965, Weis opened for business, employing a wholly nonunion staff of employees. A few days after it opened for business, Weis posted a sign on the exterior of its building prohibiting trespassing or soliciting by anyone other than its employees on its porch or parking lot. On December 17, 1965, members of Amalgamated Food Employees Union, Local 590, began picketing Weis. They carried signs stating that the Weis market was nonunion and that its employees were not "receiving union wages or other union benefits." The pickets did not include any employees of Weis, but rather were all employees of competitors of Weis. The picketing continued until December 27, during which time the number of pickets varied between four and 13 and averaged around six. The picketing was carried out almost entirely in the parcel pickup area and that portion of the parking lot immediately adjacent thereto. Although some congestion of the parcel pickup area occurred, such congestion was sporadic and infrequent. The picketing was peaceful at all times and unaccompanied by either threats or violence.

On December 27, Weis and Logan instituted an action in equity in the Court of Common Pleas of Blair County, and that court immediately issued an *ex parte* order enjoining petitioners from, *inter alia*, "[p]icketing and trespassing upon . . . . the [Weis] storeroom, porch and parcel pick-up area . . . [and] the [Logan] parking area and all entrances and exits leading to said parking area." * * *

On appeal the Pennsylvania Supreme Court, with three Justices dissenting, affirmed the issuance of the injunction on the sole ground that petitioners' conduct constituted a trespass on respondents' property.

We start from the premise that peaceful picketing carried on in a location open generally to the public is, absent other factors involving the purpose or manner of the picketing, protected by the First Amendment. * * * The case squarely presents, therefore, the question whether Pennsylvania's generally valid rules against trespass to private property can be applied in these circumstances to bar petitioners from the Weis and Logan premises. It is clear that if the shopping center premises were not privately owned but instead constituted the business area of a municipality, which they to a large extent resemble, petitioners could not be barred from exercising their First Amendment rights there on the sole ground that title to the property was in the municipality. * * * [S]treets, sidewalks, parks, and other similar public places are so historically associated with the exercise of First Amendment rights that access to them for the purpose of exercising such rights cannot constitutionally be denied broadly and absolutely. * * *

This Court has also held, in *Marsh v. Alabama*, 326 U.S. 501 (1946), that under some circumstances property that is privately owned may, at least for First Amendment purposes, be treated as though it were publicly held. * * * The similarities between the business block in *Marsh* and the shopping center in the present case are striking. The perimeter of Logan Valley Mall is a little less than 1.1 miles. Inside the mall were situated, at the time of trial, two substantial commercial enterprises with numerous others soon to follow. Immediately adjacent to the mall are two roads, one of which is a heavily traveled state highway and from both of which lead entrances directly into the mall. Adjoining the buildings in the middle of the mall are sidewalks for the use of pedestrians going to and from their cars and from building to building. In the parking areas, roadways for the use of vehicular traffic entering and leaving the mall are clearly marked out. The general public has unrestricted access to the mall property. The shopping center here is clearly the functional equivalent of the business district of Chickasaw involved in *Marsh*.

It is true that, unlike the corporation in *Marsh* the respondents here do not own the surrounding residential property and do not provide municipal services therefore. Presumably, petitioners are free to canvass the neighborhood with their message about the nonunion status of Weis Market, just as they have been permitted by the state courts to picket on the berms outside the mall. Thus, unlike the situation in *Marsh*, there is no power on respondents' part to have petitioners totally denied access to the community for which the mall serves as a business district. This fact, however, is not determinative. In *Marsh* itself the precise issue presented was whether the appellant therein had the right, under the First Amendment, to pass out leaflets in the business district, since there was no showing made there that the corporate owner would have sought to prevent the distribution of leaflets in the residential areas of the town. While it is probable that the power to prevent trespass broadly claimed in *Marsh* would have encompassed such an incursion into the residential areas, the specific facts in the case involved access to property used for commercial purposes.

We see no reason why access to a business district in a company town for the purpose of exercising First Amendment rights should be constitutionally required, while access for the same purpose to property functioning as a business district should be limited simply because the property surrounding the "business district" is not under the same ownership. Here the roadways provided for vehicular movement within the mall and the sidewalks leading from building to building are the functional equivalents of the streets and sidewalks of a normal municipal business district. The shopping center premises are open to the public to the same extent as the commercial center of a normal town. So far as can be determined, the main distinction in practice between use by the public of the Logan Valley Mall and of any other business district, were the decisions of the state courts to stand, would be that those members of the general public who sought to use the mall premises in a manner contrary to the wishes of the respondents could be prevented from so doing.

Such a power on the part of respondents would be, of course, part and parcel of the rights traditionally associated with ownership of private property. And it may well be that respondents' ownership of the property here in question gives them various rights, under the laws of Pennsylvania, to limit the use of that property by members of the public in a manner that would not be permissible were the property owned by a municipality. All we decide here is that because the shopping center serves as the community business block "and is freely accessible and open to the people in the area and those passing through," *Marsh*, 326 U.S. at 508, the State may not delegate the power, through the use of its trespass laws, wholly to exclude those members of the public wishing to exercise their First Amendment rights on the premises in a manner and for a purpose generally consonant with the use to which the property is actually put.

[Concurring opinion of Justice Douglas omitted.]

MR. JUSTICE BLACK, dissenting.

I would * * * hold that the entire injunction is valid. * * * I believe that, whether this Court likes it or not, the Constitution recognizes and supports the concept of private ownership of property. The Fifth Amendment provides that "[n]o person shall . . . be deprived of life, liberty, or property, without due process of law; nor shall private property be taken for public use, without just compensation." This means to me that there is no right to picket on the private premises of another to try to convert the owner or others to the views of the pickets. It also means, I think, that if this Court is going to arrogate to itself the power to act as the Government's agent to take a part of Weis' property to give to the pickets for their use, the Court should also award Weis just compensation for the property taken.

In affirming petitioners' contentions the majority opinion relies on *Marsh v. State of Alabama*, and holds that respondents' property has been transformed to some type of public property. But *Marsh* was never intended to apply to this kind of situation. *Marsh* dealt with the very special situation of a company-owned town, complete with streets, alleys sewers, stores, residences, and everything else that goes to make a town. The particular company town involved was Chickasaw, Alabama, which, as we stated in the opinion, except for the fact that it "is owned by the Gulf Shipbuilding Corporation . . . has all the characteristics of any other American town. The property consists of residential buildings, streets, a system of sewers, a sewage disposal plant and a 'business block' on which business places are situated." Again toward the end of the opinion we emphasized that "the town of Chickasaw does not function differently from any other town." I think it is fair to say that the basis on which the *Marsh* decision rested was that the property involved encompassed an area that for all practical purposes had been turned into a town; the area had all the attributes of a town and was exactly like any other town in Alabama. I can find very little resemblance between the shopping center involved in this case and Chickasaw, Alabama. There are no homes, there is no sewage disposal plant, there is not even a post office on this private property which the Court now considers the equivalent of a "town." Indeed, at the time this injunction was issued, there were only two stores on the property. Now there are supposed to be about 17, but they are all conceded to be "commercial establishments." The remainder of the property in the center has been laid out as a large parking lot with individually marked parking spaces provided for business customers. All I can say is that this sounds like a very strange "town" to me.

The majority opinion recognizes the problem with trying to draw too close an analogy to *Marsh*, but faces a dilemma in that *Marsh* is the only possible authority for treating admittedly privately owned property the way the majority does. Thus the majority opinion concedes that "the respondents here do not own the surrounding residential property and do not provide municipal services therefor." But that is not crucial, according to the majority, since the petitioner in *Marsh* was arrested in the business district of Chickasaw. The majority opinion then concludes that since the appellant in *Marsh* was given access to the business district of a company town, the petitioners in this case should be given access to the shopping center which was functioning as a business district. But I respectfully suggest that this reasoning completely misreads *Marsh* and begs the question. The question is, Under what circumstances can private property be treated as though it were public? The answer that *Marsh* gives is when that property has taken on all the attributes of a town, *i.e.*, "residential buildings, streets, a system of sewers, a sewage disposal plant and a 'business block' on which business places are situated." I can find nothing in *Marsh* which indicates that if one of these features is present, *e.g.*, a business district, this is sufficient for the Court to confiscate a part of an owner's private property and give its use to people who want to picket on it.

[Dissenting opinions of Justice Harlan and Justice White omitted.]

Lloyd Corporation v. Tanner

Supreme Court of the United States, 1972
407 U.S. 551

MR. JUSTICE POWELL delivered the opinion of the Court.

This case presents [a] question reserved by the Court in *Amalgamated Food Employees Union v. Logan Valley Plaza, Inc.*, 391 U.S. 308 (1968), as to the right of a privately owned shopping center to prohibit the distribution of handbills on its property when the handbilling is unrelated to the shopping center's operations. Relying primarily on *Marsh v. Alabama*, 326 U.S. 501 (1946), and *Logan Valley*, the United States District Court for the District of Oregon sustained an asserted First Amendment right to distribute handbills in petitioner's shopping center, and issued a permanent injunction restraining petitioner from interfering with such right. The Court of Appeals for the Ninth Circuit affirmed. We granted certiorari to consider petitioner's contention that the decision below violates rights of private property protected by the Fifth and Fourteenth Amendments.

Lloyd Corp., Ltd. (Lloyd), owns a large, modern retail shopping center in Portland, Oregon. Lloyd Center embraces altogether about 50 acres, including some 20 acres of open and covered parking facilities which accommodate more than 1,000 automobiles. It has a perimeter of almost one and one-half miles, bounded by four public streets. It is crossed in varying degrees by several other public streets, all of which have adjacent public sidewalks. Lloyd owns all land and buildings within the Center, except these public streets and sidewalks. There are some 60 commercial tenants, including small shops and several major department stores. * * *

The Center had been in operation for some eight years when this litigation commenced. Throughout this period it had a policy, strictly enforced, against the distribution of handbills within the building complex and its malls. No exceptions were made with respect to handbilling, which was considered likely to annoy customers, to create litter, potentially to create disorders, and generally to be incompatible with the purpose of the Center and the atmosphere sought to be preserved.

On November 14, 1968, the respondents in this case distributed within the Center handbill invitations to a meeting of the "Resistance Community" to protest the draft and the Vietnam war. The distribution, made in several different places on the mall walkways by five young people, was quiet and orderly, and there was no littering. There was a complaint from one customer. Security guards informed the respondents that they were trespassing and would be arrested unless they stopped distributing the handbills within the Center. The guards suggested that respondents distribute their literature on the public streets and sidewalks adjacent to but outside of the Center complex. Respondents left the premises as requested "to avoid arrest" and continued the handbilling outside. Subsequently this suit was instituted in the District Court seeking declaratory and injunctive relief.

I

The District Court, emphasizing that the Center "is open to the general public," found that it is "the functional equivalent of a public business district." That court then held that Lloyd's "rule prohibiting the distribution of handbills within the Mall violates . . . First Amendment rights." In a *per curiam* opinion, the Court of Appeals held that it was bound by the "factual determination" as to the character of the Center, and concluded that the decisions of this Court in *Marsh* and *Logan Valley* compelled affirmance. * * *

II

The courts below considered the critical inquiry to be whether Lloyd Center was "the functional equivalent of a public business district." This phrase was first used in *Logan Valley*, but its genesis was in *Marsh*. It is well to consider what *Marsh* actually decided. [The case] involved an economic anomaly of the past, "the company town." One must have seen such towns to understand that "functionally" they were no different from municipalities of comparable size. They developed primarily in the Deep South to meet economic conditions, especially those which existed following the Civil War. Impoverished States, and especially backward areas thereof, needed an influx of industry and capital. Corporations attracted to the area by natural resources and abundant labor were willing to assume the role of local government. Quite literally, towns were built and operated by private capital with all of the customary services and utilities normally afforded by a municipal or state government: there were streets, sidewalks, sewers, public lighting, police and fire protection, business and residential areas, churches, postal facilities, and sometimes schools. In short, as Mr. Justice Black said, Chickasaw, Alabama, had "all the characteristics of any other American town." 326 U.S., at 502. The Court simply held that where private interests were substituting for and performing the customary functions of government, First Amendment freedoms could not be denied where exercised in the customary manner on the town's sidewalks and streets. Indeed, as title to the entire town was held privately, there were no publicly owned streets, sidewalks, or parks where such rights could be exercised.

Logan Valley extended *Marsh* to a shopping center situation in a different context from the company town setting, but it did so only in a context where the First Amendment activity was related to the shopping center's operations. There is some language in *Logan Valley*, unnecessary to the decision, suggesting that the key focus of *Marsh* was upon the "business district," and that whenever a privately owned business district serves the public generally its sidewalks and streets become the functional equivalents of similar public facilities. As Mr. Justice Black's dissent in *Logan Valley* emphasized, this would be an incorrect interpretation of the Court's decision in *Marsh* * * * .

The holding in *Logan Valley* was not dependent upon the suggestion that the privately owned streets and sidewalks of a business district or a shopping center are the equivalent, for First Amendment purposes, of municipally owned streets and sidewalks. No such expansive reading of the opinion of the Court is necessary or appropriate. The opinion was carefully phrased to limit its holding to the picketing involved, where the picketing was "directly related in its purpose to the use to which the shopping center property was being put," and where the store was located in the center of a large private enclave with the consequence that no other reasonable opportunities for the pickets to convey their message to their intended audience were available.

Neither of these elements is present in the case now before the Court.

A

The handbilling by respondents in the malls of Lloyd Center had no relation to any purpose for which the center was built and being used. It is nevertheless argued by respondents that, since the Center is open to the public, the private owner cannot enforce a restriction against handbilling on the premises. The thrust of this argument is considerably broader than the rationale of *Logan Valley*. It requires a relationship, direct or indirect, between the purpose of the expressive activity and the business of the shopping center. The message sought to be conveyed by respondents was directed to all members of the public, not solely to patrons of Lloyd Center or of any of its operations. Respondents could have distributed these handbills on any public street, on any public sidewalk, in any public park, or in any public building in the city of Portland. * * *

B

A further fact, distinguishing the present case from *Logan Valley*, is that the Union pickets in that case would have been deprived of all reasonable opportunity to convey their message to patrons of the Weis store had they been denied access to the shopping center. The situation at Lloyd Center was notably different. The central building complex was surrounded by public sidewalks, totaling 66 linear blocks. All persons who enter or leave the private areas within the complex must cross public streets and sidewalks, either on foot or in automobiles. When moving to and from the privately owned parking lots, automobiles are required by law to come to a complete stop. Handbills may be distributed conveniently to pedestrians, and also to occupants of automobiles, from these public sidewalks and streets. Indeed, respondents moved to these public areas and continued distribution of their handbills after being requested to leave the interior malls. It would be an unwarranted infringement of property rights to require them to yield to the exercise of First Amendment rights under circumstances where adequate alternative avenues of communication exist. Such an accommodation would diminish property rights without significantly enhancing the asserted right of free speech. In ordering this accommodation the courts below erred in their interpretation of this Court's decisions in *Marsh* and *Logan Valley*.

III

The basic issue in this case is whether respondents, in the exercise of asserted First Amendment rights, may distribute handbills on Lloyd's private property contrary to its wishes and contrary to a policy enforced against all handbilling. In addressing this issue, it must be remembered that the First and Fourteenth Amendments safeguard the rights of free speech and assembly by limitations on *state* action, not on action by the owner of private property used nondiscriminatorily for private purposes only. * * *

Respondents contend, however, that the property of a large shopping center is "open to the public," serves the same purposes as a "business district" of a municipality, and therefore has been dedicated to certain types of public use. The argument is that such a center has sidewalks, streets, and parking areas which are functionally similar to facilities customarily provided by municipalities. It is then asserted that all members of the public, whether invited as customers or not, have the same right of free speech as they would have on the similar public facilities in the streets of a city or town.

The argument reaches too far. The Constitution by no means requires such an attenuated doctrine of dedication of private property to public use. The closest decision in theory, *Marsh v. Alabama*, involved the assumption by a private enterprise of all of the attributes of a state-created municipality and the exercise by that enterprise of semiofficial municipal functions as a delegate of the State. In effect, the owner of the company town was performing the full spectrum of municipal powers and stood in the shoes of the State. In the instant case where is no comparable assumption or exercise of municipal functions or power. * * *

We hold that there has been no such dedication of Lloyd's privately owned and operated shopping center to public use as to entitle respondents to exercise therein the asserted First Amendment rights. Accordingly, we reverse the judgment and remand the case to the Court of Appeals with directions to vacate the injunction.

MR. JUSTICE MARSHALL, with whom MR. JUSTICE DOUGLAS, MR. JUSTICE BRENNAN, and MR. JUSTICE STEWART join, dissenting.

I

The question presented by this case is whether one of the incidents of petitioner's private ownership of the Lloyd Center is the power to exclude certain forms of speech from its property. In other words, we must decide whether ownership of the Center gives petitioner unfettered discretion to determine whether or not it will be used as a public forum. * * *

[T]he District Court found that "the Mall is the functional equivalent of a public business district" within the meaning of *Marsh* and *Logan Valley*. The Court of Appeals specifically affirmed this finding, and it is overwhelmingly supported by the record.

The Lloyd Center is similar to Logan Valley Plaza in several respects: both are bordered by public roads, and the entrances of both lead directly into the public roads; both contain large parking areas and privately owned walkways leading from store to store; and the general public has unrestricted access to both. The principal differences between the two centers are that the Lloyd Center is larger than Logan Valley, that Lloyd Center contains more commercial facilities, that Lloyd Center contains a range of professional and nonprofessional services that were not found in Logan Valley, and that Lloyd Center is much more intertwined with public streets than Logan Valley. Also, as in *Marsh*, Lloyd's private police are given full police power by the city of Portland, even though they are hired, fired, controlled, and paid by the owners of the Center. This was not true in *Logan Valley*.

In 1954, when Lloyd's owners first acquired land for the Center, the city of Portland vacated about eight acres of public streets for their use. * * * From its inception, the city viewed [Lloyd Center] as a "business district" of the city and depended on it to supply much-needed employment opportunities. To insure the success of the Center, the city carefully integrated it into the pattern of streets already established and planned future development of streets around the Center. It is plain, therefore, that Lloyd Center is the equivalent of a public "business district" within the meaning of *Marsh* and *Logan Valley*. In fact, the Lloyd Center is much more analogous to the company town in *Marsh* than was the Logan Valley Plaza.

Petitioner agrees with our decision in *Logan Valley* that it is proper for courts to treat shopping centers differently from other privately owned property, like private residences. * * * The argument is made, however, that this case should be distinguished from *Logan Valley*, and this is the argument that the Court accepts.

II

As I have pointed out above, Lloyd Center is even more clearly the equivalent of a public business district than was Logan Valley Plaza. The First Amendment activity in both *Logan Valley* and the instant case was peaceful and nondisruptive; and both cases involve traditionally acceptable modes of speech. Why then should there be a different result here? The Court's answer is that the speech in this case was directed at topics of general interest—the Vietnam war and the draft—whereas the speech in Logan Valley was directed to the activities of a store in the shopping center, and that this factual difference is of constitutional dimensions. I cannot agree.

It is true that in *Logan Valley* we * * * left open the question whether "property rights could, consistently with the First Amendment, justify a bar on picketing [or handbilling] which was not . . . directly related in its purpose to the use to which the shopping center property was being put." But, I believe that the Court errs in concluding that this issue must be faced in the instant case. The District Court observed that Lloyd Center invites schools to hold football rallies, presidential candidates to give speeches, and service organizations to hold Veterans Day ceremonies on its premises. The court also observed that the Center permits the Salvation Army, the Volunteers of America, and the American Legion to solicit funds in the Mall. Thus, the court concluded that the Center was already open to First Amendment activities * * * . [I]n *Logan Valley*, * * * we specifically held that members of the public may exercise their First Amendment rights on the premises of a shopping center that is the functional equivalent of a business district if their activity is "generally consonant with the use to which the property is actually put." If the property of Lloyd Center is generally open to First Amendment activity, respondents cannot be excluded. * * *

If respondents had distributed handbills complaining about one or more stores in Lloyd Center or about the Center itself, petitioner concedes that our decision in *Logan Valley* would insulate that conduct from proscription by the Center. I cannot see any logical reason to treat differently speech that is related to subjects other than the Center and its member stores. * * *

III

* * * [I believe] that there is no legitimate way of following *Logan Valley* and not applying it to this case. But, one may suspect from reading the opinion of the Court that it is *Logan Valley* itself that the Court finds bothersome. The vote in *Logan Valley* was 6-3, and that decision is only four years old. But, I am aware that the composition of this Court has radically changed in four years. The fact remains that *Logan Valley* is binding unless and until it is overruled. There is no valid distinction between that case and this one, and, therefore, the results in both cases should be the same. * * *

We noted in *Logan Valley* that the large-scale movement of this country's population from the cities to the suburbs has been accompanied by the growth of suburban shopping centers. In response to this phenomenon, cites like Portland are providing for large-scale shopping areas within the city. It is obvious that privately owned shopping areas could prove to be greatly advantageous to cities. They are totally self-sufficient, needing no financial support from local government; and if, as here, they truly are the functional equivalent of a public business area, the city reaps the advantages of having such an area without paying for them. Some of the advantages are an increased tax base, a drawing attraction for residents, and a stimulus to further growth.

It would not be surprising in the future to see cities rely more and more on private businesses to perform functions once performed by governmental agencies. The advantage of reduced expenses and an increased tax base cannot be overstated. As governments rely on private enterprise, public property decreases in favor of privately owned property. It becomes harder and harder for citizens to find means to communicate with other citizens. Only the wealthy may find effective communication possible unless we adhere to *Marsh v. Alabama* and continue to hold that "[t]he more an owner, for his advantage, opens up his property for use by the public in general, the more do his rights become circumscribed by the statutory and constitutional rights of those who use it."

When there are no effective means of communication, free speech is a mere shibboleth. I believe that the First Amendment requires it to be a reality. Accordingly, I would affirm the decision of the Court of Appeals.

Hudgens v. National Labor Relations Board

Supreme Court of the United States, 1976
424 U.S. 507

MR. JUSTICE STEWART delivered the opinion of the Court.

A group of labor union members who engaged in peaceful primary picketing within the confines of a privately owned shopping center were threatened by an agent of the owner with arrest for criminal trespass if they did not depart. The question presented is whether this threat violated the National Labor Relations Act [NLRA]. * * *

I

The petitioner, Scott Hudgens, is the owner of the North DeKalb Shopping Center, located in suburban Atlanta, Ga. The center consists of a single large building with an enclosed mall. Surrounding the building is a parking area which can accommodate 2,640 automobiles. The shopping center houses 60 retail stores leased to various businesses. One of the lessees is the Butler Shoe Co. Most of the stores, including Butler's, can be entered only from the interior mall.

In January 1971, warehouse employees of the Butler Shoe Co. went on strike to protest the company's failure to agree to demands made by their union in contract negotiations. The strikers decided to picket not only Butler's warehouse but its nine retail stores in the Atlanta area as well, including the store in the North DeKalb Shopping Center. On January 22, 1971, four of the striking warehouse employees entered the center's enclosed mall carrying placards which read: "Butler Shoe Warehouse on Strike, AFL-CIO, Local 315." The general manager of the shopping center informed the employees that they could not picket within the mall or on the parking lot and threatened them with arrest if they did not leave. The employees departed but returned a short time later and began picketing in an area of the mall immediately adjacent to the entrances of the Butler store. After the picketing had continued for approximately 30 minutes, the shopping center manager again informed the pickets that if they did not leave they would be arrested for trespassing. The pickets departed.

The union subsequently filed with the Board an unfair labor practice charge against Hudgens, alleging interference with rights protected by the [NLRA]. Relying on this Court's decision in *Food Employees v. Logan Valley Plaza*, 391 U.S. 308 (1968), the Board entered a cease-and-desist order against Hudgens, reasoning that because the warehouse employees enjoyed a First Amendment right to picket on the shopping center property, the owner's threat of arrest violated the [NLRA]. * * *

It is, of course, a commonplace that the constitutional guarantee of free speech is a guarantee only against abridgment by government, federal or state. Thus, while statutory or common law may in some situations extend protection or provide redress against a private corporation or person who seeks to abridge the free expression of others, no such protection or redress is provided by the Constitution itself.

This elementary proposition is little more than a truism. But even truisms are not always unexceptionably true, and an exception to this one was recognized almost 30 years ago in *Marsh v. Alabama*, 326 U.S. 501 (1946). * * *

It was the *Marsh* case that in 1968 provided the foundation for the Court's decision in *Amalgamated Food Employees Union v. Logan Valley Plaza*, 391 U.S. 308 (1968). * * * The Court's opinion * * * reviewed the *Marsh* case in detail, emphasized the similarities between the business block in Chickasaw, Ala., and the Logan Valley shopping center and unambiguously concluded: "The shopping center here is clearly the functional equivalent of the business district of Chickasaw involved in *Marsh*." 391 U.S., at 318. * * *

Four years later the Court had occasion to reconsider the *Logan Valley* doctrine in *Lloyd Corp. v. Tanner*, 407 U.S. 551 (1972). * * *

The Court in its *Lloyd* opinion did not say that it was overruling the *Logan Valley* decision. Indeed a substantial portion of the Court's opinion in *Lloyd* was devoted to pointing out the differences between the two cases, noting particularly that, in contrast to the hand-billing in *Lloyd*, the picketing in *Logan Valley* had been specifically directed to a store in the shopping center and the pickets had had no other reasonable opportunity to reach their intended audience. But the fact is that the reasoning of the Court's opinion in *Lloyd* cannot be squared with the reasoning of the Court's opinion in *Logan Valley*.

It matters not that some Members of the Court may continue to believe that the *Logan Valley* case was rightly decided. Our institutional duty is to follow until changed the law as it now is, not as some Members of the Court might wish it to be. And in the performance of that duty we make clear now, if it was not clear before, that the rationale of *Logan Valley* did not survive the Court's decision in the *Lloyd* case. * * * If a large self-contained shopping center is the functional equivalent of a municipality, as *Logan Valley* held, then the First and Fourteenth Amendments would not permit control of speech within such a center to depend upon the speech's content. For while a municipality may constitutionally impose reasonable time, place, and manner regulations on the use of its streets and sidewalks for First Amendment purposes, and may even forbid altogether such use of some of its facilities, what a municipality may not do under the First and Fourteenth Amendments is to discriminate in the regulation of expression on the basis of the content of that expression. It conversely follows, therefore, that if the respondents in the *Lloyd* case did not have a First Amendment right to enter that shopping center distribute handbills concerning Vietnam, then the pickets in the present case did not have a First Amendment right to enter this shopping center for the purpose of advertising their strike against the Butler Shoe Co.

We conclude, in short, that under the present state of the law the constitutional guarantee of free expression has no part to play in a case such as this.

MR. JUSTICE STEVENS took no part in the consideration or decision of this case.

[Concurring opinions of Justice Powell and Justice White omitted.]

MR. JUSTICE MARSHALL, with whom MR. JUSTICE BRENNAN joins, dissenting.

In the final analysis, the Court's rejection of any role for the First Amendment in the privately owned shopping center complex stems, I believe, from an overly formalistic view of the relationship between the institution of private ownership of property and the First Amendment's guarantee of freedom of speech. No one would seriously question the legitimacy of the values of privacy and individual autonomy traditionally associated with privately owned property. But property that is privately owned is not always held for private use, and when a property owner opens his property to public use the force of those values diminishes. A degree of privacy is necessarily surrendered; thus, the privacy interest that petitioner retains when he leases space to 60 retail businesses and invites the public onto his land for the transaction of business with other members of the public is small indeed. And while the owner of property open to public use may not automatically surrender any of his autonomy interest in managing the property as he sees fit, there is nothing new about the notion that that autonomy interest must be accommodated with the interests of the public. As this Court noted some time ago, albeit in another context:

> "Property does become clothed with a public interest when used in a manner to make it of public consequence, and affect the community at large. When, therefore, one devotes his property to a use in which the public has an interest, he, in effect, grants to the public an interest in that use, and must submit to be controlled by the public for the

common good, to the extent of the interest he has thus created."
Munn v. Illinois, 94 U.S. 113, 126 (1877).

The interest of members of the public in communicating with one another on subjects relating to the businesses that occupy a modern shopping center is substantial. Not only employees with a labor dispute, but also consumers with complaints against business establishments, may look to the location of a retail store as the only reasonable avenue for effective communication with the public. As far as these groups are concerned, the shopping center owner has assumed the traditional role of the state in its control of historical First Amendment forums. *Lloyd* and *Logan Valley* recognized the vital role the First Amendment has to play in such cases, and I believe that this Court errs when it holds otherwise.

Notes and Questions

1. When private groups wield power normally associated with the state, why shouldn't they be subject to the same restrictions? Consider *Evans v. Newton*, 382 U.S. 296 (1966), in which the Supreme Court invalidated the exclusion of blacks from a private park. There the Court relied in part upon the public character of the facility:

> The service rendered even by a private park of this character is municipal in nature. It is open to every white person, there being no selective element other than race. Golf clubs, social centers, luncheon clubs, schools such as Tuskegee was at least in origin, and other like organizations in the private sector are often racially oriented. A park, on the other hand, is more like a fire department or police department that traditionally serves the community. Mass recreation through the use of parks is plainly in the public domain; and state courts that aid private parties to perform that public function on a segregated basis implicate the State in conduct proscribed by the Fourteenth Amendment.

Id. at 301-02.

2. On the other hand, even if one agrees that "traditionally" public activities should be subject to constitutional strictures, how does one draw the line between that which is "traditionally" public and that which is "traditionally" private? Are the shopping mall cases helpful in this regard? In what ways is a mall public? In what ways private?

3. Which of these decisions are most consistent with the rationale of *Marsh*? Are the efforts of the *Lloyd* and *Hudgens* majorities to distinguish *Marsh* persuasive? Under these later decisions, is there anything short of the precise facts in *Marsh* that would result in a determination of state action?

4. If Justice Marshall's logic in *Logan Valley* had prevailed, can you think of any principled way of limiting the scope of the decision? For example, what about a bookstore that allows people to sit on sofas and chairs to read and that provides a café and magazines, etc.? Could such a bookstore similarly be considered a substitute for the traditional town square?

5. Is an online bulletin board, listserv, or chatroom a public space where constitutional norms should prevail? Is there a coherent way of determining whether such fora serve traditional public functions or not?

6. Notice that *Hudgens* qualifies *Marsh*, requiring that a function be traditionally an *exclusive* state function in order to be subject to the Constitution. Thus, although shopping centers are generally as open to the public as parks, the *Hudgens* court views those spaces as private. Similarly, in *Jackson v. Metropolitan Edison*, 419 U.S. 345 (1974), the Court refused to impose the requirements of constitutional due process on an electric utility company despite petitioner's argument that such utilities provide an essential public service that is required by state law to be supplied on a reasonably continuous basis.

7. Return to some of the examples of nominally "private" entities discussed in Chapter Three. Are there compelling reasons to treat such actors as governmental actors? In addition to asking whether an entity performs a traditional public function, courts examine whether there is a sufficient "nexus" between a private actor and the government to justify imposing constitutional restraints. For example, what about the entanglement between ICANN and the government? In the article excerpted in Section B, Professor Froomkin makes the argument that ICANN should be treated as a state actor:

> Given that DoC called for an ICANN to exist, clothed it with authority, persuaded other government contractors to enter into agreements with it * * * and has close and continuing contacts with ICANN, a strong, but not unassailable, case can be made that ICANN is a state actor. If ICANN is a state actor, then it must comply with due process. It is highly unlikely that the procedures used to impose the UDRP on domain name registrants would meet this standard, and it is even debatable whether the UDRP itself would do so. * * *

> [D]etermining whether governmental authority may dominate an activity to such an extent that its participants should be deemed to act with the authority of the government, and, as a result, be subject to constitutional constraints, is a critical question in state action cases, and one that is primarily a question of fact. In *Edmonson v. Leesville Concrete Co.*, the Supreme Court provided three factors to be weighed: first, "the extent to which the actor relies on governmental assistance and benefits"; second, "whether the actor is performing a traditional governmental function"; and third, "whether the injury caused is aggravated in a unique way by the incidents of governmental authority."[438]

> These three tests suggest that ICANN is a state actor. First, ICANN depends very heavily on government assistance and benefits. ICANN would be irrelevant but for DoC having anointed it as NewCo and lent it control over the root. The second test focuses on the nature of the function being performed. DNS services have been a government function since the inception of the domain name system. * * * But whether DNS services can be said to be a "traditionally" governmental

---

438. 500 U.S. 614, 621-22 (1991).

function, given the relative youth of the Internet, is a little harder to say. * * * Twenty years, or even thirty, may be a little short for a "tradition," even though it is an eternity in "Internet Years." But perhaps this approach mischaracterizes the problem. For it is not ICANN that provides registry and registrar services, nor even that maintains the zone file. Rather, ICANN is fundamentally engaged in a traditional, even quintessential, government function: regulation of service providers. The fact that the objects of that regulation are relatively new types of entities is of no moment—regulation is regulation. The application of the third test, whether the harm is aggravated in a unique way by the incidents of government authority, depends on the context in which a state actor claim would arise. The factor may weigh differently in a complaint about a (would-be) top-level domain, whose access to the root is directly controlled by DoC, as opposed to a second-level domain, where the influence of DoC's control of the root is exercised through the registrars. * * *

A. Michael Froomkin, *Wrong Turn in Cyberspace: Using ICANN to Route Around the APA and the Constitution*, 50 DUKE L.J. 17, 113-14, 117-19 (2000). Is this view persuasive? If so, is Froomkin's reasoning applicable to any or all of the other nominally private entities considered in the previous section?

8. In *Lebron v. National R.R. Passenger Corp.*, 513 U.S. 374 (1995), the Supreme Court ruled that Amtrak was a state actor, based on, among other things, the fact that the government appointed a majority of Amtrak's Board of Directors. As Froomkin acknowledges, ICANN has no such formal ties to the government. Should that matter? Or is there still such a strong substantive connection between ICANN and the U.S. government that the Constitution should pose a limit to ICANN's actions? If so, how would you try to distinguish in the future between quasi-governmental entities who are to be considered state actors from those that are not? Does Froomkin provide any clues as to how he would draw that line?

9. In all of these cases, is the distinction between "public" and "private" useful? If a private property owner asks a police officer to remove a trespasser, is that a private action or a governmental action? Does the fact that the state created the private property laws in the first place make any difference? How about the fact that a court can assess whether MAPS properly included a website on its "Realtime Blackhole List? How can you tell when a private entity is acting sufficiently like a state to be subject to constitutional commands?

Paul Schiff Berman, *Cyberspace and the "State Action" Debate: The Cultural Value of Applying Constitutional Norms to "Private" Regulation*

71 U. COLO. L. REV. 1263 (2000)

Those who criticize the distinction between public and private in constitutional adjudication argue that the state action doctrine is incoherent because the state *always* plays a major role, implicitly or explicitly, in any legal relationship. First, they observe that all private actions take place against a background of laws. These laws embody state decisions either to permit or proscribe behavior. For example, legally permitted actions are permitted solely because the state has made a decision not to prohibit those actions. If such actions ultimately cause harm, it is therefore difficult to say the state has played no role.

Second, individual choices are strongly influenced by the context of state-created law. For example, a governmental zoning scheme may well be the motivating force behind an ostensibly private decision about private property. Similarly, scholars have demonstrated that the seemingly private behavior within a family is in fact heavily influenced by laws governing marriage, divorce, custody, property, and education. As Frances Olsen has observed,

> Both laissez faire and nonintervention in the family are false ideals. As long as a state exists and enforces any laws at all, it makes political choices. The state cannot be neutral or remain uninvolved, nor would anyone want the state to do so. The staunchest supporters of laissez faire always insisted that the state protect their property interests and that courts enforce contracts and adjudicate torts. They took this state action for granted and chose not to consider such protection a form of state intervention. Yet the so-called "free market" does not function except for such laws; the free market could not exist independently of the state. The enforcement of property, tort, and contract law requires constant political choices that may benefit one economic actor, usually at the expense of another. As Robert Hale pointed out more than a half century ago, these legal decisions "are bound to affect the distribution of income and the direction of economic activities." Any choice the courts make will affect the market, and there is seldom any meaningful way to label one choice intervention and the other laissez faire. When the state enforces any of these laws it must make political decisions that affect society.[54]

Third, the state plays a role in defining what even counts as a legally cognizable injury. Our property regime would permit me as a property owner to exclude a trespasser who wishes to put wallpaper over my windows, thus obstructing my view of a beautiful vista. Yet that same property regime likely would not permit me to prevent my neighbor from adding three floors to her house, causing the very same obstruction to the very same view. Thus, "[t]here is no clear distinction between a state invasion of property interests and its inevitable role in defining those interests."[55]

Fourth, even the definition of what constitutes a legally-cognizable person is dependent on law. For example, the state has chosen to treat a corporation like a person. The state has also implicitly conferred standing on human beings, but not on trees. And, of course, as anyone with knowledge of the history of slavery in this country knows, the legal definition of a human being is subject to change over time based on state decisions.

---

54. Frances E. Olsen, *The Myth of State Intervention in the Family*, 18 MICH. J.L. REFORM 835 (1985).

55. Richard S. Kay, *The State Action Doctrine, the Public-Private Distinction, and the Independence of Constitutional Law*, 10 CONST. COMMENT. 329, 335 (1993).

Finally, scholars have pointed out that the idea of a public sphere is itself a cultural construction, and that what an individual views as "public" will be a projection of his or her own values and assumptions. Accordingly, the public sphere will inevitably tend to reflect the perspective of more dominant groups within society. Or, one can flip the argument around, and similarly view the idea of a "private" sphere as a cultural construction. Because one's private choices are always made through values, language, and beliefs inherited from and influenced by the culture at large, the state will always play a constitutive role in the shaping of such choices.

Thus, the "conceptual categories in which we define what is an injury, who has caused it, and who has suffered from it are public artifacts."[61] Moreover, the distinction between public and private itself rests on cultural constructions that tend to reflect dominant players in society. Accordingly, the very determination of what is public and what is private is inevitably public.

Notes and Questions

1. Consider the argument that a state's decision *not* to act is itself a government action. For example, suppose that a state legislature considers enacting a statute that would require owners of shopping malls to permit leafleting within certain public areas of the malls. If the proposed legislation is defeated, reflecting a decision not to enact such a requirement, and a shopping center owner thereby has leafleters removed from the premises, is that removal a state action? If not, why isn't the state's decision *not* to require property owners to permit leafleting itself a state action that could be challenged under the First Amendment?

2. On the other hand, is there *no* relevance to the distinction between public and private? Aren't there certain activities that most people would say are permissible for private entities even if impermissible for the government? But if that is so, then perhaps the important question is to think of the appropriate scope of the constitutional provisions rather than simply ending the inquiry with a determination of whether the relevant action is public or private.

3. Instead of trying to draw a distinction between public and private action, might we instead consider the more fundamental question of whether or not the values embedded in the Constitution should be seen to apply to all of society, public or private? For example, employees often view restrictions on their freedom of expression or invasions of their privacy in the workplace as constitutional issues. Similarly, when large retailers decided to edit or restrict specific music albums, videos, and magazines because of their content, popular debates about this private "censorship" were framed in a language that was based on intuitions about the content of the Constitution. Finally, although private discrimination and harassment claims are technically brought pursuant to statutes, most Americans are likely to view them as constitutionally based claims. Given that core constitutional values and commitments can be threatened by private entities, might the Constitution provide a productive language for debating what to do about such threats?

---

61. *Id.* at 337.

4. Go back to the four examples of "private" regulation in the first part of this chapter: Should these actors be subject to constitutional norms? What would it mean to do so?

5. Leaving aside the Constitution, could the government by statute *require* mall owners to open their property up to leafleters? Or would such a statute itself abridge the constitutional rights of property owners? And if so, which rights would be violated? Such questions are especially important in the electronic world where cable broadcasters, Internet service providers, and others exercise substantial control over the public availability of information. We analyze these sorts of statutory responses in the next section.

SECTION C. LEGISLATIVE RESPONSES TO "PRIVATE" REGULATORY POWER

1. Regulation of Media Entities

In the previous section we considered whether constitutional norms of open access should apply to non-governmental (or quasi-governmental) entities such as shopping malls. However, even if the Constitution does not *require* that such entities obey First Amendment norms, that does not necessarily mean that government, by statute, could not *choose* to create rules guaranteeing open access. For example, consider the shopping mall cases once more. Although *Lloyd Corporation v. Tanner*, 407 U.S. 551 (1972), ultimately held that malls and shopping centers are not constitutionally required to allow leafleting, what if a state enacted a statute or adopted a constitutional provision requiring that malls of a certain size provide open access? Would such an action infringe the property rights of the owners?

In *PruneYard Shopping Center v. Robins*, 447 U.S. 74 (1980), the U.S. Supreme Court addressed a California state constitutional provision protecting speech and leafleting, if reasonably exercised, in privately owned shopping centers. The shopping center owner, relying on *Lloyd*, contended that such open access constituted an unconstitutional taking of private property by denying the property owner of a right to exclude leafleters. The Supreme Court first distinguished *Lloyd*:

> Our reasoning in *Lloyd* * * * does not *ex proprio vigore* limit the authority of the State to exercise its police power or its sovereign right to adopt in its own Constitution individual liberties more expansive than those conferred by the Federal Constitution. In *Lloyd*, there was no state constitutional or statutory provision that had been construed to create rights to the use of private property by strangers, comparable to those found to exist by the California Supreme Court here. It is, of course, well established that a State in the exercise of its police power may adopt reasonable restrictions on private property so long as the restrictions do not amount to a taking without just compensation or contravene any other federal constitutional provision. *Lloyd* held that when a shopping center owner opens his private property to the public for the purpose of

shopping, the First Amendment to the United States Constitution does not thereby create individual rights in expression beyond those already existing under applicable law.

PruneYard, 447 U.S. at 81.

The Court then rejected the takings claim raised by the property owner, noting that not every destruction or injury to property by governmental action is a "taking" in the constitutional sense:

> Rather, the determination whether a state law unlawfully infringes a landowner's property in violation of the Taking Clause requires an examination of whether the restriction on private property "forc[es] some people alone to bear public burdens which, in all fairness and justice, should be borne by the public as a whole." *Armstrong v. United States*, 364 U.S. 40, 49 (1960). This examination entails inquiry into such factors as the character of the governmental action, its economic impact, and its interference with reasonable investment-backed expectations. Here the requirement that appellants permit appellees to exercise state-protected rights of free expression and petition on shopping center property clearly does not amount to an unconstitutional infringement of appellants' property rights under the Taking Clause. There is nothing to suggest that preventing appellants from prohibiting this sort of activity will unreasonably impair the value or use of their property as a shopping center. The PruneYard is a large commercial complex that covers several city blocks, contains numerous separate business establishments, and is open to the public at large. The decision of the California Supreme Court makes it clear that the PruneYard may restrict expressive activity by adopting time, place, and manner regulations that will minimize any interference with its commercial functions. Appellees were orderly, and they limited their activity to the common areas of the shopping center. In these circumstances, the fact that they may have "physically invaded" appellants' property cannot be viewed as determinative.

PruneYard, 447 U.S. at 82-84.

PruneYard might mean that governmental efforts to open up private property to achieve greater public access will generally be constitutionally permissible. However, does this logic apply when the private property in question is a media entity—such as a radio station, a newspaper, a cable operator, or an Internet service provider—that might have First Amendment rights of its own? The following cases take up this question.

Red Lion Broadcasting Co. v. FCC

Supreme Court of the United States, 1969
395 U.S. 367

MR. JUSTICE WHITE delivered the opinion of the Court.

The Federal Communications Commission has for many years imposed on radio and television broadcasters the requirement that discussion of public issues be presented on broadcast stations, and that each side of those issues must be given fair coverage. This is known as the fairness doctrine, which originated very early in the history of broadcasting and has maintained its present outlines for some time. It is an obligation whose content has been defined in a long series of FCC rulings in particular cases. * * * Two aspects of the fairness doctrine, relating to personal attacks in the context of controversial public issues and to political editorializing, were codified more precisely in the form of FCC regulations in 1967. The two cases before us now, which were decided separately below, challenge the constitutional and statutory bases of the doctrine and component rules. *Red Lion* involves the application of the fairness doctrine to a particular broadcast, and [*United States v. Radio Television News Directors Association ("RTNDA")*] arises as an action to review the FCC's 1967 promulgation of the personal attack and political editorializing regulations, which were laid down after the *Red Lion* litigation had begun.

I.

The Red Lion Broadcasting Company is licensed to operate a Pennsylvania radio station, WGCB. On November 27, 1964, WGCB carried a 15-minute broadcast by the Reverend Billy James Hargis as part of a "Christian Crusade" series. A book by Fred J. Cook entitled "Goldwater—Extremist on the Right" was discussed by Hargis, who said that Cook had been fired by a newspaper for making false charges against city officials; that Cook had then worked for a Communist-affiliated publication; that he had defended Alger Hiss and attacked J. Edgar Hoover and the Central Intelligence Agency; and that he had now written a "book to smear and destroy Barry Goldwater." When Cook heard of the broadcast he concluded that he had been personally attacked and demanded free reply time, which the station refused. After an exchange of letters among Cook, Red Lion, and the FCC, the FCC declared that the Hargis broadcast constituted a personal attack on Cook; that Red Lion had failed to meet its obligation under the fairness doctrine * * * to send a tape, transcript, or summary of the broadcast to Cook and offer him reply time; and that the station must provide reply time whether or not Cook would pay for it. On review in the Court of Appeals for the District of Columbia Circuit, the FCC's position was upheld as constitutional and otherwise proper.

Not long after the *Red Lion* litigation was begun, the FCC issued [proposed rules], with an eye to making the personal attack aspect of the fairness doctrine more precise and more readily enforceable, and to specifying its rules relating to political editorials. After considering written comments supporting and opposing the rules, the FCC adopted them substantially as proposed. Twice amended, the rules were held unconstitutional in the *RTNDA* litigation by the Court of Appeals for the Seventh Circuit, on review of the rulemaking proceeding, as abridging the freedoms of speech and press.

As they now stand amended, the regulations [require stations to provide notification and an opportunity to respond when, "during the presentation of views on a controversial issue of public importance, an attack is made upon the honesty, character, integrity or like personal qualities of an identified person or group."] Believing that the specific application of the fairness doctrine in *Red Lion*, and the promulgation of the regulations in *RTNDA*, are both authorized by Congress and enhance rather than abridge the freedoms of speech and press protected by the First Amendment, we hold them valid and constitutional, reversing the judgment below in *RTNDA* and affirming the judgment below in *Red Lion*. * * *

III.

The broadcasters challenge the fairness doctrine and its specific manifestations in the personal attack and political editorial rules on conventional First Amendment grounds, alleging that the rules abridge their freedom of speech and press. Their contention is that the First Amendment protects their desire to use their allotted frequencies continuously to broadcast whatever they choose, and to exclude whomever they choose from ever using that frequency. No man may be prevented from saying or publishing what he thinks, or from refusing in his speech or other utterances to give equal weight to the views of his opponents. This right, they say, applies equally to broadcasters.

A.

Although broadcasting is clearly a medium affected by a First Amendment interest, * * * differences in the characteristics of new media justify differences in the First Amendment standards applied to them. For example, the ability of new technology to produce sounds more raucous than those of the human voice justifies restrictions on the sound level, and on the hours and places of use, of sound trucks so long as the restrictions are reasonable and applied without discrimination. Just as the Government may limit the use of sound-amplifying equipment potentially so noisy that it drowns out civilized private speech, so may the Government limit the use of broadcast equipment. The right of free speech of a broadcaster, the user of a sound truck, or any other individual does not embrace a right to snuff out the free speech of others. * * *

Where there are substantially more individuals who want to broadcast than there are frequencies to allocate, it is idle to posit an unabridgeable First Amendment right to broadcast comparable to the right of every individual to speak, write, or publish. If 100 persons want broadcast licenses but there are only 10 frequencies to allocate, all of them may have the same "right" to a license; but if there is to be any effective communication by radio, only a few can be licensed and the rest must be barred from the airwaves. It would be strange if the First Amendment, aimed at protecting and furthering communications, prevented the Government from making radio communication possible by requiring licenses to broadcast and by limiting the number of licenses so as not to overcrowd the spectrum.

This has been the consistent view of the Court. Congress unquestionably has the power to grant and deny licenses and to eliminate existing stations. No one has a First Amendment right to a license or to monopolize a radio frequency; to deny a station license because "the public interest" requires it "is not a denial of free speech." *National Broadcasting Co. v. United States*, 319 U.S. 190, 227 (1943).

By the same token, as far as the First Amendment is concerned those who are licensed stand no better than those to whom licenses are refused. A license permits broadcasting, but the licensee has no constitutional right to be the one who holds the license or to monopolize a radio frequency to the exclusion of his fellow citizens. There is nothing in the First Amendment which prevents the

Government from requiring a licensee to share his frequency with others and to conduct himself as a proxy or fiduciary with obligations to present those views and voices which are representative of his community and which would otherwise, by necessity, be barred from the airwaves.

This is not to say that the First Amendment is irrelevant to public broadcasting. * * * Because of the scarcity of radio frequencies, the Government is permitted to put restraints on licensees in favor of others whose views should be expressed on this unique medium. But the people as a whole retain their interest in free speech by radio and their collective right to have the medium function consistently with the ends and purposes of the First Amendment. It is the right of the viewers and listeners, not the right of the broadcasters, which is paramount. It is the purpose of the First Amendment to preserve an uninhibited marketplace of ideas in which truth will ultimately prevail, rather than to countenance monopolization of that market, whether it be by the Government itself or a private licensee. "[S]peech concerning public affairs is more than self-expression; it is the essence of self-government." *Garrison v. Louisiana*, 379 U.S. 64, 74-75 (1964). It is the right of the public to receive suitable access to social, political, esthetic, moral, and other ideas and experiences which is crucial here. That right may not constitutionally be abridged either by Congress or by the FCC.

B.

Rather than confer frequency monopolies on a relatively small number of licensees, in a Nation of 200,000,000, the Government could surely have decreed that each frequency should be shared among all or some of those who wish to use it, each being assigned a portion of the broadcast day or the broadcast week. The ruling and regulations at issue here do not go quite so far. They assert that under specified circumstances, a licensee must offer to make available a reasonable amount of broadcast time to those who have a view different from that which has already been expressed on his station. The expression of a political endorsement, or of a personal attack while dealing with a controversial public issue, simply triggers this time sharing. As we have said, the First Amendment confers no right on licensees to prevent others from broadcasting on "their" frequencies and no right to an unconditional monopoly of a scarce resource which the Government has denied others the right to use. * * *

Nor can we say that it is inconsistent with the First Amendment goal of producing an informed public capable of conducting its own affairs to require a broadcaster to permit answers to personal attacks occurring in the course of discussing controversial issues, or to require that the political opponents of those endorsed by the station be given a chance to communicate with the public. Otherwise, station owners and a few networks would have unfettered power to make time available only to the highest bidders, to communicate only their own views on public issues, people and candidates, and to permit on the air only those with whom they agreed. There is no sanctuary in the First Amendment for unlimited private censorship operating in a medium not open to all. "Freedom of the press from governmental interference under the First Amendment does not sanction repression of that freedom by private interests." *Associated Press v. United States*, 326 U.S. 1, 20 (1945).

C.

It is strenuously argued, however, that if political editorials or personal attacks will trigger an obligation in broadcasters to afford the opportunity for expression to speakers who need not pay for time and whose views are unpalatable to the licensees, then broadcasters will be irresistibly forced to self-censorship and their coverage of controversial public issues will be eliminated or at least rendered wholly ineffective. Such a result would indeed be a serious matter, for should licensees actually eliminate their coverage of controversial issues, the purposes of the doctrine would be stifled.

At this point, however, as the Federal Communications Commission has indicated, that possibility is at best speculative. The communications industry, and in particular the networks, have taken pains to present controversial issues in the past, and even now they do not assert that they intend to abandon their efforts in this regard. It would be better if the FCC's encouragement were never necessary to induce the broadcasters to meet their responsibility. And if experience with the administration of those doctrines indicates that they have the net effect of reducing rather than enhancing the volume and quality of coverage, there will be time enough to reconsider the constitutional implications. The fairness doctrine in the past has had no such overall effect.

That this will occur now seems unlikely, however, since if present licensees should suddenly prove timorous, the Commission is not powerless to insist that they give adequate and fair attention to public issues. It does not violate the First Amendment to treat licensees given the privilege of using scarce radio frequencies as proxies for the entire community, obligated to give suitable time and attention to matters of great public concern. To condition the granting or renewal of licenses on a willingness to present representative community views on controversial issues is consistent with the ends and purposes of those constitutional provisions forbidding the abridgment of freedom of speech and freedom of the press. Congress need not stand idly by and permit those with licenses to ignore the problems which beset the people or to exclude from the airways anything but their own views of fundamental questions. * * *

In view of the scarcity of broadcast frequencies, the Government's role in allocating those frequencies, and the legitimate claims of those unable without governmental assistance to gain access to those frequencies for expression of their views, we hold the regulations and ruling at issue here are both authorized by statute and constitutional. The judgment of the Court of Appeals in *Red Lion* is affirmed and that in *RTNDA* reversed and the causes remanded for proceedings consistent with this opinion.

Not having heard oral argument in these cases, MR. JUSTICE DOUGLAS took no part in the Court's decision.

Notes and Questions

1. In discussing the role of the First Amendment in the broadcast medium, the Court suggests that "the people as a whole" retain an interest in having the medium function "consistently with the ends and purposes of the First Amendment. It is the right of the viewers and listeners, not the right of

the broadcasters, which is paramount." If the relevant First Amendment stakeholders are the public and not broadcasters, would the First Amendment itself *require* a right of expressive access?

2. The Court identifies two goals of the First Amendment: to produce "an uninhibited marketplace of ideas" and to produce "an informed public capable of conducting its own affairs." Are these two goals consistent? Which, if either, does the fairness doctrine more readily serve?

3. The Court rejects the view that the fairness doctrine will inevitably prompt broadcasters to curtail coverage of controversial public issues. If there were merit to this argument, would it undermine the Court's constitutional analysis, or merely call into question the wisdom of the fairness doctrine as a matter of policy? Concern that the fairness doctrine in fact inhibited broadcasters' presentation of controversial issues in part prompted the FCC's abandonment of the doctrine in 1987. *See* In re Inquiry into Section 73.1910 of the Commission's Rules and Regulations Concerning the General Fairness Doctrine Obligations of Broadcast Licensees, 102 F.C.C.2d 143 (1985) (explaining FCC's conclusion that the fairness doctrine was no longer necessary); *Syracuse Peace Council*, 2 FCC Rcd. 5043 (1987) (largely abandoning the fairness doctrine).

4. Does the Court's rationale for upholding the fairness doctrine apply outside of the broadcast context? Consider the following case.

Miami Herald Publishing Co. v. Tornillo

Supreme Court of the United States, 1974
418 U.S. 241

MR. CHIEF JUSTICE BURGER delivered the opinion of the Court.

The issue in this case is whether a state statute granting a political candidate a right to equal space to reply to criticism and attacks on his record by a newspaper violates the guarantees of a free press.

I

In the fall of 1972, appellee, Executive Director of the Classroom Teachers Association, apparently a teachers' collective-bargaining agent, was a candidate for the Florida House of Representatives. On September 20, 1972, and again on September 29, 1972, appellant printed editorials critical of appellee's candidacy. In response to these editorials appellee demanded that appellant print verbatim his replies, defending the role of the Classroom Teachers Association and the organization's accomplishments for the citizens of Dade County. Appellant declined to print the appellee's replies and appellee brought suit in Circuit Court, Dade County, seeking declaratory and injunctive relief and actual and punitive damages in excess of $5,000. The action was premised on Florida Statute § 104.38 (1973), a "right of reply" statute which provides that if a candidate for nomination or election is assailed regarding his personal character or official record by any newspaper, the candidate has the right to demand that the newspaper print, free of cost to the candidate, any reply the candidate may make to the newspaper's charges. The reply must appear in as conspicuous a place and in the same kind of type as the charges which prompted the reply, provided it does not take up more space than the charges. Failure to comply with the statute constitutes a first-degree misdemeanor.

Appellant sought a declaration that § 104.38 was unconstitutional. After an emergency hearing requested by appellee, the Circuit Court * * * held that § 104.38 was unconstitutional as an infringement on the freedom of the press under the First and Fourteenth Amendments to the Constitution. The Circuit Court concluded that dictating what a newspaper must print was no different from dictating what it must not print. [The Florida Supreme Court reversed.] * * *

III

The challenged statute creates a right to reply to press criticism of a candidate for nomination or election. * * * The appellee and supporting advocates of an enforceable right of access to the press vigorously argue that government has an obligation to ensure that a wide variety of views reach the public. The contentions of access proponents will be set out in some detail. It is urged that at the time the First Amendment to the Constitution was ratified in 1791 as part of our Bill of Rights the press was broadly representative of the people it was serving. While many of the newspapers were intensely partisan and narrow in their views, the press collectively presented a broad range of opinions to readers. Entry into publishing was inexpensive; pamphlets and books provided meaningful alternatives to the organized press for the expression of unpopular ideas and often treated events and expressed views not covered by conventional newspapers. A true marketplace of ideas existed in which there was relatively easy access to the channels of communication.

Access advocates submit that although newspapers of the present are superficially similar to those of 1791 the press of today is in reality very different from that known in the early years of our national existence. In the past half century a communications revolution has seen the introduction of radio and television into our lives, the promise of a global community through the use of communications satellites, and the spectre of a "wired" nation by means of an expanding cable television network with two-way capabilities. The printed press, it is said, has not escaped the effects of this revolution. Newspapers have become big business and there are far fewer of them to serve a larger literate population. Chains of newspapers, national newspapers, national wire and news services, and one-newspaper towns, are the dominant features of a press that has become noncompetitive and enormously powerful and influential in its capacity to manipulate popular opinion and change the course of events. Major metropolitan newspapers have collaborated to establish news services national in scope. Such national news organizations provide syndicated "interpretive reporting" as well as syndicated features and commentary, all of which can serve as part of the new school of "advocacy journalism."

The elimination of competing newspapers in most of our large cities, and the concentration of control of media that results from the only newspaper's being owned by the same interests which own a television station and a radio station, are important components of this trend toward concentration of control of outlets to inform the public. The result of these vast changes has been to place in a few hands the power to inform the American people and shape public opinion. Much of the editorial opinion and commentary that is printed is that of syndicated columnists distributed nationwide and, as a result, we are told, on national and world issues there tends to be a homogeneity of editorial opinion, commentary, and interpretive analysis. The abuses of bias and manipulative reportage are, likewise, said to be the result of the vast accumulations of unreviewable power in the modern media empires. In effect, it is claimed, the public has lost any ability to respond or to contribute in a meaningful way to the debate on issues. The monopoly of the means of communication allows for little or no critical analysis of the media except in professional journals of very limited readership. * * *

The obvious solution, which was available to dissidents at an earlier time when entry into publishing was relatively inexpensive, today would be to have additional newspapers. But the same economic factors which have caused the disappearance of vast numbers of metropolitan newspapers, have made entry into the marketplace of ideas served by the print media almost impossible. It is urged that the claim of newspapers to be "surrogates for the public" carries with it a concomitant fiduciary obligation to account for that stewardship. From this premise it is reasoned that the only effective way to insure fairness and accuracy and to provide for some accountability is for government to take affirmative action. The First Amendment interest of the public in being informed is said to be in peril because the "marketplace of ideas" is today a monopoly controlled by the owners of the market.

Proponents of enforced access to the press take comfort from language in several of this Court's decisions which suggests that the First Amendment acts as a sword as well as a shield, that it imposes obligations on the owners of the press in addition to protecting the press from government regulation. In *Associated Press v. United States*, 326 U.S. 1, 20 (1945), the Court, in rejecting the argument that the press is immune from the antitrust laws by virtue of the First Amendment, stated:

> "The First Amendment * * * rests on the assumption that the widest possible dissemination of information from diverse and antagonistic sources is essential to the welfare of the public, that a free press is a condition of a free society. Surely a command that the government itself shall not impede the free flow of ideas does not afford non-governmental combinations a refuge if they impose restraints upon that constitutionally guaranteed freedom. Freedom to publish means freedom for all and not for some. Freedom to publish is guaranteed by the Constitution, but freedom to combine to keep others from publishing is not. Freedom of the press from governmental interference under the First Amendment does not sanction repression of that freedom by private interests." (Footnote omitted.) * * *

IV

However much validity may be found in [the] arguments [of access advocates], at each point the implementation of a remedy such as an enforceable right of access necessarily calls for some mechanism, either governmental or consensual. If it is governmental coercion, this at once brings about a confrontation with the express provisions of the First Amendment and the judicial gloss on that Amendment developed over the years.

The Court foresaw the problems relating to government-enforced access as early as its decision in *Associated Press v. United States*. There it carefully contrasted the private "compulsion to print" called for by the Association's bylaws with the provisions of the District Court decree against appellants which "does not compel AP or its members to permit publication of anything which their 'reason' tells them should not be published." 326 U.S., at 20 n.18. In *Branzburg v. Hayes*, 408 U.S. 665, 681 (1972), we emphasized that the cases then before us "involve no intrusions upon speech or assembly, no prior restraint or restriction on what the press may publish, and no express or implied command that the press publish what it prefers to withhold." * * *

We see that beginning with *Associated Press*, the Court has expressed sensitivity as to whether a restriction or requirement constituted the compulsion exerted by government on a newspaper to print that which it would not otherwise print. The clear implication has been that any such compulsion to publish that which "'reason' tells them should not be published" is unconstitutional. A responsible press is an undoubtedly desirable goal, but press responsibility is not mandated by the Constitution and like many other virtues it cannot be legislated.

Appellee's argument that the Florida statute does not amount to a restriction of appellant's right to speak because "the statute in question here has not prevented the *Miami Herald* from saying anything it wished" begs the core question. Compelling editors or publishers to publish that which "'reason' tells them should not be published" is what is at issue in this case. The Florida statute operates as a command in the same sense as a statue or regulation forbidding appellant to publish specified matter. * * *

Faced with the penalties that would accrue to any newspaper that published news or commentary arguably within the reach of the right-of-access statute, editors might well conclude that the safe course is to avoid controversy. Therefore, under the operation of the Florida statute, political and electoral coverage would be blunted or reduced. Government-enforced right of access inescapably "dampens the vigor and limits the variety of public debate," *New York Times Co. v. Sullivan*, 376 U.S. 254, 279 (1964). * * *

Even if a newspaper would face no additional costs to comply with a compulsory access law and would not be forced to forgo publication of news or opinion by the inclusion of a reply, the Florida statute fails to clear the barriers of the First Amendment because of its intrusion into the function of editors. A newspaper is more than a passive receptacle or conduit for news, comment, and advertising. The choice of material to go into a newspaper, and the decisions made as to limitations on the size and content of the paper, and treatment of public issues and public officials—whether fair or unfair—constitute the exercise of editorial control and judgment. It has yet to be demonstrated how governmental regulation of this crucial process can be exercised consistent with First Amendment guarantees of a free press as they have evolved to this time. Accordingly, the judgment of the Supreme Court of Florida is reversed.

[Concurring opinions of Justice Brennan and Justice White omitted.]

Notes and Questions

1. Although the Supreme Court heard the *Tornillo* case only five terms after *Red Lion*, it made no reference to the *Red Lion* decision. Is it possible to reconcile the two cases?

2. In rejecting the challenge to the fairness doctrine in *Red Lion*, the Court focused on the technological barriers to speakers' entry into the broadcast market: because only a finite number of broadcast frequencies are available, the government may properly require a licensee to provide access to others. To what extent could the same argument be made for economic barriers to entry into the print market? *See CBS v. Democratic Nat'l Committee*, 412 U.S. 94, 159 (1973) (Douglas, J., concurring in judgment) ("[The uniqueness of the broadcast medium] is due to engineering and technical problems. * * * But the daily papers now established are unique in the sense that it would be virtually impossible for a competitor to enter the field due to the financial exigencies of the era.").

3. Unlike in the case of the print media, the government issues licenses to broadcasters to use a particular frequency. One might argue that since the government could deny broadcasters this privilege altogether, it may take the lesser step of conditioning a license on a broadcaster's compliance with access requirements. If *Tornillo* is correct, however, and an access right interferes with a First Amendment–based right of editorial control, why is a forced access requirement not barred by the "unconstitutional conditions" doctrine, which prohibits the government from conditioning the grant of a privilege on the waiver of a constitutional right?

4. Is the rationale of *Red Lion* limited to those situations in which the resources are scarce and the channel capacity is therefore limited? If so, is there any justification for regulation of media entities when capacity is not nearly so limited? Consider the dispute over "must-carry" requirements for cable providers.

Note on Must-Carry Requirements

Unlike broadcast, which relies on the transmission and reception of electromagnetic signals, cable systems rely on a wireline connection via coaxial or fiber optic cable between a transmission facility and an individual subscriber's home. Cable systems first developed as a means of facilitating retransmission of broadcast signals where the terrain otherwise blocked reception or where the population was too sparse to support local broadcasters. Despite the connections between broadcast and cable, the FCC initially declined to regulate cable systems. In 1966, however, fearing that cable might supplant broadcast television if left unregulated, the FCC concluded that its authority to regulate broadcasting under the Communications Act of 1934 encompassed an ancillary authority to regulate cable.

Among the regulations the FCC sought to impose on cable systems were "must-carry" requirements—that is, requirements that a cable operator carry all local broadcast television signals within the cable system's service area. Courts invalidated different versions of such regulations on First Amendment grounds. *See Quincy Cable TV, Inc. v. FCC*, 768 F.2d 1434 (D.C. Cir. 1985);

Century Communications Corp. v. FCC, 835 F.2d 292 (D.C. Cir. 1987), *clarified*, 837 F.2d 517 (D.C. Cir. 1988). In 1992, Congress imposed must-carry rules on cable system operators by statute.

How do must-carry requirements differ from the requirements of the fairness doctrine at issue in *Red Lion* and from the right-of-reply statute at issue in *Tornillo*? On what grounds might the imposition of must-carry requirements survive First Amendment scrutiny after *Tornillo*? The Court considered this question in *Turner Broadcasting*.

Turner Broadcasting System, Inc. v. FCC

Supreme Court of the United States, 1994
512 U.S. 622

JUSTICE KENNEDY announced the judgment of the Court and delivered the opinion of the Court, except as to Part III-B.

I

B

* * * At issue in this case is the constitutionality of the so-called must-carry provisions, contained in §§ 4 and 5 of the [Cable Television Consumer Protection and Competition Act of 1992,] which require cable operators to carry the signals of a specified number of local broadcast television stations.

Section 4 requires carriage of "local commercial television stations," defined to include all full power television broadcasters, other than those qualifying as "noncommercial educational" stations under § 5, that operate within the same television market as the cable system. Cable systems with more than 12 active channels, and more than 300 subscribers, are required to set aside up to one-third of their channels for commercial broadcast stations that request carriage. Cable systems with more than 300 subscribers, but only 12 or fewer active channels, must carry the signals of three commercial broadcast stations. If there are fewer broadcasters requesting carriage than slots made available under the Act, the cable operator is obligated to carry only those broadcasters who make the request. If, however, there are more requesting broadcast stations than slots available, the cable operator is permitted to choose which of these stations it will carry. The broadcast signals carried under this provision must be transmitted on a continuous, uninterrupted basis and must be placed in the same numerical channel position as when broadcast over the air. Further, subject to a few exceptions, a cable operator may not charge a fee for carrying broadcast signals in fulfillment of its must-carry obligations.

Section 5 of the Act imposes similar requirements regarding the carriage of local public broadcast television stations, referred to in the Act as local "noncommercial educational television stations." A cable system with 12 or fewer channels must carry one of these stations; a system of between 13 and 36 channels must carry between one and three; and a system with more than 36 channels must carry each local public broadcast station requesting carriage. The Act requires a cable operator to import distant signals in certain circumstances but provides protection against substantial duplication of local noncommercial educational stations. As with commercial broadcast stations, § 5 requires cable system operators to carry the program schedule of the public broadcast station in its entirety and at its same over-the-air channel position.

C

Congress enacted the 1992 Cable Act after conducting three years of hearings on the structure and operation of the cable television industry. The conclusions Congress drew from its factfinding process are recited in the text of the Act itself. In brief, Congress found that the physical characteristics of cable transmission, compounded by the increasing concentration of economic power in the cable industry, are endangering the ability of over-the-air broadcast television stations to compete for a viewing audience and thus for necessary operating revenues. Congress determined that regulation of the market for video programming was necessary to correct this competitive imbalance.

In particular, Congress found that over 60 percent of the households with television sets subscribe to cable, and for these households cable has replaced over-the-air broadcast television as the primary provider of video programming. This is so, Congress found, because "[m]ost subscribers to cable television systems do not or cannot maintain antennas to receive broadcast television services, do not have input selector switches to convert from a cable to antenna reception system, or cannot otherwise receive broadcast television services." In addition, Congress concluded that due to "local franchising requirements and the extraordinary expense of constructing more than one cable television system to serve a particular geographic area," the overwhelming majority of cable operators exercise a monopoly over cable service. "The result," Congress determined, "is undue market power for the cable operator as compared to that of consumers and video programmers."

According to Congress, this market position gives cable operators the power and the incentive to harm broadcast competitors. The power derives from the cable operator's ability, as owner of the transmission facility, to "terminate the retransmission of the broadcast signal, refuse to carry new signals, or reposition a broadcast signal to a disadvantageous channel position." The incentive derives from the economic reality that "[c]able television systems and broadcast television stations increasingly compete for television advertising revenues." By refusing carriage of broadcasters' signals, cable operators, as a practical matter, can reduce the number of households that have access to the broadcasters' programming, and thereby capture advertising dollars that would otherwise go to broadcast stations.

Congress found, in addition, that increased vertical integration in the cable industry is making it even harder for broadcasters to secure carriage on cable systems, because cable operators have a financial incentive to favor their affiliated programmers. Congress also determined that the cable industry is characterized by horizontal concentration, with many cable operators sharing common ownership. This has resulted in greater "barriers to entry for new programmers and a reduction in the number of media voices available to consumers."

In light of these technological and economic conditions, Congress concluded that unless cable operators are required to carry local broadcast stations, "[t]here is a substantial likelihood that . . . additional local broadcast signals will be deleted, repositioned, or not carried"; the "marked shift in market share" from broadcast to cable will continue to erode the advertising revenue base which sustains free local broadcast television; and that, as a consequence, "the economic viability of free local broadcast television and its ability to originate quality local programming will be seriously jeopardized."

D

* * * Appellants, plaintiffs below, are numerous cable programmers and cable operators. After additional parties intervened, a three-judge District Court convened to hear the actions. * * * [T]he District Court, in a divided opinion, granted summary judgment in favor of the Government and the other intervenor-defendants, ruling that the must-carry provisions are consistent with the First Amendment. * * * This direct appeal followed.

II

There can be no disagreement on an initial premise: Cable programmers and cable operators engage in and transmit speech, and they are entitled to the protection of the speech and press provisions of the First Amendment. Through "original programming or by exercising editorial discretion over which stations or programs to include in its repertoire," cable programmers and operators "see[k] to communicate messages on a wide variety of topics and in a wide variety of formats." *Los Angeles v. Preferred Communications, Inc.*, 476 U.S. 488, 494 (1986). By requiring cable systems to set aside a portion of their channels for local broadcasters, the must-carry rules regulate cable speech in two respects: The rules reduce the number of channels over which cable operators exercise unfettered control, and they render it more difficult for cable programmers to compete for carriage on the limited channels remaining. Nevertheless, because not every interference with speech triggers the same degree of scrutiny under the First Amendment, we must decide at the outset the level of scrutiny applicable to the must-carry provisions.

A

We address first the Government's contention that regulation of cable television should be analyzed under the same First Amendment standard that applies to regulation of broadcast television. It is true that our cases have permitted more intrusive regulation of broadcast speakers than of speakers in other media. Compare *Red Lion Broadcasting Co. v. FCC*, 395 U.S. 367 (1969) (television), and *National Broadcasting Co. v. United States*, 319 U.S. 190 (1943) (radio), with *Miami Herald Publishing Co. v. Tornillo*, 418 U.S. 241 (1974) (print), and *Riley v. National Federation of Blind of N.C., Inc.*, 487 U.S. 781 (1988) (personal solicitation). But the rationale for applying a less rigorous standard of First Amendment scrutiny to broadcast regulation, whatever its validity in the cases elaborating it, does not apply in the context of cable regulation.

The justification for our distinct approach to broadcast regulation rests upon the unique physical limitations of the broadcast medium. As a general matter, there are more would-be broadcasters than frequencies available in the electromagnetic spectrum. And if two broadcasters were to attempt to transmit over the same frequency in the same locale, they would interfere with one another's signals, so that neither could be heard at all. The scarcity of broadcast frequencies thus required the establishment of some regulatory mechanism to divide the electromagnetic spectrum and assign specific frequencies to particular broadcasters. In addition, the inherent physical limitation on the number of speakers who may use the broadcast medium has been thought to require some adjustment in traditional First Amendment analysis to permit the Government to place limited content restraints, and impose certain affirmative obligations, on broadcast licensees. As we said in *Red Lion*, "[w]here there are substantially more individuals who want to broadcast than there are frequencies to allocate, it is idle to posit an unabridgeable First Amendment right to broadcast comparable to the right of every individual to speak, write, or publish." 395 U.S., at 388.

Although courts and commentators have criticized the scarcity rationale since its inception, we have declined to question its continuing validity as support for our broadcast jurisprudence and see no reason to do so here. The broadcast cases are inapposite in the present context because cable television does not suffer from the inherent limitations that characterize the broadcast medium. Indeed, given the rapid advances in fiber optics and digital compression technology, soon there may be no practical limitation on the number of speakers who may use the cable medium. Nor is there any danger of physical interference between two cable speakers attempting to share the same channel. In light of these fundamental technological differences between broadcast and cable transmission, application of the more relaxed standard of scrutiny adopted in *Red Lion* and the other broadcast cases is inapt when determining the First Amendment validity of cable regulation. * * *

Although the Government acknowledges the substantial technological differences between broadcast and cable, it advances a second argument for application of the *Red Lion* framework to cable regulation. It asserts that the foundation of our broadcast jurisprudence is not the physical limitations of the electromagnetic spectrum, but rather the "market dysfunction" that characterizes the broadcast market. Because the cable market is beset by a similar dysfunction, the Government maintains, the *Red Lion* standard of review should also apply to cable. While we agree that the cable market suffers certain structural impediments, the Government's argument is flawed in two respects. First, as discussed above, the special physical characteristics of broadcast transmission, not the economic characteristics of the broadcast market, are what underlies our broadcast jurisprudence. Second, the mere assertion of dysfunction or failure in a speech market, without more, is not sufficient to shield a speech regulation from the First Amendment standards applicable to nonbroadcast media. See, *e.g.*, *Miami Herald Publishing Co. v. Tornillo*, 418 U.S., at 248-258. * * *

B

* * * [T]he First Amendment, subject only to narrow and well-understood exceptions, does not countenance governmental control over the content of messages expressed by private individuals. Our precedents thus apply the most exacting scrutiny to regulations that suppress, disadvantage, or impose differential burdens upon speech because of its content. Laws that compel speakers to utter or distribute speech bearing a particular message are subject

to the same rigorous scrutiny. In contrast, regulations that are unrelated to the content of speech are subject to an intermediate level of scrutiny, because in most cases they pose a less substantial risk of excising certain ideas or viewpoints from the public dialogue. * * *

C

Insofar as they pertain to the carriage of full-power broadcasters, the must-carry rules, on their face, impose burdens and confer benefits without reference to the content of speech.[6] Although the provisions interfere with cable operators' editorial discretion by compelling them to offer carriage to a certain minimum number of broadcast stations, the extent of the interference does not depend upon the content of the cable operators' programming. The rules impose obligations upon all operators, save those with fewer than 300 subscribers, regardless of the programs or stations they now offer or have offered in the past. Nothing in the Act imposes a restriction, penalty, or burden by reason of the views, programs, or stations the cable operator has selected or will select. The number of channels a cable operator must set aside depends only on the operator's channel capacity; hence, an operator cannot avoid or mitigate its obligations under the Act by altering the programming it offers to subscribers. Cf. *Miami Herald Publishing Co. v. Tornillo*, 418 U.S., at 256-257 (newspaper may avoid access obligations by refraining from speech critical of political candidates).

The must-carry provisions also burden cable programmers by reducing the number of channels for which they can compete. But, again, this burden is unrelated to content, for it extends to all cable programmers irrespective of the programming they choose to offer viewers. And finally, the privileges conferred by the must-carry provisions are also unrelated to content. The rules benefit all full power broadcasters who request carriage—be they commercial or noncommercial, independent or network affiliated, English or Spanish language, religious or secular. The aggregate effect of the rules is thus to make every full power commercial and noncommercial broadcaster eligible for must-carry, provided only that the broadcaster operates within the same television market as a cable system.

It is true that the must-carry provisions distinguish between speakers in the television programming market. But they do so based only upon the manner in which speakers transmit their messages to viewers, and not upon the messages they carry: Broadcasters, which transmit over the airwaves, are

---

6. The must-carry rules also require carriage, under certain limited circumstances, of low-power broadcast stations. Under the Act, a low-power station may become eligible for carriage only if, among other things, the FCC determines that the station's programming "would address local news and informational needs which are not being adequately served by full power television broadcast stations because of the geographic distance of such full power stations from the low power station's community of license." We recognize that this aspect of § 4 appears to single out certain low-power broadcasters for special benefits on the basis of content. Because the District Court did not address whether these particular provisions are content based, and because the parties make only the most glancing reference to the operation of, and justifications for, the low-power broadcast provisions, we think it prudent to allow the District Court to consider the content-neutral or content-based character of this provision in the first instance on remand. * * *

favored, while cable programmers, which do not, are disfavored. Cable operators, too, are burdened by the carriage obligations, but only because they control access to the cable conduit. So long as they are not a subtle means of exercising a content preference, speaker distinctions of this nature are not presumed invalid under the First Amendment.

That the must-carry provisions, on their face, do not burden or benefit speech of a particular content does not end the inquiry. Our cases have recognized that even a regulation neutral on its face may be content based if its manifest purpose is to regulate speech because of the message it conveys. Appellants contend, in this regard, that the must-carry regulations are content based because Congress' purpose in enacting them was to promote speech of a favored content. We do not agree. Our review of the Act and its various findings persuades us that Congress' overriding objective in enacting must-carry was not to favor programming of a particular subject matter, viewpoint, or format, but rather to preserve access to free television programming for the 40 percent of Americans without cable.

In unusually detailed statutory findings, Congress explained that because cable systems and broadcast stations compete for local advertising revenue, and because cable operators have a vested financial interest in favoring their affiliated programmers over broadcast stations, cable operators have a built-in "economic incentive . . . to delete, reposition, or not carry local broadcast signals." Congress concluded that absent a requirement that cable systems carry the signals of local broadcast stations, the continued availability of free local broadcast television would be threatened. * * * By preventing cable operators from refusing carriage to broadcast television stations, the must-carry rules ensure that broadcast television stations will retain a large enough potential audience to earn necessary advertising revenue—or, in the case of noncommercial broadcasters, sufficient viewer contributions—to maintain their continued operation. * * * This overriding congressional purpose is unrelated to the content of expression disseminated by cable and broadcast speakers. * * *

Appellants and Justice O'Connor make much of the fact that, in the course of describing the purposes behind the Act, Congress referred to the value of broadcast programming. In particular, Congress noted that broadcast television is "an important source of local news[,] public affairs programming and other local broadcast services critical to an informed electorate," and that noncommercial television "provides educational and informational programming to the Nation's citizens." We do not think, however, that such references cast any material doubt on the content-neutral character of must-carry. That Congress acknowledged the local orientation of broadcast programming and the role that noncommercial stations have played in educating the public does not indicate that Congress regarded broadcast programming as *more* valuable than cable programming. Rather, it reflects nothing more than the recognition that the services provided by broadcast television have some intrinsic value and, thus, are worth preserving against the threats posed by cable. * * *

In short, the must-carry provisions are not designed to favor or disadvantage speech of any particular content. Rather, they are meant to protect broadcast television from what Congress determined to be unfair competition by cable systems. In enacting the provisions, Congress sought to preserve the existing structure of the Nation's broadcast television medium while permitting the concomitant expansion and development of cable television, and, in particular, to ensure that broadcast television remains available as a source of video programming for those without cable. Appellants' ability to hypothesize a content-based purpose for these provisions rests on little more than speculation and does not cast doubt upon the content-neutral character of must-carry. Indeed, "[i]t is a familiar principle of constitutional law that this Court will not strike down an otherwise constitutional statute on the basis of an alleged illicit legislative motive." *United States v. O'Brien*, 391 U.S. 367, 383 (1968).

D

Appellants advance * * * additional arguments to support their view that the must-carry provisions warrant strict scrutiny[, including the argument that] the provisions compel speech by cable operators * * * . Appellants maintain that the must-carry provisions trigger strict scrutiny because they compel cable operators to transmit speech not of their choosing. Relying principally on *Miami Herald Publishing Co. v. Tornillo*, 418 U.S. 241 (1974), appellants say this intrusion on the editorial control of cable operators amounts to forced speech which, if not *per se* invalid, can be justified only if narrowly tailored to a compelling government interest.

Tornillo affirmed an essential proposition: The First Amendment protects the editorial independence of the press. The right-of-reply statute at issue in *Tornillo* required any newspaper that assailed a political candidate's character to print, upon request by the candidate and without cost, the candidate's reply in equal space and prominence. Although the statute did not censor speech in the traditional sense—it only required newspapers to grant access to the messages of others—we found that it imposed an impermissible content-based burden on newspaper speech. Because the right of access at issue in *Tornillo* was triggered only when a newspaper elected to print matter critical of political candidates, it "exact[ed] a penalty on the basis of . . . content." *Id.*, at 256. We found, and continue to recognize, that right-of-reply statutes of this sort are an impermissible intrusion on newspapers' "editorial control and judgment." *Id.*, at 258.

We explained that, in practical effect, Florida's right-of-reply statute would deter newspapers from speaking in unfavorable terms about political candidates:

> "Faced with the penalties that would accrue to any newspaper that published news or commentary arguably within the reach of the right-of-access statute, editors might well conclude that the safe course is to avoid controversy. Therefore, under the operation of the Florida statute, political and electoral coverage would be blunted or reduced." *Id.*, at 257.

Moreover, by affording mandatory access to speakers with which the newspaper disagreed, the law induced the newspaper to respond to the candidates' replies when it might have preferred to remain silent. See *Pacific Gas & Elec. Co. v. Public Util. Comm'n of Cal.*, 475 U.S. 1, 11 (1986) (plurality opinion).

The same principles led us to invalidate a similar content-based access regulation in *Pacific Gas & Electric*. At issue was a rule requiring a privately owned utility, on a quarterly basis, to include with its monthly bills an editorial newsletter published by a consumer group critical of the utility's ratemaking practices. Although the access requirement applicable to the utility, unlike the statutory mechanism in *Tornillo*, was not triggered by speech of any particular content, the plurality held that the same strict First Amendment scrutiny applied. Like the statute in *Tornillo*, the regulation conferred benefits to speakers based on viewpoint, giving access only to a consumer group opposing the utility's practices. 475 U.S., at 13, 15. The plurality observed that in order to avoid the appearance that it agreed with the group's views, the utility would "feel compelled to respond to arguments and allegations made by [the group] in its messages to [the utility's] customers." *Id.*, at 16. This "kind of forced response," the plurality explained, "is antithetical to the free discussion that the First Amendment seeks to foster." *Ibid.*

Tornillo and *Pacific Gas & Electric* do not control this case for the following reasons. First, unlike the access rules struck down in those cases, the must-carry rules are content neutral in application. They are not activated by any particular message spoken by cable operators and thus exact no content-based penalty. Likewise, they do not grant access to broadcasters on the ground that the content of broadcast programming will counterbalance the messages of cable operators. Instead, they confer benefits upon all full-power, local broadcasters, whatever the content of their programming.

Second, appellants do not suggest, nor do we think it the case, that must-carry will force cable operators to alter their own messages to respond to the broadcast programming they are required to carry. Given cable's long history of serving as a conduit for broadcast signals, there appears little risk that cable viewers would assume that the broadcast stations carried on a cable system convey ideas or messages endorsed by the cable operator. Indeed, broadcasters are required by federal regulation to identify themselves at least once every hour, and it is a common practice for broadcasters to disclaim any identity of viewpoint between the management and the speakers who use the broadcast facility. Moreover, in contrast to the statute at issue in *Tornillo*, no aspect of the must-carry provisions would cause a cable operator or cable programmer to conclude that "the safe course is to avoid controversy," *Tornillo*, 418 U.S., at 257, and by so doing diminish the free flow of information and ideas.

Finally, the asserted analogy to *Tornillo* ignores an important technological difference between newspapers and cable television. Although a daily newspaper and a cable operator both may enjoy monopoly status in a given locale, the cable operator exercises far greater control over access to the relevant medium. A daily newspaper, no matter how secure its local monopoly, does not possess the power to obstruct readers' access to other competing publications—whether they be weekly local newspapers, or daily newspapers published in other cities. Thus, when a newspaper asserts exclusive control over its own news copy, it does not thereby prevent other newspapers from being distributed to willing recipients in the same locale.

The same is not true of cable. When an individual subscribes to cable, the physical connection between the television set and the cable network gives the cable operator bottleneck, or gatekeeper, control over most (if not all) of the television programming that is channeled into the subscriber's home. Hence, simply by virtue of its ownership of the essential pathway for cable speech, a cable operator can prevent its subscribers from obtaining access to programming it chooses to exclude. A cable operator, unlike speakers in other media, can thus silence the voice of competing speakers with a mere flick of the switch.

The potential for abuse of this private power over a central avenue of communication cannot be overlooked. The First Amendment's command that government not impede the freedom of speech does not disable the government from taking steps to ensure that private interests not restrict, through physical control of a critical pathway of communication, the free flow of information and ideas. We thus reject appellants' contention that *Tornillo* and *Pacific Gas & Electric* require strict scrutiny of the access rules in question here. * * *

III

A

* * * We agree with the District Court that the appropriate standard by which to evaluate the constitutionality of must-carry is the intermediate level of scrutiny applicable to content-neutral restrictions that impose an incidental burden on speech.

Under *O'Brien*, a content-neutral regulation will be sustained if

"it furthers an important or substantial governmental interest; if the governmental interest is unrelated to the suppression of free expression; and if the incidental restriction on alleged First Amendment freedoms is no greater than is essential to the furtherance of that interest." 391 U.S. at 377.

To satisfy this standard, a regulation need not be the least speech-restrictive means of advancing the Government's interests. "Rather, the requirement of narrow tailoring is satisfied 'so long as the . . . regulation promotes a substantial government interest that would be achieved less effectively absent the regulation.'" *Ward v. Rock Against Racism*, 491 U.S. 781, 799 (1989) (quoting *United States v. Albertini*, 472 U.S. 675, 689 (1985)). Narrow tailoring in this context requires, in other words, that the means chosen do not "burden substantially more speech than is necessary to further the government's legitimate interests." *Ibid*.

Congress declared that the must-carry provisions serve three interrelated interests: (1) preserving the benefits of free, over-the-air local broadcast television, (2) promoting the widespread dissemination of information from a multiplicity of sources, and (3) promoting fair competition in the market for television programming. None of these interests is related to the "suppression of free expression," *O'Brien*, 391 U.S. at 377. And viewed in the abstract, we have no difficulty concluding that each of them is an important governmental interest. * * *

B

That the Government's asserted interests are important in the abstract does not mean, however, that the must-carry rules will in fact advance those interests. * * * The Government's assertion that the must-carry rules are necessary to protect the viability of broadcast television rests on two essential propositions: (1) that unless cable operators are compelled to carry broadcast stations, significant numbers of broadcast stations will be refused carriage on cable systems; and (2) that the broadcast stations denied carriage will either deteriorate to a substantial degree or fail altogether. * * * Without a more substantial elaboration in the District Court of the predictive or historical evidence upon which Congress relied, or the introduction of some additional evidence to establish that the dropped or repositioned broadcasters would be at serious risk of financial difficulty, we cannot determine whether the threat to broadcast television is real enough to overcome the challenge to the provisions made by these appellants. * * *

Also lacking are any findings concerning the actual effects of must-carry on the speech of cable operators and cable programmers—*i.e.*, the extent to which cable operators will, in fact, be forced to make changes in their current or anticipated programming selections; the degree to which cable programmers will be dropped from cable systems to make room for local broadcasters; and the extent to which cable operators can satisfy their must-carry obligations by devoting previously unused channel capacity to the carriage of local broadcasters. The answers to these and perhaps other questions are critical to the narrow tailoring step of the *O'Brien* analysis, for unless we know the extent to which the must-carry provisions in fact interfere with protected speech, we cannot say whether they suppress "substantially more speech than . . . necessary" to ensure the viability of broadcast television. *Ward*, 491 U.S., at 799. Finally, the record fails to provide any judicial findings concerning the availability and efficacy of "constitutionally acceptable less restrictive means" of achieving the Government's asserted interests. See *Sable Communications of Cal., Inc. v. FCC*, 492 U.S. 115, 129 (1989).

In sum, because there are genuine issues of material fact still to be resolved on this record, we hold that the District Court erred in granting summary judgment in favor of the Government. * * * The judgment below is vacated, and the case is remanded for further proceedings consistent with this opinion.

[Opinions of Justice Blackmun, concurring, Justice Stevens, concurring in part and concurring in the judgment,[a] Justice O'Connor, concurring in part and dissenting in part, and Justice Ginsburg, concurring in part and dissenting in part, omitted.]

Notes and Questions

1. The Court concludes that the must-carry regulations are not subject to strict scrutiny in part because cable operators enjoy a monopoly power. In light of *Tornillo*'s apparent rejection of an economic justification for permitting

---

a. Justice Stevens declined to join Part III-B of Justice Kennedy's opinion, arguing that the District Court's judgment sustaining the must-carry provisions should be affirmed. Because a vote to affirm would have meant that no disposition of the appeal would have commanded the support of a majority of the Court, Justice Stevens concurred in the judgment vacating and remanding for further proceedings.

a government-enforced right of expressive access, does the Court adequately distinguish that case?

2. Does *Turner* signal a new way of understanding the ability of government to regulate the relationship between speakers and conduits? Consider the following analysis:

> Under *Turner*, (a) government may regulate (not merely subsidize) new speech sources so as to ensure access for viewers who would otherwise be without free programming and (b) government may require owners of speech sources to provide access to speakers, at least if the owners are not conventional speakers too; but (c) government must do all this on a content-neutral basis (at least as a general rule); but (d) government may support its regulation not only by reference to the provision of "access to free television programming" but also by invoking such democratic goals as the need to ensure "an outlet for exchange on matters of local concern" and "access to a multiplicity of information sources." * * * This [approach] is likely to have continuing importance in governmental efforts to control the information superhighway so as to ensure viewer and listener access.

Cass R. Sunstein, *The First Amendment in Cyberspace*, 104 YALE L.J. 1757, 1774 (1995). If courts adopted this approach with regard to, say, Internet service providers, what sorts of governmental regulations might be permissible?

3. Even though *Turner* ultimately permits the governmental regulations at issue, the Court appears to accept that the media entities have First Amendment rights comparable to individual speakers. But is there an argument that cable operators, as business entities, are significantly different from individuals, who speak as an aspect of personal autonomy? Might we therefore allow content-based (though perhaps not viewpoint-based) laws imposed on the media as long as the law does not suppress expression or undermine the media's integrity? For example, we might permit the government to require broadcasters to include children-oriented programming or to cover controversial issues (so long as there was no proscribed point of view). *See* C. Edwin Baker, Turner Broadcasting: *Content-Based Regulation of Persons and Presses*, 1994 SUP. CT. REV. 57.

On the other hand, don't the "must-carry" regulations necessarily suppress expression? After all, because of the regulations, cable operators with at least a somewhat limited number of channels (or at least a limited number of channels consumers are likely to surf through) must allocate prime channels to content preferred by Congress, rather than other content that the broadcasters (or their consumers) might prefer. Is this a proper role for government? Or, conversely, is it an inevitable role of government and not a cause for concern?

4. On remand, the district court made detailed factual findings and concluded that the must-carry provisions did in fact further the interests asserted by the government in "(1) preserving the benefits of free, over-the-air local broadcast television, (2) promoting the widespread dissemination of information from a multiplicity of sources, and (3) promoting fair competition in the market for television programming." The court also ruled that the statute was narrowly tailored. *See Turner Broadcasting Sys., Inc. v. FCC*, 910

F. Supp. 734 (D.D.C. 1995). The Supreme Court affirmed by a vote of 5-4. *See Turner Broadcasting Sys., Inc. v. FCC*, 516 U.S. 1110 (1996).

5. How would you apply the principles of *Turner* to, say, the question of how to regulate search engines? Mightn't Google be required to obey certain guidelines with regard to how it ranks or displays sites? What if the legislature tried to create statutory guidelines to prevent discriminatory rankings? Consider, for example, the recommendations made by Professor Pasquale earlier in this chapter. Would such initiatives be constitutional under *Turner*, or would they violate Google's First Amendment rights? In this regard, do you think search engines have greater First Amendment rights than the credit and bond ratings agencies discussed by Pasquale and the judge in *Search King v. Google*?

6. Do the cases addressing a right of expressive access to traditional media entities embrace a consistent view of the role of the First Amendment in fostering democratic discourse? What role *should* the government play in shaping the speech market? Consider the following view.

Owen M. Fiss, *Why the State?*

100 HARV. L. REV. 781 (1987)

Most agree that the first amendment seeks to further democracy by protecting collective self-determination * * * [, but we are] divided over the mediating principle that gives fullest expression to that ideal. * * * [The division is] between autonomy and public debate. These two principles represent different ways of understanding and furthering the democratic purposes of the first amendment. The distinction between the autonomy principle and the public debate principle is, moreover, crucial for explaining why the state has a role to play in furthering free speech values.

Those who reduce the first amendment to a limit on state action tend to regard it as a protection of autonomy. The individual is allowed to say what he or she wishes, free from interference from the state. It is as though a zone of noninterference were placed around each individual, and the state (and the state alone) were prohibited from crossing the boundary. Even in this account, however, autonomy is not protected as an end in itself, nor as a means of individual self-actualization. Rather, it is seen as a way of furthering the larger political purposes attributed to the first amendment. It is assumed that the protection of autonomy will produce a debate on issues of public importance that is, to use Justice Brennan's now classic formula, "uninhibited, robust, and wide-open."[7] Of course, rich public debate will not itself ensure self-governance, because the electorate must still listen to what is said and act on the basis of what it learns, but free debate still remains an essential precondition for democratic government, and autonomy is seen as the method of bringing that debate into being.

---

7. *New York Times Co. v. Sullivan*, 376 U.S. 254, 270 (1964).

Some may dispute this instrumental view of autonomy, but it is embraced by people as far apart on the political spectrum as Harry Kalven and Robert Bork and now dominates our thinking about the first amendment. It is rooted in the fact that the free speech guarantee appears as part of a legal instrument, the Constitution, which is for the most part concerned with establishing the structure of government. The instrumental theory also explains why speech, among the many ways of self-actualization, is singled out by the Constitution, why the autonomy protected under the first amendment could belong to institutions (CBS or the NAACP) as well as to individuals, and why speech could be preferred even when it harms someone else and thus infringes on that person's efforts at self-actualization. The linkage between autonomy and democracy also accounts for the favored position in first amendment jurisprudence of the rule against content regulation. The hope is that a rule denying the state power to silence speech on the basis of its content will produce the broadest possible debate.

In some social settings, the instrumental assumption underlying the protection of autonomy may be well founded. In a Jeffersonian democracy, for example, where the dominant social unit is the individual and power is distributed equally, autonomy might well enhance public debate and thus promote collective self-determination. But in modern society, characterized by grossly unequal distributions of power and a limited capacity of people to learn all that they must to function effectively as citizens, this assumption appears more problematic. Protecting autonomy by placing a zone of noninterference around the individual or certain institutions is likely to produce a public debate that is dominated, and thus constrained, by the same forces that dominate social structure, not a debate that is "uninhibited, robust, and wide-open."

The public debate principle, in contrast, acknowledges the problematic character of the instrumental assumption underlying the protection of autonomy and seeks to provide a foundation for the necessary corrective action. The purpose of the first amendment remains what it was under autonomy—to protect the ability of people, as a collectivity, to decide their own fate. Rich public debate also continues to appear as an essential precondition for the exercise of that sovereign prerogative. But now action is judged by its impact on public debate, a social state of affairs, rather than by whether it constrains or otherwise interferes with the autonomy of some individual or institution. The concern is not with the frustration of would-be speakers, but with the quality of public discourse. Autonomy may be protected, but only when it enriches public debate. It might well have to be sacrificed when, for example, the speech of some drowns out the voices of others or systematically distorts the public agenda.

Disfavoring state action is not the same as precluding such action altogether. Those who read the first amendment as a protection of autonomy are not necessarily committed to the absolutist position identified with Justice Black (who insisted that "no law" means "no law").[10] They sometimes allow the state to cross the boundary and interfere with autonomy in order to serve

---

10. See, e.g., New York Times Co. v. United States, 403 U.S. 713, 717-18 (1971) (Black, J., concurring).

other social interests; speakers may, for example, be silenced to preserve public order or to protect interests in reputation. What the autonomy principle does, however, is to create a very strong presumption against state interference with speech. But under the public debate principle, there is no such presumption against the state. The state stands on equal footing with other institutions and is allowed, encouraged, and sometimes required to enact measures or issue decrees that enrich public debate, even if that action entails an interference with the speech of some and thus a denial of autonomy.

Of course, the state might act wrongfully, and thereby restrict or impoverish rather than enhance public debate. We must always stand on guard against this danger, but we should do so mindful of the fact that this same danger is presented by all social institutions, private or public, and that there is no reason for presuming that the state will be more likely to exercise its power to distort public debate than would any other institution. It has no special incentive to do so; government officials like to preserve their positions and the system that brought them to power, but the same can be said of the owners and managers of so-called private enterprises, who might well use their power to protect themselves and those government officials who serve their interests. Admittedly, the state does have some unique resources at its disposal, including a monopoly over the lawful means of violence, but once we cease to think of the state as a monolith (the Leviathan) and realize that it is a network of competing and overlapping agencies, one checking another, and all being checked by private institutions, that power will appear less remarkable and less fearsome. We will come to see that the state's monopoly over the lawful infliction of violence is not a true measure of its power and that the power of an agency, like the FCC, is no greater than that of CBS. Terror comes in many forms. The powers of the FCC and CBS differ, one regulates while the other edits, but there is no reason for believing that one kind of power will be more inhibiting or limiting of public debate than the other. The state, like any other institution, can act either as a friend or enemy of speech and, without falling back on the libertarian presumption, we must learn to recognize when it is acting in one capacity rather than another.

II.

Today, public debate is dominated by the television networks and a number of large newspapers and magazines. The competition among these institutions is far from perfect, and some might argue for state intervention on a theory of market failure. There is a great deal of force to those arguments, but they obscure a deeper truth—a market, even one that is working perfectly, is itself a structure of constraint. A fully competitive market might produce a diversity of programs, formats, and reportage, but, to borrow an image of Renata Adler's, it will be the diversity of "a pack going essentially in one direction."[11]

The market constrains the presentation of matters of public interest and importance in two ways. First, the market privileges select groups, by making programs, journals, and newspapers especially responsive to their needs and

---

11. R. ADLER, RECKLESS DISREGARD 17 (1986).

desires. One such group consists of those who have the capital to acquire or own a television station, newspaper, or journal; another consists of those who control the advertising budgets of various businesses; and still another consists of those who are most able and most likely to respond enthusiastically to advertising. The number in the last group is no doubt quite large (it probably includes every nine-year-old who can bully his or her parents into purchasing one thing or another), but it is not coextensive with the electorate. To be a consumer, even a sovereign one, is not to be a citizen.

Second, the market brings to bear on editorial and programming decisions factors that might have a greater deal to do with profitability or allocative efficiency (to look at matters from a societal point of view) but little to do with the democratic needs of the electorate. For a businessman, the costs of production and the revenue likely to be generated are highly pertinent factors in determining what shows to run and when, or what to feature in a newspaper; a perfectly competitive market will produce shows or publications whose marginal cost equals marginal revenue. Reruns of I Love Lucy are profitable and an efficient use of resources. So is MTV. But there is no necessary, or even probabilistic, relationship between making a profit (or allocating resources efficiently) and supplying the electorate with the information they need to make free and intelligent choices about government policy, the structure of government, or the nature of society. This point was well understood when we freed our educational systems and our universities from the grasp of the market, and it applies with equal force to the media. * * *

Drawing on the power of taxation and its organizational advantages, the state can discharge its corrective function through the provision of subsidies. Examples of this form of state intervention include aid to public libraries, public schools, private and state universities, public broadcasting, and presidential candidates. These subsidies make an enormous contribution to public discourse and further first amendment values, although we would never know it from a reading of the first amendment that emphasizes the protection of autonomy. Autonomy is not a bar to such state activities, but it does produce a constitutional indifference, leaving these activities to suffer the vicissitudes of a politics itself dominated by the market. Under the public debate principle such action is favored and, when inaction becomes a form of action, it may also be required, although the remedial problems of implementing such an affirmative duty are acute and well known. With respect to the other form of state intervention—state action of a regulatory or prohibitory nature—the autonomy principle does have strong legal implications, and some of those are most unfortunate. The strong presumption against the state rooted in the autonomy principle has, for example, resulted in the invalidation of laws imposing ceilings on political expenditures. It has also placed a constitutional cloud over the fairness doctrine, precluding the extension of that doctrine to the print media, enfeebling its enforcement, and putting its very existence in question. Autonomy provides the proponents of deregulation with a constitutional platform that is ill deserved.

Notes and Questions

1. To what extent do the "autonomy" and "public debate" visions of the First Amendment underlie the Supreme Court's decisions in *Red Lion*, *Tornillo*, and *Turner*? Which vision do you find most convincing?

2. Professor Fiss argues that government intervention in the traditional speech marketplace is necessary not only because that market is controlled by a concentration of economically powerful interests, but because even a fully competitive market is likely to underproduce the kind of speech needed to yield an informed electorate. Even assuming that Professor Fiss's empirical assessments are correct, does his argument sufficiently take into account the risks to free expression values posed by a government-enforced right of expressive access? Why or why not? For a discussion of these perceived risks, see Martin H. Redish & Kirk J. Kaludis, *The Right of Expressive Access in First Amendment Theory: Redistributive Values and the Democratic Dilemma*, 93 Nw. U. L. Rev. 1083 (1999) (arguing that "the dangers far outweigh the limited and speculative benefits to the interests in free expression to which the right of access gives rise").

3. How does the rise of Internet speech affect the empirical foundations of Professor Fiss's argument? Does the possibility that any speaker can make his or her words available to anyone with a networked computer eliminate any argument for government intervention in the speech market?

4. One could argue that the same forces that tend to promote concentration in traditional media entities will also produce concentration among providers of Internet content. And even if diverse speakers can make their views available on matters of public importance, is it clear that those views can readily be heard? For arguments that some forms of government intervention are still required to ensure that Internet speech contributes in a meaningful way to debates over issues of public importance, see Cass Sunstein, Republic.com (2001) and Andrew J. Shapiro, The Control Revolution (1999). Do you agree that the government should play a role in shaping Internet discourse? What forms of government intervention would the First Amendment permit?

2. Open Access Requirements

As discussed in Chapter One, among the keys to the development of the Internet was the introduction of a standard protocol allowing computers to communicate with one another and allowing the resulting networks of linked computers to communicate with one another. In part because of its open architecture, the Internet presents both speakers and listeners with relatively low barriers to entry. As we have seen, advocates often argue that the Internet has flourished because it is open and unregulated and that it should remain so. The assertion that the Internet has historically been unregulated is only partly true, however; the government's regulation of the nation's telecommunications network has played an important role in the Internet's development. Of particular importance are the "common carrier" obligations that are imposed by law on providers of telecommunications services—the requirement that the provider allow third-party equipment to be connected to its network and carry the voice or data services of another provider without discrimination. Traditionally, users connected to the Internet by attaching a dial-up modem to a telephone line and contacting an Internet service provider over that line. Because of the nondiscrimination requirements the government imposes on owners of telecommunications facilities, the user and the ISP can obtain local phone service on demand.

The impact of the government's regulation of the telecommunications market on the development of the Internet is obvious. If an incumbent telephone company cannot favor its affiliated provider in the sale of its services, the market is open for service providers offering a range of services under different pricing models.

Telephone facilities, however, are no longer the primary avenue for users to access the Internet. Ordinary dial-up modems allow data to be transmitted at a maximum speed of 56 kilobits per second. Newer technologies offer much higher bandwidth connections. As users move from reliance on the "narrowband" technology of the dial-up modem to these "broadband" technologies, questions about the relationship between the owners of facilities used to transmit communications and the providers seeking access to those facilities have resurfaced.

Companies have explored several ways to provide broadband service, and two broadband technologies are now widely available. Beginning in the 1990s, many cable companies upgraded their systems to support two-way transmission of signals and now offer Internet access through cable modems. Meanwhile, telephone companies have deployed digital subscriber line (DSL) technologies, which permit the transmission of a high-bandwidth digital signal over existing copper telephone wires. Satellite and fixed wireless providers have also sought to offer broadband Internet access.

Thus far, cable companies have captured the largest share of the broadband market, and their success has prompted a sustained regulatory controversy over the terms on which Internet service providers will have access to broadband platforms. The controversy began when AT & T moved to acquire two of the nation's largest cable television companies, TCI and Media One. Each company offered, or planned to offer, broadband Internet access through an affiliated Internet service provider. In proceedings involving the FCC's review of the proposed mergers, Internet service providers and others—including telephone companies—claimed that the FCC should require cable systems to support multiple ISPs and to permit unaffiliated ISPs to compete for the business of cable subscribers. They argued, among other things, that cable-affiliated ISPs would dominate the market for broadband services and could limit users' access to certain content by providing quicker and more reliable access to content supplied by certain preferred providers.

Based on these concerns, local franchise authorities decided to impose open access requirements. For example, Portland and Multnomah County voted to approve the AT & T's efforts to take over the franchise, but only subject to the following condition:

> *Non-discriminatory access to cable modem platform.* Transferee shall provide, and cause the Franchisees to provide, non-discriminatory access

to the Franchisees' cable modem platform for providers of Internet and on-line services, whether or not such providers are affiliated with the Transferee or the Franchisees, unless otherwise required by applicable law. So long as cable modem services are deemed to be "cable services," as provided under Title VI of the Communications Act of 1934, as amended, Transferee and the Franchisees shall comply with all requirements regarding such services, including but not limited to, the inclusion of revenues from cable modem services and access within the gross revenues of the Franchisees' cable franchises, and commercial leased access requirements.

AT & T refused the condition, which resulted in a denial of the request to transfer the franchises. These open access conditions (and others like them) raise both statutory and constitutional issues.

The statutory question concerns how to classify cable modem service under the Federal Communications Act: as a "telecommunications service," 47 U.S.C. § 153(46), an "information service," *id.* § 153(20), a "cable service," *id.* § 522(6), or some combination thereof. While these distinctions may seem arcane, they have important consequences for whether cable modem service providers can be required to grant nondiscriminatory access to unaffiliated ISPs. If cable modem providers are deemed to be "cable services," then local franchising authorities, like those in Portland and Multnomah counties, are free to impose open access conditions, which they have done in some cases. A determination that such providers are "telecommunications services" means that the providers would generally be subject to *federal* common carrier requirements, which themselves also impose a form of open access. In contrast, if cable modem service is designated an "information service," then any local open access requirements are precluded, and federal open access requirements can be imposed only at the discretion of the Federal Communications Commission (FCC).

In 2002, the FCC concluded that cable broadband services are "information services" and therefore exempt from both local franchising regulation and federal open access requirements. Moreover, although the FCC does have the discretion to impose access requirements on "information services," the agency has thus far declined to do so with regard to broadband. *See* Inquiry Concerning High-Speed Access to the Internet Over Cable and Other Facilities, 17 F.C.C.R. 4798 (2002). The U.S. Supreme Court has subsequently deferred to the FCC determination as a permissible interpretation of an ambiguous statute. *See National Cable & Telecommunications Ass'n v. Brand X Internet Servs.*, 545 U.S. 967 (2005). And, in the wake of the Supreme Court's decision, the FCC issued a further order reclassifying all broadband services (both cable and DSL) as "information services." *See* In the Matters of Appropriate Framework for Broadband Access to the Internet Over Wireline Facilities, 20 F.C.C.R. 14,853 (2005).

Because the Supreme Court merely deferred to agency interpretation, nothing prevents the FCC from reclassifying broadband Internet services again at some point in the future, thereby either imposing common carrier obligations at the federal level or reopening broadband providers to local open access restrictions. Alternatively, Congress might by statute explicitly establish open access requirements on broadband providers. At whatever level open access might be imposed—by the FCC, by local franchising authorities, or by statute—cable operators would at that point likely raise constitutional objections. Accordingly, they would argue that the First Amendment prohibits the government from requiring cable operators to grant ISPs access to their systems. The resolution of this constitutional question would require courts to wrestle with how best to apply *Tornillo* and *Turner* to this context.

As the next section makes clear, the stakes underlying both the statutory and constitutional questions are high.

3. Net Neutrality Requirements

The FCC's classification of broadband Internet Service Providers as "information services," a designation that effectively exempts such providers from common carrier or open access regulation, has raised concerns about the future of the Internet. Indeed, some consumer advocacy groups contend that this new designation will make it "doubtful that the Internet of the future will remain open and accessible to all."[a] In particular, critics contend that, without further legal action, the very idea of "net neutrality"—the principle that some believe is the primary engine of the Internet's growth—will be compromised.

Recall our discussion in Chapter One about some of the elements of the Internet that have made it such an extraordinarily successful network. One of those elements is the so-called "end-to-end" principle, the idea that the infrastructure of the network remains separate from the content it carries, and all data are therefore treated equally by the carriers that transmit them. In this world of network neutrality, service providers do not discriminate among the forms of content that flows over their networks and do not compete in the content marketplace. The result of this network architecture is that, with very limited exceptions, any user with an Internet connection and a computer can visit any website, attach any device, post any content, and provide any service.

Proponents of net neutrality fear that, without any common carrier or open access restrictions in place, broadband providers may decide no longer to be passive network providers and will instead begin to regulate Internet content. They worry that this in turn could lead to a world of blocked content and/or preferential content treatment.

As to content blocking, proponents of net neutrality argue that content providers seeking to sell their own applications could block a rival application. In one celebrated example, Madison River Communications, a DSL provider, blocked its customers from using rival Voice over Internet Protocol (VoIP) Internet phone services. The FCC fined Madison River and pursued a Consent Decree pursuant to which Madison River agreed to stop blocking VoIP on its DSL lines. Significantly, however, both the fine and consent decree were enforced through the FCC's common carrier requirements. Yet, as noted

---

a. Open Internet Discussion Paper, Public Knowledge, December 1, 2005, http://www.publicknowledge.org/content/papers/20051201-open-internet-summary.

previously, the FCC has now ruled that broadband providers are *exempt* from such requirements. As a result, the sort of regulatory oversight exercised by the FCC in the Madison River case is no longer available (absent another change in the FCC's regulatory classification). As a result, critics fear that content discrimination of the sort practiced by Madison River may become the norm.

Of course, concerns about further content blocking may be overstated because a broadband provider that blocked access to too many desired applications would almost certainly find itself losing market share. On the other hand, although some broadband companies have publicly announced their opposition to content blocking, others have warned that they would soon stop permitting Internet content and application companies to use their networks for free. Meanwhile, new applications are being marketed to help service providers block selected uses of their networks (particularly those that divert large amounts of bandwith), and there is at least anecdotal evidence of efforts to block applications on certain networks or to strike deals that would render one company's application "exclusive" on a particular network.

Even absent outright blocking of content, broadband providers could develop what would effectively be a "two-tiered" system in which some content and applications would be moved along the network at higher speeds. Thus, broadband providers could extract fees from application/content companies in order to have their content transmitted at faster rates. In addition, broadband providers could offer their own content/applications at greater speeds than rival products. Thus, while stopping short of blocking an application outright, a broadband provider could decrease the available speed of an application so that the application could not effectively compete with other applications running at faster speeds. In this scenario, consumers would be left with the choice of using the broadband provider's own service, or selecting an inferior option.

Because of these concerns, proponents of net neutrality have sought Congressional legislation that would enshrine the end-to-end principle into the Communications Act. As to the wisdom of such regulation, consider the following debate.

Keeping the Internet Neutral?:
Christopher S. Yoo and Tim Wu Debate

Legal Affairs Debate Club, May 1, 2006
http://www.legalaffairs.org/webexclusive/debateclub_net-neutrality0506.msp

YOO: In recent weeks, the House and the Senate have been debating "network neutrality" legislation, which would prohibit network owners from discriminating against particular applications and content providers. I am not convinced that deviations from network neutrality will necessarily harm consumers and innovation. On the contrary, competition and innovation might be better served if policymakers embraced a "network diversity" principle that allows different network owners to pursue different approaches to routing traffic.

Simply put, deviations from network neutrality may represent nothing more than network owners' attempts to satisfy the increasingly intense and heterogeneous demands imposed by end users. The early Internet was dominated by applications such as e-mail and web browsing, in which delays of half a second were virtually unnoticeable. These are being replaced by newer applications, such as Internet telephony and streaming video, in which such delays can be catastrophic. One obvious solution would be to give a higher priority to traffic associated with time-sensitive applications. Unfortunately, this is precisely the type of discrimination between applications that network neutrality would condemn.

Another interesting innovation is the emergence of content-delivery networks like Akamai, which reportedly serves 15% of the world's Internet traffic. Suppose that an end-user in Los Angeles attempted to download a web page from CNN.com. If CNN.com hosted the content itself, this request would have to travel thousands of miles to the server in CNN's headquarters in Atlanta and back, passing any number of points of congestion along the way. Akamai minimizes delay by caching content at thousands of locations throughout the Internet and routing requests to the server that is the closest and/or the least congested. The catch from the standpoint of network neutrality is that Akamai is a commercial service available only to those who are willing to pay for it.

Employing different protocols might also provide more network options by permitting smaller networks to survive by targeting market niches, in much the same way that specialty stores survive in a world dominated by low-cost, mass-market retailers. For example, deviating from network neutrality might make it possible for three last-mile networks to coexist: one optimized for traditional Internet applications, such as e-mail and website access; a second incorporating security features to facilitate e-commerce; and a third that facilitates time-sensitive applications such as streaming media and Internet telephony. Network neutrality, in contrast, threatens to foreclose this outcome and instead forces networks to compete on price and network size—considerations that favor the largest players.

At this point, it is impossible to foresee which architecture will ultimately represent the best approach. When it is impossible to tell whether a practice would promote or hinder competition, the accepted policy response to permit the practice to go forward until actual harm to consumers can be proven. This restraint provides the room for experimentation upon which the normal competitive processes depend. It also shows appropriate humility about our ability to predict the technological future.

Wu: Network neutrality is just a way of talking about discrimination, so let's talk about discrimination, on networks or otherwise. Whether it comes to employment, networks, or just about anything else, no one really believes in systems that ban discrimination completely. In employment, for example, you want to be able to fire people who are lousy—to discriminate on the basis of ability. When government chooses who gets to vote, we accept that it can say "no" to 12-year-olds.

Yet I don't think that the fact that an absolute ban would be ridiculous undermines the case for discrimination laws. It's like what nutritionists say about fat: there are good and bad types. And what I think is going on in the network neutrality debate—the useful part of it—is getting a better grip on what amounts to good and bad forms of discrimination on information networks.

Christopher, you've done a good job of suggesting some of the reasons that types of discrimination can be useful on a network, like dealing with congestion problems and offering different types of networks altogether. These are valid points. But sometimes you seem to be arguing that based on a few good examples of discrimination, that there's no such thing as bad discrimination—particularly where network gatekeeper has market power. That is where we part company.

I'll start with the clearest network example: blocking. So yes, in general, a bell or cable company has some interest in giving you as broadly useful a network as possible, because then the product is more valuable, and the company can charge more for it. But that interest in neutrality holds true only to a point. If a product being offered over the network—say, Internet voice (VoIP) for $5/month—competes with an established revenue source (telephone service, offered at $30/month), the temptation to block it is strong. It is true that, in theory, the provider might start charging the customer $25/month extra because the network is now more valuable. But that means the costs of changing business models and establishing new consumer pricing patterns, which companies are loath to do.

Christopher, I am not sure if you would go so far to suggest that blocking is fine because either companies won't do it or will have good reasons when they do. As to whether they will, we don't have to make guesses, because incumbent providers in the United States and in many countries around the world, including Mexico, have blocked or wanted to block competition from VoIP. The United States Trade Representative's office has an ongoing practice, in fact, of trying to talk to countries and their incumbents about such blocking. They don't call it network neutrality or anything of the sort, but it is the export of network-neutrality policies.

What's bad about blocking, then? At an extreme, blocking can keep a better or cheaper product (VoIP) from coming to market at all, and often it can prevent such products from being offered in an effective form. That's a problem, in turn, because if you believe that market entry and innovation are linked to economic growth, we're ultimately talking about such policies hindering the growth rate of the country. * * *

YOO: To date, the debate has focused primarily on a type of discrimination known as "access tiering," in which network owners charge websites and application providers more for premium (i.e., higher speed) service. Access tiering could provide benefits similar to those provided by the emergence of premium mail services like FedEx. Instead of taking 3-4 days to send a letter from coast to coast, FedEx made it possible to send the same letter overnight. FedEx customers were more than happy to pay more for faster service, since it opened up new ways of doing business that were impossible when everyone paid the same amount for a single class of service.

The same logic applies to the Internet. The Internet is currently dominated by a suite of protocols known as TCP/IP. TCP/IP has two notable features: First, it routes traffic on a "first come, first served" basis that makes it impossible to guarantee how quickly a packet will arrive. Second, it also routes traffic on a "best efforts" basis that provides no guarantees that a packet will actually be delivered. Companies developing applications that depend on guaranteed throughput rates have indicated that they would willingly pay more to ensure better quality service. This has led leading technologists (such as David Farber of Carnegie Mellon) to suggest that TCP/IP may be a thirty-year-old technology that is becoming obsolete.

So what is the proper policy response if access tiering would sometimes be beneficial and sometimes not? Fortunately, the Supreme Court's antitrust jurisprudence offers useful guidance. If a practice is always harmful, it should be categorically prohibited (i.e., declared illegal per se). If a practice is always beneficial, it should be universally mandated. If a practice is sometimes harmful and sometimes beneficial, it is subjected to the so-called "rule of reason," which permits the practice to go forward until those challenging it can show a concrete competitive harm. Supreme Court precedent would thus contradict regulations that would make ambiguous practices like access tiering categorically illegal. Instead, it would seem to favor taking a middle course * * * that would allow networks to pursue different approaches unless and until they are shown to harm competition.

Even website or port blocking may not be as problematic as may appear at first glance. As suggested in my earlier post, exclusivity can provide a form of differentiation that can increase the number of providers who can survive. For example, DirecTV's exclusive access to the "NFL Sunday Ticket" package has enhanced its ability to compete with cable. The partnership between Yahoo! and SBC's (now-AT&T's) DSL service and the combination of ESPN and Sprint to offer a "mobile virtual network" may be providing similar benefits. And if 2-3 wireless broadband or broadband over powerline (BPL) providers emerge so that consumers have 4-5 last-mile broadband options (including cable modem and DSL), there would be little danger in allowing one of those networks to experiment with exclusivity arrangements. The experimenting network might find a new business model that would deliver greater value to consumers. If not, then we would expect competitors to steal business from the experimenting network until it reversed course.

In any event, the possibility of anticompetitive blocking would not support the type of general nondiscrimination mandate favored by network neutrality proponents. The only time that network owners have a plausible incentive to block a website is when they sponsor websites that compete directly with the blocked site. Conversely, network owners that do not operate auction sites have no incentive to block eBay, since doing so would simply lower the value of their network (and thus lower the amount that they can charge for it) without providing any compensating benefits. Similarly, while DSL providers may have some incentive to block VoIP, they have no plausible incentive to block services like streaming video that they do not currently offer. At most, concerns about blocking would thus support limited regulatory intervention that would only prohibit vertically integrated network owners from blocking content and applications that competed directly with their own offerings. It would not justify broad restrictions on discrimination of the kind being proposed (and currently being rejected) in Congress.

WU: A lot of the difference between Christopher's view and [my] own stems from how we think the process of innovation occurs. Christopher * * * believes that large firms—in this case, network operators—drive telecommunications innovation. * * * Christopher thinks incumbents like AT&T will rarely or perhaps never threaten innovation. Instead he views them as the driving force of the technologies of tomorrow.

I am skeptical. I think this view of incumbent behavior has been discredited, and that in general, incumbents, particularly in a monopoly position, have a strong incentive to block market entry and innovative technologies that threat their existing business model.

My faith is that economic growth is driven by market entry, and I believe that when it's careful, government can play an important role in controlling barriers to market entry that incumbents might impose. That's not to say it is easy—the challenge is to bar the worst abuses without destroying an incentive to become an incumbent in the first place. Government often gets it wrong. But Christopher's views tend toward assuming the problem away, through what I view as unrealistic assumptions about incumbent behavior.

The growth of all of the many industries on top of the Internet are a powerful testament to the vision I've described. For the Internet's design itself, and then successive FCC rules, managed to prevent infrastructure incumbents from having any influence on market entry. * * * But let's turn away from theory to the practical matter Christopher brought up: what he calls access tiering—or giving preferential treatment over the last mile.

Here's my view of what the problematic side of access tiering looks like. You have, say, AT&T with monopoly over broadband in a given area. AT&T makes an exclusive deal with Yahoo! to provide preferred search on AT&T's network. As a consequence, the Yahoo! engine loads faster than any of its competitors. I've said elsewhere it might be as if your electric company were to make a deal with Samsung so that your refrigerators from General Electric would not longer work quite so well. That's the problem I'm discussing.

There's a word for this: it's a form of discrimination called Most Favored Nation (MFN) discrimination—different treatment of like, competing products. And the problem, of course, is a distortion of competition. In our search example, the best product doesn't win, but rather the product with the best connection to AT&T, and the one that poses no threat to any of AT&T's business models.

And that returns me to the earlier discussion of innovation. The risk, as I've said elsewhere, is a market where several large companies set the pace of innovation, not the challenges of competitors. But historically—and by current economic theory—the many beat out the few. I'll take the track record of decentralized innovation.

Notes and Questions

1. Consider this debate in light of the questions of public and private regulation raised throughout the chapter. Telecommunications companies were originally subjected to "common carrier" regulations in part because the phone lines were considered a quasi-public forum, akin to a state service. Does

such a conception still make sense? For example, should Internet service providers be deemed to provide a quasi-public facility that should be subject either to constitutional norms or public regulation?

2. Neither Yoo nor Wu address the possibility that the broadband providers themselves might have rights that could be infringed by net neutrality regulation. Under *Tornillo* and *Turner*, do you think it is permissible for government to mandate end-to-end neutrality? Or do broadband providers have First Amendment rights to discriminate among content providers? Are there relevant differences between the newspaper, cable television, and Internet contexts that should affect the analysis?

3. Are there other relevant metaphors we might consider beyond newspapers and cable television service? For example, Wu has elsewhere drawn these analogies:

> In trying to figure out who's right [in the net neutrality debate], let's forget about the Internet and look at KFC. The fast-food chain discriminates. It has an exclusive deal with Pepsi, and that seems fine to pretty much everyone. Now, let's think about the nation's highways. How would you feel if I-95 announced an exclusive deal with General Motors to provide a special "rush-hour" lane for GM cars only? That seems intuitively wrong. But what, if anything, is the difference between KFC and I-95? And which is a better model for the Internet?
>
> Two obvious differences are market power and the availability of substitutes. KFC is a small fry, relatively, locked in competition with the likes of McDonald's and Popeye's. KFC sells Pepsi? So what? McDonald's sells Coke. It's a lot harder to substitute for an interstate. And if highways really did choose favorite brands, you might buy a Pontiac instead of a Toyota to get the rush-hour lane, not because the Pontiac is actually a good car. As a result, the nature of competition among car-makers would change. Rather than try to make the best product, they would battle to make deals with highways.
>
> That's what would happen if discrimination reigned on the Internet: a transformation from a market where innovation rules to one where deal-making rules. Or, a market where firms rush to make exclusive agreements with AT&T and Verizon instead of trying to improve their products. There's a deeper point here: When who you know matters more than anything, the market is no longer meritocratic and consequently becomes less efficient. At the extreme, a market where centralized actors pick favorites isn't a market at all, but a planned economy.

Tim Wu, *Why You Should Care About Net Neutrality*, SLATE, May 1, 2006, http://www.slate.com/id/2140850/. Are Wu's analogies convincing? Does your answer depend on your intuitions about barriers to entry in a given market? Does it matter that the interstate highway system is governmental whereas KFC is not?

4. What about Yoo's point concerning innovation? How might net neutrality regulation stifle progress towards developing useful Internet applications?

5. If the net neutrality concern involves improper blocking or discrimination, mightn't regulators focus on those specific examples of bad behavior, rather than a more general rule about technological access? On the other hand, are there costs to focusing on specific behaviors rather than network architecture?

6. Do you agree with Yoo that the combination of consumer choice and antitrust principles will be sufficient to discipline broadband providers? Or do you think that monopoly power (and its attendant dangers) is inevitable in this context?

7. If you think net neutrality regulation is necessary, go back and consider the other private regulators considered in this chapter. Should each of them be similarly regulated? After all, search engines can effectively block access to websites just as surely as service providers can. And certainly the Realtime Blackhole List blocks access to websites as well. Likewise, as we have seen, ICANN, through its influence over the root directories, can render a website unfindable. Should regulators or courts treat these actors differently from broadband providers? Or should we look at the Internet as a public (or quasi-public) resource and subject all incursions on public access to constitutional or regulatory scrutiny? Is that approach feasible?

8. Finally, take a moment to think about the ways in which categories of public and private, regulator and regulated, are blurred both in the net neutrality debate and throughout this chapter. Are these categories useful at all when discussing the Internet? Are they more helpful when discussing shopping malls or other non-Internet examples? And to the extent the public/private distinction seems unhelpful, what distinctions would you try to draw in seeking to determine under what circumstances governmental or constitutional regulation is appropriate?

Chapter Six

PROBLEMS OF SPEECH REGULATION

INTRODUCTION

In the previous chapter, we considered the possibility that private standard-setting bodies, corporations, and other entities might regulate behavior in cyberspace free from constitutional strictures. For example, we saw that, at least under current doctrine, search engines might be able to censor speech in ways that the government could not. The readings also raised broader questions about whether certain regulatory problems are best addressed through governmental solutions or through private approaches.

One context in which we might assume that a private approach is preferable to a governmental approach is the regulation of speech: the First Amendment, after all, is directly concerned with government censorship, and so from a constitutional perspective it appears that such governmental censorship is the primary threat. On the other hand, recall Professor Fiss's argument in Chapter Five that sometimes private entities can unduly limit access to speech. Thus, if the goal is to ensure an overall system that will be as protective of speech as possible, we must test the assumption that governmental regulations will necessarily curtail more speech than the combination of private filtering, private access controls, and private technological protection measures to protect content. Taking as an example efforts to limit children's access to sexually explicit speech, we examine government restrictions as compared with private filtering mechanisms and ask how each serves or disserves the values underlying the First Amendment.

SECTION A. GOVERNMENT REGULATION OF SEXUALLY EXPLICIT SPEECH

The First Amendment to the United States Constitution provides that "Congress shall make no law [abridging] the freedom of speech, or of the press; or the right of the people peaceably to assemble, and to petition the Government for a redress of grievances." Despite Justice Black's famous declaration that this language is absolute and does not permit any balancing of interests, the U.S. Supreme Court has never adopted Black's position. Instead, First Amendment doctrine analyzes both the type of *speech* being regulated and the type of *regulation* used. Thus, certain speech has been deemed to be of lower constitutional value and has been accorded less constitutional scrutiny. This speech includes defamation, obscenity, conspiracy, incitement, etc. In addition, courts focus on whether the relevant speech regulation is content-neutral (often referred to as a "time, place, or manner" restriction) or content-based. Content-based regulations must serve a compelling state interest and must be narrowly tailored to achieve their objective. This requirement generally scrutinizes whether the government has chosen the least restrictive means to achieve its objective.

Finally, in considering any First Amendment question, it is necessary to think more rigorously about the *rationale* for the First Amendment. Why do we think free expression is valuable and worthy of protection? Although it may seem obvious that free expression is a good thing, it is relatively difficult to agree on a reason why. Among the rationales advanced by courts and scholars are:

- *Truth/Marketplace of Ideas*. This rationale rests on the idea that "the best test of truth is the power of the thought to get itself accepted in the competition of the market." *Abrams v. United States*, 250 U.S. 616, 630 (1919) (Holmes, J., dissenting). On the other hand, the form and frequency of message presentation may have as much impact on the acceptance of an idea as its inherent quality. And, of course, markets themselves are regulated in many ways. Thus, as with economic regulation, state intervention may be necessary to correct communicative market failures.

- *Democracy/Self-Governance*. This rationale focuses on the need for free expression in order to foster democratic discourse. According to this theory, limitations on some speech would be permissible in order to better achieve the conditions for broad participation and productive debate. The problem, however, is determining who gets to make such decisions and what the criteria are for deciding how best to ensure public deliberation.

- *Personal Autonomy*. Here the emphasis is on the constitutive value of free expression as central to individual autonomy and fulfillment. On the other hand, many other (non-speech) activities may similarly contribute to self-actualization, but these are not protected by the First Amendment.

- *Fostering a Tolerant Society.* According to this theory, we protect freedom of expression because the process of tolerating multiple forms of expression provides a model for the tolerance we need in other areas of society as well.

- *Government Checking.* This is in some ways a "negative" theory. Even if we cannot agree on a rationale for free expression, so the argument goes, we may agree that any government will always have an incentive to silence opposition speech. Accordingly, we need a principle of free expression solely because we want to prevent the government from exercising discretion in the domain of speech.

Of course, these theories are not mutually exclusive, and most commentators and courts are likely to rely on some combination of these rationales. Nevertheless, as you look at cases involving free expression, it is important to consider which theory or theories are being used because the various rationales may lead to significantly different results when considering specific regulations on expression.

All of these considerations arise when assessing restrictions on so-called "indecent" material in various media. Here we are talking not about obscene material—which receives no constitutional protection—but material that is constitutionally protected as to adults, but which the government wishes to limit with respect to minors. Such "indecent" material poses a particular First Amendment problem because it is often difficult to limit access to minors without unduly restricting the constitutionally protected access of adults to that same material. The following cases all address such sexually explicit but non-obscene speech.

Ginsberg v. New York

Supreme Court of the United States, 1968
390 U.S. 629

JUSTICE BRENNAN delivered the opinion of the Court.

This case presents the question of the constitutionality on its face of a New York criminal obscenity statute which prohibits the sale to minors under 17 years of age of material defined to be obscene on the basis of its appeal to them whether or not it would be obscene to adults.

Appellant and his wife operate "Sam's Stationery and Luncheonette" in Bellmore, Long Island. They have a lunch counter, and, among other things, also sell magazines including some so-called "girlie" magazines. Appellant was prosecuted under two informations, each in two counts, which charged that he personally sold a 16-year-old boy two "girlie" magazines on each of two dates in October 1965, in violation of § 484–h of the New York Penal Law. He was tried before a judge without a jury in

Nassau County District Court and was found guilty on both counts. The judge found (1) that the magazines contained pictures which depicted female "nudity" in a manner defined in [the statute], and (2) that the pictures were "harmful to minors" in that they had, within the meaning of subsection 1(f) "that quality of . . . representation . . . of nudity . . . [which] . . . (I) predominantly appeals to the prurient, shameful or morbid interest of minors, and (ii) is patently offensive to prevailing standards in the adult community as a whole with respect to what is suitable material for minors, and (iii) is utterly without redeeming social importance for minors." He held that both sales to the 16-year-old boy therefore constituted the violation under § 484–h of "knowingly to sell . . . to a minor" under 17 of "(a) any picture . . . which depicts nudity . . . and which is harmful to minors," and "(b) any . . . magazine . . . which contains . . . [such pictures] . . . and which, taken as a whole, is harmful to minors." The conviction was affirmed without opinion by the Appellate Term, Second Department, of the Supreme Court. Appellant was denied leave to appeal to the New York Court of Appeals and then appealed to this Court. We noted probable jurisdiction. We affirm.

I.

The "girlie" picture magazines involved in the sales here are not obscene for adults. But § 484–h does not bar the appellant from stocking the magazines and selling them to persons 17 years of age or older, and therefore the conviction is not invalid under our decision in *Butler v. Michigan*, 352 U.S. 380 (1957).

Obscenity is not within the area of protected speech or press. *Roth v. United States*, 354 U.S. 476, 485 (1957). The three-pronged test of subsection 1(f) for judgment the obscenity of material sold to minors under 17 is a variable from the formulation for determining obscenity under *Roth*. * * * Appellant's primary attack upon § 484–h is leveled at the power of the State to adapt this * * * formulation to define the material's obscenity on the basis of its appeal to minors, and thus exclude material so defined from the area of protected expression. * * * [H]is contention is the broad proposition that the scope of the constitutional freedom of expression secured to a citizen to read or see material concerned with sex cannot be made to depend upon whether the citizen is an adult or a minor. He accordingly insists that the denial to minors under 17 of access to material condemned by § 484–h, insofar as that material is not obscene for persons 17 years of age or older, constitutes an unconstitutional deprivation of protected liberty. * * *

We conclude that we cannot say that the statute invades the area of freedom of expression constitutionally secured to minors. * * *

The well-being of its children is of course a subject within the State's constitutional power to regulate, and, in our view, two interests justify the limitations in § 484–h upon the availability of sex material to minors under 17, at least if it was rational for the legislature to find that the minors' exposure to such material might be harmful. First of all, constitutional interpretation has consistently recognized that the parents' claim to authority in their own household to direct the rearing of their children is basic in the structure of our society. * * * The legislature could properly conclude that parents and others, teachers for example, who have this primary responsibility for children's well-being are entitled to the support of laws designed to aid discharge of that responsibility. Indeed, subsection 1(f)(ii) of § 484–h expressly recognizes the parental role in assessing sex-related material harmful to minors according "to prevailing standards in the adult community as a whole with respect to what is suitable material for minors." Moreover, the prohibition against sales to minors does not bar parents who so desire from purchasing the magazines for their children.

The State also has an independent interest in the well-being of its youth. * * * In *Prince v. Massachusetts*, 321 U.S. 158, 165 (1944), [this Court] recognized that the State has an interest "to protect the welfare of children" and to see that they are "safeguarded from abuses" which might prevent their "growth into free and independent well-developed men and citizens." The only question remaining, therefore, is whether the New York Legislature might rationally conclude, as it has, that exposure to the materials proscribed by § 484–h constitutes such an "abuse."

Section 484–e of the law states a legislative finding that the material condemned by § 484–h is "a basic factor in impairing the ethical and moral development of our youth and a clear and present danger to the people of the state." It is very doubtful that this finding expresses an accepted scientific fact. But obscenity is not protected expression * * * . To sustain state power to exclude material defined as obscenity by § 484–h requires only that we be able to say that it was not irrational for the legislature to find that exposure to material condemned by the statute is harmful to minors. In *Meyer v. Nebraska*, 262 U.S. 390, 400 (1923), we were able to say that children's knowledge of the German language "cannot reasonably be regarded as harmful." That cannot be said by us of minors' reading and seeing sex material. To be sure, there is no lack of "studies" which purport to demonstrate that obscenity is or is not "a basic factor in impairing the ethical and moral development of . . . youth and a clear and present danger to the people of the state." But the growing consensus of commentators is that "while these studies all agree that a causal link has not been demonstrated, they are equally agreed that a causal link has not been disproved either." We do not demand of legislatures "scientifically certain criteria of legislation." *Noble State Bank v. Haskell*, 219 U.S. 104, 110 (1911). We therefore cannot say that § 484–h, in defining the obscenity of material on the basis of its appeal to minors under 17, has no rational relation to the objective of safeguarding such minors from harm.

[Concurring opinion of Justice Stewart and dissenting opinions of Justice Douglas and Justice Fortas omitted.]

FCC v. Pacifica Foundation

Supreme Court of the United States, 1978
438 U.S. 726

MR. JUSTICE STEVENS delivered the opinion of the Court (Parts I, II, III and IV-C) and an opinion in which THE CHIEF JUSTICE and MR. JUSTICE REHNQUIST joined (Parts IV-A and IV-B).

This case requires that we decide whether the Federal Communications Commission has any power to regulate a radio broadcast that is indecent but not obscene. A satiric humorist named George Carlin recorded a 12-minute monologue entitled "Filthy Words" before a live audience in a California theater. He began by referring to his thoughts about "the words you couldn't say on the public, ah, airwaves, um, the ones you definitely wouldn't say, ever." He proceeded to list those words and repeat them over and over again in a variety of colloquialisms. * * *

At about 2 o'clock in the afternoon on Tuesday, October 30, 1973, a New York radio station, owned by respondent Pacifica Foundation, broadcast the "Filthy Words" monologue. A few weeks later a man, who stated that he had heard the broadcast while driving with his young son, wrote a letter complaining to the Commission. He stated that, although he could perhaps understand the "record's being sold for private use, I certainly cannot understand the broadcast of same over the air that, supposedly, you control."

The complaint was forwarded to the station for comment. In its response, Pacifica explained that the monologue had been played during a program about contemporary society's attitude toward language and that, immediately before its broadcast, listeners had been advised that it included "sensitive language which might be regarded as offensive to some." Pacifica characterized George Carlin as "a significant social satirist" who "like Twain and Sahl before him, examines the language of ordinary people. . . . Carlin is not mouthing obscenities, he is merely using words to satirize as harmless and essentially silly our attitudes towards those words." Pacifica stated that it was not aware of any other complaints about the broadcast.

On February 21, 1975, the Commission issued a declaratory order granting the complaint and holding that Pacifica "could have been the subject of administrative sanctions." The Commission did not impose formal sanctions, but it did state that the order would be "associated with the station's license file, and in the event that subsequent complaints are received, the Commission will then decide whether it should utilize any of the available sanctions it has been granted by Congress."

In its memorandum opinion the Commission stated that it intended to "clarify the standards which will be utilized in considering" the growing number of complaints about indecent speech on the airwaves. * * * [T]he Commission found a power to regulate indecent broadcasting in two statutes: 18 U.S.C. § 1464 (1976 ed.), which forbids the use of "any obscene, indecent, or profane language by means of radio communications," and 47

U.S.C. § 303(g), which requires the Commission to "encourage the larger and more effective use of radio in the public interest." The Commission characterized the language used in the Carlin monologue as "patently offensive," though not necessarily obscene, and expressed the opinion that it should be regulated by principles analogous to those found in the law of nuisance where the "law generally speaks to *channeling* behavior more than actually prohibiting it. . . . [T]he concept of "indecent' is intimately connected with the exposure of children to language that describes, in terms patently offensive as measured by contemporary community standards for the broadcast medium, sexual or excretory activities and organs at times of the day when there is a reasonable risk that children may be in the audience."

Applying these considerations to the language used in the monologue as broadcast by respondent, the Commission concluded that certain words depicted sexual and excretory activities in a patently offensive manner, noted that they "were broadcast at a time when children were undoubtedly in the audience (i.e., in the early afternoon)," and that the prerecorded language, with these offensive words "repeated over and over," was "deliberately broadcast." In summary, the Commission stated: "We therefore hold that the language as broadcast was indecent and prohibited * * * ."

After the order issued, the Commission was asked to clarify its opinion by ruling that the broadcast of indecent words as part of a live newscast would not be prohibited. The Commission issued another opinion in which it pointed out that it "never intended to place an absolute prohibition on the broadcast of this type of language, but rather sought to channel it to times of day when children most likely would not be exposed to it." The Commission noted that its "declaratory order was issued in a specific factual context," and declined to comment on various hypothetical situations presented by the petition. It relied on its "long standing policy of refusing to issue interpretive rulings or advisory opinions when the critical facts are not explicitly stated or there is a possibility that subsequent events will alter them."

The United States Court of Appeals for the District of Columbia Circuit reversed. * * * Having granted the Commission's petition for certiorari, we must decide: * * * (4) whether the order violates the First Amendment of the United States Constitution. * * *

IV

Pacifica makes two constitutional attacks on the Commission's order. First, it argues that the Commission's construction of the statutory language [prohibiting the use of "indecent" language by means of a radio communication] broadly encompasses so much constitutionally protected speech that reversal is required even if Pacifica's broadcast of the "Filthy Words" monologue is not itself protected by the First Amendment. Second,

Pacifica argues that inasmuch as the recording is not obscene, the Constitution forbids any abridgment of the right to broadcast it on the radio.

A

The first argument fails because our review is limited to the question whether the Commission has the authority to proscribe this particular broadcast. As the Commission itself emphasized, its order was "issued in a specific factual context." That approach is appropriate for courts as well as the Commission when regulation of indecency is at stake, for indecency is largely a function of context—it cannot be adequately judged in the abstract. * * *

It is true that the Commission's order may lead some broadcasters to censor themselves. At most, however, the Commission's definition of indecency will deter only the broadcasting of patently offensive references to excretory and sexual organs and activities. While some of these references may be protected, they surely lie at the periphery of First Amendment concern. * * * Invalidating any rule on the basis of its hypothetical application to situations not before the Court is "strong medicine" to be applied "sparingly and only as a last resort." *Broadrick v. Oklahoma*, 413 U.S. 601, 613 (1973). We decline to administer that medicine to preserve the vigor of patently offensive sexual and excretory speech.

B

When the issue is narrowed to the facts of this case, the question is whether the First Amendment denies government any power to restrict the public broadcast of indecent language in any circumstances. For if the government has any such power, this was an appropriate occasion for its exercise.

The words of the Carlin monologue are unquestionably "speech" within the meaning of the First Amendment. It is equally clear that the Commission's objections to the broadcast were based in part on its content. The order must therefore fall if, as Pacifica argues, the First Amendment prohibits all governmental regulation that depends on the content of speech. Our past cases demonstrate, however, that no such absolute rule is mandated by the Constitution. * * *

The question in this case is whether a broadcast of patently offensive words dealing with sex and excretion may be regulated because of its content. Obscene materials have been denied the protection of the First Amendment because their content is so offensive to contemporary moral standards. But the fact that society may find speech offensive is not a sufficient reason for suppressing it. Indeed, if it is the speaker's opinion that gives offense, that consequence is a reason for according it constitutional protection. For it is a central tenet of the First Amendment that the government must remain neutral in the marketplace of ideas. If there were any reason to believe that the Commission's characterization of the Carlin monologue as offensive could be traced to its political content—or even to the fact that it satirized contemporary attitudes about four-letter words—First Amendment protection might be required. But that is simply not this case. These words offend for the same reasons that obscenity offends. Their place in the hierarchy of First Amendment values was aptly sketched by Mr. Justice Murphy when he said: "Such utterances are no essential part of any exposition of ideas, and are of such slight social value as a step to truth that any benefit that may be derived from them is clearly outweighed by the social interest in order and morality." *Chaplinsky v. New Hampshire*, 315 U.S. 568, 572 (1942).

Although these words ordinarily lack literary, political, or scientific value, they are not entirely outside the protection of the First Amendment. Some uses of even the most offensive words are unquestionably protected. Indeed, we may assume, *arguendo*, that this monologue would be protected in other contexts. Nonetheless, the constitutional protection accorded to a communication containing such patently offensive sexual and excretory language need not be the same in every context. It is a characteristic of speech such as this that both its capacity to offend and its "social value," to use Mr. Justice Murphy's term, vary with the circumstances. Words that are commonplace in one setting are shocking in another. To paraphrase Mr. Justice Harlan, one occasion's lyric is another's vulgarity. Cf. *Cohen v. California*, 403 U.S. 15, 25 (1971).

In this case it is undisputed that the content of Pacifica's broadcast was "vulgar," "offensive," and "shocking." Because content of that character is not entitled to absolute constitutional protection under all circumstances, we must consider its context in order to determine whether the Commission's action was constitutionally permissible.

C

We have long recognized that each medium of expression presents special First Amendment problems. And of all forms of communication, it is broadcasting that has received the most limited First Amendment protection. Thus, although other speakers cannot be licensed except under laws that carefully define and narrow official discretion, a broadcaster may be deprived of his license and his forum if the Commission decides that such an action would serve "the public interest, convenience, and necessity." Similarly, although the First Amendment protects newspaper publishers from being required to print the replies of those whom they criticize, *Miami Herald Publishing Co. v. Tornillo*, 418 U.S. 241 (1974), it affords no such protection to broadcasters; on the contrary, they must give free time to the victims of their criticism. *Red Lion Broadcasting Co. v. FCC*, 395 U.S. 367 (1969).

The reasons for these distinctions are complex, but two have relevance to the present case. First, the broadcast media have established a uniquely pervasive presence in the lives of all Americans. Patently offensive, indecent material presented over the airwaves confronts the citizen, not only in public, but also in the privacy of the home, where the individual's right to be left alone plainly outweighs the First Amendment rights of an intruder. Because the broadcast audience is constantly tuning in and out, prior warnings cannot completely protect the listener or viewer from unexpected program content. To say that one may avoid further offense by turning off the radio when he hears indecent language is like saying that the remedy for an assault is to run away after the first blow. One may hang up on an indecent phone call, but that option does not give the caller a constitutional immunity or avoid a harm that has already taken place.

Second, broadcasting is uniquely accessible to children, even those too young to read. Although [the] written message [at issue in *Cohen*] might have been incomprehensible to a first grader, Pacifica's broadcast could have enlarged a child's vocabulary in an instant. Other forms of offensive expression may be withheld from the young without restricting the expression at its source. Bookstores and motion picture theaters, for example, may be prohibited from making indecent material available to children. We held in *Ginsberg v. New York*, 390 U.S. 629 (1968), that the government's interest in the "well-being of its youth" and in supporting "parents' claim to authority in their own household" justified the regulation of otherwise protected expression. *Id.*, at 640 and 639. The ease with which children may obtain access to broadcast material, coupled with the concerns recognized in *Ginsberg*, amply justify special treatment of indecent broadcasting.

It is appropriate, in conclusion, to emphasize the narrowness of our holding. This case does not involve a two-way radio conversation between a cab driver and a dispatcher, or a telecast of an Elizabethan comedy. We have not decided that an occasional expletive in either setting would justify any sanction or, indeed, that this broadcast would justify a criminal prosecution. The Commission's decision rested entirely on a nuisance rationale under which context is all-important. The concept requires consideration of a host of variables. The time of day was emphasized by the Commission. The content of the program in which the language is used will also affect the composition of the audience, and differences between radio, television, and perhaps closed-circuit transmissions, may also be relevant. As Mr. Justice Sutherland wrote a "nuisance may be merely a right thing in the wrong place—like a pig in the parlor instead of the barnyard." *Euclid v. Ambler Realty Co.*, 272 U.S. 365, 388 (1926). We simply hold that when the Commission finds that a pig has entered the parlor, the exercise of its regulatory power does not depend on proof that the pig is obscene.

MR. JUSTICE POWELL, with whom MR. JUSTICE BLACKMUN joins, concurring in part and concurring in the judgment.

[M]y views are generally in accord with what is said in Part IV-C of MR. JUSTICE STEVENS' opinion. I therefore join that portion of his opinion. I do not join Part IV-B, however, because I do not subscribe to the theory that the Justices of this Court are free generally to decide on the basis of its content which speech protected by the First Amendment is most "valuable" and hence deserving of the most protection, and which is less "valuable" and hence deserving of less protection. In my view, the result in this case does not turn on whether Carlin's monologue, viewed as a whole, or the words that constitute it, have more or less "value" than a candidate's campaign speech. This is a judgment for each person to make, not one for the judges to impose upon him. * * *

The result turns instead on the unique characteristics of the broadcast media, combined with society's right to protect its children from speech generally agreed to be inappropriate for their years, and with the interest of unwilling adults in not being assaulted by such offensive speech in their homes. Moreover, I doubt whether today's decision will prevent any adult who wishes to receive Carlin's message in Carlin's own words from doing so, and from making for himself a value judgment as to the merit of the message and words. These are the grounds upon which I join the judgment of the Court as to Part IV.

MR. JUSTICE BRENNAN, with whom MR. JUSTICE MARSHALL joins, dissenting.

Without question, the privacy interests of an individual in his home are substantial and deserving of significant protection. In finding these interests sufficient to justify the content regulation of protected speech, however, the Court commits two errors. First, it misconceives the nature of the privacy interests involved where an individual voluntarily chooses to admit radio communications into his home. Second, it ignores the constitutionally protected interests of both those who wish to transmit and those who desire to receive broadcasts that many—including the FCC and this Court—might find offensive.

* * * I am in wholehearted agreement with my Brethren that an individual's right "to be let alone" when engaged in private activity within the confines of his own home is encompassed within the "substantial privacy interests" to which Mr. Justice Harlan referred in *Cohen*, and is entitled to the greatest solicitude. *Stanley v. Georgia*, 394 U.S. 557 (1969). However, I believe that an individual's actions in switching on and listening to communications transmitted over the public airways and directed to the public at large do not implicate fundamental privacy interests, even when engaged in within the home. Instead, because the radio is undeniably a public medium, these actions are more properly viewed as a decision to take part, if only as a listener, in an ongoing public discourse. * * * Although an individual's decision to allow public radio communications into his home undoubtedly does not abrogate all of his privacy interests, the residual privacy interests he retains vis-a-vis the communication he voluntarily admits into his home are surely no greater than those of the people present in the corridor of the Los Angeles courthouse in *Cohen* who bore witness to the words "Fuck the Draft" emblazoned across Cohen's jacket. Their privacy interests were held insufficient to justify punishing Cohen for his offensive communication.

Even if an individual who voluntarily opens his home to radio communications retains privacy interests of sufficient moment to justify a ban on protected speech if those interests are "invaded in an essentially intolerable manner," *Cohen v. California, supra,* 403 U.S., at 21, the very fact that those interests are threatened only by a radio broadcast precludes any intolerable invasion of privacy; for unlike other intrusive modes of communication, such as sound trucks, "[t]he radio can be turned off," *Lehman v. Shaker Heights,* 418 U.S. 298, 302 (1974)—and with a minimum of effort. As Chief Judge Bazelon aptly observed below, "having elected to receive public air waves, the scanner who stumbles onto an offensive program is in the same position as the unsuspecting passers-by in *Cohen* and *Erznoznik* [*v. Jacksonville,* 422 U.S. 205 (1975)]; he can avert his attention by changing channels or turning off the set. Whatever the minimal discomfort suffered by a listener who inadvertently tunes into a program he finds offensive during the brief interval before he can simply extend his arm and switch stations or flick the "off" button, it is surely worth the candle to preserve the broadcaster's right to send, and the right of those interested to receive, a message entitled to full First Amendment protection.

Notes and Questions

1. How does the New York statute at issue in *Ginsberg* define material that is "harmful to minors"? How does the definition differ from the FCC definition of "indecent" material at issue in *Pacifica*?

2. A plurality of the *Pacifica* Court concludes that sexually explicit speech "surely lie[s] at the periphery of First Amendment concern." Why do Justice Powell and Justice Blackmun reject that approach? Which view do you find more persuasive?

3. The *Ginsberg* Court sustains the New York statute in part because the statute does not affect the sale of the material in question to persons seventeen or older. To what extent should we view the New York statute as an attempt to create an "adult zone," where adults are able to obtain regulated speech but minors are not? Does the FCC's approach in *Pacifica* to indecency in broadcasting afford adults the same unfettered access to indecent speech as the New York statute at issue in *Ginsberg*? Why or why not? When the government seeks to protect minors against exposure to harmful speech, how much of a limit on adults' ability to gain access to that speech should courts allow?

4. Why should the government's power to regulate sexually explicit speech vary according to the medium in which the speech was uttered? What reasons does the Court give in *Pacifica* for concluding that speech in the broadcast medium deserves less protection than speech in other contexts? Is the Court's reasoning persuasive? Compare the metaphors. Justice Stevens views the radio program as an invasion into the privacy of the home. Justice Brennan, in contrast, likens turning on the radio to opening one's doors to public discourse. Which metaphor strikes you as more appropriate? Is either metaphor applicable to cyberspace? How would you apply this reasoning to sexually explicit speech transmitted over or displayed on the Internet?

5. Does it matter that the radio spectrum is limited and the government already plays an active role in regulating radio stations? What about the fact that the sanction at issue in *Pacifica* was not criminal punishment? Consider the following case and think about whether *Pacifica* is distinguishable.

Sable Communications of California, Inc. v. FCC

Supreme Court of the United States, 1989
492 U.S. 115

JUSTICE WHITE delivered the opinion of the Court.

The issue before us is the constitutionality of § 223(b) of the Communications Act of 1934. 47 U.S.C. § 223(b) (1982 ed., Supp. V). The statute, as amended in 1988, imposes an outright ban on indecent as well as obscene interstate commercial telephone messages. The District Court upheld the prohibition against obscene interstate telephone communications for commercial purposes, but enjoined the enforcement of the statute insofar as it applied to indecent messages. We affirm the District Court in both respects.

I

In 1983, Sable Communications, Inc., a Los Angeles-based affiliate of Carlin Communications, Inc., began offering sexually oriented prerecorded telephone messages (popularly known as "dial-a-porn") through the Pacific Bell telephone network. In order to provide the messages, Sable arranged with Pacific Bell to use special telephone lines, designed to handle large volumes of calls simultaneously. Those who called the adult message number were charged a special fee. The fee was collected by Pacific Bell and divided between the phone company and the message provider. Callers outside the Los Angeles metropolitan area could reach the number by means of a long-distance toll call to the Los Angeles area code.

In 1988, Sable brought suit in District Court seeking declaratory and injunctive relief against enforcement of the recently amended § 223(b). The 1988 amendments to the statute imposed a blanket prohibition on indecent as well as obscene interstate commercial telephone messages. Sable brought this action to enjoin the Federal Communications Commission (FCC) and the Justice Department from initiating any criminal investigation or prosecution, civil action or administrative proceeding under the statute. Sable also sought a declaratory judgment, challenging the indecency and the obscenity provisions of the amended § 223(b) as unconstitutional, chiefly under the First and Fourteenth Amendments to the Constitution.

* * * The District Court denied Sable's request for a preliminary injunction against enforcement of the statute's ban on obscene telephone messages, rejecting the argument that the statute was unconstitutional because it created a national standard of obscenity. The District Court, however, struck down the "indecent speech" provision of § 223(b), holding

that in this respect the statute was overbroad and unconstitutional and that this result was consistent with *FCC v. Pacifica Foundation*, 438 U.S. 726 (1978). "While the government unquestionably has a legitimate interest in, *e.g.*, protecting children from exposure to indecent dial-a-porn messages, § 223(b) is not narrowly drawn to achieve any such purpose. Its flat-out ban of indecent speech is contrary to the First Amendment." Therefore, the court issued a preliminary injunction prohibiting enforcement of § 223(b) with respect to any communication alleged to be "indecent."

We noted probable jurisdiction. * * *

II

* * * Congress made its first effort explicitly to address "dial-a-porn" when it added a subsection 223(b) to the 1934 Communications Act. The provision, which was the predecessor to the amendment at issue in this case, pertained directly to sexually oriented commercial telephone messages and sought to restrict the access of minors to dial-a-porn. The relevant provision * * * made it a crime to use telephone facilities to make "obscene or indecent" interstate telephone communications "for commercial purposes to any person under eighteen years of age or to any other person without that person's consent." 47 U.S.C. § 223(b)(1)(A) (1982 ed., Supp. V). The statute criminalized commercial transmission of sexually oriented communications to minors and required the FCC to promulgate regulations laying out the means by which dial-a-porn sponsors could screen out underaged callers. § 223(b)(2). The enactment provided that it would be a defense to prosecution that the defendant restricted access to adults only, in accordance with procedures established by the FCC. The statute did not criminalize sexually oriented messages to adults, whether the messages were obscene or indecent. * * *

[Over time, the FCC promulgated three sets of regulations for providers to follow in restricting access to adults. The Second Circuit invalidated the first two sets without reaching the constitutionality of the underlying legislation. The third set of regulations carried over earlier defenses for providers who restricted customer access by requiring payment by credit card or authorization by an access code. The regulations also added a new defense for providers who scrambled messages, which would be unintelligible without use of a descrambler sold only to adults.] On January 15, 1988, in *Carlin Communications, Inc. v. FCC*, 837 F.2d 546, *cert. denied*, 488 U.S. 924 (1988), the Court of Appeals for the Second Circuit held that the new regulations * * * were supported by the evidence, had been properly arrived at, and were a "feasible and effective way to serve" the "compelling state interest" in protecting minors, 837 F.2d, at 555; but the Court directed the FCC to reopen proceedings if a less restrictive technology became available. The Court of Appeals, however, this time reaching the constitutionality of the statute, invalidated § 223(b) insofar as it sought to apply to nonobscene speech.

Thereafter, in April 1988, Congress amended § 223(b) of the Communications Act to prohibit indecent as well as obscene interstate commercial telephone communications directed to any person regardless of age. The amended statute, which took effect on July 1, 1988, also eliminated the requirement that the FCC promulgate regulations for restricting access to minors since a total ban was imposed on dial-a-porn, making it illegal for adults, as well as children, to have access to the sexually explicit messages. It was this version of the statute that was in effect when Sable commenced this action. * * *

IV

[T]he District Court concluded that while the Government has a legitimate interest in protecting children from exposure to indecent dial-a-porn messages, § 223(b) was not sufficiently narrowly drawn to serve that purpose and thus violated the First Amendment. We agree.

Sexual expression which is indecent but not obscene is protected by the First Amendment; and the federal parties do not submit that the sale of such materials to adults could be criminalized solely because they are indecent. The Government may, however, regulate the content of constitutionally protected speech in order to promote a compelling interest if it chooses the least restrictive means to further the articulated interest. We have recognized that there is a compelling interest in protecting the physical and psychological well-being of minors. This interest extends to shielding minors from the influence of literature that is not obscene by adult standards. *Ginsberg v. New York*, 390 U.S. 629, 639-640 (1968). The Government may serve this legitimate interest, but to withstand constitutional scrutiny, "it must do so by narrowly drawn regulations designed to serve those interests without unnecessarily interfering with First Amendment freedoms." *Schaumburg v. Citizens for a Better Environment*, 444 U.S. 620, 637 (1980). It is not enough to show that the Government's ends are compelling; the means must be carefully tailored to achieve those ends.

In *Butler v. Michigan*, 352 U.S. 380 (1957), a unanimous Court reversed a conviction under a statute which made it an offense to make available to the general public materials found to have a potentially harmful influence on minors. The Court found the law to be insufficiently tailored since it denied adults their free speech rights by allowing them to read only what was acceptable for children. As Justice Frankfurter said in that case, "[s]urely this is to burn the house to roast the pig." *Id.*, at 383. In our judgment, this case, like *Butler*, presents us with "legislation not reasonably restricted to the evil with which it is said to deal." *Ibid.*

In attempting to justify the complete ban and criminalization of the indecent commercial telephone communications with adults as well as minors, the federal parties rely on *FCC v. Pacifica Foundation*, 438 U.S. 726 (1978), a case in which the Court considered whether the FCC has the power to regulate a radio broadcast that is indecent but not obscene. In an emphatically narrow holding, the *Pacifica* Court concluded that special treatment of indecent broadcasting was justified. *Pacifica* is readily distinguishable from these cases, most obviously because it did not involve a total ban on broadcasting indecent material. The FCC rule was not "'intended to place an absolute prohibition on the broadcast of this type of language, but rather sought to channel it to times of day when children most likely would not be exposed to it.'" *Pacifica, supra,* at 733, quoting *Pacifica Foundation,* 59 F.C.C.2d 892 (1976). The issue of a total ban was not before the Court.

The *Pacifica* opinion also relied on the "unique" attributes of broadcasting, noting that broadcasting is "uniquely pervasive," can intrude on the privacy of the home without prior warning as to program content, and is "uniquely accessible to children, even those too young to read." *Id.,* at 748-749. The private commercial telephone communications at issue here are substantially different from the public radio broadcast at issue in *Pacifica.* In contrast to public displays, unsolicited mailings and other means of expression which the recipient has no meaningful opportunity to avoid, the dial-it medium requires the listener to take affirmative steps to receive the communication. There is no "captive audience" problem here; callers will generally not be unwilling listeners. The context of dial-in services, where a caller seeks and is willing to pay for the communication, is manifestly different from a situation in which a listener does not want the received message. Placing a telephone call is not the same as turning on a radio and being taken by surprise by an indecent message. Unlike an unexpected outburst on a radio broadcast, the message received by one who places a call to a dial-a-porn service is not so invasive or surprising that it prevents an unwilling listener from avoiding exposure to it.

The Court in *Pacifica* was careful "to emphasize the narrowness of [its] holding." *Id.,* at 750. As we did in *Bolger v. Youngs Drug Products Corp.,* 463 U.S. 60 (1983), we distinguish *Pacifica* from the cases before us and reiterate that "the government may not 'reduce the adult population . . . to . . . only what is fit for children.'" 463 U.S., at 73, quoting *Butler,* 352 U.S., at 383. The federal parties nevertheless argue that the total ban on indecent commercial telephone communications is justified because nothing less could prevent children from gaining access to such messages. We find the argument quite unpersuasive. The FCC, after lengthy proceedings, determined that its credit card, access code, and scrambling rules were a satisfactory solution to the problem of keeping indecent dial-a-porn messages out of the reach of minors. The Court of Appeals, after careful consideration, agreed that these rules represented a "feasible and effective" way to serve the Government's compelling interest in protecting children.

The federal parties now insist that the rules would not be effective enough—that enterprising youngsters could and would evade the rules and gain access to communications from which they should be shielded. There is no evidence in the record before us to that effect, nor could there be since the FCC's implementation of § 223(b) prior to its 1988 amendment has never been tested over time. In this respect, the federal parties assert that in amending § 223(b) in 1988, Congress expressed its view that there was not a sufficiently effective way to protect minors short of the total ban that it enacted. The federal parties claim that we must give deference to that judgment.

* * * Beyond the fact that whatever deference is due legislative findings would not foreclose our independent judgment of the facts bearing on an issue of constitutional law, our answer is that the congressional record contains no legislative findings that would justify us in concluding that there is no constitutionally acceptable less restrictive means, short of a total ban, to achieve the Government's interest in protecting minors.

There is no doubt Congress enacted a total ban on both obscene and indecent telephone communications. But aside from conclusory statements during the debates by proponents of the bill, as well as similar assertions in hearings on a substantially identical bill the year before that under the FCC regulations minors could still have access to dial-a-porn messages, the congressional record presented to us contains no evidence as to *how* effective or ineffective the FCC's most recent regulations were or might prove to be. * * * For all we know from [the] record, the FCC's technological approach to restricting dial-a-porn messages to adults who seek them would be extremely effective, and only a few of the most enterprising and disobedient young people would manage to secure access to such messages. If this is the case, it seems to us that § 223(b) is not a narrowly tailored effort to serve the compelling interest of preventing minors from being exposed to indecent telephone messages. Under our precedents, § 223(b), in its present form, has the invalid effect of limiting the content of adult telephone conversations to that which is suitable for children to hear. It is another case of "burn[ing] the house to roast the pig." *Butler v. Michigan*, 352 U.S., at 383.

Because the statute's denial of adult access to telephone messages which are indecent but not obscene far exceeds that which is necessary to limit the access of minors to such messages, we hold that the ban does not survive constitutional scrutiny.

[Concurring opinion of Justice Scalia omitted.]

Notes and Questions

1. The Court distinguishes *Pacifica* in part on the ground that the FCC sought only to "channel" indecent speech to times when children would most likely not be exposed to it. Suppose that Congress had merely prohibited indecent interstate commercial telephone communications made between 8 a.m. and 9 p.m. How would the Court have ruled?

2. The Court concludes that the "dial-it" medium differs from the broadcast medium because a listener must take affirmative steps to receive the communication. Is this distinction persuasive? Is the Internet more like the dial-it medium or the broadcast medium?

3. Imagine that Congress had considered extensive evidence tending to show that the defenses endorsed by the FCC would be ineffective, and had made a factual finding that nothing short of a complete ban on dial-a-porn

could prevent children from gaining access to such messages. How would the Court have ruled?

Renton v. Playtime Theatres, Inc.

Supreme Court of the United States, 1986
475 U.S. 41

JUSTICE REHNQUIST delivered the opinion of the Court.

This case involves a constitutional challenge to a zoning ordinance, enacted by appellant city of Renton, Washington, that prohibits adult motion picture theaters from locating within 1,000 feet of any residential zone, single- or multiple-family dwelling, church, park, or school. Appellees, Playtime Theatres, Inc., and Sea-First Properties, Inc., filed an action in the United States District Court for the Western District of Washington seeking a declaratory judgment that the Renton ordinance violated the First and Fourteenth Amendments and a permanent injunction against its enforcement. The District Court ruled in favor of Renton and denied the permanent injunction, but the Court of Appeals for the Ninth Circuit reversed and remanded for reconsideration. We noted probable jurisdiction and now reverse the judgment of the Ninth Circuit.

In May 1980, the Mayor of Renton, a city of approximately 32,000 people located just south of Seattle, suggested to the Renton City Council that it consider the advisability of enacting zoning legislation dealing with adult entertainment uses. No such uses existed in the city at that time. Upon the Mayor's suggestion, the City Council referred the matter to the city's Planning and Development Committee. * * * In April 1981, acting on the basis of the Planning and Development Committee's recommendation, the City Council enacted Ordinance No. 3526. The ordinance prohibited any "adult motion picture theater" from locating within 1,000 feet of any residential zone, single- or multiple-family dwelling, church, or park, and within one mile of any school. The term "adult motion picture theater" was defined as "[a]n enclosed building used for presenting motion picture films, video cassettes, cable television, or any other such visual media, distinguished or characteri[zed] by an emphasis on matter depicting, describing or relating to 'specified sexual activities' or 'specified anatomical areas' . . . for observation by patrons therein."

In early 1982, respondents acquired two existing theaters in downtown Renton, with the intention of using them to exhibit feature-length adult films. The theaters were located within the area proscribed by Ordinance No. 3526. At about the same time, respondents filed the previously mentioned lawsuit challenging the ordinance on First and Fourteenth Amendment grounds, and seeking declaratory and injunctive relief. While the federal action was pending, the City Council amended the ordinance in several respects, adding a statement of reasons for its enactment and reducing the minimum distance from any school to 1,000 feet. * * * [After] the parties agreed to submit the case for a final decision on whether a permanent injunction should issue, [the District Court denied] respondents' requested permanent injunction, and entered summary judgment in favor of Renton. * * * The Court of Appeals for the Ninth Circuit reversed. * * *

In our view, the resolution of this case is largely dictated by our decision in *Young v. American Mini Theatres, Inc.*, 427 U.S. 50 (1976). There, although five Members of the Court did not agree on a single rationale for the decision, we held that the city of Detroit's zoning ordinance, which prohibited locating an adult theater within 1,000 feet of any two other "regulated uses" or within 500 feet of any residential zone, did not violate the First and Fourteenth Amendments. *Id.*, at 72-73 (plurality opinion of STEVENS, J., joined by BURGER, C.J., and WHITE and REHNQUIST, JJ.); *id.*, at 84 (POWELL, J., concurring). The Renton ordinance, like the one in *American Mini Theatres*, does not ban adult theaters altogether, but merely provides that such theaters may not be located within 1,000 feet of any residential zone, single- or multiple-family dwelling, church, park, or school. The ordinance is therefore properly analyzed as a form of time, place, and manner regulation. *Id.*, at 63, and n.18; *id.*, at 78-79 (POWELL, J., concurring).

Describing the ordinance as a time, place, and manner regulation is, of course, only the first step in our inquiry. This Court has long held that regulations enacted for the purpose of restraining speech on the basis of its content presumptively violate the First Amendment. On the other hand, so-called "content-neutral" time, place, and manner regulations are acceptable so long as they are designed to serve a substantial governmental interest and do not unreasonably limit alternative avenues of communication.

At first glance, the Renton ordinance, like the ordinance in *American Mini Theatres*, does not appear to fit neatly into either the "content-based" or the "content-neutral" category. To be sure, the ordinance treats theaters that specialize in adult films differently from other kinds of theaters. Nevertheless, as the District Court concluded, the Renton ordinance is aimed not at the *content* of the films shown at "adult motion picture theaters," but rather at the *secondary effects* of such theaters on the surrounding community. The District Court found that the City Council's *"predominate* concerns" were with the secondary effects of adult theaters, and not with the content of adult films themselves. [But the Court of Appeals] held that this was not enough to sustain the ordinance. According to the Court of Appeals, if *"a motivating factor"* in enacting the ordinance was to restrict respondents' exercise of First Amendment rights the ordinance would be invalid, apparently no matter how small a part this motivating factor may have played in the City Council's decision. This view of the law was rejected in *United States v. O'Brien*, 391 U.S. 367, 382-386 (1968), the very case that the Court of Appeals said it was applying:

> "It is a familiar principle of constitutional law that this Court will not strike down an otherwise constitutional statute on the basis of an alleged illicit legislative motive. . . .

"... What motivates one legislator to make a speech about a statute is not necessarily what motivates scores of others to enact it, and the stakes are sufficiently high for us to eschew guesswork." *Id.*, at 383-384.

The District Court's finding as to "predominate" intent, left undisturbed by the Court of Appeals, is more than adequate to establish that the city's pursuit of its zoning interests here was unrelated to the suppression of free expression. The ordinance by its terms is designed to prevent crime, protect the city's retail trade, maintain property values, and generally "protec[t] and preserv[e] the quality of [the city's] neighborhoods, commercial districts, and the quality of urban life," not to suppress the expression of unpopular views. As JUSTICE POWELL observed in *American Mini Theatres*, "[i]f [the city] had been concerned with restricting the message purveyed by adult theaters, it would have tried to close them or restrict their number rather than circumscribe their choice as to location." 427 U.S., at 82, n.4.

In short, the Renton ordinance is completely consistent with our definition of "content-neutral" speech regulations as those that "are *justified* without reference to the content of the regulated speech." *Virginia Pharmacy Board v. Virginia Citizens Consumer Council, Inc.*, 425 U.S. 748, 771 (1976) (emphasis added). The ordinance does not contravene the fundamental principle that underlies our concern about "content-based" speech regulations: that "government may not grant the use of a forum to people whose views it finds acceptable, but deny use to those wishing to express less favored or more controversial views." *Police Dept. of Chicago v. Mosley*, 408 U.S. 92, 95-96 (1972).

* * * The appropriate inquiry in this case, then, is whether the Renton ordinance is designed to serve a substantial governmental interest and allows for reasonable alternative avenues of communication. It is clear that the ordinance meets such a standard. As a majority of this Court recognized in *American Mini Theatres*, a city's "interest in attempting to preserve the quality of urban life is one that must be accorded high respect." 427 U.S., at 71 (plurality opinion); see *id.*, at 80 (POWELL, J., concurring) ("Nor is there doubt that the interests furthered by this ordinance are both important and substantial"). Exactly the same vital governmental interests are at stake here. * * *

We also find no constitutional defect in the method chosen by Renton to further its substantial interests. Cities may regulate adult theaters by dispersing them, as in Detroit, or by effectively concentrating them, as in Renton. "It is not our function to appraise the wisdom of [the city's] decision to require adult theaters to be separated rather than concentrated in the same areas. . . .[T]he city must be allowed a reasonable opportunity to experiment with solutions to admittedly serious problems." *American Mini Theatres*, 427 U.S., at 71 (plurality opinion). Moreover, the Renton ordinance is "narrowly tailored" to affect only that category of theaters shown to produce the unwanted secondary effects, thus avoiding the flaw that proved fatal to the regulations in *Schad v. Mount Ephraim*, 452 U.S. 61 (1981), and *Erznoznik v. City of Jacksonville*, 422 U.S. 205 (1975). * * *

Finally, turning to the question whether the Renton ordinance allows for reasonable alternative avenues of communication, we note that the ordinance leaves some 520 acres, or more than five percent of the entire land area of Renton, open to use as adult theater sites. * * * In our view, the First Amendment requires only that Renton refrain from effectively denying respondents a reasonable opportunity to open and operate an adult theater within the city, and the ordinance before us easily meets this requirement.

In sum, we find that the Renton ordinance represents a valid governmental response to the "admittedly serious problems" created by adult theaters. *See American Mini Theatres*, 427 U.S., at 71 (plurality opinion). Renton has not used "the power to zone as a pretext for suppressing expression," *id.*, at 84 (POWELL, J., concurring), but rather has sought to make some areas available for adult theaters and their patrons, while at the same time preserving the quality of life in the community at large by preventing those theaters from locating in other areas. This, after all, is the essence of zoning. Here, as in *American Mini Theatres*, the city has enacted a zoning ordinance that meets these goals while also satisfying the dictates of the First Amendment.

JUSTICE BLACKMUN concurs in the result.

[Dissenting opinion of Justice Brennan omitted.]

Notes and Questions

1. How does the Court distinguish an ordinance aimed at the "content" of adult films from an ordinance aimed at the "secondary effects" on the surrounding community of theaters showing such films? How does its approach differ from that of the court of appeals? Should a court assessing whether a law is aimed at secondary effects or aimed at content focus on the reach of the law or the intent of the legislators? How should a court discern that intent?

2. How might a legislature craft a law aimed at the "secondary effects" of sexually explicit speech over the Internet? Would it be possible to create an "adult zone" on the Internet?

Reno v. American Civil Liberties Union

Supreme Court of the United States, 1997
521 U.S. 844

JUSTICE STEVENS delivered the opinion of the Court.

At issue is the constitutionality of two statutory provisions enacted to protect minors from "indecent" and "patently offensive" communications on the Internet. Notwithstanding the legitimacy and importance of the congressional goal of protecting children from harmful materials, we agree with the three-judge District Court that the statute abridges "the freedom of speech" protected by the First Amendment. * * *

II

The Telecommunications Act of 1996, Pub. L. 104-104, 110 Stat. 56, was an unusually important legislative enactment. As stated on the first of its 103 pages, its primary purpose was to reduce regulation and encourage "the rapid deployment of new telecommunications technologies." The major components of the statute have nothing to do with the Internet; they were designed to promote competition in the local telephone service market, the multichannel video market, and the market for over-the-air broadcasting. The Act includes seven Titles, six of which are the product of extensive committee hearings and the subject of discussion in Reports prepared by Committees of the Senate and the House of Representatives. By contrast, Title V—known as the "Communications Decency Act of 1996" (CDA)— contains provisions that were either added in executive committee after the hearings were concluded or as amendments offered during floor debate on the legislation. An amendment offered in the Senate was the source of the two statutory provisions challenged in this case. They are informally described as the "indecent transmission" provision and the "patently offensive display" provision.

The first, 47 U.S.C. § 223(a) (1994 ed., Supp. II), prohibits the knowing transmission of obscene or indecent messages to any recipient under 18 years of age. It provides in pertinent part:

"(a) Whoever–

"(1) in interstate or foreign communications–

. . . . .

"(B) by means of a telecommunications device knowingly–

"(i) makes, creates, or solicits, and

"(ii) initiates the transmission of,

"any comment, request, suggestion, proposal, image, or other communication which is obscene or indecent, knowing that the recipient of the communication is under 18 years of age, regardless of whether the maker of such communication placed the call or initiated the communication;

. . . . .

"(2) knowingly permits any telecommunications facility under his control to be used for any activity prohibited by paragraph (1) with the intent that it be used for such activity,

"shall be fined under Title 18, or imprisoned not more than two years, or both."

The second provision, § 223(d), prohibits the knowing sending or displaying of patently offensive messages in a manner that is available to a person under 18 years of age. It provides:

"(d) Whoever–

"(1) in interstate or foreign communications knowingly–

"(A) uses an interactive computer service to send to a specific person or persons under 18 years of age, or

"(B) uses any interactive computer service to display in a manner available to a person under 18 years of age,

"any comment, request, suggestion, proposal, image, or other communication that, in context, depicts or describes, in terms patently offensive as measured by contemporary community standards, sexual or excretory activities or organs, regardless of whether the user of such service placed the call or initiated the communication; or

"(2) knowingly permits any telecommunications facility under such person's control to be used for an activity prohibited by paragraph (1) with the intent that it be used for such activity,

"shall be fined under Title 18, or imprisoned not more than two years, or both."

The breadth of these prohibitions is qualified by two affirmative defenses. See § 223(e)(5). One covers those who take "good faith, reasonable, effective, and appropriate actions" to restrict access by minors to the prohibited communications. § 223(e)(5)(A). The other covers those who restrict access to covered material by requiring certain designated forms of age proof, such as a verified credit card or an adult identification number or code. § 223(e)(5)(B).

III

On February 8, 1996, immediately after the President signed the statute, 20 plaintiffs filed suit against the Attorney General of the United States and the Department of Justice challenging the constitutionality of §§ 223(a)(1) and 223(d). * * * A second suit was then filed by 27 additional plaintiffs, the two cases were consolidated, and a three-judge District Court was convened pursuant to § 561 of the CDA. After an evidentiary hearing, that court entered a preliminary injunction against enforcement of both of the challenged provisions. * * *

The judgment of the District Court enjoins the Government from enforcing the prohibitions in § 223(a)(1)(B) insofar as they relate to "indecent" communications, but expressly preserves the Government's right to investigate and prosecute the obscenity or child pornography activities prohibited therein. The injunction against enforcement of §§ 223(d)(1) and (2) is unqualified because those provisions contain no separate reference to obscenity or child pornography.

The Government appealed under the CDA's special review provisions, and we noted probable jurisdiction. In its appeal, the Government argues that the District Court erred in holding that the CDA violated both the First Amendment because it is overbroad and the Fifth Amendment because it is vague. While we discuss the vagueness of the CDA because of its relevance to the First Amendment overbreadth inquiry, we conclude that the judgment should be affirmed without reaching the Fifth Amendment issue. We begin our analysis by reviewing the principal authorities on which the Government relies. Then, after describing the overbreadth of the CDA, we consider the Government's specific contentions, including its submission that we save portions of the statute either by severance or by fashioning judicial limitations on the scope of its coverage.

IV

In arguing for reversal, the Government contends that the CDA is plainly constitutional under three of our prior decisions: (1) *Ginsberg v. New York*, 390 U.S. 629 (1968); (2) *FCC v. Pacifica Foundation*, 438 U.S. 726 (1978); and (3) *Renton v. Playtime Theatres, Inc.*, 475 U.S. 41 (1986). A close look at these cases, however, raises—rather than relieves—doubts concerning the constitutionality of the CDA.

In *Ginsberg*, we upheld the constitutionality of a New York statute that prohibited selling to minors under 17 years of age material that was considered obscene as to them even if not obscene as to adults. We rejected the defendant's broad submission that "the scope of the constitutional freedom of expression secured to a citizen to read or see material concerned with sex cannot be made to depend on whether the citizen is an adult or a minor." 390 U.S., at 636. In rejecting that contention, we relied not only on the State's independent interest in the well-being of its youth, but also on our consistent recognition of the principle that "the parents' claim to authority in their own household to direct the rearing of their children is basic in the structure of our society."

In four important respects, the statute upheld in *Ginsberg* was narrower than the CDA. First, we noted in *Ginsberg* that "the prohibition against sales to minors does not bar parents who so desire from purchasing the magazines for their children." *Id.*, at 639. Under the CDA, by contrast, neither the parents' consent—nor even their participation—in the communication would avoid the application of the statute. Second, the New York statute applied only to commercial transactions, *id.*, at 647, whereas the CDA contains no such limitation. Third, the New York statute cabined its definition of material that is harmful to minors with the requirement that it be "utterly without redeeming social importance for minors." *Id.*, at 646. The CDA fails to provide us with any definition of the term "indecent" as used in § 223(a)(1) and, importantly, omits any requirement that the "patently offensive" material covered by § 223(d) lack serious literary, artistic, political, or scientific value. Fourth, the New York statute defined a minor as a person under the age of 17, whereas the CDA, in applying to all those under 18 years, includes an additional year of those nearest majority.

In *Pacifica*, we upheld a declaratory order of the Federal Communications Commission, holding that the broadcast of a recording of a 12-minute monologue entitled "Filthy Words" that had previously been delivered to a live audience "could have been the subject of administrative sanctions." 438 U.S., at 730 (internal quotation marks omitted). The Commission had found that the repetitive use of certain words referring to excretory or sexual activities or organs "in an afternoon broadcast when children are in the audience was patently offensive" and concluded that the monologue was indecent "as broadcast." *Id.*, at 735. * * * After rejecting respondent's statutory arguments, we confronted its [constitutional argument] * * * that since the recording was not obscene, the First Amendment forbade any abridgment of the right to broadcast it on the radio.

In the portion of the lead opinion not joined by Justices Powell and Blackmun, the plurality stated that the First Amendment does not prohibit all governmental regulation that depends on the content of speech. Accordingly, the availability of constitutional protection for a vulgar and offensive monologue that was not obscene depended on the context of the broadcast. Relying on the premise that "of all forms of communication" broadcasting had received the most limited First Amendment protection, *id.*, at 748-749, the Court concluded that the ease with which children may obtain access to broadcasts, "coupled with the concerns recognized in *Ginsberg*," justified special treatment of indecent broadcasting. *Id.*, at 749-750.

As with the New York statute at issue in *Ginsberg*, there are significant differences between the order upheld in *Pacifica* and the CDA. First, the order in *Pacifica*, issued by an agency that had been regulating radio stations for decades, targeted a specific broadcast that represented a rather dramatic departure from traditional program content in order to designate when—rather than whether—it would be permissible to air such a program in that particular medium. The CDA's broad categorical prohibitions are not limited to particular times and are not dependent on any evaluation by an agency familiar with the unique characteristics of the Internet. Second, unlike the CDA, the Commission's declaratory order was not punitive; we expressly refused to decide whether the indecent broadcast "would justify a criminal prosecution." 438 U.S., at 750. Finally, the Commission's order applied to a medium which as a matter of history had "received the most limited First Amendment protection," *id.*, at 748, in large part because warnings could not adequately protect the listener from unexpected program content. The Internet, however, has no comparable history. Moreover, the District Court found that the risk of encountering indecent material by accident is remote because a series of affirmative steps is required to access specific material.

In *Renton*, we upheld a zoning ordinance that kept adult movie theaters out of residential neighborhoods. The ordinance was aimed, not at the content of the films shown in the theaters, but rather at the "secondary effects"—such as crime and deteriorating property values—that these theaters fostered: "'It is th[e] secondary effect which these zoning ordinances attempt to avoid, not the dissemination of "offensive" speech.'" 475 U.S., at 49 (quoting *Young v. American Mini Theatres, Inc.*, 427 U.S. 50, 71, n.34 (1976)). According to the Government, the CDA is constitutional because it constitutes a sort of "cyberzoning" on the Internet. But the CDA applies broadly to the entire universe of cyberspace. And the purpose of the CDA is to protect children from the primary effects of "indecent" and "patently offensive" speech, rather than any "secondary" effect of such speech. Thus, the CDA is a content-based blanket restriction on speech, and, as such, cannot be "properly analyzed as a form of time, place, and manner regulation." 475 U.S., at 46.

These precedents, then, surely do not require us to uphold the CDA and are fully consistent with the application of the most stringent review of its provisions.

V

In *Southeastern Promotions, Ltd. v. Conrad*, 420 U.S. 546, 557 (1975), we observed that "[e]ach medium of expression . . . may present its own problems." Thus, some of our cases have recognized special justifications for regulation of the broadcast media that are not applicable to other speakers, see *Red Lion Broadcasting Co. v. FCC*, 395 U.S. 367 (1969); *FCC v. Pacifica Foundation*, 438 U.S. 726 (1978). In these cases, the Court relied on the history of extensive Government regulation of the broadcast medium; the scarcity of available frequencies at its inception; and its "invasive" nature.

Those factors are not present in cyberspace. Neither before nor after the enactment of the CDA have the vast democratic forums of the Internet been subject to the type of government supervision and regulation that has attended the broadcast industry. Moreover, the Internet is not as "invasive" as radio or television. The District Court specifically found that "[c]ommunications over the Internet do not 'invade' an individual's home or appear on one's computer screen unbidden. Users seldom encounter content 'by accident.'" It also found that "[a]lmost all sexually explicit images are preceded by warnings as to the content," and cited testimony that "'odds are slim' that a user would come across a sexually explicit sight by accident." *Ibid.* We distinguished *Pacifica* in *Sable Communications of Cal., Inc. v. FCC*, 492 U.S. 115, 128 (1989), on just this basis. * * *

Finally, unlike the conditions that prevailed when Congress first authorized regulation of the broadcast spectrum, the Internet can hardly be considered a "scarce" expressive commodity. It provides relatively unlimited, low-cost capacity for communication of all kinds. The Government estimates that "[a]s many as 40 million people use the Internet today, and that figure is expected to grow to 200 million by 1999." This dynamic, multifaceted category of communication includes not only traditional print and news services, but also audio, video, and still images, as well as interactive, real-time dialogue. Through the use of chat rooms, any person with a phone line can become a town crier with a voice that resonates farther than it could from any soapbox. Through the use of Web pages, mail exploders, and newsgroups, the same individual can become a pamphleteer.

As the District Court found, "the content on the Internet is as diverse as human thought." We agree with its conclusion that our cases provide no basis for qualifying the level of First Amendment scrutiny that should be applied to this medium.

VI

Regardless of whether the CDA is so vague that it violates the Fifth Amendment, the many ambiguities concerning the scope of its coverage render it problematic for purposes of the First Amendment. For instance, each of the two parts of the CDA uses a different linguistic form. The first uses the word "indecent," 47 U.S.C. § 223(a) (1994 ed., Supp. II), while the second speaks of material that "in context, depicts or describes, in terms patently offensive as measured by contemporary community standards, sexual or excretory activities or organs," § 223(d). Given the absence of a definition of either term, this difference in language will provoke uncertainty among speakers about how the two standards relate to each other and just what they mean. Could a speaker confidently assume that a serious discussion about birth control practices, homosexuality, the First Amendment issues raised by the Appendix to our *Pacifica* opinion, or the consequences of prison rape would not violate the CDA? This uncertainty undermines the likelihood that the CDA has been carefully tailored to the congressional goal of protecting minors from potentially harmful materials.

The vagueness of the CDA is a matter of special concern for two reasons. First, the CDA is a content-based regulation of speech. The vagueness of such a regulation raises special First Amendment concerns because of its obvious chilling effect on free speech. Second, the CDA is a criminal statute. In addition to the opprobrium and stigma of a criminal conviction, the CDA threatens violators with penalties including up to two years in prison for each act of violation. The severity of criminal sanctions may well cause speakers to remain silent rather than communicate even arguably unlawful words, ideas, and images. As a practical matter, this increased deterrent effect, coupled with the "risk of discriminatory enforcement" of vague regulations, poses greater First Amendment concerns than those implicated by the civil regulation reviewed in *Denver Area Ed. Telecommunications Consortium, Inc. v. FCC*, 518 U.S. 727 (1996).

The Government argues that the statute is no more vague than the obscenity standard this Court established in *Miller v. California*, 413 U.S. 15 (1973). But that is not so. In *Miller*, this Court reviewed a criminal conviction against a commercial vendor who mailed brochures containing pictures of sexually explicit activities to individuals who had not requested such materials. *Id.*, at 18. Having struggled for some time to establish a definition of obscenity, we set forth in *Miller* the test for obscenity that controls to this day:

> "(a) whether the average person, applying contemporary community standards would find that the work, taken as a whole, appeals to the prurient interest; (b) whether the work depicts or describes, in a patently offensive way, sexual conduct specifically defined by the applicable state law; and (c) whether the work, taken as a whole, lacks serious literary, artistic, political, or scientific value." *Id.*, at 24 (internal quotation marks and citations omitted).

Because the CDA's "patently offensive" standard (and, we assume, *arguendo*, its synonymous "indecent" standard) is one part of the three-prong *Miller* test, the Government reasons, it cannot be unconstitutionally vague.

The Government's assertion is incorrect as a matter of fact. The second prong of the *Miller* test—the purportedly analogous standard—contains a critical requirement that is omitted from the CDA: that the proscribed material be "specifically defined by the applicable state law." This requirement reduces the vagueness inherent in the open-ended term "patently offensive" as used in the CDA. Moreover, the *Miller* definition is limited to "sexual conduct," whereas the CDA extends also to include (1) "excretory activities" as well as (2) "organs" of both a sexual and excretory nature.

The Government's reasoning is also flawed. Just because a definition including three limitations is not vague, it does not follow that one of those limitations, standing by itself, is not vague. Each of *Miller*'s additional two prongs—(1) that, taken as a whole, the material appeal to the "prurient" interest, and (2) that it "lac[k] serious literary, artistic, political, or scientific value"—critically limits the uncertain sweep of the obscenity definition. The second requirement is particularly important because, unlike the "patently offensive" and "prurient interest" criteria, it is not judged by contemporary community standards. This "societal value" requirement, absent in the CDA, allows appellate courts to impose some limitations and regularity on the definition by setting, as a matter of law, a national floor for socially redeeming value. The Government's contention that courts will be able to give such legal limitations to the CDA's standards is belied by *Miller*'s own rationale for having juries determine whether material is "patently offensive" according to community standards: that such questions are essentially ones of fact.

In contrast to *Miller* and our other previous cases, the CDA thus presents a greater threat of censoring speech that, in fact, falls outside the statute's scope. Given the vague contours of the coverage of the statute, it unquestionably silences some speakers whose messages would be entitled to constitutional protection. That danger provides further reason for insisting that the statute not be overly broad. The CDA's burden on protected speech cannot be justified if it could be avoided by a more carefully drafted statute.

VII

We are persuaded that the CDA lacks the precision that the First Amendment requires when a statute regulates the content of speech. In order to deny minors access to potentially harmful speech, the CDA effectively suppresses a large amount of speech that adults have a constitutional right to receive and to address to one another. That burden on adult speech is unacceptable if less restrictive alternatives would be at least as effective in achieving the legitimate purpose that the statute was enacted to serve.

In evaluating the free speech rights of adults, we have made it perfectly clear that "[s]exual expression which is indecent but not obscene is protected by the First Amendment." *Sable*, 492 U.S., at 126. Indeed, *Pacifica* itself admonished that "the fact that society may find speech offensive is not a sufficient reason for suppressing it." 438 U.S., at 745.

It is true that we have repeatedly recognized the governmental interest in protecting children from harmful materials. But that interest does not justify an unnecessarily broad suppression of speech addressed to adults. As we have explained, the Government may not "reduc[e] the adult population * * * to * * * only what is fit for children." *Denver*, 518 U.S., at 759 (internal quotation marks omitted) (quoting *Sable*, 492 U.S., at 128). "[R]egardless of the strength of the government's interest" in protecting children, "[t]he level of discourse reaching a mailbox simply cannot be limited to that which would be suitable for a sandbox." *Bolger v. Youngs Drug Products Corp.*, 463 U.S. 60, 74-75 (1983).

The District Court was correct to conclude that the CDA effectively resembles the ban on "dial-a-porn" invalidated in *Sable*. In *Sable*, 492 U.S., at 129, this Court rejected the argument that we should defer to the congressional judgment that nothing less than a total ban would be effective in preventing enterprising youngsters from gaining access to indecent communications. *Sable* thus made clear that the mere fact that a statutory regulation of speech was enacted for the important purpose of protecting children from exposure to sexually explicit material does not foreclose inquiry into its validity. As we pointed out last Term, that inquiry embodies an "overarching commitment" to make sure that Congress has designed its statute to accomplish its purpose "without imposing an unnecessarily great restriction on speech." *Denver*, 518 U.S., at 741.

In arguing that the CDA does not so diminish adult communication, the Government relies on the incorrect factual premise that prohibiting a transmission whenever it is known that one of its recipients is a minor would not interfere with adult-to-adult communication. The findings of the District Court make clear that this premise is untenable. Given the size of the potential audience for most messages, in the absence of a viable age verification process, the sender must be charged with knowing that one or more minors will likely view it. Knowledge that, for instance, one or more members of a 100-person chat group will be a minor—and therefore that it would be a crime to send the group an indecent message—would surely burden communication among adults.

The District Court found that at the time of trial existing technology did not include any effective method for a sender to prevent minors from obtaining access to its communications on the Internet without also denying access to adults. The Court found no effective way to determine the age of a user who is accessing material through e-mail, mail exploders, newsgroups, or chat rooms. As a practical matter, the Court also found that it would be prohibitively expensive for noncommercial—as well as some commercial—speakers who have Web sites to verify that their users are adults. These limitations must inevitably curtail a significant amount of adult communication on the Internet. By contrast, the District Court found that "[d]espite its limitations, currently available *user-based* software suggests that a reasonably effective method by which *parents* can prevent their children from accessing sexually explicit and other material which parents may believe is inappropriate for their children will soon be widely available." (Emphases added.)

The breadth of the CDA's coverage is wholly unprecedented. Unlike the regulations upheld in *Ginsberg* and *Pacifica*, the scope of the CDA is not limited to commercial speech or commercial entities. Its open-ended prohibitions embrace all nonprofit entities and individuals posting indecent messages or displaying them on their own computers in the presence of minors. The general, undefined terms "indecent" and "patently offensive" cover large amounts of nonpornographic material with serious educational or other value. Moreover, the "community standards" criterion as applied to the Internet means that any communication available to a nation wide audience will be judged by the standards of the community most likely to be offended by the message. The regulated subject matter includes any of the seven "dirty words" used in the *Pacifica* monologue, the use of which the Government's expert acknowledged could constitute a felony. It may also extend to discussions about prison rape or safe sexual practices, artistic images that include nude subjects, and arguably the card catalog of the Carnegie Library.

For the purposes of our decision, we need neither accept nor reject the Government's submission that the First Amendment does not forbid a blanket prohibition on all "indecent" and "patently offensive" messages communicated to a 17-year-old—no matter how much value the message may contain and regardless of parental approval. It is at least clear that the strength of the Government's interest in protecting minors is not equally strong throughout the coverage of this broad statute. Under the CDA, a parent allowing her 17-year-old to use the family computer to obtain information on the Internet that she, in her parental judgment, deems appropriate could face a lengthy prison term. See 47 U.S.C. § 223(a)(2) (1994 ed., Supp. II). Similarly, a parent who sent his 17-year-old college freshman information on birth control via e-mail could be incarcerated even though neither he, his child, nor anyone in their home community found the material "indecent" or "patently offensive," if the college town's community thought otherwise.

The breadth of this content-based restriction of speech imposes an especially heavy burden on the Government to explain why a less restrictive provision would not be as effective as the CDA. It has not done so. The arguments in this Court have referred to possible alternatives such as requiring that indecent material be "tagged" in a way that facilitates parental control of material coming into their homes, making exceptions for messages with artistic or educational value, providing some tolerance for parental choice, and regulating some portions of the Internet—such as commercial Web sites—differently from others, such as chat rooms. Particularly in the light of the absence of any detailed findings by the Congress, or even hearings addressing the special problems of the CDA, we are persuaded that the CDA is not narrowly tailored if that requirement has any meaning at all.

VIII

In an attempt to curtail the CDA's facial overbreadth, the Government advances three additional arguments for sustaining the Act's affirmative prohibitions: (1) that the CDA is constitutional because it leaves open ample "alternative channels" of communication; (2) that the plain meaning of the CDA's "knowledge" and "specific person" requirement significantly restricts its permissible applications; and (3) that the CDA's prohibitions are "almost always" limited to material lacking redeeming social value.

The Government first contends that, even though the CDA effectively censors discourse on many of the Internet's modalities—such as chat groups, newsgroups, and mail exploders—it is nonetheless constitutional because it provides a "reasonable opportunity" for speakers to engage in the restricted speech on the World Wide Web. This argument is unpersuasive because the CDA regulates speech on the basis of its content. A "time, place, and manner" analysis is therefore inapplicable. It is thus immaterial whether such speech would be feasible on the Web (which, as the Government's own expert acknowledged, would cost up to $10,000 if the speaker's interests were not accommodated by an existing Web site, not including costs for data base management and age verification). The Government's position is equivalent to arguing that a statute could ban leaflets on certain subjects as long as individuals are free to publish books. In invalidating a number of laws that banned leafletting on the streets *regardless* of their content, we explained that "one is not to have the exercise of his liberty of expression in appropriate places abridged on the plea that it may be exercised in some other place." *Schneider v. State of N.J. (Town of Irvington)*, 308 U.S. 147, 163 (1939).

The Government also asserts that the "knowledge" requirement of both §§ 223(a) and (d), especially when coupled with the "specific child" element found in § 223(d), saves the CDA from overbreadth. Because both sections prohibit the dissemination of indecent messages only to persons known to be under 18, the Government argues, it does not require transmitters to "refrain from communicating indecent material to adults; they need only refrain from disseminating such materials to persons they know to be under 18." This argument ignores the fact that most Internet forums—including chat rooms, newsgroups, mail exploders, and the Web—are open to all comers. The Government's assertion that the knowledge requirement somehow protects the communications of adults is therefore untenable. Even the strongest reading of the "specific person" requirement of § 223(d) cannot save the statute. It would confer broad powers of censorship, in the form of a "heckler's veto," upon any opponent of indecent speech who might simply log on and inform the would-be discoursers that his 17-year-old child—a "specific person ... under 18 years of age," 47 U.S.C. § 223(d)(1)(A) (1994 ed., Supp. II)—would be present.

Finally, we find no textual support for the Government's submission that material having scientific, educational, or other redeeming social value will necessarily fall outside the CDA's "patently offensive" and "indecent" prohibitions.

IX

The Government's three remaining arguments focus on the defenses provided in § 223(e)(5). First, relying on the "good faith, reasonable, effective, and appropriate actions" provision, the Government suggests that "tagging" provides a defense that saves the constitutionality of the CDA. The suggestion assumes that transmitters may encode their indecent communications in a way that would indicate their contents, thus permitting recipients to block their reception with appropriate software. It is the requirement that the good-faith action must be "effective" that makes this defense illusory. The Government recognizes that its proposed screening software does not currently exist. Even if it did, there is no way to know whether a potential recipient will actually block the encoded material. Without the impossible knowledge that every guardian in America is screening for the "tag," the transmitter could not reasonably rely on its action to be "effective."

For its second and third arguments concerning defenses—which we can consider together—the Government relies on the latter half of § 223(e)(5), which applies when the transmitter has restricted access by requiring use of a verified credit card or adult identification. Such verification is not only technologically available but actually is used by commercial providers of sexually explicit material. These providers, therefore, would be protected by the defense. Under the findings of the District Court, however, it is not economically feasible for most noncommercial speakers to employ such verification. Accordingly, this defense would not significantly narrow the statute's burden on noncommercial speech. Even with respect to the commercial pornographers that would be protected by the defense, the Government failed to adduce any evidence that these verification techniques actually preclude minors from posing as adults. Given that the risk of criminal sanctions "hovers over each content provider, like the proverbial sword of Damocles," the

District Court correctly refused to rely on unproven future technology to save the statute. The Government thus failed to prove that the proffered defense would significantly reduce the heavy burden on adult speech produced by the prohibition on offensive displays.

We agree with the District Court's conclusion that the CDA places an unacceptably heavy burden on protected speech, and that the defenses do not constitute the sort of "narrow tailoring" that will save an otherwise patently invalid unconstitutional provision. In *Sable*, 492 U.S., at 127, we remarked that the speech restriction at issue there amounted to "'burn[ing] the house to roast the pig.'" The CDA, casting a far darker shadow over free speech, threatens to torch a large segment of the Internet community.

JUSTICE O'CONNOR, with whom THE CHIEF JUSTICE joins, concurring in the judgment in part and dissenting in part.

I write separately to explain why I view the Communications Decency Act of 1996 (CDA) as little more than an attempt by Congress to create "adult zones" on the Internet. Our precedent indicates that the creation of such zones can be constitutionally sound. Despite the soundness of its purpose, however, portions of the CDA are unconstitutional because they stray from the blueprint our prior cases have developed for constructing a "zoning law" that passes constitutional muster.

Appellees bring a facial challenge to three provisions of the CDA. The first, which the Court describes as the "indecency transmission" provision, makes it a crime to knowingly transmit an obscene or indecent message or image to a person the sender knows is under 18 years old. 47 U.S.C. § 223(a)(1)(B) (1994 ed., Supp. II). What the Court classifies as a single "'patently offensive display'" provision is in reality two separate provisions. The first of these makes it a crime to knowingly send a patently offensive message or image to a specific person under the age of 18 ("specific person" provision). § 223(d)(1)(A). The second criminalizes the display of patently offensive messages or images "in a[ny] manner available" to minors ("display" provision). § 223(d)(1)(B). None of these provisions purports to keep indecent (or patently offensive) material away from adults, who have a First Amendment right to obtain this speech. Thus, the undeniable purpose of the CDA is to segregate indecent material on the Internet into certain areas that minors cannot access.

The creation of "adult zones" is by no means a novel concept. States have long denied minors access to certain establishments frequented by adults. States have also denied minors access to speech deemed to be "harmful to minors." The Court has previously sustained such zoning laws, but only if they respect the First Amendment rights of adults and minors. That is to say, a zoning law is valid if (i) it does not unduly restrict adult access to the material; and (ii) minors have no First Amendment right to read or view the banned material. As applied to the Internet as it exists in 1997, the "display" provision and some applications of the "indecency transmission" and "specific person" provisions fail to adhere to the first of these limiting principles by restricting adults' access to protected materials in certain circumstances. Unlike the Court, however, I would invalidate the provisions only in those circumstances.

I

Our cases make clear that a "zoning" law is valid only if adults are still able to obtain the regulated speech. If they cannot, the law does more than simply keep children away from speech they have no right to obtain—it interferes with the rights of adults to obtain constitutionally protected speech and effectively "reduce[s] the adult population . . . to reading only what is fit for children." *Butler v. Michigan*, 352 U.S. 380, 383 (1957). The First Amendment does not tolerate such interference. If the law does not unduly restrict adults' access to constitutionally protected speech, however, it may be valid. In *Ginsberg v. New York*, 390 U.S. 629, 634, (1968), for example, the Court sustained a New York law that barred store owners from selling pornographic magazines to minors in part because adults could still buy those magazines.

The Court in *Ginsberg* concluded that the New York law created a constitutionally adequate adult zone simply because, on its face, it denied access only to minors. The Court did not question—and therefore necessarily assumed—that an adult zone, once created, would succeed in preserving adults' access while denying minors' access to the regulated speech. Before today, there was no reason to question this assumption, for the Court has previously only considered laws that operated in the physical world, a world that with two characteristics that make it possible to create "adult zones": geography and identity. See Lessig, Reading the Constitution in Cyberspace, 45 Emory L.J. 869, 886 (1996). A minor can see an adult dance show only if he enters an establishment that provides such entertainment. And should he attempt to do so, the minor will not be able to conceal completely his identity (or, consequently, his age). Thus, the twin characteristics of geography and identity enable the establishment's proprietor to prevent children from entering the establishment, but to let adults inside.

The electronic world is fundamentally different. Because it is no more than the interconnection of electronic pathways, cyberspace allows speakers and listeners to mask their identities. Cyberspace undeniably reflects some form of geography; chat rooms and Web sites, for example, exist at fixed "locations" on the Internet. Since users can transmit and receive messages on the Internet without revealing anything about their identities or ages, see *id.*, at 901, however, it is not currently possible to exclude persons from accessing certain messages on the basis of their identity.

Cyberspace differs from the physical world in another basic way: Cyberspace is malleable. Thus, it is possible to construct barriers in cyberspace and use them to screen for identity, making cyberspace more like the physical world and, consequently, more amenable to zoning laws. This transformation of cyberspace is already underway. *Id.*, at 888-889; *id.*, at 887 (cyberspace "is moving . . . from a relatively unzoned place to a universe that is extraordinarily well zoned"). Internet speakers (users who post material on the Internet) have begun to zone cyberspace itself through the use of "gateway" technology. Such technology requires Internet users to enter information about themselves—perhaps an adult identification number or a credit card number—before they can access certain areas of cyberspace, much like a bouncer checks a person's driver's license before admitting him to a nightclub. Internet users who access information have not attempted to zone cyberspace itself, but have tried to limit their own power to access information in cyberspace, much as a parent controls what her children watch on television by installing a lock box. This user-based zoning is accomplished through the use of screening software (such as Cyber Patrol or SurfWatch) or browsers with screening capabilities, both of which search addresses and text for keywords that are associated with "adult" sites and, if the user wishes, blocks access to such sites. *Id.*, at 839-842. The Platform for Internet Content Selection project is designed to facilitate user-based zoning by encouraging Internet speakers to rate the content of their speech using codes recognized by all screening programs. *Id.*, at 838-839.

Despite this progress, the transformation of cyberspace is not complete. Although gateway technology has been available on the World Wide Web for some time now, it is not available to *all* Web speakers, and is just now becoming technologically feasible for chat rooms and USENET newsgroups. Gateway technology is not ubiquitous in cyberspace, and because without it "there is no means of age verification," cyberspace still remains largely unzoned—and unzoneable. User-based zoning is also in its infancy. For it to be effective, (i) an agreed-upon code (or "tag") would have to exist; (ii) screening software or browsers with screening capabilities would have to be able to recognize the "tag"; and (iii) those programs would have to be widely available—and widely used—by Internet users. At present, none of these conditions is true. Screening software "is not in wide use today" and "only a handful of browsers have screening capabilities." *Shea v. Reno*, 930 F. Supp. 916, 945-946 (S.D.N.Y. 1996). There is, moreover, no agreed-upon "tag" for those programs to recognize.

Although the prospects for the eventual zoning of the Internet appear promising, I agree with the Court that we must evaluate the constitutionality of the CDA as it applies to the Internet as it exists today. Given the present state of cyberspace, I agree with the Court that the "display" provision cannot pass muster. Until gateway technology is available throughout cyberspace, and it is not in 1997, a speaker cannot be reasonably assured that the speech he displays will reach only adults because it is impossible to confine speech to an "adult zone." Thus, the only way for a speaker to avoid liability under the CDA is to refrain completely from using indecent speech. But this forced silence impinges on the First Amendment right of adults to make and obtain this speech and, for all intents and purposes, "reduce[s] the adult population [on the Internet] to reading only what is fit for children." *Butler*, 352 U.S., at 383. As a result, the "display" provision cannot withstand scrutiny.

The "indecency transmission" and "specific person" provisions present a closer issue, for they are not unconstitutional in all of their applications. As discussed above, the "indecency transmission" provision makes it a crime to transmit knowingly an indecent message to a person the sender knows is under 18 years of age. 47 U.S.C. § 223(a)(1)(B) (1994 ed., Supp II). The "specific person" provision proscribes the same conduct, although it does not as explicitly require the sender to know that the intended recipient of his indecent message is a minor. § 223(d)(1)(A). The Government urges the Court to construe the provision to impose such a knowledge requirement, and I would do so.

So construed, both provisions are constitutional as applied to a conversation involving only an adult and one or more minors—*e.g.*, when an adult speaker sends an e-mail knowing the addressee is a minor, or when an adult and minor converse by themselves or with other minors in a chat room. In this context, these provisions are no different from the law we sustained in *Ginsberg*. Restricting what the adult may say to the minors in no way restricts the adult's ability to communicate with other adults. He is not prevented from speaking indecently to other adults in a chat room (because there are no other adults participating in the conversation) and he remains free to send indecent e-mails to other adults. The relevant universe contains only one adult, and the adult in that universe has the power to refrain from using indecent speech and consequently to keep all such speech within the room in an "adult" zone.

The analogy to *Ginsberg* breaks down, however, when more than one adult is a party to the conversation. If a minor enters a chat room otherwise occupied by adults, the CDA effectively requires the adults in the room to stop using indecent speech. If they did not, they could be prosecuted under the "indecency transmission" and "specific person" provisions for any indecent statements they make to the group, since they would be transmitting an indecent message to specific persons, one of whom is a minor. The CDA is therefore akin to a law that makes it a crime for a bookstore owner to sell pornographic magazines to anyone once a minor enters his store. Even assuming such a law might be constitutional in the physical world as a reasonable alternative to excluding minors completely from the store, the absence of any means of excluding minors from chat rooms in cyberspace restricts the rights of adults to engage in indecent speech in those rooms. The "indecency transmission" and "specific person" provisions share this defect.

But these two provisions do not infringe on adults' speech in all situations. And * * * I do not find that the provisions are overbroad in the sense that they restrict minors' access to a substantial amount of speech that minors have the right to read and view. * * * Where, as here, "the parties challenging the statute are those who desire to engage in protected speech that the overbroad statute purports to punish, . . . [t]he statute may forthwith be declared invalid to the extent that it reaches too far, but otherwise left intact." *Brockett v. Spokane Arcades, Inc.*, 472 U.S. 491, 504 (1985). There is no question that Congress intended to prohibit certain communications between one adult and one or more minors. There is also no question that Congress would have enacted a narrower version of these provisions had it known a broader version would be declared unconstitutional. 47 U.S.C. § 608 ("If . . . the application [of any provision of the CDA] to any person or circumstance is held invalid, . . . the application of such provision to other persons or circumstances shall not be affected thereby"). I would therefore sustain the "indecency transmission" and "specific person" provisions to the extent they apply to the transmission of Internet communications where the party initiating the communication knows that all of the recipients are minors.

Notes and Questions

1. Does the *Reno v. ACLU* Court adequately distinguish *Ginsberg*? The Court notes that the New York statute in *Ginsberg* applied only to commercial transactions and covered only that "patently offensive" material that lacked serious literary, artistic, political, or scientific value for minors. If the result in *Ginsberg* is justified by the government's interest in protecting minors, why should it matter whether the government targets commercial transactions or all transactions? Should the fact that the CDA reaches "patently offensive" material regardless of its serious value affect the Court's analysis? Can the Court's concern with the coverage of the statute be reconciled with its approach in *Pacifica?* Can you think of material that would constitute a "patently offensive" depiction of "sexual or excretory activities or organs" but that would have serious value for minors?

2. The Court distinguishes the Internet from the broadcast medium on the ground that one must take a series of affirmative steps to access material on the Internet, and that one is therefore rarely "assaulted" by indecent or patently offensive speech. Do you agree that the risk of encountering indecent material over the Internet by accident is remote? What level of risk should mark the constitutionally significant point? Why?

3. Does the Court ultimately conclude that the CDA is vague? Do you agree with its conclusion? In its discussion of vagueness, the Court focuses on the fact that one portion of the CDA covers "indecent" material while another portion of the CDA covers "patently offensive" material. Why is the use of these two substantive standards problematic? How did the FCC define "indecent" speech in the *Pacifica* case? Should a court attribute to Congress knowledge of the administrative construction of that term, and interpret the term accordingly?

4. In its vagueness discussion, the Court observes that *Miller*'s obscenity test proscribed the "patently offensive" depiction of sexual conduct defined by applicable state law. How does *Miller*'s reliance on state law distinguish the test from the CDA's test? Do you find the Court's similar concern that the CDA reaches depictions of sexual or excretory activities or organs, as well as sexual conduct, persuasive? What about the concern that the CDA does not require that the proscribed speech lack societal value?

5. Why does the Court reject the government's argument that content providers can avoid prosecution under the CDA by "tagging" their speech as

indecent? Suppose that Congress re-passed the CDA and explicitly provided that anyone who "tagged" his or her speech as indecent would not violate the statute. Would this explicit defense save the statute? Would the tagging requirement raise other First Amendment problems?

6. Is Justice O'Connor correct that the CDA merely reflects an attempt at "cyberzoning"? What conditions would have to obtain before a court could conclude that such an effort is constitutional?

7. How would you re-write the CDA to correct the constitutional problems the Court identifies? After the Supreme Court invalidated the CDA, Congress attempted to revise the offending portions of the statute in the Child Online Protection Act. For further discussion of litigation under COPA, see *supra* p. 85 and *infra* p. 441.

SECTION B. PRIVATE FILTERING OF SEXUALLY EXPLICIT SPEECH

The ready availability of filtering and blocking technology on the Internet is one of the primary ways in which the online free speech debate differs from its realspace counterpart. Courts and commentators, however, have struggled to articulate precisely the ways in which the use or availability of those technologies should (or should not) affect the First Amendment analysis (or, more generally, our views of government versus private speech-suppressing activities). In *Reno v. American Civil Liberties Union*, for instance, *both* sides pointed to filtering technology to support their claims about the CDA: The plaintiffs argued that the CDA was overbroad because user-based filtering software would allow parents to prevent their children's access to indecent speech more effectively (and with less of a burden on adults' rights to view indecent speech) than the statute did, while the government argued that because content providers could "tag" their speech as indecent and rely on filtering software to prevent minors from gaining access to it, the CDA would therefore *not* significantly restrict adults' speech.

In this section and the one that follows, we analyze the challenges posed by filtering technology in greater depth. As you read the excerpts below, consider the advantages and the limitations of relying on private filtering (as compared to more formal law-making) to address problems relating to the distribution of offensive or indecent speech online—the ways in which filtering technology may help solve the free speech problems in cyberspace (by permitting parents, for example, to filter the information made available to their children), and the ways in which such filtering technology might itself *be* (or become) a free speech problem in cyberspace.

Jonathan Weinberg, *Rating the Net*

19 HASTINGS COMM/ENT L.J. 453 (1997)

INTRODUCTION

Internet filtering software is hot. Plaintiffs in *ACLU v. Reno* relied heavily on the existence and capabilities of filtering software (also known as blocking software) in arguing that the Communications Decency Act was unconstitutional. * * * Free speech activists see this software as the answer to the dilemma of indecency regulation, making it possible "to reconcile free expression of ideas and appropriate protection for kids."[4] Indeed, some of the strongest supporters of such software are First Amendment activists who sharply oppose direct government censorship of the net.

Internet filtering software, further, is here. As of this writing, the Platform for Internet Content Selection (PICS) working group has developed a common language for Internet rating systems, making it much easier to create and market such ratings. Two heavily-promoted ratings systems (SafeSurf and [the Recreational Software Advisory Council's] RSACi) allow content providers to rate their own World Wide Web sites in a sophisticated manner. Microsoft's World Wide Web browser incorporates a feature called Content Advisor that will block Web sites in accordance with the rules of any PICS-compliant ratings system, including SafeSurf and RSACi. Stand-alone blocking software—marketed under such trademarks as SurfWatch, Cyber Patrol, CYBERSitter, KinderGuard, Net Nanny, and Parental Guidance—is gaining increasing sophistication and popularity.

It is easy to understand the acclaim for filtering software. This software can do an impressive job at blocking access to sexually explicit material that a parent does not wish his or her child to see. The PICS standard for describing ratings systems is an important technical achievement, allowing the development and easy use of a variety of sophisticated ratings schemes.

In the midst of the general enthusiasm, though, it is worth trying to locate filtering technology's limitations and drawbacks. Blocking software is a huge step forward in solving the dilemma of sexually explicit speech on the net, but it does have costs. People whose image of the net is mediated through blocking software may miss out on worthwhile speech through deliberate exclusion, through inaccuracies in labeling inherent to the filtering process, and through the restriction of unrated sites. * * *

I. BACKGROUND

* * * Because nothing in the structure or syntax of the Web *requires* Web pages to include labels advertising their content, * * * identifying pages

---

4. Peter H. Lewis, *Microsoft Backs Ratings System for Internet*, N.Y. TIMES, Mar. 1, 1996, at D5 (quoting Daniel Weitzner, Deputy Director, Center for Democracy and Technology).

with sexually explicit material is not an easy task. First-generation blocking software compiled lists of off-limits Web pages through two methods. First, the rating services hired raters to work through individual Web pages by hand, following links to sexually explicit sites and compiling lists of URLs to be deemed off-limits to children. Second, they used string-recognition software to automatically proscribe any Web page that contained a forbidden word (such as "sex" or "xxx") in its URL.

The PICS specifications contemplate that a ratings system can be more sophisticated. A rating service may rate a document along multiple dimensions. Instead of merely rating a document as "adult" or "child-safe," it might give it separate ratings for violence, sex, nudity, and adult language. Further, along any given dimension, the rating service may choose from any number of values. Instead of simply rating a site "block" or "no-block" for violence, a rating service might assign it a rating of between one and ten for increasing amounts of violent content. * * * Finally, * * * ratings need not be assigned by the authors of filtering software. They can be assigned by the content creators themselves or by third parties * * * .

II. ACCURACY

Since blocking software first came on the market, individual content providers have complained about the ratings given to their sites. Not all of those complaints relate to problems inherent to filtering software. For example, some programs tend to block entire directories of Web pages simply because they contain a single "adult" file. That means that large numbers of innocuous Web pages are blocked merely because they are located near some *other* page with adult content. * * * Other problems arise from the wacky antics of string-recognition software. America Online's software, ever alert for four-letter words embedded in text, refused to let users register from the British town of "Scunthorpe." The University of Kansas Medical Center installed Surfwatch in its Internet kiosk, and discovered that users could not see the Web page of their own Archie R. Dykes Medical Library. For sheer wackiness, nothing can match a CYBERSitter feature that cause[d] Web browsers to white out selected *words* but display the rest of the page (so that the sentence "President Clinton opposes homosexual marriage" would be rendered "President Clinton opposes marriage"). * * *

Controversies over sites actually rated by humans are less amenable to technological solution. One dispute arose when Cyber Patrol blocked animal-rights web pages because of images of animal abuse, including syphilis-infected monkeys; Cyber Patrol classed those as "gross depiction" CyberNOTs. The situation was aggravated because Cyber Patrol, following the entire-directory approach described above, blocked *all* of the hundred or so animal welfare, animal rights, and vegetarian pages hosted at the Animal Rights Resource Site. * * * Sites discussing gay and lesbian issues are commonly blocked, even if they contain no references to sex. * * *

One might think that a better answer lies in rating systems, such as RSACi and SafeSurf, in which content providers [can] evaluate their *own* sites. An author, one might assume, could hardly disagree with a rating he chose himself. The matter, though, is not so clear. When an author evaluates his site in order to gain a rating from any PICS-compliant rating service, he must follow the algorithms and rules of that service. Jonathan Wallace, thus, in an article called *Why I Will Not Rate My Site*, asks how he is to rate "An Auschwitz Alphabet," his powerful and deeply chilling work of reportage on the Holocaust. The work contains descriptions of violence done to camp inmates' sexual organs. A self-rating system, Wallace fears, would likely force him to choose between the unsatisfactory alternatives of labeling the work as suitable for all ages, on the one hand, or "lum[ping] it together with the Hot Nude Women page" on the other.[43]

At least some of the rating services' problems in assigning ratings to individual documents are inherent. It is the nature of the process that *no* ratings system can classify documents in a perfectly satisfactory manner. Consider first how a ratings system designer might construct a ratings algorithm. She might provide an algorithm made up entirely of simple, focused questions, in which each question has a relatively easily ascertainable "yes" or "no" answer. (Example: "Does the file contain a photographic image depicting exposed male or female genitalia?") Alternatively, she might seek to afford evaluators more freedom to apply broad, informal, situationally sensitive guidelines so as to capture the overall feel of each site. (Example: "Is the site suitable for a child below the age of 13?")

In jurisprudential terms, the first approach relies on "rules" and the second on "standards." The RSACi system attempts to be rule-based. In coding its violence levels, for example, to include "harmless conflict; some damage to objects"; "creatures injured or killed; damage to objects, fighting"; "humans injured or killed with small amount of blood"; "humans injured or killed; blood and gore"; and "wanton and gratuitous violence; torture; rape," its designers have striven to devise simple, hard-edged rules, with results turning mechanically on a limited number of facts. * * * Other rating systems rely more heavily on standards. The SafeSurf questionnaire, for example, requires the self-rater to determine whether nudity is "artistic" (levels 4 through 6), "erotic" (level 7), "pornographic" (level 8), or "explicit and crude" pornographic (level 9). * * *

A problem with standards is that they are less constraining; relatively speaking, a standards-based system will lack consistency and predictability. Rules become increasingly necessary as the universe of law-appliers becomes larger, less able to rely on shared culture and values as a guide to applying standards in a relatively consistent and coherent way. * * *

---

43. Jonathan Wallace, *Why I Will Not Rate My Site* (visited Feb. 7, 1997) <http://www.spectacle.org/cda/rate.html#report>.

Let's return to the choices facing a ratings system designer as she constructs blocking software. * * * [W]hat sort of material should trigger ratings consequences? Should children have access to material about weapons making? How about hate speech? Or artistic depictions of nudity? [S]he can take two different approaches. First, she can decide all such questions herself, so that the home user need only turn the system on and all choices as to what is blocked are already made. CYBERSitter adopts this approach. This has the benefit of simplicity, but seems appropriate only if members of the target audience are in basic agreement with the rating service (and each other) respecting what sort of speech should and should not be blocked.

Alternatively, she can leave those questions for the user to answer. The ratings system designer need not decide whether to block Web sites featuring bomb-making recipes or hate speech. She can instead design the system so that the user has the power to block those sites if he chooses. Microsoft's implementation of the RSACi labels allows parents to select the levels of adult language, nudity, sex and violence that the browser will let through. Cyber Patrol allows parents to select which of the twelve CyberNOT categories to block.

Either approach, though, imposes restrictions on the categories chosen by the ratings system designer. If the system designer wishes to leave substantive choices to parents, she must create categories that correspond to the different sides of the relevant substantive questions. That is, if the designer wishes to leave users the choice whether to block sites featuring hate speech, she must break out sites featuring hate speech into a separate category or categories. If she wishes to leave the user the choice whether to block sites that depict explicit sexual behavior but nonetheless have artistic value, she must categorize those sites differently from those that do not have artistic value. On the other hand, if the system designer makes those substantive decisions herself, making her own value choices as to what material should and should not be blocked, she must create categories that correspond to those value choices. The problem is that many of these questions cleave on lines defined by standards. Many users, for example, might like to block "pornography," but allow other, more worthy, speech, even if it is sexually explicit. * * * The problem increases with the heterogeneity of the service's audience: the more heterogeneous the audience, the more categories a rating system must include to accommodate different user preferences.

With this perspective, one can better appreciate the limitations of RSAC's attempt to be rule-bound. RSACi ignores much content that some other ratings systems classify as potentially unsuitable, including speech relating to drug use, alcohol, tobacco, gambling, scatology, computer hacking and software piracy, devil worship, religious cults, militant or extremist groups, weapon making, tatooing and body piercing, and speech "grossly deficient in civility or behavior." For many observers (myself included), RSACi's narrow scope is good news because it limits the ability to block access to controversial political speech. My point, though, is that

RSACi *had to* confine its reach if it was to maintain its rule-bounded nature. * * *

In sum, rating system designers face a dilemma. If a rating service seeks to map the Web in a relatively comprehensive manner, it must rely on a relatively large group of evaluators. Such a group of evaluators can achieve fairness and consistency only if the ratings system uses simple, hard-edged categories relying on a few, easily ascertainable characteristics of each site. Such categories, though, will not categorize the Net along the lines that home users will find most useful, and will not empower those users to heed their own values in deciding what speech should and should not be blocked. To the extent that ratings system designers allow evaluators to consider more factors in a more situationally specific manner to capture the essence of each site, they will ensure inconsistency and hidden value choices as the system is applied.

III. Unrated Sites

Blocking software can work perfectly only if all sites are rated. Otherwise, the software must either exclude all unrated sites, barring innocuous speech, or allow unrated sites, letting in speech that the user would prefer to exclude. What are the prospects that a rating service will be able to label even a large percentage of the millions of pages on the Web? What are the consequences if it cannot?

First, consider rating services associated with individual manufacturers of blocking software, such as CYBERSitter and Cyber Patrol. These services hire raters to label the entire Web, site by site. The limits on their ability to do so are obvious. As the services get bigger, hiring more and more employees to rate sites, their consistency will degrade. * * * As a practical matter, providing access to all unrated sites is not an option for these rating services; it would let through too much for them to be able to market themselves as reliable screeners. Instead, they must offer users other options, dealing with unrated sites in one of two ways. First, they can seek to catch questionable content through string-recognition software. CYBERSitter, for example, offers this option. The problem with this approach, though, is that at least under current technology, string-recognition software simply doesn't work very well. This article has already mentioned America Online's travails with the town of Scunthorpe and the word "breast"; other examples are easy to find. Surfwatch, for example, blocked a page on the White House web site because its URL contains the forbidden word "couples" (http://www.whitehouse.gov/WH/kids/html/couples.html). The second option is for the rating services simply to block all unrated sites. Industry members seem to contemplate this as the necessary solution. Microsoft, for example, cautions Internet content providers that "for a rating system to be useful, the browser application must deny access to sites that are unrated." Other observers reach the same result.

What about self-rating approaches, like those of SafeSurf and RSACi? These services have the potential for near-universal reach, since they can draw on the services of an effectively unlimited number of evaluators. * * * On the other hand, self-rating services will not achieve their potential unless content providers have a sufficient incentive to participate in the ratings process in the first place. That incentive is highly uneven. Mass-market commercial providers seeking to maximize their audience reach will participate in any significant self-rating system, so as not to be shut out of homes in which parents have configured their browsers to reject all unrated sites. Many noncommercial site owners, though, may not participate. They may be indifferent to their under-18 visitors and may not wish to incur the costs of self-rating. It is still early to predict what those costs may be. For the owner of a large site containing many documents, supplying a rating for each page may be a time-consuming pain in the neck. * * *

The Internet is justly celebrated as "the most participatory form of mass speech yet developed."[102] * * * But this prospect is threatened if widespread adoption of blocking software ends up removing much of the speech of ordinary citizens, leaving the viewer little to surf but mass-market commercial programming. One hardly needs the Internet for that; we get it already from the conventional media.

In sum, blocking software could end up blocking access to a significant amount of the individual, idiosyncratic speech that makes the Internet a unique medium of mass communication. Filtering software, touted as a speech-protective technology, may instead contribute to the flattening of speech on the Internet.

IV. Children, Adults, and Blocking Software

You may protest that I am making much of little here. After all, blocking software is intended to restrict children's access to questionable sites. It won't affect what adults can see on the Internet—or will it? It seems to me that, in important respects, it will. The desire to restrict children's access has spurred the recent development of filtering technology. Widespread adoption of that software, though, will not likely leave adults unaffected.

In a variety of contexts, we can expect to see adults reaching the Internet through approaches monitored by blocking software. In the home, parents may set up filters at levels appropriate for their children, and not disable them for their own use. * * * Other people get their Internet connections through libraries; indeed, some policymakers tout libraries and other community institutions as the most promising vehicle for ensuring universal access to the Internet. The American Library Association takes the position that libraries should provide unrestricted access to information resources; it characterizes the use of blocking programs as censorship. This policy, however, is not binding on member libraries. It is likely that a substantial number of public libraries will install blocking software on their public-access terminals, including terminals intended for use by adults;

---

102. *ACLU v. Reno*, 929 F. Supp. 824, 883 (E.D. Pa. 1996) (Dalzell, J.).

indeed, some have already done so. * * * Still other people get Internet access through their employers. Corporations too, wary of risk and wasted work time, may put stringent filters in place. Some large companies worry about the possibility of being cited for sexual harassment by virtue of material that came into the office via the Internet. Even more are concerned about sports and leisure information they feel may detract from business productivity. * * * In sum, we may see home computers blocked for reasons of convenience, library computers blocked for reasons of politics, and workplace computers blocked for reasons of profit. * * *

This should affect the way we think about filtering software. Any filtering system necessarily incorporates value judgments about the speech being blocked. These value judgments are not so controversial if we think of the typical user of blocking software as a parent restricting his children's access. It is part of a parent's job, after all, to make value judgments regarding his own child's upbringing. The value judgments are much more controversial, though, if we think of the typical "blockee" as an adult using a library computer, or using a corporate computer after hours. If we are concerned about these users' access to speech, then we need to think hard about the way blocking software works, the extent to which it can be accurate, and the extent to which it is likely to exclude the sort of speech that makes the Internet worthwhile.

Notes and Questions

1. Among the difficulties that Professor Weinberg sees with filtering software is that any comprehensive rating of the web will require software writers to develop what he calls "hard-edged" rules. Why does he perceive hard-edged categories to be problematic? What is the alternative approach, and what are the problems that Weinberg sees with that approach?

2. Why do many providers of Internet content lack incentives to rate their sites? Why does Weinberg believe that filtering software will "flatten" speech?

3. Could the government *require* Internet content providers to rate their sites? Consider these two perspectives:

[A] mandatory self-rating requirement would likely be held unconstitutional. In *Riley v. Federation of the Blind*, the Court considered a requirement that professional fundraisers disclose to potential donors the percentage of charitable contributions collected over the previous twelve months that were actually turned over to charity. The Court explained that "mandating speech that a speaker would not otherwise make" necessarily alters the content of the speech and thus amounts to content-based regulation.[89] Even when a compelled statement is purely factual, the compulsion burdens protected speech and is subject to "exacting" scrutiny, subject to the rule that government cannot "dictate the content

---

89. 497 U.S. 781, 795 (1988).

of speech absent compelling necessity, and then, only by means precisely tailored."[91]

Jonathan Weinberg, *Rating the Net*, 19 HASTINGS COMM/ENT L.J. 453, 475 (1997).

The right against compelled speech * * * is not complete. [T]he Court has allowed compelled speech where it "better enable[s] the public to evaluate" the speech without causing additional misunderstandings,[100] where it causes little burden, or where the government interests are "sufficiently important" and implemented by the least restrictive means.[102] * * * The case most factually analogous to a government-imposed labeling scheme is *Meese v. Keene*, in which Keene, a distributor, challenged a regulation requiring labeling of material deemed by the State Department to be "political propaganda."[104] * * * The Supreme Court [held] that the addition of the mandatory label "plac[ed] no burden on protected expression."[106]

Whether the standard applied in *Keene* or the more traditional doctrine of compelled speech would apply to [a] PICS-enforcing statute will turn largely upon whether the speaker-producer can demonstrate a burden on protected expression. * * * How this factual "burden" determination will turn out is anyone's guess. But * * * [w]hether *Keene* applies will determine only the level of scrutiny applied * * * . [A]s I discuss below, there is reason to believe that the PICS-enforcing statute would survive intermediate and even strict scrutiny.

R. Polk Wagner, *Filters and the First Amendment*, 83 MINN. L. REV. 755, 780-83 (1999).

4. Professor Weinberg discusses the weaknesses of filtering software without necessarily advocating government restrictions on sexually explicit speech as an alternative. One could add to the catalog of difficulties Weinberg notes the observation that the development of filtering software is largely shielded from public scrutiny, because each software developer uses its own proprietary approach. Is there a plausible argument that a more transparent, governmental approach to the problem of sexually explicit speech would be preferable? In other words, if we could construct a statute regulating sexually explicit speech that would survive constitutional scrutiny, would such a regulation be preferable to the widespread implementation of filtering tools? Consider the following excerpt.

---

91. *Id.* at 798, 800.
100. *See Meese v. Keene*, 481 U.S. 465, 480 (1987).
102. *See Buckley v. Valeo*, 424 U.S. 1, 29 (1986).
104. 481 U.S. at 468. * * *
106. *Id.* at 480. * * *

Lawrence Lessig, *Code and Other Laws of Cyberspace*

Basic Books, 1999

Since the case of *Ginsberg v New York* it has been assumed that there is a class of speech that adults have a right to but children do not. States can regulate that class to ensure that such speech is channeled to the proper user.

Conceptually, then, before such a regulation could be applied, two questions must be answered:

1. Is this speech within the class of "regulable" speech?
2. Is this listener under a minium age?

Clearly, the sender is in a better position to answer question one, and the receiver is in a better position to answer question two. Yet the [Communications Decency Act] imposed the full burden of the regulation on the sender—he must determine both whether his speech is subject to regulation and whether the recipient is above the minimum age. An alternative would be to place the burden on the receiver—or more precisely, on his parents. Parents know whether they have children who should be protected from porn; if they do, they arguably should take steps to block out speech they consider inappropriate for their children.

Both solutions—placing the burden on the recipient or on the sender—require a new architecture for the Net, not at the level of the TCP/IP protocol, but in the application space. * * * Both require that changes be built into the most common suite of applications in a way that users can depend on.

What might these applications look like? Let's call the first a *zoning* solution. Speakers are zoned into a space from which children are excluded. The second is a *filtering* solution. Listeners are empowered to block speech they want to block. * * *

From a free speech perspective, how should we evaluate these two architectures? [A zoning regime] requires those who have zonable speech to place that speech behind walls; a [filtering regime, such as one implementing a PICS-based rating system,] permits listeners to adopt filters that block offending speech. The blockings of the first follow requirements in a law; the filterings of the second, while perhaps induced by law, follow from individual choice. One (zoning) looks like "censorship"; the other looks like "choice" (PICS). Thus, most people embrace the second while trashing the first.

But from a free speech perspective, this is exactly backward. As a (perhaps) unintended consequence, the PICS regime not only enables nontransparent filtering but, by producing a market in filtering technology, engenders filters for much more than *Ginsberg* speech. That, of course, was the complaint against the original CDA. But here the market, whose tastes are the tastes of the community, facilitates the filtering. Built into the filter are the norms of a community, which are broader than the narrow filter of

Ginsberg. The filtering system can expand as broadly as the users want, or as far upstream as sources want.

The zoning solution is narrower. There would be no incentive for speakers to block out listeners; the incentive of a speaker is to have more, not fewer, listeners. The only requirements to filter out listeners would be those that may constitutionally be imposed—*Ginsberg* speech requirements. Since they would be imposed by the state, these requirements could be tested against the Constitution, and if the state were found to have reached too far, it could be checked.

The difference, then, is in the generalizability of the regimes. The filtering regime would establish an architecture that could be used to filter any kind of speech, and the desires for filtering then could be expected to reach beyond a constitutional minimum; the zoning regime would establish an architecture for blocking that would not have this more general purpose.

Which regime should we prefer?

Notice the values implicit in each regime. Both are general solutions to particular problems. The filtering regime does not limit itself to *Ginsberg* speech; it can be used to rate, and filter, any Internet content. And the zoning regime is not limited to facilitating zoning only for *Ginsberg* speech. The CDA zoning solution could be used to certify any number of attributes of the user—not only age but citizenship or credit-worthiness. The * * * zoning solution could be used to advance other child protective schemes. Both have applications far beyond the specifics of porn on the Net.

In principle at least. We should be asking, however, what the incentives are to extend the solution beyond the problem. In addition, what resistance is this extended solution likely to encounter?

Here we begin to see an important difference between the two regimes. When your access is blocked because of a certificate you are holding, you want to know why. When you are told you cannot enter a certain site, the claim to exclude is checked at least by the person being excluded. Sometimes the exclusion is justified, but when it is not, it can be challenged. Zoning, then, builds into itself a system for its own limitation. A site cannot block someone from the site without that individual knowing it.

Filtering is different. If you cannot see the content, you cannot know what is being blocked. In principle at least, content could be filtered by a PICS filter somewhere upstream and you would not necessarily know this was happening. Nothing in the PICS design requires truth in blocking in the way that the zoning solution does. Thus, upstream filtering becomes easier, less transparent, and less costly with PICS.

This effect is even clearer if we take apart the components of the filtering process. Recall the two elements of filtering of solutions—labeling content, and then blocking based on that labeling. We might well argue that the labeling is the more dangerous of the two elements. If content is labeled, then it is possible to monitor who gets what without even blocking access. That might well raise greater concerns than blocking, since blocking at least puts the user on notice.

These possibilities should trouble us only if we have reason to question the value of filtering generally, and upstream filtering in particular. I believe we do. But I must confess that my concern grows out of yet another latent ambiguity in our constitutional past.

There is an undeniable value in filtering. We all filter out much more than we process, and in general it is better if we can select our filters rather than have others select them for us. If I read the *New York Times* rather than the *Wall Street Journal*, I am selecting a filter according to my understanding of the values both newspapers bring to the process of filtering. Obviously, in any particular case, there cannot be a problem with this.

But there is also a value in confronting the unfiltered. We individually may want to avoid issues of poverty or of inequality, and so we might prefer to tune those facts out of out universe. But from the standpoint of society, it would be terrible if citizens could simply tune out problems that were not theirs. Those same citizens have to select leaders to mange these very problems.

In real space we do not have to worry about this problem too much because filtering is usually imperfect. However much I'd like to ignore homelessness, I cannot go to my bank without confronting homeless people on the street; however much I'd like to ignore inequality, I cannot drive to the airport without passing through neighborhoods that remind me of how unequal a nation the United States is. All sorts of issues I'd rather not think about force themselves on me. They demand my attention in real space, regardless of my filtering choices.

This is not true for everyone. The very rich can cut themselves off from what they do not want to see. Think of the butler on a nineteenth-century English estate, answering the door and sending away those he thinks should not trouble his master. Those people lived perfectly filtered lives. And so do some today.

But on balance, most of us do not. We must confront the problems of others and think about problems that affect our society. This exposure makes us better citizens. We can better deliberate and vote on issues that affect others if we have some sense of the problems they face.

What happens, then, if the imperfections of filtering disappear? What happens if everyone can, in effect, have a butler? Would such a world be consistent with the values of the First Amendment? * * * In my view, we should not opt for perfect filtering. We should not design for the most efficient system of censoring—or at least, we should not do this in a way that allows invisible upstream filtering. Nor should we opt for perfect filtering so long as the tendency worldwide is to overfilter speech. If there is speech the government has an interest in controlling, then let that control be obvious to the users. Only when regulation is transparent is a political response possible.

Thus, between the two, my vote is for the least transformative regime. A zoning regime that enables children to self-identify is less transformative than a filtering regime that in effect requires all speech to be labeled. A zoning regime is not only less transformative but less enabling (of other regulation)—it requires the smallest change to the existing architecture of the Net and does not easily generalize to a far more significant regulation.

I would opt for a zoning regime even if it required a law and the filtering solution required only private choice. If the state is pushing for a change in the mix of law and architecture, I do not care that it is pushing with law in one context and with norms in the other. From my perspective, the question is the result, not the means—does the regime produced by these changes protect free speech values?

Others are obsessed with this distinction between law and private action. They view regulation by the state as universally suspect and regulation by private actors as beyond the scope of constitutional review. And, to their credit, most constitutional law is on their side.

But * * * I do not think we should get caught up in the lines that lawyers draw. Our question should be the values we want cyberspace to protect.

Notes and Questions

1. In Professor Lessig's terminology, what is the difference between a "zoning" regime and a "filtering" regime? Why does Lessig think that a "zoning" solution to the problem of sexually explicit speech is narrower than a "filtering" solution?

2. Recall our discussion in Chapter Three of the recently enacted Pennsylvania statute, 18 Pa. Cons. Stat. Ann. § 7622 (West 2004), which authorizes the Pennsylvania Attorney General to order Internet service providers to make websites containing child pornography inaccessible to their Pennsylvania subscribers. Is this a kind of state-imposed "filtering" scheme, under which the Attorney General filters out objectionable websites for Pennsylvania Internet users, or is it more like a "zoning" regulation, keeping objectionable content outside of Pennsylvania's borders and requiring Pennsylvania users who want to visit those "neighborhoods" to travel out-of-state in order to do so?

3. Why won't the market adequately address the concerns Lessig raises about filtering technology? Can't a user simply choose a filtering technology that most closely matches his or her own preferences?

4. What does Lessig mean by "upstream filtering"? Why would such filtering be problematic? In this regard, consider that the desire to categorize and filter out content is widespread. As we saw in the previous section, many people wish to filter unsolicited commercial e-mail. Parents want to shield their children from pornography and hate speech. And governments seek to exclude certain content from their respective territories. To the extent that this filtering is controlled only by end users, it may not be cause for undue concern. But in upstream filtering, network intermediaries can do the filtering

as long as they can be enticed or coerced to do so. Moreover, it may be difficult for end users even to know what material has been filtered out. And this filtering can take place anywhere along the line that extends from one's own computer to one's ISP to intermediate carriers to the destination's ISP to the destination server itself.

5. One of Lessig's concerns is that there are incentives to use filtering technology for purposes other than screening sexually explicit speech. What are these incentives? Why are the incentives "to extend the solution beyond the problem" greater with filtering than with zoning?

6. Do you agree with Lessig that in the case of a zoning regime, a speaker has no incentives to block more listeners than the law can constitutionally require him to block? Might a fear of liability cause the speaker to "overblock"? Or might the inconvenience of segregating sexually explicit speech prompt the content provider not to speak at all?

7. Why does Lessig think that a technology that enables "perfect" filtering is dangerous? In order to explore this question, consider the idea of the "Daily Me." MIT technology specialist Nicholas Negroponte has predicted that in the not-too-distant future we will be able to create a "Daily Me" on the Internet that will provide only the personalized news, information, and viewpoints that we have pre-selected for ourselves. *See* NICHOLAS NEGROPONTE, BEING DIGITAL 153 (1995). In this scenario, general interest newspapers, magazines, and television could become a thing of the past. Instead, people could design their own magazines and newspapers filled with only the type of content they desire and download only the television programs and movies they wish to watch.

Although this may seem like an ideal way to sort through the mass of information available on the web, some worry that such filtering could have pernicious effects because it would allow us to avoid encountering perspectives other than our own on matters of public concern. For example, Cass Sunstein argues that "the Internet creates a large risk of group polarization, simply because it makes it so easy for like-minded people to speak with one another—and ultimately to move toward extreme and sometimes even violent positions." CASS SUNSTEIN, REPUBLIC.COM 199 (2001). Over time, such filtering may damage our democracy, Sunstein argues, because a healthy democracy needs both a citizenry that has a substantial number of culturally shared experiences and a populace with the opportunity to engage in frequent unanticipated encounters among diverse people. Both of these requirements may be threatened if we all get our news and information from increasingly personalized sources.

Do you think Lessig and Sunstein are right that the ability to filter information on the Internet will result in a narrowing of the viewpoints to which individuals are exposed? Certainly there is evidence that the American populace has become increasingly polarized with regard to political issues. For example, a study released in 2003 by the Pew Research Center indicates that both Republicans and Democrats have become more intense in their political beliefs over the past ten years. *See* Evenly Divided and Increasingly Polarized: 2004 Political Landscape (2003), *available at* http://www.pewtrusts.com/pdf/ pew_research_values_110503.pdf.

On the other hand, the Internet undoubtedly allows people to access more varied sources of news, information, and political commentary than at any time in history. Thus, one might think the Internet facilitates *greater* exposure to multiple points of view. In addition, some have argued that the Internet may help counter the assimilationist tendencies of mass culture, mass politics, and economics by providing opportunities for members of minority groups both to develop their own voices within the American polity and to create new transnational communities and strengthen existing ones, thereby expanding the possible range of republics to which people might belong. For an argument along these lines, see Anupam Chander, *Whose Republic?*, 69 U. CHI. L. REV. 1472 (2002).

To the extent you consider the advent of the "Daily Me" to be problematic, what is the remedy? Can government create rules to ensure more access to a variety of viewpoints? Would some of the legislative approaches considered in Chapter Five be appropriate?

SECTION C. FILTERING TECHNOLOGY AND THE FIRST AMENDMENT

How (if at all) should First Amendment doctrine take account of the availability of filtering and blocking technologies? If cyberlaw does indeed have distinctive legal questions of its own—recall the "law of the horse" in Chapter One—this is surely one of them.

In this section, we look at three different contexts in which filtering technology and the First Amendment intersect: a federal statute criminalizing certain categories of Internet speech (*Ashcroft v. American Civil Liberties Union*), a federal subsidy to public institutions (libraries and schools) conditioned on the use of filters on their publicly-accessible Internet access points (*United States v. American Library Ass'n*), and, finally, a state statute mandating filtering by Internet service providers.

The first case concerns the constitutionality of the statute enacted shortly after the Supreme Court struck down the indecency provisions of the Communications Decency Act (in *Reno v. American Civil Liberties Union, supra* p. 409). The *Reno* Court, in concluding that the CDA was not "narrowly tailored" to accomplish its purpose and that there were other, less speech-restrictive alternatives available to Congress, had observed that "currently available *user-based* software suggests that a reasonably effective method by which *parents* can prevent their children from accessing sexually explicit and other material which parents may believe is inappropriate for their children will soon be widely available." 521 U.S. at 877 (emphases in original). In a later case, the Court explained that "[in *Reno*], the mere possibility that user-based Internet screening software would 'soon be widely available' was relevant to our rejection of an overbroad restriction of indecent cyberspeech." *United States v. Playboy Entm't Group*, 529 U.S. 803, 814 (2000). But precisely *how* was it relevant?

Ashcroft v. American Civil Liberties Union

Supreme Court of the United States, 2004
542 U.S. 656

JUSTICE KENNEDY delivered the opinion of the Court.

[After the Supreme Court struck down the CDA's "indecency" provisions in *Reno v. American Civil Liberties Union, supra* p. 409, Congress revised the offending portions in the Child Online Protection Act (COPA), Pub. L. No. 105-277, 112 Stat. 2681 (codified at 47 U.S.C. § 231), prohibiting an individual or entity from:

knowingly and with knowledge of the character of the material, in interstate or foreign commerce by means of the World Wide Web, mak[ing] any communication for commercial purposes that is available to any minor and that includes any material that is harmful to minors.

COPA defined material "harmful to minors" as

any communication, picture, image, graphic image file, article, recording, writing, or other matter of any kind that is obscene or that—

(A) the average person, applying contemporary community standards, would find, taking the material as a whole and with respect to minors, is designed to appeal to, or is designed to pander to, the prurient interest;

(B) depicts, describes, or represents, in a manner patently offensive with respect to minors, an actual or simulated sexual act or sexual contact, an actual or simulated normal or perverted sexual act, or a lewd exhibition of the genitals or post-pubescent female breast; and

(C) taken as a whole, lacks serious literary, artistic, political, or scientific value for minors.

The statute provided an affirmative defense for any provider who

in good faith, has restricted access by minors to material that is harmful to minors—

(A) by requiring use of a credit card, debit account, adult access code, or adult personal identification number;

(B) by accepting a digital certificate that verifies age; or

(C) by any other reasonable measures that are feasible under available technology.

The American Civil Liberties Union immediately filed suit challenging the constitutionality of the statute. The District Court concluded that the statute was overbroad and enjoined its enforcement. *American Civil Liberties Union v. Reno*, 31 F. Supp. 2d 473 (E.D. Pa. 1999). As we saw in Chapter Three, the court of appeals affirmed while taking a different approach, basing its conclusion that the statute violated the First Amendment on the statute's reliance on "contemporary community standards" to identify material that is "harmful to minors" in the context of Internet-based speech. *American Civil Liberties Union v. Reno*, 217 F.3d 162 (3d Cir. 2000), *supra* p. 85. The Supreme Court vacated and remanded for further consideration, *see Ashcroft v. American Civil Liberties Union*, 535 U.S. 564 (2001), *supra* p. 89, holding that "COPA's reliance on community standards to identify 'material that is harmful to minors' does not *by itself* render the statute substantially overbroad for purposes of the First Amendment." *Id.* at 574 (emphasis in original). The Court was careful, however, not to "express any view as to whether * * * the statute is unconstitutionally vague, or whether the District Court correctly concluded that the statute likely will not survive strict scrutiny analysis once adjudication of the case is completed below." *Id.*

On remand, the Third Circuit again struck down the statute as unconstitutional. *American Civil Liberties Union v. Ashcroft*, 322 F.3d 240 (3d Cir. 2003). Applying "strict scrutiny" to the Act's provisions, the court held that "the following provisions of COPA are not narrowly tailored to achieve the Government's compelling interest in protecting minors from harmful material and therefore fail the strict scrutiny test: (a) the definition of 'material that is harmful to minors,' which includes the concept of taking 'as a whole' material designed to appeal to the 'prurient interest' of minors; and material which (when judged as a whole) lacks 'serious literary' or other 'value' for minors; (b) the definition of 'commercial purposes,' which limits the reach of the statute to persons 'engaged in the business' (broadly defined) of making communications of material that is harmful to minors; and (c) the 'affirmative defenses' available to publishers, which require the technological screening of users for the purpose of age verification." *Id.* at 251.]

Content-based prohibitions, enforced by severe criminal penalties, have the constant potential to be a repressive force in the lives and thoughts of a free people. To guard against that threat the Constitution demands that content-based restrictions on speech be presumed invalid, *R. A. V.* v. *St. Paul*, 505 U.S. 377, 382 (1992), and that the Government bear the burden of showing their constitutionality. *United States* v. *Playboy Entm't Group, Inc.*, 529 U.S. 803 (2000). This is true even when Congress twice has attempted to find a constitutional means to restrict, and punish, the speech in question. * * *

This case comes to the Court on certiorari review of an appeal from the decision of the District Court granting a preliminary injunction. The Court of Appeals reviewed the decision of the District Court for abuse of discretion. Under that standard, the Court of Appeals was correct to conclude that the District Court did not abuse its discretion in granting the preliminary injunction. * * * Our reasoning in support of this conclusion, however, is based on narrower, more specific grounds than the rationale the Court of Appeals adopted. The Court of Appeals, in its opinion affirming the decision of the District Court, construed a number of terms in the statute, and held that COPA, so construed, was unconstitutional. None of those constructions of statutory terminology, however, were relied on by or necessary to the conclusions of the District Court. * * * Because we affirm the District Court's decision to grant the preliminary injunction for the reasons relied on by the District Court, we decline to consider the correctness of the other arguments relied on by the Court of Appeals.

The District Court, in deciding to grant the preliminary injunction, concentrated primarily on the argument that there are plausible, less restrictive alternatives to COPA. A statute that "effectively suppresses a large amount of speech that adults have a constitutional right to receive and to address to one another . . . is unacceptable if less restrictive alternatives would be at least as effective in achieving the legitimate purpose that the statute was enacted to serve." *Reno*, 521 U.S., at 874. When plaintiffs challenge a content-based speech restriction, the burden is on the Government to prove that the proposed alternatives will not be as effective as the challenged statute. *Id.* In considering this question, a court assumes that certain protected speech may be regulated, and then asks what is the least restrictive alternative that can be used to achieve that goal. The purpose of the test is not to consider whether the challenged restriction has some effect in achieving Congress' goal, regardless of the restriction it imposes. The purpose of the test is to ensure that speech is restricted no further than necessary to achieve the goal, for it is important to assure that legitimate speech is not chilled or punished. For that reason, the test does not begin with the status quo of existing regulations, then ask whether the challenged restriction has some additional ability to achieve Congress' legitimate interest. Any restriction on speech could be justified under that analysis. Instead, the court should ask whether the challenged regulation is the least restrictive means among available, effective alternatives.

In deciding whether to grant a preliminary injunction stage, a district court must consider whether the plaintiffs have demonstrated that they are likely to prevail on the merits. See, *e.g., Doran v. Salem Inn, Inc.*, 422 U.S. 922, 931 (1975). * * * As the Government bears the burden of proof on the ultimate question of COPA's constitutionality, respondents must be deemed likely to prevail unless the Government has shown that respondents' proposed less restrictive alternatives are less effective than COPA. Applying that analysis, the District Court concluded that respondents were likely to prevail. That conclusion was not an abuse of discretion, because on this record there are a number of plausible, less restrictive alternatives to the statute.

The primary alternative considered by the District Court was blocking and filtering software. Blocking and filtering software is an alternative that is less restrictive than COPA, and, in addition, likely more effective as a means of restricting children's access to materials harmful to them. The District Court, in granting the preliminary injunction, did so primarily because the plaintiffs had proposed that filters are a less restrictive alternative to COPA and the Government had not shown it would be likely to disprove the plaintiffs' contention at trial.

Filters are less restrictive than COPA. They impose selective restrictions on speech at the receiving end, not universal restrictions at the source. Under a filtering regime, adults without children may gain access to speech they have a right to see without having to identify themselves or provide their credit card information. Even adults with children may obtain access to the same speech on the same terms simply by turning off the filter on their home computers. Above all, promoting the use of filters does not condemn as criminal any category of speech, and so the potential chilling effect is eliminated, or at least much diminished. All of these things are true, moreover, regardless of how broadly or narrowly the definitions in COPA are construed.

Filters also may well be more effective than COPA. First, a filter can prevent minors from seeing all pornography, not just pornography posted to the Web from America. The District Court noted in its factfindings that one witness estimated that 40% of harmful-to-minors content comes from overseas. COPA does not prevent minors from having access to those foreign harmful materials. That alone makes it possible that filtering software might be more effective in serving Congress' goals. Effectiveness is likely to diminish even further if COPA is upheld, because the providers of the materials that would be covered by the statute simply can move their operations overseas. It is not an answer to say that COPA reaches some amount of materials that are harmful to minors; the question is whether it would reach more of them than less restrictive alternatives. In addition, the District Court found that verification systems may be subject to evasion and circumvention, for example by minors who have their own credit cards. Finally, filters also may be more effective because they can be applied to all forms of Internet communication, including e-mail, not just communications available via the World Wide Web.

That filtering software may well be more effective than COPA is confirmed by the findings of the Commission on Child Online Protection, a blue-ribbon commission created by Congress in COPA itself. Congress directed the Commission to evaluate the relative merits of different means of restricting minors' ability to gain access to harmful materials on the Internet. It unambiguously found that filters are more effective than age-verification requirements. See Commission on Child Online Protection (COPA), Report to Congress, at 19-21, 23-25, 27 (Oct. 20, 2000) (assigning a score for "Effectiveness" of 7.4 for server-based filters and 6.5 for client-based filters, as compared to 5.9 for independent adult-id verification, and 5.5 for credit card verification). Thus, not only has the Government failed to carry its burden of showing the District Court that the proposed alternative is less effective, but also a Government Commission appointed to consider the question has concluded just the opposite. That finding supports our conclusion that the District Court did not abuse its discretion in enjoining the statute.

Filtering software, of course, is not a perfect solution to the problem of children gaining access to harmful-to-minors materials. It may block some materials that are not harmful to minors and fail to catch some that are. Whatever the deficiencies of filters, however, the Government failed to introduce specific evidence proving that existing technologies are less effective than the restrictions in COPA. The District Court made a specific factfinding that "[n]o evidence was presented to the Court as to the percentage of time that blocking and filtering technology is over- or underinclusive." In the absence of a showing as to the relative effectiveness of COPA and the alternatives proposed by respondents, it was not an abuse of discretion for the District Court to grant the preliminary injunction. The Government's burden is not merely to show that a proposed less restrictive alternative has some flaws; its burden is to show that it is less effective. *Reno*, 521 U.S., at 874. It is not enough for the Government to show that COPA has some effect. Nor do respondents bear a burden to introduce, or offer to introduce, evidence that their proposed alternatives are more effective. The Government has the burden to show they are less so. The Government having failed to carry its burden, it was not an abuse of discretion for the District Court to grant the preliminary injunction.

One argument to the contrary is worth mentioning—the argument that filtering software is not an available alternative because Congress may not require it to be used. That argument carries little weight, because Congress undoubtedly may act to encourage the use of filters. We have held that Congress can give strong incentives to schools and libraries to use them. *United States* v. *Am. Library Ass'n*, 539 U.S. 194 (2003). It could also take steps to promote their development by industry, and their use by parents. It is incorrect, for that reason, to say that filters are part of the current regulatory status quo. The need for parental cooperation does not automatically disqualify a proposed less restrictive alternative. *Playboy Entertainment Group*, 529 U.S., at 824 ("A court should not assume a plausible, less restrictive alternative would be ineffective; and a court should not presume parents, given full information, will fail to act"). In enacting COPA, Congress said its goal was to prevent the "widespread availability of the Internet" from providing "opportunities for minors to access materials through the World Wide Web in a manner that can frustrate parental supervision or control." Congressional Findings, note following 47 U.S.C. § 231 (quoting Pub. L. 105-277, Tit. XIV, § 1402(1), 112 Stat. 2681-736). COPA presumes that parents lack the ability, not the will, to monitor what their children see. By enacting programs to promote use of filtering software, Congress could give parents that ability without subjecting protected speech to severe penalties.

The closest precedent on the general point is our decision in *Playboy Entertainment Group*. *Playboy Entertainment Group*, like this case, involved a content-based restriction designed to protect minors from viewing harmful materials. The choice was between a blanket speech restriction and a more specific technological solution that was available to parents who chose to implement it. 529 U.S., at 825. Absent a showing that the proposed less restrictive alternative would not be as effective, we concluded, the more restrictive option preferred by Congress could not survive strict scrutiny. *Id.*, at 826 (reversing because "[t]he record is silent as to the comparative effectiveness of the two alternatives"). In the instant case, too, the Government has failed to show, at this point, that the proposed less restrictive alternative will be less effective. The reasoning of *Playboy Entertainment Group,* and the holdings and force of our precedents require us to affirm the preliminary injunction. To do otherwise would be to do less than the First Amendment commands. "The starch in our constitutional standards cannot be sacrificed to accommodate the enforcement choices of the Government." *Id.,* at 830 (Thomas, J., concurring). * * *

[I]t is important to note that this opinion does not hold that Congress is incapable of enacting any regulation of the Internet designed to prevent minors from gaining access to harmful materials. The parties, because of the conclusion of the Court of Appeals that the statute's definitions rendered it unconstitutional, did not devote their attention to the question whether further evidence might be introduced on the relative restrictiveness and effectiveness of alternatives to the statute. On remand, however, the parties will be able to introduce further evidence on this point. This opinion does not foreclose the District Court from concluding, upon a proper showing by the Government that meets the Government's constitutional burden as defined in this opinion, that COPA is the least restrictive alternative available to accomplish Congress' goal. * * *

JUSTICE BREYER, with whom CHIEF JUSTICE REHNQUIST and JUSTICE O'CONNOR join, dissenting.

The Child Online Protection Act (Act), 47 U.S.C. § 231, seeks to protect children from exposure to commercial pornography placed on the Internet. It does so by requiring commercial providers to place pornographic material behind Internet "screens" readily accessible to adults who produce age verification. The Court recognizes that we should "'proceed . . . with care before invalidating the Act,'" while pointing out that the "imperative of according respect to the Congress . . . does not permit us to depart from well-established First Amendment principles." I agree with these generalities. Like the Court, I would subject the Act to "the most exacting scrutiny," *Turner Broadcasting System, Inc.* v. *FCC,* 512 U.S. 622, 642, (1994), requiring the Government to show that any restriction of nonobscene expression is "narrowly drawn" to further a "compelling interest" and that the restriction amounts to the "least restrictive means" available to further that interest, *Sable Communications of Cal., Inc.* v. *FCC,* 492 U.S. 115, 126 (1989).

Nonetheless, my examination of (1) the burdens the Act imposes on protected expression, (2) the Act's ability to further a compelling interest, and (3) the proposed "less restrictive alternatives" convinces me that the Court is wrong. I cannot accept its conclusion that Congress could have accomplished its statutory objective—protecting children from commercial pornography on the Internet—in other, less restrictive ways. * * *

II

I turn * * * to the question of "compelling interest," that of protecting minors from exposure to commercial pornography. No one denies that such an interest is "compelling." Rather, the question here is whether the Act, given its restrictions on adult access, significantly advances that interest. In other words, is the game worth the candle?

The majority argues that it is not, because of the existence of "blocking and filtering software." The majority refers to the presence of that software as a "less restrictive alternative." But that is a misnomer—a misnomer that may lead the reader to believe that all we need do is look to see if the blocking and filtering software is less restrictive; and to believe that, because in one sense it is (one can turn off the software), that is the end of the constitutional matter.

But such reasoning has no place here. Conceptually speaking, the presence of filtering software is not an *alternative* legislative approach to the problem of protecting children from exposure to commercial pornography. Rather, it is part of the status quo, *i.e.*, the backdrop against which Congress enacted the present statute. It is always true, by definition, that the status quo is less restrictive than a new regulatory law. It is always less restrictive to do *nothing* than to do *something*. But "doing nothing" does not address the problem Congress sought to address—namely that, despite the availability of filtering software, children were still being exposed to harmful material on the Internet.

Thus, the relevant constitutional question is not the question the Court asks: Would it be less restrictive to do nothing? Of course it would be. Rather, the relevant question posits a comparison of (a) a status quo that includes filtering software with (b) a change in that status quo that adds to it an age-verification screen requirement. Given the existence of filtering software, does the problem Congress identified remain significant? Does the Act help to address it? These are questions about the relation of the Act to the compelling interest. Does the Act, compared to the status quo, significantly advance the ball? (An affirmative answer to these questions will not justify "[a]ny restriction on speech," as the Court claims, ante, for a final answer in respect to constitutionality must take account of burdens and alternatives as well.)

The answers to these intermediate questions are clear: Filtering software, as presently available, does not solve the "child protection" problem. It suffers from four serious inadequacies that prompted Congress to pass legislation instead of relying on its voluntary use. First, its filtering is faulty, allowing some pornographic material to pass through without hindrance. Just last year, in *American Library Assn.*, Justice Stevens described "fundamental defects in the filtering software that is now available or that will be available in the foreseeable future." 539 U.S., at 221(dissenting opinion). He pointed to the problem of underblocking: "Because the software relies on key words or phrases to block undesirable sites, it does not have the capacity to exclude a precisely defined category of images." *Ibid.* That is to say, in the absence of words, the software alone cannot distinguish between the most obscene pictorial image and the Venus de Milo. No Member of this Court disagreed.

Second, filtering software costs money. Not every family has the $40 or so necessary to install it. By way of contrast, age screening costs * * * up to 20 cents per password or $20 per user for an identification number * * * .

Third, filtering software depends upon parents willing to decide where their children will surf the Web and able to enforce that decision. As to millions of American families, that is not a reasonable possibility. More than 28 million school age children have both parents or their sole parent in the work force, at least 5 million children are left alone at home without supervision each week, and many of those children will spend afternoons and evenings with friends who may well have access to computers and more lenient parents.

Fourth, software blocking lacks precision, with the result that those who wish to use it to screen out pornography find that it blocks a great deal of material that is valuable. As Justice Stevens pointed out, "the software's reliance on words to identify undesirable sites necessarily results in the blocking of thousands of pages that contain content that is completely innocuous for both adults and minors, and that no rational person could conclude matches the filtering companies' category definitions, such as pornography or sex." *American Library Assn., supra,* at 222 (internal quotation marks and citations omitted). Indeed, the American Civil Liberties Union (ACLU), one of the respondents here, told Congress that filtering software "block[s] out valuable and protected information, such as information about the Quaker religion, and web sites including those of the American Association of University Women, the AIDS Quilt, the Town Hall Political Site (run by the Family Resource Center, Christian Coalition and other conservative groups)." Hearing on Internet Indecency before the Senate Committee on Commerce, Science, and Transportation, 105th Cong., 2d Sess., 64 (1998). The software "is simply incapable of discerning between constitutionally protected and unprotected speech." *Id.,* at 65. It "inappropriately blocks valuable, protected speech, and does not effectively block the sites [it is] intended to block." *Id.,* at 66 (citing reports documenting overblocking).

Nothing in the District Court record suggests the contrary. No respondent has offered to produce evidence at trial to the contrary. No party has suggested, for example, that technology allowing filters to interpret and discern among images has suddenly become, or is about to become, widely available. Indeed, the Court concedes that "[f]iltering software, of course, is not a perfect solution to the problem."

In sum, a "filtering software status quo" means filtering that underblocks, imposes a cost upon each family that uses it, fails to screen outside the home, and lacks precision. Thus, Congress could reasonably conclude that a system that relies entirely upon the use of such software is not an effective system. And a law that adds to that system an age-verification screen requirement significantly increases the system's efficacy.

That is to say, at a modest additional cost to those adults who wish to obtain access to a screened program, that law will bring about better, more precise blocking, both inside and outside the home.

The Court's response—that 40% of all pornographic material may be of foreign origin—is beside the point.   Even assuming (I believe unrealistically) that *all* foreign originators will refuse to use screening, the Act would make a difference in respect to 60% of the Internet's commercial pornography. I cannot call that difference insignificant.

The upshot is that Congress could reasonably conclude that, despite the current availability of filtering software, a child protection problem exists. It also could conclude that a precisely targeted regulatory statute, adding an age-verification requirement for a narrow range of material, would more effectively shield children from commercial pornography.

Is this justification sufficient? The lower courts thought not. But that is because those courts interpreted the Act as imposing far more than a modest burden. They assumed an interpretation of the statute in which it reached far beyond legally obscene and borderline-obscene material, affecting material that, given the interpretation set forth above, would fall well outside the Act's scope. But we must interpret the Act to save it, not to destroy it. So interpreted, the Act imposes a far lesser burden on access to protected material. Given the modest nature of that burden and the likelihood that the Act will significantly further Congress' compelling objective, the Act may well satisfy the First Amendment's stringent tests. Indeed, it does satisfy the First Amendment unless, of course, there is a genuine alternative, "less restrictive" way similarly to further that objective.

III

I turn, then, to the actual "less restrictive alternatives" that the Court proposes. The Court proposes two real alternatives, *i.e.,* two potentially less restrictive ways in which Congress might alter the status quo in order to achieve its "compelling" objective.

First, the Government might "act to encourage" the use of blocking and filtering software. The problem is that any argument that rests upon this alternative proves too much. If one imagines enough government resources devoted to the problem and perhaps additional scientific advances, then, of course, the use of software might become as effective and less restrictive. Obviously, the Government could give all parents, schools, and Internet cafes free computers with filtering programs already installed, hire federal employees to train parents and teachers on their use, and devote millions of dollars to the development of better software. The result might be an alternative that is extremely effective.

But the Constitution does not, because it cannot, require the Government to disprove the existence of magic solutions, *i.e.,* solutions that, put in general terms, will solve any problem less restrictively but with equal effectiveness. Otherwise, "the undoubted ability of lawyers and judges," who are not constrained by the budgetary worries and other practical parameters within which Congress must operate, "to imagine *some* kind of slightly less drastic or restrictive an approach would make it impossible to write laws that deal with the harm that called the statute into being." *Playboy Entertainment Group*, 529 U.S., at 841 (Breyer, J., dissenting). As Justice Blackmun recognized, a "judge would be unimaginative indeed if he could not come up with something a little less 'drastic' or a little less 'restrictive' in almost any situation, and thereby enable himself to vote to strike legislation down." *Illinois Bd. of Elections* v. *Socialist Workers Party*, 440 U.S. 173, 188-189 (1979) (concurring opinion). Perhaps that is why no party has argued seriously that additional expenditure of government funds to encourage the use of screening is a "less restrictive alternative."

Second, the majority suggests decriminalizing the statute, noting the "chilling effect" of criminalizing a category of speech. To remove a major sanction, however, would make the statute less effective, virtually by definition.

IV

My conclusion is that the Act, as properly interpreted, risks imposition of minor burdens on some protected material—burdens that adults wishing to view the material may overcome at modest cost. At the same time, it significantly helps to achieve a compelling congressional goal, protecting children from exposure to commercial pornography. There is no serious, practically available "less restrictive" way similarly to further this compelling interest. Hence the Act is constitutional.

[Concurring opinion of JUSTICE STEVENS (joined by JUSTICE GINSBURG) and dissenting opinion of JUSTICE SCALIA omitted.]

Notes and Questions

1. What role does, and should, filtering technology play within the framework of the First Amendment and government regulation of speech? Professor Tom Bell suggests that the availability of filtering and other "self-help" remedies is relevant to determining both whether governmental speech restrictions are justified by a "compelling interest" and whether they represent the "least restrictive alternative" available to Congress:

> Courts in the United States * * * generally regard state action as *prima facie* justified, curbing such state action only if it evinces irrationality or an arbitrary and capricious exercise of power. Thanks to its bracingly plain demand for 'no law . . . abridging the freedom of speech,' however, the First Amendment has encouraged courts to regard state action somewhat more critically. In particular, courts applying strict scrutiny to content-based restrictions on speech have long included in their deliberations consideration of whether self-help remedies render state action superfluous. * * * Though self-help formerly affected courts' deliberations only implicitly, it has lately come to play an open and explicit role in determining the constitutionality of speech restrictions. U.S. courts have thus made clear that when it comes to restricting speech

based on its content, state agents must not try to do for us what we can do reasonably well for ourselves. * * *

Self-help's influence on free speech strict scrutiny jurisprudence offers a signal example of how changing facts can shape interpretation of the Constitution's unchanging words. * * * The[] two aspects of strict scrutiny—the "compelling interest" prong and the "least restrictive means" inquiry—have provided two openings for courts to consider self-help alternatives to state action. * * * From the very advent of the 'compelling interest' test [courts] have in practice—albeit only implicitly—cited the availability of simple and direct forms of self-help as grounds for finding state action unconstitutional. * * * [And] in the last few years, with the rise of tools empowering individuals and families to filter electronic information, courts applying strict scrutiny's "least restrictive means" test have begun to openly—and disfavorably—compare state action to alternative self-help remedies. * * * These jurisprudential phenomena, the first somewhat covert and the second very recent, * * * cast new light on First Amendment law, both clarifying old doctrines and preparing us to understand their application to new technologies.

The Supreme Court has not merely recognized the potentially revolutionary impact of pegging free speech jurisprudence to technological advances; it has embraced it:

> The Constitution exists precisely so that opinions and judgments . . . can be formed, tested, and expressed. What the Constitution says is that these judgments are for the individual to make, not for the Government to decree, even with the mandate or approval of a majority. Technology expands the capacity to choose; and it denies the potential of this revolution if we assume the Government is best positioned to make these choices for us.' [quoting *United States v. Playboy Entm't Group,* 529 U.S. 803, 818 (2000)]

Tom W. Bell, *Free Speech, Strict Scrutiny, and Self-Help: How Technology Upgrades Constitutional Jurisprudence,* 87 MINN. L. REV. 743, 744-45, 769 (2003). How would Justice Breyer respond to Professor Bell's argument? Does technology always, as the Supreme Court put it, "expand[] the capacity to choose"?

2. Does filtering actually work? How well? Is that a relevant consideration within the strict scrutiny framework? Even if you agree with Professor Bell that "when it comes to restricting speech based on its content, state agents must not try to do for us what we can do reasonably well for ourselves" and that "self-help remedies render state action superfluous" in the First Amendment context, the *effectiveness* of those remedies changes the scope of permissible state action. Are courts well-equipped to undertake such an inquiry? Should the constitutionality of a federal statute turn on the state-of-the-technology of privately-developed filtering software?

3. Professor James Boyle has observed that the result of the Supreme Court's decision in the CDA may be "to sharpen the turn to * * * filtering devices," making it unlikely that "the Internet [will be] as free, or the state as powerless, as the digerati seem to believe." James Boyle, *Foucault in*

Cyberspace: Surveillance, Sovereignty, and Hardwired Censors, 66 U. Cin. L. Rev. 177, 196 (1997). One can imagine various ways in which the government might attempt to encourage wider and more effective use of filtering software—by requiring software manufacturers to include filtering capabilities in their browsers, for instance, or by requiring website operators to "rate" their content so that filters can operate more effectively. Would such mandates be constitutional? Should the law encourage development of privately-developed technology—technology developed, Boyle suggests, "in a process effectively insulated from scrutiny"? *Id.* at 194.

The following case concerns one form such encouragement might take: conditioning the receipt of federal funds on the implementation of filters.

The Children's Internet Protection Act

In December 2000, Congress passed the Children's Internet Protection Act (CIPA), Pub. L. No. 106-554, 114 Stat. 2763, which makes the use of filtering software by elementary and secondary schools and public libraries a condition of their participation in certain federal programs. More specifically, it provides that a school or library's adoption of "Internet safety" policies involving filtering technology is a condition of both (a) receipt of federal funds for computer purchases and Internet access (under Title III of the Elementary and Secondary Education Act of 1965, 20 U.S.C. §§ 6801 *et seq.,* and the Library Services and Technology Act, 20 U.S.C. § 9134), and (b) participation in the federal "e-rate" or "universal service" program (47 U.S.C. § 254), under which telecommunications providers have to offer services at discounted rates to schools and libraries under certain circumstances. The provision governing library funding, for example, prohibits libraries from receiving money to purchase computers used to access the Internet, or to pay for direct costs associated with Internet access, unless the library:

> (i) has in place a policy of Internet safety for minors that includes the operation of a technology protection measure with respect to any of its computers with Internet access that protects against access through such computers to visual depictions that are—

> > (I) obscene;

> > (II) child pornography; or

> > (III) harmful to minors; and

> (ii) is enforcing the operation of such technology protection measure during any use of such computers by minors * * * .

CIPA § 1712(a) (codified at 20 U.S.C. § 9134(f)(1)(A)). In addition to formulating and enforcing this policy for minors, the library must have in place a general Internet safety policy for all patrons involving the use of a technology protection measure to block access to obscene materials and child pornography. *Id.* CIPA defines a "technology protection measure" as "a specific technology that blocks or filters Internet access to visual depictions" that are "obscene," "child pornography," or "harmful to minors." *Id.* § 1703(b)(1). The statute defines obscenity and child pornography by reference to federal criminal statutes, and defines material harmful to minors as

> * * * any picture, image, graphic image file, or other visual depiction that—

> (A) taken as a whole with respect to minors, appeals to a prurient interest in nudity, sex, or excretion;

> (B) depicts, describes, or represents, in a patently offensive way with respect to what is suitable for minors, an actual or simulated sexual act or sexual contact, actual or simulated normal or perverted sexual acts, or a lewd exhibition of the genitals; and

> (C) taken as a whole, lacks serious literary, artistic, political, or scientific value as to minors.

Id. § 1703(b)(2).

CIPA permits a supervisor to disable a technology protection measure when a patron seeks to use a blocked site "for bona fide research or other lawful purposes." *Id.* § 1712(a) (codified at 20 U.S.C. § 9134(f)(3)). CIPA's provisions on school funding and the e-rate program are substantially parallel to the library funding provisions, except that the e-rate provisions appear to permit a supervisor to disable a technology protection measure only when an adult seeks to use a blocked site. *See id.* § 1721(b) (codified at 47 U.S.C. § 254(h)(6)(D)).

In March 2001, a group of libraries, library patrons, and Internet content providers challenged CIPA's library provisions, seeking a declaration that the statute is unconstitutional on its face and a preliminary injunction barring its enforcement. A three-judge district court invalidated the statute. The court reasoned that a library offering Internet access creates a "designated public forum," that strict scrutiny applies to restrictions on speech within such a forum, and that a library's use of software filters could not survive that scrutiny. *See American Library Ass'n, Inc. v. United States*, 201 F. Supp. 2d 401 (E.D. Pa. 2002). The Supreme Court reversed, but no opinion commanded a majority of the Court. As you read the opinions below, ask yourself which rationale you find most persuasive.

United States v. American Library Association, Inc.

Supreme Court of the United States, 2003
539 U.S. 194

CHIEF JUSTICE REHNQUIST announced the judgment of the Court and delivered an opinion, in which JUSTICE O'CONNOR, JUSTICE SCALIA, and JUSTICE THOMAS joined.

The District Court held that Congress had exceeded its authority under the Spending Clause because, in the court's view, "any public library that complies with [the Children's Internet Protection Act (CIPA)] conditions will necessarily violate the First Amendment." *American Library Ass'n v. United States*, 201 F. Supp. 2d 401, 453 (E.D. Pa. 2002). The court acknowledged that "generally the First Amendment subjects libraries' content-based decisions about which print materials to acquire for their collections to only rational [basis] review." *Id.*, at 462. But it distinguished libraries' decisions to make certain Internet material inaccessible. "The central difference," the court stated, "is that by providing patrons with even filtered Internet access, the library permits patrons to receive speech on a virtually unlimited number of topics, from a virtually unlimited number of speakers, without attempting to restrict patrons' access to speech that the library, in the exercise of its professional judgment, determines to be particularly valuable." *Ibid.* Reasoning that "the provision of Internet access within a public library . . . is for use by the public . . . for expressive activity," the court analyzed such access as a "designated public forum." *Id.*, at 457 (citation and internal quotation marks omitted). The District Court also likened Internet access in libraries to "traditional public fora . . . such as sidewalks and parks" because it "promotes First Amendment values in an analogous manner." *Id.*, at 466.

Based on both of these grounds, the court held that the filtering software contemplated by CIPA was a content-based restriction on access to a public forum, and was therefore subject to strict scrutiny. Applying this standard, the District Court held that, although the Government has a compelling interest "in preventing the dissemination of obscenity, child pornography, or, in the case of minors, material harmful to minors," *id.*, at 471, the use of software filters is not narrowly tailored to further those interests. We noted probable jurisdiction and now reverse.

Congress has wide latitude to attach conditions to the receipt of federal assistance in order to further its policy objectives. *South Dakota v. Dole*, 483 U. S. 203, 206 (1987). But Congress may not "induce" the recipient "to engage in activities that would themselves be unconstitutional." *Id.*, at 210. To determine whether libraries would violate the First Amendment by employing the filtering software that CIPA requires, we must first examine the role of libraries in our society.

Public libraries pursue the worthy missions of facilitating learning and cultural enrichment. * * * To fulfill their traditional missions, public libraries must have broad discretion to decide what material to provide to their patrons. Although they seek to provide a wide array of information, their goal has never been to provide "universal coverage." 201 F. Supp. 2d at 421. Instead, public libraries seek to provide materials "that would be of the greatest direct benefit or interest to the community." *Ibid.* To this end, libraries collect only those materials deemed to have "requisite and appropriate quality." *Ibid.*

We have held in two analogous contexts that the government has broad discretion to make content-based judgments in deciding what private speech to make available to the public. In *Arkansas Ed. Television Comm'n v. Forbes,* 523 U. S. 666, 672-673 (1998), we held that public forum principles do not generally apply to a public television station's editorial judgments regarding the private speech it presents to its viewers. "[B]road rights of access for outside speakers would be antithetical, as a general rule, to the discretion that stations and their editorial staff must exercise to fulfill their journalistic purpose and statutory obligations." *Id.,* at 673. Recognizing a broad right of public access "would [also] risk implicating the courts in judgments that should be left to the exercise of journalistic discretion." *Id.,* at 674.

Similarly, in *National Endowment for Arts v. Finley,* 524 U. S. 569 (1998), we upheld an art funding program that required the National Endowment for the Arts (NEA) to use content-based criteria in making funding decisions. We explained that "[a]ny content-based considerations that may be taken into account in the grant-making process are a consequence of the nature of arts funding." *Id.,* at 585. In particular, "[t]he very assumption of the NEA is that grants will be awarded according to the 'artistic worth of competing applicants,' and absolute neutrality is simply inconceivable." *Ibid.* (some internal quotation marks omitted). We expressly declined to apply forum analysis, reasoning that it would conflict with "NEA's mandate . . . to make esthetic judgments, and the inherently content-based 'excellence' threshold for NEA support." *Id.,* at 586.

The principles underlying *Forbes* and *Finley* also apply to a public library's exercise of judgment in selecting the material it provides to its patrons. Just as forum analysis and heightened judicial scrutiny are incompatible with the role of public television stations and the role of the NEA, they are also incompatible with the discretion that public libraries must have to fulfill their traditional missions. Public library staffs necessarily consider content in making collection decisions and enjoy broad discretion in making them.

The public forum principles on which the District Court relied are out of place in the context of this case. Internet access in public libraries is neither a "traditional" nor a "designated" public forum. See *Cornelius v. NAACP Legal Defense & Ed. Fund, Inc.,* 473 U. S. 788, 802 (1985) (describing types of forums). First, this resource—which did not exist until quite recently—has not "immemorially been held in trust for the use of the public and, time out of mind, * * * been used for purposes of assembly, communication of thoughts between citizens, and discussing public questions." *International Soc. for Krishna Consciousness, Inc. v. Lee,* 505 U. S. 672, 679 (1992) (internal quotation marks omitted). We have "rejected the view that traditional public forum status extends beyond its historic confines." *Forbes, supra,* at 678. The doctrines surrounding traditional public forums may not be extended to situations where such history is lacking.

Nor does Internet access in a public library satisfy our definition of a "designated public forum." To create such a forum, the government must make an affirmative choice to open up its property for use as a public forum. "The government does not create a public forum by inaction or by permitting limited discourse, but only by intentionally opening a non-traditional forum for public discourse." *Cornelius, supra*, at 802. The District Court likened public libraries' Internet terminals to the forum at issue in *Rosenberger v. Rector and Visitors of Univ. of Va.*, 515 U. S. 819 (1995). In *Rosenberger*, we considered the "Student Activity Fund" established by the University of Virginia that subsidized all manner of student publications except those based on religion. We held that the fund had created a limited public forum by giving public money to student groups who wished to publish, and therefore could not discriminate on the basis of viewpoint.

The situation here is very different. A public library does not acquire Internet terminals in order to create a public forum for Web publishers to express themselves, any more than it collects books in order to provide a public forum for the authors of books to speak. It provides Internet access, not to "encourage a diversity of views from private speakers," *Rosenberger, supra,* at 834, but for the same reasons it offers other library resources: to facilitate research, learning, and recreational pursuits by furnishing materials of requisite and appropriate quality. As Congress recognized, "[t]he Internet is simply another method for making information available in a school or library." S. Rep. No. 106-141, p. 7 (1999). It is "no more than a technological extension of the book stack." *Ibid.*

The District Court disagreed because, whereas a library reviews and affirmatively chooses to acquire every book in its collection, it does not review every Web site that it makes available. Based on this distinction, the court reasoned that a public library enjoys less discretion in deciding which Internet materials to make available than in making book selections. We do not find this distinction constitutionally relevant. A library's failure to make quality-based judgments about all the material it furnishes from the Web does not somehow taint the judgments it does make. A library's need to exercise judgment in making collection decisions depends on its traditional role in identifying suitable and worthwhile material; it is no less entitled to play that role when it collects material from the Internet than when it collects material from any other source. Most libraries already exclude pornography from their print collections because they deem it inappropriate for inclusion. We do not subject these decisions to heightened scrutiny; it would make little sense to treat libraries' judgments to block online pornography any differently, when these judgments are made for just the same reason.

Moreover, because of the vast quantity of material on the Internet and the rapid pace at which it changes, libraries cannot possibly segregate, item by item, all the Internet material that is appropriate for inclusion from all that is not. While a library could limit its Internet collection to just those sites it found worthwhile, it could do so only at the cost of excluding an enormous amount of valuable information that it lacks the capacity to review. Given that tradeoff, it is entirely reasonable for public libraries to reject that approach and instead exclude certain categories of content, without making individualized judgments that everything they do make available has requisite and appropriate quality.

Like the District Court, the dissents fault the tendency of filtering software to "overblock"—that is, to erroneously block access to constitutionally protected speech that falls outside the categories that software users intend to block. Due to the software's limitations, "[m]any erroneously blocked [Web] pages contain content that is completely innocuous for both adults and minors, and that no rational person could conclude matches the filtering companies' category definitions, such as 'pornography' or 'sex.'" 201 F. Supp. 2d, at 449. Assuming that such erroneous blocking presents constitutional difficulties, any such concerns are dispelled by the ease with which patrons may have the filtering software disabled. When a patron encounters a blocked site, he need only ask a librarian to unblock it or (at least in the case of adults) disable the filter. As the District Court found, libraries have the capacity to permanently unblock any erroneously blocked site, and the Solicitor General stated at oral argument that a "library may . . . eliminate the filtering with respect to specific sites . . . at the request of a patron." With respect to adults, CIPA also expressly authorizes library officials to "disable" a filter altogether "to enable access for bona fide research or other lawful purposes." 20 U. S. C. §9134(f)(3) (disabling permitted for both adults and minors); 47 U. S. C. §254(h)(6)(D) (disabling permitted for adults). The Solicitor General confirmed that a "librarian can, in response to a request from a patron, unblock the filtering mechanism altogether," and further explained that a patron would not "have to explain . . . why he was asking a site to be unblocked or the filtering to be disabled." The District Court viewed unblocking and disabling as inadequate because some patrons may be too embarrassed to request them. But the Constitution does not guarantee the right to acquire information at a public library without any risk of embarrassment.

Appellees urge us to affirm the District Court's judgment on the alternative ground that CIPA imposes an unconstitutional condition on the receipt of federal assistance. Under this doctrine, "the government 'may not deny a benefit to a person on a basis that infringes his constitutionally protected . . . freedom of speech' even if he has no entitlement to that benefit." *Board of Comm'rs, Wabaunsee Cty. v. Umbehr*, 518 U. S. 668, 674 (1996) (quoting *Perry v. Sindermann,* 408 U. S. 593, 597 (1972)). Appellees argue that CIPA imposes an unconstitutional condition on libraries that receive E-rate and LSTA subsidies by requiring them, as a condition on their receipt of federal funds, to surrender their First Amendment right to provide the public with access to constitutionally protected speech. The Government counters that this claim fails because Government entities do not have First Amendment rights. * * *

We need not decide this question because, even assuming that appellees may assert an "unconstitutional conditions" claim, this claim would fail on the merits. Within broad limits, "when the Government appropriates public funds to establish a program it is entitled to define the limits of that program." *Rust v. Sullivan*, 500 U. S. 173, 194 (1991). * * * The E-rate and LSTA programs were intended to help public libraries fulfill their traditional role of obtaining material of requisite and appropriate quality for educational and informational purposes. Congress may certainly insist that these "public funds be spent for the purposes for which they were authorized." *Ibid.* Especially because public libraries have traditionally excluded pornographic material from their other collections, Congress could reasonably impose a parallel limitation on its Internet assistance programs. As the use of filtering software helps to carry out these programs, it is a permissible condition under *Rust*.

JUSTICE STEVENS asserts the premise that "[a] federal statute penalizing a library for failing to install filtering software on every one of its Internet-accessible computers would unquestionably violate [the First] Amendment." But—assuming again that public libraries have First Amendment rights—CIPA does not "penalize" libraries that choose not to install such software, or deny them the right to provide their patrons with unfiltered Internet access. Rather, CIPA simply reflects Congress' decision not to subsidize their doing so. To the extent that libraries wish to offer unfiltered access, they are free to do so without federal assistance. "'A refusal to fund protected activity, without more, cannot be equated with the imposition of a 'penalty' on that activity.'" *Rust, supra*, at 193 (quoting *Harris v. McRae*, 448 U. S. 297, 317, n. 19 (1980)). "'[A] legislature's decision not to subsidize the exercise of a 'fundamental' right does not infringe the right." *Rust, supra*, at 193 (quoting *Regan v. Taxation With Representation of Wash.*, 461 U. S. 540, 549 (1983)). * * *

Because public libraries' use of Internet filtering software does not violate their patrons' First Amendment rights, CIPA does not induce libraries to violate the Constitution, and is a valid exercise of Congress' spending power. Nor does CIPA impose an unconstitutional condition on public libraries. Therefore, the judgment of the District Court for the Eastern District of Pennsylvania is

Reversed.

JUSTICE KENNEDY, concurring in the judgment.

If, on the request of an adult user, a librarian will unblock filtered material or disable the Internet software filter without significant delay, there is little to this case. The Government represents this is indeed the fact. * * * If some libraries do not have the capacity to unblock specific Web sites or to disable the filter or if it is shown that an adult user's election to view constitutionally protected Internet material is burdened in some other substantial way, that would be the subject for an as-applied challenge, not the facial challenge made in this case.

JUSTICE BREYER, concurring in the judgment.

In ascertaining whether the statutory provisions are constitutional, I would apply a form of heightened scrutiny, examining the statutory requirements in question with special care. The Act directly restricts the public's receipt of information. And it does so through limitations imposed by outside bodies (here Congress) upon two critically important sources of information—the Internet as accessed via public libraries. * * * For that reason, we should not examine the statute's constitutionality as if it raised no special First Amendment concern—as if, like tax or economic regulation, the First Amendment demanded only a "rational basis" for imposing a restriction. * * *

At the same time, in my view, the First Amendment does not here demand application of the most limiting constitutional approach—that of "strict scrutiny." The statutory restriction in question is, in essence, a kind of "selection" restriction (a kind of editing). It affects the kinds and amount of materials that the library can present to its patrons. And libraries often properly engage in the selection of materials, either as a matter of necessity (*i.e.*, due to the scarcity of resources) or by design (*i.e.*, in accordance with collection development policies). To apply "strict scrutiny" to the "selection" of a library's collection (whether carried out by public libraries themselves or by other community bodies with a traditional legal right to engage in that function) would unreasonably interfere with the discretion necessary to create, maintain, or select a library's "collection" (broadly defined to include all the information the library makes available). That is to say, "strict scrutiny" implies too limiting and rigid a test for me to believe that the First Amendment requires it in this context.

Instead, I would examine the constitutionality of the Act's restrictions here as the Court has examined speech-related restrictions in other contexts where circumstances call for heightened, but not "strict," scrutiny—where, for example, complex, competing constitutional interests are potentially at issue or speech-related harm is potentially justified by unusually strong governmental interests. Typically the key question in such instances is one of proper fit. In such cases the Court has asked whether the harm to speech-related interests is disproportionate in light of both the justifications and the potential alternatives. It has considered the legitimacy of the statute's objective, the extent to which the statute will tend to achieve that objective, whether there are other, less restrictive ways of achieving that objective, and ultimately whether the statute works speech-related harm that, in relation to that objective, is out of proportion. * * *

The Act's restrictions satisfy these constitutional demands. The Act seeks to restrict access to obscenity, child pornography, and, in respect to access by minors, material that is comparably harmful. These objectives are "legitimate," and indeed often "compelling." * * * [T]he Act contains an important exception that limits the speech-related harm that "overblocking" might cause. As the plurality points out, the Act allows libraries to permit any adult patron access to an "overblocked" Web site; the adult patron need only ask a librarian to unblock the specific Web site or, alternatively, ask the librarian, "Please disable the entire filter."

The Act does impose upon the patron the burden of making this request. But it is difficult to see how that burden (or any delay associated with compliance) could prove more onerous than traditional library practices associated with segregating library materials in, say, closed stacks, or with interlibrary lending practices that require patrons to make requests that are not anonymous and to wait while the librarian obtains the desired materials from elsewhere. Perhaps local library rules or practices could further restrict the ability of patrons to obtain "overblocked" Internet material. But we are not now considering any such local practices. We here consider only a facial challenge to the Act itself.

Given the comparatively small burden that the Act imposes upon the library patron seeking legitimate Internet materials, I cannot say that any speech-related harm that the Act may cause is disproportionate when considered in relation to the Act's legitimate objectives. I therefore agree with the plurality that the statute does not violate the First Amendment, and I concur in the judgment.

JUSTICE STEVENS, dissenting.

The unchallenged findings of fact made by the District Court reveal fundamental defects in the filtering software that is now available or that will be available in the foreseeable future. Because the software relies on key words or phrases to block undesirable sites, it does not have the capacity to exclude a precisely defined category of images. * * * Given the quantity and ever-changing character of Web sites offering free sexually explicit material, it is inevitable that a substantial amount of such material will never be blocked. Because of this "underblocking," the statute will provide parents with a false sense of security without really solving the problem that motivated its enactment. Conversely, the software's reliance on words to identify undesirable sites necessarily results in the blocking of thousands of pages that "contain content that is completely innocuous for both adults and minors, and that no rational person could conclude matches the filtering companies' category definitions, such as 'pornography' or 'sex.'" 201 F. Supp. 2d at 449. In my judgment, a statutory blunderbuss that mandates this vast amount of "overblocking" abridges the freedom of speech protected by the First Amendment.

The effect of the overblocking is the functional equivalent of a host of individual decisions excluding hundreds of thousands of individual constitutionally protected messages from Internet terminals located in public libraries throughout the Nation. Neither the interest in suppressing unlawful speech nor the interest in protecting children from access to harmful materials justifies this overly broad restriction on adult access to protected speech. * * * The plurality does not reject [the district court's] findings. Instead, "[a]ssuming that such erroneous blocking presents constitutional difficulties," it relies on the Solicitor General's assurance that the statute permits individual librarians to disable filtering mechanisms whenever a patron so requests. In my judgment, that assurance does not cure the constitutional infirmity in the statute.

Until a blocked site or group of sites is unblocked, a patron is unlikely to know what is being hidden and therefore whether there is any point in asking for the filter to be removed. It is as though the statute required a significant part of every library's reading materials to be kept in unmarked, locked rooms or cabinets, which could be opened only in response to specific requests. Some curious readers would in time obtain access to the hidden materials, but many would not. Inevitably, the interest of the authors of those works in reaching the widest possible audience would be abridged. Moreover, because the procedures that different libraries are likely to adopt to respond to unblocking requests will no doubt vary, it is impossible to measure the aggregate effect of the statute on patrons' access to blocked sites. Unless we assume that the statute is a mere symbolic gesture, we must conclude that it will create a significant prior restraint on adult access to protected speech. A law that prohibits reading without official consent, like a law that prohibits speaking without consent, "constitutes a dramatic departure from our national heritage and constitutional tradition." *Watchtower Bible & Tract Soc. of N. Y., Inc. v. Village of Stratton*, 536 U. S. 150, 166 (2002).

II

The plurality incorrectly argues that the statute does not impose "an unconstitutional condition on public libraries." On the contrary, it impermissibly conditions the receipt of Government funding on the restriction of significant First Amendment rights. * * * As the plurality recognizes, we have always assumed that libraries have discretion when making decisions regarding what to include in, and exclude from, their collections. * * * [A] library's exercise of judgment with respect to its collection is entitled to First Amendment protection.

A federal statute penalizing a library for failing to install filtering software on every one of its Internet-accessible computers would unquestionably violate that Amendment. Cf. *Reno v. American Civil Liberties Union*, 521 U. S. 844 (1997). I think it equally clear that the First Amendment protects libraries from being denied funds for refusing to comply with an identical rule. An abridgment of speech by means of a threatened denial of benefits can be just as pernicious as an abridgment by means of a threatened penalty. * * *

The plurality argues that the controversial decision in *Rust v. Sullivan*, 500 U. S. 173 (1991), requires rejection of appellees' unconstitutional conditions claim. But, as subsequent cases have explained, *Rust* only involved and only applies to instances of governmental speech— that is, situations in which the government seeks to communicate a specific message. The discounts under the E-rate program and funding under the Library Services and Technology Act (LSTA) program involved in this case do not subsidize any message favored by the Government. As Congress made clear, these programs were designed "[t]o help public libraries provide their patrons with Internet access," which in turn "provide[s] patrons with a vast amount of valuable information." These programs thus are designed to provide access, particularly for individuals in low-income communities, see 47 U. S. C. §254(h)(1), to a vast amount and wide variety of private speech. They are not designed to foster or transmit any particular governmental message. * * *

The plurality's reliance on *National Endowment for Arts v. Finley*, 524 U. S. 569 (1998), is also misplaced. That case involved a challenge to a statute setting forth the criteria used by a federal panel of experts administering a federal grant program. Unlike this case, the Federal Government was not seeking to impose restrictions on the administration of a nonfederal program. * * * Also unlike *Finley*, the Government does not merely seek to control a library's discretion with respect to computers purchased with Government funds or those computers with Government-discounted Internet access. CIPA requires libraries to install filtering software on *every* computer with Internet access if the library receives *any* discount from the E-rate program or *any* funds from the LSTA program. * * *

This Court should not permit federal funds to be used to enforce this kind of broad restriction of First Amendment rights, particularly when such a restriction is unnecessary to accomplish Congress' stated goal. The abridgment of speech is equally obnoxious whether a rule like this one is enforced by a threat of penalties or by a threat to withhold a benefit.

I would affirm the judgment of the District Court.

JUSTICE SOUTER, with whom JUSTICE GINSBURG joins, dissenting.

I have no doubt about the legitimacy of governmental efforts to put a barrier between child patrons of public libraries and the raw offerings on the Internet otherwise available to them there, and if the only First Amendment interests raised here were those of children, I would uphold application of the Act. We have said that the governmental interest in "shielding" children from exposure to indecent material is "compelling," *Reno v. American Civil Liberties Union*, 521 U. S. 844, 869-870 (1997), and I do not think that the awkwardness a child might feel on asking for an unblocked terminal is any such burden as to affect constitutionality.

Nor would I dissent if I agreed with the majority of my colleagues that an adult library patron could, consistently with the Act, obtain an unblocked terminal simply for the asking. * * * [T]he unblocking provisions simply cannot be construed, even for constitutional avoidance purposes, to say that a library must unblock upon adult request, no conditions imposed and no questions asked. First, the statute says only that a library "may" unblock, not that it must. 20 U. S. C. §9134(f)(3); see 47 U.S.C. §254(h)(6)(D). In addition, it allows unblocking only for a "bona fide research or other lawful purposes," 20 U. S. C. §9134(f)(3); see 47 U.S.C. §254(h)(6)(D), and if the "lawful purposes" criterion means anything that would not subsume and render the "bona fide research" criterion superfluous, it must impose some limit on eligibility for unblocking. There is therefore necessarily some restriction, which is surely made more onerous by the uncertainty of its terms and the generosity of its discretion to library staffs in deciding who gets complete Internet access and who does not.

We therefore have to take the statute on the understanding that adults will be denied access to a substantial amount of nonobscene material harmful to children but lawful for adult examination, and a substantial quantity of text and pictures harmful to no one. As the plurality concedes, this is the inevitable consequence of the indiscriminate behavior of current filtering mechanisms, which screen out material to an extent known only by the manufacturers of the blocking software.

We likewise have to examine the statute on the understanding that the restrictions on adult Internet access have no justification in the object of protecting children. Children could be restricted to blocked terminals, leaving other unblocked terminals in areas restricted to adults and screened from casual glances. And of course the statute could simply have provided for unblocking at adult request, with no questions asked. The statute could, in other words, have protected children without blocking access for adults or subjecting adults to anything more than minimal inconvenience * * *.

The question for me, then, is whether a local library could itself constitutionally impose these restrictions on the content otherwise available to an adult patron through an Internet connection, at a library terminal provided for public use. The answer is no. A library that chose to block an adult's Internet access to material harmful to children (and whatever else the undiscriminating filter might interrupt) would be imposing a content-based restriction on communication of material in the library's control that an adult could otherwise lawfully see. This would simply be censorship. * * *

II

The Court's plurality does not treat blocking affecting adults as censorship, but chooses to describe a library's act in filtering content as simply an instance of the kind of selection from available material that every library (save, perhaps, the Library of Congress) must perform.

Public libraries are indeed selective in what they acquire to place in their stacks, as they must be. There is only so much money and so much shelf space, and the necessity to choose some material and reject the rest justifies the effort to be selective with an eye to demand, quality, and the object of maintaining the library as a place of civilized enquiry by widely different sorts of people. Selectivity is thus necessary and complex, and these two characteristics explain why review of a library's selection decisions must be limited: the decisions are made all the time, and only in extreme cases could one expect particular choices to reveal impermissible reasons (reasons even the plurality would consider to be illegitimate), like excluding books because their authors are Democrats or their critiques of organized Christianity are unsympathetic. See *Board of Ed., Island Trees Union Free School Dist. No. 26 v. Pico,* 457 U. S. 853, 870–871 (1982) (plurality opinion). Review for rational basis is probably the most that any court could conduct, owing to the myriad particular selections that might be attacked by someone, and the difficulty of untangling the play of factors behind a particular decision.

At every significant point, however, the Internet blocking here defies comparison to the process of acquisition. Whereas traditional scarcity of money and space require a library to make choices about what to acquire, and the choice to be made is whether or not to spend the money to acquire something, blocking is the subject of a choice made after the money for Internet access has been spent or committed. Since it makes no difference to the cost of Internet access whether an adult calls up material harmful for children or the Articles of Confederation, blocking (on facts like these) is not necessitated by scarcity of either money or space. In the instance of the Internet, what the library acquires is electronic access, and the choice to block is a choice to limit access that has already been acquired. Thus, deciding against buying a book means there is no book (unless a loan can be obtained), but blocking the Internet is merely blocking access purchased in its entirety and subject to unblocking if the librarian agrees. The proper analogy therefore is not to passing up a book that might have been bought; it is either to buying a book and then keeping it from adults lacking an acceptable "purpose," or to buying an encyclopedia and then cutting out pages with anything thought to be unsuitable for all adults.

The plurality claims to find support for its conclusions in the "traditional missio[n]" of the public library. The plurality thus argues, in effect, that the traditional responsibility of public libraries has called for denying adult access to certain books, or bowdlerizing the content of what the libraries let adults see. But, in fact, the plurality's conception of a public library's mission has been rejected by the libraries themselves. And no library that chose to block adult access in the way mandated by the Act could claim that the history of public library practice in this country furnished an implicit gloss on First Amendment standards, allowing for blocking out anything unsuitable for adults. * * *

To these two reasons to treat blocking differently from a decision declining to buy a book, a third must be added. Quite simply, we can smell a rat when a library blocks material already in its control, just as we do when a library removes books from its shelves for reasons having nothing to do with wear and tear, obsolescence, or lack of demand. Content-based blocking and removal tell us something that mere absence from the shelves does not.

I have already spoken about two features of acquisition decisions that make them poor candidates for effective judicial review. The first is their complexity, the number of legitimate considerations that may go into them, not all pointing one way, providing cover for any illegitimate reason that managed to sneak in. A librarian should consider likely demand, scholarly or esthetic quality, alternative purchases, relative cost, and so on. The second reason the judiciary must be shy about reviewing acquisition decisions is the sheer volume of them, and thus the number that might draw fire. Courts cannot review the administration of every library with a constituent disgruntled that the library fails to buy exactly what he wants to read.

After a library has acquired material in the first place, however, the variety of possible reasons that might legitimately support an initial rejection are no longer in play. Removal of books or selective blocking by controversial subject matter is not a function of limited resources and less likely than a selection decision to reflect an assessment of esthetic or scholarly merit. Removal (and blocking) decisions being so often obviously correlated with content, they tend to show up for just what they are, and because such decisions tend to be few, courts can examine them without facing a deluge. The difference between choices to keep out and choices to throw out is thus enormous, a perception that underlay the good sense of the plurality's conclusion in *Board of Ed., Island Trees Union Free School Dist. No. 26 v. Pico,* 457 U. S. 853 (1982), that removing classics from a school library in response to pressure from parents and school board members violates the Speech Clause.

III

There is no good reason, then, to treat blocking of adult enquiry as anything different from the censorship it presumptively is. For this reason, I would hold in accordance with conventional strict scrutiny that a library's practice of blocking would violate an adult patron's First and Fourteenth Amendment right to be free of Internet censorship, when unjustified (as here) by any legitimate interest in screening children from harmful material. On that ground, the Act's blocking requirement in its current breadth calls for unconstitutional action by a library recipient, and is itself unconstitutional.

Notes and Questions

1. To what extent does the division in the Court turn on whether a library's use of filtering software is analogous to "selecting" books for acquisition, or "removing" or "cutting out pages from" books? (Recall that this issue arose earlier in our discussion of metaphor and analogy in Chapter Two, where the court in *Mainstream Loudoun v. Board of Trustees of the Loudoun County Library,* 2 F. Supp. 2d 783 (E.D. Va. 1998) held that a public library's implementation of Internet filtering "more closely resembles * * * a collection of encyclopedias from which defendants have laboriously redacted portions deemed unfit for library patrons" than it does "an Interlibrary loan or outright book purchase.") Which analogy do you find more apt? Justices Souter and Ginsburg believe that "[a]t every significant point * * * the Internet blocking here defies comparison to the process of acquisition." Do you agree?

2. Note that CIPA requires implementation of filtering technology that screens out material meeting certain (rather complex) legal definitions. Does any such technology exist? If filtering technology necessarily screens out more than material that is obscene, child pornography, or harmful to minors, is there any way the statute can be constitutionally implemented?

3. The plurality opinion and the concurrences place great weight on the fact that a librarian can, for any patron, "unblock" an erroneously blocked site. Justice Kennedy goes so far as to say that "[i]f, on the request of an adult user, a librarian will unblock filtered material or disable the Internet software filter without significant delay, there is little to this case." Do you agree? Does the librarian's ability to unblock filtered material dispose of all First Amendment issues? Recall the concerns expressed by Professor Lessig that, depending on how filtering software operates, users may not know what sites are blocked. Suppose, for example, that a library's filtering software operated to exclude from search results any sites meeting the software's blocking criteria. How transparent does filtering have to be to render this "unblock" option a meaningful one?

4. The statute allows a patron to request disabling of the filtering software "to enable access for bona fide research or other lawful purposes." On the Justices' understanding of the statute, must a library patron actually articulate what his or her bona fide research project or other lawful purpose is? By what criteria should librarians measure what constitutes "bona fide research" or a "lawful purpose"? If you were advising a public library that received funds under the federal programs at issue, what policy on disabling access would you encourage the library to adopt?

5. Suppose that adult patrons of particular libraries have difficulty getting the libraries to disable filtering software, and bring as-applied challenges to the statute. What framework should courts use in evaluating such challenges?

6. Suppose that a local library that does *not* receive federal funds wishes to implement filtering software. How would you advise the library to write its policy?

Pennsylvania Internet Child Pornography Act

18 Pa. Cons. Stat. §§ 7621-7630

§ 7621. Definitions

The following words and phrases when used in this subchapter shall have the meanings given to them in this section unless the context clearly indicates otherwise:

"Child pornography." As described in [18 Pa. Cons. Stat. §6312] (relating to sexual abuse of children).

"Internet." The myriad of computer and telecommunications facilities, including equipment and operating software, which comprise the interconnected worldwide network of networks that employ the transmission control protocol/Internet protocol or any predecessor or successor protocols to such protocol to communicate information of all kinds by wire or radio.

"Internet service provider." A person who provides a service that enables users to access content, information, electronic mail or other services offered over the Internet.

§ 7622. Duty of Internet service provider

An Internet service provider shall remove or disable access to child pornography items residing on or accessible through its service in a manner accessible to persons located within this Commonwealth within five business days of when the Internet service provider is notified by the Attorney General pursuant to section 7628 (relating to notification procedure) that child pornography items reside on or are accessible through its service.

§ 7623. Protection of privacy

Nothing in this subchapter may be construed as imposing a duty on an Internet service provider to actively monitor its service or affirmatively seek evidence of illegal activity on its service.

§ 7624. Penalty

Notwithstanding any other provision of law to the contrary, any Internet service provider who violates section 7622 (relating to duty of Internet service provider) commits:

   (1) A misdemeanor of the third degree for a first offense punishable by a fine of $ 5,000.

   (2) A misdemeanor of the second degree for a second offense punishable by a fine of $ 20,000.

   (3) A felony of the third degree for a third or subsequent offense punishable by a fine of $ 30,000 and imprisonment for a maximum of seven years.

§ 7625. Jurisdiction for prosecution

The Attorney General shall have concurrent prosecutorial jurisdiction with the county district attorney for violations of this subchapter. No person charged with a violation of this subchapter by the Attorney General shall have standing to challenge the authority of the Attorney General to prosecute the case. If a challenge is made, the challenge shall be dismissed and no relief shall be available in the courts of this Commonwealth to the person making the challenge.

§ 7626. Application for order to remove or disable items

An application for an order of authorization to remove or disable items residing on or accessible through an Internet service provider's service shall be made to the court of common pleas having jurisdiction in writing upon the personal oath or affirmation of the Attorney General or a district attorney of the county wherein the items have been discovered and, if available, shall contain all of the following information:

   (1) A statement of the authority of the applicant to make the application.

   (2) A statement of the identity of the investigative or law enforcement officer that has, in the official scope of that officer's duties, discovered the child pornography items.

(3) A statement by the investigative or law enforcement officer who has knowledge of relevant information justifying the application.

(4) The Uniform Resource Locator providing access to the items.

(5) The identity of the Internet service provider used by the law enforcement officer.

(6) A showing that there is probable cause to believe that the items constitute a violation of section 6312 (relating to sexual abuse of children).

(7) A proposed order of authorization for consideration by the judge.

(8) Contact information for the Office of Attorney General, including the name, address and telephone number of any deputy or agent authorized by the Attorney General to submit notification.

(9) Additional testimony or documentary evidence in support of the application as the judge may require.

§ 7627. Order to remove or disable certain items from Internet service provider's service

Upon consideration of an application, the court may enter an order, including an *ex parte* order as requested, advising the Attorney General or a district attorney that the items constitute probable cause evidence of a violation of section 6312 (relating to sexual abuse of children) and that such items shall be removed or disabled from the Internet service provider's service. The court may include such other information in the order as the court deems relevant and necessary. * * *

Center for Democracy and Technology v. Pappert

United States District Court for the Eastern District of Pennsylvania, 2004
337 F. Supp. 606

DUBOIS, District Judge.

I. INTRODUCTION

In February of 2002, Pennsylvania enacted the Internet Child Pornography Act, 18 Pa. Cons. Stat. §§ 7621-7630, ("the Act"). The Act requires an Internet Service Provider ("ISP") to remove or disable access to child pornography items "residing on or accessible through its service" after notification by the Pennsylvania Attorney General. It is the first attempt by a state to impose criminal liability on an ISP which merely provides access to child pornography through its network and has no direct relationship with the source of the content. See Jonathan Zittrain, *Internet Points of Control,* 44 B.C.L. Rev. 653, 654, 672-73 (2003). * * *

Plaintiffs argue that, due to the technical limitations of the methods used by ISPs to comply with the Act, the efforts of ISPs to disable access to child pornography in response to requests by the Attorney General have led to the blocking of more than one and a half million innocent web sites not targeted by the Attorney General. Plaintiffs filed suit claiming that this blocking of innocent content, or "overblocking," violates the First Amendment to the Constitution. They also argue, *inter alia,* that the procedures provided in the Act for issuing an order to remove or disable access to child pornography are insufficient and allow for an unconstitutional prior restraint of speech. Moreover, they contend that the Informal Notice procedure developed by defendant in implementing the Act also operated as a prior restraint of speech. Finally, plaintiffs claim the Act places an impermissible burden on interstate commerce. Based on these allegations, plaintiffs ask the Court to declare the Act unconstitutional and provide related injunctive relief.

Defendant responds by arguing that the suppression of protected speech is not required by the Act and is the result of action taken by ISPs. According to defendant, ISPs have options for disabling access that would not block content unrelated to child pornography. Defendant also contends that the statutory procedures included in the Act and the Informal Notice procedure adopted by defendant in implementing the Act provide sufficient protection for the removal of child pornography from circulation. Additionally, defendant claims that the Informal Notices did not result in the prior restraint of speech because this procedure was developed with ISP input to provide for an informal and noncoercive means of advising ISPs that child pornography was accessible through their service. * * *

Based on the evidence presented by the parties at trial, the Court concludes that, with the current state of technology, the Act cannot be implemented without excessive blocking of innocent speech in violation of the First Amendment. In addition, the procedures provided by the Act are insufficient to justify the prior restraint of material protected by the First Amendment and, given the current design of the Internet * * * .

The elimination of child pornography is an important goal and those responsible for the creation or distribution of child pornography should be prosecuted to the full extent of the law. To that end, all of the ISPs involved in the case have given defendant their complete cooperation. Notwithstanding this effort, there is little evidence that the Act has reduced the production of child pornography or the child sexual abuse associated with its creation. On the other hand, there is an abundance of evidence that implementation of the Act has resulted in massive suppression of speech protected by the First Amendment. For these reasons, and the other reasons set forth in the Memorandum, the Court is ineluctably led to conclude the Act is unconstitutional. * * *

III. FINDINGS OF FACT

* * *

5. *Shared Domain Names*

Within the United States alone, there are tens of millions of separate domain names used for web sites that are, for the most part, independent of each other. * * * Web publishers can also publish on the World Wide Web without obtaining their own unique domain names for their web sites. For example, a web publisher can place content with a provider that offers to host web pages on the provider's own web site (as a sub-page under the provider's domain name). Thus, hypothetically, the Example Corporation could have a web site at the URL http://www.webhostingcompany.com/example. * * * Some web hosts allow users to create web sites using individualized subdomains of the web hosts' primary domain. Thus, hypothetically, the Example Corporation web site might be at the URL http://example.webhostingcompany.com, while another customer site might be at the URL http://acehardware.webhostingcompany.com.

Other than their existence as sub-pages or sub-domains on a providers' domains, web sites hosted as sub-pages or sub-domains are usually independent of the provider and independent of each other. * * *

6. IP Addresses and the Domain Name System

A URL such as http://www.attorneygeneral.gov or http://www.geocities.com/abwlnj/homepage.html provides enough information for a user to access the desired web site. * * * However, the URL alone is not sufficient for the user's computer to locate the web site. A user's computer must first determine the numeric Internet Protocol Address or IP address of the desired web site. Every device, or computer, using the Internet must have a unique IP address.

When a user seeks to access a particular URL, the user's computer initiates a look up through a series of global databases known as the domain name system ("DNS") to determine the IP Address of the Web Server that can provide the desired web pages. To search for the requested URL's IP address, the user's web browser must query a domain name system server ("DNS server") that has been assigned or selected within the user's computer. * * * Typically, an ISP gives its customers the IP addresses of DNS servers controlled by the ISP. * * *

Although a specific URL refers only to one specific web site, many different web sites (each with different domain names and URLs) are hosted on the same physical Web Server, and all the web sites on a server share the same IP Address. It is common for web hosting companies to offer virtual web hosting under which many web sites are hosted on the same Web Server and thus share the same IP address. * * *

Research by plaintiffs' expert Michael Clark empirically confirms the prevalence of shared IP addresses. In October-November 2003, Mr. Clark created a database of 29.5 million domain names and the IP addresses to which each domain named resolved. Using this database * * * Mr. Clark analyzed the frequency with which IP addresses were shared among domain names. * * * [A]t least fifty percent of domains shared an IP address with at least fifty other domains. * * *

One cannot determine with any certainty—using technical means—whether a given web site shares its IP address with another web site. * * *

E. ISP COMPLIANCE WITH COURT ORDERS OR INFORMAL NOTICES

* * * According to the ISPs, on most occasions, they attempted to comply with the Informal Notices by implementing either IP filtering or DNS filtering. * * *

a. DNS Filtering

* * * To perform DNS filtering, an ISP makes entries in the DNS servers under its control that prevent requests to those servers for a specific web site's fully qualified domain name (found in the requested site's URL) from resolving to the web site's correct IP address. The entries cause the DNS servers to answer the requests for the IP addresses for such domain names with either incorrect addresses or error messages. Without the correct IP addresses of the requested sites, the requests either do not proceed at all or do not reach the desired sites. * * *

b. IP Filtering

* * * To implement IP filtering, an ISP first determines the IP address to which a specific URL resolves. It then makes entries in routing equipment that it controls that will stop all outgoing requests for the specific IP address.

c. URL Filtering

URL filtering involves the placement of an additional device, or in some cases the reconfiguration of an existing "router" or other device, in the ISP's network to (a) reassemble the packets for Internet traffic flowing through its network, (b) read each http web request, and (c) if the requested URL in the web request matches one of the URLs specified in a blocking order, discard or otherwise block the http request.

3. Comparison of Filtering Methods

a. Ease of Implementation and Cost

* * * Most ISPs already have the hardware needed to implement IP filtering and IP filtering is a fairly routine aspect of the management of a network. IP filtering is used to respond to various types of attacks on a network, such as denial of service attacks and spam messages. * * * IP filtering generally does not require ISPs to purchase any new equipment and it does not have any impact on network performance. * * *

Almost all ISPs that do not outsource Internet access can utilize DNS filtering for customers that use their DNS servers. DNS filtering would be more difficult for some ISPs to implement. * * * As of February 3, 2004, AOL would have been required to make entries manually in all of its 100 DNS servers to implement a DNS block. * * * DNS filtering would require WorldCom to purchase and configure additional DNS servers in its network and potentially reconfigure the systems of millions of customers. * * *

No ISPs known to either plaintiffs' or defendant's experts utilize URL filtering to screen all World Wide Web traffic. AOL performs URL filtering on a portion of its network, but it cannot utilize URL filtering on its entire network at the present time. * * * It would take years to implement and be "extraordinarily expensive." * * * For example, an ISP would be required to purchase substantially more switches and routers to maintain the network's prior level of capacity because the switches and routers can handle less traffic if they are performing the computations necessary for URL filtering. * * *

b. Relative Effectiveness

An ISP's use of DNS filtering does not impact customers that do not use the ISP's DNS servers. Customers are not required to use the DNS server provided by their ISP. * * * IP filtering would be effective even where a user did not rely on the ISP's DNS server. * * * Although a web host can evade IP filtering by changing a web site's IP address—a technique that will not defeat DNS filtering—an ISP can track these changes and block the new IP address. Thus, it is reasonable for an ISP to chose IP filtering as a method of compliance over DNS filtering.

c. Overblocking

DNS filtering stops requests for all sub-pages under the blocked domain name. Thus, if the domain name included in the URL identified by an Informal Notice is of a Web Hosting Service that allows users to post their independent content as sub-pages on the service's site, the DNS server entries will stop requests for all of the independent pages on the service, not just the page that displays the targeted child pornography item. * * * DNS filtering stops requests for the domain name, not the IP address for the domain name; it does not disable access to any domain names that share an IP address with the targeted site unless they also share a domain name. * * *

IP filtering leads to a significant amount of overblocking. * * * [Plaintiffs' experts testified that] IP filtering "will block innocent sites to a great deal," "IP address filtering is extremely likely to block untargeted sites due to the process known as virtual hosting," and that it is "very easy to block access to additional sites" when using the IP filtering method * * * because of the prevalence of shared IP addresses * * * .

URL filtering filters out URLs down to the specific subpage. It presents no risk of disabling access to untargeted sites. Although URL filtering results in the least amount of overblocking, no ISPs are currently capable of implementing this method. Both DNS filtering and IP filtering result in overblocking. * * *

8. Methods of Evasion

a. Anonymous Proxy Servers

Internet users who want to keep their identity secret can use anonymous proxy servers or anonymizers. In the context of visiting web sites, these services route all requests through the proxy server or anonymizer, which in turn sends the request to the desired web site. Requests using these services appear to the ISP routing the request as if they are requests directed to the proxy service, not to the underlying URL to which the user actually seeks access.

The use of anonymous proxy services or anonymizers completely circumvents both of the technical blocking methods—IP filtering and DNS filtering—used by the ISPs to comply with the Informal Notices and would circumvent URL filtering as well. For example, web sites blocked by AOL could be accessed through AOL's service using the anonymizer "Proxify.com." * * *

b. The Ability of Child Pornographers to Evade Filters

* * * IP filtering can be evaded by operators of child pornography sites by changing the IP address of the web site. In one instance, the [Office of the Attorney General (OAG)] sent a second Informal Notice relating to one site because it had become available to AOL users at a different IP address after AOL blocked the original IP Address. AOL responded by blocking the second IP address as well.

Operators of child pornography sites can use a range of methods to evade DNS filtering, including: (1) using an IP address as a URL, i.e., a web site can use an IP address (or string of numbers) as the URL instead of a domain name like "www.example.com"; or (2) changing a portion of a domain name and promulgating the new domain name in hyperlinks to the web site in advertisements, search engines or newsgroups. * * *

IV. CONCLUSIONS OF LAW

* * *

B. SUBSTANTIVE FIRST AMENDMENT ISSUES

* * *

1. Burden on Speech

* * * This case is unusual in that the Act, on its face, does not burden protected speech. Facially, the Act only suppresses child pornography, which can be completely banned from the Internet. However, the action taken by private actors to comply with the Act has blocked a significant amount of speech protected by the First Amendment. *United States v. Playboy Entertainment Group,* 529 U.S. 803 (2000), relied upon by both parties, is the case that comes closest to addressing how this type of burden on protected speech should be addressed.

The federal statute at issue in *Playboy* required cable operators which provided sexually oriented programing to either fully scramble or block the channels that provided this programming, or limit the transmission of such programming to the hours between 10:00 P.M., and 6:00 A.M., referred to as "time channeling." *Id.* at 806. The Supreme Court determined that the statute was unconstitutional because the government failed to establish that the two methods for compliance identified in the challenged section were the least restrictive means for achieving the government's goal. In addressing the statute, the *Playboy* Court applied strict scrutiny because the speech targeted was defined by its content—"sexually explicit content." *Id.* at 811.

The analysis of the *Playboy* Court is particularly instructive in this case. That is so because the majority of cable operators involved in that case chose to comply with the section of the statute at issue by using time channeling notwithstanding the fact that it silenced a significant amount of protected speech, whereas the other stated method of compliance, scrambling, did not. *Id.* at 806. On that issue, the Court ruled that a reasonable cable operator could choose not to use the scrambling alternative provided by the statute because the available scrambling technology was "imprecise" and portions of the scrambled programs could be heard or seen by viewers, a phenomenon known as "signal bleed." Thus, "[a] rational cable operator, faced with the possibility of sanctions for intermittent bleeding, could well choose to time channel even if the bleeding is too momentary to pose any concern to most households." *Id.* at 821. The Court also noted that digital technology would have solved the signal bleed problem, but it was "not in wide-spread use."

The basis for the *Playboy* Court's determination that the statute was not the least restrictive means for achieving the government's goal was the fact that time channeling, deemed to be a reasonable method of compliance for cable operators, silenced "protected speech for two-thirds of the day in every home in a cable service area, regardless of the presence or likely presence of children or of the wishes of viewers." *Id.* In making this statement, the Court determined that "targeted blocking" at the request of a customer was a "less restrictive" and feasible means of furthering the government's compelling interest in the case. *Id.* at 816, 827. Targeted blocking required cable operators to block sexually-oriented channels at individual households. It was deemed to be less restrictive in that it enabled parents who did not want their child exposed to the program to block the offending channels without depriving willing viewers of the opportunity to watch a particular program. *Id.* at 815.

The Act in this case has resulted in the blocking of in excess of 1,190,000 web sites that were not targeted by the Informal Notices. Defendant argues that this overblocking does not violate the First Amendment because it resulted from decisions made by ISPs, not state actors. According to defendant, ISPs have "options for disabling access that would and will not block any, or as many, sites as Plaintiffs claim were blocked in the past" and the choice of which filtering method to use was "completely the decision of the ISPs."

The Court rejects this argument. Like the statute analyzed in *Playboy,* the Act in this case provides ISPs with discretion to choose a method of compliance although such methods are not incorporated in the Act itself. Like the time channeling in Playboy, the court concludes that ISPs could reasonably choose IP filtering and DNS filtering in order to comply with Act. And, like *Playboy,* the alternatives reasonably available to the ISPs block protected speech to a significant degree.

The two filtering methods used by the ISPs to comply with the Informal Notices and the court order—IP filtering and DNS filtering—both resulted in overblocking. IP filtering blocks all web sites at an IP address and, given the prevalence of shared IP addresses, the implementation of this method results in blocking of a significant number of sites not related to the alleged child pornography. * * *

* * * The Court will evaluate the constitutionality of the Act with respect to the technology that is currently available. * * * The URL filtering technology recommended by the OAG at trial was not available to any ISPs that received Informal Notices or a court order, with the exception of AOL. AOL's use of URL filtering was limited; it could not use URL filtering on its entire network. The evidence establishes that it would not be economical for ISPs to develop and implement URL filtering technology. Even if the ISPs invested in the development of this technology, it would take a significant amount of research and testing to implement this filtering method and none of the experts or engineers who testified were able to give a timetable for the completion of this research. Moreover, if the ISPs were able to develop the devices and software necessary to perform URL filtering, they would be required to purchase "substantially more" switches and routers to avoid "significantly" degrading the performance of their networks. * * * Thus, URL filtering is not a feasible alternative to DNS filtering and IP filtering.

As this Court reads *Playboy,* if a statute regulating speech provides distributors of speech with alternatives for compliance and the majority of distributors reasonably choose an alternative that has the effect of burdening protected speech, the statute is subject to scrutiny as a burden on speech. * * *

2. Level of Scrutiny

In determining whether a statute's burden on protected speech is constitutional, a Court must generally first decide whether to apply strict or intermediate scrutiny. Plaintiffs argue that strict scrutiny applies because the Act is a content based restriction on speech. Defendant argues that intermediate scrutiny is more appropriate because the Act only applies to child pornography, which has no protection, and the burden on protected expression is a collateral consequence of the Act. * * *

* * * Although there are strong arguments for the application of strict and intermediate scrutiny, the Court need not choose between the two because, even under the less demanding standard—intermediate scrutiny—the Act does not pass Constitutional muster. Under [intermediate scrutiny], a regulation must further an important government interest unrelated to the suppression of free expression and the incidental restriction on First Amendment freedoms must be no greater than is essential to the furtherance of that interest. *United States v. O'Brien,* 391 U.S. 367, 377 (1968). * * *

Although the prevention of child exploitation and abuse is a state interest unrelated to the suppression of free expression, defendant has not produced any evidence that the implementation of the Act has reduced child exploitation or abuse. The Act does block some users' access to child pornography; however, the material is still available to Internet users accessing the material through ISPs other than the one that blocked the web site. In addition, there are a number of methods that users and producers of child pornography can implement to avoid the filtering methods. * * * Although the inference could be drawn that making it more difficult to access child pornography reduces the incentive to produce and distribute child pornography, this burden on the child pornography business is not sufficient to overcome the significant suppression of expression that resulted from the implementation of the Act.

More than 1,190,000 innocent web sites were blocked in an effort to block less than 400 child pornography web sites, and there is no evidence that the government made an effort to avoid this impact on protected expression. * * * [A]ll the currently available technical methods of disabling access to a web site accessible through an ISP's service result in significant overblocking. The Act fails to specify any means of compliance, let alone provide guidance as to which method will minimize or avoid suppression of protected speech. This burden on protected expression is substantial whereas there is no evidence that the Act has impacted child sexual abuse. Thus, the Act cannot survive intermediate scrutiny. * * *

C. PROCEDURAL FIRST AMENDMENT ISSUES

1. Prior Restraint

The Act and Informal Notice process are not prior restraints in the traditional sense. They do not prevent speech from reaching the market place but remove material already available on the Internet from circulation. *Alexander v. United States,* 509 U.S. 544 (1993) ("The term 'prior restraint' describes orders forbidding certain communications that are issued before the communications occur.") However, they are administrative prior restraints as that term has been interpreted by the Supreme Court. According to the Court, "only a judicial determination in an adversary proceeding ensures the necessary sensitivity to freedom of expression, only a procedure requiring a judicial determination suffices to impose a valid final restraint." *Freedman v. Maryland,* 380 U.S. 51, 58 (1965). Thus, if material protected by the First Amendment is removed from circulation without these procedural protections, the seizure is invalid as a prior restraint. The Court used the term to describe a Rhode Island Commission's practice of sending letters to book distributors that asked the distributors to remove books from circulation in *Bantam Books v. Sullivan,* 372 U.S. 58 (1962) and a procedure that allowed courts to order pre-trial seizure of films alleged to be obscene in *Fort Wayne Books, Inc. v. Indiana,* 489 U.S. 46, 51-52 (1989).

In *Bantam Books,* the Court ruled on a regulatory scheme implemented by the state of Rhode Island. The state created the Rhode Island Commission to Encourage Morality in Youth, and this commission sent book distributors letters informing them that books they were distributing were "objectionable" and asking them to "cooperate" by removing this material from book stores. *Id.* at 61-63. The letters also stated that "the Attorney General will act for us in the case of non-compliance." *Id.* at 63. In response, plaintiffs stopped further circulation of copies and "instructed field men to visit retailers and to pick up all unsold copies." Although these materials were already in circulation, the Court referred to this system as a "prior administrative restraint" and ruled it was unconstitutional because there was not "an almost immediate judicial determination of the validity of the restraint" and the publisher or distributor was not entitled to notice and a hearing.

In *Fort Wayne Books v. Indiana,* 489 U.S. 46 (1989), the Court held that a finding of probable cause by a state court was not sufficient to allow seizure of material "presumptively protected by the First Amendment." "While a single copy of a book or film may be seized and retained for evidentiary purposes based on a finding of probable cause, the publication may not be taken out of circulation completely until there has been a determination of obscenity after an adversary hearing." *Id.* at 63. Like *Bantam Books,* the materials in *Fort Wayne* were already in circulation. They were removed from circulation by a state court order. According to the Court, "our cases firmly hold that mere probable cause to believe a legal violation has transpired is not adequate to remove books or films from circulation." *Id.,* at 66.

Based on the decision in *Bantam Books* and *Fort Wayne Books,* this Court concludes the procedural protections provided by the Act are inadequate. These cases require a court to make a final determination that material is child pornography after an adversary hearing before the material is completely removed from circulation. Under the Act, a judge is only required to make a finding of probable cause, he can make this determination ex parte, and there is no requirement that the publisher or distributor receive notice or an opportunity to be heard.

Additionally, as argued by plaintiffs, the Act allows for an unconstitutional prior restraint because it prevents future content from being displayed at a URL based on the fact that the URL contained illegal content in the past. Plaintiffs compare this burden to the permanent ban on the publication of a newspaper with a certain title, *Near v. Minnesota,* 283 U.S. 697 (1931), or a permanent injunction against showing films at a movie theater, *Vance v. Universal Amusement Co.,* 445 U.S. 308 (1980). * * *

There are some similarities between a newspaper and a web site. Just as the content of a newspaper changes without changing the title of the publication, the content identified by a URL can change without the URL itself changing. In fact, it is possible that the owner or publisher of material on a web site identified by a URL can change without the URL changing. Plaintiffs demonstrated this by purchasing the http://www.littleangels.tv/tr URL and converting the alleged child pornography web site into a web site dedicated to a description of this case. Moreover, an individual can purchase the rights to a URL and have no way to learn that the URL has been blocked by an ISP in response to an Informal Notice or court order.

Despite the fact that the content at a URL can change frequently, the Act does not provide for any review of the material at a URL and, other than a verification that the site was still blocked thirty days after the initial Informal Notice, the OAG did not review the content at any blocked URLs. Moreover, other than the instances in which complaints were made about blocked innocent content, ISPs have continued to maintain their blocking action. Specifically, WorldCom, Comcast, AOL, and Verizon all testified that they routinely maintain the blocks implemented in response to Informal Notices or, with respect to World Com, the court order. * * *

The fact that an ISP can challenge a judge's child pornography determination in a criminal prosecution does not save the Act. Only one ISP, WorldCom, challenged an Informal Notice and then promptly complied with a court order obtained by the OAG. An ISP has little incentive to challenge the suppression of a web site with which it has no business relationship. As stated by the Supreme Court, a statute that suppresses speech "must be tested by its operation and effect." *Near v. Minnesota*, 283 U.S. 697 (1931). The operation and effect of this Act is that speech will be suppressed when a court order is issued, and the procedural protections provided by the Act before the order can issue are insufficient to avoid constitutional infirmity. * * *

V. CONCLUSION

For the foregoing reasons, plaintiffs' Motion for Declaratory Relief and Preliminary and Permanent Injunctive Relief is granted. Pennsylvania's Internet Child Pornography Act, 18 Pa. Stat. Ann. § 7621-7630 and the Informal Notice process used by defendant to implement the Act are declared unconstitutional. Defendant is enjoined from taking any action against an ISP for failing to comply with an Informal Notice or court order under the Act.

Notes and Questions

1. The plurality in the *United States v. American Library Ass'n* case, *supra,* seemed unconcerned with the possibility that library filtering software would "overblock," while the court in *Center for Democracy and Technology v. Pappert* focused much of its constitutional analysis on this overblocking problem. What might account for this difference in approach? The fact that the former involved the provision of benefits under a quasi-voluntary government program while the latter involved mandatory blocking orders (enforced by criminal penalties)? The fact that the former was a "facial" challenge to a statute that had not yet been implemented, while the latter was a challenge to the actual application of the Pennsylvania statute? The fact that the library filters (but not the ISP filters) could be disabled by users?

2. The *Pappert* court above concludes that "URL blocking" techniques would avoid any "overblocking" of constitutionally-protected speech—but holds the statute nonetheless unconstitutional because "the evidence establishes that it would not be economical for ISPs to develop and implement URL filtering technology." Should the constitutionality of the statute depend in this fashion

on the state, and cost, of the relevant technology? Is it circular reasoning to do so, when the state, and cost, of the relevant technology are to some extent themselves dependent on the background legal regime? That is, wouldn't statutes like Pennsylvania's give ISPs an incentive to develop less expensive and more effective URL filtering techniques—thereby curing their own constitutional infirmities?

3. Professor Zittrain, in the article cited in the first paragraph of the court's opinion, writes as follows:

> Attempts to control the Internet have met with mixed success amid a vigorous and ongoing debate about the extent to which the comparatively anarchic status quo will prevail. I wish to add to that debate—in which I believe that control will trump anarchy—by examining a recent experiment in control launched by the Commonwealth of Pennsylvania to restrict the flow of illegal pornography available to its residents. This experiment, grounded in a state law by which any Internet service provider (ISP), under threat of criminal liability, can be required to block access by Pennsylvanians to a given Internet destination. The law represents a novel approach, heretofore untried by both anti-pornography champions and their conceptual siblings-in-arms, publishers seeking to limit intellectual property piracy.

> The experiment is notable for its audacious departure from the Internet's techno-political foundations. It enlists network service providers in a role that has previously—surprisingly, in retrospect—completely eluded the crossfire documented in the courses and case-books. It is also notable because, after a string of efforts resulting in something far short of total effectiveness, it portends a strategy that will work. ISPs can serve as Internet police, not only cordoning off areas from view when acting as hosts of content, but also more broadly restricting access to particular networked entities with whom their customers wish to communicate—thus determining what those customers can see, wherever it might be online. The publishers, themselves no strangers to creative and cutting-edge (if so far somewhat hapless) approaches to taming the Internet, are no doubt watching closely, and will endeavor to adapt this sort of progress on anti-pornography, should it succeed, for use in their own battles.

> A refined Pennsylvania approach—reinforced by the technical tools developed by ISPs conscripted to accommodate it—could cause a sea change in the Internet's regulability. Such a change would bring Internet usage in line much more closely with prevailing legal standards, whether concerning dissemination and use of pornography or intellectual property, or relating to other persistent problems like gambling, spam, privacy infringement, or conflicting jurisdictions.

Jonathan Zittrain, *Internet Points of Control*, 44 B.C. L. REV. 653, 654-55 (2003). Does the court's decision in *CDT v. Pappert* throw any light on Professor Zittrain's claim that this could portend a "sea change in the Internet's regulability"?

Chapter Seven

PROBLEMS OF INTERMEDIARIES

INTRODUCTION

In examining how governmental and non-governmental actors seek to influence the behavior of Internet users, we have touched upon the role of Internet service providers (ISPs) and other intermediaries. Users necessarily rely on ISPs to facilitate their access to the Internet and to host and transmit their communications. Because ISPs are the gatekeepers to the Internet, their policies can have a profound effect on its users' freedom to speak, the degree of privacy that users experience, the extent to which users are entitled to engage in anonymous or pseudonymous communication, and so on.

An ISP's policies, of course, are not simply dictated by the market. For a governmental entity that wishes to curtail certain activities, ISPs provide attractive points of "control."[a] Recall, for example, the discussion in Chapter Six of the Commonwealth of Pennsylvania's effort to curb child pornography by imposing criminal liability upon ISPs that fail to disable Pennsylvania subscribers' access to such content. *See supra* p. 468. Similarly, by imposing liability on ISPs for the activities of their users, the government can pressure ISPs to eliminate certain kinds of online behavior. ISPs and other intermediaries are important targets for regulators in another respect: to the extent that such entities serve as a repository for information, they will be a convenient point from which the government and others can extract users' identifying data and even private communications.[b]

In short, the policies and practices of intermediaries—and the laws and other forces that shape those policies and practices—will have a profound

---

a. *See, e.g.*, Jonathan Zittrain, *Internet Points of Control*, 44 B.C. L. REV. 653 (2003).

b. *See, e.g.*, Patricia L. Bellia, *Surveillance Law Through Cyberlaw's Lens*, 72 GEO. WASH. L. REV. 1375, 1456-58 (2004).

effect on the shape of the Internet. This chapter accordingly brings the role of intermediaries to the fore. Section A considers the extent to which imposing liability on intermediaries for harms caused by their users does and should shape user behavior. Section B considers the role of intermediaries as guardians of anonymity and privacy on the Internet.

SECTION A. INTERMEDIARY LIABILITY FOR ONLINE CONDUCT

The development of the Internet allows an individual speaker to make his or her words widely available, without the geographic, economic, or technological barriers to print publishing or broadcasting. Like any other speech medium, however, the Internet is value neutral: It may yield a more decentralized, diverse speech market, but we can expect some of the speech to be harmful. Indeed, one could argue that the low cost of distributing speech, coupled with other features of the Internet, makes it easier for individuals to inflict significant harm while at the same time rendering ineffective certain traditional rules that deter and allow recovery for harmful speech and activities. A speaker who wishes to circulate false information about another person has a ready means to do so even if the speaker lacks significant resources; and because the Internet can afford a speaker some degree of anonymity, it may be difficult for the person harmed by the false speech to identify the speaker or to achieve adequate compensation. One who wishes to copy and circulate copyrighted material in digital form can do so quickly, inexpensively, and without any degradation in quality. For the copyright holder, it may be difficult to identify—and expensive to pursue—individual infringers. Moreover, because dissemination of copyrighted material in digital form is so easy, from the perspective of a copyright holder even an innocent single use of copyrighted material poses a threat of harm.

Although Internet speech is inexpensive, most users must rely on a third party to facilitate their access to the network, to host content, and to transmit their communications. As those harmed by online speech or activities find the traditional rules for deterring and providing compensation for harmful speech to be ineffective, they are likely to seek compensation from these intermediaries. Under what circumstances should an Internet service provider or other intermediary be held liable for harm caused by its users?

This question represents just one facet of a broader problem that courts and legislatures grapple with in a wide range of legal contexts: When should the law impose liability on party who, although not the primary wrongdoer, might nonetheless be able to prevent a wrong or mitigate the damage that flows from it? One familiar example of this problem—variously described as the problem of of "indirect," "collateral," "vicarious," "third-party," or "secondary" liability—is the doctrine of *respondeat superior*.   Under that doctrine, courts will impute to an employer a wrong committed by an employee within the scope of his employment. In some areas of the law, indirect liability has developed as a judge-made rule.   In the copyright context, for example, courts have held—despite the absence of any explicit provision in the Copyright Act—that a mall owner may be held liable when a vendor sells counterfeit goods on the premises.[c] In other contexts, indirect liability is imposed by statute. In some states, for example, "dram shop" statutes hold bartenders liable for serving alcohol to minors or visibly intoxicated patrons who later cause injuries through drunk driving.[d] At the federal level, there are numerous examples of indirect liability in securities laws.[e]

What justifies indirect liability? As one commentator has put it, indirect liability "supplements efforts to deter primary wrongdoers directly by enlisting their associates and market contacts as de facto 'cops on the beat.'" Reinier Kraakman, *Gatekeepers: The Anatomy of a Third-Party Enforcement Strategy*, J. L. & Econ. 53, 53 (1986). But when is such liability appropriate? In answering that question, judges and legislators might consider a range of factors. Will primary enforcement efforts be sufficient to deter wrongdoing? Do third parties have adequate market incentives to deter wrongdoing even in the absence of indirect liability? Will imposing indirect liability on third parties reliably deter wrongdoing? Is imposing indirect liability fair?

Consider a classic case in which the court wrestled explicitly with the possible justifications for imposing indirect liability. Although the case involved an employer-employee relationship, the underlying policy questions are ones that recur in any context in which the law imposes liability on one party for the wrongdoing of another.

Ira S. Bushey & Sons, Inc. v. United States

United States Court of Appeals for the Second Circuit, 1968
398 F.2d 167

Friendly, Circuit Judge:

While the United States Coast Guard vessel Tamaroa was being overhauled in a floating drydock located in Brooklyn's Gowanus Canal, a seaman returning from shore leave late at night, in the condition for which seamen are famed, turned some wheels on the drydock wall. He thus opened valves that controlled the flooding of the tanks on one side of the drydock. Soon the ship listed, slid off the blocks and fell against the wall. Parts of the drydock sank, and the ship partially did—fortunately without loss of life or personal injury. The drydock owner sought and was granted

---

c. *E.g.*, Fonovisa, Inc. v. Cherry Auction, Inc., 76 F.3d 259 (9th Cir. 1996).

d. *E.g.*, 235 Ill. Comp. Stat. 5/6-21; Mich. Comp. Laws § 436.1801(3); 47 Pa. Cons. Stat. §§ 4-493(1) & 4-497.

e. *E.g.*, Securities Act of 1933, sec. 15, ch. 38, 48 Stat. 84 (codified as amended at 15 U.S.C. § 77o (2000)); Securities and Exchange Act of 1934, sec. 20, ch. 404, 48 Stat. 899 (codified as amended at 15 U.S.C. § 78t (2000)).

compensation by the District Court for the Eastern District of New York in an amount to be determined; the United States appeals. * * *

Seaman Lane, whose prior record was unblemished, returned from shore leave a little after midnight on March 14. He had been drinking heavily; the quartermaster made mental note that he was "loose." For reasons not apparent to us or very likely to Lane, he took it into his head, while progressing along the gangway wall, to turn each of three large wheels some twenty times; unhappily, as previously stated, these wheels controlled the water intake valves. After boarding ship at 12:11 A.M., Lane mumbled to an off-duty seaman that he had "turned some valves" and also muttered something about "valves" to another who was standing the engineering watch. Neither did anything; apparently Lane's condition was not such as to encourage proximity. At 12:20 A.M. a crew member discovered water coming into the drydock. By 12:30 A.M. the ship began to list, the alarm was sounded and the crew were ordered ashore. Ten minutes later the vessel and dock were listing over 20 degrees; in another ten minutes the ship slid off the blocks and fell against the drydock wall.

The Government attacks imposition of liability on the ground that Lane's acts were not within the scope of his employment. It relies heavily on § 228(1) of the Restatement of Agency 2d which says that "conduct of a servant is within the scope of employment if, but only if: * * * (c) it is actuated, at least in part by a purpose to serve the master." Courts have gone to considerable lengths to find such a purpose, as witness a well-known opinion in which Judge Learned Hand concluded that a drunken boatswain who routed the plaintiff out of his bunk with a blow, saying "Get up, you big son of a bitch, and turn to," and then continued to fight, might have thought he was acting in the interest of the ship. *Nelson v. American-West African Line*, 86 F.2d 730 (2d Cir. 1936), *cert. denied*, 300 U.S. 665 (1937). It would be going too far to find such a purpose here; while Lane's return to the Tamaroa was to serve his employer, no one has suggested how he could have thought turning the wheels to be, even if—which is by no means clear—he was unaware of the consequences.

In light of the highly artificial way in which the motive test has been applied, the district judge believed himself obliged to test the doctrine's continuing vitality by referring to the larger purposes *respondeat superior* is supposed to serve. He concluded that the old formulation failed this test. We do not find his analysis so compelling, however, as to constitute a sufficient basis in itself for discarding the old doctrine. It is not at all clear, as the court below suggested, that expansion of liability in the manner here suggested will lead to a more efficient allocation of resources. As the most astute exponent of this theory has emphasized, a more efficient allocation can only be expected if there is some reason to believe that imposing a particular cost on the enterprise will lead it to consider whether steps should be taken to prevent a recurrence of the accident. Calabresi, The Decision for Accidents: An Approach to Non-fault Allocation of Costs, 78 Harv. L. Rev. 713, 725-34 (1965). And the suggestion that imposition of liability here will lead to more intensive screening of employees rests on highly questionable premises. The unsatisfactory quality of the allocation of resource rationale is especially striking on the facts of this case. It could well be that application of the traditional rule [finding the seaman's conduct to be outside the scope of his employment] might induce drydock owners, prodded by their insurance companies, to install locks on their valves to avoid similar incidents in the future, while placing the burden on shipowners is much less likely to lead to accident prevention. It is true, of course, that in many cases the plaintiff will not be in a position to insure, and so expansion of liability will, at the very least, serve *respondeat superior*'s loss spreading function. But the fact that the defendant is better able to afford damages is not alone sufficient to justify legal responsibility, and this overarching principle must be taken into account in deciding whether to expand the reach of *respondeat superior*.

A policy analysis thus is not sufficient to justify this proposed expansion of vicarious liability. This is not surprising since *respondeat superior*, even within its traditional limits, rests not so much on policy grounds consistent with the governing principles of tort law as in a deeply rooted sentiment that a business enterprise cannot justly disclaim responsibility for accidents which may fairly be said to be characteristic of its activities. * * * Lane's conduct was not so "unforeseeable" as to make it unfair to charge the Government with responsibility. * * * Here it was foreseeable that crew members crossing the drydock might do damage, negligently or even intentionally, such as pushing a Bushey employee or kicking property into the water. Moreover, the proclivity of seamen to find solace for solitude by copious resort to the bottle while ashore has been noted in opinions too numerous to warrant citation. Once all this is granted, it is immaterial that Lane's precise action was not to be foreseen. Consequently, we can no longer accept our past decisions that have refused to move beyond the *Nelson* rule, since they do not accord with modern understanding as to when it is fair for an enterprise to disclaim the actions of its employees. * * *

The risk that seamen going and coming from the Tamaroa might cause damage to the drydock is enough to make it fair that the enterprise bear the loss. It is not a fatal objection that the rule we lay down lacks sharp contours; in the end, as Judge Andrews said in a related context, "it is all a question (of expediency,) * * * of fair judgment, always keeping in mind the fact that we endeavor to make a rule in each case that will be practical and in keeping with the general understanding of Mankind." Palsgraf v. Long Island R.R. Co., 248 N.Y. 339, 354-355 (1928) (dissenting opinion).

Notes and Questions

1. When it is clear that a tortfeasor is an employee of a particular entity (here, the United States), vicarious liability turns on whether the employee's acts were within the "scope" of his employment. In its appeal, the government invoked the "motive test" for determining the scope of employment, under which the employee's conduct must be "actuated, at least in part, by a *purpose to serve the master*." Both the district court and the court of appeals rejected the motive test, but they disagreed about what test should supplant it.

Allocative efficiency. The district court noted that "[t]he question is whether the public weal is better served by a rule shifting responsibility to employers in particular kinds of cases. * * * It is the employer who selects the worker and who may, by suitable supervision, training, psychological testing and considerate treatment, prevent him from acting in a harmful way." The court of appeals questioned this rationale: observing that "a more efficient allocation can only be expected if there is some reason to believe that imposing a particular cost on the enterprise will lead it to consider whether steps should be taken to prevent a recurrence of the accident," the court of appeals speculated that it might be more efficient for drydock owners to guard against incidents of the sort that caused the damage in this case.

Loss spreading. The district court also observed that "[t]he employer can also normally obtain insurance more cheaply than those who may be injured" and that "the employer will be financially more capable of bearing the risk than the person injured— usually an individual." The court of appeals rejected that rationale as well: "It is true, of course, that in many cases the plaintiff will not be in a position to insure, and so expansion of liability will, at the very least, serve *respondeat superior*'s loss spreading function. But the fact that the defendant is better able to afford damages is not alone sufficient to justify legal responsibility, and this overarching principle must be taken into account in deciding whether to expand the reach of *respondeat superior*."

Fairness. The court of appeals ultimately rested its holding on fairness grounds: the court believed that the instinct to impose liability rested on a "deeply rooted sentiment that a business enterprise cannot justly disclaim responsibility for accidents which may fairly be said to be characteristic of its activities."

2. Consider now the extent to which the efficiency and fairness rationales the district court and court of appeals considered in *Ira S. Bushey* point toward liability for ISPs for the harmful activities of ISP subscribers. Will direct liability alone lead to appropriate deterrence and compensation? Internet tortfeasors may be difficult to identify or lack the resources to pay for the harm caused. Are ISPs and other intermediaries in a position to monitor and control the behavior of their users? To mitigate the damage that actions of their users may cause? Will liability prompt intermediaries to internalize costs unavoidably associated with its activities?

We consider these questions more concretely in three contexts: defamation, copyright infringement, and trademark infringement and dilution.

1. Liability for Defamatory Content

Cubby, Inc. v. CompuServe, Inc.

United States District Court for the Southern District of New York, 1991
776 F. Supp. 135

LEISURE, District Judge.

CompuServe develops and provides computer-related products and services, including CompuServe Information Service ("CIS"), an on-line general information service or "electronic library" that subscribers may access from a personal computer or terminal. Subscribers to CIS pay a membership fee and online time usage fees, in return for which they have access to the thousands of information sources available on CIS. Subscribers may also obtain access to over 150 special interest "forums," which are comprised of electronic bulletin boards, interactive online conferences, and topical databases.

One forum available is the Journalism Forum, which focuses on the journalism industry. * * * One publication available as part of the Journalism Forum is Rumorville USA ("Rumorville"), a daily newsletter that provides reports about broadcast journalism and journalists. Rumorville is published by Don Fitzpatrick Associates of San Francisco ("DFA"), which is headed by defendant Don Fitzpatrick. * * * CompuServe has no opportunity to review Rumorville's contents before DFA uploads it into CompuServe's computer banks, from which it is immediately available to approved CIS subscribers. CompuServe receives no part of any fees that DFA charges for access to Rumorville, nor does CompuServe compensate DFA for providing Rumorville to the Journalism Forum; the compensation CompuServe receives for making Rumorville available to its subscribers is the standard online time usage and membership fees charged to all CIS subscribers, regardless of the information services they use. * * *

In 1990, plaintiffs Cubby, Inc. ("Cubby") and Robert Blanchard ("Blanchard") (collectively, "plaintiffs") developed Skuttlebut, a computer database designed to publish and distribute electronically news and gossip in the television news and radio industries. Plaintiffs intended to compete with Rumorville; subscribers gained access to Skuttlebut through their personal computers after completing subscription agreements with plaintiffs.

Plaintiffs claim that, on separate occasions in April 1990, Rumorville published false and defamatory statements relating to Skuttlebut and Blanchard, and that CompuServe carried these statements as part of the Journalism Forum. The allegedly defamatory remarks included a suggestion that individuals at Skuttlebut gained access to information first published by Rumorville "through some back door"; a statement that Blanchard was "bounced" from his previous employer, WABC; and a description of Skuttlebut as a "new start-up scam." Plaintiffs have asserted claims against CompuServe and Fitzpatrick under New York law for libel of Blanchard * * * . [CompuServe has moved for summary judgment, arguing that] it acted as a distributor, and not a publisher, of the statements, and cannot be held liable for the statements because it did not know and had no reason to know of the statements. * * * Plaintiffs, on the other hand, argue that the Court should conclude that CompuServe is a publisher of the statements and hold it to a higher standard of liability.

Ordinarily, "'one who repeats or otherwise republishes defamatory matter is subject to liability as if he had originally published it.'" *Cianci v. New Times Publishing Co.*, 639 F.2d 54, 61 (2d Cir. 1980) (Friendly, J.) (quoting Restatement (Second) of Torts § 578 (1977)). With respect to entities such as news vendors, book stores, and libraries, however, "New York courts have long held that vendors and distributors of defamatory publications are not liable if they neither know nor have reason to know of the defamation." *Lerman v. Chuckleberry Publishing, Inc.*, 521 F. Supp. 228, 235 (S.D.N.Y. 1981). * * *

CompuServe's CIS product is in essence an electronic, for-profit library that carries a vast number of publications and collects usage and membership fees from its subscribers in return for access to the publications. CompuServe and companies like it are at the forefront of the information industry revolution. High technology has markedly increased the speed with which information is gathered and processed; it is now possible for an individual with a personal computer, modem, and telephone line to have instantaneous access to thousands of news publications from across the United States and around the world. While CompuServe may decline to carry a given publication altogether, in reality, once it does decide to carry a publication, it will have little or no editorial control over that publication's contents. This is especially so when CompuServe carries the publication as part of a forum that is managed by a company unrelated to CompuServe.

With respect to the Rumorville publication, the undisputed facts are that DFA uploads the text of Rumorville into CompuServe's data banks and makes it available to approved CIS subscribers instantaneously. CompuServe has no more editorial control over such a publication than does a public library, book store, or newsstand, and it would be no more feasible for CompuServe to examine every publication it carries for potentially defamatory statements than it would be for any other distributor to do so. "First Amendment guarantees have long been recognized as protecting distributors of publications. . . . Obviously, the national distributor of hundreds of periodicals has no duty to monitor each issue of every periodical it distributes. Such a rule would be an impermissible burden on the First Amendment." *Lerman v. Flynt Distributing Co.*, 745 F.2d 123, 139 (2d Cir. 1984).

Technology is rapidly transforming the information industry. A computerized database is the functional equivalent of a more traditional news vendor, and the inconsistent application of a lower standard of liability to an electronic news distributor such as CompuServe than that which is applied to a public library, book store, or newsstand would impose an undue burden on the free flow of information. Given the relevant First Amendment considerations, the appropriate standard of liability to be applied to CompuServe is whether it knew or had reason to know of the allegedly defamatory Rumorville statements. * * *

Plaintiffs have not set forth any specific facts showing that there is a genuine issue as to whether CompuServe knew or had reason to know of Rumorville's contents. Because CompuServe, as a news distributor, may not be held liable if it neither knew nor had reason to know of the allegedly defamatory Rumorville statements, summary judgment in favor of CompuServe on the libel claim is granted.

Stratton Oakmont, Inc. v. Prodigy Services Co.

New York Supreme Court, 1995
1995 WL 323710

Defamation case

STUART L. AIN, Justice.

At issue in this case are statements about Plaintiffs made by an unidentified bulletin board user or "poster" on Prodigy's "Money Talk" computer bulletin board on October 23rd and 25th of 1994. These statements included [allegations that Stratton Oakmont, a securities firm, and its president, Daniel Porush, committed criminal and fraudulent acts in connection with an initial public offering]. Plaintiffs commenced this action against Prodigy, the owner and operator of the computer network on which the statements appeared, * * * alleg[ing] ten causes of action, including claims for *per se* libel. [Plaintiffs moved for partial summary judgment, arguing that Prodigy was the "publisher" of the statements in question for purposes of plaintiffs' libel claim.]

By way of background, it is undisputed that Prodigy's computer network has at least two million subscribers who communicate with each other and with the general subscriber population on Prodigy's bulletin boards. "Money Talk," the board on which the aforementioned statements appeared, is allegedly the leading and most widely read financial computer bulletin board in the United States, where members can post statements regarding stocks, investments and other financial matters. Prodigy contracts with bulletin Board Leaders, who, among other things, participate in board discussions and undertake promotional efforts to encourage usage and increase users. The Board Leader for "Money Talk" at the time the alleged libelous statements were posted was Charles Epstein.

Prodigy commenced operations in 1990. Plaintiffs base their claim that Prodigy is a publisher in large measure on Prodigy's stated policy, starting in 1990, that it was a family oriented computer network. In various national newspaper articles written by Geoffrey Moore, Prodigy's Director of Market Programs and Communications, Prodigy held itself out as an online service that exercised editorial control over the content of messages posted on its computer bulletin boards, thereby expressly differentiating itself from its competition and expressly likening itself to a newspaper. * * *

Plaintiffs further rely upon the following additional evidence in support of their claim that Prodigy is a publisher:

(A) promulgation of "content guidelines" in which, *inter alia*, users are requested to refrain from posting notes that are "insulting" and are advised that "notes that harass other members or are deemed to be in bad taste or grossly repugnant to community standards, or are deemed harmful to maintaining a harmonious online community, will be removed when brought to Prodigy's attention"; the Guidelines all expressly state that although "Prodigy is committed to open debate and discussion on the bulletin boards, . . . this doesn't mean that 'anything goes'";

(B) use of a software screening program which automatically prescreens all bulletin board postings for offensive language;

(C) the use of Board Leaders such as Epstein whose duties include enforcement of the Guidelines * * * ; and

(D) testimony by Epstein as to a tool for Board Leaders known as an "emergency delete function" pursuant to which a Board Leader could remove a note and send a previously prepared message of explanation "ranging from solicitation, bad advice, insulting, wrong topic, off topic, bad taste, etcetera."

A finding that Prodigy is a publisher is the first hurdle for Plaintiffs to overcome in pursuit of their defamation claims, because one who repeats or otherwise republishes a libel is subject to liability as if he had originally published it. In contrast, distributors such as book stores and libraries may be liable for defamatory statements of others only if they knew or had reason to know of the defamatory statement at issue. *Cubby, Inc. v. CompuServe Inc.*, 776 F. Supp. 135, 139 (S.D.N.Y. 1991). A distributor, or deliverer of defamatory material, is considered a passive conduit and will not be found liable in the absence of fault. However, a newspaper, for example, is more than a passive receptacle or conduit for news, comment and advertising. The choice of material to go into a newspaper and the decisions made as to the content of the paper constitute the exercise of editorial control and judgment, and with this editorial control comes increased liability. In short, the critical issue to be determined by this Court is whether the foregoing evidence establishes a *prima facie* case that Prodigy exercised sufficient editorial control over its computer bulletin boards to render it a publisher with the same responsibilities as a newspaper.

* * * Prodigy insists that its former policy of manually reviewing all messages prior to posting was changed "long before the messages complained of by Plaintiffs were posted." However, no documentation or detailed explanation of such a change, and the dissemination of news of such a change, has been submitted. In addition, Prodigy argues that in terms of sheer volume—currently 60,000 messages a day are posted on Prodigy bulletin boards—manual review of messages is not feasible. While Prodigy admits that Board Leaders may remove messages that violate its Guidelines, it claims in conclusory manner that Board Leaders do not function as "editors." * * *

As for legal authority, Prodigy relies on the *Cubby* case. There the defendant CompuServe was a computer network providing subscribers with computer related services or forums including an online general information service or "electronic library." One of the publications available on the Journalism Forum carried defamatory statements about the Plaintiff, an electronic newsletter. * * * The Court noted that CompuServe had no opportunity to review the contents of the publication at issue before it was uploaded into CompuServe's computer banks. Consequently, the Court found that CompuServe's product was, "in essence, an electronic for-profit library" that carried a vast number of publications, and that CompuServe had "little or no editorial control" over the contents of those publications. In granting CompuServe's motion for summary judgment, the *Cubby* court held:

A computerized database is the functional equivalent of a more traditional news vendor, and the inconsistent application of a lower standard of liability to an electronic news distributor such as CompuServe than that which is applied to a public library, book store, or newsstand would impose an undue burden on the free flow of information.

776 F. Supp. at 140.

The key distinction between CompuServe and Prodigy is two fold. First, Prodigy held itself out to the public and its members as controlling the content of its computer bulletin boards. Second, Prodigy implemented this control through its automatic software screening program, and the Guidelines which Board Leaders are required to enforce. By actively utilizing technology and manpower to delete notes from its computer bulletin boards on the basis of offensiveness and "bad taste," for example, Prodigy is clearly making decisions as to content, and such decisions constitute editorial control. That such control is not complete and is enforced both as early as the notes arrive and as late as a complaint is made does not minimize or eviscerate the simple fact that Prodigy has uniquely arrogated to itself the role of determining what is proper for its members to post and read on its bulletin boards.

Based on the foregoing, this Court is compelled to conclude that for the purposes of Plaintiffs' claims in this action, Prodigy is a publisher rather than a distributor.

Notes and Questions

1. In *Cubby*, the court essentially asks whether CompuServe is like a newspaper or a news vendor. Does either analogy capture the functions of an Internet service provider? If CompuServe cannot screen its postings, it is only because of a choice that it has made about how to construct and use its system. Should the fact that an ISP could police its system but chooses not to affect its liability?

2. Assume that you were CompuServe's general counsel at the time of Cubby's and Blanchard's complaint, and that the Rumorville publication that was the subject of the dispute remained accessible on CompuServe's system. Upon learning of Cubby and Blanchard's complaint, would you have advised CompuServe to remove the Rumorville publication in question? Why or why not? What facts would you need before making your determination?

3. What factors does the *Stratton Oakmont* court rely upon in concluding that Prodigy is a publisher rather than a distributor? Do these factors adequately distinguish the outcomes in *Cubby* and *Stratton Oakmont*?

4. How does the *Stratton Oakmont* rule affect Internet service providers' incentives to police the content available on their systems?

In 1996, Congress included in the Communications Decency Act a provision limiting service providers' liability for allowing and disallowing transmission of certain kinds of objectionable content. Although the Supreme Court struck down portions of the CDA in *Reno v. American Civil Liberties Union*, 521 U.S. 844 (1997), this provision remains intact and is set forth below.

Section 230 of the Communications Decency Act

47 U.S.C. § 230

§ 230. Protection for private blocking and screening of offensive material

(a) Findings

The Congress finds the following:

(1) The rapidly developing array of Internet and other interactive computer services available to individual Americans represent an extraordinary advance in the availability of educational and informational resources to our citizens.

(2) These services offer users a great degree of control over the information that they receive, as well as the potential for even greater control in the future as technology develops.

(3) The Internet and other interactive computer services offer a forum for a true diversity of political discourse, unique opportunities for cultural development, and myriad avenues for intellectual activity.

(4) The Internet and other interactive computer services have flourished, to the benefit of all Americans, with a minimum of government regulation.

(5) Increasingly Americans are relying on interactive media for a variety of political, educational, cultural, and entertainment services.

(b) Policy

It is the policy of the United States—

(1) to promote the continued development of the Internet and other interactive computer services and other interactive media;

(2) to preserve the vibrant and competitive free market that presently exists for the Internet and other interactive computer services, unfettered by Federal or State regulation;

(3) to encourage the development of technologies which maximize user control over what information is received by individuals, families, and schools who use the Internet and other interactive computer services;

(4) to remove disincentives for the development and utilization of blocking and filtering technologies that empower parents to restrict their children's access to objectionable or inappropriate online material; and

(5) to ensure vigorous enforcement of Federal criminal laws to deter and punish trafficking in obscenity, stalking, and harassment by means of computer.

(c) Protection for "good samaritan" blocking and screening of offensive material

(1) Treatment of publisher or speaker

No provider or user of an interactive computer service shall be treated as the publisher or speaker of any information provided by another information content provider.

(2) Civil liability

No provider or user of an interactive computer service shall be held liable on account of—

(A) any action voluntarily taken in good faith to restrict access to or availability of material that the provider or user considers to be obscene, lewd, lascivious, filthy, excessively violent, harassing, or otherwise objectionable, whether or not such material is constitutionally protected; or

(B) any action taken to enable or make available to information content providers or others the technical means to restrict access to material described in paragraph (1). * * *

(e) Effect on other laws

* * *

(2) No effect on intellectual property law

Nothing in this section shall be construed to limit or expand any law pertaining to intellectual property. * * *

(3) State law

Nothing in this section shall be construed to prevent any State from enforcing any State law that is consistent with this section. No cause of action may be brought and no liability may be imposed under any State or local law that is inconsistent with this section.

* * *

(f) Definitions

* * *

(2) Interactive computer service: The term "interactive computer service" means any information service, system, or access software provider that provides or enables computer access by multiple users to a computer server, including specifically a service or system that provides access to the Internet and such systems operated or services offered by libraries or educational institutions.

(3) Information content provider: The term "information content provider" means any person or entity that is responsible, in whole or in part, for the creation or development of information provided through the Internet or any other interactive computer service. * * *

The legislative history of the provision indicates that its sponsors sought in part to overturn the result in *Stratton Oakmont*. *See* 141 CONG. REC. 16,024-26 (1995) (remarks of Senator Coats and Senator Exon); 141 CONG. REC. 22045 (1995) (remarks of Rep. Cox); 141 CONG. REC. 22047 (remarks of Rep. Goodlatte); S. CONF. REP. No. 104-230, at 194 (1996); H.R. REP. No. 104-458, at 1130 (1996); *see also* Susan Freiwald, *Comparative Institutional Analysis in Cyberspace: The Case of Intermediary Liability for Defamation*, 14 HARV. J. L. & TECH. 569, 595, 629 & n.259 (2001).

Does section 230 affect the liability of an interactive computer service provider as a distributor, when it knows or has reason to know that a transmission or posting is defamatory? How does section 230 change a service provider's incentives to police its system and to remove content claimed to be objectionable? Consider the following cases.

Zeran v. America Online, Inc.

United States Court of Appeals for the Fourth Circuit, 1997
129 F.3d 327

WILKINSON, Chief Judge.

Kenneth Zeran brought this action against America Online, Inc. ("AOL"), arguing that AOL unreasonably delayed in removing defamatory messages posted by an unidentified third party, refused to post retractions of those messages, and failed to screen for similar postings thereafter. The district court granted judgment for AOL on the grounds that the Communications Decency Act of 1996 ("CDA")—47 U.S.C. § 230—bars Zeran's claims. Zeran appeals, arguing that § 230 leaves intact liability for interactive computer service providers who possess notice of defamatory material posted through their services. * * * Section 230, however, plainly immunizes computer service providers like AOL from liability for information that originates with third parties. * * * Accordingly, we affirm the judgment of the district court.

I.

* * * On April 25, 1995, an unidentified person posted a message on an AOL bulletin board advertising "Naughty Oklahoma T-Shirts." The posting described the sale of shirts featuring offensive and tasteless slogans related to the April 19, 1995, bombing of the Alfred P. Murrah Federal Building in Oklahoma City. Those interested in purchasing the shirts were instructed to call "Ken" at Zeran's home phone number in Seattle, Washington. As a result of this anonymously perpetrated prank, Zeran received a high volume of calls, comprised primarily of angry and derogatory messages, but also including death threats. Zeran could not change his phone number because he relied on its availability to the public in running his business out of his home. Later that day, Zeran called AOL and informed a company representative of his predicament. The employee assured Zeran that the posting would be removed from AOL's bulletin

board but explained that as a matter of policy AOL would not post a retraction. The parties dispute the date that AOL removed this original posting from its bulletin board.

On April 26, the next day, an unknown person posted another message advertising additional shirts with new tasteless slogans related to the Oklahoma City bombing. Again, interested buyers were told to call Zeran's phone number, to ask for "Ken," and to "please call back if busy" due to high demand. The angry, threatening phone calls intensified. Over the next four days, an unidentified party continued to post messages on AOL's bulletin board, advertising additional items including bumper stickers and key chains with still more offensive slogans. During this time period, Zeran called AOL repeatedly and was told by company representatives that the individual account from which the messages were posted would soon be closed. Zeran also reported his case to Seattle FBI agents. By April 30, Zeran was receiving an abusive phone call approximately every two minutes.

Meanwhile, an announcer for Oklahoma City radio station KRXO received a copy of the first AOL posting. On May 1, the announcer related the message's contents on the air, attributed them to "Ken" at Zeran's phone number, and urged the listening audience to call the number. After this radio broadcast, Zeran was inundated with death threats and other violent calls from Oklahoma City residents. Over the next few days, Zeran talked to both KRXO and AOL representatives. He also spoke to his local police, who subsequently surveilled his home to protect his safety. By May 14, after an Oklahoma City newspaper published a story exposing the shirt advertisements as a hoax and after KRXO made an on-air apology, the number of calls to Zeran's residence finally subsided to fifteen per day.

[Zeran sued AOL, which answered Zeran's complaint and then interposed 47 U.S.C. § 230 as a defense and moved for judgment on the pleadings. The district court granted AOL's motion and Zeran appeals.]

II.

A.

Because § 230 was successfully advanced by AOL in the district court as a defense to Zeran's claims, we shall briefly examine its operation here. Zeran seeks to hold AOL liable for defamatory speech initiated by a third party. He argued to the district court that once he notified AOL of the unidentified third party's hoax, AOL had a duty to remove the defamatory posting promptly, to notify its subscribers of the message's false nature, and to effectively screen future defamatory material. Section 230 entered this litigation as an affirmative defense pled by AOL. The company claimed that Congress immunized interactive computer service providers from claims based on information posted by a third party.

The relevant portion of § 230 states: "No provider or user of an interactive computer service shall be treated as the publisher or speaker of any information provided by another information content provider." 47 U.S.C. § 230(c)(1). By its plain language, § 230 creates a federal immunity to any cause of action that would make service providers liable for information originating with a third-party user of the service. Specifically, § 230 precludes courts from entertaining claims that would place a computer service provider in a publisher's role. Thus, lawsuits seeking to hold a service provider liable for its exercise of a publisher's traditional editorial functions—such as deciding whether to publish, withdraw, postpone or alter content—are barred.

The purpose of this statutory immunity is not difficult to discern. Congress recognized the threat that tort-based lawsuits pose to freedom of speech in the new and burgeoning Internet medium. The imposition of tort liability on service providers for the communications of others represented, for Congress, simply another form of intrusive government regulation of speech. Section 230 was enacted, in part, to maintain the robust nature of Internet communication and, accordingly, to keep government interference in the medium to a minimum. In specific statutory findings, Congress recognized the Internet and interactive computer services as offering "a forum for a true diversity of political discourse, unique opportunities for cultural development, and myriad avenues for intellectual activity." *Id.* § 230(a)(3). It also found that the Internet and interactive computer services "have flourished, to the benefit of all Americans, *with a minimum of government regulation.*" *Id.* § 230(a)(4) (emphasis added). Congress further stated that it is "the policy of the United States . . . to preserve the vibrant and competitive free market that presently exists for the Internet and other interactive computer services, *unfettered by Federal or State regulation.*" *Id.* § 230(b)(2) (emphasis added).

None of this means, of course, that the original culpable party who posts defamatory messages would escape accountability. While Congress acted to keep government regulation of the Internet to a minimum, it also found it to be the policy of the United States "to ensure vigorous enforcement of Federal criminal laws to deter and punish trafficking in obscenity, stalking, and harassment by means of computer." *Id.* § 230(b)(5). Congress made a policy choice, however, not to deter harmful online speech through the separate route of imposing tort liability on companies that serve as intermediaries for other parties' potentially injurious messages.

Congress' purpose in providing the § 230 immunity was thus evident. Interactive computer services have millions of users. The amount of information communicated via interactive computer services is therefore staggering. The specter of tort liability in an area of such prolific speech would have an obvious chilling effect. It would be impossible for service providers to screen each of their millions of postings for possible problems. Faced with potential liability for each message republished by their services, interactive computer service providers might choose to severely restrict the number and type of messages posted. Congress considered the weight of the speech interests implicated and chose to immunize service providers to avoid any such restrictive effect.

Another important purpose of § 230 was to encourage service providers to self-regulate the dissemination of offensive material over their services. In this respect, § 230 responded to a New York state court decision, *Stratton Oakmont, Inc. v. Prodigy Servs. Co.*, 1995 WL 323710 (N.Y. Sup. Ct. May 24, 1995). There, the plaintiffs sued Prodigy—an interactive computer service like AOL—for defamatory comments made by an unidentified party on one of Prodigy's bulletin boards. The court held Prodigy to the strict liability standard normally applied to original publishers of defamatory statements, rejecting Prodigy's claims that it should be held only to the lower "knowledge" standard usually reserved for distributors. The court reasoned that Prodigy acted more like an original publisher than a distributor both because it advertised its practice of controlling content on its service and because it actively screened and edited messages posted on its bulletin boards.

Congress enacted § 230 to remove the disincentives to self-regulation created by the *Stratton Oakmont* decision. Under that court's holding, computer service providers who regulated the dissemination of offensive material on their services risked subjecting themselves to liability, because such regulation cast the service provider in the role of a publisher. Fearing that the specter of liability would therefore deter service providers from blocking and screening offensive material, Congress enacted § 230's broad immunity "to remove disincentives for the development and utilization of blocking and filtering technologies that empower parents to restrict their children's access to objectionable or inappropriate online material." 47 U.S.C. § 230(b)(4). In line with this purpose, § 230 forbids the imposition of publisher liability on a service provider for the exercise of its editorial and self-regulatory functions.

B.

Zeran argues, however, that the § 230 immunity eliminates only publisher liability, leaving distributor liability intact. Publishers can be held liable for defamatory statements contained in their works even absent proof that they had specific knowledge of the statement's inclusion. According to Zeran, interactive computer service providers like AOL are normally considered instead to be distributors, like traditional news vendors or book sellers. Distributors cannot be held liable for defamatory statements contained in the materials they distribute unless it is proven at a minimum that they have actual knowledge of the defamatory statements upon which liability is predicated. Zeran contends that he provided AOL with sufficient notice of the defamatory statements appearing on the company's bulletin board. This notice is significant, says Zeran, because AOL could be held liable as a distributor only if it acquired knowledge of the defamatory statements' existence.

Because of the difference between these two forms of liability, Zeran contends that the term "distributor" carries a legally distinct meaning from the term "publisher." Accordingly, he asserts that Congress' use of only the term "publisher" in § 230 indicates a purpose to immunize service providers only from publisher liability. He argues that distributors are left unprotected by § 230 and, therefore, his suit should be permitted to proceed against AOL. We disagree. Assuming *arguendo* that Zeran has satisfied the requirements for imposition of distributor liability, this theory of liability is merely a subset, or a species, of publisher liability, and is therefore also foreclosed by § 230.

The terms "publisher" and "distributor" derive their legal significance from the context of defamation law. * * * Because the publication of a statement is a necessary element in a defamation action, only one who publishes can be subject to this form of tort liability. Restatement (Second) of Torts § 558(b) (1977). Publication does not only describe the choice by an author to include certain information. In addition, both the negligent communication of a defamatory statement and the failure to remove such a statement when first communicated by another party—each alleged by Zeran here under a negligence label—constitute publication.

In this case, AOL is legally considered to be a publisher. "[E]very one who takes part in the publication . . . is charged with publication." W. PAGE KEETON ET AL., PROSSER AND KEETON ON THE LAW OF TORTS § 113, at 799. Even distributors are considered to be publishers for purposes of defamation law:

> Those who are in the business of making their facilities available to disseminate the writings composed, the speeches made, and the information gathered by others may also be regarded as participating to such an extent in making the books, newspapers, magazines, and information available to others as to be regarded as publishers. They are intentionally making the contents available to others, sometimes without knowing all of the contents—including the defamatory content—and sometimes without any opportunity to ascertain, in advance, that any defamatory matter was to be included in the matter published.

Id. at 803. AOL falls squarely within this traditional definition of a publisher and, therefore, is clearly protected by § 230's immunity.

Zeran contends that decisions like *Stratton Oakmont* and *Cubby, Inc. v. CompuServe Inc.*, 776 F. Supp. 135 (S.D.N.Y. 1991), recognize a legal distinction between publishers and distributors. He misapprehends, however, the significance of that distinction for the legal issue we consider here. It is undoubtedly true that mere conduits, or distributors, are subject to a different standard of liability. As explained above, distributors must at a minimum have knowledge of the existence of a defamatory statement as a prerequisite to liability. But this distinction signifies only that different standards of liability may be applied *within* the larger publisher category, depending on the specific type of publisher concerned. * * * To the extent that decisions like *Stratton* and *Cubby* utilize the terms "publisher" and "distributor" separately, the decisions correctly describe two different standards of liability. *Stratton* and *Cubby* do not, however, suggest that distributors are not also a type of publisher for purposes of defamation law.

Zeran simply attaches too much importance to the presence of the distinct notice element in distributor liability. The simple fact of notice surely cannot transform one from an original publisher to a distributor in the eyes of the law. To the contrary, once a computer service provider receives notice of a potentially defamatory posting, it is thrust into the role of a traditional publisher. The computer service provider must decide whether to publish, edit, or withdraw the posting. In this respect, Zeran seeks to impose liability on AOL for assuming the role for which § 230 specifically proscribes liability—the publisher role.

Our view that Zeran's complaint treats AOL as a publisher is reinforced because AOL is cast in the same position as the party who originally posted the offensive messages. According to Zeran's logic, AOL is legally at fault because it communicated to third parties an allegedly defamatory statement. This is precisely the theory under which the original poster of the offensive messages would be found liable. If the original party is considered a publisher of the offensive messages, Zeran certainly cannot attach liability to AOL under the same theory without conceding that AOL too must be treated as a publisher of the statements.

Zeran next contends that interpreting § 230 to impose liability on service providers with knowledge of defamatory content on their services is consistent with the statutory purposes * * * . Zeran fails, however, to understand the practical implications of notice liability in the interactive computer service context. Liability upon notice would defeat the dual purposes advanced by § 230 of the CDA. Like the strict liability imposed by the *Stratton Oakmont* court, liability upon notice reinforces service providers' incentives to restrict speech and abstain from self-regulation.

If computer service providers were subject to distributor liability, they would face potential liability each time they receive notice of a potentially defamatory statement—from any party, concerning any message. Each notification would require a careful yet rapid investigation of the circumstances surrounding the posted information, a legal judgment concerning the information's defamatory character, and an on-the-spot editorial decision whether to risk liability by allowing the continued publication of that information. Although this might be feasible for the traditional print publisher, the sheer number of postings on interactive computer services would create an impossible burden in the Internet context. Because service providers would be subject to liability only for the publication of information, and not for its removal, they would have a natural incentive simply to remove messages upon notification, whether the contents were defamatory or not. Thus, like strict liability, liability upon notice has a chilling effect on the freedom of Internet speech.

Similarly, notice-based liability would deter service providers from regulating the dissemination of offensive material over their own services. Any efforts by a service provider to investigate and screen material posted on its service would only lead to notice of potentially defamatory material more frequently and thereby create a stronger basis for liability. Instead of subjecting themselves to further possible lawsuits, service providers would likely eschew any attempts at self-regulation.

More generally, notice-based liability for interactive computer service providers would provide third parties with a no-cost means to create the basis for future lawsuits. Whenever one was displeased with the speech of another party conducted over an interactive computer service, the offended party could simply "notify" the relevant service provider, claiming the information to be legally defamatory. In light of the vast amount of speech communicated through interactive computer services, these notices could produce an impossible burden for service providers, who would be faced with ceaseless choices of suppressing controversial speech or sustaining prohibitive liability. Because the probable effects of distributor liability on the vigor of Internet speech and on service provider self-regulation are directly contrary to § 230's statutory purposes, we will not assume that Congress intended to leave liability upon notice intact.

Blumenthal v. Drudge

United States District Court for the District of Columbia, 1998
992 F. Supp. 44

PAUL L. FRIEDMAN, District Judge.

This is a defamation case revolving around a statement published on the Internet by defendant Matt Drudge. [The statement, contained in an electronic newsletter called "the Drudge Report," claimed that White House aide Sidney Blumenthal had a history of violence against his wife, Jacqueline Jordan Blumenthal.]

I.

* * * Access to defendant Drudge's world wide web site is available at no cost to anyone who has access to the Internet at the Internet address of "www.drudgereport.com." * * * In addition, during the time period relevant to this case, Drudge had developed a list of regular readers or subscribers to whom he e-mailed each new edition of the Drudge Report. * * * [At the time of the allegedly defamatory statement, Drudge also had a license agreement with America Online ("AOL").] The agreement made the Drudge Report available to all members of AOL's service for a period of one year. In exchange, defendant Drudge received a flat monthly "royalty payment" of $3,000 from AOL. During the time relevant to this case, defendant Drudge has had no other source of income. Under the licensing agreement, Drudge is to create, edit, update and "otherwise manage" the content of the Drudge Report, and AOL may "remove content that AOL reasonably determine[s] to violate AOL's then standard terms of service." Drudge transmits new editions of the Drudge Report by e-mailing them to AOL. AOL then posts the new editions on the AOL service. Drudge also has continued to distribute each new edition of the Drudge Report via e-mail and his own web site.

Late at night on the evening of Sunday, August 10, 1997 (Pacific Daylight Time), defendant Drudge wrote and transmitted the edition of the Drudge Report that contained the alleged defamatory statement about the Blumenthals. Drudge transmitted the report from Los Angeles, California by e-mail to his direct subscribers and by posting both a headline and the full text of the Blumenthal story on his world wide web site. He then transmitted the text but not the headline to AOL, which in turn made it available to AOL subscribers. After receiving a letter from plaintiffs' counsel on Monday, August 11, 1997, defendant Drudge retracted the story through a special edition of the Drudge Report posted on his web site and e-mailed to his subscribers. At approximately 2:00 a.m. on Tuesday, August 12, 1997, Drudge e-mailed the retraction to AOL which posted it on the AOL service.

[After the Blumenthals sued Drudge and AOL, AOL moved for summary judgment, claiming that § 230 of the Communications Decency Act immunized it from any liability for Drudge's statement.]

II.

* * * In February of 1996, Congress [enacted] the Communications Decency Act of 1996. While various policy options were open to the Congress, it chose to "promote the continued development of the Internet and other interactive computer services and other interactive media" and "to preserve the vibrant and competitive free market" for such services, largely "unfettered by Federal or State regulation. . . ." 47 U.S.C. § 230(b)(1) and (2). Whether wisely or not, it made the legislative judgment to effectively immunize providers of interactive computer services from civil liability in tort with respect to material disseminated by them but created by others. In recognition of the speed with which information may be disseminated and the near impossibility of regulating information content, Congress decided not to treat providers of interactive computer services like other information providers such as newspapers, magazines or television and radio stations, all of which may be held liable for publishing or distributing obscene or defamatory material written or prepared by others. While Congress could have made a different policy choice, it opted not to hold interactive computer services liable for their failure to edit, withhold or restrict access to offensive material disseminated through their medium.

Section 230(c) of the Communications Decency Act of 1996 provides:

> No provider or user of an interactive computer service shall be treated as the publisher or speaker of any information provided by another information content provider.

The statute goes on to define the term "information content provider" as "any person or entity that is responsible, in whole or in part, for the creation or development of information provided through the Internet or any other interactive computer service." 47 U.S.C. § 230(e)(3). In view of this statutory language, plaintiffs' argument that the *Washington Post* would be liable if it had done what AOL did here—"publish Drudge's story without doing anything whatsoever to edit, verify, or even read it (despite knowing what Drudge did for a living and how he did it),"—has been rendered irrelevant by Congress.

Plaintiffs concede that AOL is a "provider . . . of an interactive computer service" for purposes of Section 230 and that if AOL acted exclusively as a provider of an interactive computer service it may not be held liable for making the Drudge Report available to AOL subscribers. They also concede that Drudge is an "information content provider" because he wrote the alleged defamatory material about the Blumenthals contained in the Drudge Report. While plaintiffs suggest that AOL is responsible along with Drudge because it had some role in writing or editing the material in the Drudge Report, they have provided no factual support for that assertion. Indeed, plaintiffs affirmatively state that "no person, other than Drudge himself, edited, checked, verified, or supervised the information that Drudge published in the Drudge Report." * * *

Plaintiffs make the additional argument, however, that Section 230 of the Communications Decency Act does not provide immunity to AOL in this case because Drudge was not just an anonymous person who sent a message over the Internet through AOL. He is a person with whom AOL contracted, whom AOL paid $3,000 a month—$36,000 a year, Drudge's sole, consistent source of income—and whom AOL promoted to its subscribers and potential subscribers as a reason to subscribe to AOL. Furthermore, the license agreement between AOL and Drudge by its terms contemplates more than a passive role for AOL; in it, AOL reserves the "right to remove, or direct [Drudge] to remove, any content which, as reasonably determined by AOL . . . violates AOL's then-standard Terms of Service. . . ." By the terms of the agreement, AOL also is "entitled to require reasonable changes to . . . content, to the extent such content will, in AOL's good faith judgment, adversely affect operations of the AOL network."

In addition, shortly after it entered into the licensing agreement with Drudge, AOL issued a press release making clear the kind of material Drudge would provide to AOL subscribers—gossip and rumor—and urged potential subscribers to sign onto AOL in order to get the benefit of the Drudge Report. The press release was captioned: "AOL Hires Runaway Gossip Success Matt Drudge." It noted that "[m]averick gossip columnist Matt Drudge has teamed up with America Online," and stated: "Giving the Drudge Report a home on America Online (keyword: Drudge) opens up the floodgates to an audience ripe for Drudge's brand of reporting. . . . AOL has made Matt Drudge instantly accessible to members who crave instant gossip and news breaks." Why is this different, the Blumenthals suggest, from AOL advertising and promoting a new purveyor of child pornography or other offensive material? Why should AOL be permitted to tout someone as a gossip columnist or rumor monger who will make such rumors and gossip "instantly accessible" to AOL subscribers, and then claim immunity when that person, as might be anticipated, defames another?

If it were writing on a clean slate, this Court would agree with plaintiffs. AOL has certain editorial rights with respect to the content provided by Drudge and disseminated by AOL, including the right to require changes in content and to remove it; and it has affirmatively promoted Drudge as a new source of unverified instant gossip on AOL. Yet it takes no responsibility for any damage he may cause. AOL is not a passive conduit like the telephone company, a common carrier with no control and therefore no responsibility for what is said over the telephone wires. Because it has the right to exercise editorial control over those with whom it contracts and whose words it disseminates, it would seem only fair to hold AOL to the liability standards applied to a publisher or, at least, like a book store owner or library, to the liability standards applied to a distributor. But Congress has made a different policy choice by providing immunity even where the interactive service provider has an active, even aggressive role in making available content prepared by others. In some sort of tacit *quid pro quo* arrangement with the service provider community, Congress has conferred immunity from tort liability as an incentive to Internet service providers to self-police the Internet for obscenity and other offensive material, even where the self-policing is unsuccessful or not even attempted.

In Section 230(c)(2) of the Communications Decency Act, Congress provided:

> No provider or user of an interactive computer service shall be held liable on account of—

> (A) Any action voluntarily taken in good faith to restrict access to or availability of material that the provider or user considers to be obscene, lewd, lascivious, filthy, excessively violent, harassing, or otherwise objectionable, whether or not such material is constitutionally protected; or

> (B) any action taken to enable or make available to information content providers or others the technical means to restrict access to material described in paragraph (1).

As the Fourth Circuit stated in *Zeran:* "Congress enacted § 230 to remove . . . disincentives to self-regulation. . . . Fearing that the specter of liability would . . . deter service providers from blocking and screening offensive material . . . § 230 forbids the imposition of publisher liability on a service provider for the exercise of its editorial and selfregulatory functions." *Zeran v. America Online, Inc.*, 129 F.3d at 331.

Any attempt to distinguish between "publisher" liability and notice-based "distributor" liability and to argue that Section 230 was only intended to immunize the former would be unavailing. Congress made no distinction between publishers and distributors in providing immunity from liability. As the Fourth Circuit has noted: "[I]f computer service providers were subject to distributor liability, they would face potential liability each time they receive notice of a potentially defamatory statement—from any party, concerning any message," and such notice-based liability "would deter service providers from regulating the dissemination of offensive material over their own services" by confronting them with "ceaseless choices of suppressing controversial speech or sustaining prohibitive liability"—exactly what Congress intended to insulate them from in Section 230. *Zeran v. America Online, Inc.*, 129 F.3d at 333. *Cf. Cubby, Inc. v. CompuServe, Inc.*, 776 F. Supp. 135, 139-40 (S.D.N.Y. 1991) (decided before enactment of Communications Decency Act). While it appears to this Court that AOL in this case has taken advantage of all the benefits conferred by Congress in the Communications Decency Act, and then some, without accepting any of the burdens that Congress intended, the statutory language is clear: AOL is immune from suit, and the Court therefore must grant its motion for summary judgment.

Notes and Questions

1. Do you agree with the *Blumenthal* court that "the statutory language is clear" in immunizing interactive computer service providers from notice-based distributor liability? While three other courts of appeals have

adopted that holding from *Zeran, see Ben Ezra, Weinstein & Co. v. America Online*, 206 F.3d 980 (10th Cir. 2003); *Batzel v. Smith*, 333 F.3d 1018 (9th Cir. 2003); *Green v. America Online*, 318 F.3d 465 (3d Cir. 2003), some courts have interpreted the statutory language differently.

In *Doe v. GTE Corp.*, 347 F.3d 655 (7th Cir. 2003), the Seventh Circuit, in dicta, noted that section 230

> bears the title "Protection for Good Samaritan blocking and screening of offensive material," hardly an apt description if its principal effect is to induce ISPs to do nothing about the distribution of indecent and offensive material via their services. Why should a law designed to eliminate ISPs' liability to the creators of offensive material end up defeating claims by the victims of tortious or criminal conduct?

The court suggested an alternative reading: that 230(c)(1) (see *supra* p. 493) be treated as merely definitional; the immunity would then only be activated by section 230(c)(2), i.e., it would only be available in the event that a provider took some action "to restrict access to or availability of material" it deemed "objectionable." This reading would leave state laws imposing duties on ISPs to screen material, and other common law actions such as defamation, in force. Similarly, in *Barrett v. Rosenthal*, 9 Cal. Rptr. 3d 142, 152 (Cal. App. 1st Dist. 2004), *review granted*, 12 Cal. Rptr. 3d 48 (2004), the California Court of Appeal held that section 230 "cannot be deemed to abrogate the common law principle that one who republishes defamatory matter originated by a third person is subject to liability if *he or she knows or has reason to know of its defamatory content*." The California Supreme Court, however, reversed and adopted the *Zeran* court's reasoning, while noting that it "share[d] the concerns of those who have expressed reservations about hte *Zeran* court's broad interpretation." *Barrett v. Rosenthal*, ___ Cal. Rptr. 3d ___, 2006 WL 3346218, at *17 (Nov. 20, 2006).

2. The *Zeran* and *Blumenthal* courts discuss two statutory purposes underlying section 230: to preserve a robust medium for communication and to remove providers' disincentives to self-regulation. Are these purposes consistent? Which does section 230 more readily serve? If subsection 230(c)(2) permits a provider to block any content it wishes, are there any other constraints that might prevent a provider from doing so?

3. In rejecting Zeran's argument that Congress intended to preserve distributor liability, the court suggests that liability upon notice will prompt providers to refrain from self-regulation. Why might notice-based liability have this effect?

4. As a matter of policy, should Congress have retained notice-based distributor liability? If the risk of defamatory speech is a natural by-product of providing Internet service, why shouldn't service providers be forced to internalize the costs of such speech? Moreover, once an ISP has notice, isn't it in an excellent position to mitigate the damage by removing the offending material? Is there any way Congress could have retained notice-based liability without prompting service providers to suppress speech immediately after receiving notice that it contained potentially defamatory material? For discussion of these issues, see, e.g., Susan Freiwald, *Comparative Institutional Analysis in Cyberspace: The Case of Intermediary Liability for Defamation*, 14 HARV. J. L. & TECH. 569, 616-21 (2001).

5. One of the Blumenthals' arguments was that Drudge's speech was effectively AOL's speech. When does an interactive computer service provider also become the "information content provider" of the material it publishes, thereby forfeiting the protection of section 230(c)(1)? Under the statute, an information content provider is one who is "responsible, in whole or in part, for the creation or development of content." Does a service provider become partly responsible for the creation or development of content when it has the power to edit material posted by a third party? When it actually exercises its power to edit such material? When it supplies the parameters for a third party's creation of content, as by developing a multiple-choice form?

For cases considering whether a service provider is an information content provider, compare *Carafano v. Metrosplash.com, Inc.*, 339 F.3d 1119, 1124-25 (9th Cir. 2003) (holding that Internet matchmaking service that hosts profiles created through multiple-choice questionnaire was an information content provider with respect to those profiles); *Ben Ezra, Weinstein, & Co. v. America Online*, 206 F.3d 980, 985-86 (10th Cir. 2000) (holding that AOL was not an information content provider with respect to inaccurate stock information even though it altered and deleted some information); and *Schneider v. Amazon.com*, 31 P.3d 37, 42 (Wash. App. Div. 1 2001) (holding that Amazon.com was not an information content provider with respect to posted book reviews even though it retained the right to edit the reviews and claims licensing rights in the posted material); with Hy Cyte Corp. v. Badbusinessbureau.com, 418 F. Supp. 2d 1142 (D. Ariz. 2005) (denying motion to dismiss where complaint alleged that defendants provided titles and editorial comments for allegedly defamatory reports posted on website).

6. Should discussion group moderators similarly be immune from defamation liability for messages written by other people and posted to the groups? Should it matter whether or not the moderators manually decide which messages to allow through? What if the moderators are very selective? Consider the following case.

Batzel v. Smith

United States Court of Appeals for the Ninth Circuit, 2003
333 F.3d 1018

BERZON, Circuit Judge.

In the summer of 1999, sometime-handyman Robert Smith was working for Ellen Batzel, an attorney licensed to practice in California and North Carolina, at Batzel's house in the North Carolina mountains. Smith recounted that while he was repairing Batzel's truck, Batzel told him that she was "the granddaughter of one of Adolf Hitler's right-hand men." Smith also maintained that as he was painting the walls of Batzel's sitting room he overheard Batzel tell her roommate that she was related to Nazi politician Heinrich Himmler. According to Smith, Batzel told him on another occasion that some of the paintings hanging in her house were inherited. To Smith, these paintings looked old and European.

After assembling these clues, Smith used a computer to look for websites concerning stolen art work and was directed by a search engine to the Museum Security Network ("the Network") website. He thereupon sent the following e-mail message to the Network:

From: Bob Smith [e-mail address omitted]
To: securma@museum-security.org [the Network]
Subject: Stolen Art

Hi there,

I am a building contractor in Asheville, North Carolina, USA. A month ago, I did a remodeling job for a woman, Ellen L. Batzel who bragged to me about being the grand daughter [sic] of "one of Adolph Hitler's right-hand men." At the time, I was concentrating on performing my tasks, but upon reflection, I believe she said she was the descendant of Heinrich Himmler.

Ellen Batzel has hundreds of older European paintings on her walls, all with heavy carved wooden frames. She told me she inherited them. I believe these paintings were looted during WWII and are the rightful legacy of the Jewish people. Her address is [omitted].

I also believe that the descendants of criminals should not be persecuted for the crimes of the [sic] fathers, nor should they benefit. I do not know who to contact about this, so I start with your organization. Please contact me via email [. . .] if you would like to discuss this matter.

Bob.

Ton Cremers, then-Director of Security at Amsterdam's famous Rijksmuseum and (in his spare time) sole operator of the Museum Security Network ("the Network"), received Smith's e-mail message. The nonprofit Network maintains both a website and an electronic e-mailed newsletter about museum security and stolen art. Cremers periodically puts together an electronic document containing: e-mails sent to him, primarily from Network subscribers; comments by himself as the moderator of an on-line discussion; and excerpts from news articles related to stolen works of art. He exercises some editorial discretion in choosing which of the e-mails he receives are included in the listserv mailing * * * . The Network's website and listserv mailings are read by hundreds of museum security officials, insurance investigators, and law enforcement personnel around the world, who use the information in the Network posting to track down stolen art.

After receiving it, Cremers published Smith's e-mail message to the Network, with some minor wording changes, on the Network listserv. He also posted that listserv, with Smith's message included, on the Network's website. * * *

After the posting, Bob Smith e-mailed a subscriber to the listserv, Jonathan Sazonoff, explaining that he had had no idea that his e-mail would be posted to the listserv or put on the web. Smith told Sazanoff:

I [was] trying to figure out how in blazes I could have posted me [sic] email to [the Network] bulletin board. I came into MSN through the back door, directed by a search engine, and never got the big picture. I don't remember reading anything about a message board either so I am a bit confused over how it could happen. Every message board to which I have ever subscribed required application, a password, and/or registration, and the instructions explained this is necessary to keep out the advertisers, cranks, and bumbling idiots like me.

Batzel discovered the message several months after its initial posting and complained to Cremers about the message. Cremers then contacted Smith via e-mail to request additional information about Smith's allegations. Smith continued to insist on the truth of his statements. He also told Cremers that if he had thought his e-mail "message would be posted on an international message board [he] never would have sent it in the first place."

Upon discovering that Smith had not intended to post his message, Cremers apologized for the confusion. He told Smith in an e-mail that "[y]ou were not a subscriber to the list and I believe that you did not realize your message would be forwarded to the mailinglist [sic]." Apparently, subscribers send messages for inclusion in the listserv to securma@x54all.nl, a different address from that to which Smith had sent his e-mail contacting the Network. Cremers further explained that he "receive[s] many e-mails each day some of which contain queries [he thinks] interesting enough to forward to the list. [Smith's] was one of those."

Batzel disputes Smith's account of their conversations. She says she is not, and never said she is, a descendant of a Nazi official, and that she did not inherit any art. Smith, she charges, defamed her not because he believed her artwork stolen but out of pique, because Batzel refused to show Hollywood contacts a screenplay he had written.

Batzel claims further that because of Cremers's actions she lost several prominent clients in California and was investigated by the North Carolina Bar Association. Also, she represents that her social reputation suffered. To redress her claimed reputational injuries she filed this lawsuit * * * .

* * *

III

California law provides for pre-trial dismissal of "SLAPPs": "Strategic Lawsuits against Public Participation." Cal. Civ. Proc. Code § 425.16. These are lawsuits that [masquerade as ordinary lawsuits] but are brought to deter common citizens from exercising their political or legal rights or to punish them for doing so. * * * [Cremers filed a motion to strike under the anti-SLAPP statute, alleging that Batzel's suit was meritless.] To resist a motion to strike pursuant to California's anti-SLAPP law, Batzel must demonstrate a probability that she will prevail on the merits of her complaint. The district court held that Batzel had made such a showing, and absent 47 U.S.C. § 230, we would be inclined to agree. * * *

To benefit from § 230(c) immunity, Cremers must first demonstrate that his Network website and listserv qualify as "provider[s] or user[s] of an *interactive computer service*." § 230(c)(1) (emphasis added). An "interactive computer service" is defined as "any information service, system, or access software provider that provides or enables computer access by multiple users to a computer server, including specifically a service or system that provides access to the Internet and such systems.

operated or services offered by libraries or educational institutions."
§ 230(f)(2). The district court concluded that only services that provide
access to the Internet as a whole are covered by this definition. But the
definition of "interactive computer service" on its face covers "any"
information services or other systems, as long as the service or system
allows "multiple users" to access "a computer server." Further, the statute
repeatedly refers to "the Internet and *other* interactive computer services,"
(emphasis added), making clear that the statutory immunity extends
beyond the Internet itself. * * *

There is, however, no need here to decide whether a listserv or website
itself fits the broad statutory definition of "interactive computer service,"
because the language of § 230(c)(1) confers immunity not just on
"providers" of such services, but also on "users" of such services.
§ 230(c)(1). There is no dispute that the Network uses interactive computer
services to distribute its on-line mailing and to post the listserv on its
website. Indeed, to make its website available and to mail out the listserv,
the Network must access the Internet through some form of "interactive
computer service." Thus, both the Network website and the listserv are
potentially immune under § 230.

Critically, however, § 230 limits immunity to information "provided
by another information content provider." § 230(c)(1). An "information
content provider" is defined by the statute to mean "any person or entity
that is responsible, in whole or in part, for the creation or development of
information provided through the Internet or any other interactive
computer service." § 230(f)(3). The reference to "*another* information
content provider" (emphasis added) distinguishes the circumstance in which
the interactive computer service itself meets the definition of "information
content provider" with respect to the information in question. The
pertinent question therefore becomes whether Smith was the sole content
provider of his e-mail, or whether Cremers can also be considered to have
"creat[ed]" or "develop[ed]" Smith's e-mail message forwarded to the
listserv.

Obviously, Cremers did not create Smith's e-mail. Smith composed
the e-mail entirely on his own. Nor do Cremers's minor alterations of
Smith's e-mail prior to its posting or his choice to publish the e-mail (while
rejecting other e-mails for inclusion in the listserv) rise to the level of
"development." * * * Because Cremers did no more than select and make
minor alterations to Smith's e-mail, Cremers cannot be considered the
content provider of Smith's e-mail for purposes of § 230.

In most cases our conclusion that Cremers cannot be considered a
content provider would end matters, but this case presents one twist on the
usual § 230 analysis: Smith maintains that he never "imagined [his]
message would be posted on an international message board or [he] never
would have sent it in the first place." The question thus becomes whether
Smith can be said to have "provided" his e-mail in the sense intended by
§ 230(c). If the defamatory information is not "provided by another
information content provider," then § 230(c) does not confer immunity on
the publisher of the information. "[P]rovided" suggests, at least, some

active role by the "provider" in supplying the material to a "provider or user of an interactive computer service." * * * Smith contends that he did not intend his e-mail to be placed on an interactive computer service for public viewing. Smith's confusion, even if legitimate, does not matter, Cremers maintains, because the § 230(c)(1) immunity should be available simply because Smith was the author of the e-mail, without more.

We disagree. Under Cremers's broad interpretation of § 230(c), users and providers of interactive computer services could with impunity intentionally post material they knew was never meant to be put on the Internet. At the same time, the creator or developer of the information presumably could not be held liable for unforeseeable publication of his material to huge numbers of people with whom he had no intention to communicate. The result would be nearly limitless immunity for speech never meant to be broadcast over the Internet.

Supplying a "provider or user of an interactive computer service" with immunity in such circumstances is not consistent with Congress's expressly stated purposes in adopting § 230. Free speech and the development of the Internet are not "promote[d]" by affording immunity when providers and users of "interactive computer service[s]" knew or had reason to know that the information provided was not intended for publication on the Internet. Quite the contrary: Users of the Internet are likely to be discouraged from sending e-mails for fear that their e-mails may be published on the web without their permission. * * * At the same time, Congress's purpose in enacting § 230(c)(1) suggests that we must take great care in determining whether another's information was "provided" to a "provider or user of an interactive computer service" for publication. Otherwise, posting of information on the Internet and other interactive computer services would be chilled, as the service provider or user could not tell whether posting was contemplated. To preclude this possibility, the focus should be not on the information provider's intentions or knowledge when transmitting content but, instead, on the service provider's or user's reasonable perception of those intentions or knowledge. We therefore hold that a service provider or user is immune from liability under § 230(c)(1) when a third person or entity that created or developed the information in question furnished it to the provider or user under circumstances in which a reasonable person in the position of the service provider or user would conclude that the information was provided for publication on the Internet or other "interactive computer service."

It is not entirely clear from the record whether Smith "provided" the e-mail for publication on the Internet under this standard. There are facts that could have led Cremers reasonably to conclude that Smith sent him the information because he operated an Internet service. On the other hand, Smith was not a subscriber to the listserv and apparently sent the information to a different e-mail account from the one at which Cremers usually received information for publication. More development of the record may be necessary to determine whether, under all the circumstances, a reasonable person in Cremers' position would conclude that the information was sent for internet publication, or whether a triable issue of fact is presented on that issue.

We therefore vacate the district court's order denying Cremers's anti-SLAPP motion and remand to the district court for further proceedings to develop the facts under this newly announced standard and to evaluate what Cremers should have reasonably concluded at the time he received Smith's e-mail. If Cremers should have reasonably concluded, for example, that because Smith's e-mail arrived via a different e-mail address it was not provided to him for possible posting on the listserv, then Cremers cannot take advantage of the § 230(c) immunities. Under that circumstance, the posted information was not "provided" by another "information content provider" within the meaning of § 230. After making such an inquiry, the district court must then evaluate whether Batzel adequately has demonstrated a probability that she will prevail on the merits of her complaint under California's anti-SLAPP statute.

Vacated in part, affirmed in part, and remanded.

GOULD, Circuit Judge, concurring in part, dissenting in part:

I respectfully dissent from the majority's analysis of the statutory immunity from libel suits created by § 230 of the Communications Decency Act (CDA). The majority gives the phrase "information provided by another" an incorrect and unworkable meaning that extends CDA immunity far beyond what Congress intended. Under the majority's interpretation of § 230, many persons who intentionally spread vicious falsehoods on the Internet will be immune from suit. This sweeping preemption of valid state libel laws is not necessary to promote Internet use and is not what Congress had in mind. * * *

The majority rule licenses professional rumor-mongers and gossip-hounds to spread false and hurtful information with impunity. So long as the defamatory information was written by a person who wanted the information to be spread on the Internet (in other words, a person with an axe to grind), the rumormonger's injurious conduct is beyond legal redress. Nothing in the CDA's text or legislative history suggests that Congress intended CDA immunity to extend so far. Nothing in the text, legislative history, or human experience would lead me to accept the notion that Congress in § 230 intended to immunize users or providers of interactive computer services who, by their discretionary decisions to spread particular communications, cause trickles of defamation to swell into rivers of harm.

The problems caused by the majority's rule all would vanish if we focused our inquiry not on the author's intent, but on the defendant's acts, as I believe Congress intended. We should hold that the CDA immunizes a defendant only when the defendant took no active role in selecting the questionable information for publication. If the defendant took an active role in selecting information for publication, the information is no longer "information provided by another" within the meaning of § 230. We should draw this conclusion from the statute's text and purposes. * * *

Under my interpretation of § 230, a company that operates an e-mail network would be immune from libel suits arising out of e-mail messages transmitted automatically across its network. Similarly, the owner, operator, organizer, or moderator of an Internet bulletin board, chat room, or listserv would be immune from libel suits arising out of messages distributed using that technology, provided that the person does not actively select particular messages for publication.

On the other hand, a person who receives a libelous communication and makes the decision to disseminate that messages to others—whether via e-mail, a bulletin board, a chat room, or a listserv—would not be immune. My approach also would further Congress's goal of encouraging "self-policing" on the Internet. * * * [I]n my view, there is no immunity under the CDA if Cremers made a discretionary decision to distribute on the Internet defamatory information about another person, without any investigation whatsoever. If Cremers made a mistake, we should not hold that he may escape all accountability just because he made that mistake on the Internet.

I respectfully dissent.

Notes and Questions

1. As the court of appeals recognizes, the immunity in section 230 covers not only "providers" of interactive computer services, but also "users" of such services. Under the court's approach, *every* Internet user is a user of an interactive computer service, and thus *every* Internet user has immunity for transmitting content "provided by another information content provider." That phrase thus takes on tremendous significance. Is the court of appeals' interpretation adequately limiting? Under what circumstances would a user reasonably conclude that information was provided for publication on the Internet? Does a user have any obligation to investigate or confirm the content provider's intentions before widely disseminating the material?

2. Consider the dissent's approach of immunizing a defendant only when the defendant "took no active role in selecting the questionable information for publication." What constitutes an "active role"? Is there any real difference between selecting information for publication and exercising discretion to remove posts, as Prodigy did in the *Stratton Oakmont* case? Does the dissent's approach simply resurrect the distinction between *Cubby* and *Stratton Oakmont* that section 230 rejected?

3. Although section 230 responded in part to the *Stratton Oakmont* decision, the statute's text does not limit the immunity to defamation cases. Courts have found service providers and others immune from suit for breach of contract, *see, e.g., Schneider v. Amazon.com*, 31 P.3d 37, 42 (Wash. App. Div. 1 2001); tortious interference with business relations, *see, e.g., id.*; invasion of privacy, *see, e.g., Carafano v. Metrosplash.com, Inc.*, 339 F.3d 1119 (9th Cir. 2003); and unfair trade practices, *see, e.g., OptInRealBig.com v. IronPort Systems, Inc.*, 323 F. Supp. 2d 1037 (N.D. Cal. 2004). Are the policy considerations the same in those contexts as in the defamation context?

2. Copyright Liability

Section 230(e)(2) of the CDA specifically states that the statute shall not be construed "to limit or expand any law pertaining to intellectual property." How, if at all, should the liability rules for service providers claimed to carry material that infringes a copyright differ from those that apply when a service provider is claimed to carry defamatory materials? Are the harms of infringing speech the same as the harms of defamatory speech (or other tortious conduct for which section 230 provides immunity)? Do service providers face the same incentives to shape the content available on their systems? To remove content claimed to infringe?

Religious Technology Center v. Netcom On-Line Communication Services

United States District Court for the Northern District of California, 1995
907 F. Supp. 1361

WHYTE, District Judge.

This case concerns an issue of first impression regarding intellectual property rights in cyberspace. Specifically, this order addresses whether the operator of a computer bulletin board service ("BBS"), and the large Internet access provider that allows that BBS to reach the Internet, should be liable for copyright infringement committed by a subscriber of the BBS.

Plaintiffs Religious Technology Center ("RTC") and Bridge Publications, Inc. ("BPI") hold copyrights in the unpublished and published works of L. Ron Hubbard, the late founder of the Church of Scientology ("the Church"). Defendant Dennis Erlich ("Erlich") is a former minister of Scientology turned vocal critic of the Church, whose pulpit is now the Usenet newsgroup alt.religion.scientology ("a.r.s."), an on-line forum for discussion and criticism of Scientology. Plaintiffs maintain that Erlich infringed their copyrights when he posted portions of their works on a.r.s. Erlich gained his access to the Internet through defendant Thomas Klemesrud's ("Klemesrud's") BBS "support.com." Klemesrud is the operator of the BBS, which is run out of his home and has approximately 500 paying users. Klemesrud's BBS is not directly linked to the Internet, but gains its connection through the facilities of defendant Netcom On-Line Communications, Inc. ("Netcom"), one of the largest providers of Internet access in the United States.

After failing to convince Erlich to stop his postings, plaintiffs contacted defendants Klemesrud and Netcom. Klemesrud responded to plaintiffs' demands that Erlich be kept off his system by asking plaintiffs to prove that they owned the copyrights to the works posted by Erlich. However, plaintiffs refused Klemesrud's request as unreasonable. Netcom similarly refused plaintiffs' request that Erlich not be allowed to gain access to the Internet through its system. Netcom contended that it would be impossible to prescreen Erlich's postings and that to kick Erlich off the Internet meant kicking off the hundreds of users of Klemesrud's BBS. Consequently, plaintiffs named Klemesrud and Netcom in their suit against Erlich [for] copyright infringement * * * .

[In an earlier opinion on plaintiffs' motion for a preliminary injunction against Erlich, the court determined that plaintiffs owned copyright in the works at issue; and that plaintiffs were likely to succeed in showing (1) that

Erlich had copied the works and (2) that Erlich was not entitled to a fair use defense. Plaintiffs also sought preliminary injunctive relief against Netcom and Klemesrud. Netcom and Klemesrud moved for summary judgment and judgment on the pleadings, respectively, claiming that even if Erlich's conduct was infringing, as a matter of law they could not be held liable for that conduct. The court's analysis of Netcom's motion follows; its conclusions with respect to Klemesrud substantially tracked its conclusions with respect to Netcom.]

I. NETCOM'S MOTION FOR SUMMARY JUDGMENT OF NONINFRINGEMENT

B. *Copyright Infringement*

   1. *Direct Infringement*

    * * * The parties do not dispute the basic processes that occur when Erlich posts his allegedly infringing messages to a.r.s. Erlich connects to Klemesrud's BBS using a telephone and a modem. Erlich then transmits his messages to Klemesrud's computer, where they are automatically briefly stored. According to a prearranged pattern established by Netcom's software, Erlich's initial act of posting a message to the Usenet results in the automatic copying of Erlich's message from Klemesrud's computer onto Netcom's computer and onto other computers on the Usenet. In order to ease transmission and for the convenience of Usenet users, Usenet servers maintain postings from newsgroups for a short period of time—eleven days for Netcom's system and three days for Klemesrud's system. Once on Netcom's computers, messages are available to Netcom's customers and Usenet neighbors, who may then download the messages to their own computers. Netcom's local server makes available its postings to a group of Usenet servers, which do the same for other servers until all Usenet sites worldwide have obtained access to the postings, which takes a matter of hours.

    Unlike some other large on-line service providers, such as CompuServe, America Online, and Prodigy, Netcom does not create or control the content of the information available to its subscribers. It also does not monitor messages as they are posted. It has, however, suspended the accounts of subscribers who violated its terms and conditions, such as where they had commercial software in their posted files. Netcom admits that, although not currently configured to do this, it may be possible to reprogram its system to screen postings containing particular words or coming from particular individuals. Netcom, however, took no action after it was told by plaintiffs that Erlich had posted messages through Netcom's system that violated plaintiffs' copyrights, instead claiming that it could not shut out Erlich without shutting out all of the users of Klemesrud's BBS. * * *

    In the present case, there is no question * * * that "copies" were created, as Erlich's act of sending a message to a.r.s. caused reproductions of portions of plaintiffs' works on both Klemesrud's and Netcom's storage devices. Even though the messages remained on their systems for at most eleven days, they were sufficiently "fixed" to constitute recognizable copies under the Copyright Act. * * * Netcom argues that Erlich, and not Netcom, is directly liable for the copying. * * * The court believes that Netcom's act of designing or implementing a system that automatically and uniformly creates temporary copies of all data sent through it is not unlike that of the owner of a copying machine who lets the public make copies with it. Although some of the people using the machine may directly infringe copyrights, courts analyze the machine owner's liability under the rubric of contributory infringement, not direct infringement. Plaintiffs' theory would create many separate acts of infringement and, carried to its natural extreme, would lead to unreasonable liability. It is not difficult to conclude that Erlich infringes by copying a protected work onto his computer and by posting a message to a newsgroup. However, plaintiffs' theory further implicates a Usenet server that carries Erlich's message to other servers regardless of whether that server acts without any human intervention beyond the initial setting up of the system. It would also result in liability for every single Usenet server in the worldwide link of computers transmitting Erlich's message to every other computer. These parties, who are liable under plaintiffs' theory, do no more than operate or implement a system that is essential if Usenet messages are to be widely distributed. There is no need to construe the Act to make all of these parties infringers. Although copyright is a strict liability statute, there should still be some element of volition or causation which is lacking where a defendant's system is merely used to create a copy by a third party. * * *

The court is not persuaded by plaintiffs' argument that Netcom is directly liable for the copies that are made and stored on its computer. Where the infringing subscriber is clearly directly liable for the same act, it does not make sense to adopt a rule that could lead to the liability of countless parties whose role in the infringement is nothing more than setting up and operating a system that is necessary for the functioning of the Internet. Such a result is unnecessary as there is already a party directly liable for causing the copies to be made. Plaintiffs occasionally claim that they only seek to hold liable a party that refuses to delete infringing files after they have been warned. However, such liability cannot be based on a theory of direct infringement, where knowledge is irrelevant. The court does not find workable a theory of infringement that would hold the entire Internet liable for activities that cannot reasonably be deterred. Billions of bits of data flow through the Internet and are necessarily stored on servers throughout the network and it is thus practically impossible to screen out infringing bits from noninfringing bits. Because the court cannot see any meaningful distinction (without regard to knowledge) between what Netcom did and what every other Usenet server does, the court finds that Netcom cannot be held liable for direct infringement.

2. *Contributory Infringement*

Netcom is not free from liability just because it did not directly infringe plaintiffs' works; it may still be liable as a contributory infringer. Although there is no statutory rule of liability for infringement committed by others,

> [t]he absence of such express language in the copyright statute does not preclude the imposition of liability for copyright infringement on certain parties who have not themselves engaged in the infringing

activity. For vicarious liability is imposed in virtually all areas of the law, and the concept of contributory infringement is merely a species of the broader problem of identifying the circumstances in which it is just to hold one individual accountable for the actions of another.

Sony Corp. v. Universal City Studios, Inc., 464 U.S. 417, 435 (1984) (footnote omitted). Liability for participation in the infringement will be established where the defendant, "with knowledge of the infringing activity, induces, causes or materially contributes to the infringing conduct of another." *Gershwin Publishing Corp. v. Columbia Artists Management, Inc.*, 443 F.2d 1159, 1162 (2d Cir. 1971).

    a.   *Knowledge of Infringing Activity*

Plaintiffs insist that Netcom knew that Erlich was infringing their copyrights at least after receiving notice from plaintiffs' counsel indicating that Erlich had posted copies of their works onto a.r.s. through Netcom's system. Despite this knowledge, Netcom continued to allow Erlich to post messages to a.r.s. and left the allegedly infringing messages on its system so that Netcom's subscribers and other Usenet servers could access them. Netcom argues that it did not possess the necessary type of knowledge because (1) it did not know of Erlich's planned infringing activities when it agreed to lease its facilities to Klemesrud, (2) it did not know that Erlich would infringe prior to any of his postings, (3) it is unable to screen out infringing postings before they are made, and (4) its knowledge of the infringing nature of Erlich's postings was too equivocal given the difficulty in assessing whether the registrations were valid and whether Erlich's use was fair. The court will address these arguments in turn.

Netcom cites cases holding that there is no contributory infringement by the lessors of premises that are later used for infringement unless the lessor had knowledge of the intended use at the time of the signing of the lease. * * * Here, Netcom not only leases space but also serves as an access provider, which includes the storage and transmission of information necessary to facilitate Erlich's postings to a.r.s. Unlike a landlord, Netcom retains some control over the use of its system. Thus, the relevant time frame for knowledge is not when Netcom entered into an agreement with Klemesrud. It should be when Netcom provided its services to allow Erlich to infringe plaintiffs' copyrights. It is undisputed that Netcom did not know that Erlich was infringing before it received notice from plaintiffs. Netcom points out that the alleged instances of infringement occurring on Netcom's system all happened prior to December 29, 1994, the date on which Netcom first received notice of plaintiffs' infringement claim against Erlich. Thus, there is no question of fact as to whether Netcom knew or should have known of Erlich's infringing activities that occurred more than 11 days before receipt of the December 28, 1994 letter.

However, the evidence reveals a question of fact as to whether Netcom knew or should have known that Erlich had infringed plaintiffs' copyrights following receipt of plaintiffs' letter. Because Netcom was arguably participating in Erlich's public distribution of plaintiffs' works, there is a genuine issue as to whether Netcom knew of any infringement by Erlich before it was too late to do anything about it. If plaintiffs can prove the knowledge element, Netcom will be liable for contributory infringement since its failure to simply cancel Erlich's infringing message and thereby stop an infringing copy from being distributed worldwide constitutes substantial participation in Erlich's public distribution of the message.

Netcom argues that its knowledge after receiving notice of Erlich's alleged infringing activities was too equivocal given the difficulty in assessing whether registrations are valid and whether use is fair. Although a mere unsupported allegation of infringement by a copyright owner may not automatically put a defendant on notice of infringing activity, Netcom's position that liability must be unequivocal is unsupportable. While perhaps the typical infringing activities of BBSs will involve copying software, where BBS operators are better equipped to judge infringement, the fact that this involves written works should not distinguish it. Where works contain copyright notices within them, as here, it is difficult to argue that a defendant did not know that the works were copyrighted. To require proof of valid registrations would be impractical and would perhaps take too long to verify, making it impossible for a copyright holder to protect his or her works in some cases, as works are automatically deleted less than two weeks after they are posted. The court is more persuaded by the argument that it is beyond the ability of a BBS operator to quickly and fairly determine when a use is not infringement where there is at least a colorable claim of fair use. Where a BBS operator cannot reasonably verify a claim of infringement, either because of a possible fair use defense, the lack of copyright notices on the copies, or the copyright holder's failure to provide the necessary documentation to show that there is a likely infringement, the operator's lack of knowledge will be found reasonable and there will be no liability for contributory infringement for allowing the continued distribution of the works on its system.

Since Netcom was given notice of an infringement claim before Erlich had completed his infringing activity, there may be a question of fact as to whether Netcom knew or should have known that such activities were infringing. Given the context of a dispute between a former minister and a church he is criticizing, Netcom may be able to show that its lack of knowledge that Erlich was infringing was reasonable. However, Netcom admits that it did not even look at the postings once given notice and that had it looked at the copyright notice and statements regarding authorship, it would have triggered an investigation into whether there was infringement.

b. *Substantial Participation*

Where a defendant has knowledge of the primary infringer's infringing activities, it will be liable if it "induces, causes or materially contributes to the infringing conduct of" the primary infringer. *Gershwin Publishing*, 443 F.2d at 1162. Such participation must be substantial.

Providing a service that allows for the automatic distribution of all Usenet postings, infringing and noninfringing, goes well beyond renting a premises to an infringer. *See Fonovisa, Inc. v. Cherry Auction, Inc.*, 847 F. Supp. 1492, 1496 (E.D. Cal. 1994) (finding that renting space at swap meet to known bootleggers not "substantial participation" in the infringers' activities). It is more akin to the radio stations that were found liable for rebroadcasting an infringing broadcast. *See, e.g., Select Theatres Corp. v. Ronzoni Macaroni Corp.*, 59 U.S.P.Q. 288, 291 (S.D.N.Y.1943). Netcom allows Erlich's infringing messages to remain on its system and be further distributed to other Usenet servers worldwide. It does not completely relinquish control over how its system is used, unlike a landlord. Thus, it is fair, assuming Netcom is able to take simple measures to prevent further damage to plaintiffs' copyrighted works, to hold Netcom liable for contributory infringement where Netcom has knowledge of Erlich's infringing postings yet continues to aid in the accomplishment of Erlich's purpose of publicly distributing the postings. Accordingly, plaintiffs do raise a genuine issue of material fact as to their theory of contributory infringement as to the postings made after Netcom was on notice of plaintiffs' infringement claim.

3. *Vicarious Liability*

Even if plaintiffs cannot prove that Netcom is contributorily liable for its participation in the infringing activity, it may still seek to prove vicarious infringement based on Netcom's relationship to Erlich. A defendant is liable for vicarious liability for the actions of a primary infringer where the defendant (1) has the right and ability to control the infringer's acts and (2) receives a direct financial benefit from the infringement. Unlike contributory infringement, knowledge is not an element of vicarious liability.

a. *Right and Ability To Control*

The first element of vicarious liability will be met if plaintiffs can show that Netcom has the right and ability to supervise the conduct of its subscribers. Netcom argues that it does not have the right to control its users' postings before they occur. Plaintiffs dispute this and argue that Netcom's terms and conditions, to which its subscribers must agree, specify that Netcom reserves the right to take remedial action against subscribers. Plaintiffs argue that under "netiquette," the informal rules and customs that have developed on the Internet, violation of copyrights by a user is unacceptable and the access provider has a duty take measures to prevent this; where the immediate service provider fails, the next service provider up the transmission stream must act. Further evidence of Netcom's right to restrict infringing activity is its prohibition of copyright infringement and its requirement that its subscribers indemnify it for any damage to third parties. Plaintiffs have thus raised a question of fact as to Netcom's right to control Erlich's use of its services.

Netcom argues that it could not possibly screen messages before they are posted given the speed and volume of the data that goes through its system. Netcom further argues that it has never exercised control over the content of its users' postings. Plaintiffs' expert opines otherwise, stating that with an easy software modification Netcom could identify postings that contain particular words or come from particular individuals. Plaintiffs further dispute Netcom's claim that it could not limit Erlich's access to Usenet without kicking off all 500 subscribers of Klemesrud's BBS. As evidence that Netcom has in fact exercised its ability to police its users' conduct, plaintiffs cite evidence that Netcom has acted to suspend subscribers' accounts on over one thousand occasions. Further evidence shows that Netcom can delete specific postings. Whether such sanctions occurred before or after the abusive conduct is not material to whether Netcom can exercise control. The court thus finds that plaintiffs have raised a genuine issue of fact as to whether Netcom has the right and ability to exercise control over the activities of its subscribers, and of Erlich in particular.

b. Direct Financial Benefit

Plaintiffs must further prove that Netcom receives a direct financial benefit from the infringing activities of its users. For example, a landlord who has the right and ability to supervise the tenant's activities is vicariously liable for the infringements of the tenant where the rental amount is proportional to the proceeds of the tenant's sales. However, where a defendant rents space or services on a fixed rental fee that does not depend on the nature of the activity of the lessee, courts usually find no vicarious liability because there is no direct financial benefit from the infringement. * * * Plaintiffs cannot provide any evidence of a direct financial benefit received by Netcom from Erlich's infringing postings. * * * There is no evidence that infringement by Erlich, or any other user of Netcom's services, in any way enhances the value of Netcom's services to subscribers or attracts new subscribers. Plaintiffs argue, however, that Netcom somehow derives a benefit from its purported "policy of refusing to take enforcement actions against its subscribers and others who transmit infringing messages over its computer networks." Plaintiffs point to Netcom's advertisements that, compared to competitors like CompuServe and America Online, Netcom provides easy, regulation-free Internet access. Plaintiffs assert that Netcom's policy attracts copyright infringers to its system, resulting in a direct financial benefit. The court is not convinced that such an argument, if true, would constitute a direct financial benefit to Netcom from Erlich's infringing activities. Further, plaintiffs' argument is not supported by probative evidence. * * * Because plaintiffs have failed to raise a question of fact on this vital element, their claim of vicarious liability fails. * * *

C. Conclusion

The court finds that plaintiffs have raised a genuine issue of fact regarding whether Netcom should have known that Erlich was infringing their copyrights after receiving a letter from plaintiffs, [and] whether Netcom substantially participated in the infringement * * *. Accordingly, Netcom is not entitled to summary judgment on plaintiffs' claim of contributory copyright infringement. However, plaintiffs' claims of direct and vicarious infringement fail. * * *

III. PRELIMINARY INJUNCTION AGAINST NETCOM AND KLEMESRUD

* * * The court finds that plaintiffs have not met their burden of showing a likelihood of success on the merits as to either Netcom or Klemesrud. The only viable theory of infringement is contributory infringement, and there is little evidence that Netcom or Klemesrud knew or should have known that Erlich was engaged in copyright infringement

of plaintiffs' works and was not entitled to a fair use defense, especially as they did not receive notice of the alleged infringement until after all but one of the postings were completed. Further, their participation in the infringement was not substantial. Accordingly, plaintiffs will not likely prevail on their claims.

Notes and Questions

1. The court based its earlier conclusion that plaintiffs were likely to succeed in showing that Erlich was not entitled to a fair use defense in part on the fact that Erlich had copied large portions of Hubbard's works without adding significant critical commentary. *See Religious Technology Ctr. v. Netcom On-line Communication Servs.*, 923 F. Supp. 1231, 1242-50 (N.D. Cal. 1995). A fair use analysis by a court involves a balancing of several factual determinations. Is a service provider faced with a claim of infringement in a good position to engage in such an analysis?

2. On the issue of direct infringement, note the district court's observation that Netcom designed a system "that *automatically* and uniformly creates temporary copies of all data sent through it." (Emphasis added.) Is a provider entitled to immunity from direct infringement even when its processes are not fully automatic? In *CoStar v. LoopNet, Inc.*, 373 F.3d 544 (4th Cir. 2004), the court considered whether LoopNet was liable for direct infringement when it allowed real estate brokers to post descriptions of real estate automatically on its web site, but cursorily reviewed all photographs before permitting them to appear on the site so as to avoid obvious copyright infringement. The court held that LoopNet's conduct with respect to the photographs "does not amount to 'copying,' nor does it add volition to LoopNet's involvement in storing the copy." *Id.* at 556. One judge dissented on this point, arguing that LoopNet's "non-passive, volitional conduct" made the *Netcom* defense unavailable. *Id.* at 557 (Gregory, J., dissenting). How would a choice between the majority and dissenting approaches affect a provider's incentives to prevent infringing material from being posted on or transmitted by its system?

3. Netcom, of course, argued that its knowledge of Erlich's infringement was "too equivocal" to support indirect liability even once it received notice from the plaintiffs, because it could not easily have determined whether Erlich had a fair use defense. Does the court ever establish what level of knowledge triggers liability? How would different rules affect a service provider's response to claims of infringement?

4. The *Netcom* court describes liability for contributory infringement as requiring that a defendant "know or have reason to know" of infringing activity. What showing should trigger the conclusion that a provider had "reason to know" of infringing activity? Does a service provider have a duty to police its system for infringing material?

5. The plaintiffs in *Netcom* argued both that Netcom should have removed infringing messages they identified *and* that Netcom (and Klemesrud) should have disabled Erlich from posting any messages. Assuming that upon receiving notice Netcom knew or had reason to know of Erlich's infringing activities, should Netcom be liable for its failure to remove the infringing posts, or for its failure to disable Erlich's access to the system altogether? How would

a court's choice between these possibilities affect Netcom's incentives to construct and police its system?

In 1998, as part of the Digital Millennium Copyright Act, Congress enacted the On-Line Copyright Infringement Liability Limitation Act, codified at 17 U.S.C. § 512. Section 512 does not immunize service providers from suit for allowing and disallowing the transmission of certain kinds of material, but it limits providers' exposure by precluding monetary liability and some forms of injunctive relief. Section 512 is far more complicated than section 230 of the CDA, in that it sets up different "safe harbors" according to the specific functions a service provider performs. The five possible "safe harbors" are set forth in subsections 512(a) through 512(e).

To qualify for any of the section 512 safe harbors, a service provider must adopt and implement a policy of terminating subscribers and account holders who are repeat infringers and must accommodate technical measures used by copyright holders to identify and protect copyrighted works. 17 U.S.C. § 512(i). Three of the most important safe harbors— subsection 512(a), for providers who act as passive conduits; subsection 512(c), for providers who store material on behalf of their users; and subsection 512(d), for information location tools—are set forth below. The statute generally defines a "service provider" as "a provider of online services or network access, or the operator of facilities therefor." *Id.* § 512(k)(1)(B). For purposes of section 512(a), the statute defines the term "service provider" narrowly, to include only "an entity offering the transmission, routing, or providing of connections for digital online communications, between or among points specified by a user, of material of the user's choosing, without modification to the content of the material sent or received." *Id.* § 512(k)(1)(A).

Section 512 of the Digital Millennium Copyright Act

17 U.S.C. § 512

§ 512. Limitations on liability relating to material online

(a) Transitory digital network communications.—A service provider shall not be liable for monetary relief, or, except as provided in subsection (j), for injunctive or other equitable relief, for infringement of copyright by reason of the provider's transmitting, routing, or providing connections for, material through a system or network controlled or operated by or for the service provider, or by reason of the intermediate and transient storage of that material in the course of such transmitting, routing, or providing connections, if—

> (1) the transmission of the material was initiated by or at the direction of a person other than the service provider;

(2) the transmission, routing, provision of connections, or storage is carried out through an automatic technical process without selection of the material by the service provider;

(3) the service provider does not select the recipients of the material except as an automatic response to the request of another person;

(4) no copy of the material made by the service provider in the course of such intermediate or transient storage is maintained on the system or network in a manner ordinarily accessible to anyone other than anticipated recipients, and no such copy is maintained on the system or network in a manner ordinarily accessible to such anticipated recipients for a longer period than is reasonably necessary for the transmission, routing, or provision of connections; and

(5) the material is transmitted through the system or network without modification of its content.

* * *

(c) Information residing on systems or networks at direction of users.—

(1) In General.—A service provider shall not be liable for monetary relief, or, except as provided in subsection (j), for injunctive or other equitable relief, for infringement of copyright by reason of the storage at the direction of a user of material that resides on a system or network controlled or operated by or for the service provider, if the service provider—

(A)(i) does not have actual knowledge that the material or an activity using the material on the system or network is infringing;

(ii) in the absence of such actual knowledge, is not aware of facts or circumstances from which infringing activity is apparent; or

(iii) upon obtaining such knowledge or awareness, acts expeditiously to remove, or disable access to, the material;

(B) does not receive a financial benefit directly attributable to the infringing activity, in a case in which the service provider has the right and ability to control such activity; and

(C) upon notification of claimed infringement as described in paragraph (3), responds expeditiously to remove, or disable access to, the material that is claimed to be infringing or to be the subject of infringing activity. * * *

(3) Elements of notification.—

(A) To be effective under this subsection, a notification of claimed infringement must be a written communication provided to the designated agent of a service provider that includes substantially the following:

(i) A physical or electronic signature of a person authorized to act on behalf of the owner of an exclusive right that is allegedly infringed.

(ii) Identification of the copyrighted work claimed to have been infringed, or, if multiple copyrighted works at a single online site are covered by a single notification, a representative list of such works at that site.

(iii) Identification of the material that is claimed to be infringing or to be the subject of infringing activity and that is to be removed or access to which is to be disabled, and information reasonably sufficient to permit the service provider to locate the material.

(iv) Information reasonably sufficient to permit the service provider to contact the complaining party, such as an address, telephone number, and, if available, an electronic mail address at which the complaining party may be contacted.

(v) A statement that the complaining party has a good faith belief that use of the material in the manner complained of is not authorized by the copyright owner, its agent, or the law.

(vi) A statement that the information in the notification is accurate, and under penalty of perjury, that the complaining party is authorized to act on behalf of the owner of an exclusive right that is allegedly infringed.

(B)(i) Subject to clause (ii), a notification from a copyright owner or from a person authorized to act on behalf of the copyright owner that fails to comply substantially with the provisions of subparagraph (A) shall not be considered under paragraph (1)(A) in determining whether a service provider has actual knowledge or is aware of facts or circumstances from which infringing activity is apparent.

(ii) In a case in which the notification that is provided to the service provider's designated agent fails to comply substantially with all the provisions of subparagraph (A) but substantially complies with clauses (ii), (iii), and (iv) of subparagraph (A), clause (i) of this subparagraph applies only if the service provider promptly attempts to contact the person making the notification or takes other reasonable steps to assist in the receipt of notification that substantially complies with all the provisions of subparagraph (A).

(d) Information Location Tools.—A service provider shall not be liable for monetary relief, or, except as provided in subsection (j), for injunctive or other equitable relief, for infringement of copyright by reason of the provider referring or linking users to an online location containing infringing material or infringing activity, by using information location tools, including a directory, index, reference, pointer, or hypertext link, if the service provider—

(1)(A) does not have actual knowledge that the material or activity is infringing;

(B) in the absence of such actual knowledge, is not aware of facts or circumstances from which infringing activity is apparent; or

(C) upon obtaining such knowledge or awareness, acts expeditiously to remove, or disable access to, the material;

(2) does not receive a financial benefit directly attributable to the infringing activity, in a case in which the service provider has the right and ability to control such activity; and

(3) upon notification of claimed infringement as described in subsection (c)(3), responds expeditiously to remove, or disable access to, the material that is claimed to be infringing or to be the subject of infringing activity, except that, for purposes of this paragraph, the information described in subsection (c)(3)(A)(iii) shall be identification of the reference or link, to material or activity claimed to be infringing, that is to be removed or access to which is to be disabled, and information reasonably sufficient to permit the service provider to locate that reference or link. * * *

(g) Replacement of Removed or Disabled Material and Limitation on Other Liability.—

(1) No liability for taking down generally.—Subject to paragraph (2), a service provider shall not be liable to any person for any claim based on the service provider's good faith disabling of access to, or removal of, material or activity claimed to be infringing or based on facts or circumstances from which infringing activity is apparent, regardless of whether the material or activity is ultimately determined to be infringing.

(2) Exception.— Paragraph (1) shall not apply with respect to material residing at the direction of a subscriber of the service provider on a system or network controlled or operated by or for the service provider that is removed, or to which access is disabled by the service provider, pursuant to a notice provided under subsection (c)(1)(C), unless the service provider—

(A) takes reasonable steps promptly to notify the subscriber that it has removed or disabled access to the material;

(B) upon receipt of a counter notification described in paragraph (3), promptly provides the person who provided the notification under subsection (c)(1)(C) with a copy of the counter notification, and informs that person that it will replace the removed material or cease disabling access to it in 10 business days; and

(C) replaces the removed material and ceases disabling access to it not less than 10, nor more than 14, business days following receipt of the counter notice, unless its designated agent first receives notice from the person who submitted the notification under subsection (c)(1)(C) that such person has filed an action seeking a court order to restrain the subscriber from engaging in infringing activity relating to the material on the service provider's system or network.

(3) Contents of counter notification.— To be effective under this subsection, a counter notification must be a written communication provided to the service provider's designated agent that includes substantially the following:

(A) A physical or electronic signature of the subscriber.

(B) Identification of the material that has been removed or to which access has been disabled and the location at which the material appeared before it was removed or access to it was disabled.

(C) A statement under penalty of perjury that the subscriber has a good faith belief that the material was removed or disabled as a result of mistake or misidentification of the material to be removed or disabled.

(D) The subscriber's name, address, and telephone number, and a statement that the subscriber consents to the jurisdiction of Federal District Court for the judicial district in which the address is located, or if the subscriber's address is outside of the United States, for any judicial district in which the service provider may be found, and that the subscriber will accept service of process from the person who provided notification under subsection (c)(1)(C) or an agent of such person.

Unlike a provider who meets the subsection 512(a) safe harbor for passive transmission, retransmission, or temporary storage, a provider seeking to meet the requirements of the subsection 512(c) safe harbor (covering providers that store materials at the direction of users) must accommodate copyright holders' complaints about specific infringing material. Under paragraph 512(c)(2), the service provider must designate an agent to receive notifications of claimed infringement. Paragraph 512(c)(3) and subsection 512(g) provide detailed rules both for this notice and for the obligations of service providers once they receive the notice. Although subsection 512(d) (covering providers offering information location tools) does not contain a provision requiring designation of an agent to receive notifications, it refers back to the so-called "notice-and-takedown" regime of subsection 512(c). Courts have thus interpreted subsection 512(d) to apply the same rules to providers as 512(c) does. If the service provider complies with all of these requirements, it is exempt from any liability to the subscriber based on removal of the material. On the other hand, a provider can ignore these procedures and take its chances in court defending a claim for contributory copyright infringement.

Section 512 creates two other safe harbors for service providers. Subsections 512(b) and (e), respectively, limit the liability of service providers for caching information and the liability of nonprofit educational institutions who act as service providers.

Despite foreclosing monetary relief, section 512 does permit some forms of injunctive relief against service providers. A court can issue an order requiring any service provider to terminate the account of an identified subscriber "who is using the provider's service to engage in infringing activity." 17 U.S.C. § 512(j)(1)(A)(ii), (B)(i). A court can also restrain a service provider who does not fit into the subsection 512(a) safe harbor from providing access to infringing material "at a particular online site" on its network and order "such other injunctive relief as the court may consider necessary to prevent or restrain infringement of copyrighted material specified in the order." *Id.* § 512(j)(1)(A)(i), (iii).

Notes and Questions

1. Does *Netcom's* holding that a provider is not liable for direct infringement when a subscriber posts infringing material survive enactment of section 512 of the DMCA? In *ALS Scan v. RemarQ Communities, Inc.*, 239 F.3d 619, 622 (4th Cir. 2001), the U.S. Court of Appeals for the Fourth Circuit characterized the DMCA as a "codification" of *Netcom*, thus implying that a provider failing to satisfy the DMCA's requirements could not rely on *Netcom's* reasoning to defend against a claim of direct infringement. The same court, however, later clarified that, whether or not it qualifies for one of the DMCA's safe harbors, a provider is not liable for direct infringement when passively storing material at the direction of users, because "Congress intended the DMCA's safe harbor for ISPs to be a floor, not a ceiling, of protection." *CoStar v. LoopNet*, 373 F.3d 544, 555 (4th Cir. 2004).

2. What is the relationship between section 512 of the DMCA and the rules for contributory infringement and vicarious liability articulated by the district court in *Netcom*? Is there any circumstance under which a provider's conduct would satisfy the requirements for contributory infringement or vicarious liability, but still fit within the section 512 safe harbors? Put another way, with respect to contributory infringement and vicarious liability theories, does section 512 merely codify *Netcom*, or does it extend *Netcom*?

In this regard, consider the relationship between the subsection 512(a) and subsection 512(c) safe harbors: even if a provider meets the requirements for contributory infringement or vicarious liability and would thus fall outside of the subsection 512(c) safe harbor, it is not liable for monetary damages if it can qualify for the subsection 512(a) safe harbor. As a result, the question whether a service provider's actions can be characterized as providing "intermediate and transient storage of . . . material in the course of . . . transmitting, routing, or providing connections" under subsection 512(a) rather than providing "storage at the direction of the user of material that resides on a system or network controlled by or operated for the service provider" under subsection 512(c) is likely to be crucial. Suppose a provider makes a USENET feed available to its subscribers and stores files related to USENET postings for 14 days. Should a court assess the service provider's protection from liability under subsection 512(a) or subsection 512(c)?

One court to consider that question reasoned as follows:

Whether AOL functioned as a conduit service provider [i.e., qualified for the subsection 512(a) safe harbor] presents a pure question of law: was the fourteen day period during which AOL stored and retained the infringing material "transient" and "intermediate" within the meaning of § 512(a)?; was "no . . . copy . . . maintained on the system or network . . . for a longer period than is reasonably necessary for the transmission, routing, or provision of connections?" The district court appropriately answered these questions in the affirmative. In doing so, the court relied upon the legislative history indicating that Congress intended the relevant language of § 512(a) to codify the result of *Netcom* (provider that stored Usenet messages for 11 days not liable for direct infringement merely for "installing and maintaining a system whereby software automatically forwards messages received from subscribers onto the Usenet, and temporary stores copies on its system"), and to extend it to claims for secondary liability.

Ellison v. Robertson, 357 F.3d 1072, 1081 (9th Cir. 2004).

Is it fair to say that Congress sought to "extend" *Netcom*'s holding to claims for secondary liability? Does the *Ellison* court appropriately grapple with the question of whether or not 14 days "is a longer period than is reasonably necessary" for purposes of subsection 512(a)?

3. Reread subsection 512(c)(1). Apart from notification substantially complying with subsection 512(c)(3), what would give rise to "actual knowledge" that material is infringing and thereby remove a provider from the subsection 512(c) safe harbor? What would constitute "facts and circumstances from which infringing activity is apparent"? One court has held that, when a copyright holder fails to give notice of infringement under subsection 512(c)(3), the relevant inquiry is not "what a reasonable person would have deduced given all the circumstances." Rather, the question is "whether the service provider deliberately proceeded in the face of blatant factors of which it was aware." *Corbis Corp. v. Amazon.com*, 351 F. Supp. 2d 1090, 1108 (W.D. Wash. 2004). Does this focus on blatantly infringing activity strike an adequate balance between protecting copyright and preserving free speech interests?

4. With regard to the notice-and-take-down process contemplated in section 512, *when* should the notice be given? For example, assume a film's copyright holder sends a letter to an ISP, notifying it that all DVD copies of her film infringe her copyright. Nearly ten months later, an infringing copy is sold over the ISP's services. Did the letter provide sufficient notice to make the ISP liable for not subsequently policing the allegedly infringing sale? In a case raising this issue, a federal court rejected such a claim, noting that the DMCA places the burden *on the copyright owner* to monitor the Internet for potentially infringing sales and does not require ISPs to monitor their services or affirmatively seek facts indicating infringing activity. Permitting a notice in advance of any infringement would, according to the court, "allow a plaintiff to shift its burden to the service provider * * * contrary to the balance crafted by Congress." *Hendrickson v. Amazon.com, Inc.*, 298 F. Supp. 2d 914, 916 (C.D. Cal. 2003).

5. Assume that a copyright holder wrongfully claims that material stored by a subscriber on a service provider's system is infringing, and the service provider disables access to the material. How does section 512 alter the subscriber's remedies? If the copyright holder provides notice that it has filed suit, the service provider cannot restore the material without exposing itself to liability. Prior to section 512's passage, what legal procedures would a copyright holder have been required to go through to achieve the same result?

Note that, in this scenario, not only will the subscriber whose material was wrongly taken down not have a cause of action against the ISP; there might not even be a cause of action against the copyright holder who incorrectly claimed infringement. Section 512(f) provides that one who "knowingly materially misrepresents" that material or activity is infringing shall be liable for damages incurred by the alleged infringer as a result of a service provider "relying upon such misrepresentation in removing or disabling access to" the material. *See, e.g., Online Policy Group v. Diebold, Inc.*, 337 F. Supp. 2d 1195 (N.D. Cal. 2004) (concluding that manufacturer of electronic voting machine materially misrepresented that plaintiffs infringed copyright interest). But at least one court has held that a copyright holder with a good faith belief that infringement occurred is not liable under section 512(f), and that there is no duty to investigate whether that belief is accurate before making a take-down request. *See Rossi v. Motion Picture Ass'n of America*, 391 F.3d 1000, 1003 (9th Cir. 2004).

6. How might technology affect the notice-and-take-down process? Consider the Automated Copyright Notice System (ACNS), a program distributed to universities by the music industry. ACNS is designed to make it easier for university officials to send e-mail notifications to individual students who are identified as participating in illegal file-sharing. The program can also automatically choke off the students' access to peer-to-peer networks, while leaving other Internet services (such as e-mail) untouched. Nevertheless, although this technology may reduce delays in issuing the various notices required under section 512, it does nothing to relieve copyright holders of the initial burden of identifying the allegedly infringing user. Moreover, technology can also make the notice-and-take-down process more difficult. For example, if someone commits infringing activity on a wireless public network, there may be no way of identifying the individual user and therefore no way of issuing a notice. How, if at all, should the law adapt to these technological considerations?

3. Trademark Liability

Gucci America, Inc. v. Hall & Associates

United States District Court for the Southern District of New York, 2001
135 F. Supp. 2d 409

Plaintiff owns the trademark and trade name "GUCCI" which is utilized on and in connection with various articles of jewelry, fashion accessories, wearing apparel and related services (the "Gucci Trademark"). Mindspring, an Internet Service Provider ("ISP"), provides Web page hosting services to [defendant Denise] Hall, (at least) at the Uniform Resource Locator ("URL") www.goldhaus.com (the "goldhaus website"). By e-mail communications dated March 26, 1999, and March 27, 1999, Mindspring allegedly was twice notified by Plaintiff that Hall was using Mindspring's services to aid in acts of trademark infringement and unfair competition, including the advertising of jewelry on the goldhaus website which bore (and infringed) the Gucci Trademark. Plaintiff alleges that, despite the emails, Mindspring continued to permit Hall to use Mindspring's Internet services to infringe Plaintiff's trademark rights, with actual knowledge of, or in reckless disregard of, Plaintiff's rights and Hall's infringement. * * *

Plaintiff asserts claims against Mindspring for direct and contributory trademark infringement under Section 32(1) of the Trademark Act of 1946 (the "Lanham Act"), 15 U.S.C. § 1114(1), false designations of origin and false descriptions and representations under Section 43(a) of the Lanham Act, 15 U.S.C. § 1125(a), and trademark infringement and unfair competition under New York common law. Mindspring's instant motion [to dismiss] is premised upon two grounds: (i) that the Communications Decency Act of 1996, 47 U.S.C. § 230 ("Section 230"), "immunizes Mindspring from liability for information posted [on the goldhaus website] by [Hall]"; and (ii) that "Plaintiff's theory of trademark infringement is barred by the First Amendment." * * *

Section 230(c)(1) provides: "No provider or user of an interactive computer service shall be treated as the publisher or speaker of any information provided by another information content provider." 47 U.S.C. § 230(c)(1). Section 230(f)(2) defines "interactive computer service" as "any information service, system, or access software provider that provides or enables computer access by multiple users to a computer server, including specifically a service or system that provides access to the Internet and such systems operated or services offered by libraries or educational institutions." *Id.* § 230(f)(2). Section 230(f)(3) defines "information content provider" as "any person or entity that is responsible, in whole or in part, for the creation or development of information provided through the Internet or any other interactive computer service." *Id.* § 230(f)(3).

Plaintiff does not dispute that Mindspring, as an ISP, is an "interactive computer service." Moreover, the complaint clearly identifies Hall as the "information content provider." Rather, Plaintiff argues that Mindspring is not immune under § 230(c)(1) from Plaintiff's claims because of the language of Section 230(e)(2): "Nothing in this section shall be construed to limit or expand any law pertaining to intellectual property." 47 U.S.C. § 230(e)(2). * * *

Section 230(e)(2) unambiguously constrains the Court to construe Section 230(c)(1) in a manner that would neither "limit or expand any law pertaining to intellectual property." 47 U.S.C. § 230(e)(2). Thus, the inquiry involves the application of existing intellectual property law. Under existing intellectual property law, publishers may, under certain circumstances, be held liable for infringement. *See* 15 U.S.C. § 1114(2)(A)(B). Moreover, the United States Supreme Court has held, under the doctrine of contributory infringement, that "if a manufacturer or distributor . . . continues to supply its product to one whom it knows or has reason to know is engaging in trademark infringement," the manufacturer or distributor itself may held be liable for infringement. *Inwood Labs., Inc. v. Ives Labs., Inc.*, 456 U.S. 844, 854 (1982); *see also Religious Technology Ctr. v. Netcom On-Line Communication Servs.*, 907 F. Supp. 1361, 1375 (N.D. Cal. 1995) (holding that an ISP with knowledge of the infringement may be held liable for contributory copyright infringement). Immunizing Mindspring from Plaintiff's claims, therefore, would "limit" the laws pertaining to intellectual property in contravention of § 230(c)(2). The plain language of Section 230(e)(2) precludes Mindspring's claim of immunity. * * *

Although Mindspring recognizes the "appeal" of the Court's reading of Section 230(e)(2), Mindspring nevertheless argues that immunity from Plaintiff's claims "would not 'limit' any law pertaining to intellectual property, since liability for trademark infringement has never previously been imposed on an ISP in this situation." * * * The Court respectfully disagrees for the reason that Mindspring's reading is in conflict with the plain language of the statute. Mindspring argues that Section 230(e)(2) directs courts to leave "the state of the law . . . as it was when the law was enacted—neither 'limited' nor 'expanded.'" However, nowhere does Section 230 state that the laws to which it refers are, as Mindspring suggests, limited to the intellectual property laws as they existed in 1996. The Court declines to incorporate or read into the statute a temporal limit. * * *

Mindspring also argues that *Lockheed Martin Corp. v. Network Solutions, Inc.*, 985 F. Supp. 949 (C.D. Cal. 1997), *aff'd*, 194 F.3d 980 (9th Cir. 1999), "rejected the application of contributory [trademark] infringement in the Internet context." Plaintiff counters that *Lockheed Martin* held only that a "domain name registrar could not be held liable [for trademark infringement] because its involvement is limited to the *registration* of the domain name and not its *use* in commerce. . . ." "Indeed," argues Plaintiff, "*Lockheed Martin* contrasted the domain name registrar's role with that of ISPs and indicated that the latter may well be liable for contributory trademark infringement." The Court agrees that *Lockheed Martin* does not foreclose the possibility that ISPs may be liable for contributory trademark infringement:

> [Network Solutions, Inc.'s] role in the Internet is distinguishable from that of an Internet service provider whose computers provide the actual storage and communications for infringing material, and who therefore might be more accurately compared to the flea market vendors in [*Fonovisa Inc. v. Cherry Auction, Inc.*, 76 F.3d 259 (9th Cir. 1996)] and [*Hard Rock Cafe Licensing Corp. v. Concession Servs., Inc.*, 955 F.2d 1143 (7th Cir. 1992)].

985 F. Supp. at 962. * * *

Mindspring suggests that certain copyright law developments, for which "[t]here have been no comparable developments in the area of trademark law," support its contention that "immunizing Mindspring under Section 230 does not limit existing trademark law in any way." Specifically, Mindspring argues that the principles of *Religious Technology Ctr. v. Netcom On-Line Communication Servs., Inc.*, 907 F. Supp. 1361 (N.D. Cal. 1995) "were incorporated into statutory law when Congress adopted . . . the Digital Millennium Copyright Act [of 1998]" ("DMCA"). Mindspring concludes that Congress, having had the opportunity (when enacting the DMCA) to alter the extent to which ISPs may assert statutory immunity from trademark infringement, "has not done so." *Id.* at 10. The Court respectfully disagrees with Mindspring's conclusion and finds that Congress' enactment of the DMCA—pertaining only to copyright infringement—two years after Section 230 was passed, lends further support to the proposition that Section 230 does not automatically immunize ISPs from all intellectual property infringement claims. To find otherwise would render the immunities created by the DMCA from copyright infringement actions superfluous. * * *

Mindspring contends that Plaintiff "is advocating the adoption of a 'trademark plaintiff's veto,' in which an ISP would be held to strict [or notice-based] liability if it does not immediately censor speech that is the subject of a dispute," and that "[t]his theory of liability conflicts with the First Amendment because it would force ISPs, who are in no position to adjudicate conflicting claims, to restrict summarily online speech." * * *

The liability limitation afforded under the "innocent infringer" defense, contained in Section 32(2) of the Lanham Act, codified at 15 U.S.C. § 1114(2) ("Section 32(2)"), appears to detract from Mindspring's argument that Plaintiff's claims "conflict[] with the First Amendment." Section 32(2) provides in pertinent part:

> (2) Notwithstanding any other provision of this Act, the remedies given to the owner of a right infringed under this Act or to a person bringing an action under section 1125(a) or (d) of this title shall be limited as follows:
>
> > (A) Where an infringer or violator is engaged solely in the business of printing the mark or violating matter for others and establishes that he or she was an innocent infringer or innocent violator, the owner of the right infringed or person bringing the action under section 1125(a) of this title shall be entitled as against such infringer or violator only to an injunction against future printing.
> >
> > (B) Where the infringement or violation complained of is contained in or is part of paid advertising matter in a newspaper, magazine, or other similar periodical or in an electronic communication as defined in section 2510(12) of title 18, United States Code, the remedies of the owner of the right infringed or person bringing the action under section 1125(a) of this title as against the publisher or distributor of such newspaper, magazine, or other similar periodical or electronic communication shall be limited to an injunction against the presentation of such advertising matter in future issues of such newspapers, magazines, or other similar periodicals or in future transmissions of such electronic communications. The limitations of this subparagraph shall apply only to innocent infringers and innocent violators. . . .

15 U.S.C. § 1114(2)(A)-(B).

Section 32(2) limits trademark plaintiffs' remedies against printers and publishers or distributors "for others" of "electronic communication[s]" who are "innocent infringers" to (prospective) injunctions against future printings or transmissions of the infringing material. Although "[t]he phrase 'innocent infringer' is not defined in the statute," it has been construed to embrace the "actual malice" standard set forth in *New York Times v. Sullivan*, 376 U.S. 254 (1964), i.e. an infringer is "innocent" unless it acted either (1) with knowledge of the infringement or (2) with reckless disregard as to whether the material infringed the trademark owner's rights. *World Wrestling Fed'n v. Posters, Inc.*, 2000 WL 1409831, at *2, *3 (N.D. Ill. Sept. 26, 2000); *NBA Properties v. Untertainment Records LLC*, 1999 WL 335147, at *14 (S.D.N.Y. May 26, 1999). Under *Sullivan*, defamation plaintiffs who show "actual malice" may, in appropriate circumstances, recover damages without running afoul of the First Amendment. *See* 376 U.S. at 279-80. That trademark plaintiffs also must meet this "heightened standard" and show "actual malice" to recover damages, *NBA Properties*, 1999 WL 335147, at *13-*16, suggests that the innocent infringer defense satisfies the requirements of the First Amendment in the context of trademark infringement.

The strictures of the "innocent infringer defense" (and the corresponding requirement that plaintiffs demonstrate "knowledge" under the contributory infringement doctrine) undermines Mindspring's argument that accepting Plaintiff's claims would subject Mindspring to "strict liability" or "notice-based liability" for trademark infringement, thereby creating a "trademark plaintiff's veto." * * * Similarly, trademark plaintiffs bear a high burden in establishing "knowledge" of contributory infringement. The Court in *Lockheed Martin*, for example, held that a trademark owner's mere assertion that its domain name is infringed is insufficient to impute knowledge of infringement. 985 F. Supp. at 963. Moreover, while "uncertainty of infringement [is] relevant to the question of an alleged contributory infringer's knowledge[,] . . . . [a] trademark owner's demand letter is insufficient to resolve this inherent uncertainty." *Id.* at 964.

Notes and Questions

1. Is the *Gucci* court correct that the "innocent infringer" doctrine and the knowledge requirement for contributory infringement are sufficient to avoid creation of a "trademark plaintiff's veto"?

2. Should a trademark owner's demand letter be sufficient to trigger a service provider's "knowledge" of trademark infringement? To trigger a service provider's duty to investigate? Is the *Gucci* court's treatment of the knowledge issue consistent with the *Netcom* court's treatment of this issue in the copyright context?

3. Gucci's claim is based upon Mindspring's role in hosting an allegedly infringing website. Claims seeking to hold intermediaries liable on trademark theories also arise in another context. Recall the discussion in Chapter Two of the use of trademarked terms to attract traffic from a rival website. In addition to using metatags in its own code, a business trying to attract traffic may purchase from a search engine the right to have an advertisement for its site "keyed" to a trademarked term, such that a link to its site will appear prominently when a user searches for term. *See supra* p. 52, note 4.

A suit against the search engine will likely involve two distinct claims: a claim of direct infringement or dilution based on the search engine's conduct in keying advertisements to the trademarked term within its own system; and a claim of indirect infringement or dilution based on the theory that the search engine is responsible for infringing or dilutive conduct by the competitor—that is, the competitor's purchase of a right to have its website keyed to the trademarked term. In considering both claims, courts have focused on whether either keying advertisements or purchasing the right to have advertisements keyed constitutes "use" of a trademark. For discussion of the range of approaches to the "use" question, see *Rescuecom Corp. v. Google, Inc.*, __ F. Supp. 2d __, 2006 WL 2811711, at *3 (N.D.N.Y. Sep. 28, 2006); *see also 1-800 Contacts v. WhenU.com, Inc.*, 414 F.3d 400 (2d Cir. 2005) (concluding that internal use of trademark to trigger "pop-up" advertisement did not constitute "use" of trademark, but distinguishing conduct of search engines). If a court concludes that purchasing a keyword constitutes "use" of a trademark, does indirect liability for the search engine automatically follow?

4. You have now studied the indirect liability rules for intermediaries whose users transmit, store, or index material alleged to be defamatory, material alleged to infringe copyrights, and material alleged to infringe trademarks. What justifies the different treatment of service providers in each of these situations? In each situation, what justifies Congress's decision to alter or preserve the common law liability rules? What liability rule(s) would best balance the interests of those harmed by objectionable content and society's interest in preserving the Internet as "a forum for a true diversity of political discourse, unique opportunities for cultural development, and myriad avenues for intellectual activity"? 47 U.S.C. § 230(a)(3).

SECTION B. INTERMEDIARY CONTROL OF INFORMATION

Section A examined examined some of the rationales for and against imposing liability on service providers and other online intermediaries. Here, we consider a different consequence of the ubiquity of Internet intermediaries: that such intermediaries provide a useful point of access to a subscriber's identity, communications, and other information. How well do real-world protections for anonymity and privacy map onto the Internet?

1. Individual Identity and Anonymity

Courts have long recognized that the First Amendment protects one's right to speak anonymously. The government cannot ban anonymous communications entirely, and efforts to control such communications have proven extremely controversial. In *McIntyre v. Ohio Elections Commission*, 514 U.S. 334 (1995), for example, the Supreme Court invalidated an Ohio statute prohibiting the distribution of anonymous campaign literature. The Court reasoned that the state's asserted justification for the prohibition—to prevent election fraud—did not justify "indiscriminately outlawing" a category of speech. The Court discussed the value of anonymity as follows:

> "Anonymous pamphlets, leaflets, brochures and even books have played an important role in the progress of mankind." *Talley v. California*, 362 U.S. 60, 64 (1960). Great works of literature have

frequently been produced by authors writing under assumed names. Despite readers' curiosity and the public's interest in identifying the creator of a work of art, an author generally is free to decide whether or not to disclose his or her true identity. The decision in favor of anonymity may be motivated by fear of economic or official retaliation, by concern about social ostracism, or merely by a desire to preserve as much of one's privacy as possible. Whatever the motivation may be, at least in the field of literary endeavor, the interest in having anonymous works enter the marketplace of ideas unquestionably outweighs any public interest in requiring disclosure as a condition of entry. Accordingly, an author's decision to remain anonymous, like other decisions concerning omissions or additions to the content of a publication, is an aspect of the freedom of speech protected by the First Amendment.

The freedom to publish anonymously extends beyond the literary realm. * * * On occasion, quite apart from any threat of persecution, an advocate may believe her ideas will be more persuasive if her readers are unaware of her identity. Anonymity thereby provides a way for a writer who may be personally unpopular to ensure that readers will not prejudge her message simply because they do not like its proponent. Thus, even in the field of political rhetoric, where "the identity of the speaker is an important component of many attempts to persuade," *City of Ladue v. Gilleo*, 512 U.S. 43, 56 (1994) (footnote omitted), the most effective advocates have sometimes opted for anonymity. * * *

The right to remain anonymous may be abused when it shields fraudulent conduct. But political speech by its nature will sometimes have unpalatable consequences, and, in general, our society accords greater weight to the value of free speech than to the dangers of its misuse.

McIntyre, 514 U.S. at 341-43, 357.

The Internet facilitates anonymous (or at least pseudonymous) communication, and it is in part for this reason that courts and commentators view the medium as revolutionary: the Internet removes barriers to ordinary citizens' meaningful participation in public discourse. As one commentator has put it:

> Although it may be an overstatement to say that the speech of ordinary [citizens] "compete[s] equally with the speech of mainstream speakers in the marketplace of ideas,"[211] it is certainly true that ordinary [citizens] need no longer win approval of the mainstream media in order to be heard and that Internet discourse is more broadly inclusive than real-world discourse.

But the Internet not only removes barriers to speaking; it also removes barriers to being heard. In a now well-known New Yorker cartoon, a picture of a dog typing at a computer reads, "On the

---

211. American Civil Liberties Union v. Reno, 31 F. Supp. 2d 473, 476 (E.D. Pa. 1999).

Internet nobody knows you're a dog." The cartoon pithily encapsulates one of the chief attractions of online anonymity. Many participants in cyberspace discussions employ pseudonymous identities, and, even when a speaker chooses to reveal her real name, she may still be anonymous for all practical purposes. For good or ill, therefore, the audience must evaluate the speaker's ideas based on her words alone. This unique feature of Internet communications promises to make public debate in cyberspace less hierarchical and discriminatory than real-world debate to the extent that it disguises status indicators such as race, class, gender, ethnicity, and age, which allow elite speakers to dominate real-world discourse.

Lyrissa Barrett Lidsky, *Silencing John Doe: Defamation and Discourse in Cyberspace*, 49 Duke L.J. 855, 895-96 (2000).

This excerpt suggests that anonymous or pseudonymous communications are central to maintaining a robust and participatory discourse on the Internet. As in other contexts, however, both law and technology—and public and private actions—will determine the degree of anonymity or pseudonymity the Internet permits. Service providers, of course, can choose the architecture of their systems, and most service providers maintain records correlating a user's alias with his or her real identity. In this respect, anonymous and pseudonymous communications on the Internet differ significantly from real-world communications, for in most instances they will be traceable through a third party. A service provider's technical ability to identify its users means that the service provider's policies and practices, as shaped by legal rules, will have a tremendous effect on the degree of anonymity or pseudonymity users actually experience. In some circumstances, a provider can voluntarily disclose a user's identity. Moreover, government officials and private parties can seek to identify subscribers engaged in wrongdoing by compelling a service provider to release a subscriber's identity.

When faced with disputes pitting a user's claimed right to remain anonymous against the governments interest in deterring or punishing wrongful conduct, how should courts respond? Is it true, as the Supreme Court suggested in *McIntyre*, that society "accords greater weight to the value of free speech than to the dangers of its misuse," and that we must accept some abuse of the right to remain anonymous? Does the appropriate balance change depending on what sort of speech is at issue? The following materials consider these questions.

In re Subpoena Duces Tecum to America Online, Inc.

Circuit Court of Virginia, 2000
52 Va. Cir. 26, 2000 WL 1210372

Klein, J.

This matter is before the Court on America Online, Inc.'s ("AOL") Motion to Quash Subpoena seeking disclosure of identifying information for four AOL Internet service subscribers.

Plaintiff Anonymous Publicly Traded Company ("APTC") seeks to learn the identities of the subscribers so that it can properly name them as defendants in an action it has instituted in the state of Indiana. AOL asserts that the First Amendment rights of its subscribers preclude APTC from obtaining the relief it seeks in this Court. For the reasons set forth in this opinion, the Motion To Quash is denied.

I. BACKGROUND

APTC filed suit in Indiana, anonymously, under the pseudonym of APTC, against five individuals ("John Does") alleging that the John Does published in Internet chat rooms certain defamatory material misrepresentations and confidential material insider information, concerning APTC, "in breach of the fiduciary duties and contractual obligations owed to [APTC]." In the Indiana proceedings, APTC sought and obtained from the court an [an order requesting the assistance of the Virginia courts in issuing a subpoena to support APTC's ability to conduct discovery]. Pursuant to Va. Code § 8.01-411, the Clerk of this Court issued a [*subpoena duces tecum* ordering] America Online Inc. to produce any and all documents from which the identity of the four AOL subscribers could be ascertained. * * *

II. ANALYSIS

AOL contends that the *subpoena duces tecum* issued by the Clerk of this Court unreasonably impairs the First Amendment rights of the John Does to speak anonymously on the Internet and therefore should be quashed pursuant to [Virginia] Supreme Court Rule 4:9(c) * * * . [T]he legal standard to be applied when ruling on a motion to quash a subpoena under Rule 4:9(c) is whether the subpoena is (1) an unreasonable request in light of all the circumstances surrounding the subpoena (2) that produces an oppressive effect on the entity challenging the subpoena. * * *

It can not be seriously questioned that those who utilize the "chat rooms" and "message boards" of AOL do so with an expectation that the anonymity of their postings and communications generally will be protected. If AOL did not uphold the confidentiality of its subscribers, as it has contracted to do, absent extraordinary circumstances, one could reasonably predict that AOL subscribers would look to AOL's competitors for anonymity. As such, the *subpoena duces tecum* at issue potentially could have an oppressive effect on AOL. * * *

As this Court has determined that the subpoena can have an oppressive effect on AOL, the sole question remaining is whether the subject subpoena is unreasonable in light of all the surrounding circumstances. Ultimately, this Court's ruling on the Motion To Quash must be governed by a determination of whether the issuance of the *subpoena duces tecum* and the potential loss of the anonymity of the John Does, would constitute an unreasonable intrusion on their First Amendment rights. * * * It is beyond question that thousands, perhaps millions, of people communicating by way of the Internet do so with a "desire to preserve as much of [their] privacy as possible." *McIntyre v. Ohio Elections Comm'n*, 514 U.S. 334, 342 (1995). * * * To fail to recognize that the First Amendment right to speak anonymously should be extended to communications on the Internet would require this Court to ignore either United States Supreme Court precedent or the realities of speech in the twenty-first century. This Court declines to do either and holds that the right to communicate anonymously on the Internet falls within the scope of the First Amendment's protections.

As AOL conceded at oral argument, however, the right to speak anonymously is not absolute. In that the Internet provides a virtually unlimited, inexpensive, and almost immediate means of communication with tens, if not hundreds, of millions of people, the dangers of its misuse cannot be ignored. The protection of the right to communicate anonymously must be balanced against the need to assure that those persons who choose to abuse the opportunities presented by this medium can be made to answer for such transgressions. Those who suffer damages as a result of tortious or other actionable communications on the Internet should be able to seek appropriate redress by preventing the wrongdoers from hiding behind an illusory shield of purported First Amendment rights. APTC's Indiana Complaint For Injunctive Relief and Damages alleges that its current and/or former employees have made defamatory material misrepresentations concerning APTC. It further alleges that the John Does have published confidential material information about APTC, in violation of the John Does' fiduciary and contractual duties to APTC, that "will cause [APTC] to continue to suffer immediate and irreparable injury, loss and damages including potentially adversely affecting the value of its publicly traded stock." * * *

[T]his Court holds that, when a subpoena is challenged under a rule akin to Virginia Supreme Court Rule 4:9(c), a court should only order a non-party, Internet service provider to provide information concerning the identity of a subscriber (1) when the court is satisfied by the pleadings or evidence supplied to that court (2) that the party requesting the subpoena has a legitimate, good faith basis to contend that it may be the victim of conduct actionable in the jurisdiction where suit was filed and (3) the subpoenaed identity information is centrally needed to advance that claim. A review of the Indiana pleadings and the subject Internet postings satisfies this Court that all three prongs of the above-stated test have been satisfied as to the identities of the subscribers utilizing the four e-mail addresses in question.

In his December 22, 1999, correspondence to the Court, counsel for AOL argued that the methodology utilized by APTC in obtaining the AOL e-mail addresses in question is far from foolproof. This Court recognizes that the methodology may be less than totally certain and that some of the postings may turn out to be from persons who owe no fiduciary or contractual duty to APTC. Nonetheless, this Court finds that the compelling state interest in protecting companies such as APTC from the potentially severe consequences that could easily flow from actionable communications on the information superhighway significantly outweigh the limited intrusion on the First Amendment rights of any innocent subscribers. * * * Accordingly, AOL's Motion to Quash is denied in its entirety.

Doe v. 2TheMart.com Inc.

United States District Court for the Western District of Washington, 2001
140 F. Supp. 2d 1088

ZILLY, District Judge.

This matter comes before the Court on the motion of J. Doe (Doe) to proceed under a pseudonym and to quash a subpoena issued [on behalf of] 2TheMart.com (TMRT) to a local internet service provider, Silicon Investor/InfoSpace, Inc. (InfoSpace). The motion raises important First Amendment issues regarding Doe's right to speak anonymously on the Internet and to proceed in this Court using a pseudonym in order to protect that right. * * *

FACTUAL BACKGROUND

There is a federal court lawsuit pending in the Central District of California in which the shareholders of TMRT have brought a shareholder derivative class action against the company and its officers and directors alleging fraud on the market. In that litigation, the defendants have asserted as an affirmative defense that no act or omission by the defendants caused the plaintiffs' injury. By subpoena, TMRT seeks to obtain the identity of twenty-three speakers who have participated anonymously on Internet message boards operated by InfoSpace. That subpoena is the subject of the present motion to quash.

InfoSpace is a Seattle based Internet company that operates a website called "Silicon Investor." The Silicon Investor site contains a series of electronic bulletin boards, and some of these bulletin boards are devoted to specific publically traded companies. InfoSpace users can freely post and exchange messages on these boards. Many do so using Internet pseudonyms, the often fanciful names that people choose for themselves when interacting on the Internet. By using a pseudonym, a person who posts or responds to a message on an Internet bulletin board maintains anonymity.

One of the Internet bulletin boards on the Silicon Investor website is specifically devoted to TMRT. * * * Some of the messages posted on the TMRT site have been less than flattering to the company. In fact, some have been downright nasty. For example, a user calling himself "Truthseeker" posted a message stating "TMRT is a Ponzi scam that Charles Ponzi would be proud of. . . . The company's CEO, Magliarditi, has defrauded employees in the past. The company's other large shareholder, Rebeil, defrauded customers in the past." Another poster named "Cuemaster" indicated that "they were dumped by their accountants . . . these guys are friggin liars . . . why haven't they told the public this yet??? Liars and criminals!!!!!" Another user, not identified in the exhibits, wrote "Lying, cheating, thieving, stealing, lowlife criminals!!!!" Other postings advised TMRT investors to sell their stock. "Look out below!!!! This stock has had it . . . get short or sell your position now while you still can." "They [TMRT] are not building anything, except extensions on their homes . . . bail out now."

TMRT, the defendant in the California lawsuit, [caused the present subpoena to be issued] to InfoSpace pursuant to Fed. R. Civ. P. 45(a)(2). The subpoena seeks, among other things, "[a]ll identifying information and documents, including, but not limited to, computerized or computer stored records and logs, electronic mail (E-mail), and postings on your online message boards," concerning a list of twenty-three InfoSpace users, including Truthseeker, Cuemaster, and the current J. Doe, who used the pseudonym NoGuano. These users have posted messages on the TMRT bulletin board or have communicated via the Internet with users who have posted such messages. The subpoena would require InfoSpace to disclose the subscriber information for these twenty-three users, thereby stripping them of their Internet anonymity.

InfoSpace notified these users by e-mail that it had received the subpoena, and gave them time to file a motion to quash. One such user who used the Internet pseudonym NoGuano now seeks to quash the subpoena.

NoGuano alleges that enforcement of the subpoena would violate his or her First Amendment right to speak anonymously. * * *

DISCUSSION

* * * The right to speak anonymously extends to speech via the Internet. Internet anonymity facilitates the rich, diverse, and far ranging exchange of ideas. The "ability to speak one's mind" on the Internet "without the burden of the other party knowing all the facts about one's identity can foster open communication and robust debate." *Columbia Ins. Co. v. Seescandy.Com*, 185 F.R.D. 573, 578 (N.D. Cal. 1999). People who have committed no wrongdoing should be free to participate in online forums without fear that their identity will be exposed under the authority of the court. *Id.*

When speech touches on matters of public political life, such as debate over the qualifications of candidates, discussion of governmental or political affairs, discussion of political campaigns, and advocacy of controversial points of view, such speech has been described as the "core" or "essence" of the First Amendment. *See McIntyre v. Ohio Elections Comm'n*, 514 U.S. 334, 346-47 (1995). Governmental restrictions on such speech are entitled to "exacting scrutiny," and are upheld only where they are "narrowly tailored to serve an overriding state interest." *Id.* at 347. However, even non-core speech is entitled to First Amendment protection. "First Amendment protections are not confined to 'the exposition of ideas[.]'" *Id.* at 346. Unlike the speech at issue in [cases such as *McIntyre*], the speech here is not entitled to "exacting scrutiny," but to normal strict scrutiny analysis.

In support of its subpoena request, TMRT argues that the right to speak anonymously does not create any corresponding right to remain anonymous after speech. In support of this contention, TMRT cites only to *Buckley v. American Const'l Law Found.*, 525 U.S. 182 (1999). TMRT argues that in *Buckley*, while the Court struck down a requirement that petition circulators wear identification badges when soliciting signatures, the Court upheld a provision of the same statute that required circulators to execute an identifying affidavit when they submitted the collected signatures to the state for counting. However, the Court's reasoning in *Buckley* does not support the contention that there is no First Amendment right to remain anonymous. It merely establishes that in the context of the submission of initiative petitions to the State, the State's enforcement interest outweighs the circulator's First Amendment protections. The right to speak anonymously is therefore not absolute. However, this right would be of little practical value if, as TMRT urges, there was no concomitant right to remain anonymous after the speech is concluded.

B.   *Applicable Legal Standard*

The free exchange of ideas on the Internet is driven in large part by the ability of Internet users to communicate anonymously. If Internet users could be stripped of that anonymity by a civil subpoena enforced under the liberal rules of civil discovery, this would have a significant chilling effect on Internet communications and thus on basic First Amendment rights. Therefore, discovery requests seeking to identify anonymous Internet users must be subjected to careful scrutiny by the courts.

As InfoSpace has urged, "[u]nmeritorious attempts to unmask the identities of online speakers . . . have a chilling effect on" Internet speech. The "potential chilling effect imposed by the unmasking of anonymous speakers would diminish if litigants first were required to make a showing in court of their need for the identifying information."   "[R]equiring litigants to make such a showing would allow [the Internet] to thrive as a forum for speakers to express their views on topics of public concern."   InfoSpace and NoGuano have accordingly urged this Court to "adopt a balancing test requiring litigants to demonstrate . . . that their need for identity information outweighs anonymous online speakers' First Amendment rights[.]" *Id.*

In the context of a civil subpoena issued pursuant to Fed. R. Civ. P. 45, this Court must determine when and under what circumstances a civil litigant will be permitted to obtain the identity of persons who have exercised their First Amendment right to speak anonymously. * * * [C]ourts that have addressed related issues have used balancing tests to decide when to protect an individual's First Amendment rights. * * * The courts in *Seescandy.Com* and *In re Subpoena Duces Tecum to America Online, Inc.*, 2000 WL 1210372 (Va. Cir. Ct. 2000) * * * required a showing of, at least, a good faith basis for bringing the lawsuit, and both required some showing of the compelling need for the discovery sought. In both cases, the need for the information was especially great because the information sought concerned J. Doe *defendants*. Without the identifying information, the litigation against those defendants could not have continued.

The standard for disclosing the identity of a non-party *witness* must be higher than that articulated in *Seescandy.Com* and *America Online, Inc.* When the anonymous Internet user is not a party to the case, the litigation can go forward without the disclosure of their identity. Therefore, non-party disclosure is only appropriate in the exceptional case where the compelling need for the discovery sought outweighs the First Amendment rights of the anonymous speaker.

[handwritten marginalia: standard for evaluating requests for ID of users]

Accordingly, this Court adopts the following standard for evaluating a civil subpoena that seeks the identity of an anonymous Internet user who is not a party to the underlying litigation. The Court will consider four factors in determining whether the subpoena should issue. These are whether: (1) the subpoena seeking the information was issued in good faith and not for any improper purpose, (2) the information sought relates to a core claim or defense, (3) the identifying information is directly and materially relevant to that claim or defense, and (4) information sufficient to establish or to disprove that claim or defense is unavailable from any other source. * * *

C. *Analysis of the Present Motion*

[The court concluded that the subpoena was not issued in bad faith, but was extremely broad; and that the information sought did not relate to a core claim or defense. Turning to whether the identifying information was directly and materially relevant to a core defense, the court reasoned as follows.]

TMRT has failed to demonstrate that the identity of the Internet users is directly and materially relevant to a core defense. These Internet users are not parties to the case and have not been named as defendants as to any claim, cross-claim or third-party claim. Therefore, unlike in *Seescandy.Com* and *America Online, Inc.*, their identity is not needed to allow the litigation to proceed.

According to the pleadings, the Internet user known as NoGuano has never posted messages on Silicon Investor's TMRT message board. At oral argument, TMRT's counsel conceded this point but stated that NoGuano's information was sought because he had "communicated" via the Internet with Silicon Investor posters such as Truthseeker. Given that NoGuano admittedly posted no public statements on the TMRT site, there is no basis to conclude that the identity of NoGuano and others similarly situated is directly and materially relevant to TMRT's defense.

As to the Internet users such as Truthseeker and Cuemaster who posted messages on the TMRT bulletin board, TMRT has failed to demonstrate that their identities are directly and materially relevant to a core defense. TMRT argues that the Internet postings caused a drop in TMRT's stock price. However, what was said in these postings is a matter of public record, and the identity of the anonymous posters had no effect on investors. If these messages did influence the stock price, they did so without *anyone* knowing the identity of the speakers.

TMRT speculates that the users of the InfoSpace website may have been engaged in stock manipulation in violation of federal securities law. TMRT indicates that it intends to compare the names of the InfoSpace users with the names of individuals who traded TMRT stock during the same period to determine whether any illegal stock manipulation occurred. However, TMRT's innuendos of stock manipulation do not suffice to overcome the First Amendment rights of the Internet users. Those rights cannot be nullified by an unsupported allegation of wrongdoing raised by the party seeking the information. * * *

[Finally, the court concluded that the messages themselves would be sufficient to establish TMRT's defense, "without encroaching on the First Amendment rights of internet users."]

TMRT has failed to demonstrate that the identify of these Internet users is directly and materially relevant to a core defense in the underlying securities litigation. Accordingly, Doe's motion to quash the subpoena is GRANTED.

Notes and Questions

1. In the *AOL* case, should the company seeking disclosure of the subscribers' identifying information have been able to proceed anonymously in doing so? AOL initially objected to the subpoena in part because APTC had failed to identify its true name in the Indiana proceedings. AOL conceded that it had complied with hundreds of similar subpoenas issued by the Virginia courts when it had been satisfied that the party seeking the information established a prima facie claim that it was the victim of tortious conduct and that the information was needed to advance the claim.

In permitting APTC to proceed, the Virginia circuit court reasoned that it was appropriate to recognize under principles of comity the Indiana court's determination that APTC should be able to engage in discovery without disclosing its name. After the Virginia circuit court denied AOL's motion to quash, AOL appealed. The Virginia Supreme Court concluded that the circuit court had abused its discretion in permitting APTC to avail itself of the coercive powers of the Virginia courts while remaining anonymous, because APTC had failed to identify the "degree and nature of the potential economic harm" it would suffer by revealing its identity. *America Online, Inc. v. Anonymous Publicly Traded Co.*, 542 S.E.2d 377 (Va. 2001). The court therefore vacated the circuit court's order denying AOL's motion to quash and remanded for further proceedings. The Virginia Supreme Court did not pass on the propriety or application of the circuit court's balancing test.

2. AOL raises the concern that the subpoena will cause it to reveal the identities of innocent subscribers owing no fiduciary or contractual duty to APTC. Does the court give adequate weight to the First Amendment interests of such subscribers? If not, how could it have done so?

3. The *TMRT* court emphasized that the subpoena in that case sought disclosure of witnesses' identities, not a defendant's identity. Should that distinction matter? What are the differences between the *AOL* and *TMRT* tests? Which test, if either, should prevail? For cases applying tests that appear closer to the *TMRT* test than to the *AOL test*, see, e.g., *Dendrite Int'l v. Doe*, 775 A.2d 756 (N.J. App. Div. 2001) (refusing to order disclosure of identity where plaintiff failed to show that allegedly defamatory statements caused harm); *Polito v. AOL Time Warner*, No. Civ.A. 03CV3218, 2004 WL 3768897 (Ct. Com. Pl. Pa. Jan. 28, 2004) (ordering disclosure of identity where plaintiff stated cognizable claim under Pennsylvania law and demonstrated centrality and necessity of obtaining identity).

4. Should a balancing test of the sort applied by the *AOL* or *TMRT* courts also apply where a defendant is claimed not to have posted allegedly defamatory speech, but rather to have engaged in copyright infringement? The following materials consider that question.

Earlier in this chapter, we discussed the structure and application of section 512 of the Digital Millennium Copyright Act, which insulates service providers from certain types of liability for transmitting, storing, or indexing infringing material. *See supra* p. 520. Subsection 512(h) of the DMCA, set forth below, permits a copyright owner to obtain a subpoena to compel a service provider to reveal the identity of a customer alleged to be infringing the owner's copyright.

Subsection 512(h) of the Digital Millennium Copyright Act

17 U.S.C. § 512

§ 512. Limitations on liability relating to material online

* * *

(h) Subpoena To Identify Infringer.—

(1) Request.—A copyright owner or a person authorized to act on the owner's behalf may request the clerk of any United States district court to issue a subpoena to a service provider for identification of an alleged infringer in accordance with this subsection.

(2) Contents of request.—The request may be made by filing with the clerk—

(A) a copy of a notification described in subsection (c)(3)(A) [*see supra* p. 521];

(B) a proposed subpoena; and

(C) a sworn declaration to the effect that the purpose for which the subpoena is sought is to obtain the identity of an alleged infringer and that such information will only be used for the purpose of protecting rights under this title.

(3) Contents of subpoena.—The subpoena shall authorize and order the service provider receiving the notification and the subpoena to expeditiously disclose to the copyright owner or person authorized by the copyright owner information sufficient to identify the alleged infringer of the material described in the notification to the extent such information is available to the service provider.

(4) Basis for granting subpoena.—If the notification filed satisfies the provisions of subsection (c)(3)(A), the proposed subpoena is in proper form, and the accompanying declaration is properly executed, the clerk shall expeditiously issue and sign the proposed subpoena and return it to the requester for delivery to the service provider.

(5) Actions of service provider receiving subpoena.—Upon receipt of the issued subpoena, either accompanying or subsequent to the receipt of a notification described in subsection (c)(3)(A), the service provider shall expeditiously disclose to the copyright owner or person

authorized by the copyright owner the information required by the subpoena, notwithstanding any other provision of law and regardless of whether the service provider responds to the notification.

(6) Rules applicable to subpoena.—Unless otherwise provided by this section or by applicable rules of the court, the procedure for issuance and delivery of the subpoena, and the remedies for noncompliance with the subpoena, shall be governed to the greatest extent practicable by those provisions of the Federal Rules of Civil Procedure governing the issuance, service, and enforcement of a subpoena duces tecum.

Does subsection 512(h) apply to *all* service providers, or merely those that store or index material on behalf of their users? Note that subsection 512(h) requires the filing of the notification required by subparagraph 512(c)(3)(A), which presumes that a copyright holder can provide "information reasonably sufficient to permit the service provider to locate the material" and disable access to it. When a service provider merely acts as a passive conduit for ˏthe transmission of content, can it meet this requirement? Consider the following case.

Recording Industry Ass'n of Am., Inc. v. Verizon Internet Servs., Inc.

United States Court of Appeals for the District of Columbia Circuit, 2003
351 F.3d 1229

GINSBURG, Chief Judge:

This case concerns the Recording Industry Association of America's use of the subpoena provision of the Digital Millennium Copyright Act, 17 U.S.C. § 512(h), to identify internet users the RIAA believes are infringing the copyrights of its members. The RIAA served two subpoenas upon Verizon Internet Services in order to discover the names of two Verizon subscribers who appeared to be trading large numbers of .mp3 files of copyrighted music via "peer-to-peer" (P2P) file sharing programs, such as KaZaA. Verizon refused to comply with the subpoenas on various legal grounds. * * *

I. BACKGROUND

Individuals with a personal computer and access to the internet began to offer digital copies of recordings for download by other users, an activity known as file sharing, in the late 1990's using a program called Napster. Although recording companies and music publishers successfully obtained an injunction against Napster's facilitating the sharing of files containing copyrighted recordings, millions of people in the United States and around the world continue to share digital .mp3 files of copyrighted recordings using P2P computer programs such as KaZaA, Morpheus, Grokster, and eDonkey. Unlike Napster, which relied upon a centralized communication architecture to identify the .mp3 files available for download, the current generation of P2P file sharing programs allow an internet user to search directly the .mp3 file libraries of other users; no web site is involved. To date, owners of copyrights have not been able to stop the use of these decentralized programs.

The RIAA now has begun to direct its anti-infringement efforts against individual users of P2P file sharing programs. In order to pursue apparent infringers the RIAA needs to be able to identify the individuals who are sharing and trading files using P2P programs. The RIAA can readily obtain the screen name of an individual user, and using the Internet Protocol (IP) address associated with that screen name, can trace the user to his ISP. Only the ISP, however, can link the IP address used to access a P2P program with the name and address of a person—the ISP's customer—who can then be contacted or, if need be, sued by the RIAA.

The RIAA has used the subpoena provisions of § 512(h) of the Digital Millennium Copyright Act (DMCA) to compel ISPs to disclose the names of subscribers whom the RIAA has reason to believe are infringing its members' copyrights. Some ISPs have complied with the RIAA's § 512(h) subpoenas and identified the names of the subscribers sought by the RIAA. The RIAA has sent letters to and filed lawsuits against several hundred such individuals, each of whom allegedly made available for download by other users hundreds or in some cases even thousands of .mp3 files of copyrighted recordings. Verizon refused to comply with and instead has challenged the validity of the two § 512(h) subpoenas it has received.

A copyright owner (or its agent, such as the RIAA) must file three items along with its request that the Clerk of a district court issue a subpoena: (1) a "notification of claimed infringement" identifying the copyrighted work(s) claimed to have been infringed and the infringing material or activity, and providing information reasonably sufficient for the ISP to locate the material, all as further specified in § 512(c)(3)(A); (2) the proposed subpoena directed to the ISP; and (3) a sworn declaration that the purpose of the subpoena is "to obtain the identity of an alleged infringer and that such information will only be used for the purpose of protecting" rights under the copyright laws of the United States. 17 U.S.C. §§ 512(h)(2)(A)-(C). If the copyright owner's request contains all three items, then the Clerk "shall expeditiously issue and sign the proposed subpoena and return it to the requester for delivery to the [ISP]." 17 U.S.C. § 512(h)(4). Upon receipt of the subpoena the ISP is "authorize[d] and order[ed]" to disclose to the copyright owner the identity of the alleged infringer. See 17 U.S.C. §§ 512(h)(3), (5). * * *

On July 24, 2002 the RIAA served Verizon with a subpoena issued pursuant to § 512(h), seeking the identity of a subscriber whom the RIAA believed to be engaged in infringing activity. * * * When Verizon refused to disclose the name of its subscriber, the RIAA filed a motion to compel production pursuant to Federal Rule of Civil Procedure 45(c)(2)(B) and § 512(h)(6) of the Act. In opposition to that motion, Verizon argued § 512(h) does not apply to an ISP acting merely as a conduit for an individual using a P2P file sharing program to exchange files. The district court rejected Verizon's argument based upon "the language and structure of the statute, as confirmed by the purpose and history of the legislation," and ordered Verizon to disclose to the RIAA the name of its subscriber.

The RIAA then obtained another § 512(h) subpoena directed to Verizon. This time Verizon moved to quash the subpoena, arguing that the district court, acting through the Clerk, lacked jurisdiction under Article III to issue the subpoena and in the alternative that § 512(h) violates the First Amendment. The district court rejected Verizon's constitutional arguments, denied the motion to quash, and again ordered Verizon to disclose the identity of its subscriber. * * *

II. ANALYSIS

* * * The issue is whether § 512(h) applies to an ISP acting only as a conduit for data transferred between two internet users, such as persons sending and receiving e-mail or, as in this case, sharing P2P files. Verizon contends § 512(h) does not authorize the issuance of a subpoena to an ISP that transmits infringing material but does not store any such material on its servers. The RIAA argues § 512(h) on its face authorizes the issuance of a subpoena to an "[internet] service provider" without regard to whether the ISP is acting as a conduit for user-directed communications. We conclude from both the terms of § 512(h) and the overall structure of § 512 that, as Verizon contends, a subpoena may be issued only to an ISP engaged in storing on its servers material that is infringing or the subject of infringing activity.

A. *Subsection 512(h) by its Terms*

* * * Verizon's statutory arguments address the meaning of and interaction between §§ 512(h) and 512(a)-(d). Having already discussed the general requirements of § 512(h), we now introduce §§ 512(a)-(d).

Section 512 creates four safe harbors, each of which immunizes ISPs from liability for copyright infringement under certain highly specified conditions. Subsection 512(a), entitled "Transitory digital network communications," provides a safe harbor "for infringement of copyright by reason of the [ISP's] transmitting, routing, or providing connections for" infringing material, subject to certain conditions, including that the transmission is initiated and directed by an internet user. Subsection 512(b), "System caching," provides immunity from liability "for infringement of copyright by reason of the intermediate and temporary storage of material on a system or network controlled or operated by or for the [ISP]," as long as certain conditions regarding the transmission and retrieval of the material created by the ISP are met. Subsection 512(c), "Information residing on systems or networks at the direction of users," creates a safe harbor from liability "for infringement of copyright by reason of the storage at the direction of a user of material that resides on a system or network controlled or operated by or for the service provider," as long as the ISP meets certain conditions regarding its lack of knowledge concerning, financial benefit from, and expeditious efforts to remove or deny access to, material that is infringing or that is claimed to be the subject of infringing activity. Finally, § 512(d), "Information location tools," provides a safe harbor from liability "for infringement of copyright by reason of the provider referring or linking users to an online location containing infringing material or infringing activity, by using information location tools" such as "a directory, index, reference, pointer, or hypertext link," subject to the same conditions as in §§ 512(c)(1)(A)-(C).

Notably present in §§ 512(b)-(d), and notably absent from § 512(a), is the so-called notice and take-down provision. It makes a condition of the ISP's protection from liability for copyright infringement that "upon notification of claimed infringement as described in [§ 512](c)(3)," the ISP "responds expeditiously to remove, or disable access to, the material that is claimed to be infringing." See 17 U.S.C. §§ 512(b)(2)(E), 512(c)(1)(C), and 512(d)(3).

Verizon argues that § 512(h) by its terms precludes the Clerk of Court from issuing a subpoena to an ISP acting as a conduit for P2P communications because a § 512(h) subpoena request cannot meet the requirement in § 512(h)(2)(A) that a proposed subpoena contain "a copy of a notification [of claimed infringement, as] described in [§ 512](c)(3)(A)." In particular, Verizon maintains the two subpoenas obtained by the RIAA fail to meet the requirements of § 512(c)(3)(A)(iii) in that they do not—because Verizon is not storing the infringing material on its server—and can not, identify material "to be removed or access to which is to be disabled" by Verizon. Here Verizon points out that § 512(h)(4) makes satisfaction of the notification requirement of § 512(c)(3)(A) a condition precedent to issuance of a subpoena: "If the notification filed satisfies the provisions of [§ 512](c)(3)(A)" and the other content requirements of § 512(h)(2) are met, then "the clerk shall expeditiously issue and sign the proposed subpoena . . . for delivery" to the ISP.

Infringing material obtained or distributed via P2P file sharing is located in the computer (or in an off-line storage device, such as a compact disc) of an individual user. No matter what information the copyright owner may provide, the ISP can neither "remove" nor "disable access to" the infringing material because that material is not stored on the ISP's servers. Verizon can not remove or disable one user's access to infringing material resident on another user's computer because Verizon does not control the content on its subscribers' computers.

The RIAA contends an ISP can indeed "disable access" to infringing material by terminating the offending subscriber's internet account. This argument is undone by the terms of the Act, however. As Verizon notes, the Congress considered disabling an individual's access to infringing material and disabling access to the internet to be different remedies for the protection of copyright owners, the former blocking access to the infringing material on the offender's computer and the latter more broadly blocking the offender's access to the internet (at least via his chosen ISP). Compare 17 U.S.C. § 512(j)(1)(A)(i) (authorizing injunction restraining ISP "from providing access to infringing material") with 17 U.S.C. § 512(j)(1)(A)(ii) (authorizing injunction restraining ISP "from providing access to a subscriber or account holder . . . who is engaging in infringing activity . . . by terminating the accounts of the subscriber or account holder"). These distinct statutory remedies establish that terminating a subscriber's account is not the same as removing or disabling access by others to the infringing material resident on the subscriber's computer.

The RIAA points out that even if, with respect to an ISP functioning as a conduit for user-directed communications, a copyright owner cannot satisfy the requirement of § 512(c)(3)(A)(iii) by identifying material to be removed by the ISP, a notification is effective under § 512(c)(3)(A) if it "includes substantially" the required information; that standard is satisfied, the RIAA maintains, because the ISP can identify the infringer based upon the information provided by the copyright owner pursuant to §§ 512(c)(3)(A)(i)- (ii) and (iv)-(vi). According to the RIAA, the purpose of § 512(h) being to identify infringers, a notice should be deemed sufficient so long as the ISP can identify the infringer from the IP address in the subpoena.

Nothing in the Act itself says how we should determine whether a notification "includes substantially" all the required information; both the Senate and House Reports, however, state the term means only that "technical errors . . . such as misspelling a name" or "supplying an outdated area code" will not render ineffective an otherwise complete § 512(c)(3)(A) notification. S. Rep. No. 105-190, at 47 (1998); H.R. Rep. No. 105-551 (II), at 56 (1998). Clearly, however, the defect in the RIAA's notification is not a mere technical error; nor could it be thought "insubstantial" even under a more forgiving standard. The RIAA's notification identifies absolutely no material Verizon could remove or access to which it could disable, which indicates to us that § 512(c)(3)(A) concerns means of infringement other than P2P file sharing. * * *

In sum, we agree with Verizon that § 512(h) does not by its terms authorize the subpoenas issued here. A § 512(h) subpoena simply cannot meet the notice requirement of § 512(c)(3)(A)(iii).

B. *Structure*

Verizon also argues the subpoena provision, § 512(h), relates uniquely to the safe harbor in § 512(c) for ISPs engaged in storing copyrighted material and does not apply to the transmitting function addressed by the safe harbor in § 512(a). Verizon's claim is based upon the "three separate cross-references" in § 512(h) to the notification described in § 512(c)(3)(A). First, as we have seen, § 512(h)(2)(A) requires the copyright owner to file, along with its request for a subpoena, the notification described in § 512(c)(3)(A). Second, and again as we have seen, § 512(h)(4) requires that the notification satisfy "the provisions of [§ 512](c)(3)(A)" as a condition precedent to the Clerk's issuing the requested subpoena. Third, § 512(h)(5) conditions the ISP's obligation to identify the alleged infringer upon "receipt of a notification described in [§ 512](c)(3)(A)." We agree that the presence in § 512(h) of three separate references to § 512(c) and the absence of any reference to § 512(a) suggests the subpoena power of § 512(h) applies only to ISPs engaged in storing copyrighted material and not to those engaged solely in transmitting it on behalf of others.

As the RIAA points out in response, however, because §§ 512(b) and (d) also require a copyright owner to provide a "notification . . . as described in [§ 512](c)(3)," the cross-references to § 512(c)(3)(A) in § 512(h) can not confine the operation of § 512(h) solely to the functions described in § 512(c), but must also include, at a minimum, the functions described in §§ 512(b) and (d). Therefore, according to the RIAA, because Verizon is mistaken in stating that "the take-down notice described in [§ 512](c)(3)(A) . . . applies exclusively to the particular functions described in [§ 512](c) of the statute," the subpoena power in § 512(h) is not linked exclusively to § 512(c) but rather applies to all the ISP functions, wherever they may be described in §§ 512(a)-(d).

Although the RIAA's conclusion is a non-sequitur with respect to § 512(a), we agree with the RIAA that Verizon overreaches by claiming the notification described in § 512(c)(3)(A) applies only to the functions identified in § 512(c). As Verizon correctly notes, however, the ISP activities described in §§ 512(b) and (d) are storage functions. As such, they are, like the ISP activities described in § 512(c) and unlike the transmission functions listed in § 512(a), susceptible to the notice and take down regime of §§ 512(b)-(d), of which the subpoena power of § 512(h) is an integral part. We think it clear, therefore, that the cross-references to § 512(c)(3) in §§ 512(b)-(d) demonstrate that § 512(h) applies to an ISP storing infringing material on its servers in any capacity—whether as a temporary cache of a web page created by the ISP per § 512(b), as a web site stored on the ISP's server per § 512(c), or as an information locating tool hosted by the ISP per § 512(d)—and does not apply to an ISP routing infringing material to or from a personal computer owned and used by a subscriber.

The storage activities described in the safe harbors of §§ 512(b)-(d) are subject to § 512(c)(3), including the notification described in § 512(c)(3)(A). By contrast, as we have already seen, an ISP performing a function described in § 512(a), such as transmitting e-mails, instant messages, or files sent by an internet user from his computer to that of another internet user, cannot be sent an effective § 512(c)(3)(A) notification. Therefore, the references to § 512(c)(3) in §§ 512(b) and (d) lead inexorably to the conclusion that § 512(h) is structurally linked to the storage functions of an ISP and not to its transmission functions, such as those listed in § 512(a).

C. *Legislative History*

In support of its claim that § 512(h) can—and should—be read to reach P2P technology, the RIAA points to congressional testimony and news articles available to the Congress prior to passage of the DMCA. These sources document the threat to copyright owners posed by bulletin board services (BBSs) and file transfer protocol (FTP) sites, which the RIAA says were precursors to P2P programs.

We need not, however, resort to investigating what the 105th Congress may have known because the text of § 512(h) and the overall structure of § 512 clearly establish, as we have seen, that § 512(h) does not authorize the issuance of a subpoena to an ISP acting as a mere conduit for the transmission of information sent by others. Legislative history can serve to inform the court's reading of an otherwise ambiguous text; it cannot lead the court to contradict the legislation itself. In any event, not only is the statute clear (albeit complex), the legislative history of the DMCA betrays no awareness whatsoever that internet users might be able directly to exchange files containing copyrighted works. That is not surprising; P2P software was "not even a glimmer in anyone's eye when the DMCA was enacted." * * *

D. *Purpose of the DMCA*

Finally, the RIAA argues Verizon's interpretation of the statute "would defeat the core objectives" of the Act. More specifically, according to the RIAA there is no policy justification for limiting the reach of § 512(h) to situations in which the ISP stores infringing material on its system, considering that many more acts of copyright infringement are committed in the P2P realm, in which the ISP merely transmits the material for others, and that the burden upon an ISP required to identify an infringing subscriber is minimal.

We are not unsympathetic either to the RIAA's concern regarding the widespread infringement of its members' copyrights, or to the need for legal tools to protect those rights. It is not the province of the courts, however, to rewrite the DMCA in order to make it fit a new and unforeseen internet architecture, no matter how damaging that development has been to the music industry or threatens being to the motion picture and software industries. The plight of copyright holders must be addressed in the first instance by the Congress * * * .

Notes and Questions

1. Is section 512(h) as clear as the Court suggests? The provision authorizes issuance of a subpoena to a "service provider," and section 512 defines the term "service provider" to include both passive conduits and providers engaged in storing, caching, or linking. *See* 17 U.S.C. § 512(k)(1). Consider the dissent's approach in *In re Charter Communications, Inc.*, 393 F.3d 771 (8th Cir. 2005), a case adopting the *Verison* court's reasoning:

> Although Charter contends that the subpoena power in the DMCA is limited by the function of the ISP, such a limitation is not to be found in a plain reading of the DMCA. To the contrary, the statute defines "service providers" in § 512(k) as all "provider[s] of online services or network access," including conduit providers who offer the "transmission . . . of material of the user's choosing, without modification." § 512(k)(1). If Congress had wanted to limit the type of ISP subject to a statutory subpoena, it could have easily specified that in § 512(h), but it did not. In the absence of such a limitation, the statute's definition of "service provider" in § 512(k)(1) controls, and it includes Charter. * * *

> Section 512(h), which creates the subpoena power, only references § 512(c)(3)(A) to indicate the kind of information which needs to be given to the clerk to request a subpoena. By referencing the elements of the notification in § 512(c)(3)(A), Congress avoided the necessity of repeating such notice details in § 512(h). The statutory requirement that storage service providers expeditiously remove or disable access to infringing materials in order to avoid secondary liability is not rooted in this notification provision, but rather in those sections of the DMCA which set

out the obligations of storage providers. *See* §§ 512(b)(2)(E), 512(c)(1)(C), 512(d)(3).

Charter's restrictive view of the subpoena power rests entirely on its reading extra words into § 512(c)(3)(A)(iii) to limit its applicability to storage ISPs. It reads the provision as if the subsection referred to material that is (1) "claimed to be infringing" and that is to be removed or access to which is to be disabled, or material that is (2) "the subject of infringing activity and that is to be removed or access to which is to be disabled." That is not what Congress said, however. To the extent that the § 512(h) cross reference to § 512(c)(3)(A)(iii) is fairly seen to be subject to different interpretations, it is ambiguous, and any ambiguity must be resolved by looking to the intent of Congress in its enactment of the legislation. * * * The suggestion that copyright holders should be left to file John Doe lawsuits to protect themselves from infringement by subscribers of conduit ISPs like Charter, instead of availing themselves of the mechanism Congress provided in the DMCA, is impractical and contrary to legislative intent. John Doe actions are costly and time consuming.

393 F.3d at 780-82 (Murphy, J., dissenting). Which approach is more persuasive?

2. Because the D.C. Circuit decided the *Verizon* case on statutory grounds, it had no occasion to address Verizon's argument that subsection 512(h) violates the First Amendment because it lacks sufficient safeguards to protect an Internet user's ability to speak and associate anonymously. Following the D.C. Circuit's decision, the RIAA began filing numerous John Doe suits and invoking the general subpoena provision of Rule 45 of the Federal Rules of Civil Procedure to compel ISPs to release identity of the subscribers. Because such lawsuits did not involve interpretation of subsection 512(h), courts could not avoid the First Amendment issue. Should courts apply one of the balancing tests adopted in cases involving the circulation of allegedly false information, or do copyright infringement disputes raise fundamentally different issues? Consider the following approach.

Sony Music Entertainment, Inc. v. Does 1-40

United States District Court for the Southern District of New York, 2004
326 F. Supp. 2d 556

CHIN, District Judge.

In this case, plaintiffs—seventeen record companies—sued forty unidentified "Doe" defendants for copyright infringement, alleging that defendants illegally downloaded and distributed plaintiffs' copyrighted or exclusively licensed songs from the Internet, using a "peer to peer" file copying network. Plaintiffs served a subpoena on non-party Internet service provider Cablevision Systems Corporation ("Cablevision"), seeking to obtain defendants' identities. Four defendants move to quash the subpoena. * * *

STATEMENT OF THE CASE

I. Facts

Plaintiffs own the copyrights and exclusive licenses to the various sound recordings at issue in this case. Plaintiffs allege that each of the forty Doe defendants, without plaintiffs' permission, used "Fast Track," an online media distribution system—or "peer to peer" ("P2P") file copying network—to download, distribute to the public, or make available for distribution "hundreds or thousands" of copyrighted sound recordings. * * *

Plaintiffs were able to identify Cablevision as the Internet service provider ("ISP") to which defendants subscribed, using a publicly available database to trace the Internet Protocol ("IP") address for each defendant. * * *

DISCUSSION

* * *

II. The Merits

* * *

Jane Doe moves to quash the subpoena based on * * * the subpoena's violation of her First Amendment right to engage in anonymous speech; * * * . [The] motions to quash raise two First Amendment issues: (1) whether a person who uses the Internet to download or distribute copyrighted music without permission is engaging in the exercise of speech; and (2) if so, whether such a person's identity is protected from disclosure by the First Amendment. * * *

A. *The First Amendment*

1. *Applicable Law*

   a. *First Amendment Protection for Anonymous Internet Speech*

The Supreme Court has recognized that the First Amendment protects anonymous speech. * * * The Internet is a particularly effective forum for the dissemination of anonymous speech. Anonymous speech, like speech from identifiable sources, does not have absolute protection. The First Amendment, for example, does not protect copyright infringement, and the Supreme Court, accordingly, has rejected First Amendment challenges to copyright infringement actions. Parties may not use the First Amendment to encroach upon the intellectual property rights of others. * * *

2. *Application*

   a. *Is Defendants' Alleged Conduct "Speech"?*

As a threshold matter, I address whether the use of P2P file copying networks to download, distribute, or make available for distribution copyrighted sound recordings, without permission, is an exercise of speech. I conclude that this conduct qualifies as speech, but only to a degree.

In contrast to many cases involving First Amendment rights on the Internet, a person who engages in P2P file sharing is not engaging in true expression. Such an individual is not seeking to communicate a thought or convey an idea. Instead, the individual's real purpose is to obtain music for free. Arguably, however, a file sharer is making a statement by downloading and making available to others copyrighted music without charge and without license to do so. Alternatively, the file sharer may be expressing himself or herself through the music selected and made available to others. Although this is not "political expression" entitled to the "broadest protection" of the First Amendment, the file sharer's speech is still entitled to "some level of First Amendment protection." *Recording Industry Ass'n of America, Inc. v. Verizon Internet Servs., Inc.*, 257 F. Supp. 2d 244, 260 (D.D.C. 2003), *rev'd on other grounds,* 351 F.3d 1229 (D.C. Cir. 2003). I conclude, accordingly, that the use of P2P file copying networks to download, distribute, or make sound recordings available qualifies as speech entitled to First Amendment protection. That protection, however, is limited, and is subject to other considerations.

> b. *Are Defendants' Identities Protected from Disclosure by the First Amendment?*

I consider next whether the Doe defendants' identities are protected from disclosure by the First Amendment. For the reasons set forth below, I conclude that the First Amendment does not bar disclosure of the Doe defendants' identities.

Cases evaluating subpoenas seeking identifying information from ISPs regarding subscribers who are parties to litigation have considered a variety of factors to weigh the need for disclosure against First Amendment interests. These factors include: (1) a concrete showing of a prima facie claim of actionable harm; (2) specificity of the discovery request; (3) the absence of alternative means to obtain the subpoenaed information; (4) a central need for the subpoenaed information to advance the claim; and (5) the party's expectation of privacy. As set forth below, each of these factors supports disclosure of defendants' identities.

> i. *Prima Facie Claim of Copyright Infringement*

Plaintiffs have made a concrete showing of a prima facie claim of copyright infringement. A prima facie claim of copyright infringement consists of two elements: "(1) ownership of a valid copyright, and (2) copying of constituent elements of the work that are original." *Arden v. Columbia Pictures Indus., Inc.*, 908 F. Supp. 1248, 1257 (S.D.N.Y. 1995) (quoting *Feist Publ'ns, Inc. v. Rural Tel. Service Co., Inc.*, 499 U.S. 340 (1991)).

Plaintiffs have alleged ownership of the copyrights or exclusive rights of copyrighted sound recordings at issue in this case sufficiently to satisfy the first element of copyright infringement. Plaintiffs have attached to the complaint a partial list of the sound recordings the rights to which defendants have allegedly infringed. Each of the copyrighted recordings on the list is the subject of a valid Certificate of Copyright Registration issued by the Register of Copyrights to one of the record company plaintiffs. Plaintiffs also allege that among the exclusive rights granted to each plaintiff under the Copyright Act are the exclusive rights to reproduce and distribute to the public the copyrighted recordings. Defendants have failed to refute in any way plaintiffs' allegations of ownership. Plaintiffs have also adequately pled the Doe defendants' infringement of plaintiffs' licenses and copyrights, thus satisfying the second element in a copyright infringement claim. Plaintiffs allege that each defendant, without plaintiffs' consent, "used, and continues to use an online media distribution system to download, distribute to the public, and/or make available for distribution to others" certain of the copyrighted recordings in Exhibit A to the complaint.

Plaintiffs have submitted supporting evidence listing the copyrighted songs downloaded or distributed by defendants using P2P systems. The lists also specify the date and time at which defendants' allegedly infringing activity occurred and the IP address assigned to each defendant at the time. Moreover, the use of P2P systems to download and distribute copyrighted music has been held to constitute copyright infringement. Accordingly, plaintiffs have sufficiently pled copyright infringement to establish a prima facie claim.

ii. *Specificity of the Discovery Request*

Plaintiffs' discovery request is also sufficiently specific to establish a reasonable likelihood that the discovery request would lead to identifying information that would make possible service upon particular defendants who could be sued in federal court. Plaintiffs seek identifying information about particular Cablevision subscribers, based on the specific times and dates when they downloaded specific copyrighted and licensed songs. Such information will enable plaintiffs to serve process on defendants.

iii. *Absence of Alternative Means to Obtain Subpoenaed Information*

Plaintiffs have also established that they lack other means to obtain the subpoenaed information by specifying in their ex parte application for expedited discovery and papers in opposition to Jane Doe's motion to quash the steps they have taken to locate the Doe defendants. These include using a publicly available database to trace the IP address for each defendant, based on the times of infringement.

iv. *Central Need for Subpoenaed Information*

Plaintiff have also demonstrated that the subpoenaed information is centrally needed for plaintiffs to advance their copyright infringement claims. Ascertaining the identities and residences of the Doe defendants is critical to plaintiffs' ability to pursue litigation, for without this information, plaintiffs will be unable to serve process.

v. *Defendants' Expectation of Privacy*

Plaintiffs are also entitled to discovery in light of defendants' minimal expectation of privacy. Cablevision's Terms of Service, to which its subscribers—including the Doe defendants—must commit, specifically prohibit the "[t]ransmission or distribution of any material in violation of any applicable law or regulation. . . . This includes, without limitation, material protected by copyright, trademark, trade secret or other intellectual property right used without proper authorization." Accordingly, defendants have little expectation of privacy in downloading and distributing copyrighted songs without permission.

In sum, defendants' First Amendment right to remain anonymous must give way to plaintiffs' right to use the judicial process to pursue what appear to be meritorious copyright infringement claims.

Notes and Questions

1. Compare the factors the *Sony* court considers with those the courts consider in *AOL* and *TMRT*. There appear to be several common elements: a plaintiff seeking disclosure of subscriber identity must demonstrate a *prima facie* showing of wrongful conduct, the centrality of the information to the case, and that the information is not available from any other source. Should the tests be the same, or does alleged copyright infringement raise different First Amendment issues than allegedly false speech?

2. In addition to relying on some of the *AOL* and *TMRT* factors, the court considers the subscribers' "expectation of privacy," which the court determines is "minimal" in light of terms of service prohibiting distribution of material in violation of law. If the mere existence of a term prohibiting unlawful conduct is enough to extinguish any expectation of privacy once there is an allegation of unlawful conduct, won't that factor always cut in favor of disclosure? Will a balancing test of this sort ever lead a court to quash a subpoena? Under what conditions? Also, to the extent that the terms of service in an online contract are used to determine reasonable expectations of privacy, should we be concerned that these contracts are not true contracts in the classic sense? Recall the discussion of this issue in Chapter Four.

3. The cases considered thus far deal with the power of a court to *compel* a service provider to identify a user, over the service provider's or the user's objection that revealing the identity will curtail the user's First Amendment rights. They do not address the situation that arises when the service provider is willing to disclose the identity voluntarily. The following materials consider the limits on voluntary disclosure.

In 1986, Congress passed the Electronic Communications Privacy Act to update federal surveillance law protections. In addition to extending federal prohibitions on wiretapping to electronic communications, Congress created a new chapter of the criminal code covering stored wire and electronic communications. *See* Electronic Communications Privacy Act of 1986, Pub. L. No. 201-202, 100 Stat. 1848, 1860–68 (codified as amended at 18 U.S.C. §§ 2701–2709, 2711–2712). Often referred to as the Stored Communications Act (SCA), the provisions prohibit unauthorized access to communications held by a service provider and impose specific requirements on government entities seeking to obtain such communications. *See* 18 U.S.C. §§ 2701, 2703. The provisions also limit government officials' access to "record[s] or other information pertaining to a subscriber to or customer of" the provider. *Id.* § 2703(c). In particular, the statute requires officials to present an administrative, grand jury, or trial subpoena to compel production of some of the information that might appear in customer records, including the customer's name, address, IP address, connection or session information, length of service, and payment information. *Id.* § 2703(c)(2). For other information in customer records, government officials must present a warrant or special court order under 18 U.S.C. § 2703(d), requiring specific and articulable facts showing reasonable grounds to believe that the information is relevant to an ongoing criminal investigation.

We discuss the SCA at greater length in Chapter Eight. For now, we consider the provisions restricting service providers' ability to disclose communications and records.

Section 2702 of the Stored Communications Act

18 U.S.C. § 2702

§ 2702. Disclosure of Contents

(a) **Prohibitions.**—Except as provided in subsection (b)—

(1) a person or entity providing an electronic communication service to the public shall not knowingly divulge to any person or entity the contents of a communication while in electronic storage by that service; and

(2) a person or entity providing remote computing service to the public shall not knowingly divulge to any person or entity the contents of any communication which is carried or maintained on that service—

(A) on behalf of, and received by means of electronic transmission from (or created by means of computer processing of communications received by means of electronic transmission from), a subscriber or customer of such service; and

(B) solely for the purpose of providing storage or computer processing services to such subscriber or customer, if the provider is not authorized to access the contents of any such communications for purposes of providing any services other than storage or computer processing; and

(3) a provider of remote computing service or electronic communication service to the public shall not knowingly divulge a record or other information pertaining to a subscriber to or customer of such service (not including the contents of communications covered by paragraph (1) or (2)) to any governmental entity.

(b) **Exceptions for disclosure of communications.**—A person or entity may divulge the contents of a communication—

(1) to an addressee or intended recipient of such communication or an agent of such addressee or intended recipient;

(2) as otherwise authorized in section 2517, 2511(2)(a), or 2703 of this title;

(3) with the lawful consent of the originator or an addressee or intended recipient of such communication, or the subscriber in the case of remote computing service;

(4) to a person employed or authorized or whose facilities are used to forward such communication to its destination;

(5) as may be necessarily incident to the rendition of the service or to the protection of the rights or property of the provider of that service; or

(6) to the National Center for Missing and Exploited Children, in connection with a report submitted thereto under section 227 of the

Victims of Child Abuse Act of 1990 [requiring service providers to report facts and circumstances from which child pornography or child exploitation crimes are apparent];

    (7) to a law enforcement agency—

        (A) if the contents—

            (i) were inadvertently obtained by the service provider; and

            (ii) appear to pertain to the commission of a crime; or

    (8) to a governmental entity, if the provider, in good faith, believes that an emergency involving danger of death or serious physical injury to any person requires disclosure without delay of communications relating to the emergency.

    (c) Exceptions for disclosure of customer records.—A provider described in subsection (a) may divulge a record or other information pertaining to a subscriber to or customer of such service (not including the contents of communications covered by subsection (a)(1) or (a)(2))—

    (1) as otherwise authorized in section 2703;

    (2) with the lawful consent of the customer or subscriber;

    (3) as may be necessarily incident to the rendition of the service or to the protection of the rights or property of the provider of that service;

    (4) to a governmental entity, if the provider in good faith, believes that an emergency involving danger of death or serious physical injury to any person requires disclosure without delay of information relating to the emergency;

    (5) to the National Center for Missing and Exploited Children, in connection with a report submitted thereto under section 227 of the Victims of Child Abuse Act of 1990; or

    (6) to any person other than a governmental entity.

    (d) Reporting of emergency disclosures.—On an annual basis, the Attorney General shall submit to the Committee on the Judiciary of the House of Representatives and the Committee on the Judiciary of the Senate a report containing—

    (1) the number of accounts from which the Department of Justice has received voluntary disclosures under subsection (b)(8); and

    (2) a summary of the basis for disclosure in those instances where—

        (A) voluntary disclosures under subsection (b)(8) were made to the Department of Justice; and

        (B) the investigation pertaining to those disclosures was closed without the filing of criminal charges.

Section 2702 covers two types of service providers: those providing an "electronic communication service" and those providing a "remote computing service." We consider the scope of those terms in greater detail in Chapter Eight, but at a minimum the terms cover providers who allow users the ability to transmit and receive communications and those that store communications on users' behalf. *Cf. Dyer v. Northwest Airlines Corps.*, 334 F. Supp. 2d 1196, 1199 (D.N.D. 2004) ("Courts have concluded that 'electronic communication service' encompasses Internet service providers as well as telecommunications companies whose lines carry internet traffic, but does not encompass businesses selling traditional products or services online.").

Note two important limitations on the statute's reach, however. First, the provisions guard against disclosures by providers who offer services to the *public*; they do not restrict the ability of any other provider (such as an employer) to voluntarily disclose any information. 18 U.S.C. § 2702(a), (b). Second, although the statute generally prohibits a public provider from disclosing the *contents* of communications to private parties or to a governmental entity not presenting the appropriate legal process, it permits disclosure of customer records "to any person other than a governmental entity," without restriction. *Id.* § 2702(c)(6). In other words, the SCA guards a subscriber's anonymity only against a *public provider's* voluntary disclosure *to a governmental entity*. For further discussion, see JAMES G. CARR & PATRICIA L. BELLIA, THE LAW OF ELECTRONIC SURVEILLANCE § 4:76 (West Group 2005).

Notes and Questions

1. When does a provider offer services "to the public"? Consider one court's approach:

> The statute does not define "public." The word "public," however, is unambiguous. Public means the "aggregate of the citizens" or "everybody" or "the people at large" or "the community at large." Black's Law Dictionary 1227 (6th ed. 1990). Thus, the statute covers any entity that provides electronic communication service (e.g., e-mail) to the community at large.

> Andersen attempts to render the phrase "to the public" superfluous by arguing that the statutory language indicates that the term "public" means something other than the community at large. It claims that if Congress wanted public to mean the community at large, it would have used the term "general public." However, the fact that Congress used both "public" and "general public" in the same statute does not lead to the conclusion that Congress intended public to have any other meaning than its commonly understood meaning. Compare 18 U.S.C. § 2511(2)(g) (using the term "general public") with id. §§ 2511(2)(a)(i), (3)(a), (3)(b), (4)(c)(ii) (using the term "public").

> Andersen argues that the legislative history indicates that a provider of electronic communication services is subject to Section 2702 even if that provider maintains the system primarily for its own use and does not provide services to the general public. This legislative history

argument is misguided. * * *   Even if the language was somehow ambiguous, the legislative history does not support Andersen's interpretation. The legislative history indicates that there is a distinction between public and proprietary. In describing "electronic mail," the legislative history stated that "[e]lectronic mail systems may be available for public use or may be proprietary, such as systems operated by private companies for internal correspondence." S. Rep. No. 99- 541, at 8 (1986), reprinted in 1986 U.S.C.C.A.N. 3555, 3562. Thus, Andersen must show that UOP's electronic mail system was available for public use.

Andersen Consulting LLP v. UOP, 991 F. Supp. 1042, 1042-43 (N.D. Ill. 1998). Even if the *Andersen* court's approach is persuasive as a matter of statutory interpretation, should section 2702 be written more broadly? Consider, for example, a university that provides all faculty, staff, and students with e-mail access. Is the university a "public" provider? Should it be?

2. Why does the SCA allow disclosure of noncontent records to private parties without restriction? Service providers could presumably set more restrictive privacy practices in their terms of service. In light of the underlying legal framework, are they likely to do so?

3. How should courts draw the line between "voluntary" disclosure pursuant to section 2702 and "compelled" disclosure pursuant to section 2703? Suppose, for example, that someone requests disclosure of information without identifying himself as a government official. Does the service provider's release of information violate section 2702? *See McVeigh v. Cohen*, 983 F. Supp. 215 (D.D.C. 1998) (suggesting that government induced violation of predecessor section to section 2702 by requesting release of subscriber information without disclosing that request was on behalf of government). Does a provider violate section 2702 when it divulges information to a governmental entity in response to defective legal process? *See Freedman v. America Online, Inc.*, 325 F. Supp. 2d 638 (E.D. Va. 2004) (finding violation of section 2702 where AOL was unaware that warrant was unsigned).

2. Communications Privacy

Thus far, we have considered how ISPs and other Internet intermediaries can supply government entities with both a path to constraining Internet users' conduct and a path to extracting users' identity. Service providers, of course, also serve as a point of access to information beyond a user's identity, including information on what website the user has visited, the contents of a user's e-mail, and so on. Although we defer discussion of broader Internet privacy issues to Chapter Eight, this brief note simply highlights the extent to which the ordinary functioning of Internet intermediaries can transform (and threaten) communications privacy.

Until use of e-mail and the Internet became widespread, most conversational communications were transient (as in the case of telephone calls and oral conversations) and most written communications were ultimately maintained in the hands of the recipient (as in the case of physical mail). Although third parties might be involved in the process of helping a communication reach its destination—the phone company connecting the call or the Postal Service or other carrier delivering a letter or package—the role of the third party ended once the communication ended or reached its recipient. Communications were thus highly protected, both by the Supreme Court's interpretation of the Fourth Amendment to require a warrant for the acquisition of communications in transit, *see Katz v. United States*, 389 U.S. 347 (1967), and by the fact that letters and packages would physically be held in the recipient's home rather than by a third party. In addition, while details of certain real-world transactions (such as purchases, movie rentals, and library borrowing) might be accessible to particular third parties (such as a credit card company, the video store, or the library), no single party could record or aggregate all transactional information.

Widespread use of the Internet has transformed these models. Consider one commentator's description (circa 2004) of the communications environment:

Today, sixty-three percent of U.S. adults—126 million people—use the Internet. Internet users are found in every segment of the population. Individuals use the Internet to communicate with friends, family, and colleagues. They use it to seek out information about every imaginable topic. Individuals use it to store photos, documents, and diaries. They use it to organize rallies and demonstrations. Individuals use it to shop, to bank, and to barter. They use it from home and from work, and for work and for play.

The information flowing across the Internet reflects this diversity of activity. Broken into tiny packets of data, text, voice, sounds, and images flow across the Internet backbone. Forty-three million individuals in the United States reported that they listened to music online in 2001. On a typical day, over 7.5 million individuals will listen to a video or audio clip. Online gaming is responsible for nine percent of Internet traffic. With over eleven percent of long-distance telephone calls passing over the Internet at some point in their journey, many individuals will be engaged in real-time voice communications online. Wedding, birth, graduation, vacation, and other personal photos are part of the 880 million photos available using Google's image search. * * *

Home is now the dominant site of Internet access for U.S. Internet users. Increasing numbers of individuals report using the Internet for fun and for leisure activities. * * * Over 112 million individuals use the Internet to search for information: ninety-one million to seek out information about personal interests; seventy-three million to seek out health information; sixty-six million to seek out government information; forty-seven million to seek out political information; and thirty-five million to seek out information on religion.

E-mail remains the dominant online activity engaged in by Internet users surpassing purchasing activities by thirty-two percent. Approximately 102 million U.S. individuals use e-mail, with about 60 million using it on any given day. Fifty-two million US individuals have used instant messaging, with over 10 million using it on a typical day. Twenty-one million U.S. individuals have created content on the Internet, including pages for Web sites, "blogs," online diaries, or postings to bulletin boards or newsgroups. The content individuals create ranges from movies, short stories, and news reports to journals, family trees, and photo albums. * * *

These data points and trends illustrate the extent to which the Internet has infiltrated personal life. They speak to the increasingly personal nature of individuals' online activities, conversations, and information searches. The Internet is now used as a storage site for personal photos, a meeting place for social clubs, and is a primary personal communication system for millions of individuals. If an activity can be done without leaving the house and physically interacting with another individual, someone somewhere has found a way to do it online. As broadband connections are available in more homes, the use of the Internet for personal, rather than business, activities will accelerate. In analyzing the adequacy of existing privacy protections and proposing revisions, the personal nature of today's online activities should be a core consideration.

Deirdre K. Mulligan, *Reasonable Expectations in Electronic Communications: A Critical Analysis*, 72 GEO. WASH. L. REV. 1557, 1575–77 (2004).

In the environment Professor Mulligan describes, service providers and other intermediaries have access to a wide range of communications and data that were once transient, held in the home, or scattered among various third parties. To the extent that e-mails supplant phone calls, they replace transient communications with more permanent ones, because service providers routinely store incoming and outgoing messages. To the extent that e-mails supplant correspondence by letter, they replace communications maintained (if at all) by the final recipient with communications routinely maintained by a service provider. To the extent that online activities such as shopping, reading, researching personal issues, and storing personal documents supplant similar activities in the physical world, they leave a trail of such activities not with multiple unrelated third parties, but with third parties capable of integrating the information—the ISP or a third-party advertiser with a widespread network of partner websites.

In such an environment, ISPs and other intermediaries essentially become the guardians of privacy. As discussed earlier, section 2702 of the Stored Communications Act prohibits public providers of an electronic communication service or a remote computing service from disclosing the contents of communications except in compliance with appropriate legal process. But who fits the provider definitions? What constitutes the "contents" of a communication? And what constitutes appropriate legal process? As we turn to broader questions of privacy in Chapter Eight, keep in mind the crucial role that Internet intermediaries will necessarily play in safeguarding or undermining privacy online.

Chapter Eight

PROBLEMS OF PRIVACY AND SURVEILLANCE

INTRODUCTION

In Chapter Seven, we explored how Internet service providers and other intermediaries can serve as repositories for private information—and thus as convenient targets for government and private entities seeking to acquire users' identifying data and even their private communications. In this chapter, we consider problems of privacy and surveillance more directly.

The relationship between technology and privacy is a complex one, and questions about why and how the law should protect information privacy are not unique to the Internet context. At a theoretical level, scholars do not agree on what "privacy" is, why it should be protected, and how such protection should be balanced against other values, such as access to information, free speech, national security, and efficient law enforcement. At a practical level, privacy law—even the narrower category of information privacy law—can consist of a hodgepodge of constitutional protections, federal and state statutory provisions, common law rules, and so on. We must ask, then, whether the development of digital technology and the widespread use of the Internet presents any specific challenges for understanding privacy and for striking an appropriate balance between privacy and other values. More broadly, does studying problems of privacy and surveillance in the Internet context offer any lessons for understanding and addressing such problems in other contexts?

Commentators and privacy advocates argue that the problems of information privacy are indeed more acute in cyberspace than in real space. Consider four specific challenges:

Scope and diversity of content. The Internet has become an essential medium of communication and has assumed a vital role in our lives. E-mail accounts reveal extensive and detailed information about our interests, political opinions, religious beliefs, personal relationships, and actions. Our e-mail thus contains a far richer body of data than telephone calls. Even a list of Internet sites we visit can reveal far more about our preferences and interests than the substance of a phone call.

Storage. Computer storage, once costly and bulky, is now increasingly inexpensive and convenient. The development of cheap storage has already led computer users—individuals as well as businesses—to retain more information than was previously possible. For example, when the Supreme Court held in *Katz v. United States*, 389 U.S. 347 (1967), that warrantless eavesdropping on conversations violated the Fourth Amendment, a telephone company would have been highly unlikely to retain a recorded copy of a call, even if it legally and technically could have made the recording. As e-mail communications have supplanted some telephone conversations, they have replaced transient telephone communications with semi-permanent electronic communications. Indeed, the development of Voice over Internet Protocol (VoIP) telephony raises the prospect that even copies of telephone conversations can readily be stored.

Network storage. The significance of increased storage may lie not only in the fact that such storage is possible, but also where the storage occurs—often on a network server rather than on an individual user's hard drive. A user's e-mail provider, for example, might hold copies of incoming and outgoing communications, copies of "opened" or downloaded e-mails that a user chooses not to delete, and backup copies of all of these. As we will discuss, storing communications on a network rather than on one's hard drive can have tremendous legal consequences. The robust protections the Fourth Amendment provides against warrantless searches of the home do not necessarily apply to communications stored outside of the home. In addition, employers that act as service providers have ready access to tools to monitor their employees' e-mail communications and other Internet activities.

Aggregation and disclosure. The development of digital technology and widespread use of computer networks also facilitate the collection and aggregation of information from a variety of sources. As Professor Julie Cohen has put it, "Collections of information about, and identified to, individuals have existed for decades. The rise of a networked society, however, has brought with it intense concern about the personal and social implications of such databases—now, in digital form, capable of being rapidly searched, instantly distributed, and seamlessly combined with other data sources to generate ever more comprehensive records of individual attributes and activities."[a] The concern is not only with these activities in and of themselves, but with the ease with which information collected by third parties can then pass into the hands of the government.[b]

How (if at all) should the law respond to these four challenges? Section A sets the context for this discussion by introducing different

---

a. Julie E. Cohen, *Examined Lives: Informational Privacy and the Subject as Object*, 52 STAN. L. REV. 1373 (2000).

b. *See, e.g.,* Daniel J. Solove, *Digital Dossiers and the Dissipation of Fourth Amendment Privacy*, 75 S. CAL. L. REV. 1083 (2002).

conceptions of privacy and exploring the values that privacy is thought to serve. As you read these materials, ask yourself whether there is anything about the Internet that makes privacy more or less important in this context than it is in other contexts. Section B then considers the special problems of government surveillance that the Internet presents. Section C turns to private conduct, focusing specifically on employers' access to their employees' communications and the collection and aggregation of "transactional" data.

SECTION A. FRAMING PRIVACY

Daniel J. Solove, *Conceptualizing Privacy*

90 CAL. L. REV. 1087 (2002)

I

A CRITIQUE OF THE CONCEPTIONS OF PRIVACY

What is privacy? We all have some intuitive sense that there are certain aspects of life that are "private" and view these aspects of life as related to each other. But what does it mean when we say that these aspects of life are "private"?

This question is very important for making legal and policy decisions. Many recognize the importance of privacy for freedom, democracy, social welfare, individual well-being, and other ends. Many also assert it is worth protecting at significant cost. * * * Society's commitment to privacy often entails restraining or even sacrificing interests of substantial importance, such as freedom of speech and press, efficient law enforcement, access to information, and so on. Why is privacy valuable enough to make significant trade-offs to protect it? To answer this question, we need to have some notion of what privacy is. When we protect "privacy," what are we protecting? * * *

In this section, I explore the philosophical and legal discourse to assess the conceptions that attempt to isolate a common denominator of privacy. * * * [E]ach of the conceptions has significant limitations if it is to serve as a conceptual account of privacy in general. * * *

1.   The Right to Be Let Alone

In 1890, Samuel Warren and Louis Brandeis penned their famous article, *The Right to Privacy*,[43] hailed by a multitude of scholars as the foundation of privacy law in the United States. * * * Warren and Brandeis defined privacy as the "right to be let alone," a phrase adopted from Judge Thomas Cooley's famous treatise on torts in 1880.[47] * * *

The formulation of privacy as the right to be let alone merely describes an attribute of privacy. Understanding privacy as being let alone fails to

---

43. Samuel D. Warren & Louis D. Brandeis, *The Right to Privacy*, 4 HARV. L. REV. 193 (1890).

47. THOMAS M. COOLEY, LAW OF TORTS (2d ed. 1888). * * *

provide much guidance about how privacy should be valued vis-à-vis other interests, such as free speech, effective law enforcement, and other important values. * * * As many commentators lament, defining privacy as the right to be let alone is too broad. For example, legal scholar Anita Allen explains: "If privacy simply meant 'being let alone,' any form of offensive or harmful conduct directed toward another person could be characterized as a violation of personal privacy. A punch in the nose would be a privacy invasion as much as a peep in the bedroom."[62] * * *

2. Limited Access to the Self

A number of theorists conceptualize privacy as "limited access" to the self. This conception recognizes the individual's desire for concealment and for being apart from others. In this way, it is closely related to the right-to-be-let-alone conception, and is perhaps a more sophisticated formulation of that right. * * *

Without a notion of what matters are private, limited-access conceptions do not tell us the substantive matters for which access would implicate privacy. Certainly not all access to the self infringes upon privacy—only access to specific dimensions of the self or to particular matters and information. As a result, the theory provides no understanding of the degree of access necessary to constitute a privacy violation. How much control we should have over access to the self? Proponents of the limited-access conception could respond that privacy is a continuum between absolutely no access to the self and total access. If privacy is such a continuum, then the important question is where the lines should be drawn—that is, what degree of access should we recognize as reasonable? This question can only be answered with an understanding of what matters are private and the value of privacy. Like the right-to-be-let-alone conception, the limited-access conception suffers from being too broad and too vague. * * *

3. Secrecy

One of the most common understandings of privacy is that it constitutes the secrecy of certain matters. Under this view, privacy is violated by the public disclosure of previously concealed information. According to Judge Richard Posner:

> [T]he word "privacy" seems to embrace at least two distinct interests.
> One is the interest in being left alone—the interest that is invaded by
> the unwanted telephone solicitation, the noisy sound truck, the music
> in elevators, being jostled in the street, or even an obscene theater
> billboard or shouted obscenity. . . . The other privacy interest,
> concealment of information, is invaded whenever private information
> is obtained against the wishes of the person to whom the information
> pertains.[84]

The latter privacy interest, "concealment of information," involves secrecy. * * * Posner sees privacy as a form of self-interested economic

---

62. ANITA L. ALLEN, UNEASY ACCESS: PRIVACY FOR WOMEN IN A FREE SOCIETY 7 (1988).
84. RICHARD A. POSNER, THE ECONOMICS OF JUSTICE 272-73 (1981).

behavior, concealing true but harmful facts about oneself for one's own gain. * * * "[W]hen people today decry lack of privacy," Posner argues, "what they want, I think, is mainly something quite different from seclusion; they want more power to conceal information about themselves that others might use to their disadvantage."[87] * * *

In a variety of legal contexts, the view of privacy as secrecy often leads to the conclusion that once a fact is divulged in public, no matter how limited or narrow the disclosure, it can no longer remain private. Privacy is thus viewed as coextensive with the total secrecy of information. For example, the Court's Fourth Amendment jurisprudence adheres to the notion that matters that are no longer completely secret can no longer be private. * * * In a series of cases, the Court has held there can be no "reasonable expectation of privacy" in things exposed to the public, even if it is highly unlikely that anybody will see or discover them. As the Court observed in Katz: "What a person knowingly exposes to the public, even in his own home or office, is not a subject of Fourth Amendment protection."[88] * * *

A number of theorists have claimed that understanding privacy as secrecy conceptualizes privacy too narrowly. * * * We often expect privacy even when in public. Not all activities we deem as private occur behind the curtain. The books we read, the products we buy, the people we associate with—these are often not viewed as secrets, but we nonetheless view them as private matters. * * * Therefore, while most theorists would recognize the disclosure of certain secrets to be a violation of privacy, many commonly recognized privacy invasions do not involve the loss of secrecy. Secrecy as the common denominator of privacy makes the conception of privacy too narrow.

4. *Control Over Personal Information*

One of the most predominant theories of privacy is that of control over personal information. According to Alan Westin: "Privacy is the claim of individuals, groups, or institutions to determine for themselves when, how, and to what extent information about them is communicated to others."[111] Numerous other scholars have articulated similar theories. * * *

The control-over-information [conception] can be viewed as a subset of the limited access conception. The theory's focus on information, however, makes it too narrow a conception, for it excludes those aspects of privacy that are not informational, such as the right to make certain fundamental decisions about one's body, reproduction, or rearing of one's children.

Additionally, the theory is too vague because proponents of the theory often fail to define the types of information over which individuals should have control * * * [and] [w]hat is meant by "control" over information. * * * Frequently, control is understood as a form of ownership in information.

---

87. *Id.* at 271. * * *

88. Katz v. United States, 389 U.S. 347, 351 (1967).

111. ALAN F. WESTIN, PRIVACY AND FREEDOM 7 (1967).

For example, Westin concludes that "personal information, thought of as the right of decision over one's private personality, should be defined as a property right."[123] * * *   Given the unique nature of information, the extension of [property] concepts to personal information does not come without some difficulties. * * * Personal information is often formed in relationships with others, with all parties to that relationship having some claim to that information. For example, individuals are not the lone creators of their web-browsing information, for most of that information is created from the interaction between the user and website. Often, the market value of information is not created exclusively by the labor of the individual to whom it relates but in part by the third party that compiles the information. For example, the value of personal information for advertisers and marketers emerges in part from their consolidation and categorization of that information. * * * [Defining] "control" * * * as a form of ownership [makes] the conception falter in a number of respects. * * *

5. *Personhood*

Another theory of privacy views it as a form of protecting personhood. Building upon Warren and Brandeis's notion of "inviolate personality," Paul Freund coined the term "personhood" to refer to "those attributes of an individual which are irreducible in his selfhood."[149] The theory of privacy as personhood differs from the theories discussed earlier because it is constructed around a normative end of privacy, namely the protection of the integrity of the personality. This theory is not independent of the other theories, and it often is used in conjunction with the other theories to explain why privacy is important, what aspects of the self should be limited, or what information we should have control over.

a. *Individuality, Dignity, and Autonomy*

What is personhood? What aspects of the self does privacy protect? According to Edward Bloustein, privacy protects individuality.[150] Privacy is a unified and coherent concept protecting against conduct that is "demeaning to individuality," "an affront to personal dignity," or an "assault on human personality."[153] Jeffrey Reiman also recognizes a personhood component to privacy: "The right to privacy . . . protects the individual's interest in becoming, being, and remaining a person."[154] * * *

Theories of privacy as personhood, however, fail to elucidate what privacy is because the theories often do not articulate an adequate definition of personhood. * * * Personhood theories are also too broad. Our personalities are not purely private; indeed, there is much that is unique to the self that we readily display and express in public. An artistic work is often an expression of the deepest recesses of an artist's existence; yet art

---

123. [*Id.* at 324].

149. Paul Freund, AMERICAN LAW INSTITUTE, 52ND ANNUAL MEETING 42-43 (1975).

150. Edward J. Bloustein, *Privacy as an Aspect of Human Dignity: An Answer to Dean Prosser*, 39 N.Y.U. L. REV. 962, 971 (1964).

153. *Id.* at 974.

154. Jeffrey H. Reiman, *Privacy, Intimacy, and Personhood*, in PHILOSOPHICAL DIMENSIONS OF PRIVACY 300, 314 (Ferdinand David Schoeman ed., 1984).

is rarely exclusively a private affair. [Ruth] Gavison, for example, criticizes Bloustein's dignity conception because "there are ways to offend dignity and personality that have nothing to do with privacy."[155] She elaborates: "Having to beg or sell one's body in order to survive are serious affronts to dignity, but do not appear to involve loss of privacy."[156]

Further, theories of privacy as personhood tell us why we value privacy (to protect individuality, dignity, and autonomy), but their usual focus on limiting state intervention in our decisions often gives too little attention to the private sector. Merely restricting state interference is not always sufficient to protect privacy. * * *

b. *Antitotalitarianism*

In his influential article, *The Right of Privacy*, Jed Rubenfeld has provided a sophisticated account of the problems of the personhood theory of privacy.[177] * * * Rubenfeld offers an alternative conception, defining the right to privacy as "the fundamental freedom not to have one's life too totally determined by a progressively more normalizing state."[183] Rubenfeld claims that privacy protects against a "creeping totalitarianism, an unarmed occupation of individuals' lives."[184] Privacy "is to be invoked only where the government threatens to take over or occupy our lives—to exert its power in some way over the totality of our lives."[185] As Rubenfeld elaborates, "[t]he anti-totalitarian right to privacy . . . prevents the state from imposing on individuals a defined identity."[186]

Although Rubenfeld's critique of the personhood conception is certainly warranted, he fails in his attempt to abandon a personhood conception. If privacy concerns only those exercises of state power that threaten the "totality of our lives," then it is difficult to conceive of anything that would be protected. * * * Rubenfeld's critique of personhood forbids him to sketch any conception of identity that the law should protect, for to do so would be to seize from individuals their right to define themselves. By abandoning any attempt to define a conception of identity, Rubenfeld's conception of privacy collapses into a vague right to be let alone. * * *

6. *Intimacy*

An increasingly popular theory understands privacy as a form of intimacy. This theory appropriately recognizes that privacy is not just essential to individual self-creation, but also to human relationships. As Daniel Farber correctly notes, one virtue of privacy as intimacy is that it "expand[s] moral personhood beyond simple rational autonomy."[190] The theory views privacy as consisting of some form of limited access or control,

---

155. Ruth Gavison, *Privacy and the Limits of Law*, 89 YALE L.J. 421, 438 (1980).

156. *Id.*

177. Jed Rubenfeld, *The Right of Privacy*, 102 HARV. L. REV. 737, 737 (1989).

183. *Id.* at 784.

184. *Id.*

185. *Id.* at 787.

186. *Id.* at 794.

190. Daniel A. Farber, *Book Review, Privacy, Intimacy, and Isolation by Julie C. Inness*, 10 CONST. COMMENT. 510, 516 (1993).

and it locates the value of privacy in the development of personal relationships. * * * How is "intimate" information to be defined? * * * Without limitations in scope, the word "intimacy" is merely a different word for "privacy," and is certainly not sufficient as a way to determine which matters are private.

On the other hand, privacy-as-intimacy theories are too narrow because they focus too exclusively on interpersonal relationships and the particular feelings engendered by them. * * *

II

RECONCEPTUALIZING PRIVACY: A PRAGMATIC APPROACH

* * * I contend that privacy problems involve disruptions to certain practices. By "practices," I am referring broadly to various activities, customs, norms, and traditions. Examples of practices include writing letters, talking to one's psychotherapist, engaging in sexual intercourse, making certain decisions, and so on. Privacy is a dimension of these practices, and under my approach, privacy should be understood as part of these practices rather than as a separate abstract conception. * * *

When I speak of privacy as a dimension of practices, I understand privacy to be an important (sometimes essential) constitutive part of particular practices. Understanding privacy requires us to look to the specific ways in which privacy manifests itself within practices and the degree to which privacy is linked to the purposes. When we state that we are protecting "privacy," we are claiming to guard against disruptions to certain practices. Privacy invasions disrupt and sometimes completely annihilate certain practices. Practices can be disrupted in certain ways, such as interference with peace of mind and tranquility, invasion of solitude, breach of confidentiality, loss of control over facts about oneself, searches of one's person and property, threats to or violations of personal security, destruction of reputation, surveillance, and so on.

There are certain similarities in particular types of disruptions as well as in the practices that they disrupt; but there are differences as well. We should conceptualize privacy by focusing on the specific types of disruption and the specific practices disrupted rather than looking for the common denominator that links all of them. * * *

Turning our focus from disruptions to the practices they disrupt, we often refer to aspects of these practices as "private matters." * * * [A]s I have argued, we should seek to understand practices rather than classify certain matters as public or private * * * . It is reductive to carve the world of social practices into two spheres, public and private, and then attempt to determine what matters belong in each sphere. * * * [T]he matters we consider private change over time. While some form of dichotomy between public and private has been maintained throughout the history of Western civilization, the matters that have been considered public and private have metamorphosed throughout history due to changing attitudes, institutions, living conditions, and technology. * * *

One might object to my approach because of its evolving nature. If there is no consistent set of practices that should be considered private, how are we to determine what to protect as private? We must make such determinations by evaluating practices empirically, historically, and normatively. Empirical and descriptive claims as to the current cultural understandings of privacy are very important in conceptualizing privacy. A conception of privacy must be responsive to social reality since privacy is an aspect of social practices. Since practices are dynamic, we must understand their historical development. Looking historically at practices deepens our understanding of the role that privacy has played in them and the effects that disruptions to them might cause.

However, privacy is not simply an empirical and historical question that measures the collective sense in any given society of what is and has long been considered to be private. Without a normative component, a conception of privacy can only provide a status report on existing privacy norms rather than guide us toward shaping privacy law and policy in the future. If we focus simply on people's current expectations of privacy, our conception of privacy would continually shrink given the increasing surveillance in the modern world. Similarly, the government could gradually condition people to accept wiretapping or other privacy incursions, thus altering society's expectations of privacy. On the other hand, if we merely seek to preserve those activities and matters that have historically been considered private, then we fail to adapt to the changing realities of the modern world. * * *

We want certain matters to be private, even if we need to create this privacy through the use of law. * * * Therefore, determining what the law should protect as private depends upon a normative analysis, which requires us to examine the value of privacy in particular contexts.

Notes and Questions

1. Professor Solove outlines several conceptions of what privacy is. Which conceptions, if any, provide useful models for protecting Internet privacy? Consider this question in light of the many types of communications and data about a person that may reside on some computer network: personal communications (stored by one's service provider or that of a recipient); logs of web browsing activities; financial information; subscriber information; and so on. Can a single conception of privacy capture the interests at stake with respect to each type of information?

2. Professor Solove views privacy problems as involving the "disruption" of certain social practices. Is this a helpful description of Internet-related privacy problems? Consider, for example, the data generated by a user's successive interactions with different websites. Does collection and aggregation of that data disrupt any social practices?

3. Professor Solove's conception of privacy accounts for the fact that social practices change over time. Is such a recognition helpful in light of rapidly changing technology? In other words, must a social practice take hold before disruption of that practice becomes a privacy problem? Is it a sufficient answer to say that privacy has a normative component as well?

4. The excerpt above outlines different conceptions of what privacy is, but not why it should be protected. For Professor Solove's discussion of that point,

see Solove, *supra*, at 1144-46. Is there anything specific about the Internet that makes protecting privacy particularly important?   Consider the following perspectives.

Paul M. Schwartz, *Privacy and Democracy in Cyberspace*

52 VAND. L. REV. 1609 (1999)

Cyberspace is our new arena for public and private activities.   It reveals information technology's great promise: to form new links between people and to marshal these connections to increase collaboration in political and other activities that promote democratic community.   In particular, cyberspace has a tremendous potential to revitalize democratic self-governance at a time when a declining level of participation in communal life endangers civil society in the United States.

Yet, information technology in cyberspace also affects privacy in ways that are dramatically different from anything previously possible.   By generating comprehensive records of online behavior, information technology can broadcast an individual's secrets in ways that she can neither anticipate nor control.   Once linked to the Internet, the computer on our desk becomes a potential recorder and betrayer of our confidences. In the absence of strong privacy rules, cyberspace's civic potential will never be attained.   At present, however, no successful standards, legal or otherwise, exist for limiting the collection and utilization of personal data in cyberspace. * * *

The absence of privacy on the Internet reflects a deeper current, namely the establishment of the managerial data processing model in cyberspace. * * * The utilization of information technology in cyberspace will act as a powerful negative force in two ways.   First, as currently configured, it will discourage unfettered participation in deliberative democracy in the United States.   Second, the current use of information technology on the Internet can harm an individual's capacity for self-governance. These two negative effects are significant because our nation's political order is based both on democratic deliberation and on individuals who are capable of forming and acting on their notions of the good. * * *

From the civic republican perspective, the true promise of the Internet will not be as a place for electronic commerce, but as a forum for deliberative democracy. Cyberspace appears as the answer to their search for a new hospitable space. * * * Cyberspace can provide a space for "civic forums," where, to cite Frank Michaelman's general formulation, "the critical and corrective rigors of actual democratic discourses" can occur.[250] * * * [C]yberspace offers the promise to fulfill [Benjamin Barber's]

---

250. Frank Michelman, *How Can the People Ever Make the Laws? A Critique of Deliberative Democracy, in* DELIBERATIVE DEMOCRACY: ESSAYS ON REASON AND POLITICS 145, 165 (James Bowman & William Rehg eds., 1997).

call for a "free space in which democratic attitudes are cultivated and democratic behavior is conditioned."[251]

This framework offers a fruitful basis for understanding why certain proposals regarding the future development of cyberspace are so important. For example, Stephen Doheny-Farina has pointed to some of the trends already mentioned, such as the setting up of virtual community bulletin boards, and has described them as proof of the promise of the "wired neighborhood."[252] In his view, there is a critical need for a proliferation of civic networks that originate locally and organize community information and culture to foster responsibility and pride in our neighborhoods. Beyond the idea of such local networks, Laura Gurak views cyberspace as an electronic place of speed and simultaneity that allows people with common values to gather around an issue and take effective political action.[254] While Doheny-Farina is interested in the potential of a wired neighborhood, Gurak explores the potential of interest communities that are national and international in scope. * * *

In the absence of strong rules for information privacy, Americans will hesitate to engage in cyberspace activities—including those that are most likely to promote democratic self-rule. Current polls already indicate an aversion on the part of some people to engage even in basic commercial activities on the Internet. Yet, deliberative democracy requires more than shoppers; it demands speakers and listeners. But who will speak or listen when this behavior leaves finely-grained data trails in a fashion that is difficult to understand or anticipate? Put differently, when widespread and secret surveillance becomes the norm, the act of speaking or listening takes on a different social meaning. * * *

Information privacy rules must evaluate the demands for personal data along with the need for restrictions on access that will encourage speech. If cyberspace is to be a place where we develop our commonality through democratic discourse, the right kinds of rules must shape the terms and conditions under which others have access to our personal data. The issue is of the highest importance; the Internet's potential to improve democracy will be squandered unless we safeguard the kinds of information use that democratic community requires. * * *

Beyond democratic deliberation, information use in cyberspace poses an important threat to a second value necessary for life in a democracy. * * * [D]emocracy requires more than group deliberation at a town square located either in Real Space or in cyberspace. It requires individuals with an underlying capacity to form and act on their notions of the good in deciding how to live their lives. This anti-totalitarian principle stands as a bulwark against any coercive standardization of the individual. Yet, a considerable difficulty arises in identifying the kinds of government

---

251. BENJAMIN R. BARBER, A PLACE FOR US: HOW TO MAKE SOCIETY CIVIL AND DEMOCRACY STRONG 6 (1998).

252. STEPHEN DOHENY-FARINA, THE WIRED NEIGHBORHOOD 125 (1996).

254. LAURA J. GURAK, PERSUASION AND PRIVACY IN CYBERSPACE: THE ONLINE PROTESTS OVER LOTUS MARKETPLACE AND THE CLIPPER CHIP 8 (1997).

or group behavior that raises a threat to personal self-governance. Part of the problem is that autonomy is a notoriously slippery concept. Even more to the point, however, communal life requires something beyond isolated decisionmaking—self-governance takes place in individuals who are not located on discrete behavioral islands, but are tied to others and necessarily open to influence through outside persuasion. * * *

Self-determination is a capacity that is embodied and developed through social forms and practices. The threat to this quality arises when private or government action interferes with a person's control of her reasoning process. * * * [P]hysical coercion or false statements of fact corrupt decisionmaking by commandering the listener's mind to produce an outcome that the speaker desires. Autonomy manipulation on the Internet reaches a similar result in a different fashion. Its perfected surveillance of naked thought's digital expression short-circuits the individual's own process of decisionmaking.

George Orwell carried out the classic analysis of how surveillance can exert this negative pressure. In the novel *1984*, first published in 1949, Orwell imagined a machine called the "telescreen."[292] This omnipresent device broadcasted propaganda on a nonstop basis and allowed the state officials, the "Thought Police," to observe the populace. Computers on the Internet are reminiscent of the telescreen; under current conditions, it is impossible to know if and when the cyber-Thought Police are plugged in on any individual wire. To extend Orwell's thought, one can say that as habit becomes instinct and people on the Internet gain a sense that their every mouse click and key stroke might be observed, the necessary insulation for individual self-determination will vanish. * * *

Information processing coerces decisionmaking when it undermines an individual's ability to make choices about participation in social and political life. This analysis also reveals the considerable positive role that privacy on the Internet can play in our society. * * * [T]he Internet, if accompanied by the right kind of rules for access to personal data, has a tremendous potential to become a space for individual deliberations about identity.

Julie E. Cohen, *Examined Lives: Informational Privacy and the Subject as Object*

52 STAN. L. REV. 1373 (2000)

It is conventional to justify trade in personally-identified data with reference to individual liberty. Yet * * * on sustained examination the concern with the individuals who are data subjects proves relatively superficial. The rhetorics of liberty mask the fact that, at a more fundamental level, data privacy discourse has been driven by concerns for the autonomy of those who would objectify individuals—with the rights of the data processor as owner, trader, vendor, speaker, chooser. If we are

---

292. GEORGE ORWELL, 1984 at 6 (Penguin Books 1954) (1949).

serious about fostering individual freedom in reality as well as in rhetoric, this is an odd result. What is needed, instead, is a dynamic theory of informational privacy—one that focuses on the conditions for meaningful autonomy in fact. * * *

Prevailing market-based approaches to data privacy policy—including "solutions" in the form of tradable privacy rights or heightened disclosure requirements before consent—treat preferences for informational privacy as a matter of individual taste, entitled to no more (and often much less) weight than preferences for black shoes over brown or red wine over white. But the values of informational privacy are far more fundamental. A degree of freedom from scrutiny and categorization by others promotes important noninstrumental values, and serves vital individual and collective ends.

First, informational autonomy comports with important values concerning the fair and just treatment of individuals within society. From Kant to Rawls, a central strand of Western philosophical tradition emphasizes respect for the fundamental dignity of persons, and a concomitant commitment to egalitarianism in both principle and practice. Advocates of strong data privacy protection argue that these principles have clear and very specific implications for the treatment of personally-identified data: They require that we forbid data-processing practices that treat individuals as mere conglomerations of transactional data, or that rank people as prospective customers, tenants, neighbors, employees, or insureds based on their financial or genetic desirability. The drafters of the European Data Protection Directive agreed with this characterization; the Directive is explicitly grounded in "the fundamental rights and freedoms of natural persons."

Arguably, however, the leap from normative first principles to the European model of fair information practice requires further explanation. In theory, at least, a market model of tradable privacy rights is fully consistent with first-order normative commitments to dignity and equality, in that it treats each individual as an autonomous, rational actor and presumes that all individuals are equally capable of ascertaining and pursuing the goals that will maximize their own happiness. * * * [But] individuals experience substantially less choice about data-processing practice, and enjoy substantially less agency, than the rational-actor model predicts. The disjunction arises because the rational-actor model (even modified to acknowledge preferences for privacy as legitimate) devotes no attention to how individuals attain autonomy in fact—that is, to how we develop the capacity and facility for choice.

Autonomous individuals do not spring full-blown from the womb. We must learn to process information and to draw our own conclusions about the world around us. We must learn to choose, and must learn something before we can choose anything. Here, though, information theory suggests a paradox: "Autonomy" connotes an essential independence of critical faculty and an imperviousness to influence. But to the extent that information shapes behavior, autonomy is radically contingent upon environment and circumstance. The only tenable resolution—if "autonomy" is not to degenerate into the simple, stimulus-response behavior sought by direct marketers—is to underdetermine environment. Autonomy in a contingent world requires a zone of relative insulation from outside scrutiny and interference—a field of operation within which to engage in the conscious construction of self. The solution to the paradox of contingent autonomy, in other words, lies in a second paradox: To exist in fact as well as in theory, autonomy must be nurtured.

A realm of autonomous, unmonitored choice, in turn, promotes a vital diversity of speech and behavior. The recognition that anonymity shelters constitutionally-protected decisions about speech, belief, and political and intellectual association—decisions that otherwise might be chilled by unpopularity or simple difference—is part of our constitutional tradition. But the benefits of informational autonomy (defined to include the condition in which no information is recorded about nonanonymous choices) extend to a much wider range of human activity and choice. We do not experiment only with beliefs and associations, but also with every other conceivable type of taste and behavior that expresses and defines self. The opportunity to experiment with preferences is a vital part of the process of learning, and learning to choose, that every individual must undergo. * * *

The point is not that people will not learn under conditions of no-privacy, but that they will learn differently, and that the experience of being watched will constrain, ex ante, the acceptable spectrum of belief and behavior. Pervasive monitoring of every first move or false start will, at the margin, incline choices toward the bland and the mainstream. The result will be a subtle yet fundamental shift in the content of our character, a blunting and blurring of rough edges and sharp lines. * * * The condition of no-privacy threatens not only to chill the expression of eccentric individuality, but also, gradually, to dampen the force of our aspirations to it.

As the foregoing discussion shows, there are compelling theoretical and practical justifications for legislating strong data privacy protection that creates and preserves a zone of informational autonomy for individuals.

Notes and Questions

1. Professor Schwartz predicted, *circa* 1999, that "the true promise of the Internet will not be as a place for electronic commerce, but as a forum for deliberative democracy," and that "[i]n the absence of strong rules for information privacy, Americans will hesitate to engage in cyberspace activities." Were these predictions borne out?

2. Both Professor Schwartz and Professor Cohen are concerned about the consequences (as Cohen puts it) of the Internet's "no-privacy" condition. What consequences of the no-privacy condition does each foresee? How do their views differ? Each focuses to some degree on the consequences that inadequate privacy protections have for Internet users' "autonomy." What does each mean by autonomy, and why does each see it as worth protecting?

3. Do Schwartz and Cohen simply have an idealized vision of the Internet and the need for privacy? Both seem to believe that privacy is worth protecting regardless of users' preferences, and both seem to believe that some form of government intervention may be necessary. Consider, however, the following contrary view:

Dozens of bills are pending in Congress to regulate Internet privacy, often based on the assumption that privacy fears are stifling the growth of the Internet. * * * Consumers may tell survey takers they fear for their privacy, but their behavior belies it. Of more interest is how much consumers will pay—in time or money—for the corresponding benefits. * * * [O]nline businesses will invest in privacy when it's profitable. * * * Consumer behavior will tell companies what level of privacy to provide. Let the market continue unimpeded rather than chase phantom consumer fears through unnecessary regulation.

Eric Goldman, *The Privacy Hoax*, FORBES, Oct. 14, 2002, at 42. Which view is more persuasive?

4. All of the perspectives discussed above focus largely on the privacy threats posed by private parties such as data processors. What additional concerns arise when the claimed privacy invasion results from government activities? Does such surveillance pose other threats to the democratic process? For an argument that it does, see Peter P. Swire, *The System of Foreign Intelligence Surveillance Law*, 72 GEO. WASH. L. REV. 1306, 1317-20 (2004). The next section considers these issues.

SECTION B. GOVERNMENT SURVEILLANCE

As discussed in Chapter Four, the Fourth Amendment protects against government surveillance of communications in some circumstances. In particular, as *Katz v. United States* illustrates, the government cannot invade a zone in which a person has a reasonable expectation of privacy without prior judicial authorization based on a showing of probable cause. 389 U.S. 347 (1967). But when it comes to the Internet, *Katz* raises more questions than it answers. Does one have a reasonable expectation of privacy in electronic communications as well as telephonic communications and oral conversations? Does one have a reasonable expectation in information that a service provider might retain about a user, such as logs of a subscriber's web browsing? How does the Fourth Amendment apply to communications stored by a third-party service provider? Does the *Katz* framework apply when the government seeks communications for national security purposes rather than law enforcement purposes?

In 1968, Congress responded to *Katz* and other decisions by setting up procedures for law enforcement officials to follow in order to obtain appropriate judicial authorization for wiretapping and eavesdropping. Enacted as Title III of the Omnibus Crime Control and Safe Streets Act ("Title III", often referred to as the "Wiretap Act"), the procedures are codified as amended at 18 U.S.C. §§ 2510-2522. Because many of the questions above were unforeseen when the Court decided *Katz* and

Congress enacted the Wiretap Act,[c] the statute did no more than regulate the "interception" of telephone and oral conversations—it did not cover communications more broadly. Moreover, although *Katz* is the foundation for the reasonable expectation of privacy test, there remains no established method for determining when an expectation of privacy is reasonable. Does the reasonableness of an expectation of privacy depend on the legal protection afforded to communications? The public's opinion that communications are invulnerable? The societal importance of the communications system involved?

Electronic communications thus began to develop against the backdrop of Fourth Amendment uncertainty and a statutory gap. Congress responded in 1986 by enacting the Electronic Communications Privacy Act. That statute extended the reach of the Wiretap Act to prohibit the interception of electronic communications.[d] In addition, ECPA added protection for *stored* electronic communications, generally prohibiting private and government access to such communications while establishing procedures for government access. Finally, ECPA imposed limits on private and governmental access to dialing and signaling information associated with incoming and outgoing communications. Protection of electronic communications is thus largely statutory, based on Congress's understanding in 1986 of what level of privacy the law should accord various categories of communications.

Although electronic communications systems were already in use when Congress enacted ECPA in 1986, Congress did not necessarily foresee subsequent technological developments, including the development of the Internet, the widespread use of e-mail, the dramatic increase in storage capacity, or the capability to aggregate communications from disparate sources. These technological changes have placed tremendous pressure on the statutory categories Congress created and have brought to the fore unanswered questions about *Katz*'s application. In addition, the Court in *Katz* and Congress in the Wiretap Act presumed a relatively clear boundary between criminal investigations and national security investigations. To the extent that boundary becomes more porous, it places still more pressure on the constitutional and statutory surveillance law framework.

In framing issues of Internet surveillance, it is useful to begin with the core context in which *Katz* was decided and the Wiretap Act was adopted—the *prospective, real-time* acquisition of the *contents* of communications in a *criminal* investigation—and then to consider activities outside of that

---

c. The *Katz* Court did reserve the question whether application of the Fourth Amendment should differ between criminal investigations and national security investigations, and Congress excepted national security investigations from the original scope of the Wiretap Act. *See Katz*, 389 U.S. at 358 n.23; *infra* p. 626.

d. Because ECPA amended the Wiretap Act, courts and commentators on occasion refer to the amended statute as ECPA, or as Title I of the ECPA (reflecting the portion of ECPA containing the amendments). Since the amended statute covers far more than electronic communications, and to avoid confusion with other portions of ECPA discussed later in this section, we follow the more common practice of referring to the amended statute as Title III or the federal Wiretap Act.

highly protected core. As will become clear, the constitutional and statutory distinctions at every turn are highly contested.

1. Prospective Acquisition of Contents

Berger v. New York

Supreme Court of the United States, 1967
388 U.S. 41

MR. JUSTICE CLARK delivered the opinion of the Court.

This writ tests the validity of New York's permissive eavesdrop statute, N.Y. Code Crim. Proc. § 813-a, under the Fourth . . . and Fourteenth Amendments. * * *

Section 813-a authorizes the issuance of an "ex parte order for eavesdropping" upon "oath or affirmation of a district attorney, or of the attorney-general or of an officer above the rank of sergeant of any police department of the state or of any political subdivision thereof . . . ." The oath must state "that there is reasonable ground to believe that evidence of crime may be thus obtained, and particularly describing the person or persons whose communications, conversations or discussions are to be overheard or recorded and the purpose thereof, and . . . identifying the particular telephone number or telegraph line involved." The judge "may examine on oath the applicant and any other witness he may produce and shall satisfy himself of the existence of reasonable grounds for the granting of such application." The order must specify the duration of the eavesdrop—not exceeding two months unless extended—and "[a]ny such order together with the papers upon which the application was based, shall be delivered to and retained by the applicant as authority for the eavesdropping authorized therein."

While New York's statute satisfies the Fourth Amendment's requirement that a neutral and detached authority be interposed between the police and the public, the broad sweep of the statute is immediately observable. * * * The Fourth Amendment commands that a warrant issue not only upon probable cause supported by oath or affirmation, but also "particularly describing the place to be searched, and the persons or things to be seized." New York's statute lacks this particularization. It merely says that a warrant may issue on reasonable ground to believe that evidence of crime may be obtained by the eavesdrop. It lays down no requirement for particularity in the warrant as to what specific crime has been or is being committed, nor "the place to be searched," or "the persons or things to be seized" as specifically required by the Fourth Amendment. The need for particularity and evidence of reliability in the showing required when judicial authorization of a search is sought is especially great in the case of eavesdropping. * * * [The statute] actually permits general searches by electronic devices, the truly offensive character of which was first condemned in *Entick v. Carrington*, 19 How. St. Tr. 1029 (K.B. 1765), and which were then known as "general warrants." The use of the latter was a motivating factor behind the Declaration of Independence. * * *

[E]avesdropping is authorized without requiring belief that any particular offense has been or is being committed; nor that the "property" sought, the conversations, be particularly described. The purpose of the probable-cause requirement of the Fourth Amendment, to keep the state out of constitutionally protected areas until it has reason to believe that a specific crime has been or is being committed, is thereby wholly aborted. Likewise the statute's failure to describe with particularity the conversations sought gives the officer a roving commission to "seize" any and all conversations. It is true that the statute requires the naming of "the person or persons whose communications, conversations or discussions are to be overheard or recorded * * *." But this does no more than identify the person whose constitutionally protected area is to be invaded rather than "particularly describing" the communications, conversations, or discussions to be seized. As with general warrants this leaves too much to the discretion of the officer executing the order.

Secondly, authorization of eavesdropping for a two-month period is the equivalent of a series of intrusions, searches, and seizures pursuant to a single showing of probable cause. Prompt execution is also avoided. During such a long and continuous (24 hours a day) period the conversations of any and all persons coming into the area covered by the device will be seized indiscriminately and without regard to their connection with the crime under investigation. Moreover, the statute permits, and there were authorized here, extensions of the original two-month period—presumably for two months each—on a mere showing that such extension is "in the public interest." Apparently the original grounds on which the eavesdrop order was initially issued also form the basis of the renewal. This we believe insufficient without a showing of present probable cause for the continuance of the eavesdrop.

Third, the statute places no termination date on the eavesdrop once the conversation sought is seized. This is left entirely in the discretion of the officer. Finally, the statute's procedure, necessarily because its success depends on secrecy, has no requirement for notice as do conventional warrants, nor does it overcome this defect by requiring some showing of special facts. On the contrary, it permits uncontested entry without any showing of exigent circumstances. Such a showing of exigency, in order to avoid notice would appear more important in eavesdropping, with its inherent dangers, than that required when conventional procedures of search and seizure are utilized. Nor does the statute provide for a return on the warrant thereby leaving full discretion in the officer as to the use of seized conversations of innocent as well as guilty parties. In short, the statute's blanket grant of permission to eavesdrop is without adequate judicial supervision or protective procedures.

[Concurring opinions of Justice Douglas and Justice Stewart and dissenting opinions of Justice Black, Justice Harlan, and Justice White omitted.]

Notes and Questions

1. What aspects of New York's eavesdropping statute does the Court find deficient under the Fourth Amendment?

2. Portions of the Wiretap Act, as amended, are set forth below. As you read the statute, consider the ways in which it meets or exceeds the requirements the Court outlined in *Berger* and in *Katz v. United States, supra* p. 201. Consider also how the law distinguishes between wire and oral communications on the one hand and electronic communications on the other. Are the distinctions justified?

Interception of Wire, Oral, and Electronic Communications

Title III of the Omnibus Crime Control and Safe Streets Act of 1968, as amended

18 U.S.C. §§ 2510-2522

§ 2510. Definitions

As used in this chapter—

(1) "wire communication" means any aural transfer made in whole or in part through the use of facilities for the transmission of communications by the aid of wire, cable, or other like connection between the point of origin and the point of reception (including the use of such connection in a switching station) furnished or operated by any person engaged in providing or operating such facilities for the transmission of interstate or foreign communications or communications affecting interstate or foreign commerce;

(2) "oral communication" means any oral communication uttered by a person exhibiting an expectation that such communication is not subject to interception under circumstances justifying such expectation, but such term does not include any electronic communication;

* * *

(4) "intercept" means the aural or other acquisition of the contents of any wire, electronic, or oral communication through the use of any electronic, mechanical, or other device;

* * *

(8) "contents", when used with respect to any wire, oral, or electronic communication, includes any information concerning the substance, purport, or meaning of that communication;

* * *

(12) "electronic communication" means any transfer of signs, signals, writing, images, sounds, data, or intelligence of any nature transmitted in whole or in part by a wire, radio, electromagnetic, photoelectronic or photooptical system that affects interstate or foreign commerce, but does not include—

(A) any wire or oral communication * * * .

§ 2511. Interception and disclosure of wire, oral, or electronic communications prohibited

(1) Except as otherwise specifically provided in this chapter any person who—

(a) intentionally intercepts, endeavors to intercept, or procures any other person to intercept or endeavor to intercept, any wire, oral, or electronic communication; * * *

shall be punished as provided in subsection (4) or shall be subject to suit as provided in subsection (5). * * *

(2) * * *

(f) Nothing contained in this chapter or chapter 121 or 206 of this title, or section 705 of the Communications Act of 1934, shall be deemed to affect the acquisition by the United States Government of foreign intelligence information from international or foreign communications, or foreign intelligence activities conducted in accordance with otherwise applicable Federal law involving a foreign electronic communications system, utilizing a means other than electronic surveillance as defined in section 101 of the Foreign Intelligence Surveillance Act of 1978, and procedures in this chapter or chapter 121 and the Foreign Intelligence Surveillance Act of 1978 shall be the exclusive means by which electronic surveillance, as defined in section 101 of such Act, and the interception of domestic wire, oral, and electronic communications may be conducted.

§ 2518. Procedure for interception of wire, oral, or electronic communications

(1) Each application for an order authorizing or approving the interception of a wire, oral, or electronic communication under this chapter shall be made in writing upon oath or affirmation to a judge of competent jurisdiction and shall state the applicant's authority to make such application.

          * * *

(3) Upon [an appropriate application to a judge of a court of competent jurisdiction,] the judge may enter an ex parte order, as requested or as modified, authorizing or approving interception of wire, oral, or electronic communications within the territorial jurisdiction of the court in which the judge is sitting (and outside that jurisdiction but within the United States in the case of a mobile interception device authorized by a Federal court within such jurisdiction), if the judge determines on the basis of the facts submitted by the applicant that—

(a) there is probable cause for belief that an individual is committing, has committed, or is about to commit a particular offense enumerated in section 2516 of this chapter;

(b) there is probable cause for belief that particular communications concerning that offense will be obtained through such interception;

(c) normal investigative procedures have been tried and have failed or reasonably appear to be unlikely to succeed if tried or to be too dangerous;

(d) except as provided in subsection (11), there is probable cause for belief that the facilities from which, or the place where, the wire, oral, or electronic communications are to be intercepted are being used, or are about to be used, in connection with the commission of such offense, or are leased to, listed in the name of, or commonly used by such person.

(4) Each order authorizing or approving the interception of any wire, oral, or electronic communication under this chapter shall specify—

(a) the identity of the person, if known, whose communications are to be intercepted;

(b) the nature and location of the communications facilities as to which, or the place where, authority to intercept is granted;

(c) a particular description of the type of communication sought to be intercepted, and a statement of the particular offense to which it relates;

(d) the identity of the agency authorized to intercept the communications, and of the person authorizing the application; and

(e) the period of time during which such interception is authorized, including a statement as to whether or not the interception shall automatically terminate when the described communication has been first obtained. * * *

(5) No order entered under this section may authorize or approve the interception of any wire, oral, or electronic communication for any period longer than is necessary to achieve the objective of the authorization, nor in any event longer than thirty days. * * * Extensions of an order may be granted, but only upon * * * the court making the findings required by subsection (3) of this section. The period of extension shall be no longer than the authorizing judge deems necessary to achieve the purposes for which it was granted and in no event for longer than thirty days. Every order and extension thereof shall contain a provision that the authorization to intercept shall be executed as soon as practicable, shall be conducted in such a way as to minimize the interception of communications not otherwise subject to interception under this chapter, and must terminate upon attainment of the authorized objective, or in any event in thirty days. * * *

(6) Whenever an order authorizing interception is entered pursuant to this chapter, the order may require reports to be made to the judge who issued the order showing what progress has been made toward achievement of the authorized objective and the need for continued interception. * * *

(8)(a) The contents of any wire, oral, or electronic communication intercepted by any means authorized by this chapter shall, if possible, be recorded on tape or wire or other comparable device. The recording of the contents of any wire, oral, or electronic communication under this subsection shall be done in such way as will protect the recording from editing or other alterations. Immediately upon the expiration of the period of the order, or extensions thereof, such recordings shall be made available to the judge issuing such order and sealed under his directions. * * *

(d) Within a reasonable time but not later than ninety days after the filing of an application for an order of approval under section 2518(7)(b) which is denied or the termination of the period of an order or extensions thereof, the issuing or denying judge shall cause to be served, on the persons named in the order or the application, and such other parties to intercepted communications as the judge may determine in his discretion that is in the interest of justice, an inventory which shall include notice of—

(1) the fact of the entry of the order or the application;

(2) the date of the entry and the period of authorized, approved or disapproved interception, or the denial of the application; and

(3) the fact that during the period wire, oral, or electronic communications were or were not intercepted. * * *

(10)(a) Any aggrieved person in any trial, hearing, or proceeding in or before any court, department, officer, agency, regulatory body, or other authority of the United States, a State, or a political subdivision thereof, may move to suppress the contents of any wire or oral communication intercepted pursuant to this chapter * * * .

(11) The requirements of subsections (1)(b)(ii) and (3)(d) of this section relating to the specification of the facilities from which, or the place where, the communication is to be intercepted do not apply if [, among other things, the judge finds probable cause to believe that the person's actions could have the effect of thwarting interception from a specified facility].

Notes and Questions

1. To what extent does Congress's decision to adopt privacy protections shape—or limit—individuals' reasonable expectations of privacy for Fourth Amendment purposes? Recall the Supreme Court's conclusion in *Kyllo v. United States*, 533 U.S. 27 (2001), that law enforcement officials cannot employ a sense-enhancing technology that reveals information about the home, at least unless the technology is in wide public use. Is a federal prohibition, such as the general prohibition in the Wiretap Act on uses of devices to intercept communications, enough create a reasonable expectation of privacy? *Cf. California v. Greenwood*, 486 U.S. 35, 44 (1988) (holding that a provision of state law cannot create a reasonable expectation of privacy). For further discussion, see Patricia L. Bellia, *Surveillance Law Through Cyberlaw's Lens*, 72 GEO. WASH. L. REV. 1375, 1387-88 (2004).

2. The excerpt above sets forth the Wiretap Act's general prohibition on interception of wire, oral, and electronic communications, as well as the most important law enforcement exception, which authorizes courts to issue a special order permitting law enforcement officials to intercept the contents of communications. Other exceptions allow service providers to intercept communications in the normal course of their business, allow a party to a communication to intercept that communication, and allow law enforcement officials to intercept a communication with the consent of one party. In

addition, the statute contains an exception allowing certain high officials in the U.S. Department of Justice to proceed with an interception if an "emergency situation" requires that communications be acquired before a court order "can, with due diligence, be obtained." 18 U.S.C. § 2518(7). The provision requires that the government apply for a full Title III order within forty-eight hours.

3. As previously noted, the Wiretap Act originally protected only wire and oral communications. Congress added protection against interception of electronic communications in 1986. Obviously, much has changed since 1986 with respect to our use of electronic communications. Does Congress's enactment of statutes such as the Wiretap Act and its amendments adequately account for potential changes in technology? How might Congress create privacy protections without tying those protections to specific technologies?

4. Section 2518(3), set forth above, outlines the findings a judge must make before approving an interception order. Additional requirements appear in section 2516 and section 2518(1), which establish the circumstances under which the government can apply for an order. Some of these provisions have interesting implications for our consideration of the appropriate scope of privacy protection for wire and oral communications on the one hand and electronic communications on the other. Under section 2516(1), only certain designated federal officials—all high officials in the Justice Department—can approve an application for a Title III order to intercept wire or oral communications in a federal investigation. The statute authorizes such an application only when the interception will provide evidence of certain enumerated felonies, including various violent crimes, terrorism-related offenses, drug offenses, fraud, and racketeering. In contrast, section 2516(3) authorizes any attorney for the federal government to apply for a Title III order to intercept electronic communications, and any federal felony can provide the predicate for such an interception. What accounts for the different statutory treatment? Do you see any other ways in which the Wiretap Act treats wire and oral communications on the one hand and electronic communications on the other hand differently? Are the differences justified?

5. Despite the differences between the Wiretap Act's treatment of wire communications and its treatment of electronic communications, the Act's protections of electronic communications are fairly strong. But when do those protections apply? In *United States v. Councilman*, 418 F.3d 67 (1st Cir. 2005) (en banc), the Court of Appeals for the First Circuit confirmed that the Wiretap Act prohibits the ongoing acquisition of electronic communications while en route to the recipient, even if the communications are briefly stored at a point along the transmission path. As the next set of materials shows, almost everything else is up for grabs.

2. Retrospective Acquisition of Stored Communications

Berger and *Katz* dealt with government agents' prospective, real-time acquisition of communications as they occurred. Unsurprisingly, in the Wiretap Act, Congress was also centrally concerned with real-time surveillance. The statute defines "intercept" as the "acquisition of the contents" of a communication "through the use of any electronic, mechanical, or other device." 18 U.S.C. § 2510(4). To intercept those types of communications that the Wiretap Act was first enacted to cover—wire and oral communications—law enforcement officials would have had to acquire a communication as it was occurring, whether by listening to it or recording it. The Wiretap Act's prohibition on interception was thus naturally understood to govern the acquisition of communications in transit.

The widespread use of electronic communications, of course, raises important questions about the constitutional and statutory constraints on government conduct. Unlike a wire or oral communication, which generally no longer exists after it reaches the intended recipient (except perhaps in the case of stored voice mail), an electronic communication can be stored at any one of a number of points along a transmission path. Most important for our purposes, a copy of an electronic communication will often be held in the hands of a third party, such as an Internet service provider offering e-mail services.

Does the Constitution protect against the retrospective acquisition of stored communications to the same extent that it protects against prospective acquisition of communications? Does a subscriber have an expectation of privacy in personal communications stored with a third-party service provider? Does it matter whether the provider is an ISP that offers services to the general public, as opposed to an employer? Are the service provider's e-mail monitoring policies or practices relevant to determining whether one has an expectation of privacy against government monitoring?

Consider how the following cases bear on those questions.

United States v. Miller

Supreme Court of the United States, 1976
425 U.S. 435

MR. JUSTICE POWELL delivered the opinion of the Court.

[Respondent Miller allegedly conspired to defraud the United States of tax revenues through the operation of an unregistered still. In connection with an investigation of Miller, federal agents presented two grand jury subpoenas to the presidents of banks where Miller maintained accounts. The subpoenas required the presidents to appear before the grand jury to produce records of accounts in Miller's name. The banks provided the agents with copies of checks, deposit slips, financial statements, and monthly statements. The banks had maintained these records in compliance with the Bank Secrecy Act of 1970, 12 U.S.C. § 1829b(d). The banks did not advise Miller that the subpoenas had been served. After Miller and four others were indicted, Miller moved to suppress the bank records. The district court denied the motion, and the court of appeals reversed.]

In *Hoffa v. United States*, 385 U.S. 293, 301-302 (1966), the Court said that "no interest legitimately protected by the Fourth Amendment" is implicated by governmental investigative activities unless there is an intrusion into a zone of privacy, into "the security a man relies upon when he places himself or his property within a constitutionally protected area." The Court of Appeals, as noted above, assumed that respondent had the necessary Fourth Amendment interest * * * . We think that the Court of Appeals erred in finding the subpoenaed documents to fall within a protected zone of privacy.

On their face, the documents subpoenaed here are not respondent's "private papers." Unlike the claimant in *Boyd v. United States*, 116 U.S. 616 (1886), respondent can assert neither ownership nor possession. Instead, these are the business records of the banks. As we said in *California Bankers Assn. v. Shultz*, 416 U.S. 21, 48-49 (1974), "[b]anks are . . . not . . . neutrals in transactions involving negotiable instruments, but parties to the instruments with a substantial stake in their continued availability and acceptance." The records of respondent's accounts, like "all of the records [which are required to be kept pursuant to the Bank Secrecy Act,] pertain to transactions to which the bank was itself a party." *Id.*, at 52.

Respondent argues, however, that the Bank Secrecy Act introduces a factor that makes the subpoena in this case the functional equivalent of a search and seizure of the depositor's "private papers." * * * [R]espondent contends that the combination of the recordkeeping requirements of the Act and the issuance of a subpoena to obtain those records permits the Government to circumvent the requirements of the Fourth Amendment by allowing it to obtain a depositor's private records without complying with the legal requirements that would be applicable had it proceeded against him directly. Therefore, we must address the question whether the compulsion embodied in the Bank Secrecy Act as exercised in this case creates a Fourth Amendment interest in the depositor where none existed before. * * *

Respondent urges that he has a Fourth Amendment interest in the records kept by the banks because they are merely copies of personal records that were made available to the banks for a limited purpose and in which he has a reasonable expectation of privacy. He relies on this Court's statement in *Katz v. United States*, 389 U.S. 347, 353 (1967), quoting *Warden v. Hayden*, 387 U.S. 294, 304 (1967), that "we have . . . departed from the narrow view" that "'property interests control the right of the Government to search and seize,'" and that a "search and seizure" become unreasonable when the Government's activities violate "the privacy upon which [a person] justifiably relie[s]." But in *Katz* the Court also stressed that "[w]hat a person knowingly exposes to the public . . . is not a subject of Fourth Amendment protection." 389 U.S., at 351. We must examine the nature of the particular documents sought to be protected in order to determine whether there is a legitimate "expectation of privacy" concerning their contents.

* * * [W]e perceive no legitimate "expectation of privacy" in the contents [of the documents]. The checks are not confidential communications but negotiable instruments to be used in commercial transactions. All of the documents obtained, including financial statements and deposit slips, contain only information voluntarily conveyed to the

banks and exposed to their employees in the ordinary course of business. The lack of any legitimate expectation of privacy concerning the information kept in bank records was assumed by Congress in enacting the Bank Secrecy Act, the expressed purpose of which is to require records to be maintained because they "have a high degree of usefulness in criminal tax, and regulatory investigations and proceedings." 12 U.S.C. § 1829b(a)(1).

The depositor takes the risk, in revealing his affairs to another, that the information will be conveyed by that person to the Government. *United States v. White*, 401 U.S. 745, 751-752 (1971). This Court has held repeatedly that the Fourth Amendment does not prohibit the obtaining of information revealed to a third party and conveyed by him to Government authorities, even if the information is revealed on the assumption that it will be used only for a limited purpose and the confidence placed in the third party will not be betrayed. This analysis is not changed by the mandate of the Bank Secrecy Act that records of depositors' transactions be maintained by banks. * * *

We hold that the District Court correctly denied respondent's motion to suppress, since he possessed no Fourth Amendment interest that could be vindicated by a challenge to the subpoenas.

[Dissenting opinions of Justice Brennan and Justice Marshall omitted.]

United States v. Barr

United States District Court for the Southern District of New York, 1985
605 F. Supp. 114

LASKER, District Judge.

Harold Barr moves to suppress evidence obtained from the Affiliated Answering Service ("Affiliated"). The issue presented is whether the circumstances surrounding the government's acquisition of mail through the use of a grand jury subpoena were such that they constituted a warrantless seizure in violation of the fourth amendment. We hold Barr's fourth amendment rights were not violated. * * *

During the course of an investigation into the suspected narcotics and narcotics-related activities of Barr the government learned that Barr employed Affiliated to receive mail and telephone messages for him. On June 4, 1984 a grand jury subpoena duces tecum was served on Affiliated. The subpoena requested production on June 12, 1984 of mail addressed to "Larry Freeman", an alleged alias for Harold Barr. Rather than bring the mail to the grand jury on that date, Affiliated complied with the subpoena immediately, that is, on June 4th. On June 11, 1984 the government secured a search warrant and opened the mail which had been delivered by Affiliated pursuant to the subpoena.

Barr argues that the mail should be suppressed because the government impermissibly used a subpoena duces tecum to obtain his mail in the first place, in circumvention of the warrant requirement. The government answers that "the subpoena duces tecum issued to Affiliated on June 1, 1984 was a wholly proper use of the subpoena process."

Although the fourth amendment prohibits the issuance of subpoenas duces tecum which are overbroad, *Hale v. Henkel*, 201 U.S. 43 (1906), a subpoena which compels production of evidence is generally not considered to be a "seizure" within the meaning of the Constitution, that is, a taking which cannot be undertaken without the authority of a warrant. *United States v. Dionisio*, 410 U.S. 1 (1973). In comparing the grand jury subpoena process with fourth amendment seizures the *Dionisio* Court relied upon the diminished compulsion attendant in grand jury subpoenas as the critical distinguishing factor. *United States v. Dionisio*, 410 U.S. at 9-10.

The * * * distinction between the compulsion exerted by a subpoena and a seizure lies in the different nature of the two legal processes. Quoting with approval a decision of Judge Friendly, the Dionisio court stated:

> [A seizure] is abrupt, is effected with force or the threat of it and often in demeaning circumstances, and, in the case of arrest, results in a record involving stigma. A subpoena is served in the same manner as other legal process; it involves no stigma whatever; if the time for appearance is inconvenient, this can generally be altered; and it remains at all times under the control and supervision of a court.

Id. (quoting *United States v. Doe (Schwartz)*, 457 F.2d 895, 898 (2d Cir. 1972))

Despite the diminished compulsion of the subpoena process, however, a grand jury subpoena is not a "talisman that dissolves all constitutional protections." *Id.* at 11. Further, "the rule has long been established that a subpoena duces tecum may not be used in such a way as to impinge upon Fourth Amendment rights." *United States v. Re*, 313 F. Supp. 442, 448 (S.D.N.Y. 1970). * * *

As a threshold showing, to invoke the fourth amendment successfully a defendant must demonstrate a reasonable expectation of privacy in the papers subpoenaed. *Katz v. United States*, 389 U.S. 347, 361 (1967) (Harlan, J., concurring); *cf. United States v. Miller*, 425 U.S. 435, 442 (1976) ("[w]e must examine the nature of the particular documents sought to be protected in order to determine whether there is a legitimate 'expectation of privacy' concerning their contents"). * * * The government asserts that the mail it obtained from Affiliated was "business and financial correspondence" and "junk mail" and not "personal correspondence."

However, we do not interpret the decisions which hold that there is no reasonable expectation of privacy in corporate or other public records as precluding an individual's privacy interest in mail which relates to, for instance, his personal financial matters. Barr's personal mail is a type of property in which Barr ordinarily could have had a legitimate privacy expectation.

Beyond the determination of the simple proposition whether the property seized is of a nature which the fourth amendment generally protects, no bright line rule determines when a subpoena infringes upon fourth amendment rights. The evaluation must be made from the facts of each particular case. A review of the few relevant cases in this circuit demonstrates that, as in *Dionisio*, the focus of the inquiry relates to the level of compulsion present when the subpoena duces tecum is served. * * *

Although * * * the line between a permissible and an impermissible level of compulsion is not bright, guiding principles have evolved which aid in determining when a fourth amendment violation has occurred. Whether, and under what circumstances the person on whom process is served consents to the release of the items is a factor in evaluating the existence of a fourth amendment infraction. Clearly, a subpoena does not authorize the seizure of materials by the use of force or threats of violence, regardless of who has possession of the items or is charged with compliance.

A subpoena duces tecum may violate the fourth amendment if government agents improperly impinge on the defendant's right to contest the subpoena's validity or a court's authority to quash, alter or enforce it. Whether the defendant has notice of the subpoena is related to the opportunity to challenge the subpoena and is also a factor to be considered. Nonetheless, a mere lack of notice, standing alone, does not establish a violation. Indeed, the decisions indicate that the importance of notice as a factor diminishes when the defendant demonstrates an intent to tamper with or destroy documents or when there are no grounds upon which to assert a successful motion to quash.

Further, * * * a defendant may be deemed to have constructive notice of the subpoena when he chooses to relinquish control of his property to another person if, when served with a subpoena, the person who has custody of the items can notify the defendant, consult an attorney or move to quash the subpoena.

Applying these principles to the case at hand we find Barr's fourth amendment rights not to have been violated. Barr does not argue, nor has he produced any evidence which indicates that Affiliated's compliance with the subpoena duces tecum was by other than voluntary consent. The agents who served the subpoena did not coerce compliance by force or threats or overstep their legal authority. Indeed, Affiliated chose to comply with the subpoena immediately although compliance was not called for until eight days after the date of service.

Although * * * Barr did not have notice of the subpoena duces tecum, a motion to quash the subpoena on fourth amendment grounds would not have been successful in any event. The subpoena was not overly broad nor, as we have concluded, did the subpoena process in this case constitute an illegal seizure. Further, irrespective of any lack of notice at the time the subpoena was served, Barr has now had ample opportunity, which he is by this motion utilizing, to raise any alleged infirmities in the subpoena process which he would have challenged in a motion to quash. Moreover, Affiliated was free to consult counsel or move to quash the subpoena in Barr's absence.

Finally, we do not accept Barr's argument that Affiliated, as a "bailee" (of Barr's mail), "could not legally permit the government to inspect or take the . . . mail without incurring liability for conversion . . . ." Whatever were the contractual terms between Barr and Affiliated vis-a-vis the handling of Barr's mail, the government was not bound by them.

Notes and Questions

1. Although a subpoena, like a search warrant, is a form of legal process that law enforcement officials can present to obtain access to materials, the requirements for issuance of a subpoena differ significantly from the requirements for issuance of a warrant. Whereas a judge must find probable cause that a search warrant will yield evidence or fruits of a crime, a subpoena can issue merely upon a showing that documents or testimony are likely to be relevant to an ongoing criminal investigation. In addition, although the subpoenas in *Miller* and *Barr* were issued by a grand jury, in some circumstances a subpoena may be issued by an entity entirely outside of the court system—as when a statute authorizes use of an administrative subpoena by a federal official. The determination whether an individual has an expectation of privacy in certain items, or whether placement of the items in the hands of a third party eliminates that expectation, is therefore a crucial one for Fourth Amendment purposes.

2. *Miller* and *Barr* actually present two possible theories for why stored communications are not entitled to the same constitutional protection as communications in transit. *Miller* suggests that placing materials in the hands of a third party eliminates any expectation of privacy, whereas *Barr* suggests that searching for evidence and compelling production of evidence are simply distinct procedures, with the expectation of privacy that is fully determinative of the former having no bearing on the latter. Is either theory persuasive?

3. Is there an argument that acquisition of stored e-mail is just as invasive as a real-time interception of communications? Consider the following perspective:

> When monitors gain access to stored e-mails, they effectively conduct continuous surveillance for the period that the correspondence spans. Online surveillance of stored e-mails can be at least as hidden as wiretapping, if not more. Finally, it seems at least as likely that acquisition of stored e-mails will be indiscriminate in the sense that it discloses information about innocent people or innocent activities.

Susan Freiwald, *Online Surveillance: Remembering the Lessons of the Wiretap Act*, 56 ALA. L. REV. 9, 81 (2004). For cases recognizing an expectation of privacy in stored communications, see *United States v. Maxwell*, 45 M.J. 406 (C.A.A.F. 1996), and *United States v. Long*, 64 M.J. 57 (C.A.A.F. 2006).

4. In light of *Miller*, how should legislatures protect the privacy of stored communications against government acquisition? As noted earlier, Congress considered this question in 1986 and included in ECPA protections for electronic communications, including those stored with a service provider. Did Congress view stored electronic communications as being subject to a reasonable expectation of privacy?

Stored Communications and Transactional Records Access

Title II of the Electronic Communications Privacy Act of 1986, as amended
18 U.S.C. §§ 2701-2709, 2711-2712

§ 2701. Unlawful access to stored communications

(a) Offense.—Except as provided in subsection (c) of this section whoever—

(1) intentionally accesses without authorization a facility through which an electronic communication service is provided; or

(2) intentionally exceeds an authorization to access that facility;

and thereby obtains, alters, or prevents authorized access to a wire or electronic communication while it is in electronic storage in such system shall be punished as provided in subsection (b) of this section. * * *

(c) Exceptions.—Subsection (a) does not apply with respect to conduct authorized— * * *

(3) in section 2703, 2704, or 2518 of this title.

§ 2703. Required disclosure of customer communications or records

(a) Contents of wire or electronic communications in electronic storage.—A governmental entity may require the disclosure by a provider of electronic communication service of the contents of a wire or electronic communication, that is in electronic storage in an electronic communications system for one hundred and eighty days or less, only pursuant to a warrant issued using the procedures described in the Federal Rules of Criminal Procedure by a court with jurisdiction over the offense under investigation or equivalent State warrant. A governmental entity may require the disclosure by a provider of electronic communications services of the contents of a wire or electronic communication that has been in electronic storage in an electronic communications system for more than one hundred and eighty days by the means available under subsection (b) of this section.

(b) Contents of wire or electronic communications in a remote computing service.—

(1) A governmental entity may require a provider of remote computing service to disclose the contents of any wire or electronic communication to which this paragraph is made applicable by paragraph (2) of this subsection—

(A) without required notice to the subscriber or customer, if the governmental entity obtains a warrant issued using the procedures described in the Federal Rules of Criminal Procedure by a court with jurisdiction over the offense under investigation or equivalent State warrant; or

(B) with prior notice from the governmental entity to the subscriber or customer if the governmental entity—

(i) uses an administrative subpoena authorized by a Federal or State statute or a Federal or State grand jury or trial subpoena; or

(ii) obtains a court order for such disclosure under subsection (d) of this section;

except that delayed notice may be given pursuant to section 2705 of this title.

(2) Paragraph (1) is applicable with respect to any wire or electronic communication that is held or maintained on that service—

(A) on behalf of, and received by means of electronic transmission from (or created by means of computer processing of communications received by means of electronic transmission from), a subscriber or customer of such remote computing service; and

(B) solely for the purpose of providing storage or computer processing services to such subscriber or customer, if the provider is not authorized to access the contents of any such communications for purposes of providing any services other than storage or computer processing. * * *

(d) Requirements for court order.—A court order for disclosure under subsection (b) or (c) may be issued by any court that is a court of competent jurisdiction and shall issue only if the governmental entity offers specific and articulable facts showing that there are reasonable grounds to believe that the contents of a wire or electronic communication, or the records or other information sought, are relevant and material to an ongoing criminal investigation. In the case of a State governmental authority, such a court order shall not issue if prohibited by the law of such State. * * *

* * *

§ 2711. Definitions for chapter

As used in this chapter—

(1) the terms defined in section 2510 of this title have, respectively, the definitions given such terms in that section;

(2) the term "remote computing service" means the provision to the public of computer storage or processing services by means of an electronic communications system; * * *

[18 U.S.C. § 2510. Definitions]

(12) "electronic communication" means any transfer of signs, signals, writing, images, sounds, data, or intelligence of any nature transmitted in whole or in part by a wire, radio, electromagnetic, photoelectronic or photooptical system that affects interstate or foreign commerce, but does not include—

(A) any wire or oral communication * * * .

(15) "electronic communication service" means any service which provides to users thereof the ability to send or receive wire or electronic communications; * * *

(17) "electronic storage" means—

(A) any temporary, intermediate storage of a wire or electronic communication incidental to the electronic transmission thereof; and

(B) any storage of such communication by an electronic communication service for purposes of backup protection of such communication; * * * .

To understand these provisions (often referred to as the Stored Communications Act (SCA)), and their relationship to the Fourth Amendment, it is necessary to discuss three statutory terms that dictate what communications the SCA covers and what protection those communications receive.

First, recall that the Wiretap Act prohibits the "intercept[ion]" of wire, oral, and electronic communications. The SCA, in contrast, prohibits the "acquisition" of electronic communications in certain circumstances. Can the statutory term "intercept" be interpreted to cover the acquisition of stored communications, notwithstanding the separate statutory framework that the SCA creates for such communications?

Second, the SCA provides greater protection for communications that are "in electronic storage" than for those that are not * * * . Electronic storage describes "any *temporary, intermediate* storage of a wire or electronic communication *incidental* to the electronic transmission thereof; and . . . any storage of such communication by an electronic communication service for purposes of *backup protection* of such communication." 18 U.S.C. § 2510(17) (2000). Does the term "electronic storage" cover all communications that we might intuitively regard as "stored," or does it cover a smaller subset of those communications? What should it cover?

Third, the statute divides service providers into two categories: those that offer an "electronic communication service" and those that offer a "remote computing service." An electronic communication service is a service that "provides to users thereof the ability to send or receive wire or electronic communications." *Id.* § 2510(15). A remote computing service is "the provision to the public of computer storage or processing services." *Id.* § 2711(2). How should a service provider such as America Online be classified? It certainly offers users the ability the ability to send or receive communications, but it also offers certain storage functions. Can the provider's classification change depending upon the type of communication involved? At the time ECPA was enacted, many companies outsourced data storage and processing functions, and the remote computing service category likely referred to entities performing those functions. Now that the concept of the remote computer service is somewhat dated, and providers can easily combine transmission and storage functions, how should courts interpret the statutory terms?

As we will see, how court interpret these terms determines how much protection the surveillance law framework provides to stored communications. First, if stored communications cannot be "intercept[ed]," they are outside the *Berger, Katz,* and Wiretap Act core of highest protection. Second, the SCA assigns the greatest level of protection to communications that are in "electronic storage" with the provider of an "electronic communication service." The term electronic storage would clearly cover communications held by a service provider and not yet retrieved by a subscriber, such as an unopened e-mail. The difficulty is how to deal with a variety of other communications that a service provider holds on a user's behalf, such as a copy of a sent e-mail or an e-mail that a subscriber opens but does not delete.

What light do the following cases shed on the interpretation of these terms? As you consider the cases, keep two features of the federal surveillance law statutes in mind. First, because the Wiretap Act and the SCA cover both government conduct and private conduct, the statutory terms are frequently interpreted in cases where private parties, not government agents, are claimed to have violated the statute. When the conduct of government agents is involved, different interpretations of the SCA might raise Fourth Amendment questions. A court choosing among those interpretations might allow the "constitutional avoidance" canon—under which a court will avoid choosing an interpretation of a statute that raises constitutional questions—to guide its decision. *See Jones v. United States,* 526 U.S. 227, 239 (1999). In cases involving private conduct, however, courts are less likely to use the constitutional avoidance canon as a guide to statutory interpretation. Indeed, in criminal cases involving private conduct, the rule of lenity might lead to the opposite conclusion.

Second, because the Wiretap Act and the SCA each apply to wire communications as well as electronic communications, courts can interpret key terms in cases involving wire communications without foreseeing the implications of such decisions for electronic communications, and vice versa.

a. What Constitutes an "Interception"?

United States v. Smith

United States Court of Appeals for the Ninth Circuit, 1998
151 F.3d 1051

O'SCANNLAIN, Circuit Judge.

In this appeal from an insider securities trading conviction, we must decide difficult evidentiary issues involving an illegal interception of voicemail * * * . [An employee correctly guessed the password to her co-worker's voicemail box, retrieved an incriminating message from Smith, and passed it onto federal authorities. The district court suppressed the voicemail after concluding that it was obtained in violation of the Wiretap Act, but declined to suppress additional evidence that Smith claims the government derived from the voicemail. Smith challenges that ruling on appeal.]

[T]he government maintains * * * that the district court erred in concluding that [the Wiretap Act] governs this case in the first place. The government contends that a separate section of Title 18—§ 2701—applies to situations like the one presented here and thus controls the evidentiary question. * * *

When the Fifth Circuit observed that the Wiretap Act "is famous (if not infamous) for its lack of clarity," *Steve Jackson Games, Inc. v. United States Secret Service,* 36 F.3d 457, 462 (5th Cir. 1994), it might have put the matter too mildly. Indeed, the intersection of the Wiretap Act and the Stored Communications Act is a complex, often convoluted, area of the law. This case turns, at least in part, on issues at the very heart of that intersection. Smith insists that the Wiretap Act controls. The district court agreed. Section 2515 provides, in relevant part, that "[w]henever any *wire . . . communication* has been *intercepted,* no part of the contents of such communication and no evidence derived therefrom may be received in evidence in any trial." 18 U.S.C. § 2515 (emphasis added). Section 2510(1) defines "wire communication" as "any aural transfer made in whole or in part through the use of facilities for the transmission of communications by the aid of wire, cable, or other like connection" and expressly includes within its scope "any *electronic storage* of such communication." 18 U.S.C. § 2510(1) (emphasis added).[e] Section 2510(4) defines "intercept" as "the aural or other acquisition of the contents of any wire . . . communication through the use of any electronic, mechanical, or other device." 18 U.S.C. § 2510(4).

In view of the rather broad definitions supplied in § 2510, Smith argues, the voicemail message * * * seems rather plainly to fit within the language of the exclusionary provision of § 2515. For starters, the message itself, which Smith left in the voicemail system via telephone, was a "wire communication"; it was an "aural transfer," made using a wire facility (the telephone line), and was subsequently "electronic[ally] stor[ed]" within the voicemail system. In addition, [the co-worker's] act of recording the message with a handheld audiotape-recording "device" constituted an "aural or other acquisition"—and, hence, an "interception"—of the message. It is clear, Smith insists, that § 2515 applies. The government's response: Not so fast.

Section 2701, which is part of the Stored Communications Act, provides for the criminal punishment of anyone who "intentionally accesses without authorization a facility through which an electronic communication service is provided . . . and thereby obtains . . . access to a wire . . . communication while it is in storage in such system." 18 U.S.C. § 2701. There is no doubt that the voicemail message at issue is a "wire communication." We have also already observed that the message was in

---

e. Section 209 of he USA PATRIOT Act of 2001, Pub. L. No. 107-56, 115 Stat. 272, 283, eliminated the "electronic storage" portion of the wire communication definition. *See infra* p. 605.

"storage" within [the] voicemail system. When [the co-worker] * * * retrieved and recorded Smith's message, the government argues, she violated § 2701's prohibition on "access[ing]" stored wired communications. Consequently, the government argues, the voicemail message fits within § 2701.

The fact that § 2701, as well as § 2515, appears to apply to the voicemail message is significant, the government argues, because, unlike the Wiretap Act, the Stored Communications Act does *not* provide an exclusion remedy. * * * If the voicemail message at issue is subject to the strictures of the Stored Communications Act, then suppression is not an available remedy. If, however, it is subject to the Wiretap Act, then suppression is quite explicitly available. In other words, with respect to this case, the Wiretap Act and the Stored Communications Act appear, on their faces, to be mutually exclusive statutes (with mutually exclusive remedial schemes). Unfortunately, at least at first glance, Congress seems to have defied the laws of semantics and managed to make the voicemail message here at issue simultaneously subject to both.

In an effort to alleviate the apparent textual tension, the government endeavors to take the voicemail message at issue outside the scope of § 2515 by narrowly interpreting the word "intercept." * * * [T]he government insists that the term "intercept[ion]" in § 2515 necessarily connotes contemporaneity; that is, it "mean[s] listening to a conversation as it is taking place." In *United States v. Turk,* 526 F.2d 654, 658 (5th Cir. 1976), the Fifth Circuit held that the word "intercept" does not include "the replaying of a previously recorded conversation." Rather, it "require[s] participation by the one charged with an 'interception' in the contemporaneous acquisition of the communication through the use of the device." *Id.* Consequently, according to the government, there exists a fairly distinct division of regulatory labor, with the Wiretap Act governing the retrieval of wire communications *while in progress* and the Stored Communications Act governing the retrieval of wire communications *while in storage.* This case, the government maintains, is within the latter category, not the former.

The government's explanation encounters problems, however. Most significantly, although the government's proposed definition of "intercept" might comport with the term's ordinary meaning—"to take, seize or stop by the way or *before arrival at the destined place,*" see, e.g., *Webster's Third New International Dictionary* 1176 (1986) (emphasis added)—in this case, ordinary meaning does not control. * * * When, as here, the meaning of a word is clearly explained in a statute, courts are not at liberty to look beyond the statutory definition. And as the *Turk* court itself frankly acknowledged, "[n]o explicit limitation of coverage to contemporaneous 'acquisitions' appears in the Act." *Turk,* 526 F.2d at 658.

The government cites a slew of cases that it claims supports its narrow definition of "intercept" as requiring contemporaneity. The lion's share of those cases, however, concern electronic communications, not wire communications. See *Steve Jackson Games,* 36 F.3d 457; *Wesley College v. Pitts,* 974 F. Supp. 375 (D. Del. 1997); *Bohach v. City of Reno,* 932 F. Supp.

1232 (D. Nev. 1996); *United States v. Reyes,* 922 F. Supp. 818 (S.D.N.Y.1996). The distinction is critical, because unlike the definition of "wire communication," *see* 18 U.S.C. § 2510(1), the definition of "electronic communication" does *not* specifically include stored information. Rather, the statute defines "electronic communication" simply as the "*transfer* of signs, signals, writing, images, sounds, data, or intelligence." 18 U.S.C. § 2510(12) (emphasis added). Consequently, in cases concerning "electronic communication[s]"—the definition of which specifically includes "transfer[s]" and specifically excludes "storage"—the "narrow" definition of "intercept" fits like a glove; it is natural to except non-contemporaneous retrievals from the scope of the Wiretap Act. In fact, a number of courts adopting the narrow interpretation of "interception" have specifically premised their decisions to do so on the distinction between § 2510's definitions of wire and electronic communications. As the Fifth Circuit put the matter in *Steve Jackson Games,* an electronic-communications case:

> Congress' use of the word "transfer" in the definition of "electronic communication," and its omission in that definition of the phrase "any electronic storage of such communication" (part of the definition of "wire communication") reflects that Congress did not intend for "intercept" to apply to "electronic communications" when those communications are in "electronic storage."

Steve Jackson Games, 36 F.3d at 461-62.

In a case involving wire communications, like this one, the narrow definition of "intercept" is much harder to swallow. If, as the government insists, the term "intercept" necessarily implies contemporaneous acquisition, then the portion of § 2510(1) that specifically explains "wire communication" as including stored information is rendered essentially meaningless because messages in electronic storage cannot, by definition, be acquired contemporaneously.[12] We cannot accept such an interpretation, which flies in the face of "the cardinal rule of statutory interpretation that no provision [of a statute] should be construed to be entirely redundant." *Kungys v. United States,* 485 U.S. 759, 778 (1988). * * * Consequently, we conclude that the government's attempt to divide the statutory provisions cleanly between those concerning in-progress wire communications (*e.g.,* § 2515) and those concerning in-storage wire communications (*e.g.,* § 2701) is not a viable one.

It is not necessary, as the government assumes, either to rewrite or to ignore congressionally approved language to make sense of the Stored Communications Act and the Wiretap Act. Rather, the two statutes "admit[] a reasonable construction which gives effect to all of [their] provisions." *Jarecki v. G.D. Searle & Co.,* 367 U.S. 303, 307, 859 (1961). The terms "intercept" and "access" are not, as the government claims, temporally different, with the former, but not the latter, requiring contemporaneity;

---

12. Of course, that would not necessarily be the case if there were *other* portions of the Wiretap Act, § 2511 for instance, in which the "storage" element of the "wire communication" definition might remain viable. Every mention in the Act of "wire communication," however, refers in some manner or another to that communication's "intercept[ion]."

rather, the terms are conceptually, or qualitatively, different. The word "intercept" entails *actually* acquiring the contents of a communication, whereas the word "access" merely involves *being in position* to acquire the contents of a communication. In other words, "access[ ]" is, for all intents and purposes, a lesser included offense (or tort, as the case may be) of "intercept[ion]." As applied to the facts of this case, [Smith's co-worker] might have violated the Stored Communications Act's prohibition on "access[ing]" by simply making unauthorized use of [the] voicemail password and roaming about [the company's] automated voicemail system, even had she never recorded or otherwise "intercepted" the contents of any given message. Once she retrieved and recorded Smith's message, however, she crossed the line between the Stored Communications Act and the Wiretap Act and violated the latter's prohibition on "interception]." * * *

[O]ur reading of the Acts explains their contrasting penalty schemes. If, for instance, a hypothetical hacker were merely to "access[ ]" a communication facility (*i.e.*, put himself in position to acquire a wire communication), he could be either sued for civil damages under § 2707 or criminally prosecuted under § 2701(b), which provides for incarceration for a period of up to *two* years. If, however, he were to go further, and actually to "intercept[ ]" (*i.e.*, acquire) a wire communication, he may be sued for civil damages under § 2520 or criminally prosecuted under § 2511, which provides for incarceration for a period of up to *five* years. The fact that criminal violations of the Wiretap Act are punished more severely than those of the Stored Communications Act reflects Congress's considered judgment regarding the relative culpability that attaches to violations of those provisions and supports our conclusion that a violation of the latter is, conceptually, a "lesser included offense" of the former. * * * [O]ur construction explains the absence of an exclusion remedy among the Stored Communications Act's provisions. Obviously, the act of merely "access [ing]" a communications facility would not alone produce the contents of any wire communication that might be suppressed; hence, an exclusion provision in the Stored Communications Act is unnecessary. The actual "intercept[ion]" of a wire communication, however, could yield suppressible evidence; hence, pursuant to § 2515, the contents of any such communication illegally intercepted may not be introduced in any official proceeding. Finally, and perhaps most importantly, our interpretation permits the Wiretap Act and the Stored Communications Act to coexist peacefully; that is, it prevents us from having simply to ignore a congressional enactment or a portion thereof.

We thus reject the government's interpretation in favor of what we believe to be a more holistically sound approach to this confusing area of the law. Pursuant to that approach, we conclude that [the co-worker's] act of retrieving and recording Smith's voicemail message constituted an "intercept[ion]," and is therefore governed, not by the Stored Communications Act but, instead, by the Wiretap Act and the exclusionary rule of § 2515. Consequently, we conclude that the district court was correct to suppress the tape of the voicemail message.

[Although the court of appeals treated the applicability of the Wiretap Act as a "threshold issue," it ultimately declined to suppress the evidence because it concluded that the government did not in fact derive the evidence from the voicemail.]

Notes and Questions

1. Is the *Smith* court's reading of the statutes persuasive? Consider first the court's conclusion that the term interception must cover acquisition of stored communications, because otherwise the inclusion of "electronic storage" in the definition of "wire communication" would be meaningless. The court acknowledged that the phrase would not be meaningless if there were other portions of the Wiretap Act in which the "storage" element of the wire communication definition would remain viable. But the court may have overlooked a key feature of the pre-USA PATRIOT Act statutory scheme: that the SCA contained no procedure for government acquisition of stored wire communications, other than a reference to the Wiretap Act. Including the term "electronic storage" in the Wiretap Act definition thus emphasized the procedure that law enforcement officials had to follow to gain access to voicemail messages.

Consider also the court's conclusion that the SCA covers conduct that puts one in a position to acquire the contents of a communication, whereas the Wiretap Act covers the actual acquisition. Does the statutory language support that argument? Why or why not?

2. The *Smith* court appears to concede that, under its approach, "interception" means two different things—that it includes the acquisition of stored wire communications but excludes the acquisition of electronic communications. Is such an approach plausible? If the interpretation should be uniform, does that counsel in favor of a broader interpretation or a narrower interpretation? The Ninth Circuit found itself in precisely this dilemma in the following case.

Konop v. Hawaiian Airlines, Inc. ("Konop I")

United States Court of Appeals for the Ninth Circuit, 2001
236 F.3d 1035, *withdrawn*, 262 F.3d 972, *superseded*, 302 F.3d 868

BOOCHEVER, Circuit Judge:

Konop, a pilot for Hawaiian, maintained a website where he posted bulletins critical of his employer, its officers, and the incumbent union, Air Line Pilots Association ("ALPA"). Many of those criticisms related to Konop's opposition to labor concessions which Hawaiian sought from ALPA. Because ALPA supported giving management concessions to the existing collective bargaining agreement, Konop encouraged others via his website to consider alternative union representation. Konop controlled access to his website by requiring visitors to log in with a user name and password. Konop provided user names to certain Hawaiian employees, but not to managers or union representatives. To obtain a password and view the site, an eligible employee had to register and consent to an agreement not to disclose the site's contents.

About December 14, 1995, Hawaiian vice president James Davis ("Davis") contacted Hawaiian pilot Gene Wong ("Wong") and asked permission to use Wong's name to access Konop's site. * * * When Davis accessed the site using Wong's name, he presumably clicked a button indicating that he was Wong and agreed to Konop's terms and conditions. * * *

Konop filed suit alleging numerous [claims] arising out of Davis' viewing and use of his website[, including a claim that Davis' conduct violated the Wiretap Act. The district court granted summary judgment to Hawaiian on the Wiretap Act claim.] * * *

Protection against eavesdropping on modern electronic communications was added to the Wiretap Act and enacted in the Stored Communications Act by the Electronic Communications Privacy Act of 1986.   Title I of the ECPA amended the Wiretap Act to prohibit unauthorized "interception" of "electronic communications." 18 U.S.C. § 2511. Title II of the ECPA created the Stored Communications Act, which prohibits unauthorized "access" to "a facility through which an electronic communication service is provided." *Id.* at § 2701. * * *

The Fifth Circuit has characterized the Wiretap Act as "famous (if not infamous) for its lack of clarity." *Steve Jackson Games, Inc. v. United States Secret Serv.,* 36 F.3d 457, 462 (5th Cir. 1994). We have noted that the Fifth Circuit "might have put the matter too mildly. Indeed, the intersection of the Wiretap Act and the Stored Communications Act is a complex, often convoluted, area of the law." *United States v. Smith,* 155 F.3d 1051, 1055 (9th Cir. 1998), *cert. denied,* 525 U.S. 1071 (1999) (citations omitted).

Our way through this statutory thicket begins with the Wiretap Act as it was written and interpreted prior to its amendment by the ECPA. As originally enacted, the Wiretap Act sanctioned "any person who ... willfully intercepts, endeavors to intercept, or procures any other person to intercept, any wire or oral communication. . . ." 18 U.S.C.A. § 2511(a) (1970).   The Wiretap Act defined "wire communication" as "any communication made in whole or in part through the use of facilities for the transmission of communications by the aid of wire, cable, or other like connection." *Id.* at § 2510(1). An "oral communication" meant "any oral communication uttered by a person exhibiting an expectation that such communication is not subject to interception under circumstances justifying such expectation." *Id.* at § 2510(2). "Intercept" was defined as "the aural acquisition of the contents of any wire or oral communication through the use of any electronic, mechanical, or other device." *Id.* at § 2510(4).

The term "intercept" received a narrow construction in the influential case of *United States v. Turk,* 526 F.2d 654 (5th Cir. 1976). At issue in *Turk* was whether police intercepted a communication when they played back a tape of a telephone call that had been previously recorded by a third party. The Fifth Circuit held no unlawful interception occurred.   The court explained that the logic and policy of the Wiretap Act "require participation by the one charged with an 'interception' in the contemporaneous acquisition of the communication." *Id.* at 658.

A requirement that transmission and acquisition be contemporaneous would be fatal to Konop's claim that Hawaiian violated the Wiretap Act by gaining unauthorized access to his website. There is ordinarily a period of latency between the initial transmission of information for storage on a web server, and the acquisition of that information by its recipients. If interception requires that acquisition and transmission occur contemporaneously, then unauthorized downloading of information stored on a web server cannot be interception.

The law by which such acts of downloading are judged has changed significantly, however, since *Turk* read its contemporaneity requirement into the Wiretap Act. The variety of acts constituting interception was expanded by Title I of the ECPA from "aural acquisition" of protected communications to "aural *or other* acquisition" of protected communications. 18 U.S.C. § 2510(4) (1986) (emphasis added). The ECPA also reclassified and redefined the types of communications protected from interception. The definition of "wire communication" was narrowed from "any communication" made over the wires to "any *aural* transfer" made over the wires, *id.* at § 2510(1) (emphasis added), but the definition was also expanded to include "any electronic storage of such communication." *Id.* In addition, the ECPA added a catch-all category of "electronic communication" defined, with certain exceptions, as "any transfer of signs, signals, writing, images, sounds, data, or intelligence of any nature transmitted in whole or in part by a wire, radio, electromagnetic, photoelectronic or photooptical system. . . ." *Id.* at § 2510(12).

In *United States v. Smith,* 155 F.3d 1051 (9th Cir. 1998), *cert. denied,* 525 U.S. 1071 (1999), we considered the effect of these amendments on the meaning of "intercept" under the Wiretap Act. We also considered the relation of interception to the new offense of unauthorized access to stored communications facilities under the Stored Communications Act. At issue in *Smith* was whether the Wiretap Act required suppression of a tape of phone messages retrieved without authorization from the defendant's voice mailbox.

The government argued in *Smith* that the ECPA was not intended to repudiate *Turk* 's requirement that acquisition must be contemporaneous with transmission to constitute interception under the Wiretap Act. Instead, maintained the government, Congress intended ECPA Titles I and II to establish a distinction between the strong protection of communications in transmission afforded by the Wiretap Act (which provides for suppression of unauthorized intercepted wire communications, *see* 18 U.S.C. § 2518(10)(a)), and the weaker protection of communications in storage afforded by the Stored Communications Act (which does not provide for suppression, *see* 18 U.S.C. § 2708).

Rejecting these arguments, we found *Turk*'s narrow definition of "intercept" difficult to square with the amended Wiretap Act's definition of "wire communication." If "the term 'intercept' necessarily implies contemporaneous acquisition, then the portion of § 2510(1) that specifically defines 'wire communication' as including stored information is rendered essentially meaningless because messages in electronic storage cannot, by definition, be acquired contemporaneously." *Smith,* 155 F.3d at 1058.

The terms "intercept" under the Wiretap Act and "access" under the Stored Communications Act, we concluded, are not "temporally different, with the former, but not the latter, requiring contemporaneity; rather the terms are conceptually, or qualitatively, different." *Id.*

> The word "intercept" entails actually acquiring the contents of a communication, whereas the word "access" merely involves being in position to acquire the contents of a communication. In other words, "access" is, for all intents and purposes, a lesser included offense (or tort, as the case may be) of "interception."

Id. (alterations omitted). Under this scheme, the Wiretap Act and the Stored Communications Act do not discriminate between wire communications based on whether they are in transit or storage, but instead attach different consequences to invasions of privacy based on degrees of intrusion.

If *Smith's* definition of "intercept" applies to electronic communications, then a person's unauthorized acquisition of the contents of a secure website would constitute an interception in violation of the Wiretap Act. The only circuit court to have decided the issue, however, has held that "intercept" does not mean the same thing when applied to electronic communications as when applied to wire communications. The Fifth Circuit, in *Steve Jackson Games v. United States Secret Service,* 36 F.3d 457 (5th Cir. 1994), concluded that, with respect to electronic communications, Congress intended the ECPA to carry forward the *Turk* definition of "intercept" as contemporaneous acquisition. The court noted that the ECPA defines "electronic communication" as a "transfer" of signals, and that "unlike the definition of 'wire communication,' the definition of 'electronic communication' does not include electronic storage of such communications." *Id.* at 461.

We endorsed the reasoning of *Steve Jackson Games* in *Smith,* and this would ordinarily end our inquiry. Though electronic communications were not at issue in *Smith,* and our endorsement of *Steve Jackson Games* in that case was therefore not essential to our holding, we do not lightly reconsider persuasive dicta, even if they do not bind us. But confronting the issue squarely for the first time in this case, we find ourselves unpersuaded that Congress intended one definition of "intercept" to govern "wire communications," and another to govern "electronic communications."

We first note that the Wiretap Act provides but a single definition of "intercept," and that definition does not expressly contain or suggest the contemporaneity requirement read into it by *Turk.* The textual basis for the Fifth Circuit's conclusion in *Steve Jackson Games,* that stored electronic communications are not protected from interception under the Wiretap Act, is that the statute defines "electronic communication" as a "transfer" of information without expressly including storage of information. In contrast, the corresponding definition of "wire communication" does expressly include storage of information. It is plausible, however, that the express inclusion of stored communications in the definition of "wire communication" was intended not for purposes of contrast, but for clarification. The language was a late subcommittee addition to the draft ECPA to ensure that voice mail and similar stored wire communications would be protected as wire communications.

This addition was necessary because * * * wire communication does not necessarily include storage of that communication. Electronic communication, on the other hand, cannot successfully be completed without being stored. Therefore, it was not necessary for Congress to explicitly include the concept of storage in its definition of electronic communication.

* * * In other instances, where Congress has provided lesser protection for electronic communications, it has done so straightforwardly, and for discernable reasons. Electronic communication service providers must divulge communications in certain circumstances as an incident to their services, for example, and the Wiretap Act expressly permits them to do so. *See* 18 U.S.C. § 2511(3)(b). No expectation of privacy attaches to electronic communications made available through facilities readily available to the public, and interception of such communications is also expressly permitted under the Wiretap Act. *See* 18 U.S.C. § 2511(2)(g)(i). A suggestion by the Justice Department resulted in a provision emphasizing the unavailability of suppression, where not constitutionally required, as a remedy for unlawful interception of electronic communications. *See* 18 U.S.C. § 2518(10)(c).

No similarly straightforward provision of the Wiretap Act affords stored electronic communications a lesser degree of protection from interception than stored wire communications. We know of no reason why Congress might have wished to do so. An electronic communication in storage is no more or less private than an electronic communication in transmission. Distinguishing between the two for purposes of protection from interception is "irrational" and "an insupportable result given Congress' emphasis of individual privacy rights during passage of the ECPA." Thomas Greenberg, *E-Mail and Voice Mail: Employee Privacy and the Federal Wiretap Statute,* 44 AM. U. L. REV. 219, 248-49 (1994). * * *

We believe that Congress intended the ECPA to eliminate distinctions between protection of private communications based on arbitrary features of the technology used for transmission. * * * It makes no more sense that a private message expressed in a digitized voice recording stored in a voice mailbox should be protected from interception, but the same words expressed in an e-mail stored in an electronic post office pending delivery should not.

We conclude that it would be equally senseless to hold that Konop's messages to his fellow pilots would have been protected from interception had he recorded them and delivered them through a secure voice bulletin board accessible by telephone, but not when he set them down in electronic text and delivered them through a secure web server accessible by a personal computer. We hold that the Wiretap Act protects electronic communications from interception when stored to the same extent as when in transit.

Konop v. Hawaiian Airlines, Inc. ("Konop II")

United States Court of Appeals for the Ninth Circuit, 2002
302 F.3d 868

BOOCHEVER, Circuit Judge.

On January 8, 2001, we issued an opinion, reversing the district court's decision on Konop's claims under the Wiretap Act * * *. Hawaiian filed a petition for rehearing, which became moot when we withdrew our previous opinion. We now affirm the judgment of the district court with respect to Konop's Wiretap Act claims * * *.[2]

As we have previously observed, the intersection of [the Wiretap Act and the Stored Communications Act] "is a complex, often convoluted, area of the law." *United States v. Smith*, 155 F.3d 1051, 1055 (9th Cir. 1998). In the present case, the difficulty is compounded by the fact that the ECPA was written prior to the advent of the Internet and the World Wide Web. As a result, the existing statutory framework is ill-suited to address modern forms of communication like Konop's secure website. Courts have struggled to analyze problems involving modern technology within the confines of this statutory framework, often with unsatisfying results. We observe that until Congress brings the laws in line with modern technology, protection of the Internet and websites such as Konop's will remain a confusing and uncertain area of the law. * * *

Konop argues that Davis' conduct constitutes an interception of an electronic communication in violation of the Wiretap Act. The Wiretap Act makes it an offense to "intentionally intercept [ ] . . . any wire, oral, or electronic communication." 18 U.S.C. § 2511(1)(a). * * * "Intercept" is defined as "the aural or other acquisition of the contents of any wire, electronic, or oral communication through the use of any electronic, mechanical, or other device." *Id.* § 2510(4). Standing alone, this definition would seem to suggest that an individual "intercepts" an electronic communication merely by "acquiring" its contents, regardless of when or under what circumstances the acquisition occurs. Courts, however, have clarified that Congress intended a narrower definition of "intercept" with regard to electronic communications.

In *Steve Jackson Games, Inc. v. United States Secret Service*, 36 F.3d 457 (5th Cir. 1994), the Fifth Circuit held that the government's acquisition of email messages stored on an electronic bulletin board system, but not yet retrieved by the intended recipients, was not an "interception" under the Wiretap Act. The court observed that, prior to the enactment of the ECPA, the word "intercept" had been interpreted to mean the acquisition of a communication contemporaneous with transmission. *Id.* at 460 (*citing United States v. Turk*, 526 F.2d 654, 658 (5th Cir. 1976)). The court further observed that Congress, in passing the ECPA, intended to retain the previous definition of "intercept" with respect to wire and oral

---

2. The Wiretap Act and SCA have since been amended by the Uniting and Strengthening America by Providing Appropriate Tools Required to Intercept and Obstruct Terrorism Act (USA PATRIOT Act), Pub.L. No. 107- 56, 115 Stat. 272 (October 26, 2001).

communications, while amending the Wiretap Act to cover interceptions of electronic communications. The court reasoned, however, that the word "intercept" could not describe the exact same conduct with respect to wire and electronic communications, because wire and electronic communications were defined differently in the statute. Specifically, the term "wire communication" was defined to include storage of the communication, while "electronic communication" was not. The court concluded that this textual difference evidenced Congress' understanding that, although one could "intercept" a *wire* communication in storage, one could not "intercept" an *electronic* communication in storage:

> Critical to the issue before us is the fact that, unlike the definition of "wire communication," the definition of "electronic communication" does not include electronic storage of such communications. . . . Congress' use of the word "transfer" in the definition of "electronic communication," and its omission in that definition of the phrase "any electronic storage of such communication" . . . reflects that Congress did not intend for "intercept" to apply to "electronic communications" when those communications are in "electronic storage."

Steve Jackson Games, 36 F.3d at 461-62. The *Steve Jackson* Court further noted that the ECPA was deliberately structured to afford electronic communications *in storage* less protection than other forms of communication. *See Steve Jackson Games,* 36 F.3d at 462-64.

The Ninth Circuit endorsed the reasoning of *Steve Jackson Games* in *United States v. Smith,* 155 F.3d at 1051. The question presented in *Smith* was whether the Wiretap Act covered wire communications in storage, such as voice mail messages, or just wire communications in transmission, such as ongoing telephone conversations. Relying on the same textual distinction as the Fifth Circuit in *Steve Jackson Games,* we concluded that wire communications in storage could be "intercepted" under the Wiretap Act. We found that Congress' inclusion of storage in the definition of "wire communication" militated in favor of a broad definition of the term "intercept" with respect to wire communications, one that included acquisition of a communication subsequent to transmission. We further observed that, *with respect to wire communications only,* the prior definition of "intercept"— acquisition contemporaneous with transmission—had been overruled by the ECPA. On the other hand, we suggested that the narrower definition of "intercept" was still appropriate with regard to electronic communications:

> [I]n cases concerning "electronic communications"—the definition of which specifically includes "transfers" and specifically excludes "storage"— the "narrow" definition of "intercept" fits like a glove; it is natural to except non-contemporaneous retrievals from the scope of the Wiretap Act. In fact, a number of courts adopting the narrow interpretation of "interception" have specifically premised their decisions to do so on the distinction between § 2510's definitions of wire and electronic communications.

Smith, 155 F.3d at 1057 (citations and alterations omitted).

We agree with the *Steve Jackson* and *Smith* courts that the narrow definition of "intercept" applies to electronic communications. Notably, Congress has since amended the Wiretap Act to eliminate storage from the definition of wire communication, *see* USA PATRIOT Act § 209, 115 Stat. at 283, such that the textual distinction relied upon by the *Steve Jackson* and *Smith* courts no longer exists. This change, however, supports the analysis of those cases. By eliminating storage from the definition of wire communication, Congress essentially reinstated the pre-ECPA definition of "intercept"—acquisition contemporaneous with transmission—with respect to wire communications. The purpose of the recent amendment was to reduce protection of voice mail messages to the lower level of protection provided other electronically stored communications. *See* H.R. Rep. 107-236(I), at 158-59 (2001). When Congress passed the USA PATRIOT Act, it was aware of the narrow definition courts had given the term "intercept" with respect to electronic communications, but chose not to change or modify that definition. To the contrary, it modified the statute to make that definition applicable to voice mail messages as well. Congress, therefore, accepted and implicitly approved the judicial definition of "intercept" as acquisition contemporaneous with transmission.

We therefore hold that for a website such as Konop's to be "intercepted" in violation of the Wiretap Act, it must be acquired during transmission, not while it is in electronic storage.[6] This conclusion is consistent with the ordinary meaning of "intercept," which is "to stop, seize, or interrupt in progress or course before arrival." *Webster's Ninth New Collegiate Dictionary* 630 (1985). More importantly, it is consistent with the structure of the ECPA, which created the SCA for the express purpose of addressing "access to *stored* . . . electronic communications and transactional records." S. Rep. No. 99-541 at 3 (emphasis added). The level of protection provided stored communications under the SCA is considerably less than that provided communications covered by the Wiretap Act. Section 2703(a) of the SCA details the procedures law enforcement must follow to access the contents of stored electronic communications, but these procedures are considerably less burdensome and less restrictive than those required to obtain a wiretap order under the Wiretap Act. Thus, if Konop's position were correct and acquisition of a

---

6. The dissent, amici, and several law review articles argue that the term "intercept" must apply to electronic communications in storage because storage is a necessary incident to the transmission of electronic communications. Email and other electronic communications are stored at various junctures in various computers between the time the sender types the message and the recipient reads it. In addition, the transmission time of email is very short because it travels across the wires at the speed of light. It is therefore argued that if the term "intercept" does not apply to the *en route* storage of electronic communications, the Wiretap Act's prohibition against "intercepting" electronic communications would have virtually no effect. While this argument is not without appeal, the language and structure of the ECPA demonstrate that Congress considered and rejected this argument. Congress defined "electronic storage" as "any temporary, intermediate storage of a wire or electronic communication incidental to the electronic transmission thereof," 18 U.S.C. § 2510(17)(A), indicating that Congress understood that electronic storage was an inherent part of electronic communication. Nevertheless, as discussed above, Congress chose to afford stored electronic communications less protection than other forms of communication.

stored electronic communication were an interception under the Wiretap Act, the government would have to comply with the more burdensome, more restrictive procedures of the Wiretap Act to do exactly what Congress apparently authorized it to do under the less burdensome procedures of the SCA. Congress could not have intended this result. As the Fifth Circuit recognized in *Steve Jackson Games,* "it is most unlikely that Congress intended to require law enforcement officers to satisfy the more stringent requirements for an intercept in order to gain access to the contents of stored electronic communications." *Id.*

Because we conclude that Davis' conduct did not constitute an "interception" of an electronic communication in violation of the Wiretap Act, we affirm the district court's grant of summary judgment against Konop on his Wiretap Act claims. * * *

REINHARDT, Circuit Judge, concurring in part, dissenting in part.

I dissent * * * from [the holding] that the term "intercept" in the Wiretap Act, as applied to electronic communications, refers solely to *contemporaneous* acquisition. I conclude instead that "stored electronic communications" are subject to the statute's intercept prohibition as well.

Because I recognize that any reading of the relevant statutory provisions raises some difficulties and introduces some inconsistencies, the question becomes: which reading is more coherent and more consistent with Congressional intent? The majority reasons, and I agree, that stored electronic communications are covered under the definition of "electronic communications" in the Wiretap Act. However, having made that determination, the majority proceeds to introduce unnecessary confusion and incoherence into the statute by holding that "intercept" encompasses only *contemporaneous* acquisition of electronic communications, and thus that it is not possible to "intercept" a stored electronic communication. We have already rejected just such a contemporaneity requirement with respect to the acquisition of stored wire communications, and there is no justification for reviving it with respect to stored electronic communications. *United States v. Smith,* 155 F.3d 1051, 1057 n.11, 1058 (9th Cir. 1998).

* * * To read a contemporaneity requirement into the definition of "intercept" renders the prohibition against the electronic communication interception largely superfluous, and violates the precept against interpreting one provision of a statute to negate another. The nature of electronic communication is that it spends infinitesimal amounts of time "en route," unlike a phone call. Therefore, in order to "intercept" an electronic communication, one ordinarily obtains one of the copies made en route or at the destination. These copies constitute "stored electronic communications," as acknowledged by the majority. 18 U.S.C. § 2510(17)(A)(" 'electronic storage' means . . . any temporary, intermediate storage of a wire or electronic communication incidental to the electronic transmission thereof"). If intercept is defined as solely contemporaneous acquisition, then in contravention of Congressional intent, at most all

acquisitions of the contents of electronic communications would escape the intercept prohibition entirely. * * * [2]

This is a case of first impression in this circuit, and there is no binding authority on the regulation of stored electronic communications. There are no Supreme Court cases interpreting the provisions of the Wiretap Act and the Stored Communications Act as they relate to electronic communications, and the court of appeals decisions, in our circuit and others, either do not deal with stored electronic communications, or are superseded by changes in law and technology, or both. *United States v. Turk* predates the addition of the electronic provisions and language to the statute, and therefore is of little relevance. 526 F.2d 654 (5th Cir. 1976). More important, its contemporaneity requirement was expressly repudiated in *United States v. Smith.* 155 F.3d 1051, 1057 n. 11, 1058 (9th Cir. 1998) ("[T]o the extent that *Turk* stands for a definition of "intercept" that necessarily entails contemporaneity, it has . . . been statutorily overruled."). *Steve Jackson Games* is the only circuit court case that involves stored electronic communications. * * * *Steve Jackson Games* is rendered somewhat obsolete by the growth of the Internet, a phenomenon that the judges deciding that case could not have meaningfully incorporated into their reading of the statute. In particular, it would have been impossible to anticipate the expectations of privacy that people would develop regarding the Internet, expectations that are crucial to interpreting the statutory scheme consistent with Congressional intent to protect privacy interests. The other cases cited by the majority are district court cases, not binding on this court; they also have little persuasive value because they rely on the flawed reasoning of *Steve Jackson Games* and on the contemporaneity requirement that this court has rejected. Although this court in *United States v. Smith* correctly recognized the access/intercept distinction, our opinion contained unfortunate dicta regarding electronic communications. 155 F.3d at 1057. Because the case involved wire, not electronic, communications, those statements are not binding upon us.

Notes and Questions

1. Which of the *Konop* decisions is more persuasive as a matter of statutory interpretation? Note the *Konop II* court's observation that the USA PATRIOT Act of 2001 eliminated "electronic storage" from the definition of wire communications. Should that change have dictated a change in the court's approach? Why or why not?

2. Which of the *Konop* decisions is more persuasive as a matter of policy? Consider this argument:

---

2. In its interpretation of the term "intercept," the majority relies in part on legislative history from the USA Patriot Act. As the Supreme Court has cautioned, however, "'the *views of a subsequent Congress form a hazardous basis for inferring the intent of an earlier* one.'" *Consumer Product Safety Comm'n v. GTE Sylvania, Inc.,* 447 U.S. 102, 117 (1980)(quoting *United States v. Price,* 361 U.S. 304, 313 (1960)). Such subsequent legislative history will "rarely override a *reasonable interpretation* of a statute that can be gleaned from its language and legislative history prior to its enactment." *Id.* at 118 n.13, (emphasis added).

By merely waiting perhaps a nano-second for an e-mail to reach its destination, law enforcement monitors may easily avoid the super-warrant requirements for dynamic content interceptions. Privacy of online communications therefore depends heavily on the agents' timing, rather than on meaningful differences in either the information acquired or the intrusiveness of the procedures. The [*Konop I* court] recognized this anomaly * * *. The original panel's laudable attempt to make sense of the statute and give appreciable scope to the category of highly regulated dynamic content interceptions ended in failure.

Susan Freiwald, *Online Surveillance: Remembering the Lessons of the Wiretap Act*, 56 ALA. L. REV. 9, 55-56 (2004). Do you agree that the original panel's decision was "laudable"? Why or why not?

3. The *Smith, Konop I*, and *Konop II* cases reflect a recurring theme: that courts experience a great deal of confusion in applying the Wiretap Act and the SCA. How *should* courts resolve complex interpretive questions in a changing technological context? Is it enough for a court to recognize that the purpose of the statute is to protect privacy, and to take that purpose as a mandate to "update" the statutory language? Are there any dangers to such an approach? For discussion of this approach in surveillance law cases, see Patricia L. Bellia, *Spyware and the Limits of Surveillance Law*, 20 BERKELEY TECH. L.J. 1283, 1318-43 (2005).

b. What Constitutes "Electronic Storage"?

The Stored Communications Act treats communications differently depending on whether they are held "in electronic storage" by the provider of an "electronic communication service," or instead are held outside of electronic storage, either by the provider of a "remote computing service" (a term encompassing only providers offering services to the public) or by a provider outside of the terms of the SCA. The Wiretap Act, and by incorporation the Stored Communications Act, defines "electronic storage" as "any temporary, intermediate storage of a wire or electronic communication incidental to the electronic transmission thereof," or in the alternative as "any storage of such communication by an electronic communication service for purposes of backup protection of such communication." 18 U.S.C. § 2510(17). How does this term map onto the current communications system? Consider first a very controversial government interpretation, followed by two cases wrestling with the term.

U.S. Department of Justice, Criminal Division, Computer Crime and Intellectual Property Section, Searching and Seizing Computers and Obtaining Electronic Evidence in Criminal Investigations

July 2002, available at http://www.cybercrime.gov/s&smanual2002.pdf

The mismatch between the everyday meaning of "electronic storage" and its narrow statutory definition has been a source of considerable confusion. It is crucial to remember that "electronic storage" refers only to temporary storage, made in the course of transmission, by a provider of electronic communication service. * * * To determine whether a communication is in "electronic storage," it helps to identify the communication's final destination. A copy of a communication is in "electronic storage" only if it is a copy of a communication created at an intermediate point that is designed to be sent on to its final destination. For example, e-mail that has been received by a recipient's service provider but has not yet been accessed by the recipient is in "electronic storage." At that stage, the copy of the stored communication exists only as a temporary and intermediate measure, pending the recipient's retrieval of the communication from the service provider.

Once the recipient retrieves the e-mail, however, the communication reaches its final destination. If a recipient then chooses to retain a copy of the accessed communication on the provider's system, the copy stored on the network is no longer in "electronic storage" because the retained copy is no longer in "temporary, intermediate storage . . . incidental to . . . electronic transmission." 18 U.S.C. § 2510(17). Rather, because the process of transmission to the intended recipient has been completed, the copy is simply a remotely stored file.

As a practical matter, whether a communication is held in "electronic storage" by a provider governs whether that service provides [electronic communication service (ECS)] with respect to the communication. The two concepts are coextensive: a service provides ECS with respect to a communication if and only if the service holds the communication in electronic storage. Thus, it follows that if a communication is not in temporary, intermediate storage incidental to its electronic transmission, the service cannot provide ECS for that communication. Instead, the service must provide either "remote computing service," * * * or else neither ECS nor RCS.

Fraser v. Nationwide Mutual Ins. Co.

United States District Court for the Eastern District of Pennsylvania, 2001
135 F. Supp. 2d 623, *rev'd on other grounds*, 352 F.3d 107 (3rd Cir. 2003)

BRODY, District Judge.

This is one of the few cases that has required a court to interpret the wiretapping acts in the context of recent electronic communication technology. Here, there is a claim that the * * * Stored Communications Act * * * cover[s] retrieval of a person's e-mail from post-transmission storage. * * *

Nationwide is a family of insurance companies doing business across the country and headquartered in Columbus, Ohio. Fraser joined Nationwide as an employee in 1986. Subsequently, on or about March 1, 1986, Fraser signed the standard Agent's Agreement to become an exclusive career agent with Nationwide. * * * Fraser was committed under the agreement to represent Nationwide exclusively in the sale and service of insurance. Such exclusive representation is defined in the Agreement to mean "that you will not solicit or write policies of insurance in companies other than those parties to this Agreement, either directly or indirectly, without written consent of these Companies." * * *

On January 23, 1990, Fraser entered into an Agency Office Automation Lease Agreement with Nationwide whereby Fraser leased computer hardware and software from Nationwide for use in the automation of his office and insurance business. * * *

[Beginning in June of 1996, Fraser engaged in a variety of activities, including participating in the formation of a Pennsylvania chapter of the Nationwide Insurance Independent Contractors Association ("NIICA") (an organization that sought to lobby legislatures for increased state regulation of the insurance industry to protect agents'), filing a complaint concerning certain of Nationwide's business practices with the Pennsylvania Insurance Department and the Pennsylvania Legislature, and drafting a letter to Nationwide's competitors soliciting their interest in acquiring the business of policyholders served by Nationwide's Pennsylvania agents.]

Nationwide did not know whether or not this letter drafted by Fraser had actually been sent to Nationwide's competitors. On August 27, 1998, Nationwide's director of electronic communications in Columbus, Gregory Ricker, in the presence of Nationwide's assistant general counsel, Randall Orr, searched Nationwide's electronic file server for e-mail communication indicating whether or not the letter had been sent. Ricker opened the stored e-mail of Fraser and other agents. Ricker ultimately found an exchange of e-mails from August 25, 1998 between Fraser and Lon McAllister, an agent of Nationwide at the time, indicating that the letter had been sent to at least one competitor. * * * This e-mail was retrieved from McAllister's file of already received and discarded messages stored on the server. The messages retrieved from Nationwide's storage site had already been sent by Fraser and received by McAllister. On September 2, 1998, Nationwide cancelled Fraser's Agent's Agreement. * * *

[Fraser alleges] that Nationwide * * * retrieved his e-mail from Nationwide's electronic storage sites, in violation of * * * the Stored Communications [Act]. * * *

This decision requires a basic understanding of how electronic communication, and in particular, how e-mail communication works. Transmission of e-mail from the sender to the recipient through an electronic communication system ("the system") is indirect. First, an individual authorized to use the system logs on to the system to send a message. After a message is sent, the system stores the message in temporary or intermediate storage. I will refer to this storage as "intermediate storage". After a message is sent, the system also stores a copy of the message in a separate storage for back-up protection, in the event that the system crashes before transmission is completed. I will refer to this storage as "back-up protection storage". In the course of transmission from the sender to the recipient, a message passes through both intermediate and back-up protection storage.

Transmission is completed when the recipient logs on to the system and retrieves the message from intermediate storage. After the message is retrieved by the intended recipient, the message is copied to a third type of storage, which I will call "post-transmission storage." A message may remain in post-transmission storage for several years. * * *

The Stored Communications Act, which prohibits unauthorized "access" to an electronic communication while it is in "electronic storage" similarly provides protection for private communication only during the course of transmission. "Electronic storage" is defined under the Act as:

> "(A) any temporary, intermediate storage of a wire or electronic communication incidental to the electronic transmission thereof; and

> (B) any storage of such communication by an electronic communication service for purposes of backup protection of such communication."

18 U.S.C. § 2510(17). Part (A) of the definition fits what I previously defined as "intermediate storage". It is clear that the Stored Communications Act covers a message that is stored in intermediate storage temporarily, after the message is sent by the sender, but before it is retrieved by the intended recipient.

Part (B) of the definition refers to what I previously defined as back-up protection storage, which protects the communication in the event the system crashes before transmission is complete. The phrase "for purposes of backup protection of such communication" in the statutory definition makes clear that messages that are in post-transmission storage, after transmission is complete, are not covered by part (B) of the definition of "electronic storage". Therefore, retrieval of a message from post-transmission storage is not covered by the Stored Communications Act. The Act provides protection only for messages while they are in the course of transmission.

The facts of this case are that Nationwide retrieved Fraser's e-mail from storage after the e-mail had already been sent and received by the recipient. Nationwide acquired Fraser's e-mail from post-transmission storage. Therefore, Nationwide's conduct is not prohibited under the Stored Communications Act.

Theofel v. Farey-Jones

United States Court of Appeals for the Ninth Circuit, 2004
359 F.3d 1066

KOZINSKI, Circuit Judge:

We consider whether defendants violated federal electronic privacy and computer fraud statutes when they used a "patently unlawful" subpoena to gain access to e-mail stored by plaintiffs' Internet service provider.

Plaintiffs Wolf and Buckingham, officers of Integrated Capital Associates, Inc. (ICA), are embroiled in commercial litigation in New York against defendant Farey-Jones. In the course of discovery, Farey-Jones sought access to ICA's e-mail. He told his lawyer Iryna Kwasny to subpoena ICA's ISP, NetGate. * * * Kwasny ordered production of "[a]ll copies of emails sent or received by anyone" at ICA, with no limitation as to time or scope. NetGate, which apparently was not represented by counsel, explained that the amount of e-mail covered by the subpoena was substantial. But defendants did not relent. NetGate then took what might be described as the "Baskin-Robbins" approach to subpoena compliance and offered defendants a "free sample" consisting of 339 messages. It posted copies of the messages to a NetGate website where, without notifying opposing counsel, Kwasny and Farey-Jones read them. Most were unrelated to the litigation, and many were privileged or personal. * * *

Wolf, Buckingham and other ICA employees whose e-mail was included in the sample also filed this civil suit against Farey-Jones and Kwasny. They claim defendants violated the Stored Communications Act * * *. The Stored Communications Act provides a cause of action against anyone who "intentionally accesses without authorization a facility through which an electronic communication service is provided . . . and thereby obtains, alters, or prevents authorized access to a wire or electronic communication while it is in electronic storage." 18 U.S.C. §§ 2701(a)(1), 2707(a). * * *

Defendants ask us to [hold] that the messages they accessed were not in "electronic storage" and therefore fell outside the Stored Communications Act's coverage. See 18 U.S.C. § 2701(a)(1). The Act defines "electronic storage" as "(A) any temporary, intermediate storage of a wire or electronic communication incidental to the electronic transmission thereof; and (B) any storage of such communication by an electronic communication service for purposes of backup protection of such communication." Id. § 2510(17), incorporated by id. § 2711(1). Several courts have held that subsection (A) covers e-mail messages stored on an ISP's server pending delivery to the recipient. See In re DoubleClick, Inc. Privacy Litig., 154 F. Supp. 2d 497, 511-12 (S.D.N.Y.2001); Fraser v. Nationwide Mut. Ins. Co., 135 F. Supp. 2d 623, 635-36 (E.D. Pa. 2001); cf. Steve Jackson Games, Inc. v. U.S. Secret Serv., 36 F.3d 457, 461-62 (5th Cir. 1994) (messages stored on a BBS pending delivery). Because subsection (A) applies only to messages in "temporary, intermediate storage," however, these courts have limited that subsection's coverage to messages not yet delivered to their intended recipient. See DoubleClick, 154 F. Supp. 2d at 512; Fraser, 135 F. Supp. 2d at 636.

Defendants point to these cases and argue that messages remaining on an ISP's server after delivery no longer fall within the Act's coverage. But, even if such messages are not within the purview of subsection (A), they do fit comfortably within subsection (B). There is no dispute that messages remaining on NetGate's server after delivery are stored "by an electronic communication service" within the meaning of 18 U.S.C. § 2510(17)(B). The only issue, then, is whether the messages are stored "for purposes of backup protection." 18 U.S.C. § 2510(17)(B). We think that, within the ordinary meaning of those terms, they are.

An obvious purpose for storing a message on an ISP's server after delivery is to provide a second copy of the message in the event that the user needs to download it again—if, for example, the message is accidentally erased from the user's own computer. The ISP copy of the message functions as a "backup" for the user. Notably, nothing in the Act requires that the backup protection be for the benefit of the ISP rather than the user. Storage under these circumstances thus literally falls within the statutory definition.

One district court reached a contrary conclusion, holding that "backup protection" includes only temporary backup storage pending delivery, and not any form of "post-transmission storage." *See Fraser,* 135 F. Supp. 2d at 633- 34, 636. We reject this view as contrary to the plain language of the Act. In contrast to subsection (A), subsection (B) does not distinguish between intermediate and post-transmission storage. Indeed, *Fraser's* interpretation renders subsection (B) essentially superfluous, since temporary backup storage pending transmission would already seem to qualify as "temporary, intermediate storage" within the meaning of subsection (A). By its plain terms, subsection (B) applies to backup storage regardless of whether it is intermediate or post-transmission.

The United States, as amicus curiae, disputes our interpretation. It first argues that, because subsection (B) refers to "any storage of *such* communication," it applies only to backup copies of messages that are themselves in temporary, intermediate storage under subsection (A). The text of the statute, however, does not support this reading. Subsection (A) identifies a type of communication ("a wire or electronic communication") and a type of storage ("temporary, intermediate storage . . . incidental to the electronic transmission thereof"). The phrase "such communication" in subsection (B) does not, as a matter of grammar, reference attributes of the type of storage defined in subsection (A). The government's argument would be correct if subsection (B) referred to "a communication in such storage," or if subsection (A) referred to a communication in temporary, intermediate storage rather than temporary, intermediate storage of a communication. However, as the statute is written, "such communication" is nothing more than shorthand for "a wire or electronic communication."

The government's contrary interpretation suffers from the same flaw as *Fraser*'s: It drains subsection (B) of independent content because virtually any backup of a subsection (A) message will itself qualify as a message in temporary, intermediate storage. The government counters that the statute requires only that the underlying message be temporary, not the backup. But the lifespan of a backup is necessarily tied to that of the underlying message. Where the underlying message has expired in the normal course, any copy is no longer performing any backup function. An ISP that kept permanent copies of temporary messages could not fairly be described as "backing up" those messages.

The United States also argues that we upset the structure of the Act by defining "electronic storage" so broadly as to be superfluous and by rendering irrelevant certain other provisions dealing with remote computing services. The first claim relies on the argument that any copy of a message necessarily serves as a backup to the user, the service or both. But the mere fact that a copy *could* serve as a backup does not mean it is stored for that purpose. We see many instances where an ISP could hold messages not in electronic storage—for example, e-mail sent to or from the ISP's staff, or messages a user has flagged for deletion from the server. In both cases, the messages are not in temporary, intermediate storage, nor are they kept for any backup purpose.

Our interpretation also does not render irrelevant the more liberal access standards governing messages stored by remote computing services. *See* 18 U.S.C. §§ 2702(a)(2), 2703(b). The government's premise is that a message stored by a remote computing service "solely for the purpose of providing storage or computer processing services to [the] subscriber," *id.* §§ 2702(a)(2)(B), 2703(b)(2)(B), would also necessarily be stored for purposes of backup protection under section 2510(17)(B), and thus would be subject to the more stringent rules governing electronic storage. But not all remote computing services are also electronic communications services and, as to those that are not, section 2510(17)(B) is by its own terms inapplicable. The government notes that remote computing services and electronic communications services are "often the same entities," but "often" is not good enough to make the government's point. Even as to remote computing services that are also electronic communications services, not all storage covered by sections 2702(a)(2)(B) and 2703(b)(2)(B) is also covered by section 2510(17)(B). A remote computing service might be the only place a user stores his messages; in that case, the messages are not stored for backup purposes.

Finally, the government invokes legislative history. It cites a passage from a 1986 report indicating that a committee intended that messages stored by a remote computing service would "continue to be covered by section 2702(a)(2)" if left on the server after user access. H.R.Rep. No. 647, 99th Cong., at 65 (1986). The cited discussion addresses provisions relating to remote computing services. We do not read it to address whether the electronic storage provisions also apply. *See id.* at 64-65. The committee's statement that section 2702(a)(2) would "continue" to cover e-mail upon access supports our reading. If section 2702(a)(2) applies to e-mail even before access, the committee could not have been identifying an exclusive source of protection, since even the government concedes that unopened e-mail is protected by the electronic storage provisions.

The government also points to a subsequent, rejected amendment that would have made explicit the electronic storage definition's coverage of opened e-mail. *See* H.R.Rep. No. 932, 106th Cong., at 7 (2000). This sort of legislative history has very little probative value; Congress might have rejected the amendment precisely because it thought the definition already applied. * * *

We acknowledge that our interpretation of the Act differs from the government's and do not lightly conclude that the government's reading is erroneous. Nonetheless, for the reasons above, we think that prior access is irrelevant to whether the messages at issue were in electronic storage. Because plaintiff's e-mail messages were in electronic storage regardless of whether they had been previously delivered, the district court's decision cannot be affirmed on this alternative ground.

Notes and Questions

1. To reach the conclusion that the SCA prohibited Farey-Jones' conduct, the court of appeals in *Theofel* had to address a number of threshold issues. Section 2701(a) requires a showing that a defendant gained unauthorized access to a facility through which an electronic communication service is provided. Assuming the relevant "facilities" in this case are NetGate's mail servers or the website on which NetGate provided the e-mails, in what sense was Farey-Jones' access to them "unauthorized"? Indeed, in what sense did Farey-Jones gain access to the mail servers at all? Would the case have been decided differently if NetGate had simply mailed copies of the correspondence to Farey-Jones?

2. Was the *Theofel* court correct to conclude that merely choosing not to delete a communication is the same thing as "backing up" that communication? Does the statute actually cover *user* backups, or *service provider* backups?

3. Note that the *Theofel* court does not conclude that messages can be in backup protection forever. Rather, the court states that "[w]here the underlying message has expired in the normal course, any copy is no longer performing any backup function. An ISP that kept permanent copies of temporary messages could not fairly be described as 'backing up' those messages." How should courts apply this distinction?

4. As a matter of statutory interpretation, the key dispute between the Justice Department and the *Fraser* court on the one hand and the *Theofel* court on the other is whether communications accessed by a user but retained on a provider's server are in "electronic storage" as the Wiretap Act and SCA define the term. Which approach is more persuasive as a matter of statutory interpretation? Consider the following perspectives, one an attack on the Justice Department's approach and another an attack on the *Theofel* court's approach:

> [The Justice Department's approach] rests on a strained reading of a statutory term designed to cover practices in 1986 that are no longer applicable. It asserts, illogically, that a computer morphs from one type of service into another type when an e-mail is read, just for that e-mail. The approach conflicts with the ECPA's legislative history, which indicates that the government would need warrants for e-mails stored 180 days or less, because Congress viewed such information as constitutionally protected. * * *

> Again drawing upon the outmoded ["remote computing service"] term that no court has ever defined, the Justice Department further teaches that an e-mail, once read, falls entirely out of the ECPA's protections if it resides on a service that does not offer e-mail to the general public. In other words, the Justice Department claims that users of e-mail provided by private employers, such as companies and universities, have absolutely no protection from government demands for their e-mail messages once the messages have been read. This would mean that a large proportion of e-mails in existence today are completely unprotected.* * *

> According to the Justice Department, e-mails are entitled to the short-term storage protections for stored content acquisitions only when they are sitting on a server waiting to be retrieved. Once they are retrieved—even if it is immediately after they arrive—they are subject to

the long-term storage protections if they reside on a public system, but to no protections at all if they reside on a private system. Were it not for the history of outlandish interpretations of restrictions on wiretapping, these arguments would be hard to believe. Unfortunately, Congress has not managed to reassert that the ECPA is designed to protect privacy rather than eliminate it.

Susan Freiwald, *Online Surveillance: Remembering the Lessons of the Wiretap Act*, 56 ALA. L. REV. 9, 58-59 (2004).

> An understanding of the structure of the SCA indicates that the backup provision of the definition of electronic storage exists only to ensure that the government cannot make an end-run around the privacy-protecting ECS rules by attempting to access backup copies of unopened e-mails made by the ISP for its administrative purposes. ISPs regularly generate backup copies of their servers in the event of a server crash or other problem, and they often store these copies for the long term. Section 2510(17)(B) provides that backup copies of unopened e-mails are protected by the ECS rules even though they are not themselves incident to transmission; without this provision, copies of unopened e-mails generated by this universal ISP practice would be unprotected by the SCA. * * *

> *Theofel* * * * sets up a distinction that * * * is unworkable in practice. *Theofel* suggests that each e-mail has a definable "lifespan," during which a service provider or user may need a copy of the e-mail. During that time, the copy is in "electronic storage" and the ECS rules apply. Eventually the e-mail will "expire[ ] in the normal course," at which time the e-mail is no longer in electronic storage and the ECS protections no longer apply. * * * The apparently subjective nature of the line makes it all the less likely from the standpoint of statutory interpretation: investigators must be able to classify a file before they know what legal process they must obtain to compel it, and normally they cannot tell when a user or service provider no longer needs the file or is storing it for backup purposes.

Orin S. Kerr, *A User's Guide to the Stored Communications Act, and a Legislator's Guide to Amending It*, 72 GEO. WASH. L. REV. 1208, 1217 n.61 (2004). How should courts construe the "electronic storage" term? Are Professor Freiwald's arguments best directed to courts or Congress? Does Professor Kerr's approach provide sufficient protection as a normative matter?

3. Acquisition of Noncontent Information

Thus far, we have examined how the Fourth Amendment and federal statutes apply to the contents of communications. The Wiretap Act grants a high level of protection against the interception of the contents of electronic communications, whereas the SCA grants less protection against the acquisition of communications in electronic storage and even less protection still to the contents of electronic communications not in electronic storage. For courts, the difficult task has been to decide what sorts of Internet communications fit within each statutory category—a task that is complicated greatly by the fact that Congress enacted ECPA long before the Internet flourished. The electronic surveillance law framework presents another difficult question: What protection does the law grant against acquisition of information that is not neatly categorized as the "contents" of a communication? That is, once we move beyond communications that are essentially conversational—such as the telephone calls at issue in *Katz* and the e-mails that supplant such calls—what protection applies?

Once again, technological changes have largely outpaced legal changes. Consider what noncontent data a telephone service provider would have had available to it at the time of the *Katz* decision: dialing information necessary to connect a call and personal and other information necessary to bill the subscriber. The development of the Internet may well expand that category of information available, in that a service provider might not only have information on the recipient's of a user's e-mails, but also a detailed record of the user's web surfing activity.

To what degree should the law protect this information, as a matter of constitutional law and as a matter of statutory law? As you read the following case, ask yourself whether its logic applies to electronic communications.

Smith v. Maryland

Supreme Court of the United States, 1979
442 U.S. 735

MR. JUSTICE BLACKMUN delivered the opinion of the Court.

This case presents the question whether the installation and use of a pen register[1] constitutes a "search" within the meaning of the Fourth Amendment, made applicable to the States through the Fourteenth Amendment.

I

On March 5, 1976, in Baltimore, Md., Patricia McDonough was robbed. She gave the police a description of the robber and of a 1975 Monte Carlo automobile she had observed near the scene of the crime. After the robbery, McDonough began receiving threatening and obscene phone calls from a man identifying himself as the robber. On one occasion, the caller asked that she step out on her front porch; she did so, and saw the 1975 Monte Carlo she had earlier described to police moving slowly past her home. On March 16, police spotted a man who met McDonough's description driving a 1975 Monte Carlo in her neighborhood. By tracing the license plate number, police learned that the car was registered in the name of petitioner, Michael Lee Smith.

---

1. "A pen register is a mechanical device that records the numbers dialed on a telephone by monitoring the electrical impulses caused when the dial on the telephone is released. It does not overhear oral communications and does not indicate whether calls are actually completed." *United States v. New York Tel. Co.,* 434 U.S. 159, 161 n. 1 (1977). A pen register is "usually installed at a central telephone facility [and] records on a paper tape all numbers dialed from [the] line" to which it is attached. *United States v. Giordano,* 416 U.S. 505, 549 n. 1 (1974) (opinion concurring in part and dissenting in part).

The next day, the telephone company, at police request, installed a pen register at its central offices to record the numbers dialed from the telephone at petitioner's home. The police did not get a warrant or court order before having the pen register installed. The register revealed that on March 17 a call was placed from petitioner's home to McDonough's phone. On the basis of this and other evidence, the police obtained a warrant to search petitioner's residence.   The search revealed that a page in petitioner's phone book was turned down to the name and number of Patricia McDonough;   the phone book was seized.   Petitioner was arrested * * * .

Petitioner was indicted in the Criminal Court of Baltimore for robbery. By pretrial motion, he sought to suppress "all fruits derived from the pen register" on the ground that the police had failed to secure a warrant prior to its installation. The trial court denied the suppression motion, holding that the warrantless installation of the pen register did not violate the Fourth Amendment. [The Maryland Court of Appeals affirmed.] * * *

II

A

The Fourth Amendment guarantees "[t]he right of the people to be secure in their persons, houses, papers, and effects, against unreasonable searches and seizures." In determining whether a particular form of government-initiated electronic surveillance is a "search" within the meaning of the Fourth Amendment, our lodestar is *Katz v. United States*, 389 U.S. 347 (1967). * * * Consistently with *Katz*, this Court uniformly has held that the application of the Fourth Amendment depends on whether the person invoking its protection can claim a "justifiable," a "reasonable," or a "legitimate expectation of privacy" that has been invaded by government action. * * * This inquiry, as Mr. Justice Harlan aptly noted in his *Katz* concurrence, normally embraces two discrete questions. The first is whether the individual, by his conduct, has "exhibited an actual (subjective) expectation of privacy," 389 U.S., at 361—whether, in the words of the *Katz* majority, the individual has shown that "he seeks to preserve [something] as private." *Id.*, at 351. The second question is whether the individual's subjective expectation of privacy is "one that society is prepared to recognize as 'reasonable,'" *id.*, at 361—whether, in the words of the *Katz* majority, the individual's expectation, viewed objectively, is "justifiable" under the circumstances. *Id.*, at 353.

B

In applying the *Katz* analysis to this case, it is important to begin by specifying precisely the nature of the state activity that is challenged. The activity here took the form of installing and using a pen register. Since the pen register was installed on telephone company property at the telephone company's central offices, petitioner obviously cannot claim that his "property" was invaded or that police intruded into a "constitutionally protected area." Petitioner's claim, rather, is that, notwithstanding the absence of a trespass, the State, as did the Government in *Katz*, infringed a "legitimate expectation of privacy" that petitioner held. Yet a pen register differs significantly from the listening device employed in *Katz*, for pen registers do not acquire the contents of communications. This Court recently noted:

> "Indeed, a law enforcement official could not even determine from the use of a pen register whether a communication existed. These devices do not hear sound. They disclose only the telephone numbers that have been dialed—a means of establishing communication. Neither the purport of any communication between the caller and the recipient of the call, their identities, nor whether the call was even completed is disclosed by pen registers." *United States v. New York Tel. Co.*, 434 U.S. 159, 167 (1977).

Given a pen register's limited capabilities, therefore, petitioner's argument that its installation and use constituted a "search" necessarily rests upon a claim that he had a "legitimate expectation of privacy" regarding the numbers he dialed on his phone.

This claim must be rejected. First, we doubt that people in general entertain any actual expectation of privacy in the numbers they dial. All telephone users realize that they must "convey" phone numbers to the telephone company, since it is through telephone company switching equipment that their calls are completed. All subscribers realize, moreover, that the phone company has facilities for making permanent records of the numbers they dial, for they see a list of their long-distance (toll) calls on their monthly bills. In fact, pen registers and similar devices are routinely used by telephone companies "for the purposes of checking billing operations, detecting fraud and preventing violations of law." *United States v. New York Tel. Co.*, 434 U.S., at 174-175. Electronic equipment is used not only to keep billing records of toll calls, but also "to keep a record of all calls dialed from a telephone which is subject to a special rate structure." *Hodge v. Mountain States Tel. & Tel. Co.*, 555 F.2d 254, 266 (9th Cir. 1977) (concurring opinion). Pen registers are regularly employed "to determine whether a home phone is being used to conduct a business, to check for a defective dial, or to check for overbilling." Note, *The Legal Constraints upon the Use of the Pen Register as a Law Enforcement Tool*, 60 Cornell L. Rev. 1028, 1029 (1975) (footnotes omitted). Although most people may be oblivious to a pen register's esoteric functions, they presumably have some awareness of one common use: to aid in the identification of persons making annoying or obscene calls. Most phone books tell subscribers, on a page entitled "Consumer Information," that the company "can frequently help in identifying to the authorities the origin of unwelcome and troublesome calls." Telephone users, in sum, typically know that they must convey numerical information to the phone company; that the phone company has facilities for recording this information; and that the phone company does in fact record this information for a variety of legitimate business purposes. Although subjective expectations cannot be scientifically gauged, it is too much to believe that telephone subscribers, under these circumstances, harbor any general expectation that the numbers they dial will remain secret.

Petitioner argues, however, that, whatever the expectations of telephone users in general, he demonstrated an expectation of privacy by his own conduct here, since he "us[ed] the telephone *in his house* to the exclusion of all others." But the site of the call is immaterial for purposes of analysis in this case. Although petitioner's conduct may have been calculated to keep the *contents* of his conversation private, his conduct was not and could not have been calculated to preserve the privacy of the number he dialed. Regardless of his location, petitioner had to convey that number to the telephone company in precisely the same way if he wished to complete his call. The fact that he dialed the number on his home phone rather than on some other phone could make no conceivable difference, nor could any subscriber rationally think that it would.

Second, even if petitioner did harbor some subjective expectation that the phone numbers he dialed would remain private, this expectation is not "one that society is prepared to recognize as 'reasonable.'" *Katz v. United States*, 389 U.S., at 361. This Court consistently has held that a person has no legitimate expectation of privacy in information he voluntarily turns over to third parties. E.g., *United States v. Miller*, 425 U.S., 435, 442-444 (1976). In *Miller*, for example, the Court held that a bank depositor has no "legitimate 'expectation of privacy'" in financial information "voluntarily conveyed to . . . banks and exposed to their employees in the ordinary course of business." 425 U.S., at 442. The Court explained:

> "The depositor takes the risk, in revealing his affairs to another, that the information will be conveyed by that person to the Government. . . . This Court has held repeatedly that the Fourth Amendment does not prohibit the obtaining of information revealed to a third party and conveyed by him to Government authorities, even if the information is revealed on the assumption that it will be used only for a limited purpose and the confidence placed in the third party will not be betrayed."

Id., at 443. Because the depositor "assumed the risk" of disclosure, the Court held that it would be unreasonable for him to expect his financial records to remain private.

This analysis dictates that petitioner can claim no legitimate expectation of privacy here. When he used his phone, petitioner voluntarily conveyed numerical information to the telephone company and "exposed" that information to its equipment in the ordinary course of business. In so doing, petitioner assumed the risk that the company would reveal to police the numbers he dialed. * * *

We therefore conclude that petitioner in all probability entertained no actual expectation of privacy in the phone numbers he dialed, and that, even if he did, his expectation was not "legitimate." The installation and use of a pen register, consequently, was not a "search," and no warrant was required.

MR. JUSTICE POWELL took no part in the consideration or decision of this case.

[Dissenting opinions of Justice Stewart and Justice Marshall omitted.]

Notes and Questions

1. The *Smith* Court's reasoning that the Fourth Amendment does not require law enforcement officials to obtain a warrant before installing a pen register was based on the fact that the defendant necessarily conveyed the number he dialed to a third party to complete his call. With respect to Internet-based communications, what information is analogous to the dialing information picked up by a conventional pen register or trap and trace device? E-mail addresses? What about the URL of the websites an Internet user visits?

2. Does a user reveal more information to complete online transactions than to complete telephone calls? Consider, for example, a user searching the Barnes & Noble website for a book on "breast cancer." The URL of the page displaying the search results will likely contain the search terms, as in the example http://search.barnesandnoble.com/booksearch/results.asp?WRD= breast+cancer&userid=[* * *]. For Fourth Amendment purposes, is the resulting URL "content" in which a user has a reasonable expectation of privacy, or is it merely an address analogous to a phone number?

3. As in the case of communications in transit and stored communications, Congress has introduced a layer of statutory protection for information associated with the addressing and routing of communications. The provisions, appearing at 18 U.S.C. §§ 3121-3127, were originally enacted in 1986 as part of the ECPA. When enacted in 1986, the prohibitions and permissions were expressed in terms of the use of two devices—"pen registers," used to capture information associated with outgoing calls, and "trap and trace" devices, used to capture information associated with incoming calls.

The development of computer technology complicated application of these statutory provisions. First, the provisions clearly presumed (following *Smith*) that a telephone user lacks an expectation of privacy in the telephone number of an incoming or outgoing call, for they allowed government agents to acquire such information without a warrant based on probable cause. One could argue, however, that the Fourth Amendment analysis of the routing and addressing information associated with electronic communications should differ from the analysis of dialing and signaling information associated with a telephone call. Second, despite the fact that the provisions were part of ECPA, they focused principally on telephone communications rather than electronic communications. For example, the pen register definition provision referred to "the numbers dialed or otherwise transmitted on the telephone line." 18 U.S.C. § 3127(3) (2000). The focus on telephone numbers raised the possibility that the information associated with electronic communications was outside the statute. The government construed the provisions to cover information associated with electronic communications but to authorize government access on a standard less than probable cause. Uncertainty nevertheless surrounded law enforcement officials' ability to access such information. If the Fourth Amendment protected the information in spite of *Smith*, then the statutory procedures were insufficient. If the Fourth Amendment did not protect the information, and if the statutory prohibitions did not apply, then nothing limited law enforcement officials' acquisition of the information.

In October 2001, in section 216 the USA PATRIOT Act, Pub. L. No. 107-56, 115 Stat. 272, 288, Congress dramatically revised the pen register and trap and trace provisions to update the technologies to which they apply. As you read the provisions, consider whether the statute adequately protects information associated with electronic communications. Is such information analogous to dialing and signaling information associated with a telephone call? Why or why not?

Pen Registers and Trap and Trace Devices

Title III of the Electronic Communications Privacy Act of 1986, as amended
18 U.S.C. §§ 3121-3127

§ 3121. General prohibition on pen register and trap and trace device use; exception

(a) In general.—Except as provided in this section, no person may install or use a pen register or a trap and trace device without first obtaining a court order under section 3123 of this title * * * .

* * *

§ 3123. Issuance of an order for a pen register or a trap and trace device

(a) In general.—

(1) **Attorney for the Government**.– Upon an application made under section 3122(a)(1) [by an attorney for the federal government to a federal court], the court shall enter an ex parte order authorizing the installation and use of a pen register or trap and trace device anywhere within the United States, if the court finds that the attorney for the Government has certified to the court that the information likely to be obtained by such installation and use is relevant to an ongoing criminal investigation. The order, upon service of that order, shall apply to any person or entity providing wire or electronic communication service in the United States whose assistance may facilitate the execution of the order. Whenever such an order is served on any person or entity not specifically named in the order, upon request of such person or entity, the attorney for the Government or law enforcement or investigative officer that is serving the order shall provide written or electronic certification that the order applies to the person or entity being served.

(2) **State investigative or law enforcement officer**.– Upon an application made under section 3122(a)(2) [by a state official to a state court], the court shall enter an ex parte order authorizing the installation and use of a pen register or trap and trace device within the jurisdiction of the court, if the court finds that the State law enforcement or investigative officer has certified to the court that the information likely to be obtained by such installation and use is relevant to an ongoing criminal investigation. * * *

(b) Contents of order.—An order issued under this section—

(1) shall specify—

(A) the identity, if known, of the person to whom is leased or in whose name is listed the telephone line or other facility to which the pen register or trap and trace device is to be attached or applied;

(B) the identity, if known, of the person who is the subject of the criminal investigation;

(C) the attributes of the communications to which the order applies, including the number or other identifier and, if known, the location of the telephone line or other facility to which the pen register or trap and trace device is to be attached or applied, and, in the case of an order authorizing installation and use of a trap and trace device under subsection (a)(2), the geographic limits of the order; and

(D) a statement of the offense to which the information likely to be obtained by the pen register or trap and trace device relates; and

(2) shall direct, upon the request of the applicant, the furnishing of information, facilities, and technical assistance necessary to accomplish the installation of the pen register or trap and trace device under section 3124 of this title.

(c) Time period and extensions.—

(1) An order issued under this section shall authorize the installation and use of a pen register or a trap and trace device for a period not to exceed sixty days.

(2) Extensions of such an order may be granted, but only upon an application for an order under section 3122 of this title and upon the judicial finding required by subsection (a) of this section. The period of extension shall be for a period not to exceed sixty days. * * *

§ 3127. Definitions for chapter

As used in this chapter—

(1) the terms "wire communication", "electronic communication", "electronic communication service", and "contents" have the meanings set forth for such terms in section 2510 of this title;* * *

(3) the term "pen register" means a device or process which records or decodes dialing, routing, addressing, or signaling information transmitted by an instrument or facility from which a wire or electronic communication is transmitted, provided, however, that such information shall not include the contents of any communication * * * ;

(4) the term "trap and trace device" means a device or process which captures the incoming electronic or other impulses which identify the originating number or other dialing, routing, addressing, and signaling information reasonably likely to identify the source of a wire or electronic communication, provided, however, that such information shall not include the contents of any communication; * * * .

[18 U.S.C. § 2510. Definitions.]

* * *

(8) "contents", when used with respect to any wire, oral, or electronic communication, includes any information concerning the substance, purport, or meaning of that communication; * * * .

Notes and Questions

1. Like the Wiretap Act and the SCA, the prohibitions on the use of pen registers and trap and trace devices exempt certain uses, such as the use of a device by a service provider to perform service checks or the use of a device when a user consents. In addition, law enforcement officials can use a pen register or trap and trace device in an emergency situation, so long as they acquire an order within forty-eight hours.

2. How does the showing that an applicant must make before applying for a pen register or trap and trace order differ from that required for a Wiretap Act order? From that required for retrieval of stored communications? What process must a court go through before granting an order under the pen register and trap and trace provisions? Are the differences in the statutory schemes justified?

3. Return to the example above of the case in which a URL incorporates a search term such as "breast cancer." Whether such information lawfully be acquired through use of a pen register or trap and trace device turns on whether it constitutes "content." Does it? Should it?

Note on the Customer Records Provisions of the Stored Communications Act

In addition to providing procedures for law enforcement access to the contents of communications, the Stored Communications Act provides avenues for the government to compel production of certain information analogous to that covered by the pen register and trap and trace statute. Section 2703(c) of the SCA essentially creates two categories of information. First, the government is entitled to receive certain basic subscriber information when it presents (1) an administrative or grand jury subpoena; (2) a "2703(d)" order, requiring demonstration to a court of "specific and articulable" facts showing "reasonable grounds to believe" that the records are relevant to an ongoing investigation; (3) or a warrant. 18 U.S.C. § 2703(c) (2000 & Supp. IV 2004). The type of information available through these methods includes a user's name, address, length of service and type of service used, telephone number or temporary IP address, and payment information, as well as "local and long distance telephone connection records, or records of session times and durations." 18 U.S.C. § 2703(c)(2)(C) (Supp. IV 2004). Notably excluded from this category is a log of a user's electronic communications. Second, the government is entitled receive any other information pertaining to a subscriber, not including contents, if it presents a provider with a warrant or a 2703(d) order. It remains unclear what information, other than the basic subscriber information available through a subpoena, is "information pertaining to a subscriber" but not "the contents of communications." Would a log of

URLs qualify? What about a list of terms entered into a search engine? *Cf.* Gonzales v. Google, 234 F.R.D. 674 (N.D. Cal. 2006) (declining to opine on application of ECPA to government's civil subpoena seeking sample of 5,000 entries in Google's search query log and 50,000 URLs from Google's index).

4. National Security Investigations

In *Katz v. United States,* the Supreme Court declined to address whether the Fourth Amendment applies to national security investigations in the same way that it applies to criminal investigations, observing that "[w]hether safeguards other than prior authorization by a magistrate would satisfy the Fourth Amendment in a situation involving the national security is a question not presented by this case." 389 U.S. 347, 358 n.23 (1967). Three Justices, however, sparred over this point in concurring opinions. Justice White stated as follows:

> In joining the Court's opinion, I note the Court's acknowledgment that there are circumstance in which it is reasonable to search without a warrant. In this connection, in footnote 23 the Court points out that today's decision does not reach national security cases. Wiretapping to protect the security of the Nation has been authorized by successive Presidents. The present Administration would apparently save national security cases from restrictions against wiretapping. We should not require the warrant procedure and the magistrate's judgment if the President of the United States or his chief legal officer, the Attorney General, has considered the requirements of national security and authorized electronic surveillance as reasonable.

389 U.S. at 518 (White, J., concurring). Justice Douglas, joined by Justice Brennan, replied:

> While I join the opinion of the Court, I feel compelled to reply to the separate concurring opinion of my Brother WHITE, which I view as a wholly unwarranted green light for the Executive Branch to resort to electronic eavesdropping without a warrant in cases which the Executive Branch itself labels "national security" matters.
>
> Neither the President nor the Attorney General is a magistrate. In matters where they believe national security may be involved they are not detached, disinterested, and neutral as a court or magistrate must be. Under the separation of powers created by the Constitution, the Executive Branch is not supposed to be neutral and disinterested. Rather it should vigorously investigate and prevent breaches of national security and prosecute those who violate the pertinent federal laws. The President and Attorney General are properly interested parties, cast in the role of adversary, in national security cases. They may even be the intended victims of subversive action. Since spies and saboteurs are as entitled to the protection of the Fourth Amendment as suspected gamblers like petitioner, I cannot agree that where spies and saboteurs are involved adequate protection of Fourth Amendment

rights is assured when the President and Attorney General assume both the position of adversary-and-prosecutor and disinterested, neutral magistrate.

There is, so far as I understand constitutional history, no distinction under the Fourth Amendment between types of crimes. * * * [T]he Fourth Amendment draws no lines between various substantive offenses. The arrests on cases of "hot pursuit" and the arrests on visible or other evidence of probable cause cut across the board and are not peculiar to any kind of crime. I would respect the present lines of distinction and not improvise because a particular crime seems particularly heinous.

Id. at 515-16 (Douglas, J., concurring).

In debating the applicability of the warrant requirement to surveillance for national security purposes in *Katz*, none of the Justices specified precisely what was meant by "national security," and in particular whether any leeway the President should have to order warrantless surveillance would apply only to foreign targets, or also would apply to domestic targets. As enacted, the Wiretap Act preserved whatever preexisting authority the President might have to authorize wiretaps for national security purposes:

Nothing contained in this chapter * * * shall limit the constitutional power of the President to take such measures as he deems necessary to protect the Nation against actual or potential attack or other hostile acts of a foreign power, to obtain foreign intelligence information deemed essential to the security of the United States, or to protect national security information against foreign intelligence activities. Nor shall anything contained in this chapter be deemed to limit the constitutional power of the President to take such measures as he deems necessary to protect the United States against the overthrow of the Government by force or other unlawful means, or against any other clear and present danger to the structure or existence of the Government.

18 U.S.C. § 2511(3) (1976).

The Supreme Court addressed the constitutionality of the use of warrantless electronic surveillance against a purely *domestic* group in *United States v. United States District Court of the Eastern District of Michigan*, commonly known as the *Keith* case (for the name of the district court judge against whom the Government sought a writ of mandamus, Damon J. Keith of the Eastern District of Michigan). As you read the case, consider both the breadth of the government's arguments as to domestic threats to national security, and the space that the Court gave Congress to legislate with respect to foreign threats to national security.

United States v. United States District Court for the Eastern District of Michigan

Supreme Court of the United States, 1972
407 U.S. 297

MR. JUSTICE POWELL delivered the opinion of the Court.

This case arises from a criminal proceeding in the United States District Court for the Eastern District of Michigan, in which the United States charged three defendants with conspiracy to destroy Government property in violation of 18 U.S.C. § 371. One of the defendants, Plamondon, was charged with the dynamite bombing of an office of the Central Intelligence Agency in Ann Arbor, Michigan.

During pretrial proceedings, the defendants moved to compel the United States to disclose certain electronic surveillance information and to conduct a hearing to determine whether this information "tainted" the evidence on which the indictment was based or which the Government intended to offer at trial. In response, the Government filed an affidavit of the Attorney General, acknowledging that its agents had overheard conversations in which Plamondon had participated. The affidavit also stated that the Attorney General approved the wiretaps "to gather intelligence information deemed necessary to protect the nation from attempts of domestic organizations to attack and subvert the existing structure of the Government." The logs of the surveillance were filed in a sealed exhibit for in camera inspection by the District Court.

On the basis of the Attorney General's affidavit and the sealed exhibit, the Government asserted that the surveillance was lawful, though conducted without prior judicial approval, as a reasonable exercise of the President's power (exercised through the Attorney General) to protect the national security. The District Court held that the surveillance violated the Fourth Amendment, and ordered the Government to make full disclosure to Plamondon of his overheard conversations.

The Government then filed in the Court of Appeals for the Sixth Circuit a petition for a writ of mandamus to set aside the District Court order, which was stayed pending final disposition of the case. * * * [T]hat court held that the surveillance was unlawful and that the District Court had properly required disclosure of the overheard conversations. We granted certiorari.

[The Court first rejected the Government's argument that 18 U.S.C. § 2511(3) in fact authorized the surveillance. The Court concluded:] [N]othing in § 2511(3) was intended to expand or to contract or to define whatever presidential surveillance powers existed in matters affecting the national security. * * * [T]he statute is not the measure of the executive authority asserted in this case. Rather, we must look to the constitutional powers of the President. * * *

It is important at the outset to emphasize the limited nature of the question before the Court. This case raises no constitutional challenge to electronic surveillance as specifically authorized by Title III * * * . Nor is there any question or doubt as to the necessity of obtaining a warrant in the surveillance of crimes unrelated to the national security interest. Further, the instant case requires no judgment on the scope of the President's surveillance power with respect to the activities of foreign powers, within or without this country. The Attorney General's affidavit in this case states that the surveillances were "deemed necessary to protect the nation from attempts of *domestic* organizations to attack and subvert the existing structure of Government" (emphasis supplied). There is no evidence of any involvement, directly or indirectly, of a foreign power.

Our present inquiry, though important, is therefore a narrow one. It addresses a question left open by *Katz v. United States*, 389 U.S. 347, 358 n.23 (1967):

> Whether safeguards other than prior authorization by a magistrate would satisfy the Fourth Amendment in a situation involving the national security . . . .

The determination of this question requires the essential Fourth Amendment inquiry into the "reasonableness" of the search and seizure in question, and the way in which that "reasonableness" derives content and meaning through reference to the warrant clause.

We begin the inquiry by noting that the President of the United States has the fundamental duty, under Art. II, § 1, of the Constitution, to "preserve, protect and defend the Constitution of the United States." * * * But a recognition of these elementary truths does not make the employment by Government of electronic surveillance a welcome development—even when employed with restraint and under judicial supervision. * * * National security cases, moreover, often reflect a convergence of First and Fourth Amendment values not present in cases of "ordinary" crime. Though the investigative duty of the executive may be stronger in such cases, so also is there greater jeopardy to constitutionally protected speech. * * *

As the Fourth Amendment is not absolute in its terms, our task is to examine and balance the basic values at stake in this case: the duty of Government to protect the domestic security, and the potential danger posed by unreasonable surveillance to individual privacy and free expression. If the legitimate need of Government to safeguard domestic security requires the use of electronic surveillance, the question is whether the needs of citizens for privacy and the free expression may not be better protected by requiring a warrant before such surveillance is undertaken. We must also ask whether a warrant requirement would unduly frustrate the efforts of Government to protect itself from acts of subversion and overthrow directed against it.

* * * Fourth Amendment freedoms cannot properly be guaranteed if domestic security surveillances may be conducted solely within the discretion of the Executive Branch. The Fourth Amendment does not contemplate the executive officers of Government as neutral and disinterested magistrates. Their duty and responsibility are to enforce the laws, to investigate, and to prosecute. But those charged with this investigative and prosecutorial duty should not be the sole judges of when to utilize constitutionally sensitive means in pursuing their tasks. The

historical judgment, which the Fourth Amendment accepts, is that unreviewed executive discretion may yield too readily to pressures to obtain incriminating evidence and overlook potential invasions of privacy and protected speech.

It may well be that, in the instant case, the Government's surveillance of Plamondon's conversations was a reasonable one which readily would have gained prior judicial approval. But this Court "has never sustained a search upon the sole ground that officers reasonably expected to find evidence of a particular crime and voluntarily confined their activities to the least intrusive means consistent with that end." *Katz, supra,* at 356-357. The Fourth Amendment contemplates a prior judicial judgment, not the risk that executive discretion may be reasonably exercised. This judicial role accords with our basic constitutional doctrine that individual freedoms will best be preserved through a separation of powers and division of functions among the different branches and levels of Government. The independent check upon executive discretion is not satisfied, as the Government argues, by "extremely limited" post-surveillance judicial review. Indeed, post-surveillance review would never reach the surveillances which failed to result in prosecutions. Prior review by a neutral and detached magistrate is the time-tested means of effectuating Fourth Amendment rights. * * *

The Government argues that the special circumstances applicable to domestic security surveillances necessitate a further exception to the warrant requirement. It is urged that the requirement of prior judicial review would obstruct the President in the discharge of his constitutional duty to protect domestic security. We are told further that these surveillances are directed primarily to the collecting and maintaining of intelligence with respect to subversive forces, and are not an attempt to gather evidence for specific criminal prosecutions. It is said that this type of surveillance should not be subject to traditional warrant requirements which were established to govern investigation of criminal activity, not ongoing intelligence gathering.

The Government further insists that courts "as a practical matter would have neither the knowledge nor the techniques necessary to determine whether there was probable cause to believe that surveillance was necessary to protect national security." These security problems, the Government contends, involve "a large number of complex and subtle factors" beyond the competence of courts to evaluate.

As a final reason for exemption from a warrant requirement, the Government believes that disclosure to a magistrate of all or even a significant portion of the information involved in domestic security surveillances "would create serious potential dangers to the national security and to the lives of informants and agents. . . . Secrecy is the essential ingredient in intelligence gathering; requiring prior judicial authorization would create a greater 'danger of leaks . . . , because in addition to the judge, you have the clerk, the stenographer and some other officer like a law assistant or bailiff who may be apprised of the nature' of the surveillance."

These contentions in behalf of a complete exemption from the warrant requirement, when urged on behalf of the President and the national security in its domestic implications, merit the most careful consideration. We certainly do not reject them lightly, especially at a time of worldwide ferment and when civil disorders in this country are more prevalent than in the less turbulent periods of our history. There is, no doubt, pragmatic force to the Government's position.

But we do not think a case has been made for the requested departure from Fourth Amendment standards. The circumstances described do not justify complete exemption of domestic security surveillance from prior judicial scrutiny. Official surveillance, whether its purpose be criminal investigation or ongoing intelligence gathering, risks infringement of constitutionally protected privacy of speech. Security surveillances are especially sensitive because of the inherent vagueness of the domestic security concept, the necessarily broad and continuing nature of intelligence gathering, and the temptation to utilize such surveillances to oversee political dissent. We recognize, as we have before, the constitutional basis of the President's domestic security role, but we think it must be exercised in a manner compatible with the Fourth Amendment. In this case we hold that this requires an appropriate prior warrant procedure.

We cannot accept the Government's argument that internal security matters are too subtle and complex for judicial evaluation. Courts regularly deal with the most difficult issues of our society. There is no reason to believe that federal judges will be insensitive to or uncomprehending of the issues involved in domestic security cases. Certainly courts can recognize that domestic security surveillance involves different considerations from the surveillance of "ordinary crime." If the threat is too subtle or complex for our senior law enforcement officers to convey its significance to a court, one may question whether there is probable cause for surveillance.

Nor do we believe prior judicial approval will fracture the secrecy essential to official intelligence gathering. The investigation of criminal activity has long involved imparting sensitive information to judicial officers who have respected the confidentialities involved. Judges may be counted upon to be especially conscious of security requirements in national security cases. Title III * * * already has imposed this responsibility on the judiciary in connection with such crimes as espionage, sabotage, and treason, each of which may involve domestic as well as foreign security threats. Moreover, a warrant application involves no public or adversary proceedings: it is an ex parte request before a magistrate or judge. Whatever security dangers clerical and secretarial personnel may pose can be minimized by proper administrative measures, possibly to the point of allowing the Government itself to provide the necessary clerical assistance.

Thus, we conclude that the Government's concerns do not justify departure in this case from the customary Fourth Amendment requirement of judicial approval prior to initiation of a search or surveillance. Although some added burden will be imposed upon the Attorney General, this inconvenience is justified in a free society to protect constitutional values. Nor do we think the Government's domestic surveillance powers will be impaired to any significant degree. A prior warrant establishes presumptive validity of the surveillance and will minimize the burden of justification in post-surveillance judicial review. By no means of least importance will be the reassurance of the public generally that indiscriminate wiretapping and bugging of law-abiding citizens cannot occur.

We emphasize, before concluding this opinion, the scope of our decision. As stated at the outset, this case involves only the domestic aspects of national security. We have not addressed and express no opinion as to, the issues which may be involved with respect to activities of foreign powers or their agents. * * *

Moreover, we do not hold that the same type of standards and procedures prescribed by Title III are necessarily applicable to this case. We recognize that domestic security surveillance may involve different policy and practical considerations from the surveillance of "ordinary crime." The gathering of security intelligence is often long range and involves the interrelation of various sources and types of information. The exact targets of such surveillance may be more difficult to identify than in surveillance operations against many types of crime specified in Title III. Often, too, the emphasis of domestic intelligence gathering is on the prevention of unlawful activity or the enhancement of the Government's preparedness for some possible future crisis or emergency. Thus, the focus of domestic surveillance may be less precise than that directed against more conventional types of crime.

Given those potential distinctions between Title III criminal surveillances and those involving the domestic security, Congress may wish to consider protective standards for the latter which differ from those already prescribed for specified crimes in Title III. Different standards may be compatible with the Fourth Amendment if they are reasonable both in relation to the legitimate need of Government for intelligence information and the protected rights of our citizens. It may be that Congress, for example, would judge that the application and affidavit showing probable cause need not follow the exact requirements of § 2518 but should allege other circumstances more appropriate to domestic security cases; that the request for prior court authorization could, in sensitive cases, be made to any member of a specially designated court (e.g., the District Court for the District of Columbia or the Court of Appeals for the District of Columbia Circuit); and that the time and reporting requirements need not be so strict as those in § 2518.

The above paragraph does not, of course, attempt to guide the congressional judgment but rather to delineate the present scope of our own opinion. We do not attempt to detail the precise standards for domestic security warrants any more than our decision in *Katz* sought to set the refined requirements for the specified criminal surveillances which now constitute Title III. We do hold, however, that prior judicial approval is required for the type of domestic security surveillance involved in this case and that such approval may be made in accordance with such reasonable standards as the Congress may prescribe.

Notes and Questions

1. The Court concluded that the Government's concerns about the special problems of national security surveillance did not justify a departure from the Fourth Amendment's requirement of judicial approval. The Court went on to say that different standards for judicial approval may be appropriate in national security investigations than in criminal investigations. Are the variances that the Court suggests appropriate ones?

2. Because the *Keith* decision did not foreclose warrantless surveillance in cases involving foreign powers or their agents, the government continued to conduct such surveillance against such targets. In challenges to the use in criminal cases of evidence derived from such surveillance, several courts of appeals concluded that wiretaps for the purpose of gathering foreign intelligence information were lawful despite the absence of a warrant. *See, e.g., United States v. Truong Dinh* Hung, 629 F.2d 908 (4th Cir. 1980); United *States v. Buck*, 548 F.2d 871, 875 (9th Cir. 1977); *United States v. Butenko*, 494 F.2d 593, 605 (3rd Cir. 1974) (en banc); *United States v. Brown*, 484 F.2d 418, 425 (5th Cir. 1973).

3. Congress did not take up the Court's invitation to establish special judicial approval procedures for all national security cases. In 1978, however, Congress passed the Foreign Intelligence Surveillance Act (FISA), creating a special judicial approval procedure for "foreign intelligence" surveillance. FISA repealed the reservation clause of 18 U.S.C. § 2511(3). It added a new provision preserving any pre-existing Executive authority to acquire "foreign intelligence information" by means "other than electronic surveillance" as defined by FISA. 18 U.S.C. § 2511(2)(f). The provision also made the Wiretap Act, the SCA, the pen/trap statute, and FISA the "exclusive means by which electronic surveillance [as defined in FISA], and the interception of domestic wire, oral, and electronic communications may be conducted." 18 U.S.C. § 2511(2)(f); *see supra* p. 580. Surveillance concerning purely domestic threats to national security thus must proceed under ordinary criminal investigation authorities, while surveillance to gather foreign intelligence information can proceed under FISA. Some of FISA's key provisions are set forth below.

Foreign Intelligence Surveillance, Subchapter I, Electronic Surveillance

Foreign Intelligence Surveillance Act of 1978, as amended
50 U.S.C. §§ 1801-1811

§ 1803. Designation of judges

(a) Court to hear applications and grant orders; record of denial; transmittal to court of review

The Chief Justice of the United States shall publicly designate 11 district court judges from seven of the United States judicial circuits of whom no fewer than 3 shall reside within 20 miles of the District of Columbia who shall constitute a court which shall have jurisdiction to hear applications for and grant orders approving electronic surveillance anywhere within the United States under the procedures set forth in this chapter, * * * .

(b) Court of review; record, transmittal to Supreme Court

The Chief Justice shall publicly designate three judges, one of whom shall be publicly designated as the presiding judge, from the United States district courts or courts of appeals who together shall comprise a court of review which shall have jurisdiction to review the denial of any application made under this chapter. If such court determines that the application was properly denied, the court shall immediately provide for the record a written statement of each reason for its decision and, on petition of the United States for a writ of certiorari, the record shall be transmitted under seal to the Supreme Court, which shall have jurisdiction to review such decision. * * *

(d) Tenure

Each judge designated under this section shall so serve for a maximum of seven years and shall not be eligible for redesignation * * *.

§ 1804. Applications for court orders

(a) Submission by Federal officer; approval of Attorney General; contents

Each application for an order approving electronic surveillance under this subchapter shall be made by a Federal officer in writing upon oath or affirmation to a judge having jurisdiction under section 1803 of this title. Each application shall require the approval of the Attorney General based upon his finding that it satisfies the criteria and requirements of such application as set forth in this subchapter. It shall include—

(1) the identity of the Federal officer making the application;

(2) the authority conferred on the Attorney General by the President of the United States and the approval of the Attorney General to make the application;

(3) the identity, if known, or a description of the target of the electronic surveillance;

(4) a statement of the facts and circumstances relied upon by the applicant to justify his belief that—

(A) the target of the electronic surveillance is a foreign power or an agent of a foreign power; and

(B) each of the facilities or places at which the electronic surveillance is directed is being used, or is about to be used, by a foreign power or an agent of a foreign power;

(5) a statement of the proposed minimization procedures;

(6) a detailed description of the nature of the information sought and the type of communications or activities to be subjected to the surveillance;

(7) a certification or certifications by the Assistant to the President for National Security Affairs or an executive branch official or officials designated by the President from among those executive officers employed in the area of national security or defense and

appointed by the President with the advice and consent of the Senate—

>(A) that the certifying official deems the information sought to be foreign intelligence information;

>(B) that a significant purpose of the surveillance is to obtain foreign intelligence information;

>(C) that such information cannot reasonably be obtained by normal investigative techniques;

>(D) that designates the type of foreign intelligence information being sought according to the categories described in section 1801(e) of this title; and

>(E) including a statement of the basis for the certification that—

>>(i) the information sought is the type of foreign intelligence information designated; and

>>(ii) such information cannot reasonably be obtained by normal investigative techniques;

(8) a statement of the means by which the surveillance will be effected and a statement whether physical entry is required to effect the surveillance;

(9) a statement of the facts concerning all previous applications that have been made to any judge under this subchapter involving any of the persons, facilities, or places specified in the application, and the action taken on each previous application;

(10) a statement of the period of time for which the electronic surveillance is required to be maintained, and if the nature of the intelligence gathering is such that the approval of the use of electronic surveillance under this subchapter should not automatically terminate when the described type of information has first been obtained, a description of facts supporting the belief that additional information of the same type will be obtained thereafter; and

(11) whenever more than one electronic, mechanical or other surveillance device is to be used with respect to a particular proposed electronic surveillance, the coverage of the devices involved and what minimization procedures apply to information acquired by each device.

* * *

§ 1805. Issuance of order

(a) Necessary findings

Upon an application made pursuant to section 1804 of this title, the judge shall enter an ex parte order as requested or as modified approving the electronic surveillance if he finds that—

>(1) the President has authorized the Attorney General to approve applications for electronic surveillance for foreign intelligence information;

(2) the application has been made by a Federal officer and approved by the Attorney General;

(3) on the basis of the facts submitted by the applicant there is probable cause to believe that—

(A) the target of the electronic surveillance is a foreign power or an agent of a foreign power: *Provided,* That no United States person may be considered a foreign power or an agent of a foreign power solely upon the basis of activities protected by the first amendment to the Constitution of the United States; and

(B) each of the facilities or places at which the electronic surveillance is directed is being used, or is about to be used, by a foreign power or an agent of a foreign power;

(4) the proposed minimization procedures meet the definition of minimization procedures under section [1801(h)] of this title; and

(5) the application which has been filed contains all statements and certifications required by section 1804 of this title and, if the target is a United States person, the certification or certifications are not clearly erroneous on the basis of the statement made under section 1804(a)(7)(E) of this title and any other information furnished under section 1804(d) of this title. * * *

As passed, FISA was limited to "electronic surveillance" to obtain "foreign intelligence information." *See* 50 U.S.C. §§ 1803(a), 1804(a)(7)(A)- (B) (2000). The term "electronic surveillance" has a complex definition, but essentially regulates acquisition of the *contents* of "*wire communications*" (and in some cases "radio communications") through the monitoring of persons or the installation of surveillance devices within the United States. *See id.* § 1801(f). Both "content" and "wire communication," however, are defined more broadly than the same terms in the Wiretap Act. In FISA, the term "content" covers "any information concerning the *identity of the parties to such communication or the existence*, substance, purport, or meaning of that communication," *id.* § 1801(n) (emphasis added); the corresponding definition in the Wiretap Act covers "information concerning the substance, purport, or meaning of that communication." 18 U.S.C. § 2510(8) (2000). The term "wire communication" in FISA encompasses electronic communications as well as those containing the human voice, *see* 50 U.S.C. § 1801(*l*) (2000); "wire communication" and "electronic communication" are separately defined in the Wiretap Act. *See* 18 U.S.C. §§ 2510(1), (12) (2000 & Supp. IV 2004).

The term "foreign intelligence information" in FISA covers two broad categories of information. Section 1801(e)(2) of FISA includes information that might be described as "positive" (or "affirmative") foreign intelligence information—information with respect to a foreign power or foreign territory that relates to "the national defense or the security of the United States" or "the conduct of the foreign affairs of the United States." 50

U.S.C. § 1801(e)(2) (2000). Section 1801(e)(1) covers information that might be described as "counterintelligence" (or "protective") information—information relating to the United States' ability to protect against "grave hostile acts of a foreign power or an agent of a foreign power," "sabotage or international terrorism by a foreign power or an agent of a foreign power," or "clandestine intelligence activities" by a foreign power or an agent of a foreign power. *Id.* § 1801(e)(1).

Apart from "electronic surveillance" and "foreign intelligence information," the other limitation on the scope of FISA is the definition of the terms "foreign power" and "agent of a foreign power." Executive officials can only seek, and the FISA court can only grant, applications for surveillance targeting a foreign power or an agent of a foreign power. *See id.* §§ 1804(a)(4)(A), 1805(a)(3)(A). For discussion of these terms, see Patricia L. Bellia, *The "Lone Wolf" Amendment and the Future of Foreign Intelligence Surveillance Law*, 50 VILL. L. REV. 425, 427-28, 439-40 (2005).

Notes and Questions

1. Numerous courts upheld the constitutionality under the Fourth Amendment of FISA as enacted in 1978. How do FISA's procedures differ from those in Title III? Consider the following analysis:

> With limited exceptions not at issue here, both Title III and FISA require prior judicial scrutiny of an application for an order authorizing electronic surveillance. And there is no dispute that a FISA judge satisfies the Fourth Amendment's requirement of a "neutral and detached magistrate."

> The statutes differ to some extent in their probable cause showings. Title III allows a court to enter an ex parte order authorizing electronic surveillance if it determines on the basis of the facts submitted in the government's application that "there is probable cause for belief that an individual is committing, has committed, or is about to commit" a specified predicate offense. FISA by contrast requires a showing of probable cause that the target is a foreign power or an agent of a foreign power. We have noted, however, that where a U.S. person is involved, an "agent of a foreign power" is defined in terms of criminal activity. Admittedly, the definition of one category of U.S.-person agents of foreign powers—that is, persons engaged in espionage and clandestine intelligence activities for a foreign power—does not necessarily require a showing of an imminent violation of criminal law. Congress clearly intended a lesser showing of probable cause for these activities than that applicable to ordinary criminal cases. And with good reason—these activities present the type of threats contemplated by the Supreme Court in *Keith* when it recognized that the focus of security surveillance "may be less precise than that directed against more conventional types of crime" even in the area of domestic threats to national security. *Keith*, 407 U.S. at 322. Congress was aware of Keith's reasoning, and recognized that it applies a fortiori to foreign threats. * * * FISA applies only to certain carefully delineated, and particularly serious, foreign threats to national security.

Turning then to the first of the particularity requirements, while Title III requires probable cause to believe that particular communications concerning the specified crime will be obtained through the interception, FISA instead requires an official to designate the type of foreign intelligence information being sought, and to certify that the information sought is foreign intelligence information. When the target is a U.S. person, the FISA judge reviews the certification for clear error, but this standard of review is not, of course, comparable to a probable cause finding by the judge. Nevertheless, FISA provides additional protections to ensure that only pertinent information is sought. The certification must be made by a national security officer—typically the FBI Director—and must be approved by the Attorney General or the Attorney General's Deputy. Congress recognized that this certification would assure written accountability within the Executive Branch and provide an internal check on Executive Branch arbitrariness. In addition, the court may require the government to submit any further information it deems necessary to determine whether or not the certification is clearly erroneous.

With respect to the second element of particularity, although Title III generally requires probable cause to believe that the facilities subject to surveillance are being used or are about to be used in connection with the commission of a crime or are leased to, listed in the name of, or used by the individual committing the crime, FISA requires probable cause to believe that each of the facilities or places at which the surveillance is directed is being used, or is about to be used, by a foreign power or agent. In cases where the targeted facilities are not leased to, listed in the name of, or used by the individual committing the crime, Title III requires the government to show a nexus between the facilities and communications regarding the criminal offense. The government does not have to show, however, anything about the target of the surveillance; it is enough that "an individual"—not necessarily the target—is committing a crime. On the other hand, FISA requires probable cause to believe the target is an agent of a foreign power (that is, the individual committing a foreign intelligence crime) who uses or is about to use the targeted facility. Simply put, FISA requires less of a nexus between the facility and the pertinent communications than Title III, but more of a nexus between the target and the pertinent communications.

There are other elements of Title III that at least some circuits have determined are constitutionally significant—that is, necessity, duration of surveillance, and minimization. Both statutes have a "necessity" provision, which requires the court to find that the information sought is not available through normal investigative procedures. * * * The statutes also have duration provisions; Title III orders may last up to 30 days, while FISA orders may last up to 90 days for U.S. persons. This difference is based on the nature of national security surveillance, which is "often long range and involves the interrelation of various sources and types of information." *Keith*, 407 U.S. at 322. * * * And where Title III requires minimization of what is acquired, as we have discussed, for U.S. persons, FISA requires minimization of what is acquired, retained, and disseminated. * * *

Title III requires notice to the target (and, within the discretion of the judge, to other persons whose communications were intercepted) once the surveillance order expires. FISA does not require notice to a person whose communications were intercepted unless the government "intends to enter into evidence or otherwise use or disclose" such communications in a trial or other enumerated official proceedings. As the government points out, however, to the extent evidence obtained through a FISA surveillance order is used in a criminal proceeding, notice to the defendant is required. * * *

Based on the foregoing, it should be evident that while Title III contains some protections that are not in FISA, in many significant respects the two statutes are equivalent, and in some, FISA contains additional protections. * * * [We] note that to the extent a FISA order comes close to meeting Title III, that certainly bears on its reasonableness under the Fourth Amendment.

In re Sealed Case, 310 F.3d 717, 737–41 (For. Intell. Surv. Ct. Rev. 2002). Do you agree with the court's analysis of the Fourth Amendment significance (or lack thereof) of the differences between the two types of orders?

2. Note that section 1804(a)(7)(B) requires certification that "*a significant purpose* of the surveillance is to obtain foreign intelligence information." (Emphasis added.) Congress adopted the "significant purpose" language in section 218 of the USA PATRIOT Act in 2001. Pub. L. No. 107-56, 115 Stat. 272, 291. As enacted, FISA required certification that "the purpose" of the surveillance was to obtain foreign intelligence information. *See* 50 U.S.C. § 1804(a)(7)(B) (2000). Drawing upon pre-FISA cases, however, defendants challenging FISA surveillance maintained that such surveillance could proceed only where "the *primary* purpose" of the surveillance was to obtain foreign intelligence information. Although no court squarely addressed this question, concern that FISA or the Fourth Amendment would be so construed prompted successive Attorneys General to adopt guidelines limiting information-sharing between counterintelligence and criminal investigators and prosecutors within the FBI and the Justice Department. *See* Patricia L. Bellia, *The "Lone Wolf" Amendment and the Future of Foreign Intelligence Surveillance Law*, 50 VILL. L. REV. 425, 453 (2005). The guidelines were designed to prevent contacts within the Justice Department that might trigger a court's conclusion that the primary objective of surveillance was not to gather "foreign intelligence" information. Should either the Fourth Amendment or FISA limit use of FISA-derived evidence in criminal proceedings? Were the Attorney General Guidelines based on a misreading of FISA? For an argument that they were, see *In re Sealed Case*, 310 F.3d 717, 722–28 (For. Intell. Surv. Ct. Rev. 2002).

3. In shifting the required certification from "the purpose" to "a significant purpose," Congress sought to eliminate any strict separation between counterintelligence and criminal investigators and prosecutors. Does the shift call into question the constitutionality of FISA? One could argue that FISA as passed in 1978 reflected a shared understanding of participants in the legislative process of the contours of the Fourth Amendment in the foreign intelligence context. *See* Patricia L. Bellia, *The "Lone Wolf" Amendment and the Future of Foreign Intelligence Surveillance Law*, 50 VILL. L. REV. 425, 452 (2005). If so, should courts regard FISA's original standards as quasi-constitutional?

4. In December 2005, *The New York Times* reported that the President had authorized the National Security Agency to engage in program of warrantless electronic surveillance of international telephone calls and Internet communications, including some communications between U.S. persons and others outside the United States. According to some reports, the NSA's activities involved copying calls and communications at telecommunications switches in the United States. The Justice Department defended the surveillance by claiming that the broad authorization for the use of military force Congress adopted following the September 11, 2001, attacks permitted the program. The Justice Department also argued that construing FISA to prohibit the President's actions would raise serious separation of powers questions, and that the NSA activities were consistent with the Fourth Amendment:

> Whether Congress may interfere with the President's constitutional authority to collect foreign intelligence information through interception of communications reasonably believed to be linked to the enemy poses a difficult constitutional question. * * * Congress recognized at the time [of FISA's passage] that the enactment of a statute purporting to eliminate the President's ability, even during peacetime, to conduct warrantless electronic surveillance to collect foreign intelligence was near or perhaps beyond the limit of Congress's Article I powers. * * * [I]ntelligence gathering is at the heart of the executive functions.

> * * *

> [T]he Supreme Court repeatedly has made clear in situations involving "special needs" that go beyond a routine interest in law enforcement, the warrant requirement is inapplicable. * * * Foreign intelligence collection, especially in the midst of an armed conflict in which the adversary has already launched catastrophic attacks within the United States, fits squarely within the area of "special needs, beyond the normal need for law enforcement" where the Fourth Amendment's touchstone of reasonableness can be satisfied without resort to a warrant. The Executive Branch has long maintained that collecting foreign intelligence is far removed from the ordinary criminal law enforcement action to which the warrant requirement is particularly suited.

U.S. Dep't of Justice, Legal Authorities Supporting the Activities of the National Security Agency Described by the President (Jan. 19, 2006). Are these arguments persuasive? To what extent are the executive power and Fourth Amendment issues intertwined?

Note on Acquisition of Stored Communications and Non-Content Information in National Security Investigations

Although FISA's provisions are not identical to the Wiretap Act's, agents seeking to intercept electronic communications under FISA must go through a fairly rigorous process. How must agents in a foreign intelligence investigation proceed when they are not intercepting the contents of electronic communications, but instead seek to acquire stored communications or non-content information—that is, information governed in the criminal context by the Stored Communications Act or the pen register statute?

For use of pen registers and trap and trace devices, the answer is relatively straightforward. In 1998, Congress added a new title to FISA granting judges of the Foreign Intelligence Surveillance Court or specially designated magistrate judges the authority to approve applications for use of pen reisters and trap and trace devices. Intelligence Authorization Act for Fiscal Year 1999, § 402(b), Pub. L. No. 105-272, 112 Stat. 2396, 2405 (1998) (codified as amended at 50 U.S.C. §§ 1841-1846 (2000 & Supp. IV 2004)). The provisions were thought to be necessary in view of FISA's broad definition of "contents" as covering the "identity of the parties" to, or the "existence of," the communication: Without separate pen/trap authority, investigators needed full FISA orders to install such devices. The pen/trap provisions required certification that use of the device would yield information that was "relevant" to an ongoing foreign intelligence or international terrorism investigation—a standard that roughly tracked that of the analogous criminal law authority. The provisions also went beyond the analogous criminal law provisions in requiring the application to demonstrate "reason to believe" that the targeted communications device had been or would be used in connection with a suspected international terrorist, spy, foreign power, or agent of a foreign power. 50 U.S.C. § 1842(c)(3) (2000). The USA PATRIOT Act eliminated the latter requirement. Pub. L. No. 107-56, § 214(a)(3), 115 Stat. 272, 286 (codified at 50 U.S.C. § 1842(c) (2000 & Supp. IV 2004)). That is, agents seeking approval of a pen/trap device under FISA need to show that the information sought is relevant to a foreign intelligence investigation, but not that the specific communications device targeted is about to be used by or in communication with a foreign power, agent of a foreign power, terrorist, or spy.

For stored communications and customer records covered by the Stored Communications Act, the corresponding foreign intelligence authorities are more complicated. First, FISA contains provisions authorizing physical searches, 50 U.S.C. §§ 1821-1829 (2000 & Supp. IV 2004), defined to include "physical intrusion within the United States into premises or property (including examination of the interior of property by technical means) that is intended to result in a seizure, reproduction, inspection, or alteration of information, material, or property under circumstances in which a person has a reasonable expectation of privacy and a warrant would be required for law enforcement purposes," *id.* § 1821(5). The provisions essentially authorize the FISA equivalent of a search warrant, under substantive standards largely tracking those governing FISA electronic surveillance. Whether the physical search provisions can or should be interpreted to govern compelled acquisition of communications from service providers remains unclear. *Cf.* U.S. Internet Service Provider Association, *Electronic Evidence Compliance—A Guide for Internet Service Providers*, 18 BERKELEY TECH. L.J. 945, 973 (2003) (discussing FISA physical search orders in context of requests for customer records).

Second, the SCA itself contains a provision authorizing the FBI to issue so-called "national security letters" to compel providers of wire and electronic communications services to release certain "transactional" records concerning a subscriber's account, including "the name, address, length of service, and * * * toll billing records." 18 U.S.C. § 2709 (2000 & Supp. IV 2004). As passed in 1986, the provision permitted the FBI to issue NSLs upon written certification that certain records sought were relevant to an "authorized foreign counterintelligence investigation" and that there were specific and articulable facts linking the information sought to a foreign power or an agent of a foreign power under FISA. Electronic Communications Privacy Act of 1986, Pub. L. No. 99-508, § 201, 100 Stat. 1848, 1867 (codified at 18 U.S.C. § 2709(b)(2) (2000)). Section 505(a)(2)(B) of the USA PATRIOT Act deleted the second requirement. Pub. L. No. 107-56, 115 Stat. 272, 365 (2001). As enacted in 1986, section 2709 also contained a nondisclosure provision prohibiting a service provider from disclosing "to any person" that the FBI sought or obtained access to information under the provision. 18 U.S.C. § 2709(c) (2000 & Supp. IV 2004). That provision was amended in 2006 to permit disclosure for the purpose of obtaining legal assistance to comply with or challenge the request. *See* 18 U.S.C.A. § 2709(c) (West Supp. 2006).

Third, FISA contains a provision authorizing applications to the FISC for orders compelling production of certain records and "tangible things." 50 U.S.C.A. § 1861 (West 2006). The provision is the successor to one adopted in 1998 covering the acquisition of certain travel-related records, namely records of a common carrier, vehicle rental facility, physical storage facility, or public accommodation facility. *See* 50 U.S.C. § 1862 (2000). The substantive showing for an order compelling production of such records was similar to that for pen registers and trap and trace devices, requiring a showing of "relevance" to a foreign intelligence or international terrorism investigation and specific and articulable facts giving reason to believe that the records concerned a foreign power or an agent of a foreign power. *Id.*

Section 215 of the USA PATRIOT Act, however, dramatically changed the scope of this authority: rather that extending to travel-related records, the provision permitted orders for the production of "any tangible things, including books, records, papers, documents, and other items) for an investigation" to obtain foreign intelligence information or protect against terrorism or clandestine intelligence activities. *See* 50 U.S.C. § 1861 (Supp. IV 2004). Read literally, section 215 might have provided an avenue for investigators to compel production of the contents of communications outside of the parameters of the physical search provisions of FISA or the procedures of the SCA. When Congress reauthorized the USA PATRIOT Act in 2006, it narrowed the provision, authorizing the government to apply to obtain the production of any "tangible things (including books, records, papers, documents, and other items)," but requiring the government's application to the FISC to establish:

> reasonable grounds to believe that the tangible things sought are relevant to an authorized investigation * * * conducted in accordance with subsection (a)(2) of this section to obtain foreign intelligence information not concerning a United States person or to protect against international terrorism or clandestine intelligence activities, such things being presumptively relevant to an authorized

investigation if the applicant shows in the statement of the facts that they pertain to—

(i) a foreign power or an agent of a foreign power;

(ii) the activities of a suspected agent of a foreign power who is the subject of such authorized investigation; or

(iii) an individual in contact with, or known to, a suspected agent of a foreign power who is the subject of such authorized investigation * * * .

50 U.S.C.A. § 1861(b)(2)(A) (West. Supp. 2006). The scope of the provision—and particularly whether it applies to compelled production of communications from a provider for foreign intelligence purposes—remains unclear.

The compelled production of communications and records under FISA and the SCA's NSL authority of course raises many of the same constitutional and policy issues as compelled production of communications and records under the SCA. For the most part, courts have not yet had occasion to address these issues fully. One court, however, considered a service provider's challenge to the constitutionality of section 2709 as it existed prior to 2006. Although Congress altered the nondisclosure provision following the decision in this case, the court's approach to the Fourth Amendment questions at issue may continue to be important.

Doe v. Ashcroft

United States District Court for the Southern District of New York, 2004
334 F. Supp. 2d 471, *vacated on other grounds*, 449 F.3d 415 (2d Cir. 2006)

MARRERO, District Judge.

Plaintiffs in this case challenge the constitutionality of 18 U.S.C. § 2709. That statute authorizes the Federal Bureau of Investigation ("FBI") to compel communications firms, such as internet service providers ("ISPs") or telephone companies, to produce certain customer records whenever the FBI certifies that those records are "relevant to an authorized investigation to protect against international terrorism or clandestine intelligence activities." The FBI's demands under § 2709 are issued in the form of national security letters ("NSLs"), which constitute a unique form of administrative subpoena cloaked in secrecy and pertaining to national security issues. The statute bars all NSL recipients from ever disclosing that the FBI has issued an NSL.

The lead plaintiff, called "John Doe" ("Doe") for purposes of this litigation, is described in the complaint as an internet access firm that received an NSL. * * * Plaintiffs contend that § 2709's broad subpoena power violates [the Fourth Amendment]. They argue that § 2709 is unconstitutional on its face and as applied to the facts of this case. [Plaintiff argues that] § 2709 gives the FBI extraordinary and unchecked power to obtain private information without any form of judicial process * * * . The parties have cross-moved for summary judgment on all claims.

For the reasons explained below, the Court grants Plaintiffs' motion. The Court concludes that § 2709 violates the Fourth Amendment because, at least as currently applied, it effectively bars or substantially deters any judicial challenge to the propriety of an NSL request. In the Court's view, ready availability of judicial process to pursue such a challenge is necessary to vindicate important rights guaranteed by the Constitution or by statute. * * *

After receiving a call from an FBI agent informing him that he would be served with an NSL, Doe received a document, printed on FBI letterhead, which stated that, "pursuant to Title 18, United States Code (U.S.C.), Section 2709" Doe was "directed" to provide certain information to the Government. As required by the terms of § 2709, in the NSL the FBI "certif[ied] that the information sought [was] relevant to an authorized investigation to protect against international terrorism or clandestine intelligence activities." Doe was "further advised" that § 2709(c) prohibited him, or his officers, agents, or employees, "from disclosing to *any person* that the FBI has sought or obtained access to information or records under these provisions." Doe was "requested to provide records responsive to [the] request *personally*" to a designated individual, and to not transmit the records by mail or even mention the NSL in *any* telephone conversation.

After a subsequent conversation with the same FBI agent, Doe decided to consult ACLU lawyers. * * * Doe has not complied with the NSL request, and has instead engaged counsel to bring the present lawsuit.

Section 2709 And The Fourth Amendment[118]

The Fourth Amendment prohibits the Government from conducting "unreasonable searches and seizures," which generally means that any search or seizure must be performed pursuant to a valid warrant based upon probable cause. As the Second Circuit has declared: "It is fundamental that governmental searches and seizures without warrant or probable cause are per se unreasonable under the Fourth Amendment unless they fall within one of the Amendment's few established and well-delineated exceptions." *United States v. Streifel*, 665 F.2d 414, 419-20 (2d Cir. 1981). The Fourth Amendment's protection against unreasonable searches applies to administrative subpoenas, even though issuing a subpoena does not involve a literal physical intrusion or search. In so

---

118. To be clear, the Fourth Amendment rights at issue here belong to the person or entity receiving the NSL, not to the person or entity to whom the subpoenaed records pertain. Individuals possess a limited Fourth Amendment interest in records which they voluntarily convey to a third party. *See Smith v. Maryland*, 442 U.S. 735, 742-46 (1979); *United States v. Miller*, 425 U.S. 435, 440-43 (1976). Nevertheless, as discussed below, many potential NSL recipients may have particular interests in resisting an NSL, *e.g.*, because they have contractually obligated themselves to protect the anonymity of their subscribers or because their own rights are uniquely implicated by what they regard as an intrusive and secretive NSL regime. For example, since the definition of "wire or electronic communication service provider," 18 U.S.C. § 2709(a), is so vague, the statute could (and may currently) be used to seek subscriber lists or other information from an association that also provides electronic communication services (e.g., email addresses) to its members, or to seek records from libraries that many, including the *amici* appearing in this proceeding, fear will chill speech and use of these invaluable public institutions. * * *

doing, the Supreme Court explained that the Fourth Amendment is not "confined literally to searches and seizures as such, but extends as well to the orderly taking under compulsion of process."

However, because administrative subpoenas are "at best, constructive searches," there is no requirement that they be issued pursuant to a warrant or that they be supported by probable cause. *Gimbel v. Federal Deposit Ins. Corp. (In re Gimbel)*, 77 F.3d 593, 596 (2d Cir. 1996). Instead, an administrative subpoena needs only to be "reasonable," which the Supreme Court has interpreted to mean that (1) the administrative subpoena is "within the authority of the agency;" (2) that the demand is "not too indefinite;" and (3) that the information sought is "reasonably relevant" to a proper inquiry. *United States v. Morton Salt Co.*, 338 U.S. 632, 652 (1950).

While the Fourth Amendment reasonableness standard is permissive in the context of administrative subpoenas, the constitutionality of the administrative subpoena is predicated on the availability of a neutral tribunal to determine, after a subpoena is issued, whether the subpoena actually complies with the Fourth Amendment's demands. In contrast to an actual physical search, which must be justified by the warrant and probable cause requirements occurring *before* the search, an administrative subpoena "is regulated by, and its justification derives from, [judicial] process" available *after* the subpoena is issued. *United States v. Bailey (In re Subpoena Duces Tecum)*, 228 F.3d 341, 348 (4th Cir. 2000).

Accordingly, the Supreme Court has held that an administrative subpoena "may not be made and enforced" by the administrative agency; rather, the subpoenaed party must be able to "obtain judicial review of the reasonableness of the demand prior to suffering penalties for refusing to comply." *See v. City of Seattle*, 387 U.S. 541, 544-45 (1967). In sum, longstanding Supreme Court doctrine makes clear that an administrative subpoena statute is consistent with the Fourth Amendment when it is subject to "judicial supervision" and "surrounded by every safeguard of judicial restraint."

Plaintiffs contend that § 2709 violates this Fourth Amendment process-based guarantee because it gives the FBI alone the power to issue as well as enforce its own NSLs, instead of contemplating some form of judicial review. Although Plaintiffs appear to concede that the statute does not authorize the FBI to literally enforce the terms of an NSL by, for example, unilaterally seizing documents or imposing fines, Plaintiffs contend that § 2709 has the *practical* effect of coercing compliance.

Specifically, Plaintiffs stress that the statute has no provision for judicial enforcement or review, and that theoretically any judicial review an NSL recipient sought would violate the express terms of the non-disclosure provision. For example, if an NSL recipient thought that an NSL request was unreasonable or otherwise unlawful—because, for instance, the underlying investigation was not duly "authorized," was initiated "solely on the basis of activities protected by the first amendment to the Constitution of the United States," or did not involve "international terrorism or clandestine intelligence activities," as § 2709 demands—he would have no specific statute under which to challenge the request. More fundamentally, the literal terms of the non-disclosure provision would bar the recipient from even consulting an attorney to file such a challenge. Even if he were to challenge the NSL on his own, the recipient would necessarily have to disclose the fact of the NSL's issuance to the clerk of court and to the presiding judge, again, in violation of the literal terms of the non-disclosure provision.

Rather than dispute the Plaintiffs' interpretation of the relevant constitutional doctrine, the Government's response to these arguments endeavors to heavily repair the statute * * * . The course the Government urges poses several conceptual difficulties for the Court. * * * [I]t is at odds with statutory construction principle and case law * * * dealing with comparable competing interpretations deriving from different statutes. * * * for the Court to give effect to the Government's construction in the face of apparently conflicting, or at best very ambiguous legislative designs, would implicate severe concerns over the proper separation of powers. * * *

Despite these severe reservations, in the final analysis the Court need not resolve Plaintiffs' facial challenge to § 2709 on Fourth Amendment grounds * * * . [E]ven if the Court were to accept that the FBI's authority to issue and enforce NSLs pursuant to § 2709 *means* what the Government says it means, the Court's inquiry would not end there with a ruling in favor of the Government. Investing those provisions with the reading the Government accords them does not address the Plaintiffs' distinct claim that *in practice* § 2709 in all or the vast majority of actual cases, by virtue of the statute's unwarranted application by the FBI, *operates* otherwise. The Court concludes that the operation of § 2709 renders it unconstitutional, notwithstanding that, at least in a theoretical sense, a possible reading of portions of the statute as the Government propounds, through extensive judicial tinkering with its silences, may be posited to withstand a Fourth Amendment facial challenge. In particular, deficiencies in the application of § 2709 pertain to the very core issues—access to legal advice and availability of judicial process to enforce and contest the law—upon which Plaintiffs' Fourth Amendment facial challenge is grounded. Because the Court agrees that those protections are vital to satisfy Fourth Amendment standards, it finds the manner in which § 2709 has been applied unwarranted.

The crux of the problem is that the form NSL, like the one issued in this case, which is preceded by a personal call from an FBI agent, is framed in imposing language on FBI letterhead and which, citing the authorizing statute, orders a combination of disclosure *in person* and in complete secrecy, essentially coerces the reasonable recipient into immediate compliance. Objectively viewed, it is improbable that an FBI summons invoking the authority of a certified "investigation to protect against international terrorism or clandestine intelligence activities," and phrased in tones sounding virtually as biblical commandment, would not be perceived with some apprehension by an ordinary person and therefore elicit passive obedience from a reasonable NSL recipient. The full weight of this ominous writ is especially felt when the NSL's plain language, in a measure that enhances its aura as an expression of public will, prohibits disclosing the issuance of the NSL to "any person." Reading such strictures, it is also highly unlikely that an NSL recipient reasonably would know that he may have a right to contest the NSL, and that a process to do so may exist through a judicial proceeding.

Because neither the statute, nor an NSL, nor the FBI agents dealing with the recipient say as much, all but the most mettlesome and undaunted NSL recipients would consider themselves effectively barred from consulting an attorney or anyone else who might advise them otherwise, as well as bound to absolute silence about the very existence of the NSL. Furthermore, it is doubtful that an NSL recipient, not necessarily a lawyer, would be willing to undertake any creative exercises in statutory construction to somehow reach the Government's proposed reading of § 2709, especially because that construction is not apparent from the plain language of the statute, the NSL itself, or accompanying government communications, and any penalties for non-compliance or disclosure are also unspecified in the NSL or in the statute. For the reasonable NSL recipient confronted with the NSL's mandatory language and the FBI's conduct related to the NSL, resistance is not a viable option.

The evidence in this case bears out the hypothesis that NSLs work coercively in this way. The ACLU obtained, via the Freedom of Information Act ("FOIA"), and presented to the Court in this proceeding, a document listing all the NSLs the Government issued from October 2001 through January 2003. Although the entire substance of the document is redacted, it is apparent that hundreds of NSL requests were made during that period. Because § 2709 has been available to the FBI since 1986 (and its financial records counterpart in RFPA since 1978), the Court concludes that there must have been hundreds more NSLs issued in that long time span. The evidence suggests that, until now, none of those NSLs was ever challenged in any court. First, the Department of Justice explicitly informed the House Judiciary Committee in May 2003 that there had been *no* challenges to the propriety or legality of any NSLs. Second, the Government's evidence in this case conspicuously lacks any suggestion either that the Government has ever had to resort to a judicial enforcement proceeding for any NSL, or that any recipient has ever resisted an NSL request in such a proceeding or via any motion to quash.

To be sure, the Court recognizes that many other reasons may exist to explain the absence of challenges to NSLs: the communications provider who receives the NSL ordinarily would have little incentive to contest the NSL on the subscriber's behalf; the standard of review for administrative subpoenas similar to NSLs is so minimal that most such NSLs would likely be upheld in court; litigating these issues is expensive; and many citizens may feel a civic duty to help the FBI's investigation and thus may willingly comply. Nevertheless, the Court finds it striking that, in all the years during which the FBI has been serving NSLs, the evidence suggests that, until now, no single NSL recipient has ever sought to quash such a directive. The Court thus concludes that in practice NSLs are essentially unreviewable because, as explained, given the language and tone of the statute as carried into the NSL by the FBI, the recipient would consider himself, in virtually every case, obliged to comply, with no other option but to immediately obey and stay quiet.

The Government responds that Doe's arguments on this point are undermined by the very fact that Doe himself consulted an attorney and brought this challenge. The Court disagrees for several reasons. First, so far as the evidence shows, Doe's decision to challenge the NSL is a lone exception in the otherwise consistent record. The constitutional bar marking the limits the Government can permissibly reach in curtailing personal freedoms in the name of national security should not be raised to heights at which all but the most powerfully endowed would feel impelled to remain cowered or content, and none but the well-heeled could stand tall enough to take on a law enforcer's coercive order. If the Court were to take up the Government's invitation and reject Doe's as-applied challenge to the statute until one of the NSL recipients who actually felt intimidated enough by the NSL was moved to bring suit, such a day may never arrive. Moreover, in such a prospect the NSL recipient would presumably have already turned over the requested information to the FBI, further defeating the purpose of subsequent resistance.

Second, the Court finds support for its analysis in caselaw which, in testing the validity of a Government policy or law, recognizes the importance of appreciating its practical effect on a reasonable person, especially as evidenced by the methods and terms the Government employs to convey what it demands and to elicit the desired compliance. * * * Here, the Court concludes it would be * * * naive to conclude that § 2709 NSLs, given their commandeering warrant, do anything short of coercing all but the most fearless NSL recipient into immediate compliance and secrecy. * * *

[T]he Court here concludes that what is, in practice, an implicit obligation of automatic compliance with NSLs violates the Fourth Amendment right to judicial access, even if hypothetically the law were construed to imply such access.

Recognizing from the preceding discussion the reality that § 2709 effectively keeps § 2709 NSLs out of litigation altogether, the Court concludes that supplying a judicial gloss to § 2709 but failing to address the practical effects of the unparalleled level of secrecy and coercion fostered by the FBI's implementation of the statute would be completely academic. That is the Court is reluctant to fashion a "remedy" which has no effect beyond being printed in the Federal Supplement.

[The Court also concluded that the non-disclosure provision of § 2709(c) violated the First Amendment and could not be severed from the remainder of the statute.]

Notes and Questions

1. Re-read the court's description in footnote 118 of the Fourth Amendment interests at stake in the case. Do you agree with its characterization?

2. In analogizing NSLs to administrative subpoenas, the court states that such subpoenas are constructive searches, and implies that no inquiry into an expectation of privacy is necessary. Do you agree? What are the implications of such an argument?

3. In March 2006, Congress passed the USA PATRIOT Improvement and Reauthorization Act, which altered section 2709 and added new procedures governing judicial review of the FBI's requests for information through NSLs. Section 2709(c) now explicitly permits an NSL recipient to disclose the letter to "those to whom such disclosure is necessary to comply with the request or an attorney to obtain legal advice or legal assistance with respect to the request." 18 U.S.C.A. § 2709(c) (West Supp. 2006). The new review procedures allow the target of an NSL to petition a court to modify the request "if compliance would be unreasonable, oppressive, or otherwise unlawful" and to set aside any nondisclosure requirement. 18 U.S.C.A. § 3511 (West Supp. 2006). Do these changes adequately address the court's concerns in *Doe v. Ashcroft*? Do they make judicial review more likely as a practical matter?

SECTION C. PRIVATE ACQUISITION OF COMMUNICATIONS AND DATA

Many of the criminal law authorities discussed in the previous section—including the Wiretap Act, the Stored Communications Act, and the pen/trap statute—constrain private as well as governmental activities. Indeed, several of the cases we read construing key statutory provisions concerned private rather than government conduct. Here we consider how the law protects the privacy of communications and data against *private* acquisition in two specific scenarios that present particular problems in the Internet context. The first involves *employer* monitoring of employee communications. Employers often operate a proprietary communications system for their own business purposes. They are unlikely to have privacy policies analogous to those that a provider of services to the public might have, and yet communications held on an employer's system may be just as revealing as those held by a public provider. What protections do such communications receive? Second, as an Internet user surfs the web, she generates a trail of data about the websites she has visited. That data trail may be exposed not only to her service provider, but also to others, visible and not so visible, with whom she transacts business. How, if at all, should the law protect such data?

1. Employer Monitoring

In practice, the federal statutes we have considered thus far afford little protection against acquisition of personal communications when an employer monitors communications through facilities the employer provides. Each statute contains an exception for some conduct undertaken by a service provider: The Wiretap Act exempts conduct by a service provider that is incident to the rendition of service, 18 U.S.C.

§ 2511(2)(a)(i); the SCA exempts conduct authorized by the person or entity providing an electronic communication service, 18 U.S.C. § 2701(c)(1); and the pen/trap statute exempts a service provider's use of a pen register or trap and trace device to protect its rights or property, 18 U.S.C. § 3121(b)(1).

In addition, the statutes exempt activities undertaken with the consent of a party to a communication. *See* 18 U.S.C. § 2511(2)(d) (exempting interception of communication where one party has given prior consent, unless communication is intercepted for criminal or tortious purpose); 18 U.S.C. § 2701(c)(3) (exempting acquisition of stored communication when conduct is authorized by user of communication service with respect to a communication of or intended for that user); 18 U.S.C. § 3121(b)(3) (exempting use of a pen register or trap and trace device where the consent of the user has been obtained). Accordingly, an employer may attempt to secure an employee's prior consent, by requiring the employee to click a banner or by some other means, to avoid liability under the statute.

Are the exemptions necessary to protect the rights and property of an employer? Should the law recognize greater privacy rights in personal communications against monitoring by an employer? Consider the following cases.

Fraser v. Nationwide Mutual Insurance Co.

United States Court of Appeals for the Third Circuit, 2003
352 F.3d 107

AMBRO, Circuit Judge.

Richard Fraser, an independent insurance agent for Nationwide Mutual Insurance Company, was terminated by Nationwide as an agent. We decide whether * * * he is entitled to damages * * * for Nationwide's alleged unauthorized access to his e-mail account * * * .

This dispute stems from Nationwide's September 2, 1998 termination of Fraser's Agent's Agreement (the "Agreement"). It provided that Fraser sell insurance policies as an independent contractor for Nationwide on an exclusive basis. The relationship was terminable at will by either party. The parties disagree on the reason for Fraser's termination. * * * Nationwide argues * * * that it terminated Fraser because he was disloyal. It points out that Fraser drafted a letter to two competitors * * * expressing * * * dissatisfaction with Nationwide and seeking to determine whether [the competitors] would be interested in acquiring the policyholders of [Nationwide's independent contractor] agents * * * . Fraser claims that the letters only were drafted to get Nationwide's attention and were not sent. (Were the letters sent, however, they would constitute a violation of the "exclusive representation" provision of Fraser's Agreement with Nationwide.)

When Nationwide learned about these letters, it claims that it became concerned that Fraser might also be revealing company secrets to its competitors. It therefore searched its main file server—on which all of

Fraser's e-mail was lodged—for any e-mail to or from Fraser that showed similar improper behavior. Nationwide's general counsel testified that the e-mail search confirmed Fraser's disloyalty. Therefore, on the basis of the two letters and the e-mail search, Nationwide terminated Fraser's Agreement. * * *

Fraser argues that, by accessing his e-mail on its central file server without his express permission, Nationwide violated [the Wiretap Act], which prohibits "intercepts" of electronic communications such as e-mail. The statute defines an "intercept" as "the aural or other acquisition of the contents of any wire, electronic, or oral communication through the use of any electronic, mechanical, or other device." 18 U.S.C. § 2510(4). Nationwide argues that it did not "intercept" Fraser's e-mail within the meaning of [the Wiretap Act] because an "intercept" can only occur contemporaneously with transmission and it did not access Fraser's e-mail at the initial time of transmission. On this matter of statutory interpretation * * * we agree with Nationwide. Every circuit court to have considered the matter has held that an "intercept" under [the Wiretap Act] must occur contemporaneously with transmission. * * * While Congress's definition of "intercept" does not appear to fit with its intent to extend protection to electronic communications, it is for Congress to cover the bases untouched. We adopt the reasoning of our sister circuits and therefore hold that there has been no "intercept" * * * .

Fraser also argues that Nationwide's search of his e-mail violated [the SCA]. That [statute] creates civil liability for one who "(1) intentionally accesses without authorization a facility through which an electronic communication service is provided; or (2) intentionally exceeds an authorization to access that facility; and thereby obtains, alters, or prevents authorized access to a wire or electronic communication while it is in electronic storage in such system." 18 U.S.C. § 2701(a). The statute defines "electronic storage" as "(A) any temporary, intermediate storage of a wire or electronic communication incidental to the electronic transmission thereof; and (B) any storage of such communication by an electronic communication service for purposes of backup protection of such communication." Id. § 2510(17).

The District Court granted summary judgment in favor of Nationwide, holding that [the SCA] does not apply to the e-mail in question because the transmissions were neither in "temporary, intermediate storage" nor in "backup" storage. Rather, according to the District Court, the e-mail was in a state it described as "post-transmission storage." We agree that Fraser's e-mail was not in temporary, intermediate storage. But to us it seems questionable that the transmissions were not in backup storage—a term that neither the statute nor the legislative history defines. Therefore, while we affirm the District Court, we do so through a different analytical path, assuming without deciding that the e-mail in question was in backup storage.

18 U.S.C. § 2701(c)(1) excepts from [the SCA] seizures of e-mail authorized "by the person or entity providing a wire or electronic communications service." There is no circuit court case law interpreting

this exception. However, in *Bohach v. City of Reno*, 932 F. Supp. 1232 (D. Nev. 1996), a district court held that the Reno police department could, without violating [the SCA], retrieve pager text messages stored on the police department's computer system because the department "is the provider of the 'service'" and "service providers [may] do as they wish when it comes to accessing communications in electronic storage." *Id*. at 1236. Like the court in *Bohach*, we read § 2701(c) literally to except from [the SCA's] protection all searches by communications service providers. Thus, we hold that, because Fraser's e-mail was stored on Nationwide's system (which Nationwide administered), its search of that e-mail falls within § 2701(c)'s exception to [the SCA].

Smyth v. Pillsbury Co.

United States District Court for the Eastern District of Pennsylvania, 1996
914 F. Supp. 97

WEINER, District Judge.

In this diversity action, plaintiff, an at-will employee, claims he was wrongfully discharged from his position as a regional operations manager by the defendant. Presently before the court is the motion of the defendant to dismiss pursuant to Rule 12(b)(6) of the Federal Rules of Civil Procedure. For the reasons which follow, the motion is granted. * * *

Defendant maintained an electronic mail communication system ("e-mail") in order to promote internal corporate communications between its employees. Defendant repeatedly assured its employees, including plaintiff, that all e-mail communications would remain confidential and privileged. Defendant further assured its employees, including plaintiff, that e-mail communications could not be intercepted and used by defendant against its employees as grounds for termination or reprimand.

In October 1994, plaintiff received certain e-mail communications from his supervisor over defendant's e-mail system on his computer at home. In reliance on defendant's assurances regarding defendant's e-mail system, plaintiff responded and exchanged e-mails with his supervisor. At some later date, contrary to the assurances of confidentiality made by defendant, defendant, acting through its agents, servants and employees, intercepted plaintiff's private e-mail messages made in October 1994. On January 17, 1995, defendant notified plaintiff that it was terminating his employment effective February 1, 1995, for transmitting what it deemed to be inappropriate and unprofessional comments over defendant's e-mail system in October, 1994.

As a general rule, Pennsylvania law does not provide a common law cause of action for the wrongful discharge of an at-will employee such as plaintiff. Pennsylvania is an employment at-will jurisdiction and an employer "may discharge an employee with or without cause, at pleasure, unless restrained by some contract." *Henry v. Pittsburgh & Lake Erie Railroad Co.*, 139 Pa. 289, 297, 21 A. 157, 157 (1891). However, in the most limited of circumstances, exceptions have been recognized where discharge of an at-will employee threatens or violates a clear mandate of public policy This recognized public policy exception is an especially narrow one. *Burkholder v. Hutchison*, 403 Pa. Super. 498, 589 A.2d 721, 724 (1991). * * *

Plaintiff claims that his termination was in violation of "public policy which precludes an employer from terminating an employee in violation of the employee's right to privacy as embodied in Pennsylvania common law." In support for this proposition, plaintiff directs our attention to a decision by our Court of Appeals in *Borse v. Piece Goods Shop, Inc.*, 963 F.2d 611 (3d Cir. 1992). In *Borse*, the plaintiff sued her employer alleging wrongful discharge as a result of her refusal to submit to urinalysis screening and personal property searches at her work place pursuant to the employer's drug and alcohol policy. After rejecting plaintiff's argument that the employer's drug and alcohol program violated public policy encompassed in the United States and Pennsylvania Constitutions, our Court of Appeals stated "our review of Pennsylvania law reveals other evidence of a public policy that may, under certain circumstances, give rise to a wrongful discharge action related to urinalysis or to personal property searches. Specifically, we refer to the Pennsylvania common law regarding tortious invasion of privacy." *Id.* at 620.

The Court of Appeals in *Borse* observed that one of the torts which Pennsylvania recognizes as encompassing an action for invasion of privacy is the tort of "intrusion upon seclusion." As noted by the Court of Appeals, the Restatement (Second) of Torts defines the tort as follows:

> One who intentionally intrudes, physically or otherwise, upon the solitude or seclusion of another or his private affairs or concerns, is subject to liability to the other for invasion of his privacy, if the intrusion would be highly offensive to a reasonable person.

RESTATEMENT (SECOND) OF TORTS § 652B. Liability only attaches when the "intrusion is substantial and would be highly offensive to the 'ordinary reasonable person.'" *Borse*, 963 F.2d at 621 (citation omitted). Although the Court of Appeals in *Borse* observed that "[t]he Pennsylvania courts have not had occasion to consider whether a discharge related to an employer's tortious invasion of an employee's privacy violates public policy", the Court of Appeals predicted that in any claim where the employee claimed that his discharge related to an invasion of his privacy "the Pennsylvania Supreme Court would examine the facts and circumstances surrounding the alleged invasion of privacy. If the court determined that the discharge was related to a substantial and highly offensive invasion of the employee's privacy, [the Court of Appeals] believe that it would conclude that the discharge violated public policy." *Id.* at 622. In determining whether an alleged invasion of privacy is substantial and highly offensive to a reasonable person, the Court of Appeals predicted that Pennsylvania would adopt a balancing test which balances the employee's privacy interest against the employer's interest in maintaining a drug-free workplace. *Id.* at 625. Because the Court of Appeals in *Borse* could "envision at least two ways in which an employer's drug and alcohol program might violate the public policy protecting individuals from tortious invasion of privacy by private actors," *id.* at 626, the Court vacated the district court's order dismissing the plaintiff's complaint and remanded the case to the district court with directions to grant *Borse* leave to amend the Complaint to allege how the defendant's drug and alcohol program violates her right to privacy.

Applying the Restatement definition of the tort of intrusion upon seclusion to the facts and circumstances of the case sub judice, we find that plaintiff has failed to state a claim upon which relief can be granted. In the first instance, unlike urinalysis and personal property searches, we do not find a reasonable expectation of privacy in e-mail communications voluntarily made by an employee to his supervisor over the company e-mail system notwithstanding any assurances that such communications would not be intercepted by management. Once plaintiff communicated the alleged unprofessional comments to a second person (his supervisor) over an e-mail system which was apparently utilized by the entire company, any reasonable expectation of privacy was lost. Significantly, the defendant did not require plaintiff, as in the case of an urinalysis or personal property search to disclose any personal information about himself. Rather, plaintiff voluntarily communicated the alleged unprofessional comments over the company e-mail system. We find no privacy interests in such communications.

In the second instance, even if we found that an employee had a reasonable expectation of privacy in the contents of his e-mail communications over the company e-mail system, we do not find that a reasonable person would consider the defendant's interception of these communications to be a substantial and highly offensive invasion of his privacy. Again, we note that by intercepting such communications, the company is not, as in the case of urinalysis or personal property searches, requiring the employee to disclose any personal information about himself or invading the employee's person or personal effects. Moreover, the company's interest in preventing inappropriate and unprofessional comments or even illegal activity over its e-mail system outweighs any privacy interest the employee may have in those comments.

In sum, we find that the defendant's actions did not tortiously invade the plaintiff's privacy and, therefore, did not violate public policy. As a result, the motion to dismiss is granted.

Notes and Questions

1. In *Fraser*, the court of appeals concluded that Nationwide's conduct fell within the § 2701(c)(1) exception without considering Nationwide's computer usage or privacy policies, and in particular whether Nationwide reserved the right to monitor communications. Should the employer's policies factor into the analysis? How would you revise § 2701(c)(1) to take account of such policies?

2. Does Nationwide's right as a service provider to inspect communications extend to purely personal communications of its employees? Is access to such communications necessary for an employer to protect its rights or property? Are there other justifications for an employer's broad right of access?

3. The court in *Smyth* observes that the employer "intercepted" plaintiff's "private e-mail messages." Do the facts of the case bear this out? How might the court have decided the case more narrowly?

4. Assume that the employer had acquired communications between plaintiff and a fellow employee rather than between plaintiff and his supervisor. Would the result of the case have been the same? What additional facts would you need to know before making a determination?

5. Will an employee ever have a reasonable expectation of privacy in communications over the company e-mail system? In what circumstances? Assume an employer promulgates an "acceptable use" policy, in which it notifies employees that monitoring may occur. Would such a policy eliminate any expectation of privacy?

6. Recent legislative proposals would require companies to provide notice that they are engaging in monitoring of employees' communications. Is notice sufficient to protect employees' privacy interests? Why are employers likely to oppose such a requirement?

7. *Smyth* involved employer monitoring of communications transmitted and stored on the *employer's* network. What result should obtain when the employee places the communications he or she wishes to remain confidential on a third party's network in a password-restricted location? Consider the following case.

Konop v. Hawaiian Airlines, Inc. ("Konop II")

United States Court of Appeals for the Ninth Circuit, 2002
302 F.3d 868

BOOCHEVER, Circuit Judge.

[The facts of this case and discussion of Konop's Wiretap Act claim appear at p. 603.]

Konop also argues that, by viewing his secure website, Davis accessed a stored electronic communication without authorization in violation of the SCA. The SCA makes it an offense to "intentionally access[] without authorization a facility through which an electronic communication service is provided . . . and thereby obtain[] . . . access to a wire or electronic communication while it is in electronic storage in such system." 18 U.S.C. § 2701(a)(1). The SCA excepts from liability, however, "conduct authorized . . . by a user of that service with respect to a communication of or intended for that user." 18 U.S.C. § 2701(c)(2). The district court found that the exception in section 2701(c)(2) applied because Wong and Gardner consented to Davis' use of Konop's website. It therefore granted summary judgment to Hawaiian on the SCA claim.

The parties agree that the relevant "electronic communications service" is Konop's website, and that [information on] the website was in "electronic storage." In addition, for the purposes of this opinion, we accept the parties' assumption that Davis' conduct constituted "access without authorization" to "a facility through which an electronic communication service is provided."

We therefore address only the narrow question of whether the district court properly found Hawaiian exempt from liability under § 2701(c)(2). Section 2701(c)(2) allows a person to authorize a third party's access to an electronic communication if the person is 1) a "user" of the "service" and 2) the communication is "of or intended for that user." *See* 18 U.S.C. § 2701(c)(2). A "user" is "any person or entity who– (A) uses an electronic communications service; and (B) is duly authorized by the provider of such service to engage in such use." 18 U.S.C. § 2510(13).

The district court concluded that Wong and Gardner had the authority under § 2701(c)(2) to consent to Davis' use of the website because Konop put Wong and Gardner on the list of eligible users. This conclusion is consistent with other parts of the Wiretap Act and the SCA which allow intended recipients of wire and electronic communications to authorize third parties to access those communications. In addition, there is some indication in the legislative history that Congress believed "addressees" or "intended recipients" of electronic communications would have the authority under the SCA to allow third parties access to those communications. *See* H.R. Rep. No. 99-647, at 66-67 (1986) (explaining that "an addressee [of an electronic communication] may consent to the disclosure of a communication to any other person" and that "[a] person may be an 'intended recipient' of a communication . . . even if he is not individually identified by name or otherwise").

Nevertheless, the plain language of § 2701(c)(2) indicates that only a "user" of the service can authorize a third party's access to the communication. The statute defines "user" as one who 1) *uses* the service and 2) is duly authorized to do so. Because the statutory language is unambiguous, it must control our construction of the statute, notwithstanding the legislative history. *See United States v. Daas*, 198 F.3d 1167, 1174 (9th Cir. 1999). The statute does not define the word "use," so we apply the ordinary definition, which is "to put into action or service, avail oneself of, employ." *Webster's* at 1299; *see Daas*, 198 F.3d at 1174 ("If the statute uses a term which it does not define, the court gives that term its ordinary meaning.").

Based on the common definition of the word "use," we cannot find any evidence in the record that Wong ever used Konop's website. There is some evidence, however, that Gardner may have used the website, but it is unclear when that use occurred. At any rate, the district court did not make any findings on whether Wong and Gardner actually used Konop's website—it simply assumed that Wong and Gardner, by virtue of being eligible to view the website, could authorize Davis' access. The problem with this approach is that it essentially reads the "user" requirement out of § 2701(c)(2). Taking the facts in the light most favorable to Konop, we must assume that neither Wong nor Gardner was a "user" of the website at the time he authorized Davis to view it. We therefore reverse the district court's grant of summary judgment to Hawaiian on Konop's SCA claim.

[Opinion of Judge Reinhardt, concurring in part and dissenting in part, omitted.]

Notes and Questions

1. Under the court of appeals' approach, when will use of someone else's password violate the SCA? Rather than giving Davis his password, could Wong have obtained access to Konop's site and then conveyed all of the information on it to Davis without violating the SCA? If so, then why should Davis's use of Wong's password violate the SCA?

2. Recall the discussion above about what constitutes "electronic storage": a "temporary, intermediate" storage that is "incidental to the transmission" of a communication, or storage for purposes of "backup protection." 18 U.S.C. § 2510(17). Here, the parties apparently assumed that information on Konop's website was in "electronic storage." Do you agree? If not, when *should* information on a website be treated as information in "electronic storage"?

3. In evaluating Konop's claims under the SCA, the court of appeals accepts the parties' position that Konop's website constitutes an "electronic communication service." If you had served as counsel to Hawaiian Airlines and Davis, would you have made this concession? What are the implications of adopting this view of the statute? The SCA, of course, was passed long before websites even existed. If every website is an electronic communication service, do the restrictions that a website owner seeks to impose on others' use of his or her site thereby have the force of federal law? Suppose that Konop had not used password protection on his site, but instead had simply included the banner on his home page prohibiting any member of Hawaiian Airlines' management from viewing the website. If Davis had viewed the site anyway, would his actions have constituted unauthorized access? Why or why not?

4. Even assuming that a website is an "electronic communication service," what is the "facility" through which that service is provided? The Internet? The server that hosts Konop's site? In what sense was Davis's access to either of these "facilities" unauthorized?

5. Questions about the degree to which a website owner can limit access to his or her site arise not only when an employee seeks to shield private communications from his employer, but also when a company attempts to control its competitors' use of data. We take up those issues in Chapter Nine.

2. Transaction-Based Monitoring:
Online Profiling and the Collection and Use of Personal Data

Claims that problems of control over personal information are more acute in cyberspace than in real space often highlight the ability of online advertisers and others to track users' movements across different websites, thereby developing a detailed profile of the user's activities and interests—a profile sometimes associated with personal information about that user. Professor Jerry Kang describes the problem this way:

> [I]magine the following two visits to a mall, one in real space, the other in cyberspace. In real space, you drive to a mall, walk up and down its corridors, peer into numerous shops, and stroll through

corridors of inviting stores. Along the way, you buy an ice cream cone with cash. You walk into a bookstore and flip through a few magazines. Finally, you stop at a clothing store and buy a friend a silk scarf with a credit card. In this narrative, numerous persons interact with you and collect information along the way. For instance, while walking through the mall, fellow visitors visually collect information about you, if for no other reason than to avoid bumping into you. But such information is general—e.g., it does not pinpoint the geographical location and time of the sighting—is not in a format that can be processed by a computer, is not indexed to your name or another unique identifier, and is impermanent, residing in short-term human memory. You remain a barely noticed stranger. One important exception exists: The scarf purchase generates data that are detailed, computer-processable, indexed by name, and potentially permanent.

By contrast, in cyberspace, the exception becomes the norm: Every interaction is like the credit card purchase. The best way to grasp this point is to take seriously, if only for a moment, the metaphor that cyberspace is an actual place, a computer-constructed world, a virtual reality. In this alternate universe, you are invisibly stamped with a bar code as soon as you venture outside your home. There are entities called "road providers," who supply the streets and ground you walk on, who track precisely where, when, and how fast you traverse the lands, in order to charge you for your wear on the infrastructure. As soon as you enter the cyber-mall's domain, the mall begins to track you through invisible scanners focused on your bar code. It automatically records which stores you visit, which windows you browse, in which order, and for how long. The specific stores collect even more detailed data when you enter their domain. For example, the cyber-bookstore notes which magazines you skimmed, recording which pages you have seen and for how long, and notes the pattern, if any, of your browsing. It notes that you picked up briefly a health magazine featuring an article on St. John's Wort, read for seven minutes a newsweekly detailing a politician's sex scandal, and flipped ever-so-quickly through a tabloid claiming that Elvis lives. Of course, whenever any item is actually purchased, the store, as well as the credit, debit, or virtual cash company that provides payment through cyberspace, takes careful notes of what you bought—in this case, a silk scarf, red, expensive.

All these data generated in cyberspace are detailed, computer-processable, indexed to the individual, and permanent. While the mall example does not concern data that appear especially sensitive, the same extensive data collection takes place as we travel through other cyberspace domains—for instance: to research health issues and politics; to communicate to individuals, private institutions, and the state; and to pay our bills and manage our finances. Moreover, the data collected in these various domains can be aggregated to produce telling profiles of who we are, as revealed by what we do and say. The very technology that makes cyberspace possible also makes detailed, cumulative, invisible observation of our selves possible. * * *

Jerry Kang, *Information Privacy in Cyberspace*, 50 STAN. L. REV. 1193, 1198-99 (1998).

We can identify two different privacy concerns that these tracking activities raise: concerns about the gathering of data, and concerns about use or disclosure of the data once collected. The theoretical questions posed by any invocation of a right of privacy in this context are particularly difficult, because in many cases the entity against which a privacy right is asserted is actually a party to the communication—not an outsider, such as the government or an employer—and one might presume that a party to a communication may do as it wishes with the information it receives, including aggregating it with other information or revealing it to others.

Although commentators generally agree that U.S. law does little to constrain the collection and dissemination of personal data, they disagree over whether greater recognition of a "right" to privacy would be beneficial—and, if it would be, what form such a right should take. Much of the skepticism of the value of greater recognition of privacy rights comes from the law and economics literature, which often takes the view that privacy restrictions are not socially beneficial because, among other things, they preclude fully informed trades and increase transaction costs.[f] In addition, commentators taking a property rights–based approach have argued that the concept of privacy only has meaning to the extent that it can be reduced to a property interest.[g]

Even those scholars who argue that courts and legislatures must provide greater protections of personal data offer a wide range of perspectives on what form such protections should take. These different perspectives stem in part from different views of what kind of interests privacy protects—for example, a property interest, or an interest in secrecy, or an interest in individual autonomy. Recall our discussion in Section A of what privacy protects and why. In this section, we examine how the law protects information privacy in transaction-based settings and consider whether the existing protections are sufficient. As you read the materials below, ask yourself what conception of privacy current law reflects. If you favor additional protections, what form should they take?

Online Profiling: A Report to Congress

United States Federal Trade Commission, June 2000

A.   *Overview*

* * * Currently, tens of billions of banner ads are delivered to consumers each month as they surf the World Wide Web. Often, these ads

---

f. *See, e.g.*, Richard A. Posner, *The Right of Privacy*, 12 GA. L. REV. 393, 399 (1978); George J. Stigler, *An Introduction to Privacy in Economics and Politics*, 9 J. LEGAL STUD. 623 (1980). *But see* Richard S. Murphy, *Property Rights in Personal Information: An Economic Defense of Privacy*, 84 GEO. L. REV. 2381 (1996) (arguing that law and economics literature overstates the costs of greater judicial and statutory recognition of privacy rights).

g. *See, e.g.*, Judith Jarvis Thomson, *The Right to Privacy*, in PHILOSOPHICAL DIMENSIONS OF PRIVACY: AN ANTHOLOGY 272 (Ferdinand David Schoeman ed., 1984).

are not selected and delivered by the Web site visited by a consumer, but by a network advertising company that manages and provides advertising for numerous unrelated Web sites. DoubleClick, Engage, and 24/7 Media, three of the largest Internet advertising networks, all estimate that over half of all online consumers have seen an ad that they delivered.

In general, these network advertising companies do not merely supply banner ads; they also gather data about the consumers who view their ads. This is accomplished primarily by the use of "cookies"[11] and "Web bugs" which track the individual's actions on the Web.[12] Among the types of information that can be collected by network advertisers are: information on the Web sites and pages within those sites visited by consumers; the time and duration of the visits; query terms entered into search engines; purchases; "click-through" responses to advertisements; and the Web page a consumer came from before landing on the site monitored by the particular ad network (the referring page). All of this information is gathered even if the consumer never clicks on a single ad.

The information gathered by network advertisers is often, but not always, anonymous, i.e., the profiles are frequently linked to the identification number of the advertising network's cookie on the consumer's computer rather than the name of a specific person. This data is generally referred to as non-personally identifiable information ("non-PII"). In some circumstances, however, the profiles derived from tracking consumers' activities on the Web are linked or merged with personally identifiable information ("PII"). This generally occurs in one of two ways when consumers identify themselves to a Web site on which the network advertiser places banner ads. First, the Web site to whom personal information is provided may, in turn, provide that information to the network advertiser. Second, depending upon how the personal information is retrieved and processed by the Web site, the personally identifying information may be incorporated into a URL string that is automatically transmitted to the network advertiser through its cookie.

Once collected, consumer data can be analyzed and combined with demographic and "psychographic" data from third-party sources, data on

---

11. A cookie is a small text file placed on a consumer's computer hard drive by a Web server. The cookie transmits information back to the server that placed it and, in general, can be read only by that server.

12. "Web bugs" are also known as "clear GIFs" or "1-by-1 GIFs." Web bugs are tiny graphic image files embedded in a Web page, generally the same color as the background on which they are displayed which are invisible to the naked eye. The Web bug sends back to its home server (which can belong to the host site, a network advertiser or some other third party): the IP (Internet Protocol) address of the computer that downloaded the page on which the bug appears; the URL (Uniform Resource Locator) of the page on which the Web bug appears; the URL of the Web bug image; the time the page containing the Web bug was viewed; the type of browser that fetched the Web bug; and the identification number of any cookie on the consumer's computer previously placed by that server. Web bugs can be detected only by looking at the source code of a Web page and searching in the code for 1-by-1 IMG tags that load images from a server different than the rest of the Web page. At least one expert claims that, in addition to disclosing who visits the particular Web page or reads the particular email in which the bug has been placed, in some circumstances, Web bugs can also be used to place a cookie on a computer or to synchronize a particular email address with a cookie identification number, making an otherwise anonymous profile personally identifiable. * * *

the consumer's offline purchases, or information collected directly from consumers through surveys and registration forms. This enhanced data allows the advertising networks to make a variety of inferences about each consumer's interests and preferences. The result is a detailed profile that attempts to predict the individual consumer's tastes, needs, and purchasing habits and enables the advertising companies' computers to make split-second decisions about how to deliver ads directly targeted to the consumer's specific interests.

The profiles created by the advertising networks can be extremely detailed. A cookie placed by a network advertising company can track a consumer on any Web site served by that company, thereby allowing data collection across disparate and unrelated sites on the Web. Also, because the cookies used by ad networks are generally persistent, their tracking occurs over an extended period of time, resuming each time the individual logs on to the Internet. When this "clickstream" information is combined with third-party data, these profiles can include hundreds of distinct data fields.

Although network advertisers and their profiling activities are nearly ubiquitous, they are most often invisible to consumers. All that consumers see are the Web sites they visit; banner ads appear as a seamless, integral part of the Web page on which they appear and cookies are placed without any notice to consumers.[21] Unless the Web sites visited by consumers provide notice of the ad network's presence and data collection, consumers may be totally unaware that their activities online are being monitored.

B. *An Illustration of How Network Profiling Works*

Online consumer Joe Smith goes to a Web site that sells sporting goods. He clicks on the page for golf bags. While there, he sees a banner ad, which he ignores as it does not interest him. The ad was placed by USAad Network. He then goes to a travel site and enters a search on "Hawaii." USAad Network also serves ads on this site, and Joe sees an ad for rental cars there. Joe then visits an online bookstore and browses through books about the world's best golf courses. USAad Network serves ads there, as well. A week later, Joe visits his favorite online news site, and notices an ad for golf vacation packages in Hawaii. Delighted, he clicks on the ad, which was served by the USAad Network. Later, Joe begins to wonder whether it was a coincidence that this particular ad appeared and, if not, how it happened.

* * * Embedded in the HTML code that Joe's browser receives from the sporting goods site is an invisible link to the USAad Network site which delivers ads in the banner space on the sporting goods Web site. Joe's browser is automatically triggered to send an HTTP request to USAad which reveals the following information: his browser type and operating system; the language(s) accepted by the browser; the address of the referring Web page (in this case, the home page of the sporting goods site);

---

21. Most Internet browsers can be configured to notify users that a cookie is being sent to their computer and to give users the option of rejecting the cookie. The browsers' default setting, however, is to permit placement of cookies without any notification.

and the identification number and information stored in any USAad cookies already on Joe's computer. Based on this information, USAad will place an ad in the pre-set banner space on the sporting goods site's home page. The ad will appear as an integral part of the page. If an USAad cookie is not already present on Joe's computer, USAad will place a cookie with a unique identifier on Joe's hard drive. Unless he has set his browser to notify him before accepting cookies, Joe has no way to know that a cookie is being placed on his computer. When Joe clicks on the page for golf bags, the URL address of that page, which discloses its content, is also transmitted to USAad by its cookie.

When Joe leaves the sporting goods site and goes to the travel site, also serviced by USAad, a similar process occurs. The HTML source code for the travel site will contain an invisible link to USAad that requests delivery of an ad as part of the travel site's page. Because the request reveals that the referring site is travel related, USAad sends an advertisement for rental cars. USAad will also know the identification number of its cookie on Joe's machine. As Joe moves around the travel site, USAad checks his cookie and modifies the profile associated with it, adding elements based on Joe's activities. When Joe enters a search for "Hawaii," his search term is transmitted to USAad through the URL used by the travel site to locate the information Joe wants and the search term is associated with the other data collected by the cookie on Joe's machine. USAad will also record what advertisements it has shown Joe and whether he has clicked on them.

This process is repeated when Joe goes to the online bookstore. Because USAad serves banner ads on this site as well, it will recognize Joe by his cookie identification number. USAad can track what books Joe looks at, even though he does not buy anything. The fact that Joe browsed for books about golf courses around the world is added to his profile.

Based on Joe's activities, USAad infers that Joe is a golfer, that he is interested in traveling to Hawaii someday, and that he might be interested in a golf vacation. Thus, a week later, when Joe goes to his favorite online news site, also served by USAad, the cookie on his computer is recognized and he is presented with an ad for golf vacation packages in Hawaii. The ad grabs his attention and appeals to his interests, so he clicks on it.

Notes and Questions

1. Assume that a network advertiser engages in profiling, but does not gather personally identifiable information. What are the benefits of such profiling? Why might online profiling be troubling even when it does not involve collection of personally identifiable information?

2. How is online profiling different from any other profiling that might occur in real space—as, for example, when one's grocery store purchases cause the store's computer to generate a coupon for a future purchase?

3. The FTC report observes that network advertisers place cookies "without any notice to consumers." In terms of notice, are cookies placed by a network advertiser any more troubling than cookies placed by the website on which the banner ad appears? Why wouldn't we assume that a user is aware that banner ads are supplied by third parties?

4. Do cookies placed in connection with "clear GIFs" or "web bugs" raise any concerns different from those that cookies placed in connection with banner ads raise? Why or why not?

5. Does the capture of a URL or other communications by a network advertiser violate statutory protections of electronic communications? Consider the following case.

In re DoubleClick Inc. Privacy Litigation

United States District Court for the Southern District of New York, 2001
154 F. Supp. 2d 497

BUCHWALD, District Judge.

Plaintiffs bring this class action on behalf of themselves and all others similarly situated against defendant DoubleClick, Inc. ("defendant" or "DoubleClick") seeking injunctive and monetary relief for injuries they have suffered as a result of DoubleClick's purported illegal conduct. Specifically, plaintiffs bring * * * claims under * * * 18 U.S.C. § 2701, *et seq.* [and] * * * 18 U.S.C. § 2510, *et seq.* * * * Now pending is DoubleClick's [motion to dismiss].

DOUBLECLICK'S TECHNOLOGY AND SERVICES

DoubleClick provides the Internet's largest advertising service. Commercial Web sites often rent out online advertising "space" to other Web sites. In the simplest type of arrangement, the host Web site (e.g., Lycos.com) rents space on its webpages to another Web site (e.g., TheGlobe.com) to place a "hotlink" banner advertisement ("banner advertisement"). When a user on the host Web site "clicks" on the banner advertisement, he is automatically connected to the advertiser's designated Web site.

DoubleClick acts as an intermediary between host Web sites and Web sites seeking to place banner advertisements. It promises client Web sites that it will place their banner advertisements in front of viewers who match their demographic target. For example, DoubleClick might try to place banner advertisements for a Web site that sells golf clubs in front of high-income people who follow golf and have a track record of making expensive online purchases. DoubleClick creates value for its customers in large part by building detailed profiles of Internet users and using them to target clients' advertisements.

DoubleClick compiles user profiles utilizing its proprietary technologies and analyses in cooperation with its affiliated Web sites. DoubleClick is affiliated with over 11,000 Web sites for which and on which it provides targeted banner advertisements. * * * When users visit any of these DoubleClick-affiliated Web sites, a "cookie" is placed on their hard drives. Cookies are computer programs commonly used by Web sites to store useful information such as usernames, passwords, and preferences, making it easier for users to access Web pages in an efficient manner. However, Plaintiffs allege that DoubleClick's cookies collect "information that Web users, including plaintiffs and the Class, consider to be personal and private, such as names, e-mail addresses, home and business addresses, telephone numbers, searches performed on the Internet, Web pages or sites visited on the Internet and other communications and information that users would not ordinarily expect advertisers to be able to collect." * * *

A. *Targeting Banner Advertisements*

DoubleClick's advertising targeting process involves three participants and four steps. The three participants are: (1) the user; (2) the DoubleClick-affiliated Web site; (3) the DoubleClick server. For the purposes of this discussion, we assume that a DoubleClick cookie already sits on the user's computer with the identification number "# 0001."

In Step One, a user seeks to access a DoubleClick-affiliated Web site such as Lycos.com. The user's browser sends a communication to Lycos.com (technically, to Lycos.com's server) saying, in essence, "Send me your homepage." * * *

In Step Two, Lycos.com receives the request, processes it, and returns a communication to the user saying "Here is the Web page you requested." The communication has two parts. The first part is a copy of the Lycos.com homepage, essentially the collection of article summaries, pictures and hotlinks a user sees on his screen when Lycos.com appears. The only objects missing are the banner advertisements; in their places lie blank spaces. The second part of the communication is an IP-address link to the DoubleClick server. This link instructs the user's computer to send a communication automatically to DoubleClick's server.

In Step Three, as per the IP-address instruction, the user's computer sends a communication to the DoubleClick server saying "I am cookie # 0001, send me banner advertisements to fill the blank spaces in the Lycos.com Web page." This communication contains information including the cookie identification number, the name of the DoubleClick-affiliated Web site the user requested, and the user's browser type.

Finally, in Step Four, the DoubleClick server identifies the user's profile by the cookie identification number and runs a complex set of algorithms based, in part, on the user's profile, to determine which advertisements it will present to the user. It then sends a communication to the user with banner advertisements saying "Here are the targeted banner advertisements for the Lycos.com homepage." Meanwhile, it also updates the user's profile with the information from the request.

DoubleClick's targeted advertising process is invisible to the user. His experience consists simply of requesting the Lycos.com homepage and, several moments later, receiving it complete with banner advertisements.

B. *Cookie Information Collection*

DoubleClick's cookies only collect information from one step of the above process: Step One. The cookies capture certain parts of the communications that users send to DoubleClick-affiliated Web sites. They collect this information in three ways: (1) "GET" submissions, (2) "POST" submissions, and (3) "GIF" submissions.

GET information is submitted as part of a Web site's address or "URL," in what is known as a "query string." For example, a request for a hypothetical online record store's selection of Bon Jovi albums might read: *http:// recordstore.hypothetical.com/search?terms=bonjovi.* The URL query string begins with the "?" character meaning the cookie would record that the user requested information about Bon Jovi.

Users submit POST information when they fill in multiple blank fields on a webpage. For example, if a user signed up for an online discussion group, he might have to fill in fields with his name, address, email address, phone number and discussion group alias. The cookie would capture this submitted POST information.

Finally, DoubleClick places GIF tags on its affiliated Web sites. GIF tags are the size of a single pixel and are invisible to users. Unseen, they record the users' movements throughout the affiliated Web site, enabling DoubleClick to learn what information the user sought and viewed.

Although the information collected by DoubleClick's cookies is allegedly voluminous and detailed, it is important to note three clearly defined parameters. First, DoubleClick's cookies *only* collect information concerning users' activities *on DoubleClick-affiliated Web sites*. Thus, if a user visits an unaffiliated Web site, the DoubleClick cookie captures no information. Second, plaintiff does not allege that DoubleClick ever attempted to collect *any* information other than the GET, POST, and GIF information submitted by users. DoubleClick is never alleged to have accessed files, programs or other information on users' hard drives. Third, DoubleClick will not collect information from any user who takes simple steps to prevent DoubleClick's tracking. As plaintiffs' counsel demonstrated at oral argument, users can easily and at no cost prevent DoubleClick from collecting information from them. They may do this in two ways: (1) visiting the DoubleClick Web site and requesting an "opt-out" cookie; and (2) configuring their browsers to block any cookies from being deposited. * * *

Once DoubleClick collects information from the cookies on users' hard drives, it aggregates and compiles the information to build demographic profiles of users. Plaintiffs allege that DoubleClick has more than 100 million user profiles in its database. Exploiting its proprietary Dynamic Advertising Reporting & Targeting ("DART") technology, DoubleClick and its licensees target banner advertisements using these demographic profiles. * * *

CLAIM I. TITLE II OF THE ECPA

Title II ("Title II") of the Electronic Communications Privacy Act ("ECPA"), 18 U.S.C. § 2701 et seq. ("§ 2701"), aims to prevent hackers from obtaining, altering or destroying certain stored electronic communications. It creates both criminal sanctions and a civil right of action against persons who gain unauthorized access to communications facilities and thereby access electronic communications stored incident to their transmission. Title II specifically defines the relevant prohibited conduct as follows:

"(a) Offense. Except as provided in subsection (c) of this section whoever (1) intentionally accesses without authorization a facility through which an electronic [communication] service is provided; or (2) intentionally exceeds an authorization to access that facility; and thereby obtains . . . access to a wire or electronic communication while it is in electronic storage in such system shall be punished. . . ."

Plaintiffs contend that DoubleClick's placement of cookies on plaintiffs' hard drives constitutes unauthorized access and, as a result, DoubleClick's collection of information from the cookies violates Title II. However, Title II contains an exception to its general prohibition.

> "(c) Exceptions.—Subsection (a) of this section does not apply with respect to conduct authorized . . . (2) by a user of that [electronic communication] service with respect to a communication of or intended for that user;"

DoubleClick argues that its conduct falls under this exception. It contends that the DoubleClick-affiliated Web sites are "users" of the Internet and that all of plaintiffs' communications accessed by DoubleClick's cookies have been "of or intended for" these Web sites. Therefore, it asserts, the Web sites' authorization excepts DoubleClick's access from § 2701(a)'s general prohibition. * * *

Assuming that the communications are considered to be in "electronic storage," it appears that plaintiffs have adequately pled that DoubleClick's conduct constitutes an offense under § 2701(a), absent the exception under § 2701(c)(2). Therefore, the issue is whether DoubleClick's conduct falls under § 2701(c)(2)'s exception. This issue has three parts: (1) what is the relevant electronic communications service?; (2) were DoubleClick-affiliated Web sites "users" of this service?; and (3) did the DoubleClick-affiliated Web sites give DoubleClick sufficient authorization to access plaintiffs' stored communications "intended for" those Web sites?

A. *"Internet Access" is the relevant electronic communications service.*

Obviously, in a broad sense, the "Internet" is the relevant communications service. However, for the purposes of this motion, it is important that we define Internet service with somewhat greater care and precision. Plaintiff, at turns, argues that the electronic communications service is "Internet access" and "the ISP [Internet Service Provider]." The difference is important. An ISP is *an entity* that provides access to the Internet; examples include America Online, UUNET and Juno. Access to the Internet is *the service* an ISP provides. Therefore, the "service which provides to users thereof the ability to send or receive wire or electronic communications" is "Internet access."

B. *Web Sites are "users" under the ECPA.*

The ECPA defines a "user" as "any person or entity who (A) uses an electronic communication service; and (B) is duly authorized by the provider of such service to engage in such use." 18 U.S.C. § 2510(13). On first reading, the DoubleClick-affiliated Web sites appear to be users—they are (1) "entities" that (2) use Internet access and (3) are authorized to use Internet access by the ISPs to which they subscribe. However, plaintiffs make two arguments that Web sites nevertheless are not users. Both are unpersuasive.

First, plaintiffs argue that "[t]he most natural reading of 'user' is the person who has signed up for Internet access, which means the individual plaintiffs and Class members—*not* the Web servers." * * * [This argument] rests on the erroneous assumption that only human users "sign[] up for Internet access," not Web sites or servers. * * * [A]ll people and entities that utilize Internet access subscribe to ISPs or are ISPs. Although the vast majority of people who sign up for Internet access from consumer-focused ISPs such as America Online and Juno are individuals, every Web site, company, university, and government agency that utilizes Internet access also subscribes to an ISP or is one. These larger entities generally purchase "Internet access" in bulk from ISPs, often with value-added services and technologically advanced hardware. Nevertheless, they purchase the same underlying Internet access as individual users. Therefore, plaintiffs fail to distinguish class members from Web sites and servers based on whether they subscribe to an ISP for Internet access.

Second, plaintiffs argue that "[t]he individual plaintiff ('user') owns the personal computer ('facility'), while the Web sites she visits do not. [And that] [u]nder basic property and privacy notions, therefore, only she can authorize access to her own messages stored on that facility." Again, plaintiffs seem to ignore the statute's plain language. The general rule under § 2701(a) embodies plaintiffs' position that only those authorized to use a "facility" may consent to its access. Nevertheless, Congress explicitly chose to make § 2701(a)'s general rule subject to § 2701(c)(2)'s exception for access authorized by authors and intended recipients of electronic communications. Thus, plaintiffs' argument is essentially that this Court should ignore § 2701(c)(2) because Congress failed to take adequate account of "basic property and privacy notions." However, it is not this Court's role to revisit Congress' legislative judgments. * * *

C.   *All of the communications DoubleClick has accessed through its cookies have been authorized or have fallen outside of Title II's scope.*

Because plaintiffs only allege that DoubleClick accessed communications from plaintiffs to DoubleClick-affiliated Web sites, the issue becomes whether the Web sites gave DoubleClick adequate authorization under § 2701(c)(2) to access those communications. This issue, in turn, has two parts: (1) have the DoubleClick-affiliated Web sites authorized DoubleClick to access plaintiffs' communications to them?; and (2) is that authorization sufficient under § 2701(c)(2)?

1.   *The DoubleClick-affiliated Web sites have consented to DoubleClick's interception of plaintiffs' communications.*

* * * Examining DoubleClick's technological and commercial relationships with its affiliated Web sites, we find it implausible to infer that the Web sites have not authorized DoubleClick's access. In a practical sense, the very reason clients hire DoubleClick is to target advertisements based on users' demographic profiles. DoubleClick has trumpeted this fact in its advertising, patents and Securities and Exchange filings. True, officers of certain Web sites might not understand precisely how DoubleClick collects demographic information through cookies and records plaintiffs' travels across the Web. However, that knowledge is irrelevant to the authorization at issue—Title II in no way outlaws collecting personally identifiable information or placing cookies, qua such. All that the Web sites must authorize is that DoubleClick access plaintiffs' communications to them. [As described earlier,] the DoubleClick-affiliated Web sites actively notify DoubleClick each time a plaintiff sends them an electronic

communication (whether through a page request, search, or GIF tag). The data in these notifications (such as the name of the Web site requested) often play an important role in determining which advertisements are presented to users. Plaintiffs have offered no explanation as to how, in anything other than a purely theoretical sense, the DoubleClick-affiliated Web sites could have played such a central role in the information collection and not have authorized DoubleClick's access. * * *

2.   *DoubleClick is authorized to access plaintiffs' GET, POST and GIF submissions to the DoubleClick-affiliated Web sites.*

Plaintiffs' GET, POST and GIF submissions to DoubleClick-affiliated Web sites are all "intended for" those Web sites. In the case of the GET and POST submissions, users voluntarily type in information they wish to submit to the Web sites, information such as queries, commercial orders, and personal information. GIF information is generated and collected when users use their computer "mouse" or other instruments to navigate through Web pages and access information. Although the users' requests for data come through clicks, not keystrokes, they nonetheless are voluntary and purposeful. Therefore, because plaintiffs' GET, POST and GIF submissions to DoubleClick-affiliated Web sites are all "intended for" those Web sites, the Web sites' authorization is sufficient to except DoubleClick's access under § 2701(c)(2).

3.   *To the extent that the DoubleClick cookies' identification numbers are electronic communications, (1) they fall outside of Title II's scope, and (2) DoubleClick's access to them is otherwise authorized.*

Plaintiffs argue that even if DoubleClick's access to plaintiffs' GET, POST and GIF submissions is properly authorized under § 2701(c)(2), the cookie identification numbers that accompany these submissions are not because they are never sent to, or through, the Web sites. However, this argument too is unavailing.

(a)   *The Cookies' identification numbers are not in "electronic storage" and therefore are outside Title II's scope.*

Putting aside the issue of whether the cookie identification numbers are electronic communications at all, DoubleClick does not need anyone's authority to access them. The cookies' long-term residence on plaintiffs' hard drives places them outside of § 2510(17)'s definition of "electronic storage" and, hence, Title II's protection. Section 2510(17) defines "electronic storage" as:

"(A) any *temporary, intermediate storage* of a wire or electronic communication incidental to the electronic transmission thereof; and

(B) any storage of such communication *by an electronic communication service* for the purpose of backup protection of such communication." (emphasis added)

Clearly, the cookies' residence on plaintiffs' computers does not fall into § 2510(17)(B) because plaintiffs are not "electronic communication service" providers.

Section 2510(17)(A)'s language and legislative history make evident that "electronic storage" is not meant to include DoubleClick's cookies either. Rather, it appears that the section is specifically targeted at communications temporarily stored by electronic communications services incident to their transmission—for example, when an email service stores a message until the addressee downloads it. The statute's language explicitly refers to "temporary, intermediate" storage. Webster's Dictionary defines "temporary" as "lasting for a limited time," and "intermediate" as "being or occurring at the middle place . . . ." *Webster's Third New International Dictionary* 2353, 1180 (1993). In other words, Title II only protects electronic communications stored "for a limited time" in the "middle" of a transmission, i.e. when an electronic communication service temporarily stores a communication while waiting to deliver it. * * *

Turning to the facts of this case, it is clear that DoubleClick's cookies fall outside § 2510(17)'s definition of electronic storage and, hence, § 2701's scope. * * *

> (b) *If the DoubleClick cookies' identification numbers are considered stored electronic communications, they are "of or intended for" DoubleClick and DoubleClick's acquisition of them does not violate Title II.*

Even if we were to assume that cookies and their identification numbers were "electronic communication[s] . . . in electronic storage," DoubleClick's access is still authorized. Section 2701(c)(2) excepts from Title II's prohibition access, authorized by a "user," to communications (1) "of" (2) "or intended for" that user. In every practical sense, the cookies' identification numbers are internal DoubleClick communications—both "of" and "intended for" DoubleClick. DoubleClick creates the cookies, assigns them identification numbers, and places them on plaintiffs' hard drives. The cookies and their identification numbers are vital to DoubleClick and meaningless to anyone else. * * * [B]ecause the identification numbers are "of or intended for" DoubleClick, it does not violate Title II for DoubleClick to obtain them from plaintiffs' electronic storage.

Claim II. Wiretap Act

Plaintiffs' second claim is that DoubleClick violated the Federal Wiretap Act ("Wiretap Act"), 18 U.S.C. § 2510, et seq. The Wiretap Act provides for criminal punishment and a private right of action against:

> "any person who—(a) intentionally intercepts, endeavors to intercept, or procures any other person to intercept or endeavor to intercept wire, oral, or electronic communication [except as provided in the statute]." 18 U.S.C. § 2511.

For the purposes of this motion, DoubleClick concedes that its conduct, as pled, violates this prohibition. However, DoubleClick claims that its actions fall under an explicit statutory exception:

> "It shall not be unlawful under this chapter for a person not acting under color of law to intercept a wire, oral, or electronic communication where such person is a party to the communication or where one of the parties to the communication has given prior consent to such interception *unless such communication is intercepted for the purpose of committing any criminal or tortious act in violation of the*

Constitution or laws of the United States or any State." 18 U.S.C. § 2511(2)(d) ("§ 2511(2)(d)") (emphasis added).

DoubleClick argues once again that the DoubleClick-affiliated Web sites have consented to its interceptions and, accordingly, that its conduct is exempted from the Wiretap Act's general prohibition as it was from the Title II's. Plaintiffs deny that the Web sites have consented and argue that even if the Web sites do consent, the exception does not apply because DoubleClick's purpose is to commit "criminal or tortious act[s]."

As a preliminary matter, we find that the DoubleClick-affiliated Web sites are "parties to the communication[s]" from plaintiffs and have given sufficient consent to DoubleClick to intercept them. In reviewing the case law and legislative histories of Title II and the Wiretap Act, we can find no difference in their definitions of "user" (Title II) and "parties to the communication" (Wiretap Act) or "authorize" (Title II) and "consent" (Wiretap Act) that would make our analysis of the Web sites' consent under Title II inapplicable to the Wiretap Act. Therefore, the issue before us is: assuming that DoubleClick committed every act alleged in the Amended Complaint, could this evince a "criminal or tortious" purpose on DoubleClick's part?

In light of the DoubleClick-affiliated Web sites' consent, plaintiffs must allege "either (1) that the primary motivation, or (2) that a determinative factor in the actor's [DoubleClick's] motivation for intercepting the conversation was to commit a criminal [or] tortious . . . act." *United States v. Dale,* 991 F.2d 819, 841-42 (D.C. Cir. 1993). * * *

Plaintiffs attempt to meet § 2511(2)(d)'s "purpose" requirement by arguing that their six non–Wiretap Act claims against DoubleClick "plead conduct that has underlying it a tortious purpose and/or that translates into tortious acts." In other words, by virtue of its tortious acts, DoubleClick must have had a tortious purpose. * * * In the instant case, plaintiffs clearly allege that DoubleClick has committed a number of torts. However, nowhere have they alleged that DoubleClick's "primary motivation" or a "determining factor" in its actions has been to injure plaintiffs tortiously. * * * [W]e find that plaintiffs have failed to allege that DoubleClick has intercepted plaintiffs' communications for a "criminal or tortious" purpose.

Notes and Questions

1. Re-read 18 U.S.C. § 2701(a). What is it designed to prohibit? The court states that it "appears that the plaintiffs have adequately pled that DoubleClick's conduct constitutes an offense under § 2701(a)." Do you agree? What is the "facility through which an electronic communication service is provided" that DoubleClick has accessed without authorization? What "electronic communication" did DoubleClick obtain from "electronic storage"?

2. Under the court's reading of the consent exceptions in § 2701(c) and § 2511(2)(d), the consent of the website that engaged DoubleClick's services is sufficient to preclude liability. Should the law instead require the consent of the user of the website? Why or why not?

3. Consider the substantive predicate for liability under the second cause of action the court discusses, 18 U.S.C. § 2511. As the court notes, DoubleClick concedes that its conduct, as pled, violates this provision. If you were DoubleClick's lawyer, would you have made this concession? What communications did DoubleClick intercept, and what "device" did DoubleClick use to intercept them?

4. *DoubleClick* is one of several cases addressing challenges under federal statutes to the use of cookies. *See Chance v. Avenue A*, 165 F. Supp. 2d 1153 (W.D. Wash. 2001) (rejecting challenge to advertiser's use of cookies); *In re Intuit Privacy Litigation*, 138 F. Supp. 2d 1272 (C.D. Cal. 2001) (rejecting Title III and Computer Fraud and Abuse Act (CFAA), 18 U.S.C. § 1030, claims against website operator that placed cookies, but denying motion to dismiss ECPA claim); *In re Pharmatrak, Inc. Privacy Litigation*, 220 F. Supp. 2d 4 (D. Mass. 2002) (rejecting Title III, ECPA, and CFAA claims against company that planted cookies to track data on behalf of pharmaceutical company clients), *rev'd*, 329 F.3d 9 (1st Cir. 2003) (reversing grant of summary judgment on Title III claim).

For our purposes, what is interesting is that courts have largely accepted the framework that plaintiffs' lawyers have created for bringing claims under Title III, the stored communications access provisions of ECPA, and the CFAA. The point of contention in the cases is typically whether one party *consented* to the use of cookies to track data, thus triggering the statutory exceptions—not whether the federal statutes cover this sort of conduct in the first place. Since the adoption of the statutes well pre-dated the use of cookies, we can legitimately ask whether courts should interpret the statutes to cover the conduct in question, and whether the statutes are adequate to address privacy concerns raised by the use of cookies. For further discussion, see Patricia L. Bellia, *Spyware and the Limits of Surveillance Law*, 20 BERKELEY TECH. L.J. 1283, 1318-43 (2005).

5. The plaintiffs' claims in *DoubleClick* mainly challenged DoubleClick's collection of information, not its subsequent use and disclosure of that information. To what extent does the law regulate the use and disclosure of personal data? Consider the following case.

Dwyer v. American Express Co.

First District Appellate Court of Illinois, 1995
652 N.E.2d 1351

JUSTICE BUCKLEY delivered the opinion of the court:

Plaintiffs, American Express cardholders, appeal the circuit court's dismissal of their claims for invasion of privacy and consumer fraud against defendants, American Express Company, American Express Credit Corporation, and American Express Travel Related Services Company, for their practice of renting information regarding cardholder spending habits. * * *

[D]efendants categorize and rank their cardholders into six tiers based on spending habits and then rent this information to participating merchants as part of a targeted joint-marketing and sales program. For example, a cardholder may be characterized as "Rodeo Drive Chic" or

"Value Oriented." In order to characterize its cardholders, defendants analyze where they shop and how much they spend, and also consider behavioral characteristics and spending histories. Defendants then offer to create a list of cardholders who would most likely shop in a particular store and rent that list to the merchant.

Defendants also offer to create lists which target cardholders who purchase specific types of items, such as fine jewelry. The merchants using the defendants' service can also target shoppers in categories such as mail-order apparel buyers, home-improvement shoppers, electronics shoppers, luxury lodgers, card members with children, skiers, frequent business travelers, resort users, Asian/European travelers, luxury European car owners, or recent movers. Finally, defendants offer joint-marketing ventures to merchants who generate substantial sales through the American Express card. Defendants mail special promotions devised by the merchants to its cardholders and share the profits generated by these advertisements.

On May 14, 1992, Patrick E. Dwyer filed a class action against defendants. * * * Plaintiffs have alleged that defendants' practices constitute an invasion of their privacy * * * .

There are four branches of the privacy invasion tort identified by the Restatement (Second) of Torts. These are: (1) an unreasonable intrusion upon the seclusion of another; (2) an appropriation of another's name or likeness; (3) a public disclosure of private facts; and (4) publicity which reasonably places another in a false light before the public. (Restatement (Second) of Torts §§ 652B, 652C, 652D, 652E, at 378-94 (1977).) Plaintiffs' complaint includes claims under the first and second branches.

As a preliminary matter, we note that a cause of action for intrusion into seclusion has never been recognized explicitly by the Illinois Supreme Court. [Another Illinois appellate court recognizing the cause of action] set out four elements which must be alleged in order to state a cause of action: (1) an unauthorized intrusion or prying into the plaintiff's seclusion; (2) an intrusion which is offensive or objectionable to a reasonable man; (3) the matter upon which the intrusion occurs is private; and (4) the intrusion causes anguish and suffering. * * *

Plaintiffs' allegations fail to satisfy the first element, an unauthorized intrusion or prying into the plaintiffs' seclusion. The alleged wrongful actions involve the defendants' practice of renting lists that they have compiled from information contained in their own records. By using the American Express card, a cardholder is voluntarily, and necessarily, giving information to defendants that, if analyzed, will reveal a cardholder's spending habits and shopping preferences. We cannot hold that a defendant has committed an unauthorized intrusion by compiling the information voluntarily given to it and then renting its compilation.

Plaintiffs claim that because defendants rented lists based on this compiled information, this case involves the disclosure of private financial information and most closely resembles cases involving intrusion into private financial dealings, such as bank account transactions. * * * However, we find that this case more closely resembles the sale of magazine subscription lists * * * . Defendants rent names and addresses after they create a list of cardholders who have certain shopping tendencies; they are not disclosing financial information about particular cardholders. These lists are being used solely for the purpose of determining what type of advertising should be sent to whom. * * *

Considering plaintiffs' appropriation claim, the elements of the tort are: an appropriation, without consent, of one's name or likeness for another's use or benefit. (Restatement (Second) of Torts § 652C (1977).) * * *

Plaintiffs claim that defendants appropriate information about cardholders' personalities, including their names and perceived lifestyles, without their consent. Defendants argue that their practice does not adversely affect the interest of a cardholder in the "exclusive use of his own identity," using the language of the Restatement. Defendants also argue that the cardholders' names lack value and that the lists that defendants create are valuable because "they identify a useful aggregate of potential customers to whom offers may be sent." * * *

[W]e * * * find that plaintiffs have not stated a claim for tortious appropriation because they have failed to allege the first element. Undeniably, each cardholder's name is valuable to defendants. The more names included on a list, the more that list will be worth. However, a single, random cardholder's name has little or no intrinsic value to defendants (or a merchant). Rather, an individual name has value only when it is associated with one of defendants' lists. Defendants create value by categorizing and aggregating these names. Furthermore, defendants' practices do not deprive any of the cardholders of any value their individual names may possess. * * *

Affirmed.

RAKOWSKI and CAHILL, JJ., concur.

Notes and Questions

1. With respect to the plaintiffs' claim of unreasonable intrusion upon seclusion, should it matter whether American Express provides information on its use and disclosure practices? Should American Express's use and disclosure policies affect a court's analysis of whether the plaintiffs "voluntarily" provided their personal information to American Express?

2. With respect to the plaintiffs' appropriation claim, does the court properly measure the "value" of what the plaintiffs seek to protect? Should the court have measured the "value" of the plaintiffs' names to the plaintiffs, rather than the defendant? Should the court have measured the "value" of individual profiles, rather than individual names? Why or why not?

Note on the Federal Trade Commission Act and the Children's Online Privacy Protection Act

Although courts have largely rejected claims that a company's information disclosure practices violate a right to privacy protected under state tort law, claims under consumer protection statutes have fared somewhat better. For example, the Federal Trade Commission has taken enforcement action against Internet companies in a number of high-profile cases, alleging that companies' privacy policies are misleading, and that their information collection and disclosure practices therefore violate the Federal Trade Commission Act's prohibition on unfair and deceptive trade practices. 15 U.S.C. § 45(a).

In 1997, for example, the FTC brought a complaint against the operators of the GeoCities website. GeoCities required new members, including children, to fill out an application form that collected certain mandatory and optional data. GeoCities' privacy statement explicitly stated that the site would not share the information with anyone without users' permission.   The FTC charged that GeoCities had "sold, rented, or otherwise marketed or disclosed" the information, including information collected from children, to third parties, who then sent GeoCities members unsolicited advertisements. In addition, the FTC alleged that GeoCities, in promotions targeting children, represented that it would collect and maintain certain information in connection with an application for membership in the GeoKidz Club and in connection with a contest entry form.   The FTC alleged that the information was in fact collected and maintained by a third party.

In 1999, the FTC entered a consent decree against GeoCities. *In the Matter of GeoCities*, FTC Docket No. C-3850. The FTC's order required GeoCities to take a number of steps with respect to the collection and use of personal identifying information. Apart from requiring GeoCities not to make any misrepresentations about its collection or use of such information, the FTC prohibited GeoCities from collecting personal identifying information from any child if GeoCities "has actual knowledge that such child does not have his or her parent's permission to provide the information." The order required GeoCities to adopt a procedure "by which it obtains express parental consent" before collecting information about a child. GeoCities could satisfy this requirement by acquiring the parent's e-mail address from the child and instructing the parent to view information on GeoCities' practices and provide consent.

For all consumers from whom GeoCities collected personal identifying information—adults and children—the FTC required GeoCities to provide notice that such information had been collected and to provide a means by which the consumers could view and remove such information.

While the *GeoCities* case was still pending, Congress adopted the Children's Online Privacy Protection Act of 1998 (COPPA), 15 U.S.C. §§ 6501-6506, to curb perceived abuses in the collection and disclosure of personal information concerning children under the age of thirteen. COPPA, along with the FTC rule implementing it, places strict collection and disclosure limitations on the operators of websites or online services directed at children or that knowingly collect personal data from children under thirteen. *See* 16 C.F.R. § 312. To comply with COPPA, an operator of a website or online service generally must: (1) provide notice on the website or online service of its information collection, use, and disclosure practices; (2) obtain "verifiable parental consent" for the collection, use, and/or disclosure of personal information from children; (3) provide a reasonable means for a parent to review the personal information collected from a child and to refuse to permit its further use or maintenance; (4) limit collection of personal information for a child's online participation in a game, prize offer, or other activity to information that is reasonably necessary for the activity; and (5) establish and maintain reasonable procedures to protect the confidentiality, security, and integrity of the personal information collected from children. To obtain "verifiable parental consent" for the collection, use, and disclosure of information is to ensure that before personal information is collected from a child, a parent receives notice of the operator's practices with respect to personal information and authorizes any collection, use, or disclosure. Under the FTC's implementing regulation, methods satisfying the authorization requirement would include:

> providing a consent form to be signed by the parent and returned to the operator by postal mail or facsimile; requiring a parent to use a credit card in connection with a transaction; having a parent call a toll-free telephone number staffed by trained personnel; using a digital certificate that uses public key technology; and using e-mail accompanied by a PIN or password obtained through one of the verification methods listed in this paragraph.

16 C.F.R. § 312.5(b)(2).

Notes and Questions

1. COPPA only covers the collection, use, and disclosure of information regarding children; the United States has no comprehensive regulation of information practices regarding adults. The FTC has, however, developed a set of "core principles" it believes website operators and third-party advertisers (as well as other entities outside of the Internet context) should follow.

Under these principles, operators should: provide *notice* of their information practices before collecting personal information; give consumers *choice* about whether and how personal information should be used for purposes beyond those for which the information was provided; provide consumers with *access* to the data so as to be able to contest its accuracy and completeness; and ensure the *security* of data, so that the data remains accurate and protected from unauthorized disclosure. Finally, fair information practices—whether adopted through legislation or as part of a self-regulatory effort—should include an enforcement component to identify and impose sanctions for noncompliance. *See* Federal Trade Comm'n, *Online Profiling: A Report to Congress, Part 2 (Recommendations)* (July 2000).

Do the FTC principles adequately take into account the privacy threats in the online context? Recall the principles that Professor Cohen argued should form the basis for data privacy legislation. How do the FTC's principles differ? What conception of privacy underlies the FTC principles?

2. The FTC principles could be implemented as part of a self-regulatory program by online companies or as part of a legislative effort. Is self-regulation sufficient? Why or why not?

3. Note that the FTC principles leave major issues unresolved. For example, if website operators wish to follow the FTC principles and offer users a choice about the circumstances under which personal information will be disclosed, how should they require users to manifest their consent? By opting

in to a particular use? Or by declining to opt out? In other words, should the default rule be that the website is free to disclose the information, or not? Which default rule would lead to clearer policies on information disclosure? How would the different default rules affect the availability of content on the Internet? Why?

4.   Unlike the United States, the European Union has developed a comprehensive scheme regulating the collection, processing, and reuse of personal data. *See* Directive 95/46/EC of the European Parliament and of the Council of 24 October 1995 on the Protection of Individuals with regard to the Processing of Personal Data and on the Free Movement of Such Data. Article 6 of the Directive obligates member states to provide that personal data must be "collected for specified, explicit, and legitimate purposes and not further processed in a way incompatible with those purposes." Under Article 7, member states must provide that personal data may be processed only if

(a)   the data subject has unambiguously given his consent; or

(b)   processing is necessary for the performance of a contract to which the data subject is party or in order to take steps at the request of the data subject prior to entering into a contract; or

(c)   processing is necessary for compliance with a legal obligation to which the controller is subject; or

(d)   processing is necessary in order to protect the vital interests of the data subject; or

(e)   processing is necessary for the performance of a task carried out in the public interest or in the exercise of official authority vested in the controller or in a third party to whom the data are disclosed; or

(f)   processing is necessary for the purposes of the legitimate interests pursued by the controller or by the third party or parties to whom the data are disclosed, except where such interests are overridden by the interests for fundamental rights and freedoms of the data subject * * * .

Article 25 of the Directive requires member states to provide that the "transfer to a third country of personal data * * * may take place only if * * * the third country in question ensures an adequate level of protection." U.S. and European Union officials negotiated "safe harbor" principles allowing U.S. firms to collect and process data on Europeans as long as they abide by certain fair information practices. *See* U.S. Department of Commerce, Safe Harbor Privacy Principles (July 21, 2000), *available at* http://www.export.gov/safe harbor/SHPRINCIPLESFINAL.htm.

What are the advantages and disadvantages of a comprehensive approach such as that taken by the European Union? What underlying conception of privacy does the Directive reflect?

5. Can technology supplement or supplant statutory privacy protections? Even among advocates of greater privacy protections, there is much controversy over the development of the Platform for Privacy Preferences (P3P), a technological standard designed to give users greater control over what information they disclose to third parties. P3P, developed by the World Wide Web Consortium, is somewhat like the Platform for Internet Content Selection (PICS) standard discussed in Chapter Six. The standard, developed by a private organization, is designed to build into the architecture of the Internet

a means for consumers to signal their preferences about information collection and disclosure. Professor Lessig describes the architectural approach to protecting privacy this way:

> What is needed * * * is a machine-to-machine protocol for negotiating privacy protections. The user sets her preferences once—specifies how she would negotiate privacy and what she is willing to give up—and from that moment on, when she enters a site, the site and her machine negotiate. Only if the machines can agree will the site be able to obtain her personal data.

> The kernel to this architecture is a project sponsored by the World Wide Web Consortium. Dubbed P3P, the project's aim is to facilitate an architecture within which users can express their preferences and negotiate the use of data about them. * * * My aim is not to endorse this particular privacy architecture. * * * My point instead is [that] we could imagine an architecture, tied to a market, that protects privacy rights in a way that real space cannot, but that architecture cannot emerge on its own. It needs the push of law.

> The law would be a kind of property right in privacy. Individuals must have both the ability to negotiate easily over privacy rights and the entitlement to privacy as a default. That is property's purpose: it says to those who want, you must negotiate before you can take. P3P is the architecture to facilitate that negotiation; the law is the rule that says negotiation must occur.

LAWRENCE LESSIG, CODE AND OTHER LAWS OF CYBERSPACE 160 (1999). Is Lessig's position on P3P consistent with his position on PICS? Can you construct an argument for why this sort of technological solution might be appropriate in the privacy context, but not in the speech context? For Lessig's defense of his position, see *id.* at 181-82. Do you agree with Lessig that PICS would be a useful technological architecture? If so, recall Chapter Four: how might law be used to encourage development and deployment of this architecture?

6. For criticism of an architectural approach to protecting privacy, see, for example, Marc Rotenberg, *Fair Information Practices and the Architecture of Privacy (What Larry Doesn't Get)*, 2001 STAN. TECH. L. REV. 1:

> The problems with P3P have now been widely reported. Technical experts have noted that the protocols are complex, difficult to implement, and unlikely to enable consumer to protect privacy. Privacy experts have emphasized that the standard is intended to enable collection of personal information rather than the protection of personal information. Industry analysts have also found shortcomings in the P3P proposal. * * *

> Perhaps the most significant criticism of the regime is the extent to which it codes the preferences of the P3P designer as opposed to say the general public. Who decides, for example, what basic elements should be made available to others? And why should techniques that ultimately shift burdens to the consumer be adopted? Do consumers really want to negotiate over privacy preferences? Wouldn't consumers prefer to disclose the minimal amount of personal information necessary to a transaction as Fair Information Practices generally?

It is possible to answer these questions with a general defense that P3P is "a work in progress," and that some of these problems may be resolved over time, though there is in fact little indication that such a process is progressing. But the larger question for Lessig is why should individuals settle for a cyberspace architecture that leaves them isolated in the marketplace to negotiate over privacy protection when there is a rich tradition of Fair Information Practices and an emerging architecture of privacy that seems far more likely to safeguard privacy interests.

7.   To embrace an architectural solution such as P3P, must one view privacy as protecting a property right? Is P3P inconsistent with the autonomy-based approach to privacy that Professor Cohen takes? Why or why not? *See* Julie E. Cohen, *Examined Lives, Informational Privacy, and the Subject as Object*, 52 STAN. L. REV. 1373, 1432 (2000).

Chapter Nine

PROBLEMS OF INFORMATION ENCLOSURE

INTRODUCTION

Throughout this book, we have seen that many of the problems of law and policy we encounter in cyberspace involve questions about who will control information, and what tools—legal and technological—will facilitate or hinder that control. In Chapter Two, for example, we considered eBay's efforts to invoke the trespass to chattels cause of action to control the terms on which competitors could use its auction site. *eBay, Inc. v. Bidder's Edge*, 100 F. Supp. 2d 1058 (N.D. Cal. 2000). Chapter Four examined how the development of digital technology both impedes and enhances the efforts of copyright holders to control uses of their works. In particular, we saw that courts have allowed contract law rather than copyright law to dictate the extent of a content provider's control over information, *see ProCD v. Zeidenberg*, 86 F.3d 1447 (7th Cir. 1996); that copyright holders can enclose information with technological protection mechanisms; and that Congress has backed those mechanisms with the force of law by prohibiting their circumvention in some circumstances.

We consider here a new wrinkle on problems of control over information. Web servers and other networked computers can hold a range of data, some of it protected by copyright law and some of it not. A content provider seeking to limit use of the information it provides via a computer network has an extra weapon in its arsenal: It can claim not only that it has the right to control the use of its *content*, but also that it has the right to control the uses of the *computer system or network resources* that host the content. This, of course, was precisely the sort of claim we encountered in Chapter Two in the *eBay* case—eBay successfully argued that it was entitled to an injunction on a trespass to chattels theory because Bidder's Edge's access to eBay's servers was unauthorized.

How should the law treat these sorts of hybrid claims for protection of information and protection of network·resources? Companies pursuing such claims typically invoke a variety of legal doctrines, including copyright law, contract law, trespass to chattels, and statutory prohibitions on illegal access to computer systems. Section A frames the debate over how courts should treat these claims; Sections B through D explore courts' current approaches.

SECTION A. THE "CYBERPROPERTY" CONTROVERSY

In Chapter Four, when we explored the use of private mechanisms (such as contract law backed by technological protection measures) to control information, we saw that the weight of scholarship opposes any approach that substitutes private decisions for the legislative choices reflected in the Copyright Act. Do hybrid claims seeking protection of information and protection of network resources raise the same concerns? Does the fact that the owner of a computer system must invest in equipment and develop a business model mean that she should have a greater right to control access to that equipment, even if control over information will inevitably result? Are owners of network computer systems likely to undervalue the benefits of preserving open access to the system? Consider the following discussion.

Patricia L. Bellia, *Defending Cyberproperty*

79 N.Y.U. L. Rev. 2164 (2004)

Although the various legal doctrines that plaintiffs invoke to block unwanted uses of network computing resources are distinct, each doctrine involves the same underlying claim: that the system owner should have the right to set the terms of access to the resource, a default conventionally known as property-rule protection. * * * I refer to the various doctrinal routes to controlling the terms of access collectively as "cyberproperty" claims. * * *

Under a property rule, the law recognizes an entitlement holder's right to enjoin any unwanted uses of a protected asset, whether or not the use will cause harm. Because the entitlement holder can block any unwanted use, she can set the terms of access to a resource, requiring potential users of the system to negotiate for access. Protecting network computing resources under a property rule would allow the resource owner to weigh the costs and benefits of particular uses and determine which uses to allow. In contrast, under a liability-rule approach, the would-be user has the right to utilize the entitlement holder's asset, subject to terms determined by a third party (typically, a court or legislature). A liability-rule approach to network resources would allow access against the property owner's wishes but might require payment of damages for certain harmful activities. Applying either type of rule with respect to network resources could in theory yield the same level of access. For example, even if a website owner can set the terms of access (a property-rule approach), she may choose to allow all access that does not impair her system, on the theory that such access will be beneficial. This approach would result in the same degree of openness as would a liability rule that allowed access but required a user to pay for any harm to the system. Thus, in choosing between property-rule protection and liability-rule protection for resources, the issue is not only *what level of access* to network resources is appropriate, but also *who should decide* what level of access is appropriate—the resource owner or a third party (such as a court or legislature). * * *

1. The Competing Interests in Cyberproperty Claims

Before evaluating the normative arguments against granting a network resource owner a right to exclude unwanted uses, we should identify the competing interests at stake in cyberproperty disputes. These competing interests are well illustrated by the trespass-to-chattels cases * * * .

First, the law must provide sufficient protection of a network resource owner's investments—both in physical equipment and in the development of a business model—to generate appropriate incentives for productive activities. [Early trespass-to-chattels decisions] reflect courts' sensitivity to this problem. In *CompuServe* [*v. Cyber Promotions*, 962 F. Supp. 1015 (S.D. Ohio 1997), a case involving a service provider's attempt to enjoin defendants from sending spam], the defendants had essentially shifted to CompuServe (and its subscribers) some of the costs of transmitting bulk e-mail, and CompuServe's lawsuit reflected an effort to shift those costs back to the defendants. If the law required ISPs to bear the full cost of the transmission of unsolicited commercial e-mail, they would be less likely to provide such services. Similarly, companies such as eBay are less likely to develop online business models if they cannot protect against a competitor's free riding.

Second, the public has an interest in open access to information and open avenues for speech. If a company such as eBay can control access to its servers, it can also control access to the information those servers hold. eBay may have objected to Bidder's Edge's extraction and aggregation of its data in part because it feared that Bidder's Edge (though not a direct competitor) would draw customers away from its site. But search engines and comparative shopping utilities work in precisely the same way as Bidder's Edge, by using software programs to recursively query sites and aggregating and organizing the resulting data for users. Granting a website owner the power to block a competitor's robots also grants the site owner the ability to block a search engine's robots, thus raising the possibility that property-rule protection for systems will curtail one of the most publicly beneficial features of the Internet. Likewise, as evidenced by the *[Intel Corp. v. Hamidi* case], power to control access to mail servers can translate easily into a power to curtail objectionable speech. The California Supreme

Court's sympathy with Hamidi's defense appeared to stem from its concern that Intel was seeking to suppress dissent about its policies-that the case implicated free-speech interests, albeit at the level of policy rather than at the level of the Constitution.

Third, even setting aside questions about how information available on the Internet is ultimately used and about the extent to which the Internet provides open avenues for speech, society has an interest in the scale of the network itself. The Internet reflects what economists term "network effects" or positive "network externalities": Access to the network becomes more valuable as it becomes more widespread. Consider an analogy to a telephone system. With only a few subscribers, such a system has very little value. As subscribership grows, however, the value of the system to each subscriber increases. Similarly, each user's access to the Internet becomes more valuable as use of the Internet becomes more widespread. When a service provider or website owner blocks unwanted access, the service provider essentially closes a portion of the network and thereby limits the network's scale.

Finally, assuming the law does permit system owners to enforce some restrictions on the use of network resources, users have an interest in fair notice of the conditions of access. Most Internet resources appear to users to be available without any restrictions on access, in the sense that there is no technical impediment (such as a password restriction) to users sending e-mail to most mail servers or retrieving files from most web servers. Because the lack of any technical impediment to access can signal the resource owner's consent to the use in question, the law must require a resource owner to provide adequate notice of deviations from an open access condition. In *CompuServe* and *eBay*, of course, the defendants had actual notice of the system owners' objection to the unwanted use. Both cases also raised, but did not resolve, questions about the adequacy of alternative forms of notice—in CompuServe's case, a policy available on its network prohibiting unsolicited commercial e-mail, and in eBay's case, a user agreement that prohibited automated queries of its system.

2.   *"Overpropertization" Critiques and Their Limitations*

The question then becomes: What sort of legal protection for network resources best balances the competing interests identified above? To date, most scholars have rejected property-rule protection in the Internet context. The next two subsections evaluate the arguments against property-rule protection. * * *

a.   Cyberproperty Claims as Enclosure of Intellectual Property

As noted, one of the difficulties raised by cyberproperty claims is that a right to control access to the physical equipment of a network translates into far broader powers—for example, the ability to block speech or to control access to and uses of information. It is intellectual property law—specifically copyright law—that ordinarily establishes the extent to which one can control uses of informational goods. The control that copyright law provides, moreover, is incomplete. Accordingly, scholars fear that recognizing a system owner's right to block unwanted uses of network resources will shift informational goods from a copyright regime of incomplete protection to a property regime of complete protection. As I will show, however, there are two problems with this argument. First, the argument assumes that the incentives that intellectual property law provides for the development of informational goods are sufficient for the development of online business models. Second, taken to its logical conclusion, the anti-enclosure position points to a fully mandatory access approach, under which sites could not use password protection or any other sort of technical self-help to block unwanted uses. Scholars do not seem to embrace that conclusion. Yet, in accepting that system owners may use some technical measures to "close" access to a site, scholars do not explain why technical limitations on access are permissible, but other limitations are not.

A significant and growing body of literature on developments in copyright law suggests that the public domain is shrinking, as informational goods traditionally treated as part of the "commons" achieve legal protection as private property. * * * The normative concerns scholars raise with respect to cyberproperty claims fit within the context of this larger debate. Applying trespass-to-chattels doctrine in a dispute over access to a web server or similar system may allow the system owner to restrict access to and use of material made available on that system, regardless of whether copyright law protects the material. For example * * * copyright protection does not extend to facts or insufficiently original compilations of factual information, such as the white pages of a telephone directory. If similar information were held on a website, and a court recognized a system owner's right to block unwanted uses through trespass to chattels or another claim, the court would effectively grant to system owners a right to control information broader than that granted by copyright law. Likewise, the Computer Fraud and Abuse Act, the federal analogue to state trespass claims, prohibits unauthorized access to "information," regardless of whether intellectual property law protects the material in question. If a system owner can block any use of material on a website based on the objection that the system owner did not authorize access to its computer system, the CFAA provides an alternative cause of action when copyright protection is unavailable. Similarly, if a court applies contract principles to enforce a system owner's "terms of use," and allows the agreement to govern even when its terms are inconsistent with copyright law, the terms of use displace more limited copyright protections. In such a case, the owner's right may sound in contract rather than property, but if courts do not carefully scrutinize whether the user had notice of and manifested assent to the contract terms, the owner's contract rights take on the characteristics of property rights.

Scholars thus argue that if intellectual property law does not protect particular material, then other doctrines and methods should not; otherwise the balance that intellectual property law strikes between providing incentives to create and preserving public access will be undermined. In other words, by granting protection above and beyond intellectual property law, a cyberproperty rule grants benefits to producers that go further than necessary to incentivize production of the underlying work. It effectively becomes a transfer of wealth from consumers to producers. * * *

Cyberproperty critics attach paramount importance to the interest in preserving open access to information. As for the role of the law in providing incentives for investments in the development of an online business, however, the anti-enclosure position simply seems to presume that the incentives copyright law supplies are sufficient—that any incentives above those copyright law provides simply transfer wealth from consumers to producers. When we focus on the interest in open access to the exclusion of the interest in providing incentives, however, it becomes difficult to say why the law should even grant a system owner a right to block uses that cause physical harm to a system. In other words, if all websites should remain part of a "commons," it is unclear why a private party should have a right of action even if her computer system is harmed. The fact that most scholars do accept that a system owner can block uses that will cause harm to her system suggests that scholars are in fact more sensitive to the incentive issues than their predominant focus on the preservation of open access would at first suggest. But once we recognize that some protection of a system is necessary to guard investments in an online business model, it is unclear why the law should recognize physical harm and not economic harm. The anti-enclosure position simply provides no basis for accepting one harm rule and rejecting another.

Second, even if intellectual property law does provide the relevant incentive structure, relying on intellectual property law to displace application of cyberproperty claims faces another problem. In particular, taken to its logical conclusion, the anti-enclosure position would suggest that systems connected to the Internet cannot use password protection to control access to their websites. I know of no scholar who advocates this sort of fully mandatory open-access approach. Scholars do criticize the DMCA on the ground that, in prohibiting circumvention of technical measures to control access to a copyrighted work, it puts the force of law behind a copyright holder's terms of access; some scholars go so far as to argue that would-be users should have the right to circumvent technical measures to gain access to a work to make a fair use. Scholars do not, however, suggest that a website must remain open to all would-be users. Rather, they seem to view the decision to disallow some access—by "closing" sections of the site—as a permissible and legitimate choice. The question is why the decision to limit access through password protection is permissible, but the decision to impose other kinds of limitations is not. The anti-enclosure story simply cannot answer that question.

Relatedly, an approach that relied wholly on the contours of intellectual property law to establish when access to a system is permissible would prohibit a website owner from using other sorts of self-help measures to control the circumstances under which others gain access to the site. For example, eBay's * * * efforts to block requests for data based on the IP address of the computer seeking the data, or efforts to redirect requests for information to a main page rather than an interior page, would be illegitimate because, like a legal right to exclude unwanted uses, such self-help measures allow enclosure of information that copyright law does not protect. Again, I know of no scholar who suggests that these sorts of self-help measures are impermissible. * * *

In sum, although arguments challenging enclosure trends make many compelling points with respect to intellectual property law, those arguments ultimately cannot explain why courts should reject cyberproperty claims. Scholars seem to assume that intellectual property law provides adequate incentives for the development and delivery of web content. Even if they are correct, their argument points to a position that no one ultimately takes—that system owners cannot use even the most basic technical protections.

b.   Bargaining and Valuation Problems Under a Property-Rule Approach

As the discussion above suggests, arguments relying on the balance intellectual property law strikes between control and access do not conclusively establish the case for rejecting cyberproperty claims. I turn here to other normative arguments scholars offer to explain why granting system owners the right to exclude unwanted uses will result in overpropertization. In particular, scholars offer three main reasons why recognizing cyberproperty claims will curtail productive uses of the Internet. First, they claim, Internet transactions are sufficiently complex that granting resource owners a right to exclude unwanted uses of their systems will prevent optimal uses. Second, if resource owners are left to balance the competing interests at stake, they will be likely to undervalue the benefits of open access. Finally, scholars fear that if system owners are granted a right to exclude, they will exercise that right in an anticompetitive manner. I highlight problems with each of these arguments.

First, scholars seem to assume that protecting network resources through a property-rule approach is the equivalent of setting a default rule of closed access, regardless of a system's technical configuration. That assumption, of course, factors heavily into scholars' assessment of when users must negotiate for access and thus of whether productive uses of the Internet are likely to occur. A default rule of closed access, however, is not an inevitable feature of a property-rule approach. Removing that assumption undermines much of the force of the scholarly critiques. Second, like the intellectual property critique, some of the arguments logically lead to a fully mandatory access rule that few commentators actually would advocate. Finally, although it is difficult to gauge the risk of anticompetitive conduct, concerns about such conduct are difficult to reconcile with existing cyberproperty cases. In addition, it is possible to respond to such concerns without entirely rejecting property rule forms of protection.

Notes and Questions

1. The excerpt above is not designed to make a conclusive case that a property-rule approach to protecting networked computers is appropriate; rather, it is intended to summarize and critique the prevailing position that the balance struck by copyright law should control. What is the affirmative case for a property rule approach in this context? According to the conventional view of how the legal system should protect entitlements, property rules are favored when transaction costs—including the costs of identifying and

bargaining with the parties to the dispute, and the costs of obtaining information on how the parties value a particular entitlement—are low. Do those conditions obtain here? How would multiple users seeking access to a site under terms different from those offered in a website's policy negotiate access to the system?

2. One of the difficulties with arguing against property rule protection for computer systems is that those who would reject a property rule approach would also likely accept technical restrictions—such as password protection—on a particular site. How can scholars' embrace of an open access approach be reconciled with recognition that password protection may sometimes be appropriate? Is it enough to say that one who chooses password protection forgoes some of the benefits of maintaining a fully open site, whereas those who open their sites to public use cannot benefit from a large-scale network while refusing to bear the costs associated with it?

3. Is there any danger in this context that technological protection measures will end up displacing legal ones? In other words, might a system owner who believes that the law is not providing enough protection to her system seek to achieve through technical measures the property-rule protection that she cannot achieve through law? For discussion of this question, see Patricia L. Bellia, *Defending Cyberproperty*, 79 N.Y.U. L. REV. 2164, 2261-72 (2004).

SECTION B. STATE LAW CLAIMS: TRESPASS AND CONTRACT

eBay v. Bidder's Edge provides an example of a case in which a court wrestled with whether to apply property-rule or liability-rule protection to a computer system. eBay sought a property-rule approach that would allow it to exclude unwanted uses. Bidder's Edge sought a liability-rule approach, arguing that eBay should not have a right to block uses that are not damaging or that do not violate copyright law. In other words, eBay sought to force Bidder's Edge to negotiate for access to its system; Bidder's Edge sought to have the court (by virtue of a rule allowing harmless uses) or Congress (by virtue of copyright protections) set the terms of access.

The court granted eBay a fairly broad right to exclude unwanted uses of its system:

> Although eBay appears unlikely to be able to show a substantial interference at this time, such a showing is not required. Conduct that does not amount to a substantial interference with possession, but which consists of intermeddling with or use of another's personal property, is sufficient to establish a cause of action for trespass to chattel. * * * [I]t is undisputed that eBay's server and its capacity are personal property, and that BE's searches use a portion of this property. Even if, as BE argues, its searches use only a small amount of eBay's computer system capacity, BE has nonetheless deprived eBay of the ability to use that portion of its personal property for its own

purposes. The law recognizes no such right to use another's personal property.

eBay, Inc. v. Bidder's Edge, 100 F. Supp. 2d 1058, 1070-71 (N.D. Cal. 2000). Is that approach sound? Moreover, what triggers a content providers right to block unwanted uses? Actual notice to the user that its access to the system is unwelcome? A user's acceptance of "terms of use" governing the site? Consider the following cases.

Ticketmaster Corporation v. Tickets.com, Inc.

United States District Court for the Central District of California, 2003
2003 U.S. Dist. LEXIS 6483

HUPP, District Judge.

Both [Ticketmaster Corporation ("TM")] and [Tickets.com, Inc. ("TX")] are in the business of selling tickets to all kinds of "events" (sports, concerts, plays, etc.) to the public. They are in heavy competition with one another, but operate in distinctive ways. TM is the largest company in the industry. It sells tickets by the four methods of ticket selling—venue box office, retail outlets, by telephone, and over the internet. * * * TX at the time of the events considered in this motion was primarily (but not exclusively) an internet seller. Both TM and TX maintain a web page reachable by anyone with an internet connection. Each of their web pages has many subsidiary (or interior) web pages which describe one event each and provide such basic information as to location, date, time, description of the event, and ticket prices. * * *

TM principally does business by exclusive contracts with the event providers or their producers, and its web pages only list the events for which TM is the exclusive ticket seller. TX also sells tickets to a number of events * * * . At [relevant times, however,] its web pages attempted to list all events for which tickets were available whether or not TX sold the tickets. * * * When TX could not sell the tickets, it listed ticket brokers who sold at premium prices. * * * Until early 2000, in situations where TM was the only source of tickets, TX provided a "deep link" by which the customer would be transferred to the interior web page of TM's web site, where the customer could purchase the ticket from TM. This process of "deep linking" is the subject of TM's complaint in this action, of which there [are] now left the contract, copyright, and trespass theories. [TX moves for summary judgment on all three theories.]

Starting in 1998 and continuing to July 2001, when it stopped the practice, TX employed an electronic program called a "spider" or "crawler" to review the internal web pages (available to the public) of TM. The "spider" "crawled" through the internal web pages to TM and electronically extracted the electronic information from which the web page is shown on the user's computer. The spider temporarily loaded this electronic information into the Random Access Memory ("RAM") of TX's computers for a period of from 10-15 seconds. TX then extracted the factual information (event, date, time, tickets prices, and URL) and discarded the rest (which consisted of TM identification, logos, ads, and other information which TX did not intend to use; much of this discarded material was protected by copyright). The factual information was then organized in the TX format to be displayed on the TX internal web page. The TX internal web page carried no TM identification and had only the factual information about the event on it * * * plus any information or advertisement added by TX. From March 1998 to early 2000, the TX user was provided the deep linking option * * * to go directly from the TX web site to the relevant TM interior web page. This option stopped (or was stopped by TM) in early 2000. For an unknown period afterward, the TX customer was given the option of linking to the TM home page, from which the customer could work his way to the interior web page in which he was interested. * * *

The contract aspect of the case derives from a notice placed on the home page of the TM web site which states that anyone going beyond that point into the interior web pages of the web site accepts certain conditions, which include, relevant to this case, that all information obtained from the web site is for the personal use of the user and may not be used for commercial purposes. * * * [T]here has been developed evidence that TX was fully familiar with the conditions TM claimed to impose on users, including a letter from TM to TX which quoted the conditions (and a reply by TX stating that it did not accept the conditions). Thus, there is sufficient evidence to defeat summary judgment on the contract theory if knowledge of the asserted conditions of use was had by TX, who nevertheless continued to send its spider into the TM interior web pages, and if it is legally concluded that doing so can lead to a binding contract. * * * As a result, the TX motion for summary judgment on the contract issue is denied.

The trespass to chattels issue requires adapting the ancient common law action to the modern age. * * * [Lower court] cases discussing the chattel theory * * * tend to support the proposition that mere invasion or use of a portion of the web site by a spider is a trespass (leading at least to nominal damages), and that there need not be an independent showing of direct harm either to the chattel (unlikely in the case of a spider) or tangible interference with the use of the computer being invaded. However, scholars and practitioners alike have criticized the extension of the trespass to chattels doctrine to the internet context, noting that this doctrinal expansion threatens basic internet functions (i.e., search engines) and exposes the flaws inherent in applying doctrines based in real and tangible property to cyberspace. Pending appellate guidance, this court comes down on the side of requiring some tangible interference with the use or operation of the computer being invaded by the spider. [The] RESTATEMENT (SECOND) OF TORTS § 219 requires a showing that "the chattel is impaired as to its condition, quality, or value." Therefore, unless there is actual dispossession of the chattel for a substantial time (not present here), the elements of the tort have not been made out. Since the spider does not cause physical injury to the chattel, there must be some evidence that the * * * utility of the computer (or computer network) being "spiderized" is adversely affected by the use of the spider. No such evidence is presented here. This court respectfully disagrees with other district courts' finding that mere use of a spider to enter a publically available web site to gather information, without more, is sufficient to fulfill the harm requirement for trespass to chattels.

TM complains that the information obtained by the use of the spider was valuable (and even that it was sold by TX), and that it spent time and money attempting to frustrate the spider, but neither of these items shows damage to the computers or their operation. One must keep in mind that we are talking about the common law tort of trespass, not damage from breach of contract or copyright infringement. The tort claim may not succeed without proof of tort-type damage. Plaintiff TM has the burden to show such damage. None is shown here. The motion for summary judgment is granted to eliminate the claim for trespass to chattels. * * *

The copyright issues are more difficult. They divide into three issues. The first is whether the momentary resting in the TX computers of [information copied from TM's computers] constitutes actionable copyright infringement. The second is whether the URLs, which were copied and used by TX, contain copyrightable material. The third is whether TX's deep linking caused the unauthorized public display of TM event pages.

In examining these questions, we must keep in mind a prime theorem of copyright law—facts, as such, are not subject to copyright protection. What is subject to copyright protection is the manner or mode of expression of those facts. Thus, addresses and telephone numbers contained in a directory do not have copyright protection, *Feist Publications v. Rural Tel. Serv. Co.*, 499 U.S. 340 (1991), despite the fact that time, money, and effort went into compiling the information. Similarly, in this case, the existence of the event, its date and time, and its ticket prices, are not subject to copyright. Anyone is free to print (or show on the internet) such information. Thus, if TX had sat down a secretary at the computer screen with instructions manually to go through TM's web sites and pick out and write down purely factual information about the events, and then feed it into the TX web pages (using the TX distinctive format only), no one could complain. The objection is that the same thing was done with an electronic program. * * * [TX's] spider picks up the electronic [signals] and loads them momentarily (for 10 to 15 seconds) into the RAM of the TX computers, where a program [extracts] the factual data (not protected) [and places it] into the TX format for its web pages * * * . Thus, the actual copying (if it can be called that) is momentary while the non-protected material, all open to the public, is extracted.

Is this momentary resting of the electronic symbols from which a TM web page could be (but is not) constructed fair use where the purpose is to obtain nonprotected facts? The court thinks the answer is "yes". There is not much law in point. However, there are two Ninth Circuit cases which shed light on the problem. They are *Sony Computer Entm't, Inc. v. Connectix Corp.*, 203 F.3d 596 (9th Cir. 2000), and *Sega Enters. v. Accolade, Inc.*, 977 F.2d 1510 (9th Cir. 1992). In each of these cases, the alleged infringer attempted to get at non-protected source code by reverse engineering of the plaintiff's copyrighted software. In doing so, the necessary method was to copy the software and work backwards to derive the unprotected source code. The copied software was then destroyed. In each case, this was held to be fair use since it was necessary to temporarily copy the software to obtain the non-protected material. There may be a difference with this case, however; at least TM claims so. It asserts in its points and authorities that taking the temporary copy in this case was not the only way to obtain the unprotected information, and that TX was able to, and in actuality did, purchase such information from certain third-parties. Both *Sony* and *Sega* stated that the fair use was justified because reverse engineering (including taking a temporary copy) was the only way the unprotected information could be obtained. Although this court recognizes that the holdings of *Sony* and *Sega* were limited to the specific context of "disassembling" copyrighted object code in order to access unprotected elements contained in the source code, this court believes that the "fair use" doctrine can be applied to the current facts.

* * * In determining whether a challenged use of copyrighted material is fair, a court must keep in mind the public policy underlying the Copyright Act: to secure a fair return for an author's creative labor and to stimulate artistic creativity for the general good. This court sees no public policy that would be served by restricting TX from using spiders to temporarily download TM's event pages in order to acquire the unprotected, publicly available factual event information. The rest of the event page information (which consisted of TM identification, logos, ads, and other information) was discarded and not used by TX and is not exposed to the public by TX. In temporarily downloading TM's event pages to its RAM through the use of spiders, TX was not exploiting TM's creative labors in any way: its spiders gathered copyrightable and non-copyrightable information alike but then immediately discarded the copyrighted material. It is unlikely that the spiders could have been programmed to take only the factual information from the TM web pages without initially downloading the entire page.

Consideration of the fair use factors listed in 17 USC § 106 supports this result. First, TX operates its site for commercial purposes, and this fact tends to weigh against a finding of fair use. *Campbell v. Acuff-Rose Music*, 510 U.S. 569, 585 (1994). TX's use of the data gathered from TM's event pages was only slightly transformative. As for the second factor, the nature of the copyrighted work, the copying that occurred when spiders download the event page, access the source code for each page, and extract the factual data embedded in the code, is analogous to the process of copying that the *Sony* court condoned * * *. Third, because TX's final product—the TX web site—did not contain any infringing material, the "amount and substantiality of the portion used" is of little weight. The fourth factor (the effect on the market value of the copyrighted work) is, of course nil, and weighs towards finding fair use. TM's arguments and evidence regarding loss of advertising revenue * * * are not persuasive.

The second copyright problem is whether the URLs (Uniform Resource Locator) are subject to copyright protection. The URLs are copied by TX and, while TX was deep hyper-linking to TM interior web pages, were used by TX to allow the deep-linking (by providing the electronic address of the particular relevant TM interior web page). * * * TM contends that, although the URLs are strictly functional, they are entitled to copyright protection because there are several ways to write the URL, and, thus, original authorship is used. The court disagrees. A URL is simply an address, open to the public, like the street address of a building, which, if known, can enable the user to reach the building. There is nothing sufficiently original to make the URL a copyrightable item, especially the way it is used. There appear to be no cases holding the URLs to be subject to copyright. On principle, they should not be.

The third copyright problem is whether TX's deep linking caused the unauthorized public display of TM event pages in violation of TM's exclusive rights of reproduction and display under 17 U.S.C. § 106. The Ninth Circuit in *Kelly v. Arriba Soft Corp.*, 280 F.3d 934 (9th Cir. 2002), recognized that inline linking and framing of full-sized images of plaintiff's copyrighted photographs within the defendant's web site violated the plaintiff's public display rights. In that case, defendant's web site contained links to plaintiff's photographs (which were on plaintiff's publicly available website). Users were able to view plaintiff's photographs within the context of defendant's site: Plaintiff's images were "framed" by the defendant's window, and were thus surrounded by defendant web page's text and advertising. * * * TM alleges that when a user was deep-linked from the TX site to a TM event page, a smaller window was opened. The smaller window was described as containing a page from the TM web site which was "framed" by the larger window. At the time of the preliminary injunction motion, TX stated that whether "framing" occurs or not depends on the settings on the user's computer, over which TX has no control. Thus, framing occurred on some occasions but not on others. However, TX says that it "did not try to disguise a sale by use of frames occurring on the Tickets.com website." TX further states that when users were linked to TM web pages, the TM event pages were clearly identified as belonging to TM.

[E]ven if the TM interior web site page was "framed" within the TX web page, this case is distinguishable from *Kelly*. In *Kelly*, the defendant's site would display a variety of "thumbnail" images as a result of the user's search. By clicking on the desired thumbnail image, a user could view the "Images Attributes" page, which displayed the original full-size image, a description of its dimensions, a link to the originating web site, and defendant's banner and advertising. The full-size image was not technically located on defendant's web site, but was taken directly from the originating web site. However, only the image itself, and not any other part of the originating web site, was displayed on the "Images Attributes" page. The Ninth Circuit determined that by importing plaintiff's images into its own web page, and by showing them in the context of its own site, defendant infringed upon plaintiff's exclusive public display right.

In this case, a user on the TX site was taken directly to the originating TM site, containing all the elements of that particular TM event page. Each TM event page clearly identified itself as belonging to TM. Moreover, the link on the TX site to the TM event page contained the following notice: "Buy this ticket from another online ticketing company. Click here to buy tickets. These tickets are sold by another ticketing company. Although we can't sell them to you, the link above will take you directly to the other company's web site where you can purchase them." Even if the TM site may have been displayed as a smaller window that was literally "framed" by the larger TX window, it is not clear that, as matter of law, the linking to TX event pages would constitute a showing or public display in violation of 17 U.S.C. § 106(5). Accordingly, summary judgment is granted on the copyright claims of TM and it is eliminated from this action.

Register.com, Inc. v. Verio, Inc.

United States Court of Appeals for the Second Circuit, 2004
356 F.3d 393

LEVAL, Circuit Judge.

Defendant, Verio, Inc. ("Verio") appeals from an order * * * granting the motion of plaintiff Register.com, Inc. ("Register") for a preliminary injunction. The court's order enjoined Verio from * * * accessing Register's computers by use of automated software programs performing multiple successive queries; and * * * using data obtained from Register's database of contact information of registrants of Internet domain names to solicit the registrants for the sale of web site development services by electronic mail, telephone calls, or direct mail. We affirm.

BACKGROUND

This plaintiff Register is one of over fifty companies serving as registrars for the issuance of domain names on the world wide web. As a registrar, Register issues domain names to persons and entities preparing to establish web sites on the Internet. Web sites are identified and accessed by reference to their domain names.

Register was appointed a registrar of domain names by the Internet Corporation for Assigned Names and Numbers, known by the acronym "ICANN." ICANN is a private, non-profit public benefit corporation which was established by agencies of the U.S. government to administer the Internet domain name system. To become a registrar of domain names, Register was required to enter into a standard form agreement with ICANN, designated as the ICANN Registrar Accreditation Agreement, November 1999 version (referred to herein as the "ICANN Agreement").

Applicants to register a domain name submit to the registrar contact information, including at a minimum the applicant's name, postal address, telephone number, and electronic mail address. The ICANN Agreement, referring to this registrant contact information under the rubric "WHOIS information," requires the registrar * * * to preserve it, update it daily, and provide for free public access to it through the Internet as well as through an independent access port, called port 43.

* * * An entity making a WHOIS query through Register's Internet site or port 43 would receive a reply furnishing the requested WHOIS information, captioned by a legend devised by Register, which stated,

> By submitting a WHOIS query, you agree that you will use this data only for lawful purposes and that under no circumstances will you use this data to . . . support the transmission of mass unsolicited, commercial advertising or solicitation via email.

The terms of that legend tracked * * * the ICANN Agreement in specifying the restrictions Register imposed on the use of its WHOIS data.

Subsequently, as explained below, Register amended the terms of this legend to impose more stringent restrictions on the use of the information gathered through such queries.

In addition to performing the function of a registrar of domain names, Register also engages in the business of selling web-related services to entities that maintain web sites. These services cover various aspects of web site development. In order to solicit business for the services it offers, Register sends out marketing communications. Among the entities it solicits for the sale of such services are entities whose domain names it registered. However, during the registration process, Register offers registrants the opportunity to elect whether or not they will receive marketing communications from it.

The defendant Verio, against whom the preliminary injunction was issued, is engaged in the business of selling a variety of web site design, development and operation services. In the sale of such services, Verio competes with Register's web site development business. To facilitate its pursuit of customers, Verio undertook to obtain daily updates of the WHOIS information relating to newly registered domain names. To achieve this, Verio devised an automated software program, or robot, which each day would submit multiple successive WHOIS queries through the port 43 accesses of various registrars. Upon acquiring the WHOIS information of new registrants, Verio would send them marketing solicitations by email, telemarketing and direct mail. To the extent that Verio's solicitations were sent by email, the practice was inconsistent with the terms of the restrictive legend Register attached to its responses to Verio's queries.

At first, Verio's solicitations addressed to Register's registrants made explicit reference to their recent registration through Register. This led some of the recipients of Verio's solicitations to believe the solicitation was initiated by Register (or an affiliate), and was sent in violation of the registrant's election not to receive solicitations from Register. Register began to receive complaints from registrants. Register in turn complained to Verio and demanded that Verio cease and desist from this form of marketing. Register asserted that Verio was harming Register's goodwill, and that by soliciting via email, was violating the terms to which it had agreed on submitting its queries for WHOIS information. Verio responded to the effect that it had stopped mentioning Register in its solicitation message.

In the meantime, Register changed the restrictive legend it attached to its responses to WHOIS queries. * * * [I]ts new legend undertook to bar mass solicitation "via direct mail, electronic mail, or by telephone." * * * Register wrote to Verio demanding that it cease using WHOIS information derived from Register not only for email marketing, but also for marketing by direct mail and telephone. Verio ceased using the information in email marketing, but refused to stop marketing by direct mail and telephone.

Register brought this suit on August 3, 2000, and moved for a temporary restraining order and a preliminary injunction. * * * On December 8, 2000, the district court entered a preliminary injunction. The injunction barred Verio from * * * "[a]ccessing Register.com's computers and computer networks in any manner, including, but not limited to, by software programs performing multiple, automated, successive queries, provided that nothing in this Order shall prohibit Verio from accessing Register.com's WHOIS database in accordance with the terms and conditions thereof * * * ." Verio appeals from that order.

DISCUSSION

A.   *Verio's enforcement of the restrictions placed on Register by the ICANN Agreement*

Verio conceded that it knew of the restrictions Register placed on the use of the WHOIS data and knew that, by using Register's WHOIS data for direct mail and telemarketing solicitations, it was violating Register's restrictions. Verio's principal argument is that Register was not authorized to forbid Verio from using the data for direct mail and telemarketing solicitation because the ICANN Agreement prohibited Register from imposing any "terms and conditions" on use of WHOIS data, "except as permitted by ICANN-adopted policy," which specified that Register was required to permit "any lawful purpose, except . . . mass solicitation[ ] via email."

Register does not deny that the restrictions it imposed contravened this requirement of the ICANN Agreement. Register contends, however, that the question whether it violated * * * its Agreement with ICANN is a matter between itself and ICANN, and that Verio cannot enforce the obligations placed on Register by the ICANN Agreement. * * * ICANN intervened in the district court as an amicus curiae and strongly supports Register's position, opposing Verio's right to invoke Register's contractual promises to ICANN. * * * We are persuaded by the arguments Register and ICANN advance. * * *

B.   *Verio's assent to Register's contract terms*

Verio's next contention assumes that Register was legally authorized to demand that takers of WHOIS data from its systems refrain from using it for mass solicitation by mail and telephone, as well as by email. Verio contends that it nonetheless never became contractually bound to the conditions imposed by Register's restrictive legend because, in the case of each query Verio made, the legend did not appear until after Verio had submitted the query and received the WHOIS data. Accordingly, Verio contends that in no instance did it receive legally enforceable notice of the conditions Register intended to impose. Verio therefore argues it should not be deemed to have taken WHOIS data from Register's systems subject to Register's conditions.

Verio's argument might well be persuasive if its queries addressed to Register's computers had been sporadic and infrequent. If Verio had submitted only one query, or even if it had submitted only a few sporadic queries, that would give considerable force to its contention that it obtained the WHOIS data without being conscious that Register intended to impose conditions, and without being deemed to have accepted Register's conditions. But Verio was daily submitting numerous queries, each of which resulted in its receiving notice of the terms Register exacted.

Furthermore, Verio admits that it knew perfectly well what terms Register demanded. Verio's argument fails.

The situation might be compared to one in which plaintiff P maintains a roadside fruit stand displaying bins of apples. A visitor, defendant D, takes an apple and bites into it. As D turns to leave, D sees a sign, visible only as one turns to exit, which says "Apples—50 cents apiece." D does not pay for the apple. D believes he has no obligation to pay because he had no notice when he bit into the apple that 50 cents was expected in return. D's view is that he never agreed to pay for the apple. Thereafter, each day, several times a day, D revisits the stand, takes an apple, and eats it. D never leaves money.

P sues D in contract for the price of the apples taken. D defends on the ground that on no occasion did he see P's price notice until after he had bitten into the apples. D may well prevail as to the first apple taken. D had no reason to understand upon taking it that P was demanding the payment. In our view, however, D cannot continue on a daily basis to take apples for free, knowing full well that P is offering them only in exchange for 50 cents in compensation, merely because the sign demanding payment is so placed that on each occasion D does not see it until he has bitten into the apple.

Verio's circumstance is effectively the same. Each day Verio repeatedly enters Register's computers and takes that day's new WHOIS data. Each day upon receiving the requested data, Verio receives Register's notice of the terms on which it makes the data available—that the data not be used for mass solicitation via direct mail, email, or telephone. Verio acknowledges that it continued drawing the data from Register's computers with full knowledge that Register offered access subject to these restrictions. Verio is no more free to take Register's data without being bound by the terms on which Register offers it, than D was free, in the example, once he became aware of the terms of P's offer, to take P's apples without obligation to pay the 50 cent price at which P offered them.

Verio seeks support for its position from cases that have dealt with the formation of contracts on the Internet. An excellent example, although decided subsequent to the submission of this case, is *Specht v. Netscape Communications Corp.*, 306 F.3d 17 (2d Cir. 2002). The dispute was whether users of Netscape's software, who downloaded it from Netscape's web site, were bound by an agreement to arbitrate disputes with Netscape, where Netscape had posted the terms of its offer of the software (including the obligation to arbitrate disputes) on the web site from which they downloaded the software. We ruled against Netscape and in favor of the users of its software because the users would not have seen the terms Netscape exacted without scrolling down their computer screens, and there was no reason for them to do so. The evidence did not demonstrate that one who had downloaded Netscape's software had necessarily seen the terms of its offer.

Verio, however, cannot avail itself of the reasoning of *Specht*. In *Specht*, the users in whose favor we decided visited Netscape's web site one time to download its software. Netscape's posting of its terms did not compel the conclusion that its downloaders took the software subject to those terms because there was no way to determine that any downloader had seen the terms of the offer. There was no basis for imputing to the downloaders of Netscape's software knowledge of the terms on which the software was offered. This case is crucially different. Verio visited Register's computers daily to access WHOIS data and each day saw the terms of Register's offer; Verio admitted that, in entering Register's computers to get the data, it was fully aware of the terms on which Register offered the access.

Verio's next argument is that it was not bound by Register's terms because it rejected them. Even assuming Register is entitled to demand compliance with its terms in exchange for Verio's entry into its systems to take WHOIS data, and even acknowledging that Verio was fully aware of Register's terms, Verio contends that it still is not bound by Register's terms because it did not agree to be bound. In support of its claim, Verio cites a district court case from the Central District of California, *Ticketmaster Corp. v. Tickets.com, Inc.*, No. CV99-7654, 2000 WL 1887522 (C.D. Cal. Aug. 10, 2000), in which the court rejected Ticketmaster's application for a preliminary injunction to enforce posted terms of use of data available on its website against a regular user. Noting that the user of Ticketmaster's web site is not required to check an "I agree" box before proceeding, the court concluded that there was insufficient proof of agreement to support a preliminary injunction. *Id.* at *5.

We acknowledge that the *Ticketmaster* decision gives Verio some support, but not enough. In the first place, the Ticketmaster court was not making a definitive ruling rejecting Ticketmaster's contract claim. It was rather exercising a district court's discretion to deny a preliminary injunction because of a doubt whether the movant had adequately shown likelihood of success on the merits.

But more importantly, we are not inclined to agree with the *Ticketmaster* court's analysis. There is a crucial difference between the circumstances of *Specht,* where we declined to enforce Netscape's specified terms against a user of its software because of inadequate evidence that the user had seen the terms when downloading the software, and those of *Ticketmaster,* where the taker of information from Ticketmaster's site knew full well the terms on which the information was offered but was not offered an icon marked, "I agree," on which to click. Under the circumstances of *Ticketmaster,* we see no reason why the enforceability of the offeror's terms should depend on whether the taker states (or clicks), "I agree."

We recognize that contract offers on the Internet often require the offeree to click on an "I agree" icon. And no doubt, in many circumstances, such a statement of agreement by the offeree is essential to the formation of a contract. But not in all circumstances. While new commerce on the Internet has exposed courts to many new situations, it has not fundamentally changed the principles of contract. It is standard contract doctrine that when a benefit is offered subject to stated conditions, and the offeree makes a decision to take the benefit with knowledge of the terms of the offer, the taking constitutes an acceptance of the terms, which accordingly become binding on the offeree.

Returning to the apple stand, the visitor, who sees apples offered for 50 cents apiece and takes an apple, owes 50 cents, regardless whether he did or did not say, "I agree." The choice offered in such circumstances is to take the apple on the known terms of the offer or not to take the apple. As we see it, the defendant in *Ticketmaster* and Verio in this case had a similar choice. Each was offered access to information subject to terms of which they were well aware. Their choice was either to accept the offer of contract, taking the information subject to the terms of the offer, or, if the terms were not acceptable, to decline to take the benefits. * * *

D.   *Trespass to chattels*

Verio also attacks the grant of the preliminary injunction against its accessing Register's computers by automated software programs performing multiple successive queries. This prong of the injunction was premised on Register's claim of trespass to chattels. Verio contends the ruling was in error because Register failed to establish that Verio's conduct resulted in harm to Register's servers and because Verio's robot access to the WHOIS database through Register was "not unauthorized." We believe the district court's findings were within the range of its permissible discretion.

"A trespass to a chattel may be committed by intentionally . . . using or intermeddling with a chattel in the possession of another," RESTATEMENT (SECOND) OF TORTS § 217(b) (1965), where "the chattel is impaired as to its condition, quality, or value," *id.* § 218(b).

The district court found that Verio's use of search robots, consisting of software programs performing multiple automated successive queries, consumed a significant portion of the capacity of Register's computer systems. While Verio's robots alone would not incapacitate Register's systems, the court found that if Verio were permitted to continue to access Register's computers through such robots, it was "highly probable" that other Internet service providers would devise similar programs to access Register's data, and that the system would be overtaxed and would crash. We cannot say these findings were unreasonable.

Nor is there merit to Verio's contention that it cannot be engaged in trespass when Register had never instructed it not to use its robot programs. As the district court noted, Register's complaint sufficiently advised Verio that its use of robots was not authorized and, according to Register's contentions, would cause harm to Register's systems. * * *

The ruling of the district court is hereby AFFIRMED.

Notes and Questions

1. Recall the approaches to trespass to chattels that we encountered in Chapter Two. Does the *Ticketmaster* court's treatment of the trespass issue differ, and if so, how? Which approach do you find more persuasive? Why shouldn't Ticketmaster's efforts to frustrate Tickets.com's activities count as harm for purposes of the trespass to chattels claim?

2. Should the law grant Ticketmaster a more robust right to control its computer system, so that Ticketmaster could exclude any use that it finds

detrimental? What are the benefits of a broader right to exclude? What harms would flow from such a rule?

3. The district court in *Ticketmaster* discusses the Ninth Circuit's conclusion in *Kelly v. Arriba Soft Corp.* that "in-line linking" to or "framing" of Kelly's copyrighted images violates Kelly's copyright. 280 F.3d 934, 947 (9th Cir. 2002). The *Ticketmaster* court distinguishes that conclusion in part on the ground that Arriba Soft "import[ed]" Kelly's image, while a Tickets.com user "was taken directly to the originating TM site." In both cases, however, the alleged infringer's site simply instructed the user's browser to communicate with the copyright holder's site and display portions of it. How might you argue that Tickets.com's conduct is in fact more harmful than Arriba Soft's conduct?

In *Kelly*, the Ninth Circuit ultimately withdrew the opinion discussed by the *Ticketmaster* court. In its new opinion, the Ninth Circuit avoided resolving whether Arriba Soft's linking to or framing of the full-size images violated Kelly's copyright, concluding that, since the parties did not request summary judgment on the issue, the district court erred in granting summary judgment to Arriba Soft. *Kelly v. Arriba Soft Corp.*, 336 F.3d 811, 822 (9th Cir. 2003).

4. In 2003, the German Federal Supreme Court—similarly to the court in *Ticketmaster*—ruled that deep links from a news search engine directly to articles in a publisher's website do not violate German copyright or competition law. *See Handelsblatt v. Paperboy*, Federal Supreme Court of Germany (Bundesgerichtshof). The court stressed the importance of deep links for the Internet and held that it is up to plaintiffs to use technological self-help if they object to such linking. The court did not, however, answer the further question of whether circumventing any such technological self-help would be illegal. If deep-linking is so important to the Internet, why do you think the court appeared willing to countenance the idea of websites blocking such links through technological means?

5. As the court of appeals notes, Register.com never imposed conditions on the method of access to its data—for example, by barring robots. Rather, it sought to restrict the subsequent *use* of the data. Should this fact have affected the court's analysis of Register.com's trespass and contract claims? In what way? Was it sufficient, in seeking injunctive relief, for Register.com simply to file a complaint objecting to Verio's practices? Would Register.com be entitled to damages on its trespass claim?

6. In both *Ticketmaster* and *Register.com*, the defendants sought access to *factual* information—material not protected under copyright law. Does recognizing a trespass claim or a contract claim where copyright protection is unavailable undermine the balance copyright law strikes between providing authors with an incentive to create and preserving the availability of information? Why or why not?

SECTION C. THE COMPUTER FRAUD AND ABUSE ACT

The state trespass cause of action at issue in *eBay, Ticketmaster*, and *Register.com* has a federal statutory analogue, the federal Computer Fraud and Abuse Act (CFAA). 18 U.S.C. § 1030.[a] That statute contains several provisions outlawing unauthorized access to computer systems. When Congress passed the first version of this statute in 1984, it clearly sought to target hacking activities. As initially enacted, the statute protected a fairly narrow range of computers, none of which were available to the general public: those containing national security information; those containing financial data; and those operated by or on behalf of the government. *See* Counterfeit Access Device and Computer Fraud and Abuse Act of 1984, Pub. L. No. 98-473, 98 Stat. 2190. A major amendment in 1986 expanded the range of computers covered and added new offenses, Computer Fraud and Abuse Act of 1986, Pub. L. No. 99-474, § 2, 100 Stat. 1213-16, and Congress further expanded the statute's scope with amendments in 1994 and 1996. At each turn, however, the debate over the statute's passage and the accompanying legislative reports reflect a primary concern with protecting security and confidentiality; there is no indication that Congress intended to extend the statute's coverage to publicly available information on computers.[b]

Despite Congress's primary focus on hacking activities, the language of the statute is now quite broad, in that it prohibits knowingly or intentionally "access[ing] a computer without authorization" or "exceed[ing] authorized access" and obtaining certain information. For example, section 1030(a)(2) prohibits the acquisition of information from a financial institution, from the U.S. government, or from any "protected computer," defined to include any computer used in interstate or foreign commerce or communication. Other provisions prohibit persons from accessing a computer without authorization and using it to further fraudulent activity, *id.* § 1030(a)(4), and prohibit persons from transmitting codes or commands to a computer that cause damage, *id.* § 1030(a)(5)(i). The statute carries criminal penalties, but also authorizes a person "who suffers damage or loss by reason of a violation" of the statute to maintain a civil action against the violator. *Id.* § 1030(g). Several of the statute's key provisions are set forth below. As you read them, consider whether the statute should cover access to information in circumstances where a content provider generally makes information accessible to the public but seeks to limit its subsequent use.

Computer Fraud and Abuse Act

18 U.S.C. § 1030

§ 1030. Fraud and related activity in connection with computers

(a) Whoever—

---

a. Technically, the title Computer Fraud and Abuse Act refers to the 1986 amendments to 18 U.S.C. § 1030, *see* Computer Fraud and Abuse Act of 1986, Pub. L. No. 99-474, § 2, 100 Stat. 1213-16, but courts commonly use it to describe 18 U.S.C. § 1030 as a whole.

b. *See* Patricia L. Bellia, *Defending Cyberproperty*, 79 N.Y.U. L. REV. 2164, 2253-58 (2004).

(1) having knowingly accessed a computer without authorization or exceeding authorized access, and by means of such conduct having obtained information that has been determined by the United States Government pursuant to an Executive order or statute to require protection against unauthorized disclosure for reasons of national defense or foreign relations, or any restricted data, as defined in paragraph y of section 11 of the Atomic Energy Act of 1954, with reason to believe that such information so obtained could be used to the injury of the United States, or to the advantage of any foreign nation willfully communicates, delivers, transmits, or causes to be communicated, delivered, or transmitted, or attempts to communicate, deliver, transmit or cause to be communicated, delivered, or transmitted the same to any person not entitled to receive it, or willfully retains the same and fails to deliver it to the officer or employee of the United States entitled to receive it;

(2) intentionally accesses a computer without authorization or exceeds authorized access, and thereby obtains—

(A) information contained in a financial record of a financial institution, or of a card issuer as defined in section 1602(n) of title 15, or contained in a file of a consumer reporting agency on a consumer, as such terms are defined in the Fair Credit Reporting Act (15 U.S.C. 1681 et seq.);

(B) information from any department or agency of the United States; or

(C) information from any protected computer if the conduct involved an interstate or foreign communication;

(3) intentionally, without authorization to access any nonpublic computer of a department or agency of the United States, accesses such a computer of that department or agency that is exclusively for the use of the Government of the United States or, in the case of a computer not exclusively for such use, is used by or for the Government of the United States and such conduct affects that use by or for the Government of the United States;

(4) knowingly and with intent to defraud, accesses a protected computer without authorization, or exceeds authorized access, and by means of such conduct furthers the intended fraud and obtains anything of value, unless the object of the fraud and the thing obtained consists only of the use of the computer and the value of such use is not more than $5,000 in any 1-year period;

(5)(A)(i) knowingly causes the transmission of a program, information, code, or command, and as a result of such conduct, intentionally causes damage without authorization, to a protected computer;

(ii) intentionally accesses a protected computer without authorization, and as a result of such conduct, recklessly causes damage; or

(iii) intentionally accesses a protected computer without authorization, and as a result of such conduct, causes damage; and

(B) by conduct described in clause (i), (ii), or (iii) of subparagraph (A), caused (or, in the case of an attempted offense, would, if completed, have caused)—

(i) loss to 1 or more persons during any 1-year period (and, for purposes of an investigation, prosecution, or other proceeding brought by the United States only, loss resulting from a related course of conduct affecting 1 or more other protected computers) aggregating at least $5,000 in value;

(ii) the modification or impairment, or potential modification or impairment, of the medical examination, diagnosis, treatment, or care of 1 or more individuals;

(iii) physical injury to any person;

(iv) a threat to public health or safety; or

(v) damage affecting a computer system used by or for a government entity in furtherance of the administration of justice, national defense, or national security;

(6) knowingly and with intent to defraud traffics (as defined in section 1029) in any password or similar information through which a computer may be accessed without authorization, if—

(A) such trafficking affects interstate or foreign commerce; or

(B) such computer is used by or for the Government of the United States; [or]

(7) with intent to extort from any person any money or other thing of value, transmits in interstate or foreign commerce any communication containing any threat to cause damage to a protected computer;

shall be punished as provided in subsection (c) of this section.

(b) Whoever attempts to commit an offense under subsection (a) of this section shall be punished as provided in subsection (c) of this section. * * *

(e) As used in this section—

(1) the term "computer" means an electronic, magnetic, optical, electrochemical, or other high speed data processing device performing logical, arithmetic, or storage functions, and includes any data storage facility or communications facility directly related to or operating in conjunction with such device, but such term does not include an automated typewriter or typesetter, a portable hand held calculator, or other similar device;

(2) the term "protected computer" means a computer—

(A) exclusively for the use of a financial institution or the United States Government, or, in the case of a computer not exclusively for such use, used by or for a financial institution or the United States Government and the conduct constituting the offense affects that use by or for the financial institution or the Government; or

(B) which is used in interstate or foreign commerce or communication, including a computer located outside the United States that is used in a manner that affects interstate or foreign commerce or communication of the United States; * * *

(6) the term "exceeds authorized access" means to access a computer with authorization and to use such access to obtain or alter information in the computer that the accesser is not entitled so to obtain or alter; * * *

(8) the term "damage" means any impairment to the integrity or availability of data, a program, a system, or information; * * *

(11) the term "loss" means any reasonable cost to any victim, including the cost of responding to an offense, conducting a damage assessment, and restoring the data, program, system, or information to its condition prior to the offense, and any revenue lost, cost incurred, or other consequential damages incurred because of interruption of service; * * *

(g) Any person who suffers damage or loss by reason of a violation of this section may maintain a civil action against the violator to obtain compensatory damages and injunctive relief or other equitable relief. A civil action for a violation of this section may be brought only if the conduct involves 1 of the factors set forth in clause (i), (ii), (iii), (iv), or (v) of subsection (a)(5)(B). Damages for a violation involving only conduct described in subsection (a)(5)(B)(i) are limited to economic damages. No action may be brought under this subsection unless such action is begun within 2 years of the date of the act complained of or the date of the discovery of the damage. No action may be brought under this subsection for the negligent design or manufacture of computer hardware, computer software, or firmware. * * *

Because the "protected computer" definition is broad enough to capture any Internet-connected computer, efforts to limit application of the statute to nonpublic information must come from other sources—perhaps from a narrow interpretation of "access"; from a narrow interpretation of what it means for access to "exceed" what is authorized or to be "without authorization"; or from other structural or policy considerations.

The first case to consider what it means to access a system "without authorization" or to "exceed[]" what has been authorized involved transmission of a worm that caused significant damage to a number of computers. At the time, the CFAA did not have a prohibition equivalent to what is now section 1030(a)(5)(A)(i), which bars the transmission of a file that causes damage without authorization, regardless of whether the sender is authorized to access the system in the first place. Despite the change in the statute, the court's interpretation continues to be relevant to interpretation of unauthorized access provisions. Is the interpretation correct?

United States v. Morris

United States Court of Appeals for the Second Circuit, 1991
928 F.2d 504

JON O. NEWMAN, Circuit Judge.

In the fall of 1988, Morris was a first-year graduate student in Cornell University's computer science Ph.D. program. Through undergraduate work at Harvard and in various jobs he had acquired significant computer experience and expertise. When Morris entered Cornell, he was given an account on the computer at the Computer Science Division. This account gave him explicit authorization to use computers at Cornell. Morris engaged in various discussions with fellow graduate students about the security of computer networks and his ability to penetrate it.

In October 1988, Morris began work on a computer program, later known as the Internet "worm" or "virus." The goal of this program was to demonstrate the inadequacies of current security measures on computer networks by exploiting the security defects that Morris had discovered. * * * Morris designed the program to spread across a national network of computers after being inserted at one computer location connected to the network. Morris released the worm into [the] Internet * * * .

Morris sought to program the Internet worm to spread widely without drawing attention to itself. The worm was supposed to occupy little computer operation time, and thus not interfere with normal use of the computers. Morris programmed the worm to make it difficult to detect and read, so that other programmers would not be able to "kill" the worm easily.

Morris also wanted to ensure that the worm did not copy itself onto a computer that already had a copy. Multiple copies of the worm on a computer would make the worm easier to detect and would bog down the system and ultimately cause the computer to crash. Therefore, Morris designed the worm to "ask" each computer whether it already had a copy of the worm. If it responded "no," then the worm would copy onto the computer; if it responded "yes," the worm would not duplicate. However, Morris was concerned that other programmers could kill the worm by programming their own computers to falsely respond "yes" to the question. To circumvent this protection, Morris programmed the worm to duplicate itself every seventh time it received a "yes" response. As it turned out, Morris underestimated the number of times a computer would be asked the question, and his one-out-of-seven ratio resulted in far more copying than he had anticipated. The worm was also designed so that it would be killed when a computer was shut down, an event that typically occurs once every week or two. This would have prevented the worm from accumulating on one computer, had Morris correctly estimated the likely rate of reinfection. * * *

Morris identified four ways in which the worm could break into computers on the network:

(1) through a "hole" or "bug" (an error) in send mail, a computer program that transfers and receives electronic mail on a computer;

(2) through a bug in the "finger demon" program, a program that permits a person to obtain limited information about the users of another computer;

(3) through the "trusted hosts" feature, which permits a user with certain privileges on one computer to have equivalent privileges on another computer without using a password; and

(4) through a program of password guessing, whereby various combinations of letters are tried out in rapid sequence in the hope that one will be an authorized user's password, which is entered to permit whatever level of activity that user is authorized to perform.

On November 2, 1988, Morris released the worm from a computer at the Massachusetts Institute of Technology. MIT was selected to disguise the fact that the worm came from Morris at Cornell. Morris soon discovered that the worm was replicating and reinfecting machines at a much faster rate than he had anticipated. Ultimately, many machines at locations around the country either crashed or became "catatonic." When Morris realized what was happening, he contacted a friend at Harvard to discuss a solution. Eventually, they sent an anonymous message from Harvard over the network, instructing programmers how to kill the worm and prevent reinfection. However, because the network route was clogged, this message did not get through until it was too late. Computers were affected at numerous installations, including leading universities, military sites, and medical research facilities. The estimated cost of dealing with the worm at each installation ranged from $200 to more than $53,000.

Morris was found guilty, following a jury trial, of violating 18 U.S.C. § 1030(a)(5)(A). He was sentenced to three years of probation, 400 hours of community service, a fine of $10,050, and the costs of his supervision.

DISCUSSION

* * * Section 1030(a)(5)(A) covers anyone who

(5) intentionally accesses a Federal interest computer without authorization, and by means of one or more instances of such conduct alters, damages, or destroys information in any such Federal interest computer, or prevents authorized use of any such computer or information, and thereby

(A) causes loss to one or more others of a value aggregating $1,000 or more during any one year period; * * *

Morris contends that his conduct constituted, at most, "exceeding authorized access" rather than the "unauthorized access" that the subsection punishes. Morris argues that there was insufficient evidence to convict him of "unauthorized access" * * * .

We assess the sufficiency of the evidence under the traditional standard. Morris was authorized to use computers at Cornell, Harvard, and

Berkeley, all of which were on Internet. As a result, Morris was authorized to communicate with other computers on the network to send electronic mail (send mail), and to find out certain information about the users of other computers (finger demon). The question is whether Morris's transmission of his worm constituted exceeding authorized access or accessing without authorization.

[The first federal statute dealing with computer crimes was passed in 1984, Pub. L. No. 98-473 (codified at 18 U.S.C. § 1030 (Supp. II 1984)). The specific provision under which Morris was convicted was added in 1986, Pub. L. No. 99-474, along with some other changes.] The [report of the Senate Judiciary Committee accompanying the 1986 Act] stated that section 1030(a)(5)(A), like the new section 1030(a)(3) [also adopted in 1986], would "be aimed at 'outsiders,' i.e., those lacking authorization to access any Federal interest computer." S. Rep. No. 99-432, at 10 (1986). But the Report also stated, in concluding its discussion on the scope of section 1030(a)(3), that it applies "where the offender is completely outside the Government, . . . *or where the offender's act of trespass is interdepartmental in nature.*" *Id.* at 8 (emphasis added).

Morris [argues] that his actions can be characterized only as exceeding authorized access, since he had authorized access to a federal interest computer. However, * * * Congress contemplated that individuals with access to some federal interest computers would be subject to liability under the computer fraud provisions for gaining unauthorized access to other federal interest computers.

The evidence permitted the jury to conclude that Morris's use of the send mail and finger demon features constituted access without authorization. While a case might arise where the use of send mail or finger demon falls within a nebulous area in which the line between accessing without authorization and exceeding authorized access may not be clear, Morris's conduct here falls well within the area of unauthorized access. Morris did not use either of those features in any way related to their intended function. He did not send or read mail nor discover information about other users; instead he found holes in both programs that permitted him a special and unauthorized access route into other computers.

Moreover, the jury verdict need not be upheld solely on Morris's use of send mail and finger demon. As the District Court noted, in denying Morris' motion for acquittal,

> Although the evidence may have shown that defendant's initial insertion of the worm simply exceeded his authorized access, the evidence also demonstrated that the worm was designed to spread to other computers at which he had no account and no authority, express or implied, to unleash the worm program. Moreover, there was also evidence that the worm was designed to gain access to computers at which he had no account by guessing their passwords. Accordingly, the evidence did support the jury's conclusion that defendant accessed without authority as opposed to merely exceeding the scope of his authority.

In light of the reasonable conclusions that the jury could draw from Morris's use of send mail and finger demon, and from his use of the trusted hosts feature and password guessing, his challenge to the sufficiency of the evidence fails. * * *

It is true that a primary concern of Congress in drafting subsection (a)(5) was to reach those unauthorized to access any federal interest computer. The Senate Report stated, "[T]his subsection [(a)(5)] will be aimed at 'outsiders,' i.e., those lacking authorization to access any Federal interest computer." Senate Report at 10. But the fact that the subsection is "aimed" at such "outsiders" does not mean that its coverage is limited to them. Congress understandably thought that the group most likely to damage federal interest computers would be those who lack authorization to use any of them. But it surely did not mean to insulate from liability the person authorized to use computers at the State Department who causes damage to computers at the Defense Department. Congress created the misdemeanor offense of subsection (a)(3) to punish intentional trespasses into computers for which one lacks authorized access; it added the felony offense of subsection (a)(5) to punish such a trespasser who also causes damage or loss in excess of $1,000, not only to computers of the United States but to any computer within the definition of federal interest computers. With both provisions, Congress was punishing those, like Morris, who, with access to some computers that enable them to communicate on a network linking other computers, gain access to other computers to which they lack authorization and either trespass, in violation of subsection (a)(3), or cause damage or loss of $1,000 or more, in violation of subsection (a)(5). * * *

CONCLUSION

For the foregoing reasons, the judgment of the District Court is affirmed.

Notes and Questions

1. In amending the CFAA in 1994, Congress added a provision covering the transmission of harmful code and otherwise rewrote section 1030(a)(5). *See* Pub. L. No. 103-322, § 290001(b). Conduct such as Morris's would likely be covered by what is now (after further amendments in 2001) section 1030(a)(5)(A)(i), which prohibits a person from "knowingly caus[ing] the transmission of a program, information, code, or command, and as a result of such conduct, intentionally caus[ing] damage, without authorization, to a protected computer." In other words, whether an individual transmitting a worm or virus would be "access[ing]" a computer "without authorization," or merely "exceeding authorized access," would no longer be at issue. Other portions of the statute continue to use these terms, however, so the *Morris* court's interpretation of what it means to proceed "without authorization" remains relevant.

2. In arguing that he did not access the send mail and finger demon programs "without authorization," Morris attempted to draw an insider/outsider distinction, suggesting that the provision under which he was charged covered only access "without authorization" rather than "exceed[ing]

authorized access." How did the court respond to this argument? Is its answer persuasive? For a case accepting an insider/outsider distinction, see *In re Am. Online, Inc. Version 5.0 Software Litig.*, 168 F. Supp. 2d 1359, 1370-71 (S.D. Fla. 2001).

3. The court states that Morris did not use the send mail and finger demon features "in any way related to their intended function." Should the line between accessing a computer without authorization and exceeding authorized access depend on the "intended function" of a system? How is a potential user to know what the limits of a system's "intended functions" are? What other line might you draw?

4. Is an "intended function" analysis helpful when the issue is whether content providers should be permitted to dictate the scope of authorized access to portions of their systems that are, in technical terms, publicly accessible? Consider the following case.

America Online, Inc. v. LCGM, Inc.

United States District Court for the Eastern District of Virginia, 1998
46 F. Supp. 2d 444

LEE, District Judge.

This matter is before the Court on plaintiff's Motion for Summary Judgment * * * . AOL, an Internet service provider located in the Eastern District of Virginia, provides a proprietary, content-based online service that provides its members (AOL members) access to the Internet and the capability to receive as well as send e-mail messages. * * * AOL alleges that defendants, in concert, sent unauthorized and unsolicited bulk e-mail advertisements ("spam") to AOL customers. AOL's Unsolicited Bulk E-mail Policy and its Terms of Service bar both members and nonmembers from sending bulk e-mail through AOL's computer systems. * * *

Plaintiff alleges that defendants harvested, or collected, the e-mail addresses of AOL members in violation of AOL's Terms of Service. Defendants have admitted to maintaining AOL memberships to harvest or collect the e-mail addresses of other AOL members. Defendants have admitted to maintaining AOL accounts and to using the AOL Collector and E-mail Pro/Stealth Mailer extractor programs to collect the e-mail addresses of AOL members, alleging that they did so in targeted adult AOL chat rooms. Defendants have admitted to using this software to evade AOL's filtering mechanisms. * * * Plaintiff alleges that defendants' actions injured AOL by consuming capacity on AOL's computers, causing AOL to incur technical costs, impairing the functioning of AOL's e-mail system, forcing AOL to upgrade its computer networks to process authorized e-mails in a timely manner, damaging AOL's goodwill with its members, and causing AOL to lose customers and revenue. Plaintiff asserts that between the months of December 1997 and April 1998, defendants' unsolicited bulk e-mails generated more than 450,000 complaints by AOL members. * * *

COUNT III: EXCEEDING AUTHORIZED ACCESS IN VIOLATION OF THE COMPUTER FRAUD AND ABUSE ACT

The facts before the Court establish that defendants violated 18 U.S.C. § 1030(a)(2)(C) of the Computer Fraud and Abuse Act, which prohibits individuals from "intentionally accessing] a computer without authorization or exceed[ing] authorized access, and thereby obtain[ing] information from any protected computer if the conduct involved an interstate or foreign communication." Defendants' own admissions satisfy the Act's requirements. Defendants have admitted to maintaining an AOL membership and using that membership to harvest the e-mail addresses of AOL members. Defendants have stated that they acquired these e-mail addresses by using extractor software programs. Defendants' actions violated AOL's Terms of Service, and as such [were] unauthorized. Plaintiff contends that the addresses of AOL members are "information" within the meaning of the Act because they are proprietary in nature. Plaintiff asserts that as a result of defendants' actions, it suffered damages exceeding $5,000, the statutory threshold requirement.

COUNT IV: IMPAIRING COMPUTER FACILITIES IN VIOLATION OF THE COMPUTER FRAUD AND ABUSE ACT

The undisputed facts establish that defendants violated 18 U.S.C. § 1030(a)(5)(C)[°] of the Computer Fraud and Abuse Act, which prohibits anyone from "intentionally access[ing] a protected computer without authorization, and as a result of such conduct, caus[ing] damage." * * * Defendants have admitted to utilizing software to collect AOL members' addresses. These actions were unauthorized because they violated AOL's Terms of Service. Defendants' intent to access a protected computer, in this case computers within AOL's network, is clear under the circumstances. Defendants' access of AOL's computer network enabled defendants to send large numbers of unsolicited bulk e-mail messages to AOL members.

In addition to defendants' admissions, plaintiff alleges that by using the domain information "aol.com" in their e-mails, defendants and their "site partners" camouflaged their identities, and evaded plaintiff's blocking filters and its members' mail controls. Defendants have admitted to using extractor software to evade AOL's filtering mechanisms. As a result of these actions, plaintiff asserts damages to its computer network, reputation and goodwill in excess of the minimum $5,000 statutory requirement. * * *

[T]he Court grants plaintiff's Motion for Summary Judgment [with respect to these counts].

---

c. The 2001 amendment to the CFAA renumbered subparagraphs 1030(a)(5)(A)-(C) as subparagraphs 1030(a)(5)(A)(i)-(iii) and imported into section 1030(a)(5)(B) language substantially similar to that previously appearing in the definition of "damage" in section 1030(e)(8). *See* USA PATRIOT Act of 2001, Pub. L. No. 107-56, § 814(a), 115 Stat. 272, 382-83 (1001).

Notes and Questions

1. Why does the court conclude that the harvesting of e-mail addresses of AOL members constitutes exceeding authorized access? Is the court's reasoning persuasive?

2. Suppose that LCGM had not used a software extraction program to obtain addresses, but instead had acquired addresses by participating in and monitoring chat rooms. Would such an act also have exceeded authorized access for purposes of AOL's Count III claim that the acquisition of addresses violates section 1030(a)(2)(C)? What additional facts would you need to make this determination?

3. What must AOL prove in connection with its Count IV claim that the sending of bulk e-mail violates section 1030(a)(5)(C) (now appearing at section 1030(a)(5)(A)(iii))? On what basis does the court conclude that the defendants gained access to AOL's system without authorization? Would the result have been the same if the defendants had merely sent e-mail, without also using the software to extract AOL members' addresses? Why or why not?

EF Cultural Travel BV v. Explorica, Inc.

United States Court of Appeals for the First Circuit, 2001
274 F.3d 577

COFFIN, Senior Circuit Judge.

Appellant Explorica, Inc. ("Explorica") and several of its employees challenge a preliminary injunction issued against them for alleged violations of the Computer Fraud and Abuse Act ("CFAA"), 18 U.S.C. § 1030. We affirm the district court's conclusion that appellees will likely succeed on the merits of their CFAA claim, but rest on a narrower basis than the court below.

I. BACKGROUND

Explorica was formed in 2000 to compete in the field of global tours for high school students. Several of Explorica's employees formerly were employed by appellee EF, which has been in business for more than thirty-five years. EF and its partners and subsidiaries make up the world's largest private student travel organization.

Shortly after the individual defendants left EF in the beginning of 2000, Explorica began competing in the teenage tour market. The company's vice president (and former vice president of information strategy at EF), Philip Gormley, envisioned that Explorica could gain a substantial advantage over all other student tour companies, and especially EF, by undercutting EF's already competitive prices on student tours. Gormley considered several ways to obtain and utilize EF's prices: by manually keying in the information from EF's brochures and other printed materials; by using a scanner to record that same information; or, by manually searching for each tour offered through EF's website. Ultimately, however, Gormley engaged Zefer [Corp.], Explorica's Internet consultant, to design a computer program called a "scraper" to glean all of the necessary information from EF's website. Zefer designed the program in three days.

The scraper has been likened to a "robot," a tool that is extensively used on the Internet. Robots are used to gather information for countless purposes, ranging from compiling results for search engines such as Yahoo! to filtering for inappropriate content. The widespread deployment of robots enables global Internet users to find comprehensive information quickly and almost effortlessly.

Like a robot, the scraper sought information through the Internet. Unlike other robots, however, the scraper focused solely on EF's website, using information that other robots would not have. Specifically, Zefer utilized tour codes whose significance was not readily understandable to the public. With the tour codes, the scraper accessed EF's website repeatedly and easily obtained pricing information for those specific tours. The scraper sent more than 30,000 inquiries to EF's website and recorded the pricing information into a spreadsheet.

Zefer ran the scraper program twice, first to retrieve the 2000 tour prices and then the 2001 prices. All told, the scraper downloaded 60,000 lines of data, the equivalent of eight telephone directories of information. Once Zefer "scraped" all of the prices, it sent a spreadsheet containing EF's pricing information to Explorica, which then systematically undercut EF's prices. Explorica thereafter printed its own brochures and began competing in EF's tour market. * * * [After the development and use of the scraper came to light during state court litigation, EF] filed this action, alleging [, among other things,] violations of the CFAA * * * .

On May 30, 2001, the district court granted a preliminary injunction against Explorica based on the CFAA, which criminally and civilly prohibits certain access to computers. *See* 18 U.S.C. § 1030(a)(4). The court found that EF would likely prove that Explorica violated the CFAA when it used EF's website in a manner outside the "reasonable expectations" of both EF and its ordinary users. The court also concluded that EF could show that it suffered a loss, as required by the statute, consisting of reduced business, harm to its goodwill, and the cost of diagnostic measures it incurred to evaluate possible harm to EF's systems, although it could not show that Explorica's actions physically damaged its computers. In a supplemental opinion the district court further articulated its "reasonable expectations" standard and explained that copyright, contractual and technical restraints sufficiently notified Explorica that its use of a scraper would be unauthorized and thus would violate the CFAA.

The district court first relied on EF's use of a copyright symbol on one of the pages of its website and a link directing users with questions to contact the company, finding that "such a clear statement should have dispelled any notion a reasonable person may have had that the 'presumption of open access' applied to information on EF's website." The court next found that the manner by which Explorica accessed EF's website likely violated a confidentiality agreement between appellant Gormley and EF, because Gormley provided to Zefer technical instructions concerning the creation of the scraper. Finally, the district court noted without elaboration that the scraper bypassed technical restrictions embedded in the website to acquire the information. The court therefore let stand its earlier decision granting the preliminary injunction. Appellants contend that the district court erred in taking too narrow a view of what is authorized under the CFAA and similarly mistook the reach of the confidentiality agreement. Appellants also argue that the district court erred in finding that appellees suffered a "loss," as defined by the CFAA * * * .

III. THE COMPUTER FRAUD AND ABUSE ACT

Although appellees alleged violations of three provisions of the CFAA, the district court found that they were likely to succeed only under section 1030(a)(4). That section provides

> [Whoever] knowingly and with intent to defraud, accesses a protected computer without authorization, or exceeds authorized access, and by means of such conduct furthers the intended fraud and obtains anything of value . . . shall be punished.

18 U.S.C. § 1030(a)(4). Appellees allege that the appellants knowingly and with intent to defraud accessed the server hosting EF's website more than 30,000 times to obtain proprietary pricing and tour information, and confidential information about appellees' technical abilities. At the heart of the parties' dispute is whether appellants' actions either were "without authorization" or "exceed[ed] authorized access" as defined by the CFAA. We conclude that because of the broad confidentiality agreement appellants' actions "exceed[ed] authorized access," and so we do not reach the more general arguments made about statutory meaning, including whether use of a scraper alone renders access unauthorized.

A.   *"Exceeds authorized access"*

Congress defined "exceeds authorized access," as accessing "a computer with authorization and [using] such access to obtain or alter information in the computer that the accesser is not entitled so to obtain or alter." 18 U.S.C. § 1030(e)(6). EF is likely to prove such excessive access based on the confidentiality agreement between Gormley and EF. Pertinently, that agreement provides:

> Employee agrees to maintain in strict confidence and not to disclose to any third party, either orally or in writing, any Confidential or Proprietary Information . . . and never to at any time (i) directly or indirectly publish, disseminate or otherwise disclose, deliver or make available to anybody any Confidential or Proprietary Information or (ii) use such Confidential or [P]roprietary Information for Employee's own benefit or for the benefit of any other person or business entity other than EF.
>
> * * *
>
> As used in this Agreement, the term "Confidential or Proprietary Information" means (a) any trade or business secrets or confidential information of EF, whether or not reduced to writing . . . ; (b) any technical, business, or financial information, the use or disclosure of which might reasonably be construed to be contrary to the interests of EF. . . .

The record contains at least two communications from Gormley to Zefer seeming to rely on information about EF to which he was privy only because of his employment there. First, in an email to Zefer employee Joseph Alt exploring the use of a scraper, Gormley wrote: "[m]ight one of the team be able to write a program to automatically extract prices . . . ? I could work with him/her on the specification." Gormley also sent the following email to Zefer employee John Hawley:

> Here is a link to the page where you can grab EF's prices. There are two important drop down menus on the right. . . . With the lowest one you select one of about 150 tours. * * * You then select your origin gateway from a list of about 100 domestic gateways (middle drop down menu). When you select your origin gateway a page with a couple of tables comes up. One table has 1999- 2000 prices and the other has 2000-2001 prices. * * * On a high speed connection it is possible to move quickly from one price table to the next by hitting backspace and then the down arrow.

This documentary evidence points to Gormley's heavy involvement in the conception of the scraper program. Furthermore, the voluminous spreadsheet containing all of the scraped information includes the tour codes, which EF claims are proprietary information. Each page of the spreadsheet produced by Zefer includes the tour and gateway codes, the date of travel, and the price for the tour. An uninformed reader would regard the tour codes as nothing but gibberish. Although the codes can be correlated to the actual tours and destination points, the codes standing alone need to be "translated" to be meaningful. * * *

Here, * * * there is ample evidence that Gormley provided Explorica proprietary information about the structure of the website and the tour codes. To be sure, gathering manually the various codes through repeated searching and deciphering of the URLs theoretically may be possible. Practically speaking, however, if proven, Explorica's wholesale use of EF's travel codes to facilitate gathering EF's prices from its website reeks of use—and, indeed, abuse—of proprietary information that goes beyond any authorized use of EF's website.

Gormley voluntarily entered a broad confidentiality agreement prohibiting his disclosure of any information "which might reasonably be construed to be contrary to the interests of EF." Appellants would face an uphill battle trying to argue that it was not against EF's interests for appellants to use the tour codes to mine EF's pricing data. If EF's allegations are proven, it will likely prove that whatever authorization Explorica had to navigate around EF's site (even in a competitive vein), it exceeded that authorization by providing proprietary information and know-how to Zefer to create the scraper. Accordingly, the district court's finding that Explorica likely violated the CFAA was not clearly erroneous. * * * We agree with the district court that appellees will likely succeed on the merits of their CFAA claim under 18 U.S.C. §1030(a)(4). Accordingly, the preliminary injunction was properly ordered.

Notes and Questions

1. Would the result in this case have been the same if operation of the "scraper" had not relied on the tour codes? Is the court of appeals correct to conclude that Gormley's confidentiality agreement provides the basis for concluding that Explorica exceeded authorized access to EF's system? Why or why not?

2. Suppose that development of the scraper tool had not depended on the use of confidential information. Would use of the scraper alone render access "unauthorized" within the meaning of the CFAA? What additional information would you need to make a determination? The district court rested its holding that Explorica violated the CFAA on its conclusion that Explorica used EF's web site in a manner outside of EF's "reasonable expectations." What notifies a potential user of the site owner's "reasonable expectations"? How does the district court's standard for determining authorized access differ from the standard applied in *AOL*? From the standard applied in *Morris*?

3. In a separate appeal, Zefer Corp. also challenged the district court's preliminary injunction. The court of appeals concluded that Zefer was not necessarily aware that Explorica and Gormley relied on confidential information in providing Zefer with the specifications for development of the scraper tool. As a result, the court of appeals had to consider directly the district court's "reasonable expectations" test. The court rejected that test:

> We agree with the district court that lack of authorization may be implicit, rather than explicit. * * * But we think that in general a reasonable expectations test is not the proper gloss on subsection (a)(4) and we reject it [as] neither prescribed by the statute nor prudentially sound.

> Our basis for this view is not, as some have urged, that there is a "presumption" of open access to Internet information. The CFAA, after all, is primarily a statute imposing limits on access and enhancing control by information providers. Instead, we think that the public website provider can easily spell out explicitly what is forbidden and, consonantly, that nothing justifies putting users at the mercy of a highly imprecise, litigation-spawning standard like "reasonable expectations." If EF wants to ban scrapers, let it say so on the webpage or a link clearly marked as containing restrictions.

EF Cultural Travel BV v. Zefer Corp., 318 F.3d 58, 63 (1st Cir. 2003). Because EF's terms of use did not prohibit scrapers, the court of appeals concluded that there was no basis for an independent preliminary injunction against Zefer. The court nevertheless affirmed the preliminary injunction insofar as it prohibited Zefer, like any other third party, from acting on behalf of or in concert with Explorica to use the scraper to access EF's information.

Under the court of appeals' approach in *Zefer Corp.*, are there any limitations on the restrictions a web site owner can impose on use of his or her site? Suppose that EF's terms of use not only barred scraper tools, but also excluded competitors from looking at its site to extract prices to compile a database manually. Would violation of this term of use constitute "unauthorized access" for purposes of the CFAA?

4. Compare the scope of conduct rendered unlawful by the CFAA, as interpreted by the court of appeals, to the scope of conduct reachable under a

trespass cause of action in real space. Is there any analogue to the CFAA for conduct in real space?

5. How should courts interpret the unauthorized access provisions of the CFAA? For perspectives on this issue, see Patricia L. Bellia, *Defending Cyberproperty*, 79 N.Y.U. L. REV. 2164, 2253-2258 (2004) (arguing that CFAA's unauthorized access provisions should cover only breach of technical restrictions on computer systems); Orin S. Kerr, *Cybercrime's Scope: Interpreting "Access" and "Authorization" in Computer Misuse Statutes*, 78 N.Y.U. L. REV. 1596, 1599-1600, 1644-64 (2003) (reaching same conclusion but finding limitation in "without authorization" language rather than "access" language). As currently interpreted, do the provisions provide content providers with an end-run around the limits of copyright law? *See* Christine D. Galbraith, *Access Denied: Improper Use of the Computer Fraud and Abuse Act to Control Information on Publicly Accessible Internet Websites*, 63 MD. L. REV. 320, 324 (2004) (arguing that "by allowing website owners to protect information that is not protectable under copyright law, the CFAA unconstitutionally overrides the delicate balance of rights between authors and the public.").

SECTION D. THE DIGITAL MILLENNIUM COPYRIGHT ACT'S ANTI-CIRCUMVENTION AND ANTI-TRAFFICKING RESTRICTIONS

In Chapter Four, we introduced another controversial statute that arguably allows a copyright holder to link efforts to control information with a claim against unauthorized access to information on a computer system: the Digital Millennium Copyright Act of 1998 (DMCA). More specifically, we considered how the DMCA's "anti-circumvention" and "anti-trafficking" provisions—17 U.S.C. §§ 1201(a)(1)(A), 1201(a)(2), and 1201(b)(1), all excerpted at p. 246—might supplement or supplant existing copyright rules governing when a company can market devices that facilitate infringement.

To what extent does the DMCA act as the same sort of hybrid cause of action as trespass, contract, and the CFAA—allowing a content provider to control access to information by claiming a right to exclude unwanted uses from a computer network? Certainly, the DMCA differs from a statute such as the CFAA or a trespass cause of action in an important way: it specifically requires that a content provider deploy a "technological measure" that "effectively controls access" to the work to trigger's the statute's protection. Understanding how the DMCA relates to other causes of action in this context, therefore, requires us to analyze what exactly it means for a technological measure to "control access" to a copyright-protected work, and what it means for that technological measure to be "effective." How strong must a technological measure be? To the extent that courts protect *weak* technological controls, the cause of action it provides may be closer than expected to others we have considered, for a weak technological control will function in much the same way as a step taken by a content provider that does no more than notify a user of the limitations on use of the system.

The question of what it means for a technological measure to "control access" to a work has arisen most prominently in disputes involving manufacturers that use a technological measure in connection with software installed on a particular product. For example, many printers contain a computer chip with software that activates upon installation of a cartridge; the software tells the printer whether the cartridge is running low on ink. Among other things, such an approach allows the manufacturer to control which "aftermarket" products—such as a replacement ink cartridge—will work with the original product. Does circumvention of a technological measure in this context—to produce a competing aftermarket product, for example—constitute violation of the DMCA?

These sorts of technological mechanisms may become increasingly relevant in the Internet context as the rise of broadband-connected PCs makes it easier for software manufacturers and others to deploy content as a *service* rather than a *product*, requiring constant communication with its source.[d] What does the following case imply for the use of technological mechanisms in that context?

Lexmark International, Inc. v. Static Control Components, Inc.

United States Court of Appeals for the Sixth Circuit, 2004
387 F.3d 522

SUTTON, Circuit Judge.

This copyright dispute involves two computer programs * * * . The first computer program, known as the "Toner Loading Program," calculates toner level in printers manufactured by Lexmark International. The second computer program, known as the "Printer Engine Program," controls various printer functions on Lexmark printers. * * * [T]he Digital Millennium Copyright Act (DMCA), 17 U.S.C. § 1201 *et seq.*, was enacted in 1998 and proscribes the sale of products that may be used to "circumvent a technological measure that effectively controls access to a work" protected by the copyright statute.

[This statute] became relevant to these computer programs when Lexmark began selling discount toner cartridges for its printers that only Lexmark could re-fill and that contained a microchip designed to prevent Lexmark printers from functioning with toner cartridges that Lexmark had not re-filled. In an effort to support the market for competing toner cartridges, Static Control Components (SCC) mimicked Lexmark's computer chip and sold it to companies interested in selling remanufactured toner cartridges.

---

d. For further discussion of this trend, see the excerpt from Jonathan Zittrain, *The Generative Internet*, 119 HARV. L. REV. 1974 (2006), in Chapter Ten.

Lexmark brought this action to enjoin the sale of SCC's computer chips * * * . It claimed that SCC's chip violated the DMCA by circumventing a technological measure designed to control access to the Toner Loading Program. And it claimed that SCC's chip violated the DMCA by circumventing a technological measure designed to control access to the Printer Engine Program.

After an evidentiary hearing, the district court decided that Lexmark had shown a likelihood of success on each claim and entered a preliminary injunction against SCC. As we view Lexmark's prospects for success on each of these claims differently, we vacate the preliminary injunction and remand the case for further proceedings.

I.

A.

Headquartered in Lexington, Kentucky, Lexmark is a leading manufacturer of laser and inkjet printers and has sold printers and toner cartridges for its printers since 1991. * * * Static Control Components * * * makes a wide range of technology products, including microchips that it sells to third-party companies for use in remanufactured toner cartridges.

The Two Computer Programs. * * * The first program at issue is Lexmark's "Toner Loading Program," which measures the amount of toner remaining in the cartridge based on the amount of torque (rotational force) sensed on the toner cartridge wheel. The Toner Loading Program relies upon eight program commands—"add," "sub" (an abbreviation for subtract), "mul" (multiply), "pct" (take a percent), "jump," "if," "load," and "exit"—to execute one of several mathematical equations that convert the torque reading into an approximation of toner level. If the torque is less than a certain threshold value, the program executes one equation to calculate the toner level, and if the torque equals or exceeds that threshold, the program executes a different equation to calculate the toner level. * * *

The second program is Lexmark's "Printer Engine Program." The Printer Engine Program occupies far more memory than the Toner Loading Program and translates into over 20 printed pages of program commands. The program controls a variety of functions on each printer—e.g., paper feed and movement, and printer motor control. Unlike the Toner Loading Program, the Printer Engine Program is located within Lexmark's printers. * * * Neither program is encrypted and each can be read (and copied) directly from its respective memory chip.

Lexmark's Prebate and Non-Prebate Cartridges. Lexmark markets two types of toner cartridges for its laser printers: "Prebate" and "Non-Prebate." Prebate cartridges are sold to business consumers at an up-front discount. In exchange, consumers agree to use the cartridge just once, then return the empty unit to Lexmark; a "shrink-wrap" agreement on the top of each cartridge box spells out these restrictions and confirms that using the cartridge constitutes acceptance of these terms. Non-Prebate cartridges are sold without any discount, are not subject to any restrictive agreements and may be re-filled with toner and reused by the consumer or a third-party remanufacturer.

To ensure that consumers adhere to the Prebate agreement, Lexmark uses an "authentication sequence" that performs a "secret handshake" between each Lexmark printer and a microchip on each Lexmark toner cartridge. Both the printer and the chip employ a publicly available encryption algorithm known as "Secure Hash Algorigthm-1" or "SHA-1," which calculates a "Message Authentication Code" based on data in the microchip's memory. If the code calculated by the microchip matches the code calculated by the printer, the printer functions normally. If the two values do not match, the printer returns an error message and will not operate, blocking consumers from using toner cartridges that Lexmark has not authorized.

SCC's Competing Microchip. SCC sells its own microchip—the "SMARTEK" chip—that permits consumers to satisfy Lexmark's authentication sequence each time it would otherwise be performed, *i.e.,* when the printer is turned on or the printer door is opened and shut. SCC's advertising boasts that its chip breaks Lexmark's "secret code" (the authentication sequence), which "even on the fastest computer available today . . . would take years to run through all of the possible 8-byte combinations to break." SCC sells these chips to third-party cartridge remanufacturers, permitting them to replace Lexmark's chip with the SMARTEK chip on refurbished Prebate cartridges. These recycled cartridges are in turn sold to consumers as a low-cost alternative to new Lexmark toner cartridges.

Each of SCC's SMARTEK chips also contains a copy of Lexmark's Toner Loading Program, which SCC claims is necessary to make its product compatible with Lexmark's printers. The SMARTEK chips thus contain an identical copy of the Toner Loading Program that is appropriate for each Lexmark printer, and SCC acknowledges that it "slavishly copied" the Toner Loading Program "in the exact format and order" found on Lexmark's cartridge chip. A side-by-side comparison of the two data sequences reveals no differences between them.

The parties agree that Lexmark's printers perform a second calculation independent of the authentication sequence. After the authentication sequence concludes, the Printer Engine Program downloads a copy of the Toner Loading Program from the toner cartridge chip onto the printer in order to measure toner levels. Before the printer runs the Toner Loading Program, it performs a "checksum operation," a "commonly used technique" to ensure the "integrity" of the data downloaded from the toner cartridge microchip. Under this operation, the printer compares the result of a calculation performed on the data bytes of the transferred copy of the Toner Loading Program with the "checksum value" located elsewhere on the toner cartridge microchip. If the two values do not match, the printer assumes that the data was corrupted in the program download, displays an error message and ceases functioning. If the two values do match, the printer continues to operate.

The Lawsuit. On December 30, 2002, Lexmark filed a complaint in the United States District Court for the Eastern District of Kentucky seeking to enjoin SCC (on a preliminary and permanent basis) from distributing the

SMARTEK chips. * * * [I]t alleged that SCC violated the DMCA by selling a product that circumvents access controls on the Toner Loading Program [and] that SCC violated the DMCA by selling a product that circumvents access controls on the Printer Engine Program.

* * *

IV.

A.

Enacted in 1998, the DMCA has three liability provisions. The statute first prohibits the circumvention of "a technological measure that effectively controls access to a work protected [by copyright]." 17 U.S.C. § 1201(a)(1). The statute then prohibits selling devices that circumvent access-control measures:

> No person shall manufacture, import, offer to the public, provide, or otherwise traffic in any technology, product, service, device, component, or part thereof, that—
>
>   (A) is primarily designed or produced for the purpose of circumventing a technological measure that effectively controls access to a [copyrighted work];
>
>   (B) has only limited commercially significant purpose or use other than to circumvent a technological measure that effectively controls access to a [copyrighted work]; or
>
>   (C) is marketed by that person or another acting in concert with that person with that person's knowledge for use in circumventing a technological measure that effectively controls access to a [copyrighted work].

Id. § 1201(a)(2). The statute finally bans devices that circumvent "technological measures" protecting "a right" of the copyright owner. *Id.* § 1201(b). The last provision prohibits devices aimed at circumventing technological measures that allow some forms of "access" but restrict other uses of the copyrighted work, such as streaming media, which permits users to view or watch a copyrighted work but prevents them from downloading a permanent copy of the work.

The statute also contains three "reverse engineering" defenses.[e] A

---

e. The "reverse engineering" provision mentioned in the text states as follows:

    (f) Reverse engineering.—(1) Notwithstanding the provisions of subsection (a)(1)(A), a person who has lawfully obtained the right to use a copy of a computer program may circumvent a technological measure that effectively controls access to a particular portion of that program for the sole purpose of identifying and analyzing those elements of the program that are necessary to achieve interoperability of an independently created computer program with other programs, and that have not previously been readily available to the person engaging in the circumvention, to the extent any such acts of identification and analysis do not constitute infringement under this title.

    (2) Notwithstanding the [anti-trafficking prohibitions], a person may develop and employ technological means to circumvent a technological measure, or to circumvent protection afforded by a technological measure, in order to enable the identification and analysis under paragraph (1), or for the purpose of enabling

person may circumvent an access control measure "for the sole purpose of identifying and analyzing those elements of the program that are necessary to achieve interoperability of an independently created computer program with other programs, and that have not previously been readily available to [that person]." 17 U.S.C. § 1201(f)(1). A person "may develop and employ technological means" that are "necessary" to enable interoperability. *Id.* § 1201(f)(2). And these technological means may be made available to others "solely for the purpose of enabling interoperability of an independently created computer program with other programs." *Id.* § 1201(f)(3). All three defenses apply only when traditional copyright infringement does not occur and only when the challenged actions (in the case of the third provision) would not violate other "applicable law[s]." *Id.*

In filing its complaint and in its motion for a preliminary injunction, Lexmark invoked the second liability provision—the ban on distributing devices that circumvent access-control measures placed on copyrighted works. *See id.* § 1201(a)(2). According to Lexmark, SCC's SMARTEK chip is a "device" marketed and sold by SCC that "circumvents" Lexmark's "technological measure" (the SHA-1 authentication sequence, not the checksum operation), which "effectively controls access" to its copyrighted works (the Toner Loading Program and Printer Engine Program). Lexmark claims that the SMARTEK chip meets all three tests for liability under § 1201(a)(2): (1) the chip "is primarily designed or produced for the purpose of circumventing" Lexmark's authentication sequence, 17 U.S.C. § 1201(a)(2)(A); (2) the chip "has only limited commercially significant purpose or use other than to circumvent" the authentication sequence, *id.* § 1201(a)(2)(B); and (3) SCC "market[s]" the chip "for use in circumventing" the authentication sequence, *id.* § 1201(a)(2)(C). The district court agreed and concluded that Lexmark had shown a likelihood of success under all three provisions.

B.

We initially consider Lexmark's DMCA claim concerning the Printer Engine Program, which (the parties agree) is protected by the general copyright statute. In deciding that Lexmark's authentication sequence "effectively controls access to a work protected under [the copyright provisions]," the district court relied on a definition in the DMCA saying that a measure "effectively controls access to a work" if, "in the ordinary

---

interoperability of an independently created computer program with other programs, if such means are necessary to achieve such interoperability, to the extent that doing so does not constitute infringement under this title.

(3) The information acquired through the acts permitted under paragraph (1), and the means permitted under paragraph (2), may be made available to others if the person referred to in paragraph (1) or (2), as the case may be, provides such information or means solely for the purpose of enabling interoperability of an independently created computer program with other programs, and to the extent that doing so does not constitute infringement under this title or violate applicable law other than this section.

(4) For purposes of this subsection, the term "interoperability" means the ability of computer programs to exchange information, and of such programs mutually to use the information which has been exchanged. * * *

course of operation," it "requires the application of information, or a process or treatment, with the authority of the copyright owner, to gain access to the work." 17 U.S.C. § 1201(a)(3). Because Congress did not explain what it means to "gain access to the work," the district court relied on the "ordinary, customary meaning" of "access": "the ability to enter, to obtain, or to make use of," (quoting *Merriam-Webster's Collegiate Dictionary* 6 (10th ed. 1999)). Based on this definition, the court concluded that "Lexmark's authentication sequence effectively 'controls access' to the Printer Engine Program because it controls the consumer's ability to *make use of* these programs."

We disagree. It is not Lexmark's authentication sequence that "controls access" to the Printer Engine Program. It is the purchase of a Lexmark printer that allows "access" to the program. Anyone who buys a Lexmark printer may read the literal code of the Printer Engine Program directly from the printer memory, with or without the benefit of the authentication sequence, and the data from the program may be translated into readable source code after which copies may be freely distributed. No security device, in other words, protects access to the Printer Engine Program Code and no security device accordingly must be circumvented to obtain access to that program code.

The authentication sequence, it is true, may well block one form of "access"— the "ability to . . . make use of" the Printer Engine Program by preventing the printer from functioning. But it does not block another relevant form of "access"—the "ability to [ ] obtain" a copy of the work or to "make use of" the literal elements of the program (its code). Because the statute refers to "control[ling] access to a work protected under this title," it does not naturally apply when the "work protected under this title" is otherwise accessible. Just as one would not say that a lock on the back door of a house "controls access" to a house whose front door does not contain a lock and just as one would not say that a lock on any door of a house "controls access" to the house after its purchaser receives the key to the lock, it does not make sense to say that this provision of the DMCA applies to otherwise-readily-accessible copyrighted works. Add to this the fact that the DMCA not only requires the technological measure to "control[ ] access" but also requires the measure to control that access "effectively," 17 U.S.C. § 1201(a)(2), and it seems clear that this provision does not naturally extend to a technological measure that restricts one form of access but leaves another route wide open. *See also id.* § 1201(a)(3) (technological measure must "*require* [ ] the application of information, or a process or a treatment . . . to gain access to the work") (emphasis added).

Nor are we aware of any cases that have applied this provision of the DMCA to a situation where the access-control measure left the literal code or text of the computer program or data freely readable. * * *

Lexmark defends the district court's contrary ruling on several grounds. Lexmark [argues] that several cases have embraced a "to make use of" definition of "access" in applying the DMCA. While Lexmark is partially correct, these cases (and others as well) ultimately illustrate the liability line that the statute draws and in the end explain why access to the Printer Engine Program is not covered.

In the essential setting where the DMCA applies, the copyright protection operates on two planes: in the literal code governing the work and in the visual or audio manifestation generated by the code's execution. For example, the encoded data on CDs translates into music and on DVDs into motion pictures, while the program commands in software for video games or computers translate into some other visual and audio manifestation. In the cases upon which Lexmark relies, restricting "use" of the work means restricting consumers from making use of the copyrightable expression in the work. As shown above, the DMCA applies in these settings when the product manufacturer prevents all access to the copyrightable material and the alleged infringer responds by marketing a device that circumvents the technological measure designed to guard access to the copyrightable material.

The copyrightable expression in the Printer Engine Program, by contrast, operates on only one plane: in the literal elements of the program, its source and object code. Unlike the code underlying video games or DVDs, "using" or executing the Printer Engine Program does not in turn create any protected expression. Instead, the program's output is purely functional: the Printer Engine Program [controls a number of operations in the Lexmark printer]. And unlike the code underlying video games or DVDs, no encryption or other technological measure prevents access to the Printer Engine Program. Presumably, it is precisely because the Printer Engine Program is not a conduit to protectable expression that explains why Lexmark (or any other printer company) would not block access to the computer software that makes the printer work. Because Lexmark's authentication sequence does not restrict access to this literal code, the DMCA does not apply.

Lexmark next argues that access-control measures may "effectively control access" to a copyrighted work within the meaning of the DMCA even though the measure may be evaded by an "'enterprising end-user.'" Doubtless, Lexmark is correct that a precondition for DMCA liability is not the creation of an impervious shield to the copyrighted work. Otherwise, the DMCA would apply only when it is not needed.

But our reasoning does not turn on the *degree* to which a measure controls access to a work. It turns on the textual requirement that the challenged circumvention device must indeed circumvent *something,* which did not happen with the Printer Engine Program. Because Lexmark has not directed any of its security efforts, through its authentication sequence or otherwise, to ensuring that its copyrighted work (the Printer Engine Program) cannot be read and copied, it cannot lay claim to having put in place a "technological measure that effectively controls access to a work protected under [the copyright statute]." 17 U.S.C. § 1201(a)(2)(B).

Nor can Lexmark tenably claim that this reading of the statute fails to respect Congress's purpose in enacting it. Congress enacted the DMCA to implement the Copyright Treaty of the World Intellectual Property Organization, and in doing so expressed concerns about the threat of "massive piracy" of digital works due to "the ease with which [they] can be copied and distributed worldwide virtually instantaneously." S. REP. NO. 105-190, at 8 (1998). As Congress saw it, "copyrighted works will most likely be encrypted and made available to consumers once payment is made for access to a copy of the work. [People] will try to profit from the works of others by decoding the encrypted codes protecting copyrighted works, or engaging in the business of providing devices or services to enable others to do so." H.R. REP. NO. 105-551, pt. 1, at 10. Backing with legal sanctions "the efforts of copyright owners to protect their works from piracy behind digital walls such as encryption codes or password protections," *Universal City Studios v. Corley,* 273 F.3d 429, 435 (2d Cir. 2001), Congress noted, would encourage copyright owners to make digital works more readily available.

Nowhere in its deliberations over the DMCA did Congress express an interest in creating liability for the circumvention of technological measures designed to prevent consumers from using consumer goods while leaving the copyrightable content of a work unprotected. In fact, Congress added the interoperability provision in part to ensure that the DMCA would not diminish the benefit to consumers of interoperable devices in the consumer electronics environment."

C.

In view of our conclusion regarding the Printer Engine Program, we can dispose quickly of Lexmark's DMCA claim regarding the Toner Loading Program. The SCC chip does not provide "access" to the Toner Loading Program but replaces the program. And to the extent a copy of the Toner Loading Program appears on the Printer Engine Program, Lexmark fails to overcome the same problem that undermines its DMCA claim with respect to the Printer Engine Program: Namely, it is not the SCC chip that permits access to the Printer Engine Program but the consumer's purchase of the printer. * * *

D.

The district court also rejected SCC's interoperability defense—that its replication of the Toner Loading Program data is a "technological means" that SCC may make "available to others" "solely for the purpose of enabling interoperability of an independently created computer program with other programs." 17 U.S.C. § 1201(f)(3). In rejecting this defense, the district court said that "SCC's SMARTEK microchips cannot be considered independently created computer programs. [They] serve no legitimate purpose other than to circumvent Lexmark's authentication sequence and . . . cannot qualify as independently created when they contain exact copies of Lexmark's Toner Loading Programs."

Because the issue could become relevant at the permanent injunction stage of this dispute, we briefly explain our disagreement with this conclusion. In particular, the court did not explain why it rejected SCC's testimony that the SMARTEK chips do contain other functional computer programs beyond the copied Toner Loading Program data. * * * Lexmark contends that [there is no] "credible evidence" that "independently created computer programs" exist on the SMARTEK chip. Yet Lexmark bears the burden of establishing its likelihood of success on the merits of the DMCA claims. Because Lexmark has offered no reason why the testimony of SCC's experts is not "credible evidence" on this point and has offered no evidence of its own to dispute or even overcome the statements of [SCC's witnesses], SCC also has satisfied the "independently created computer programs" requirement and may benefit from the interoperability defense, at least in the preliminary injunction context.

Lexmark argues alternatively that if independently created programs do exist, (1) they must have existed prior to the "reverse engineering" of Lexmark's Toner Loading Program, and (2) the technological means must be "necessary or absolutely needed" to enable interoperability of SCC's SMARTEK chip with Lexmark's Printer Engine Program. As to the first argument, nothing in the statute precludes simultaneous creation of an interoperability device and another computer program; it just must be "independently" created. As to the second argument, the statute is silent about the degree to which the "technological means" must be necessary, if indeed they must be necessary at all, for interoperability. The Toner Loading Program copy satisfies any such requirement, however, because without that program the checksum operation precludes operation of the printer (and, accordingly, operation of the Printer Engine Program), unless the checksum value located elsewhere on the chip is modified—which appears to be a computational impossibility without the contextual information that Lexmark does not disclose.

Notes and Questions

1. How does the court define what it means to "control access" to a copyright-protected work? Do you agree with its approach?

2. How does the court distinguish use of the programs at issue in this case from the use of video games or movies on DVDs? Is its distinction persuasive?

3. One key to the court's holding is that the Lexmark programs on the toner cartridge and in the printer itself are not encrypted; the authentication measure simply allows the cartridge to communicate with the printer. In other words, the authentication sequence controls access to the functional programs in the toner and on the computer, not to ordinary content. Does the court's focus on encryption provide an adequate limiting principle? Isn't it possible for Lexmark to encrypt is programs and thereby overcome the limitation in the court's holding?

4. Could the court simply have said that the DMCA does not apply to aftermarket products? What would be the appropriate textual hook for such an argument? *See* Anti-Circumvention Rulemaking Hearing 44-56, at http://www.copyright.gov/1201/2003/hearings/transcript-may9.pdf (testimony of Professor Jane Ginsburg) (arguing that anti-circumvention provision does not cover "circumvention of a technological measure that controls access to a work not protected under [the Copyright] title. And if we're talking about ball point pen cartridges, printer cartridges, garage doors and so forth, we're talking about works not protected under this title.").

In *Chamberlain Group, Inc. v. Skylink Technologies*, 381 F.3d 1178 (Fed. Cir. 2004), the court reached a similar result to the *Lexmark* court, holding that the DMCA's antitrafficking provisions did not prohibit the sale of a universal garage door opener that worked with models installed by a rival company. Rather than focusing on the "work" that is the subject of the access control (in the *Lexmark* case, the programs located in the printer and in the toner cartrdige), the *Chamberlain* court addressed the *purpose* of the access that the technological measure controls. More specifically, it required a connection between the access control and the prevention of infringement under the Copyright Act. *See id.* at 1197. If the use that the access control forestalls is an infringing one, then the DMCA protects it; if not, the DMCA does not apply.

Is this approach persuasive?

5. Does either the *Lexmark* approach or the *Chamberlain* approach adequately guard against content providers' use of the DMCA to achieve a level of protection that copyright law does not provide? Under conventional accounts of the purpose of copyright, the copyright law is thought to grant the author a limited monopoly in his or her creation while preserving certain rights—such as fair use and the right to exploit the work once it is in the public domain—for the public. To what extent does the DMCA upset this balance by allowing copyright holders to use technological protection measures to "enclose" copyrighted works and thereby divest the public of its rights? *See* Yochai Benkler, *Free as the Air to Common Use: First Amendment Constraints on Enclosure of the Public Domain*, 74 N.Y.U. L. REV. 354 (1999). For an economic analysis of the effects of the DMCA's anti-circumvention and anti-trafficking provisions, and an argument that a narrower rule would achieve the benefits Congress intended for copyright owners while preserving fair uses, see Pamela Samuelson & Suzanne Scotchmer, *The Law and Economics of Reverse Engineering*, 111 YALE L.J. 1575 (2002).

6. Do *Lexmark* and *Chamberlain* signal that courts can find limiting principles in the DMCA when dealing with content, as opposed to durable goods such as toner cartridges and garage door openers? How would the next case fare under either the *Lexmark* approach or the *Chamberlain* approach?

Davidson & Assoc. v. Jung

United States Court of Appeals for the Eighth Circuit, 2005
422 F.3d 630

SMITH, Circuit Judge.

Davidson & Associates, Inc. d/b/a Blizzard Entertainment ("Blizzard") and Vivendi Universal Games, Inc. ("Vivendi"), owner of copyrights in computer game software and online gaming service software sued Ross Combs ("Combs"), Rob Crittenden ("Crittenden"), Jim Jung ("Jung"), and Internet Gateway, Inc. ("Internet Gateway") (collectively referred to as "Appellants"), for breach of contract, circumvention of copyright protection system, and trafficking in circumvention technology. * * * The district court granted summary judgment in favor of Blizzard and Vivendi. * * * We affirm.

I. *Background*

A. *Factual Background*

Blizzard, a California corporation and subsidiary of Vivendi, creates and sells software games for personal computers. This appeal concerns the particular Blizzard games "StarCraft," "StarCraft: Brood War," "WarCraft II: Battle.net Edition," "Diablo," and "Diablo II: Lord of Destruction." Combs and Crittenden are computer programmers, Jung is a systems administrator, and Internet Gateway is an Internet service provider based in St. Peters, Missouri. Jung is also the president, co-owner, and day-to-day operator of Internet Gateway.

In January 1997, Blizzard officially launched "Battle.net," a 24-hour online-gaming service available exclusively to purchasers of its computer games. The Battle.net service has nearly 12 million active users who spend more that 2.1 million hours online per day. Blizzard holds valid copyright registrations covering Battle.net and each of its computer games at issue in this litigation. Battle.net is a free service that allows owners of Blizzard games to play each other on their personal computers via the Internet. Battle.net mode allows users to create and join multi-player games that can be accessed across the Internet, to chat with other potential players, to record wins and losses and save advancements in an individual password-protected game account, and to participate with others in tournament play featuring elimination rounds. Players can set up private "chat channels" and private games on Battle.net to allow players to determine with whom they wish to interact online. These Battle.net mode features are only accessible from within the games.

Like most computer software, Blizzard's games can be easily copied and distributed over the Internet. Blizzard has taken steps to avoid piracy by designing Battle.net to restrict access and use of the Battle.net mode feature of the game. Each time a user logs onto Battle.net, a Battle.net server examines the user's version of the game software. If a Blizzard game does not have the latest software upgrades and fixes, the Battle.net service updates the customer's game before allowing the game to play in Battle.net mode.

With the exception of "Diablo," each authorized version of a Blizzard game comes with a "CD Key." A CD Key is a unique sequence of alphanumeric characters printed on a sticker attached to the case in which the CD-ROM was packaged. To log on to Battle.net and access Battle.net mode, the game initiates an authentication sequence or "secret handshake" between the game and the Battle.net server. In order to play the Blizzard game contained on a CD-ROM, a user must first install the game onto a computer and agree to the terms of the End User License Agreement ("EULA") and Terms of Use ("TOU"), both of which prohibit reverse engineering. At the end of both the EULA and TOU, Blizzard includes a button with the text, "I Agree" in it, which the user must select in order to proceed with the installation. Users are also required to enter a name and the CD Key during installation of Battle.net and Blizzard games.

The users of Battle.net have occasionally experienced difficulties with the service. To address their frustrations with Battle.net, a group of non-profit volunteer game hobbyists, programmers, and other individuals formed a group called the "bnetd project." The bnetd project developed a program called the "bnetd.org server" that emulates the Battle.net service and permits users to play online without use of Battle.net. The bnetd project is a volunteer effort and the project has always offered the bnetd program for free to anyone. Combs, Crittenden, and Jung were lead developers for the bnetd project.

The bnetd project was organized and managed over the Internet through a website, www.bnetd.org, that was made available to the public through equipment provided by Internet Gateway. The bnetd.org emulator provides a server that allows gamers unable or unwilling to connect to Battle.net to experience the multi-player features of Blizzard's games. The bnetd.org emulator also provides matchmaking services for users of Blizzard games who want to play those games in a multi-player environment without using Battle.net. Bnetd.org attempted to mirror all of the user-visible features of Battle.net, including online discussion forums and information about the bnetd project, as well as access to the program's computer code for others to copy and modify.

To serve as a functional alternative to Battle.net, bnetd.org had to be compatible with Blizzard's software. In particular, compatibility required that bnetd.org speak the same protocol language that the Battle.net speaks. By speaking the same protocol language, the bnetd programs would be interoperable with Blizzard games. Once game play starts, a user perceives no difference between Battle.net and the bnetd.org.

By necessity, Appellants used reverse engineering to learn Blizzard's protocol language and to ensure that bnetd.org worked with Blizzard games. Combs used reverse engineering to develop the bnetd.org server, including a program called "tcpdump" to log communications between Blizzard games and the Battle.net server. Crittenden used reverse engineering to develop the bnetd.org server, including using a program called "Nextray." Crittenden also used a program called "ripper" to take Blizzard client files that were compiled together in one file and break them into their component parts. Crittenden used the ripper program to determine how Blizzard games displayed ad banners so that bnetd.org could display ad banners to users in the format that Blizzard uses on the Battle.net service. Combs tried to disassemble a Blizzard game to figure out how to implement a feature that allowed bnetd.org to protect the password that a user enters when creating an account in Battle.net mode. Crittenden made an unauthorized copy of a Blizzard game in order to test the interoperability of the bnetd.org server with multiple games.

Blizzard designed its games to connect only to Battle.net servers. To enable a Blizzard game to connect to a bnetd.org server instead of a Battle.net server, bnetd had to modify the computer file that contained the Internet address of the Battle.net servers. As part of the bnetd project, Combs participated in the development of a utility program called "BNS" to allow Blizzard games to connect to bnetd.org servers more easily. Through the BNS program, the game sends the bnetd.org server information about its CD Key. An individual can thus play one of the Blizzard games at issue over the Internet via bnetd.org rather than

Battle.net. According to Blizzard, the EULAs and TOUs prohibit this activity.

Bnetd.org has important operational differences from Battle.net. When bnetd.org receives the CD Key information, unlike Battle.net, it does not determine whether the CD Key is valid or currently in use by another player. The bnetd.org server computer code always sends the game an "okay" reply regardless of whether the CD Key is valid or currently in use by another player. The bnetd .org emulator always allows the Blizzard games to access Battle.net mode features even if the user does not have a valid or unique CD Key. Blizzard did not disclose the methods it used to generate CD Keys or to confirm the validity of CD Keys.

Combs, Crittenden, and Jung used Blizzard games to log into bnetd .org. Crittenden was aware that unauthorized versions of Blizzard games were played on bnetd.org. Jung knew that the bnetd.org emulator did not require that Blizzard games provide valid CD Keys. Combs suspected that the bnetd.org emulator would not know the difference between a real game and a pirated game. Combs and Crittenden either sent portions of the bnetd software to Jung to place on the www.bnetd.org website for download or put the software on the website themselves. Combs made the bnetd software available on his website located at www.cs.nmsu.edu /~rcombs/sc/. Also distributed was the BNS utility program which allowed Blizzard games to connect to bnetd.org. The source code was made available as an "open source" application, meaning that others were free to copy the source code and distribute it with or without modifications. Because the bnetd.org source code was freely available, others developed additional Battle.net emulators based on the bnetd.org source code. Binary versions of the bnetd.org were distributed which made it more convenient for users to set up and access the emulator program. Internet Gateway has donated space on its computers for use by the bnetd project. Internet Gateway also hosted a bnetd.org server that anyone on the Internet could access and use to play Blizzard games in Battle.net mode. * * *

II. *Discussion*

A. *Preemption*

* * * Conflict preemption applies when there is no express preemption but (1) it is impossible to comply with both the state and federal law or when (2) the state law stands as an obstacle to the accomplishment and execution of the full purposes and objectives of Congress. Appellants, relying upon *Vault v. Quaid Software Ltd.*, 847 F.2d 255, 268-70 (5th Cir. 1988), argue that the federal Copyright Act preempts Blizzard's state law breach-of-contract claims. We disagree.

In *Vault*, plaintiffs challenged the Louisiana Software License Enforcement Act, which permitted a software producer to impose contractual terms upon software purchasers provided that the terms were set forth in a license agreement comporting with the statute. *Id.* at 268. "Enforceable terms [under the Louisiana statute] include the prohibition of: (1) any copying of the program for any purpose; and (2) modifying and/or adapting the program in any way, including adaptation by reverse engineering, decompilation or disassembly." *Id.* at 269 (citation omitted).

The Louisiana statute defined reverse engineering, decompiling or disassembling as "any process by which computer software is converted from one form to another form which is more readily understandable to human beings, including without limitation any decoding or decrypting of any computer program which has been encoded or encrypted in any manner." *Id.* (citation omitted). The Fifth Circuit held that the Louisiana statute conflicted with the rights of computer program owners under the Copyright Act, specifically 17 U.S.C. § 117, which permits a computer program owner to make an adaptation of a program provided that the adaption is either created as an essential step in the utilization of the computer program in conjunction with a machine or is for archival purpose only. *Id.* at 270.

Unlike in *Vault,* the state law at issue here neither conflicts with the interoperability exception under 17 U.S.C. § 1201(f) nor restricts rights given under federal law. Appellants contractually accepted restrictions on their ability to reverse engineer by their agreement to the terms of the TOU and EULA. "[P]rivate parties are free to contractually forego the limited ability to reverse engineer a software product under the exemptions of the Copyright Act[,]" *Bowers v. Baystate Techs, Inc.,* 320 F.3d 1317, 1325-26 (Fed. Cir. 2003), and "a state can permit parties to contract away a fair use defense or to agree not to engage in uses of copyrighted material that are permitted by the copyright law if the contract is freely negotiated." *Id.* at 1337 (Dyk, J., dissenting). While *Bowers* [involved] express preemption * * * rather than conflict preemption, their reasoning applies here with equal force. By signing the TOUs and EULAs, Appellants expressly relinquished their rights to reverse engineer. Summary judgment on this issue was properly granted in favor of Blizzard and Vivendi.

B.   *DMCA Claims and Interoperability Exception*

* * * The DMCA contains three provisions targeted at the circumvention of technological protections. The first is § 1201(a)(1), the anti-circumvention provision. This provision prohibits a person from "circumvent[ing] a technological measure that effectively controls access to a work protected under [Title 17, governing copyright]." The Librarian of Congress is required to promulgate regulations every three years exempting from this subsection individuals who would otherwise be "adversely affected" in "their ability to make noninfringing uses." 17 U.S.C. § 1201(a)(1)(B)-(E). Section 1201(a)(1) differs from the second and third provisions in that it targets the use of a circumvention technology, not the trafficking in such a technology.

The second and third provisions are §§ 1201(a)(2) and 1201(b)(1), the "anti-trafficking provisions." These sections are similar, except that § 1201(a)(2) covers those who traffic in technology that can circumvent "a technological measure *that effectively controls access* to a work protected under" Title 17, whereas § 1201(b)(1) covers those who traffic in technology that can circumvent "protection afforded by a technological measure *that effectively protects a right of a copyright owner* under" Title 17. 17 U.S.C. §§ 1201(a)(2) & (b)(1). (Emphases added.) In other words, although both sections prohibit trafficking in a circumvention technology, the focus of

§ 1201(a)(2) is circumvention of technologies designed to *prevent access* to a work, and the focus of § 1201(b)(1) is circumvention of technologies designed to *permit access* to a work but *prevent copying* of the work or some other act that infringes a copyright. *See* S. REP. NO. 105-190, at 11-12 (1998).

The district court determined that Appellants's reverse engineering violated § 1201(a)(1) as well as § 1201(a)(2). We agree.

1. *Anti-Circumvention Violation*

Section 1201(a)(1) provides that "[n]o person shall circumvent a technological measure that effectively controls access to a work protected under this title." The term "circumvent a technological measure" "means to descramble a scrambled work, to decrypt an encrypted work, or otherwise to avoid, bypass, remove, deactivate, or impair a technological measure, without the authority of the copyright owner." 17 U.S.C. § 1201(3)(A). "Effectively controls access to a work" means that the measure, in the ordinary course of its operation, requires the application of information, or a process or a treatment, with the authority of the copyright owner, to gain access to the work. 17 U.S.C. § 1201(3)(B).

Blizzard games, through Battle.net, employed a technological measure, a software "secret handshake" (CD key), to control access to its copyrighted games. The bnetd.org emulator developed by Appellants allowed the Blizzard game to access Battle.net mode features without a valid or unique CD key. As a result, unauthorized copies of the Blizzard games were played on bnetd.org servers. After Appellants distributed the bnetd program, others developed additional Battle.net emulators based on the bnetd source code. Appellants's distribution of binary versions of the bnetd program facilitated set up and access to the emulator program.

Relying on *Lexmark Int'l, Inc. v. Static Control Components, Inc.,* 387 F.3d 522 (6th Cir. 2004), Appellants argue that Battle.net mode is a strictly functional process that lacks creative expression, and thus DMCA protections do not apply. *Lexmark Int'l, Inc.,* concerned two computer programs: the first was known as the "Toner Loading Program" and the second was known as the "Printer Engine Program." DMCA anti-circumvention claims were brought after Lexmark's authentication sequence contained in its printer cartridges were allegedly circumvented. The district court in that case held that Lexmark's authentication sequence effectively controlled access to the programs because it controlled the consumers' ability to make use of those programs. The Sixth Circuit reversed, holding that it was not Lexmark's authentication sequence that controlled access to the programs, but the purchase of a Lexmark printer that allowed access to the program. "No security device, in other words, protects access to the . . . program and no security device accordingly must be circumvented to obtain access to that program code." *Id.* at 547.

Here, Battle.net's control measure was not freely available. Appellants could not have obtained a copy of Battle.net or made use of the literal elements of Battle.net mode without acts of reverse engineering, which allowed for a circumvention of Battle.net and Battle.net mode. Unlike in *Lexmark Int'l, Inc.,* Battle.net mode codes were not accessible by simply purchasing a Blizzard game or logging onto Battle.net., nor could data from the program be translated into readable source code after which copies were freely available without some type of circumvention. Appellants misread *Lexmark Int'l, Inc.* and we are unpersuaded that summary judgment on the anti-circumvention violations was improperly granted in favor of Blizzard and Vivendi.

2. *Anti-trafficking Violations*

Section 1201(a)(2) provides that:

> No person shall manufacture, import, offer to the public, provide, or otherwise traffic in any technology, product, service, device, component, or part thereof, that . . . is primarily designed or produced for the purpose of circumventing a technological measure that effectively controls access to a work protected under this title; . . . has only limited commercially significant purpose or use other than to circumvent a technological measure that effectively controls access to a work protected under this title; *or* . . . is marketed by that person or another acting in concert with that person with that person's knowledge for use in circumventing a technological measure that effectively controls access to a work protected under this title.

17 U.S.C. § 1201(a)(2). The bnetd.org emulator had limited commercial purpose because its sole purpose was to avoid the limitations of Battle.net. There is no genuine issue of material fact that Appellants designed and developed the bnetd.org server and emulator for the purpose of circumventing Blizzard's technological measures controlling access to Battle.net and the Blizzard games. Summary judgment was properly granted in favor of Blizzard and Vivendi on the anti-trafficking violations.

3. *Interoperability Exception*

The DMCA contains several exceptions, including one for individuals using circumvention technology "for the sole purpose" of trying to achieve "interoperability" of computer programs through reverse engineering. *See* 17 U.S.C. § 1201(f). Subsection (f)(4) defines interoperability as "the ability of computer programs to exchange information, and such programs mutually to use the information which has been exchanged." 17 U.S.C. § 1201(f)(4). Appellants argue that the interoperability exception applies to any alleged infringement of Blizzard games and Battle.net. To successfully prove the interoperability defense under § 1201(f), Appellants must show: (1) they lawfully obtained the right to use a copy of a computer program; (2) the information gathered as a result of the reverse engineering was not previously readily available to the person engaging in the circumvention; (3) the sole purpose of the reverse engineering was to identify and analyze those elements of the program that were necessary to achieve interoperability of an independently created computer program with other programs; and (4) the alleged circumvention did not constitute infringement. *See* 17 U.S.C. § 1201(f).

Appellants's circumvention in this case constitutes infringement. As detailed earlier, Blizzard's secret handshake between Blizzard games and Battle.net effectively controlled access to Battle.net mode within its games. The purpose of the bnetd.org project was to provide matchmaking services for users of Blizzard games who wanted to play in a multi-player environment without using Battle.net. The bnetd.org emulator enabled users of Blizzard games to access Battle.net mode features without a valid or unique CD key to enter Battle.net. The bnetd.org emulator did not determine whether the CD key was valid or currently in use by another player. As a result, unauthorized copies of the Blizzard games were freely played on bnetd.org servers. Appellants failed to establish a genuine issue of material fact as to the applicability of the interoperability exception. The district court properly granted summary judgment in favor of Blizzard and Vivendi on the interoperability exception.

Notes and Questions

1. Assume that the defendants lawfully obtained the copies of the Blizzard and Battle.net programs that they reverse engineered. Why would the conduct not fall within the reverse engineering exception? Even if the bdnet.org server does not block the participation of users whose copies of the software are infringing, does that make the defendants' use infringing as well?

2. On the other hand, is the defendants' conduct in this case different from the defendants' conduct in *Real Networks, Inc. v. Streambox, Inc.*, 2000 WL 127311 (W.D. Wash. 2000), or *Universal City Studios v. Corley*, 273 F.3d 429 (2d Cir. 2001), discussed in Chapter Four? In *Real Networks*, Streambox bypassed controls that limited access to and copying of streaming video hosted on Real Networks' servers. In *Corley*, the defendants made available the means for users to bypass encryption on and view and make copies of DVDs. The bdnet.org server allows games to be played without authentication from the Battle.net server. Even if all copies of the game were non-infringing, isn't the bdnet.org server allowing users to circumvent an access control that would otherwise prevent the games to be played—just as in *Corley* the defendants made available technology that allowed DVDs to be viewed on noncompliant DVD players, and just as Streambox allowed access to content protected by a technological measure?

3. Should the court instead have looked to whether the program running on the bdnet.org server infringed the Battle.net program? Would a reverse-engineering exception make sense if it didn't take into account whether the resulting program is infringing?

Chapter Ten

PROBLEMS OF CULTURAL CHANGE

INTRODUCTION

Legal rules never exist in a vacuum. Rather, law responds to cultural change. While that is true in every legal field, it is perhaps easier to see with regard to online interaction. Indeed, if one simply read the federal reporters chronologically, cover to cover, since 1995, it would be obvious that a major cultural shift had occurred. Prior to 1995, one would find only a handful of cases with the word "Internet" in them; then, decisions began to appear (complete with lengthy explanations of the technology underlying the Internet and the world wide web); and now, legal decisions involving online interaction are commonplace (although as we have seen in previous chapters, many of the legal issues remain difficult to solve). Indeed, as one commentator has pointed out, "[t]he idea that we are moving toward an 'information age' * * * has now passed from iconoclasm through orthodoxy to cliché."[a]

Significantly, although law *responds* to cultural change, law also helps *produce* cultural change. Indeed, law is not simply an instrument for dispensing justice, but a constitutive societal force that shapes social relations, constructs meaning, and defines categories of behavior. Thus, law cannot be distinguished from the rest of social life; rather, "law permeates social life, and its influence is not adequately grasped by treating law as a type of external, normative influence on independent, ongoing activities."[b] Legal categories tend to define the parameters for social interaction and construct the categories we use unconsciously as we go about our daily lives. "Law talk" gets dispersed throughout the culture and becomes part of the

---

a. JAMES BOYLE, SHAMANS, SOFTWARE, AND SPLEENS: LAW AND THE CONSTRUCTION OF THE INFORMATION SOCIETY 1 (1996).

b. Bryant G. Garth & Austin Sarat, *Justice and Power in Law and Society Research: On the Contested Careers of Core Concepts, in* JUSTICE AND POWER IN SOCIOLEGAL STUDIES 1, 3 (Bryant G. Garth & Austin Sarat eds., 1997).

currency of our personal and professional interactions. Thus, "[w]e experience the rule of law not just when the policeman stops us on the street or when we consult a lawyer on how to create a corporation. The rule of law shapes our experience of meaning everywhere and at all times. It is not alone in shaping meaning, but it is rarely absent."[c] In short, law symbolically reflects and reinforces deep cultural attitudes, fears, or beliefs.

In this last chapter of the book, therefore, we take a step back and try to understand the many complex cultural changes brought about by the rise of online interaction as well as the role law plays in shaping our understanding of those changes. This broader view of law can provide a distinctive framework for recontextualizing established legal doctrine or reconceiving intractable policy debates and accordingly is essential for lawyers and policymakers who are fashioning rules that will shape social life amidst cultural change.

SECTION A. CYBERSPACE AS METAPHOR

The Internet, perhaps because it has seemed to herald a new world order of interconnection and decentralization, has provided a potent series of metaphors for understanding life in the information age. Even the word "cyberspace" itself conjures up a sense of being in some place that both is and is not the "real" world. In addition, cyberspace has become a *site* for metaphors, and discussions of the Internet are frequently permeated with references to "highways," "frontiers," "global conversations," and the like.

The metaphors we project onto cyberspace have powerful consequences for the way we formulate public policy regarding online interaction. For example, if the Internet is seen as the embodiment of postmodern theory, then we are apt to view the idea of distinct authors with their own intellectual property rights as outmoded. Similarly, if cyberspace is viewed as the newest iteration of the American frontier mythology, then the idea of "taming" it with legal regulation might seem anathema. Finally, if the Internet is conceptualized as the repository of humanity's collective wisdom, captured in a space that is nether dead nor alive, legal regulation must contend with an almost spiritual sense of the sanctity of the dialogue taking place over the interconnected wires.

The following three readings explore some of these metaphorical formulations. As you read each, think first about the degree to which you think the metaphor is apt and second about how the metaphor chosen might affect one's view of online interaction and the proper regulatory framework for such interaction.

---

c. Paul Kahn, The Cultural Study of Law: Reconstructing Legal Scholarship 124 (1999).

Sherry Turkle, *Life on the Screen*

Touchstone Books, 1994

In a surprising and counter-intuitive twist, * * * the mechanical engines of computers have been grounding the radically nonmechanical philosophy of postmodernism. The online world of the Internet is not the only instance of evocative computer objects and experiences bringing postmodernism down to earth. One of my students at MIT dropped out of a course I teach on social theory, complaining that the writings of the literary theorist Jacques Derrida were simply beyond him. He found that Derrida's dense prose and far-flung philosophical allusions were incomprehensible. The following semester I ran into the student in an MIT cafeteria. "Maybe I wouldn't have to drop out now," he told me. In the past month, with his roommate's acquisition of new software for his Macintosh computer, my student had found his own key to Derrida. That software was a type of hypertext, which allows a computer user to create links between related texts, songs, photographs, and video, as well as to travel along the links made by others. Derrida emphasized that writing is constructed by the audience as well as by the author and that what is absent from the text is as significant as what is present. The student made the following connection:

> Derrida was saying that the messages of the great books are no more written in stone than are the links of a hypertext. I look at my roommate's hypertext stacks and I am able to trace the connections he made and the peculiarities of how he links things together. . . . And the things he might have linked but didn't. The traditional texts are like [elements in] the stack. Meanings are arbitrary, as arbitrary as the links in a stack.

"The cards in a hypertext stack," he concluded, "get their meaning in relation to each other. It's like Derrida. The links have a reason but there is no final truth behind them."

* * * The student's story shows how technology is bringing a set of ideas associated with postmodernism—in this case, ideas about the instability of meanings and the lack of universal and knowable truths—into everyday life. In recent years, it has become fashionable to poke fun at postmodern philosophy and lampoon its allusiveness and density. Indeed, I have done some of this myself. But * * * through experiences with computers, people come to a certain understanding of postmodernism and to recognize its ability to usefully capture certain aspects of their own experience, both online and off.

In *The Electronic Word*, the classicist Richard A. Lanham argues that open-ended screen text subverts traditional fantasies of a master narrative, or definitive reading, by presenting the reader with possibilities for changing fonts, zooming in and out, and rearranging and replacing text. The result is "a body of work active not passive, a canon not frozen in perfection but volatile with contending human motive." Lanham puts technology and post modernism together and concludes that the computer is a "fulfillment of social thought." But I believe the relationship is better thought of as a two-way process. Computer technology not only "fulfills the postmodern aesthetic" as Lanham would have it, heightening and concretizing the postmodern experience, but helps the aesthetic hit the street as well as the seminar room. Computers embody postmodern theory and bring it down to earth.

As recently as ten to fifteen years ago, it was almost unthinkable to speak of the computer's involvement with ideas about unstable meanings and unknowable truths. The computer had a clear intellectual identity as a calculating machine. Indeed, when I took an introductory programming course at Harvard in 1978, the professor introduced the computer to the class by calling it a giant calculator. Programming, he reassured us, was a cut and dried technical activity whose rules were crystal clear.

These reassurances captured the essence of * * * the modernist computational aesthetic. The image of the computer as calculator suggested that no matter how complicated a computer might seem, what happened inside it could be mechanically unpacked. Programming was a technical skill that could be done a right way or a wrong way. * * * In other words, computational ideas were presented as one of the great modern metanarratives, stories of how the world worked that provided unifying pictures and analyzed complicated things by breaking them down into simpler parts. The modernist computational aesthetic promised to explain and unpack, to reduce and clarify. Although the computer culture was never monolithic, always including dissenters and deviant subcultures, for many years its professional mainstream (including computer scientists, engineers, economists, and cognitive scientists) shared this clear intellectual direction. Computers, it was assumed, would become more powerful, both as tools and as metaphors, by becoming better and faster calculating machines, better and faster analytical engines. * * *

[These past decades, however, have seen] changes in what computers do *for* us and in what they do *to* us—to our relationships and our ways of thinking about ourselves.

We have become accustomed to opaque technology. As the processing power of computers increased exponentially, it became possible to use that power to build graphical user interfaces, commonly known by the acronym GUI, that hid the bare machine from its user. The new opaque interfaces—most specifically, the Macintosh iconic style of interface, which simulates the space of a desktop as well as communication through dialogue—represented more than a technical change. These new interfaces modeled a way of understanding that depended on getting to know a computer through interacting with it, as one might get to know a person or explore a town.

The early personal computers of the 1970s and the IBM PC of the early 1980s presented themselves as open, "transparent," potentially reducible to their underlying mechanisms. These were systems that invited users to imagine that they could understand its "gears" as they turned, even if very few people ever tried to reach that level of understanding. * * *

In contrast, the 1984 introduction of the Macintosh's iconic style presented the public with simulations (the icons of file folders, a trash can, a desktop) that did nothing to suggest how their underlying structure could be known. It seemed unavailable, visible only through its effects. As one user said, "The Mac looked perfect, finished. To install a program on my DOS machine, I had to fiddle with things. It clearly wasn't perfect. With the Mac, the system told me to stay on the surface." This is the kind of involvement with computers that has come to dominate the field; no longer associated only with the Macintosh, it is nearly universal in personal computing.

We have learned to take things at interface value. We are moving toward a culture of simulation in which people are increasingly comfortable with substituting representations of reality for the real. We use a Macintosh-style "desktop" as well as one on four legs. We join virtual communities that exist only among people communicating on computer networks as well as communities in which we are physically present. We come to question simple distinctions between real and artificial. In what sense should one consider a screen desktop less real than any other? The screen desktop I am currently using has a folder on it labeled "Professional Life." It contains my business correspondence, date book, and telephone directory. Another folder, labeled "Courses," contains syllabuses, reading assignments, class lists, and lecture notes. A third, "Current Work," contains my research notes and this book's drafts. I feel no sense of unreality in my relationship to any of these objects. The culture of simulation encourages me to take what I see on the screen "at (inter)face value." In the culture of simulation, if it works for you, it has all the reality it needs.

The habit of taking things at interface value is new, but it has gone quite far. For example, a decade ago, the idea of a conversation with a computer about emotional matters, the image of a computer psychotherapist, struck most people as inappropriate or even obscene. Today, several such programs are on the market, and they tend to provoke a very different and quite pragmatic response. People are most likely to say, "Might as well try it. It might help. What's the harm?"

We have used our relationships with technology to reflect on the human. A decade ago, people were often made nervous by the idea of thinking about computers in human terms. Behind their anxiety was distress at the idea that their own minds might be similar to a computer's "mind." This reaction against the formalism and rationality of the machine was romantic.

I use this term to analogize our cultural response to computing to nineteenth century Romanticism. * * * This response emphasized not only the richness of human emotion but the flexibility of human thought and the degree to which knowledge arises in subtle interaction with the environment. Humans, it insists, have to be something very different from mere calculating machines.

In the mid-1980s, this romantic reaction was met by a movement in computer science toward the research and design of increasingly "romantic machines." These machines were touted not as logical but as biological, not as programmed but as able to learn from experience. The researchers who worked on them said they sought a species of machine that would prove as unpredictable and undetermined as the human mind itself. The cultural presence of these romantic machines encouraged a new discourse; both persons and objects were reconfigured, machines as psychological objects, people as living machines. * * *

In the past decade, the changes in the intellectual identity and cultural impact of the computer have taken place in a culture still deeply attached to the quest for a modernist understanding of the mechanisms of life. Larger scientific and cultural trends, among them advances in psychopharmacology and the development of genetics as a computational biology, reflect the extent to which we assume ourselves to be like machines whose inner workings we can understand. "Do we have our emotions," asks a college sophomore whose mother has been transformed by taking antidepressant medication, "or do our emotions have us?" To whom is one listening when one is "listening to Prozac"? The aim of the Human Genome Project is to specify the location and role of all the genes in human DNA. The Project is often justified on the grounds that it promises to find the pieces of our genetic code responsible for many human diseases so that these may be better treated, perhaps by genetic reengineering. But talk about the Project also addresses the possibility of finding the genetic markers that determine human personality, temperament, and sexual orientation. As we contemplate reengineering the genome, we are also reengineering our view of ourselves as programmed beings. Any romantic reaction that relies on biology as the bottom line is fragile, because it is building on shifting ground. Biology is appropriating computer technology's older, modernist models of computation while at the same time computer scientists are aspiring to develop a new opaque, emergent biology that is closer to the postmodern culture of simulation.

Today, more lifelike machines sit on our desktops, computer science uses biological concepts, and human biology is recast in terms of deciphering a code. With descriptions of the brain that explicitly invoke computers and images of computers that explicitly invoke the brain, we have reached a cultural watershed. The rethinking of human and machine identity is not taking place just among philosophers but "on the ground," through a philosophy in everyday life that is in some measure both provoked and carried by the computer presence. * * *

Computers don't just do things for us, they do things to us, including to our ways of thinking about ourselves and other people. * * * [I]t is computer screens where we project ourselves into our own dramas, dramas in which we are producer, director, and star. Some of these dramas are private, but increasingly we are able to draw in other people. Computer screens are the new location for our fantasies, both erotic and intellectual. We are using life on computer screens to become comfortable with new ways of thinking about evolution, relationships, sexuality, politics, and identity.

Notes and Questions

1. What does Professor Turkle mean when she writes that our conception of computers has shifted from a modern to a postmodern one? What are the differences she sees between older computer interfaces and the graphical user interface most common today? Do you think it changes a child's perception of the world to manipulate virtual "folders" on a virtual "desktop"? How does this relate to what Turkle calls a "culture of simulation"?

2. In what way is the hypertext linking system that is employed over the world wide web an embodiment of postmodern philosophy?

3. Do you think the lines between computers and human beings are becoming increasingly blurred, as Turkle suggests? In what ways do we now tend to think of the human body as a machine? In what ways do we think of computers as alive?

4. Does looking at the Internet as an embodiment of postmodernism change your intuitions about how one might try to regulate online interaction? For example, should language in chat rooms be treated the same as language in "real" space? What about the ownership of ideas? Should online relationships be considered distinct from face-to-face encounters? If a person commits a "cyber-rape," should that be considered speech or an act? Does thinking about the choice between the two complicate our understanding of the relationship between speech and action in the offline context?

Alfred C. Yen, *Western Frontier or Feudal Society?: Metaphors and Perceptions of Cyberspace*

17 BERKELEY TECH. L.J. 1207 (2002)

The application of metaphor to the Internet is entirely sensible. It is an unavoidable and useful human habit to compare unfamiliar objects to familiar ones. People use apt metaphors because they stimulate the imagination, drawing attention to patterns and possibilities that would otherwise have escaped attention. If perceptions stimulated by metaphor become sufficiently ingrained, people may adopt them as reality and make them the basis for future beliefs and actions. At the same time, however, it is important to separate the application of metaphor from the complete apprehension of reality. Metaphors work because they provide perspective, but the adoption of one perspective necessarily omits insights offered by other perspectives. Accordingly, insight gets lost when one metaphor assumes enough prominence to crowd other ones out, especially if the prominent metaphor has misleading qualities. It therefore makes sense to develop and use a balanced set of metaphors when studying any object.

* * * [M]etaphors shape the perception of Internet reality. Of the many metaphors that have been applied to the Internet, the most prominent and influential has been the imagination of the Internet as a separate, new physical place known as "cyberspace" and its comparison to America's Western Frontier. * * * Events of the 20th century and America's internalization of the frontier thesis have created conditions ripe for the application of the Western Frontier metaphor to the Internet. The upheavals of the twentieth century—two world wars, the Viet Nam experience, and the moral struggles of the civil rights movement—have contributed to a collective sense that America needs to revisit its fundamental values in order to chart its future course. Under the frontier thesis, such renewal would ordinarily occur in the wilderness of the Western Frontier, land that is now largely civilized. Even where significant tracts of land remain uninhabited, the state extends its reach, making it impossible for brave individuals to found new communities on values developed in the absence of the state.

Not surprisingly, Americans have been looking for a new frontier. Widely accepted national boundaries make the occupation of new lands impossible and rule out the possibility of actual land-based frontiers. Space and the ocean are candidates to be new frontiers, but so far the technical obstacles are too great. The Internet, however, appears to be just the ticket, and a number of American writers have promoted it that way—not just for America, but potentially the world. Cyberspace may be virtual space, but its characteristics resemble a romanticized * * * Western Frontier, where the state seems largely absent. This seeming absence makes cyberspace a dangerous wilderness characterized by free pornography, "spam," identity theft, rampant copyright infringement, gambling, and hacking. Its technological nature also makes cyberspace a difficult place to negotiate. Only computer-savvy settlers really know how to survive there. At the same time, cyberspace contains abundant free land that bestows huge fortunes and social opportunities to those sufficiently brave and industrious to venture into its virtual wilderness. Founders of new "dot-coms," venture capitalists, and even ordinary investors participate in an Internet gold rush that has gone through a cycle of boom and bust. Others risk being stalked in order find love and friendship. For them, the very technology that distributes pornography, pirated software, and junk e-mail also unites them with others previously separated by physical geography. They are pioneers who found diverse new communities in the wilderness of cyberspace. Modern individuals who follow these Internet pioneers by logging on to the Internet therefore participate in the creation of a more prosperous and better society.

The Western Frontier metaphor provides an inspiring account of the Internet, but this account does not offer neutral truth beyond debate. Instead, the Western Frontier metaphor operates as propaganda supporting minimal regulation of the Internet. * * *

[Frederick Jackson Turner first advanced the "frontier thesis" in 1893, thereby attributing the development of American society and American virtues to the Western Frontier.[22] According to Turner, the Western Frontier ensured American freedom and prosperity precisely because resources were abundant and the state was absent. The Western Frontier metaphor constructs the Internet the same way. The minimally regulated Internet offers freedom and prosperity because cyberspace has a lot of "land" and very few state-imposed laws. In Turner's romanticized West, people who faced oppression could easily find freedom by moving further west. That freedom allowed self-sufficient individuals to succeed precisely because the absence of the state allowed them to create better lives and civic institutions on their own. Internet users who feel oppressed can do the same thing by clicking a mouse. In fact, an Internet user can find a place of his own more easily than a Western pioneer could because there are no physical distances to cross in cyberspace. Cyberspace is therefore an improved version of the American West where the state can only inhibit self-sufficient individuals from ensuring their own freedom and prosperity. Accordingly, it would be wise to apply minimal regulation to the Internet. Granted, this perspective would not necessarily rule out all Internet regulation, but it does create a basic presumption against regulation beyond the recognition of basic property rights and the enforcement of contract. * * *

It is therefore instructive to note that the Western Frontier metaphor's history is, at best, incomplete. * * * [T]he operating image of the Western Frontier metaphor is one where the virtuous prevail and evil is wiped out. Unfortunately, the West was not such place. Genocide, racism, and personal exploitation in the name of progress comprise a significant portion of Western Frontier history, but popular culture has cemented a romanticized version of the West that ignores or discounts this reality.

This makes the Western Frontier metaphor problematic because it encourages ignorance of the very real possibility that the Internet will foster undesirable social developments. Internalization of the Western Frontier metaphor creates the belief that minimal legal regulation "naturally" works well for the Internet, when effective legal regulation might have prevented the myriad social problems of the actual Western Frontier. * * * Continued application of the * * * metaphor creates an incomplete and misleading influence on policy and crowds out other metaphors that offer alternate perspectives on the Internet. Minimal regulation of the Internet might then pass from one of many possible strategies to an unquestionable "truth" protected by an unchallenged Western Frontier ideology. We must therefore begin imagining the Internet from new perspectives that challenge the Western Frontier metaphor, and it is to this task that this Article now turns by offering feudal society as a metaphor for the Internet.

---

22. Frederick Jackson Turner, *The Significance of the Frontier in American History, in* REPORT OF THE AMERICAN HISTORICAL ASSOCIATION FOR 1893, at 199-227 (1894), *reprinted in* FREDERICK JACKSON TURNER, THE FRONTIER IN AMERICAN HISTORY 1-38 (1st ed. Henry Holt & Co. 1920).

* * * The feudal character of cyberspace emerges from the hierarchical privatization of its government associated with the granting of Internet domains. In particular, [the Internet Corporation for Assigned Names and Numbers (ICANN)] is a private entity that controls a most precious commodity—cyberspace "land" in the form of domain names. Like a feudal king, ICANN grants "cyberfiefs" to those who promise to pay money and abide by ICANN's rules in exchange for Internet domains. Recipients of cyberfiefs need only comply with minimal technical standards such as TCP/IP before making their cyberfiefs operational. ICANN distributes these cyberfiefs in a manner reminiscent of the methods used by feudal kings. * * * ICANN divides the available "cyberland" into [Top-Level Domains (TLDs)] such as .com, .edu, and .org. It then delegates the management of TLDs to TLD managers like VeriSign Global Registry Services. TLD managers then deal with various Internet domain name registrars, who in turn deal with general public. This pattern of distribution makes TLD managers' status analogous to tenants-in-chief and domain name registrars' status analogous to mesne lords, and it effectively creates a class of "cyberlords" that includes TLD managers, registrars, ISPs, businesses, and others who obtain and exploit significant interests in "cyberland."

The hierarchical distribution of cyberfiefs means that, as in feudal society, every interest in cyberland is held from a superior computer operator who functions as lord over vassal or serf. This hierarchical distribution of cyberfiefs affects cyberspace in the same way that the granting of fiefs affected medieval Europe. State power becomes an incident of private property that gets fragmented through delegation to numerous private parties. This occurs because cyberlords generally delegate powers of government whenever they grant a cyberfief. Like feudal monarchs, they must do so because the Internet has become too unwieldy for any attempt to manage all aspects of its operation. New cyberlords therefore face very few restrictions on how they operate their computers. Cyberlords can post whatever content they like on their computers, permit or refuse communications from particular individuals and domains, limit the number of users their computers serve, or observe the behavior of users. The political nature of these powers becomes even clearer upon examination of the role that cyberlords play in the ability of individuals to enter and experience cyberspace.

Ordinary individuals generally get Internet access by purchasing service from a commercial Internet Service Provider ("ISP") or employers who act as ISPs. The typical ISP is a cyberlord who sells access to the Internet through a computer or computers for which he has registered one or more domain names. Such an ISP typically provides the individual with a connection for the user's personal computer, an e-mail account, and hosting for the individual's web page on the ISP's Internet server. The ISP also takes complete control of the user's existence in cyberspace as soon as she logs on.

If the ISP chooses to do nothing, the user can employ whatever software she desires to experience cyberspace as she sees fit. She can view movie trailers, read about history, send e-mail, or "chat" with her friends. However, the ISP has the power and authority to alter this experience in whatever way it desires. For example, ISPs sometimes offer their users proprietary content such as news, stock quotes, or games. Like city planners, they can create meeting places, facilitate travel through cyberspace, and control the size of crowds. ISPs can also keep their users from visiting certain parts of cyberspace, censor what they say and read, review their e-mail, monitor their behavior, and enforce codes of conduct. Moreover, an ISP can enforce its will because it controls the user's ability to enter cyberspace. An ISP can "sentence" users who defy its rules by denying access to certain materials, logging them off for specified amounts of time, deleting files kept on the ISP's server, or even terminating the user's account completely. Moreover, it can do these things arbitrarily without providing notice, a hearing, or any other form of due process. In "real space," the power to behave this way rests with the state. In cyberspace, however, it belongs to the cyberlord.

Almost every cyberlord exercises the same power as ISPs by dictating the experience of those who connect to his computer. In some cases, the appearance of the virtual state is clear because the cyberlord creates a virtual community that comes with a governing "constitution." In other cases, the appearance of state power seems nonexistent because the site offers users a limited experience such as pure text or technical connection to the Internet's backbone. However, it is still the cyberlord's choice, and not her inability, to offer the limited experience. The private power to shape and control the user's experience still remains. * * *

The modern cyberlord faces management problems similar to those confronted by feudal lords. A cyberlord who wishes to earn a fortune in cyberspace has to acquire a cyberfief, but possession of a cyberfief is not enough to ensure prosperity. Like the feudal lord, the cyberlord needs to attract and hold people to make his cyberfief economically productive. This happens at every level of the Internet's feudal hierarchy. At the top, large cyberlords who provide direct connection to the Internet's backbone look for other cyberlords who can profitably utilize Internet bandwidth. At the bottom, cyberlords try to attract ordinary individuals to do the same, but it is at this level that the cyberlord's business turns to exploitation.

At first blush, one might think that cyberlords could profit only if they somehow get their users to pay for the privilege of communicating with the cyberlord's computer. This sometimes happens. For example, Internet users generally pay ISPs a fee in return for their Internet service. However, the cyberlord that limits herself to the collection of user fees is unlikely to maximize profits. Users in cyberspace are consumers in real space, and each of a cyberlord's users represents an opportunity to sell or advertise something. ISPs and other web site operators must therefore attract and retain as many users as they can while connecting their users' "cyberlives" to profits whenever possible. A profit maximizing strategy starts with the realization that users experience cyberspace through their computers, that the cyberlord controls what the computer displays, and that the users' attention, activities, and personal presence become resources that generate revenue for cyberlords.

The most obvious way to accomplish this is displaying advertisements to the user, which many commercial ISPs and web site operators do. * * * The savvy cyberlord can increase the revenue raised from advertisements by diligently collecting information about his users. Sometimes this information is voluntarily disclosed in exchange for services. For example, ISPs sometimes offer to track a user's stocks or pay her bills online. This can provide valuable clues about a user's wealth. Additionally, users leave many clues about themselves as they move through cyberspace. Some visit web sites devoted to sports. Others go to virtual bookstores. Still others look for stock tips. Cyberlords who record this information can direct advertisements to targeted audiences. * * *

Really astute cyberlords, however, can accomplish even more by turning their users' personalities into sources of revenue. Of all the things that attract and hold people in cyberspace, human interaction has proven highly effective. This can hardly be surprising. After all, in real space, people generally form their most powerful and long lasting relationships with other people. Thus, a clever cyberlord provides users the opportunity to chat or otherwise interact in "real time" with fellow users in the hope that these users will develop cyberspace relationships. Cyberlords who control access to such users can sell that access. Indeed, the value of such access increases with the number of users available and the intensity of the personal relationships formed. An individual who "sees" a dear friend only in cyberspace will pay more to maintain that connection and will spend more time connected to the cyberlord's site. The increased time spent in cyberspace makes the individual more available for exposure to advertisements and other commercial opportunities controlled by the cyberlord. Moreover, the user's increased presence itself attracts more users who in turn increase the value of the access controlled by the cyberlord. * * *

The foregoing shows that cyberlords manage their cyberfiefs like feudal manors. Like feudal serfs, "cyberserfs" live "cyberlives" managed by their lord for the lord's financial gain. As such, the cyberserf becomes an asset owned by the cyberlord's business. Indeed, as the term "buying eyeballs" suggests, cyberlords sometimes acquire existing cyberfiefs because they deem the cyberserfs valuable. Even when businesses are not being bought and sold, cyberlords remain keenly aware that their relationships with cyberserfs are valuable assets that can be "rented" to others. This does not, however, mean that cyberlords routinely abuse their cyberserfs. Just like their medieval counterparts, cyberlords have to limit the exploitation of their cyberserfs because overexploitation will drive cyberserfs to join the cybermanors of his competitors.

The Feudal Society metaphor challenges the Western Frontier metaphor by diverting attention from romanticized images of the West to the darker ones of feudal Europe. Like America's Western Frontier, medieval Europe had abundant land that governments found difficult to control. However, these conditions did not give rise to a happy European version of the Western Frontier experience. Instead, Europe endured three centuries of feudal rule that declined only as the evolving modern state expanded its regulation of otherwise private feudal arrangements. The Feudal Society metaphor contradicts the idea that plentiful land and minimal government regulation ensure widespread freedom and prosperity. Indeed, the metaphor implies that such conditions support the fragmentation of political authority and the private exercise of political power. By doing so, the metaphor draws attention to the many instances where, as in medieval Europe, weak states created political vacuums ultimately filled by powerful individuals and clans who governed for private gain. These historical examples make it difficult to accept the Western Frontier metaphor's historical prediction of a glorious future in cyberspace. Rather than presume that things will work out simply because cyberspace resembles the romanticized Western Frontier, society must choose the kind of cyberspace that it will have.

Admittedly, one basis for rejecting this idea is that the institutions and practices emerging in cyberspace do not perfectly mirror those of feudal Europe. Armed retainers do not exist in cyberspace, and cyberserfs do not face the same degree of subordination that medieval serfs endured. However, metaphors may provide insight without perfectly describing the things they illuminate. The Western Frontier metaphor offers insight despite its imperfections. The Feudal Society metaphor does likewise by suggesting a very complicated future for the denizens of a cyberspace dominated by unregulated private ordering. Instead of being free and prosperous, these denizens may find themselves controlled and exploited by superiors in a technological hierarchy of power. In order to prevent this, a society should use the Feudal Society metaphor to find examples of emerging feudal practices, and then focus on these problems and how they can be blunted by the application of law.

Notes and Questions

1. In what ways does Professor Yen think the mythology of the American frontier has affected our understanding of the Internet and its possible regulation? Is the frontier metaphor a useful one? Why or why not? On what bases does Yen challenge the application of the American frontier metaphor?

2. Does it make sense to think of cyberspace in terms of *American* utopian thought? In what ways might we say that the Internet is American? Might that change? If so, do you think the frontier metaphor will decline as well? What about the *Yahoo!* case, discussed in Chapter Three? Does your intuition in that case depend in part on whether you adopt the frontier metaphor Yen describes?

3. Why does Yen think feudalism offers a better metaphor for understanding online regulation? Do you agree that the metaphor is apt? What are the regulatory consequences of his choice of metaphor?

4. Are there important differences between feudal serfs and "cyberserfs"? Consider the Realtime Blackhole List, discussed in Chapter Five. The premise of Post's argument concerning the list was that various cyber-actors (whether individuals, service providers, or system operators) would be able to leave one "cyberfiefdom" and migrate to another one easily. Yen's feudalism metaphor encourages us to assume the opposite. To what degree are the barriers to exit the same or different in feudal society as compared to online activity?

5. How does Yen's feudalism metaphor relate to broader conceptions of "community"? After all, a feudal understanding of the Internet implies various isolated and insular communities. Think of instances in the preceding chapters when the idea of community has been invoked. Are those evocations of community problematic? Would Yen accept them? For further discussions of cyberspace communities, see Section B, *infra*.

Jonathan Rosen, *The Talmud and the Internet*

Farrar, Straus & Giroux, 2000

Not long after my grandmother died, my computer crashed and I lost the journal I had kept of her dying. I'd made diskette copies of everything else on my computer—many drafts of a novel, scores of reviews and essays and probably hundreds of articles, but I had not printed out, backed up or made a copy of the diary. No doubt this had to do with my ambivalence about writing and where it leads, for I was recording not only my feelings but also the concrete details of her death. How the tiny monitor taped to her index finger made it glow pink. How mist from the oxygen collar whispered through her hair. How her skin grew swollen and wrinkled, like the skin of a baked apple, yet remained astonishingly soft to the touch. Her favorite songs—"Embraceable You" and "Our Love Is Here to Stay"—that she could no longer hear but that we sang to her anyway. The great gaps in her breathing. The moment when she was gone and the nurses came and bound her jaws together with white bandages.

I was ashamed of my need to translate into words the physical intimacy of her death, so while I was writing it, I took comfort in the fact that my journal did and did not exist. It lived in limbo, much as my grandmother had as she lay unconscious. My unacknowledged journal became, to my mind, what the Rabbis in the Talmud call a *goses*: a body between life and death, neither of heaven nor of earth. But then my computer crashed and I wanted my words back. I mourned my journal alongside my grandmother. That secondary cyber loss brought back the first loss and made it final. The details of her dying no longer lived in a safe interim computer sleep. My words were gone.

Or were they? Friends who knew about computers assured me that in the world of computers, nothing is ever really gone. If I cared enough about retrieving my journal, there were places I could send my ruined machine where the indelible imprint of my diary, along with everything else I had ever written, could be skimmed off the hard drive and saved. It would cost a fortune, but I could do it.

The idea that nothing is ever lost is something one hears a great deal when people speak of computers. "Anything you do with digital technology," my Internet handbook warns, "will leave automatically documented evidence for other people or computer systems to find." There is of course something ominous in that notion. But there is a sort of ancient comfort in it, too.

"All mankind is of one author and is one volume," John Donne wrote in one of his most beautiful meditations. "When one man dies, one chapter is not torn out of the book, but translated into a better language; and every chapter must be so translated." I'd thought of that passage when my grandmother died and had tried to find it in my old college edition of Donne, but I couldn't, so I'd settled for the harsher comforts of Psalm 121—more appropriate for my grandmother in any case. But Donne's passage, when I finally found it (about which more later), turned out to be as hauntingly beautiful as I had hoped. It continues:

> God employs several translators; some pieces are translated by age, some by sickness, some by war, some by justice, but God's hand is in every translation, and his hand shall bind up all our scattered leaves again for that library where every book shall lie open to one another.

At the time I had only a dim remembered impression of Donne's words, and I decided that, as soon as I had the chance, I would find the passage on the Internet. I hadn't yet used the Internet much beyond E-mail, but I had somehow gathered that universities were all assembling vast computer-text libraries and that anyone with a modem could scan their contents. Though I had often expressed cynicism about the Internet, I secretly dreamed it would turn out to be a virtual analogue to John Donne's heaven.

There was another passage I wished to find—not on the Internet but in the Talmud, which, like the Internet, I also think of as being a kind of terrestrial version of Donne's divine library, a place where everything exists, if only one knows how and where to look. I'd thought repeatedly about the Talmudic passage I alluded to earlier, the one that speaks of the *goses*, the soul that is neither dead nor alive. I suppose the decision to remove my grandmother from the respirator disturbed me—despite her "living will" and the hopelessness of the situation—and I tried to recall the conversation the Rabbis had about the ways one can—and cannot—allow a person headed towards death to die.

The Talmud tells a story about a great Rabbi who is dying, he has become a *goses*, but he cannot die because outside all his students are praying for him to live and this is distracting to his soul. His maidservant climbs to the roof of the hut where the Rabbi is dying and hurls a clay vessel to the ground. The sound diverts the students, who stop praying. In that moment, the Rabbi dies and his soul goes to heaven. The servant, too, the Talmud says, is guaranteed her place in the world to come.

The story, suggesting the virtue of letting the dead depart, was comforting to me, even though I know that the Talmud is ultimately inconclusive on end-of-life issues, offering , as it always does, a number of arguments and counterarguments, stories and counterstories. Not to mention the fact that the Talmud was finalized in the early sixth century, long before certain technological innovations complicated questions of life and death. I also wasn't sure I was remembering the story correctly. Was I retelling the story in a way that offered me comfort but distorted the original intent? I am far from being an accomplished Talmud student and did not trust my skills or memory. But for all that, I took enormous consolation in recalling that the Rabbis had in fact discussed the matter.

"Turn it and turn it for everything is in it," a Talmudic sage famously declared. The sage, with the improbable name of Ben Bag Bag, is quoted only once in the entire Talmud, but his words have a mythic resonance. Like the Greek Ouroboros—the snake who swallows its own tail—Ben Bag Bag's words appear in the Talmud and refer to the Talmud, a self-swallowing observation that seems to bear out the truth of the sage's observation. The Talmud is a book and is not a book, and the Rabbi's phrase flexibly found its way into it because, oral and written both, the Talmud reached out and drew into itself the world around it, even as it declared itself the unchanging word of God.

Though it may seem sacrilegious to say so, I can't help feeling that in certain respects the Internet has a lot in common with the Talmud. The Rabbis referred to the Talmud as a yam, a sea—and though one is hardly intended to "surf" the Talmud, something more than oceanic metaphors links the two verbal universes. Vastness and an uncategorizable nature are in part what define them both. When Maimonides, the great medieval codifier and philosopher, wanted to extract from the Talmud's peculiar blend of stories, folklore, legalistic arguments, anthropological asides, biblical exegesis, and intergenerational rabbinic wrangling some basic categories and legal conclusions, he was denounced as a heretic for disrupting the very chaos that, in some sense, had come to represent a divine fecundity. Eventually, Maimonides was forgiven, and his work, the *Mishneh Torah*, is now one of the many cross-referenced sources on a printed page of Talmud—absorbed by the very thing it sought to replace.

The Mishnah itself—the legalistic core of the Talmud—is divided into six broad orders that reflect six vast categories of Jewish life, but those six categories are subdivided into numerous subcategories called tractates that range over a far vaster number of subjects often impossible to fathom from the names of the orders they appear in. The Hebrew word for tractate is *masechet*, which means, literally, "webbing." As with the World Wide Web, only the metaphor of the loom, ancient and inclusive, captures the reach and the randomness, the infinite interconnectedness of words.

I have often thought, contemplating a page of Talmud, that it bears a certain uncanny resemblance to a home page on the Internet, where nothing is whole in itself but where icons and text boxes are doorways through which visitors pass into an infinity of cross-referenced texts and conversations. Consider a page of Talmud. There are a few lines of Mishnah, the conversation the Rabbis conducted (for hundreds of years before it was codified around 200 C.E.) about a broad range of legalistic questions stemming from the Bible but ranging into a host of other matters as well. Underneath these few lines begins the Gemarah, the conversation *later* Rabbis had about the conversation *earlier* Rabbis had in the Mishnah. Both the Mishnah and the Gemarah evolved orally over so many hundreds of years that, even in a few lines of text, Rabbis who lived generations apart participate and give the appearance, both within those discrete passages as well as by juxtaposition on the page, of speaking directly to each other. The text includes not only legal disputes but fabulous stories, snippets of history and anthropology and biblical interpretations. Running in a slender strip down the inside of the page is the commentary of Rashi, the medieval exegete, commenting on both the Mishnah and the Gemarah, and the biblical passages (also indexed elsewhere on the page) that inspired the original conversation. Rising up on the other side of the Mishnah and the Gemarah are the tosefists, the Rashi's descendants and disciples, who comment on Rashi's work, as well as on everything Rashi commented on himself. The page is also cross-referenced to other passages of the Talmud, to various medieval codes of Jewish law (that of Maimonides, for example), and to the *Shulkhan Arukh*, the great sixteenth-century codification of Jewish law by Joseph Caro. And one should add to this mix the student himself, who participates in a conversation that began over two thousand years ago.

Now all this is a far cry from the assault of recipes, news briefs, weather bulletins, chat rooms, university libraries, pornographic pictures, Rembrandt reproductions and assorted self-promotional verbiage that drifts untethered through cyberspace. The Talmud was produced by the moral imperative of Jewish law, the free play of great minds, the pressures of exile, the self-conscious need to keep a civilization together and a driving desire to identify and follow the unfolding word of God. Nobody was trying to buy airline tickets or meet a date. Moreover, the Talmud, after hundreds of years as an oral construct, was at last written down, shaped by (largely) unknown editors, masters of erudition and invention who float through its precincts and offer anonymous, ghostly promptings—posing questions, suggesting answers and refutations—so that one feels, for all its multiplicities, an organizing intelligence at work.

And yet when I look at a page of Talmud and see all those texts tucked intimately and intrusively onto the same page, like immigrant children sharing a single bed, I do think of the interrupting, jumbled culture of the Internet. For hundreds of years, responses to, questions on virtually every aspect of Jewish life, winged back and forth between scattered Jews and various centers of Talmudic learning. The Internet is also a world of unbounded curiosity, of argument and information, where anyone with a modem can wander out of the wilderness for a while, ask a question and receive an answer. I take comfort in thinking that a modern technological medium echoes an ancient one.

For me, I suppose, the Internet makes actual a certain disjointed approach to reading I had already come to understand was part of my encounter with books and with the world. I realized this forcefully when I went looking for the John Donne passage that comforted me after the death of my grandmother. I'd tried to find that passage in my Modern Library *Complete Poetry and Selected Prose* without success. I knew the lines, I confess, not from a college course but from the movie version of *84, Charing Cross Road* with Anthony Hopkins and Anne Bancroft. The book, a 1970 best-seller, is a collection of letters written by an American woman who loves English literature and a British book clerk who sells her old leather-bound editions of Hazlitt and Lamb and Donne, presumably bought up cheap from the libraries of great houses whose owners are going broke after the war. The book itself is a comment on the death of a certain kind of print culture. The American woman loves literature but she also writes for television, and at one point she buys Walter Savage Landor's *Imaginary Conversations* so she can adapt it for the radio.

In any event, I checked out *84, Charing Cross Road* from the library in the hope of finding the Donne passage, but it wasn't in the book. It's alluded to in the play that was adapted from the book (I found that too), but it isn't reprinted, there's just a brief discussion of Donne's Sermon 15 (of which the American woman complains she's been sent an abridged version; she likes her Donne sermons whole). So I rented the movie again, and there was the passage, read beautifully in voice-over by Anthony Hopkins, but without attribution, so there was no way to look it up. Unfortunately, the passage was also abridged so that, when I finally turned to the Web, I found myself searching for the line "All mankind is of one volume" instead of "All mankind is of one author and is one volume."

My Internet search was initially no more successful than my library search. I had thought that summoning books from the vast deep was a matter of a few key-strokes, but when I visited the Web site of the Yale library, I found that most of its books do not yet exist as a computer text. I'd somehow believed the world had grown digital, and though I'd long feared and even derided this notion, I now found how disappointed and frustrated I was that it hadn't happened. As a last-ditch effort, I searched the phrase "God employs many translators." And there it was!

The passage I wanted finally came to me, as it turns out, not as part of a scholarly library collection but simply because someone who loves John Donne had posted it on his home page. (At the bottom of the passage was the charming sentence "This small thread has been spun by . . ." followed by the man's name and Internet address.) For one moment, there in dimensionless, chilly cyberspace, I felt close to my grandmother, close to

John Donne, and close to some stranger who, as it happens, designs software for a living.

The lines I sought were from Meditation 17 in *Devotions upon Emergent Occasions*, which happens to be the most famous thing Donne ever wrote, containing as it does the line "never send to know for whom the bell tolls; it tolls for thee." My search had led me from a movie to a book to a play to a computer and back to a book (it was, after all, in my Modern Library edition, but who knew that it followed from "No man is an Island"?). I had gone through all this to retrieve something that an educated person thirty years ago could probably have quoted by heart. Then again, these words may be as famous as they are only because Hemingway lifted them for his book title. Literature has been in a plundered, fragmentary state for a long time.

Still, if the books had all been converted into computer text, and if Donne and Hemingway and *84, Charing Cross Road* had come up together and bumped into each other on my screen, I wouldn't have minded. Perhaps there is a spirit in books that lets them live beyond their actual bound bodies.

This is not to say that I do not fear the loss of the book as object, as body. Donne imagined people who die becoming like books, but what happens when books die? Are they reborn in some new ethereal form? Is it out of the ruined body of the book that the Internet is growing? This would account for another similarity I feel between the Internet and the Talmud, for the Talmud was also born partly out of loss.

The Talmud offered a virtual home for an uprooted culture, and grew out of the Jewish need to pack civilization into words and wander out into the world. The Talmud became essential for Jewish survival once the Temple—God's pre-Talmud home—was destroyed, and the Temple practices, those bodily rituals of blood and fire and physical atonement, could no longer be performed. When the Jewish people lost their home (the land of Israel) and God lost His (the Temple), then a new way of being was devised and Jews became the people of the book and not the people of the Temple or the land. They became the people of the book because they had no place else to live. That bodily loss is frequently overlooked, but for me it lies at the heart of the Talmud, for all its plentitude. The Internet, which we are continually told binds us all together, nevertheless engenders in me a similar sense of Diaspora, a feeling of being everywhere and nowhere. Where else but in the middle of Diaspora do you need a home page? * * *

[W]e are passing, books and people both, through the doors of the computer age and entering a new sort of global Diaspora in which we are everywhere—except home. But I suppose that writing, in any form, always has about it a ghostliness, an unsatisfactory, disembodied aspect, and it would be unfair to blame computers or the Internet for enhancing what has always been disappointing about words. Does anyone really want to be a book in John Donne's heaven?

A few weeks after my computer crashed, I gave in and sent it to a fancy place in Virginia where—for more money than the original cost of the machine—technicians were in fact able to lift off of my hard drive the ghostly impression of everything I had ever written on my computer during seven years of use. It was all sent to me on separate diskettes and on a single, inclusive CD-ROM. I immediately found the diskette with my journal and, using my wife's computer, set about printing it out.

As it turns out, I'd written in my journal only six or seven times in the course of my grandmother's two-month illness. Somehow I'd imagined myself chronicling the whole ordeal in the minutest recoverable detail. Instead, I was astonished at how paltry, how sparse my entries really were. Where were the long hours holding her hand? The one-way conversations—what had I said? The slow, dreamlike afternoons with the rest of my family, eating and talking in the waiting area? Where, most of all, was my grandmother? I was glad to have my journal back, of course, and I'd have paid to recover it again in a second. But it was only when I had my own scant words before me at last that I realized how much I'd lost.

Notes and Questions

1. In what ways does Rosen think the Talmud is like the Internet? Why does he think that the Talmud is related to homelessness? Is the act of communicating online similarly multivocal and rootless?

2. Think about Turkle's observation that computers and online interaction are changing the way we think about the difference between being alive and dead. In what ways do Rosen's thoughts about his grandmother reflect this perspective?

3. How does John Donne's phrase "[n]o man is an island" relate to online interaction? Are we more connected in an online world or less? What about Rosen's connection with the person who posted the poem? Can legal regulation have an effect on this sense of connection?

4. Is it significant that Rosen remembers the lines from Donne's poem not from the poem itself but from a movie? What about the fact that the movie has the poem slightly incorrect? Would it matter whether the website Rosen finds actually has the poem "correct"? How would Rosen even know?

5. Should Donne's descendants be able to prevent the software engineer from posting the poem? What would be lost if they could? On the other hand, what would be lost if they could not? If Donne were still alive, would that alter the discussion? Why should that be relevant?

6. Do you think that the Internet will ultimately replace books? Or will the nature of books change? In what ways?

7. Rosen emphasizes the dialogic nature of the Talmud. Is the Internet also dialogic? Are there ways in which law could encourage its dialogic properties?

SECTION B. CYBERSPACE, COMMUNITY, AND GLOBALIZATION

The rise of the Internet has rekindled discussion about the idea of community itself. It has been argued that the development of the printing press helped create the modern nation-state by promoting a common vernacular language, thereby encouraging a conception of shared community among widely dispersed peoples. Likewise, scholars have asked whether the advent of online communication will have a similarly far-reaching affect on the nature of modern communities.

Such discussion is also part of a broader conversation about globalization, a word that has come to signify the increasing flow of capital, information, and people across territorial borders. Obviously, the Internet facilitates connection (and possibly communion) among people who are unconnected by either time and space. The question for those interested in community is whether or not the two people engaging in this online colloquy come to feel connected in any way that we might recognize as community. Or, conversely, does online communication encourage people to *retreat* from their face-to-face communities and sit at home alone in front of computer screens?

Similar contrasts are available when thinking about political communities. For example, one might be concerned about growing insularity online, whereby only those with like interests or political affiliation communicate with each other. On this account, the rise of the Internet limits our access to genuinely public space, where we would be forced to encounter and grapple with people and perspectives outside our daily consciousness. On the other hand, one could argue that the ready availability of multiple news sources, personal opinions, web logs and so forth form an important alternative to the homogenization of mass culture. Indeed, according to one study, half of those who participate in online groups say that the Internet has helped them to become acquainted with people they might not otherwise have met, while a quarter say that the Internet has helped them connect with people from racial, ethnic, or economic backgrounds different from their own.[d]

The following materials offer possible ways of thinking about community in an increasingly globalized world. As you read them, you should ask yourself what you think about the possibility of online communities and the challenge they pose to geographical or other communities. In addition, consider the policy consequences that might flow from each viewpoint. Are there actions governments could or should take to try to increase the salutary effects of the Internet on political community

---

d. John B. Horrigan, *Online Communities, Networks That Nurture Long-Distance Relationships and Local Ties* (2001), *available at* http://www.pewInternet.org/reports/pdfs/ PIP_Communities_Report.pdf.

or to minimize the dangers? Or do the readings imply that government action is irrelevant to these trends?

Paul Schiff Berman, *The Globalization of Jurisdiction*
151 U. PA. L. REV. 311 (2002)

In recent years, anthropologists and others have increasingly challenged the assumed correlation between a people, a culture, and a physical place. Historically, anthropology had been premised on the idea that a world of human differences could be conceptualized as a diversity of separate societies each with its own culture. * * * The implicit starting point was the presumed existence of separate, individuated worldviews that could be associated with particular "peoples", "tribes", or "nations."

This individuated conception of community, still so powerful in legal discussions, no longer fits the understanding of anthropologists, or the practice of ethnography. "In place of such a world of separate, integrated cultural systems . . . political economy turned the anthropological gaze in the direction of social and economic processes that connected even the most isolated of local settings with a wider world."[530] As many commentators have observed, cultural difference no longer can be based on territory because of the mass migrations and transnational culture flows of late capitalism. * * * Accordingly, * * * one can see increasing efforts to explore the "intertwined processes of place making and people making in the complex cultural politics of the nation-state."[536] * * *

Indeed, "[a]lthough the color map of the political world displays a neat and ordered pattern of interlocking units (with only a few lines of discord), it is not surprising that the real world of national identities is one of blotches, blends, and blurs."[553] First, many people inhabit border areas * * * . Such people may feel an affiliation with the state controlling the area, the nation with which most inhabitants identify, or the borderland itself. Second, many others live a life of border *crossings*—migrant workers, nomads, and members of the transnational business and professional elite. For these people, it may be impossible to find a unified cultural identity. For example, "[w]hat is 'the culture' of farm workers who spend half a year in Mexico and half in the United States?"[556] Finally, many people cross borders on a relatively permanent basis—immigrants, refugees, exiles, and expatriates. For them, the disjuncture of place and culture is especially

---

530. Akhil Gupta & James Ferguson, *Culture, Power, Place: Ethnography at the End of an Era, in* CULTURE, POWER, PLACE: EXPLORATIONS IN CRITICAL ANTHROPOLOGY 1, 2 (Akhil Gupta & James Ferguson eds., 1997).

536. *Id.* at 4.

553. David H. Kaplan, *Territorial Identities and Geographic Scale, in* NESTED IDENTITIES: NATIONALISM, TERRITORY, AND SCALE 31, 35 (Guntram H. Herb & David H. Kaplan eds., 1999).

556. Gupta & Ferguson, *supra* note 530, at 34.

clear. Immigrants invariably transport their own culture with them to the new location and, almost as invariably, shed certain aspects of that culture when they come in contact with their new communities.   Diasporas therefore are both "transnational" because members of a single diaspora may live in many different countries, and "extremely national" in their continued cultural and political loyalty to a homeland.[558] * * * By creating communities of interest rather than place, diasporas (the number of which is increasing due largely to labor immigration) pose an implicit threat to territorially based nation-states.   In sum, we see that "[p]rocesses of migration, displacement and deterritorialization are increasingly sundering the fixed association between identity, culture, and place."[563] * * *

We can see the everyday effects of deterritorialization in all areas of the world and all sectors of the economy. For example, the "local" shopping mall is not truly experienced as truly local at all, because nearly "everyone who shops there is aware both that most of the shops are chain stores," identical to stores elsewhere and that the mall itself closely resembles innumerable other malls around the globe.[566] Thus, while experiencing a "local" place, we recognize the absent forces that structure our experience. Such forces include the steady decline in local ownership of public spaces, which can itself be linked to the globalization of capital.

Similarly, we may feel the growing significance of "remote" forces on our lives, whether those forces are multinational corporations, world capital markets, or distant bureaucracies such as the European Union. As John Tomlinson has observed: "People probably come to include distant events and processes more routinely in their perceptions of what is significant for their own personal lives. This is one aspect of what deterritorialization may involve: the ever-broadening horizon of relevance in people's routine experience . . . ."[568]   The increased access to media also affects deterritorialization because one is no longer limited to the perspectives offered from within one's "home culture." Thus, the "typical" life of a suburban family in the United States may become as familiar to world citizens inundated by American film and television as their own "home" life. And, of course, those with less power to influence the processes of globalization—those forced to cross borders for work, those bankrupted through global competition, those affected by environmental degradation, and many others—experience this deterritorialization in even more insidious ways.

Ironically, as actual places and localities become ever more blurred and indeterminate, *ideas* of culturally and ethnically distinct places become perhaps even more important. Imagined communities attach themselves to

---

558. Kaplan, *supra* note 553, at 34.

563. Akhil Gupta, *The Song of the Nonaligned World: Transnational Identities and the Reinscription of Space in Late Capitalism, in* CULTURE, POWER, PLACE: EXPLORATIONS IN CRITICAL ANTHROPOLOGY 179, 196 (Akhil Gupta & James Ferguson eds., 1997).

566. ANTHONY GIDDENS, THE CONSEQUENCES OF MODERNITY 140-41 (1990).

568. JOHN TOMLINSON, GLOBALIZATION AND CULTURE 115 (1999).

imagined places; displaced peoples cluster around remembered or idealized homelands in a world that seems increasingly to deny such firm territorialized anchors in their actuality. * * *

[One way of thinking about community in this changing social context is to consider the idea of] community as truly global and plural—a cosmopolitan community. * * * "If people can get * * * emotional * * * about relations with fellow nationals they never see face-to-face, then now that print capitalism has become electronic- and digital-capitalism, and now that this system is so clearly transnational, it would be strange if people did *not* get emotional in much the same way, if not necessarily to the same degree, about others who are *not* fellow nationals, people bound to them by some transnational sort of fellowship."[754] * * *

Indeed, a cosmopolitan perspective may cause us to feel connected to others in a way that breeds empathy and, perhaps, political engagement. Cosmopolitans recognize that "[w]e are connected to all sorts of places, causally if not always consciously, including many that we have never traveled to, that we have perhaps only seen on television—including the place where the television itself was manufactured."[755] If we truly feel that connection, we may be more likely to concern ourselves with the plight of those who manufactured the product.

Cosmopolitanism can be traced at least as far back as the Stoics, who argued that each of us dwells in two communities: "the local community of our birth, and the community of human argument and aspiration that 'is truly great and truly common, in which we look neither to this corner nor to that, but measure the boundaries of our nation by the sun.'"[756] Recognizing the dangers of factionalism that come from allegiance to the political life of a group, the Stoics contended that only by placing primary allegiance in the world community can mutual problems be addressed.

Martha Nussbaum has recently elaborated on the Stoic ideal in an essay touting the cosmopolitan perspective. According to Nussbaum, cosmopolitanism does not require one to give up local identifications, which, she acknowledges, "can be a source of great richness in life."[757] Rather, following the stoics, she suggests that we think of ourselves as surrounded by a series of concentric circles. "The first one encircles the self, the next takes in the immediate family, then follows the extended family, then, in order, neighbors or local groups, fellow city-dwellers, and fellow countrymen—and we can easily add to this list groupings based on ethnic, linguistic, historical, professional, gender, or sexual identities. Outside all

---

754. Bruce Robbins, *Introduction Part I: Actually Existing Cosmopolitanism, in* Cosmopolitics: Thinking and Feeling Beyond the Nation 1, 7 (Pheng Cheah & Bruce Robbins eds., 1998).

755. *Id.* at 3.

756. Martha C. Nussbaum, *Patriotism and Cosmopolitanism, in* Martha C. Nussbaum et al., For Love of Country: Debating the Limits of Patriotism 3, 7 (Joshua Cohen ed., 1996) (quoting Roman playwright Lucius Annaeus Seneca).

757. *Id.* at 9.

these circles is the largest one, humanity as a whole."[758] The task then, is to draw the circles together. Therefore, we need not relinquish special affiliations and identifications with the various groups. * * *

In this vision, people could be "cosmopolitan patriots,"[761] accepting their responsibility to nurture the culture and politics of their home community, while at the same time recognizing that such cultural practices are always shifting, as people move from place to place. "The result would be a world in which each local form of human life was the result of long-term and persistent processes of cultural hybridization—a world, in that respect, much like the world we live in now."[762] * * *

Iris Young has used the ideal of the "unoppressive city" as a model for a similarly multifaceted understanding of community.[763] She argues that "community" is always a politically problematic term because "those motivated by it will tend to suppress differences among themselves or implicitly to exclude from their political groups persons with whom they do not identify."[764] Thus "[t]he desire for community relies on the same desire for social wholeness and identification that underlies racism and ethnic chauvinism on the one hand and political sectarianism on the other."[765] Instead, she envisions ideal city life as the "'being-together' of strangers."[766] These strangers may remain strangers and continue to "experience the other as other."[767] Indeed, they do not necessarily seek an overall group identification and loyalty. Yet, they are open to "unassimilated otherness."[768] They belong to various distinct groups or cultures, and they are constantly interacting with other groups. But they do so without seeking either to assimilate or to reject those others. Such interactions instantiate an alternative kind of community, one that is never a hegemonic imposition of sameness but that nevertheless prevents different groups from ever being completely outside one another. In a city's public spaces, Young argues, we see glimpses of this ideal: "The city consists in a great diversity of peoples and groups, with a multitude of subcultures and differentiated activities and functions, whose lives and movements mingle and overlap in public spaces."[771] In this vision, there can be community without sameness, shifting affiliations without ostracism.

Although Young does not refer to her vision as cosmopolitan, it fits comfortably within the alternative understanding of community I am

---

758. *Id.*

761. Kwame Anthony Appiah, *Cosmopolitan Patriots, in* COSMOPOLITICS: THINKING AND FEELING BEYOND THE NATION 91, 91 (Pheng Cheah & Bruce Robbins eds., 1998).

762. *Id.* at 92.

763. *See* Iris Marion Young, *The Ideal of Community and the Politics of Difference, in* FEMINISM/POSTMODERNISM 300, 317 (Linda J. Nicholson ed., 1990).

764. *Id.* at 300.

765. *Id.* at 302.

766. *Id.* at 318.

767. *Id.*

768. *Id.* at 319.

771. *Id.*

sketching here. Cosmopolitanism is emphatically not a model of international citizenship in the sense of international harmonization and standardization, but instead is a recognition of multiple refracted differences where (as in Young's ideal city) people acknowledge links with the "other" without demanding assimilation or ostracism. Cosmopolitanism seeks "flexible citizenship,"[773] in which people are permitted to shift identities amid a plurality of possible affiliations and allegiances. These allegiances could also include non-territorial communities, like those found in Internet chatrooms. The cosmopolitan worldview shifts back and forth from the rooted particularity of personal identity to the global possibility of multiple overlapping communities. "Instead of an ideal of detachment, actually existing cosmopolitanism is a reality of (re)attachment, multiple attachment, or attachment at a distance."[774]

Thus, cosmopolitanism forms perhaps the strongest alternative vision to the territorially bounded sovereignty of the nation-state.

Anupam Chander, *Whose Republic?*

69 U. Chi. L. Rev. 1479 (2002)

The Internet * * * is crucial to the project of deepening democracy to include marginalized groups. * * * Cyberspace helps give members of minority groups a fuller sense of citizenship—a right to a practice of citizenship that better reflects who they are. It does so by helping to counter the assimilationist tendencies of mass culture, mass politics, and economics. In this way, cyberspace plays an important role in the multicultural project of including everyone in political and civic society.

At the same time, cyberspace is helping to create new types of republics. Through cyberspace we see the creation of new transnational communities and the strengthening of existing ones. It advances, for example, the creation of transnational environmental, feminist, libertarian, and even, ironically enough, antiglobalization movements.

Cyberspace may also support the project of modern cosmopolitans by bringing people all over the world into daily contact with one another. This kind of interaction will bolster the cosmopolitan goal of diminishing the importance of national borders in favor of an enhanced sense of our common humanity. Cyberspace may ultimately help make us think of ourselves as first and foremost "citizens of the world." * * *

[G]eneral interest intermediaries provide shared experiences that focus almost exclusively on the concerns and experiences of the dominant group. In this way, the [daily visions] offered by the traditional mass media den[y] minorities a sense of full membership in the general polity. If these

---

773. *See* Aihwa Ong, Flexible Citizenship: The Cultural Logics of Transnationality 10 (1999).

774. Robbins, *supra* note 754, at 3.

groups were forced to rely on traditional popular media * * * they would find little that would affirm their interests, their concerns, or their way of life. To the extent the media of the majority exposes individuals to a diversity of voices, that diversity is in fact quite limited in scope.

The primary avenues for shared experiences today can be found in the entertainment industry, the educational system, economic life, and the political process. Thus, it seems appropriate to examine what sort of shared experiences these realms in fact offer.

Even today, at the start of a new century, primetime television fails to reflect the diversity of America. The poor and working class are almost invisible; Latinos are rare and Latinas are rarer; Asian-American families do not exist; immigrants appear occasionally, but only to drive cabs. * * * The paucity of examples to the contrary proves the basic point.

Moreover, the shared experiences available in traditional spaces tend to be ones that confirm the feelings of the dominant group. This is unsurprising because they tend to be the rituals and works created by and for this group. Consider mainstream movies, for example. Could James Bond be played by a black man? Could Superman be gay? The icons of culture promote the heroism and superiority of the heterosexual white male. Media corporations believe such favoritism to be economically profitable, perhaps because the economically powerful part of society prefers it. While there are specialized works created for niche groups (for example, magazines like *The Economist, The Nation, Ebony, Ms.,* and *The American Spectator*), these are not * * * mass information intermediaries * * * .

The discrepancy pervades not only the media, but politics and business as well. To the extent that our elected officials offer subjects of a shared experience, there too we find that that experience excludes significant sections of society. The U.S. Senate has no member who is African-American or Latino. The only Asian-Americans ever to sit in this august body are from Hawaii. Despite two centuries of shared experiences, democracy has not yet produced an American president who is not a white man. There has never been a minority woman on the United States Supreme Court, nor a Latino or an Asian-American man. American business may be somewhat better, but still there are disproportionately few titans of industry who reflect the diversity of America. While subjective and certainly flawed, Entertainment Weekly's annual ranking of the most powerful people in American entertainment suggests the skewed distribution of power in that industry: of the 136 individuals ranked in the most recent list, only ten appear to be members of racial minorities. Only one racial minority (Oprah Winfrey) appears in the top ten positions, and only two (Winfrey and Denzel Washington) appear in the top fifty. The gender distribution is also skewed: of the 136 individuals, only twenty-eight are women (only three of whom are racial minorities). * * *

For groups marginalized by mainstream society, the Internet offers a way to find community. American indigenous peoples can discuss issues of interest to many tribes at NativeWeb.org. A gay youth growing up in a small town can find support through the Internet, despite a hostile local setting. Sikh Americans might find community in cyberspace. Cyberspace offers a respite from the median consumer perspective of mainstream media. Here is the world's diversity, in its full glory (and, at times, disgrace). While cyberspace is no substitute for a society in which minorities are not required to cover, at least it allows minorities to find each other and, through the Web, lend each other support. Minority groups can also build coalitions with other minority groups. Of course, all this is possible even without the Internet, but the Internet serves importantly to reduce the costs of social and political mobilization.

A fundamental design principle of the Internet—"end-to-end design"— facilitates minority participation. The principle holds that the intelligence in the network lies principally at its endpoints. Rather than relying upon centralized authorities, the Internet depends upon the contributions of its end users. The World Wide Web deepens this design principle: an important democratizing feature of the Web is that it enables anyone to become a content provider on the Internet even with little capital equipment or technical knowledge. Tim Berners-Lee, the inventor of the Web, insisted that an editor be built into the Web browser, thereby allowing the user not only to view websites, but to create them. Moreover, unlike a specialty newspaper or magazine, the content of a website becomes relatively widely accessible because of the increasing ubiquity of the Internet. In this way, even minority communities that are not well endowed with resources can use the Web to communicate widely. The Internet and the Web thus allow an end user to make an end run around the mainstreaming of mass media intermediaries. This is not to deny that much of the Web has come to follow a centralized, mass media content producer-consumer model, with a few commercial websites receiving a large percentage of website visitors. Yet, minorities who desire to find (or create) their own communities on the Web can readily do so. The Web thus brings us closer to the ideal of a "semiotic democracy," in which all individuals have the power to participate in the process of meaning-making.

Unfortunately, the price of pluralism is the existence of many points of view and communities that we may find personally distasteful. But if we are to allow for diversity, we cannot just limit diverse views to those that do not trouble mainstream sensibility. It is difficult to distinguish, as a matter of state policy, "extremist" enclaves from other heterodox ones. And further, it is unclear whether extremism is necessarily an evil that a healthy democracy should attempt to stamp out: is moderation a virtue when it comes to whether women should have the right to an abortion? Many people might feel strongly yes, but others, similarly certain, might feel no. In order to find a view "extreme," one must have a metric for judging views, a metric which typically is defined according to the dominant understandings in society. * * *

On China.com, people of Chinese descent can find a community dedicated to their special concerns. Tinig.com allows young Filipino netizens across the world to find each other, converse in Tagalog or English, and address the many issues of the Filipino diaspora. Tsinoy.com focuses on Filipinos of Chinese descent. People of Scottish descent might congregate online at ElectricScotland.com, which seeks to "bring[ ] Scots and Scots' descendants together from around the world." The Irish diaspora might find information about "roots" and "traditions" at IrishAbroad.com. Yahoo! lists more than a thousand websites devoted to "cultures" from Acadians to Zimbabweans. Many of these sites allow chats among the participants, provide bulletin boards for discussion, and organize special community events. People can read newspapers from their homelands on a daily basis and even listen to radio stations. The Internet thus makes it easier for people living in diaspora to maintain ties to family and homeland.

At the same time, the Internet helps create a sense of community among people with shared interests, even if they share no common homeland. E-mail makes it possible to communicate personally with people worldwide for free (on the significant assumption that one has access to the Internet). The relationships of friendship and colleagueship nurtured via e-mail form some of the essential foundations of community life. Individuals interested in a particular topic can register to participate in "listservs," through which they can discuss issues via e-mails distributed to all participants. Often such listservs draw people from all over the world who share a common interest. Cyberlaw professors, for example, can participate in CyberProf, hosted at the University of California, Berkeley. Listservs often serve as forums for lively debates * * * .

But the Internet fosters more than interpersonal relationships. Business and politics can be conducted through the Web. Economic and political ties are created, sustained, and strengthened through this medium. Via the Web, diasporas can learn about problems in the homeland and can channel aid as appropriate. The welcoming message at a website oriented towards the Nigerian diaspora reads: "Are you a Nigerian? Do you want to help Nigeria?" Rediff.com encourages diaspora Indians (who are often much richer than their families in India) to purchase gifts for loved ones back "home," even offering to send gifts to your "Valentine in India." It is not fanciful to think that some countries might offer Internet voting to their diasporas in order to enhance their diasporas' sense of commitment to their homelands.

In a globalized world, we see the rise of nations that transcend the geographic borders of their states—nations based not necessarily on formal ties of citizenship but on strong bonds of loyalty. We also see the rise of new political communities that are not centered on a state, but that participate effectively in international discourse nonetheless. The Internet helps nurture such transnational bonds, whether of diasporas or of other interest-based communities. * * *

Admittedly, citizenship has often been thought of as a geographically-bound concept. But in today's globalized world, the diaspora can make significant contributions to its far-off homeland. The migrant Filipino who works abroad, for example, is now valorized as an "economic hero" of the nation.

We should not be afraid that such transnational relationships will devalue domestic citizenship and make people poorer citizens at "home." * * * [W]e are capable of membership in more than one nation, [and] citizenship should not be seen as a zero-sum game. Moreover, if we begin to understand jurisdiction as invented and therefore subject to reinvention, we can try to engineer new forms of jurisdiction, loosened perhaps from territorial bounds. We should welcome a world in which individuals have the freedom and capability to participate meaningfully in real and virtual communities simultaneously * * * .

Michele Wilson, *Community in the Abstract: A Political and Ethical Dilemma?*

From THE CYBERCULTURES READER, Thomson Publishing Services, 2000

In an age when people have more capacity—through technologically aided communication—to be interconnected across space and time than at any other point in history, the postmodern individual in contemporary Western society is paradoxically feeling increasingly isolated and is searching for new ways to understand and experience meaningful togetherness. Nostalgia contributes to this search. Re-presented memories of 1950s-style communities where moral, social and public order "flourished" are contrasted with present social forms, which are portrayed as chaotic, morally impoverished and narcissistic. However, and at least in theory, there is also a desire to formulate more enriching ways of experiencing ourselves "in relation" which escape the difficulties of earlier, restrictive forms of community.

Many are looking for a form of "being together" which can be seen as valued and, indeed, necessary. In turning to technology, we are presented with the possibility of virtual communities as a potential solution. Virtual communities—or communities experienced through technological mediation over the Internet and possibly enhanced in the future by virtual reality technologies—are represented by some as a form of postmodern community. These virtual communities are depicted as the answer to the theorist's search for a less exclusionary or repressive experience of community. Perhaps this will prove to be the case. But other theorists are uneasy about whether the unique, "liberatory" and interconnective potential of the virtual will provide a vision for future communities. This is not to claim that celebrations of such a form of community are positing it as the only form to be practiced or experienced, since to some degree "earlier" forms will still continue to exist. How the relations between old and new forms are modeled requires further elaboration and critical attention. * * *

What I want to suggest is that, through the withdrawal of community from an embodied, political and social area—either to lodge within a philosophical abstraction or to become a disembodied, technologically enabled interaction—an ethical or political concern for the Other is rendered impotent and unrealizable. "Community" is then produced as an ideal rather than as a reality, or else it is abandoned altogether.

[Investigating] the political and ethical implications of the rise of cultures of disembodiment * * * requires separating the applications of information and communication technologies into the areas of administration, surveillance and communications. There is, of course, significant overlap between these areas. For the sake of simplicity I shall be referring to two "types" of computer technology: the system technologies or databases used by the public and private sectors, and the Internet.

Databases are used by institutions to accumulate, combine and create information on all facets of life (including people's personal lives). These systems operate from diverse, decentred locations, often with different intentions or orientations. Database systems are becoming increasingly interconnected and sophisticated, taking on the form of a global information system capable of infinite analysis, profiling and information combinations. This has consequences for the subjectivity of social actors through the creation of a technologized Panopticon. The Western individual increasingly experiences her/his life as monitored by technology: being caught on speed camera; captured on video while shopping; monitored for work efficiency by technological surveillance techniques; and taking a loan which is recorded, linked with other financial transactions and purchasing practices, and related to demographic statistics. These are just a few examples of contemporary surveillance. The continuous but often unverifiable surveillance has implications * * * for the instigation of normalization practices. The power of normalization refers to the process by which a subject self-imposes or interiorizes particular norms and behaviours to conform to a self-perceived (but socially constructed) understanding of normality. * * *

Databases are perceived as a means to assist the surveyor. Given that the surveyor is usually an institution of some description, viewing those outside (or working within) its system, images of Orwell's Big Brother—or many "little brothers"—are ominously invoked. The technology is oriented towards attaining control through information storage and analysis. Within the data field, information itself becomes an entity. Detached from its referent subject, it is able to be moved, manipulated and transformed.

The Internet also enables information to be moved, transformed and manipulated, bringing into question the issues of authorship and authenticity of material. In contrast to system databases, however, the Internet is depicted as a liberating technology. Its information is accessible to many users and it is interactive in form. The Internet enables the extension of many everyday activities. It is utilized for information collection, discussion of both academic and social topics, dissemination of views and undertaking financial transactions. Like databases, the Internet is unimpeded by state boundaries and is increasingly accessible on a global scale. It is a diverse, decentred communications system with unlimited input—in as much as anybody who is connected to a network can participate in the system—resulting in seemingly uncontrolled and unpredictable development. This is viewed by some institutions as potentially threatening, leading to media exposure of "illegitimate" or socially destructive activities on the Internet, and attempts by politicians to grapple with this issue through discussions of censorship and guidelines. * * *

[T]he application to the technology of such terms as *controlling* or *liberating* is arbitrary. Obviously, the technology itself is neither controlling or liberating, but the social and cultural uses to which it is put may well be. In so far as the Internet operates as an interconnected database, it has as much potential for bringing about panoptical kinds of recognition relations as it has for enhancing an experience of freedom and mobility. * * *

Virtual communities are formed and function within cyberspace—the space that exists within the connections and networks of communication technologies. They are presented by growing numbers of writers as exciting new forms of community which *liberate* the individual from the social constraints of embodied identity and from the restrictions of geographically embodied space; which *equalize* through the removal of embodied hierarchical structures; and which promote a sense of connectedness (or *fraternity*) among interactive participants. They are thereby posited as the epitome of a form of post-modern community within which multiplicity of self is enhanced and difference proliferates uninhabited by external, social structures. * * *

Participants in virtual communities can * * * escape their own embodied identities and accordingly can also escape any social inequities and attitudes relating to various forms of embodiment. Race, gender or physical disability is indiscernible over the Internet. Any basis for enacting discrimination is removed, freeing access to participation and granting each participant equal status within the network.

Liberation may also be achieved from the constraints of geographical space in so far as the physical location of the "body" of the [individual] is overcome through the extension of interaction in cyberspace * * * . Thus virtual communities are also seen as a way of overcoming the inherent isolation of contemporary life where people do not know their physical neighbours, are not involved in their local township decisions and possibly work from home. This "solution" overlooks the physically isolated nature of participation, where only the mind is extended into the mutual interaction. It is worth noting that virtual community participants often feel the need to reinforce/complement their disembodied relations by simulating, at the level of ritual, more embodied or sensorial contacts. For example, participants on the WELL—a virtual community on the Internet— have regular face-to-face picnics and social gatherings. The participants develop a more complete understanding of each other at such gatherings.

The perception of anonymity is presented as a further "plus" by proponents of virtual community. Liberated from the normative gaze of both institutions and society, identity cannot be verified and attached to the embodied user and behaviour is not constrained by "real space" norms and values. The degree of anonymity actually achieved is questionable, and will prove increasingly so as information providers and commercial interests devise more effective means of accumulating information about network users. Additionally, the chaos within some communities—as a consequence of anonymity being equated with a lack of accountability—has led them to require participants to provide stable identification. On the WELL, for example, participants are obliged to link all presentations of self with an unchanging referent user-ID, thus enabling identities to be verified. The need for a kind of order within community interaction has prompted such communities to sacrifice liberatory aspects of anonymity in favour of accountability. The recording and archiving of interactions also creates the "historical trace" of a character, decreasing the ability for that character to interact unidentified by past behaviours or statements. * * *

Virtual communities are celebrated as providing a space and form for a new experience of community. This experience is depicted as multiple, liberating, equalizing and thus providing a richer experience of togetherness. However, a critical examination of these understandings reveals, paradoxically, a "thinning" of the complexities of human engagement to the level of one-dimensional transactions and a detaching of the user from the political and social responsibilities of the "real space" environment. * * * In their desire to avoid placing restrictive or totalizing tendencies on the experience or understanding of community, theorists of both technological and non-technological orientation have removed community from a tangible, embodied or concrete possibility, relegating it either to the sphere of ontological, pre-political, pre-historical existence; or to an experiential existence within the nodes of a computer network system. This general movement towards a separation or abstraction of community from the political possibilities of real space removes any necessity for direct, embodied, political action. The depth of commitment to others within a community also declines, questioning the possibility of responsibility for the Other. * * * [A] concern for the Other is vital for any valid experience of community. But in the case of virtual communities such an ethic is far from apparent.

James Grimmelmann, *Virtual Worlds as Comparative Law*

2004-05 N.Y. L. Sch. L. Rev. 147

I would like to take seriously the claims of virtual world games to be genuinely new societies, at least for awhile. Societies have laws, so why should virtual societies be any different? My topic, then, will not be the law of virtual worlds, but rather law in virtual worlds. If lawyers can learn from studying the legal systems of common law and civil law countries, perhaps we can also learn from studying the legal systems of virtual law worlds.

In some cases, these legal systems track our own surprisingly well. In other cases, the contrasts are striking. Both the similarities and differences between real-life law and virtual law are instructive. They can teach us something about what is really going on in virtual worlds, and they can teach us something about what is really going on in our own world.

This Article is therefore a thought experiment; an attempt to lay the necessary conceptual foundations for talking coherently about "in-game" law. I will identify four recurring problems in virtual worlds, and discuss what we might gain by thinking about these problems as legal ones. * * *

Virtual Property

If one had to choose a single canonical feature of multiplayer online games, there would be no contest. Property is invariably among the first features implemented in any game. * * * Further, virtual property has been an enormous success in two related ways. First, these propertized spaces have been commercial successes as games because people enjoy fiddling with virtual property enough to play games that feature it. Second, this virtual property has been a success as property. A Chinese court has considered such property real enough to order its restitution and players in general consider it reliable enough to sustain a large and lucrative trade in virtual items. * * *

We might * * * ask * * * how this new form of property functions within the "legal" context of the virtual worlds that define it. * * * [C]ode-based property rights can be, and often are, absolute. If I "own" an enchanted sword, I am guaranteed to be the only player who can use that sword. No other player can use my virtual personalty, let alone take it from me. The game's interface typically won't even have a command allowing another player to attempt to use the sword; such a concept is inexpressible within the game's interface. * * * Of course, * * * much of the value of property rights, even highly secure ones, comes from their granularity. Unless they match the uses people wish to make of things, many productive transactions will be foregone as too risky or impossible to express. There is a natural pressure on designers to provide more detailed code-based property rules than the simple "possession-is-all rule."

Getting these details right, however, is a startlingly complex affair. Take the example of virtual homeownership, a feature supported in many games. * * * [E]very major game that allows ownership of real estate also gives owners the ability to choose who is allowed entry. In property law terms, such games take the virtual fee simple and carve out a new estate—let us call it the "right of visit." The right of visit is perpetual, non-transferable, and subject to revocation by the owner of the underlying fee simple. Thanks to this right, owners can use homes for parties. The ability to pass out rights of visit makes the underlying virtual fee simple more valuable.

While the right of visit solves one problem of coarse property rights, it exposes another. It is not a priori obvious how personal property should interact with the right of visit. * * * If a guest with a right of visit enters a house and drops an item, does it remain theirs, become the homeowner's, or become a res nullius? What if the owner revokes the right of visit while a guest is in the home and carrying items picked up inside? What if the owner sells the house with items and guests inside? Some answers to these questions seem better than others. For example, no game of which I am aware follows the rule that items dropped inside a dwelling become the property of the owner. My point is that these questions inevitably come up, no matter how complex the system of code-based property rights may be. And they can become quite complex. For example, Dark Age of Camelot defines ten separate estates: Visitor, Guest, Resident, Tenant, Acquaintance, Associate, Friend, Ally, and Partner, in addition to owner. Further, each of these roles can be customized with respect to a number of permissions, and homeowners can use various kinds of special objects with their own special rules.

This form of radiating complexity is of course by no means unique to software. As intricate as these rules may be, they pale in comparison to the Internal Revenue Code. The process of writing down exceptions and exceptions to exceptions can produce systems of breathtaking intricacy. However, there is a crucial difference between a highly-detailed system of legal rules and a highly-detailed system of software rules; one rooted in the fundamental distinction between law and software. A law depends on humans for its enforcement, which means that human cognitive biases will inevitably creep into the enforcement process as a law is applied to particular cases. Thus, as the complexity of a legal doctrine increases, so does its indeterminacy. As the number of provisions touching a given point of law increases, so to do the opportunities to pick and choose, to shade one statutory interpretation or another. The cumulative effect of many small ambiguities can be enormous. Complexity inherently begets ambiguity and creates space for creative lawyering and judicial discretion.

But in the world of software, increasing complexity does not bring with it increased discretion. This is so because software operates by itself: the only human in a position to determine its decisions is its programmer. Even as code-based property rights become increasingly complex, with more exceptions and special cases, they never become any less hard-nosed in their application. The tests are always binary and objective. * * * Software, by its nature, does not have discretion in the same sense that a judge does. We can commit decisions to a computer, but we cannot commit decisions to the reasoned discretion of the computer. In telling a computer which factors it should take into account and how it should weight them, we pre-decide every possible case. * * *

[Another important property issue involves] cases that are curiosities in the real world, [but] are of central importance in many online games. In the large crop of quasi-medieval games, with their strongly fantastic overtones, the capture of wild animals is nothing less than the principal source of wealth. The single most profitable "industry" is hunting monsters and looting their corpses. Unsurprisingly, the property rules governing acquisition by capture are highly worked out, and yet essentially every game that supplies code-based property to the killers of monsters sees these code-based rules supplanted by understandings among players.

For example, EverQuest automatically awards the experience produced by killing a monster to that team of players which has done the most damage to the monster. Therefore, at a code level, EverQuest propertizes the experience to the people who have done the majority of the work of the kill and turns the treasure into unowned property which can be claimed by any finder. Among the EverQuest player community, however, this rule is not considered normatively binding. Instead, a group which is actively engaged in fighting a monster, even if it has done little damage, is considered to have a prospecting property right because attacking the monster (unless the first group abandons the effort) is considered "kill stealing" and is taboo. Sony considers kill stealers to be engaged in "griefing," a term usually understood to mean deliberately annoying other players, and will suspend their accounts if it receives too many complaints.

Now, compare this rule to Asheron's Call's rules on kills. There, experience is divided up in direct proportion to the amount of damage a player does, so that if three players each independently do equal damage, each receives a third of the experience. These rules might have been written deliberately to fix EverQuest's normative problem. By allowing partial though not majority wounders to keep experience in proportion to the damage they deal, these rules create no danger of later hunters taking away the work that earlier hunters have done. Yet despite this rule, Asheron's Call still has a kill stealing problem, in the sense that players feel the need to define a code of conduct that forbids kill stealing and to complain to the gamemaker when other players violate that code. Players get upset when other, more powerful, groups come in, like bullies at the beach kicking sand in the faces of the weaklings and stealing their beautiful monsters. It seems that the kind of hot pursuit necessary to establish a normative right to the spoils is quite weak. One need not have immanent success, or even substantial progress, or even, perhaps, a high likelihood of ultimate success.

Every game has a property rule on the spoils of killing monsters embodied in its software. Players, however, will deviate from this rule based on their own social understandings. The idea that customary interactions will frequently depart from the law on point is not a new one. Robert Ellickson's study of norms among neighboring ranchers makes this point quite forcefully. His observation that people will often ignore an inappropriate or inefficient legal rule has a special force in games, where the "law" is enforced through software. A judge might at least hope to sort through conflicting versions of a story, while software is necessarily blind to the social meaning of events. * * *

The problem here is that, almost by definition, multiplayer games are endowed by their players with a rich layer of social meaning. Players make friendships, tell jokes, and fill out their virtual existences with their own ideas and interpretations. The game's code (and even often the game's designers) is ignorant of it all. If every iota of this meaning were reduced to code, there would be no game. The gaming conception of "possession-as-property" depends fundamentally on players having a meaningful social understanding of property. Probing those social understandings is a large and open topic for further study.

Wealth, Status, and Contract

Reliable contract law—along with reliable property law—is the intuitive basis of a functional market economy. If property gives individuals economic security, then contract allows them to put their property to use through productive exchange. But, while online games have quite strong protections for property, they have nothing that we would recognize as a comparable body of contracts law. Most games have no way to draft any contract more complex than an immediate sale of goods for cash.

This anomaly is even more striking in that most virtual worlds possess a fully-functioning market economy, complete with merchants, long distance trade, arbitrage, and recognizable macroeconomic trends. We need an account of how these extensive economies flourish without the promissory protections that we think of as being central to contract law. * * *

Even representing contracts in a computer intelligible form is a near intractable problem. Enormous effort and expense have been poured into automating contracts between businesses in the real world, but even there, code is still at least five centuries behind history. * * * Enforcing them is even more complex. After all, in deciding a contractual dispute, the decisionmaker is necessarily dealing with rules written by the parties themselves and specific to the case at hand. Determining whether conduct constitutes compliance or breach requires understanding of the communicatory, contextual meanings of that conduct. Such basic contractual issues as waiver, curing defects in nonconforming goods, and assurance will not be capable of automatic enforcement until we have true artificial intelligence.

But this is hardly the end of the matter. Property norms in games are enforced by players and designers as well as through code. Kill-stealers are attacked, shunned, and even expelled from games. It seems at least plausible that oath-breakers could be similarly disciplined. In fact, it is not so much that oath-breakers in games roam freely as that very little ever reaches the stage of oaths. There is something about virtual worlds that does not mix well with contracting.

We might plausibly ask how much practical difference rich contractual protection would make. The single most important commercial transaction—the present sale of goods—can be handled without formal contracts. Even in the complete absence of trust, two characters can meet, open up a window to display their offers, and then, when each has "inspected" the other's goods, click to confirm the trade and move on. The common contingencies many contracts are drafted to avoid are simply not possibilities. For example, there is typically no danger of defective goods because items in games typically don't have hidden attributes. In fact, many games, recognizing the centrality of cash sales of goods on hand, have implemented special facilities for these common transactions.

If we think about the other kinds of transactions for which we use contract law extensively in the real world, their underlying motivations are often absent in game worlds. There is comparatively little practical use to contracts for sales at some later time because game worlds are highly predictable. The harvests are reliable, monsters appear in set locations and on set schedules, there are no natural disasters, and no political turmoil ever threatens property or closes off the main roads. There is also little practical use for the large institutional contracts used in the real world to mobilize capital and put it to productive use because games lack major investment opportunities of the sort that would require contractual borrowing. There are no mines, factories, aqueducts, or other capital intensive projects capable of paying for themselves. Nor, for that matter, do we see family-relations contracts. Players frequently "marry" each other in-game, but they almost never draw up premarital agreements.

This last example is suggestive. To generalize it slightly, it seems that games frequently have rules, either in code or in player norms, governing status and adjustments to status. The game allows players to pick one profession or another, and players devise extensive lists of qualifications as prerequisites for joining guilds. Yet games do not seem to exhibit a particularly rich contractual penumbra around these incidents of status. The dissatisfied spouse declares himself "divorced," the dissatisfied guild expels an unruly member, and the game does not negotiate at all with the dissatisfied farmer. Self-help and ongoing negotiation are more the order of the day than enforceable agreements.

One model, then, would be that games represent worlds that are relational rather than contractual. Certainly the extensive gift economies that flow through many games, often coexisting quite comfortably with market economies, express something of this sense. The norm of generosity to newbies is quite pervasive. Even in Ultima Online's early Wild West days, when new players were considered easy marks, they were often still the beneficiaries of repeated gifts from more experienced players.

Guilds, where patron-client networks are perhaps strongest, also illustrate this through their relationship with their members. While guilds have been compared to organized crime gangs, it might be more accurate to think of them as quasi-feudal. Certainly, the tendency among top EverQuest guilds towards evaluating members for periods that verge on indentured servitude in exchange for spoils and protection has something of the lord-vassal relationship.

Perhaps we cannot see contract law when we look at games because the contract is not the right abstraction for expressing the nature of relationships in virtual worlds.   In terms of Henry Maine's famous dichotomy, it is at least plausible to claim that these games are worlds of "status," not of "contract."   In a formal sense, everything pertaining to a character is wrapped up in a few thousand bytes of data stored on one of the game's servers. Who is Adelaida? What are her legal rights? How does the game treat her? Those thousand bytes of status supply all the answers. This status defines most of her position within player society as well. Her appearance, her level, her experience—all of these qualities are visible, objective, and inalienable. She can hide her wealth or transfer it, but it too is a number on a server somewhere. Most factors that would draw other players to her are inherent in herself, not in her relationships with others. * * *

Virtual Criminal Law and Administration

* * * When we look at the mechanisms by which players might enforce their notions of fair play and good behavior, an odd paradox emerges. The set of unpleasant and wrongful acts players might wish to deter is identical to the set of unpleasant and effective sanctions available as deterrence. To prevent violence, annoyance, and non-cooperation, players can engage in violence, annoyance, or non-cooperation.

* * * I submit that whoever understands the nature of guilds will understand the nature of community and community norm-enforcement in modern virtual worlds.   Every major game has some variant on the guild concept.   EverQuest has guilds and raid parties, Asheron's Call has allegiance hierarchies, Star Wars Galaxies has player associations, and many games have more complex systems. Across these disparate games, guilds almost always have several important features in common: the games make some explicit provision for their existence, the powers granted to them by the games are very weak, and yet they are somehow key to the social energy of a virtual world.

Scholars of virtual worlds need to develop theories about the emergent properties of guilds. We need an account of why guilds seem to be so important in server-level politics and of how players inside guilds interact. Further, we need to understand how game software becomes social, specifically, how the choices made by game designers in creating guild systems turn into the surprisingly prominent guilds we know and love. An account of this form, I believe, will tell us what is really going on as the Sims Shadow Government and the Sims Mafia struggle to define what is "right" and what is "griefing" in The Sims Online.

First, there is the null hypothesis that people join guilds for the same reason they join any other group. On this view, guilds don't present any special problems; they're just another example of general phenomena in the study of social groups. People are hard-wired to be social, so any software environments capable of supporting sociability will intrinsically also support, and indeed create, social groups. Guilds will often be created by people who know each other in real life. Accordingly, there is no important way in which they differ from other groups.

This description is useful in reminding us that not every aspect of guild life is unique to guilds and that not every feature of guilds requires a purposive explanation. Nonetheless, its explanatory power is weak. We need an explanation that makes sense of the fact that where there is code-level support for guilds, they tend very strongly to displace other, potentially competing, social groups.

We might, for example, understand guilds as groups optimized to minimize transaction costs. Based on this view, players form guilds to help them accomplish important tasks cooperatively. The hard part about cooperation is making sure that others are playing along. A guild's real "use" is its ability to reduce the difficulty of knowing the many other players on the server to the simpler task of knowing only the players in your guild. Larger size guilds allow for larger in-game challenges, but they are increasingly more difficult to organize. Here, the code-level features are the kernels around which social groups crystallize

It is also important to pay attention to the negotiations and relations among guilds. Take for example, the coordination problem for EverQuest raids. In a raid, a group of players go to a highly dangerous area and systematically kill the monsters there. Good raid strategy involves close coordination and patience. If a raiding party draws the attention of too many monsters at once, it is likely to be slaughtered. For this reason, it is safer and easier for one group to raid a given area than for two distinct groups to try at the same time. The structure of EverQuest raids thus creates a classic coordination problem for which websites have emerged to handle the necessary cooperation. These raid calendars allow raiding parties to reserve zones for future raids. Since these sites are entirely independent of the game itself, they have available to them only those sanctions that guilds can enforce against other guilds. The most notable of these sanctions, of course, is the ability to ruin another group's raid with well-timed interference, drawing monsters out into open combat before the raiding group is prepared to fight them.

I suspect that we are witnessing the bottom-up emergence of governing institutions in games, as catalyzed by whatever code-level features the games offer for guild formation. Of course, what we currently have is quasi-feudal: allegiance hierarchies which start to become powerful entities in their own right. * * * The political relationship between these increasingly powerful guilds and game designers also needs explication. There is something incongruous about the trend towards increasingly important guild extensions. "Player towns," essentially guild-owned gated communities, are one of the most hyped features hurtling towards the market. Other games are trying to devise richer political systems, including elections, mayors, factions in conflict, explicit patron-client relationships, and other simulations of real-world governments and states. Within limits, it seems almost as though new games are in a race to create territorial sovereigns in their games' code.

And yet, the question arises: If a game had a rich enough social universe, why would it need any of these features? Isn't the need to implement elections in code a sign that the game is too flat to allow players to institute their own elections? Conversely, isn't there something artificial about an election held through game code? Is anything really at stake, or is it just another quest for players in the same way that killing a dragon in the mountains would be? * * *

The God Problem

Whether the designers who control game software and game servers are called "gods," "wizards," "sysops," or "GMs," players are inescapably in their hands and at their mercy. * * * Virtual worlds are not democratic. It is true that the designers could hold elections among players and promise to be bound by the results, but such promises can always be broken. At the end of the day, all such referenda are never more than advisory. To put this point another way, at least since Locke, the legitimacy of republican government has been intertwined with the right of revolution. If the government refuses to obey the results of an election, it must expect the citizenry to rise up and depose. But there is no way to depose the designers of a game.

This is not to say that game designers are entirely free to act as tyrants. If they do, players will leave the game. If we have respect for players' autonomy, their continued willingness to play must count for something. Indeed, any game dependent on players for its revenue will have very strong incentives not to frustrate the strong desires of a majority for too long. Players, as a single collective group, have power over designers through their exit option. It is the virtual equivalent of emigration. * * *

Another perspective on the "unlimited" power of game designers comes from looking at the rise of real-life markets in virtual items. In the real world, those who make investments in a country expose themselves to uniquely "sovereign" risks because of the danger that the government might alter the laws under which they claim to hold assets. Players find themselves in a similar relationship with games because they are largely without recourse if the designers change the game's rules mid-stream. However, like investors, they can bring a game to its knees if they collectively choose to withdraw their support. I am not suggesting that we might actually apply the international law of sovereign expropriations to games. I am instead suggesting that this example of "unlimited" power from the real world provides a useful analogy for thinking about the powers of game designers.

Speaking loosely, we might call multiplayer games tourist economies because their principal wealth-creating activity is providing pleasure for those who choose to vacation there. Their incorporeal nature means that they can't make tangible goods capable of being exported and that anything "made" in-game must stay there. On the other hand, most games see capital, or hard currency, flowing inexorably inwards. Players invest by paying monthly fees to its government, the designers. That government supplies various services by converting the capital supplied by players into game infrastructure. New areas of the map, items available for purchase and the merchants who sell them, and those infinitely respawning monster sites are all tourist-industry infrastructure.

The "investors" in a game are in an interesting position. They cannot remove capital from the game once it has been spent on internal improvements. There are no goods susceptible to export and their original investment partner, the game's designers, will not be willing to unwind the investment. The best that a player-investor can do is to make profits within the game's economy and then find a new player-investor willing to step into her shoes. Positions cannot be liquidated, only transferred. To leave a game, an individual player-investor must find another player-investor in an offshore market who wishes to invest in the game to the same degree as the leaving player-investor

This fact leads to * * * various observations about the practical influence of "eBayers." By allowing players to buy their way into or out of a game with hard (real world) currency, these markets tamper with the political climate of their games. On the one hand, allowing the liquidation of one's stake in a game makes players less bought-in to a game and less susceptible to its control. After all, as long as the game has not actually suspended your account, you can always turn around, convert your character and assets into cash, and walk away. The effective threats that other players can make against you are that much weaker.

Further, by allowing players to purchase their way into a game, the presence of an offshore market changes the list of real-world attributes that influence in-game success. Without such markets, one's success is mostly a function of one's skill in playing and one's willingness to devote time to the game. Where they exist, however, wealthy players can leapfrog over poorer ones, purchasing the symbols of success, rather than winning them directly. * * *

For now, the calculus of a game designer is rather simple: maximize the number of players, and therefore settle disputes in whichever way will cause the fewest people to leave in annoyance. * * * But many games are starting to break out of this form of equality. They hope to capture for themselves some of the money that currently goes to other players from those who buy their way in. * * * Such changes undo the rough identity between the notions of "citizen" and "investor." The great mass of low-paying regular players are now useful principally to the extent that they keep the high-rollers happy. If driving away five $10 per month players causes a $100 per month player to double her spending, the game administration will happily make such a trade.

Whether such changes will be stabilizing or destabilizing is a fascinating question that requires us to think about the relationship between real and virtual economies—between real and virtual societies.

Thinking of the "god problem" from an international law perspective on investors makes clear that it is hardly a one-sided power dynamic. The players may have as much to fear from other players' influence on game designers as they do from the whimsy of the designers themselves. * * *

Conclusion

There are two themes running throughout this article that I would like to highlight. First, there are questions of power: Who can do what to whom? In various combinations, I have asked what players and designers can do to, for, or with each other. Second, there are questions of meaning: How do people understand the significance of various features and behaviors in these virtual worlds?

I believe that because of the virtuality of these worlds, these two questions are intertwined. Establishing the social understandings that make a virtual society possible is both an act of laying out its power relations and an act of agreeing upon its semiotics. In its own way, each of the four topics discussed illustrates one aspect of the way in which these two questions relate to each other. They may even be the same question.

Of course, these questions are also familiar to real world lawyers and scholars. The answers to these questions become more salient when they are analyzed in the context of online virtual worlds. It is my hope that from this reflection we may gain insight into answering these questions in the virtual world we inhabit offline.

Notes and Questions

1. How would you define "community"? What are its key attributes? Do you think communities are important (or even necessary) to human life? Why or why not?

2. In what ways do you think the Internet fosters community? In what ways might online interaction impede the formation of community affiliations?

3. What is cosmopolitanism? Is it a useful model for thinking about community? Are Professor Berman and Professor Chander right that territorially based communities are not the only significant community affiliations that exist? If so, how might legal regulation adapt to account for this change?

4. Is Iris Young's model of the "unoppresive city" a useful ideal? If so, does online interaction help foster any of these ideals?

5. Is Chander right that online interaction permits members of minority groups more space to pursue alternative community formulations? Or do you agree with Wilson that community unmoored to physical connection is not an alternative to face-to-face community identity?

6. Consider the modern nation-state. Why are such states conceptualized as communities? After all, members of even the smallest nation-state will never know most of their fellow-members, meet them, or even hear of them. Could we say, therefore, that the nation-state is a community that is *imagined* through a social psychological process? Yet if communities are based not on fixed attributes such as geographical proximity, shared history, or face-to-face interaction, but instead on symbolic identification and social psychology, then

what reason is there to privilege nation-state communities over other possible community identifications that people might share? Does Berman's cosmopolitan view challenge the nation-state? Does it render the nation-state irrelevant?

7. Wilson argues that community affiliation unmoored to physical location "removes any necessity for direct, embodied, political action." Do you agree? What about global environmental or human rights movements that have used the Internet to share information and build international political coalitions? Are these networks appropriately thought of as communities?

8. Wilson also challenges the liberatory story of the Internet by focusing on the way that the technology facilitates increasing centralized control of information and therefore more intrusive government surveillance. Can you think of examples of this surveillance? Does the possibility of increasing mechanisms for control undermine Berman's or Chander's visions? Why or why not?

9. Consider Grimmelmann's approach. Does it make sense to you to think of virtual worlds as distinct places, with laws and social networks of their own? Would Wilson think that players in these virtual games constitute a community?

10. If we do think of virtual worlds as societies with significant legal and quasi-legal arrangements, what then? Does studying such worlds illuminate features of law in physical space? Might virtual worlds provide useful experiments in alternative legal arrangements? Or are the code-based parameters of these games so different that no useful lessons can be learned?

11. In thinking about virtual worlds, recall the problems of jurisdiction and sovereignty discussed in Chapter Three. Are virtual worlds an area where it makes sense to think of the online environment itself as a legal jurisdiction? If not, how should territorially based courts resolve disputes engendered by such worlds? Or should they simply dismiss any such disputes as non-justiciable disagreements about a "game"? *See, e.g., Ga. High Sch. Ass'n v. Waddell*, 285 S.E. 2d 7, 9 (Ga. 1981)(holding that a dispute over a referee's decision affecting the outcome of a high school football game was nonjusticiable). *But see PGA Tour, Inc. v. Martin*, 532 U.S. 661, 690 (2001) (ruling that a golf association had violated the Americans with Disabilities Act by preventing a partially disabled golfer from using a golf cart to compete). Grimmelman notes that these virtual worlds generate hundreds of thousands of dollars in economic transactions on eBay and elsewhere. Given the economic stakes, is it inevitable that courts will be called upon to resolve disputes over these trades or purchases? If so, what law should be used?

SECTION C. CYBERSPACE AND THE FORMATION OF LAW AND POLICY

Finally, we consider the possible effect of the Internet on the way in which legal and policy decisions themselves might be reached. For example, what are the core attributes that make the Internet so popular, and how can such attributes be retained even as more and more people interact online? Are there governance models in cyberspace that are different from those that tend to be employed in the offline context, and if so, are those governance models attractive or repugnant? What is the appropriate role for government policy-making? If government control wanes, should we be concerned about the increasing power of non-governmental entities? Most important, do questions of online law and policy formation illuminate more general issues concerning the variety of ways that legal norms develop and the appropriate allocation of law-making authority?

Jonathan Zittrain, *The Generative Internet*
119 HARV. L. REV. 1974 (2006)

The Internet today is exceptionally generative. It can be leveraged: its protocols solve difficult problems of data distribution, making it much cheaper to implement network-aware services. It is adaptable in the sense that its basic framework for the interconnection of nodes is amenable to a large number of applications, from e-mail and instant messaging to telephony and streaming video. This adaptability exists in large part because Internet protocol relies on few assumptions about the purposes for which it will be used and because it efficiently scales to accommodate large amounts of data and large numbers of users. It is easy to master because it is structured to allow users to design new applications without having to know or worry about the intricacies of packet routing. And it is accessible because, at the functional level, there is no central gatekeeper with which to negotiate access and because its protocols are publicly available and not subject to intellectual property restrictions. Thus, programmers independent of the Internet's architects and service providers can offer, and consumers can accept, new software or services

How did this state of affairs come to pass? * * * The network's design is perhaps best crystallized in a seminal 1984 paper entitled End-to-End Arguments in System Design. As this paper describes, the Internet's framers intended an hourglass design, with a simple set of narrow and slow-changing protocols in the middle, resting on an open stable of physical carriers at the bottom and any number of applications written by third parties on the top. The Internet hourglass, despite having been conceived by an utterly different group of architects from those who designed or structured the market for PCs, thus mirrors PC architecture in key respects. The network is indifferent to both the physical media on which it operates and the nature of the data it passes, just as a PC OS is open to running upon a variety of physical hardware "below" and to supporting any number of applications from various sources "above." * * *

Two further historical developments assured that an easy-to-master Internet would also be extraordinarily accessible. First, the early Internet consisted of nodes primarily at university computer science departments, U.S. government research units, and select technology companies with an interest in cutting-edge network research. These institutions collaborated on advances in bandwidth management and tools for researchers to use for communication and discussion. But consumer applications were nowhere to be found until the Internet began accepting commercial interconnections without requiring academic or government research justifications, and the population at large was solicited to join. This historical development—the withering away of the norms against commercial use and broad interconnection that had been reflected in a National Science Foundation admonishment that its contribution to the functioning Internet backbone be used for noncommercial purposes—greatly increased the Internet's generativity. It opened development of networked technologies to a broad, commercially driven audience that individual companies running proprietary services did not think to invite and that the original designers of the Internet would not have thought to include in the design process.

A second historical development is easily overlooked because it may in retrospect seem inevitable: the dominance of the Internet as the network to which PCs connected, rather than the emergence of proprietary networks analogous to the information appliances that PCs themselves beat. The first large-scale networking of consumer PCs took place through self-contained "walled garden" networks like CompuServe, The Source, and Prodigy. Each network connected its members only to other subscribing members and to content managed and cleared through the network proprietor. For example, as early as 1983, a home computer user with a CompuServe subscription was able to engage in a variety of activities—reading news feeds, sending e-mail, posting messages on public bulletin boards, and participating in rudimentary multiplayer games (again, only with other CompuServe subscribers). But each of these activities was coded by CompuServe or its formal partners, making the network much less generatively accessible than the Internet would be. Although CompuServe entered into some development agreements with outside software programmers and content providers, even as the service grew to almost two million subscribers by 1994, its core functionalities remained largely unchanged.

The proprietary services could be leveraged for certain tasks, and their technologies were adaptable to many purposes and easy to master, but consumers' and outsiders' inability to tinker easily with the services limited their generativity. They were more like early video game consoles than PCs: capable of multiple uses, through the development of individual "cartridges" approved by central management, yet slow to evolve because potential audiences of developers were slowed or shut out by centralized control over the network's services.

The computers first attached to the Internet were mainframes and minicomputers of the sort typically found within university computer science departments, and early desktop access to the Internet came through specialized nonconsumer workstations, many running variants of the UNIX OS. As the Internet expanded and came to appeal to nonexpert participants, the millions of PCs in consumer hands were a natural source of Internet growth. * * *

As PC users found themselves increasingly able to access the Internet, proprietary network operators cum content providers scrambled to reorient their business models away from corralled content and toward accessibility to the wider Internet. These online service providers quickly became mere ISPs, with their users branching out to the thriving Internet for programs and services. * * *

The resulting Internet is a network that no one in particular owns and that anyone can join. * * * Both noncommercial and commercial enterprises have taken advantage of open PC and Internet technology, developing a variety of Internet-enabled applications and services, many going from implementation to popularity (or notoriety) in a matter of months or even days. Yahoo!, Amazon.com, eBay, flickr, the Drudge Report, CNN.com, Wikipedia, MySpace: the list of available services and activities could go into the millions, even as a small handful of Web sites and applications account for a large proportion of online user activity. Some sites, like CNN.com, are online instantiations of existing institutions; others, from PayPal to Geocities, represent new ventures by formerly unestablished market participants. Although many of the offerings created during the dot-com boom years—roughly 1995 to 2000—proved premature at best and flatly ill-advised at worst, the fact remains that many large companies, including technology-oriented ones, ignored the Internet's potential for too long.

Significantly, the last several years have witnessed a proliferation of PCs hosting broadband Internet connections. The generative PC has become intertwined with the generative Internet, and the whole is now greater than the sum of its parts. A critical mass of always-on computers means that processing power for many tasks, ranging from difficult mathematical computations to rapid transmission of otherwise prohibitively large files, can be distributed among hundreds, thousands, or millions of PCs. Similarly, it means that much of the information that once needed to reside on a user's PC to remain conveniently accessible—documents, e-mail, photos, and the like—can instead be stored somewhere on the Internet. So, too, can the programs that a user might care to run.

This still-emerging "generative grid" expands the boundaries of leverage, adaptability, and accessibility for information technology. It also raises the ante for the project of cyberlaw because the slope of this innovative curve may nonetheless soon be constrained by some of the very factors that have made it so steep. Such constraints may arise because generativity is vulnerability in the current order: the fact that tens of millions of machines are connected to networks that can convey reprogramming in a matter of seconds means that those computers stand exposed to near-instantaneous change. This kind of generativity keeps publishers vulnerable to the latest tools of intellectual property infringement, crafted ever more cleverly to evade monitoring and control, and available for installation within moments everywhere. It also opens PCs to the prospect of mass infection by a computer virus that exploits either user ignorance or a security vulnerability that allows code from the network to run on a PC without approval by its owner. Shoring up these vulnerabilities will require substantial changes in some aspects of the grid, and such changes are sure to affect the current level of generativity. Faced with the prospect of such changes, we must not fight an overly narrow if well-intentioned battle simply to preserve end-to-end network neutrality or to focus on relative trivialities like domain names and cookies. Recognizing the true value of the grid—its hypergenerativity—along with the magnitude of its vulnerabilities and the implications of eliminating those vulnerabilities, leads to the realization that we should instead carefully tailor reforms to address those vulnerabilities with minimal impact on generativity. * * *

To appreciate the power of the new and growing Internet backlash—a backlash that augurs a dramatically different, managed Internet of the sort that content providers and others have unsuccessfully strived to bring about—one must first identify three powerful groups that may find common cause in seeking a less generative grid: regulators (in part driven by threatened economic interests, including those of content providers), mature technology industry players, and consumers. These groups are not natural allies in technology policy, and only recently have significant constituencies from all three sectors gained momentum in promoting a refashioning of Internet and PC architecture that would severely restrict the Internet's generativity. * * *

Looking to the grid's future gives us a sense of what regulators and consumers want, as well as when these groups' interests and views will largely align, or at least will not paralyzingly conflict.

1. *Information Appliances.* — An "information appliance" is one that will run only those programs designated by the entity that built or sold it. In the taxonomy of generativity, an information appliance may have the leverage and adaptability of a PC, but its accessibility for further coding is strictly limited.

There are already several Internet-aware mainstream information appliances. A flagship example is TiVo, a digital video recorder that connects to a user's cable, satellite, or antenna feed to record television programs. TiVo also connects to a phone line or Internet connection to download program information daily. It is thus both a product and a service. Consumers who have TiVo nearly uniformly love it, and many say they would not want to watch television without it.

The designers of TiVo did not write its software from scratch; they implemented it on top of the highly generative GNU/Linux OS. Most TiVo owners do not realize that they have purchased a form of PC. There is no sign that an OS—in the generative sense of something open to third-party programs—is present. Users interact with TiVo using a remote control, and the limitations on TiVo's use are not easy to circumvent. Such limitations include the inability to create standardized digital output: TiVo's recorded programs cannot be copied over to a PC without TiVo's own DRM-restricted software.

TiVo works as reliably as a traditional appliance because its makers know, with much greater certainty than most PC manufacturers, the uses to which it can be put. This certainty is good for TiVo and its partner hardware manufacturers because it gives TiVo complete control over the combined product/service that it provides. It is good for consumers because they find TiVo useful and trustworthy. It is also satisfying to regulators because TiVo was designed to prevent contributions to the peer-to-peer problem. * * * TiVo's recorded shows may only be saved to a standard VCR or DVD, or in a copy-protected PC format, rather than, as would be trivial for the manufacturer to allow, digitally to a consumer's PC hard drive in an unprotected format or over the Internet to an arbitrary destination. Even though many consumers would no doubt like such a feature, TiVo has likely refrained from offering it in part because it has relationships with content providers and in part because of fears of secondary copyright liability. * * *

TiVo heralds growth in Internet-aware appliances that exploit the generativity of OSs and networks but that are not themselves generative to consumers or other end users. This lack of generativity does not alone bespeak a major shift in the fundamentals of the Internet/PC grid, though it does perhaps make for some lost collective potential. Consumers who might otherwise buy a television-aware PC—and who might find themselves pleasantly surprised that it can be adapted to uses that they did not contemplate at the time of purchase—instead will buy TiVos. In turn, there is less incentive for some coders to create new uses because the audience of people who might benefit from those uses has decreased. * * *

Similar patterns may be found for other new information appliances. For example, smartphones are mobile cellular telephones that are designed to surf the Internet and handle nontelephonic tasks like taking pictures and maintaining calendars and to-do lists. Some smartphones like the Palm Treo are based on general-purpose handheld computers and then add telephonic functionality; they can run applications from third parties, possibly to the chagrin of cellular operators whose service is subject to disruption should Treos be compromised by malicious code. Others, including some phones by Cingular, run a version of Windows, but are configured by the cellular carriers who sell them to run only specially "signed" software: customers cannot simply double-click their way to running software not approved by the cellular carrier. Beyond smartphones, some information appliances are more closely related to the PC. For example, the Xbox is a powerful video game console produced by Microsoft. As a general-purpose device it has capacity for non-gaming applications, but, unlike a PC running Windows, it is generatively far less accessible: third-party hardware and software add-ons must be licensed by Microsoft, and some portion of profits from their sale must be shared with Microsoft as royalties.

2. *The Appliancized PC.* — The PC is heading in the direction of these information appliances. The first step that OS makers have taken as a natural response to threats from viruses and worms is to caution users before they run unfamiliar code for the first time. Users have found that they can compromise their PCs simply by visiting the wrong webpage, by clicking on executable e-mail attachments, or by downloading malicious software. Microsoft Windows presents a security warning when a user tries to run "unknown" software, defined as software without a digital certificate recognized by Microsoft. In the most recent version of Windows (Windows XP), when a user attempts to run such an unknown program, or when one tries to execute automatically—perhaps when the user visits a webpage—the user is presented with the warning: "The publisher could not be verified. Are you sure you want to run this software?" * * * Businesses can readily configure employees' computers to run only approved applications; so, too, can libraries, schools, and parents. This not only screens out some undesirable content, but also locks down the PC for uses that couldbe quite positive, even if not explicitly approved by the machines' custodians. * * *

It helps to juxtapose this developing architecture with another new feature in OSs that is possible now that networking is so ubiquitous: automatic updating. This new feature, which appears in the latest Microsoft and Apple OSs and in many individual pieces of software, takes account of the fact that more and more PCs have always-on broadband Internet connections. From the moment the computer is first connected to the Internet, the feature is enabled for some software. For others, including Windows XP, the feature is off, but the computer prompts the user to turn it on. With automatic updating, the computer regularly checks—typically daily—for updates from the OS publisher and from the makers of any software installed on the PC. At first blush, this function is innocuous enough; it takes advantage of the networkability and adaptability of the PC to obtain the most recent security patches as they become available.

* * * But * * * automatic updating opens the door to an utter transformation of the way the Internet grid works. With automatic updating, the OS and attendant applications become services rather than products. This transformation holds appeal for software makers, who can request or require consumers to subscribe to regular updates, much as those who purchase antivirus software are asked to subscribe annually to virus definition updates after a one-year grace period. Further, such updates help reduce software piracy: if a consumer does not validate his or her copy of the software or OS, the manufacturer can deactivate the software from a distance or can configure it to cease functioning if not properly renewed.

Automatic updating works in concert with appliancization, allowing manufacturers to see when their software has been hacked or altered--and to shut down or reinstall the original OS when they have. Exactly this happened with the Hughes DirecTV satellite receiver information appliance. Just before the Super Bowl in 2001, consumers who had hacked their

DirecTV receivers to receive smartcard access found their receivers suddenly no longer working: the satellite had broadcast not only programming for people to watch, but programming for the receiver to obey. The receiver checked for particular hacks and, if they were found, self-destructed, rendering the affected cards entirely useless. By some reports, the last few computer bytes of the hacked smartcards were rewritten to read "Game Over."

Automatically updating software on PCs is becoming more common at the same time as the Internet itself becomes a host for highly controlled software. The emergence of the PC/Internet grid makes it easier for applications to be developed to run on remote servers rather than on the PC itself. A PC or information appliance equipped with only a web browser can now access a range of service—a development variously known as application streaming, web services, and Web 2.0. On one view, this development is generatively neutral, merely shifting the locus of generative software writing to a server on the Internet rather than on the PC itself--perhaps even avoiding the generative damage caused by PC lockdown. This shift, however, undermines distributed PC processing power for novel peer-to-peer applications. It also carries many, but not all, of the drawbacks of automatic updating. From a security standpoint, a service updated at one location on the Internet may be much less likely to interfere with the user's enjoyment of a service offered elsewhere by another provider—unlike an automatic update by one PC application that can harm a concurrent PC application or disrupt the overall operation of the PC. However, this very isolation of services can also prevent generative building of software on other software. * * * Consumers deciding between security-flawed generative PCs and safer but more limited information appliances (or appliancized PCs) may consistently undervalue the benefits of future innovation (and therefore of generative PCs). The benefits of future innovation are difficult to perceive in present-value terms, and few consumers are likely to factor into their purchasing decisions the history of unexpected information technology innovation that promises so much more just around the corner.

From the regulators' point of view, automatic updating presents new gatekeeping opportunities. Updates can be and have been used by manufacturers not only to add functionality, but also to take it away, at times apparently because of legal concerns. For example, an earlier version of Apple's iTunes software permitted users to stream their music on the Internet, without permitting them to copy each others' music permanently. Apple subsequently thought better of the feature, and in a later automatic update trimmed iTunes to permit streaming only to those on one's local network.

* * * MP3 players, including the iPod, are increasingly being used for radio-like broadcasts. Through so-called "podcasting," an owner of an MP3 player can lawfully download, for listening purposes, a number of selected programs from the Internet at large. The iTunes streaming feature could have been a significant contributor to the popular uptake of podcasting

because it could have allowed people to share their favorite broadcasts widely. But because Apple withdrew the feature, its potential impact cannot be known. Although Apple's withdrawal was voluntary, many more generative developments might be lost as a result of legally compelled restrictions on such features.

* * * To be sure, there is no basis on which to insist flatly that any tradeoff between regulability and generativity should favor the latter. But this is a false dichotomy if we can make the grid more secure without sacrificing its essential generative characteristics. Making progress on the security problem is difficult because the distributed nature of the Internet and individual ownership of PCs do not induce participants to internalize their negative security externalities. * * * ISPs are not held economically accountable when their subscribers' computers fall victim to viruses. Similarly, individual users may not care if their compromised machines cause trouble for other, faraway users. Locking down the PC, although attractive from a regulatory point of view, is undesirable because of its effect on innovation: technical innovation will slow as third parties are squeezed out of the development cycle, and intellectual and artistic innovation will slow as some of the technical innovations forestalled are quite possibly ones that would enhance valuable expressive activities. * * *

To evaluate the different paths information technology might take, we must bear in mind key contributors to its success: those who are creative and are inspired to express that creativity, whether through producing new code or code-enabled art. Amateurs, who produced applications that others overlooked, played a vital role in the rise of the Internet and the PC. * * * In this sense, of course, "amateurs" are those who do what they do because they love to do it. The availability of tools through which amateurs could express creativity meant that code was written by parties other than those who had chosen lives of professional codewriting. Today, thanks to networked information technology and the recursively generative code produced in large part by amateurs, art can be produced and shared by people other than professional artists, citizens can engage in far-ranging dialogues with others whom they would not otherwise encounter, and people can work together from the four corners of the globe to produce intellectual projects of social and economic significance.

The most important opportunities for such creativity ought to be retained as the Internet evolves. But this will require those who support creative communities to make an important concession. They will have to face the reality that a free and open Internet, including open PCs distributed among tens of millions of consumers, is simply not possible unless the most pressing demands of countervailing regulatory forces are satisfied. It is now an opportune time for thoughtful interventions in law and code. Matters are still in flux, and no stakeholder is too invested in any of the most locked-down versions of the postdiluvian Internet. Intervention can preserve and maybe even enhance generativity while making necessary progress toward stability. * * *

[First,] those who favor end-to-end principles because they favor generativity must realize that failure to take action at the network level may close some parts of the grid because consumers may demand, and PC manufacturers may provide, locked-down endpoint environments that promise security and stability with minimum user upkeep. * * * Put simply, complete fidelity to end-to-end may cause users to embrace the digital equivalent of gated communities. Gated communities offer safety and stability to residents and a manager to complain to when something goes wrong. But from a generative standpoint, digital gated communities are prisons. Their confinement is less than obvious because what they block is generative possibility: the ability of outsiders to offer code and services to users, giving users and producers an opportunity to influence the future without a regulator's permission. If digital gated communities become the norm, highly skilled Internet users of the sort who predominated in the mid-1980s will still be able to enjoy generative computing on platforms that are not locked down, but the rest of the public will not be brought along for the ride. For those using locked-down endpoints, the freedom in the middle of the network is meaningless.

Thus, strict loyalty to end-to-end neutrality should give way to a new generativity principle, a rule that asks that modifications to the PC/Internet grid be made when they will do the least harm to its generative possibilities. Under such a principle, for example, it may be preferable in the medium term to screen out viruses through ISP-operated network gateways rather than through constantly updated PCs. Although such network screening theoretically opens the door to additional filtering that may be undesirable, this risk should be balanced against the very real risks to generativity inherent in PCs operated as services rather than products.

* * * [Second,] OS makers or security firms may block the deployment of individual PC applications on behalf of PC users who crave security, creating broader bottlenecks to application deployment by anyone other than centralized kingmakers. The puzzle, then, is how to avoid these bottlenecks, whether coming from government or from private code-filtering schemes, while conceding that PC users can no longer be expected to exercise meaningful choice about code without help. A worthy Internet governance project to retain consumer choice without creating a new bottleneck could take the form of a grassroots campaign or public interest organization with participation from Internet architects. This project could set up a technical architecture to label applications and fragments of executable code, coupled with an organization to apply such labels nondiscriminatorily. Alternatively, the project could establish a distributed architecture by which the individual decisions about whether to run a given application, and the subsequent results, could serve as advice to others contemplating whether to run such code. The history of the Internet is seasoned with successful organizations devoted to such ends even though ideological views and regulatory agendas are often embedded in technical decisions. Public interest "underwriters' laboratories" for the Internet would reduce consumer demand for evaluations by OS makers or ISPs.

Precisely because the lines separating viruses, spyware, poorly written software, and flat rent extraction by software authors are so blurry, they are best adjudicated using the sorts of quasi-public mechanisms that have served Internet development in the past. The alternative is to see such power accrete in a handful of private firms with incentives to become gatekeepers for purposes other than security.

* * * [Third, a]s the capacity to inflict damage increases with the Internet's reach and with the number of valuable activities reliant upon it, the imperatives to take action will also increase. Intermediaries will be called to supervise because they provide a service capable of filtering user behavior. Preemptive reductions in PC or Internet generativity may also arise as it becomes easier to implement such changes over the grid.

One way to reduce pressure on institutional and technological gatekeepers is to make direct responsibility more feasible. Forthcoming piecemeal solutions to problems such as spam take this approach. ISPs are working with makers of major PC e-mail applications to provide for forms of sender authentication. A given domain can, using public key encryption tools, authenticate that it is indeed the source of e-mail attributed to it. With Microsoft's Sender ID or something like it, e-mail purporting--but not proving--to be from a user at yahoo.com can be filtered as spam so easily that it will no longer be worthwhile to send. This regime will hold ISPs more accountable for the e-mail they permit their networks to originate because they will find themselves shunned by other ISPs if they permit excessive anonymous spam. This opportunity for more direct liability reduces the pressure on those processing incoming e-mail—both the designated recipients and their ISPs—to resort to spam filtration heuristics that may unintentionally block legitimate e-mail.

The same principle can be applied to individuals' uses of the Internet that are said to harm legally protected interests. From the point of view of generativity, music industry lawsuits against individual file sharers inflict little damage on the network and the PC themselves, even if they are bad policy because the underlying substantive law demarcating the protected interest is itself ill-advised--as I believe it is. The Internet's future may be brighter if technical processes are refined to permit easier identification of Internet users, alongside legal processes—and perhaps technical limitations—to ensure that such identification is only made with good cause. * * *

The modern Internet is at a point of inflection. This Article argues that its generativity, and that of the PC, has produced extraordinary progress in information technology, which in turn has led to extraordinary progress in the development of forms of artistic and political expression. Internet architects and regulatory authorities have applauded this progress, but they are increasingly concerned by its excesses. The experimentalist spirit that fostered maximum generativity is out of place now that we rely upon the Internet and PCs for applications that we deem vital.

The challenge facing those interested in a vibrant global Internet is to maintain the core of that experimentalist spirit in the face of growing pressures. One path leads to a velvet divorce, creating two separate Internets with distinct audiences: a return to the quiet backwater for the original experimentalist Internet that would restart the generative cycle among researchers and hackers distinct from consumers who live with a new, controlled Internet experience. Two Internets would consign the existing grid to an appliancized fate, in which little new happens as existing technology players incrementally modify existing applications without the competitive pressure of grid-enabled innovation arbitrage.

The alternative paths that this Article advocates try to maintain the fundamental generativity of the existing grid while taking seriously the problems that fuel enemies of the Internet free-for-all. It requires charting an intermediate course to make the grid more secure—and to make some activities to which regulators object more regulable—in order to continue to enable the rapid deployment of the sort of amateur programming that has made the Internet such a stunning success.

Crippling generative accessibility and adaptability by transforming the PC into an information appliance is undesirable. So, too, are hamfisted clamps by ISPs upon network traffic in an effort to beat back viruses and other PC security threats, even as complete fidelity to end-to-end neutrality may on balance harm the generative information technology environment. Some limits are inevitable, and this Article attempts to point to ways in which these limits might be most judiciously applied. The key is to set such limits through thoughtful adjustments to accessibility that do not themselves spawn new centralized gatekeepers. The right interventions will preserve the public's ability to adopt new technologies from all corners, creating rough accountability for those who wish to introduce software to the world and for individuals who put that software to certain uses, while enabling those who maintain generative technologies—the Internet architects, ISPs, and OS publishers—to keep those technologies open and to ensure that those who wish to contribute to the global information grid can do so without having to occupy the privileged perches of established firms or powerful governments.

Notes and Questions

1. Why does Zittrain think that the Internet is "generative"? What does he mean by generativity? How did such generativity arise? Why does Zittrain think generativity is desirable? What are the disadvantages of generativity?

2. Why does Zittrain believe that the generative Internet is at risk of disappearing? Do you agree?

3. What does Zittrain mean by an "appliancized" Internet and PC? And what's wrong with products such as TiVo or services such as automatic updating? What dangers does Zittrain identify?

4. If users seem to prefer a more "locked down" Internet that provides better safer functionality, why shouldn't this preference be honored? How would Zittrain respond?

5. We considered the end-to-end net neutrality debate in Chapter Five. Why does Zittrain think those advocating neutrality are misguided?

6. What are Zittrain's proposals for keeping the Internet more generative? Do you think they would be helpful? Are they sufficient?

7. Why does Zittrain reject the cyberlibertarian vision of an unregulated Internet? How do his generativity-based principles differ?

8. Although Zittrain proposes ways of keeping the Internet generative, he does not discuss in great detail how such policy decisions will be made. He does suggest that a grassroots effort to rate lines of code would be a "worthwhile governance project," but otherwise offers little sense of how his proposals would be adopted. How do you think Zittrain would respond to this concern? If, as seems clear, Zittrain is willing to have a more regulated Internet (as long as it preserves generativity), how is this regulation to occur, and who does the regulating?

David G. Post, *Governing Cyberspace*

43 Wayne L. Rev. 155 (1997)

Cyberspace may herald what Walter Wriston called, some years back, the "twilight of sovereignty,"[21] quite possibly the final days of a governance system relying on individual sovereign states as primary law-making authority, a system that has served us, often for better and sometimes for worse, for the last half millennium. This is an exciting, and a slightly terrifying prospect, a radical transformation of the legal landscape to which we have all become accustomed. What will take its place?

There are, appropriately enough given the binary nature of the information traveling in cyberspace, two radically different processes through which order can emerge in this environment. I have, only somewhat facetiously, referred elsewhere to them by name: Hamilton and Jefferson. Hamilton involves an increasing degree of centralization of control, achieved by means of increasing international coordination among existing sovereigns, through multi-lateral treaties and/or the creation of new international governing bodies along the lines of the World Trade Organization, the World Intellectual Property Organization, and the like. If choice of law is hopelessly confused, in other words, we can eliminate the choice by imposing a single, uniform legal standard world-wide.

Jefferson invokes a radical decentralization of law-making, the development of processes that do not *impose* order on the electronic world but through which order can emerge. Some of these decentralized processes

---

21. *See* Walter Wriston, The Twilight of Sovereignty (1992).

will look familiar to us as a kind of "electronic federalism." In this model, individual network access providers, rather than territorially based states, become the essential units of governance; users in effect delegate the task of rule-making to them—confer sovereignty on them—and choose among them according to their own individual views of the constituent elements of an ordered society. The "law of the Internet" thus emerges, not from the decision of some higher authority, but as the aggregate of the choices made by individual system operators about what rules to impose, and by individual users about which online communities to join. Mobility—our ability to move unhindered into and out of these individual networks with their distinct rule-sets—is a powerful guarantee that the resulting distribution of rules is a just one; indeed, our very conception of what constitutes justice may change as we observe the kind of law that emerges from uncoerced individual choice.

To illustrate, and to bring this discussion back down to earth, consider the facts of * * * *Cyber Promotions, Inc. v. America Online*[29] * * * . The defendant, America Online, is, of course, a large commercial online service provider. Like most online service providers, America Online offers a service to its subscribers—the ability to receive, and to send, electronic mail, not merely to other America Online subscribers but over the Internet—a "gateway" between the closed America Online system and the open, worldwide Internet. Cyber Promotions, Inc., the plaintiff, is a bulk e-mail operation, offering businesses the opportunity to send electronic mail containing commercial solicitations to millions of recipients at a minuscule fraction of the cost of such promotional activities in the real world.

America Online claims that many of its subscribers have complained about receiving this "virtual junk mail"—or "spam," as it is sometimes called in online parlance. In response, it configured its Internet gateway to reject any and all electronic mail that arrives bearing a Cyber Promotions return address. Cyber Promotions cried foul (and filed suit), claiming that America Online's actions improperly interfere with its "freedom of speech," its ability to engage in commercial activity on the net.

In a stunningly wrongheaded move, the trial court initially issued a preliminary ruling siding with Cyber Promotions, ordering America Online to open up its mail gateway to incoming mail from the Cyber Promotions site, at least pending a full trial. Wrongheaded because what America Online has done here is precisely what Internet governance requires. It has, in effect, promulgated a rule about junk e-mail. Those who believe it is a good rule can remain as members of the America Online community, and those who believe it is otherwise (including those who believe it is infringing some right of entities like Cyber Promotion) can move elsewhere, to any one of the hundreds of other providers of Internet mail service, each of whom may define "junk mail" in very different ways (or, of course, not at all). We can be reasonably confident that the rule imposed by America

---

29. 948 F. Supp. 456 (E.D. Pa. 1996).

Online is an expression of their subscribers' collective desires to order their electronic world in a certain way, because America Online's ability to "impose" rules contrary to that collective will is severely constrained by the ability of its subscribers to move somewhere else—to "vote with their electrons."

This is a kind of market for law and, like all markets, it is a powerful information-processing device. We could engage in an abstract argument within some centralized Hamiltonian process about whether there exists some "right" to send unsolicited bulk e-mail, and perhaps impose some uniform rule on the global network regarding this practice. But even aside from the difficulty of reaching consensus among the sovereign governments of the world in regard to the scope of that right, consider the possibility that the decentralized Jeffersonian market for rules is a better indicator of the views of the participants in these transactions on this question than is a vote in, say, the International Telecommunications Union, that the process that records the aggregate of uncoerced voluntary choices among communities with different rule-sets is a superior device for answering the question "what is the 'best' rule?" It is true, of course, that if many Internet service providers implement a rule similar to America Online's, and if those service providers flourish and attract many subscribers, the activities of entities like Cyber Promotions will be drastically curtailed. But if many Internet service providers implement a similar rule, and if those service providers flourish and attract many subscribers, who would venture to say—who has the right to say—that that isn't the best rule to deal with this problem? * * *

The Jeffersonian mode of law-making has, at its heart, the sovereignty of the individual, the recognition that individual choice—consent of the governed—is the firmest basis on which to build political order. The extent to which it is allowed to flourish on the global network in the coming years is the central question we face as we engage in our collective conversation about the way that this new territory is going to be settled.

Notes and Questions

1. Like Zittrain, Post sees the Internet as generative and wants to preserve generativity. What then is the difference between Zittrain's vision of Internet regulation and Post's?

2. To the extent Post's Jefferson approach relies on private property and contract rules, how are such rules to be enforced? If the answer is that territorially based nation-states must do the enforcing, has Post truly offered an alternative legal model?

3. Post asserts that, if users want a different "law" from the one America Online (AOL) offers, they can simply migrate to a different service provider. This vision assumes, however, that there will always be other, substantively different, options available. If AOL dominates the market or other service providers offer the same terms, no other viable alternative will exist. Will a sovereign government then need to enforce antitrust or consumer protection

laws to insure the existence of legitimate alternatives? If so, which sovereign and whose laws?

4. Would Zittrain embrace Post's idea that individual private entities should construct their own "law"? Why or why not?

5. Both Zittrain and Post acknowledge that it is difficult to predict the outcomes of their normative visions because, almost by definition, the product of an unpredictable set of interactions among millions of users around the globe cannot be discerned in advance. This uncertainty almost inevitably means that the drawbacks of their proposals are easier to see than the potential benefits. Is this a shortcoming of their models or is the unpredictability precisely what should be embraced? What about the argument that law is useful only to the extent that it creates greater certainty? Are Zittrain's and Post's visions (different though they are) fundamentally "anti-law"? Or is there a different understanding of legal norms at play here?

Robert McChesney, *So Much for the Magic of Technology and the Free Market: The World Wide Web and the Corporate Media System*

From THE WORLD WIDE WEB AND CONTEMPORARY CULTURAL THEORY, Routledge, 2000

One of the striking characteristics of the World Wide Web is that there has been virtually no public debate over how it should develop; a consensus of "experts" simply decided that it should be turned over to the market. Indeed, the antidemocratic nature of Web policy making is explained or defended on very simple grounds: the Web is to be and should be regulated by the free market. This is the most rational, fair, and democratic regulatory mechanism ever known to humanity, so by all rights it should be automatically applied to any and all areas of social life where profit can be found. No debate is necessary to establish the market as the reigning regulatory mechanism, because the market naturally assumes that role unless the government intervenes and prevents the market from working its magic. Indeed, by this logic, any public debate over Web policy can only be counterproductive, because it could only lead us away from a profit-driven system. Public meddling would allow unproductive bureaucrats to interfere with productive market players.

Combining the market with the Web, we are told, will allow entrepreneurs to compete as never before, offering wonderful new products at ever lower prices. It will provide a virtual cornucopia of choices for consumers, and empower people all over the world in a manner previously unimaginable. Enterprise will blossom as the multitudes become online entrepreneurs. It will be a capitalist Valhalla. Nowhere will the cyber-market revolution be more apparent than in the realm of media and communication. When anyone can put something up on the Web, the argument goes, and when the Web effectively converges with television, the value of having a television or cable network will approach zero. Eventually the control of any distribution network will be of no value as all media convert to digital formats. Production studios, too, will have less leverage as the market will be opened to innumerable new players. Even governments will, in the end, find its power untamable.

As a consequence, the likely result of the digital revolution will be the withering—perhaps even the outright elimination—of the media giants and a flowering of a competitive commercial media marketplace the likes of which have never been seen. Indeed, the rise of the Web threatens not only the market power of the media giants but also the very survival of the telecommunication and computer software giants.

It is ironic that as the claims about the genius of the market have grown in conventional discourse over the past two decades, the need to provide empirical evidence for the claims has declined. The market has assumed mythological status, becoming a religious totem to which all must pledge allegiance or face expulsion to the margins. The mythology of the market is so widely embraced to some extent because it has some elements of truth. It is formally a voluntary mechanism, without direct coercion, and it permits an element of consumer choice. But the main reason it has vaulted to the top of the ideological totem pole is because it serves the interests of the most dominant elements of our society. And the free market mythology harms few if any powerful interests, so it goes increasingly unchallenged. As this mythology of the free market is the foundation of almost the entire case for the lack of any public debate on the course—and therefore for the privatization and commercialization—of the Web, it demands very careful scrutiny.

The claim that the market is a fair, just, and rational allocator of goods and services is premised on the notion that the market is based on competition. This competition constantly forces all economic actors to produce the highest-quality product for the lowest possible price, and it rewards those who work the hardest and the most efficiently. Therefore, these new technologies will permit hungry entrepreneurs to enter markets, slay corporate dinosaurs, lower prices, improve products, and generally do good things for humanity. And just when these newly successful entrepreneurs are riding high on the hog, along will come some plucky upstart (probably with a new technology) to teach them a lesson and work the magic of competition yet again. This is the sort of pabulum that is served up to those Americans who lack significant investments in the economy. It provides an attractive image for the way our economy works—making it seem downright fair and rational—but it has little to do with how the economy actually operates. Corporate executives will even invoke this rhetoric in dealing with Congress or the public and, at a certain level, they may even believe it. Yet their actions speak louder than words.

The truth is that for those atop our economy the key to success is based in large part on eliminating competition. I am being somewhat facetious, because in the end capitalism is indeed a war of one against all, since every capitalist is in competition with all others. But competition is also something successful capitalists (the kind that remain capitalists) learn to avoid like the plague. The less competition a firm has, the less risk it faces and the more profitable it tends to be. All investors and firms rationally desire to be in as monopolistic a position as possible. In general, most markets in the United States in the twentieth century have gravitated not to monopoly status, but to oligopolistic status. This means that a small handful of firms—ranging from two or three to as many as a dozen or so— thoroughly dominate the market's output and maintain barriers to entry that effectively keep new market entrants at bay * * * . In pricing and output, oligopolistic markets are far closer to being monopolistic markets than they are the competitive markets described in capitalist folklore. * * *

So how should we expect the World Wide Web to develop in this model of the free market? Exactly as it has so far. Despite now having the technological capacity to compete, the largest firms are extremely reticent about entering new markets and forcing their way into existing and highly lucrative communication markets. Thus the local telephone companies have tended to avoid providing pay television over their wires, and the cable companies have avoided providing telephone services over their lines. This is no conspiracy. There have been a few, and will no doubt be more, attempts by these firms and others to cross over and compete in new markets. But it will be done selectively, usually targeting affluent markets that are far more attractive to these firms. Most important, no existing giant will attempt to enter another market unless they are reasonably certain that they will have a chance to win their own monopoly, or at least have a large chunk of a stable oligopoly with significant barriers to entry. * * * In general, new firms are ill-equipped to challenge giant firms in oligopolistic markets due to entry barriers. The role of small firms in the classic scenario is to conduct the research, development, and experimentation that large firms deem insufficiently profitable, then, when a small firm finds a lucrative new avenue, it sells out to an existing giant. Some of the impetus for technological innovation comes from these small firms, eager to find a new niche in which they can grow away from the shadows of the corporate giants in existing industries. It is in times of technological upheaval, as now, with the World Wide Web and digital communication, that brand new industries are being formed and there is an opportunity for new giants to emerge.

It is safe to say that some new communications giants will be established during the coming years, much as Microsoft attained gigantic status during the eighties and nineties. But most of the great new fortunes will be made by start-up firms who develop a profitable idea and then sell out to one of the existing giants. (Witness Microsoft, which spent over $2 billion between 1994 and 1997 to purchase or take a stake in some fifty communication companies.) Indeed, this is conceded to be the explicit goal of nearly all the start-up Web and telecommunications firms, who are founded with the premise of an "exit scenario" through their sale to a giant. * * *

There are a couple of other aspects of capitalism that do not comport to the mythology. First, when free-market mythologists criticize the *heavy* *hand* of government, what they really mean by heavy hand is that government might actually represent the interests of the citizenry versus those of business. When governments spend billions subsidizing industries or advocating the interests of business, not a peep is heard about the evils of "big government." Government policies play a decisive role in assisting corporate profitability and dominance in numerous industries, not the least of which is communications. Most of the communications industry associated with the technology revolution—particularly the Web—grew directly out of government subsidies. Indeed, at one point fully 85 percent of research and development in the U.S. electronics industry was subsidized by the federal government, although the eventual profits accrued to private firms. * * *

Understanding the crucial importance of the government undercuts also the myth that the market exists "naturally," independent of the government, blindly rewarding the most efficient performers. Government policies are instrumental in determining who the winners will and will not be, and those policies are often derived in an antidemocratic and corrupt manner. * * *

The two most important corporate sectors regarding the Web are telecommunications and computers. Each of these sectors is more immediately threatened by the World Wide Web than are the dominant media firms. In the case of the seven or eight massive telecommunications firms that dominate the U.S. telephone industry, the Web poses a threat to its very existence. The new technology of Internet protocol (IP) telephony threatens to open the way to vastly less expensive communication and the possibility of newfound competition. The telecommunications giant Sprint has gone so far as to revamp its entire network to operate by IP standards. More important, the very notion of voice telephony is in the process of being superseded by the digital data networks that send voice as only a small portion of its data delivery. In this sense, the big telecommunications firms may appear like giant dinosaurs made irrelevant by the Web.

Yet the giant telecommunications firms have a few distinct assets with which to play. First, they already have wires into people's businesses and homes and these wires are suitable for carrying Web traffic. Second, the World Wide Web "backbone" of fiber-optic trunk lines is owned by several of the largest U.S. telecommunications firms, including WorldCom-MCI, AT&T, GTE and Sprint. These factors make the telecommunication firms ideally suited to become Internet service providers (ISPs) to business and consumers, already an area with a proven market. Indeed, with the entry of the large telecommunication companies into the ISP sector, the *Financial Times* wrote that the "Internet small fry" were "on the road to oblivion." It added: "The situation is very much like the PC market 10 years ago where a lot of smaller PC dealers went out of business."

With regard to being an ISP, as in other facets of telecommunication, size means a great deal for establishing a competitive advantage. Hence, the dominant trend in the late 1990s has been a wave of massive mergers among the largest telecommunications firms, not only in the United States but globally. The second asset these firms enjoy is a great deal of cash flow, which permits them to engage in more aggressive acquisitions than perhaps any other Web-related firms. The consensus of opinion in the business community is that early in the twenty-first century as few as four to six firms will dominate the entirety of global telecommunications.

The other major contender in providing Web access is the cable television industry; in the United States that means the five or six companies that have monopolies over more than 80 percent of the nation. By the summer of 1998 the Federal Communications Commission (FCC) effectively abandoned the notion that the ISP market could ever be remotely competitive. It granted the regional Bell companies the right to restrict the use of their wires to their own ISP services, rather than make them available to all users at a fair price. By doing so, the FCC hopes to encourage at least two viable ISP services—one telephone based, the other cable based—in each market, rather than have it become a monopoly. * * *

So ironically, the most striking feature of digital communication may well be not that it has opened up competition in communication markets, but that it has made it vastly easier, attractive, and necessary for firms to consolidate and strike alliances across the media, telecommunications, and computer sectors. * * *

Indeed, by the end of the 1990s the possibility of new Web content providers emerging to slay the traditional media appears more farfetched than ever before. In 1998 there was a massive shakeout in the online media industry, as smaller players could not remain afloat. Forrester Research estimated that the cost of an "average-content" website increased threefold to $3.1 million by 1998, and would double again by 2000. "While the big names are establishing themselves on the Internet," the *Economist* wrote in 1998, "the content sites that have grown organically out of the new medium are suffering." Even a firm with the resources of Microsoft flopped in its attempt to become an online content provider, abolishing its operation in early 1998. "It's a fair comment to say that entertainment on the Internet did not pan out as expected," said a Microsoft executive. As telecommunications and computer firms work to develop Web content, they now turn to partnerships with the corporate media giants.

We can now see that those who forecast that the media giants would smash into the World Wide Web "iceberg" exaggerated the power of technology and failed to grasp the manner in which markets actually work. In addition to having deep pockets and a lengthy time, the media giants enjoy five other distinct advantages over those who might intrude into their territory. First, they have digital programming from their other ventures that they can plug into the Web at little extra cost. This in itself is a huge advantage over firms that have to create original content from scratch. Second, to generate an audience, they can and do promote their websites incessantly on their traditional media holdings; thus bringing their audiences to their sites on the Web. * * *

Third, as advertising develops on the Web, the media giants are poised to seize most of these revenues. Online advertising amounted to $900 million in 1997, and some expect it to reach $5 billion by the year 2000. It is worth noting that this will still be no more than 3 percent of all U.S. ad spending that year, suggesting again how long a path it will be to an era of Web dominance. The media giants have long and close relationships with the advertising industry, and work closely with them to make Web advertising viable. The evidence suggests that in the commercialized Web, advertisers will have increased leverage over content, in the same manner their influence has increased in television in the 1990s. A common form of Web advertising is "sponsorships," whereby for a flat sum ranging from $100,000 to $1 million annually, the advertiser, its agency and the host Web network work together to develop "advertorials." The media giants also have another concrete advantage in their dealings with major advertisers: they can and do arrange to have them agree to do a portion of their business on their Web.

Fourth, as the possessors of the hottest "brands," the media firms have the leverage to get premier location from browser software makers and portals. Microsoft Internet Explorer offers 250 high-lighted channels, the "plum positions" belonging to Disney and Time Warner, and similar arrangements are taking place with Netscape and Pointcast. Fifth—and this relates to their deep pockets—the media giants are aggressive investors in start-up Web media companies. Approximately one-half of the venture capital for Web content start-up companies comes from established media firms. The Tribune Company, for example, owns stakes in fifteen Web companies, including the portals AOL, Excite!, and the women-targeted iVillage. If some new company shows commercial promise, the media giants will be poised to capitalize upon, not be buried by, that promise. * * *

We might want to ponder what all of this means for the nature of journalism on the Web. This is really a fundamental issue; if the Web fails to produce a higher caliber of journalism and stimulate public understanding and activity, the claim that it is a boon for democracy is severely weakened. Many have chronicled the deplorable state of commercial journalism at the hand of the media giants. There is little reason to expect a journalistic renaissance online. At present the trend for online journalism is to accentuate the worst synergistic and profit-hungry attributes of commercial journalism, with its emphasis on trivia, celebrities, and consumer news. One observer characterized the news offerings on AOL, drawn from all the commercial giants, as less a "market-place of ideas" than "a shopping mall of notions."

This does not mean that there are no considerable advantages or differences between the emerging digital world and what preceded it. Even if the Web becomes primarily a commercial medium for electronic commerce, e-mail, and commercial news and entertainment fare, it will also be a haven for all sorts of interactive activities that never existed in the past. In particular, the Web's openness permits a plethora of voices to speak and be heard worldwide at relatively minimal expense. This is indeed a communications revolution, and one that is being taken advantage of by countless social and political organizations that heretofore were marginalized. In 1998, for example, the global and largely secretive negotiations for a Multilateral Agreement on Investment (MAI) were undercut when a flurry of Web communication created a groundswell of popular opposition. The MAI was barely covered in the commercial media, and to the extent that it was the coverage was favorable to a global bill of rights for investors and corporations. Yet this point should not be exaggerated. As a rule, journalism is not something that can be undertaken piecemeal by amateurs working in their spare time. It is best done by people who make a living at it, and who have training, experience, and resources. Journalism also requires institutional support (from commercial and governmental attack) to survive and prosper. Corporate media giants have failed miserably to provide a viable journalism, and as they dominate journalism online there is no reason to expect anything different. In this context, it should be no surprise that the leading product of Web journalism is none other than Matt Drudge, who, as *The Economist* puts it, "spares himself the drudgery of fact-checking." * * *

It may turn out, as a few Web experts suggest, that portals will prove to have been a flash in the pan. As the president of InfoSeek has put it, "The Internet's still in the Stone Age." Yet however it develops, the following comment from the president of Time, Inc. seems fairly accurate: "I believe the electronic revolution is simply one new form of communications that will find its place in the food chain of communications and will not displace or replace anything that already exists, just as television did not replace radio, just as cable did not replace network television, just as the VCR did not replace the movie theatres." The evidence so far suggests that media giants will be able to draw the Web into their existing empires. While the Web is in many ways revolutionizing the way we lead our lives, it is a revolution that does not appear to include changing the identity and nature of those in power.

Notes and Questions

1. Why does McChesney think that entrenched corporate powers will maintain their dominance in the online world? Does his argument challenge either Zittrain's vision of generativity or Post's conception of decentralized law-making? How might each respond to McChesney's arguments?

2. To the extent that you agree with McChesney's critique of what he refers to as free market "mythology" with regard to cyberspace, does that also force you to question the same mythology in the offline world, or are there fundamental differences between the way corporations can consolidate power online?

3. Why does McChesney think that competition alone will not constantly generate creative alternatives, as free market theory might suggest? Do you agree with his critique? Consider Post's argument about how easily new

corporations can enter the market online. Does that undercut McChesney's point? How might he respond?

4. Does McChesney suggest any way to combat the entrenchment of oligopolistic power that he identifies? Does his argument necessarily envision a role for government in law formation? On the other hand, he also seems to suggest that government regulation tends to support business interests. In this regard, consider the net neutrality debate in Chapter Five. Would McChesney find *both* governmental and non-governmental law-making problematic? If so, are there any realistic alternatives? Do either Zittrain or Post offer useful responses?

Index

References are to pages.

ANONYMITY
Electronic Communications Privacy Act
and, 555–558
freedom of speech and, 532–541
subscriber identity, compelled disclosure by
ISP, 532–557
subscriber identity, voluntary disclosure by
ISP, 555–558

**ANTICYBERSQUATTING
CONSUMER PROTECTION ACT
(ACPA)**
generally, 170, 185, 192, 196, 285–288, 291
in rem jurisdiction, 169–186

ARCHITECTURE
regulation through, 6–8, 10, 12–14,
297–299
Platform for Internet Content Selection
(PICS), 423, 427, 675
Platform for Privacy Preferences (P3P),
675

AUTONOMY
generally, 19, 323, 345, 372–376, 390
First Amendment and, 372–376
privacy and, 570–574

BROWSEWRAP LICENSES, 215–220

CALEA
See Communications Assistance for Law
Enforcement Act.

CDA
See Communications Decency Act.

CFAA
See Computer Fraud and Abuse Act.

**CHILD ONLINE PROTECTION ACT
(COPA),** 85–94, 426, 441–454, 457,
458, 462, 465

**CHILDREN'S INTERNET
PROTECTION ACT (CIPA),** 62,
452–465

**CHILDREN'S ONLINE PRIVACY
PROTECTION ACT (COPPA),**
673–674

CIPA
See Children's Internet Protection Act.

CLICKWRAP LICENSES, 211–214, 216,
219

CODE
See Architecture.

**COMMUNICATIONS ASSISTANCE
FOR LAW ENFORCEMENT ACT
(CALEA),** 282–283

**COMMUNICATIONS DECENCY ACT
(CDA)**
immunity provisions, 486–511
indecency, regulation of, 409–425

COMPUTER CRIME
Computer Fraud and Abuse Act, 698–713
cross-border searches, 64, 149-157, 163-165

**COMPUTER FRAUD AND ABUSE
ACT,** 698-713

CONTRACTS, ONLINE
browsewrap licenses, 215–220
clickwrap agreements, 211–214, 216, 219
enforceability of form contracts, 211–227
forum selection clauses, 227

unconscionability, 223–224

CONTROL OF DATA, COMMERCIAL
Computer Fraud and Abuse Act,698–713
trespass to chattels, 23–43, 687–697

COPA
See Child Online Protection Act.

COPPA
See Children's Online Privacy Protection
    Act.

COPYRIGHT
generally, 228–230
challenges of digital technology, 228–230
Digital Millennium Copyright Act, anti-
    circumvention and anti-trafficking
    provisions, 237, 246–254, 714–731
Digital Millennium Copyright Act,
    immunity provisions, 251–252
digital music, 255–281
fair use, effect of digital rights management
    systems on, 231–235, 237
fair use, effect of DMCA on, 251–252
freedom of speech and, 291–301
infringement,
        contributory infringement, 239-245,
            260-264, 271, 274, 276, 514-519
        direct infringement, 243, 257, 259-262,
            269, 270, 513, 514 519, 525, 526,
            531
        vicarious liability, 240, 262, 263, 265,
            270, 485, 515, 517, 518, 525
infringement-facilitating devices, 239–253
intermediary liability, 271, 511–526
peer-to-peer file sharing, 265–280
preemption of contractual terms, 213, 214
technological protection measures, 228–237

CULTURE AND CYBERLAW
community and globalization,753–776
law and culture, relationship between,
    733–734, 776–790
metaphors and formation of policy, 734–752

CYBERLAW
as integrated field of study, 1–12

CYBERSPACE
history and development of, 13–20
unique features, 15–19

CYBERSQUATTING, 170, 185, 192, 196,
    285–288, 291

DATA MINING
See Privacy, data mining.

DEFAMATION
intermediary liability for, 486–511
jurisdiction and, 159–164

**DIGITAL MILLENNIUM COPYRIGHT
    ACT**
anti-circumvention and anti-trafficking
    provisions, 237, 246–254, 714–731
fair use and, 251–252
section 512 safe harbor, 525–530

DIGITAL MUSIC, 265–290

**DIGITAL RIGHTS MANAGEMENT
    SYSTEMS**
See Copyright; technological protection
    measures

DOMAIN NAMES
Anticybersquatting Consumer Protection
    Act, 170, 185, 192, 196, 285–288, 291
domain name system, 188–192, 301–303
ICANN Uniform Dispute Resolution Policy,
    204–206
in rem jurisdiction and, 169-186
personal jurisdiction and, 170–174
use of trademark in, 48, 54, 55

DORMANT COMMERCE CLAUSE
application to internet, 64, 105–112

DUE PROCESS
See Personal Jurisdiction.

ECPA
See Electronic Communications Privacy
    Act.

**ELECTRONIC COMMUNICATIONS
    PRIVACY ACT**
anonymity and, 532–557
data mining and, 5-6, 9, 6546–654
employer monitoring and, 648–656
government surveillance and, 575–647
pen registers and trap and trace devices,
    616–625
stored communications access, 580–588
See also Electronic Surveillance; Privacy.

ELECTRONIC SURVEILLANCE
Electronic Communications Privacy Act,
    576, 589, 592, 599-605, 616, 621, 625,
    664, 665, 670, 215, 554, 576, 590, 599,
    622, 641, 664
Fourth Amendment constraints on,
    577–582
interception of communications, 575–583

non-content information, 622–625, 639–642

pen registers and trap and trace devices, 616–624, 639–642

stored communications access, 580–588

See also Privacy; Fourth Amendment.

E-MAIL

employer monitoring, 648–656

government surveillance and, 575–647

unsolicited commercial e-mail,
dormant commerce clause and, 104–111
Realtime Blackhole List, 318–326
trespass to chattels and, 30–43

ENFORCEMENT OF JUDGMENTS

See Jurisdiction, Power to Enforce.

FILTERING

available technology, 427

effect on speech, 432–440

limitations of technology, 427–432

Platform for Internet Content Selection (PICS), 423, 427, 675

private ordering in cyberspace, 426–439

use in public settings, 452–465

FIRST AMENDMENT

See Freedom of Speech.

FOURTH AMENDMENT

cross-border searches, 64, 149–157, 163–165

electronic surveillance and, 577–582

extraterritorial application of, 157–165

reasonable expectation of privacy
generally, 196–199
effect of technology on, 296–211

See also Electronic Surveillance; Title III.

FREEDOM OF SPEECH

access to media entities, 351–361, 377–380

anonymity, 532–541

community standards and, 84-87, 89-94, 96, 395, 411, 415, 416, 441, 442, 489

extraterritorial regulation of speech, 98–105

fairness doctrine, 352–357

filtering technology and, 440–478

First Amendment background, 389–390

"harmful to minors" speech, regulation of,
generally, 391–394
Child Online Protection Act, 85–94

indecent speech, regulation of,
generally, 390–425
broadcast medium, 394–400
Communications Decency Act, 409–426
zoning, 422–425

must–carry requirements, 362–371

open access requirements, 377–380

sexually explicit speech, regulation of,
generally, 390–426
blocking by ISPs, 466–478
Child Online Protection Act, 84–93, 441–451
Children's Internet Protection Act, 452–465
Communications Decency Act, 409–425

GEOGRAPHY AND SOVEREIGNTY

generally, 63–192

personal jurisdiction and, 112–136

theoretical debate over regulation of internet, 65–82

GOVERNMENT SURVEILLANCE

See Electronic Surveillance.

ICANN

See Internet Corporation for Assigned Names and Numbers (ICANN)

INTERMEDIARY LIABILITY

common law approach, 482–485

Communications Decency Act, 486–491, 512–519

copyright claims, 511–526

defamation claims, 486–511

Digital Millennium Copyright Act, 520–527

file exchange systems, 225–282

trademark claims, 527–532

INTERNET

history and development of, 13–20

unique features, 15–19

INTERNET CORPORATION FOR ASSIGNED NAMES AND NUMBERS (ICANN)

domain name disputes and, 186–192, 301–307, 346–47332–333, 362–371

legitimacy of, 187–192, 301–307, 346–347

state action doctrine and, 346–347

Uniform Dispute Resolution Policy, 304–306

INTERNET GOVERNANCE

ICANN, 187–192, 301–307, 346–347

standard–setting bodies, 359–362

INTERNET SERVICE PROVIDERS

copyright infringement, liability for, 511–526

defamation, liability for, 456–511

open access requirements, 330–380

See also Intermediary Liability.

JURISDICTION
adjudicate, jurisdiction to, 112–137
articulation of community norms and, 137–148
challenges posed by internet, 117–125
definition of community and, 84-87, 89–94, 96, 395, 411, 415, 416, 441, 442, 489
effects doctrine, 64, 71, 72, 78, 81
extraterritorial criminal investigation, 149–157
extraterritoriality, 64
in rem jurisdiction, 304–306
judgment recognition and, 137–142
personal jurisdiction,
    generally, 112–114
    domain name disputes and, 166–184
    due process considerations, 112–114
    "effects" as basis for, 84-87, 89–94, 96, 115–117, 395, 411, 415, 416, 441, 442, 489
    minimum contacts, 112–148
    online interaction and, 119–125
    "targeting" as basis for, 115–117, 129–136
power to enforce, 83, 137–142
prescribe, jurisdiction to, 84–112
trademark law and, 64

LIBRARIES
filtering of sexually explicit speech, 67–61, 452–465

METAPHORS AND ANALOGIES
role in formation of policy, 734–752
role in judicial decisions, 21–61

METATAGS
use of trademark in, 44–54

ONLINE CONTRACTS
See Contracts, Online.

P3P
See Platform for Privacy Preferences (P3P).

PEN REGISTERS AND TRAP AND TRACE DEVICES, 616–624, 639–642

PERSONAL JURISDICTION
generally, 112–114
domain name disputes and, 166–184
due process considerations, 112–114
"effects" as basis for, 84-87, 89–94, 96, 115–117, 395, 411, 415, 416, 441, 442, 489 minimum contacts, 112–148
online interaction and, 119–125
"targeting" as basis for, 115–117, 129–136

PICS
See Platform for Internet Content Selection (PICS).

PLATFORM FOR INTERNET CONTENT SELECTION (PICS), 423, 427,675

PLATFORM FOR PRIVACY PREFERENCES (P3P), 675
PORNOGRAPHY
See Freedom of Speech; Sexually Explicit Content.

PRIVACY
Children's Online Privacy Protection Act, 673–674
communications, privacy of, 575–674
cookies and web bugs, 656–672
data mining, 656–672
Electronic Communications Privacy Act, application to private parties, 648–656
    stored communications, 586–615
employer monitoring, 648–656
EU Data Protection Directive, 672–673
Federal Trade Commission and, 672–673
online profiling, 605–606, 656–672
Platform for Privacy Preferences (P3P), 675
state tort claims, 651–653, 670–672, 563–574
theoretical basis for protection of, 563–574
See also Electronic Surveillance.
See also Fourth Amendment.

REGULATION OF THE INTERNET
feasibility of, 6–10, 75–93, 234–241
geography and sovereignty and, 75–93
ICANN, 225–231, 363–371
law and technology, relationship between, 233–333
legitimacy of, 75–93, 234–241
private entities, power of, 358–392
private ordering in cyberspace, 237–239, 303–312, 383–392, 429–443, 657–681
See also Internet Governance.

SEXUALLY EXPLICIT CONTENT
Child Online Protection Act, 85–94, 426, 441–454, 457, 458, 462, 465
Communications Decency Act, 409–425
community standards and, 84-87, 89–94, 96, 395, 411, 415, 416, 441, 442, 489
filtering, 432–440
"harmful to minors" speech, regulation of, 85–94, 391–394

indecent speech, regulation of, 390–425
zoning, 422–425

SPAM
See Unsolicited Commercial E-Mail.

STATE ACTION DOCTRINE
generally, 327–350
application to ICANN, 346–347
criticism of, 348–350

STORED COMMUNICATIONS ACT
See Electronic Communications Privacy
    Act.

TITLE III
government surveillance, 579–583
interception of communications, 593–608
private parties, application to, 593–608,
    654–656
See also Electronic Surveillance, Privacy.

TRADEMARKS
Anticybersquatting Consumer Protection
    Act, 170, 185, 192, 196, 285–288, 291
consumer confusion,
    generally, 44, 50, 52, 55, 62, 288
    domain names, 48, 54, 55
    initial interest confusion, 44–48
    metatags, 44–53
cybersquatting,170, 185, 192, 196, 285–288,
    291
function of, 44, 48
geography and, 64, 68, 169, 170
statutory provisions, 44

technological innovation, effect of
    trademark law on, 284–292
use in domain name, 44–56, 171–183
use in metatags, 44–53

TRESPASS TO CHATTELS
generally, 23–43
controlling access to data, 687–697

UCITA
See Uniform Computer Information
    Transactions Act.

UDRP
See Uniform Dispute Resolution Policy.

**UNIFORM COMPUTER
    INFORMATION TRANSACTIONS
    ACT (UCITA),** 677–681

**UNIFORM DISPUTE RESOLUTION
    POLICY (UDRP),** 187, 287, 288, 291,
    302, 304–306, 347

**UNSOLICITED COMMERCIAL E-
    MAIL**
dormant commerce clause and, 104–111
Realtime Blackhole List, 318–326
trespass to chattels and, 30–43

USA PATRIOT ACT, 594, 598, 603, 605,
    607, 621, 638, 640, 641, 708

WIRETAP ACT
See Title III.